Lecture Notes in Computer Science 16115

The series Lecture Notes in Computer Science (LNCS), including its subseries Lecture Notes in Artificial Intelligence (LNAI) and Lecture Notes in Bioinformatics (LNBI), has established itself as a medium for the publication of new developments in computer science and information technology research, teaching, and education.

LNCS enjoys close cooperation with the computer science R & D community, the series counts many renowned academics among its volume editors and paper authors, and collaborates with prestigious societies. Its mission is to serve this international community by providing an invaluable service, mainly focused on the publication of conference and workshop proceedings and postproceedings. LNCS commenced publication in 1973.

Jiajia Li · Richard Chbeir · Lei Li ·
Chuanyu Zong · Yanfeng Zhang ·
Mengxuan Zhang
Editors

Web and Big Data

9th International Joint Conference, APWeb-WAIM 2025
Shenyang, China, August 28–30, 2025
Proceedings, Part III

Springer

Editors
Jiajia Li
Shenyang Aerospace University
Shenyang, China

Lei Li
The Hong Kong University of Science and Technology (Guangzhou)
Guangzhou, China

Yanfeng Zhang
Northeastern University
Shenyang, China

Richard Chbeir
University of Pau and Pays de l'Adour
Anglet, France

Chuanyu Zong
Shenyang Aerospace University
Shenyang, China

Mengxuan Zhang
Australian National University
Canberra, ACT, Australia

ISSN 0302-9743 ISSN 1611-3349 (electronic)
Lecture Notes in Computer Science
ISBN 978-981-95-5718-9 ISBN 978-981-95-5719-6 (eBook)
https://doi.org/10.1007/978-981-95-5719-6

This Springer imprint is published by the registered company Springer Nature Singapore Pte Ltd.
The registered company address is: 152 Beach Road, #21-01/04 Gateway East, Singapore 189721, Singapore

Preface

This volume (LNCS 16115) and its companion volumes (LNCS 16113, LNCS 16114, and LNCS 16116) contain the proceedings of the 9th Asia-Pacific Web (APWeb) and Web-Age Information Management (WAIM) Joint Conference on Web and Big Data, called APWeb-WAIM. Researchers and practitioners from around the world came together at this leading international forum to share innovative ideas, original research findings, case study results, and experienced insights in the areas of the World Wide Web and big data. The topics covered include web technologies, database systems, information management, software engineering, knowledge graphs, recommendation systems, and big data.

The 9th APWeb-WAIM conference was held in Shenyang from August 28 to August 30, 2025. As an Asia-Pacific flagship conference focusing on research, development, and applications related to Web information management, APWeb-WAIM builds on the successes of APWeb and WAIM. Previous APWeb conferences were held in Beijing (1998), Hong Kong (1999), Xi'an (2000), Changsha (2001), Xi'an (2003), Hangzhou (2004), Shanghai (2005), Harbin (2006), Huangshan (2007), Shenyang (2008), Suzhou (2009), Busan (2010), Beijing (2011), Kunming (2012), Sydney (2013), Changsha (2014), Guangzhou (2015), and Suzhou (2016). WAIM conferences were held in Shanghai (2000), Xi'an (2001), Beijing (2002), Chengdu (2003), Dalian (2004), Hangzhou (2005), Hong Kong (2006), Huangshan (2007), Zhangjiajie (2008), Suzhou (2009), Jiuzhaigou (2010), Wuhan (2011), Harbin (2012), Beidaihe (2013), Macau (2014), Qingdao (2015), and Nanchang (2016). The APWeb-WAIM conferences were held in Beijing (2017), Macau (2018), Chengdu (2019), Tianjin (2020), Guangzhou (2021), Nanjing (2022), Wuhan (2023), and Jinhua (2024). With the ever-growing importance of appropriate methods in these data-rich times and the rapid development of web-related technologies, APWeb-WAIM will continue to be a flagship conference in this field.

The high-quality program documented in these proceedings would not have been possible without the authors who chose APWeb-WAIM for disseminating their findings. APWeb-WAIM 2025 received a total of 472 research paper submissions. After the double-blind review process (each paper received at least three review reports), the conference accepted 136 regular research papers, resulting in an acceptance rate of 28.8%. In addition, the conference accepted 15 short research papers, 4 industry papers, and 13 demonstrations. The contributed papers address a wide range of topics, such as big data analytics, advanced database and web applications, data mining and applications, graph data and social networks, information extraction and retrieval, knowledge graphs, natural language processing, trusted and interpretable AI, LLM for data management, uncertain data, machine learning, cloud computing, distributed systems, recommender systems, security and blockchain, privacy and trust, and spatial and temporal data. We are grateful to these distinguished scientists for their invaluable contributions to the conference program.

We would like to express our gratitude to all individuals, institutions, and sponsors that supported APWeb-WAIM 2025. We are deeply thankful to the Program Committee members for lending their time and expertise to the conference. We also acknowledge the support of the other members of the organizing committee, all of whom helped make APWeb-WAIM 2025 a success. We are grateful for the guidance of the honorary chairs (Yannis Manolopoulos and Ge Yu), the steering committee representative (Yanchun Zhang), and the general chairs (Guoren Wang, Mahmoud Barhamgi, and Liang Zhao) for their guidance and support. Thanks also go to the program committee chairs (Jiajia Li, Richard Chbeir, and Lei Li), industry chairs (Xiaochun Yang, Kai Zheng, and Yu Yang), workshop chairs (Ye Yuan, Linlin Ding, and Ningning Cui), tutorial chairs (Jianxin Li, Wen Hua, and Guohui Ding), demo chairs (Yunjun Gao, Bin Yang, and Saeid Hosseini), publicity chairs (Hongzhi Wang, Bolong Zheng, Rui Zhu, and Yang Cao), publication chairs (Chuanyu Zong, Yanfeng Zhang, and Mengxuan Zhang), sponsorship chairs (Zhonglong Zheng and Haofen Wang), web chairs (Tao Qiu and Huanjie Zhu), local chairs (Keyan Cao, Xin Bi, Shan Huang, and Mo Li), CCF TCIS liaison (Xin Wang), and CCF TCDB liaison (Yueguo Chen).

August 2025

Jiajia Li
Richard Chbeir
Lei Li
Chuanyu Zong
Yanfeng Zhang
Mengxuan Zhang

Organization

Honorary Chairs

Yannis Manolopoulos	Aristotle University of Thessaloniki, Greece
Ge Yu	Northeastern University, China

General Chairs

Guoren Wang	Beijing Institute of Technology, China
Mahmoud Barhamgi	Qatar University, Qatar
Liang Zhao	Shenyang Aerospace University, China

Program Committee Chairs

Jiajia Li	Shenyang Aerospace University, China
Richard Chbeir	University of Pau & Pays Adour, France
Lei Li	Hong Kong University of Science and Technology (Guangzhou), China

Industry Track Chairs

Xiaochun Yang	Northeastern University, China
Kai Zheng	University of Electronic Science and Technology of China, China
Yu Yang	Education University of Hong Kong, China

Workshop Chairs

Ye Yuan	Beijing Institute of Technology, China
Linlin Ding	Liaoning University, China
Ningning Cui	Chang'an University, China

Tutorial Chairs

Jianxin Li	Edith Cowan University, Australia
Wen Hua	Hong Kong Polytechnic University, China
Guohui Ding	Shenyang Aerospace University, China

Demo Chairs

Yunjun Gao	Zhejiang University, China
Bin Yang	East China Normal University, China
Saeid Hosseini	Sohar University, Oman

Publicity Chairs

Hongzhi Wang	Harbin Institute of Technology, China
Bolong Zheng	Huazhong University of Science and Technology, China
Rui Zhu	Shenyang Aerospace University, China
Yang Cao	Institute of Science Tokyo, Japan

Publication Chairs

Chuanyu Zong	Shenyang Aerospace University, China
Yanfeng Zhang	Northeastern University, China
Mengxuan Zhang	Australian National University, Australia

Sponsorship Chairs

Zhonglong Zheng	Zhejiang Normal University, China
Haofen Wang	Tongji University, China

Web Chairs

Tao Qiu	Shenyang Aerospace University, China
Huaijie Zhu	Sun Yat-sen University, China

Local Chairs

Keyan Cao	Shenyang Jianzhu University, China
Xin Bi	Northeastern University, China
Shan Huang	Dalian Minzu University, China
Mo Li	Liaoning University, China

CCF TCIS Liaison

Xin Wang	Tianjin University, China

CCF TCDB Liaison

Yueguo Chen	Renmin University of China, China

Steering Committee Representative

Yanchun Zhang	Zhejiang Normal University, China & Victoria University, Australia

Program Committee members

Alexandros Karakasidis	University of Macedonia, Greece
Antonio Corral	University of Almería, Spain
Aoqian Zhang	Beijing Institute of Technology, China
Baokang Zhao	National University of Defense Technology, China
Benzhao Tang	Guangzhou University, China
Bingyan Liu	Beijing University of Posts and Telecommunications, China
Bo Lu Dalian	Minzu University, China
Bo Ning	Dalian Maritime University, China
Bohan Li	Nanjing University of Aeronautics and Astronautics, China
Boyang Li	Beijing Institute of Technology, China
Boyu Ruan	Hong Kong University of Science and Technology, China
Chao Kong	Anhui Polytechnic University, China

Chaokun Wang	Tsinghua University, China
Chenchen Li	Liaoning Normal University, China
Chenchen Sun	Chang'an University, China
Chuanyu Zong	Shenyang Aerospace University, China
Chunyan Zhao	East China Normal University, China
Derong Shen	Northeastern University, China
Dian Ouyang	Guangzhou University, China
Dong Yuan	University of Sydney, Australia
Fei Hao	Shaanxi Normal University, China
Fengmei Jin	Hong Kong Polytechnic University, China
Guiyang Jiang	Ocean University of China, China
Hangxu Ji	Northeastern University, China
Haolong Xiang	Nanjing University of Information Science and Technology, China
Hongzhi Wang	Harbin Institute of Technology, China
Hua Dai	Nanjing University of Posts and Telecommunications, China
Huaijie Zhu	Sun Yat-sen University, China
Huaming Chen	University of Sydney, Australia
Jia Xu	Guangxi University, China
Jiaheng Wei	Hong Kong University of Science and Technology (Guangzhou), China
Jiake Ge	Tianjin University, China
Jian Chen	Harbin Institute of Technology, China
Jianke Yu	University of Technology Sydney, Australia
Jianwei Wang	University of New South Wales, Australia
Jianye Yang	Guangzhou University, China
Jiaxin Jiang	National University of Singapore, Singapore
Jiaying Wang	Shenyang University of Technology, China
Jie Shao	University of Electronic Science and Technology of China, China
Jie Zhao	Chang'an University, China
Jinbao Li	Qilu University of Technology, China
Jing Li	Guangzhou University, China
Jing Zhang	Shenyang Aerospace University, China
Jingxian Cheng	Chang'an University, China
Jun Pang	Wuhan University of Science and Technology, China
Jun Song	Newcastle University, UK
Junhua Fang	Soochow University, China
Junhua Zhang	University of New South Wales, Australia
Kai Wang	Shanghai Jiao Tong University, China

Kaiqi Zhang	Harbin Institute of Technology, China
Keyan Cao	Shenyang Jianzhu University, China
Laurent d'Orazio	University of Rennes, France
Lei Li	Hong Kong University of Science and Technology (Guangzhou), China
Jiajia Li	Shenyang Aerospace University, China
Liangwei Zheng	University of Adelaide, Australia
Lingbin Guo	Tianjin University, China
Linlin Ding	Liaoning University, China
Lonji Huang	Suzhou University of Technology, China
Lu Chen	Zhejiang University, China
Mariam Dedabrishvili	International Black Sea University, Georgia
Meng Wang	Xi'an Polytechnic University, China
Meng-xiang Wang	China National Institute of Standardization, China
Mengxuan Zhang	Australian National University, Australia
Miao Xu	University of Queensland, Australia
Minghao Zhao	East China Normal University, China
Minghe Yu	Northeastern University, China
Mo Li	Liaoning University, China
Na Guo	Shenyang Aerospace University, China
Ning Wang	Guangzhou University, China
Ningning Cui	Chang'an University, China
Peng Tang	Shandong University, China
Pengfei Zhang	Anhui University of Science and Technology, China
Pingfu Chao	Soochow University, China
Qiange Wang	National University of Singapore, Singapore
Qing Liu	Zhejiang University, China
Qingbo Zhang	Northeastern University, China
Renjun Hu	East China Normal University, China
Rui Zhu	Shenyang Aerospace University, China
Ruiyuan Li	Chongqing University, China
Sana Sellami	Aix-Marseille University, France
Sandro Bimonte	INRAE, France
Sanghyun Park	Yonsei University, South Korea
Senzhang Wang	Central South University, China
Sergey Stupnikov	FRC CSC RAS, Russia
Han Huang	Dalian Minzu University, China
Shangqi Lu	Hong Kong University of Science and Technology (Guangzhou), China
Shanshan Yao	Shanxi University, China
Sheng Wang	Wuhan University, China

ShiJie Sun	Chang'an University, China
Shikai Guo	Dalian Maritime University, China
Shiyu Yang	Guangzhou University, China
Shizhuo Deng	Northeastern University, China
Shuai Xu	Nanjing University of Aeronautics and Astronautics, China
Shufeng Gong	Northeastern University, China
Shunmei Meng	Nanjing University of Science and Technology, China
Shunyang Li	University of New South Wales, Australia
Sijia Ruan	Beijing Institute of Technology, China
Suiming Guo	Jinan University, China
Tao Qiu	Shenyang Aerospace University, China
Tianxing Wu	Southeast University, China
Tianyi Li	Aalborg University, Denmark
Tiezheng Nie	Northeastern University, China
Vjeran Strahoja	University of Zagreb, Croatia
Wei Han	China University of Geosciences (Wuhan), China
Wei Li	Harbin Engineering University, China
Wei Liu	Sun Yat-sen University, China
Wei Song	Wuhan University, China
Wei Wang	Hong Kong University of Science and Technology (Guangzhou), China
Wei Emma Zhang	University of Adelaide, Australia
Weikai Yang	Hong Kong University of Science and Technology (Guangzhou), China
Wen Qu	Liaoning Normal University, China
Wenbin Guo	Tianjin University, China
Wenchao Jiang	Guangdong University of Technology, China
Wenhao Liang	University of Adelaide, Australia
Wenjian Qin	Shenzhen Institutes of Advanced Technology, China
Wentao Li	University of Leicester, UK
Xiang Lian	Kent State University, USA
Xiang Zhao	National University of Defense Technology, China
Xiangmin Zhou	RMIT University, Australia
Xiangyu Ke	Zhejiang University, China
Xianji Cui	Dalian Minzu University, China
Xiao Pan	Shijiazhuang Tiedao University, China
Xiaofeng Ding	Huazhong University of Science and Technology, China
Xiaojing Liu	Anhui University of Science & Technology, China

Xiaojun Xie	Nanjing Agricultural University, China
Xiaoling Wang	East China Normal University, China
Xiaowang Zhang	Tianjin University, China
Xiaoyang Wang	University of New South Wales, Australia
Xiaoyun Liu	Hong Kong Polytechnic University, China
Xin Bi	Northeastern University, China
Xin Cao	University of New South Wales, Australia
Xin Hu	Chang'an University, China
Xin Xie	Tianjin University, China
Xubo Wang	University of Technology Sydney, Australia
Xuliang Zhu	Shanghai Jiao Tong University, China
Xuyun Zhang	Macquarie University, Australia
Yajun Yang	Tianjin University, China
Yakun Chen	University of Technology Sydney, Australia
Yanda Wang	Nanjing Normal University, China
Yanfeng Zhang	Northeastern University, China
Yang-Sae Moon	Kangwon National University, South Korea
Yanping Wu	University of Technology Sydney, Australia
Yaoshu Wang	Shenzhen Institute of Computing Sciences, Shenzhen University, China
Ye Zhu	Deakin University, Australia
Yicong Li	Nanjing University of Aeronautics and Astronautics, China
Yifan Zhu	Zhejiang University, China
Yifu Tang	Swinburne University of Technology, Australia
Yiping Teng	Shenyang Aerospace University, China
Yishu Wang	Northeastern University, China
Yizhang He	University of New South Wales, Australia
Yong Zhang	Tsinghua University, China
Youwen Zhu	Nanjing University of Aeronautics and Astronautics, China
Yu Liu	University of International Relations, China
Yu Liu	Beijing Jiaotong University, China
Yu Yan	Harbin Institute of Technology, China
Yu Yang	Education University of Hong Kong, China
Yu-Xuan Qiu	Beijing Institute of Technology, China
Yuan Li	North China University of Technology, China
Yuanbo Xu	Jilin University, China
Yuanhang Yu	University of Technology Sydney, Australia
Yudong Zhang	University of Science and Technology of China, China
Yulang Ma	Northeastern University, China

Yunpeng Chai	Renmin University of China, China
Yuren Mao	Zhejiang University, China
Yurong Cheng	Beijing Institute of Technology, China
Yushuai Li	Aalborg University, Denmark
Yutong Han	Dalian Minzu University, China
Yuwen Peng	Wuhan University, China
Yuxiang Zeng	Beihang University, China
Yuxuan Liang	Hong Kong University of Science and Technology (Guangzhou), China
Zemin Chao	Harbin Institute of Technology, China
Anzhen Zhang	Shenyang Aerospace University, China
Zhao Li	Tianjin University, China
Zhaokang Wang	Nanjing University of Aeronautics and Astronautics, China
Zhaonian Zou	Harbin Institute of Technology, China
Zhen Song	Northeastern University, China
Zhen Tan	National University of Defense Technology, China
Zhengyi Yang	University of New South Wales, Australia
Zhenying He	Fudan University, China
Zhibin Wang	Nanjing University, China
Zhikun Zhang	Zhejiang University, China
Zhiqiang Zhang	Zhejiang University of Finance and Economics, China
Zhiyu Liang	Harbin Institute of Technology, China
Zhiyuan Wen	Hong Kong Polytechnic University, China
Zhongyang Wang	Shenyang Jianzhu University, China
Zi Chen	Nanjing University of Aeronautics and Astronautics, China
Ziqiang Yu	Yantai University, China
Ziquan Fang	Zhejiang University, China
Zirui Chen	Tianjin University, China
Zishuo Ding	Hong Kong University of Science and Technology (Guangzhou), China
Ziyi Liu	Hong Kong University of Science and Technology, China

Contents

Data Mining II

Machine Learning II

Graph Data Management and Analytics II

Big Data Management

Data Mining II

TimeMultiformer: Attention-Based Collaborative Feature and Temporal Dependencies Learning for Multivariate Time Series Imputation

Zhaoqin Wang, Qian Ma(✉), Hui Li, Qiao Ning, Furui Zhan, and Shikai Guo

School of Information Science and Technology, Dalian Maritime University, Dalian 116026, China
maqian@dlmu.edu.cn

Abstract. Multivariate time series data generated in fields such as transportation, economics, and healthcare can support various analytical tasks. However, due to the common occurrence of missing data in real-world scenarios, existing work faces significant challenges in ensuring data interpretability and effectively conducting specific tasks like advanced analysis and pattern recognition. Traditional missing value imputation methods struggle to effectively capture temporal dependencies in time series data. Although deep learning-based approaches (e.g., Transformer) demonstrate advantages in modeling long-range dependencies, they generally suffer from two critical limitations: (1) inadequate consideration of unequal time intervals between adjacent observations; (2) deficiencies in joint modeling of temporal and feature dependencies. To address these gaps, this paper proposes an attention-based framework named TimeMultiformer. The framework innovatively integrates Transformer and iTransformer architectures to accurately capture temporal dependencies and inter-variable feature dependencies, respectively. Specifically, it introduces a time lag matrix to explicitly model the impact of historical observations on current imputation and employs a diagonal-masked multi-head attention mechanism to mitigate the model's over-reliance on current time-step information, thereby enhancing the capture of long-range dependencies. Additionally, through a joint data imputation learning strategy, TimeMultiformer exhibits superior performance in time series imputation tasks. Extensive experiments on four real-world datasets demonstrate that TimeMultiformer outperforms state-of-the-art methods in time series imputation both quantitatively and qualitatively, with the mean absolute error (MAE) reduced by 2%–16%, root mean square error (RMSE) reduced by 10%–26%, and the average reduction of mean relative error (MRE) exceeding 10%. The source code of this project is publicly available at: https://github.com/wzq-come-on/TimeMultiformer.git.

Keywords: multivariate time series · Transformer · iTransformer · Missing data imputation

J. Li et al. (Eds.): APWeb-WAIM 2025, LNCS 16115, pp. 3–18, 2026.
https://doi.org/10.1007/978-981-95-5719-6_1

1 Introduction

Multivariate time series [28] are ubiquitous in the real world, being extensively generated and utilized across diverse domains including transportation science [10] and meteorology [18,24]. Each time series not only possesses temporal characteristics but also contains variables that may be interrelated or independent. Through the analysis and mining of multivariate time series, associations and patterns between different variables can be revealed, providing more comprehensive information for decision-making. However, missing values (MVs) are introduced into multivariate time series due to sensor failures during data acquisition, communication errors, and unexpected malfunctions. These MVs severely compromise data interpretability and pose challenges to advanced analytical tasks such as classification and clustering. According to statistics, over 40% of datasets provided by the commonly used UCI[1] database are incomplete.

With the rapid advancements in deep learning and neural networks in recent years, numerous deep learning-based time series imputation methods have been proposed, such as GAIN [25], E^2GAN [14], DeepMVI [2], BRITS [3], etc. Notably, in the field of time series data processing, Transformer can directly model dependency relationships between any positions in a sequence (regardless of their temporal distance) through its self-attention mechanism. This characteristic grants the Transformer unique advantages in handling time series data. Moreover, Transformer effectively leverages both global information (e.g., historical trends) and local context (e.g., adjacent data points) for imputation inference. This dual capability enables the Transformer to excel in time series imputation, offering more accurate and reliable results.

Owing to its superior capability in capturing global dependencies, various Transformer-based time series imputation models have been proposed, such as Informer [29] and SAITS [7]. However, most existing approaches face two limitations: (1) **It does not account for the issue of unequal time intervals between two valid adjacent observations.** In time series data, observations are not always recorded at consistent intervals, leading to variable time lags between two complete observations. This variability implies that the influence of past observations on current values should be adjusted based on the length of these time lags. Therefore, it is essential to consider these changing time lags to accurately model the temporal dynamics and ensure that the influence of past observations is appropriately weighted according to the actual time elapsed. (2) **It inadequately explores the feature dependencies within the multivariate time series.** While most existing works have extensively developed methods to capture temporal dependencies, the importance of feature dependencies has often been overlooked. However, the feature dependencies are crucial for accurate multivariate imputation, as they can significantly enhance the understanding of complex relationships between different variables and improve the overall quality of the imputation process.

[1] https://archive.ics.uci.edu/.

To address these issues, we propose a novel TimeMultiformer framework for multivariate time series imputation. The proposed TimeMultiformer integrates Transformer and iTransformer architectures, where the Transformer component captures temporal dependencies while the iTransformer models the inter-variable (feature) dependencies. Moreover, we introduce a time lag matrix, as detailed in Definition 4, to serve as an input for the TimeMultiformer model. This matrix allows the model to apply a variable influence from past data, effectively accommodating the changing time intervals between observations. We validated the effectiveness of our model on four real-world datasets, demonstrating that it achieves substantial improvements in both imputation tasks and downstream classification tasks compared to previous models. Our main contributions are summarized as follows:

- We propose TimeMultiformer, a novel multivariate time series imputation model that comprehensively leverages attention mechanisms. The proposed model, built upon Transformer and iTranformer, can more accurately capture both temporal and feature dependencies.
- We model a time lag matrix to reflect the impact of the past observed values on the current imputation. By including the time lag matrix as part of TimeMultiformer's input, the model can effectively capture changing temporal correlations among observations.
- We conducted extensive experiments on four real-world datasets, quantitatively and qualitatively evaluating TimeMultiformer to validate the effectiveness of the proposed algorithm.

2 Related Work

In recent years, various missing value imputation methods have been proposed. However, due to space constraints, this paper focuses solely on the most directly relevant works for time series imputation. Based on the typical models, we classify the existing works into the following categories: (1) RNN-based imputation methods, e.g., GRU-D [5], BRITS [3], and M-RNN [26], excel at capturing temporal information for time series imputation. But they are difficult to model long-term temporal dependencies, and thereby degrade performance. (2) GAN-based imputation methods, e.g., GAIN [25], E^2GAN [14], and NAOMI [12], explore the generability of the GANs for time series imputation. However, GANs commonly encounter non-convergence and mode collapse issues, necessitating the design of refined training pipelines to stabilize the adversarial learning process. (3) VAE-based imputation methods, e.g., MIVAE [16], GP-VAE [8], and MIWAE [17], enhance the capture of complex spatiotemporal dependencies through probabilistic modeling. While they have inherent advantages in explicit probabilistic modeling, their generative capability is constrained by the representational power of the latent space. (4) Attention-based imputation methods, e.g., CDSA [15], DeepMVI [2], and SAITS [7], utilize self-attention techniques to model time series. Attention-based models usually outperform other models due to their advantages in handling remote dependencies and parallel processing capabilities. However, they increase the computational cost when dealing with long sequences, which can lead to slower training and inference.

3 Problem Statement

In this section, we first introduce the notations and definitions used in this paper and describe our research objectives.

Definition 1. *We denote the multivariate time series as* $\mathbf{X} = (\mathbf{x}_{t_1}, \mathbf{x}_{t_2}, \cdots, \mathbf{x}_{t_n}) \in \mathbb{R}^{n \times d}$*, representing a sequence of observations arriving at time points* $\mathbf{T} = (t_1, t_2, \cdots, t_n)$*. Each* $\mathbf{x}_{t_i}$ *is a d-dimensional observation of* $\mathbf{X}$*, and* $x_{t_i}^j$ *denotes the* j*th variable of* $\mathbf{x}_{t_i}$*. Notably, if any observation* $x_{t_i}^j$ *is missing, the time series* $\mathbf{X}$ *is considered incomplete.*

Definition 2. *The mask matrix* $\mathbf{M} \in \mathbb{R}^{n \times d}$ *is defined to indicate the missingness of the multivariate time series* $\mathbf{X}$*. Each entry* $m_{t_i}^j$ *in* $\mathbf{M}$ *corresponds to the presence or absence of the value* $x_{t_i}^j$*, defined such that* $m_{t_i}^j = 1$ *when* $x_{t_i}^j$ *is observed and* $m_{t_i}^j = 0$ *otherwise.*

Definition 3. *The artificial mask matrix* $\mathbf{I} \in \mathbb{R}^{n \times d}$ *is used to characterize the status of artificial masking for missing values in the multivariate time series* $\mathbf{X}$*. Each element* $i_{t_i}^j$ *in the matrix* $\mathbf{I}$ *corresponds to indicating whether the value* $x_{t_i}^j$ *is artificially masked, defined such that* $i_{t_i}^j = 1$ *when* $x_{t_i}^j$ *is artificially masked, and* $i_{t_i}^j = 0$ *otherwise.*

In this paper, we assume that the data missing mechanism follows Missing Completely at Random (MCAR), meaning that any feature dimension $x_{t_i}^j$ (where $1 \leq j \leq d$) at time point $t_i \in \mathbf{T}$ may exhibit missingness. Notably, due to the presence of Missing Values (MV), the time intervals between consecutive valid observations exhibit dynamic variability. Such variable time delay information serves as a critical indicator for characterizing the strength of temporal correlations. Thus, we define a time lag matrix followed by [14].

Definition 4. *A time lag matrix* $\Delta \in \mathbb{R}^{n \times d}$ *indicates the time intervals between two adjacent observations, where the mathematical formulation for each individual time lag* $\delta_{t_i}^j$ *within* $\boldsymbol{\Delta}$ *is defined as:*

$$\delta_{t_i}^j = \begin{cases} t_i - t_{i-1} & \text{if } m_{t_{i-1}}^j = 1 \,\&\, i > 0 \\ \delta_{t_{i-1}}^j + t_i - t_{i-1} & \text{if } m_{t_{i-1}}^j = 0 \,\&\, i > 0 \\ 0 & \text{if } i == 0 \end{cases} \tag{1}$$

MTS Imputation. Given an incomplete multivariate time series $\mathbf{X}$, the MTS imputation is to generate a complete time series $\widetilde{\mathbf{X}}$ by replacing the missing values in $\mathbf{X}$ with plausible ones (close to the ground truth) through an MV imputation model $\mathbf{M}(\mathbf{X}, \mathbf{M}, \boldsymbol{\Delta})$.

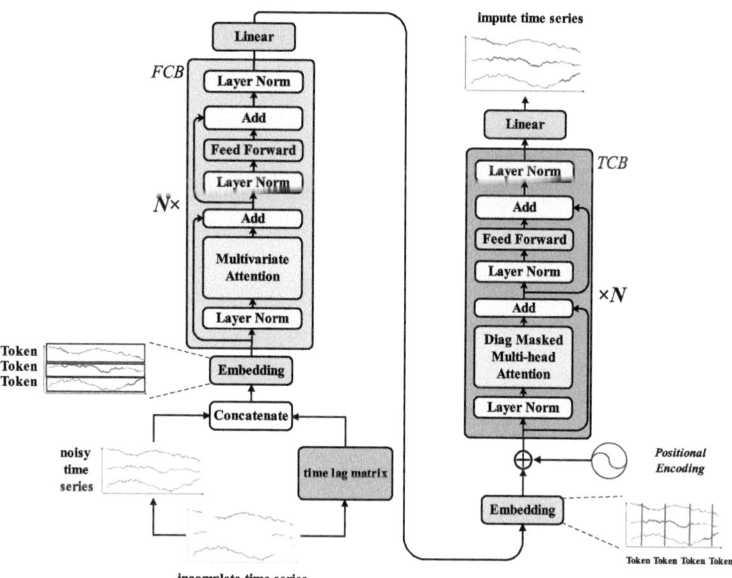

Fig. 1. Architectural Overview of the TimeMultiformer Model: The framework consists of two core components: the Feature Dependencies Learning Net (FDLN) and the Temporal Dependencies Learning Net (TDLN).

4 Methodology

In this section, we first outline the proposed TimeMultiformer. Then, we present the details of each component of the model.

4.1 TimeMultiformer-An Overview

As shown in Fig 1, the proposed TimeMultiformer employs a collaborative architecture of Transformer and iTransformer to construct a Feature Dependencies Learning Net (FDLN) and a Temporal Dependencies Learning Net (TDLN). It overcomes the limitations of traditional time-series modeling methods through a dual-pathway modeling mechanism. TimeMultiformer first utilizes FDLN to learn feature dependencies. Taking the time series of each feature as input, this module addresses the issue of data misalignment caused by unequal sampling intervals of adjacent observations by introducing a time lag matrix as an additional input. Subsequently, TDLN is employed, with the observations composed of all features at each timestamp serving as input, to learn temporal dependencies. Moreover, to mitigate the model's over-reliance on the current time-step information during data imputation, we modify the Transformer by adopting a diagonal masking mechanism [19]. By suppressing the diagonal elements of the attention map, the model is compelled to focus on other time steps, thereby enabling precise capture of temporal dependencies and feature correlations and enhancing imputation performance.

Compared with the standard Transformer [22], which incurs information loss in the feature dimension due to global attention calculations along the sequence dimension, and the iTransformer [11], which struggles to capture long-range temporal patterns when performing attention mapping in the feature dimension, this architecture innovatively enables the modeling of cross-variable correlations and temporal dependencies.

4.2 Feature Dependencies Learning Net (FDLN)

Network Input: Given an incomplete multivariate time series $\mathbf{X}$, the FDLN takes as input the noise matrix $\widetilde{\mathbf{X}}$ and the time lag matrix Δ computed from $\mathbf{X}$. Specifically, we first generate a random noise matrix $\mathbf{Z} \in \mathbb{R}^{n \times d}$, where each element $z_{t_i}^j \sim \mathcal{N}(0, 1)$, and fill the missing values in $\mathbf{X}$ with entries from $\mathbf{Z}$, such that $\widetilde{\mathbf{X}} = \mathbf{M} \odot \mathbf{X} + (1 - \mathbf{M}) \odot \mathbf{Z}$ (unlike most approaches that directly fill missing values with zeros). This noise matrix aids the model in learning more effectively.

Network Architecture: As illustrated in Fig 1, the FDLN comprises an Embedding layer and N stacked Feature Capture Blocks (FCBs), where each block consists of self-attention, feed-forward network, normalization layer, etc. The architecture closely resembles that of the iTransformer encoder. Then, we concatenate $\widetilde{\mathbf{X}}$ and Δ, feed them into the embedding layer, and obtain the FDLN input $\mathbf{X}_I$ as shown below.

$$\mathbf{X}_I = \text{Embedding}(\text{Concat}(\overline{\mathbf{X}}, \Delta)) \tag{2}$$

Secondly, as previously described, the network contains N stacked FCBs. Inspired by Vaswani et al., the FCB innovatively treats the full time series of each variable as independent processes. We take $\mathbf{X}_I$ as the input to the FCBs and obtain $\mathbf{X}_F$, as shown in the following equation:

$$\mathbf{X}_F = \text{FCBs}(\mathbf{X}_I) \tag{3}$$

Notably, the task of generating the predicted sequence is essentially delegated to linear layers—which has been proven effective by previous work [6]. Therefore, we ultimately utilize linear layers to generate the imputation results of the Feature Dependencies Learning Network (FDLN). The formula is as follows:

$$\mathbf{X}_{FDLN} = LN(\mathbf{X}_F) \tag{4}$$

4.3 Temporal Dependencies Learning Net (TDLN)

Network Input: In this study, the imputed matrix generated by the Feature Dependencies Learning Net $\mathbf{X}_{FDLN}$ serves as the input to the Temporal Dependencies Learning Net.

Network Architecture: As shown in the Fig. 1, the Temporal Dependencies Learning Net comprises a Positional encoding layer, N Temporal Capture Blocks(TCBs), and a linear layer, with an architecture closely resembling that of the Transformer.

Positional Encoding: Since the self-attention mechanism lacks inherent awareness of the position or order of each observation, a positional encoding layer is introduced to provide the model with information about the positions of observations in the time series. Incorporating relative positional encoding facilitates capturing temporal dependencies and feature correlations between observations.

Specifically, for the i-th observation x_{ti} in the time series X, the computation of its positional encoding is as follows:

$$\text{PE}(\mathbf{x}_{t_i}) = \begin{cases} sin(w_k \cdot i), & \text{if} i == 2k \\ cos(w_k \cdot i), & \text{if} i == 2k+1 \end{cases} \tag{5}$$

where $w_k = \frac{1}{10000^{\frac{2k}{d_m}}}$, and d_m represents the number of dimensions of the exported position encoding.

Temporal Capture Blocks: As described previously, the Temporal Dependencies Learning Net contains N Temporal Capture Blocks. Each block is composed of a diagonally masked multi-head attention sub-block, a feed-forward sub-block, as well as components like the layer normalization layer and the residual connection layer. Inspired by SAITS [7], we employ diagonally masked multi-head attention (DiagMaskedMHA)—an improvement based on the single-head attention mechanism proposed by Vaswani et al. [22] in 2017—to replace traditional multi-head attention. The specific formula for DiagMaskedMHA is as follows:

$$\begin{aligned} &\text{DiagMaskedMHA}(Q, K, V) \\ &\qquad = Concat(head_1, head_2, \cdots, head_h)W^O \end{aligned} \tag{6}$$

where Q is the query vector, K is the key vector, and V is the value vector, which respectively correspond to dimensions d_k, d_k, and d_v. Additionally, h denotes the number of heads, and W^O is the output transformation matrix. The output of the i-th head, head$_i$, is defined as follows:

$$\begin{aligned} head_i &= \text{DiagMaskedAttn}(Q_i, K_i, V_i) \\ &= \text{Softmax}\left(\text{DiagMask}\left(\frac{Q_i K_i^T}{\sqrt{d_k}}\right)\right) V_i \end{aligned} \tag{7}$$

where $Q_i = QW_i^Q$, $K_i = KW_i^K$, and $V_i = VW_i^V$, with (W_i^Q, W_i^K, W_i^V) denoting the weight matrices for the i-th head's (Q, K, V), respectively. Unlike traditional MHA, where Head$_i$ = Softmax $\left(\frac{Q_i K_i^\top}{\sqrt{d_k}}\right) V$, DiagMaskedMHA modifies the design by setting the diagonal values of the score matrix $\left(\frac{Q_i K_i^\top}{\sqrt{d_k}}\right)$ to $-\infty$, ensuring that the corresponding weights approach zero after applying the softmax function. The specific functional formula for DiagMaskedMHA is as follows:

$$\text{DiagMask}\left(\frac{QK^T}{\sqrt{d_k}}\right) = \left(\frac{QK^T}{\sqrt{d_k}}\right) \cdot A_m \tag{8}$$

$$A_m(i,j) = \begin{cases} -\infty & \text{if} i = j \\ 1 & \text{if} i \neq j \end{cases} \tag{9}$$

The DiagMask operation ensures that the estimation of missing values (MV) depends solely on other observations, thereby preventing them from being influenced by their own estimation.

The DiagMaskedMHA module proposed in this study achieves the joint capture of temporal dependencies and feature correlations through a single attention operation. However, the internal structure of the classical multi-head attention mechanism, dominated by linear transformations, exhibits limitations in representational capacity when modeling complex data patterns compared to nonlinear transformations.

To address this, we introduce a feed-forward sub-block after the DiagMaskedMHA sub-module, enhancing the overall representational learning efficiency of the model through nonlinear enhancement.

The Feed-Forward sub-block designed in this study adopts a two-layer cascaded fully connected architecture, characterized by a position-aware independent feature evolution mechanism. Specifically, the module consists of two fully connected layers with independent parameters, where each neuron responds exclusively to the input vector at the corresponding temporal position—i.e., performing parallel and independent processing (position-wise processing) on the feature vector of each time step in the input sequence. This design preserves the integrity of local temporal features while enabling deep reconstruction of the feature space through nonlinear transformations. Given the input feature vector $\mathbf{x}_f \in \mathbb{R}^d$ to the current feed-forward sub-module, its specific definition is as follows:

$$\text{FFN}(\mathbf{x}_f) = \text{ReLU}(\mathbf{x}_f \cdot \mathbf{W}_1 + \mathbf{b}_1) \cdot \mathbf{W}_2 + \mathbf{b}_2 \tag{10}$$

where W_1, W_2, b_1, and b_2 are learnable parameters. As shown in the formula, the feed-forward sub-block plays a crucial role in learning the output distribution, thereby facilitating time series imputation.

Additionally, layer normalization and residual connections are key components of the Transformer. The formula for layer normalization is as follows:

$$\text{LayerNorm}(\mathbf{x}_L) = \frac{\mathbf{x}_L - \mu}{\sigma} \cdot \mathbf{W}_L + \mathbf{b}_L \tag{11}$$

where μ and σ denote the mean and standard deviation of $\mathbf{x}_L$, respectively, and W_L and b_L are trainable parameters.

Residual connections serve primarily to optimize model training by duplicating the information from the previous layer: one copy is directly transmitted to the next layer, while the other is processed through the current layer. The two results—i.e., the direct transmission and the transformed output of the current layer—are summed to form the input for the next layer. This design ensures that at least the information from the previous layer is preserved, thereby enhancing model performance.

The data processing flow of TDLN can be summarized as follows:

$$\mathbf{X}_{PE} = \text{PE}(\mathbf{X}_{FDLN}) \tag{12}$$

$$\mathbf{X}_S = \text{TCBs}(\mathbf{X}_{PE}) \tag{13}$$

$$\widehat{\mathbf{X}} = \mathbf{X}_{TDLN} = LN(\mathbf{X}_S) \tag{14}$$

Among them, in Eq 12, $\mathbf{X}_{PE}$ represents the output of $\mathbf{X}_{FDLN}$ after positional encoding. $\mathbf{X}_S$ in Eq 13 denotes the output after passing through N Temporal Capture Blocks. $\widehat{\mathbf{X}}$ in Eq 14 signifies the final output of the entire model.

4.4 Loss Functions of Learning Objectives

To facilitate model training, we propose a joint data imputation learning task based on SAITS [7]. As illustrated in the figure, the joint data imputation learning task consists of an Observed Value Imputation Task and an Artificial Mask Imputation Task. Both tasks employ the MAE loss function defined in Eq. 19 (denoted as ℓ_{MAE}), which takes three input parameters: estimation, target, and mask and calculates the mean absolute error (MAE) between the estimation and target at positions indicated by the mask.

As shown in Eq. 15, $\mathcal{L}_{\text{OVIT}}$ is calculated by summing the losses of $\mathbf{X}_{FDLN}$ and $\mathbf{X}_{TDLN}$. To prevent it from dominating the gradient direction due to excessively large magnitude, its final value is normalized by a weighting factor of 2 (i.e., taking the arithmetic mean of the two). As shown in Eq. 16, $\mathcal{L}_{\text{AMIT}}$ is the loss calculated over the mask vector I for the final imputed matrix $\widehat{\mathbf{X}}$. As shown in Eq. 17, the final loss $\mathcal{L}$ is obtained by summing $\mathcal{L}_{\text{OVIT}}$ and $\mathcal{L}_{\text{AMIT}}$ in a certain proportion. Here, μ and λ serve as hyperparameters that regulate the weights of each component of the loss function.

$$\mathcal{L}_{\text{OVIT}} = \frac{1}{2}\left(\ell_{\text{MAE}}\left(\mathbf{X}_{FDLN}, \mathbf{X}, \hat{M}\right) + \ell_{\text{MAE}}\left(\mathbf{X}_{TDLN}, \mathbf{X}, \hat{M}\right)\right) \tag{15}$$

$$\mathcal{L}_{\text{AMIT}} = \ell_{\text{MAE}}\left(\widehat{\mathbf{X}}, \mathbf{X}, I\right) \tag{16}$$

$$\mathcal{L} = \mu\mathcal{L}_{\text{OVIT}} + \lambda\mathcal{L}_{\text{AMIT}} \tag{17}$$

4.5 Imputation

Given an incomplete time series $\mathbf{X}$, we reconstruct the complete time series $\hat{\mathbf{X}}$ using TimeMultiformer. With the joint data imputation learning mechanism, the estimates at corresponding positions in $\hat{\mathbf{X}}$ are ultimately used to impute the missing parts in $\mathbf{X}$, and the resulting complete imputed time series is denoted as:

$$\tilde{X} = \mathbf{X} \odot \mathbf{M} + \widehat{\mathbf{X}} \odot (1 - \mathbf{M}) \tag{18}$$

5 Experiments

5.1 Experimental Settings

Datasets: We adopt four real-world time series datasets, i.e., PhysioNet-2012 (PhysioNet 2012 Mortality Prediction Challenge) [9], Air-Quality (Beijing Multi-Site Air-Quality) [27], Electricity (Electricity Load Diagrams) [21], and ETT [1] (Electricity Transformer Temperature) to conduct experiments.
Algorithms for Comparison: We evaluate the proposed TimeMultiformer against nine state-of-the-art time series imputation algorithms, including Median, Last, GRUI-GAN [13], E^2GAN [14], M-RNN [26], GP-VAE [8], BRITS [3], Transformer [22], SAITS [7] and MTSCI [30]. The Median and Last are two naive imputation methods in which missing values (MVs) are replaced by the median of the training set and the last observed value, respectively. GRUI-GAN and E^2GAN are state-of-the-art GAN-based time series imputation methods proposed by Luo et al. [13,14]. M-RNN, GP-VAE, and BRITS are autoregressive imputation models that leverage RNNs to capture temporal correlations. Transformer and SAITS represent the latest attention-based time series imputation frameworks, which process input data in parallel and globally.
Model Settings: We implement the proposed TimeMultiformer using PyTorch, building extensively upon established methodologies for model architecture design. The hyperparameter settings of TimeMultiformer are detailed in Table 1. Here, the parameter n_groups denotes the number of Temporal Capture Blocks, depth represents the number of Feature Capture Blocks, and n_head stands for the number of heads in the multi-head attention mechanism. Although the model achieves satisfactory performance with the final parameter configuration described in this table, there remains potential for further optimization. All models were trained with the Adam optimizer on NVIDIA RTX A6000 GPUs.
Measurements: We employ three evaluation metrics—mean absolute error (MAE), root mean square error (RMSE), and mean relative error (MRE)—to assess the missing value (MV) imputation performance of different models. Notably, imputation errors are calculated exclusively for the missing values specified by the mask matrix **M**.

$$\mathrm{MAE}(\mathbf{X}, \widetilde{\mathbf{X}}, \mathbf{M}) = \frac{\sum_{t_i=t_1}^{t_n} \sum_{j=1}^{d} \left| \left(x_{t_i}^j - \widetilde{x}_{t_i}^j \right) \cdot m_{t_i}^j \right|}{\sum_{t_i=t_1}^{t_n} \sum_{j=1}^{d} m_{t_i}^j} \tag{19}$$

$$\mathrm{RMSE}(\mathbf{X}, \widetilde{\mathbf{X}}, \mathbf{M}) = \sqrt{\frac{\sum_{t_i=t_1}^{t_n} \sum_{j=1}^{d} \left[\left(x_{t_i}^j - \widetilde{x}_{t_i}^j \right)^2 \cdot m_{t_i}^j \right]}{\sum_{t_i=t_1}^{t_n} \sum_{j=1}^{d} m_{t_i}^j}} \tag{20}$$

$$\mathrm{MRE}(\mathbf{X}, \widetilde{\mathbf{X}}, \mathbf{M}) = \frac{\sum_{t_i=t_1}^{t_n} \sum_{j=1}^{d} \left| \left(x_{t_i}^j - \widetilde{x}_{t_i}^j \right) \cdot m_{t_i}^j \right|}{\sum_{t_i=t_1}^{t_n} \sum_{j=1}^{d} \left| \widetilde{x}_{t_i}^j \cdot m_{t_i}^j \right|} \tag{21}$$

Table 1. Hyper-parameters Settings

Hyper-parameters	PhysioNet-2012	Air-Quality	ETT(m1)	Electricity
batch_size	128	128	128	128
lr	0.0005	0.0001	0.001	0.0002
d_k	32	128	32	128
d_model	512	1024	1024	1024
d_v	64	64	32	128
epochs	1000	10000	10000	1000
n_group	2	2	2	5
depth	1	1	2	2
n_head	8	4	1	8

5.2 Comparison with Baselines

First, we present the imputation errors measured by three metrics (MAE, RMSE, and MRE) on four datasets with a 10% missing rate. As shown in Table 2, recent deep-learning-based imputation models generally outperform the Median and Last methods, which validates the effectiveness of deep learning models in time series imputation. Additionally, in most scenarios, attention-based models (e.g., Transformer and SAITS) generally surpass pure generative adversarial network (GAN)-based models (i.e., GRUI-GAN and E^2GAN) and recurrent neural network (RNN)-based models (i.e., M-RNN, GP-VAE, and BRITS). The TimeMultiformer model proposed in this paper, constructed upon Transformer and iTransformer, demonstrates robust performance by accurately capturing temporal and feature dependencies, achieving a general performance improvement of approximately 10% compared to other attention-based models. Due to the high dimensionality and long time series characteristics of the Electricity dataset, GRUI-GAN and E^2GAN encounter the problem of loss explosion and thus fail to produce interpolation results. When running the MTSCI based on diffusion models, it brings an extremely high computational load, leading to excessive GPU resource occupation and long operation time. Therefore, the relevant experimental results are not presented on this dataset for the time being.

Next, to further demonstrate the superiority of TimeMultiformer, Table 3 presents the imputation performance of several state-of-the-art models on the Electricity dataset across different missing rates (20%~70%). It is obvious that the imputation errors of all deep learning-based imputation models gradually increase as the missing rate rises, which is because there is less valid information available for multivariate imputation.

5.3 Applications in Classification

Given the widespread presence of missing values (MVs) in real-world datasets, tasks such as classification and pattern recognition face significant challenges. To

Table 2. Performance comparison for Imputation

Method	PhysioNet-2012	Air-Quality
Median	0.725/0.985/103.1%	0.761/1.173/107.2%
Last	0.850/1.188/118.3%	0.948/1.389/129.1%
GRUI-GAN	0.760/1.021/107.0%	0.766/1.155/108.1%
E^2GAN	0.698/0.944/99.1%	0.752/1.124/105.7%
M-RNN	0.521/0.765/74.9%	0.302/0.651/42.0%
GP-VAE	0.410/0.655/57.1%	0.273/0.632/38.3%
BRITS	0.259/0.780/36.5%	0.159/0.554/22.6%
Transformer	0.197/0.466/27.5%	0.168/0.571/23.3%
SAITS	0.186/0.431/26.6%	0.143/0.336/20.3%
MTSCI	**0.142**/0.389/**24.6%**	0.140/0.408/19.7%
TimeMultiformer	0.184/**0.319**/ 27.8%	**0.118/0.303/16.7%**
Method	ETT(m1)	Electricity
Median	1.151/1.862/139.9%	2.088/2.739/112.1%
Last	0.977/1.257/95.9%	0.988/1.497/51.3%
GRUI-GAN	0.603/0.710/94.2%	/
E^2GAN	0.558/0.688/87.0%	/
M-RNN	0.389/0.446/32.1%	1.231/1.848/65.8%
GP-VAE	0.277/0.322/15.9%	1.113/1.591/58.9%
BRITS	0.133/0.264/12.8%	0.881/1.333/46.3%
Transformer	0.121/0.193/11.8%	0.877/1.327/45.6%
SAITS	0.098/0.151/9.3%	0.796/1.232/42.6%
MTSCI	0.238/0.379/18.6%	/
TimeMultiformer	**0.084/0.125/8.0%**	**0.572/0.945/30.6%**

further evaluate the effectiveness of TimeMultiformer, we conducted a real-world data classification experiment using the PhysioNet-2012 dataset. The rationale of the experimental design is that improved input data quality (specifically, the imputation results generated by our model) should enhance the performance of subsequent classification tasks, with the imputed data serving as the input for these tasks. We developed an RNN-based classifier with configurations identical to those used in SAITS.

Figure 2 reports the classification results of data imputed by existing methods and data processed by TimeMultiformer (we use three metrics to evaluate the classification results: ROC-AUC [4], PR-AUC [20], and F1-score [23]). The results show that TimeMultiformer achieves the best performance across all metrics. Compared with the latest state-of-the-art (SOTA) model, it significantly improves ROC-AUC, PR-AUC, and F1-score by 0.7%, 3.8%, and 1.4%, respectively. The results demonstrate the superiority and general applicability of the proposed TimeMultiformer.

Table 3. Performance comparison of different methods on the Electricity dataset across varying missing rates from 20% to 70% is presented. The reported metrics are MAE/RMSE/MRE, where lower values indicate better performance.

Method	20%	30%	40%
GP-VAE	1.120/1.497/59.9%	1.012/1.540/56.2%	1.090/1.567/58.1%
BRITS	0.933/1.412/49.9%	0.942/1.433/50.4%	0.988/1.489/53.9%
Transformer	0.851/1.325/45.4%	0.857/1.331/45.6%	0.878/1.389/46.9%
SAITS	0.763/1.187/40.8%	0.790/1.223/42.3%	0.869/1.314/46.7%
TimeMultiformer	**0.587/0.999/31.4%**	**0.725/1.106/40.2%**	**0.833/1.274/45.1%**
Method	50%	60%	70%
GP-VAE	1.089/1.567/58.6%	1.103/1.621/59.1%	1.042/1.601/55.7%
BRITS	1.021/1.528/55.1%	1.103/1.606/59.1%	1.092/1.611/58.6%
Transformer	0.901/1.418/48.2%	0.898/1.412/48.1%	0.908/1.432/48.7%
SAITS	0.876/1.377/46.9%	**0.892**/1.328/**47.9%**	**0.898**/1.273/**48.1%**
TimeMultiformer	**0.875/1.312/46.9%**	0.903/**1.283**/48.5%	0.907/**1.263**/48.8%

Table 4. Ablation Experiment results with each part of modifications

Model	PhysioNet-2012	Air-Quality
Base	0.304/0.466/45.8%	0.129/0.330/18.3%
Base + DiagMask	0.298/0.447/45.0%	0.129/0.330/18.3%
Base + DiagMask + Δ	0.319/0.474/48.1%	0.128/0.316/18.2%
TimeMultiformer	**0.189/0.327/28.5%**	**0.118/0.303/16.7%**
Model	ETT(m1)	Electricity
Base	0.129/0.200/12.3%	0.864/1.379/46.3%
Base + DiagMask	0.159/0.244/15.2%	0.845/1.331/45.3%
Base + DiagMask + Δ	0.127/0.196/12.1%	0.848/1.2583/45.5%
TimeMultiformer	**0.084/0.130/8.0%**	**0.572/0.945/30.6%**

5.4 Ablation Study

To improve the imputation accuracy, TimeMultiformer incorporates three key mechanisms: (1) It takes the time lag information Δ as part of the input to capture the temporal dependencies in sequential data. (2) It adopts the joint data imputation learning strategy (manually masking some observed values) to enhance the model's robustness against incomplete data. (3) It uses the diagonally masked multi-head attention mechanism in imputation to effectively model the long-range dependencies within the sequence. In this subsection, we conduct ablation experiments to verify the effectiveness of each design in improving the missing value (MV) imputation accuracy.

Table 4 presents the ablation results on four real-world datasets. The baseline model excluding all three proposed designs (denoted as 'Base' in the table)

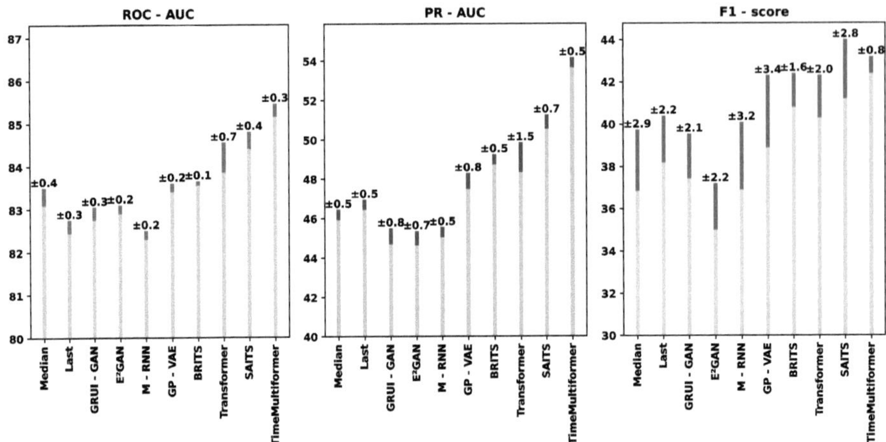

Fig. 2. Downstream Classification Results on PhysioNet-2012 Metrics are based on five independent runs, reported as means ± standard deviations. Light colors denote means, and dark regions represent standard deviations in the figure. Higher values indicate better performance.

exhibits the lowest imputation accuracy, confirming the necessity of these mechanisms. Starting from the base model, iterative integration of each design progressively enhances performance, with TimeMultiformer achieving optimal results once all components are combined. These findings validate the individual contributions of each design in improving missing value (MV) imputation accuracy.

Additionally, we implemented a single iTransformer, serving as the feature dependencies learning net component of TimeMultiformer. As shown in Table 5, TimeMultiformer exhibits further performance gains when integrated with the temporal capture network component.

Table 5. Ablation Experiment Results without Temporal Dependencies Learning Net

Model	PhysioNet-2012	Air-Quality
iTransformer	0.299/0.436/44.6%	0.134/0.339/19.1%
TimeMultiformer	**0.189/0.327/28.5%**	**0.118/0.303/16.7%**
Model	ETT(m1)	Electricity
iTransformer	0.144/0.212/13.8%	0.588/0.988/31.2%
TimeMultiformer	**0.084/0.130/8.0%**	**0.572/0.945/30.6%**

6 Conclusion

This paper proposes TimeMultiformer, an attention-based model that enhances time series imputation accuracy through the collaborative design of feature and temporal dependencies learning net. Trained with a joint optimization strategy, the model outperforms existing methods in imputation tasks. When compared to state-of-the-art (SOTA) models, TimeMultiformer significantly reduces errors across four real-world datasets: mean absolute error (MAE) by 2%-16%, root mean square error (RMSE) by 10%-26%, and mean relative error (MRE) with an average reduction exceeding 10%, achieving the current optimal imputation accuracy for time series data. Downstream classification experiments further demonstrate that the complete data imputed by TimeMultiformer directly improves the performance of classification tasks. Despite the aforementioned advantages, TimeMultiformer still has room for further improvement. In the future, we will explore lightweight attention variants or dynamic pruning strategies to reduce redundant computations while maintaining imputation accuracy. Secondly, the current framework assumes that the missing patterns in time series are random, but actual data often contain non-random or structured missingness. In future work, we will also consider more missing patterns.

References

1. Asuncion, A., Newman, D., et al.: Uci machine learning repository (2007)
2. Bansal, P., Deshpande, P., Sarawagi, S.: Missing value imputation on multidimensional time series. CoRR abs/ arXiv: 2103.01600 (2021)
3. Cao, W., Wang, D., Li, J., Zhou, H., Li, L., Li, Y.: Brits: bidirectional recurrent imputation for time series. Adv. Neural Inform. Process. Syst. **31** (2018)
4. Carrington, A.M., et al.: Deep roc analysis and auc as balanced average accuracy, for improved classifier selection, audit and explanation. IEEE Trans. Pattern Anal. Mach. Intell. **45**(1), 329–341 (2022)
5. Che, Z., Purushotham, S., Cho, K., Sontag, D., Liu, Y.: Recurrent neural networks for multivariate time series with missing values. Sci. Rep. **8**(1), 6085 (2018)
6. Das, A., Kong, W., Leach, A., Mathur, S., Sen, R., Yu, R.: Long-term forecasting with tide: Time-series dense encoder. arXiv preprint arXiv:2304.08424 (2023)
7. Du, W., Côté, D., Liu, Y.: Saits: self-attention-based imputation for time series. Expert Syst. Appl. **219**, 119619 (2023)
8. Fortuin, V., Baranchuk, D., Rätsch, G., Mandt, S.: Gp-vae: deep probabilistic time series imputation. In: International Conference on Artificial Intelligence and Statistics, pp. 1651–1661. PMLR (2020)
9. Goldberger, A.L., et al.: Physiobank, physiotoolkit, and physionet: components of a new research resource for complex physiologic signals. Circulation **101**(23), e215–e220 (2000)
10. Lin, Q., Kuang, H., Zhang, X.: Design and implementation of big data forecasting system based on intelligent transportation. IEEE Trans. Consumer Electron. **70**(1), 1286–1293 (2024). https://doi.org/10.1109/TCE.2023.3319639
11. Liu, Y., Hu, T., Zhang, H., Wu, H., Wang, S., Ma, L., Long, M.: itransformer: inverted transformers are effective for time series forecasting. arXiv preprint arXiv:2310.06625 (2023)
12. Liu, Y., Yu, R., Zheng, S., Zhan, E., Yue, Y.: Naomi: non-autoregressive multiresolution sequence imputation. Adv. Neural Inform. Process. Syst. **32** (2019)
13. Luo, Y., Cai, X., Zhang, Y., Xu, J., et al.: Multivariate time series imputation with generative adversarial networks. Adv. Neural Inform. Process. Syst. **31** (2018)

14. Luo, Y., Zhang, Y., Cai, X., Yuan, X.: E2gan: End-to-end generative adversarial network for multivariate time series imputation. In: Proceedings of the 28th International Joint Conference on artificial Intelligence, pp. 3094–3100. AAAI Press Palo Alto, CA, USA (2019)
15. Ma, J., Shou, Z., Zareian, A., Mansour, H., Vetro, A., Chang, S.F.: Cdsa: cross-dimensional self-attention for multivariate, geo-tagged time series imputation. arXiv preprint arXiv:1905.09904 (2019)
16. Ma, Q., Li, X., Bai, M., Wang, X., Ning, B., Li, G.: Mivae: multiple imputation based on variational auto-encoder. Eng. Appl. Artif. Intell. **123**, 106270 (2023)
17. Mattei, P.A., Frellsen, J.: Miwae: deep generative modelling and imputation of incomplete data sets. In: International Conference on Machine Learning, pp. 4413–4423. PMLR (2019)
18. Shi, X., Chen, Z., Wang, H., Yeung, D.Y., Wong, W.K., Woo, W.c.: Convolutional lstm network: a machine learning approach for precipitation nowcasting. Adv. Neural Inform. Process. Syst. **28** (2015)
19. Shin, J., Lee, Y., Yoon, S., Jung, K.: Fast and accurate deep bidirectional language representations for unsupervised learning. arXiv preprint arXiv:2004.08097 (2020)
20. Sofaer, H.R., Hoeting, J.A., Jarnevich, C.S.: The area under the precision-recall curve as a performance metric for rare binary events. Methods Ecol. Evol. **10**(4), 565–577 (2019)
21. Trindade, A.: ElectricityLoadDiagrams20112014. UCI Machine Learning Repository (2015). https://doi.org/10.24432/C58C86
22. Vaswani, A., et al.: Attention is all you need. Adv. Neural Inform. Process. Syst.**30** (2017)
23. Yacouby, R., Axman, D.: Probabilistic extension of precision, recall, and f1 score for more thorough evaluation of classification models. In: Proceedings of the First Workshop on Evaluation and Comparison of NLP Systems, pp. 79–91 (2020)
24. Yi, X., Zheng, Y., Zhang, J., Li, T.: St-mvl: filling missing values in geo-sensory time series data. In: Proceedings of the 25th International Joint Conference on Artificial Intelligence (2016)
25. Yoon, J., Jordon, J., Schaar, M.: Gain: missing data imputation using generative adversarial nets. In: International Conference on Machine Learning, pp. 5689–5698. PMLR (2018)
26. Yoon, J., Zame, W.R., van der Schaar, M.: Estimating missing data in temporal data streams using multi-directional recurrent neural networks. IEEE Trans. Biomed. Eng. **66**(5), 1477–1490 (2018)
27. Zhang, S., Guo, B., Dong, A., He, J., Xu, Z., Chen, S.X.: Cautionary tales on air-quality improvement in Beijing. Proc. Royal Soc. A: Math. Phys. Eng. Sci. **473**(2205), 20170457 (2017)
28. Zhenxin, L., Fengming, Z., Ying, W., Qian, T., Chao, L.: Method of missing data imputation for multivariate time series. Syst. Eng. Electron. **40**(01), 225–230 (2018)
29. Zhou, H., et al.: Informer: beyond efficient transformer for long sequence time-series forecasting. In: Proceedings of the AAAI Conference on Artificial Intelligence, vol. 35, pp. 11106–11115 (2021)
30. Zhou, J., Li, J., Zheng, G., Wang, X., Zhou, C.: Mtsci: a conditional diffusion model for multivariate time series consistent imputation. In: Proceedings of the 33rd ACM International Conference on Information and Knowledge Management, pp. 3474–3483 (2024)

Heterogeneous Graph-Enhanced Temporal Prediction with Adaptive Monitoring for Industrial Chain Data

Xinran Su, Yongjiao Sun(✉), and Hangxu Ji

School of Computer Science and Engineering, Northeastern University, Shenyang 110819, China

sunyongjiao@mail.neu.edu.cn

Abstract. With the increasing complexity of industrial chains, intelligent monitoring methods for industrial chain data have become essential for economic security and high-quality industrial development. Industrial chain data has temporal and heterogeneous characteristics, requiring intelligent systems that can forecast trends and adjust monitoring strategies in response to anomalies. Current trend prediction methods struggle to model complex heterogeneous interactions between variables, while existing adaptive monitoring approaches lack sensitivity to abnormal trends and cannot efficiently sample multiple variables synchronously. To address these challenges, we propose: (1) HGAN-TPMLP, a trend prediction algorithm combining heterogeneous graph representation learning with a Patch-based MLP structure and temporal causal convolution, improving both short-term feature sensitivity and long-range forecasting; (2) HTAAM, an adaptive monitoring method including HGAN-GRU for trend anomaly detection and EATSA for time-synchronized adaptive sampling based on anomaly scores. Experiments demonstrate that our methods significantly improve prediction accuracy on industrial chain data while reducing unnecessary data transmission and enhancing anomaly coverage, making them well-suited for complex industrial environments.

Keywords: Industrial chain · Heterogeneous graph · Multivariate time series forecasting · Graph neural network · Adaptive monitoring

1 Introduction

With the growing complexity of industrial chain networks, the multi-source heterogeneous data generated by corporate economic activities have become critical information carriers for portraying the operational status of industrial chains. This data—covering transaction logs, logistics traces, and information exchanges—directly reveals the interaction patterns and dependency structures among entities in the chain. Detecting trend changes and anomalies in such data enables the early identification of potential industrial chain risks and shifts in market structure. In the industrial chain network, raw material suppliers, logistics and storage centers, and downstream retailers form close collaborative relationships through complex transportation and information channels. Once logistics nodes experience delivery delays, or when factory actual inventory deviates

J. Li et al. (Eds.): APWeb-WAIM 2025, LNCS 16115, pp. 19–33, 2026.
https://doi.org/10.1007/978-981-95-5719-6_2

from shipping plans, it may trigger chain disruptions in production schedules across numerous enterprises throughout the network. The trend monitoring and anomaly detection of industrial chain data can effectively identify these abnormal phenomena and maintain the stable operation of the industrial chain system.

Industrial chain data is distributed throughout the upstream and downstream of the industrial chain, exhibiting highly dispersed characteristics. This dispersion causes industrial chain data to display significant features including dynamic evolution, multi-source heterogeneity, non-uniform sampling, and complex relational structures. In particular, upstream suppliers and downstream distributors often collect data using different temporal granularities. Furthermore, as a complex system, the overall operational status of industrial chains requires coordinated observation across multiple dimensions to be accurately captured. Non-synchronized sampling leads to inconsistent sampling frequencies and misaligned temporal baselines across dimensions, making it difficult to construct complete system state snapshots. Moreover, anomalies in a single component often propagate to other components within short time intervals, and non-synchronized sampling may miss critical cross-dimensional anomaly propagation processes. These inherent complexities pose severe challenges to traditional deep learning methods in the field of temporal trend prediction and adaptive monitoring. Mainstream time series models such as LSTM and TCN are built on the basic assumption of fixed time intervals, which significantly limits their effectiveness when processing non-uniform sampling data in industrial chains. Although graph representation learning can effectively handle structural and semantic information, traditional graph neural networks like GCN struggle to effectively capture the multiple relationships and temporal evolution features in industrial chains, limiting their ability to perform trend prediction on industrial chain data. Additionally, traditional adaptive monitoring methods lack sensitivity to abnormal trends, focusing primarily on data variation amplitude rather than trend abnormality, making it difficult to precisely monitor and sample critical periods with potential risks.

Industrial chain trend monitoring faces the following major challenges: (1) Industrial chain data exhibits heterogeneity, making it difficult to effectively distinguish trends across different data types. (2) Industrial chain data possesses dynamic evolutionary characteristics, with each component following specific business cycles and fluctuation patterns, making it challenging to effectively capture evolutionary patterns across multiple time scales. (3) The synchronized adaptive sampling of multidimensional industrial chain data remains a significant challenge, hindering the system's ability to gain a macro perspective on trend changes while maintaining efficient resource utilization.

To address the above challenges, this research proposes a novel Temporal Heterogeneous Graph Learning-based Trend Monitoring framework (THeGraL-TM) that integrates node and semantic attention mechanisms with advanced temporal modeling techniques, aimed at effectively predicting trends and detecting anomalies in industrial chain evolution patterns. The framework can be divided into three key components: (1) Heterogeneous graph-based trend prediction. By leveraging a heterogeneous graph attention network combined with a patch-based MLP architecture, we construct a lightweight yet powerful model that effectively captures both complex relationships between variables and temporal patterns. (2) Heterogeneous trend anomaly detection. We design a trend anomaly detection module that integrates graph representation learning with gated recurrent units to identify abnormal trends accurately while minimizing false alarms. (3) Adaptive monitoring mechanism. We combine trend prediction and anomaly detection to develop an adaptive sampling strategy that dynamically adjusts monitoring frequency based on anomaly scores, enabling time-synchronized sampling across multiple dimensions. The main contributions of this study are as follows:

- We propose a new trend prediction method (HGAN-TPMLP) that fuses heterogeneous graph attention networks with temporal convolutional patch-based MLP, which captures dynamic heterogeneous correlations between variables while maintaining computational efficiency. This approach significantly improves prediction accuracy for industrial chain data.
- We propose a neural anomaly detection module (HGAN-GRU) combining heterogeneous graph attention with gated recurrent units, enabling the model to simultaneously capture spatial information exchange between nodes and their temporal evolution characteristics, enhancing the ability to identify long and short-term anomaly patterns in industrial chains.
- We develop an adaptive monitoring framework (HTAAM) that integrates trend prediction, anomaly detection, and adaptive sampling to achieve time-synchronized monitoring across multiple dimensions of industrial chain data, focusing on abnormal trends while significantly reducing data transmission costs.
- We conduct extensive experiments on real-world industrial chain datasets, demonstrating that our framework significantly outperforms existing methods in both prediction accuracy and anomaly detection. Our adaptive monitoring approach effectively covers abnormal periods while reducing overall sampling by up to 95%, proving its practicality in industrial chain monitoring scenarios.

2 Related Work

2.1 Multivariate Time Series Forecasting

Multivariate time series forecasting (MTSF) has evolved significantly from traditional statistical methods like ARIMA [1] and exponential smoothing to advanced deep learning approaches. Early deep learning models for MTSF included recurrent architectures like LSTM [2] and GRU [3], which effectively captured temporal dependencies but struggled with computational efficiency and parallelization. Graph Neural Networks (GNNs) [4] have emerged as powerful tools for modeling relationships between variables in MTSF tasks. Gao et al. [5] proposed MTGNN, which automatically learns dependency relationships between variables through a graph learning module. GAT-LSTM [6] combines graph attention with LSTM for traffic network prediction, while SGST-GNN [7] uses spatial convolution with temporal units for power system load forecasting. Transformer-based models have also gained prominence in time series forecasting. While standard Transformers aren't inherently suited for time series data, specialized variants like Informer [8], TFT [9], and Autoformer [10] have achieved remarkable results. Recently, MLP-based approaches have shown promising performance with reduced computational complexity. Notable examples include PatchTST [11], which applies the patch concept to time series, and Google's TSMixer [12] and TiDE [13], which employ efficient MLP structures for multivariate forecasting.

2.2 Heterogeneous Graph Learning

Heterogeneous graphs contain multiple types of nodes and edges, better representing complex real-world relationships than homogeneous graphs. Meta-paths, defined as relationship sequences connecting different node types, are essential for capturing semantic dependencies in heterogeneous graphs. Heterogeneous Graph Neural Networks (HGNNs) have been developed to effectively process such complex structures. The Heterogeneous Graph Attention Network (HGAN) [14] employs meta-path-based attention to weight different types of neighbors, while the Heterogeneous Graph Transformer (HGT) [15] enhances expressiveness through type-aware attention mechanisms. Chen et al. proposed MFGNN [16], which combines graph neural networks with channel fusion mechanisms for improved prediction, and MAGNN [17], which maintains temporal correlations across different time scales without requiring predefined knowledge of variable relationships.

2.3 Adaptive Monitoring

Adaptive monitoring dynamically adjusts sampling frequencies based on data changes, optimizing resource usage while maintaining monitoring quality. Early approaches included server-side filtering adjustments [18], which performed poorly with changing data distributions. More sophisticated methods like DDASA [19] improved efficiency while ensuring accuracy, and user-driven adaptive sampling [20] allowed customization based on energy-saving requirements. For resource-constrained IoT environments, Trihinas et al. developed the ADMin framework [21], using probabilistic weighted exponential moving average (PEWMA) for frequency adjustment, and later the AdaM framework [22], which combines adaptive sampling with filtering based on trend changes and confidence levels. Recent research has explored federated learning [23] to reduce data transmission by training models on edge devices, and prediction-based methods [24] that transmit data only when necessary for target node selection. While adaptive monitoring has progressed from statistical methods to intelligent approaches, challenges remain in computational resource optimization and processing large-scale heterogeneous data, highlighting the need for further research in deep learning integration and practical application scenarios.

3 Preliminaries

This section presents the formal definitions of key concepts and the problem statement for our research on industrial chain data monitoring.

Definition 1 (Industrial Chain Risk Factor Data). *Industrial chain risk factor data represents multivariate time-series data collected from multiple channels, formally denoted as* $D = \{d_1, d_2, \ldots, d_T\}$*, where* $d_t \in \mathbb{R}^n$ *is an n-dimensional vector at time t representing values from various risk factors across logistics, capital flow, and information flow channels. Each variable in* d_t *can be continuous (e.g., inventory levels, transaction amounts) or categorical (e.g., status indicators).*

Definition 2 (Time-Series Heterogeneous Graph). *A time-series heterogeneous graph for industrial chain data is a dynamic structure denoted as* $G_{TS} = (V, E, N, R, T)$*, where* $T = \{t_1, t_2, \ldots, t_T\}$ *is the sequence of time points,* V *is the set of nodes representing risk factor variables,* E *represents the set of edges between nodes,* N *is the set of node types (logistics, capital flow, information flow), and* R *is the set of relationship types between variables. Each node* $v_i \in V$ *has a type mapping* $\phi_N(v_i) \in N$ *and each edge* $e_{ij} \in E$ *has a relationship type* $\phi_R(e_{ij}) \in R$*. This graph structure captures both static topological relationships and dynamic temporal dependencies among risk factors.*

Trend Prediction Problem: Given historical industrial chain risk factor data $D_{1:t}$ and its corresponding time-series heterogeneous graph G_{TS}, develop a prediction model M_P that accurately forecasts future values $\hat{D}_{t+1:t+h}$ for horizon h, effectively capturing complex heterogeneous relationships among variables.
Adaptive Monitoring Problem: Given prediction results $\hat{D}_{t+1:t+h}$ and a trend anomaly detection mechanism M_A, determine the optimal sampling interval I_t for each time step that satisfies: maximizing anomaly coverage rate while minimizing overall sampling rate; ensuring synchronized sampling across all risk factor variables; and dynamically adjusting sampling frequency based on detected anomalies rather than simple data fluctuations. The solution requires integrating heterogeneous graph learning with time-series prediction and anomaly detection to enable effective time-synchronized adaptive monitoring with focused attention on abnormal trends.

4 Methodology

This section presents our HGAN-TPMLP (Heterogeneous Graph Attention Network with Temporal Convolutional Patch-based Multi-Layer Perceptron) framework for industrial chain data trend prediction. We first formulate the multivariate time series prediction problem, then detail our architecture with its two key components: heterogeneous graph representation learning and temporal patch-based prediction.

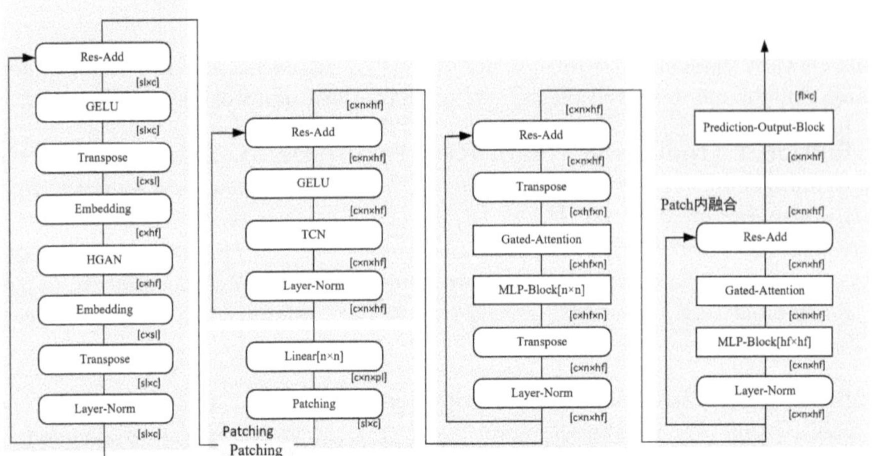

Fig. 1. Overall architecture of the proposed HGAN-TPMLP model.

4.1 Problem Formulation

We formulate industrial chain trend prediction as a multivariate time series forecasting task. Given historical observations $X_{sl \times c} \in \mathbb{R}^{sl \times c}$, where sl denotes the sequence length (lookback window) and c represents the number of variables (channels), our goal is to predict future values $\hat{Y}_{fl \times c} \in \mathbb{R}^{fl \times c}$ for a horizon of length fl:

$$\hat{Y}_{fl \times c} = \mathcal{M}_{MTSF}(X_{sl \times c}) \tag{1}$$

where $\mathcal{M}_{MTSF}$ represents our multivariate time series forecasting model. The model is trained end-to-end using mean squared error:

$$\mathcal{L}_{MSE} = \frac{1}{fl \times c} \sum_{i=1}^{fl} \sum_{j=1}^{c} (Y_{ij} - \hat{Y}_{ij})^2 \tag{2}$$

Unlike standard forecasting approaches, industrial chain data exhibits complex heterogeneous relationships between variables across different channels (logistics, capital flow, information flow). These relationships form a heterogeneous graph structure that must be effectively leveraged to achieve accurate predictions.

4.2 Model Architecture

The HGAN-TPMLP model comprises two main components, as illustrated in Fig. 1: (1) a heterogeneous graph attention network (HGAN) that captures complex variable relationships, and (2) a temporal convolutional patch-based MLP (TPMLP) that efficiently models temporal dynamics.

Heterogeneous Graph Attention Network. The HGAN module captures the complex relationships between variables by modeling them as a heterogeneous graph. Each variable is represented as a node with a specific type (logistics, capital flow, or information flow), while edges represent relationships between variables.

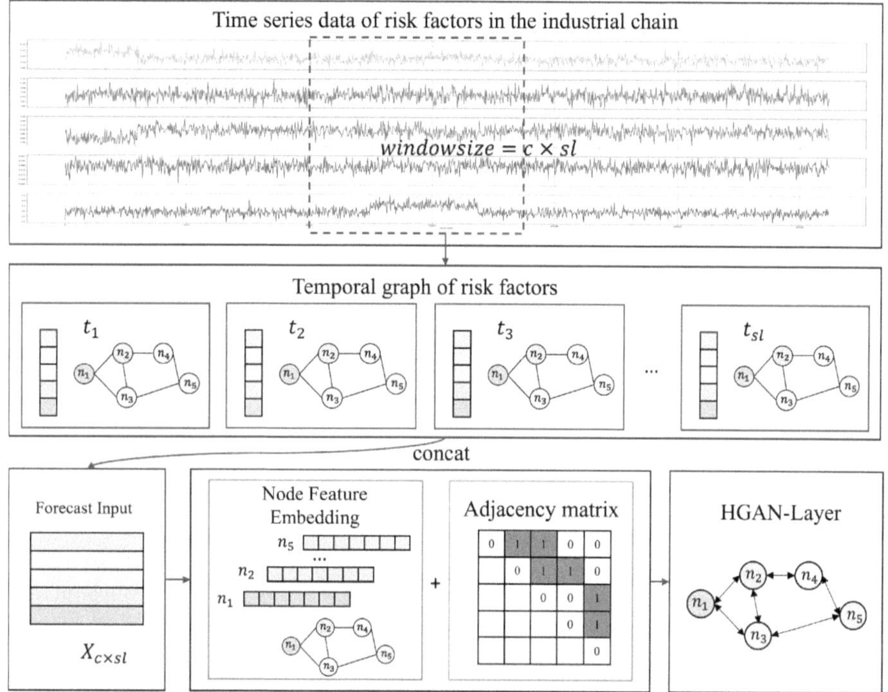

Fig. 2. Modeling process of HGAN module temporal heterogeneous graph

The modeling process of temporal heterogeneous graph for industrial chain data is shown in Fig. 2. Given the input $X_{sl \times c}$, HGAN processes the variable relationships by first obtaining initial representations for each variable node. For each node i, we obtain its initial representation $h_i \in \mathbb{R}^{hf}$, where hf is the hidden feature dimension. These representations are then enhanced through two levels of attention-based aggregation:

Node-Level Aggregation: For each node i with relationship type r, we compute attention coefficients with its neighbors:

$$\alpha_{ij}^{(r)} = \frac{\exp\left(\text{LeakyReLU}\left(a^{(r)T}\left[W^{(r)}h_i \parallel W^{(r)}h_j\right]\right)\right)}{\sum_{k \in \mathcal{N}_i^{(r)}} \exp\left(\text{LeakyReLU}\left(a^{(r)T}\left[W^{(r)}h_i \parallel W^{(r)}h_k\right]\right)\right)} \tag{3}$$

where $W^{(r)}$ is a learnable weight matrix for relationship r, $\|$ denotes concatenation, and $a^{(r)}$ is a learnable attention vector. The node representation is then updated by aggregating features from its neighbors:

$$h_i^{(r)} = \sigma\left(\sum_{j\in\mathcal{N}_i^{(r)}} \alpha_{ij}^{(r)} W^{(r)} h_j\right) \tag{4}$$

where σ is the LeakyReLU activation function.
Semantic-Level Aggregation: To fuse information from different relationship types, we compute importance weights for each relationship:

$$\beta_r = \frac{\exp\left(q^T \cdot \mathrm{ReLU}\left(W_r \sum_{i\in V} h_i^{(r)}\right)\right)}{\sum_{r'\in\mathcal{R}} \exp\left(q^T \cdot \mathrm{ReLU}\left(W_{r'} \sum_{i\in V} h_i^{(r')}\right)\right)} \tag{5}$$

where q is a global context vector and W_r is a transformation matrix. The final node representation is:

$$h_i = \sum_{r\in\mathcal{R}} \beta_r h_i^{(r)} \tag{6}$$

After aggregation, node representations are transformed back to the original dimensions, producing enhanced features $X_{sl\times c}^{\mathcal{G}}$ that incorporate heterogeneous graph information.

Temporal Convolutional Patch-Based MLP. The TPMLP module processes the graph-enhanced features $X_{sl\times c}^{\mathcal{G}}$ to generate forecasts through the following components:
Patching: We divide the temporal dimension into non-overlapping patches of length pl, transforming $X_{sl\times c}^{\mathcal{G}}$ into shape $[c \times n \times pl]$, where $n = sl/pl$ represents the number of patches. This enables efficient local feature extraction.
Multi-scale Temporal Causal Convolution: To capture local temporal patterns at multiple scales, we apply 1D causal convolutions with different kernel sizes ($k \in \{3, 5, 7\}$) to each patch:

$$\hat{x}_t = \sum_{\tau=0}^{k-1} w_\tau x_{t-\tau} \tag{7}$$

where w_τ represents learnable convolution weights. The causal nature ensures no information leakage from future time steps.
Patch Embedding: After convolution, each patch is embedded into a higher-dimensional space through a linear projection: $[c \times n \times pl] \rightarrow [c \times n \times hf]$.
Patch Processing: We employ two complementary fusion modules:

1) *Inter-Patch Fusion* processes information across patches to capture long-term dependencies. For each variable, we apply an MLP-Block along the patch dimension:

$$\text{MLP-Block}(X) = \text{LayerNorm}(X + \text{Dropout}(\text{Linear}(\text{GELU}(\text{Linear}(X))))) \quad (8)$$

2) *Intra-Patch Fusion* processes information within each patch to extract fine-grained features, applying a similar MLP Block along the feature dimension.

Both fusion modules incorporate a Gated Attention (GA) mechanism to selectively emphasize important features:

$$g_i = \sigma((W_g x + b_g)_i), \quad \alpha_i = \frac{\exp((W_a x + b_a)_i)}{\sum_{j=1}^{hf} \exp((W_a x + b_a)_j)} \quad (9)$$

$$y = \sum_{i=1}^{hf} \alpha_i g_i x_i \quad (10)$$

where g_i represents gate values, α_i denotes attention weights, and W_g, W_a, b_g, b_a are learnable parameters.

Forecast Generation: Finally, the processed features are transformed through a prediction head to produce forecasts:

$$\hat{Y}_{fl \times c} = \text{Linear}(\text{GELU}(\text{Linear}(\text{Reshape}(X)))) \quad (11)$$

The combination of heterogeneous graph representation learning and temporal patch-based prediction allows our model to effectively capture both complex variable relationships and temporal dynamics, resulting in accurate forecasting for industrial chain data.

5 Experiments

This section presents comprehensive experimental evaluations of our proposed HGAN-TPMLP model. We first describe the experimental setup, including datasets, implementation details, and evaluation metrics. We then evaluate our model through comparison experiments on industrial chain data and public datasets, followed by ablation studies to validate each component's contribution.

5.1 Experimental Setup

Environment and Datasets. All experiments were conducted on a server with dual Intel Xeon Silver 4310 CPUs @ 2.10 GHz, dual NVIDIA GeForce RTX 4090 24 GB GPUs, 128 GB 3200 MHz RAM, running Linux with Python as the development language.

We conducted experiments on both industrial chain data and public datasets:

- **Supply**: An industrial chain dataset containing 61 variables with 31,200 time points sampled hourly, split in a 7:2:1 ratio for training, validation, and testing.

- **Weather**: 21 variables with 52,695 time points at 10-minute intervals.
- **ETT** datasets: ETTh1 and ETTh2 (hourly data) and ETTm1 and ETTm2 (15-minute data), each containing 7 variables.
- **Traffic**: 862 variables with 17,544 time points recorded hourly.

Hyperparameters and Metrics. Key hyperparameters include: training epochs (100), batch size (32), dropout rates {0.1, 0.3, 0.5, 0.7, 0.9}, hidden dimensions {64, 128}, patch lengths {8, 16}, input sequence length (512), and prediction horizons {96, 192, 336, 720}.

We use Mean Absolute Error (MAE) and Mean Squared Error (MSE) as evaluation metrics:

$$\mathrm{MAE} = \frac{1}{fl \times c} \sum_{i=1}^{fl} \sum_{j=1}^{c} |Y_{ij} - \hat{Y}_{ij}| \tag{12}$$

$$\mathrm{MSE} = \frac{1}{fl \times c} \sum_{i=1}^{fl} \sum_{j=1}^{c} (Y_{ij} - \hat{Y}_{ij})^2 \tag{13}$$

where Y_{ij} and $\hat{Y}_{ij}$ represent the ground truth and predicted values, respectively, for the i-th time step of the j-th variable, fl is the forecast length, and c is the number of variables.

5.2 Results on Industrial Chain Data

We compare our HGAN-TPMLP model with three state-of-the-art baseline models: TFT, Autoformer, and Informer. Table 1 presents the performance on the Supply dataset across different prediction horizons.

Table 1. Prediction performance on the Supply dataset

Horizon	HGAN-TPMLP		TFT		Autoformer		Informer	
	MSE	MAE	MSE	MAE	MSE	MAE	MSE	MAE
96	**0.719**	**0.633**	1.055	0.801	1.044	0.805	1.197	0.856
192	**0.863**	**0.714**	1.045	0.799	1.055	0.811	1.152	0.843
336	**0.825**	**0.694**	1.073	0.803	1.192	0.863	1.254	0.884
720	**0.941**	**0.757**	1.037	0.795	1.054	0.807	1.059	0.804

As shown in Fig. 3, HGAN-TPMLP consistently outperforms all baseline models across different prediction horizons. The improvement is particularly significant in MSE, with reductions of 31.9%, 17.4%, 30.8%, and 9.3% for horizons 96, 192, 336, and 720, respectively, compared to the best-performing baseline. This demonstrates the effectiveness of our approach in modeling the complex relationships in industrial chain data.

5.3 Results on Public Datasets

To evaluate the generalizability of our approach, we tested a variant of our model (TPMLP, without the heterogeneous graph component) on multiple public datasets that lack predefined graph structures. Table 2 presents the results across different datasets and prediction horizons.

Table 2. Prediction performance on public datasets

Dataset	Horizon	TPMLP		TFT		Autoformer		Informer	
		MSE	MAE	MSE	MAE	MSE	MAE	MSE	MAE
Weather	96	**0.196**	**0.258**	0.441	0.474	0.249	0.329	0.354	0.405
	192	**0.288**	**0.332**	0.699	0.599	0.325	0.370	0.419	0.434
	336	**0.344**	**0.386**	0.693	0.596	0.351	0.391	0.583	0.543
	720	**0.242**	**0.296**	1.038	0.753	0.415	0.426	0.916	0.705
ETTh1	96	**0.375**	**0.425**	0.674	0.634	0.435	0.446	0.941	0.769
	192	**0.416**	**0.451**	0.858	0.704	0.456	0.457	1.007	0.786
	336	**0.470**	**0.467**	0.900	0.731	0.486	0.487	1.038	0.784
	720	**0.596**	**0.586**	0.745	0.666	0.515	0.517	1.144	0.857
ETTh2	96	**0.168**	**0.283**	0.409	0.505	0.332	0.368	1.549	0.952
	192	**0.214**	**0.327**	0.953	0.651	0.426	0.434	3.729	1.542
	336	**0.235**	**0.347**	1.006	0.709	0.477	0.479	4.215	1.642
	720	**0.295**	**0.401**	1.187	0.816	0.453	0.490	3.656	1.619
ETTm1	96	**0.408**	**0.419**	0.752	0.626	0.510	0.492	0.626	0.560
	192	**0.513**	**0.483**	0.752	0.649	0.514	0.495	0.725	0.619
	336	**0.658**	**0.543**	0.810	0.674	0.510	0.492	1.005	0.741
	720	**0.944**	**0.653**	0.849	0.694	0.527	0.493	1.133	0.845
ETTm2	96	0.556	0.513	0.386	0.472	**0.205**	**0.293**	0.355	0.462
	192	0.550	0.513	0.739	0.626	**0.278**	**0.336**	0.595	0.586
	336	0.540	0.514	0.477	0.494	**0.343**	**0.379**	1.270	0.871
	720	0.579	0.527	0.523	0.537	**0.414**	**0.419**	3.001	1.267
Traffic	96	**0.395**	**0.287**	0.678	0.362	0.597	0.371	0.733	0.410
	192	**0.405**	**0.289**	0.664	0.355	0.607	0.382	0.777	0.435
	336	**0.416**	**0.295**	0.679	0.354	0.623	0.387	0.776	0.434
	720	**0.453**	**0.317**	0.610	0.325	0.639	0.395	0.827	0.466

The results demonstrate that TPMLP achieves state-of-the-art performance on most datasets, particularly on Weather, ETTh1, ETTh2, and Traffic, across almost all forecasting horizons. On ETTm1, TPMLP consistently outperforms all baselines in terms of MSE. Only on ETTm2 does Autoformer show better performance. These results highlight that even without the heterogeneous graph component, our temporal patching and MLP design effectively capture temporal patterns in diverse time series data.

5.4 Ablation Study

To evaluate the contribution of each component in our HGAN-TPMLP model, we conducted ablation studies by removing key components: (1) TPMLP: removing the heterogeneous graph attention network (HGAN); (2) Patch-MLP: further removing the temporal convolutional network (TCN) from TPMLP. Table 3 presents the results on the Supply dataset.

Table 3. Ablation study results on the Supply dataset

Horizon	HGAN-TPMLP		TPMLP		Patch-MLP	
	MSE	MAE	MSE	MAE	MSE	MAE
96	**0.719**	**0.633**	0.742	0.669	0.763	0.695
192	**0.863**	**0.714**	0.907	0.731	0.928	0.764
336	**0.825**	**0.694**	0.854	0.712	0.873	0.729
720	**0.941**	**0.757**	0.972	0.773	0.965	0.771

As shown in Fig. 4, the full HGAN-TPMLP model consistently outperforms its ablated versions across all prediction horizons. We observe that: (1) Removing HGAN leads to performance degradation, confirming the importance of heterogeneous graph modeling for capturing complex variable relationships in industrial chain data; (2) Further removing the temporal convolution component causes additional performance declines, highlighting its effectiveness in capturing local

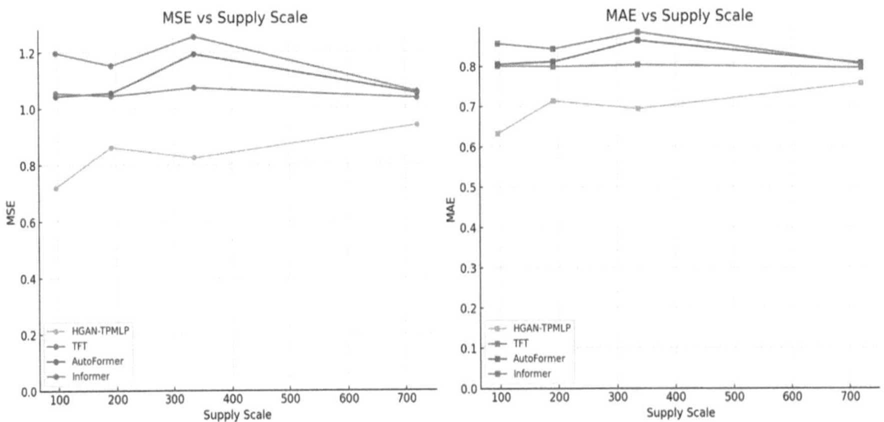

Fig. 3. Performance comparison on Supply dataset across different prediction horizons

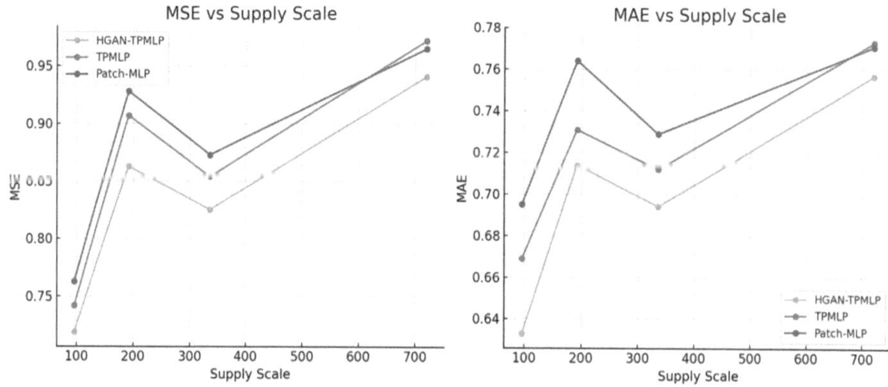

Fig. 4. Ablation study results across different prediction horizons

temporal patterns. These results validate that both HGAN and TCN components contribute significantly to the model's overall performance.

6 Conclusion from Experimental Results

The experimental results clearly demonstrate the effectiveness of our proposed HGAN-TPMLP model for multivariate time series forecasting in industrial chain data. The model significantly outperforms state-of-the-art baseline methods across various prediction horizons. The ablation studies confirm that both the heterogeneous graph attention network and temporal convolutional components contribute substantially to prediction accuracy. Furthermore, even without the graph component, our TPMLP model generalizes well to public datasets, achieving competitive or superior performance. These findings highlight the importance of effectively modeling both temporal patterns and heterogeneous relationships in complex industrial chain data, and validate our design choices for the HGAN-TPMLP architecture.

7 Conclusion

In this paper, we proposed a comprehensive framework for industrial chain data monitoring, including the HGAN-TPMLP prediction model and the HTAAM adaptive monitoring method. Extensive experiments on industrial chain datasets demonstrate that our approach achieves superior performance in trend prediction, anomaly detection, and adaptive monitoring. The HGAN-TPMLP model effectively captures heterogeneous relationships between variables and temporal patterns, resulting in more accurate predictions. The HTAAM framework enables efficient monitoring by focusing resources on anomalous periods, significantly reducing data transmission while maintaining high anomaly coverage.

Acknowledgments. This research is supported by the National Key R&D Program of China under Grant No. 2022YFB3304300; and the NSFC under Grant No. 62402096, 62302084, U2441237 and U23A20297; and the Guangdong Basic and Applied Basic Research Foundation under Grant No. 2023A1515110268.

References

1. Shumway, R.H., Stoffer, D.S.: Arima models. In: Time Series Analysis and Its Applications: with R Examples, pp. 75–163 (2017)
2. Yong, Yu., Si, X., Changhua, H., Zhang, J.: A review of recurrent neural networks: LSTM cells and network architectures. Neural Comput. **31**(7), 1235–1270 (2019)
3. Dey, R., Salem, F.M.: Gate-variants of gated recurrent unit (GRU) neural networks. In: 2017 IEEE 60th International Midwest Symposium on Circuits and Systems (MWSCAS), pp. 1597–1600. IEEE (2017)
4. Wu, Z., Pan, S., Chen, F., Long, G., Zhang, C., Yu, P.S.: A comprehensive survey on graph neural networks. IEEE Trans. Neural Netw. Learn. Syst. **32**(1), 4–24 (2020)
5. Gao, J., Zhang, X., Tian, L., Liu, Y., Wang, J., Li, Z., Xiaohua, H.: MTGNN: multi-task graph neural network based few-shot learning for disease similarity measurement. Methods **198**, 88–95 (2022)
6. Zhao, J., Yan, Z., Zhou, Z.Z., Chen, X., Bing, W., Wang, S.: A ship trajectory prediction method based on gat and LSTM. Ocean Eng. **289**, 116159 (2023)
7. Lee, J., Liu, Y., Yu, L.: SGST: an open source semantic geostreaming toolkit. In: Proceedings of the 2nd ACM SIGSPATIAL International Workshop on GeoStreaming, pp. 17–20 (2011)
8. Zhou, H., et al.: Informer: beyond efficient transformer for long sequence time-series forecasting. In: Proceedings of the AAAI Conference on Artificial Intelligence, vol. 35, pp. 11106–11115 (2021)
9. Weimer, P.K.: The TFT a new thin-film transistor. Proc. IRE **50**(6), 1462–1469 (1962)
10. Haixu, W., Jiehui, X., Wang, J., Long, M.: AutoFormer: decomposition transformers with auto-correlation for long-term series forecasting. Adv. Neural. Inf. Process. Syst. **34**, 22419–22430 (2021)
11. Huang, X., Tang, J., Shen, Y.: Long time series of ocean wave prediction based on PATCHTST model. Ocean Eng. **301**, 117572 (2024)
12. Ekambaram, V., Jati, A., Nguyen, N., Sinthong, P., Kalagnanam, J.: TSMIXER: lightweight MLP-mixer model for multivariate time series forecasting. In: Proceedings of the 29th ACM SIGKDD Conference on Knowledge Discovery and Data Mining, pp. 459–469 (2023)
13. Stammer, D., et al.: Accuracy assessment of global barotropic ocean tide models. Rev. Geophys. **52**(3), 243–282 (2014)
14. Guo, J., et al.: HGAN: hierarchical graph alignment network for image-text retrieval. IEEE Trans. Multimedia **25**, 9189–9202 (2023)
15. Abe, K., Nomura, N., Suzuki, S.: Biofilms: hot spots of horizontal gene transfer (HGT) in aquatic environments, with a focus on a new HGT mechanism. FEMS Microbiol. Ecol. **96**(5), fiaa031 (2020)
16. Ye, W., Li, J., Cai, X.: MFGNN: multi-scale feature-attentive graph neural networks for molecular property prediction. J. Comput. Chem. **46**(3), e70011 (2025)

17. Xinyu, F., Zhang, J., Meng, Z., King, I.: MAGNN: Metapath aggregated graph neural network for heterogeneous graph embedding. In: Proceedings of the Web Conference, vol. 2020, pp. 2331–2341 (2020)
18. Dykes, S.G., Robbins, K.A., Jeffery, C.L.: An empirical evaluation of client-side server selection algorithms. In: Proceedings IEEE INFOCOM 2000. Conference on Computer Communications. Nineteenth Annual Joint Conference of the IEEE Computer and Communications Societies (Cat. No. 00CH37064), vol. 3, pp. 1361–1370. IEEE (2000)
19. Shu, T., Xia, M., Chen, J., De Silva, C.: An energy efficient adaptive sampling algorithm in a sensor network for automated water quality monitoring. Sensors **17**(11), 2551 (2017)
20. Kim-Hung, L., Le-Trung, Q.: User-driven adaptive sampling for massive internet of things. IEEE Access **8**, 135798–135810 (2020)
21. Mishra, A.K., Tyagi, A.K., Dananjayan, S., Rajavat, A., Rawat, H. and Rawat, A.: Revolutionizing government operations: the impact of artificial intelligence in public administration. Convers. Artif. Intell., 607–634 (2024)
22. Huang, H.-H., Shu, J., Liang, Y.: MUMA: a multi-omics meta-learning algorithm for data interpretation and classification. IEEE J. Biomed. Health Inform. **28**(4), 2428–2436 (2024)
23. Abreha, H.G., Hayajneh, M., Serhani, M.A.: Federated learning in edge computing: a systematic survey. Sensors **22**(2), 450 (2022)
24. Płaczek, B.: Prediction-based data reduction with dynamic target node selection in IoT sensor networks. Futur. Gener. Comput. Syst. **152**, 225–238 (2024)

Finding Maximum Common Subgraphs Efficiently Through Dynamic Bidirectional Vertex Selection

Yicheng Hu[1(✉)], Xibo Sun[1], and Qiong Luo[1,2]

[1] Hong Kong University of Science and Technology, Hong Kong, China
yicheng.hu@connect.ust.hk, {xsunax,luo}@cse.ust.hk
[2] Hong Kong University of Science and Technology (Guangzhou), Guangzhou, China

Abstract. Finding the Maximum Common Subgraph (MCS) in two graphs is NP-hard, and MCS algorithms adopt heuristics to improve time performance. In particular, the state-of-the-art branch-and-bound MCS algorithms, including McSplit, McSplit+RL, McSplit+LL, and McSplit+DAL, apply heuristics in selecting vertices to match from the two input graphs. However, they always select a vertex from the first graph to match with a set of candidate vertices from the second graph. This fixed order of the two graphs is not necessarily the best, because the number of candidates for a single vertex may vary. Therefore, we propose a bidirectional vertex selection method in which each time a single vertex is dynamically selected from either the first or the second graph depending on the number of candidate vertices to match in the other graph. This way the search space is reduced and the search time performance is improved. We have evaluated our method on a real-world chemical molecular graph dataset as well as other datasets. The results show that our proposed approach can find more non-trivial MCS than the best of McSplit family algorithms.

Keywords: Data mining · Exact algorithms · Maximum Common Subgraph

1 Introduction

The Maximum common subgraph is an indicator of the similarity between two graphs. Such similarity testing is applied in software development [4], image mining [6], and molecular matching and comparisons [3]. Due to the NP-hard nature of the maximum common subgraph problem, it is difficult to find MCS in scenarios that require online response. Hence, we study how to solve the maximum common subgraph problem more efficiently.

Prior work on the maximum common subgraph problem, includes exact approaches and inexact approaches. Inexact approaches aim to obtain a close-to-optimal solution within a given time limit. Recent studies on inexact approaches

J. Li et al. (Eds.): APWeb-WAIM 2025, LNCS 16115, pp. 34–50, 2026.
https://doi.org/10.1007/978-981-95-5719-6_3

utilize graph neural networks (GNN) to approximate the solution [9,18]. In contrast, exact approaches aim to find the optimal solution to the problem. The first class of exact algorithms utilize a clique-based approach, which constructs a compatibility graph (modular product), and finds the maximum clique in the compatibility graph [7,8]. The best clique-based MCS solver [13] is implemented based on the maximum clique algorithm [17]. The MCS problem can also be solved using constraint programming. Vismara et al. proposed an approach to solve connected MCS using constraint programming [19]. Then the approach is further refined to solve both connected and unconnected MCS [16]. Hoffmann et al. adapted the approach of finding subgraph isomorphism to finding MCS [5]. Bahiense et al. applied integer programming [1]. Branch and bound algorithms are also applied to find MCS [15]. Recently, a branch and bound algorithm, McSplit [14], has become the state of the art in finding MCS, and a series of variants of this algorithm have been proposed [10,11,21]. We call these four variants, McSplit family algorithms.

The maximum common subgraph problem can be further divided into two categories. The maximum common induced subgraph problem requires the solution to be an induced subgraph of the original graphs. The maximum common edge subgraph problem focuses on a solution that has a maximum number of edges. Following previous studies on molecular similarity [2,3], we focus on the maximum common induced subgraph (denoted as MCS) problem. The MCS problem has several variants by considering (1) whether the vertices and edges are labelled; (2) whether the input graphs are directed; (3) whether the solution MCS must be connected. For instance, the retrosynthetic molecular similarity problem is a labelled, undirected and unconnected MCS problem, where each atom element is a vertex label, and each bond type is an edge label. The McSplit family algorithm can support different MCS problem variants, except the connected directed MCS problem.

We explore in-depth the search scheme adopted by McSplit family algorithms. The algorithms utilize a data structure named label class. Each label class consists of two lists of candidate vertices, each list contains vertices from one graph, and the algorithms select a pair of vertices, one from each list within the same label class for mapping. However, we observe that they use a static vertex selection scheme in the search. Specifically, in McSplit family algorithms, the search for a vertex mapping pair always selects the first vertex from the candidate vertices list of the first input graph and the second vertex from the other candidate vertices list. Through step-by-step trace of the execution of the algorithms, we discover that this static vertex selection scheme is often ineffective in reducing the search space, leading to a longer search time.

To address this limitation, we propose bidirectional vertex selection (BVS) to apply a dynamic vertex selection scheme within a label class when mapping each pair of vertices from two graphs. The new vertex selection scheme selects the first and second vertex for mapping depending on the difference in the lengths of candidate vertices lists within a label class. We find that this new vertex selection scheme helps reduce the search space further. We apply bidirectional vertex selection on McSplit family algorithms and test our BVS algorithms on molecular graphs, we name our new approach BVS algorithms. Our experiment shows that BVS algorithms outperform the McSplit family algorithms. The source code and experiment data are published at https://anonymous.4open.science/r/MCS_BVS-8995/.

2 Problem Definition

The definition of the MCS problem is briefly discussed here. Given a graph $G = (V, E)$, V and E represent the set of vertices and the set of edges of graph G. two vertices u and v are adjacent if there is an edge between them, i.e., $e(u, v) \in E$. The graph $G' = (V', E')$ is an induced subgraph of G if and only if: (1) $V' \subseteq V$, (2) $E' = \{(u, v) \mid \forall u, v \in V', (u, v) \in E\}$.

Given two graphs $G_1 = (V_1, E_1), G_2 = (V_2, E_2)$, if $G'_1 = (V'_1, E'_1)$ is an induced subgraph of G_1, and $G'_2 = (V'_2, E'_2)$ is an induced subgraph of G_2, and there exists a bijection $\varnothing : V'_1 \rightarrow V'_2$ such that for any $u', v' \in V'_1$, $e(u', v') \in E_1$ if and only if $e(\varnothing(u'), \varnothing(v')) \in E_2$. Then G'_1 and G'_2 are a common subgraph of G_1 and G_2. In the case of a labelled MCS problem, $\forall v \in V'_1$, v and $\varnothing(v)$ must have the same vertex label, and $\forall e(u, v) \in E'_1$, $e(u, v)$ and $e(\varnothing(u), \varnothing(v))$ must have the same edge label.

The maximum common subgraph problem aims to find an induced common subgraph $[G'_1 = (V'_1, E'_1), G'_2 = (V'_2, E'_2)]$ of a pair of input graphs $[G_1, G_2]$, such that no other induced common subgraph of the input graphs pair has a larger size than $|V'_1|$. Let $V'_1 = \{v_1, v_2, v_3, ..., v_m\}$, the solution of MCS is denoted as a list of matched vertex pairs, i.e., $\{(v_1, \varnothing(v_1)), (v_2, \varnothing(v_2)), (v_3, \varnothing(v_3)), ..., (v_m, \varnothing(v_m))\}$. The solution of MCS is not unique, the goal of MCS is to find one solution.

3 The McSplit Family Algorithms

The McSplit family algorithms include the original version of the McSplit algorithms (denoted as McSplit) [14], and three successors, McSplit+RL [10], McSplit+LL [21] and McSplit+DAL [11]. They all share the same algorithm framework developed by the McSplit algorithm.

3.1 McSplit Algorithm

This section will describe the approach adopted by the McSplit Algorithm. McSplit adopts the usual branch and bound framework, it explores all possible mappings between the vertices of two input graphs using **exhaustive tree search**, where each search node in the search tree is a mapping between a pair of vertices from input graphs.

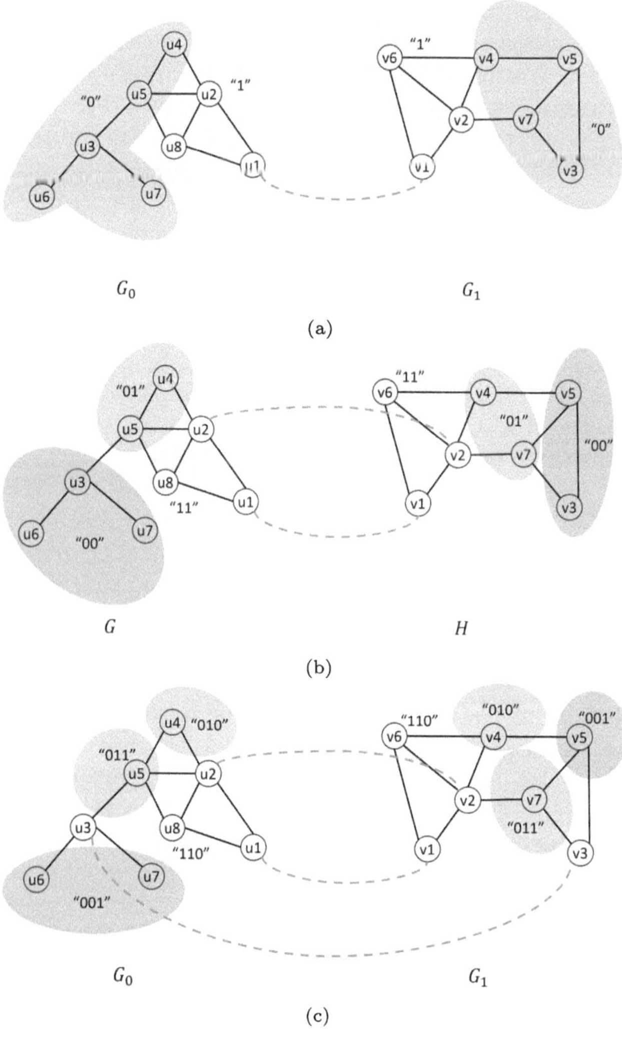

Fig. 1. Label Class used in McSplit Family Algorithms.

Label Class. To facilitate the searching process and reduce the search space, McSplit introduced the **label class** data structure, as illustrated in Fig. 1. A label class consists of two lists of candidate vertices labelled with a bit string, each list of candidate vertices is from one input graph, and any two vertices taken from two lists respectively can be added into the mapping. The vertices in different label classes are mutually exclusive, by only considering the mappings within the same label class, McSplit effectively reduce the search space.

We take the examples in Fig. 1 to demonstrate the concept of label class. Suppose we initially mapped vertex u_1 in G_0 to vertex v_1 in G_1, denoted as

(u_1, v_1) (Fig. 1(a)). To further construct an MCS, we can add a new pair of vertices (u_n, v_n) into the current mapping, if u_n is adjacent (resp., not adjacent) to vertex u_1 and v_n is adjacent (resp., not adjacent) to vertex v_1. The remaining unexplored vertices in each graph can thus be divided into 2 groups, the group of vertices that are adjacent to vertex u_1 (v_1), and the other group that are not. We assign a bit string of **1** (resp., **0**) to represent the group with vertices adjacent (resp., not adjacent) to u_1 and v_1. Vertices from both graphs that are assigned with the same bit string are said to belong to the same label class. A pair of vertices within the same label class, one from each graph, is an eligible mapping pair to be added into the current MCS in the next step of exploration. Each time when we expand the mapping, we split each current label class into two sub label classes and append an additional bit to its bit string. In Fig. 1(a), the selected mapping (u_1, v_1) generates two label classes, label class **"1"** in yellow and **"0"** in red. In 1(b), we map vertex u_2 to v_2 that belong to label class **"1"**, and that creates three sub label classes **"00"**, **"01"** and **"11"**. Note that the label class **"10"** is empty, hence we remove it. We continue this "select vertex to map -> split label classes based on mapping" procedure recursively to reach a maximal result and then trace back. The benefit of label class is intuitive that we do not need to explore the mapping of vertices from different label classes, thus reducing search steps.

Label class also provides a way to prune the search tree by estimating an upper bound to the current mapping. In Fig. 1(c), the label class **"001"** has two vertices from G_0, u_6 and u_7, and one vertex from G_1, v_5. Therefore, there is at most one mapping within this label class we can add to the current mapping. To be more general, suppose the current mapping is C, where $C = \{(u_1, v_1), (u_2, v_2), ..., (u_n, v_n)\}$. A label class is denoted as $\langle U, V \rangle$, and the number of new mappings that can be added to the current mapping is $min(|U|, |V|)$. Suppose L is the set of all current label classes, where $L = \{\langle U, V \rangle_1, \langle U, V \rangle_2, ..., \langle U, V \rangle_l\}$, the upper bound when the search proceeds with the current mapping is represented with the following formula:

$$UB(L, C) = |C| + \sum_{\langle U,V \rangle_i \in L} min(|U|, |V|) \tag{1}$$

Exhaustive Tree Search. Algorithm 1 describes the core recursive searching process adopted by McSplit family algorithms. The searching process can be constructed using a search tree, where each recursive call to the procedure is a search node in the search tree. In each recursive call, the procedure first decides whether to prune the current search branch by calculating the upper bound of the current search branch. It then exhaustively explores all child search branches when selecting a pair of vertices into the current mapping by certain heuristics and when excluding this pair of vertices from the current mapping.

There are three heuristics adopted by the algorithm. At Line 6, a heuristic is used to pick a label class (**heuristic1**); at Line 7, a heuristic is used to pick a vertex for mapping from the first input graph (**heuristic2**); at Line 9, a heuristic

Algorithm 1. Exhaustive tree search procedure.

Input:
L: the set of all label classes
C: current mapping
incumbent: largest mapping found

procedure SOLVE($L, C, incumbent$)
    if $|C| > |incumbent|$ **then**
        $incumbent \leftarrow C$
    $upperBound \leftarrow UB(L, C)$
    if $upperBound \leq |incumbent|$ **then return**

    $\langle U, V\rangle \leftarrow$ SELECTLABELCLASS(L)
    $u \leftarrow$ SELECTFIRSTVERTEX(U)
    while there is still vertex in V not tried **do**
        $v \leftarrow$ SELECTSECONDVERTEX(V)
        $C' \leftarrow C \cup \{u, v\}$
        $L' \leftarrow$ SPLITLABELCLASSES(L, u, v)
        SOLVE($L', C', incumbent$)

    $U' \leftarrow U \setminus \{u\}$
    $L' \leftarrow L \setminus \langle U, V\rangle \cup \langle U', V\rangle$
    SOLVE($L', C, incumbent$)

is used to pick a vertex for mapping with the first selected vertex from the second input graph (**heuristic3**). The latter two heuristics, the vertex selection heuristics, are the major differences between McSplit, McSplit+RL, McSplit+LL and McSplit+DAL. In McSplit, a label class $\langle U, V\rangle$ is chosen by considering the label class with the smallest $max(|U|, |V|)$ (**heuristic1**). McSplit selects the first vertex that has the largest degree in U (**heuristic2**), and the second vertex by decreasing order of vertex degrees in V (**heuristic3**).

3.2 Reward-Based McSplit Algorithms

Suppose the current search node has the set of label classes L, and after a pair of vertices (u, v) are added to the current mapping, the algorithm explores its child search node. Suppose the child search node has a set of label classes L' after the label classes split operations. McSplit+RL defines the reward on the mapping of (u, v), $R(u, v)$ as follows for reinforcement learning:

$$R(u, v) = \sum_{\langle U,V\rangle_i \in L} min(|U|, |V|) - \sum_{\langle U',V'\rangle_i \in L'} min(|U'|, |V'|) \tag{2}$$

The Algorithm maintains a score list S_p, and S_k for the first and second input graph, respectively, where $S_p(u)$ (resp., $S_k(v)$) records the cumulative reward of vertex u (resp., v). All entries in the two score lists are initialized to 0, and when a mapping (u, v) is selected, their corresponding entries in the score lists are updated as follows:

$$S_p(u) \leftarrow S_p(u) + R(u, v) \tag{3}$$
$$S_k(v) \leftarrow S_k(v) + R(u, v) \tag{4}$$

At each search node, after a label class $\langle U, V\rangle$ is selected, the algorithm first selects a vertex $u \in U$ that has the highest cumulative reward $S_p(u)$ (**heuristic2**), and selects the second vertex $v \in V$ by decreasing order of value $S_k(v)$ (**heuristic3**).

In McSplit+LL, the algorithm maintains the score list of the first input graph S_p, and a score table S_t. Each entry of the score table $S_t(u, v)$ stores the cumulative reward of the mapping (u, v). At each search node, the first vertex u will be selected based on the value $S_p(u)$ (**heuristic2**), while the second vertex v will be selected by decreasing order of value $S_t(u, v)$ (**heuristic3**).

McSplit+DAL also uses S_p and $S_t(u, v)$ as the two vertex selection heuristics. However, the algorithm slightly modifies the reward function as follows:

$$R(u, v) = \sum_{\langle U,V\rangle_i \in L} min(|U|, |V|) - \sum_{\langle U',V'\rangle_i \in L'} min(|U'|, |V'|) + |L'| \tag{5}$$

The function adds the number of label classes as a positive reward. A branching leading to more and smaller label classes is preferred.

4 Proposed BVS Algorithms

4.1 Bidirectional Vertex Selection

The McSplit family algorithms adopt a static vertex selection scheme as **heuristic1** and **heuristic2** always select vertex from the candidate vertices list from the first and the second graph respectively. In this section, we detail why this static scheme is not effective in reducing search upper bound, and how we apply bidirectional vertex selection at every search node to dynamically determine the vertex selection order based on the length difference of the candidate vertices lists within a label class.

To demonstrate the concept, we only focus on a single label class. Consider a label class that is selected using **heuristic1** under the current search node in the search tree. Consider the situation that the label class selected at the current search node has the following vertices $\langle\{v_1, v_3, v_5, v_9\}, \{u_1, u_3, u_5\}\rangle$, where vertices v_n are from the first input graph, and vertices u_n are from the second input graph. Suppose vertex v_1 is selected using **heuristic2**. Then the remaining searches under the current search branch can be represented by different search nodes that are the direct children of the current search node. Each vertex of $\{u_1, u_3, u_5\}$ mapped to v_1 will become a new search node, corresponding to Line 12 of Algorithm 1, and the algorithm will perform a depth-first search on all of these search nodes. In the end, a new child search node will also be created by not considering vertex v_1, corresponding to Line 15. This last search node will have the current label class changed to $\langle\{v_3, v_5, v_9\}, \{u_1, u_3, u_5\}\rangle$. At each search node, the algorithm will estimate an upper bound to prune the search tree at Line 4. Suppose the current mapping has a size of 2, then the upper bound at both the current search node and the last child search node will be 5, because there are at least 3 vertices from either input graph in both label classes. We denote this example as **case 1**.

Now, we revisit the current search node with a little modification. Suppose the label class selected has the following vertices $\langle\{u_1, u_3, u_5\}, \{v_1, v_3, v_5, v_9\}\rangle$, where the order of input graphs are swapped. If vertex u_1 is selected using **heuristic2**, likewise, each vertex of $\{v_1, v_3, v_5, v_9\}$ mapped to u_1 will become a child search node, and the last child search node will have the current label class changed to $\langle\{u_3, u_5\}, \{v_1, v_3, v_5, v_9\}\rangle$. Therefore, this last child search node will have an upper bound of 4, since the minimum number of vertices from the first input graph is reduced to 2. Because this last child search node has a lower upper bound than in **case 1**, the branch under this child search node could be pruned earlier. We denote this example as **case 2**.

However, although the last child search node in **case 2** has a tighter bound, it has one more child search node because the number of vertices mapped to vertex u_1 in **case 2** is more than that to vertex v_1 in **case 1**. We address this problem by considering all mappings in a single label class. To simplify the analysis, we focus on the current label class only, and we assume that the current label class will not be split at Line 11 of Algorithm 1.

Suppose we have a label class $\langle U, V\rangle$, where $m = |U|$, and $n = |V|$. Suppose the current mapping is C, and $c = |C|$. Suppose the best solution found so far is *incumbent*, and $b = |incumbent|$. No matter how the search tree is constructed, the algorithm will eventually exhaustively explore all possible mappings with vertices from U to V. Therefore, the number of mappings explored is $m \times n$. This exploration process is equivalent to a nested loop, where vertices from the first input graph are iterators of the outer loop and vertices from the second graph are iterators of the inner loop. Line 12 of Algorithm 1 advances the inner iterator, and Line 15 advances the outer iterator. Now, we consider the effect of pruning. We will finish the exploration of the current label class when either of the following conditions is met: $c + m <= b$ or $c + n <= b$. We consider the case where currently $c + m$ and $c + n$ are both greater than b, otherwise it is trivial. The number of mappings to explore within the current label class is then $[m - (b - c)] \times n$, simplified to $m \times n - (b - c) \times n$. We can easily see that when $m < n$, the number of mappings to explore under this domain class is smaller.

Based on this observation, we revise the vertex selection heuristics on the McSplit family algorithms. Suppose a label class $\langle U, V\rangle$ is selected under the current search node, we will select the first vertex from U and the second vertex from V only if $|U| <= |V|$, otherwise we select the first and second vertex from V and U respectively. We name it **bidirectional vertex selection (BVS)** to indicate that we lift the constraint on the original probe order that vertices in the first input graph always probe against vertices in the second input graph.

Referring to Algorithm 1, BVS performs the described condition check between Line 6 and Line 7, the subsequent vertex selections, and thus the sub-branches to be explored will differ from the original algorithm. Bidirectional vertex selection dynamically selects which candidate vertices list to choose the vertex for mapping at each search node based on the difference in candidate list length within the selected label class. The effect of bidirectional vertex selection is only visible within the current search node, the behavior of all descendants of the current search node will be unchanged and the optimality of the solution is unaffected due to the symmetrical nature of the MCS problem. To be consistent with the bidirectional vertex selection behavior, we also revise **heuristic1**. Using small-scale experiments, we modify **heuristic1** to break ties by selecting the label class $\langle U, V\rangle$ that contains a vertex with the largest degree in the smaller set of U or V, and breaks the second-layer ties by selecting the label class $\langle U, V\rangle$ that has a smaller $min(|U|, |V|)$.

4.2 Revision of Reward-Based Vertex Selection Scheme

We modify the reward-based McSplit algorithms to adapt to bidirectional vertex selection. McSplit+LL only maintains the score list S_p of the first input graph, we also add a score list S_q for the second input graph, and use the corresponding score list for selection based on whether the first vertex selected is from the first or the second input graph.

In addition, after applying bidirectional vertex selection, we modify the original vertex reward accumulation scheme in McSplit+LL to better capture the ability of each vertex to reduce the search upper bound.

We first show that the original vertex reward accumulation scheme adopted by McSplit+LL is unfair. In Sect. 4.1, at each search node, we have divided the children search nodes into two categories. Suppose the first vertex selected is u, then the first type of children search nodes are those that mapped u to the vertex in another input graph, and the second type is the search node that considers not taking vertex u into the mapping. The upper bound reduction of the first type of children search nodes should be affected by both vertices mapped equally. However, the reward accumulation scheme of McSplit+LL does not treat the two vertices mapped equally. For example, suppose u from the first input graph is mapped to v from the second input graph. The upper bound reduction by adding the mapping (u, v) is equally affected by both u and v, and this reward is accumulated in score list $S_p(u)$ and the score table $S_t(u, v)$. Thus, the score list S_p records only the reward obtained by each vertex from the first input graph for being as the first mapped vertex. On the other hand, after we applied bidirectional vertex selection, we use another score list S_q to record the reward obtained by each vertex from the second input graph for being as the first mapped vertex. The reward of the mapping (u, v) is not recorded in S_q.

To capture the mapping reward equally. We create two other score lists S_{p2} and S_{q2}. They record the cumulative reward of each vertex in two input graphs for being selected as the second mapped vertex. For each mapping (u, v) explored during searching, we accumulate the reward to $S_p(u)$, $S_t(u, v)$, $S_{q2}(v)$, or $S_q(u), S_t(u,v), S_{p2}(v)$ depending on which graph vertices u and v belong to. During vertex selection, instead of selecting the candidate vertex u with the highest reward from $S_p(u)$ or $S_q(u)$, we select the candidate vertex with the highest reward sum from $S_p(u)+S_{p2}(u)$ or $S_q(u)+S_{q2}(u)$. As a side note, for each mapping (u,v), instead of accumulating the reward using $S_{q2}(v)$ (resp., $S_{p2}(v)$), we can accumulate the reward directly to $S_q(v)$ (resp., $S_p(v)$) because the rewards are added up during vertex selection, and we do not need two additional score lists. However, the original McSplit+LL implements a reward thresholding operation on S_p when one of the reward values in S_p exceeds a manually set threshold. Through small-scale experiments, we observed that using two separate reward lists for each input graph performs slightly better under the influence of reward thresholding. We make the same modification to McSplit+DAL, as it shares the same reward accumulation scheme as McSplit+LL.

5 Experimental Evaluation

We perform the experiments on a computer with dual Intel Xeon E5-2683 v4 CPUs. Each algorithm runs on a dedicated CPU core and each algorithm is applied a memory limit of 6 GBytes. All algorithms are implemented in C++ and compiled using g++ 13.2.0 with O3 optimization level. The algorithms tested in experiments are McSplit, McSplit+RL, McSplit+LL, McSplit+DAL and McSplitBVS, McSplit+RLBVS, McSplit+LLBVS, McSplit+DALBVS. We apply bidirectional vertex selection on the latter four algorithms. For each pair of input graphs, we set a time limit of 1000 s following previous work [14]. If the algorithm cannot find the MCS of a pair of graphs within the time limit, it will be regarded as a failure.

We compare the performance of these algorithms on finding MCS on chemistry molecular graphs using two datasets, USPTO-50K and USPTO-MIT [12]. Both datasets are widely used in retrosynthesis prediction. The USPTO-50K dataset contains 50K retrosynthesis reactions, and USPTO-MIT contains around 479K reactions, both datasets are extracted from the chemistry reactions published in US patents, organized in a text format called SMILES [20]. To simulate retrosynthesis application, we use the size of MCS to indicate the similarity between the reactants and the product of each reaction. Because the MCS algorithms take two graphs as the input, we preprocess the datasets to merge the reactants into a graph, and save each reactant and product graph in the DIMACS format. We select 1000 reactions from each of the two datasets for our experiments. We use the product of reactant graph size and product graph size as the reaction size. Since most of the reactions in the two datasets can be solved within one millisecond, we select the largest 1000 reactions. After filtering, USPTO-MIT and USPTO-50K contain reactions with an average reaction size of 7824 and 2656 respectively. The two filtered datasets represent relatively complex and simple retrosynthesis similarity tasks respectively.

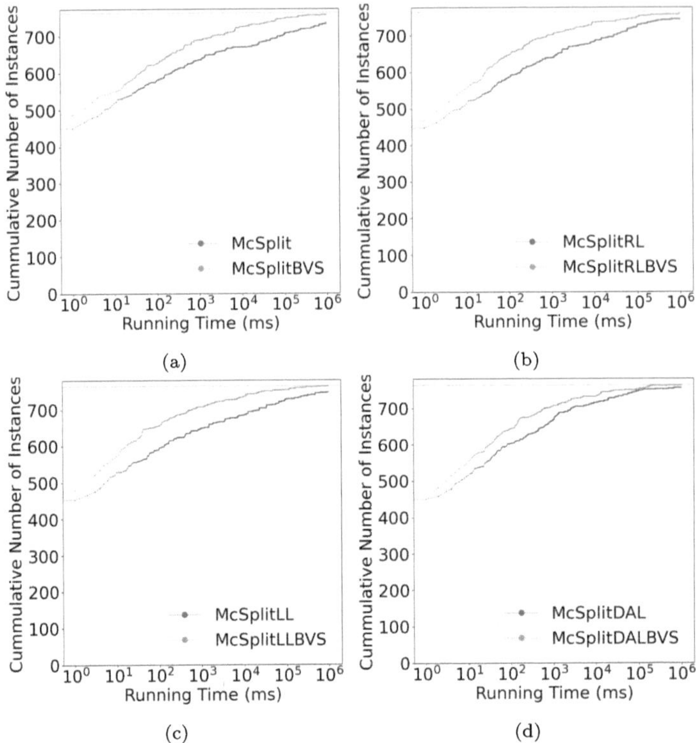

Fig. 2. Performance of BVS algorithms compared to McSplit family algorithms on USPTO-MIT dataset.

5.1 On Molecular Graph Datasets

Following the conventions of experiments in McSplit, we evaluate the performance of algorithms by plotting the cumulative number of instances solved (y-axis) against the time limit (x-axis) in the log scale. If we set a particular time limit, the algorithm that can solve more instances within this time limit is better. We plot the results for instances that can be solved by some algorithms within 1000 s. Figure 2 shows the comparison between each of our BVS algorithms and the original McSplit family algorithms on the USPTO-MIT dataset, and Fig. 3 for the USPTO-50K dataset. When plotting the results, we discard the instances that all algorithms can solve in less than 1 millisecond since these instances are trivial and make no performance difference between these algorithms.

We observe that, overall BVS algorithms outperform McSplit family algorithms in these two datasets. In particular, the extent to which BVS algorithms outperform McSplit family algorithms becomes larger when the size of input graphs increase, as the advantage of BVS algorithms in Fig. 2 is larger than that in Fig. 3. In addition, we observe that when the given time limit approaches

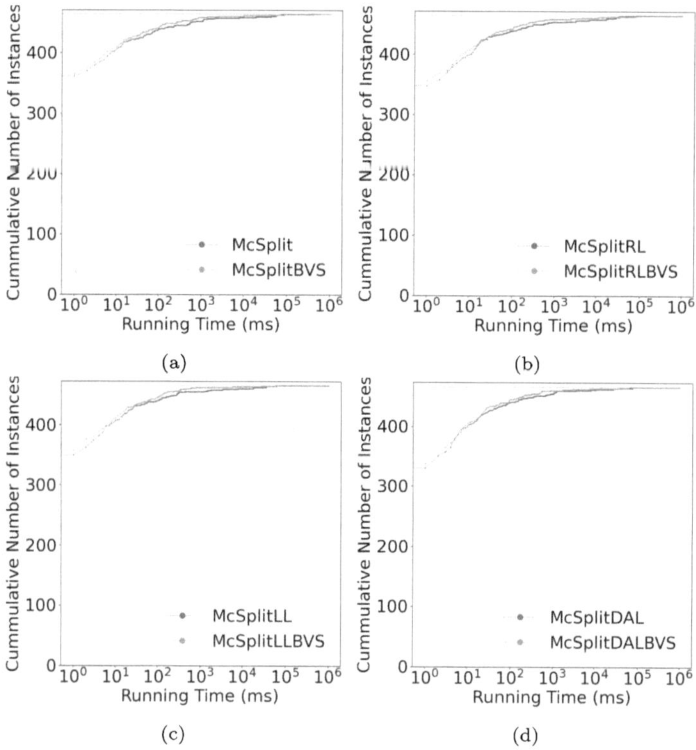

Fig. 3. Performance of BVS algorithms compared to McSplit family algorithms on USPTO-50K dataset.

10^6ms, the performance advantage of BVS algorithms becomes smaller on both datasets.

Because we also modified the reward-based vertex selection scheme (Sect. 4.2) for McSplit+LLBVS and McSplit+DALBVS to better accommodate bidirectional vertex selection, we also experimented only adopting BVS while excluding the modification on the reward-based vertex selection scheme on molecular graph datasets (Fig. 4). It shows that on faster instances, the BVS algorithms without this modification are more efficient, while for instances that take longer time, BVS algorithms with this modification slightly outperform their counterparts, but not evident. A possible reason could be the extra execution burden added by the modified reward-based vertex selection scheme, while this reward is not significant when the search ends very shortly. On the other hand, it proves that bidirectional vertex selection alone is the major contributor of the performance gain.

To explore the effectiveness of BVS algorithms further, we select the best performing algorithms among the original McSplit family algorithms, McSplit+LL and McSplit+DAL, and the best performing algorithm among the BVS algorithms, McSplit+LLBVS. For each instance solved, we plot the number of

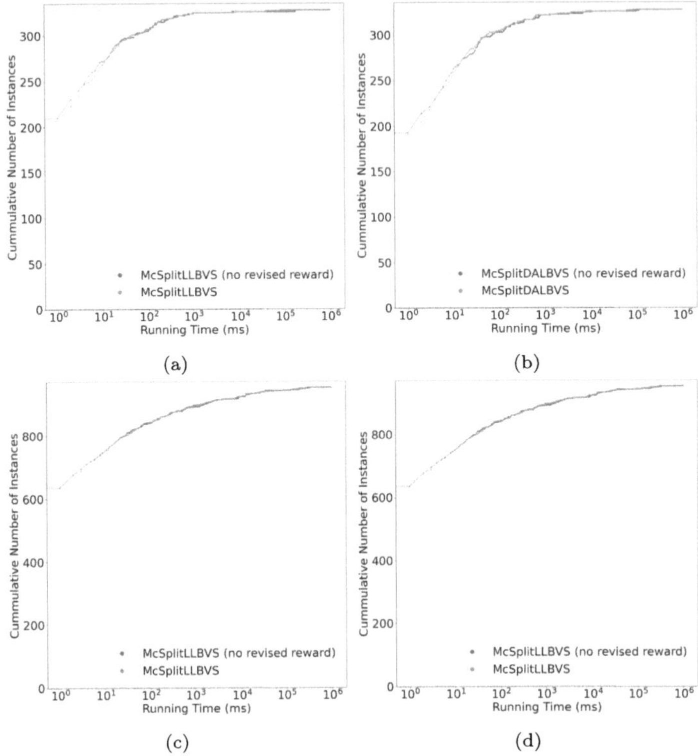

Fig. 4. Performance of BVS algorithms with and without revised reward-based vertex selection scheme on USPTO-50K ((a)(b)) and USPTO-MIT dataset ((c)(d)).

search nodes explored in McSplit+LLBVS as the y-coordinate, and that in McSplit+DAL/McSplit+LL as the x-coordinate in Fig. 5. We can see that on both datasets, most points fall on the McSplit+LL/McSplit+DAL side, indicating that McSplit+LLBVS explores fewer search nodes to end the search in most cases.

5.2 On Random Datasets

We also benchmark BVS algorithms and McSplit family algorithms using a randomly generated dataset [14]. The dataset contains randomly generated regular and irregular meshes and bounded valence graphs with different densities to simulate different types of graphs that exist in different research fields. This dataset is widely used in evaluating MCS algorithms in previous works. We adopt similar settings as the experiments conducted by McSplit. We benchmark algorithms on over 4000 instances, with each input graph size varied between 15 and 50. We solve the vertex and edge labelled, unconnected and directed MCS problem, as well as the vertex and edge labelled, unconnected and undirected MCS problem. We find that each BVS algorithm performs slightly better than its original

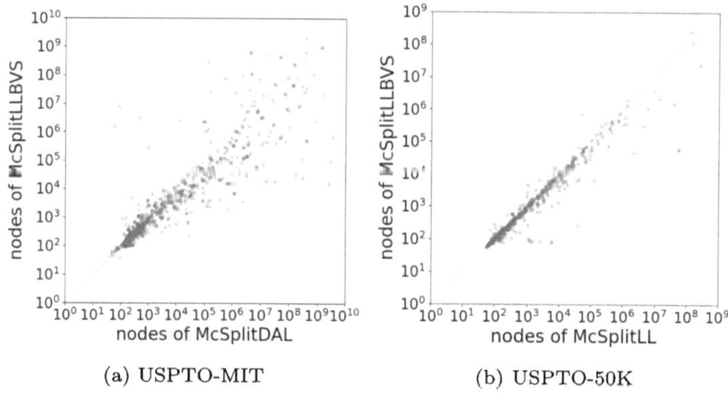

(a) USPTO-MIT (b) USPTO-50K

Fig. 5. Number of per-instance search nodes explored by both algorithms.

McSplit family algorithm, but the performance difference is small. Figure 6(a) and Fig. 6(b) show that when solving vertex and edge labelled, unconnected and directed MCS on the random graph dataset, McSplitBVS explores fewer search nodes and completes search more quickly.

However, when we compare McSplit to any other original McSplit family algorithms or BVS algorithms, McSplit always performs better in terms of search time. In Fig. 6(c) and Fig. 6(d), we use McSplit+DALBVS as an example. While McSplit+DALBVS explores slightly fewer nodes than McSplit most of the time, McSplit completely outperforms McSplit+DALBVS in search time. When we compare the algorithms pairwise, we observe that McSplit(BVS) mostly take less time to search than McSplit+RL(BVS), and McSplit+RL(BVS) mostly takes less time to search than McSplit+LL(BVS) and McSplit+DAL(BVS). Nevertheless, the difference in number of per-instance nodes searched is much smaller than the difference in the per-instance search time. We recognize that both McSplit+LL(BVS) and McSplit+DAL(BVS) have slightly more complex implementations than McSplit+RL(BVS), and McSplit+RL(BVS) is slightly more complex than McSplit(BVS). Hence, we attribute the differences in running time to their implementations complexity.

5.3 Discussions

In Figs. 5 and 6, the performance advantage of BVS algorithms becomes larger when the number of searched nodes is greater. When the number of search nodes of an instance is around 10^2 to 10^3, BVS algorithms perform almost the same as original McSplit family algorithms. When the number of search nodes of an instance is over 10^5, BVS algorithms search fewer nodes most of the time. In addition, we also evaluate the algorithms to solve the vertex and edge unlabelled MCS problem on the USPTO-50K dataset. We notice that even when running on the same dataset, the BVS algorithms have greater performance advantages when solving the unlabelled MCS than labelled MCS, because solving unlabelled

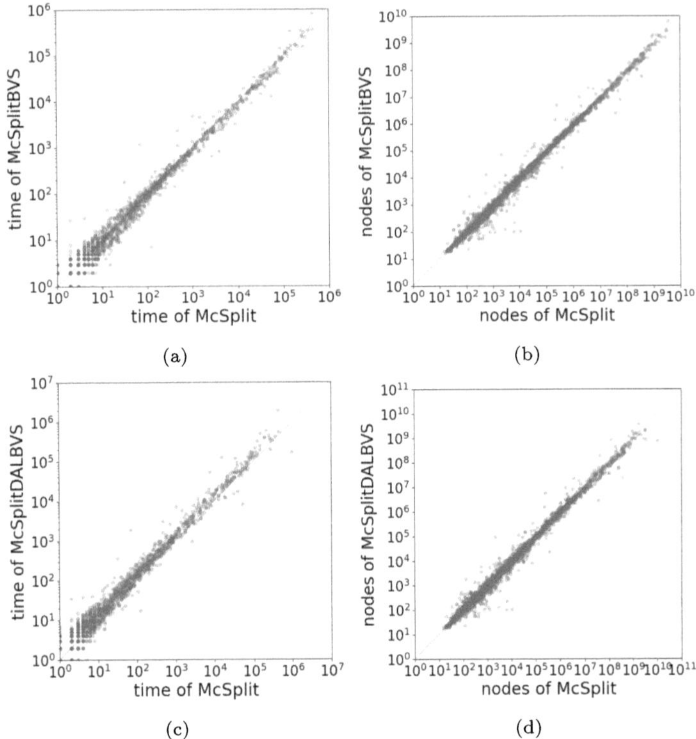

Fig. 6. Number of per-instance search nodes and search time (ms) explored by McSplit-BVS vs McSplit ((a)(b)), and McSplit+DALBVS vs McSplit ((c)(d)).

MCS generally requires the algorithm to explore more search nodes. Likewise, Fig. 5(a) and Fig. 5(b) show that solving instances in USPTO-MIT requires more search nodes than USPTO-50K. In comparison, if the instances require only a small number of search nodes, then there are no distinctive differences in terms of the number of search nodes between these algorithms. In this case, an algorithm with simpler implementation, such as McSplit(BVS) is faster. Otherwise, BVS algorithms make a considerable improvement over original McSpilt family algorithms.

6 Conclusion

Through an in-depth analysis of the exhaustive tree search process of McSplit family algorithms, we address the limitations of the static vertex selection scheme adopted by these algorithms. We propose a new dynamic vertex selection scheme, bidirectional vertex selection, to overcome the limitations. This new scheme reduces the upper bound of the search tree further by utilizing the list length difference in a label class, and it ends the search with a smaller number of search nodes, thus making the search process more efficient. We also address the unfairness nature of the reward accumulation scheme of reward-based McSplit algorithms and revise it to a fair scheme. On top of the McSplit family algorithms, we implement BVS algorithms. Experimental results show that BVS algorithms outperform McSplit family algorithms on both molecular graphs and random graphs. The performance advantage is especially large on large molecular graphs. In the future, we will expand the scope of bidirectional vertex selection on graphs of other domains with different features.

References

1. Bahiense, L., Manić, G., Piva, B., De Souza, C.C.: The maximum common edge subgraph problem: A polyhedral investigation. Discret. Appl. Math. **160**(18), 2523–2541 (2012)
2. Cao, Y., Jiang, T., Girke, T.: A maximum common substructure-based algorithm for searching and predicting drug-like compounds. Bioinformatics **24**(13), i366–i374 (2008)
3. Ehrlich, H.C., Rarey, M.: Maximum common subgraph isomorphism algorithms and their applications in molecular science: a review. Wiley Interdisc. Rev.: Comput. Mol. Sci. **1**(1), 68–79 (2011)
4. Hjort Blindell, G., Castañeda Lozano, R., Carlsson, M., Schulte, C.: Modeling universal instruction selection. In: Principles and Practice of Constraint Programming: 21st International Conference, CP 2015, Cork, Ireland, August 31–September 4, 2015, Proceedings 21, pp. 609–626. Springer (2015)
5. Hoffmann, R., McCreesh, C., Reilly, C.: Between subgraph isomorphism and maximum common subgraph. In: Proceedings of the AAAI Conference on Artificial Intelligence, vol. 31 (2017)
6. Jiang, H., Ngo, C.W.: Image mining using inexact maximal common subgraph of multiple args. In: International Conference on Visual Information System, vol. 2, p. 3 (2003)
7. Koch, I.: Enumerating all connected maximal common subgraphs in two graphs. Theoret. Comput. Sci. **250**(1–2), 1–30 (2001)
8. Levi, G.: A note on the derivation of maximal common subgraphs of two directed or undirected graphs. Calcolo **9**(4), 341–352 (1973)
9. Li, Y., Gu, C., Dullien, T., Vinyals, O., Kohli, P.: Graph matching networks for learning the similarity of graph structured objects. In: International Conference on Machine Learning, pp. 3835–3845. PMLR (2019)
10. Liu, Y., Li, C.M., Jiang, H., He, K.: A learning based branch and bound for maximum common subgraph related problems. Proc. AAAI Conf. Artif. Intell. **34**(03), 2392–2399 (2020). https://doi.org/10.1609/aaai.v34i03.5619
11. Liu, Y., Zhao, J., Li, C.M., Jiang, H., He, K.: Hybrid learning with new value function for the maximum common induced subgraph problem. In: Proceedings of the AAAI Conference on Artificial Intelligence, vol. 37, pp. 4044–4051 (2023)
12. Lowe, D.M.: Extraction of chemical structures and reactions from the literature. Ph.D. thesis, University of Cambridge (2012)
13. McCreesh, C., Ndiaye, S.N., Prosser, P., Solnon, C.: Clique and constraint models for maximum common (connected) subgraph problems. In: Principles and Practice of Constraint Programming: 22nd International Conference, CP 2016, Toulouse, France, September 5-9, 2016, Proceedings 22, pp. 350–368. Springer (2016)

14. McCreesh, C., Prosser, P., Trimble, J.: A partitioning algorithm for maximum common subgraph problems. In: Proceedings of the Twenty-Sixth International Joint Conference on Artificial Intelligence (2017). https://doi.org/10.24963/ijcai.2017/99
15. McGregor, J.J.: Backtrack search algorithms and the maximal common subgraph problem. Software: Practice and Experience **12**(1), 23–34 (1982)
16. Ndiaye, S.N., Solnon, C.: Cp models for maximum common subgraph problems. Principles and Practice of Constraint Programming – CP 2011 pp. 637–644 (2011). https://doi.org/10.1007/978-3-642-23786-7_48
17. Prosser, P.: Exact algorithms for maximum clique: a computational study. Algorithms **5**(4), 545–587 (2012)
18. Roy, I., Chakrabarti, S., De, A.: Maximum common subgraph guided graph retrieval: late and early interaction networks. Adv. Neural. Inf. Process. Syst. **35**, 32112–32126 (2022)
19. Vismara, P., Valery, B.: Finding maximum common connected subgraphs using clique detection or constraint satisfaction algorithms. In: Modelling, Computation and Optimization in Information Systems and Management Sciences: Second International Conference MCO 2008, Metz, France-Luxembourg, September 8-10, 2008. Proceedings, pp. 358–368. Springer (2008)
20. Weininger, D.: Smiles, a chemical language and information system. 1. introduction to methodology and encoding rules. J. Chem. Inform. Comput. Sci. **28**(1), 31–36 (1988)
21. Zhou, J., He, K., Zheng, J., Li, C.M., Liu, Y.: A strengthened branch and bound algorithm for the maximum common (connected) subgraph problem. In: Proceedings of the Thirty-First International Joint Conference on Artificial Intelligence (2022). https://doi.org/10.24963/ijcai.2022/265

TD-LTNet: Temporal-Decay LSTM-Transformer Network for Mobile Video QoE Prediction

Linfang Peng[1], Guoquan Zhang[2], Jin Qian[3], Yanjun Kang[2], Fanxi Bi[2], and Pingfu Chao[1](✉)

[1] School of Computer Science and Technology, Soochow University, Suzhou, China

20235227125@stu.suda.edu.cn

[2] Beijing Xiaomi Mobile Software Co., Ltd., Beijing, China

[3] Hainan University, Haikou, China

Abstract. Thanks to the global popularity of short video apps, the video streaming service has become the most dominant traffic in mobile networks. However, the strong demands on large throughput and real-time efficiency make the video streaming service hard to maintain its high Quality of Experience (QoE), especially during high mobility events, like high-speed trains and subways. Therefore, it is crucial to analyze and predict the QoE beforehand to ensure quick adjustments. However, while existing machine/deep learning approaches analyze historical temporal patterns to forecast network conditions, they suffer from two critical limitations: (1) insufficient emphasis on temporally decaying features in recent observations, and (2) interference from pervasive video preloading mechanisms that distort real-time stall detection. To address these challenges, we propose **TD-LTNet** (Temporal-Decay LSTM-Transformer Network), a hybrid framework integrating sequential modeling with adaptive attention mechanisms for subway network environments. Specifically, our framework includes a Temporal-Decay Multi-Head Attention (TDMA) mechanism that effectively prioritizes time-sensitive patterns through learnable decay factors, and an Adaptive Window Attention Pooling (AWAP) module that dynamically segments input sequences and suppresses preloading-induced pseudo-features via multi-scale attention fusion.

Experiments demonstrate superior prediction accuracy and real-time performance compared to conventional methods, offering an efficient solution for QoE optimization in subway network systems.

Keywords: Time series prediction · Mobile network optimization · Transformer · LSTM

1 Introduction

The rapid proliferation of video platforms has positioned Quality of Experience (QoE) optimization as a critical research frontier in both academic and industrial

J. Li et al. (Eds.): APWeb-WAIM 2025, LNCS 16115, pp. 51–66, 2026.
https://doi.org/10.1007/978-981-95-5719-6_4

domains. QoE directly reflects user perception regarding service quality, with its core objective being to determine whether users encounter video lag. Providing users with high-quality video experiences is of paramount importance [2]. Accurate assessment of online user experience enables network providers to optimize network configurations and improve service quality, while simultaneously delivering smoother, more personalized and more reliable digital experiences to end users in real time. However, achieving such goal is extremely challenging from the operating system perspectives, as the direct data labels (the lagging screens) from the apps are not provided.

Temporal modeling has shown potential in other tasks (such as financial forecasting [1,5], traffic forecasting [14,25] and fault prediction [11,23]), but QoE prediction faces unique challenges:

(1)Temporal Modeling: Imbalance of short-term and long-term dependencies and temporal decay effect. Deep learning models face challenges in capturing both short-term and long-term dependencies in temporal data. While RNNs/LSTMs can model short-term dependencies (e.g., second-level delay fluctuations), they suffer from the vanishing gradient problem, limiting their ability to learn long-range patterns. For instance, as demonstrated in [28], the prediction error in LSTM models accumulates by 42% when forecasting tunnel network states beyond 30-time steps. Transformers, on the other hand, theoretically support long-range dependencies via self-attention. However, when applied directly to subway network data, their performance degrades because they lack a time-decay prior—treating historically irrelevant signals and recent critical states equally, which reduces prediction timeliness. Furthermore, subway network states exhibit a temporal decay effect: their influence on stalling follows an exponential decay pattern, where more recent data is significantly more critical. Existing methods (e.g., the sliding average strategy in [8]) fail to explicitly model this decay, causing delayed responses to sudden network deterioration, such as instantaneous congestion in high-density areas.

(2)Interference in Video Preloading: Confusion between pseudo anomalies and real stalls. Video preloading strategies can cause two types of interference. One is feature space confusion: preloading-induced traffic surges and real stall events exhibit highly overlapping feature distributions. Traditional sliding window methods (e.g., the 10-second window statistics in [8]) struggle to distinguish between them. Another is time window misalignment: The unpredictable duration of preload behaviors introduces boundary noise when fixed window segmentation is applied. Existing models process raw window data directly, causing preloading-induced pseudo-anomalies to degrade the Quality of Experience (QoE) in stall prediction.

To address the aforementioned issues, we propose **TD-LTNet (Temporal-Decay LSTM-Transformer Network)**, a hybrid architecture integrating the long-sequence temporal dependency modeling capability of LSTM with the global pattern recognition ability of Transformer. Our key contributions include:

1. We propose TD-LTNet, a novel collaborative architecture that effectively integrates LSTM and Transformer networks. This composite design leverages

LSTM for local temporal modeling and Transformer for global dependencies, addressing the fundamental tension between short-term and long-term patterns in time series prediction.
2. We introduce a **Temporal-Decay Multi-Head Attention** mechanism that explicitly incorporates temporal weighting into network status modeling. By integrating temporal decay factors with relative positional encoding, this innovation enables a more accurate representation of time-sensitive patterns in network behavior.
3. We develop an **Adaptive Window Attention Pooling** module that employs a dual-focus attention mechanism. This solution simultaneously maintains attention within local windows while preserving inter-window relationships, allowing the model to precisely identify and emphasize features from non-preloaded data segments.
4. We conduct extensive experiments on real-world datasets against different baseline models across various look-back windows, and our model achieves the best performance consistently.

2 Related Work

2.1 Evaluation of QoE

Current research approaches QoE from two perspectives: **(1) Application layer methods:** Focus on adaptive bitrate (ABR) algorithms (e.g. Netflix dynamic bitrate selection [4]) and preload strategies to minimize perceived buffering. However, these methods often ignore the underlying network dynamics, leading to misclassification ing-induced pseudo-stutter as true network congestion. Lightweight terminal-side models (e.g., LSTM-based predictors [29]) rely on the characteristics of the application layer but do not capture cross-layer dependencies, limiting their accuracy in complex scenarios. **(2) Modem-Layer Methods:** directly map network metrics (rsrp, snr, latency) to QoE using statistical regression [7] or deep learning (e.g. CNN-LSTM [26]). Although these models capture the dynamics of the physical layer, they overlook user perception nuances and struggle with data imbalance. This dichotomy creates a research gap where neither approach fully captures both network dynamics and user experience.

2.2 Time Series Prediction

Time series prediction in the field of video stall prediction mainly goes through two stages of evolution: **(1) Machine learning methods:** Algorithms like SVM and Random Forests were introduced to handle nonlinear features (Zhou et al. [31]). Models such as XGBoost and LightGBM could make predictions based on artificially constructed time series features. **(2) Deep Learning Methods:** Traditional time series prediction models primarily used Recurrent Neural Networks (RNNs) and their variants (e.g., LSTM and GRU) to capture short-term temporal dependencies. For example, S Bilotta [3] utilized LSTMs to model network traffic fluctuations. Transformers, with their self-attention mechanisms, excelled in long-sequence modeling (e.g., Informer [31] improved prediction efficiency through sparse attention). Recent hybrid architectures (e.g., [6]) combine LSTM feature extraction with Transformer processing, **though none address both temporal decay and preloading interference.**

2.3 Temporal Modeling and Attention Mechanisms

Current position encoding methods for Transformers exhibit notable limitations in video stall prediction. While Relative Position Encoding (RPE) [22] improves upon absolute encoding [24] by modeling relative distances, it fails to incorporate temporal decay effects - a critical oversight given the time-sensitive nature of network states. Recent attempts [21] to introduce decay weights remain disconnected from RPE, missing the opportunity to jointly optimize position and temporal importance.

Inspired by window attention developments in CV [15] and NLP domains, we adapt these techniques for temporal data. Traditional sliding window approaches [30] demonstrate limited effectiveness when processing streaming data with dynamically changing preloading boundaries. While hierarchical windowing [27] and MoE variants [17] offer improvements, they still struggle with preloading interference. Our work bridges these gaps by: **(1) unifying decay-aware position encoding, and (2) developing adaptive windowing that respects both temporal patterns and preloading artifacts.**

3 Preliminary

3.1 Definitions

Definition 1 (Quality of Experience (QoE)). Given a mobile video streaming session under fluctuating wireless conditions, the *Quality of Experience (QoE)* is defined as the end-user's perceived playback **continuity**, i.e. whether the video plays without any stall (playback interruption).

Our primary objective is to utilize historical network feature data to forecast future network quality. This predictive capability facilitates timely network intervention decisions, thereby optimizing network performance. In Sect. 4 of this paper, we present a detailed description of the model design. Section 5 delves into the specifics of the dataset used and presents the experimental results. This comprehensive analysis ensures that our approach is both methodologically sound and empirically validated.

Definition 2 (Temporal Dependency). Given a multivariate time series $\mathbf{S} = \{s_t\}_{t=1}^{T}$ of network metrics, a *Temporal Dependency* refers to the influence that a past observation $s_{t-\tau}$ exerts on a future value s_t across a time lag τ.

In this work the dependency strength decays exponentially with τ, encoding the domain prior that recent measurements carry more predictive information than distant ones. Building on this, in Sect. 4.2 of this paper, we provide a detailed introduction to our approach of incorporating a temporal decay factor to give greater emphasis to recent data trends.

Definition 3 (Look-back Window). Given a univariate or multivariate time series $\mathbf{S} = \{s_t\}_{t=1}^{T}$, a *Look-back Window* of size L refers to the subset of observations $\{s_{t-L+1}, s_{t-L+2}, \ldots, s_{t-1}, s_t\}$ that are considered when making a prediction or analysis at time step t.

The look-back window encompasses historical data points, which are used to provide the model with information about recent trends and patterns. In the experimental section of this paper, we also compare the impact of different look-back windows on the results.

3.2 Problem Statement

Let $\mathbf{S} = \{\, \mathbf{s}_t \in \mathbb{R}^M \mid t = 1, \ldots, T\}$ denote a realâĂŞtime multivariate sequence of M lower-layer network metrics (*e.g.*, rsrp, snr, ulRateBps, dlRateBps...) captured from a mobile video client in the subway environment. At the decision instant t, the player has already observed the *look-back window* $\mathbf{X}_t = \left[\mathbf{s}_{t-L+1}, \ldots, \mathbf{s}_t\right] \in \mathbb{R}^{L\times M}$, where L is a fixed past horizon (5 s sampling $\Rightarrow L = 15$ corresponds to one minute). Accordingly, the research problem addressed in this paper is characterized by three key components:
Prediction Target. We denote by $y_t \in \{0, 1\}$ the ground-truth label indicating whether a *buffer-underflow stall* will occur during the forthcoming prediction horizon Δ (here $\Delta = 4$ s). A stall event is recorded if the render buffer becomes empty at any moment within $(t, t + \Delta]$.
Learning Objective. Given a training set $\mathcal{D} = \{(\mathbf{X}_t^{(n)}, y_t^{(n)})\}_{n=1}^{N}$ extracted with a sliding window over multiple sessions, we seek a predictor $f_\theta : \mathbb{R}^{L\times M} \to \{0, 1\}$ parameterized by θ such that

$$\hat{y}_t = f_\theta(\mathbf{X}_t) \approx y_t, \qquad \forall (\mathbf{X}_t, y_t) \in \mathcal{D}. \tag{1}$$

Due to the rarity of stall events, which constitute approximately 16% of the total windows, we aim to minimize the weighted binary cross-entropy loss:

$$\mathcal{L}(\theta) = -\sum_{(\mathbf{X},y)\in\mathcal{D}} \Big[\alpha\, y \log \hat{p}_\theta(\mathbf{X}) + \beta\,(1-y) \log(1 - \hat{p}_\theta(\mathbf{X}))\Big], \tag{2}$$

with $\alpha > \beta$ to counter class imbalance, subject to an operational *false-positive-rate* constraint FPR $\le \varepsilon$ ($\varepsilon = 20\%$ in subway deployment).
Key Challenges: To achieve the aforementioned objectives, three technical challenges must be overcome, including:

1. **Temporal locality.** Recent measurements have a stronger influence than distant ones, and ignoring this decay can lead to a slower response.
2. **Preloading interference.** Preloaded chunks introduce traffic spikes whose feature patterns overlap genuine stalls, causing label noise.
3. **Real-time constraint.** The model must output $\hat{y}_t$ within one sampling interval (4 s) to be actionable by the adaptive bitrate controller.

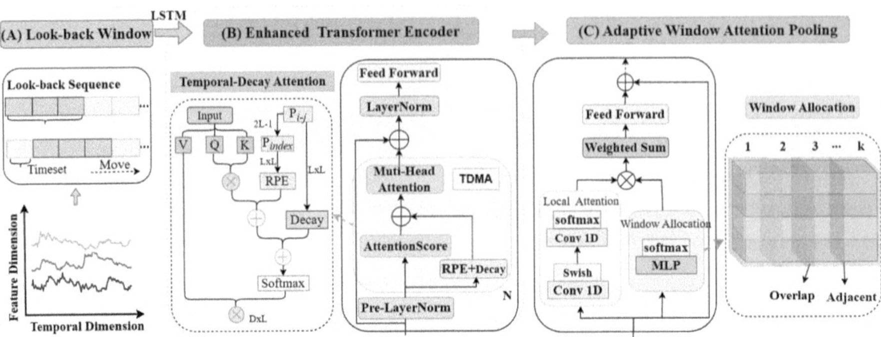

Fig. 1. Overview of TD-LTNet. (A) QoS Data with sliding window, (B) Enhanced Transformer Encoder, which contains Temporal-Decay Multi-Head Attention(left is the details of Temporal-Decay Attention), (C) Adaptive Window Attention Pooling(left is a flowchart of Adaptive Window Attention Pooling, and right is a schematic of Window Allocation).

4 Methodology

4.1 Framework Overview

The proposed **TD-LTNet** is a hybrid neural architecture designed for real-time network stall prediction in dynamic subway environments. As illustrated in Fig. 1, after transforming the QoS data of the time series into a fixed look-back window sequence and processing them through an LSTM model, the sequence undergoes two critical steps for enhanced temporal feature extraction:

1. **Enhanced Transformer Encoder**: Combines multi-head self-attention with temporal-decay factors and relative positional encoding to dynamically adjust attention weights, prioritizing recent network states while maintaining precise timing relationships across the entire sequence (Sect. 4.2).
2. **Adaptive Window Attention Pooling**: Implements an intelligent windowing mechanism that automatically segments sequences into optimal windows, applying attention both within and across windows to maximize feature extraction while maintaining computational efficiency (Sect. 4.3).

4.2 Enhanced Transformer Encoder

In sequential modeling tasks, the fundamental assumption of **temporal locality** [18] dictates that recent events typically exert a stronger influence on current predictions than distant historical events. This prior knowledge is particularly critical in time-sensitive applications such as video stall prediction, where network jitter or packet loss occurring milliseconds before a playback frame has a substantially greater impact than similar events seconds earlier. The most recent measurements usually hold the strongest causal signal for the next step, whereas a vanilla Transformer initially treats every past time-stamp equally. Thus, we introduce a **Temporal-Decay Multi-Head Attention (TDMA)** incorporating *Relative Positional Encoding* [22] and *Temporal Decay factors* to achieve hierarchical feature abstraction. Figure 1 (B) shows full details.

1) Relative Positional Encoding. Traditional positional encodings in Transformers are insufficient for modeling temporal decay in sequential data. We utilize relative position encoding to compute the relative position difference $|i-j|$ between query key pairs, which also facilitates the combination with our designed time decay factor function. A learnable parameter matrix $\mathbf{P} \in \mathbb{R}^{H\times(2L-1)}$ (where H is the number of attention heads and L is the maximum sequence length) generates positional biases, enhancing sensitivity to element distances:

$$\text{AttnScoreTemp}_{i,j} = \frac{Q_i K_j^T}{\sqrt{d_k}} + P_{h,i-j}. \tag{3}$$

2) Temporal Decay Factor. We employ the natural logarithm function (ln) to enhance the sensitivity of the model to temporal distances, which emphasizes the significance of more recent events over older ones. In conjunction with the natural logarithm, we employ the hyperbolic tangent function (tanh) to compress the input values within the range of [-1,1], thus controlling the nonlinear characteristics of decay and preventing the model from assigning disproportionately large or small weights to events based on their temporal distance. This combination ensures both temporal resolution and numerical stability in attention weight calculation. A learnable scalar γ imposes an exponential decay constraint on the attention scores for each individual attention head, initialized to 1.0 and optimized through backpropagation with gradient clipping (max norm=5.0). This design allows the model to automatically learn optimal temporal decay patterns from data while maintaining numerical stability. Different attention heads learn distinct γ values, enabling multi-scale temporal modeling. Here, ϵ serves as a very small stabilizing constant:

$$\text{Decay}_{i,j} = -\gamma \cdot \ln\left(1 + (i-j)\cdot \tanh\left(\frac{i-j}{\epsilon}\right)\right), \tag{4}$$

$$\text{AttnScore}_{i,j} \leftarrow \text{AttnScoreTemp}_{i,j} + \text{Decay}_{i,j}. \tag{5}$$

The encoder comprises N stacked layers, each containing pre-normalized multi-head attention, a feed-forward network (FFN), and residual connections.

4.3 Adaptive Window Attention Pooling

In short video scenarios, the data typically incorporates preloading mechanisms, which may compromise the prediction accuracy for real-time data. To address this, we propose **Adaptive Window Attention Pooling (AWAP)**, which effectively extracts and fuses features from input sequences. Specifically, the input sequence is partitioned into multi-scale window blocks (e.g., short/medium/long windows). The module subsequently calculates both inter-block and intra-block attention weights to prioritize non-preloaded real-time data in the model focus. This design also prevents temporal information fragmentation caused by fixed windowing strategies. The exploration is systematically divided into three interconnected steps as follows:

1) Dynamic Window Allocation. The adaptive window allocation mechanism endows the model with the capability to dynamically partition spatiotemporal perception areas. As shown in Fig. 1 (C), by dividing the input sequence into windows, the model can effectively handle sequences of varying lengths and complexities. The flexibility to allow overlapping windows is particularly advantageous as it enables the model to capture dependencies that span across multiple segments of the sequence. This overlapping capability ensures that the model does not miss critical transitions or patterns that might be obscured when considering only strictly non-overlapping segments.

This module abandons the prior assumption of preset window sizes and generates window allocation weight matrices through a learnable convolutional network. Let the input sequence be $X \in \mathbb{R}^{B\times T\times d}$ (where B is the batch size, T is the time step length, and d is the feature dimension):

$$\mathbf{W}_{\text{assign}} = \text{Softmax}\left(\text{Conv1D}\left(\text{GELU}\left(\text{Conv1D}\left(\mathbf{X}^{\top}\right)\right)\right)\right) \in \mathbb{R}^{B\times K\times T}, \tag{6}$$

where K is the preset number of windows, and the softmax normalizes along the temporal axis. A 1D convolution with kernel_size=1 has a receptive field that contains only the current time step. It is equivalent to a fully connected layer that shares weights on all time steps. This means that which window a time step is assigned to depends entirely on the feature vectors of the time step itself, and is independent of its neighboring time steps. The two-layer network plus a nonlinear activation function (GELU) gives it the ability to learn nonlinear mappings. This is the lightest convolution operation with low computational cost, and for abrupt transitions that need to be accurately segmented, a large kernel may smooth the boundaries and lead to inaccurate localization.

There are two theoretical limitations to the current window assignment weight calculation. One is the paradox of static kernel dynamics. Although the convolutional kernel parameters are obtained through training, their inference phase remains fixed. This is fundamentally different from fully dynamic attentional mechanisms, which we classify as semi-dynamic designs, retaining part of the input during inference through batch normalization (BN) layer dependencies. Second, traditional Softmax forces all window probabilities to sum up to 1, which may inhibit response to unexpected events. This is consistent with the "probabilistic dilution effect" reported in the literature [19]. Gumbel-Softmax-based optimization methods can alleviate this problem.

2) Local Attention Mechanism. The Local Attention Mechanism computes position-wise importance scores that highlight semantically relevant elements within the sequence. This operates in conjunction with window assignments to focus attention within meaningful segments. And the collaborative optimization of local attention and global features constructs a multi-level feature representation system. The module refines features through a dual parallel attention mechanism. The local attention branch uses a gated convolutional network to extract fine-grained patterns:

$$\alpha = \text{Softmax}\left(\text{Conv1D}\left(\text{Swish}\left(\text{Conv1D}\left(\mathbf{X}^{T}\right)\right)\right)\right) \in \mathbb{R}^{B\times 1\times T}, \tag{7}$$

where the swish activation

$$\text{swish}(x) = x \cdot \sigma(x) \tag{8}$$

introduces nonlinearity while maintaining gradient flow, particularly beneficial for capturing local temporal patterns. The module ensures three key properties:

1. **Locality:** Each α_t depends primarily on features within a receptive field of size Δ through the convolutional operators;
2. **Content Sensitivity:** The switch-gated transformation allows non-linear dependency on input features ($\frac{\partial \alpha_t}{\partial X_{t-d}} \neq 0$ for $|d| \leq \Delta$);
3. **Normalization:** The softmax constraint prevents attention dominance by single timesteps.

3) Fusion Layer. The Fusion Layer hierarchically combines information from all windows to produce a fixed-dimensional representation. This stage transforms the window-level features into a unified representation while preserving information from all partitions.Given window assignments $\mathbf{W} \in \mathbb{R}^{B\times K\times T}$ and attention weights $\boldsymbol{\alpha} \in \mathbb{R}^{B\times 1\times T}$, we first compute window features:

$$\mathbf{V} = (\mathbf{W} \odot \boldsymbol{\alpha})\mathbf{X} \in \mathbb{R}^{B\times K\times D}, \tag{9}$$

where $\odot$ denotes element-wise multiplication and the product implements weighted pooling. And we choose learned Fusion:

$$\boldsymbol{\mu} = \mathbf{U}^{\top}\text{vec}(\mathbf{V}) + \mathbf{b}, \quad \mathbf{U} \in \mathbb{R}^{KD\times D}, \tag{10}$$

The final output incorporates residual connections and normalization:

$$\text{Output} = \text{LayerNorm}\left(\boldsymbol{\mu} + \frac{1}{T}\sum_{t=1}^{T}\mathbf{X}_t\right). \tag{11}$$

The proposed AWAP architecture exhibits three key characteristics that enable effective sequence modeling: (1) Hierarchical aggregation that systematically combines local window-level features with global sequence information through its multi-stage processing pipeline; (2) Architectural flexibility through configurable fusion strategies that adapt to different application requirements; (3) Enhanced training stability via residual connections that maintain gradient flow. The synergistic operation of these three components enables AWAP to dynamically adapt to input sequences while maintaining efficient computation and rich representational capacity. The window assignments provide structure, the local attention provides focus within windows, and the fusion layer ensures comprehensive information integration.

5 Experiment

5.1 Dataset and Preprocessing

Data Collection and Characteristics. The dataset comprises 25 raw network metrics (such as rsrp, rsrq, ulRateBps, dlRateBps...) collected from all subway systems between September 2024 and March 2025, with binary annotations (1 for Stall, 0 for Normal). Data is collected through intelligent monitoring systems deployed in subway cities across the country. The data is pre-processed by the edge computing nodes and then transmitted back to the central cloud platform via a dedicated metro network. The collection covers more than 80% of the operating lines in each city. Each data segment is 2 min long, with data sampled every 4 s, resulting in 31 consecutive time-series data points per segment. The entire dataset comprises 98,299 such segments. The dataset is complete, with no missing values, indicating a high level of data quality. Data preprocessing involves outlier handling, normalization, and removal of irrelevant features. Table 1 shows the sample data, with the last column being the label. The proportion of stall events ranges from 16%, which is relatively low, highlighting a class imbalance within the dataset. It should be noted that our experimental data do not explicitly distinguish between different mobility scenarios (e.g., cellular density, train speed intervals, etc.), which may lead to insufficient evaluation of model performance in extreme scenarios. This will be addressed in future work through multi-city cross-scenario joint experiments.

Table 1. Data Samples contains 25 columns and 3,047,269 rows of data.

TimeStamp	Rat	Rsrp	Rsrq	Snr	DlRateBps	UlRateBps	...	AvgRtt	DataStall
4106092547	20	−92	−14	6	36	14	...	39583	0
4106092547	20	−82	−11	14	33	13	...	44997	1
...	...	...	...	...	...	...	...	...	...
23597064	13	−85	−6	21	23	6	...	114961	0

5.2 Baselines

The baseline models considered in this study encompass both traditional machine learning algorithms and deep learning architectures:

1. **XGBoost(XGB):** An efficient and scalable implementation of gradient boosting framework that has proven to be highly effective in various machine learning tasks [9].
2. **LightGBM(LGBM):** A gradient boosting framework optimized for distributed and efficient training, known for its speed and performance [13].

3. **Recurrent Neural Networks(RNN):** A class of artificial neural networks designed to process sequential data by maintaining a memory of previous inputs through hidden states.
4. **Long Short-Term Memory(LSTM):** A type of Recurrent Neural Network (RNN) designed to handle the vanishing gradient problem, making it suitable for learning long-term dependencies in sequential data [12].
5. **Fully Convolutional Network(FCN):** A neural network architecture that uses only convolutional layers, well-suited for tasks like image segmentation where spatial hierarchies are crucial [16].
6. **TransformerEncoder(Trans):** A component of the Transformer model that relies on self-attention mechanisms to process sequences, particularly effective for tasks involving long-range dependencies [24].
7. **ConvTran:** A transformer-based model for multivariate time series classification that enhances positional awareness and feature extraction. It introduces time Absolute Position Encoding (tAPE) to better capture temporal order by adjusting embeddings based on series length and dimension [10].

5.3 Metrics

To capture the multiâĂŞfaceted requirements of mobile-video stall prediction, we adopt three complementary metrics: Accuracy, F1-score (F1), and False-Positive Rate (FPR).

Accuracy is a common metric used to evaluate the performance of classification models, representing the proportion of correctly predicted samples out of the total number of samples. The formula for calculating accuracy is as follows:

$$\text{Accuracy} = \frac{TP + TN}{TP + TN + FP + FN}, \tag{12}$$

where TP (True Positives) denotes the number of true positive instances, TN (True Negatives) denotes the number of true negative instances, FP (False Positives) represents the number of false positive instances, and FN (False Negatives) indicates the number of false negative instances.

F1-Score is a metric used to evaluate the performance of models when dealing with imbalanced datasets, and it is the harmonic mean of Precision and Recall. The formula for calculating the F1-Score is as follows:

$$F1 = 2 \cdot \frac{\text{Precision} \cdot \text{Recall}}{\text{Precision} + \text{Recall}}, \tag{13}$$

where Precision is the ratio of true positives to the sum of true and false positives, and Recall (or Sensitivity) is the ratio of true positives to the sum of true positives and false negatives. A higher F1-Score indicates better performance. Given the class imbalance in our dataset, where the proportion of stall (cardinality) data samples is significantly larger than that of non-stall samples, the

F1-Score offers a more precise and comprehensive evaluation of model performance compared to using accuracy as the sole metric.

False Positive Rate (FPR) is the ratio of false positives to the total number of actual negatives and is given by:

$$FPR = \frac{FP}{FP + TN}, \tag{14}$$

which isolates the fraction of normal sessions that are incorrectly flagged as stalls. A low FPR is indispensable for large-scale deployment. In practical application scenarios, every false positive can trigger unnecessary bitrate downgrades or pre-fetch retransmissions, incurring tangible OPEX and energy overheads. So we need to monitor the FPR.

5.4 Experimental Results

In this section, we conduct a comprehensive performance evaluation of the proposed method, comparing it against multiple established prediction approaches documented in the literature [9,12,13,16,20,24]. Since the size of the look-back window can affect the performance of different models, we choose the look-back window sizes 10, 15, and 20. To ensure a fair and accurate comparison, we have aligned our evaluation criteria. This includes utilizing the same datasets, pre-processing steps, and performance metrics. We use L2 regularization and determine the model parameters through 10-fold hierarchical cross-validation. To prevent overfitting, we use 0.1 dropout in the neural network and apply early stopping.

Table 2. Results under varying look-back window(%).

Model	Seq = 10			Seq = 15			Seq = 20		
	F1	Acc	FPR	F1	Acc	FPR	F1	Acc	FPR
LGBM	52.18	70.20	34.94	54.01	81.13	28.18	51.95	75.99	25.97
XGB	54.87	74.71	28.43	55.89	80.86	23.2	53.87	79.62	20.42
FCN	54.82	78.94	20.51	57.82	77.19	15.75	53.22	79.81	19.23
RNN	54.76	79.50	19.39	58.04	78.55	18.42	52.7	80.03	18.54
LSTM	54.66	79.79	20.52	58.52	78.84	18.1	54.96	81.41	15.72
Trans	55.98	79.65	19.89	58.86	79.80	20.25	54.75	81.38	17.11
ConvTrans	56.35	78.75	19.31	58.58	79.12	18.58	54.97	82.17	17.17
Ours	**56.52**	**80.61**	**18.09**	**60.23**	**82.72**	**15.01**	**55.49**	**82.52**	**15.32**

Main Result. Table 2 presents the experimental results, showing the performance metrics of various models on our dataset across different look-back windows, specifically 10, 15, and 20. The metrics evaluated include Accuracy (denoted as Acc), F1-score (denoted as F1), and False Positive Rate (denoted as FPR). These evaluation metrics collectively quantify the predictive performance across different look-back windows (denoted as Seq).

1) Compared with various predictive models, including machine learning models with engineered temporal features and deep learning models, our proposed model demonstrates superior predictive performance in terms of Accuracy, F1, and FPR. Particularly compared to the machine learning model XGBoost with engineered temporal features, our model shows the best improvement in F1 by 7. 7% when the look-back windows are 15, and reduces the FPR by 35.3%. When compared to the latest deep learning models, our performance is slightly better.
2) Comparative analysis of look-back windows demonstrates that our model achieves optimal performance at input length 15. The accuracy improves from 80.61% to 82.72% (+2.11% points, representing a 2.6% relative gain) compared to length 10, while slightly outperforming length 20. Similar improvements are observed in F1-score and false positive rate (FPR). These results demonstrate that while longer historical windows do not guarantee better QoE prediction performance for video stalling events, selecting an appropriately sized look-back window (15 timesteps in our case) achieves optimal balance by effectively capturing relevant temporal patterns while preserving predictive power for future states.

Computational Complexity Analysis. We use FLOPs/Sequence to measure the complexity and exclude the interference of Batch Size to ensure the fairness of comparison. The transformer's self-attention mechanism is $\mathcal{O}((T^2 \cdot H + T \cdot H^2))$ (L denotes the number of transformer layers, T denotes the sequence length, and H denotes the hidden dimension), which is a well-established trade-off for state-of-the-art sequence modeling. The AWAP module $\mathcal{O}((T^2 \cdot H + K \cdot T \cdot H))$ operates in linear time, providing computational efficiency for long sequences. Optimization of efficiency is achieved through a triple design: (1) extraction of local features in a convolutional way, (2) sparse windows for dynamic focus, and (3) fusion of features at the layer level. Experiments show that this design leads to an improvement in the F1 score. Notably, despite AWAP's asymptotically better linear scaling, its actual FLOPs for our experiments are higher than a single Transformer layer.

Ablation Studies. In order to verify the effect of our proposed two modules, we conduct additional experiments, ablation experiments to verify the effect of different modules:

(1) w/o TDMA: Remove Temporal-Decay Multi-Head Attention.

(2) w/o AWAP: Remove Adaptive Window Attention Pooling.
(3) w/o All: LSTM-Transformer combined with Relative Position Encoding.
(4) APE: LSTM-Transformer combined with Absolute Position Encoding.

Table 3. Performance comparison under different look-back windows. **Bold** indicates the best values in each column(%).

Method	Seq = 10			Seq = 15			Seq = 20		
	Acc	F1	FPR	Acc	F1	FPR	Acc	F1	FPR
Ours	**80.61**	**56.52**	18.09	**82.72**	**60.23**	**15.01**	**82.52**	**55.49**	**15.32**
w/o EDA	80.08	56.33	19.02	81.05	59.31	17.94	81.13	54.56	17.39
w/o AWAP	80.59	56.22	**17.94**	80.97	59.68	18.36	81.49	54.64	16.76
w/o ALL	80.13	56.25	18.87	80.40	59.18	19.20	81.31	53.64	16.57
APE	80.25	55.91	18.42	79.45	58.37	20.61	79.31	53.33	20.21

We conducted ablation experiments with inputs of length 10, 15 and 20 and Table 3 illustrates the impact of each module. It can be observed that: (1) Removing the TDMA module leads to a slight degradation in both F1-score and accuracy, along with an increased FPR, highlighting the importance of temporal decay mechanisms for effective time-series modeling; (2) Eliminating the AWAP module results in reduced F1-score, which confirms that AWAP contributes significantly to overall performance. Even though removing this module may slightly affect FPR performance in 10 of the sequences, it remains a valuable component of the model architecture; and (3) the removal of both modules causes significant accuracy deterioration, underscoring their collective importance for model effectiveness. These findings validate two key design principles: first, that data points closer to the prediction horizon have a greater influence on performance, and second, that segmented processing of preloaded data is essential. Finally, compared to the baseline LSTM-TransformerEncoder model (using Absolute Positional Encoding), our proposed architecture with both modules shows consistent and substantial improvements across all metrics.

6 Conclusion

This paper proposed a general framework for time series prediction, TD-LTNet, which was designed based on LSTM and Transformer encoder. Considering that data closer to the prediction point is more important in time series tasks, we designed a temporal decay multi-head attention module to assign different weights based on relative positional distance, thereby establishing temporal dependencies. Additionally, to address the preloading scenario in short videos, we introduced adaptive window attention pooling. This mechanism dynamically divided the input time series into multiple window blocks, ensuring the model prioritizes non-preloaded data. These innovative mechanisms collectively enabled TD-LTNet to achieve superior predictive performance while improving adaptability across diverse subway lines and operational scenarios. Future work will explore the application of TD-LTNet to other time-series prediction tasks to demonstrate model generalization capabilities.

References

1. Forecasting economic and financial time-series with non-linear models. Int. J. Forecast. **20**(2), 169–183 (2004). forecasting Economic and Financial Time Series Using Nonlinear Methods
2. Barakabitze, A.A., et al.: QOE management of multimedia streaming services in future networks: a tutorial and survey. IEEE Commun. Surv. Tutorials **22**(1), 526–565 (2019)
3. Bilotta, S., Collini, E., Nesi, P., Pantaleo, G.: Short-term prediction of city traffic flow via convolutional deep learning. IEEE Access **10**, 113086–113099 (2022)
4. Blog, N.T.: Dynamic optimizer — a perceptual video encoding optimization framework (2021)
5. Cao, J., Li, Z., Li, J.: Financial time series forecasting model based on CEEMDAN and LSTM. Phys. A **519**, 127–139 (2019)
6. Cao, K., Zhang, T., Huang, J.: Advanced hybrid LSTM-transformer architecture for real-time multi-task prediction in engineering systems. Sci. Rep. **14**(1), 4890 (2024)
7. Casas, P., et al.: Predicting QOE in cellular networks using machine learning and in-smartphone measurements, pp. 1–6 (2017)
8. Chang, C.I., Wang, Y., Chen, S.Y.: Anomaly detection using causal sliding windows. IEEE J. Sel. Top. Appl. Earth Observ. Remote Sens. **8**(7), 3260–3270 (2015)
9. Chen, T., Guestrin, C.: XGBoost: a scalable tree boosting system. In: Proceedings of the 22nd ACM SIGKDD International Conference on Knowledge Discovery and Data Mining, pp. 785–794 (2016)
10. Foumani, N.M., Tan, C.W., Webb, G.I., Salehi, M.: Improving position encoding of transformers for multivariate time series classification. Data Min. Knowl. Disc. **38**(1), 22–48 (2024)
11. Gao, J., Wang, H., Shen, H.: Task failure prediction in cloud data centers using deep learning. In: 2019 IEEE International Conference on Big Data *BigData*, pp. 1111–1116. IEEE (2019)
12. Hochreiter, S., Schmidhuber, J.: Long short-term memory. Neural Comput. **9**(8), 1735–1780 (1997)
13. Ke, G., et al.: LightGBM: a highly efficient gradient boosting decision tree. In: Advances in Neural Information Processing Systems, vol. 30 (2017)
14. Lippi, M., Bertini, M., Frasconi, P.: Short-term traffic flow forecasting: an experimental comparison of time-series analysis and supervised learning. IEEE Trans. Intell. Transp. Syst. **14**(2), 871–882 (2013)
15. Liu, Z., et al.: SWIN transformer: Hierarchical vision transformer using shifted windows. In: Proceedings of the IEEE/CVF International Conference on Computer Vision, pp. 10012–10022 (2021)
16. Long, J., Shelhamer, E., Darrell, T.: Fully convolutional networks for semantic segmentation. In: Proceedings of the IEEE Conference on Computer Vision and Pattern Recognition, pp. 3431–3440 (2015)

17. Lu, E., et al.: MOBA: mixture of block attention for long-context LLMS. arXiv preprint arXiv:2502.13189 (2025)
18. Ma, X., et al.: MEGA: moving average equipped gated attention. arXiv preprint arXiv:2209.10655 (2022)
19. Niculae, V., Martins, A., Blondel, M., Cardie, C.: SparseMAP: differentiable sparse structured inference. In: Dy, J., Krause, A. (eds.) Proceedings of the 35th International Conference on Machine Learning. Proceedings of Machine Learning Research, vol. 80, pp. 3799–3808. PMLR (2018). https://proceedings.mlr.press/v80/niculae18a.html
20. Rumelhart, D.E., Hinton, G.E., Williams, R.J.: Learning representations by back-propagating errors. Nature **323**(6088), 533–536 (1986)
21. Shao, R., et al.: Earlier tokens contribute more: learning direct preference optimization from temporal decay perspective. arXiv preprint arXiv:2502.14340 (2025)
22. Shaw, P., Uszkoreit, J., Vaswani, A.: Self-attention with relative position representations. arXiv preprint arXiv:1803.02155 (2018)
23. Thi Minh Phuong, H., Vu Thu Nguyet, P., Huu Nhat Minh, N., Thi My Hanh, L., Thanh Binh, N.: A comparative study of handling imbalanced data using generative adversarial networks for machine learning based software fault prediction. Appl. Intell. **55**(4), 1–34 (2025)
24. Vaswani, A., et al.: Attention is all you need. In: Advances in Neural Information Processing Systems, vol. 30 (2017)
25. Wei, X., et al.: Attention-based spatial-temporal synchronous graph convolution networks for traffic flow forecasting. Appl. Intell. **55**(6), 516 (2025)
26. Wen, H., Yu, J., Pan, G., Chen, X., Zhang, S., Xu, S.: A hybrid CNN-LSTM architecture for high accurate edge-assisted bandwidth prediction. IEEE Wirel. Commun. Lett. **11**(12), 2640–2644 (2022)
27. Xiang, X., Tian, Y., Zhang, Y., Fu, Y., Allebach, J.P., Xu, C.: Zooming Slowmo: an efficient one-stage framework for space-time video super-resolution. arXiv preprint arXiv:2104.07473 (2021)
28. Ye, B.L., Zhang, M., Li, L., Liu, C., Wu, W.: A survey of traffic flow prediction methods based on long short-term memory networks. IEEE Intell. Transport. Syst. Mag. (2024)
29. Zhang, H., Dong, L., Gao, G., Hu, H., Wen, Y., Guan, K.: DeepQOE: a multimodal learning framework for video quality of experience (QOE) prediction. IEEE Trans. Multimedia (2020)
30. Zhang, L., Lin, J., Karim, R.: Sliding window-based fault detection from high-dimensional data streams. IEEE Trans. Syst. Man Cybern. Syst. **47**(2), 289–303 (2016)
31. Zhou, H., et al.: Informer: beyond efficient transformer for long sequence time-series forecasting. In: Proceedings of the AAAI Conference on Artificial Intelligence, vol. 35, pp. 11106–11115 (2021)

FACKT: A Fault-Aware Model for Code Knowledge Tracing

Mengshuang Zhou, Qing Zhou(✉), Wenyuan Xia, Ying Jiang, Cifa Lin, and Subo Zhao

College of Computer Science, Chongqing University, Chongqing 401331, China
{202314021006,xiawenyuan,202414021014T,lincifa, 202414131171}@stu.cqu.edu.cn, tzhou@cqu.edu.cn

Abstract. Programming skills are an essential competency in today's digital age. As online judgement systems have gained popularity, students are contributing vast amounts of behavioral data through programming exercises. Traditional knowledge tracing can be employed to predict students' performance in programming. Nevertheless, these methods frequently fall short by neglecting the role of code faults in modeling programming learning state. Furthermore, they fail to capture the dynamic and semantic characteristics of source code due to reliance on general-purpose code representation techniques. In this study, we propose a novel method called Fault-Aware Code Knowledge Tracing (FACKT), which integrates a dual-LSTM architecture with attention mechanisms and memory decay theory to track the evolution of both fault patterns and knowledge states of students. Moreover, by incorporating test case analysis with Large Language Models (LLMs), FACKT autonomously generates fault types, thereby enriching the code representation. Experimental results indicate that FACKT achieves an 8.3% improvement in AUC and a 3.5% increase in ACC compared to baseline methods. Ablation studies further demonstrate the effectiveness of modeling the fault evolution process. Additionally, we publicly release FACKT_2024, a dataset comprising 74,269 code submissions from university students.

Keywords: Code Knowledge Tracing · Programming Education · Code Faults

1 Introduction

The continuous development of the Internet and computer technology has pushed the transformation of traditional education to smart education, and has put forward new requirements for programming skills. Recently, various types of online programming learning platforms, such as Online Judge (OJ) systems, have facilitated large-scale, self-directed learning as well as accumulated a large amount of learning interactions. How-ever, they also led to a lack of personalized teaching since instructors cannot keep track of students' programming skills in time. Therefore, modeling students' behavioral data from OJ systems to assess the mastery level of programming skills and enable personalized instruction has emerged as a critical research issue in Educational Data Mining (EDM).

J. Li et al. (Eds.): APWeb-WAIM 2025, LNCS 16115, pp. 67–80, 2026.
https://doi.org/10.1007/978-981-95-5719-6_5

Knowledge Tracing (KT) is an educational analytics technique initially proposed by A.T. Corbett et al. [1], which aims to model students' knowledge mastery by analyzing their historical response data, and to predict their future performance on exercises. This foundational work has given rise to a variety of KT models based on traditional probabilistic methods [2, 3] and deep neural network.

Current researches on KT primarily focus on conventional objective questions, such as multiple-choice math problems, which have clearly defined and unique correct answers. However, when applied to programming education, existing methods exhibit two critical limitations: (1) Existing methods predominantly neglect the impact of code faults on modeling students' programming learning state. As shown in Fig. 1, programming learning is iterative. Students generate and detect faults through multiple attempts, then either resolve them via system feedback and debugging, or reinforce faults through incorrect operations, or even introduce new bugs. Furthermore, students make different code faults on the same questions, and gain different inspirations from mistakes. This phenomenon suggests that the experience of making programming faults significantly affects future performance. But existing KT researches primarily focus on modeling knowledge state evolution, which limits the predictive accuracy of Code Knowledge Tracing (CKT) tasks. (2) Existing methods fail to adequately capture the rich dynamic and semantic information embedded in student codes. To achieve open- ended programming questions, students must develop solutions that satisfy all test cases. For each submitted code, it reflects a student's programming knowledge and ap-plication skills. Current CKT methods typically rely on general-purpose code representation techniques (e.g., Code2vec [4], ASTNN [5]) to capture code features. However, these methods primarily focus on static structural features instead of dynamic and semantic features, resulting in incomplete feature representation of programming learning behaviors, ultimately constraining model performance.

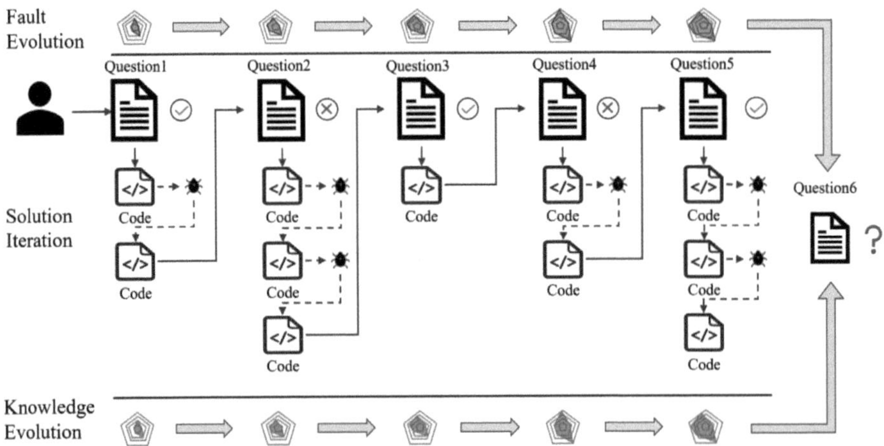

Fig. 1. The process of code knowledge tracing.

To address these limitations, this study makes the following key contributions:

1. We propose Fault-Aware Code knowledge Tracing (FACKT), a novel CKT framework that use a dual-LSTM architecture to simultaneously trace the dynamic evolution of students' knowledge state and fault patterns, which enhances prediction accuracy in CKT tasks.
2. We introduce a dual feature extraction method from the code syntax to the semantic level, by leveraging testcases and prompt engineering techniques with Large Language Models (LLMs) to generate fault types autonomously.
3. We construct a dataset FACKT_2024 with fine-grained fault labels for CKT. And carrying out extensive experiments to validate our methods, achieving an 8.3% increase in AUC and 3.52% enhancement in ACC compared to baseline methods.

2 Related Work

2.1 Knowledge Tracing

Nowadays, extensive researches aim to observe, represent, and quantify a student's knowledge state [6], known as knowledge tracing (KT). Traditional probabilistic KT models [1–3], like Bayesian Knowledge Tracing (BKT) [1], assume learning follows a Markov process, estimating learners' latent knowledge state through observed performance. These models offer good interpretability, but suffer from inherent theoretical and practical limitations which need to rely on theoretical assumptions for manual feature engineering.

Thanks to the adaptive learning capability and powerful feature representation learning of deep neural networks, KT models based on deep learning networks have achieved significant performance. Deep Knowledge Tracing (DKT) [7] models students' learning processes as sequential data, then employs Recurrent Neural Network (RNN) and Long Short-Term Memory (LSTM) to predict the response at the next time step. Moreover, according to the different backbone networks, memory networks based KT models [8], attention mechanism based KT models [9, 10], and graph neural networks based KT models [11] have emerged. However, these models cannot meet the demands of programming education due to the specificity of programming questions and the complexity of students' codes.

To dynamically trace learners' the mastery level of programming knowledge, researchers have conducted extensive explorations. Early studies rarely focused on source code itself; instead, they relied on historical exam scores or log data to identify potential learning difficulties [12, 13]. Recent work has shifted toward analyzing submitted code. Code-DKT [14] argues that source code includes complex semantic expressions and structured problem-solving logic. It pioneers the integration of DKT with Code2vec [4] to automatically extract and select domain-specific code features, achieving significant performance gains. Existing researches further optimize KT models through incorporating additional features, or modeling students' knowledge state in different ways, or improving the prediction module. For example, PKT-ATTN [15] employs attention mechanisms to extract multi-skill features from submitted code, reflecting the diverse programming skills tested in each question. PDKT [16] models double-sequence through problem embeddings and code embeddings. TIKTOC [17] refines CKT into predicting whether code passes individual testcase, and generates the open-ended code.

GPPKT [18] leverages knowledge graphs to encode concept-exercise relationships and uses Variational Autoencoders (VAE) to incorporate student learning abilities and latent representations of personalized solution sequences.

Furthermore, several researches have specifically investigated knowledge tracing within individual programming question. Jiang et al. [19] utilize Abstract Syntax Tree (AST) to measure the similarity between intermediate solutions and optimal solutions, then based on this similarity to predict future performance. PST [20] designs Code Information Graph (CIG) to represent the code feature, and Code Tracing Graph (CTG) to measure the changes between the consecutive submissions. Then the model predicts performance through iterative updates. While the above methods are capable of extracting structure features from source code, they ignore the dynamic and semantic features of student code. Moreover, existing CKT methods demonstrate low accuracy in predicting future performance due to the high difference between students' experience of making faults. Therefore, in this study we incorporate the code fault evolution process and complete code features to assess students' mastery of programming learning.

2.2 Large Language Model

Recent advancements in language models have significantly facilitated the automation of software engineering tasks, including code generation [21], automated program repair [22], and programming concept recognition [23]. To enhance the generalization capabilities of LLMs for specific tasks, researchers typically employ two primary paradigms: fine-tuning or prompt engineering. Prompt engineering, in particular, involves crafting specialized instructions to guide LLMs responses. The specificity of these prompts can substantially influence both the content and quality of the generated outputs [24]. Demonstrating this approach, Julian et al. [25] utilizes Codex with carefully engineered prompts to improve bug detection capabilities, successfully correcting errors in both Java and Python programs.

Some researches utilize the remarkable capabilities of LLMs to improve the performance of CKT tasks. ECKT [26] employs LLMs to generate detailed problem descriptions and knowledge concepts from student code, which enhances the model's understanding of programming concepts. Inspired by these foundations, we combine prompt engineering with LLMs to identify latent semantic features in student code and generate fault type automatically, to enrich the feature expression of the source code.

3 Methodology

3.1 Problem Definition

In the process of programming learning, student $s \in S$ has a historical learning sequence $LS_t = \{s_1, s_2, s_3, ..., s_t\} = \{(q_1, c_1, r_1), (q_2, c_2, r_2), (q_3, c_3, r_3), ..., (q_t, c_t, r_t)\}$, where $s_t = (q_t, c_t, r_t)$ represents the code c_t submitted by the student for a given question q_t in the t step, and r_t denote the OJ system's feedback result for a submission. If the code c_t meet the requirement of q_t i.e. get the Accepted (AC) result, r_t equals to 1; otherwise r_t equals to 0. In the light of the historical programming exercise process LS_t of each student from programming exercise process step 1 to N, the goal of CKT is to assess the student's programming proficiency state and subsequently predict the probability of solving a new programming task q_{t+1} correctly at the next time step $t + 1$.

3.2 Model Overview

The main structure of FACT is shown in Fig. 2. Specifically, it consists of four parts: code-fault extraction module, code-knowledge extraction module, fault and knowledge evolution module, and prediction module. The code-fault extraction module, as shown in Fig. 2(a), executes student code against test cases, and leverage the semantic reasoning capabilities of LLMs to extract both dynamic execution features and deep semantic features of the code. The code-knowledge extraction module (See Fig. 2(b)) identifies latent relationships between programming knowledge concepts and code structures, and generates embedded representations of code-knowledge. The outputs of first two modules are then fed into the fault and knowledge evolution module (See Fig. 2(c)), which employs a dual-LSTM architecture to simultaneously model the temporal dynamics of both fault patterns and knowledge mastery. Finally, as shown in Fig. 2(d), the prediction module forecasts students' future programming performance based on their programming learning status. The above four modules are elaborated in the following sections.

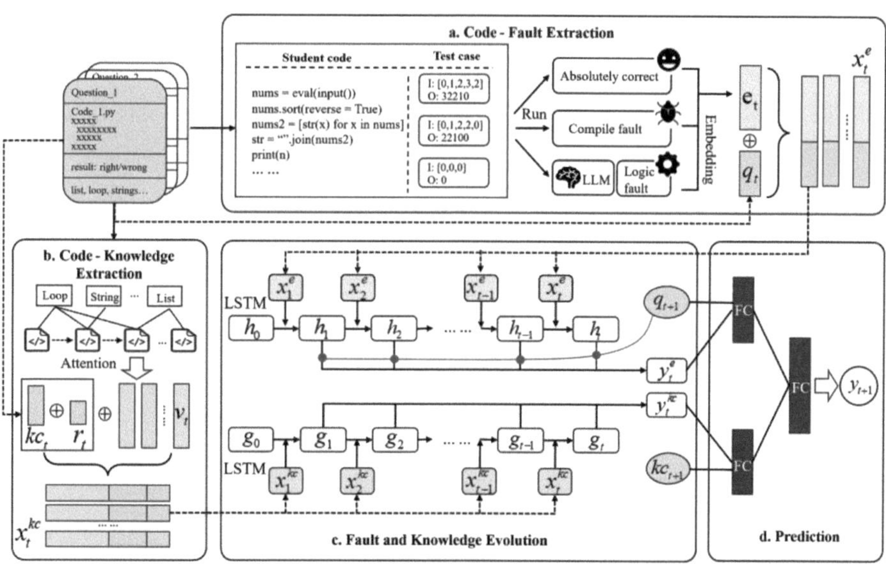

Fig. 2. The architecture of FACKT.

3.3 Code-Fault Extraction Module

In this module, code fault types are identified automatically by extracting the dynamic and semantic features from students' codes. Most of the existing CKT methods generally adopt code representation method based on code structure features, which can effectively model the hierarchical syntactic relationships in programming languages. However, the codes written by students during programming practice also contains other rich features. For instance, the compile faults occurred during code execution, and the logic faults caused by various semantic issues, both can prevent the code from passing all test cases. These faults objectively reflect the cognitive state of learners in terms of their mastery of programming concepts and problem-solving abilities.

In order to efficiently extract code features, we first execute the target code against a carefully designed set of test cases. If the actual output matches the expected output across all test cases, the code is labeled as "correct." If execution triggers a compile fault, the code is annotated with fine-grained labels corresponding to the specific error type. Additionally, if the code runs without com-pile faults but produces mismatched outputs, it is preliminarily labeled as a "logical error" for subsequent finer classification. Through systematic code analysis and error diagnosis, we identified and categorized 9 compile faults and 8 logical faults, as shown in Table 1.

Table 1. Fault types.

Compile faults	Logic faults
TypeError	Wrong solution strategy
FunctionError	Loop fault
AttributeError	Condition fault
Variable misuse	IO process fault
IndexError	List misuse
SyntaxError	Variable misuse
IOError	Function misuse
RecursionError	File fault
Module error	

Given the demonstrated reasoning capabilities of LLMs in software engineer-ing tasks, we employ LLMs to automatically identify and classify code samples containing logical faults, avoiding the limitations of high cost and inefficiency associated with manual annotation. Specifically, we leverage prompt engineering techniques to dynamically encapsulate raw information, optimizing the process through role assignment, task-specific constraints, and other enhancement strategies. The raw information includes the problem description, input-output example pairs, reference correct code, erroneous student code, and a predefined set of logic faults. These multimodal inputs are integrated into a structured prompt template. Then, we assign a role of Python programming expert at the beginning of the prompt, providing the model with a professional knowledge context. Subsequently, the model is guided via a zero-shot approach to simulate the human cognitive process of program debugging. By comparing the correct code with the erroneous code, the model identifies discrepancies and detects abnormal patterns in the erroneous code. Finally, we introduce a display command: "Infer the most likely fault type by analyzing the minimum repair strategy backwards," to enable automated error classification and labeling.

Figure 3 illustrates a typical example of the application of the method. We ex-tract 500 error codes from the datasets and perform manual cross-validation of the fault labels generated by proposed method. Among these, 89.4% of the fault types are consistent with those confirmed by human experts. The remaining 10.6% show some deviation, but there is still a certain degree of correlation. For example, when iterating through a list in a loop, the experts consider it a loop fault, while LLMs classify it as a list misuse fault. However, both classifications are justifiable.

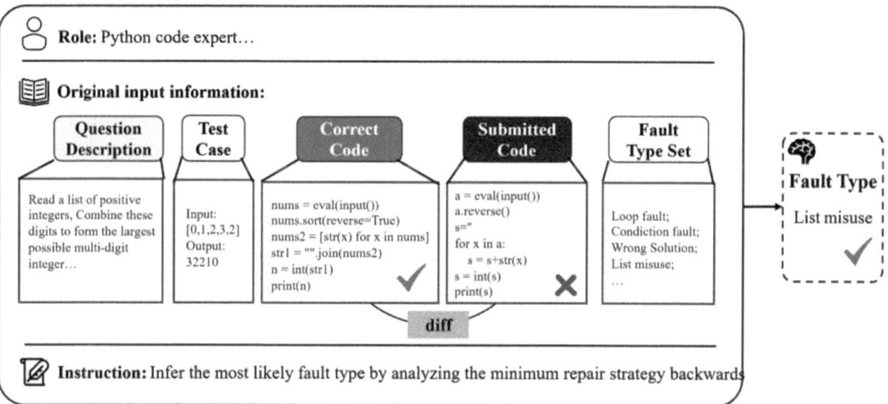

Fig. 3. The example of generating fault type.

Finally, based on the generated fault type labels with dynamic and semantic features, utilizing one-hot encoding to compute embedding representations $e_t \in \mathbb{R}^{m \times d_e}$, where m represents the total number of error types, d_e denotes the feature dimension.

3.4 Code-Knowledge Extraction Module

This module is designed to analyze the interaction between code and program-ming knowledge concepts, aiming to identify the specific concepts applied in student code. Unlike objective question, programming questions are subjective and usually have multiple solutions, and it is difficult to establish a strict one-to-one or one-to-many relationship between the questions and knowledge concepts. To address this issue, we introduce code-knowledge extraction module.

Specifically, we first transform the student code into an Abstract Syntax Tree (AST). The AST is an abstract representation that uses a tree structure to represent the syntactic structure of the source code, where each node in the tree represents a syntactic unit. Following the approach of Code2vec [2], the AST is parsed to generate a list of triples. Each triple consists of the start node, the end node, and the path of nodes connecting the two, forming a set of path contexts $T = \{(x^j_{start}, p^j, x^j_{end})\}_{j=1}^N$, where N denotes the number of path contexts. Next, we embed the nodes and paths respectively, and concatenate the embedding vectors of the triple in sequence as follows:

$$pathsembed_t = \text{Concat}([E_n(x^j_{start}), E_p(p^j), E_n(x^j_{end})])_{j=1}^N \tag{1}$$

where $E_n(\cdot)$ refers to the node embedding matrix, $E_p(\cdot)$ refers to the path embedding matrix, Concat$(\cdot)$ is the concatenating operation. Then, the vector $pathsembed_t$ feed into a linear layer and a Tanh activation function, yielding the representation vector C_t for each path context in the code.

$$C_t = \text{Tanh}[\text{Linear}(pathsembed_t)] \tag{2}$$

Finally, we use attention to compute similarity weights α_{ij} between knowledge concepts and path contexts, then aggregated. The matrix of hidden relationship $H_t \in \mathbb{R}^{|kc| \times d_v}$ between all concepts and code is calculated as:

$$\begin{aligned} \alpha_{ij} &= \text{Softmax}[KC_i \cdot (C_t^j)^T] \\ H_t^i &= \sum_{j=1}^{N} \alpha_{ij} \cdot C_t^j \end{aligned} \tag{3}$$

where KC is the vector of knowledge concepts, $|kc|$ is the total number of knowledge concepts. In addition, we further compute the average hidden states to obtain the overall code-knowledge interaction feature v_t as follows:

$$v_t = \frac{\text{Sum}(M_t \odot H_t)}{|kc_t|} \tag{4}$$

where $|kc_t|$ is the total number of knowledge concepts contained in the current question q_t, $M_t \in \{0, 1\}^{|kc| \times d_v}$ is a mask matrix expanded from the relevant knowledge concepts id, Sum$(\cdot)$ means to sum the matrix by column.

3.5 Fault and Knowledge Evolution Module

In this module, we introduce a dual-LSTM structure with attention mechanism and exponential decay to trace the evolution of programming faults and knowledge concepts. We may notice that the process of programming practice is iterative. As students accumulate and apply knowledge through repeated at-tempts, they simultaneously generate, resolve, or reinforce faults. Moreover, the evolution of knowledge and the evolution of faults are not entirely complementary. Therefore, combining the change of code-fault feature and code-knowledge feature v_t, we can gain a more comprehensive understanding of students' programming learning state.

Initially, we concatenate the code-fault features with the programming question vector q_t encoded by CodeBERT [27] to form the fault sequence $X_t^e = \{x_1^e, x_2^e, x_3^e, ..., x_t^e\}$, and concatenate the code-knowledge features with both knowledge concepts KC_t and results r_t to construct the knowledge sequence $X_t^{kc} = \{x_1^{kc}, x_2^{kc}, x_3^{kc}, ..., x_t^{kc}\}$. These two representations are fed as inputs to two separate LSTMs respectively. In our implementation, the hidden vectors, h_0, g_0 along with C_0^h, C_0^g, are randomly initialized. Then the outputs of LSTMs at time step t are current latent state h_t^e, g_t^{kc}, with g_t^{kc} is directly used as the knowledge evolution state y_t^{kc}:

$$x_t^e = \text{Concat}(e_t, q_t), x_t^{kc} = \text{Concat}(KC_t, v_t, r_t) \tag{5}$$

$$h_t^e = \text{LSTM}(X_t^e), y_t^{kc} = g_t^{kc} = \text{LSTM}(X_t^{kc}) \tag{6}$$

According to the intuition that similar questions have similar solution strategies, and similar solution strategies in turn make or avoid similar faults. To improve the accuracy of prediction at next time step $t + 1$, we use attention to assign higher weight to the more relevant historical experience, which is more similar to the current question q_{t+1} as follows:

$$S_t^h = [W_q(q_{t+1}) + b_p](h_t^e)^T \tag{7}$$

Furthermore, the Ebbinghaus Forgetting Curve illustrates that learning is temporal and memories decay [28], which say that a learner's performance in the distant past is not as informative as recent performance when predicting their response to the current question. Therefore, we add a multiplicative exponential decay term to the similarity matrix before computing normalized attention weights:

$$attn\_e = \text{Softmax}[\exp(-\theta \cdot d) \odot S_t^h] \tag{8}$$

where $\theta > 0$ is an exponential decay hyperparameter, $d = [t-1, t-2, ..., 1, 0]$ is the distance measure between time steps t and historical sequence. Subsequently, by calculating weighted sum, we obtain the students' current state of faults evolution y_t^e:

$$y_t^e = \sum_{k=1}^{t} attn\_e^{(k)} \cdot (h_t^e)^{(k)} \tag{9}$$

3.6 Prediction Module

This module we combine the fault evolution state and knowledge evolution state, then process them through two Fully Connected Neural Networks (FCNNs) to generate the final prediction. Specifically, we first concatenate the fault evolution state with the next question q_{t+1}, and concatenate the knowledge evolution state with the concepts of the next question kc_{t+1}. Then, feed them into two FCNNs to obtain the similarity between the current fault evolution state and the future question, as well as the similarity between the current knowledge evolution state and the future knowledge concepts. Finally, we concatenate the two similarities and use another FCNN, with a Sigmoid activation function to obtain the final predicted probability $pred_{t+1}$ as follows:

$$pred_{i+1} = \sigma[FC(FC(y_t^e \oplus q_{t+1}) \oplus FC(y_t^{kc} \oplus kc_{t+1}))] \tag{10}$$

where $\sigma(\cdot)$ is Sigmoid activation function, $FC(\cdot)$ represents Fully Connected Neural Networks, $\oplus$ is the concatenating operation. Similar to the general classification problem, we choose the cross-entropy log loss between the prediction and ground truth $y_k \in \{0, 1\}$ to optimize the model parameters. Then the loss of our method is defined as follows:

$$L = -\sum_{k=1}^{t} [y_k \cdot \log(pred_k) + (1 - y_k) \cdot \log(1 - pred_k)] \tag{11}$$

4 Experiments

4.1 Datasets

Existing benchmark datasets for CKT primarily cover statical programming languages such as C/C++ and Java, while datasets for dynamical languages like Python remain relatively scarce. Moreover, most publicly available datasets lack complete and authentic code data, which cannot support the fine-grained annotations, such as code faults types and programming knowledge concepts.

Table 2. Data statistics of FACKT_2024.

Statistics	CG_Python2024
# of students	197
# of questions	158
# of submitted codes	74269
Avg. Codes of students	377
AC rate	34.41%
Compile faults rate	37.14%
Logic faults rate	28.45%

To bridge the gap, we construct a Pythonbased dataset FACKT_2024, which is collected from CourseGrading[1], an OJ system for programming training in many universities. By randomly selecting the complete submission records of students from two teaching classes in the 2024 academic year and performing data cleaning, we obtained 74,269 code submissions from 197 students across 158 programming questions. For each record, it contains question description, related concept, submitted code, the judging result and so on. Additionally, the complete statistics of all the datasets is shown in Table 2.

4.2 Baseline Model

To validate the effectiveness of the FACKT model, we selected the following representative CKT methods as baselines for comparison. The descriptions of each baseline model are as follows:

- Code-DKT [14] utilizes attention to extract code features for code knowledge tracing, which enhances DKT.
- PKT-ATTN [15] employs LSTM to model learning process, with attention mechanism to extract multi-skill features from code submissions.
- PDK [16] leverages problem embeddings and source code embeddings to implement a double-sequence RNN architecture for effective CKT. Specifically, since the model's code embedding method PLCodeBERT is not publicly available, we adopt CodeBERT to generate code embeddings.

[1] https://course.educg.net/acm/

4.3 Experiment Settings

In the experiments, the FACKT_2024 dataset is divided into training, validation and test sets with a ratio of 60%-20%-20%. We segment the student's learning sequence into multiple subsequences with a fixed length of 100. The embed-ding dimensions for question descriptions, knowledge concepts, fault types are set to 128. We set batch size, learning rate, and the regularization term to 8, 0.001, 0.00025, respectively. The layer and hidden state dimension of LSTM are 2 and 64. The exponential decay hyperparameter is tuned among $\{0.01, 0.05, 0.1, 0.5\}$. We use Adam as the default optimizer. In addition, we select AUC and ACC values as evaluation metrics. The dataset and our code are available at https://github.com/fackt2024/fackt.

4.4 Performance Comparative Study

As shown in Table 3, the proposed FACKT method significantly outperforms the other three baselines in terms of performance. Specifically, in classification performance, FACT achieves at least an 8.3% improvement in the AUC metric compared to the baseline models. And in terms of prediction accuracy, the ACC of our proposed method is boosted by an additional at least 3.52%. We attribute this improvement to the fact that baseline models only consider binary exercise result, while FACKT achieves more precise feature representation by fine-grained identification of code faults. Moreover, FACKT innovatively traces fault evolution, exploring the intrinsic link between fault patterns and learning state, thus better modeling the change of programming skills and significantly improving prediction performance.

Table 3. The AUC and ACC results on different models.

Methods	AUC	ACC
Code-DKT	0.6814	0.6924
PKT-ATTN	0.6873	0.7014
PDKT	0.6908	0.7035
FACKT	0.7738	0.7387

Additionally, we conducted experiments across $\theta = \{0.01, 0.05, 0.1, 0.5\}$ to investigate the impact of different exponential decay hyperparameters θ on model performance. As shown in Fig. 4, when the value of θ is 0.1, the FACKT gets the best performance.

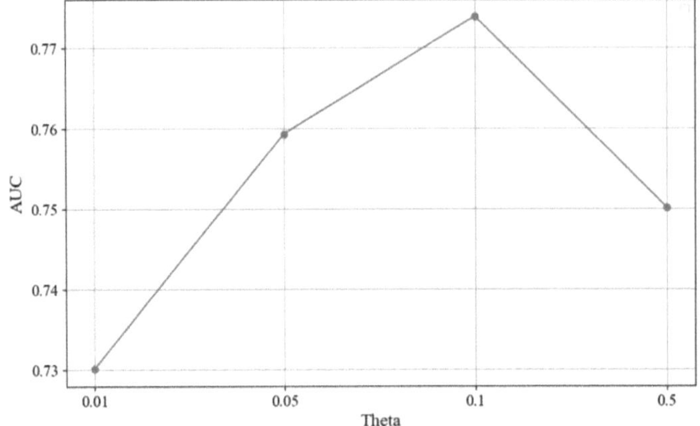

Fig. 4. Effect of the hyperparameters θ

4.5 Ablation Study

In this experiment, we design three variants, each removing one module from the complete FACKT, to evaluate the impact of each module on overall model performance:

- FACKT-KC removes code-knowledge extraction module, and only traces the evolution of code faults.
- FACLT-ATTN removes the attention mechanism in fault evolution process.
- FACKT-D removes the memory decay term in fault evolution process.

Table 4. The result of ablation experiments

Methods	AUC	ACC
FACKT-KC	0.7402	0.7185
FACKT-ATTN	0.7289	0.7116
FACKT-D	0.7572	0.7282
FACKT	0.7738	0.7387

Table 4 presents the result of ablation study, showing that the variants failed to perform at the optimal level of the full FACKT. Notably, removing the attention mechanism in fault evolution led to the most significant performance drop (-4.49% AUC, -2.71% ACC), which highlighting the critical role of similar historical experience of making faults. Moreover, the FACKT-KC still outperforms the best baseline (+4.94% AUC, + 1.5% ACC), with AUC = 0.7408 and ACC = 0.7185, further validating the effectiveness of fault evolution process.

5 Conclusion

In this study, we propose FACKT, a novel CKT method that incorporates code fault evolution process to achieve comprehensive learning state tracing, addressing limitations in existing methods. Furthermore, by extracting the dynamic and semantic features of students' code, the feature expression of the code has been enriched. Experimental results on the fine-grained annotated FACKT_2024 dataset demonstrate that FACKT improves classification performance and prediction accuracy, consistently outperforming existing CKT baselines. These findings validate the effectiveness of integrating fault evolution analysis into knowledge tracing process.

Our study contributes to the development of personalized assistance in programming education, may enable instructors to monitor students' programming learning state in real-time, and accurately identify common code fault patterns. It can also provide data support for differentiated instructional strategies and optimizing curriculum design.

In the future, we will enhance FACKT with more efficient and automated methods for code fault feature extraction. Also, we will consider incorporating additional behavioral features.

Disclosure of Interests. The authors declare no Conflict of interest.

References

1. Corbett, A.T., Anderson, J.R.: Knowledge tracing: modelling the acquisition of procedural knowledge. User Model. User-Adapt. Interact. **4**(4), 253–278 (1995)
2. Cen, H., Koedinger, K., Junker, B.: Learning factors analysis–a general method for cognitive model evaluation and improvement. In: International Conference on Intelligent Tutoring Systems, pp. 164–175. Springer, Heidelberg (2006)
3. Baker, F.B.: The basics of item response theory. ERIC (2001)
4. Alon, U., Zilberstein, M., Levy, O., Yahav, E.: code2vec: learning distributed representations of code. Proc. ACM Program. Lang. **3**(POPL), 1–29 (2019)
5. Zhang, J., Wang, X., Zhang, H., Sun, H., Wang, K., Liu, X.: A novel neural source code representation based on abstract syntax tree. In: 2019 IEEE/ACM 41st International Conference on Software Engineering (ICSE), pp. 783–794. IEEE (2019)
6. Abdelrahman, G., Wang, Q., Nunes, B.: Knowledge tracing: a survey. ACM Comput. Surv. **55**(11), 1–37 (2023)
7. Piech, C., et al.: Deep knowledge tracing. Adv. Neural Inf. Process. Syst. **28** (2015)
8. Zhang, J., Shi, X., King, I., Yeung, D.Y.: Dynamic key-value memory networks for knowledge tracing. In: Proceedings of the 26th International Conference on World Wide Web, pp. 765–774 (2017)
9. Ghosh, A., Heffernan, N., Lan, A.S.: Context-aware attentive knowledge tracing. In: Proceedings of the 26th ACM SIGKDD International Conference on Knowledge Discovery & Data Mining, pp. 2330–2339 (2020)
10. Yin, Y., et al.: Tracing knowledge instead of patterns: stable knowledge tracing with diagnostic transformer. In: Proceedings of the ACM Web Conference 2023, pp. 855–864 (2023)
11. Nakagawa, H., Iwasawa, Y., Matsuo, Y.: Graph-based knowledge tracing: modeling student proficiency using graph neural network. In: IEEE/WIC/ACM International Conference on Web Intelligence, pp. 156–163 (2019)

12. Castro-Wunsch, K., Ahadi, A., Petersen, A.: Evaluating neural networks as a method for identifying students in need of assistance. In: Proceedings of the 2017 ACM SIGCSE Technical Symposium on Computer Science Education, pp. 111–116 (2017)
13. Gao, G., Marwan, S., Price, T.W.: Early performance prediction using interpretable patterns in programming process data. In: Proceedings of the 52nd ACM Technical Symposium on Computer Science Education, pp. 342–348 (2021)
14. Shi, Y., Chi, M., Barnes, T., Price, T.: Code-dkt: a code-based knowledge tracing model for programming tasks. arXiv preprint arXiv:2206.03545 (2022)
15. Zhu, M., Han, S., Yuan, P., Lu, X.: Enhancing programming knowledge tracing by interacting programming skills and student code. In: LAK22: 12th International Learning Analytics and Knowledge Conference, pp. 438–443 (2022)
16. Zhu, R., et al.: Programming knowledge tracing: a comprehensive dataset and a new model. In: 2022 IEEE International Conference on Data Mining Workshops (ICDMW), pp. 298–307. IEEE (2022)
17. Duan, Z., Fernandez, N., Hicks, A., Lan, A.: Test case-informed knowledge tracing for open-ended coding tasks. In: Proceedings of the 15th International Learning Analytics and Knowledge Conference, pp. 238–248 (2025)
18. Pan, J., Dong, Z., Yan, L., Cai, X.: Knowledge graph and personalized answer sequences for programming knowledge tracing. Appl. Sci. **14**(17), 7952 (2024)
19. Jiang, B., Wu, S., Yin, C., Zhang, H.: Knowledge tracing within single programming practice using problem-solving process data. IEEE Trans. Learn. Technol. **13**(4), 822–832 (2020)
20. Li, R., et al.: Pst: measuring skill proficiency in programming exercise process via programming skill tracing. In: Proceedings of the 45th International ACM SIGIR Conference on Research and Development in Information Retrieval, pp. 2601–2606 (2022)
21. Yang, A.Z., Le Goues, C., Martins, R., Hellendoorn, V.: Large language models for test-free fault localization. In: Proceedings of the 46th IEEE/ACM International Conference on Software Engineering, pp. 1–12 (2024)
22. Jin, M., et al.: Inferfix: end-to-end program repair with llms. In: Proceedings of the 31st ACM Joint European Software Engineering Conference and Symposium on the Foundations of Software Engineering, pp. 1646–1656 (2023)
23. Tran, A., Li, L., Rama, E., Angelikas, K., MacNeil, S.: Using large language models to automatically identify programming concepts in code snippets. In: Proceedings of the 2023 ACM Conference on International Computing Education Research, vol. 2, pp. 22–23 (2023)
24. Si, C., et al.: Prompting gpt-3 to be reliable. arXiv preprint arXiv:2210.09150 (2022)
25. Prenner, J.A., Babii, H., Robbes, R.: Can openai's codex fix bugs? An evaluation on quixbugs. In: Proceedings of the Third International Workshop on Automated Program Repair, pp. 69–75 (2022)
26. Yu, Y., Zhou, Y., Zhu, Y., Ye, Y., Chen, L., Chen, M.: Eckt: enhancing code knowledge tracing via large language models. In: Proceedings of the Annual Meeting of the Cognitive Science Society, vol. 46 (2024)
27. Feng, Z., et al.: Codebert: a pre-trained model for program ming and natural languages. arXiv preprint arXiv:2002.08155 (2020)
28. Ebbinghaus, H.: [image] memory: a contribution to experimental psychology. Ann. Neurosci. **20**(4), 155 (2013)

UCPM-CPI: A United Co-Location Pattern Mining Algorithm Based on Correlated Participation Index

Lijin Tang[1], Lizhen Wang[2](✉), and Dongsheng Wang[3]

[1] School of Information Science and Engineering, Yunnan University, Kunming 650091, China
tanglijin@stu.ynu.edu.cn

[2] School of Science and Technology, Dianchi College, Kunming 650228, China
lzhwang@ynu.edu.cn

[3] University of Electronic Science and Technology of China, Chengdu 611731, China
202411081626@std.uestc.edu.cn

Abstract. Spatial co-location patterns reveal associations among spatial features and serve as critical tools for discovering and understanding complex spatial phenomena. However, existing studies overlook the adverse effects of isolated instances on prevalence measures and fail to capture asymmetric combinatorial dependencies between spatial features, which results in the omission of valuable co-location information. To solve these problems, we propose a revised prevalence measure called correlated participation index (CPI). It reduces the influence of isolated instances while preserving the anti-monotonicity property. In addition, we propose the concept of united co-location pattern (UCP) and define distinct prevalence types to represent hierarchical and directional combinations of features, which enrich the semantic expressiveness of co-location patterns. We further develop a united co-location mining algorithm based on CPI, called UCPM-CPI, and design pruning strategies to optimize its computational efficiency. Extensive experiments on real-world datasets demonstrate the effectiveness and efficiency of the proposed algorithm.

Keywords: Spatial data mining · united co-location pattern · isolated instance · correlated participation index · asymmetric combinatorial dependency

1 Introduction

With the rapid development of spatial information technologies, spatial data are growing rapidly in volume and variety. To extract valuable information and uncover hidden knowledge from these data, spatial data mining techniques continue to advance steadily. Among them, spatial co-location pattern mining has emerged as a significant research direction due to its ability to reveal implicit geographic correlations among different spatial features [1]. Specifically, a spatial co-location pattern is a set of spatial features whose instances frequently appear in close proximity in space [2]. Nowadays, co-location pattern mining has been widely applied in various fields, including ecological conservation [3], urban planning [4], and public health [5].

J. Li et al. (Eds.): APWeb-WAIM 2025, LNCS 16115, pp. 81–96, 2026.
https://doi.org/10.1007/978-981-95-5719-6_6

Spatial co-location pattern mining is an extension of association rule mining based on transactional data, where most existing studies adopt the participation index (PI) as the prevalence measure [6]. By computing the ratio between the number of participating instances and the total number of instances for each spatial feature, PI quantifies the contribution of each feature within a pattern and reflects the significance of a pattern. However, due to the heterogeneity of spatial data and the variability in distance threshold settings, some instances may not neighbor any instances of other features. These are referred to as isolated instances. Clearly, isolated instances are scattered across the spatial domain and do not participate in any valid co-location pattern. It means that isolated instances offer no positive contribution to pattern prevalence and should be excluded when defining prevalence measures. Unfortunately, this issue has been largely ignored in current co-location research. Taking the PI as an example, its denominator includes all instances of a spatial feature, even those that are isolated. This inclusion can lead to underestimation of prevalence, causing some genuinely prevalent patterns to be wrongly filtered out, thereby compromising the completeness of the mining results and may missing substantial practical value.

Moreover, with the increasing diversity of spatial datasets, the demands for spatial data analysis are becoming more complex and differentiated. While traditional spatial co-location patterns are effective in characterizing the co-existence relationships among spatial objects, they fall short in capturing richer associative dependencies and asymmetric compositional relationships. Specifically, certain combinations of spatial features can promote or induce the co-location of other features in a given area, exhibiting hierarchical and directional characteristics. These combinatorial dependencies are common in complex spatial phenomena such as urban development and ecosystem evolution, offering valuable insights into latent relationships within spatial data. For example, the feature set {hospital, pharmacy, restaurant} is often considered a classic co-location pattern. However, such pattern not account for the underlying combinatorial dependencies and more intricate prevalence characteristics inherent in the data. Based on a statistical analysis of point-of-interest (POI) datasets from several cities, we observe that the combination of hospitals and pharmacies is more likely to facilitate the co-location of restaurants, with a probability exceeding 75%. In comparison, the hospital-restaurant pair exerts less influence on pharmacies, while the pharmacy-restaurant pair contributes little to the presence of hospitals with less than 15% probability. Different combinations of the same features may exhibit distinct prevalence levels, indicating that the co-location of spatial features depends on their hierarchical dependencies and demonstrates inherent directionality. Meanwhile, instances of feature combinations may also be isolated and should be considered. Treating feature combinations as a whole also facilitates the discovery of larger-size patterns involving rare features.

Based on these insights, we propose a revised prevalence measure that accounts for isolated instances, termed the Correlated Participation Index (CPI). The CPI inherits the definitional framework of the PI while refining the denominator calculation. This design not only eliminates the influence of isolated instances but also preserves the anti-monotonicity property essential for efficient pattern mining. Second, we propose the concepts of united feature and united co-location patterns (UCPs) to characterize combinatorial dependencies among spatial features. Furthermore, we develop a CPI-based united co-location mining algorithm (UCPM-CPI) with tailored pruning strategies to improve computational efficiency.

The main contributions of this paper are summarized as follows. (i) The CPI is proposed as an enhancement to the existing prevalence measure, which account for the impact of isolated instances while preserving anti-monotonicity. (ii) United features and UCPs are introduced, along with a dedicated mining algorithm, UCPM-CPI. Tailored pruning strategies are designed to accelerate the mining process, and the prevalence of UCP is further categorized into multiple-levels. (iii) Extensive experiments are conducted on real-world spatial datasets to validate the effectiveness and efficiency of the proposed algorithm and pruning strategies.

2 Related Work

Spatial co-location pattern mining is analogous to frequent itemset mining in transactional data, as both aim to discover frequent co-existence relationships among objects. However, unlike transactional data, spatial data lacks the concept of "transactions", making it impossible to directly apply frequent itemset mining methods to spatial co-location mining. To address this challenge, Shekhar and Huang et al. [7] pioneered a co-location mining approach. They introduced table instances as a substitute for "transactions" in traditional itemset mining and defined the participation index to measure the prevalence of co-locations. Subsequently, an increasing number of studies have been devoted to the exploration and advancement of co-location mining [8–10]. These algorithms rely on table instances to discover co-location patterns. Beyond these, several novel and efficient approaches have been proposed. For instance, Yang et al. [11] introduced a method based on column calculation, which avoids generating table instances by directly searching for participating instances, thereby improving efficiency. Later, Li et al. [12] proposed a grid-clique-based approach, which accelerates the search for participating instances without verifying neighbor relationships between instances, further enhancing algorithmic efficiency.

Except mining classic co-locations and improving their efficiency, many researchers have conducted studies on different types of spatial data or mining objectives to discover more interesting and application-worthy co-locations. Yao et al. [4] incorporated the distance decay effect into prevalence measurement and refined the participation index. Ouyang et al. [13] defined a fuzzy participation index for discovering patterns from fuzzy objects. Li et al. [14] considered the value differences of spatial features and proposed high-utility co-locations. To avoid missing potentially interesting patterns, Wang et al. [15] relaxed the strict clique constraint in traditional co-location mining and introduced sub-prevalent co-location mining based on a star participation index. Chan et al. [16] accounted for shared relationships among spatial instances and proposed a novel measure called Fraction-Score to more precisely quantify the contribution of participating instances to pattern prevalence. Yang et al. [17] considered both the number of feature instances and the heterogeneity of their spatial distribution, proposing a mixed prevalence measure that reduces bias in prevalence assessment while effectively identifying patterns with rare features. Li et al. [18] defined a relative distribution coefficient to distinguish and measure the prevalence of global and regional co-locations, enabling efficient mining of multi-level co-location patterns.

However, existing researches on prevalence measures have yet to address the negative impact of isolated instances, and there are no reports on the combinatorial dependencies among spatial features. This paper attempts to provide complementary insights into these issues.

3 Background Concepts and Proposed Definitions

3.1 Fundamentals of Spatial Co-location Patterns

To facilitate later discussions, we first revisit the fundamental concepts and their formal representations in co-location mining. Given a spatial dataset *D*, the set of its *n* **spatial features** is denoted as $F = \{f_1, f_2, \ldots, f_n\}$. The set of **spatial instances** for all features is denoted as $S = \{s_1, s_2, \ldots, s_m\}$, where each *s* represents a specific instance of a feature f_i in space, expressed as a triple $<$ feature type, id, location $>$. Two instances from different features satisfy the **spatial neighbor relationship** *R* if their distance (typically Euclidean) does not exceed a given distance threshold *d*. A **spatial co-location pattern** *c* is a nonempty subset of *F*, i.e., $c \subseteq F$, where instances of different features in *c* are frequently neighboring with each other. The number of features in *c* is called the **size** of *c*. A set of instances *RI*(*c*) is a **row instance** of *c* if it covers all features in *c* and any two instances in *RI*(*c*) satisfy the neighbor relationship *R*, i.e., instances of *RI*(*c*) form a clique. The collection of all row instances of *c* forms its **table instance** *T*(*c*). For a feature $f \in c$, an instance *s* is considered a **participating instance** of f_i in *c* if it appears in at least one row instance *RI*(*c*). The set of all such instances is denoted as *Obj*(*c*, f_i). To quantify co-location prevalence, Shekhar et al. [7] introduced the **participation ratio** (**PR**) and **participation index** (**PI**), which are defined as $PR(c, f_i) = \frac{|Obj(c, f_i)|}{|T(\{f_i\})|}$ and $PI(c) = min_{i=1}^{k}(PR(c, f_i))$ respectively. An example is shown in Fig. 1. The dataset contains four features with 18 instances in total, and lines between instances indicate spatial neighbor relationships.

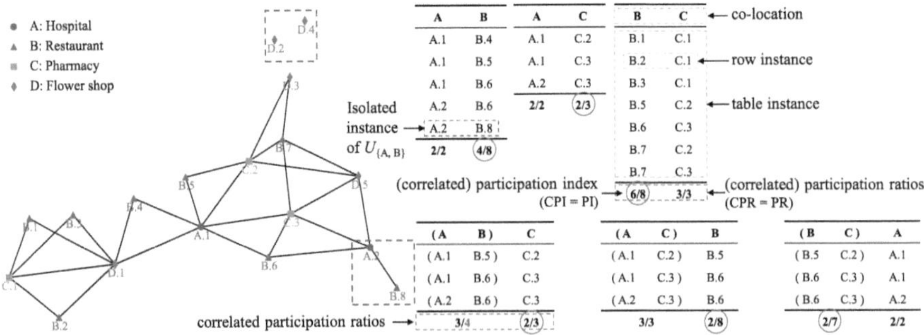

Fig. 1. Example of spatial datasets and partial table instances.

3.2 Correlated Participation Index

Before introducing the concept of correlated participation index, it is necessary to first clarify the notion of isolated instances.

Definition 1. Given a distance threshold d, if an instance of a feature f is not neighboring any instance of other features, it is termed an **isolated instance**. The set of all isolated instances of f is denoted as $I(f)$.

In Fig. 1, instances D.2 and D.4 are typical examples of isolated instances. Since isolated instances are not neighboring any instances of other features, they offer no positive contribution to the prevalence of co-location patterns. Therefore, PR and PI can be refined by removing isolated instances from the calculation. The revised measure is defined as follows.

Definition 2. For a feature f_i in a co-location pattern c, the ratio of the number of participating instances to the number of non-isolated instances of f_i is called the **Correlated Participation Rate (CPR)**, denoted as $CPR(c, f_i)$: $CPR(c, f_i) = \frac{|Obj(c, f_i)|}{|T(\{f_i\})| - |I(f_i)|}$.

Definition 3. The minimum correlated participation rate among all features in a co-location pattern c is defined as the **Correlated Participation Index (CPI)**, denoted as CPI(c). The formula is $CPI(c) = min_{i=1}^{k}(CPR(c, f_i))$.

According to the above definitions, if a feature contains isolated instances, its CPR exceeds its PR since the CPR excludes the count of isolated instances from the denominator. Consequently, the CPI of patterns are no less than their traditional PI, which helps identify previously misclassified non-prevalent patterns due to the isolated instances. We refer to such patterns as **boundary co-location patterns**.

Furthermore, since the CPI inherits the definitional structure of the traditional PI, it requires only the identification of isolated instances once the distance threshold is fixed. This ensures that the CPI retains the anti-monotonicity property and remains fully compatible with all existing PI-based co-location mining algorithms. Additionally, the process of identifying isolated instances can be integrated into neighborhood relationship discovery, introducing negligible impact on algorithmic efficiency.

3.3 United Co-location Pattern

Due to the complex combinatorial dependencies among spatial features, different feature combinations exhibit varying capacities to attract other features into co-location, which manifests as hierarchical structures and directional tendencies in co-location expansions. However, traditional co-location patterns merely describe co-existence phenomena, overlooking these dependencies. To explore such relationships, we first define the combinations of features as united features.

Definition 4. A **united feature** is abstracted from a prevalent co-location pattern c, denoted as U_c, where U_c equals c. The instances of U_c are the row instances of c.

As shown in Fig. 1, the united feature $U_{\{A, B\}}$ exists with the following instances: {A.1, B.4}, {A.1, B.5}, {A.1, B.6}, {A.2, B.6}, {A.2, B.8}. Moreover, instances of the united features may also be isolated, e.g., {A.2, B.8} is considered an isolated instance of $U_{\{A, B\}}$ because it does not neighbor instances of other features (i.e., it fails to form a larger clique) and is therefore excluded from the formation of larger-size patterns.

To facilitate distinction, this paper refers to features other than united features as **basic features** (i.e., normal spatial features). A united feature is essentially a co-location pattern, meaning that the combination of features is not random but must be based on the frequent co-existence of their instances, which makes the definition well-grounded. Additionally, as a united feature, it can further combine with other features to form larger-size patterns, termed united co-location patterns below.

Definition 5. A binary tuple composed of a united feature U_c and a basic feature f_i constitutes a **united co-location pattern (UCP)**, denoted as $< U_c, f_i >$ and $f_i \notin U_c$.

In real-world scenarios, combinations of spatial features typically expand incrementally. That is, existing feature combinations usually attract other features into co-existence one by one, while it is relatively rare for one feature combination to directly attract another combination into co-location. The definition of UCPs excludes combinations between united features to simplify the problem.

It is important to emphasize that the UCPs $<$ {A, B}, C $>$, $<$ {A, C}, B $>$, and $<$ {B, C}, A $>$ in Fig. 1 convey different meanings. Each is formed by a different united feature in combination with another basic feature, thus representing distinct co-location relationships. Intuitively, these patterns reflect a certain hierarchical structure, which differentiates them from the traditional co-location pattern {A, B, C}. Regarding prevalence measurement, UCPs follow a similar approach to traditional ones. However, considering the presence of isolated instances, we adopt the CPI as the prevalence measure, which better aligns with real-world application.

Definition 6. For a UCP $< U_c, f_i >$, if $CPI(< U_c, f_i >)$ is not less than a given prevalence threshold, the pattern is considered prevalent.

It should be noted that when computing the CPI of a UCP, the united feature U_c is treated as a whole, i.e., $CPI(< U_c, f_i >) = min(CPR(< U_c, f_i >, U_c), CPR(< U_c, f_i >, f_i))$. The calculation details of the CPI for selected UCPs are shown in Fig. 1. Under Definition 6, the UCPs $<$ {A, B}, C $>$, $<$ {A, C}, B $>$, and $<$ {B, C}, A $>$ may exhibit different prevalence levels, thereby revealing the directional dependencies in co-location relationships. Taking the case in Fig. 1 as an example, if the prevalence threshold is set to 0.3, only $<$ {A, B}, C $>$ is prevalent, reflecting that the combination of hospitals and restaurants attracts pharmacies to co-locate. In contrast, the traditional co-location pattern {A, B, C} is non-prevalent because $PI(\{A, B, C\}) = min(2/2, 2/8, 2/5) = 1/4 < 0.3$, which is inconsistent with the statistical observations mentioned in Sect. 1.

To characterize the hierarchical and directional properties of feature combinations and facilitate further analysis, we classify the group of UCPs sharing the same basic features by comparing their prevalence with the corresponding traditional co-location.

Definition 7. Given a co-location pattern c, if all of its corresponding UCPs $\{< c - \{f_i\}, f_i > | f_i \in c\}$ are prevalent, then c is called a **fully united co-location pattern (FUCP)**. If at least one of these UCPs is not prevalent, then c is called a **partially united co-location pattern (PUCP)**. If exactly one of them is prevalent, then c is called a **singly united co-location pattern (SUCP)**.

Since 2-size UCPs are equivalent to traditional co-location patterns, all 2-size co-location patterns are FUCPs. It is only in larger-size patterns (i.e., size 3 and above) that partially united and singly united patterns emerge. These patterns may carry important semantic information. Specifically, partially united patterns indicate that several features are not attracted to co-locate by any combination of the others, while the other features tend to co-locate under their influence. This suggests that these non-attracted features may serve as key components of the pattern. In the case of a singly united pattern, the basic feature that is attracted to co-locate may be a rare feature (i.e., one with very few instances in the dataset). This is because united features help reduce instance quantity disparities between features, thereby preventing meaningful patterns from being overlooked by the PI. The practical value of these patterns will be further analyzed and demonstrated using real-world datasets in Sect. 5.

4 United Co-location Pattern Mining Algorithm

4.1 Basic Mining Approach

Considering that UCPs are gradually expanded from united features which are themselves co-location patterns, this process aligns with size-by-size pattern mining frameworks. Based on this foundation, we design the United Co-location Pattern Mining with CPI (UCPM-CPI) algorithm. UCPM-CPI takes a spatial dataset, a distance threshold, and a prevalence threshold as inputs. It employs a generate-and-test framework to discover all prevalent UCPs. The pseudocode of UCPM-CPI is detailed in **Algorithm 1**.

Algorithm 1: UCPM-CPI

Input: (a) Spatial dataset D; (b) Prevalence threshold *min_prev*; (c) Distance threshold d.
Output: A set of prevalent UCPs.
Variables: C_k: set of k-size candidate UCPs; T_k: set of table instances of UCPs in C_k; II_k: set of k-size isolated instances; P_k: set of k-size prevalent UCPs; FP_k, PP_k, SP_k: set of k-size FUCPs, PUCPs, SUCPs separately.
Steps:

```
NL = gen_neighbor_list(D, d)
initialize k = 1, Pk = F, FPk = Pk
While FPk not empty do
k = k+1
Ck = gen_candidates(FPk-1, F, k)
Tk = gen_table_instances(Ck, NL)
IIk = get_isolated_instances(Tk)
calculate_CPI(Ck, IIk)
Pk = select_prevalent_patterns(Ck, min_prev)
FPk, PPk, SPk = classify_prevalent_patterns(Pk)
End While
Return union(P1, P2, ...,Pk)
```

The mining process in Algorithm 1 consists of four main phases. First, the algorithm scans the spatial dataset to establish neighborhood relationships based on the distance threshold, while all spatial features are recorded as prevalent 1-size patterns (Steps 1–2). To generate candidate k-size UCPs ($k > 1$), the (k-1)-size FUCPs are treated as united features and combined with basic features (not already included) as defined in Definition 5 (Step 5). Next, the algorithm searches for the table instances of each candidate pattern using the recorded neighborhood relationships, filters out the isolated instances of the united features, and calculates the CPI for each candidate (Steps 6–8). Finally, candidates with CPI values meeting or exceeding the prevalence threshold are selected as prevalent UCPs (Step 9) and subsequently categorized (Step 10). The value of k is incremented, and the process repeated until no new candidates can be generated, at which point the algorithm terminates.

It should be noted that all 1-size and 2-size prevalent co-location patterns are FUCPs. Practically, FUCPs are chosen as new united features because all of their subsets are prevalent, such tightly connected groups are more likely to attract other features into co-locations. Meanwhile, when searching for table instances of candidate UCPs, those with the same set of spatial features are computed only once, as their table instances are essentially identical under the clique relationship constraint. They only need to be distinguished later during the calculation of the CPI. Moreover, the isolated instances of united features are identified through the table instances, because these isolated instances are strictly excluded from table instances of larger-size patterns.

4.2 Optimization Strategy

In traditional size-by-size mining algorithms, the anti-monotonicity property of prevalence measures is typically leveraged to reduce candidate patterns and improve computational efficiency. Unfortunately, although the CPI satisfies anti-monotonicity in traditional co-location mining, it does not retain this property in the context of united co-location pattern mining. In fact, this limitation also applies to other potential prevalence measures. Because the denominator of the CPR for the united feature U_c is determined by the number of row instances of its corresponding pattern c, and some of these row instances may be isolated, making the denominator unpredictable. For instance, in the scenario illustrated in Fig. 1, $CPI(<\{\mathrm{B}, \mathrm{D}\}, \mathrm{C}>) = 3/4$, which is greater than $CPI(<\mathrm{B}, \mathrm{D}>) = 2/3$, clearly violating the anti-monotonicity property. As a result, the Apriori-based pruning strategies are incompatible with united co-location pattern mining, and alternative methods are needed to reduce the pattern search space. Through rigorous analysis, we discover that UCPs exhibit partial anti-monotonicity.

Lemma 1. Given a k-size FUCP c and a larger-size FUCP c', for any basic feature f not contained in either c and c', it holds that $CPR(< c', f >, f) \leq CPR(< c, f >, f)$.

Proof 1. Since the row instances of UCPs form clique relationships, any instance s of spatial feature f that appears in the row instances of pattern $<c', f>$ must also appear in the row instances of pattern $< c,f >$. The reverse, however, does not necessarily hold. Meanwhile, the number of isolated instances of f remains constant across UCP sizes, as they are identified during dataset traversal. Therefore, $CPR(< c, f >, f)$ satisfies anti-monotonicity according to the definition of CPR.

Based on Lemma 1, we design an algorithm that prunes larger-size candidate patterns by searching the CPR values of smaller-size ones. To minimize the search time, we introduce a composite hash structure called CPR-hash for storing CPR values. In CPR-hash, each candidate pattern serves as a primary key, and its value is a nested inner hash that separately records the CPR values of the united feature and the basic feature within the pattern. For the UCP < {A, B}, C > in Fig. 1, its corresponding inner hash contains two key-value pairs: one for the united feature $U_{\{A, B\}}$ and its CPR value, and another for the basic feature C and its CPR value. This structure allows efficient access to CPR values, facilitating subsequent computations. The CPR-hash is updated during the prevalent pattern selecting step in Algorithm 1.

The pseudocode of the pruning algorithm is shown in **Algorithm 2**. The algorithm takes a *k*-size (*k* > 2) candidate pattern $< c, f >$, the CPR-hash table, and the prevalence threshold as inputs. It first constructs the (*k*-1)-size sub-patterns containing basic feature *f*. For each sub-pattern, it retrieves the CPR value of *f* from the CPR-hash. If the CPR is not found or is less than the given threshold, the candidate pattern is pruned and the algorithm terminates. Otherwise, the algorithm continues to check the remaining (*k*-1)-size sub-patterns containing *f*, until all sub-patterns have been examined. Clearly, Algorithm 2 is applied during the candidate pattern generation phase of Algorithm 1. Only unpruned candidate UCPs are retained for subsequent prevalence validation.

Algorithm 2: Candidate Pruning

Input: (a) Candidate co-location *C*; (b) Correlated participation ratio hash table *CPR-hash*; (c) Prevalence threshold *min_prev*.

Output: Boolean flag indicating whether the candidate is pruned.

Steps:

sub_patterns_set = gen_sub_patterns(*C*)
f = *C*[len(*C*)-1] // *f* is the basic feature in candidate *C*
for *sub_pattern* in *sub_patterns_set*:
if *CPR_hash*[*sub_pattern*] not found: **return** True
else if *CPR_hash*[*sub_pattern*][*f*] < *min_prev*: **return** True
else: **return** False

In addition to the pruning strategy based on partial anti-monotonicity, a heuristic pruning strategy can be applied when constructing the table instances of a *k*-size (*k* > 2) candidate pattern $< c, f >$. Specifically, the participating instances of the basic feature *f* in the (*k*-1)-size sub-patterns can be leveraged to narrow the search space. Formally, $Obj(< c', f >, f) \subseteq \cap_{i=1}^{k+1} Obj(< c_i, f >, f)$, where *c'* is a *k*-size FUCP, and each c_i is its (*k*-1)-size sub-pattern excluding feature *f* and is also a FUCP. This relationship holds inherently due to the clique constraint in table instances, and it effectively reduces the search space for feature *f*. For example, in the UCP < {A, B}, C >, *Obj*(<{A, B}, C >, C) must be a subset of the intersection of *Obj*(<A, C >, C) and *Obj*(<B, C >, C). This means that when constructing table instances, the search scope for feature C is reduced from all instances of C to that intersection. Concurrently, an upper bound of *CPR*(<{A, B}, C >, C) can be easily estimated for further pruning.

4.3 Algorithm Discussion

In this section, we discuss the completeness, correctness, and time complexity of the proposed algorithm.

Completeness means that all prevalent UCPs can be identified by UCPM-CPI. As shown in Algorithm 1, candidate patterns at each size are generated by united features with other basic features. This combination covers all possible cases defined by the UCP. Meanwhile, the pruning strategy filters out non-prevalent candidates early without mistakenly removing prevalent patterns, which are proofed in Sect. 4.2. Therefore, the algorithm is complete because the candidate set includes all prevalent UCPs, and subsequent prevalence validation guarantees no patterns are missed.

Correctness means that all prevalent UCPs discovered by the algorithm satisfy the prevalence threshold. First, the table instances are correctly computed via neighbor relationship validation for all relevant instances of candidate patterns in Algorithm 1 and the heuristic pruning method in Sect. 4.2 preserves table instance integrity. Second, isolated instances are identified based on table instances, meaning the counting of all isolated instances is also correct. Thus, the CPR can be calculated correctly, ensuring the correctness of the CPI. During the subsequent prevalent pattern selecting phase, candidate patterns with the CPI below the given threshold are discarded, only truly prevalent patterns are retained. In conclusion, the algorithm is correct.

Based on the above analysis, it is evident that under the same input, the mining results of UCPM-CPI encompass those of traditional co-location patterns. This is mainly due to two factors. First, the candidate UCPs cover all possible feature combinations, naturally including all traditional candidate co-location patterns. Second, the CPI is always greater than or equal to the traditional PI (discussed in Sect. 3.2). Therefore, UCPM-CPI produces a superset of traditional co-location patterns.

The time complexity of the proposed algorithm consists of several parts. First, for Algorithm 1, the worst-case time complexity of generating the spatial neighbor relationships is $O(|S|^2)$, and that of generating all candidate UCPs is $O(|\mathcal{P}_{\text{FUCPs}}| \times |F| \times \max K)$, where $\mathcal{P}_{\text{FUCPs}}$ is the set of all FUCPs and $\max K$ is the maximum iteration count. Table instance construction is the most time-consuming step, requiring traversal of all instances of both the united features and basic features to validate neighbor relationships. Isolated instances can be identified immediately after generating row instances. Thus, for a group of candidate patterns C_k, the worst-case complexity for table instance construction and isolated instance detection is $O(|C_k| \times |S_{Uc}| \times |S_f| \times k^2\ logk)$, where $|S_{Uc}|$ and $|S_f|$ denote the number of instances of the united features and basic features in C_k, respectively. For a k-size candidate pattern c, computing its CPI takes $O(|T(c)| \times k)$. Filtering out prevalent UCPs from C_k has a complexity of $O(|C_k|)$, and classifying the prevalent patterns P_k requires $O(|P_k| \times k\ logk)$. For Algorithm 2, determining whether a candidate k-size pattern c should be pruned takes $O((k\text{-}1)^2\ log(k\text{-}1))$, mainly due to subpatterns construction overhead. In summary, the algorithm exhibits a worst-case time complexity of $max(O(|S|^2), O(|\mathcal{P}_{\text{FUCPs}}| \times |F| \times |S_{Uc}| \times |S| \times \max K^3 log\ \max K))$, which is higher than Join-based [8] because of the increased number of possible feature combinations. However, due to the pruning strategies, the actual runtime is significantly lower than this upper bound.

5 Experimental Results and Analysis

5.1 Experimental Setup

The experiments primarily utilized two real-world datasets: a vegetation dataset from the Gaoligong Mountains and a POI dataset from the Futian District of Shenzhen. The urban POI data was sourced from Amap (AutoNavi Map), from which 26 common features were selected and adapted for algorithmic processing. Key parameters of these datasets are summarized in Table 1. For parameter settings, the default distance threshold was set to 1000 m for the sparse vegetation data of Gaoligong Mountain and 100 m for the dense POI data of Futian District, with a uniform prevalence threshold of 0.3. Based on these settings, we conducted comparative analyses of the results generated by traditional co-location pattern mining algorithms and the proposed UCPM-CPI algorithm, to evaluate the effectiveness of the CPI and UCPs. All algorithms discussed in this paper were implemented in Python and executed on a Windows 11 machine equipped with a 3.70 GHz Intel Core i7 processor and 16 GB RAM.

Table 1. Main parameters of the two real-world datasets.

Dataset	Number of features	Number of instances	Instances per feature
Gaoligong Mountain	25	13,349	1 ~ 2,866
Futian, Shenzhen POI	26	28,055	7 ~ 7,446

5.2 Effectiveness of the UCPM-CPI Algorithm

UCPs can identify asymmetric combinational dependencies among spatial features and are capable of discovering larger-size patterns involving rare features, while the CPI can reveal boundary patterns in spatial data. To evaluate their practical effectiveness, we applied both the UCPM-CPI and the traditional co-location mining approach (e.g., Join-based [8]) to the two real-world datasets using default parameters.

Visibly, the UCPM-CPI algorithm identified significantly more UCPs than the traditional method, with patterns of larger-size, as shown in Fig. 2. This is partly because the CPI can detect boundary co-location patterns, and partly due to the hierarchical and directional properties of feature combinations, which leads to the emergence of many seemingly "redundant" patterns with distinct semantic meanings.

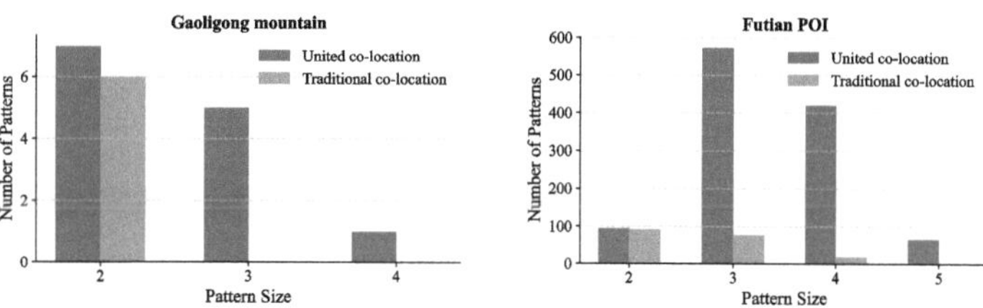

Fig. 2. Comparison of the number of discovered patterns.

Considering the large number of UCPs discovered in the Futian POI dataset (nearly one thousand) and the space constraints, we present only the complete mining results on the Gaoligong Mountain dataset, which include the identified patterns and their prevalence scores, as shown in Table 2. Clearly, the UCPs fully cover the traditional co-location patterns, which is consistent with the analysis in Sect. 4.3. Additionally, enabled by the CPI, the boundary patterns {Mix, Arr} and {Yun, Oth-BF, Ald} are also included and both are classified as FUCPs. We visualized the instance distribution of the boundary pattern {Yun, Oth-BF, Ald}, as shown in Fig. 3(a). It is evident that numerous isolated instances exist, and instances of different features within the pattern exhibit substantial neighboring relationships, which confirms the rationality of the boundary pattern formation. Notably, the CPI values of < {Yun, Oth-BF}, Ald >, < {Oth-BF, Ald}, Yun >, and < {Yun, Ald}, Oth-BF > exhibit marked differences. This indicates that the combination {Yun, Oth-BF} has a stronger pull in attracting Ald into co-location. In Fig. 3(a), this is reflected by the fact that most Ald instances are located near both Yun and Oth-BF, whereas Oth-BF instances are less often co-located with both Yun and Ald, with some Oth-BF instances even being isolated. Similar observations apply to the pattern < {Oth-BF, Ald}, Yun >. Despite these differences, all of the above patterns have CPI values exceeding the predefined prevalence threshold of 0.3, so {Yun, Oth-BF, Ald} is still identified as a FUCP. In addition, three SUCPs (underlined in the table) appear in the results, each involving a rare feature. Particularly, the pattern {Abi, Hem, Lar} is previously identified in a study on rare-feature patterns [17] using identical dataset and distance threshold. This demonstrates that UCPM-CPI can discover large-size co-location patterns with rare features.

Table 2. Mining results on the Gaoligong Mountain dataset.

Traditional co-location	United co-location
{Yun, Oth-BF}: 0.6240	< Yun, Oth-BF >: 0.6357
{Oth-BF, Ald}: 0.4503	**< {Yun, Oth-BF}, Ald >: 0.6188**
{Yun, Ald}: 0.4375	< {Abi, Hem}, Lar >: 0.5714
{Abi, Hem}: 0.4156	< Abi, Hem >: 0.4889
{Arr, Abi}: 0.3664	< Yun, Ald >: 0.4637
{Oth-BF, Hem}: 0.3511	< Oth-BF, Ald >: 0.4587
	< Arr, Abi >: 0.4310
	< Oth-BF, Hem >: 0.3831
	< {Abi, Oth-BF, Ald}, Oth-B >: 0.3372
	< Mix, Arr >: 0.3231
	< {Oth-BF, Hem}, Spr >: 0.3208
	< {Oth-BF, Ald}, Yun >: 0.3084
	< {Yun, Ald}, Oth-BF >: 0.3024

* Yun: Yunnan Pine(1959); Oth-BF: Other Broad-leaved Forest(2072); Ald: Alder(802); Abi: Abies(2866); Hem: Hemlock(2176); Lar: Larch(56); Arr: Arrow Bamboo(1288); Mix: Mixed

Shrubs(1282); Spr: Spruce(53);Oth-B: Other Bamboo(109); (number): the number of instances per feature.

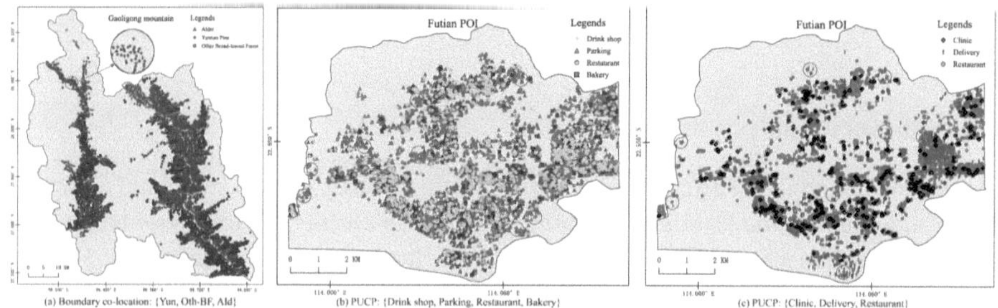

(a) Boundary co-location: {Yun, Oth-BF, Ald} (b) PUCP: {Drink shop, Parking, Restaurant, Bakery} (c) PUCP: {Clinic, Delivery, Restaurant}

Fig. 3. Instance distribution visualization of some co-location patterns.

In the Futian POI dataset, UCPM-CPI also discovered several boundary patterns, such as {Attraction, Park} and {Restaurant, Residence area, Store}. Likewise, the algorithm identified a large number of FUCPs, such as {Drink shop, Restaurant}, as well as SUCPs involving rare features, such as < {Restaurant, Toilet}, Mall >. For brevity, these valuable patterns are not elaborated further here. We focus on PUCPs to analyze their implicit semantic meanings. Take the one with the highest average CPI, {Drink shop, Parking, Restaurant, Bakery}, as an example. Traditional co-location mining algorithms failed to detect this pattern. UCPM-CPI identifies two prevalent combinations: < {Drink shop, Parking, Restaurant}, Bakery > and < {Parking, Restaurant, Bakery}, Drink shop >, while other two combinations are not prevalent. Detailed analysis reveals that {Drink shop, Parking, Bakery} only forms a PUCP because the combination {Drink shop, Bakery} struggles to attract parking lots development nearby, and thus cannot form larger-size patterns. Similarly, while {Drink shop, Restaurant, Bakery} can form a FUCP, it also exhibits weak attraction to parking lots. Figure 3(b) shows the instance distributions of these four features. It is clear that drink shops and bakeries are often located near parking lots and restaurants, but the reverse does not necessarily hold, i.e., a lot of parking lots and restaurants exist without drink shops or bakeries nearby, as indicated by the red circles (500 m diameter) in Fig. 3(b). This analysis suggests that Parking and Restaurant are likely the key features that drive the partially-united property of the pattern {Drink shop, Parking, Restaurant, Bakery}. Consequently, in commercial site selection, locating bakeries or drink shops near existing parking lots and restaurants may lead to better economic outcomes.

In addition, extensive experiments show that traditional co-location patterns are a subset of the FUCPs in most cases under the same input. In other words, traditional co-location patterns assume equal combinatorial dependencies among spatial features, which clearly inconsistent with reality. Such as, for the traditional co-location pattern {Clinic, Delivery, Restaurant} discovered in the Futian POI dataset, UCPM-CPI finds that the patterns < {Clinic, Delivery}, Restaurant > and < {Clinic, Restaurant}, Delivery > are prevalent, while < {Delivery, Restaurant}, Clinic > is not. This means that {Clinic, Delivery, Restaurant} is a PUCP. This difference in prevalence highlights the key role of the feature Clinic in the pattern, i.e., wherever a clinic exist, deliveries and restaurants are very likely to appear nearby, but not necessarily the other way around. This situation is clearly illustrated in Fig. 3(c).

In summary, the proposed UCPs effectively capture the asymmetric co-location relationships among spatial features, revealing their hierarchical and directional dependencies.

5.3 Efficiency Analysis of Pruning

To evaluate the practical effectiveness of the pruning strategies, we conducted comparative experiments on the Gaoligong Mountain dataset, selecting the Join-based algorithm [8] as the baseline since the UCPM-CPI adopts a similar mining framework.

First, we analyzed the difference in the number of candidate patterns. Since 2-size candidate patterns are essentially all pairwise combinations of features, their counts remain constant for a given dataset. Therefore, Fig. 4 illustrates only the counts of 3-size and larger-size candidate patterns under parameter variations. When varying the distance threshold, the prevalence threshold was fixed at 0.4; when varying the prevalence threshold, the distance threshold was fixed at 1400 m. It is clear that increasing the distance threshold leads to more candidate patterns, as more instances are considered neighboring, resulting in more combinations of features. Conversely, a higher prevalence threshold filters out more small-size candidate patterns, causing the number of large-size patterns to drop quickly. Figure 4 demonstrates that the proposed pruning algorithm (Algorithm 2) consistently filters out about two-thirds of candidate patterns and is robust to changes in both distance and prevalence thresholds.

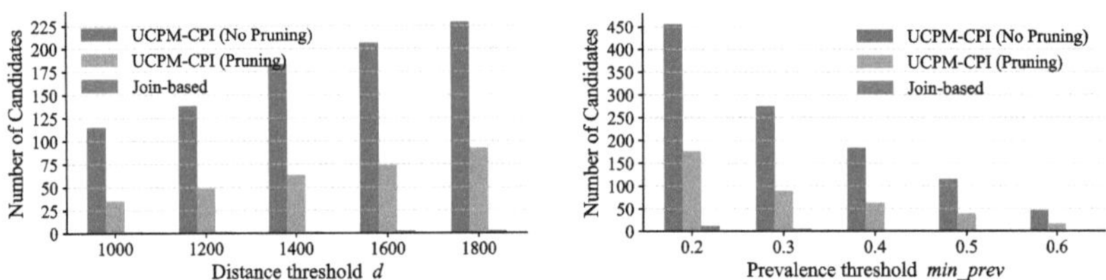

Fig. 4. Number of candidate patterns generated by different methods.

Notably, the pruned UCPM-CPI algorithm still generates much more candidate patterns than the Join-based algorithm. This is primarily due to the abundance of UCPs with identical spatial feature compositions. However, the heuristic pruning method based on participating instances avoids unnecessary table instance computations in advance, further optimizing algorithmic efficiency. Figure 5(a) illustrates the runtime of the algorithms under varying distance and prevalence thresholds, while Fig. 5(b) shows the number of patterns discovered under these conditions. Fixed parameter settings align with those in Fig. 4. It is clear that compared to the prevalence threshold, the distance threshold has a greater impact on the time efficiency of UCPM-CPI. Because increasing the distance threshold leads to a sharp rise in the number of instance cliques, requiring extensive neighbor validation and table instance computations, but the prevalence threshold mainly affects the number of candidate patterns. Without pruning, the runtime of UCPM-CPI grows exponentially with larger distance thresholds, while raising the prevalence threshold leads to only a slight reduction in runtime. Overall, the time efficiency of the unpruned UCPM-CPI is much lower than that of the Join-based algorithm. After incorporating the pruning strategies, UCPM-CPI achieves substantially lower time costs and becomes less sensitive to parameter changes. Remarkably, its runtime becomes slightly lower than Join-based while discovering more valuable patterns.

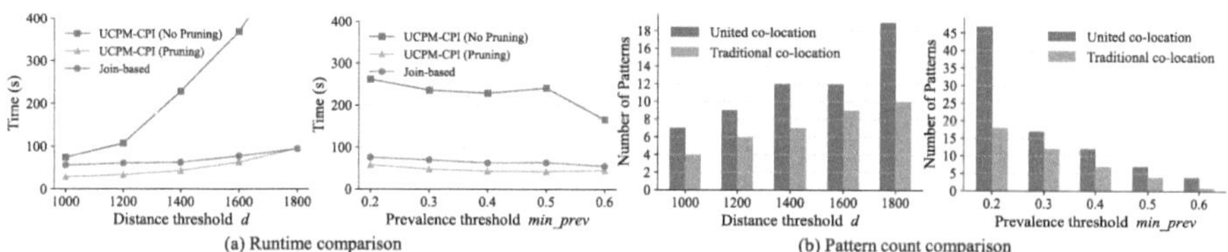

Fig. 5. Runtime and number of patterns with varying parameters.

In summary, the proposed pruning strategies are proven effective in optimizing the runtime efficiency of the UCPM-CPI algorithm to a certain extent, though there is still room for further improvement.

6 Conclusion

In this paper, we first propose an improved prevalence measure called Correlated Participation Index (CPI), which addresses and corrects the negative impact of isolated instances in spatial datasets on the prevalence measure. The CPI helps uncover previously overlooked boundary co-location in traditional co-location pattern mining. Second, we introduce United Co-location Patterns along with a prevalence-based classification framework to capture the hierarchical and directional combination dependencies among spatial features, thereby enriching the semantic information of co-location patterns. In addition, we integrate the CPI with united co-location pattern mining and present the UCPM-CPI algorithm along with corresponding pruning strategies. We also discuss the algorithm's completeness, correctness, and complexity. During the experimental evaluation, we validate the effectiveness of the CPI and united co-location patterns using real-world datasets with different spatial distributions, and analyze the performance of the proposed pruning strategies.

Although the proposed pruning strategies improve the runtime efficiency of the UCPM-CPI algorithm, the overall process remains inherently time-consuming. In future work, we will focus on improving the efficiency of united co-location pattern mining, for example, by designing new pruning strategies or incorporating parallel computing frameworks. In addition, exploring regional united co-location patterns is also an interesting task.

Acknowledgements. This work was supported by the National Natural Science Foundation of China (62276227, 62266050, 62306266), and the Yunnan Fundamental Research Projects (202201AS070015, 202401AT070450).

References

1. Jia, T., Cai, C., Li, X., Luo, X., Zhang, Y., Yu, X.: Dynamical community detection and spatiotemporal analysis in multilayer spatial interaction networks using trajectory data. Geogr. Inf. Syst. **36**, 1719–1740 (2022)
2. Yang, P., Wang, L., Wang, X., Zhou, L.: SCPM-CR: A novel method for spatial co-location pattern mining with coupling relation consideration. IEEE Trans. Knowl. Data Eng. **34**, 5979–5992 (2022)
3. Lu, J., Wang, L., Fang, Y., Zhao, J.: Mining strong symbiotic patterns hidden in spatial prevalent co-location patterns. Knowl. Based Syst. **146**, 190–202 (2018)
4. Yao, X., Chen, L., Peng, L., Chi, T.: A co-location pattern-mining algorithm with a density-weighted distance thresholding consideration. Inf. Sci. (Ny) **396**, 144–161 (2017)
5. Yao, X., Jiang, X., Wang, D., Yang, L., Peng, L., Chi, T.: Efficiently mining maximal co-locations in a spatial continuous field under directed road networks. Inf. Sci. (Ny) **542**, 357–379 (2021)
6. Wang, L., Fang, Y., Zhou, L.: Preference-Based Spatial Co-location Pattern Mining. Springer, Singapore (2022)
7. Shekhar, S., Huang, Y.: Discovering spatial co-location patterns: a summary of results. In: Advances in Spatial and Temporal Databases, pp. 236–256. Springer, Heidelberg (2001)
8. Huang, Y., Shekhar, S., Xiong, H.: Discovering colocation patterns from spatial data sets: a general approach. IEEE Trans. Knowl. Data Eng. **16**, 1472–1485 (2004)
9. Yoo, J.S., Shekhar, S.: A joinless approach for mining spatial colocation patterns. IEEE Trans. Knowl. Data Eng. **18**, 1323–1337 (2006)
10. Wu, P., Wang, L., Zou, M.: A maximal ordered ego-clique based approach for prevalent co-location pattern mining. Inf. Sci. (Ny) **608**, 630–654 (2022)
11. Yang, P., Wang, L., Wang, X., Zhou, L.: A spatial co-location pattern mining approach based on column calculation. Sci. Sin. Inf. **52**, 1053 (2022)
12. Li, J., Wang, L., Chen, H., Sun, Z.: dGridED-SCPM: a grid-clique-based approach for efficiently mining spatial co-location patterns. Expert Syst. Appl. **261**, 125471 (2025)
13. Ouyang, Z., Wang, L., Wu, P.: Spatial co-location pattern discovery from fuzzy objects. Int. J. Artif. Intell. Tools **26**, 1750003 (2017)
14. Li, Y., Wang, L., Yang, P., Li, J.: EHUCM: an efficient algorithm for mining high utility co-location patterns from spatial datasets with feature-specific utilities. In: Lecture Notes in Computer Science, pp. 185–191. Springer, Cham (2021)
15. Wang, L., Bao, X., Zhou, L., Chen, H.: Mining maximal sub-prevalent co-location patterns. World Wide Web. **22**, 1971–1997 (2019)
16. Chan, H.K.-H., Long, C., Yan, D., Wong, R.C.-W., Lu, H.: Fraction-score: a generalized support measure for weighted and maximal co-location pattern mining. IEEE Trans. Knowl. Data Eng. **36**, 1582–1596 (2024)
17. Yang, P., Wang, L., Zhou, L., Chen, H.: Mining spatial co-location patterns with a mixed prevalence measure. IEEE Trans. Neural Netw. Learn. Syst. **35**, 7845–7859 (2024)
18. Li, J., Wang, L., Yang, P., Zhou, L.: A novel algorithm for efficiently mining spatial multi-level co-location patterns. IEEE Trans. Knowl. Data Eng. **36**, 4361–4374 (2024)

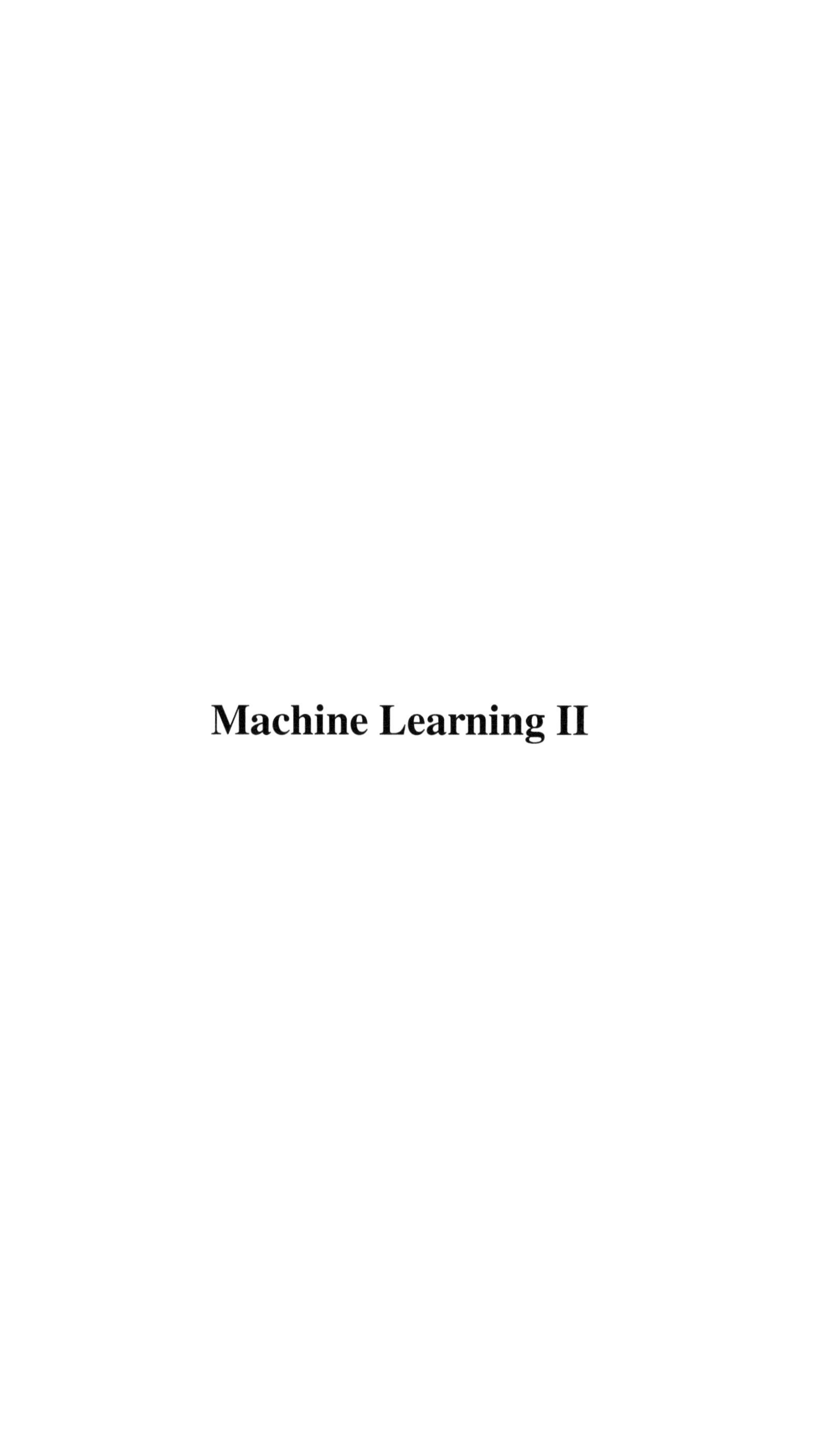

Machine Learning II

A Cross-Modal Fusion Method for Short Video Fake News Detection via MambaFormer

Chunyu Zhang, Liyuan Zhang, Jiachen Ma, Wei Zhang, and Yong Liu(✉)

School of Computer and Big Data, Heilongjiang University, Harbin, China
{2231986,2231976}@s.hlju.edu.cn,
{majiachen,zhangwei_jsj,liuyong123456}@hlju.edu.cn

Abstract. The rapid growth of short video platforms has accelerated the dissemination of fake news in the form of videos. Compared to traditional fake news, short video fake news integrates multi-modal information such as text, audio, and video. However, existing fake news detection methods face significant challenges in processing long-sequence data like videos and uncovering the inherent relationships between diverse modalities. To address the above problems, we propose a short video fake news detection based on MambaFormer method called SVFDMF. Specifically, SVFDMF alternates between mamba layers, multi-head attention mechanisms, and adaptive normalization layers to effectively extract long-sequence features from modalities such as video and audio while preserving temporal structural information. In addition, we design a Transformer-based cross-modal fusion mechanism to capture more complex inter-modal correlations. Extensive experimental results demonstrate that our proposed method outperforms existing methods. The code is available at https://github.com/SVFDMF-main/SVFDMF.

Keywords: Short Video · Fake News Detection · Multi-modal · MambaFormer

1 Introduction

Short video platforms (e.g., TikTok) have become major global channels for information acquisition, entertainment, and social interaction [1]. With a steadily growing user base, short videos have emerged as one of the most popular forms of content consumption. However, the openness and low entry barriers of these platforms have also made them fertile ground for the rapid spread of false information, thereby amplifying the impact of fake news [2]. The dissemination of rumors can have far-reaching consequences—not only undermining political stability, but also posing serious threats to public safety [3], and the broader online ecosystem [4,5].

Short video news refers to false, exaggerated, or misleading information disseminated through short video platforms, often encompassing fabricated news,

J. Li et al. (Eds.): APWeb-WAIM 2025, LNCS 16115, pp. 99–114, 2026.
https://doi.org/10.1007/978-981-95-5719-6_7

maliciously falsified content, or pseudoscientific claims. Unlike traditional formats, short videos integrate multi-modal data, including text, images, audio, and video, significantly complicating fake news detection. The unique characteristics of fake news propagation in short videos are summarized as follows: **(1)** The multi-modal nature of short videos limits the effectiveness of text-only detection approaches. **(2)** Fake news content is often meticulously crafted, making it challenging to identify through direct content analysis. **(3)** Short video news is inherently more persuasive and shareable than text-based counterparts, enabling rapid and extensive dissemination to diverse audiences [2,6]. Consequently, developing efficient and accurate detection methods for short video fake news is essential for preserving societal stability and harmony.

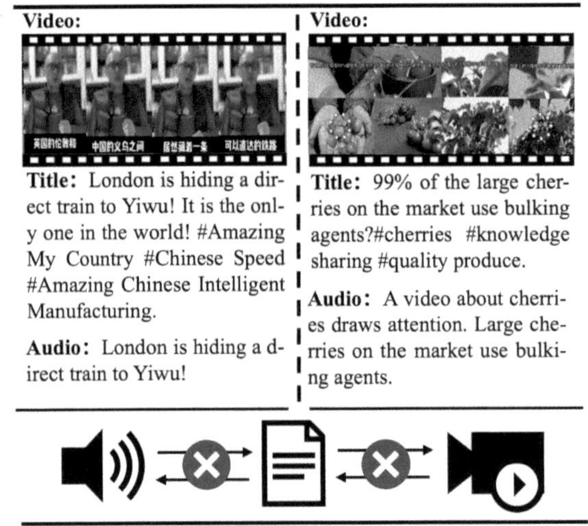

Fig. 1. The two examples in the FakeSV dataset demonstrate that short videos are long sequence data and multi-modal, which are not well connected each other.

Existing fake news detection methods primarily rely on text-image modal analysis [7–9]. While some studies incorporate video-based modalities [10,11], significant challenges persist. As shown in Fig. 1: (1) Traditional approaches struggle to effectively process long-sequence data, such as videos, leading to sub-optimal recognition accuracy. (2) Limited utilization of intrinsic relationships among modalities results in inadequate multi-modal fusion. Therefore, accurately handling long-sequence data and enhancing multi-modal integration are pivotal challenges in advancing fake news detection in short videos.

To address these problems, we propose a cross-modal fusion method for short video fake news detection via MambaFormer called SVFDMF, which effectively integrates multi-modal data and processes long-sequence information. SVFDMF alternates between Mamba layers, multi-head self-attention mechanisms, and adaptive normalization layers, enabling precise extraction of long-sequence features while preserving temporal structural information. Furthermore, a Transformer-based cross-modal fusion mechanism is introduced to capture intricate inter-modal relationships. By mapping different modalities into a shared high-dimensional space, aligning their features, and embedding temporal information, the proposed model ensures comprehensive feature integration.

Our main contributions are as follows:

- We propose the MambaFormer, which alternates Mamba layers, multi-head self-attention, and adaptive normalization layers to address the challenges of processing long-sequence data and preserving temporal structures, enabling effective feature extraction for short videos.
- We propose a Transformer-based cross-modal fusion mechanism that effectively captures complex inter-modal correlations, enabling seamless integration of textual, visual, and audio features in short videos for enhanced feature representation.
- We conducted extensive experiments on the FakeTT and FakeSV datasets, show casing the clear superiority of SVFDMF over existing methods in detecting fake news in short videos.

2 Related Works

2.1 Fake News Detection

Far behind text-image fake news detection, significant progress has been made with well-designed neural networks to model various types of text-image correlations [24–26]. With the rise of short video platforms, fake news creators have shifted toward fabricating videos to spread misinformation. To address this, researchers have proposed diverse methods for short-video fake news detection. For instance, Hou et al. [10] combined SVM classification with speech features and user engagement, while Choi et al. [13] employed adversarial neural networks to extract irrelevant features. Qi et al. [14] utilized a cross-modal converter to extract relationships between text, audio, and video, and constructed the FakeSV dataset to support short-video fake news detection.

Although these methods have achieved notable results, challenges remain in processing long-sequence video data and improving multi-modal fusion. To address these issues, we propose SVFDMF, a novel approach that alternates Mamba layers with self-attention layers to efficiently process text, image, and audio information.

2.2 State Space Models and Mamba

State Space Models (SSMs) have demonstrated strong potential in sequence modeling, and with the development of efficient algorithms, Mamba has achieved notable success across various domains. A promising research direction is the integration of Mamba with Transformers for language modeling [16]. For instance, Fei et al. [17] introduced a novel diffusion model for text-to-image generation, leveraging a unique architecture that combines Transformer and Mamba components. Inspired by this approach, this paper proposes a MambaFormer-based method for fake news detection in short videos. By alternating Mamba layers with attention mechanisms, the model efficiently processes video, audio, and text information. This multi-layer architecture effectively captures the detailed features of each modality, thereby enhancing detection performance in this challenging domain.

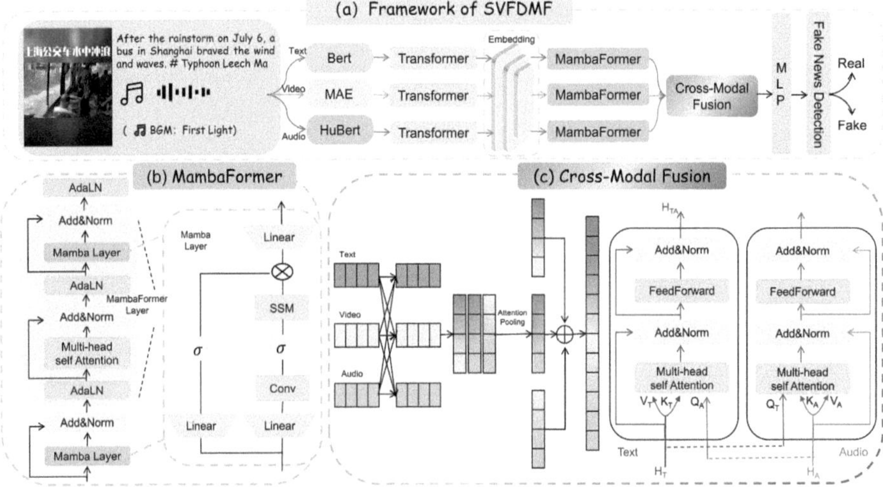

Fig. 2. Overview of the proposed SVFDMF. (a) Overall framework: Employs a Transformer for intra-modal feature extraction, MambaFormer for state-space-based feature refinement, and a cross-modal Transformer for feature fusion, culminating in MLP classification. (b) MambaFormer module: Leverages SSMs to refine spatiotemporal features. (c) Cross-modal fusion: Integrates multi-modal representations via Transformer.

3 Proposed Method

3.1 Framework

Figure 2(a) details the overall architecture of the proposed SVFDMF. To model the different features of the input news video, we first extract features from multiple modalities, including text, video, and audio. The Transformer with a self-attention mechanism is then used to capture correlations within each modality. The data from different modalities are subsequently mapped to a shared high-dimensional vector space, enabling inter-modal feature alignment. Fixed sine-cosine position encoding is added to the initial features to help the model understand the temporal relationships between the different modality features. Next, the MambaFormer is employed to process the text, video, and audio data, capturing detailed information. This architecture alternates between Mamba Layers, Self-Attention Mechanisms, and Adaptive Normalization Layers (AdaLN). Finally, the features are fused using a cross-modal Transformer and non-linear mapping via an MLP before performing the final classification.

3.2 Feature Extraction

Text. The information in the title and text is mostly incomplete and often the embedded text information in the video is comprehensive. We extract the text from the video and feed it into the pre-trained BERT [18] with the combination of title and text to extract the text features H_T=$[t_1,t_2,...,t_m]$, where t_i denotes the feature of the *i-th* word and m denotes the text-length.
Video. Video is a main modality in short video news, which can convey rich contextual information through the combination of moving images and sound. We use the pre-trained MAE [19] to extract video features H_V=$[v_1,v_2,...,v_n]$, where v_i denotes the feature of the *i-th* frame in the video and n is the number of frames in the video.
Audio. Audio is a new modality compared to traditional fake news detection methods, which provides semantic features, environments and background music. We use the pre-trained Hubert [20] to extract audio features H_A=$[a_1,a_2,...,a_p]$, where a_i denotes the feature of the *i-th* audio frame and p represents the number of audio frames.

After extracting the features, the single-modal features are modeled with self-attention using a Transformer to capture the global information within the modality.

3.3 Embedding Layer

In Embedding Layer, we use token embedding and temporal embedding to implement the model. Token embedding is processed to achieve dimensional unity, which facilitates the subsequent processing and fusion of individual modalities in the neural network. The temporal embedding uses sine and cosine functions to provide positional information. Because it enhances the model to recognize the position of elements in the input sequence, it is beneficial to improve the overall model performance and comprehension. Embedding layer can be represented as:

$$E = E_{token}(X) + E_{temporal}(C) \tag{1}$$

where E is the output of the Embedding layer and X and C are the inputs of a single modality. These two modules can facilitate the subsequent MambaFormer and cross-modal Transformer to process data.

3.4 MambaFormer

As shown in Fig. 2(b), the data is first processed by the Mamba Layer, which consists of two Linear Layers. The first Linear Layer maps the input features to appropriate dimensions and applies convolution for local feature extraction. The output is then passed through an activation function and sent to the SSM, which captures long-range dependencies. The second Linear Layer integrates the SSM output with a multiplicative gate, followed by another activation function, producing the final output. The Mamba Layer enables the model to capture the temporal structure of the input data, model intra-modal dependencies, and generate a structured feature representation for subsequent processing. It can be expressed as:

$$H = Mamba(E) \tag{2}$$

where H represents the mixed Token and Temporal Embedding. Figure 2(b) also illustrates the overall structure of MambaFormer, which alternates between the Mamba Layer, Multi-head Attention, and AdaLN. The Mamba Layer, using SSMs, is optimized for processing long time-series data (e.g., video and audio) while preserving temporal structure and extracting global features. The Multi-head Self-Attention mechanism captures contextual relationships between positions in the input sequence, improving global feature learning across modalities. To mitigate the risk of vanishing gradients in deeper networks, we employ AdaLN, an adaptive normalization method that adjusts its parameters dynamically during training. This enhances gradient flow and accelerates convergence, especially when handling data from diverse modalities like text, audio, and video. By alternating Mamba Layer, Multi-head Attention, and AdaLN, MambaFormer effectively captures complex relationships in multimodal data, improving model expressiveness, stability, and convergence speed.

3.5 Cross-Modal Fusion

Correlations between different modalities are essential for understanding video semantics. For instance, acoustic features from the audio modality can provide cues that help capture key information in the text features. Conversely, text features can assist in selecting keyframes from visual features, while visual features can complement and support textual features. The cross-modal fusion model utilizes a cross-modal Transformer to capture complementary information across textual, visual, and audio features. These features can interact across modalities, with information from other modalities enhancing the resulting cross-modal representations. Specifically, the query vectors from each modality are passed to the multi-head attention block of the other modalities.

As shown in Fig. 2(c), the text feature H_T and audio feature H_A are used to obtain the text-audio feature H_{TA}. Similarly, the text-video feature H_{TV} and video-audio feature H_{VA} are obtained in the same manner. Taking H_{TA} as an example, the formulas are as follows:

$$H_{TA} = \left(\Big\Vert_{h=1}^{H} softmax\left(\frac{Q_{\text{TA}} K_{\text{TA}}^{\top}}{\sqrt{d}} \right) V_{\text{TA}} \right) W_V^{\top}, \tag{3}$$

where Q_{TA}=$H_T W_Q$, K_{TA}=$H_A W_K$, V_{TA}=$H_A W_V$. W_Q,W_K and W_V are learnable linear transformation matrices. And H is the number of attention heads, W_V^T is the output linear transformation matrix.

Subsequently, we apply AttentionPooling to the text-audio feature H_{TA}, text-video feature H_{TV}, and video-audio feature H_{VA} to obtain weighted features. These weighted features are then concatenated to form a final fused feature vector as follows:

$$H_{concat} = [H_{TA}; H_{TV}; H_{VA}] \tag{4}$$

where H_{concat} represents the feature vector obtained after concatenating H_{TA}, H_{TV}, and H_{VA}.

3.6 Fake News Detection

The concated feature vectors are inputted into the MLP for nonlinear mapping. The MLP Layer consists of three fully connected layers and a RELU activation function to obtain the final multi-modal vector X_q. We project the multi-modal feature vector X_q through a fully connected layer with the softmax activation into the target space to distinguish real news videos from fake news videos and generate the corresponding probability distributions as follows:

$$p = softmax(W_p X_q + b_p) \tag{5}$$

where W_p is the weight matrix, b_p is the bias term. And p=$[p_0$,$p_1]$ is the predicted probability vector, where p_0 and p_1 denote the predicted probabilities with labels 0 (real news video) and 1 (fake news video) respectively.

$$L_{Fake\_News} = -\sum_{i=1}^{N} [(1 - Y)\log(p_0) + Y\log(p_1)] \tag{6}$$

where $Y \in \{0, 1\}$, N is the number of samples and p_0, p_1 are the probabilities of real and fake news respectively.

4 Experiments

4.1 Datasets

To validate the effectiveness of the proposed method, we conducted extensive experiments on the FakeSV [14] and FakeTT [15] datasets. **FakeSV** is the largest publicly available Chinese dataset for fake news detection in short videos, comprising manually annotated news videos collected from Chinese short video platforms. **FakeTT** is an English dataset designed to evaluate fake news detection in English-speaking contexts. It includes videos sourced from TikTok, focusing on events reported on fact-checking websites, with all samples manually annotated. The statistics of these two datasets are summarized in Table 1.

4.2 Experimental Setup

Our model uses Transformer and MambaFormer with 16 heads and dimension 512, with a Dropout set to 0.1 to prevent over-fitting. Feature fusion compresses cross-modal features to the input dimension via ReLU and MLP of Linear functions, training is done using Adam optimizer with decreasing learning rate with batch, batch size 16, and experiments are done on dual NVIDIA RTX 3080x2 GPUs with PyTorch. The experiments use Accuracy(Acc.), Macro Precision (Prec.), Macro Recall(Recall) and Macro F1 Score (F1) as evaluation metrics.

Table 1. Statistics of the two datasets.

Dataset	Fake	Real	Total
FakeSV	1810	1814	3624
FakeTT	1172	819	1991

4.3 Baselines

We conducted a comprehensive comparison between the proposed SVFDMF and a set of state-of-the-art baselines. These included multi-modal large language models (MLLMs), traditional methods based on handcrafted features and neural network-based techniques. This broad comparison framework ensures a fair and rigorous evaluation of the effectiveness and robustness of our proposed method.

MLLMs Methods:

- GPT-4 [21] is a powerful LLMs currently available for predicting and extracting on-screen text based on video news headlines.
- GPT-4o [22] autoregressive omnimodal model capable of receiving any combination of text, audio, image and video as input and generating any combination of text, audio and image as output.
- VideoLLAma2 [23] improves the performance of video and audio-oriented tasks by enhancing spatial-temporal modeling and audio comprehension.

Handcrafted Features-Based Methods:

- HCFC-Hou [10] exploits linguistic features of speech, acoustic-emotional features, and user engagement to complete the statistics of the data and classify it by SVM.
- HCFE-Medina [11] extracts video title features and the first 100 hundred comments and uses a traditional machine learning classifier.

Neural networks-based methods:

- TikTec [12] proposes a multi-modal fake news detection framework that guides the feature learning of visual frames through the extracted speech text information while introducing a co-attention module to achieve efficient fusion of visual and speech information.
- FANVM [13] constructs an adversarial neural network to efficiently extract topic-independent features and extracts features such as comments, titles and videos.
- SVFEND [14] uses cross-modal Transformer to extract relationships between text and audio, and text and video.
- FakingRecipe [15] detects fake news on short video platforms from the perspective of the creative process and designs creative process-aware detectors.

4.4 Overall Performance

Table 2 shows the performance comparison between SVFDMF and the baseline methods: **(1)** Some methods base-d on the LLMs underperform the dedicated Fake News Detection Models, as LLMs are more concerned with the linguistic patterns of the large dataset, and it is difficult to effectively capture fake information, VideoLLAma2 is always judged as true in FakeSV and false in FakeTT. **(2)** Neural network-based methods usually outperform artificial feature-based methods, TikTec shows that artificial methods still have advantages in specific scenarios. **(3)** SVFDMF outperforms all baselines on both FakeSV and FakeTT datasets in terms of accuracy, improving by 2.47% and 3.79%, proving its effectiveness in short video fake news detection.

4.5 Feature Extraction Experiment

We did perform an experiment using CLIP for feature extraction, and the results in Table 3 show that our approach outperforms CLIP. This is because the SVFDMF model extracts features from both text and video, leveraging Transformer mechanisms to strengthen temporal dependencies between video frames, and using MambaFormer to further enhance feature fusion. While CLIP excels at learning relationships between images and text, it may not fully capture the temporal sequence information inherent in videos, which is crucial for effective fake news detection in short videos.

4.6 Ablation Study

To evaluate the performance of the SVFDMF component, we conducted multiple ablation experiments from different perspectives.

The first group is based on the different components of SVFDMF, and the variants are defined as follows: (1)w/o ST: Remove the self-attention mechanism. (2)w/o Emb: Remove the Embedding Layer module. (3)w/o MF: Remove

Table 2. Comparison results on FakeSV and FakeTT datasets.

Dataset	Methods	Accuracy	Macro F1	Fake			Real		
				Prec	Recall	F1	Prec	Recall	F1
FakeSV	GPT-4	75.46	74.30	86.18	74.22	79.76	61.76	77.78	68.85
	GPT-4o	73.93	73.44	76.29	77.84	77.06	70.77	68.91	69.83
	VideoLLAma2	58.79	58.35	47.26	63.28	54.11	70.98	55.99	62.60
	HCFC-Hou	74.91	73.61	73.46	86.51	79.46	77.72	60.08	67.77
	HCFC-Medina	76.38	75.83	77.50	81.58	79.49	74.77	69.75	72.17
	TikTec	73.43	73.26	78.37	72.70	75.43	68.08	74.37	71.08
	FANVM	79.52	78.81	78.64	87.17	82.68	80.98	69.75	74.94
	SVFEND	80.88	80.54	85.82	77.63	81.52	74.53	**83.61**	78.81
	FakingRecipe	85.35	84.83	83.33	**92.11**	87.50	88.35	76.47	81.98
	SVFDMF (Ours)	**87.82 (+2.47%)**	**87.54 (+2.71%)**	**87.19**	91.78	**89.42**	**88.74**	82.77	**85.65**
FakeTT	GPT-4	62.21	62.17	**88.89**	46.32	60.90	49.00	89.91	63.43
	GPT-4o	66.56	65.47	63.00	82.89	71.59	73.74	49.66	59.35
	VideoLLAma2	66.32	48.70	91.75	68.99	78.76	12.09	40.74	18.64
	HCFC-Hou	73.24	72.00	56.93	78.79	66.10	87.04	70.50	77.90
	HCFC-Medina	62.54	62.23	46.24	80.81	58.82	84.92	53.50	65.64
	TikTec	66.22	65.08	49.32	72.73	58.78	82.35	63.00	71.39
	FANVM	71.57	70.21	55.15	75.76	63.83	85.28	69.50	76.58
	SVFEND	77.14	75.63	62.33	78.79	69.57	87.91	76.33	81.69
	FakingRecipe	79.15	77.74	64.75	**81.82**	72.18	**89.74**	77.83	83.30
	SVFDMF (Ours)	**82.94 (+3.79%)**	**80.49 (+2.75%)**	75.53	71.12	**73.58**	86.34	**88.50**	**87.41**

Table 3. Feature Extraction Experiment

Methods	FakeSV		FakeTT	
	Acc	F1	Acc	F1
SVFDMF	**87.82**	**87.54**	**82.94**	**80.49**
CLIP	84.89	83.60	80.21	77.90

the MambaFormer module. (4)w/o CT: Remove the cross-modal fusion module. The experimental results are shown in Table 4(a), from which we can draw the following conclusions:

- All variants performed lower than SVFDMF, demonstrating the importance of each component to the overall performance.
- The removal of the self-attention module degraded the performance, verifying its effectiveness in modal correlation capture.
- The removal of the embedding degraded the performance, demonstrating its role in modal alignment and timing modeling.
- Removal of the MambaFormer performance decreases, demonstrating its usefulness in capturing intra-modal local and global information.
- Removal of cross-modal fusion (replaced by concating) performance decreases, suggesting that cross-modal fusion enhances modal interaction.

The second group is based on the number of modalities in the data, and the variants are defined as follows: (1)w/o T: Remove the text modal. (2)w/o V: Remove the video modal. (3)w/o A: Remove the audio modal. The experimental results are shown in Table 4(b), from which we can draw the following conclusions:

- The performance of all variants is lower than that of the full SVFDMF, demonstrating the importance of each modality to the overall performance.
- Text is the most effective for fake news detection, probably because video contains a lot of textual information and audio carries semantic cues.
- Audio plays the least role, because it focuses more on emotion and sound information capture.

The third group is based on different components in mambaformer, and the variants are defined as follows: (1)w/o Mamba: Remove the mamba layer in the MambaFormer. (2)w/o MA: Remove the multi-head attention mechanism in the MambaFormer. (3)w/o AdaLN: Remove the AdaLN module in the MambaFormer. The experimental results are shown in Table 4(c), from which we can draw the following conclusions:

- Removing Mamba leads to a substantial decline in feature extraction performance, particularly on the FakeSV dataset, where Mamba plays a pivotal role in enhancing both the model's ability to characterize complex patterns and its overall training effectiveness.
- Removing multi-attention results in a slight decrease in performance, probably because Mamba and AdaLN still play a feature extraction and normalization.
- Removing AdaLN results in a notable degradation in model performance, particularly on the FakeTT dataset, where the absence of AdaLN disrupts stable gradient propagation, thereby impairing the model's learning capability and overall effectiveness.

4.7 Analysis of Pooling Operation

To evaluate the performance of different feature pooling methods on the FakeSV and FakeTT datasets, we conducted a series of pooling experiments, with the results shown in Fig. 3. The results indicate that none of the alternative methods outperform the original SVFDMF, highlighting the superior performance of the AttentionPooling method we employed. While WeightedPooling and MaxPooling do not perform as well as SVFDMF, they still demonstrate some advantages in fusing features from different layers. In contrast, the overall performance of MeanPooling and MinPooling is notably poor, likely due to their inability to effectively capture the complex features of multi-modal data, which makes them less suitable for this task.

Table 4. Ablation Study on FakeSV and FakeTT datasets.

	Methods	FakeSV		FakeTT	
		Acc	F1	Acc	F1
	SVFDMF	**87.82**	**87.54**	**82.94**	**80.49**
(a)	w/o ST	86.72	86.45	80.27	78.30
	w/o Emb	86.35	85.98	81.61	79.68
	w/o MF	85.98	85.22	80.27	80.15
	w/o CT	85.61	85.41	80.60	78.98
(b)	w/o T	74.72	74.05	70.23	67.94
	w/o V	84.69	84.30	79.93	78.43
	w/o A	86.53	86.25	80.60	78.72
(c)	w/o Mamba	86.61	86.37	81.27	80.08
	w/o MA	86.42	86.21	81.60	79.39
	w/o AdaLN	86.72	86.43	81.61	78.85

Table 5. Analysis of computational efficiency after applying mixed-precision training (Times: training time per epoch).

Methods	FakeSV			FakeTT		
	Acc	F1	Times	Acc	F1	Times
SVFDMF	**87.82**	**87.54**	126 s	**82.94**	**80.49**	79 s
autocast	87.68	86.56	**102 s**	82.79	79.24	**64 s**

4.8 Computational Efficiency

When dealing with multiple modalities (text, audio, video), the model can incur significant computational costs, particularly during the training phase. Multimodal learning typically requires substantial memory and processing power. To mitigate this, we used mixed-precision training, which accelerates the training process and reduces memory usage by converting certain computations to lower precision. The results, shown in Table 5, show that this approach maintains a similar performance to standard training while reducing the training time per epoch by 19.99% approximately. This experiment confirms that our method is computationally efficient without compromising the quality of the results.

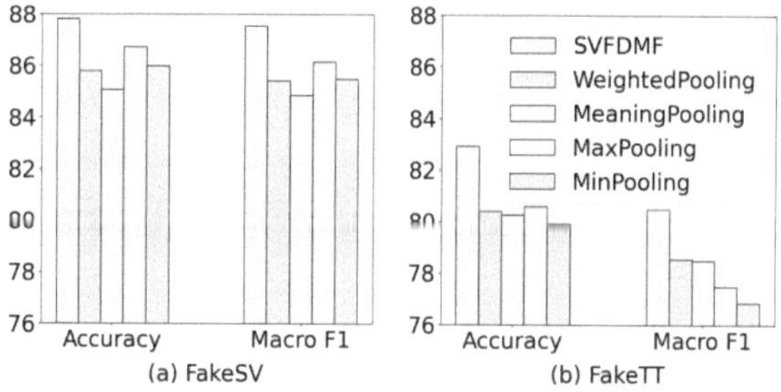

Fig. 3. Performance analysis of different pooling methods on FakeSV and FakeTT Datasets.

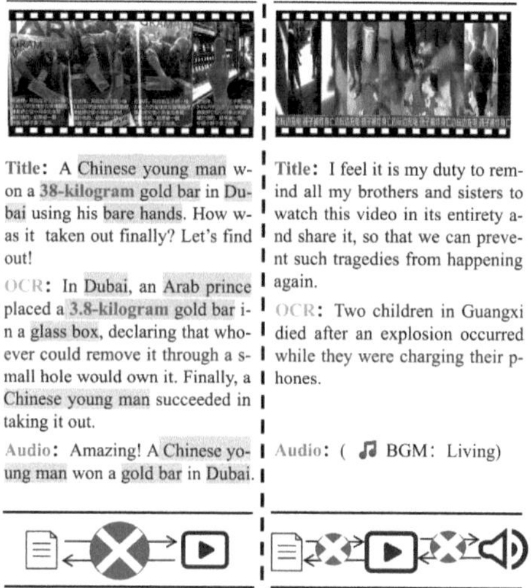

Fig. 4. Case Analysis. The left side shows a successful case, while the right side displays a failure case.

5 Case Studies

5.1 Successful Case

We conducted a visualization of entities across video, text, and audio modalities by highlighting them in distinct colors—red for video entities and yellow for text and audio entities—as illustrated on the left side of Fig. 4. This multimodal visualization reveals evident semantic inconsistencies between modalities. For instance, while the textual content references a 38-kilogram gold bar, the corresponding video depicts one weighing only 3.8 kg. Such a discrepancy casts doubt on the credibility of the news and serves as compelling evidence of misinformation. This example underscores the effectiveness of our model in detecting fake news by leveraging cross-modal inconsistencies.

5.2 Failure Case

Despite the inclusion of sophisticated interaction layers, such as Transformers and Mambaformer, designed to bolster modality relationships, there exist instances where the inter-modal connections remain obscure, thereby impeding seamless integration. Particularly in scenarios where certain modal information (e.g., text) is less relevant to the task, the cross-modal fusion mechanism may underperform, potentially undermining model accuracy. As illustrated on the right side of Fig. 4, such cases highlight the failure of the fusion process to adequately exploit the unique strengths of each modality, resulting in suboptimal model performance.

Conclusion

In this work, we propose SVFDMF, an innovative framework for detecting fake news in short videos, specifically designed to tackle the challenges associated with long-sequence data processing and intricate inter-modal correlations. By leveraging Mamba layers, multi-head self-attention, adaptive normalization, and a Transformer-based cross-modal fusion module, SVFDMF enables comprehensive extraction and effective integration of multi-modal representations. Extensive experiments validate that our approach consistently outperforms existing state-of-the-art methods, highlighting its robustness and superior detection capabilities.

Acknowledgments. This work was supported by the National Natural Science Foundation of China (No. 6247074060), the Natural Science Foundation of Heilongjiang Province in China (No. PL2024F029), the Fundamental Research Funds for Province-owned Higher Education Institutions in Heilongjiang Province (2021-KYYWF-0043, 2023-KYYWF-1463, 2024-KYYWF-0115) and Doctoral Postdoctoral Funding Project in Heilongjiang Province.

References

1. Vaswani, A., et al.: Attention is all you need. In: Advances in Neural Information Processing Systems, vol. 30 (2017)
2. Sundar, S.S., Molina, M.D., Cho, E.G.: Seeing is believing: Is video modality more powerful in spreading fake news via online messaging apps? J. Comput.-Mediat. Commun. **26**(5), 301–319 (2021)
3. Naeem, S.B., Bhatti, R.: The COVID19 ‘infodemic’: a new front for information professionals. Health Inform. Libraries J. **37**(3), 233–239 (2020)
4. Niu, S., Lu, Z., Zhang, A.X., Cai, J., Griggio, C.F., Heuer, H.: Building credibility, trust, and safety on video-sharing platforms. In: Extended Abstracts of the 2023 CHI Conference on Human Factors in Computing Systems (2023)
5. Bu, Y., Sheng, Q., Cao, J., Qi, P., Wang, D., Li, J.: Combating online misinformation videos: Characterization, detection, and future directions. In: Proceedings of the 31st ACM International Conference on Multimedia, pp. 8770–8780 (2023)

6. Wu, Y., Zhan, P., Zhang, Y., Wang, L., Xu, Z.: Multimodal fusion with coattention networks for fake news detection. In: Findings of the Association for Computational Linguistics: ACL-IJCNLP 2021, pp. 2560–2569 (2021)
7. Zhou, Y., Ying, Q., Qian, Z., Li, S., Zhang, X.: Multimodal fake news detection via CLIP guided learning. In: IEEE International Conference on Multimedia and Expo (ICME), pp. 2825–2830 (2023)
8. Zeng, Z., Wu, M., Li, G., Li, X., Huang, Z., Sha, Y.: Correcting the bias: mitigating multimodal inconsistency contrastive learning for multimodal fake news detection. In: IEEE International Conference on Multimedia and Expo (ICME), pp. 2861–2866 (2023)
9. Zhou, Y., Yang, Y., Ying, Q., Qian, Z., Zhang, X.: Multi-modal fake news detection on social media via multi-grained information fusion. In: Proceedings of the ACM International Conference on Multimedia Retrieval (ICMR), pp. 343–352. ACM (2023)
10. Hou, R., Pérez-Rosas, V., Loeb, S., Mihalcea, R.: Towards automatic detection of misinformation in online medical videos. In: Proceedings of the 2019 International Conference on Multimodal Interaction, pp. 235–243 (2019)
11. Serrano, J.C.M., Papakyriakopoulos, O., Hegelich, S.: NLP-based feature extraction for the detection of COVID-19 misinformation videos on YouTube. In: 1st Workshop on NLP for COVID-19 at ACL 2020 (2020)
12. Shang, L., Kou, Z., Zhang, Y., Wang, D.: A multimodal misinformation detector for COVID-19 short videos on TikTok. In: IEEE International Conference on Big Data, pp. 899–908 (2021)
13. Choi, H., Ko, Y.: Using topic modeling and adversarial neural networks for fake news video detection. In: Proceedings of the 30th ACM International Conference on Information and Knowledge Management (CIKM), pp. 2950–2954 (2021)
14. Qi, P., et al.: FakeSV: a multimodal benchmark with rich social context for fake news detection on short video platforms. In: Proceedings of the AAAI Conference on Artificial Intelligence, vol. 37(12), 14444–14452 (2023)
15. Bu, Y., Sheng, Q., Cao, J., Qi, P., Wang, D., Li, J.: FakingRecipe: detecting fake news on short video platforms from the perspective of creative process. In: Proceedings of the 32nd ACM International Conference on Multimedia, pp. 1351–1360 (2024)
16. Park, J., et al.: Can Mamba learn how to learn? A comparative study on in-context learning tasks. arXiv preprint arXiv:2402.04248 (2024)
17. Fei, Z., Fan, M., Yu, C., Li, D., Zhang, Y., Huang, J.: Dimba: transformer-Mamba diffusion models. arXiv preprint arXiv:2406.01159 (2024)
18. Cui, Y., Che, W., Liu, T., Qin, B., Yang, Z.: Pre-training with whole word masking for Chinese BERT. IEEE/ACM Transactions on Audio, Speech, and Language Processing **29**, 3504–3513 (2021)
19. He, K., Chen, X., Xie, S., Li, Y., Dollár, P., Girshick, R.: Masked autoencoders are scalable vision learners. In: Proceedings of the IEEE/CVF Conference on Computer Vision and Pattern Recognition, pp. 16000–16009 (2022)
20. Hsu, W.-N., Bolte, B., Tsai, Y.-H.H., Lakhotia, K., Salakhutdinov, R., Mohamed, A.: HuBERT: Self-supervised speech representation learning by masked prediction of hidden units. IEEE/ACM Transactions on Audio, Speech, and Language Processing **29**, 3451–3460 (2021)
21. Achiam, J., Adler, S., Agarwal, S., et al.: GPT-4 Technical Report. arXiv preprint arXiv:2303.08774 (2023)
22. Hurst, A., Lerer, A., Goucher, A.P., et al.: GPT-4o System Card. arXiv preprint arXiv:2410.21276 (2024)

23. Cheng, Z., Leng, S., Zhang, H., et al.: VideoLLaMA 2: Advancing spatial-temporal modeling and audio understanding in video-LLMs. arXiv preprint arXiv:2406.07476 (2024)
24. Ma, J., Liu, Y., Liu, M., Han, M.: Curriculum contrastive learning for fake news detection. In: Proceedings of the 31st ACM International Conference on Information & Knowledge Management, pp. 4309–4313 (2022)
25. Ma, J., Dai, J., Liu, Y., Han, M., Ai, C.: Contrastive learning for rumor detection via fitting beta mixture model. In: Proceedings of the 32nd ACM International Conference on Information and Knowledge Management, pp. 4160–4164 (2023)
26. Ma, J., Liu, Y., Han, M., Hu, C., Ju, Z.: Propagation structure fusion for rumor detection based on node-level contrastive learning. IEEE Transactions on Neural Networks and Learning Systems (2023)

A Lightweight Pavement Defect Detection Method Based on Multi-branch Attention with Contextual Guidance

Keyan Cao[1,2](✉), Jiayin Chen[1], Zhongyang Wang[1,2], and Xinlei Wang[1,2]

[1] School of Computer Science and Engineering, Shenyang Jianzhu University, Shenyang 110168, China
caokeyan@sjzu.edu.cn

[2] Liaoning Provincial Key Laboratory of Big Data Management and Analysis of Urban Construction, Shenyang 110168, China

Abstract. The present paper addresses multi-scale target imbalance, background noise interference, and edge deployment needs in pavement defect detection within complex road scenarios. The following proposal is hereby submitted: Initially, the Cascaded Channel Group Attention (CCGA) module is employed to reconfigure the Cross-Stage Partial Spatial Attention (C2PSA) with cascading grouped attention, thereby enabling multi-branch feature decoupling. This process is undertaken to enhance the accuracy of small targets and overlapping defect detection. Secondly, the Channel-Transposed Kernel Collaborative Attention (CKCA) module employs multi-head grouped self-attention with a learnable temperature to enhance crack classification and reduce the amount of computation. Thirdly, a lightweight Context-GuidedBlock-based downsampling module retains fine crack features via multi-branch context fusion and adaptive pooling. Furthermore, the P2 detection head, equipped with a two-layer cavity and dynamic convolution, enhances the detection of small targets through high-resolution feature fusion and dynamic weighting. The RDD2022 dataset was utilized in a series of experiments, which yielded enhancements of 2.4%, 2.6%, and 5.8% in mAP@50, precision, and recall, respectively. These enhancements were effective in reducing missed detections and false alarms, thereby supporting real-time road inspection and intelligent highway development.

Keywords: Multi-scale target detection · Attention mechanism optimization · Pavement defect recognition

1 Introduction

1.1 Background and Significance of the Study

The global situation concerning road safety is still critical. According to the World Health Organization (WHO), approximately 90% of road traffic fatalities occur in low- and middle-income countries, with pavement defects (e.g., cracks,

J. Li et al. (Eds.): APWeb-WAIM 2025, LNCS 16115, pp. 115–129, 2026.
https://doi.org/10.1007/978-981-95-5719-6_8

potholes) being a significant contributing factor. China, which possesses one of the most extensive road networks, had 5.4 million km of asphalt pavement in 2024, with annual maintenance costs exceeding 72 billion yuan [7]. It is anticipated that this figure will increase in 2025, with defect-related traffic accidents projected to exceed 16% [15]. In this domain, the performance of mainstream detection models is often constrained by the complexity of environmental conditions, leading to suboptimal mean mAP@0.5 scores. This limitation compromises the precision of all-day detection, reduces the clarity of road surface imaging and feature interpretation, and increases analytical errors. The challenges under discussion can be traced back to three fundamental issues. Firstly, there are deficiencies in multi-scale feature fusion, where the current feature pyramid provides an inadequate encoding of micro-crack semantics [24], resulting in weaker micro-crack responses [23]. Secondly, there is limited transferability, as the features of cross-regional road paving materials vary by up to $\pm 15\%$ across RDD2022 subsets [3]. Thirdly, there is poor resistance to environmental disturbances, where rain and fog reduce image SNR to 2.8 dB, while traditional CNNs' local connectivity limits accurate segmentation of defective backgrounds [1]. The enhancement of the accuracy, efficiency, and adaptability of road surface defect detection remains a critical objective.

The present study proposes a target detection method to overcome the problems of uneven distribution of multi-scale targets and insufficient robustness to complex backgrounds. The method is designed to enhance the detection of small-size defects and resistance to interference. The method under discussion is rooted in YOLO11 and incorporates the CCGA module to combat complex background interference. In addition, it incorporates the CKCA mechanism and the ContextGuidedDown downsampling module. The integration of these components serves to enhance the accuracy, speed, and versatility of road defect detection. The primary contributions encompass the following three aspects:

The proposal of a new feature enhancement module, CCGA, is put forward as a solution to the issue of suboptimal performance in the detection of small objects. The functionality of the module is such that it can reconfigure the feature extraction mechanism located in the final layer of the backbone network. The effect of this is to enhance the ability of the system to capture object details and features. The model's localization accuracy and multi-scale feature discrimination for defective regions are enhanced, whilst concomitantly reducing computational complexity.

A new module, CKCA, is hereby proposed to address deficiencies in cross-channel interaction efficiency and adaptability to dynamic environments. The approach under discussion divides feature maps into multi-head groups by channel and models cross-channel global dependencies through transposed matrix multiplication. The resulting system provides both high-precision and low-latency benefits for pavement defect detection.

In the third instance, a more concise ContextGuidedBlock is adopted to replace the downsampled ordinary convolutional layer. This development improves the model's running speed without compromising accuracy. Furthermore, a P2 dynamic detection head structure is introduced, which detects and localizes small targets more effectively through a specialized P2 layer, thereby improving the accuracy of small target detection.

1.2 Related Work

Commonly used two-stage such as Region-based Convolutional Neural Network (R-CNN) series [9] algorithms. The first stage model is simple, efficient and fast, but has low detection accuracy for small targets. The second stage model has high accuracy but is computationally intensive and slow. experiments by Ping et al. [18] show that the YOLOv3 model has the best performance in pavement defects detection, with fast and reliable results; Liu et al. [12] combine 3D ground-penetrating radar with the YOLO algorithm for detecting structural damage to pavements, which can detect potential damage in advance but at a higher cost; Baek et al. [5] use the YOLO model for pavement pothole image gray processing and inputting it into the YOLO algorithm, which can detect potential damage in advance, but at a higher cost. Baek et al. [5] processed pothole images in grayscale and input them into the YOLO detection mode, which improved the detection speed but reduced the model generalization ability and robustness; Fang Wan et al. [22] proposed a lightweight road defect detection algorithm YOLO-LRDD, which utilizes a new backbone network, Shuffle-ECANet, and reduces the model size while maintaining the accuracy and is suitable for the deployment of mobile devices, and Xu Yu et al. proposed the YOLO algorithm for asphalt pavement defect detection, which is suitable for mobile devices. YOLOv 5-PD for asphalt pavement defect detection, which integrates large kernel convolution and channel attention mechanisms to improve performance. The model achieves an inference speed of 41 FPS and a 73.3% improvement in mAP, which exceeds the existing models. Existing pavement defect detection suffers from difficulties such as insufficient dataset, uneven light intensity, and easy to miss detection of small targets, etc. The YOLO algorithm has been developed to YOLO11, which has significant advantages in detection accuracy and speed. Therefore, we choose to use the YOLO11 framework to optimize the model to further improve the accuracy of the algorithm.

2 Proposed Methodology

2.1 Model Overview

The present study proposes a lightweight downsampling module, based on the ContextGuidedBlock, which has been designed to reduce computational volume while retaining the fine-grained features of cracks. The proposal of a P2 detection head with double-layer cavity convolution and full-dimensional dynamic convolution is presented, with the objective being to enhance the detection accuracy of small targets by leveraging high-resolution feature fusion and dynamic weight adjustment. As illustrated in Fig. 1, the network structure is delineated as follows.

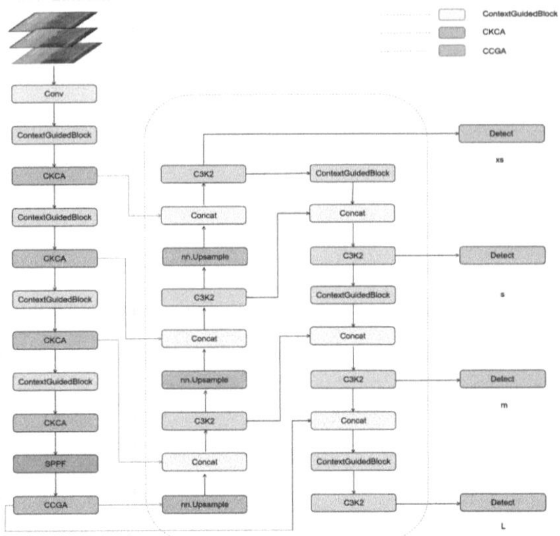

Fig. 1. Network structure diagram of this method

2.2 CCGA Module Structure Design and Feature Enhancement Mechanism

The present study proposes a novel feature enhancement module, CCGA, to address the challenges of variable target scales, fuzzy texture features, and background noise interference in road surface defect detection. This module has been shown to enhance the model's capacity for localization accuracy in defective regions, as well as its multi-scale feature discrimination capability. This enhancement is achieved through the reconfiguration of the final layer of the backbone network's feature extraction mechanism.

Module Architecture Design. In this paper, we propose a CCGA module to improve detection efficiency. The CCGA module follows the cross-stage partial (CSP) design pattern of C2PSA [19] and employs the three-stage cascade grouped attention initiative [13] to strengthen the location-sensitive attention module. First, we apply the grouped channel attention mechanism to reduce background interference. Then, we use spatial location coding to improve the localization of defective regions. In addition, we use the tensor product operation to combine the weighting matrix with C2PSA features to improve the detection of small and mutually occluded targets (Fig. 2).

These Modifications Yield Three Effective Improvements: (1) Multi-branch feature decoupling: The input feature map is divided into two groups of branches using the CSP structure, where the main branch performs shallow feature extraction via stacking Bottleneck layers, and the auxiliary branch employs the cascade grouped attention mechanism. The channels are divided into subspaces by

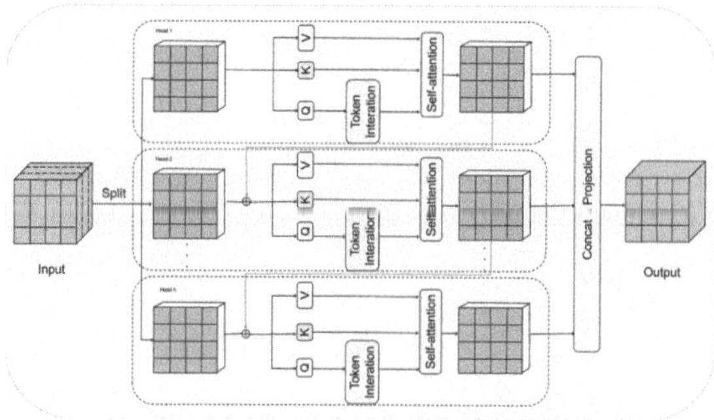

Fig. 2. Cascade Group Attention Architecture Diagram

grouped convolution (experimentally verified to be optimal when $k=4$), with each subspace independently calculating hybrid attention weights in the channel space.

$$Attn_i = \sigma\left(DWConv\left(F_i\right) \oplus Conv_{1\times 1}\left(F_i\right)\right) \quad (i = 1, \ldots, k) \tag{1}$$

where F_i denotes the i group of sub-features, σ represents the Sigmoid activation function, and $DWConv$ indicates depthwise separable convolution.

(2) Cascade attention fusion: A two-stage cascade strategy is employed, where the first stage calibrates the attention of each subspace locally, and the second stage generates global attention through cross-group feature interactions.

$$F_{fused} = \sum_{i=1}^{k} Attn_i \odot F_i + FFN\left(Concat(Attn_1, \ldots, Attn_k)\right) \tag{2}$$

In the equation, $\odot$ denotes element-wise multiplication, and the feed-forward network (FFN) employs a two-layer fully connected architecture to achieve non-linear mapping.

(3) Residual connection optimization: to avoid gradient degradation of the deep network, an adaptive residual connection strategy is designed to perform constant mapping when the number of input and output channels matches, otherwise 1×1 convolution is used for dimension alignment. To optimize the gradient propagation and facilitate the training of the network.

Feature enhancement mechanism analysis. Dynamic convolution Omni-Dimensional Dynamic Convolution (ODConv) [8] improves the feature enhancement mechanism to optimize the road defect detection analysis; from the perspective of multi-granularity detection, the P3 branch with 1/8 resolution focuses on the extraction of tiny defect features, and the P5 branch captures the macro spalling features with 1/32 resolution to realize the integration of multi-granularity features; Explaining the principle of feature optimization of the CCGA module can effectively Explaining the principle of feature optimization of the CCGA module can effectively improve the detection ability of road defects.

2.3 CKCA Module Design Principles

For the CKCA module, we draw inspiration from the FreqFormer [6] architecture and introduce a novel Channel Transposed Attention (Fig. 3) in the backbone C3K2. The novel architecture class of the CTA attention mechanism is used for channel dimensional interactions, which is different from the classical channel attention mechanism. It divides the feature map into multiple parts based on channel dimensions. Specifically, the feature map is divided into multiple parts based on the channel dimension, and it adopts the channel transposition means to reach the cross-channel global association modeling with the help of matrix transposition operation. This is essential to realize the cross-channel feature aggregation by using the channel dimensional attention mechanism [20]. The fusion of the C3K2 module first does a good job of structural calibration and location planning, The C3K2 module relies on the standard convolution and lightweight branching parallel processing to complete the feature segmentation and fusion, and its channel diversion and CTA multi-head allocation is naturally complementary; CTA and C3K2 are combined in the feature splicing layer, and the attention weights are modeled based on the intermediate output before feature transformation; the dynamic weights are adjusted to adapt to the long-tailed distribution pattern of the pavement defects, and the weights are redistributed to enhance the ability to capture the defect features of the low occupancy ratio, which is especially suitable for the detection needs of the high number of channels. CKCA is mainly aimed at the two major problems of the significant heterogeneity of the channels in the detection of pavement defects (e.g., differences of response of cracks between different materials) and bottleneck of computational efficiency. The application of the CKCA module mainly makes the following contributions:

Adopt a Multi-head Grouping Strategy. Divide the input feature maps into groups by channel dimension (defaultH = 8), and each group independently performs transpose matrix multiplication (Eq. 3) to establish cross-channel global dependencies:

$$Attn_h(F) = Softmax\left(\frac{(F_h W_q)(F_h W_k)^T}{\sqrt{d_k}}\right)(F_h W_v) \tag{3}$$

where F_h denotes the sub-features of the -th group, and W_q, W_k, W_v are learnable projection matrices. For feature reorganization enhancement: adaptation to heterogeneous channel features is improved by cross-head information fusion (Eq. 4):

$$F_{out} = Concat(Attn_1, Attn_2, \ldots, Attn_H)\, W_o \tag{4}$$

Computational Complexity Optimization. Traditional channel attention defects: mechanisms such as SENet achieve feature calibration through global channel compression excitation, but its $O(C^2)$ complexity is computationally expensive in high-channel-count scenarios (e.g., C3K2's 512 channels). To reduce the computational complexity CTA reduces the computational complexity from $O(C^2)$ to $O(C^2/H)$ (is the number of heads) by grouping and transposition operations. The grouping parallel computing feature is highly compatible with the GPU tensor core architecture, enabling hardware acceleration adaptation.

Dynamic Feature Calibration Capability. Enhanced environmental adaptability: CTA dynamically adjusts the channel response strength via self-attention weights, elevating the activation weights of defect-related channels under complex lighting conditions (e.g., strong reflections) and adverse weather (e.g., rain and fog).

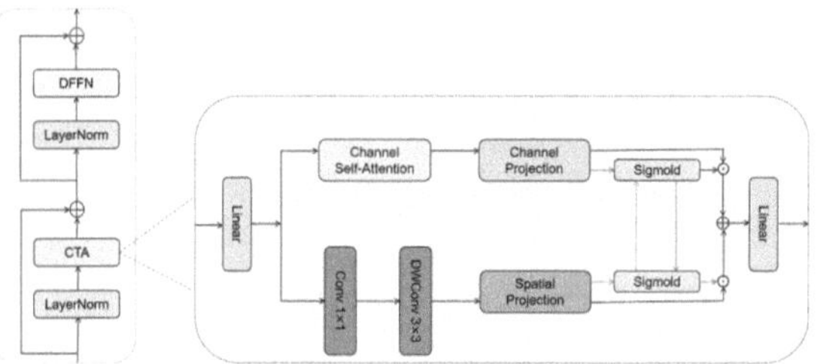

Fig. 3. Channel transposition attention

The C3K2 module in the basic YOLO11 network is derived from the C2F module. Its implementation is controlled by a setting in the code: when the c3k parameter is set to FALSE, the C3K2 module functions as a C2F module; when it is TRUE, the standard Bottleneck module is replaced with the C3 module. Additionally, we have enhanced the design of the CKCA module within the C3K2 structure. A comparison of the three modules is shown in Fig. 4.

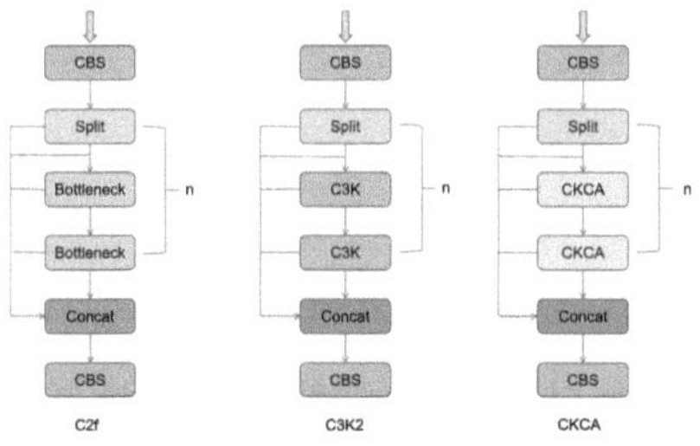

Fig. 4. Comparison of C2f, C3K2, CKCA

2.4 Pavement Defect Detection Method Based on Context-Guided Down Module Design Improvement Models

The traditional model adopts a downsampling approach combining standard convolution with maximum pooling, which results in a significant loss of fine-grained feature information. For pavement cracks and other targets with long-tailed distributions, we use the lightweight context-guided Downsample in CGNet [25]. The core idea of this module originates from the Context Guided Block (CG block) proposed in CGNet, which becomes a lightweight model by fusing local features, surrounding context, and global context. This fusion forms the theoretical basis of lightweight downsampling. Specifically, the context-guided downsampling method, termed ContextGuided, is derived from a 2023 technical report in the field of computer vision. This work combines CGNet's context-guided mechanism with adaptive pooling to design a specialized downsampling module, which serves as a multi-scale feature extraction component tailored for target detection tasks. Its core design concepts include multi-branch context fusion and lightweight structural features. The contextual information from different receptive fields is captured by parallel convolutional branches (e.g., 3×3 standard convolution, 5×5 cavity convolution) to address scale variation problems in pavement defect detection (Eq. 5). Grouped convolution and channel rearrangement techniques are utilized to enhance inter-channel information interaction while maintaining computational efficiency. Additionally, edge feature enhancement preserves texture details via residual connections, making this approach particularly suitable for edge-sensitive feature extraction of pavement cracks, potholes, and similar defects [16]. Let the input feature map $X \in R^{C \times H \times W}$, Processing by parallel branching:

$$\begin{cases} Y_{local} = Conv_{3\times3}(X) \\ Y_{context} = DilatedConv_{3\times3}(X, d = 2) \\ Y_{gate} = \sigma\left(Conv_{1\times1}\left([AvgPool(X), MaxPool(X)]\right)\right) \end{cases} \tag{5}$$

where d denotes the null rate and σ is the Sigmoid function.

The final output of fusion features:

$$Y_{out} = Y_{gate} \odot (Y_{local} \oplus Y_{context}) \tag{6}$$

where $\odot$ denotes element-by-element multiplication and $\oplus$ denotes feature splicing (Fig. 5).

2.5 Role of the P2 Detection Head in the Model

The P2 detection head is a critical module designed for small objects, using high-resolution feature maps to accurately capture microscopic features such as reticulation defects while supporting multi-scale feature fusion and lightweight processing. This design overcomes the limitations of traditional detection heads, where the detection of small targets decreases with increasing mesh depth [21].

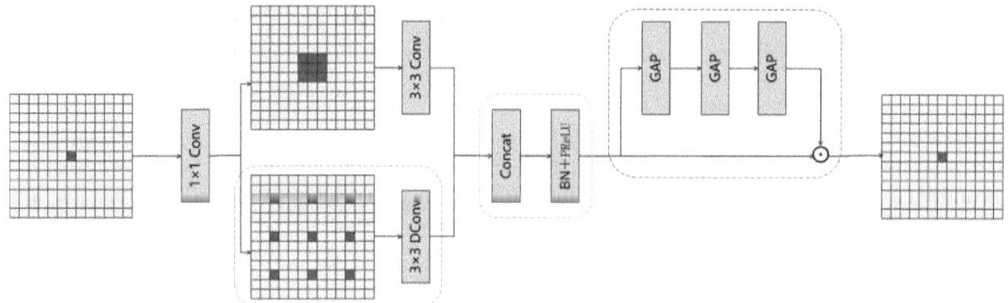

Fig. 5. Structure of Context Guided Block module

It cooperates with deeper layers (P4/P5), exploiting FPN and PAN architectures for enhanced semantic information [11], enabling multi-scale detection and addressing target size variability. Key innovations include a two-layer cascaded cavity convolution module with multi-scale 3×3 kernels (expansion ratios 1, 3, and 5) for shallow feature extraction, and a full-dimensional ODConv that dynamically adjusts weights across four dimensions - kernel space, input channels, output channels, and number of kernels - via a multi-dimensional attention mechanism to improve the network's focus on faulty regions.

3 Results and Discussion

3.1 Dataset

The present study employs the publicly available road damage detection dataset RDD2022 [2], which encompasses images from six countries. To validate the Chinese subset of RDD2022 [4], which encompasses Guangdong's hot and humid climate and Heilongjiang's freezing and thawing road conditions, a total of 4,378 images were selected based on the structure and characteristics of Chinese road pavements. The dataset under consideration encompasses five distinct categories of detection objects: namely, vertical cracks (D00), horizontal cracks (D10), mesh cracks (D20), potholes (D40), and repair works. As illustrated in Fig. 8, the five categories of data are displayed, along with their respective distributions. The images were obtained through two distinct methodologies: firstly, a camera mounted on a motorcycle, and secondly, an unmanned aerial vehicle (UAV). The images have a resolution of 512 × 512 pixels (Fig. 6 and Table 1).

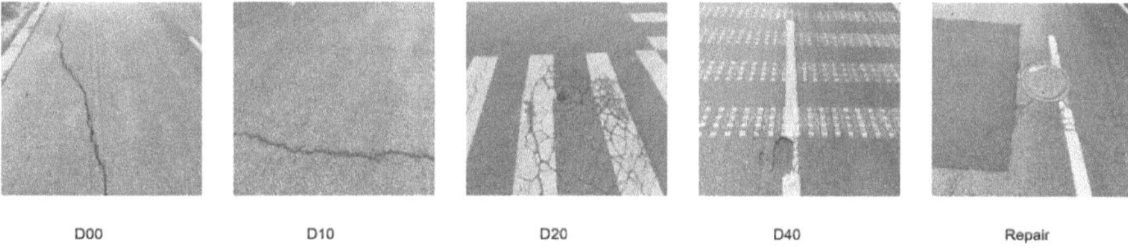

Fig. 6. Five types of detection targets

Table 1. Distribution of the five types of data

Class	D00	D10	D20	D40	Re-pair
Train	2414	1394	559	185	643
Test	504	375	154	53	142
Val	494	343	136	44	164

3.2 Experimental Environment and Parameter Settings

The experimental setup utilized a system equipped with an NVIDIA RTX 4090 (24 GB) GPU, an Intel Xeon Gold 6430 CPU with 16 cores, 120 GB of RAM, PyTorch 2.1.0 as the deep learning framework, Python 3.10 running on Ubuntu 22.04, and CUDA version 12.1. The parameter settings are summarized in the table below (Table 2).

Table 2. Training parameter settings

Hyperparameters	Value
Learning Rate	0.01
Image Size	512×512
Momentum	0.937
Optimizer	SGD
Epoch	450
Batch Size	16
Works	4

3.3 Experimental Process and Results

First, the selected road defect dataset was converted into the format required for training and divided into training, validation, and test sets in a ratio of 6:2:2. Next, YOLO11 was used as the baseline model and the enhancements introduced in Sect. 2.2 were applied to improve its performance. Finally, the model was trained in the environment described in Sect. 3.2. Figures a and b (Fig. 8) show the confusion matrices derived from the detection results of the original and improved models, respectively. The accuracy and completeness curves of the improved model exceed those of the original model. This indicates that the improved model performs better over several types of road defects (Fig. 7).

3.4 Ablation Experiments

The present study involved the execution of ablation experiments, wherein each enhanced component was integrated into the original model on an individual

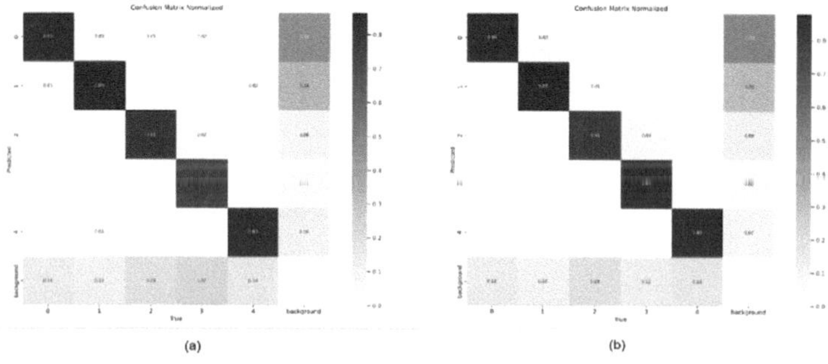

Fig. 7. (a) Confusion matrix of the baseline model.(b) Confusion matrix of our model

basis, to conduct a comprehensive analysis of their respective contributions. The results are presented in Table 3, where A denotes the YOLO11 model with the CCGA module, B the model with the enhanced neck, C the model with the C3K2 optimization, and E the model incorporating all three modules along with the P2 detection layer.

Table 3. Ablation experiment

Method	CCGA	CKCA	ContextGuideDown	P2	P	R	mAP@0.5	Parameters/M
YOLO11					0.837	0.724	0.818	25.8
A	✓				0.838	0.767	0.830	25.59
B		✓			0.855	0.754	0.835	25.9
A+B	✓	✓			0.813	0.769	0.816	25.64
C			✓		0.850	0.741	0.821	35.3
A+C	✓		✓		0.816	0.784	0.833	35.0
B+C		✓	✓		0.834	0.777	0.831	35.35
A+B+C	✓	✓	✓		0.838	0.753	0.832	35.11
E	✓	✓	✓	✓	0.863	0.782	0.842	36.1

The results show that Model A improves mAP@0.5 by 1.2% over the original, with a 0.29% reduction in parameters, confirming the effectiveness of the CCGA module in extracting fine features. Model B achieves a 1.7% increase in mAP@0.5, demonstrating that the improved neck effectively integrates multi-scale features for more robust pavement defect detection. The 0.3% increase in mAP@0.5 for Model C indicates efficient extraction of key features. Model E, with the addition of a small target detection head, improves detection accuracy, increasing precision by 2.6%, recall by 5.8%, and overall mAP@0.5 by 2.4%. The P-R curves in Fig. 9 visualize these improvements, with the axes showing recall and precision, and the top right corner showing the AP for each defect type and the overall map (Table 4)

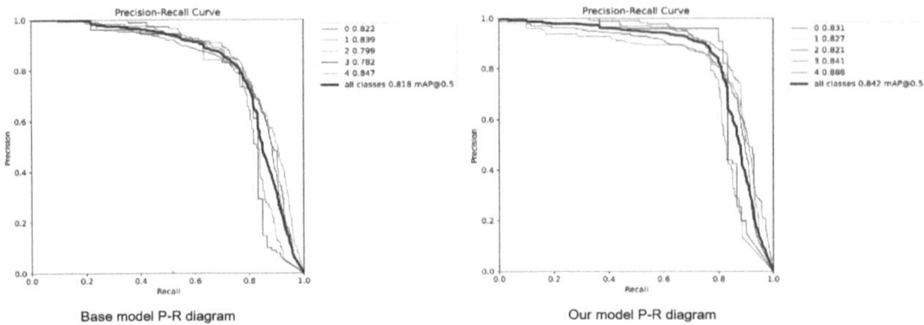

Fig. 8. Comparison of base model P-R diagrams and improved model P-R diagrams

3.5 Comparison of Experiments and Results of Different Models

Table 4. Comparison experiments with mainstream algorithms

Models	mAP@0.5/%	Para(M)	GFLOPs	FPS
Faster-RCNN [17]	0.691	83.0	940.97	9
SSD	0.680	52.6	62.74	35
YOLOv3	0.824	103.6	282.2	67
YOLOv3-tiny	0.761	86.8	213.6	222
YOLOv5	0.813	25.3	7.1	45
YOLOv5s	0.828	91.2	24.1	156
YOLOv5-MobileNetv3 [10]	0.781	78.1	9.9	82
Efficientdet [14]	0.498	38.7	5.2	27
YOLOv6	0.773	42.3	11.8	104
YOLOv8	0.809	30.1	8.2	38
YOLOv8-Ghost	0.793	17.1	5.1	92
YOLOv9	0.834	72.8	27.4	76
YOLOv10	0.802	26.9	8.2	36
YOLO12	0.808	25.83	6.3	107
Rt-DETR	0.798	20.2	57.3	65
Ours	0.842	36.1	13.7	73

Our model is better suited to scenarios with dense small targets and complex backgrounds and improves anti-interference capabilities. It outperforms traditional two-stage models (e.g. Faster-RCNN, SSD) and lightweight schemes (e.g. YOLOv3-tiny) in balancing precision and recall. Among single-stage detectors, YOLOv10 and YOLOv8 have the fastest speeds and fewest parameters, but lower accuracy with high leakage and false alarms, which limits their use in precise detection. YOLO12 achieves high accuracy but at high FPS, making it less suitable for mobile use.

In terms of computational complexity, the parameters and GFLOPs reflect the cost of the model. Our model performs best, with both 73 GFLOPs and 36.1 million parameters - far less than similar models. This increases efficiency on resource-constrained devices, reduces costs, and improves field detection by more accurately identifying multiple defects and reducing errors.

Although Rt-DETR speeds up processing with fewer parameters, its accuracy is slightly lower. although it does not outperform others in terms of accuracy and recall, its overall performance remains strong. Our method outperforms many benchmarks, achieving an average accuracy of 0.842 at a threshold of 0.5, enabling efficient detection and localization of road defects. Its defect screening, lightweight design, speed, and overall performance have excellent practical value and potential to improve the accuracy and efficiency of pavement detection.

3.6 Visualization

We compare the performance of our algorithm with YOLOv3, YOLOv5, YOLOv8, YOLOv9, YOLOv10, and YOLOv12 for road defect localization and detection over five defect types. This comparison aims to visualize the effectiveness of our method relative to these models. Figure 9 illustrates the detection results.

Fig. 9. Detection results of different defect types.

4 Conclusion

In this study, we propose a model for pavement defect detection. First, to address the limited sensitivity of fuzzy texture features, we design a novel module, CCGA, which compensates for the lack of detail sensitivity, enhances computational efficiency, and improves robustness against complex backgrounds, thereby building a stronger feature extraction foundation for pavement defect detection. Second, to mitigate the problem of severe background noise interference, we introduce the CKCA module, in which the CTA mechanism, aided by channel transposition and a multiple grouping strategy, decomposes the input features into H-attentional subspaces. It then performs matrix transposition multiplication within each subspace to establish cross-channel long-range dependencies. Finally, to reduce the computational complexity of the original model, the context-guided block minimizes the computational cost while preserving fine-grained crack features through multi-branch context fusion and adaptive pooling. The joint design of CKCA and the ContextGuidedDown module realizes deployment on edge devices, further optimizing computation, increasing interference resistance, and enabling lightweight multi-scale feature enhancement by adding the P2 branch to the existing P3-P5 detection heads. This is achieved through lightweight design and dynamic anchor assignment based on the combined optimization of CCGA and P2 head.

However, the current experiment has limitations. The dataset may not fully capture the diversity of real-world road conditions. Future work should increase the size and diversity of the dataset to improve the generalization capability of the model. In addition, other strategies, including the integration of other advanced technologies, can be explored to improve overall performance.

References

1. Aloysius, N., Geetha, M.: A review on deep convolutional neural networks. In: 2017 International Conference on Communication and Signal Processing (ICCSP), pp. 0588–0592. IEEE (2017)
2. Arya, D., et al.: Rdd2022-the multi-national road damage dataset released through crddc'2022. In: 2022 IEEE International Conference on Big Data (Big Data), vol. 10, p. m9 (2022)
3. Arya, D., et al.: Deep learning-based road damage detection and classification for multiple countries. Autom. Constr. **132**, 103935 (2021)
4. Arya, D., Maeda, H., Ghosh, S.K., Toshniwal, D., Sekimoto, Y.: Rdd 2022: a multinational image dataset for automatic road damage detection. Geosci. Data J. **11**(4), 846–862 (2024)
5. Baek, J.W., Chung, K.: Pothole classification model using edge detection in road image. Appl. Sci. **10**(19), 6662 (2020)
6. Dai, T., Wang, J., Guo, H., Li, J., Wang, J., Zhu, Z.: Freqformer: frequency-aware transformer for lightweight image super-resolution. In: Proceedings of the International Joint Conference on Artificial Intelligence, pp. 731–739 (2024)
7. Du, A., Ghavidel, A.: Parameterized deep reinforcement learning-enabled maintenance decision-support and life-cycle risk assessment for highway bridge portfolios. Struct. Saf. **97**, 102221 (2022)

8. Gao, J., Liang, J., Li, J., Sun, W., Qu, G.: White-light endoscopic colorectal lesion detection based on improved yolov7. Biomed. Signal Process. Control **90**, 105897 (2024)
9. Girshick, R.: Fast r-cnn. In: Proceedings of the IEEE International Conference on Computer Vision, pp. 1440–1448 (2015)
10. Guo, G., Zhang, Z.: Road damage detection algorithm for improved yolov5. Sci. Rep. **12**(1), 15523 (2022)
11. Lin, T.Y., Dollár, P., Girshick, R., He, K., Hariharan, B., Belongie, S.: Feature pyramid networks for object detection. In: Proceedings of the IEEE Conference on Computer Vision and Pattern Recognition, pp. 2117–2125 (2017)
12. Liu, C., Wu, Y., Liu, J., Han, J.: Mti-yolo: a light-weight and real-time deep neural network for insulator detection in complex aerial images. Energies **14**(5), 1426 (2021)
13. Liu, X., Peng, H., Zheng, N., Yang, Y., Hu, H., Yuan, Y.: Efficientvit: memory efficient vision transformer with cascaded group attention. In: Proceedings of the IEEE/CVF Conference on Computer Vision and Pattern Recognition, pp. 14420–14430 (2023)
14. Naddaf-Sh, S., Naddaf-Sh, M.M., Kashani, A.R., Zargarzadeh, H.: An efficient and scalable deep learning approach for road damage detection. In: 2020 IEEE International Conference on Big Data (Big Data), pp. 5602–5608. IEEE (2020)
15. National Highway Traffic Safety Administration: National highway traffic safety administration technical report dot hs **811**, 095 (2008)
16. Pham, V., Nguyen, D., Donan, C.: Road damage detection and classification with yolov7. In: 2022 IEEE International Conference on Big Data (Big Data), pp. 6416–6423. IEEE (2022)
17. Pham, V., Pham, C., Dang, T.: Road damage detection and classification with detectron2 and faster r-cnn. In: 2020 IEEE International Conference on Big Data (Big Data), pp. 5592–5601. IEEE (2020)
18. Ping, P., Yang, X., Gao, Z.: A deep learning approach for street pothole detection. In: 2020 IEEE Sixth International Conference on Big Data Computing Service and Applications (BigDataService), pp. 198–204. IEEE (2020)
19. Sapkota, R., Qureshi, R., Flores-Calero, M., Badgujar, C., Nepal, U., Poulose, A., Zeno, P., Bhanu Prakash Vaddevolu, U., Yan, P., Karkee, M., et al.: Yolov10 to its genesis: A decadal and comprehensive review of the you only look once series. arXiv:2406.19407 (2024)
20. Song, J., Xie, J., Wang, Q., Shen, T.: An improved yolo-based method with lightweight c3 modules for object detection in resource-constrained environments. J. Supercomput. **81**(5), 702 (2025)
21. Sun, Z., Zhu, L., Qin, S., Yu, Y., Ju, R., Li, Q.: Road surface defect detection algorithm based on yolov8. Electronics **13**(12), 2413 (2024)
22. Wan, F., Sun, C., He, H., Lei, G., Xu, L., Xiao, T.: Yolo-lrdd: a lightweight method for road damage detection based on improved yolov5s. EURASIP J. Adv. Signal Process. **2022**(1), 98 (2022)
23. Wang, S., Tang, W.: Pavement crack segmentation algorithm based on local optimal threshold of cracks density distribution. In: Proceedings of the 7th International Conference on Advanced Intelligent Computing, pp. 298–302 (2011)
24. Wang, X., Gao, H., Jia, Z., Li, Z.: Bl-yolov8: an improved road defect detection model based on yolov8. Sensors **23**(20), 8361 (2023)
25. Wu, T., Tang, S., Zhang, R., Zhang, Y.: Cgnet: a light-weight context guided network for semantic segmentation. arXiv e-prints pp. arXiv–1811 (2018)

A Hierarchical Reinforcement Learning Method Based on Decision Frequency and Internal Reward Mechanism

Cong Wang[1], Mingqiang Li[1], Yuewei Wang[1(✉)], Xiaopan Zhang[2], Xiaohui Huang[1], Binhao Li[2], Jianxin Li[3], and Yunliang Chen[1]

[1] School of Computer Science, China University of Geosciences, Wuhan, China
yuewei.w@cug.edu.cn

[2] School of Computer Science and Artificial Intelligence, Wuhan University of Technology, Wuhan, China

[3] School of Business and Law, Edith Cowan University, Perth, Australia

Abstract. Wargames require participants to make real-time reasoning and decisions based on complex battlefield environment changes, facing severe challenges brought by large-scale decision spaces and rapidly changing battlefield situations. In recent years, many reinforcement learning algorithms have been continuously applied to wargames to simulate confrontational situations. However, existing methods have not yet provided satisfactory solutions for wargames and have certain limitations. In this context, we propose a hierarchical decision reinforcement learning algorithm based on decision frequency and internal reward mechanism. The algorithm divides decisions into three layers, decomposes complex tasks to reduce decision complexity, and compresses the action space to accelerate convergence. In addition, the decision frequency and internal reward mechanism are introduced to improve decision stability and guide learning. To verify the performance of the algorithm, experiments are designed for wargame scenarios. The experimental results show that the hierarchical structure enables the agent to effectively learn strategies and accelerate convergence.

Keywords: Wargames · Reinforcement learning · Decision frequency · Internal reward mechanism

1 Introduction

As a real-time simulation and reasoning activity for the complex battlefield environment changes, the wargames can realize the perception of the battlefield environment and assist the command decision-making, which is a very valuable tool in the military field. The scenario usually covers a wealth of strategic and tactical elements, ranging from troop deployment, firepower utilization to resource management, requiring participants to make reasonable decisions in a dynamically changing situation. With the development of artificial intelligence,

J. Li et al. (Eds.): APWeb-WAIM 2025, LNCS 16115, pp. 130–145, 2026.
https://doi.org/10.1007/978-981-95-5719-6_9

reinforcement learning is applied to wargames to learn the optimal strategy through the interaction between intelligent agents and the game environment, so as to achieve decision-making for complex battlefield situations and enhance their ability to explore and optimize military strategies in the game [1]. Some artificial intelligence research institutions have trained intelligent agents that have demonstrated high-level decision-making capabilities in wargames and achieved remarkable results [2].

The hierarchical task decision-making in war games has distinct characteristics, and the goals at different levels are significantly different. The strategic layer focuses on macro layout, such as strike missions, the campaign layer focuses on combat plans, and the execution layer is specific to the specific micro actions of each unit. From the time scale, high-level decisions focus on the long-term, and low-level decisions focus on immediate changes. In this scenario, hierarchical reinforcement learning is used for multi-level decision-making, and the reasonable hierarchical division of decisions effectively distinguishes decisions at different levels such as strategy and tactics, leading to efficient solutions for problems at different levels, and achieving accurate simulation and effective decision-making of complex battlefield environments. However, existing research on hierarchical reinforcement learning has difficulties in delineating the state and action space between levels, leading to poor information transfer, complex cross-level coordination, and irrational allocation of rewards to each level, which makes it difficult to quickly adapt to dynamically changing situations and make effective decisions.

To address these limitations, a hierarchical decision reinforcement learning algorithm (HDDQN) based on decision frequency and internal reward mechanism is proposed in this paper. The algorithm divides the entire decision process into three layers, namely the high-level controller, the mid-level controller and the low-level controller. The high-level controller is responsible for macro decisions, the mid-level controller makes more detailed decisions, and the low-level performs specific actions. By decomposing complex tasks into multiple subtasks, each of which is completed by different layers, the decision complexity of multi-agents is reduced. The main contributions of this paper are summarized as follows:

1) A three-level cascade control hierarchical structure is designed. The high-level controller is responsible for macro decisions and determining strategic directions; the mid-level controller formulates more detailed operational plans based on the high-level decisions; and the low-level controller is responsible for executing specific unit actions. Through the top-down strategy transmission mechanism, the action space is effectively compressed, and the efficiency and accuracy of decision-making are improved.
2) The decision frequency and internal reward mechanism are designed. The decision step size is used in the high-level and mid-level controllers to control their decision frequency, while the low-level controller changes every moment. Internal rewards are given to the mid-level and low-level controllers for completing their respective actions. This mechanism improves the stability of decision making, accelerates and guides the learning process.
3) In order to verify the effectiveness and performance of the method, a case study of hierarchical decision-making reinforcement learning based on

wargame simulation is proposed. This case study uses 2D maps, 4 combat units, 11 action types and score feedback to simulate the battlefield, and the rationality of the method is ensured through rigorous fusion experiments, parameter sensitivity verification and benchmark comparison experiments.

The rest of this paper is organized as follows. Section 2 describes related work, Sect. 3 introduces the objects and goals of this paper based on war game simulation, Sect. 4 details the method proposed in this paper, Sect. 5 shows the experimental results and analyzes the algorithm performance, and finally, Sect. 6 summarizes the conclusions of this study and proposes future development directions.

2 Related Work

In traditional machine learning algorithms, Lee et al. [3] proposed a machine learning-based model in multiplayer online battle arena (MOBA) games, using an object bounty mechanism to predict regression wins. Jisun Lee and Yoonho Seo [1] proposed a Q-learning algorithm based on strategic artificial potential fields for path planning in complex battlefield environments.

Deep reinforcement learning combines the advantages of deep learning and traditional reinforcement learning. By using deep neural networks to approximate state-value functions or state-action-value functions, it can effectively handle problems with large state spaces and action spaces [4]. Xinwei Wang et al. [5] proposed an air combat maneuver decision-making method based on deep reinforcement learning to solve the maneuver decision-making problem in complex environments. Hyunsang Cho et al. [6] proposed an integrated perception and communication system assisted by an aerial reconfigurable intelligent surface based on deep reinforcement learning to enhance environmental situational awareness. Zhao et al. [7] proposed an intelligent auxiliary decision-making method based on deep reinforcement learning, aiming to provide real-time and efficient decision support for complex and changing environments. Palma et al. [8] proposed a novel system designed to cope with the strategic complexity of six-sided chess and counter-games by combining the latest advances in recurrent neural networks with the reliable modern reinforcement learning algorithm AlphaZero.

Based on the existing multi-agent reinforcement learning research, the multi-agent reinforcement learning algorithm takes into account the interaction and cooperation between multiple agents, and each agent achieves the global optimal goal by learning its own strategy [9]. Shi Ding et al. [10] proposed a collaborative simulation algorithm based on improved multi-agent reinforcement learning, which solved the problem of multi-agent collaborative decision-making in complex battlefield environments. Wang et al. [11] proposed a framework based on hierarchical multi-agent reinforcement learning to solve complex decision-making problems in war games. Chen et al. [12] proposed a multi-agent confrontation algorithm based on MADDPG, which solved the challenges of reinforcement learning algorithm application caused by algorithm convergence difficulties and sparse real rewards in large-scale state and action spaces. Kim et al. [13] proposed an algorithm based on multi-agent deep reinforcement learning and communication network for the coordinated of UAVs in large-scale environments.

Although multi-agent reinforcement learning algorithms have shown greater advantages in battlefield decision-making, when faced with large-scale and complex battlefields, their cross-layer decisions are inconsistent, strategy conflicts occur frequently, and convergence is difficult. Hierarchical reinforcement learning algorithms can decompose complex tasks to accelerate learning. Nield et al. [14] combined hierarchical reinforcement learning with multi-layer perceptrons (MLPs) to receive high-order inputs to improve learning speed and performance. Zhang et al. [15] proposed a novel hierarchical reinforcement learning model for MOBA games, where agents execute macro strategies through imitation learning and perform micro operations through reinforcement learning.

3 Problem Definition

In this section, we will take wargame simulation as the starting point, briefly describe the operation objects and goals of the simulation, and demonstrate the status and actions of reinforcement learning in wargame simulation.

Wargames are conducted on a $2D$ map. In this game, players from two camps control their own battle chess pieces to complete tasks and get higher scores. The chess pieces of each camp player are the same, and there are three types of chess pieces, including reconnaissance aircraft, ships, and nuclear submarines. Each type of chess piece has four attributes: fuel, ammunition, speed, and height. The score s_i of each chess piece is related to its attack effect F_{attack} and hit rate P, that is, $s_i = f(F^i_{attack}|P^i)$. Under the premise of a high hit rate, the higher the attack effect, the higher the score, and vice versa.

For the attack of chess pieces, the attack effect F_{attact} is related to their distance Δx and height difference Δh. The specific formula is as follows 1.

$$F^i_{\text{attack}} = \begin{cases} f(\Delta x^i, \Delta h^i) & \text{if } \Delta x^i \leq D^i_{\max} \; and \; \Delta h^i \leq H^i_{\max} \\ 0 & \text{otherwise} \end{cases} \tag{1}$$

Among them, $D^i_{\max}$ is the maximum horizontal attack distance of each chess piece, and Δh^i is the maximum vertical attack distance.

The hit rate P is related to the oil volume O, the detection object C_e, the distance D from the opponent's chess piece, and the height Δh. The formula is as follows 2:

$$P = k \times \frac{O}{O_{\max}} \times \frac{1}{\Delta x} \times \frac{1}{1 + |\Delta h|} \times C_e \tag{2}$$

Each parameter needs to satisfy the following constraints:

1. $0 \leq O \leq O_{\max}$, the fuel volume cannot be negative and cannot exceed the maximum fuel volume of the missile.
2. $\Delta x > 0$, the distance cannot be 0 or negative.

3. $\Delta h \geq 0$, the height cannot be negative, and Δh must be within the missile's flight altitude range.
4. $C_e \in \{0, 1\}$, $C_e = 1$ indicates that the enemy chess piece has been detected, and $C_e = 0$ indicates that it has not been detected.
5. $0 < k \leq 1$, used to make a reasonable overall adjustment to the hit rate so that it conforms to the hit probability range in actual scenarios.

The goal of the game is to get a higher score, which is the sum of the scores of each chess piece. r and b are used to distinguish the red and blue chess pieces, so the optimization formula for the red camp score is represented by s_r, and the red chess pieces are represented by $s_{i,r} = f(F^{i,r}_{attack}|P^{i,r})$. The number of chess pieces in each camp is N. Specifically, the optimization goal of the red camp score is shown in formula 3, and the blue camp is similar:

$$\text{Maximize } s_r = \sum_{i=1}^{N} f(F^{i,r}_{attack}|P^{i,r}) - \sum_{j=1}^{N} f(F^{j,b}_{attack}|P^{j,b}) \tag{3}$$

Since the decision-making task of war game simulation can be regarded as a Markov decision process, its state and action can be expressed as follows:

State Space: As shown in Fig. 1, the state consists of the following four parts, namely the number of chess pieces in the area, the number of weapons, the remaining fuel and the number of chess pieces. On the entire $2D$ map, it is necessary to divide multiple areas and count the number of chess pieces in a certain area.

Action Space: Each chess piece has about eleven actions, including do nothing, moving, formation moving, anti-submarine reconnaissance, formation anti-submarine reconnaissance, attack, formation attack, anti-submarine attack, formation anti-submarine attack, take-off and return. Among them, the take-off and return actions are exclusive to the anti-submarine aircraft chess piece, and other chess pieces do not have them.

Wargame simulations use a rigorous system of rules, symbolic chess pieces, and a concrete chessboard to build a basic framework for simulating wars. During the simulation process, commanders need to convert strategic deployments into actionable game actions based on the battlefield situation and in combination with multi-dimensional parameters such as simulation rules, force attributes, and routes. This process requires commanders to have both a strategic macro perspective and a tactical micro perspective, and to be able to make flexible decisions and efficiently allocate resources in combination with complex battlefield situations within the framework of rules.

4 Proposed Method

4.1 The Framework of HDDQN

The three-level cascade control hierarchical structure proposed in this paper consists of three layers, as shown in the Fig. 1, namely the high-level controller, the

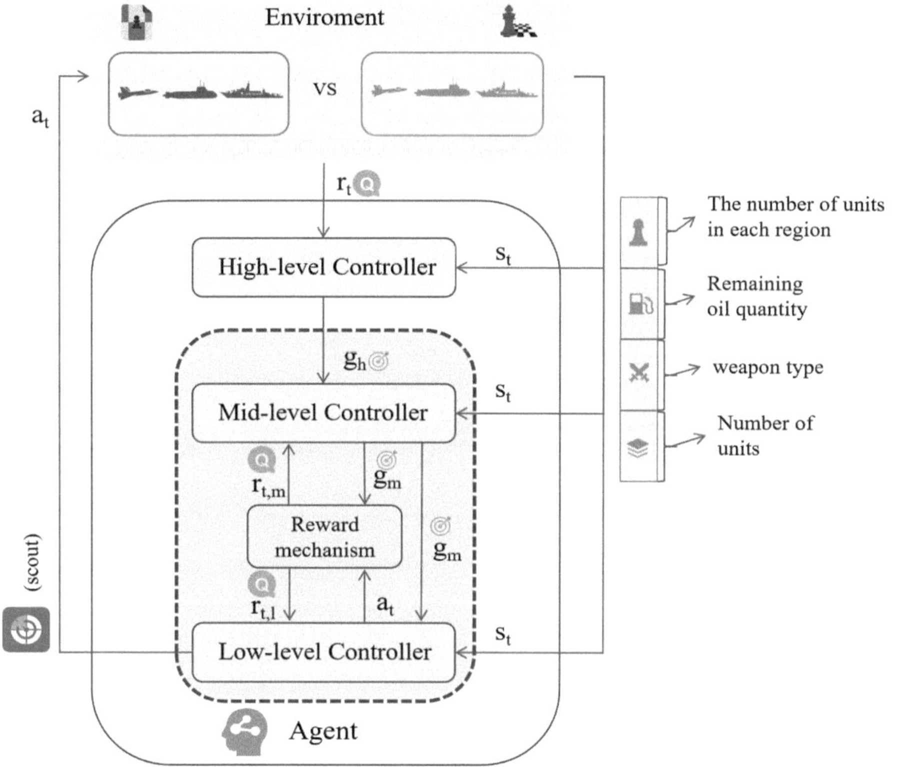

Fig. 1. Hierarchical reinforcement learning framework

mid-level controller and the low-level controller. The high-level receives the state $s \in S$ and is responsible for making macro decisions, determining the macro goal g_h to be executed, and planning the execution direction of the task as a whole; the mid-level receives s and the macro goal g_h specified by the high-level, and further divides the sub-goal g_m; and the low-level receives s and the sub-goal g_m specified by the mid-level strategy, and makes specific action decisions $a \in \mathcal{A}$. The above three-layer structure all uses the DDQN network, as shown in the Fig. 2. As can be seen from the figure, DDQN contains an online network and a target network. The online network is used to calculate the current state in real time, and it will continuously adjust parameters according to environmental feedback and the update instructions of the optimizer. The target network is relatively fixed, and its parameters are regularly copied and updated from the online network to calculate the target Q value. At the same time, the experience replay mechanism is adopted. The state transition tuple (S_t, A_t, R_t, S_{t+1}) generated by the interaction between the agent and the environment is stored in the experience replay buffer.

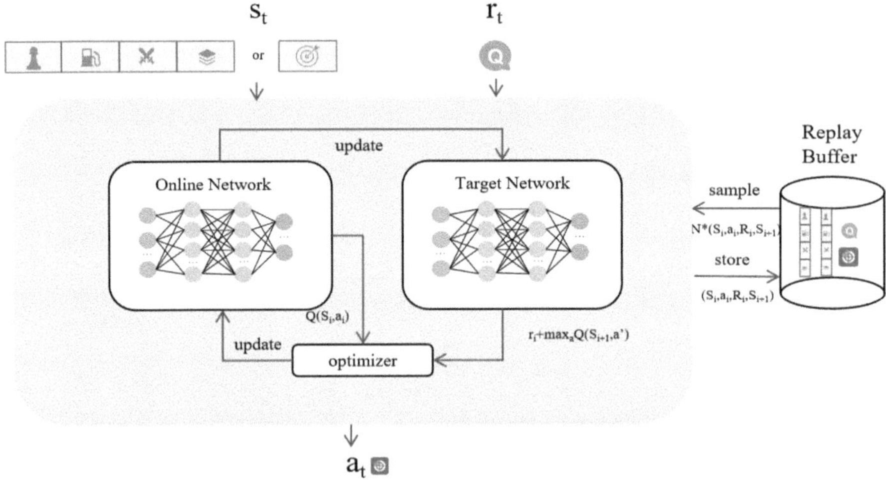

Fig. 2. DDQN network architecture

In terms of decision-making frequency, the high-level focuses on long-term strategy with low-frequency decision-making, the mid-level adjusts the frequency rhythm, and the low-level high-frequency decision-making ensures flexibility, and global coordination is achieved through hierarchical interaction. In terms of the reward mechanism, the high-level accumulates rewards for each step under the decision-making time, the mid-level accumulates rewards for each step and internal rewards, and the low-level is composed of rewards for each step and internal rewards. This hierarchy fits the command system. The high-level provides goals for the low-level, reduces the complexity of the problem, and improves decision-making efficiency and adaptability through hierarchical decision-making. It has military characteristics and algorithm innovation.

4.2 High-Level Controller

In the hierarchical decision reinforcement learning architecture, the decision frequencies of each layer show differentiated characteristics. The high-level controller takes the state s_t given by the environment as input, and the DDQN network of this layer makes the sub-goal g_h at that moment. Given that the lower-level execution entity takes a certain amount of time to achieve the macro goal, the high-level strategy is allowed to make decisions at a lower frequency, measured in time steps N_h, as shown in Fig. 3. When the sub-goal is completed, the reward r_h of the sub-goal is accumulated, which is the score fed back by the game environment. Finally, based on the four-tuple $(s_t,\ g_h,\ r_h,\ s_{t+N_h})$ collected in the experience replay buffer, the Q value is calculated using the following update formula 4 to update the network:

$$Q_h(s, g_h) = \max_{\pi_{g_h}} \mathbb{E}\left[\sum_{t'=t}^{t+N_h} r_h + \gamma \max_{g'_h} Q_h(s_{t+N_h}, g'_h)\right] \tag{4}$$

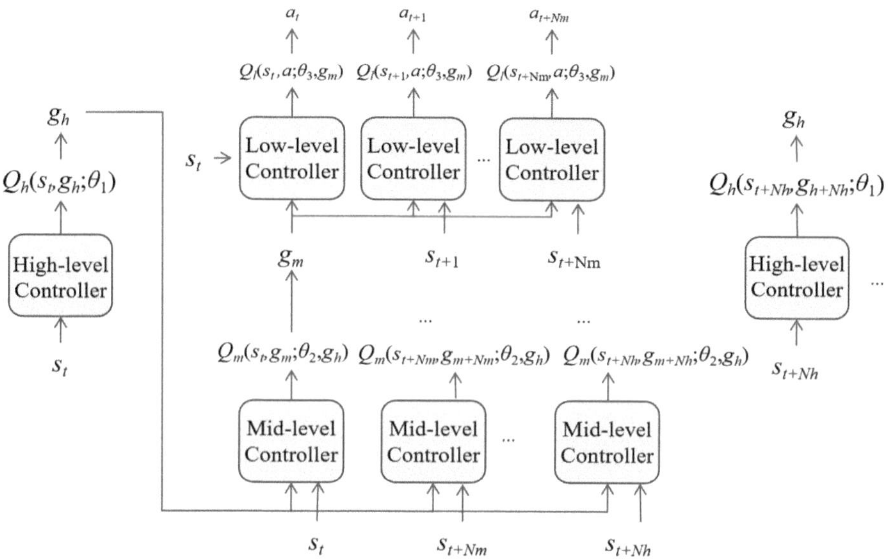

Fig. 3. Details of three-layer network decision-making

4.3 Mid-Level Controller

The mid-level controller is the key link between the high-level and low-level layers. As shown in Fig. 3, this layer takes the environment state s_t and the sub-goal g_h given by the high-level layer as input. The DDQN network of this layer further divides the high-level goal, which is recorded as g_m. Since the decision-making at the intermediate level is essentially a further interpretation and implementation of the high-level macro directives, and needs to maintain a certain degree of consistency and stability, it is also appropriate for this level to adopt a lower-frequency decision-making mode, measured by the time step of N_m, in order to ensure that the formulation of the sub-objectives not only meets the high-level strategic intent, but also has the practical operability. When the sub-goal of this layer is executed to completion, the reward r_m of the sub-goal is accumulated according to the internal reward function $f_m(g_m)$ of this layer. Finally, according to the four-tuple (s_t, g_m, r_m, s_{t+N_m}) collected in the experience replay buffer, the value function of this layer is used to update the network of this layer.

$$Q_m(s, g_m; g_h) = \max_{\pi_{g_m}} \mathbb{E}\left[\sum_{t'=t}^{t+N_m} r_m + \gamma \max_{g'_m} Q_m(s_{t+N_m}, g'_m; g_h)\right] \tag{5}$$

4.4 Low-Level Controller

Algorithm 1. The framework of HDDQN

Initialize environment, high-level π_h, mid-level π_m, and low-level π_l;
Initialize the number of episodes N, high-level and mid-level decision-making steps N_h, N_m;
for episode = 1 to N **do**
  $s_t \leftarrow$ environment;
  $g_h \sim \pi_h(s_t)$; ▷ High-level controller makes the goal
  $g_m \sim \pi_m(s_t, g_h)$; ▷ Mid-level controller makes the sub-goal
  $t_h, t_m, r_h, r_m, r_l \leftarrow 0$;
  for $t = 1, 2, ...$ **do**
    $a_t \sim \pi_l(s_t, g_m)$; ▷ Low-level execution
    $s_{t+1}, r_t \leftarrow$ environment ,a, $r_l \leftarrow r_t + f_l(a_t)$;
    Store (s_t, a_t, r_l, s_{t+1}) in the low-level controller replay buffer;
    $r_h \leftarrow r_h + r_t, r_m \leftarrow r_m + r_t + f_m(g_m)$;
    Update the low-level controller network using the Eq. 6;
    if $t_m \geq N_m$ **then**
      Store (s_t, g_m, r_m, s_{t+1}) in the mid-level controller replay buffer;
      Update the mid-level controller network using the Eq. 5;
      $g_m \sim \pi_m(s_{t+1})$ ▷ Update the mid-level goal
      $t_m, r_m \leftarrow 0$;
    else
      $t_m \leftarrow t_m + 1$
    end if
    if $t_h \geq N_h$ **then**
      Store (s_t, g_h, r_h, s_{t+1}) in the high-level controller replay buffer;
      Update the high-level controller network using the Eq. 4;
      $g_h \sim \pi_h(s_{t+1})$ ▷ Update the high-level goal
      $t_h, r_h \leftarrow 0$;
    else
      $t_h \leftarrow t_h + 1$
    end if
    $s_t \leftarrow s_{t+1}$
  end for
end for

In the low-level controller, as shown in Fig. 3, the environment state s_t and the mid-level sub-goal g_m are used as inputs, and the DDQN network of this layer selects the action a_t with the highest Q value. Since this layer can perform atomic actions and directly operate the movement and attack of chess pieces, a strategy can be changed at every moment to complete the mid-level subgoals. When the action of this layer is completed, the reward r_l of the action is obtained according to the internal reward function $f_l(a_t)$ of this layer. Finally, the quadruple (s_t, a_t, r_l, s_{t+1}) collected from the experience replay buffer is used to update the network of this layer using the value function of this layer. The three-level decision-making process and rewards of the overall algorithm is shown in Algorithm 1.

$$Q_m(s, a; g_m) = \max_{\pi_a} \mathbb{E}\left[\sum_{t'=t}^{t+1} r_l + \gamma \max_{g'_m} Q_m(s_{t+1}, a_{t+1}; g_m)\right] \tag{6}$$

5 Experiments

In this section, ablation experiments and decision frequency sensitivity experiments are designed to analyze the effectiveness of the proposed method. Finally, HDDQN competes with the baseline algorithm and compares the results from multiple aspects to further verify the performance of the hierarchical decision reinforcement learning algorithm.

5.1 Experimental Setup

The experiment uses Python programming language and PyTorch deep learning framework. The computer configuration is CPU 11th Gen Intel(R) Core(TM) i7-11700K @ 3.60 GHz, graphics card is NVIDlA GeForce GTX 960, and memory is 64 GB. In this experiment, each algorithm was trained in the war game for 500 episodes, with 300 steps per episode and a time interval of 30 s. Since DDQN is used as the basic network structure, most of the parameters come from this structure. The basic parameters of DDQN are shown in Table 1. In the experiment, the following baseline algorithms were selected for comparison with the algorithm in this paper:

1) PPO [16], a policy gradient reinforcement learning algorithm, improves the stability of training by limiting the policy update amplitude.
2) Rule, an intelligent agent built based on established tactics, whose decision follows a preset rule system, providing a reference benchmark with clear rule guidance.
3) SAC [17], the algorithm combines the policy gradient and value function estimation algorithms to learn the optimal strategy by maximizing the expected reward and policy entropy.
4) TD3 [18], the algorithm improves the stability of learning in continuous action space by using two critic networks and delayed policy updates.
5) DQN [19], a reinforcement learning algorithm that combines Q-learning and deep learning, uses neural networks to approximate Q functions.

6) DDQN [20], an improved version of DQN, solves the problem of overestimation of Q values by using an online network to select actions and a target network to evaluate the action.

Table 1. Parameter Settings

Parameter Name	Value	Description
batch_size	16	The maximum size of the data batch sampled from replay buffer
buffer_size	100	The maximum capacity of the experience replay buffer
learning_rate	1.00E-04	The learning rate of the neural network
greedy_epsilon	0.9	The exploration rate of the greedy strategy
gamma	0.98	The discount factor for future rewards
target_net_update	10	The update frequency of the target network

5.2 Experimental Results

In order to deeply explore the contribution of each layer structure to the overall performance in the hierarchical decision reinforcement learning algorithm, this study designed a set of ablation experiments. In the hierarchical decision reinforcement learning algorithm, each layer adopts the DDQN structure. By gradually removing the other two layers of structure and comparatively analyzing their performance in a specific task, the mechanism of the role of hierarchical structure in the reinforcement learning task is revealed. During the experiment, the deduction scores of the baseline model (HDDQN) and the ablation model (DDQN) during the training process are collected respectively, and the experimental results are shown in Fig. 4. During the training process, the deduction score of each time step is recorded to observe the learning process of the model.

The figure shows the average score change curves of HDDQN and DDQN during the training process. From Fig. 4, we can see that in the early stage of training, HDDQN has a high score spike and then falls back, while DDQN has a low and negative initial score. Throughout the 500 training iterations, the average score of HDDQN is mostly positive and the fluctuation is relatively stable, with a fast convergence speed. On the contrary, the average score of DDQN fluctuates greatly, frequently switches between positive and negative, is generally low, and converges slowly. Therefore, compared with the single-layer structure, the hierarchical structure in the hierarchical decision reinforcement learning algorithm can enable the model to obtain higher scores more stably during the training process, indicating that the hierarchical structure not only improves the performance of the model in reinforcement learning tasks through

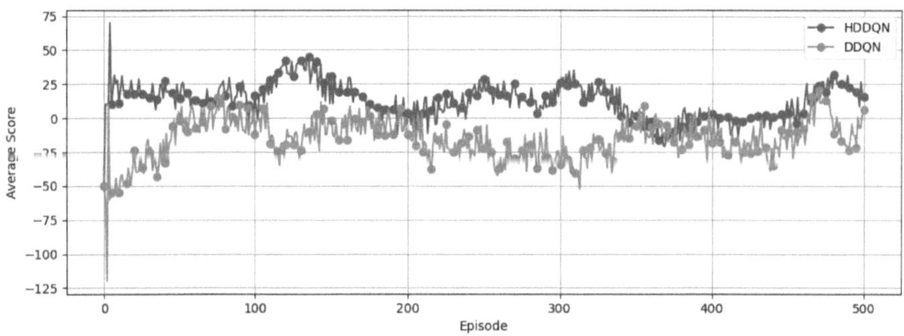

Fig. 4. Average score curves of HDDQN and DDQN

the collaborative cooperation of each layer, but also accelerates the convergence speed, which has a positive contribution to the overall performance.

In addition, in order to explore the impact of decision frequency parameters in the hierarchical decision reinforcement learning algorithm on model performance, this study designed a set of sensitivity experiments. The decision frequency parameters of the hierarchical decision reinforcement learning algorithm mainly include the high-level decision time step h_{step} and the mid-level decision time step m_{step}. These two parameters determine the time intervals for high-level and mid-level decisions in the reinforcement learning process, which have an important impact on the strategy learning and execution efficiency of the algorithm.

In the experiment, different variants were obtained based on different parameter combinations. The names of each variant and the parameter combinations are shown in Table 2:

Table 2. Parameter settings for different variants

Variant Name	Parameter Settings
HDDQN_M1	$h_{step} = 10$, $m_{step} = 5$
HDDQN_M2	$h_{step} = 6$, $m_{step} = 3$
HDDQN_M3	$h_{step} = 4$, $m_{step} = 2$

Based on these three variants, they were trained for 500 episodes respectively, and the score of each variant was recorded in each episode. The average score result curve of 500 episodes is shown in Fig. 5.

As can be seen from the figure, in the early stage of training, the three models all experienced fluctuations to varying degrees. HDDQN_M1 has a large drop at the beginning, while HDDQN_M2 and HDDQN_M3 are relatively flat. During the entire 500 training iterations, the average score of HDDQN_M2 is relatively high in most stages and the fluctuation is relatively small. The average scores

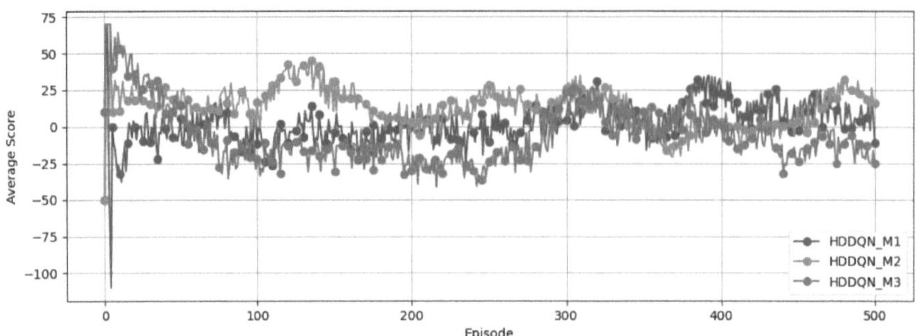

Fig. 5. Average score curves of HDDQN_M1, HDDQN_M2 and HDDQN_M3

of HDDQN_M1 and HDDQN_M3 fluctuate greatly and the overall values are relatively unstable. Therefore, in the hierarchical decision reinforcement learning algorithm, different combinations of decision frequency parameters have a certain impact on model performance. Among them, the parameter combination of $h_{step} = 6$ and $m_{step} = 3$ performs relatively better in this experimental scenario, which enables the model to obtain higher scores more stably during the training process, indicating that the appropriate high-level and mid-level decision time step settings are helpful to improve the performance and stability of the model in reinforcement learning tasks.

Finally, in order to fully evaluate the performance of the trained HDDQN model in the actual combat exercise, we tested the model with the trained PPO model, Rule, SAC model, TD3 model and DQN model. PPO, SAC, TD3 and DQN models were trained for the same episodes and were tested with HDDQN after fully optimizing the model parameters. In the actual combat exercise, HDDQN played 50 rounds with PPO, Rule, SAC, TD3 and DQN, respectively, and each episode of the game recorded the win, draw or loss results of each model. The results of the 50 episodes are shown in Table 3.

Table 3. Performance Comparison Between HDDQN and Baseline Algorithms

Metric	PPO	Rule	SAC	TD3	DQN
Wins	42(3)	29(11)	25(13)	45(5)	38(4)
Draws	5(5)	10(10)	12(12)	0(0)	8(8)
Losses	3(42)	11(29)	13(25)	5(45)	4(38)
Win Rate	**84%**(6%)	**58%**(22%)	**50%**(26%)	**90%**(10%)	**76%**(8%)

The values without brackets in the table are the values of HDDQN under win, draw, loss and win rate, and the values with brackets are the values of the combat models (PPO, rules, SAC, TD3 and DQN) under different indicators. As can be seen from the table, in the war game between HDDQN and PPO, HDDQN won 42 games, accounting for 84% of the total number of games, while PPO only won 3 games, with a win rate of 6%. This shows that in the confrontation with the PPO model, the HDDQN model showed a clear advantage, and was able to make decisions more effectively and guide reasoning to victory. When HDDQN played against Rule, HDDQN won 29 games, with a win rate of 58%, which is higher than the 22% win rate of Rule. It can be seen that compared with agent based on fixed tactics and rules, the HDDQN model has stronger adaptability and decision-making flexibility. Although Rule can also respond with established rules in certain scenarios, HDDQN has better overall performance and can flexibly take different decisions to win in a complex and ever-changing war game environment. In the battle against the SAC model, HDDQN won 25 games, with a winning rate of 50%, which is the lowest among many models. In the battle against TD3, HDDQN performed well, with a winning rate of 90%. In the battle against DQN, HDDQN won 38 games and lost 4 games, with a winning rate of 76%, which is higher than DQN. HDDQN adopts a three-layer structure. In the experimental results, HDDQN is far ahead in terms of winning rate and stability.

6 Conclusions

Based on wargames, this paper proposes a hierarchical decision-making reinforcement learning algorithm framework based on decision frequency and internal reward mechanism. The framework adopts a three-level cascade control hierarchical structure to decompose complex tasks into multiple sub-goals, effectively reducing the complexity of decision-making. The high-level is responsible for macro-decision-making, the mid-level formulates specific strategies, and the low-level performs specific actions. In addition, the differentiated design of decision frequencies at different levels enables the algorithm to quickly adapt to local dynamic changes while maintaining macro-stability, further improving decision-making efficiency and learning speed. The mid-level and low-level controllers design internal reward mechanisms to enhance the autonomous decision-making ability and learning efficiency of each layer. In the experiment, the algorithm proposed in this paper showed a strong advantage in the game, verifying the significant advantages of the hierarchical structure and internal reward mechanism in improving the performance of the algorithm, and proving the efficiency and practicality of the framework in complex tasks. However, the algorithm framework still needs to be further improved. The setting of decision frequency and internal reward affects the performance of the algorithm. In the future, we will explore the problem of adaptively changing the decision frequency and internal reward distribution of each layer.

Acknowledgements. The work was supported by the "CUG Scholar" Scientific Research Funds at China University of Geosciences (Wuhan) (Project No. 2023080)

References

1. Lee, J., Seo, Y.: Q-learning based on strategic artificial potential field for path planning enabling concealment and cover in ground battlefield environments. Appl. Intell. **54**(13), 7170–7200 (2024)
2. Boron, J., Darken, C.: Developing combat behavior through reinforcement learning in wargames and simulations. In: 2020 IEEE Conference on Games (CoG), pp. 728–731 (2020)
3. Lee, J., Kim, N.: Development of machine learning-based indicators for predicting comeback victories using the bounty mechanism in moba games. Electronics **14**(7), 1–25 (2025)
4. BarroseSá, G.C., Madeira, C.A.G.A.: Deep reinforcement learning in real-time strategy games: a systematic literature review: deep reinforcement learning in real-time strategy games. Appl. Intell. **55**(4), 1–16 (2025)
5. Wang, X., et al.: Deep reinforcement learning-based air combat maneuver decision-making: literature review, implementation tutorial and future direction. Artif. Intell. Rev. **57**(1) (2023)
6. Cho, H., Yoo, S., Jung, B.C., Kang, J.: Enhancing battlefield awareness: an aerial ris-assisted isac system with deep reinforcement learning. In: MILCOM 2024 - 2024 IEEE Military Communications Conference (MILCOM), pp. 469–474 (2024)
7. Zhao, X.Y., Yang, M., Peng, C., Wang, C.: Research on intelligent operational assisted decision-making of naval battlefield based on deep reinforcement learning. In: Proceedings of the 3rd International Conference on Advanced Information Science and System (2022)
8. Palma, G., Santos, P.A., Dias, J.: Playing hex and counter wargames using reinforcement learning and recurrent neural networks (2025)
9. Wang, Y., Wang, Y., Tian, F., Ma, J., Jin, Q.: Intelligent games meeting with multi-agent deep reinforcement learning: a comprehensive review. Artif. Intell. Rev. **58**(6), 165 (2025)
10. Shi, D., Yan, X., Gong, L., Zhang, J., Guan, D., Wei, M.: Multi-agent cooperative combat simulation in naval battlefield with reinforcement learning. J. Syst. Simul. **35**(4), 786–796 (2023)
11. Wang, H., Tang, H., Hao, J., Hao, X., Fu, Y., Ma, Y.: Large scale deep reinforcement learning in war-games. In: 2020 IEEE International Conference on Bioinformatics and Biomedicine (BIBM), pp. 1693–1699 (2020)
12. Chen, W., Nie, J.: A maddpg-based multi-agent antagonistic algorithm for sea battlefield confrontation. Multimedia Syst. **29**, 2991–3000 (2022)
13. Kim, G.S., Lee, S., Woo, T., Park, S.: Cooperative reinforcement learning for military drones over large-scale battlefields. IEEE Trans. Intell. Veh. 1–11 (2024)
14. Niel, R., Krebbers, J., Drugan, M.M., Wiering, M.A.: Hierarchical reinforcement learning for real-time strategy games. In: 10th International Conference on Agents and Artificial Intelligence, pp. 470–477 (2018)
15. Zhang, Z., et al.: Hierarchical reinforcement learning for multi-agent moba game (2019)
16. Schulman, J., Wolski, F., Dhariwal, P., Radford, A., Klimov, O.: Proximal policy optimization algorithms, pp. 1–12. arXiv preprint arXiv:1707.06347 (2017)
17. Haarnoja, T., Zhou, A., Abbeel, P., Levine, S.: Soft actor-critic: off-policy maximum entropy deep reinforcement learning with a stochastic actor. In: Proceedings of the 35th International Conference on Machine Learning, vol. 80, pp. 1861–1870 (2018)

18. Fujimoto, S., van Hoof, H., Meger, D.: Addressing function approximation error in actor-critic methods. In: Proceedings of the 35th International Conference on Machine Learning, vol. 80, pp. 1587–1596 (2018)
19. Mnih, V., et al.: Human-level control through deep reinforcement learning. Nature **518**(7540), 529–533 (2015)
20. Van Hasselt, H., Guez, A., Silver, D.: Deep reinforcement learning with double q-learning. In: Proceedings of the AAAI Conference on Artificial Intelligence, vol. 30 (2016)

A Soluble Solids Content Prediction Method for Blueberries Based on Differential Enhancement and Multi-scale Feature Fusion

Bingxin Peng, Zhaokui Li(✉), Jiaxu Guo, Yan Wang, Hang Meng, Jing Tian, and Mingtai Qi

School of Computer Science, Shenyang Aerospace University, Shenyang, China
{pengbingxin,menghang,tianjing,qimingtai}@stu.sau.edu.cn,
{lzk,jiaxu,wy4615}@sau.edu.cn

Abstract. Hyperspectral imaging technology provides an effective means for non-destructive detection of soluble solids content (SSC) in blueberries. However, multiple interference factors, including the diversity of fruit biological characteristics and differences during the data acquisition process, significantly affect the predictive performance of models. To address this challenge, this study proposes a differential enhancement and multi-scale feature fusion framework. This framework extracts gradient dynamic features and curvature characteristics of spectral curves through a multi-order differential feature enhancement module, achieving hierarchical fusion of static spectral and local dynamic features, thereby improving the model's robustness against multiple interference factors. Simultaneously, by combining a multi-scale feature extraction network, it promotes deep fusion of information at different scales and enhances feature representation capabilities. Experimental results on 13 sets of blueberry datasets demonstrate that the proposed method significantly outperforms existing models in SSC prediction performance, validating its effectiveness and superiority.

Keywords: Hyperspectral imaging · Soluble solids content (SSC) · Differential enhancement · Multi-scale feature fusion · Non-destructive detection

1 Introduction

Blueberries possess numerous health benefits including prevention of brain and nervous system aging, vision protection, heart strengthening, and immune system enhancement [1]. Consequently, blueberry quality is crucial for meeting consumer demands. Among the various indicators used to assess blueberry quality, soluble solids content (SSC) represents a key factor. SSC primarily consists of sugars, acids, vitamins, and other soluble substances, with its level directly affecting the taste and flavor of blueberries. Additionally, SSC reflects, to a certain extent, the maturity and nutritional status of blueberries, as well-ripened and

J. Li et al. (Eds.): APWeb-WAIM 2025, LNCS 16115, pp. 146–161, 2026.
https://doi.org/10.1007/978-981-95-5719-6_10

nutrient-rich blueberries typically exhibit higher SSC levels. Therefore, accurate detection of SSC is significant for scientifically and comprehensively evaluating blueberry quality, while also providing valuable reference data for blueberry production, sales, and consumer selection. In traditional detection methods, SSC is assessed through manual measurements conducted in the laboratory, a process that is not only time-consuming and expensive but also destructive to the blueberry samples used for analysis. Thus, developing rapid, non-destructive, and environmentally friendly SSC detection technologies has become an inevitable choice to overcome the limitations of traditional laboratory testing, which is time-consuming, costly, and sample-destructive.

In recent years, hyperspectral imaging technology has gradually emerged as an efficient non-destructive detection method, providing effective solutions for the non-destructive assessment of agricultural product quality. Significant progress has already been achieved in the non-destructive quality inspection of fruits such as tomatoes, plums [2,3]. However, the diversity of biological characteristics such as seasonality, variety, and origin of fruits affects the interaction between light and matter, resulting in high variability in fruits, thereby reducing the prediction accuracy and robustness of models [4,5], significantly limiting the practical application of hyperspectral imaging technology in agricultural detection scenarios. In existing studies, Tian et al. [6] constructed three types of SSC prediction models (separate location model, global locations model and average spectra model) and four types of surface location classification models to mitigate the influence of fruit surface feature. Bai et al. [7] established a multiple-origin SSC prediction model for apples from multiple geographical regions has been developed by combining spectral fingerprint feature extraction, origin recognition, model search strategies, optimal wavelength selection, and deep learning with multivariate regression analysis to reduce sensitivity to geographical origin. Fan et al. [8] applied the slope and bias (S/B) correction method to eliminate the impact of seasonal diversity. Although these models can specifically reduce the influence of single biological characteristics, they struggle to comprehensively address complex and diverse biological characteristic differences. Additionally, during the actual model development process, the collected datasets are often affected by differences in acquisition conditions (such as light source degradation, manual measurement bias, etc.), introducing more uncertainties and thereby posing greater challenges to model prediction.

To address the above challenges, this study constructed 13 sets of blueberry datasets containing different seasons, varieties, and acquisition parameters, and on this basis, proposed a soluble solids content prediction method for blueberries based on differential enhancement and multi-scale feature fusion (DEMF). The specific innovations are as follows:

1) A differential enhancement and multi-scale feature fusion prediction framework for non-destructive detection of soluble solids in blueberries is proposed. This framework constructs an end-to-end robust learning model by integrating multi-order differential feature enhancement and multi-scale feature extraction networks. The model can effectively address the complexity

challenges posed by blueberry datasets with different biological characteristics and acquisition parameters.

2) A multi-order differential feature enhancement strategy is designed, which uses discrete differential operators to extract gradient dynamic features and curvature characteristics of spectral curves, and hierarchically fuses these dynamic features with the original spectral data. This fusion method not only retains the static information of the original spectrum but also incorporates local dynamic information of spectral changes, providing a more comprehensive spectral feature representation for the model, enhancing its ability to identify subtle spectral differences, and thereby improving the accuracy of SSC prediction.
3) A novel multi-scale feature extraction network is constructed, which integrates the improved Inception-ResNet-A structure with a self-attention mechanism. The improved Inception-ResNet-A structure is responsible for extracting multi-scale local features under different receptive fields, while the self-attention mechanism is used to capture long-range dependencies between bands, achieving adaptive global information fusion. This deep fusion mechanism effectively enhances the model's feature representation capability, enabling it to better capture key spectral information related to SSC, thus improving the model's predictive performance.

2 Materials

2.1 Data Preparation and Acquisition

The blueberries used in this study were obtained through both online (sourced from Dandong, Liaoning and Yuxi, Yunnan) and offline (local fruit stores in Shenyang, Liaoning) purchases. As shown in Table 1, to simulate complex scenarios in practical applications, this study comprehensively considered the diversity of blueberry biological characteristics (seasons and varieties) and differences in the data acquisition process, collecting 13 sets of blueberry datasets with multiple interference factors, comprising a total of 2,165 blueberry samples with diameters ranging from 13 to 14 mm.

Specifically, the 13 datasets collected in this study spanned across 2022, 2023, and 2024; seasonal characteristics included summer, autumn, and winter; varieties included multiple known or unknown cultivars; hyperspectral image acquisition environments are divided into two categories: non-darkroom (datasets 1–9) and darkroom (datasets 10–13); SSC measurements employed the grinding method (datasets 1–9: crushing samples followed by filtering juice through gauze and measuring with a refractometer) and the syringe compression method (datasets 10–13: compressing samples with a syringe followed by filtering juice through gauze and measuring with a refractometer). All samples were measured in triplicate, and the average value was taken as the final SSC value to ensure data reliability.

The hardware system used for data acquisition in this study consisted of a push-broom hyperspectral camera (GaiaSky-mini2, with a spectral range of 393.7–1001.4 nm, comprising 176 bands, and a spectral resolution of 3.5 nm Âś

Table 1. Blueberry datasets containing multiple interference factors

ID	Date (t)	Season	Variety	Darkroom	Mask Threshold	SSC Range	Number (n)
1	2022-10-15	Autumn	Unknown	✗	[0.4, 0.75]	[8.7, 16.7]	180
2	2022-10-21	Autumn	Unknown	✗	[0.4, 0.75]	[8.9, 16.6]	210
3	2022-10-28	Autumn	Unknown	✗	[0.4, 0.75]	[7.7, 19.8]	170
4	2022-11-04	Autumn	Unknown	✗	[0.4, 0.75]	[8.8, 18.6]	220
5	2023-02-17	Winter	Emerald	✗	[0.4, 0.75]	[10.7, 19.0]	230
6	2023-02-27	Winter	Emerald	✗	[0.3, 0.6]	[10.7, 17.5]	160
7	2023-06-14	Summer	H5	✗	[0.3, 0.6]	[9.0, 17.0]	230
8	2023-07-04	Summer	Legacy	✗	[0.3, 0.6]	[9.7, 19.3]	216
9	2023-07-21	Summer	H5	✗	[0.3, 0.6]	[6.8, 19.0]	180
10	2024-09-24	Autumn	Unknown	✓	[0.5, 0.72]	[6.9, 12.7]	139
11	2024-09-25	Autumn	Unknown	✓	[0.5, 0.72]	[7.2, 13.2]	80
12	2024-09-26	Autumn	Unknown	✓	[0.5, 0.72]	[7.4, 12.9]	80
13	2024-09-27	Autumn	Unknown	✓	[0.5, 0.72]	[8.9, 16.3]	70
Total(N)							**2165**

0.5 nm), four 50W halogen lamps, a conveyor belt, and a computer (see Fig. 1). The conveyor belt speed was set to 2.0 cm/s, and the camera height was 29 cm. Prior to spectral acquisition, the halogen lamps were adjusted and preheated for 30 min to ensure uniform and stable illumination in the scanning area.

Fig. 1. Hyperspectral image acquisition system hardware used for blueberries

Before image acquisition, this study obtained a white background reference image using a white polytetrafluoroethylene board and a dark background reference image by covering the camera lens with an opaque lens cap. These two reference images were used for reflectance calibration of the acquired hyperspectral images, with the reflectance calibration formula as follows:

$$R_c = \frac{I_{\text{original}} - I_{\text{dark}}}{I_{white} - I_{\text{dark}}} \times R_{white} \tag{1}$$

where R_c represents the calibrated hyperspectral image, $I_{original}$ is the original hyperspectral image, I_{white} is the white background reference image, I_{dark} is the dark background reference image, and R_{white} is the reflectance of the white polytetrafluoroethylene board (approximately 100%).

2.2 Spectral Extraction

The spherical appearance of blueberries results in uneven light distribution on their surface, leading to varying reflectance in different regions. As shown in Fig. 2, spectral curves from different regions exhibit distinct differences: the green line corresponding to the highlight area shows the highest reflectance, the blue line representing the central area has moderate reflectance, the red line displaying the edge area has lower reflectance, while the azure line indicating the background area spectrum shows significant differences from the fruit regions. To obtain representative spectral features of blueberries, this study employed a binary mask method based on reflectance thresholds to extract the average spectrum of effective regions. The specific process is illustrated in Fig. 2: first, a single-band grayscale image was generated at the 904.5 nm band where reflectance differences are significant; then, a reflectance threshold range [0.30, 0.60] was set based on visual assessment, and a binary mask was generated accordingly (regions with reflectance between 0.30 and 0.60 were set to 1, and other regions to 0); subsequently, this mask was used to eliminate the background areas, high-reflectance highlight areas, and low-reflectance edge areas from the original hyperspectral image, retaining regions of interest with moderate reflectance; finally, the average of all pixel values within the regions of interest for each band was calculated to obtain representative values for each band, thereby constructing a complete average spectral curve.

After extracting the average spectra of all blueberry samples, the dataset $D_t = \{(\mathbf{x}_1, y_1), \ldots, (\mathbf{x}_n, y_n)\}$ was obtained, where D_t represents the dataset collected on date t (see Table 1), $\mathbf{x}_k \in \mathbb{R}^{1 \times b}$ denotes the spectral features of the k-th blueberry sample, b is the number of bands, n is the number of samples, y_k is the SSC measurement value of the k-th blueberry sample, and $k \in [1, n]$.

3 Methods

3.1 Differential Enhancement and Multi-scale Feature Fusion Framework

Figure 3 illustrates the DEMF framework proposed in this study. This framework extracts gradient dynamic features and curvature characteristics of spectral curves through a multi-order differential feature enhancement module, achieving

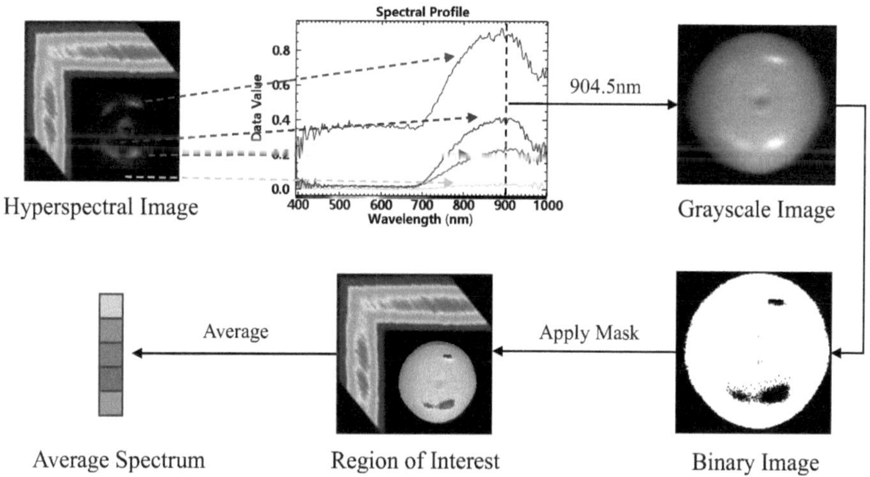

Fig. 2. Flowchart of average spectrum extraction

hierarchical fusion of static spectral and local dynamic features, thereby enhancing model robustness against multiple interference factors. Simultaneously, by incorporating a multi-scale feature extraction network, the framework promotes deep fusion of information at different scales, strengthening feature expressiveness.

3.2 Multi-order Differential Feature Enhancement Module

To improve the accuracy of SSC prediction under multiple interference factors, this study designed a multi-order differential feature enhancement module (MDFE). This module utilizes discrete differential operators to extract gradient dynamic features and curvature characteristics of spectral curves, and hierarchically fuses these dynamic features with the original spectral data. This fusion approach not only preserves the static information of the original spectrum but also incorporates local dynamic information of spectral changes, providing the model with a more comprehensive spectral feature representation. This enhances the model's ability to identify subtle spectral differences, thereby improving the accuracy of SSC prediction. The implementation steps of this strategy are as follows:

First, first-order differential operation is performed on the original spectral features $\mathbf{x}_i \in \mathbb{R}^{1\times b}$. Mathematically, this corresponds to an approximation of the first-order derivative of the spectral curve, characterizing the rate of change properties of local bands. The element-wise calculation form of first-order difference is defined as:

$$\Delta x_{i,j} = x_{i,j+1} - x_{i,j}, \quad (1 \leq i \leq N, 1 \leq j < b) \tag{2}$$

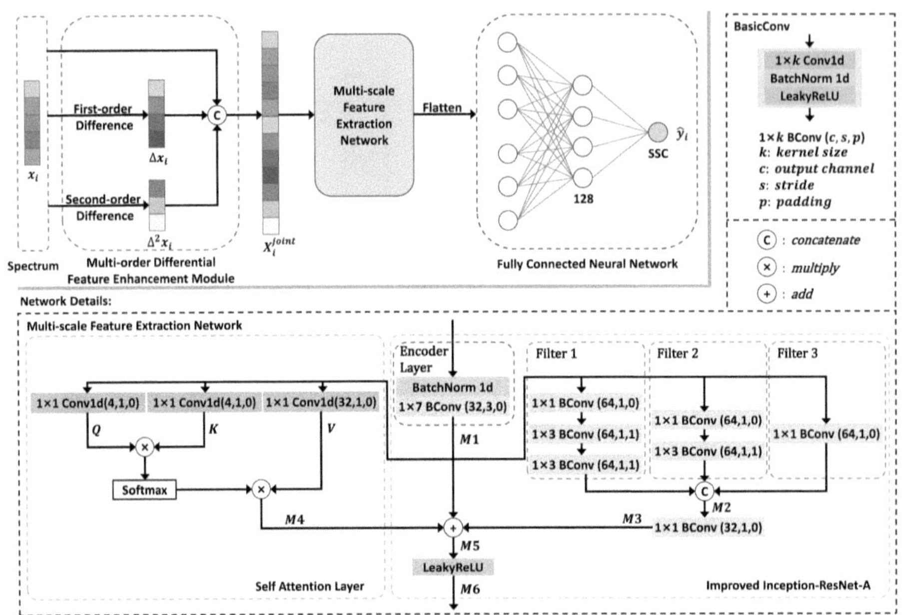

Fig. 3. The proposed DEMF framework.

The corresponding vectorized representation is:

$$\Delta \mathbf{x}_i = [x_{i2} - x_{i1},\ x_{i3} - x_{i2},\ \ldots,\ x_{ib} - x_{i,b-1}] \tag{3}$$

where $\Delta x_{i,j}$ represents the reflectance of the first-order differential feature of the i-th sample at the j-th band, $x_{i,j}$ represents the reflectance of the original spectral feature of the i-th sample at the j-th band, N is the total number of samples, b is the number of spectral bands, and $\Delta \mathbf{x}_i \in \mathbb{R}^{1\times(b-1)}$ is the first-order differential feature of the i-th sample.

To further capture the evolution patterns of spectral gradients, second-order differential operations are performed based on the first-order differential features $\Delta \mathbf{x}_i$. Mathematically, this corresponds to an approximation of the second-order derivative of the spectral curve, characterizing the curvature properties of local band changes. The recursive calculation process for the second-order difference is defined as:

$$\begin{aligned}\Delta^2 x_{i,j} &= \Delta x_{i,j+1} - \Delta x_{i,j} \\ &= (x_{i,j+2} - x_{i,j+1}) - (x_{i,j+1} - x_{i,j}) \\ &= x_{i,j+2} - 2x_{i,j+1} + x_{i,j}, \quad (1 \le i \le N,\ 1 \le j < b-1)\end{aligned} \tag{4}$$

The corresponding vectorized representation is:

$$\Delta^2 \mathbf{x}_i = [x_{i3} - 2x_{i2} + x_{i1},\ x_{i4} - 2x_{i3} + x_{i2},\ \ldots,\ x_{ib} - 2x_{i,b-1} + x_{i,b-2}] \tag{5}$$

where $\Delta^2 x_{i,j}$ represents the reflectance of the second-order differential feature of the i-th sample at the j-th band, and $\Delta^2 \mathbf{x}_i \in \mathbb{R}^{1\times(b-2)}$ is the second-order differential feature of the i-th sample.

Finally, a joint representation vector is constructed by concatenating the original spectral features $\mathbf{x}_i$, first-order differential features $\Delta \mathbf{x}_i$, and second-order differential features $\Delta^2 \mathbf{x}_i$ along the feature dimension, achieving hierarchical fusion of dynamic features and original spectral data:

$$\mathbf{X}_i^{\text{joint}} = \left[\mathbf{x}_i;\ \Delta \mathbf{x}_i;\ \Delta^2 \mathbf{x}_i\right] \in \mathbb{R}^{1\times(3b-3)} \tag{6}$$

3.3 Multi-scale Feature Extraction Network

To enhance the performance of SSC prediction under multiple interference factors, this study constructed a multi-scale feature extraction network as a feature extractor. This network integrates an improved Inception-ResNet-A (IIRA) structure with a self-attention mechanism. The improved Inception-ResNet-A structure is responsible for extracting multi-scale local features under different receptive fields, while the self-attention mechanism captures long-range dependencies between bands, achieving adaptive global information fusion. This deep fusion mechanism effectively enhances the feature representation capability of the model, enabling it to better capture key spectral information related to SSC, thereby improving the predictive performance of the model.

As shown in Fig. 3, the blue blocks in IIRA represent BasicConv, with detailed operations displayed in the upper right corner. The joint representation vector $\mathbf{X}_i^{\text{joint}}$ obtained through MDFE first passes through an encoder layer to obtain $M1$. The core function of the encoder layer is to compress, abstract, and efficiently represent the input features. $M1$ is then input into three different filters and one self-attention layer. The outputs of the three filters are concatenated along the channel dimension to obtain $M2$, which is then input into a BasicConv to obtain $M3$. This process achieves fusion, dimensionality reduction, and non-linear enhancement of multi-scale features. The self-attention layer projects $M1$ into a query matrix Q, a key matrix K, and a value matrix V through three independent convolutional layers. Subsequently, Q and K undergo matrix multiplication followed by softmax normalization to obtain an attention weight matrix, which is then multiplied with the value matrix V to obtain the attention-weighted feature $M4$. Afterward, through residual connections, $M1$, $M3$, and $M4$ are added at corresponding positions to obtain $M5$. Finally, $M5$ is passed through the LeakyReLU activation function to obtain $M6$ as the output of the multi-scale feature extraction network.

The mathematical representation of the self-attention layer is:

$$\mathbf{M4} = \text{Softmax}\left(\mathbf{QK}^\top\right) \cdot \mathbf{V} \tag{7}$$

where $\mathbf{Q} \in \mathbb{R}^{d_k}$, $\mathbf{K} \in \mathbb{R}^{d_k}$, and $\mathbf{V} \in \mathbb{R}^{d_v}$ are the query, key, and value matrices, respectively, d_k is the dimension of $\mathbf{K}$, and d_v is the dimension of $\mathbf{V}$. Unlike traditional self-attention mechanisms, this study did not adopt a scaling factor

($\frac{1}{\sqrt{d_k}}$) to scale $\mathbf{QK}^\top$. This aims to avoid the suppression of low-amplitude but critical feature correlations in the attention weight matrix by traditional scaling factors and to reduce effective signal degradation caused by numerical range compression, thereby maintaining more complete semantic fidelity in global feature interaction.

3.4 Fully Connected Neural Network and Loss Function

As shown in Fig. 3, the output of the multi-scale feature extraction network is flattened and input into a 3-layer fully connected neural network to achieve SSC prediction. The network's hidden layers employ batch normalization, LeakyReLU, and dropout (with a dropout probability of 0.2), with the final output layer result $\hat{y}_i$ serving as the predicted SSC value. This study uses the Huber loss as the model's loss function, with the mathematical expression as follows:

$$L_\delta = \frac{1}{S}\sum_{i=1}^{S}\left[\mathbb{I}_{|y_i-\hat{y}_i|\leq\delta}\cdot\frac{1}{2}(y_i-\hat{y}_i)^2+\mathbb{I}_{|y_i-\hat{y}_i|>\delta}\cdot\left(\delta|y_i-\hat{y}_i|-\frac{1}{2}\delta^2\right)\right] \tag{8}$$

where L_δ is the loss value for one training epoch, S is the number of training samples, $\mathbb{I}$ is an indicator function (1 when the condition is met, 0 otherwise), y_i is the measured SSC value of the i-th sample, $\hat{y}_i$ is the predicted SSC value of the i-th sample, and δ is the threshold controlling the switch of the loss function from mean squared error (MSE) to mean absolute error (MAE), with a value of 0.4. The training objective of the model is to minimize this loss function.

4 Experiments

4.1 Dataset and Experimental Setup

Due to interference from multiple factors such as the diversity of blueberry biological characteristics (season and variety) and differences in the data acquisition process, datasets collected on different dates exhibit significant distribution differences. Additionally, in the process of extracting average spectra from blueberry datasets for each date, the manual selection of bands and thresholds inevitably introduces subjective bias, further increasing the difficulty of cross-date prediction. Therefore, this study chose to divide the training, validation, and test sets according to acquisition dates to correctly evaluate the generalization ability of the model.

In this experiment, 220 blueberry samples collected on November 4, 2022, were randomly selected as the test set, with the training and validation sets derived from data collected on other dates. The DEMF framework proposed in this study and all comparison models (except for PLS, which used 10-fold cross-validation) employed 12-fold cross-validation to determine the optimal hyperparameter combination, with the best model selected for final testing based on validation results. Unlike traditional K-fold cross-validation experiments that divide training and validation sets based on stratified sampling strategies, this study divided training and validation sets according to data acquisition dates.

Model performance was evaluated using the coefficient of determination (R^2), mean squared error (MSE), and mean absolute error (MAE). The input blueberry features were standardized using Standard Scaler, while SSC values were not normalized or standardized. During model training, the batch_size was set to 32 and the number of epochs to 100. The Rectified Adam optimizer was used with an initial learning rate of 1e-5 and a weight_decay coefficient of 0.01. The OneCycleLR strategy was employed for dynamic learning rate adjustment, with a maximum learning rate (max_lr) of 0.01. OneCycleLR follows a triangular learning rate policy, non-linearly increasing the learning rate from its initial value to max_lr and then gradually decreasing it within the specified training epochs.

4.2 Comparative Experiments

The DEMF framework proposed in this study was compared with PLS [9], CNN [10], DeepSpectra [11], MBA [12], SpectraNet32 [13], SpectraNet53 [14], and RN-TLDL [15], with the hyperparameters of all models determined through cross-validation. Specifically, for the PLS model, 10-fold cross-validation was used to determine the optimal number of latent variables, with the maximum number of latent variables set to 50. Other deep learning methods divided training and validation sets according to data acquisition dates for 12-fold cross-validation, ultimately selecting hyperparameters $epoch \in \{75, 100, 125, 155, 175\}$, $lr \in \{0.0001, 0.001, 0.01, 0.1, 0.5\}$, and $weight\_decay \in \{0.0001, 0.001, 0.01, 0.1, 0.5\}$ based on the average results of 12 cross-validation sets.

Table 2 shows the comparative performance results of various models in the SSC prediction task under multiple interference factors after cross-validation optimization. The experimental results indicate that the DEMF framework proposed in this paper outperforms comparison models on all evaluation metrics, demonstrating extremely strong prediction advantages and generalization capabilities. Specifically, in terms of the testing R^2 metric, DEMF showed improvements of 0.1703, 0.6702, 0.6835, 1.2238, 0.6942, 0.2631, and 0.4705 compared to PLS, CNN, DeepSpectra, MBA, SpectraNet32, SpectraNet53, and RN-TLDL, respectively. Meanwhile, DEMF also achieved lower testing MSE and testing MAE metrics than the comparison models, fully demonstrating the prediction advantages of the DEMF framework proposed in this study for SSC under multiple interference factors.

Figure 4 compares the SSC prediction performance of various models on the test set through scatter plots. The horizontal and vertical coordinates of the scatter plots correspond to the measured and predicted SSC values, respectively, where the black solid line (y=x) represents the ideal reference line, and the orange solid line is the actual regression fitting line. The degree of fit between these two lines intuitively reflects the prediction accuracy of the model. From the figure, it can be observed that the orange fitting line of the proposed DEMF framework is closest to the reference line, and the data points are most concentrated along

Table 2. Performance comparison of various models in the SSC prediction task

Model	Training R^2	Training MSE	Training MAE	Testing R^2	Testing MSE	Testing MAE
PLS	0.8651	0.7182	0.6667	0.4840	1.7490	1.1214
CNN	0.8935	0.5608	0.5884	−0.0159	3.4438	1.6137
DeepSpectra	0.8651	0.7083	0.6590	−0.0292	3.4890	1.6100
MBA	0.8894	0.4946	0.5519	−0.5695	5.3203	2.0567
SpectraNet32	0.9053	0.5028	0.5497	−0.0399	3.5252	1.6776
SpectraNet53	0.8840	0.6150	0.6105	0.3912	2.0638	1.2228
RN-TLDL	0.6386	1.9228	1.0930	0.1838	2.7669	1.2966
DEMF	0.7625	1.1265	0.8270	**0.6543**	**1.1720**	**0.9158**

the diagonal line, demonstrating superior prediction performance compared to other models.

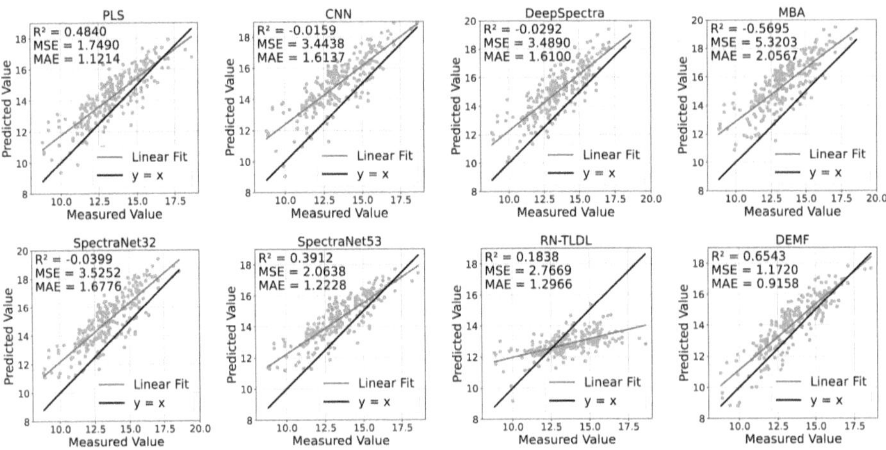

Fig. 4. Scatter plots of prediction results of various models on the test set

4.3 Parameter Selection

Figure 5 shows the cross-validation and test performance of the DEMF framework proposed in this study under different epochs, lr, and weight_decay values. The horizontal axis represents the hyperparameter values, while the vertical axis shows the coefficient of determination R^2 of the model under the corresponding hyperparameters. The blue line displays the average R^2 results on the validation set from 12 cross-validation experiments, while the red line presents the R^2 performance on the final test set. The results indicate that the cross-validation results are optimal when epoch is 100, lr is 0.01, and weight_decay is 0.01.

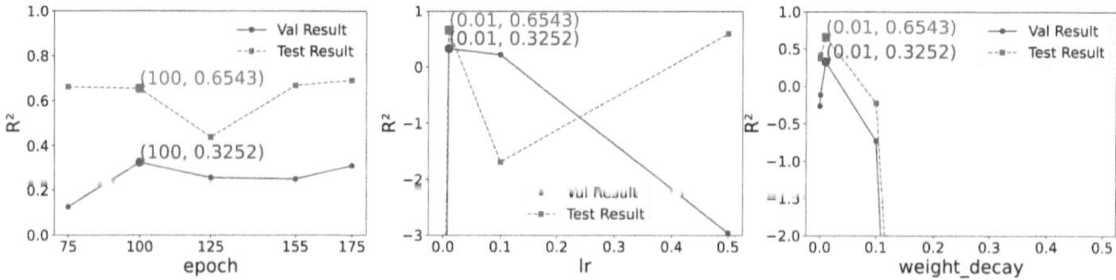

Fig. 5. Cross-validation and test performance of the DEMF framework under different epochs, lr, and weight_decay values

4.4 Ablation Experiments

The DEMF framework proposed in this paper is built upon the IIRA [12] as the base network, integrating self-attention mechanisms and the MDFE module.

As can be seen from the DEMF framework diagram (see Fig. 3), the base network IIRA is constructed based on CNN, indicating that it can only focus on local information of features while lacking global feature information learning. Therefore, by introducing a self-attention mechanism, the model is able to capture global dependencies between spectral bands during feature learning, allowing each band to comprehensively consider contextual information from other bands during representation, thereby strengthening the model's understanding of the overall spectral structure.

Figure 6 compares the original spectral features of all blueberry samples with the spectral features enhanced using MDFE. It can be observed that after MDFE enhancement, the feature dimension expanded from the original 176 dimensions to 525 dimensions, introducing spectral gradient dynamic features and curvature features extracted by discrete differential operators. Compared to the original spectral features, the enhanced spectral features provide the model with a more comprehensive spectral feature representation, improving the model's ability to identify subtle spectral differences, thereby enhancing the accuracy of SSC prediction.

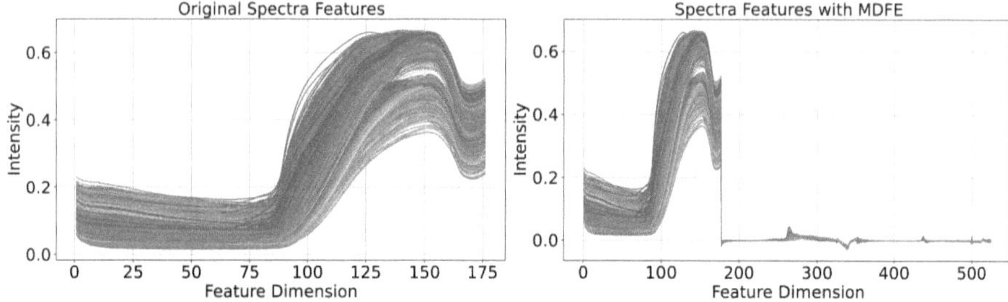

Fig. 6. Comparison of original spectral features and MDFE-enhanced spectral features for all blueberry samples

To verify the effectiveness of each module, ablation experiments were conducted as shown in Table 3. The experimental results indicate that introducing the MDFE module on top of the base network IIRA increased testing R^2 by 0.1178 and decreased testing MSE and testing MAE by 0.399 and 0.0981, respectively. Further introducing the self-attention mechanism (SA) on this basis increased testing R^2 by another 0.0933 and decreased testing MSE and testing MAE by another 0.3163 and 0.1086, respectively. This progressive performance improvement demonstrates that the rich feature representation introduced by MDFE makes an important contribution to improving the model's SSC prediction performance, while the self-attention mechanism effectively strengthens the model's perception of global spectral semantics by modeling long-distance dependencies between spectral bands, further enhancing the model's prediction performance for SSC under multiple interference factors.

Table 3. Ablation experiment results verifying the effectiveness of each module

IIRA	MDFE	SA	Training R^2	Training MSE	Training MAE	Testing R^2	Testing MSE	Testing MAE
✓			0.6515	1.6116	0.9845	0.4432	1.8873	1.1225
✓	✓		0.7716	1.0556	0.7909	0.5610	1.4883	1.0244
✓	✓	✓	0.7625	1.1265	0.8270	**0.6543**	**1.1720**	**0.9158**

To verify that not using a scaling factor in the self-attention mechanism can reduce effective signal degradation caused by numerical range compression, thereby maintaining more complete semantic fidelity in global feature interaction, ablation experiments were conducted as shown in Table 4. The experimental results indicate that the DEMF framework without the scaling factor ($\frac{1}{\sqrt{d_k}}$) showed superior performance on the test set. Compared to the setting with the scaling factor, its testing R^2 metric increased by 0.1601, while testing MSE and testing MAE decreased by 0.5427 and 0.1913, respectively.

Table 4. Ablation experiment results on the impact of scaling factor ($\frac{1}{\sqrt{d_k}}$) in self-attention mechanism on DEMF framework performance

$\frac{1}{\sqrt{d_k}}$	Training R^2	Training MSE	Training MAE	Testing R^2	Testing MSE	Testing MAE
w	0.7677	1.0906	0.8186	0.4942	1.7147	1.1071
w/o	0.7625	1.1265	0.8270	**0.6543**	**1.1720**	**0.9158**

4.5 Runtime Efficiency and Computational Resource Requirements

The training process employed an NVIDIA GeForce RTX 4090 graphics card, with the DEMF framework consuming 658MiB of GPU memory during training. The MDFE module is executed during the data preprocessing stage prior to training and does not affect inference time. The multi-scale feature extraction network contains 0.7612M parameters, with an inference time of 1.7520ms per batch and 0.0197 GFLOPs per batch. The self-attention layer comprises 0.0013M parameters, with an inference time of 0.2376ms per batch and 0.0006 GFLOPs per batch.

5 Conclusion

This study addresses the inadequate prediction accuracy and generalization capability of existing models in blueberry SSC detection tasks due to interference from multiple factors, including the diversity of fruit biological characteristics (season and variety) and differences in the data acquisition process, by proposing a differential enhancement and multi-scale feature fusion framework. This framework extracts gradient dynamic features and curvature characteristics of spectral curves through a multi-order differential feature enhancement module, achieving hierarchical fusion of static spectral and local dynamic features, thereby enhancing model robustness against multiple interference factors. Simultaneously, by incorporating a multi-scale feature extraction network, the framework promotes deep fusion of information at different scales, strengthening feature expressiveness. Experimental results on 13 sets of blueberry datasets demonstrate that the proposed method significantly outperforms existing models in SSC prediction performance, validating its effectiveness and superiority.

Acknowledgments. This work was supported in part by the National Natural Science Foundation of China under Grant 62171295, in part by the Applied Basic Research Project of Liaoning Province under Grant 2023JH2/101300204, in part by the Fund of CAS Key Laboratory of Forest Ecology and Silviculture, Institute of Applied Ecology, Chinese Academy of Sciences under Grant KLFES-2035, and in part by the Fundamental Research Funds for the Universities of Liaoning Province under Grant LJ212410143091.

Declaration of Interests. The authors have no competing interests to declare that are relevant to the content of this article.

References

1. Yi, M., Zhao, C., Liao, F., et al.: Classification of blueberry varieties based on improved EfficientNet. In: 2022 4th International Academic Exchange Conference on Science and Technology Innovation (IAECST), pp. 411–415. IEEE (2022). https://doi.org/10.1109/IAECST57965.2022.10062152
2. Zhao, M., Cang, H., Chen, H., et al.: Determination of quality and maturity of processing tomatoes using near-infrared hyperspectral imaging with interpretable machine learning methods. Lwt. **183**, 114861 (2023). https://doi.org/10.1016/j.lwt.2023.114861
3. Zhou, C., Zhang, X., Liu, Y., et al.: Research on hyperspectral regression method of soluble solids in green plum based on one-dimensional deep convolution network. Spectrochimica Acta Part A Mol. Biomol. Spectrosc. **303**, 123151 (2023). https://doi.org/10.1016/j.saa.2023.123151
4. Silva, R., Freitas, O., Melo-Pinto, P.: Evaluating the generalization ability of deep learning models: an application on sugar content estimation from hyperspectral images of wine grape berries. Expert Syst. Appl. **250**, 123891 (2024). https://doi.org/10.1016/j.eswa.2024.123891
5. Zheng, W., Bai, Y., Luo, H., et al.: Self-adaptive models for predicting soluble solid content of blueberries with biological variability by using near-infrared spectroscopy and chemometrics. Postharvest Biol. Technol. **169**, 111286 (2020). https://doi.org/10.1016/j.postharvbio.2020.111286
6. Tian, X., Wang, Q., Li, J., et al.: Non-destructive prediction of soluble solids content of pear based on fruit surface feature classification and multivariate regression analysis. Infrared Phys. Technol. **92**, 336–344 (2018). https://doi.org/10.1016/j.infrared.2018.06.019
7. Bai, Y., Xiong, Y., Huang, J., et al.: Accurate prediction of soluble solid content of apples from multiple geographical regions by combining deep learning with spectral fingerprint features. Postharvest Biol. Technol. **156**, 110943 (2019). https://doi.org/10.1016/j.postharvbio.2019.110943
8. Fan, S., Li, J., Xia, Y., et al.: Long-term evaluation of soluble solids content of apples with biological variability by using near-infrared spectroscopy and calibration transfer method. Postharvest Biol. Technol. **151**, 79–87 (2019). https://doi.org/10.1016/j.postharvbio.2019.02.001
9. Wold, S., Sjöström, M., Eriksson, L.: PLS-regression: a basic tool of chemometrics[J]. Chemom. Intell. Lab. Syst. **58**(2), 109–130 (2001). https://doi.org/10.1016/S0169-7439(01)00155-1
10. Zhang, C., Wu, W., Zhou, L., et al.: Developing deep learning based regression approaches for determination of chemical compositions in dry black goji berries (Lycium ruthenicum Murr.) using near-infrared hyperspectral imaging. Food Chem. **319**, 126536 (2020). https://doi.org/10.1016/j.foodchem.2020.126536
11. Zhang, X., Lin, T., Xu, J., et al.: DeepSpectra: an end-to-end deep learning approach for quantitative spectral analysis. Anal. Chimica Acta **1058**, 48–57 (2019). https://doi.org/10.1016/j.aca.2019.01.002
12. Li, Z., Zhang, J., Li, W., et al.: A quantitative spectra analysis framework combining mixup and band attention for predicting soluble solid content of blueberries. In: International Conference on Knowledge Science, Engineering and Management. Cham: Springer Nature Switzerland 2023, pp. 366–373 (2023). https://doi.org/10.1007/978-3-031-40292-0_30

13. Martins, J.A., Rodrigues, D., Cavaco, A.M., et al.: Estimation of soluble solids content and fruit temperature in 'Rocha' pear using Vis-NIR spectroscopy and the SpectraNet–32 deep learning architecture. Postharvest Biol. Technol. **199**, 112281 (2023). https://doi.org/10.1016/j.postharvbio.2023.112281
14. Martins, J.A., Guerra, R., Pires, R., et al.: SpectraNet–53: a deep residual learning architecture for predicting soluble solids content with VIS–NIR spectroscopy. Comput. Electron. Agricult. **197**, 106945 (2022). https://doi.org/10.1016/j.compag.2022.106945
15. Li, F., Sun, D., Li, Z., et al.: Research on quantitative analysis method of Blueberry soluble solids using transformer. In: Intelligent Information Processing Industrialization Branch of China High-Tech Industrialization Research Association. Proceedings of the 18th National Conference on Signal and Intelligent Information Processing and Applications. School of Computer Science, Shenyang Aerospace University, pp. 536–543+577 (2024). https://doi.org/10.26914/c.cnkihy.2024.050433

MedDPA: Multi-scale Decomposition and Prototype-Based Channel Aggregation for Medical Time Series Classification

Xiaotian Gu, Pengfei Wang, Yiqiao Wang, Xiaoling Wang(✉), and Tianwen Qian

School of Computer Science and Technology, East China Normal University, Shanghai, China
{xtgu,pfwang,yqwang_01}@stu.ecnu.edu.cn, {xlwang,twqian}@cs.ecnu.edu.cn

Abstract. Medical time series (MedTS) data, including Electroencephalography (EEG) and Electrocardiography (ECG), are widely utilized in clinical diagnosis and physiological monitoring. With the rapid advancement of deep learning, various models have been applied to MedTS classification. However, existing approaches still have significant limitations. From a temporal perspective, many methods fail to capture both local fluctuations and long-term trends simultaneously, which are essential for identifying disease-related patterns. In terms of spatial modeling, most approaches overlook redundant and noisy information across channels, leading to suboptimal performance and reduced generalization ability. To address these issues, we propose MedDPA, a multi-scale framework based on MLP for MedTS classification. MedDPA explicitly separates short-term fluctuations and long-term trends through a decomposition module. We also introduce a prototype-based channel aggregation module to suppress noise and reduce redundancy while preserving essential information. Finally, we integrate multi-scale features through a dual-direction fusion strategy and dynamically adjust the contribution of each scale. Our method is evaluated on multiple real-world EEG and ECG datasets. Results demonstrate that MedDPA outperforms 10 baselines across different metrics, validating its effectiveness, robustness, and potential for real-world applications.

Keywords: Medical Time Series · Time Series Classification · Multi-Scale Modeling

1 Introduction

Medical time series refers to physiological signal sequences that are continuously recorded at a fixed sampling rate. These signals are widely used in scenarios such as disease diagnosis, motion detection, and brain-computer interfaces (BCIs) [10]. For example, Electroencephalography (EEG), which records the brain's electrical activity via electrodes placed on the scalp, has been extensively applied

J. Li et al. (Eds.): APWeb-WAIM 2025, LNCS 16115, pp. 162–178, 2026.
https://doi.org/10.1007/978-981-95-5719-6_11

to tasks such as epilepsy detection [36] and Alzheimer's disease recognition [20]. While Electrocardiography (ECG) records electrical activity of cardiac muscle, which is crucial for the detection of cardiovascular diseases such as arrhythmias [24] and myocardial infarction [22]. Notably, due to limitations in sensor stability and acquisition environments, MedTS are often accompanied by severe noise and artifacts [13], posing additional challenges for analysis.

Traditional methods for MedTS classification mainly rely on hand-crafted features [29]. Although these approaches offer good interpretability, the design of such features is highly dependent on domain expertise. In addition to hand-crafted features, early research also explored statistical methods for MedTS modeling [4]. However, these methods often make strong assumptions about data distribution, thereby limiting their capacity to model nonlinear and noisy signals. In recent years, various deep learning methods have been applied to time series analysis, including MedTS classification [34,35,43].

Despite these advancements, existing models still face critical limitations in modeling temporal and spatial characteristics of MedTS: (i) **Temporal Perspective: Insufficient Multi-Scale Modeling and Integration.** Multi-scale and multi-period features are essential, as some disease-related patterns may only appear in specific frequency bands [1]. Accurately capturing and integrating these features is crucial for identifying disease-specific patterns. However, CNN- and GNN-based approaches are limited by their small receptive fields and struggle with long-term dependencies [7,8]. More recently, the Transformer-based method Medformer [34] has attempted to address this by partitioning sequences into fixed-length patches. However, this approach requires extensive tuning and lacks adaptability. Moreover, MedTS components differ in physiological meaning: trend components reflect long-term states like baseline heart rate [16], while seasonal components capture short-term cycles such as EEG rhythms or cardiac activity [2,25], thus requiring separate processing. (ii) **Spatial Perspective: Interference from Redundant Information between Channels.** Cross-channel information is critical in MedTS analysis [34], but current MLP-based models often overlook redundancy and noise between channels. This makes them prone to overfitting noise and reduces generalization. Additionally, most existing approaches are designed for general classification tasks and fail to address MedTS-specific phenomena, such as slow potential drifts [26]. This limitation reduces their clinical applicability.

To tackle these limitations, we propose **MedDPA**, a multi-scale decomposition and dynamic channel aggregation framework for MedTS classification, which aims to align with the temporal and spatial characteristics of physiological signals. Our approach consists of three key modules: a multi-scale decomposition module to separate local fluctuations from global trends at different scales, a prototype-based channel aggregation module to suppress redundant information interference, and a dual-direction multi-scale fusion module to integrate information across scales. Our main contributions are summarized as follows:

- We propose a novel MLP-based framework for MedTS classification, which effectively captures features across scales through downsampling, decompo-

sition and dual-direction fusion. A learnable weighting mechanism is also introduced to adaptively adjust the contribution of each scale.
- Prototype-based channel aggregation is performed at each scale to obtain scale-specific representations, and a codebook is employed to reduce noise and redundancy in MedTS.
- Extensive experiments on multiple public datasets show that MedDPA achieves the highest average ranking across all evaluation metrics and datasets, demonstrating its superior performance, generalization ability, and potential for real-world applications.

2 Related Work

2.1 Medical Time Series Classification

Medical time series, as dynamic signals reflecting changes in human physiological states, play a key role in disease diagnosis [16], health monitoring [33], and biometric authentication [27]. Traditional methods for MedTS classification mainly relied on hand-crafted feature extraction techniques and classical machine learning algorithms. For example, a previous study used wavelet transform combined with Support Vector Machine (SVM) to detect epileptic seizures from EEG signals [29]. Another study employed a sequential forward floating search algorithm based on linear discriminant analysis for arrhythmia classification using ECG data [18]. Although these methods offer certain interpretability, they struggle to capture complex and nonlinear patterns within the data.

With the advancement of deep learning, CNN have shown significant promise in MedTS classification. HS-CNN [7] reduced the time and effort of designing hand-crafted features by using multiple convolution scales to extract features and expand training data. TS-HCL [41] used hierarchical contrastive learning and domain label smoothing to tackle the challenge of unsupervised domain adaptation. With the application of Transformer in time series analysis, EEG Conformer [28] combined convolution with self-attention mechanism, significantly outperforming traditional CNN models in EEG decoding tasks. More recently, Medformer [34] introduced a multi-granularity patching strategy to model temporal patterns across different scales. However, its performance is highly related to the choice of patch size, reducing general applicability.

2.2 Multilayer Perceptrons for Time Series

Multilayer Perceptrons (MLPs), as a fundamental deep learning architecture, have recently demonstrated remarkable potential in time series analysis tasks [15]. Classical MLP inherently lacks the capability to capture temporal dependencies in time series data. To address this limitation, researchers have proposed a series of enhanced MLP variants to improve its modeling ability. DLinear [38] decomposed time series into trend and seasonal components and processed them with linear layers respectively, demonstrating that simple MLP structures can efficiently handle various time series prediction tasks. LightTS [39] adopted a lightweight MLP structure with moving average layers to construct a highly efficient forecasting framework. TimeMixer [32] used a multi-scale mixing architecture to tackle the intricate temporal variations, but ignored channel correlations.

For multivariate time series, TSMixer [6] applied MLP layers in time and feature dimensions respectively. This design effectively integrated temporal and channel information, achieving strong performance in multivariate time series forecasting tasks. In addition, FreTS [37] pointed out that modeling only in the time domain is insufficient due to the inherent complexity of time series data, and proposed to learn forecasting mappings in the frequency domain. Expanding on this idea, WPMixer [21] employed multi-resolution wavelet decomposition to capture complex patterns in both time and frequency domains. These methods demonstrate that MLP-based architectures have great potential for time series modeling and are emerging as a competitive alternative to more complex models.

3 Problem Formulation

Consider a MedTS dataset consisting of N samples, denoted as $\mathcal{D} = \{(\mathbf{x}^{(i)}, y^{(i)})\}_{i=1}^{N}$. Each sample $\mathbf{x}^{(i)} \in \mathbb{R}^{T \times C}$ represents a multivariate time series, where T denotes the number of timestamps and C represents the number of channels. The corresponding label $y^{(i)} \in \{1, 2, \ldots, K\}$ indicates the disease type or physiological state, with a total of K classes. The objective is to learn a mapping function $\mathcal{F} : \mathbb{R}^{T \times C} \rightarrow \mathbb{R}^{K}$. We frame this task as a supervised classification problem, optimizing the cross-entropy loss. Formally, for a given sample $\mathbf{x}^{(i)}$, the goal is to predict the label $y^{(i)}$, which can be written as:

$$\hat{y}^{(i)} = \mathcal{F}(\mathbf{x}^{(i)}; \theta), \tag{1}$$

where $\hat{y}^{(i)}$ is the predicted label for i-th sample, θ is the learnable parameters.

4 Methodology

In MedDPA, we first downsample the original sequence to obtain representations at different time scales. For each scale, we further decompose the sequence into seasonal and trend components. Second, we designed a channel aggregation module to extract features from each channel and aggregate them. A learnable codebook is also introduced to reduce noise and redundancy across channels. Third, to handle the differences between trend and seasonal components at different scales, we use a dual-direction information fusion module to integrate information at different scales. Finally, we fuse the output of each scale through learnable weights, enabling the model to select the most relevant scale-specific information under different pathological conditions. The overall architecture of MedDPA is illustrated in Fig. 1.

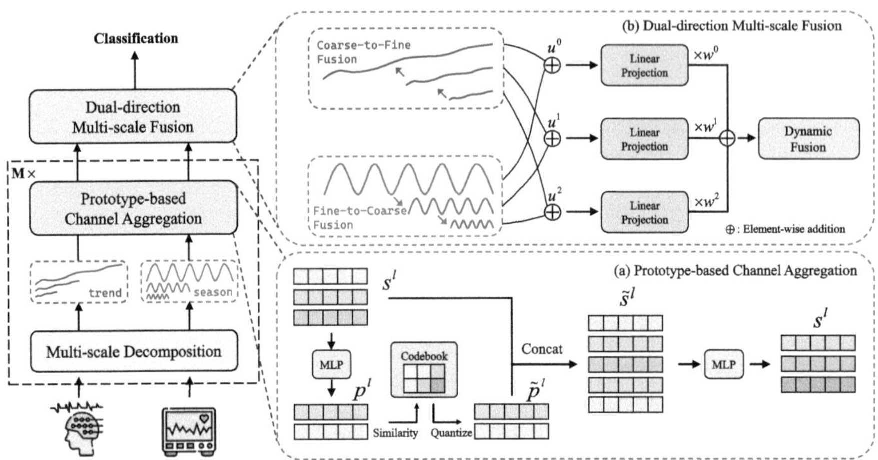

Fig. 1. The overall architecture of MedDPA.

4.1 Multi-scale Decomposition Module

In order to capture both short-term local patterns and long-term global trends, we use average pooling to perform multi-scale downsampling on the input time series data. For a sample $\mathbf{x}$, the downsampling process can be expressed as:

$$\mathbf{x}^l = \text{AvgPool}(\mathbf{x}^{l-1}), \quad l \in \{1, \cdots, L\}, \tag{2}$$

where $\mathbf{x}^l \in \mathbb{R}^{\lfloor \frac{T}{2^l} \rfloor \times C}$, and L denotes the number of downsampling layers. Each downsampled sequence $\mathbf{x}^l$ is then embedded into a hidden representation, which can be formulated as:

$$h^l = \text{Embed}(\mathbf{x}^l), \quad h^l \in \mathbb{R}^{\lfloor \frac{T}{2^l} \rfloor \times d}, \tag{3}$$

where d is the dimension of the hidden layer.

After downsampling, we perform series decomposition to obtain the trend and seasonal components for each scale. For MedTS, the trend component reflects changes in long-term physiological state, such as the baseline heart rate in ECG. These changes are usually determined by regulatory mechanisms and have low short-term variability [16]. In contrast, the seasonal component captures short-term periodic fluctuations, such as α and β band activity in EEG signals or cardiac cycles in ECG [2,25]. Motivated by these physiological characteristics, we use temporal average pooling with a padding operation to decompose complex non-stationary sequences into more tractable trend and seasonal components.

Specifically, for the l-th scale, we decompose the input time series data h^l to obtain its seasonal component s^l and trend component t^l. The decomposition process can be expressed as:

$$s^l, t^l = \text{SeriesDecomp}(h^l, k). \tag{4}$$

We apply a moving average filter with a sliding window of size k to the input sequence. This operation smooths out short-term fluctuations and extracts the long-term trend component. To reduce boundary effects, symmetric padding is used. The seasonal component is then obtained by subtracting the extracted trend from the original sequence.

4.2 Prototype-Based Channel Aggregation Module

To preserve informative patterns while suppressing redundancy, we propose a prototype-based channel aggregation module with a learnable codebook. In the previous module, the input sequence was downsampled and decomposed into seasonal and trend components. In this module, the aggregation is performed only on the seasonal component s at each scale l, and the reasoning for this choice will be explained later in this section. Specifically, we first apply a MLP layer to extract a prototype representation from the input features:

$$p^l = \text{MLP}_1(s^l), \tag{5}$$

where $\text{MLP}_1 : \mathbb{R}^d \to \mathbb{R}^{d'}$ is a projection, d' is the dimension of the prototype representation, and $p^l \in \mathbb{R}^{\lfloor \frac{T}{2^l} \rfloor \times d'}$. While p^l captures key information from each channel, it still may contain redundant elements. To further compact the representation, we introduce a learnable *Codebook* to reduce redundancy. The codebook C consists of M learnable prototype, each with a dimension of d':

$$C = \{c_1, c_2, \dots, c_M\}, \quad c_i \in \mathbb{R}^{d'}. \tag{6}$$

The codebook is randomly initialized and updated during training. For each $p_i^l \in \mathbb{R}^{d'}$, we compute the similarity between p_i^l and all c, and then use a softmax operation with a temperature parameter τ to generate soft weights:

$$\text{sim}(p_i^l, c_j) = p_i^l \cdot c_j^\top, \tag{7}$$

$$\alpha_{ij} = \frac{\exp(\text{sim}(p_i^l, c_j) \times \tau)}{\sum_{k=1}^{M} \exp(\text{sim}(p_i^l, c_k) \times \tau)}. \tag{8}$$

Here, τ controls the sharpness of softmax. We fix τ to 2 across all datasets. Using these weights, we compute a weighted sum of codebook vectors to obtain the quantized representation $\tilde{p}_i^l$:

$$\tilde{p}_i^l = \sum_{j=1}^{N} \alpha_{ij} c_j. \tag{9}$$

This mechanism is similar to Vector Quantization (VQ) [30], where each prototype vector is learnable and updated during training to capture common patterns in the input data. In MedTS, signals from different electrodes may exhibit strong spatial correlations [5]. Encouraging them to share similar c can reduce the model's sensitivity to channel variations.

After quantization, we concatenate the quantized representation $\tilde{p}^l$ with the original seasonal component s^l to obtain an enhanced representation. We then apply another MLP layer to fuse the concatenated features and project them back to the original hidden dimension d:

$$\tilde{s}^l = \text{Concat}(s^l, \tilde{p}^l), \tag{10}$$

$$s^l \leftarrow \text{MLP}_2(\tilde{s}^l), \tag{11}$$

where $\text{MLP}_2 : \mathbb{R}^{d'+d} \rightarrow \mathbb{R}^d$.

It is worth noting that the trend component mainly contains low-frequency components, such as slow potential drifts in EEG [26] and baseline wander in ECG [14], which exhibit channel-specific variations [26]. Channel aggregation may mix or erase the unique long-term trend information of a channel, thereby reducing the model's ability to capture features. In contrast, the seasonal component often contains rhythmic or periodic patterns, such as heartbeat cycles in ECG and brain oscillations in EEG. These patterns tend to have similarities between different channels [3,23]. Therefore, we apply channel aggregation module only to the seasonal component, while keeping the trend component unchanged. Our ablation studies demonstrate the effectiveness of this method.

4.3 Dual-Direction Multi-scale Fusion Module

To effectively utilize both seasonal and trend components at different scales, we design a dual-direction multi-scale fusion module. In previous modules, each scale of the time series was decomposed into seasonal and trend components. However, these two components exhibit distinct temporal dynamics in medical time series: the seasonal component captures local fluctuations, while the trend component reflects global patterns.

Specifically, for seasonal components, let the high-resolution feature representation be s^i, and the module progressively integrates local details through a series of downsampling and fusion operations:

$$s^{i+1} = \text{GELU}(\text{DownSample}(s^i)) + s^{i+1}. \tag{12}$$

In this way, high-resolution, periodic local information can be progressively integrated across layers to form a representative seasonal feature. For trend components, let the trend representation of the low-resolution layer be t^{i+1}, and the module transfers macroscopic trend information to the higher-resolution layer through upsampling and fusion strategies:

$$t^i = \text{GELU}(\text{UpSample}(t^{i+1})) + t^i. \tag{13}$$

This design makes use of the guiding role of coarse-grained global information in modeling fine-grained trends, thereby helping suppress noise and enhance the robustness of trend features.

After dual-direction fusion, we combine the seasonal and trend components at each scale via element-wise addition to obtain a set of multi-scale representations

$\mathcal{U} = \{u^0, u^1, \ldots, u^L\}$, where u^0 corresponds to the finest scale. For each scale i, we apply a scale-specific projection function to map the representations to a unified dimension to obtain logits $P^i \in \mathbb{R}^K$, where K is the number of classes. To integrate predictions from different scales, we introduce a learnable weight vector $\mathbf{w} = [w^0, w^1, \ldots, w^L]$ to adaptively adjust the magnitude of the contribution of each scale. The final classification output is computed as a weighted sum of logits:

$$\hat{\mathbf{w}} = \text{Softmax}(\mathbf{w}), \tag{14}$$

$$\hat{y} = \text{Softmax}(\sum_{k=0}^{L} \hat{w}^k P^k), \tag{15}$$

where $\hat{\mathbf{w}}$ denotes the normalized importance scores obtained via the softmax function, and $\hat{y}$ is the predicted probabilities.

This design allows the model to simultaneously focus on short-term pathological features at fine scales and long-term trends at coarse scales. Moreover, the weight distribution offers an interpretable perspective by revealing the relative importance of different temporal resolutions for disease classification. This design not only improves accuracy but also provides valuable insights for clinical interpretation.

5 Experiments

5.1 Experimental Setup

In this section, we evaluate our proposed model on four real-world medical time series datasets, including three EEG datasets and one ECG dataset. For data preprocessing, data augmentation, and train-validation-test split, we follow the previous work [34].

Datasets. (1) **APAVA** [9] consists of 5,967 EEG samples from 23 subjects, recorded using 16 channels at a sampling rate of 256 Hz. Each sample is labeled with a binary indicator denoting whether the subject has Alzheimer's disease. (2) **TDBrain** [31] includes 6,240 EEG samples from 72 subjects, recorded using 33 channels at 256 Hz. Each sample is labeled with a binary indicator denoting the presence or absence of Parkinson's disease. (3) **ADFTD** [19] contains 69,762 EEG samples from 88 subjects, recorded using 19 channels at 256 Hz. It provides a three-class label indicating whether the subject is healthy, has frontotemporal dementia, or Alzheimer's disease. (4) **PTB** [11] includes 64,356 ECG samples from 198 subjects, recorded using 15 channels at 250 Hz. Each sample is labeled as either Myocardial Infarction (MI) or non-MI.

Baselines. We compare the proposed MedDPA with 10 state-of-the-art time series models, which are selected from two categories: (1) Transformer-based models, including Crossformer [40], FEDformer [43], Informer [42], iTransformer [17], and Medformer [34]. (2) MLP-based models, including DLinear [38], FreTS [37], LightTS [39], SOFTS [12], and TSMixer [6].

Implementation. All experiments are implemented in PyTorch 2.1.2 and conducted on a server equipped with six NVIDIA RTX A6000 GPUs. We evaluate model performance using six metrics: accuracy, precision, recall, F1 Score, AUROC, and AUPRC. Training and evaluation are conducted on fixed training, validation, and test splits. We adopt the hyperparameter settings used in Medformer. Each model is trained with five different random seeds, and the mean and standard deviation of all metrics are reported.

5.2 Main Results

Settings. Our experiments include two different evaluation settings. In the **subject-dependent** setting, the training, validation, and test sets are split based on samples. Due to the consistency of individual physiological signals, the model can learn subject-specific patterns, resulting in higher accuracy. However, this limits the model's ability to generalize. In the **subject-independent** setting, the training, validation, and test sets are split based on subjects, better simulating real-world applications. It evaluates the generalization ability across different individuals, which is critical for clinical applications. However, large individual differences between subjects reduce the model's accuracy, and personalized features may be overlooked, leading to reduced recognition accuracy for some special individuals.

Results of Subject-Dependent. Since evaluation under this setting is generally easier than the subject-independent setting, we only evaluate the ADFTD dataset for a simple comparison. As shown in Table 1, our method outperforms all baselines across all six metrics, achieving an F1 score of 98.62%.

Results of Subject-Independent. Table 2 shows the results under the subject-independent setting. Overall, our method achieves 17 top-1 out of 24 in total across four datasets, demonstrating strong robustness. For the APAVA dataset, it has few subjects and high variability. Our model achieves significant improvements of 15.01%, 18.71%, and 18.32% in accuracy, recall, and F1 score over the second-best method, showing that our method can effectively separate individual-specific fluctuations from shared temporal patterns in small datasets. On the other hand, TDBrain contains more channels and higher inter-channel redundancy, our prototype-based aggregation compresses redundant signals into representative patterns, achieving the best performance. It is worth noting that

Table 1. Result of subject-dependent setup. The best result is highlighted in bold, and the second best is underlined.

Datasets	Models	Accuracy	Precision	Recall	F1 score	AUROC	AUPRC
ADFTD-Dep	Crossformer	89.35±1.32	89.00±1.44	88.79±1.37	88.88±1.40	97.52±0.58	95.45±1.03
	FEDformer	77.24±1.71	76.35±1.77	76.08±1.43	76.15±1.63	91.31±1.02	84.43±1.57
	Informer	91.61±0.30	91.34±0.39	91.26±0.35	91.27±0.30	98.41±0.07	96.92±0.15
	iTransformer	64.76±0.43	62.36±0.45	62.01±0.38	61.97±0.39	81.46±0.34	68.76±0.47
	Medformer	<u>97.80 ± 0.64</u>	<u>97.68 ± 0.68</u>	<u>97.74 ± 0.66</u>	<u>97.71 ± 0.67</u>	<u>99.87 ± 0.07</u>	<u>99.72 ± 0.13</u>
	DLinear	39.18±0.57	34.95±0.65	34.39±0.46	32.69±0.59	50.35±0.29	34.06±0.29
	FreTS	48.16±1.17	44.91±1.05	43.75±0.76	42.83±0.84	63.03±0.89	45.54±0.71
	LightTS	66.77±0.33	65.91±0.41	64.68±0.66	65.07±0.54	83.34±0.39	72.39±0.58
	SOFTS	66.09±0.49	64.15±0.55	64.06±0.38	64.09±0.46	82.55±0.28	71.04±0.43
	TSMixer	93.81±0.58	93.50±0.62	93.50±0.63	93.49±0.60	99.02±0.16	98.08±0.29
	MedDPA	**98.67±0.15**	**98.63±0.15**	**98.61±0.19**	**98.62±0.16**	**99.91±0.03**	**99.82±0.05**

all models underperform on the ADFTD dataset, likely due to substantial inter-subject variability in rhythmic features. The decomposition process may exacerbate this variability, resulting in performance degradation.

In addition, we plot the heatmap of rankings across all metrics. As shown in Fig. 2, our method achieves the best average ranking across all metrics, further highlighting its strong generalization ability.

5.3 Ablation Study

To evaluate the effectiveness of each proposed module, we conduct ablation experiments on the APAVA and TDBrain datasets. For clarity, "w/o" stands for "without", and "w" stands for "with" in Table 3. As shown in the table, removing the series decomposition module or the channel aggregation module leads to significant performance drops, confirming the importance of both temporal decomposition and channel correlation modeling. Removing the codebook also leads to performance degradation, indicating its role in reducing redundant information. Moreover, applying channel aggregation to the trend component also results in worse performance, indicating that modeling long-term trend correlations across channels may harm the representation quality. Finally, the dual-direction fusion strategy outperforms both one-direction alternatives, highlighting the importance of dual-direction information flow between coarse and fine scales for capturing both global trend and local details. These results demonstrate the contributions of each component in our framework.

Table 2. Result of subject-independent setup. The best result is highlighted in bold, and the second best is underlined.

Datasets	Models	Accuracy	Precision	Recall	F1 score	AUROC	AUPRC
APAVA-Indep	Crossformer	73.57±3.17	78.52±3.37	68.64±3.72	68.54±4.44	72.69±4.88	71.98±4.69
	FEDformer	74.44±2.03	74.24±1.65	72.94±3.49	72.87±3.23	83.70±1.97	82.97±2.27
	Informer	73.46±2.51	75.04±4.23	69.94±2.35	70.35±2.56	71.43±2.86	72.18±2.91
	iTransformer	74.55±1.66	74.77±2.10	71.76±1.72	72.30±1.79	85.59±1.55	84.39±1.57
	Medformer	73.88±3.39	74.10±4.41	71.20±3.09	71.71±3.32	75.79±4.96	76.86±5.29
	DLinear	53.66±0.41	50.31±0.43	50.27±0.38	49.79±0.40	49.57±0.42	49.36±0.32
	FreTS	66.50±0.42	66.94±0.36	61.58±0.66	60.75±0.95	76.41±1.98	75.44±1.94
	LightTS	63.12±3.79	64.93±7.53	57.94±2.46	56.17±2.01	64.99±4.27	64.81±4.29
	SOFTS	73.11±1.37	73.84±1.81	69.83±1.79	70.22±1.85	81.71±2.56	80.60±2.78
	TSMixer	76.67±5.86	77.71±7.29	73.76±5.94	74.48±6.29	86.03±7.15	85.86±7.37
	MedDPA	**89.34±1.05**	**89.91±0.81**	**88.06±1.32**	**88.73±1.19**	**96.02±0.56**	**96.12±0.54**
TDBrain-Indep	Crossformer	82.15±1.96	82.42±1.92	82.15±1.96	82.11±1.98	91.36±1.53	91.67±1.50
	FEDformer	77.58±2.03	77.70±1.95	77.58±2.03	77.56±2.05	86.49±1.92	86.47±2.12
	Informer	87.58±2.19	88.29±1.74	87.58±2.19	87.52±2.24	96.23±0.64	96.38±0.61
	iTransformer	75.04±1.07	75.07±1.07	75.04±1.07	75.04±1.07	83.74±0.78	84.06±0.92
	Medformer	89.10±1.19	89.18±1.15	89.10±1.19	89.10±1.20	96.31±0.33	96.41±0.31
	DLinear	55.90±1.01	56.68±1.18	55.90±1.01	54.59±1.43	59.41±1.10	58.12±1.11
	FreTS	77.54±1.99	77.62±2.01	77.54±1.99	77.53±1.99	87.33±1.46	87.67±1.47
	LightTS	79.85±4.05	80.79±3.64	79.85±4.05	79.67±4.19	90.44±2.87	90.68±2.74
	SOFTS	64.17±2.57	67.53±2.12	64.17±2.57	62.29±3.38	79.47±2.17	77.90±2.73
	TSMixer	79.52±1.33	79.81±1.28	79.52±1.33	79.47±1.34	88.85±1.36	89.03±1.41
	MedDPA	**91.04±3.44**	**91.76±2.76**	**91.04±3.44**	**90.98±3.51**	**96.89±0.99**	**96.95±0.91**
ADFTD-Indep	Crossformer	49.84±1.60	45.34±1.46	45.68±1.41	45.31±1.50	65.86±1.09	47.87±1.19
	FEDformer	44.32±1.77	43.75±1.54	44.52±0.92	43.67±1.36	63.05±1.38	45.20±1.41
	Informer	46.51±1.43	44.84±2.25	42.51±0.88	42.57±1.05	64.37±1.00	45.87±1.51
	iTransformer	52.07±0.66	46.46±0.89	46.83±0.78	46.53±0.81	66.98±0.85	49.41±0.72
	Medformer	52.24±1.10	50.60±1.09	**49.49±1.49**	49.11±1.63	**69.18±1.38**	49.59±1.18
	DLinear	40.15±0.61	36.28±0.62	34.28±0.23	32.79±0.50	50.19±0.20	33.99±0.22
	FreTS	47.23±0.81	44.40±1.47	42.39±0.83	41.89±0.77	60.78±1.09	45.35±1.40
	LightTS	46.51±1.37	44.43±1.28	43.13±0.86	43.29±0.90	60.74±0.87	43.78±1.01
	SOFTS	49.32±0.46	45.62±0.41	44.82±0.14	**49.32±0.46**	63.57±0.26	46.60±0.20
	TSMixer	51.61±1.07	49.23±1.88	48.23±1.80	48.36±1.93	68.22±1.07	**50.73±1.50**
	MedDPA	**54.05±0.45**	**51.38±3.82**	45.24±0.22	48.17±0.09	65.11±0.59	48.88±0.37
PTB-Indep	Crossformer	80.77±1.78	83.88±0.66	72.66±3.33	74.64±3.59	89.20±0.67	87.99±0.96
	FEDformer	74.73±3.52	76.54±4.97	63.79±5.36	63.91±6.80	83.93±4.41	79.89±5.50
	Informer	78.75±0.92	82.86±0.50	69.25±1.48	71.04±1.70	**92.66±0.37**	**90.34±0.45**
	iTransformer	83.02±0.67	**87.52±0.83**	75.18±1.40	77.73±1.34	90.54±1.28	90.24±1.06
	Medformer	79.90±1.15	81.98±0.98	71.76±1.92	73.71±2.09	92.36±0.89	90.12±1.09
	DLinear	74.41±1.43	74.89±1.99	64.09±2.26	64.74±2.83	88.21±0.55	84.15±0.72
	FreTS	79.61±2.13	85.21±0.78	70.08±3.61	71.87±4.19	89.73±0.44	88.25±0.43
	LightTS	75.17±1.97	76.86±2.06	64.81±3.33	65.45±4.31	89.61±1.82	84.59±1.53
	SOFTS	81.51±1.00	85.57±0.53	73.19±1.59	75.53±1.73	90.58±1.21	89.26±0.81
	TSMixer	81.65±0.64	85.10±2.19	73.81±1.60	76.04±1.52	91.37±0.68	89.97±0.51
	MedDPA	**83.48±1.31**	84.23±0.64	**77.67±2.38**	**79.57±2.15**	92.37±0.19	88.23±0.82

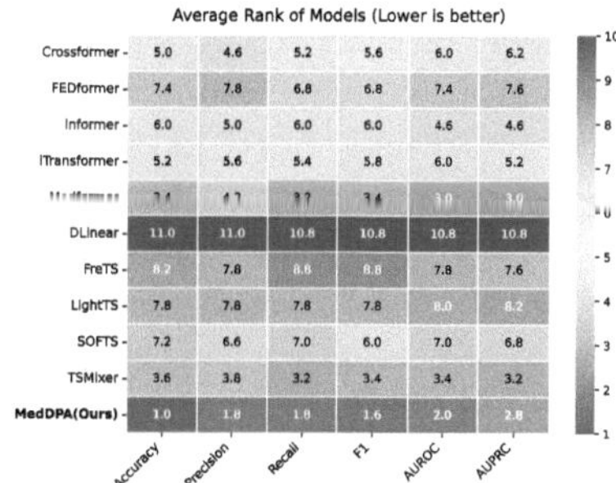

Fig. 2. Average rank across all metrics.

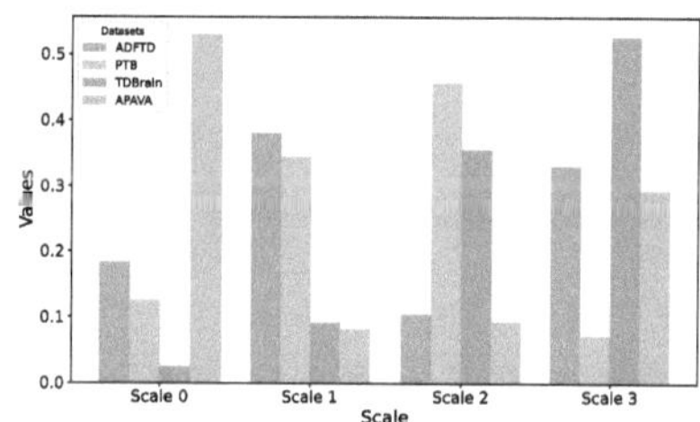

Fig. 3. Scale weights across datasets.

5.4 Additional Experiments

Study of Scale Contributions. We compare the contribution of each scale to the final result across different datasets, as shown in Fig. 3, where scale 0 represents the finest-grained scale. Higher values indicate greater contribution of a given scale. It shows that the contribution of features at different scales varies significantly across datasets. In the TDBrain dataset, coarser-grained features are more important, which may be due to Parkinson's disease being associated with low-frequency EEG rhythms and long-duration activity patterns. In contrast, in the PTB dataset, the coarsest scale has the lowest contribution, possibly because key ECG features, such as the QRS complex and ST segment, are short in duration and lie in high-frequency components. Additionally, for the similar Alzheimer's disease classification datasets, APAVA and ADFTD, the importance of scale 2 and scale 3 is nearly identical. This demonstrates the importance of adaptive weighting in handling diverse disease scenarios.

Table 3. Ablation study results on APAVA and TDBrain.

Datasets	APAVA				TDBrain			
Variants	Accuracy	Precision	Recall	F1 score	Accuracy	Precision	Recall	F1 score
w/o Decomposition	72.24	77.36	67.09	66.78	88.39	88.80	88.39	88.35
w/o Channel Agg	75.10	80.90	70.27	70.48	80.39	85.11	80.39	79.52
w/o Codebook	87.85	88.83	86.26	87.02	89.56	90.93	89.56	89.47
w Trend Agg	85.70	88.80	82.96	84.23	88.96	90.34	88.96	88.82
Coarse-to-Fine	84.28	85.19	82.29	83.15	90.21	91.19	90.21	90.15
Fine-to-Coarse	85.27	85.65	83.77	84.38	83.69	83.48	82.65	82.95
MedDPA	**89.34**	**89.91**	**88.06**	**88.73**	**91.04**	**91.76**	**91.04**	**90.98**

Study of Size of Codebooks. As shown in the Fig. 4, increasing the codebook size within a reasonable range enhances the expressiveness of the prototype representation. This is because a larger codebook provides more prototype vectors, allowing the model to better capture diverse and fine-grained patterns across channels, thereby enhancing the expressiveness ability of the aggregated features. However, an overly large codebook introduces redundancy, which not only degrades performance but also increases model complexity, leading to high computational cost. Therefore, there exists a trade-off between expressiveness and efficiency, and selecting an appropriate codebook size is critical for achieving optimal performance.

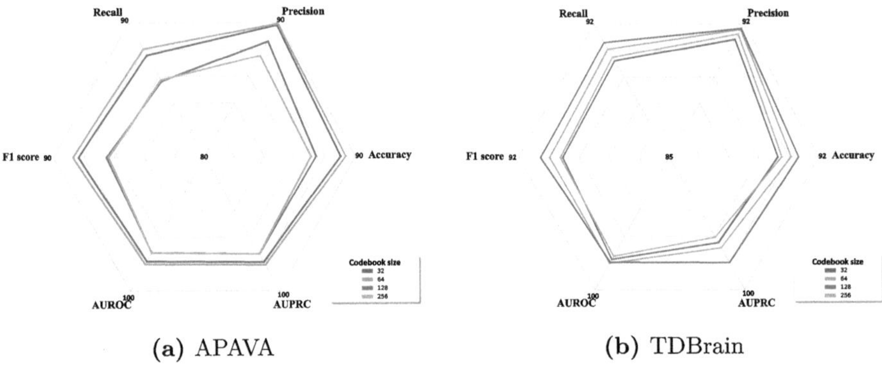

(a) APAVA (b) TDBrain

Fig. 4. Effect of different codebook sizes. (a) and (b) correspond to APAVA and TDBrain datasets respectively.

Study of Number of DownSampling Layers. Figure 5 shows the effect of different numbers of downsampling layers on classification performance. Too few layers may cause the model to fail to fully capture sufficient multi-scale features, weakening global pattern modeling. In contrast, too many layers may result in the loss of subtle yet important signals, especially when processing high temporal resolution data such as EEG. Overall, our results indicate that an appropriate number of downsampling layers can achieve a good balance between local and global features, leading to the best performance in our task.

Model Efficiency. Our MedDPA model demonstrates excellent efficiency, exhibiting consistently low memory and time consumption. Figure 6 presents the memory and time usage of different models on the TDBrain dataset under the same experimental settings, the downsampling layers and codebook size are set to 2 and 128 respectively. It can be observed that although MLP-based models consume fewer resources, they generally suffer from inferior performance. In contrast, Transformer-based models tend to achieve better accuracy but at

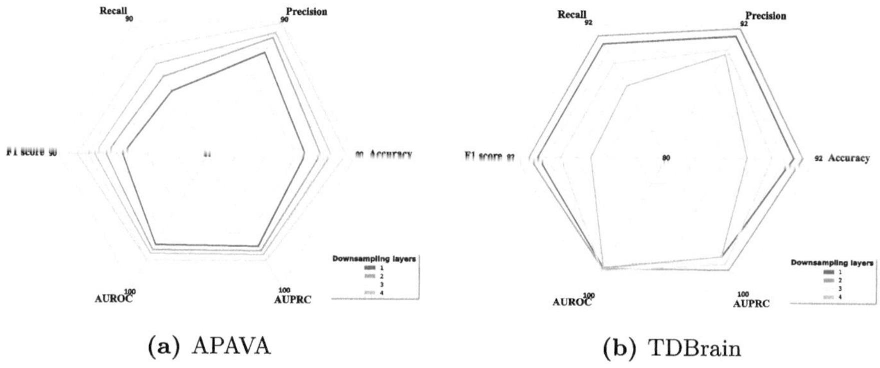

(a) APAVA

(b) TDBrain

Fig. 5. Effect of different downsampling layers. (a) and (b) correspond to APAVA and TDBrian datasets respectively.

the cost of significantly higher memory and time overhead. MedDPA strikes a favorable balance between accuracy and efficiency, highlighting its potential for real-time applications.

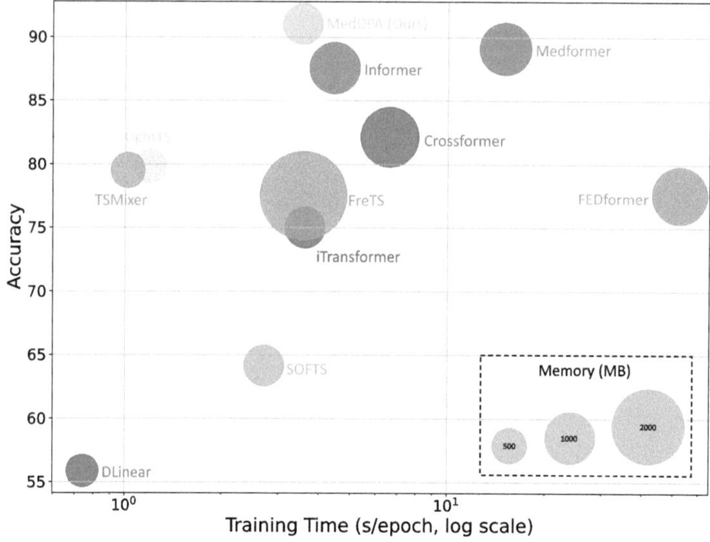

Fig. 6. Memory and time consumption of different models on TDBrain.

6 Conclusion

This paper presents MedDPA, an MLP-based model designed for MedTS classification. From the temporal perspective, we introduce a multi scale decomposition module to explicitly model local fluctuations and global trends. A dual-direction fusion strategy is also employed to integrate information across different temporal scales and adaptively balance their contributions. From the spatial perspective, we propose a prototype-based channel aggregation module with a learnable codebook to reduce noise and redundancy between channels while preserving meaningful patterns. Extensive experiments show consistent performance improvements across multiple datasets, highlighting the superiority, robustness, and applicability of the proposed method in real-world healthcare settings.

Acknowledgements. This work was supported by NSFC grant (No. 62136002 and 62477014), Ministry of Education Research Joint Fund Project (8091B042239), and Fundamental Research Funds for the Central Universities.

References

1. Al-Zaiti, S.S., et al.: Machine learning for ECG diagnosis and risk stratification of occlusion myocardial infarction. Nat. Med. **29**(7), 1804–1813 (2023)
2. Başar, E.: A review of alpha activity in integrative brain function: fundamental physiology, sensory coding, cognition and pathology. Int. J. Psychophysiol. **86**(1), 1–24 (2012)
3. Başar, E.: Brain oscillations in neuropsychiatric disease. Dialogues Clin. Neurosci. **15**(3), 291–300 (2013)
4. Cao, J., et al.: Unsupervised eye blink artifact detection from EEG with Gaussian mixture model. IEEE J. Biomed. Health Inform. **25**(8), 2895–2905 (2021)
5. Chaddad, A., Wu, Y., Kateb, R., Bouridane, A.: Electroencephalography signal processing: a comprehensive review and analysis of methods and techniques. Sensors **23**(14), 6434 (2023)
6. Chen, S.A., Li, C.L., Arik, S.O., Yoder, N.C., Pfister, T.: Tsmixer: an all-MLP architecture for time series forecasting. Trans. Mach. Learn. Res. (2023)
7. Dai, G., Zhou, J., Huang, J., Wang, N.: Hs-CNN: a CNN with hybrid convolution scale for EEG motor imagery classification. J. Neural Eng. **17**(1), 016025 (2020)
8. Demir, A., Koike-Akino, T., Wang, Y., Haruna, M., Erdogmus, D.: EEG-GNN: graph neural networks for classification of electroencephalogram (EEG) signals. In: 2021 43rd Annual International Conference of the IEEE Engineering in Medicine & Biology Society (EMBC), pp. 1061–1067. IEEE (2021)
9. Escudero, J., Abásolo, D., Hornero, R., Espino, P., López, M.: Analysis of electroencephalograms in Alzheimer's disease patients with multiscale entropy. Physiol. Meas. **27**(11), 1091 (2006)
10. Faust, O., Hagiwara, Y., Hong, T.J., Lih, O.S., Acharya, U.R.: Deep learning for healthcare applications based on physiological signals: a review. Comput. Methods Programs Biomed. **161**, 1–13 (2018)
11. Goldberger, A.L., et al.: Physiobank, physiotoolkit, and physionet: components of a new research resource for complex physiologic signals. Circulation **101**(23), e215–e220 (2000)
12. Han, L., Chen, X.Y., Ye, H.J., Zhan, D.C.: Softs: efficient multivariate time series forecasting with series-core fusion. In: The Thirty-eighth Annual Conference on Neural Information Processing Systems (2024)

13. Lai, C.Q., Ibrahim, H., Abdullah, M.Z., Abdullah, J.M., Suandi, S.A., Azman, A.: Artifacts and noise removal for electroencephalogram (EEG): a literature review. In: 2018 IEEE Symposium on Computer Applications & Industrial Electronics (ISCAIE), pp. 326–332. IEEE (2018)
14. Li, Q., Mark, R.G., Clifford, G.D.: Robust heart rate estimation from multiple asynchronous noisy sources using signal quality indices and a Kalman filter. Physiol. Meas. **29**(1), 15 (2007)
15. Liu, X., Wang, W.: Deep time series forecasting models: a comprehensive survey. Mathematics **12**(10), 1504 (2024)
16. Liu, X., Wang, H., Li, Z., Qin, L.: Deep learning in ECG diagnosis: a review. Knowl.-Based Syst. **227**, 107187 (2021)
17. Liu, Y., et al.: itransformer: inverted transformers are effective for time series forecasting. In: The Twelfth International Conference on Learning Representations (2024)
18. Mar, T., Zaunseder, S., Martínez, J.P., Llamedo, M., Poll, R.: Optimization of ECG classification by means of feature selection. IEEE Trans. Biomed. Eng. **58**(8), 2168–2177 (2011)
19. Miltiadous, A., et al.: A dataset of scalp EEG recordings of Alzheimer's disease, frontotemporal dementia and healthy subjects from routine EEG. Data **8**(6), 95 (2023)
20. Miltiadous, A., et al.: Alzheimer's disease and frontotemporal dementia: a robust classification method of EEG signals and a comparison of validation methods. Diagnostics **11**(8), 1437 (2021)
21. Murad, M.M.N., Aktukmak, M., Yilmaz, Y.: Wpmixer: efficient multi-resolution mixing for long-term time series forecasting. In: Proceedings of the AAAI Conference on Artificial Intelligence, vol. 39, pp. 19581–19588 (2025)
22. Padhy, S., Dandapat, S.: Third-order tensor based analysis of multilead ECG for classification of myocardial infarction. Biomed. Signal Process. Control **31**, 71–78 (2017)
23. Palva, S., Palva, J.M.: New vistas for α-frequency band oscillations. Trends Neurosci. **30**(4), 150–158 (2007)
24. Rajpurkar, P., Hannun, A.Y., Haghpanahi, M., Bourn, C., Ng, A.Y.: Cardiologist-level arrhythmia detection with convolutional neural networks. arXiv preprint arXiv:1707.01836 (2017)
25. Rasti-Meymandi, A., Ghaffari, A.: A deep learning-based framework for ECG signal denoising based on stacked cardiac cycle tensor. Biomed. Signal Process. Control **71**, 103275 (2022)
26. Rockstroh, B., Müller, M., Wagner, M., Cohen, R., Elbert, T.: probing the nature of the CNV. Electroencephalogr. Clin. Neurophysiol. **87**(4), 235–241 (1993)
27. Shams, T.B., Hossain, M.S., Mahmud, M.F., Tehjib, M.S., Hossain, Z., Pramanik, M.I.: EEG-based biometric authentication using machine learning: a comprehensive survey. ECTI Trans. Electr. Eng. Electron. Commun. **20**(2), 225–241 (2022)
28. Song, Y., Zheng, Q., Liu, B., Gao, X.: EEG conformer: convolutional transformer for EEG decoding and visualization. IEEE Trans. Neural Syst. Rehabil. Eng. **31**, 710–719 (2022)
29. Subasi, A.: EEG signal classification using wavelet feature extraction and a mixture of expert model. Expert Syst. Appl. **32**(4), 1084–1093 (2007)
30. Van Den Oord, A., Vinyals, O., et al.: Neural discrete representation learning. Adv. Neural Inf. Process. Syst. **30** (2017)

31. Van Dijk, H., Van Wingen, G., Denys, D., Olbrich, S., Van Ruth, R., Arns, M.: The two decades brainclinics research archive for insights in neurophysiology (TDBrain) database. Sci. Data **9**(1), 333 (2022)
32. Wang, S., et al.: Timemixer: decomposable multiscale mixing for time series forecasting. In: The Twelfth International Conference on Learning Representations (2024)
33. Wang, X., Ren, Y., Luo, Z., He, W., Hong, J., Huang, Y.: Deep learning-based EEG emotion recognition: current trends and future perspectives. Front. Psychol. **14**, 1126994 (2023)
34. Wang, Y., Huang, N., Li, T., Yan, Y., Zhang, X.: Medformer: a multi-granularity patching transformer for medical time-series classification. In: The Thirty-Eighth Annual Conference on Neural Information Processing Systems (2024)
35. Wu, H., Hu, T., Liu, Y., Zhou, H., Wang, J., Long, M.: Timesnet: temporal 2D-variation modeling for general time series analysis. In: The Eleventh International Conference on Learning Representations (2023)
36. Xin, Q., Hu, S., Liu, S., Zhao, L., Zhang, Y.D.: An attention-based wavelet convolution neural network for epilepsy EEG classification. IEEE Trans. Neural Syst. Rehabil. Eng. **30**, 957–966 (2022)
37. Yi, K., et al.: Frequency-domain MLPS are more effective learners in time series forecasting. Adv. Neural. Inf. Process. Syst. **36**, 76656–76679 (2023)
38. Zeng, A., Chen, M., Zhang, L., Xu, Q.: Are transformers effective for time series forecasting? In: Proceedings of the AAAI Conference on Artificial Intelligence, vol. 37, pp. 11121–11128 (2023)
39. Zhang, T., et al.: Less is more: fast multivariate time series forecasting with light sampling-oriented MLP structures. arXiv preprint arXiv:2207.01186 (2022)
40. Zhang, Y., Yan, J.: Crossformer: transformer utilizing cross-dimension dependency for multivariate time series forecasting. In: The Eleventh International Conference on Learning Representations (2023)
41. Zhong, B., Wang, P., Wang, X.: Ts-HCL: hierarchical layer-wise contrastive learning for unsupervised domain adaptation on time-series. In: Asia-Pacific Web (APWeb) and Web-Age Information Management (WAIM) Joint International Conference on Web and Big Data, pp. 31–45. Springer (2024)
42. Zhou, H., et al.: Informer: beyond efficient transformer for long sequence time-series forecasting. In: Proceedings of the AAAI Conference on Artificial Intelligence, vol. 35, pp. 11106–11115 (2021)
43. Zhou, T., Ma, Z., Wen, Q., Wang, X., Sun, L., Jin, R.: Fedformer: frequency enhanced decomposed transformer for long-term series forecasting. In: International Conference on Machine Learning, pp. 27268–27286. PMLR (2022)

Knowledge Graph and Hypergraph Enabled Semantic Modeling for Dual-Intent Recommendation

Xianji Cui, Jinhua Zhang, Yan Lan, and Shan Huang(✉)

Dalian Minzu University, Dalian, China
huangshan@dlnu.edu.cn

Abstract. Recommendation systems rely on modeling user behavior to deliver personalized suggestions, with latent intention disentanglement being pivotal for performance enhancement. However, two challenges remain: 1) insufficient multidimensional semantic fusion for fine-grained intention representation; 2) implicit feedback sparsity limiting intention characterization. To address these issues, this paper proposes a dual-intent recommendation framework integrating knowledge graph and hypergraph modeling semantics (KHSDIR), comprising three modules: First, a hypergraph of user-item-group interactions is constructed to characterize social semantics, while linking item-side knowledge graphs to represent entity semantics; Second, social-semantic-enhanced user representations and knowledge-aware item representations are utilized to model collective intentions (capturing common preferences) and individual intentions (capturing personalized preferences), with a designed dual-intent fusion mechanism to achieve fine-grained characterizations; Finally, to mitigate the impact of data sparsity and enable better intention disentangling, graph contrastive regularization techniques are employed, along with a knowledge-based multi-view contrast and bidirectional intention-aware contrast mechanism to further constrain the consistency among users, items and intentions. Experiments on four datasets demonstrate that the KHSDIR has superiority over state-of-the-art methods, providing new insights for disentangled intention modeling.

Keywords: Recommender Systems · Intent Modeling · Knowledge Graph · Hypergraph Modeling · Contrastive Learning

1 Introduction

Recommendation systems provide personalized recommendation services based on user interests [1]. As a classic paradigm in recommendation systems, Collaborative Filtering (CF) [2] based on user-item interaction matrices [3] to model features. Like LightGCN [4] that leverage Graph Convolutional Networks (GCN) to mine high-order interaction patterns, techniques such as NCL [5] and LightGCL [6] that optimize embedding representations via Contrastive Learning (CL),

J. Li et al. (Eds.): APWeb-WAIM 2025, LNCS 16115, pp. 179–196, 2026.
https://doi.org/10.1007/978-981-95-5719-6_12

and HCCF [7] that employ graph structures to model high-order relationships, continuously advancing the development of recommendation algorithms.

In recent years, intention-aware recommendation has made significant progress by exploring the driving factors behind user behavior. Existing studies tend to disentangle user multiple intention representations, such as DICE [9], DGCF [10], and DCCF [11]. Building on these efforts, BIGCF [12] has further decoupled intentions into collective and individual dimensions, and proposes the concepts of collective intentions (i.e., peer influence) and individual intentions (i.e., individual characteristics).

While existing intention modeling has advanced recommendation optimization, key limitations remain: **(1) It overlooks the synergy of multidimensional semantics in user decision making.** User decisions are driven by social contexts (e.g. peer influence) and objective item features (e.g. individual characteristics), social semantics and entity semantics. Group-based recommendation has demonstrated that its rich social semantics positively impact the characterization of high-quality user embeddings [13,14]; Knowledge Graphs (KG) rely on their powerful semantic representation and knowledge correlation capabilities, are widely applied in the recommendation field [15–17], and demonstrate that the entity semantic information can supplement item representations with contextual semantics [18]. Figure 1 illustrates a semantic-influenced recommendation process.

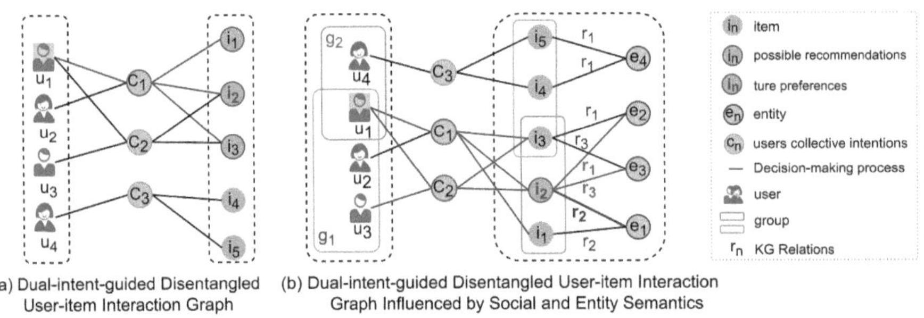

Fig. 1. A recommendation process influenced by multidimensional semantics.

Figure 1(b) demonstrates that integrating dual-intent modeling of social and entity semantics—compared to the framework in Fig. 1(a)—enhances recommendation accuracy and interpretability. The reason is that under the influence of dual-intent-guided recommendations, it further takes into account the social relationship u_3 of u_1 and the $\{i_2, r_2, e_1\}$ characteristics of i_2 that distinguish it from i_3. Existing studies on intention modeling have failed to effectively integrate the social semantics with KG entity semantic correlations.

(2) Sparse data constrains intention representation and induces redundancy [12,17]. Sparse implicit feedback renders intention modeling susceptible to noise. Although self-supervised intention modeling mitigates this via data augmentation [5,19], random perturbations often disrupt structural semantics, inducing representational bias in intentions.

The KHSDIR model is proposed, with the following contributions:

1. **Multidimensional Semantic Enhancement:** Aiming at the problem of incomplete dual-intent disentanglement caused by insufficient multidimensional semantic fusion, social semantics are modeled through hypergraphs, and entity semantics are characterized by combining KG, with a multi-layer propagation mechanism adopted to achieve semantic encoding.

2. **Intent Disentanglement and Fusion:** To disentangle dual intents, embedding representations are enhanced with multidimensional semantics, a dynamic gating mechanism is proposed for supplementing individual intention modeling, and a dual-intent fusion mechanism is utilized to realize user and item representations.

3. **Intention-aware Contrastive Learning Mechanism:** To alleviate the intention representation noise caused by data sparsity, Graph Contrastive Regularization (GCR) and a bidirectional intention-aware CL are leveraged, and knowledge-based multi-view CL is proposed to enhance intention representations.

4. **Experimental Validation:** Experiments on four datasets demonstrate that KHSDIR improves recommendation performance compared with existing state-of-the-art methods, validating the effectiveness of fusing multidimensional semantics to disentangle intentions in complex scenarios.

2 Related Work

Technically, we review the evolution of recommendation systems from traditional CF to deep neural network-driven high-order representation learning.

Semantic Enhancement of CF and Graph Structure Modeling
Early CF method fail to capture semantic correlations for quality embeddings [3,20]. GCN-based models like LightGCN [4] and NGCF [21] model high-order interactions through neighborhood aggregation mechanisms to learn graph-structured data. CGSL [22] model leverages prototype-based CL to capture underlying semantic structures, thereby enhancing the quality of embeddings. However, their reliance on bipartite graphs restricts external semantic integration. While hypergraphs enable structured social semantic representation [23], they underutilize item-side attribute semantics.

KG bridge the semantic integration gap. Models such as KGIN [17] use KG embedding for relation-aware aggregation, KGAN [16] employs knowledge grouping for interpretable recommendation, and KGAT [24] fuses user-item interactions with heterogeneous KG. These methods enhance user-item associations via semantic reasoning, demonstrating KG' efficacy in enriching item semantics and alleviating data sparsity.

Intention Modeling and Disentanglement:
Intention-aware recommendation employs disentanglement to separate user intentions for interpretability. Models like DGCF [10], DCCF [11], and ICLRec [19]. Leveraging hypergraphs for high-order dependencies, HCCF [7] combines hypergraphs with self-supervised CL to enhance latent intentions. Leveraging rich interpretable knowledge in KG, KHIM [8] designs hierarchical user intent modeling to extract universal and personalized preferences from attribute tuples at global and local levels, respectively. Causal reasoning methods (e.g. DICE [9], BIGCF [12]) separate user interests from consistencies via causal embeddings. BIGCF further distinguishes collective and individual intentions causally and strengthens representations through graph reconstruction. Existing approaches miss fine-grained semantic distinctions in intentions and fail to explicitly disentangle their origins, hindering granular modeling.

Self-supervised Learning for Recommendation Enhancement
Self-supervised learning (SSL) enhances model discriminability. Models like NCL [5] construct contrastive objectives via graph neighborhoods and semantic similarities, LightGCL [6] improves CL with singular value decomposition, IHGCL [25] model integrates CL with intent modeling, enhancing recommendations by capturing intents embedded in meta-paths. While these methods strengthen intention representation robustness, complex data augmentation introduces noise, causing representation bias.

3 Methodology

3.1 Problem Formulation

Interaction Data: In recommendation scenario, let $U = \{u_1, u_2, \ldots, u_J\}$, $I = \{i_1, i_2, \ldots, i_K\}$, and $G = \{g_1, g_2, \ldots, g_T\}$ denote users, items, and groups sets, with sizes J, K and T respectively. The interaction matrix $R \in \mathbb{R}^{J \times K}$ is defined as $R_{jk} = 1$ if u_j interacted with i_k, otherwise, $R_{jk} = 0$. Define the hypergraph as $HG = (V, B, H)$, where V is the vertex set and B is the hyperedge set. Its incidence matrix $H = [h_{vb}] \in \mathbb{R}^{|V| \times |b|}$ satisfies $h_{vb} = 1$ if hyperedge b connects vertex v, otherwise $h_{vb} = 0$. $X \in \mathbb{R}^{(J+T) \times T}$ and $Y \in \mathbb{R}^{(K+T) \times T}$ are constructed from user-group and item-group interactions, respectively. Let $KG = \{(h, r, t) \mid h, t \in \delta, r \in \mathfrak{R}\}$, where h, r and t corresponds to the head entity, relation, and tail entity in a knowledge triple, δ and $\mathfrak{R}$ represent the entity and relation sets, respectively.

Recommendation Task: Abstracting user-item interactions as a bipartite graph, transforming the recommendation task into predicting edge existence probability in the interaction graph:

$$P(\hat{R}|E^{(0)}, R) = \prod_{u \in U} \prod_{i \in I} P(\hat{R}_{ui}|e_u, e_i) \tag{1}$$

where $E^{(0)} = \{E_U^{(0)}, E_I^{(0)}\}$ is the initial embedding and $\hat{R}$ is the reconstructed interaction graph. User-item interactions are influenced by social semantics and entity semantics and driven by intentions. Thus, such influences should be considered in prediction, the KHSDIR model leverages this to predict likelihood.

3.2 KHSDIR Model

KHSDIR is proposed, which models multidimensional semantic information through hypergraphs and KG, uses the semantics to enhance collective and individual intentions modeling, integrates dual intentions to characterize user and item embeddings, and makes predictions, as shown in Fig. 2.

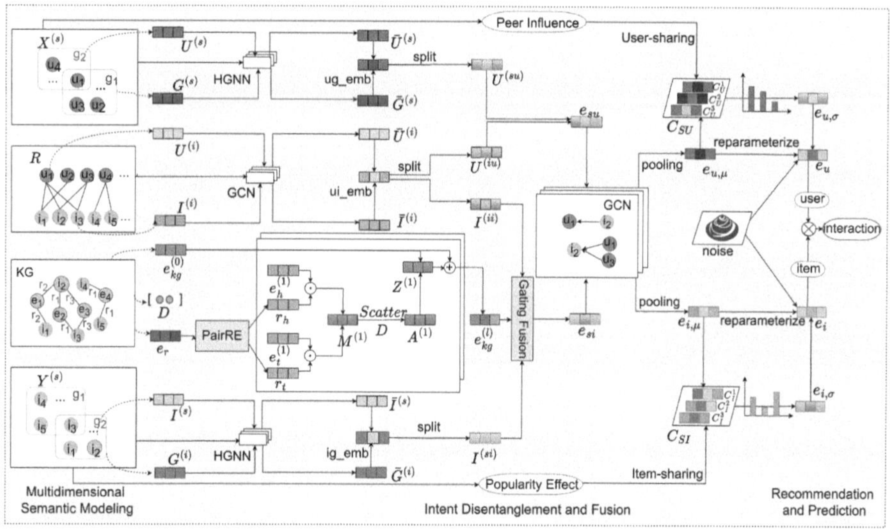

Fig. 2. The KHSDIR model architecture diagram.

Multidimensional Semantic Modeling. The Semantic Modeling models social and entity semantics to support for dual-intent representations.

(1)Social Semantic Modeling: Group information is integrated to model the multivariate relationships among users, items, and groups. Given the complexity of tripartite interactions, hypergraphs are employed to construct the interactions.

We model the hypergraph to store social semantics and utilize $UG^{(s)} = (V^{(s)}, B^{(s)}, H^{(s)})$ to model the user-group interactions, where the nodes in this hypergraph include all users and groups $V^{(s)} = U \bigcup G$. Based on the definition of hypergraphs, $X^{(s)} = [h_{va}^{(s)}] \in \mathbb{R}^{(J+T)\times T}$ is defined as the user-group hypergraph matrix. Similarly, the item-group hypergraph is defined as $IG^{(s)} = (V^{(s)}, B^{(s)}, H^{(s)})$, with the matrix $Y^{(s)} \in \mathbb{R}^{(K+T)\times T}$. Hypergraph Neural Networks (HGNNs) [26] are employed for semantic propagation. It collects node features via hyperedges, generates messages through nonlinear transformations, and updates node features using a propagation mechanism. By integrating group features, the propagation of social semantic signals at the group level is achieved.

(2)Entity Semantic Modeling: KG is constructed to enhance the semantic representation of item entities. Leveraging the PairRE method [27], entity and relation vector embeddings in real space are learned.

KG entity embeddings are initialized as $e_{kg}^{(0)}$. For each edge, the embeddings of the head and tail entity are denoted as $e_h^{(0)}$ and $e_t^{(0)}$ (i.e., extracted from $e_{kg}^{(0)}$), respectively. The edge index matrix is denoted as D, and the embedding vector of the relation type is e_r. Relation embeddings are projected into the Euclidean space as pairwise vectors for each layer l:

$$r_h = W_r^{head} e_r, \quad r_t = W_r^{tail} e_r \tag{2}$$

where W_r^{head} and W_r^{tail} are mapping functions from relation types to projection spaces. Next, element-wise multiplication $\odot$ is used to fuse entity embeddings with relation projections, generating edge-level semantic messages $M^{(l)}$. Moreover, sparse aggregation is employed to aggregate edge messages to the head entities based on the edge index matrix D, thereby achieving neighborhood information integration:

$$M^{(l)} = e_h^{(l-1)} \odot r_h + e_t^{(l-1)} \odot r_t, \quad A^{(l)} = Scatter(M^{(l)}, D) \tag{3}$$

The Scatter function groups $M^{(l)}$ according to head entity indices and computes their mean. Finally, the aggregated neighborhood embeddings $A^{(l)}$ and entity embeddings $e_{kg}^{(l-1)}$ are concatenated and fed into a linear transformation layer:

$$Z^{(l)} = LeakyReLU\left(W_a^{(l)} \left[e_{kg}^{(l-1)} \parallel A^{(l)}\right]\right), \quad e_{kg}^{(l)} = e_{kg}^{(l-1)} + Z^{(l)} \tag{4}$$

where $\parallel$ denotes the concatenation operation, $W_a^{(l)}$ is the weight matrix. An activation function (LeakyReLU) is introduced for non-linearity, historical information is retained through residual connections, and finally, $e_{kg}^{(l)}$ is obtained via these residual connections. This process enhances the semantic representation of item entities by integrating KG structural information.

Intent Disentanglement and Fusion. This section integrates social and entity semantics to encode social and interest features of users and items. Collective intention parameters are then abstracted from group information, enabling intention disentanglement and dynamic fusion.

(1) Multidimensional Semantic-aware Individual Intention Modeling: It is posited that each user, item, and group contains dual information of social-side and interest-side [23]. Thus, group-side embeddings and individual-side embeddings for users and items are derived.

In the embedding layer, U, I and G are defined to represent the raw embeddings of users, items, and groups, respectively. Dual information from these raw embeddings is extracted to obtain the social-side and interest-side representations of items, $i_k^{(s)}$ and $i_k^{(i)}$, similarly, the social-side and interest-side embeddings for users u_j and groups g_t are obtained as $u_j^{(s)}$, $u_j^{(i)}$ and $g_t^{(s)}$, $g_t^{(i)}$, respectively.

Based on the item-group hypergraph matrix $Y^{(s)}$ and HGNNs, we enhance the social-side representations $I^{(s)}(i_k^{(s)} \in I^{(s)})$, $G^{(i)}(g_t^{(i)} \in G^{(i)})$ of items and groups to obtain fused social semantic representations $\bar{I}^{(s)}$ and $\bar{G}^{(i)}$. The updated social-side representations are updated through the following methods:

$$\bar{I}^{(s)}, \bar{G}^{(i)} = HGNN_{\Theta}\left(\left[I^{(s)} \parallel G^{(i)}\right], Y^{(s)}\right) \tag{5}$$

The $\bar{I}^{(s)}$ and $\bar{G}^{(i)}$ are concatenated to form a comprehensive embedding, which is then split according to the number of items and groups. Then, the item-group-side embeddings $I^{(si)}$ are obtained. By analogy, the user-group-side embeddings $U^{(su)}$ is derived. Then, the user interest-side embeddings $U^{(i)}(u_j^{(i)} \in U^{(i)})$, item interest-side embeddings $I^{(i)}(i_k^{(i)} \in I^{(i)})$, and R are fed into a GCN to obtain the updated user-individual-side embeddings $U^{(iu)}$ and item-individual-side embeddings $I^{(ii)}$.

The above process realizes the embedding update incorporating social semantic information. Give in that interaction prediction depends on both history and entity semantics, therefore, in the individual intention modeling, the item knowledge-enhanced embedding $K^{(l)} = e_{kg}^{(l)}$ is utilized, which is derived from the entity semantic modeling module. To effectively fuse item information from different sources, this paper integrates $I^{(ii)}$, $I^{(si)}$, and $K^{(l)}$ via a dynamic gating mechanism. Given that the contributions of different semantic information sources vary significantly across scenarios, the dynamic gating mechanism adaptively adjusts weight allocation. It enhances the model's adaptability and robustness in complex interaction scenarios by learning the importance weights of each information source in an end-to-end manner. Details are as follows:

We define a fusion gate module that concatenates three embeddings as inputs to the fusion gate, yielding a fusion gate weight vector:

$$g = \sigma\left(W_g\left[I^{(ii)} \parallel I^{(si)} \parallel K^{(l)}\right] + b\right) \tag{6}$$

where $\left[I^{(ii)} \parallel I^{(si)} \parallel K^{(l)}\right]$ is the input feature, W_g is the weight matrix of the linear layer, b is the bias vector, σ is the Sigmoid activation function, and the output is a scalar gating weight $g \in (0, 1)$. The item embeddings are weighted and fused according to the fusion gate weights to yield the final item embedding:

$$e_{si} = g \cdot \left[I^{(ii)} \parallel I^{(si)}\right] + (1 - g) \cdot (W_k K^{(l)}) \tag{7}$$

where W_k is the dimension transformation matrix that maps the d-dimensional knowledge-enhanced embedding $K^{(l)}$ to a 2d-dimensional space, and $\cdot$ denotes scalar multiplication. Through the above fusion approach, the weights are dynamically adjusted to fully leverage item information from different sources, further enhancing the model's ability to understand items. In the meanwhile, user embeddings e_{su} are obtained by concatenating $U^{(su)}$ and $U^{(iu)}$.

With the support of variational inference, e_{si} and e_{su} are employed to perform high-order relational aggregation via LightGCN and encoded based on a Gaussian distribution, the final individual intention embedding representations of users and items $e_{u,\mu}$ and $e_{i,\mu}$ are obtained.

(2) Social Semantic-enhanced Collective Intention Modeling: Intention modeling explicitly captures the alignment between individual traits and group commonalities. Collective intentions are extracted from hypergraphs, leveraging embedded social semantics to enhance user-item commonalities. Consequently, abstracted collective intention sets C_{SU} and C_{SI} are obtained for users and items, respectively. By calculating the correlation scores between individual intention embeddings and collective intentions, the likelihood of user interactions influenced by collective intentions —$P(C_{SU}^k|e_{u,\mu})$ and $P(C_{SI}^k|e_{i,\mu})$—is quantified, with $k \in K$ defining the size of the intention set.

(3) Dual-intent Fusion Mechanism: To achieve the in-depth fusion of dual intentions. The affinity between user-item interactions and each intention is calculated via collective intentions $P(C_{SU}^k|e_{u,\mu})$ and $P(C_{SI}^k|e_{i,\mu})$, and the personalized intention embeddings of users and items, $e_{u,\sigma}$ and $e_{i,\sigma}$, are obtained.

$$e_{u,\sigma} = \sum_{k \in |K|} P(C_{SU}^k \mid e_{u,\mu}) \cdot C_{SU}^k,\; e_{i,\sigma} = \sum_{k \in |K|} P(C_{SI}^k \mid e_{i,\mu}) \cdot C_{SI}^k \tag{8}$$

Based on the variational inference, the encoded individual and personalized intention embeddings are regarded as Gaussian distribution parameters. The mean $e_{u,\mu}$ reflects likelihood, and the variance $e_{u,\sigma}$ quantifies uncertainty.

Recommendation and Prediction. Reparameterization is employed to circumvent the backpropagation problem:

$$e_u = e_{u,\mu} + e_{u,\sigma} \otimes \varepsilon_u,\; e_i = e_{i,\mu} + e_{i,\sigma} \otimes \varepsilon_i \tag{9}$$

where ε_u and ε_i are the introduced noise variable; $\otimes$ denotes the element-wise product. The inner product calculation is performed using the user and item embeddings, thereby achieving prediction:

$$P(\hat{R}_{ui}|e_u, e_i) = Sigmoid(e_u^T e_i) \tag{10}$$

where e_u and e_i are the dual-intent embedded representations of users and items, respectively, and $\hat{R}_{ui}$ is the reconstructed interaction matrix between users and items.

Contrastive Learning Mechanism Design. To tackle implicit data sparsity's impact on intention representation, an intention-aware CL mechanism is introduced for recommendation. Through the application of regularization and InfoNCE loss, the CL mechanism depicted in Fig. 3 is proposed.

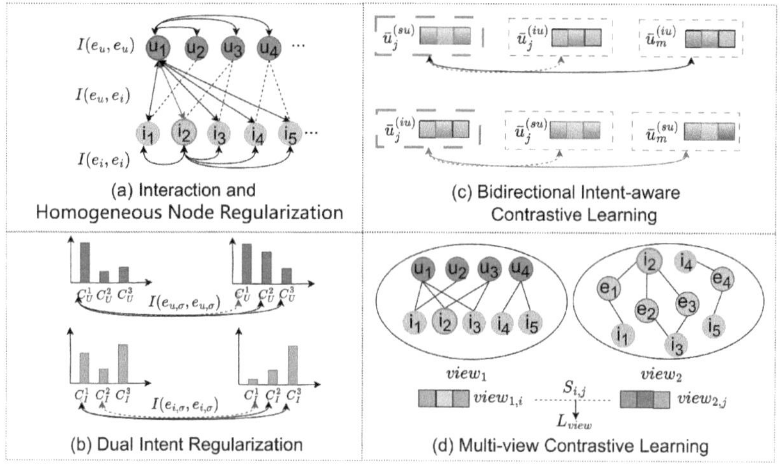

Fig. 3. Intention-aware contrastive learning mechanism.

(1) Graph Contrastive Regularization: To address embedding concentration and the Matthew effect caused, interaction and homogeneous node regularization are employed, $I(e_u, e_i)$, $I(e_u, e_u)$ and $I(e_i, e_i)$. To address the issue of intention redundancy in dual-intent modeling, employ dual intent regularization $I(e_{u,\sigma}, e_{u,\sigma})$ and $I(e_{i,\sigma}, e_{i,\sigma})$. The above process is shown in Figs. 3(a) and 3(b). From this addition, L_{int} is obtained.

(2) Bidirectional Intent-aware Contrastive Learning: Since the model incorporates dual intentions with semantic representations, it is necessary to minimize the distance between the user's group and individual side embeddings, as shown in Fig. 3(c). Contrastive losses are designed from the individual perspectives of users:

$$L_{bcl}^{(user)_1} = -\sum_{u_j \in U} \log \frac{\exp(\text{sim}(\bar{u}_j^{(su)}, \bar{u}_j^{(iu)})/\tau)}{\sum_{u_m \in U/u_j} \exp(\text{sim}(\bar{u}_j^{(su)}, \bar{u}_m^{(iu)})/\tau)} \tag{11}$$

where $\bar{u}_j^{(su)}$ denotes the user-group-side embedding, $\bar{u}_j^{(iu)}$ denotes the user-individual-side embedding, U is the set of users, U/u_j is the set of users excluding u_j, τ represents a predefined coefficient, and sim(,) denotes the cosine similarity. Similarly, obtain the group representation of perspectives of users $L_{bcl}^{(user)_2}$, and generate them to get the total user-side loss $L_{bcl}^{(user)}$. The item loss $L_{bcl}^{(item)}$ is calculated in the same manner. This design achieves structured separation and unification of social-semantic-integrated embedding representations.

(3) Knowledge-based Multi-view Contrastive Learning: To align the original item representations with knowledge-enhanced semantics, two complementary views are constructed. We normalize the original item embedding matrix to obtain the original item $view_1$. Meanwhile, leveraging the multi-layer propagation mechanism of KG information, the knowledge-enhanced $view_2$ is obtained. Then the pairwise similarity matrix S is computed as: $S_{ij} = \frac{\langle view_{1,i}, view_{2,j} \rangle}{\tau}$. where $\langle , \rangle$ denotes the dot product, $view_{1,i}$ represents the vector representation of the i-th item in $view_1$. A symmetric contrastive loss is employed:

$$L_{view} = \frac{1}{2N} \sum_{i=1}^{N} (-\log \frac{\exp(s_{ii})}{\sum_{j=1}^{N} \exp(s_{ij})} - \log \frac{\exp(s_{ii})}{\sum_{j=1}^{N} \exp(s_{ji})}) \tag{12}$$

where N denotes the number of items in a batch. The above process is shown in Fig. 3(d). This bidirectional objective maximizes mutual information between corresponding items while minimizing agreement with negative samples, effectively aligning knowledge and item representations.

3.3 Multi-task Joint Training

To enhance the model's generalization ability, a multi-task joint training strategy is employed to jointly optimize the recommendation and CL tasks. For the recommendation task, the negative log-likelihood loss is adopted and defined as L_{rec}. The three tasks—the recommendation task, GCR task, and CL task—are jointly optimized. The total training loss is defined as:

$$L_{total} = L_{rec} + \lambda_1 L_{int} + \lambda_2 L_{bcl}^{(user)} + \lambda_3 L_{bcl}^{(item)} + \lambda_4 L_{view} \tag{13}$$

4 Experiments

This section presents the experimental settings and results of the KHSDIR model, addressing the following research questions:

RQ 1: How does KHSDIR's performance compare with existing recommendation methods?
RQ 2: What are the impacts of KHSDIR components on model performance?
RQ 3: How do various hyperparameter settings affect model performance?

Table 1. Statistical data of the datasets.

Dataset	Mafengwo	Weeplaces	Steam	MOOC
Users	1269	1501	11099	14321
Groups	972	4651	1085	184
Items	999	6406	2351	3603
User-Group Interactions	5574	12258	57654	18767
User-Item Interactions	8676	43942	444776	301577
Group-Item Belongings	2540	6033	22318	8147

4.1 Experimental Settings

Datasets. To validate the model's effectiveness, three datasets with group information—Mafengwo, Steam, and Weeplaces [23]—are employed. Mafengwo and Weeplaces record users' social network travel histories, while Steam captures player-game interaction histories. Their statistical details are presented in Table 1.

The MOOC dataset is derived from MOOCCube. Inspired by the GroupIM model's [28] user grouping method, it groups users and extracts 4,069 entities and four types of relationship data related to interactive items from MOOCCube, constructing 14,412 triples. All explicit feedback in the data is converted into implicit feedback. Recall@K and NDCG@K are used to evaluate the performance.

Baselines. The KHSDIR model is compared with the following baselines to validate its effectiveness.

Traditional MF Recommendation:

(1) MF [3]: It regards user-item interactions as isolated data instances and only uses ID embeddings for inner product prediction.

GCN-based Recommendation:

(2) LightGCN [4]: By removing redundant operations in the GCN, it aggregates user-item interaction information for lightweight graph propagation.
(3) GTN [29]: It achieves the adaptive generation of heterogeneous graph and representation learning through an graph propagation mechanism.

Based on Intention Modeling Recommendation:

(4) DICE [9]: It proposes a framework for separating user interests and consistencies and uses the Bayesian Personalized Ranking loss function to decouple intention representations.
(5) DCCF [11]: By learning disentangled representations with global context, it extracts latent intention information from self-supervised signals.

(6) HCCF [7]: It models the high-order dependency relationships by constructing hypergraph and combines SSL to enhance intention representations.
(7) ICLRec [19]: It proposes an intentional CL method. It learns the intention distribution by modeling and clustering user behavior sequences and optimizes the model using SSL.
(8) BIGCF [12]: It subdivides the motivations of user-item interactions into collective and individual intentions, and enhances representation learning via graph reconstruction.

Based on Contrastive Learning Recommendation:

(9) NCL [5]: It improves performance through structural and semantic CL.
(10) LightGCL [6]: It conducts graph enhancement via SVD to address the limitations of random perturbations and heuristic strategies in existing methods.

Hyperparameter Settings. The model is implemented in the PyTorch. The embedding and batch size of the model are set to 32 and 10240, respectively. The default optimizer is Adam with a learning rate of $1e^{-3}$, initialized by the Xavier method. The number of GCN and KG information propagation layers are set in {1,2,3,4}, and the number of intentions K is selected from {4,8,16,32,64}. The GCR weight λ_1 range from {0.2,0.3,0.4,0.5}, and the loss weights λ_2, λ_3, and λ_4 undergo grid search in {0,0.0001,0.001,0.01,0.1,1}. For the four datasets of Mafengwo, Steam, Weeplaces, and MOOC, the number of latent intents |K| is set to 16, 8, 16, and 8, respectively; the number of training epochs is set to 50, 100, 200, and 50, respectively; the number of GCN and KG information propagation layers is set to 2; and the GCR weight λ_1 is set to 0.2.

4.2 Performance Comparisons(RQ1)

This section presents a comparison between KHSDIR and baselines, results shown in Table 2. Given data constraints, the Mafengwo, Weeplaces, and Steam datasets are used to assess the impact of social semantics, the MOOC dataset is used to evaluate the effects of multidimensional semantics on model performance.

Comparison with GCN-based Models: KHSDIR outperforms LightGCN and GTN across all metrics, highlighting that KHSDIR leverages hypergraphs to model group information, introducing social semantics. Its iterative GCN approach for capturing tuple-level collaborative relationships better captures users' dynamic preferences.

Comparison with Intention-Aware Models: Compared with DICE and DCCF, the KHSDIR model demonstrates significant performance improvement. On the Steam dataset, its N@10 score (0.7445) surpasses DICE and HCCF by 71.19% and 36.86%, respectively. This highlights that, KHSDIR's approach of integrating multidimensional semantics can enhance dual-intention representations. The HCCF model demonstrates excellent performance in handling the

Table 2. Performance comparison on different datasets (Bold values indicate the best performance)

Dataset	Metric	MF	LightGCN	GTN	DICE	DCCF	HCCF	ICLRec	BIGCF	NCL	LightGCL	**KHSDIR**
Mafengwo	R@5	0.0086	0.1005	0.0572	0.0340	0.0454	0.1964	0.1981	0.2473	0.3008	0.2078	**0.4237**
	R@10	0.0221	0.1744	0.1190	0.0474	0.0657	0.2350	0.3090	0.3130	0.4552	0.3599	**0.5000**
	R@20	0.0297	0.2584	0.1728	0.0788	0.1016	0.2871	0.4646	0.3457	**0.6447**	0.5507	0.6262
	N@5	0.0287	0.2009	0.1420	0.0228	0.0337	0.1494	0.1135	0.1766	0.2076	0.1855	**0.7660**
	N@10	0.0320	0.2168	0.1533	0.0270	0.0402	0.1592	0.1497	0.1986	0.2575	0.2448	**0.7182**
	N@20	0.0319	0.2337	0.1611	0.0349	0.0489	0.1777	0.1892	0.2069	0.3098	0.3090	**0.7025**
Weeplaces	R@5	0.0014	0.0105	0.0056	0.0570	0.0253	0.1454	0.0245	0.1446	0.2209	0.1538	**0.2318**
	R@10	0.0020	0.0128	0.0098	0.0834	0.0336	0.2043	0.0412	0.2132	**0.3770**	0.2244	0.3225
	R@20	0.0043	0.0211	0.0141	0.1142	0.0474	0.2944	0.0629	0.2903	**0.5072**	0.3103	0.4563
	N@5	0.0103	0.0398	0.0365	0.0638	0.0291	0.1668	0.0197	0.1630	0.1812	0.1737	**0.6357**
	N@10	0.0082	0.0333	0.0333	0.0709	0.0309	0.1735	0.0250	0.1788	0.2300	0.1901	**0.5830**
	N@20	0.0078	0.0310	0.0288	0.0813	0.0354	0.2071	0.0305	0.2050	0.2671	0.2186	**0.5700**
Steam	R@5	0.0070	0.0594	0.0640	0.3599	0.1005	**0.4184**	0.3863	0.2582	0.1223	0.3866	0.2776
	R@10	0.0148	0.1034	0.1000	0.4630	0.1342	**0.5308**	0.4989	0.3176	0.1758	0.4510	0.4323
	R@20	0.0278	0.1595	0.1475	0.5542	0.1755	**0.6260**	0.5832	0.3801	0.2498	0.5099	0.5509
	N@5	0.0333	0.2205	0.2294	0.4150	0.1305	0.5396	0.2982	0.3142	0.0950	0.5154	**0.7796**
	N@10	0.0344	0.2140	0.2104	0.4349	0.1362	0.5440	0.3346	0.3208	0.1140	0.5041	**0.7445**
	N@20	0.0377	0.2140	0.2054	0.4590	0.1474	0.5607	0.3560	0.3357	0.1366	0.5097	**0.7231**
MOOC	R@5	0.0060	0.0309	0.0329	0.0025	0.0184	0.0358	0.2558	0.4333	0.3186	0.3249	**0.4550**
	R@10	0.0115	0.0446	0.0471	0.0042	0.0304	0.0474	0.3959	0.5569	0.4596	0.4532	**0.6006**
	R@20	0.0188	0.0626	0.0679	0.0073	0.0469	0.0664	0.5246	0.6714	0.6181	0.5880	**0.7320**
	N@5	0.0393	0.1927	0.1991	0.0283	0.1443	0.2387	0.1527	0.4319	0.3580	0.5808	**0.7898**
	N@10	0.0403	0.1685	0.1764	0.0265	0.1328	0.2080	0.1980	0.4662	0.3979	0.5839	**0.7884**
	N@20	0.0411	0.1522	0.1630	0.0251	0.1223	0.1848	0.2305	0.4996	0.4470	0.6004	**0.8039**

Steam dataset, which can be attributed to its hypergraph structure module and cross-view hypergraph contrastive pattern.

Comparison with Contrastive Learning for Recommendation: Compared with NCL and LightGCL, the KHSDIR model demonstrates performance improvements in most cases across four datasets, which is attributed to its self-supervised CL mechanism. This mechanism implements alignment and uniformity constraints in the embedding space, alleviating the restriction of data sparsity on intent representation while avoiding complex data augmentation. The good performance of NCL on the Weeplace dataset benefits from its use of the semantic CL paradigm, which integrates latent node correlations into the embedding representation.

4.3 Ablation Studies(RQ2)

A series of KHSDIR variants is constructed to validate the model's effectiveness:

KHSDIR-SS: removes the social semantic influence; KHSDIR-SE: removes the entity semantic influence; KHSDIR-DI: removes the dual-intent fusion mechanism; KHSDIR-CL: removes the bidirectional CL design; KHSDIR-GCR:

removes the GCR; KHSDIR-VL: removes the knowledge-aware multi-view CL. Figure 4 shows the ablation results on the MOOC dataset.

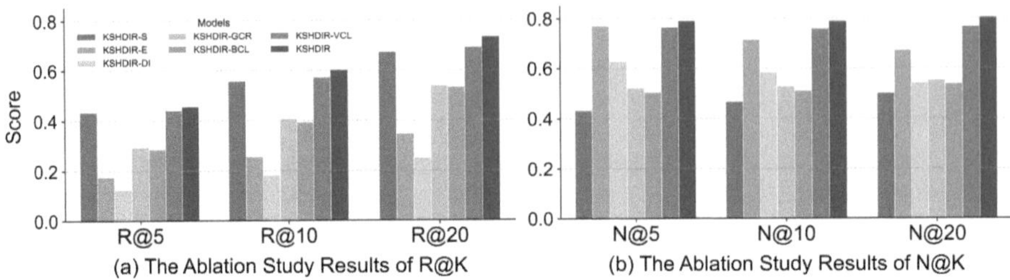

Fig. 4. Ablation study of KHSDIR on R@K and N@K.

Ablation experiments reveal: **1) The cruciality of integrating multidimensional semantic information:** Removing social and entity semantic modeling significantly degrades model performance. Experimental results illustrate that lacking these semantics impairs the model's ability to capture user interests and item characteristics. **2)The necessity of the dual-intent fusion mechanism:** Omitting this mechanism leads to significant performance degradation. As Fig. 4(b) shows, N@K drops by 20.55%, 26.07%, and 32.65% compared to the original model. This highlights that separating user/item features from group influence and popularity effects enables capturing fine-grained preference differences. **3)The role of the contrastive learning mechanism:** Removing GCR, the bidirectional contrastive, and the multi-view contrastive module decreases R@20 by 26.56%, 27.46%, and 5.77%, respectively. This validates that mechanism enhances the model's discriminative ability for intention modeling.

4.4 Hyperparameter Sensitivities(RQ3)

We conduct experiments on the MOOC dataset to investigate the impact of the number of intentions K, regularization weight λ_1 , GCN layers, and the KG propagation layers on the model's performance.

The K value represents the granularity of intent partitioning. As shown in Figs. 5(a) and 5(b), when the K value is small, the model cannot sufficiently capture diverse intents. As the K value increases and matches the semantic granularity of the MOOC dataset, the indicator values all show an upward trend. However, an excessively large K value leads to a decline in model performance. This is because too many intents blur the boundaries between intents, weakening the model's discriminative ability.

The contrastive learning mechanism is key to enhancing the model's discriminative ability under data sparsity. To regulate its strength, as shown in Figs. 5(c) and 5(d), the model performs best when $\lambda_1 = 0.2$, effectively suppressing representation collapse in sparse interactions. Excessively large λ_1 harms performance

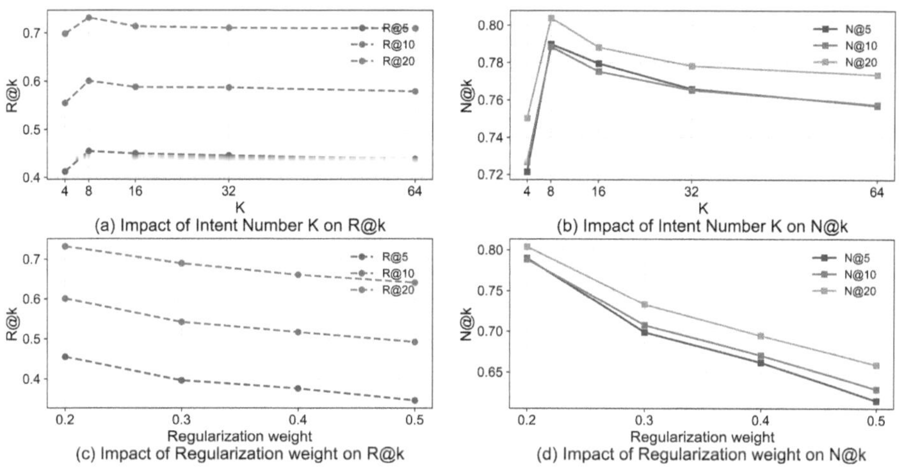

Fig. 5. Impact of K and regularization weight λ_1 on KHSDIR's performance

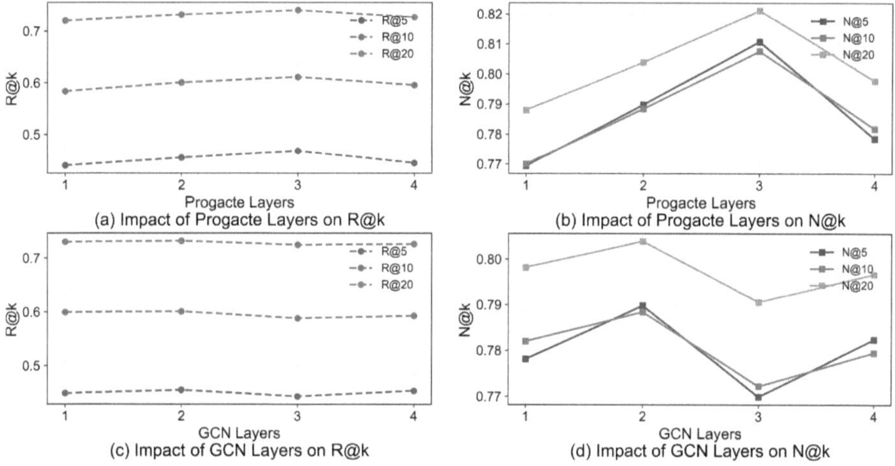

Fig. 6. Impact of GCN and propagation layers on KHSDIR's performance

by over-suppressing meaningful collaborative signals and breaking semantic associations between intents.

The performance curve of KHSDIR versus layers is shown in Figs. 6. Shallow layers ($L = 1$) only capture first-order neighborhood information, failing to model high-order collaborative relationships, leading to insufficient semantic fusion. The optimal layer ($L = 2$) balances local-global information: GCN layers aggregate hypergraph social semantics via 2-layer propagation to enhance intent disentanglement, while KG progacte layers fuse entity-relationship-entity knowledge via 2-layer propagation to supplement item semantics. Deep layers

($L > 2$) cause over-smoothing and noise accumulation, degrading performance. Considering time complexity, this study sets both the layers to 2.

5 Conclusions and Future Work

We propose a dual-intent recommendation framework that integrates KG and hypergraph modeling semantics (KHSDIR). By synergizing social and entity semantic information, it dynamically models collective and individual intentions. The dual-intent fusion mechanism refines user and item embeddings, boosting recommendation performance. Additionally, an intention-aware contrastive mechanism is employed to ensure consistency among users, items, and intentions, offering novel solutions for intention disentangling in complex scenarios. Experiments on four datasets confirm its effectiveness.

For future research, enhancing intention decoupling via multimodal knowledge fusion and modeling the temporal dynamics of users using causal reasoning are planned.

Acknowledgments. This study was funded by Fundamental Research Funds for the Central Universities (044420250025).

Declaration of Interest. The authors have no competing interests to declare that are relevant to the content of this article.

References

1. Ying, R., He, R., Chen, K., Eksombatchai, P., Hamilton, W. L., Leskovec, J.: Graph convolutional neural networks for web-scale recommender systems. In: Proceedings of the 24th ACM SIGKDD International Conference on Knowledge Discovery & Data Mining, pp. 974–983. https://doi.org/10.1145/3219819.3219890
2. Wu, Q., Zhang, H., Gao, X., Yan, J., Zha, H.: Towards open-world recommendation: an inductive model-based collaborative filtering approach. In: International Conference on Machine Learning (ICML), pp. 11329–11339. PMLR (2021b). https://doi.org/10.48550/arXiv.2007.04833
3. He, X., Zhang, H., Kan, M.-Y., Chua, T.-S.: Fast matrix factorization for online recommendation with implicit feedback. In: Proceedings of the 39th International ACM SIGIR Conference on Research and Development in Information Retrieval, pp. 549–558 (2016). https://doi.org/10.1145/2911451.2911489
4. He, X., Deng, K., Xiangwang, Y., Li, Y., Zhang, M.: LightGCN: simplifying and powering graph convolution network for recommendation. In: Proceedings Ofthe 43rd International ACM SIGIR Conference on Research and Development in Information Retrieval (SIGIR), pp. 639–648 (2020). https://doi.org/10.1145/3397271.3401063
5. Lin, Z., Tian, C., Hou, Y., Zhao, W.X.: Improving graph collaborative filtering with neighborhood-enriched contrastive learning. In: Proceedings of the ACM Web Conference 2022, pp. 2320–2329 (2022). https://doi.org/10.1145/3485447.3512104

6. Cai, X., Huang, C., Xia, L., Ren, X.: LightGCL: simple yet effective graph contrastive learning for recommendation. In: The Eleventh International Conference on Learning Representations (ICLR) (2023). https://doi.org/10.48550/arXiv.2302.08191
7. Xia, L., Huang, C., Xu, Y., Zhao, J., Yin, D., Huang, J.: Hypergraph contrastive collaborative filtering. In: Proceedings of the 45th International ACM SIGIR Conference on Research and Development in Information Retrieval, pp. 70–79 (2022). https://doi.org/10.1145/3477495.3532058
8. Zeng, J., Wang, N., Li, J.: Knowledge-driven hierarchical intents modeling for recommendation. Expert Syst. Appl. **259**, 125361 (2025). https://doi.org/10.1016/j.eswa.2024.125361
9. Zheng, Y., Gao, C., Li, X., He, X., Li, Y., Jin, D.: Disentangling user interest and conformity for recommendation with causal embedding. In: Proceedings of the Web Conference 2021, pp. 2980–2991 (2021). https://doi.org/10.1145/3442381.3449788
10. Wang, X., Jin, H., Zhang, A., He, X., Xu, T., Chua, T.-S.: Disentangled graph collaborative filtering. In: Proceedings of the 43rd International ACM SIGIR Conference on Research and Development in Information Retrieval, pp. 1001–1010 (2020). https://doi.org/10.1145/3397271.3401137
11. Ren, X., Xia, L., Zhao, J., Yin, D., Huang, C.: Disentangled contrastive collaborative filtering. In: Proceedings of the 46th International ACM SIGIR Conference on Research and Development in Information Retrieval, pp. 1137–1146 (2023). https://doi.org/10.1145/3539618.3591665
12. Zhang, Y., Sang, L., Zhang, Y.: Exploring the individuality and collectivity of intents behind interactions for graph collaborative filtering. In: Proceedings of the 47th International ACM SIGIR Conference on Research and Development in Information Retrieval, pp. 1253–1262 (2024). https://doi.org/10.1145/3626772.3657738
13. Cao, D., He, X., Miao, L., An, Y., Yang, C., Hong, R.: Attentive group recommendation. In: The 41st International ACM SIGIR Conference on Research & Development in Information Retrieval, pp. 645–654 (2018). https://doi.org/10.1145/3209978.3209998
14. Chen, T., Yin, H., Long, J., Nguyen, Q.V.H., Wang, Y., Wang, M.: Thinking inside the box: learning hypercube representations for group recommendation. In: Proceedings of the 45th International ACM SIGIR Conference on Research and Development in Information Retrieval, pp. 1664–1673 (2022). https://doi.org/10.1145/3477495.3532066
15. Yang, Y., Huang, C., Xia, L., Li, C.: Knowledge graph contrastive learning for recommendation. In: Proceedings of the 45th International ACM SIGIR Conference on Research and Development in Information Retrieval, pp. 1434–1443 (2022). https://doi.org/10.1145/3477495.3532009
16. Zhang, H., Shen, X., Yi, B., Wang, W., Feng, Y.: KGAN: knowledge grouping aggregation network for course recommendation in MOOCs. Expert Syst. Appl. **211**, 118344 (2023). https://doi.org/10.1016/j.eswa.2022.118344
17. Wang, X., Huang, T., Wang, D., Yuan, Y., Liu, Z., He, X., Chua, T.S.: Learning intents behind interactions with knowledge graph for recommendation. In: Proceedings of the Web Conference 2021, pp. 878–887 (2021). https://doi.org/10.1145/3442381.3450133
18. Li, S., Yang, B., Li, D.: Entity-driven user intent inference for knowledge graph-based recommendation. Appl. Intell. **53**(9), 10734–10750 (2023). https://doi.org/10.1007/s10489-022-04048-4

19. Chen, Y., Liu, Z., Li, J., McAuley, J., Xiong, C.: Intent contrastive learning for sequential recommendation. In: Proceedings of the ACM Web Conference 2022, pp. 2172–2182 (2022). https://doi.org/10.1145/3485447.3512090
20. Wang, X., et al.: Multi-component graph convolutional collaborative filtering. In: AAAI, vol. 34, pp. 6267–6274 (2020). https://doi.org/10.1609/aaai.v34i04.6094
21. Wang, X., He, X., Wang, M., Feng, F., Chua, T.-S.: Neural graph collaborative filtering. In: Proceedings of the 42nd International ACM SIGIR Conference on Research and Development in Information Retrieval, pp. 165–174 (2019). https://doi.org/10.1145/3331184.3331267
22. Wen, M., Wang, H., Li, W., Fan, Z., Yu, X.: Contrastive graph semantic learning via prototype for recommendation. Inf. Sci. **699**, 121799 (2025). https://doi.org/10.1016/j.ins.2024.121799
23. Wu, X., Xiong, Y., Zhang, Y., Jiao, Y., Zhang, J.: Dual intents graph modeling for user-centric group discovery. In: Proceedings of the 32nd ACM International Conference on Information and Knowledge Management, pp. 2716–2725 (2023). https://doi.org/10.1145/3583780.3614855
24. Wang, X., He, X., Cao, Y., Liu, M., Chua, T.S.: KGAT: knowledge graph attention network for recommendation. In: Proceedings of the 25th ACM SIGKDD International Conference on Knowledge Discovery & Data Mining, pp. 950–958 (2019). https://doi.org/10.1145/3292500.3330989
25. Sang, L., Wang, Y., Zhang, Y., Zhang, Y., Wu, X.: Intent-guided heterogeneous graph contrastive learning for recommendation. IEEE Trans. Knowl. Data Eng. (2025). https://doi.org/10.48550/arXiv.2407.17234
26. Feng, Y., You, H., Zhang, Z., Ji, R., Gao, Y.: Hypergraph neural networks. In: Proceedings of the AAAI Conference on Artificial Intelligence, vol. 33, no. 01, pp. 3558–3565 (2018). https://doi.org/10.1609/aaai.v33i01.33013558
27. Chao, L., He, J., Wang, T., Chu, W.: PairRE: knowledge graph embeddings via paired relation vectors (2020). arXiv preprint: arXiv:2011.03798
28. Sankar, A., Wu, Y., Wu, Y., Zhang, W., Yang, H., Sundaram, H.: GroupIM: a mutual information maximization framework for neural group recommendation. In: Proceedings of the 43rd International ACM SIGIR Conference on Research and Development in Information Retrieval, pp. 1279–1288 (2020). https://doi.org/10.1145/3397271.3401116
29. Fan, W., Liu, X., Jin, W., Zhao, X., Tang, J., Li, Q.: Graph trend filtering networks for recommendation. In: Proceedings of the 45th International ACM SIGIR Conference on Research and Development in Information Retrieval, pp. 112–121 (2022). https://doi.org/10.1145/3477495.3531985

GK-SMOTE: A Hyperparameter-Free Noise-Resilient Gaussian KDE-Based Oversampling Approach

Mahabubur Rahman Miraj[1], Hongyu Huang[1], Ting Yang[1], Jinxue Zhao[1], Nankun Mu[1(✉)], and Xinyu Lei[2]

[1] College of Computer Science, Chongqing University, Chongqing 400044, China
miraj@stu.cqu.edu.cn, nankun.mu@cqu.edu.cn

[2] Department of Computer Science, Michigan Technological University, Houghton, MI 49931, USA

Abstract. Imbalanced classification is a significant challenge in machine learning, especially in critical applications like medical diagnosis, fraud detection, and cybersecurity. Traditional oversampling techniques, such as SMOTE, often fail to handle label noise and complex data distributions, leading to reduced classification accuracy. In this paper, we propose GK-SMOTE, a hyperparameter-free, noise-resilient extension of SMOTE, built on Gaussian Kernel Density Estimation (KDE). GK-SMOTE enhances class separability by generating synthetic samples in high-density minority regions, while effectively avoiding noisy or ambiguous areas. This self-adaptive approach uses Gaussian KDE to differentiate between safe and noisy regions, ensuring more accurate sample generation without requiring extensive parameter tuning. Our extensive experiments on diverse binary classification datasets demonstrate that GK-SMOTE outperforms existing state-of-the-art oversampling techniques across key evaluation metrics, including MCC, Balanced Accuracy, and AUPRC. The proposed method offers a robust, efficient solution for imbalanced classification tasks, especially in noisy data environments, making it an attractive choice for real-world applications.

Keywords: Oversampling · Hyperparameter-free · Noise-Resilient

1 Introduction

Imbalanced classification has emerged as a prominent challenge in data mining and machine learning due to the uneven distribution of instances across classes in real-world datasets [1]. In such cases, the majority class dominates, while the minority class, which often contains more significant instances, is underrepresented. This phenomenon is particularly prevalent in critical applications such as medical diagnostics, network intrusion detection, and bankruptcy prediction [2]. Traditional classification methods tend to optimize for overall accuracy by minimizing loss functions, which often results in a bias towards the majority

J. Li et al. (Eds.): APWeb-WAIM 2025, LNCS 16115, pp. 197–212, 2026.
https://doi.org/10.1007/978-981-95-5719-6_13

class. In datasets with a large majority-to-minority class ratio (e.g., 99:1), even a simple classifier that labels all instances as belonging to the majority class can achieve an artificially high accuracy of 99%. However, this leads to poor performance on the minority class, which is crucial in many practical contexts, such as medical diagnoses, where the identification of patients with a disease is far more important than identifying non-diseased individuals [1].

To address these challenges, various strategies have been developed, falling into three primary categories: data-level methods, algorithm-level methods, and cost-sensitive methods. Among these, data-level methods, particularly oversampling techniques, have gained significant traction due to their simplicity and adaptability [3]. Oversampling increases the representation of the minority class without discarding valuable data from the majority class, unlike under-sampling techniques. Additionally, oversampling methods, such as SMOTE (Synthetic Minority Over-sampling Technique), have been found to perform better than under-sampling when evaluated using metrics like the area under the ROC curve (AUC). SMOTE creates synthetic samples by interpolating between adjacent instances in the feature space, enhancing classifier performance by balancing the class distribution. However, SMOTE has notable limitations, especially when dealing with noisy data [4].

Recent research indicates that the imbalance ratio alone is insufficient to explain the deterioration in classification performance; factors such as data complexity and label noise play more significant roles [5]. Label noise, which refers to inaccurately labeled instances, is a common issue in real-world datasets [6]. SMOTE's interpolation approach can exacerbate the negative effects of label noise, especially in the regions near decision boundaries, by generating noisy and overlapping samples. This reduces the separability between classes and harms classifier performance [4]. Therefore, there is an urgent need for more robust oversampling techniques that address both label noise and complex data distributions. In response, this work introduces GK-SMOTE, a self-adaptive, Gaussian Kernel Density Estimation (KDE)-based robust version of SMOTE. GK-SMOTE aims to improve classification performance in imbalanced datasets with label noise. Key innovations include:

- Using Gaussian KDE to assess the local density of minority samples and categorize them into safe and borderline areas. This helps in generating synthetic samples that improve class separability and mitigate label noise.
- Adapting the density-based approach to focus on high-density regions of the minority class, ensuring that synthetic samples are created in areas where they enhance classification performance, while avoiding noisy regions.
- Maintaining simplicity and efficiency by leveraging the same k-nearest neighbors used in KDE for sample generation, facilitating integration into existing workflows without the need for additional parameters.
- Extensive validation on various binary classification benchmark datasets with varying degrees of label noise, demonstrating the superior performance of GK-SMOTE over other advanced oversampling techniques based on evaluation

metrics such as MCC (Matthews Correlation Coefficient), Balanced Accuracy (BAc), and AUPRC (Area Under Precision-Recall Curve).

By targeting label noise and improving class separability, GK-SMOTE offers a robust solution for handling imbalanced datasets, yielding more reliable classification of minority class instances.

2 Related Work

2.1 State of the Art Oversampling Methods

Over-sampling techniques such as SMOTE and its variants have become fundamental for addressing imbalanced datasets in machine learning. SMOTE generates synthetic minority class samples through interpolation between neighboring instances, improving class balance, but struggles with noisy data and label inaccuracies, often resulting in reduced performance when label noise is present [4]. Borderline-SMOTE extends SMOTE by focusing on the decision boundary and generating synthetic samples in regions near the class boundary, which is particularly effective for classes that are not easily separable but still falls short when label noise is present, as it does not explicitly address noise robustness [7]. ADASYN (Adaptive Synthetic Sampling) further extends SMOTE by adaptively generating samples in low-density regions to improve classifier performance by focusing on difficult-to-classify instances, but similarly suffers from issues when noisy labels are present, as it does not fully address label noise [8]. AB-SMOTE (Adaptive Borderline-SMOTE) enhances SMOTE by introducing a weighting mechanism that focuses on minority class instances near the decision boundary, improving data complexity handling and class separability but not fully addressing label noise [9]. Safe-Level-SMOTE filters safe regions for synthetic sample generation to mitigate the adverse effects of noise but still lacks noise robustness and struggles in environments with high label noise, limiting its applicability in real-world scenarios where label noise is common [10]. Km-SMOTE improves SMOTE by using clustering methods such as K-means to generate synthetic samples based on centroids, aiding class separability and data complexity, but it does not directly address the problem of label noise, which may result in generating noisy samples in noisy environments [11]. Despite these advancements, these methods still fail to fully address label noise, limiting their robustness in noisy environments.

2.2 Gaussian-Based SMOTE Methods

Gaussian-based oversampling methods, such as GMF-SMOTE [12], NGOS [13], MGD [14], HGDO [15], and GDO [16], have been developed to improve noise robustness and sampling efficiency. GMF-SMOTE utilizes Gaussian mixture models to filter out noisy data before generating synthetic samples, improving performance in noisy environments by focusing on areas with better class separability and reducing the risk of generating noisy samples [12]. NGOS (noise gaussian oversampling) [13] and MGD (multivariate gaussian distribution) also use Gaussian distributions to avoid generating samples in noisy regions, effectively handling noisy environments to some extent [14]. However, these methods still require hyperparameter tuning, which can be computationally expensive and inefficient, particularly in high-dimensional settings. HGDO (hypergraph Gaussian distribution oversampling) [15] and GDO aim to leverage Gaussian distributions for more robust noise handling, showing better performance in complex data environments compared to traditional methods [16]. However, they still suffer from the need for hyperparameter tuning, making them less user-friendly and harder to integrate into practical applications, with their computational inefficiency in high-dimensional spaces being a limiting factor in real-world use cases. Among these methods, GK-SMOTE stands out as the most robust solution to label noise, as it leverages Gaussian Kernel Density Estimation (KDE) to focus on high-density regions of the minority class while avoiding noisy areas. Unlike GMF-SMOTE [12] and NGOS [13], GK-SMOTE is fully hyperparameter-free, making it more user-friendly and adaptable to practical applications. This unique feature ensures that GK-SMOTE strikes a balance between robustness, efficiency, and simplicity, enabling it to handle imbalanced datasets with label noise effectively, and providing a more reliable and efficient solution for real-world imbalanced classification problems, particularly in noisy environments where other methods may struggle as shown in the Table: 1.

Table 1. Comparison of Oversampling Methods with GK-SMOTE

Oversampling Methods	Noise Robustness	Handle Label Noise	Data Complexity	Compute Efficiency	Hyperparameter Methods	Gaussian KDE Based Methods
SMOTE [4]	×	×	×	×	×	×
Borderline-SMOTE [7]	×	×	×	×	×	×
ADASYN [8]	×	×	✓	×	×	×
AB-SMOTE [9]	✓	×	✓	✓	×	×
Km-SMOTE [11]	✓	×	✓	×	×	×
Safe-Level-SMOTE [10]	✓	×	✓	×	×	×
GMF-SMOTE [12]	✓	×	✓	✓	×	×
NGOS [13]	✓	×	✓	✓	✓	×
MGD [14]	✓	✓	✓	✓	✓	×
HGDO [15]	✓	✓	✓	✓	✓	×
GDO [16]	✓	✓	✓	✓	✓	×
GK-SMOTE	✓	✓	✓	✓	✓	✓

3 Proposed Framework of GK-SMOTE

We propose GK-SMOTE, a robust and adaptive extension of the traditional SMOTE (Synthetic Minority Over-sampling Technique), designed to address the challenges of class imbalance and label noise in machine learning. By leveraging Gaussian Kernel Density Estimation (KDE), GK-SMOTE creates synthetic data that avoids the common pitfalls of standard SMOTE, such as introducing noise or class overlap. The GK-SMOTE framework, outlined in Fig. 1, follows a structured process to generate synthetic samples while enhancing class separability. It starts with processing the imbalanced training set and calculating the class imbalance ratio (IR) between the majority class (Q) and the minority class (P). A noise filtering step is applied, followed by density calculation to differentiate minority samples based on their location within the dataset, helping to distinguish those near decision boundaries from those in safe regions. The framework then clusters the minority samples into borderline and safe categories using 2-means clustering, ensuring a targeted oversampling process. Synthetic samples are generated through interpolation using the k-nearest neighbors (k-NN) algorithm, and further refined with Gaussian KDE, focusing on high-density regions of the minority class to improve class separability. To evaluate the generated synthetic data, GK-SMOTE uses 10-fold cross-validation, ensuring robust performance across multiple folds, with results averaged for final performance metrics. This method operates hyperparameter-free, eliminating the need for manual tuning of parameters and ensuring computational efficiency by using the same k-NN algorithm for both clustering and oversampling.

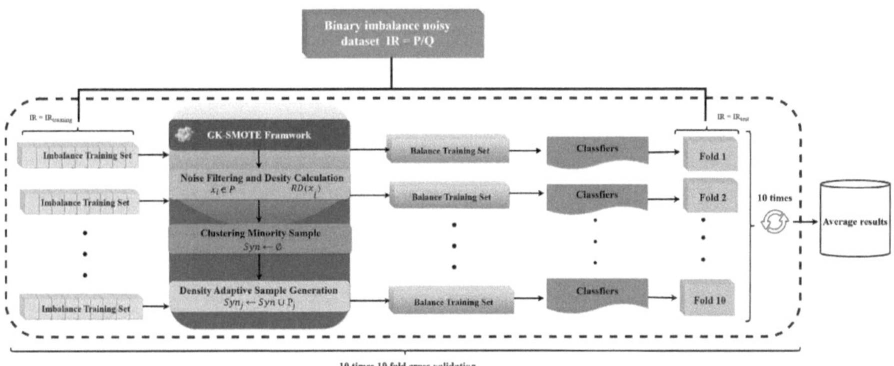

Fig. 1. GK-SMOTE Framework.

3.1 GK-SMOTE Algorithm

A key motivation behind the GK-SMOTE algorithm is the observation that the spatial distribution of minority class samples significantly influences their reliability for synthetic instance generation. In particular, the variation in distances between each minority sample and its k-nearest neighbors, whether from the majority or minority class forms the foundation for adaptive classification into three categories: noisy, borderline, and safe. As illustrated in Fig. 2, minority class samples (red points) are evaluated based on their neighborhood structure in relation to the majority class (blue points), using Gaussian Kernel Density

Estimation (KDE) with $k = 3$. In the noise case shown in Fig. 2(a), the minority sample A is surrounded predominantly by majority samples (A4, A5, A6), and is relatively distant from its own class neighbors (A1, A2, A3). KDE assigns such points a low density score, identifying them as unreliable for oversampling due to potential label noise and high overlap with the majority class. In contrast, safe samples like C, shown in Fig. 2(c), are enclosed by minority samples (C1, C2, C3) and distant from majority instances (C4, C5, C6). KDE assigns high probability density to such points, making them highly suitable for generating synthetic samples. Borderline samples, such as B in Fig. 2(b), lie near the class decision boundary and exhibit a mixed neighborhood (majority neighbors: B4, B5, B6; minority neighbors: B1, B2, B3). These receive intermediate KDE density values, reflecting their transitional position. Unlike traditional methods that rely on distance-based relative density, GK-SMOTE uses KDE probability to systematically and adaptively categorize samples. It prioritizes synthetic generation in safe, high-density regions while minimizing oversampling in noisy, low-density regions. This KDE-driven sampling not only enhances class separability but also mitigates the risk of overfitting and label noise. As demonstrated in Table 2, this algorithmic strategy allows GK-SMOTE to dynamically adjust sampling behavior across varying data distributions, making it a self-adaptive and noise-resilient framework for imbalanced classification problems.

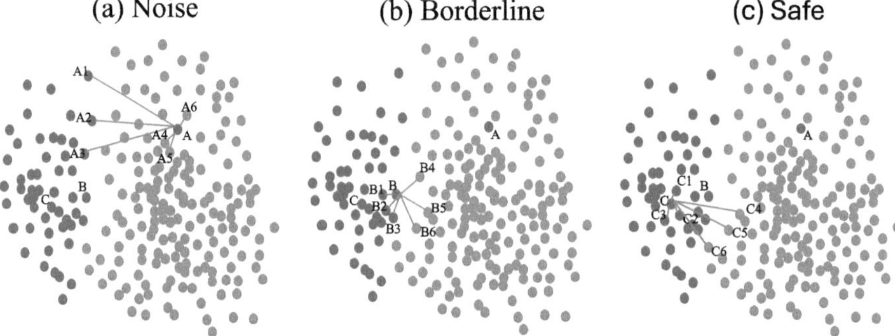

Fig. 2. Illustration of distances between each type of minority sample and its k-nearest majority/minority neighbors.

Definition 1. Given a dataset $D \subseteq \mathbb{R}^d$ and a data point $p \in D$, the function $d(p, q)$ represents the Euclidean distance between points p and q. Traditional distance-based methods often fail to capture the true data distribution, particularly in imbalanced datasets. To address this, Gaussian Kernel Density Estimation (KDE) is employed to estimate the probability density function (PDF) of a given sample p, providing an adaptive measure of local density. The KDE-based probability density estimate for p is given by:

$$\hat{f}(p) = \frac{1}{|N(p, D)|} \sum_{q \in N(p,D)} K_h(d(p, q)), \tag{1}$$

where $K_h(\cdot)$ is the Gaussian kernel function with bandwidth h, and $N(p, D)$ is the set of nearest neighbors of p in D. This adaptive and probabilistic density estimation allows for a flexible characterization of local density, distinguishing between noisy, borderline, and safe samples.

Definition 2. For a dataset $D \subseteq \mathbb{R}^d$ consisting of a minority class D^+ and a majority class D^-, we define homogeneous and heterogeneous neighbors for any minority sample $p \in D^+$ using KDE-based density estimates. Homogeneous neighbors are minority samples that lie in high-density regions relative to p, while heterogeneous neighbors are majority samples that reduce the density estimate of p. These neighbors are defined as:

$$HON(p) = \{q \mid q \in D^+, \hat{f}(q) \geq \hat{f}(p)\}, \tag{2}$$

$$HEN(p) = \{q \mid q \in D^-, \hat{f}(q) > \hat{f}(p)\}, \tag{3}$$

This classification helps identify safe and noisy regions in the dataset for effective oversampling.

Definition 3. After estimating the KDE-based probability densities, minority samples are categorized adaptively into safe, borderline, and noisy samples based on their KDE density values. Noisy samples are those with a low $\hat{f}(p)$, indicating their presence in sparse regions or overlapping areas with the majority class. Borderline samples are those with intermediate densities, lying near the decision boundary with a mix of homogeneous and heterogeneous neighbors. Safe samples have high $\hat{f}(p)$, indicating clear separation from the majority class. GK-SMOTE adapts to these classifications through three steps:

- Noise Filtering with KDE: Noisy samples with low KDE values are removed before oversampling.
- Density-Based Clustering: KDE-driven clustering replaces traditional methods to separate safe and borderline samples without requiring fixed parameters.
- Density-Adaptive Synthetic Sample Generation: Synthetic samples are generated based on the KDE probability distribution, ensuring placement in high-density regions.

3.2 Computational Complexity Analysis

To analyze the computational efficiency of GK-SMOTE, we consider three key operations. First, the KDE Probability Estimation dynamically estimates density for all samples with a complexity of $\mathcal{O}(nN)$, where n is the number of minority samples and N is the total dataset size. Second, the Density-Based Clustering

Table 2. GK-SMOTE Algorithm

Input: Training set $D = P \cup Q$, where P is the minority samples, Q is the majority samples.
IR: The expected imbalance ratio.
k: Number of nearest neighbors.
Output: Syn: Synthesized minority samples.

$P' \leftarrow \emptyset, \quad N \leftarrow \left\lfloor \frac{|Q|}{IR} \right\rfloor - |P|$ // Total number of minority samples to be synthesized

// **Step 1: Noise Filtering and Density Calculation**
For each minority sample $x_i \in P$:
Compute k nearest neighbors;
Count number m of majority samples in k nearest neighbors;
If $m = k$ then:
Filter x_i from P;
Else:
$P' \leftarrow P' \cup \{x_i\}$;
$RD(x_i) \leftarrow$ Calculate KDE-based density of x_i;

// **Step 2: Clustering Minority Samples**
Apply 2-means clustering on $RD(P')$ to obtain clusters C_A and C_B;
Assign P_A, P_B as minority samples corresponding to C_A and C_B, respectively;
$Syn \leftarrow \emptyset$;

// **Step 3: Density-Adaptive Sample Generation**
For each cluster P_j, $j \in \{A, B\}$:
$N_j \leftarrow \frac{|P_j|}{|P|} \cdot N$; // Number of minority samples to be synthesized in P_j
For each sample $x_i \in P_j$:
$w_i \leftarrow \frac{k - w_i}{k}$;
$w_i \leftarrow \frac{w_i}{\sum_i w_i}$;
$N_i \leftarrow w_i \cdot N_j$;
Populate($N_i, x, narray$);

$Syn_j \leftarrow Syn_j \cup$ generated samples by each minority sample in P_j;
return $Syn = Syn_A \cup Syn_B$;

applies KDE-driven clustering on the density vector with a complexity of $\mathcal{O}(nt)$, where t is the number of iterations for convergence. Third, the Adaptive Synthetic Sample Generation generates synthetic samples based on KDE density, with a complexity of $\mathcal{O}(ns)$, where s is the number of synthetic samples. Therefore, the overall computational complexity of GK-SMOTE is $\mathcal{O}(nN + nt + ns)$, demonstrating its efficiency and scalability across different imbalanced datasets.

4 Experiments

4.1 Dataset Selection

We evaluate the effectiveness of the proposed GK-SMOTE method using 27 real-world datasets from the UCI Machine Learning Repository[1], employed for binary classification tasks. Nine datasets are intrinsically imbalanced (breast_tissue2, ecoli, heart, iris, libra, pima, segment, vehicle, and wine), while the remaining 18 datasets are artificially imbalanced by increasing the imbalance ratio (IR), defined as:

$$IR = \frac{\#\text{Majority samples}}{\#\text{Minority samples}}.$$

Each dataset is split into 75% for training and 25% for testing. The majority and minority samples are partitioned separately to address class imbalance. To assess GK-SMOTE's robustness in imbalanced learning with label noise, controlled levels of noise (10%, 20%, and 30%) are introduced, where minority class labels are randomly flipped to the majority class, and vice versa, based on the noise rate c. This process alters the class distribution in both training and testing sets (Table 3).

Table 3. Description of UCI Datasets

Data	#Dim	#Sample	#Maj	#Min	IR	Data	#Dim	#Sample	#Maj	#Min	IR
breast_tissue2	9	88	70	18	3.89	symguide3	22	1041	947	94	10.07
ecoli	8	336	284	52	5.46	splice	60	620	517	51	10.14
heart	13	270	150	120	1.25	mushrooms	112	4628	4208	420	10.02
iris	4	150	100	50	2	isolet5	617	858	780	78	10
libra	90	360	288	72	4	codrna	8	41674	39690	3969	10
pima	8	768	500	268	1.87	avila	10	11695	10632	1063	10
segment	16	2310	1980	330	6	letter	16	11057	10052	1005	10
vehicle	18	846	647	199	3.25	susy	18	23752	21593	2159	10
wine	13	178	107	71	1.51	mocap	33	48023	46852	4685	10
symguide1	4	4400	4000	400	10	poker	10	49804	48828	4882	10
breastcancer	10	532	444	44	10.09	nomao	119	25852	24621	2462	10
creditApproval	15	459	383	38	10.08	magic	10	13665	12332	1233	10
votes	16	320	267	26	10.27	skin	3	196139	194198	1941	100.05
						Online_Retail	7	541909	531285	10624	50.01

4.2 Assessment Metrics

To provide a more balanced evaluation, we use three metrics: Matthews Correlation Coefficient (MCC), Balanced Accuracy (BAc), and Area Under the Precision-Recall Curve (AUPRC), as shown in Eqs. 4, 5 and 6. These metrics

[1] http://archive.ics.uci.edu/ml/index.php.

evaluate both class-wise performance and the classifier's ability to predict minority class instances effectively.

$$MCC = \frac{tp \times tn - fp \times fn}{\sqrt{(tp + fp)(tp + fn)(tn + fp)(tn + fn)}}, \tag{4}$$

$$Balance\ Accuracy\ (BAc) = \frac{1}{2}\left(\frac{tp}{tp + fn} + \frac{tn}{tn + fp}\right), \tag{5}$$

$$AUPRC = \int_0^1 P(R), dR, \tag{6}$$

MCC considers all confusion matrix components, Balanced Accuracy (BAc) adjusts for imbalance, AUPRC focuses on the minority class.

4.3 Comparison Methods and Experiment Setup

This method introduces noise evenly across both classes, with slight IR variations due to rounding. We compare oversampling techniques' effectiveness across various models using default hyperparameters. SMOTE, Borderline-SMOTE, ADASYN, and AB-SMOTE use $k_{\text{nn}} \in \{3, 5, 20\}$, while k-means SMOTE includes

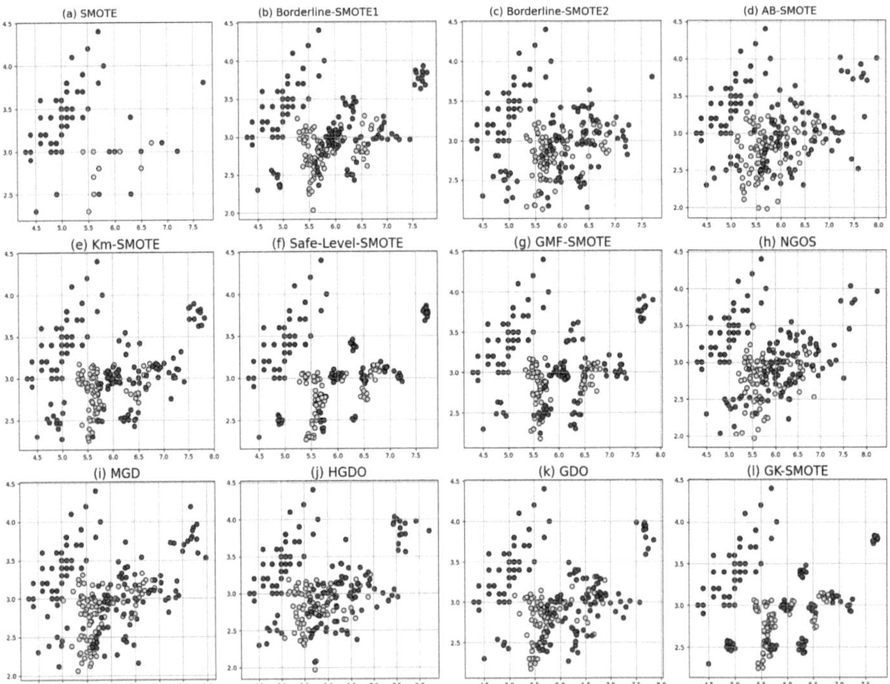

Fig. 3. Visual comparison of synthetic sample generation by various oversampling methods, including GK-SMOTE.

parameters like $k \in \{2, 20, 50, 100\}$ and interpolation ratio ($irt \in \{1, 1.5\}$). GMF-SMOTE and NGOS include Gaussian mixture model ($gmm \in \{0.1, 0.5, 1.0\}$) and interpolation ratio (irt). MGD, HGDO, and GDO incorporate Gaussian distribution weights ($gd \in \{0.1, 0.5, 1.0\}$) and hypergraph identification weights ($hg \in \{1.0, 2.0, 3.0\}$). GK-SMOTE uses a KDE-based approach to adaptively generate synthetic samples based on local density variations, eliminating the need for fixed parameter tuning.

4.4 Basic Classifier Selection

We evaluated five classifiers from the scikit-learn library such as Random Forest (RF), LightGBM, Logistic Regression (LR), KNN, and Decision Tree (DT) on imbalanced datasets using 10-fold cross-validation. These classifiers were tested with SMOTE, Borderline-SMOTE, and others oversampling method inducing GK-SMOTE. Performance was compared using MCC, Balanced Accuracy (BAc), and AUPRC to identify the best classifier for handling imbalanced data with GK-SMOTE.

5 Results

5.1 Visualization Comparison on Synthetic Dataset

To evaluate the effectiveness of various oversampling techniques, we generated scatter plots visualizing the synthetic data produced by SMOTE, Borderline-SMOTE (SMOTE1 and SMOTE2), AB-SMOTE, Km-SMOTE, Safe-Level-SMOTE, GMF-SMOTE, NGOS, MGD, HGDO, GDO, and the proposed GK-SMOTE, as illustrated in Fig. 3. In each plot, blue, red, and gray dots represent majority, minority, and synthetic samples, respectively. The visualizations show that GMF-SMOTE and GK-SMOTE generate well-separated synthetic samples that maintain class balance and reduce overlap. While methods like Borderline-SMOTE and AB-SMOTE tend to generate samples near decision boundaries potentially enhancing classification in borderline regions, they also introduce a higher risk of overlap. In contrast, GK-SMOTE consistently produces more distinct, well-clustered class regions, effectively avoiding noisy samples and highlighting its superiority in preserving class separability for improved classification performance in imbalanced settings.

5.2 Experimental Comparison and Results Analysis

Results under No Label Noise ($\gamma = 0$): Under noise-free conditions, GK-SMOTE consistently achieved the best performance across all classifiers and evaluation metrics. For the MCC metric, GK-SMOTE significantly outperformed SMOTE across every classifier, with improvements of 19.9% for Random Forest, 28.4% for LightGBM, 25.4% for Logistic Regression, 41.0% for KNN, and 27.4% for Decision Tree. These results highlight GK-SMOTE's strong ability to enhance the classifiers' discriminative power in distinguishing between classes in imbalanced datasets. In terms of BAc, GK-SMOTE also demonstrated substantial gains over SMOTE, improving performance by 35.9% for Random Forest, 30.5% for LightGBM, 37.7% for Logistic Regression, 31.5% for KNN, and 27.3% for Decision Tree, indicating its effectiveness in balancing classification performance across majority and minority classes. Furthermore, for the AUPRC, GK-SMOTE achieved enhancements of 25.0% for Random Forest, 20.8% for LightGBM, 26.3% for Logistic Regression, 24.5% for KNN, and 26.3% for Decision Tree, suggesting improved sensitivity and precision in identifying minority class instances. These findings, as shown in Fig. 4(a) and Table 4 (Tab a), confirm GK-SMOTE's superior performance under clean-label conditions, consistently

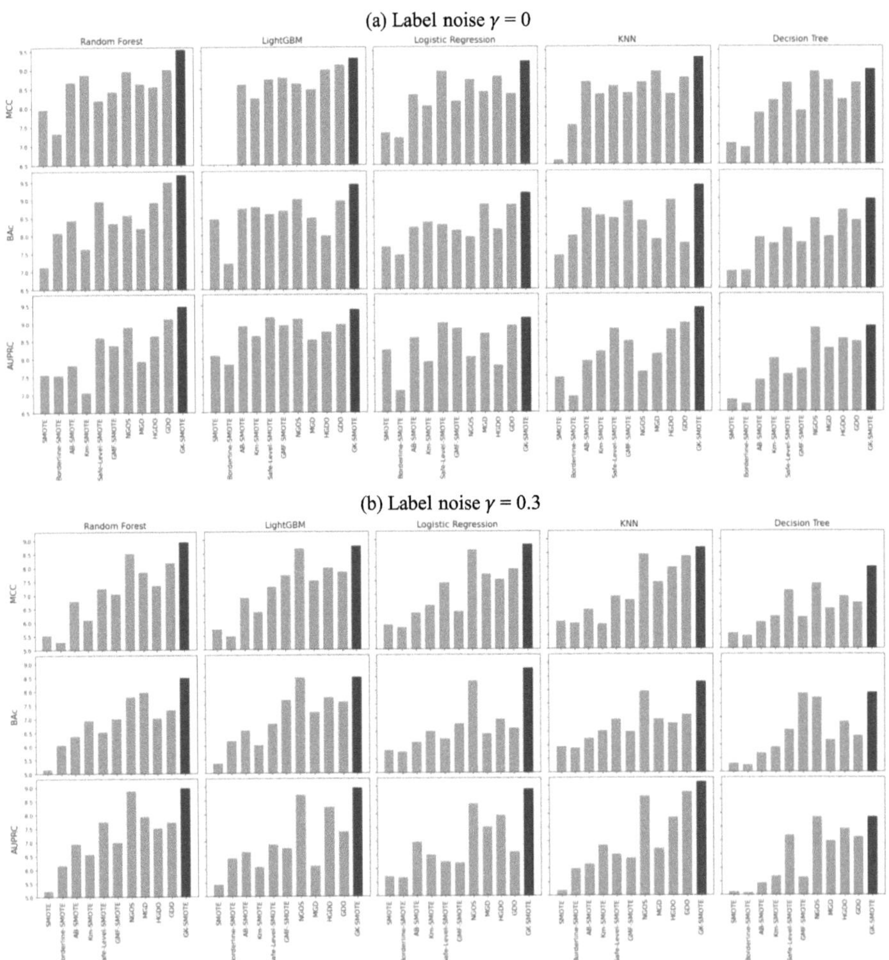

Fig. 4. Bar plots comparing of oversampling methods across classifiers under varying label noise levels such as (a) no label noise $\gamma = 0$ and (b) label noise $\gamma = 0.3$.

outperforming both traditional and advanced oversampling methods across all classifiers and evaluation metrics.

Results under Label Noise ($\gamma = 0.3$): Even in the presence of 30% label noise, GK-SMOTE maintained top-tier performance across all classifiers and evaluation metrics. For the MCC) metric, GK-SMOTE showed substantial improvements over SMOTE, achieving gains of 61.3% for Random Forest, 53.6% for LightGBM, 32.7% for Logistic Regression, 57.0% for KNN, and 55.2% for Decision Tree. These results reflect GK-SMOTE's robustness and stability in handling noisy data environments. Regarding BAc, GK-SMOTE again demonstrated superior performance with improvements of 64.9% for Random Forest, 58.9% for LightGBM, 47.4% for Logistic Regression, 53.1% for KNN, and 49.1% for Decision Tree, indicating its strong ability to maintain balanced classification outcomes under label noise. In terms of AUPRC, GK-SMOTE outperformed all other methods, delivering enhancements of 70.9% for Random Forest, 64.7% for LightGBM, 66.2% for Logistic Regression, 61.2% for KNN, and 52.5% for Deci-

Table 4. Comparing the performance of eleven oversampling methods, including the proposed GK-SMOTE, across five classifiers under two conditions: (Tab a) no label noise $\gamma = 0$ and (Tab b) label noise $\gamma = 0.3$. The evaluation metrics include MCC, Balanced Accuracy (BAc), and AUPRC. Here AUC: AUPRC; GBM: LightGBM; SMT: SMOTE; BSM: Borderline-SMOTE; ASM: AB-SMOTE; KMS: Km-SMOTE; SSM: Safe-Level SMOTE; GSM: GMF-SMOTE; NGO: NGOS; HGD: HGDO; GKS: GK-SMOTE

Tab a															
	MCC					BAc					AUC				
	RF	GBM	LR	KNN	DT	RF	GBM	LR	KNN	DT	RF	GBM	LR	KNN	DT
SMT	7.957	6.213	7.346	6.611	7.045	7.132	8.456	7.675	7.428	6.995	7.564	8.078	8.244	7.471	6.843
BSM	7.334	6.072	7.216	7.525	6.944	8.085	7.228	7.451	7.978	6.996	7.538	7.835	7.102	6.934	6.712
ASM	8.672	8.612	8.338	8.664	7.845	8.427	8.749	8.219	8.748	7.926	7.825	8.923	8.583	7.925	7.381
KSM	8.868	8.245	8.041	8.336	8.171	7.625	8.788	8.365	8.545	7.748	7.063	8.626	7.911	8.188	7.994
SSM	8.194	8.736	8.945	8.552	8.634	8.959	8.597	8.289	8.469	8.187	8.598	9.167	9.001	8.824	7.531
GSM	8.429	8.786	8.165	8.367	7.901	8.339	8.693	8.125	8.942	7.778	8.372	8.942	8.849	8.476	7.693
NGO	8.957	8.634	8.725	8.654	8.921	8.568	9.019	7.955	8.397	8.438	8.897	9.121	8.051	7.614	8.856
MGD	8.636	8.476	8.417	8.933	8.698	8.195	8.488	8.865	7.875	7.939	7.931	8.528	8.696	8.115	8.269
HGD	8.551	8.989	8.821	8.348	8.198	8.925	7.985	8.168	8.982	8.685	8.642	8.763	7.803	8.799	8.537
GDO	8.998	9.118	8.354	8.778	8.631	9.497	8.967	8.845	7.765	8.393	9.115	8.961	8.927	8.991	8.452
GKS	9.538	9.301	9.214	9.313	8.976	9.698	9.429	9.191	9.399	8.991	9.461	9.388	9.146	9.421	8.897
Tab b															
	MCC					BAc					AUC				
	RF	GBM	LR	KNN	DT	RF	GBM	LR	KNN	DT	RF	GBM	LR	KNN	DT
SMT	5.531	5.732	5.892	5.998	5.542	5.152	5.344	5.814	5.937	5.302	5.208	5.445	5.732	5.185	5.112
BSM	5.292	5.482	5.784	5.931	5.453	6.043	6.188	5.763	5.882	5.239	6.157	6.389	5.681	5.982	5.077
ASM	6.794	6.899	6.319	6.422	5.963	6.372	6.567	6.126	6.246	5.679	6.935	6.629	6.971	6.151	5.438
KSM	6.092	6.372	6.611	5.891	6.169	6.948	6.032	6.514	6.518	5.899	6.563	6.073	6.502	6.842	5.693
SSM	7.241	7.286	7.421	6.919	7.128	6.522	6.803	6.246	6.927	6.541	7.731	6.896	6.263	6.509	7.183
GSM	7.055	7.716	6.362	6.783	6.145	6.996	7.663	6.788	6.487	7.871	6.983	6.754	6.21	6.366	5.65
NGO	8.514	8.688	8.622	8.461	7.384	7.787	8.489	8.351	7.958	7.715	8.853	8.698	8.371	8.624	7.848
MGD	7.841	7.514	7.751	7.436	6.459	7.951	7.225	6.432	6.946	6.172	7.921	6.124	7.523	6.711	6.965
HGD	7.355	7.992	7.544	7.973	6.917	7.014	7.763	6.953	6.787	6.837	7.507	8.257	7.944	7.853	7.429
GDO	8.165	7.835	7.926	8.387	6.686	7.316	7.586	6.624	7.102	6.314	7.712	7.372	6.614	8.779	7.118
GKS	8.921	8.775	8.815	8.702	7.994	8.486	8.497	8.799	8.312	7.902	8.957	8.951	8.892	9.132	7.849

sion Tree. These AUPRC improvements highlight GK-SMOTE's effectiveness in preserving both precision and recall for minority classes, even under noisy conditions. As illustrated in Fig. 4(b) and Table 4 (Tab b), GK-SMOTE continues to outperform all baseline and state-of-the-art oversampling techniques, reinforcing its robustness and adaptability in complex, real-world imbalanced classification scenarios.

Dataset Performance Analysis: Among the 27 datasets evaluated in our study, GK-SMOTE achieved superior performance on 21 datasets under both noise-free ($\gamma = 0$) and noisy ($\gamma = 0.3$) conditions. These datasets included many with high imbalance ratios (IR), which traditionally present greater classification challenges. GK-SMOTE's consistent performance across these datasets highlights its generalization and robustness in handling imbalanced learning scenarios.

5.3 Statistical Analysis

To rigorously evaluate the statistical significance of the performance differences among oversampling methods, we employed a non-parametric Friedman test followed by the Nemenyi post-hoc test under two distinct conditions: (a) no label noise ($\gamma = 0$) and (b) moderate label noise ($\gamma = 0.3$). Figure 5 shows

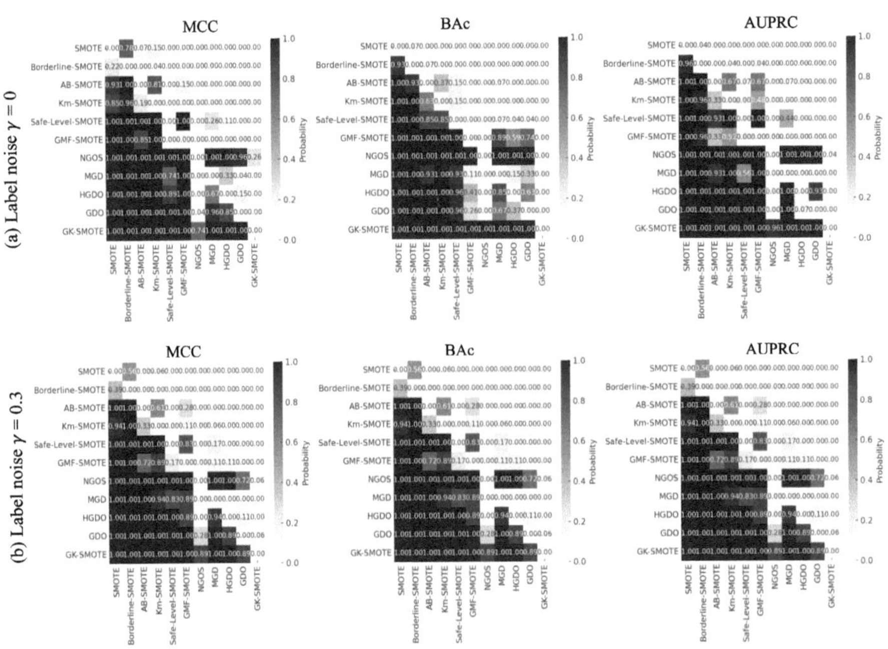

Fig. 5. Heatmaps of p-values for MCC, BAc, and AUPRC across oversampling methods under (a) no label noise $\gamma = 0$ and (b) label noise $\gamma = 0.3$ in Random Forest (RF).

p-value heatmaps for the Random Forest (RF) classifier across three key evaluation metrics: MCC, BAc, and AUPRC. Each heatmap summarizes pairwise comparisons between oversampling methods, where darker blue cells indicate statistically significant differences with $p < 0.05$. The results clearly show that under $\gamma = 0$, GK-SMOTE achieves statistically significant superiority ($p < 0.05$) over 100% (11 out of 11) of the competing methods across all three metrics. When label noise increases to $\gamma = 0.3$, GK-SMOTE retains this significance for 100% of comparisons in MCC and 90.9% (10 out of 11) in both BAc and AUPRC, further confirming its robustness. These statistical findings reinforce that GK-SMOTE consistently performs better than other state-of-the-art and Gaussian-based oversampling techniques. These consistent results demonstrate GK-SMOTE's resilience to label noise and its statistically validated advantage in classification performance.

6 Conclusion

This paper presents GK-SMOTE, a robust and hyperparameter-free oversampling method for handling imbalanced datasets with label noise. Leveraging Gaussian Kernel Density Estimation (KDE), GK-SMOTE effectively identifies dense minority regions while avoiding noisy areas, thereby enhancing class separability and mitigating noise impact. Experimental results demonstrate that GK-SMOTE consistently outperforms state-of-the-art methods, including SMOTE, Borderline-SMOTE, AB-SMOTE, km-SMOTE, and Safe-level-SMOTE, as well as modern Gaussian-based techniques such as GMF-SMOTE, NGOS, MGD, HGDO, and GDO, confirming its superior robustness, efficiency, and classification performance. Its simplicity and computational efficiency make GK-SMOTE well-suited for real-world noisy and imbalanced scenarios. In conclusion, GK-SMOTE offers an effective, user-friendly solution for improving classification accuracy without hyperparameter tuning. Future work may explore its extension to multi-class imbalances and broader model applications.

Acknowledgment. This work was supported by the National Natural Science Foundation of China under Grant 62272073.

References

1. Liu, Z., Li, Y., Chen, N., Wang, Q., Hooi, B., He, B.: A survey of imbalanced learning on graphs: problems, techniques, and future directions. IEEE Trans. Knowl. Data Eng. (2025)
2. Chen, W., Yang, K., Yu, Z., et al.: A survey on imbalanced learning: latest research, applications and future directions. Artif. Intell. Rev. **57**, 137 (2024). https://doi.org/10.1007/s10462-024-10759-6
3. Zhang, R., Lu, S., Yan, B., Yu, P., Tang, X.: A density-based oversampling approach for class imbalance and data overlap. Comput. Ind. Eng. **186**, 109747 (2023)

4. Chawla, N.V., Bowyer, K.W., Hall, L.O., Kegelmeyer, W.P.: SMOTE: synthetic minority over-sampling technique. J. Artif. Intell. Res. **16**, 321–357 (2002)
5. Carvalho, M., Pinho, A.J., Brás, S.: Resampling approaches to handle class imbalance: a review from a data perspective. J. Big Data **12**(1), 71 (2025)
6. Cinar, A.C.: A synergistic oversampling technique with differential evolution and safe level synthetic minority oversampling. Appl. Soft Comput. **112819** (2025)
7. Han, H., Wang, W.Y., Mao, B.H.: Borderline-SMOTE: a new over-sampling method in imbalanced data sets learning. In: International Conference on Intelligent Computing, pp. 878–887. Springer, Berlin, Heidelberg (2005)
8. He, H., Bai, Y., Garcia, E.A., Li, S.: ADASYN: adaptive synthetic sampling approach for imbalanced learning. In: 2008 IEEE International Joint Conference on Neural Networks (IEEE World Congress on Computational Intelligence), pp. 1322–1328. IEEE (2008)
9. Majzoub, H.A., Elgedawy, I.: AB-SMOTE: an affinitive borderline SMOTE approach for imbalanced data binary classification. Int. J. Mach. Learn. Comput. **10**(1), 31–37 (2020)
10. Bunkhumpornpat, C., Sinapiromsaran, K., Lursinsap, C.: Safe-Level-SMOTE: safe-level-synthetic minority over-sampling technique for handling the class imbalanced problem. In: Theeramunkong, T., Kijsirikul, B., Cercone, N., Ho, T.-B. (eds.) PAKDD 2009. LNCS (LNAI), vol. 5476, pp. 475–482. Springer, Heidelberg (2009). https://doi.org/10.1007/978-3-642-01307-2_43
11. Guo, C., Ma, Y., Xu, Z., Cao, M., Yao, Q.: An improved oversampling method for imbalanced data–SMOTE based on Canopy and K-means. In: 2019 Chinese Automation Congress (CAC), pp. 1467–1469. IEEE (2019)
12. Xu, Z., Shen, D., Kou, Y., Nie, T.: A synthetic minority oversampling technique based on Gaussian mixture model filtering for imbalanced data classification. IEEE Trans. Neural Netw. Learn. Syst. **35**(3), 3740–3753 (2022)
13. Shao, X., Yan, Y.: Noise-robust Gaussian distribution based imbalanced oversampling. In: International Conference on Algorithms and Architectures for Parallel Processing, pp. 221–234. Springer, Singapore (2023)
14. Xie, J., Zhu, M., Hu, K., Zhang, J.: Instance hardness and multivariate Gaussian distribution-based oversampling technique for imbalance classification. Pattern Anal. Appl. **26**(2), 735–749 (2023)
15. Jia, L., Wang, Z., Sun, P., Wang, P.: HGDO: an oversampling technique based on hypergraph recognition and Gaussian distribution. Inf. Sci. **679**, 120891 (2024)
16. Xie, Y., Qiu, M., Zhang, H., Peng, L., Chen, Z.: Gaussian distribution based oversampling for imbalanced data classification. IEEE Trans. Knowl. Data Eng. **34**(2), 667–679 (2020)

Robust Ensemble Learning via *t*-Tilted Loss: A Noise-Resistant Framework

Junru Luo(✉), Xinyu Xu, and Wenya Shi

School of Computer Science and Artificial Intelligence, Changzhou University, Changzhou 213159, China
luojunru@cczu.edu.cn

Abstract. The performance of machine learning models largely depends on the choice of the loss function. Traditional loss functions perform well in many tasks but may be limited when handling complex data distributions or noisy environments. To address this, this paper proposes an ensemble algorithm based on the t-tilted loss. The t-tilted loss adjusts its values to generate a series of decision makers with different preferences and decision boundaries, which are then effectively combined to enhance a model's generalization ability in noisy datasets. The experiments cover both regression and classification datasets, incorporating different noise ratios to simulate real-world noise conditions. Experimental results show that the ensemble algorithm based on t-tilted loss significantly improves model accuracy in noisy environments and outperforms traditional ensemble methods. Therefore, this study offers new insights into noise-robust learning and provides a theoretical foundation for further improving ensemble algorithms.

Keywords: Robust Optimization · Ensemble Learning · Machine Learning

1 Introduction

In machine learning applications, data noise has consistently been a key factor challenging model performance [12]. Noise primarily arises from mislabeled data, outliers, or measurement errors, and is prevalent across various task domains, such as image classification [33], natural language processing (NLP) [3], and financial risk prediction [25].

This challenge has driven research into noise-resistant methods [1]. In low-noise scenarios, data preprocessing techniques are typically employed, such as removing noisy data through outlier detection [27], or generating adversarial samples through data augmentation [13]. In high-noise environments, dynamic optimization at both the algorithmic and model levels is required, such as noise filtering through knowledge distillation with a teacher-student model [16] or mitigating noise interference through curriculum learning, which progressively shifts from easy to hard tasks [15].

J. Li et al. (Eds.): APWeb-WAIM 2025, LNCS 16115, pp. 213–230, 2026.
https://doi.org/10.1007/978-981-95-5719-6_14

The high computational cost of complex models has prompted researchers to improve noise robustness through the design of loss functions. A commonly adopted approach is the Huber loss [24], a smooth regression loss designed to reduce the influence of outliers during training. Another prevalent strategy involves modifying the cross-entropy loss, as seen in Peer Loss [21] and Normalized Cross-Entropy (NCE) Loss [22], both aimed at enhancing robustness to label noise. Additionally, Tilted Empirical Risk Minimization (TERM) [17] incorporates a parameter t into the empirical risk minimization (ERM) framework to dynamically reshape the loss function and adaptively down-weight outliers, thereby effectively suppressing the impact of noise. The mathematical formulation of TERM is as follows:

$$R = \frac{1}{t} \log\left(\frac{1}{N} \sum_{i \in [N]} \exp\big(t\, \ell\big(f(\mathbf{x}_i; \theta),\, y_i\big)\big) \right), \tag{1}$$

where $f(x_i; \theta)$ is the prediction function with parameters θ, $\ell\big(f(x_i; \theta), y_i\big)$ measures the gap between the output and the label y_i, and N is the total number of training samples.

However, in real-world settings, the true noise distribution is typically unknown in advance, complicating the design of fixed-loss functions and highlighting the need for adaptive strategies [18,30,39]. While the TERM framework demonstrates promising robustness by employing a t-tilted loss to dynamically adjust sample weights through the parameter t, its reliance on cross-validation or hyperparameter optimization to determine the optimal t introduces notable limitations—such as computational inefficiency and suboptimal generalization due to t's sensitivity to the noise distribution. Specifically, TERM's static adjustment mechanism cannot adapt to unknown or shifting noise distributions in high-noise environments. A review of the history of machine learning reveals that ensemble learning constitutes a canonical approach for enhancing overall model stability and generalization performance by combining the strengths of multiple weak learners and mitigating their individual weaknesses. For instance, methods such as Bagging [4], Boosting [9], and Random Forest [5] have been extensively validated as effective means of addressing overfitting, noise, and outliers. Consequently, introducing the ensemble paradigm into the TERM framework emerges as a natural and powerful avenue for improvement.

Building on this idea, we now describe ETERM's two-stage learning framework in detail. In the first stage, we train linear base models using the TERM robust loss function and generate diversity among the base models by setting different values of t. This approach leverages the unique characteristics of the TERM loss function at different t values to enhance the model's adaptability to noise. Compared to other ensemble methods, this diversity-promoting strategy better captures noise patterns, thus reducing the risk of overfitting. In the second stage, base models' predictions and residual patterns are fed into a nonlinear aggregator, which learns to correct errors that linear combinations alone cannot capture. The advantage of this fusion strategy lies in the combination of linear and nonlinear models, which allows for a more comprehensive adaptation to noise and avoids issues such as the lack of model architecture diversity commonly seen in traditional ensemble methods. Empirical results demonstrate that ETERM consistently outperforms other methods.

The main contributions of this paper are as follows:

1. We propose ETERM, an algorithm that trains linear base models with varying t values to promote model diversity while leveraging their efficiency and interpretability. By integrating ensemble learning with a robust loss function, ETERM improves both noise robustness and generalization performance.
2. We conduct extensive experiments on both classification and regression tasks using datasets contaminated with varying levels of synthetic and real-world-inspired noise. The results consistently demonstrate that ETERM outperforms conventional ensemble methods and individual robust models in terms of accuracy, robustness and stability.

The structure of this paper is organized as follows: Sect. 2 reviews robust loss functions and noise-resistant regression methods and their shortcomings; Sect. 3 presents the t-tilted loss for generating diverse base models and a nonlinear second-stage learner; Sect. 4 reports experiments on regression and classification tasks with method comparisons; and Sect. 5 concludes and outlines future work on adaptive parameter tuning and large-scale deployment.

2 Related Work

Data noise poses a significant challenge in machine learning, and robust loss functions have become a central strategy to mitigate its effects. Existing methods fall into two categories. First, some approaches depend on estimating noise characteristics to correct loss functions. For example, Patrini et al. [28] estimate the noise transition matrix using a small set of clean anchor samples, applying forward correction to predicted probabilities and backward correction to loss gradients for unbiased learning. Liu and Tao [20] compute the density ratio β between noisy and true label distributions and reweight the empirical risk accordingly. Yu et al. [38] incorporate noise transition estimation into federated learning by periodically updating noise rates and correcting predictions during local training. Next, inherently robust losses require no prior noise-distribution knowledge. Theoretical results show that 0âĂŞ1 loss and mean absolute error (MAE) are noise-tolerant, unlike cross-entropy (CE) [11]. This insight has led to the development of hybrid loss functions. For example, generalized cross-entropy (GCE) combines MAE and CE [40], while asymmetric losses such as AGCE, AEL, and AUL apply different smoothing and weighting mechanisms to reduce the influence of easily classified samples under noisy labels [42]. Beyond loss design, algorithmic methods have also been proposed. For instance, MS-ADMM [36] combines Huber loss with adaptive step sizes for faster convergence, while kernel-based robust regression [8] adopts an l_s-loss with iteratively reweighted least squares (IRLS) to resist noise.

In addition to robust loss functions, several studies have explored distributed robust optimization frameworks to handle noise during training. One representative formulation is $\min_x \max_{u\in U} f(x,u)$, which aims to improve robustness and computational efficiency in distributed settings [7,23]. Qi et al. [29] introduce a KL-divergence term to transform this minâĂŞmax problem into a pure minimization, thereby reducing computational cost. Zhu et al. [43] propose an adaptive label loss with minimal overhead, while Zhou et al. [41] develop a robust curriculum learning strategy that detects clean labels and self-corrects noisy ones through dynamic sampling and temporal consistency.

Robust optimization has demonstrated broad applicability across domains in noisy environments. Wang et al. [35] develop the RIES scheduling model, which treats data uncertainty as decision-making noise to support agricultural energy pollution reduction. Tang et al. [32] apply confidence-threshold calibration to enhance memristor system reliability under noise. Liu et al. [19] propose the SOP method, using sparse regularization to combat label noise in over-parameterized networks. Sun et al. [31] introduce EKML for few-shot text classification, leveraging external knowledge, contrastive learning, and adversarial networks to boost meta-learning robustness. Xie et al. [37] present UTWAA, which injects a few words into inputs to reveal classifier vulnerability to adversarial noise.

Collectively, these studies highlight the central challenge of designing noise-resilient methods. Whether through label-noise rates, robust objectives, or min-max optimization, developing effective solutions remains challenging yet highly relevant, as evidenced by the increasing number of new approaches in recent years.

3 Method

Ensemble learning reduces variance, improves generalization, and enhances robustness by aggregating weak learners. We propose a two-stage noise-robust framework that integrates TERM with stacking. In stage one, K linear base learners are trained on bootstrap-sampled subsets, each using a distinct tilted t_k to emphasize high- or low-loss samples. In stage two, a meta-learner optimally combines their outputs. This synergy between tilt-induced diversity and stacking markedly boosts adaptability, accuracy, and stability under high noise.

To enhance the model's robustness against noisy data, we introduce a diversity-driven training mechanism in the first stage. Let the full training set be $\mathcal{D} = \{(\mathbf{x}_i, y_i) \mid i = 1, \ldots, N\}$, from which we generate K distinct subsets $\{\mathcal{D}_k\}$ by the Bootstrap method. We then apply TERM to each $\mathcal{D}_k$ with its own tilted parameter t_k, dynamically reweighting samples based on their loss magnitude to improve adaptability to specific tasks and noisy environments (see Eq. (1)).

As shown in ETERM, we update the model parameters θ by minimizing this t-tilted loss via weighted gradient descent, where predictions—under our linear base learners $f(\mathbf{x}_i;\theta) = \mathbf{x}_i^T\theta$—are first fed into the loss $\ell(f(\mathbf{x}_i;\theta), y_i)$ and its gradient $\nabla_\theta \ell(f(\mathbf{x}_i;\theta), y_i)$. The t-tilted loss over the current parameters is then calculated as follows:

$$R_k(\theta) = \frac{1}{t_k} \log\left(\frac{1}{|\mathcal{D}_k|} \sum_{(\mathbf{x}_i, y_i) \in \mathcal{D}_k} \exp\big(t_k\, \ell(f(\mathbf{x}_i;\theta);\, y_i)\big) \right). \tag{2}$$

Let $\ell_i(\theta) = \ell(f(\mathbf{x}_i;\theta), y_i)$, then Eq. (2) can be rewritten as

$$R_k(\theta) = \frac{1}{t_k} \log Z_k(\theta), \tag{3}$$

where $Z_k(\theta) = \frac{1}{|\mathcal{D}_k|} \sum_{i \in \mathcal{D}_k} \exp\big(t_k\, \ell_i(\theta)\big)$. Differentiating $R_k(\theta)$ with respect to θ gives:

$$\nabla_\theta R_k(\theta) = \frac{1}{t_k\, Z_k(\theta)} \nabla_\theta Z_k(\theta) = \sum_{i \in \mathcal{D}_k} \frac{\exp\big(t_k\, \ell_i(\theta)\big)}{\sum_{j \in \mathcal{D}_k} \exp\big(t_k\, \ell_j(\theta)\big)} \nabla_\theta \ell_i(\theta), \tag{4}$$

revealing a soft-max weighting term. Noting that

$$\sum_{j \in \mathcal{D}_k} e^{t_k\, \ell_j(\theta)} = |\mathcal{D}_k|\, e^{t_k R_k(\theta)}, \tag{5}$$

we obtain the per-sample importance weight:

$$w_i(t_k;\theta) = \frac{\exp\big(t_k\, \ell_i(\theta)\big)}{\sum_{j \in \mathcal{D}_k} \exp\big(t_k\, \ell_j(\theta)\big)} = \exp\big(t_k [\ell_i(\theta) - R_k(\theta)]\big). \tag{6}$$

$w_i(t_k;\theta)$ is based on the current parameter θ in each iteration and quantifies the contribution of each sample. The parameters are then updated through weighted gradient descent, where α is the learning rate:

$$\theta \leftarrow \theta - \frac{\alpha}{|\mathcal{D}_k|} \sum_{(\mathbf{x}_i, y_i) \in \mathcal{D}_k} w_i(t_k;\theta)\, \nabla_\theta\, \ell\big(f(\mathbf{x}_i;\theta),\, y_i\big). \tag{7}$$

The tilted parameter t in TERM plays a pivotal role in model training by dynamically reshaping the loss landscape, thereby controlling the relative emphasis placed on high-loss and low-loss samples. Specifically, varying t values induce distinct sample weight distributions. A larger t amplifies the influence of high-loss (potentially noisy) samples, while a smaller t prioritizes low-loss regions. By randomly sampling diverse t values across base learners, we enforce heterogeneity in their learned loss distributions, effectively promoting model diversity. This deliberate variation ensures that each learner captures complementary patterns of the data, some robust to noise and others sensitive to outliers. Integrating these learners through ensemble aggregation then mitigates individual biases, enhancing both stability and robustness—particularly in noisy settings.

In the second stage, the core of the ensemble lies in fusing the outputs of multiple base learners. For the i-th sample, each linear base learner first computes $\hat{y}_i^{(k)} = \mathbf{x}_i^\top \theta_k$.

These predictions from all base learners are first collected into a vector $\mathbf{h}_i = \left[\hat{y}_i^1, \hat{y}_i^2, \ldots, \hat{y}_i^K\right]^\top$.

To capture potential nonlinear relationships among these predictions, $\mathbf{h}_i$ is mapped to a higher-dimensional feature space using a second-order polynomial expansion:

$$\text{Poly}(\mathbf{h}_i) = \left[1,\ \{h_{ij}\}_{j=1}^K,\ \{h_{ij}^2\}_{j=1}^K,\ \{h_{ij}h_{i\ell}\}_{1 \le j < \ell \le K}\right]^\top. \tag{8}$$

Algorithm: ETERM

Input: training set $\mathcal{D}_{\text{train}}$, number of base learners K

Stage 1: Train K base learners
for $k = 1$ **to** K:
  Samples the subset D_k from the training dataset D_{train} using Bootstrap
  For each subset D_k, randomly sample a tilted parameter $t_k \in \mathbb{R}$
  Initialize parameters θ_k
  for $t = 1$ **to** T:
    Compute the sample losses $\ell_i(\theta_k)$ and the t-tilted loss $R_k(\theta_k)$ in Eq.(2)
    Compute sample weights:

$$w_i(t_k; \theta_k) = \exp\Big(t_k\left[\ell_i(\theta_k) - R_k(\theta_k)\right]\Big)$$

    Update parameters:

$$\theta_k \leftarrow \theta_k - \frac{\alpha}{|\mathcal{D}_k|} \sum_{(\mathbf{x}_i, y_i) \in \mathcal{D}_k} w_i(t_k; \theta_k)\, \nabla_{\theta_k} \ell\big(f(\mathbf{x}_i; \theta_k), y_i\big)$$

  end for
  Compute the base-learner output $\hat{y}_i^{(k)} = \theta_k^\top \mathbf{x}_i$
end for

Stage 2: Train ensemble model
for each $(\mathbf{x}_i, y_i) \in \mathcal{D}_{\text{train}}$:
  Generate base outputs: $\mathbf{h}_i = [\hat{y}_i^1, \hat{y}_i^2, \ldots, \hat{y}_i^K]$
  Feature expansion: $\mathbf{h}_i' = \text{Poly}(\mathbf{h}_i)$
  Build the second-stage training set: $\mathcal{D}_{\text{ensemble}} = \{(\mathbf{h}_i', y_i)\}$
  Train the model M in training set $\mathcal{D}_{\text{ensemble}}$
end for

The expanded feature vector $\mathbf{h}_i' = \text{Poly}(\mathbf{h}_i)$, together with its real label y_i, forms the training set $\mathcal{D}_{\text{ensemble}}$ for the second stage learner M. Then we choose the non-linear meta learner M according to the task. For classification, we use XGBoost with a logistic-loss objective; for regression, we employ a two-layer MLP trained to minimize MSE using SGD. Training on $\mathcal{D}_{\text{ensemble}}$ proceeds as follows. First, we sample a mini-batch of examples and perform a forward pass through the meta-learner. Next, we compute the task-specific loss and back-propagate gradients. We then update the model parameters. These steps are repeated until validation performance converges or early stopping is triggered. The final model M thus implicitly learns the optimal nonlinear combination and interaction weights for the base learners' outputs.

Combining robust loss functions with ensemble learning leverages their complementary strengths. Specifically, TERM mitigates outlier influence by adaptively reweighting samples based on losses. Meanwhile, ensemble learning enhances robustness by aggregating predictions from multiple base learners, each trained with a different tilted parameter t, thereby introducing diverse sensitivities to noise. This fusion reduces volatility, lowers prediction variance, and improves stability and generalization. As a result, the framework retains noise control from robust loss functions while adapting to various noise distributions using ensemble strategies.

In practice, the first stage assigns a unique tilted parameter t to each base learner, which is independently trained on a subset of randomly sampled data. This 'diverse-t and diverse-data' strategy promotes model diversity: Some learners focus more on low-loss samples to suppress outliers, while others prioritize high-loss samples to capture the underlying noise patterns. In the second stage, the outputs of these diverse models are transformed through polynomial expansion into a high-dimensional feature space. A nonlinear second-stage learner is then trained to automatically assign weights to each base learner, down-weighting those that are more affected by noise and emphasizing those with greater stability. This entire process requires no manual hyperparameter tuning and dynamically adapts to unknown noise conditions, thereby simplifying model selection while significantly enhancing noise suppression and prediction accuracy.

4 Experiments

This section evaluates the robustness of the ETERM algorithm under noisy conditions in both regression and classification tasks. Compared with classical ensemble methods and robust learning algorithms, ETERM demonstrates strong predictive performance in most scenarios. All datasets are publicly available from the UCI repository.[1]

4.1 Toy Experiments

To illustrate the observed robustness, we first present a controlled toy experiment that demonstrates the effect of different t-tilted losses on noise. As shown in Fig. 1, a one-dimensional quadratic function $y = 0.5x^2 - x + 1$ was sampled at 300 clean points and corrupted by 20 outliers drawn from a heavy-tailed distribution. When training a linear regression model with ETERM, different choices of t significantly impact the model predictions.

As shown in Fig. 2, increasing the number of base learners enables the ensemble to better capture data characteristics under different t-tilted objectives,

[1] https://archive.ics.uci.edu/ml/index.php.

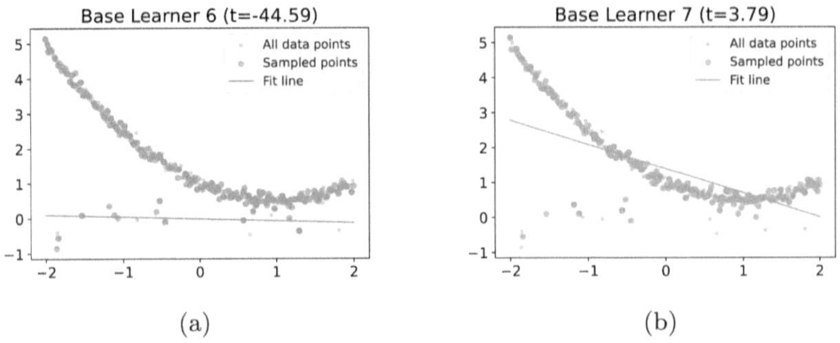

(a) (b)

Fig. 1. TERM Models with Variable t-Values on a Toy Dataset.

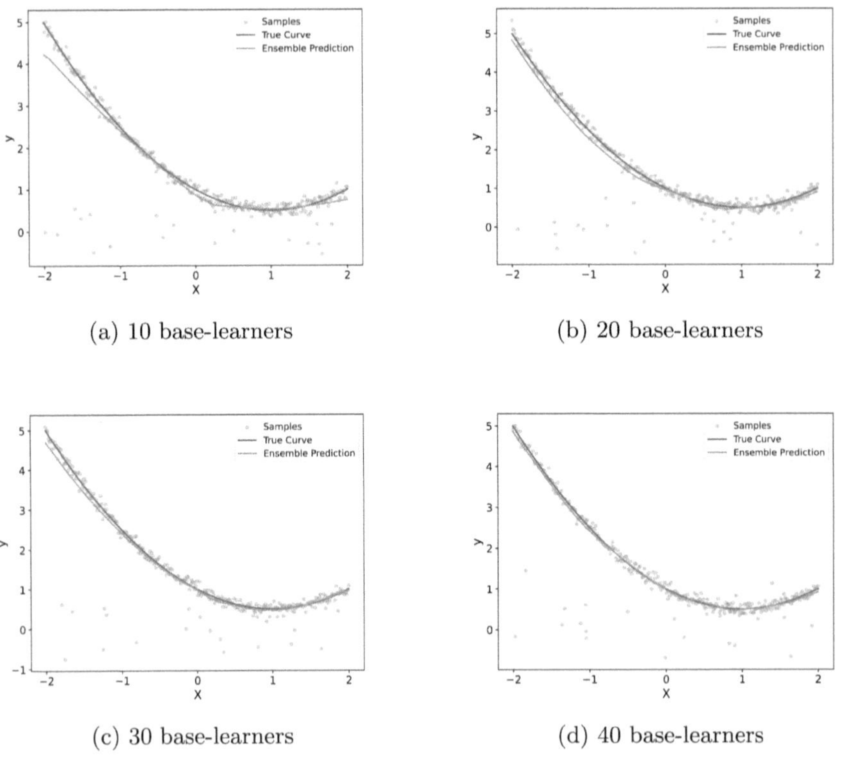

(a) 10 base-learners (b) 20 base-learners

(c) 30 base-learners (d) 40 base-learners

Fig. 2. Impact of the Number of Base Learners on Ensemble Performance.

thereby improving robustness and overall performance.As shown in Fig. 3,When K increases from 10 to 15, the RMSE decreases markedly, indicating that in this range the addition of base learners yields the most significant noise-suppression benefit. Further raising K to 25 causes the RMSE to plateau, suggesting that model performance has essentially reached its optimum and that marginal gains begin to diminish. Beyond $K = 30$, both RMSE and training time change neg-

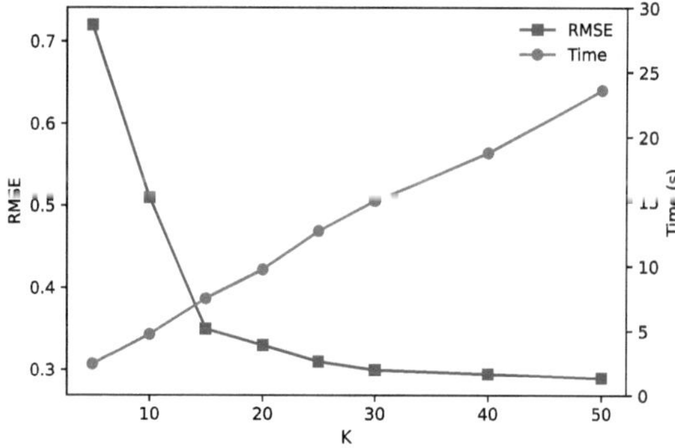

Fig. 3. RMSE and Computation Time vs. Number of Base Learners.

ligibly compared to $K = 50$, implying that performance saturation has been reached while computational cost continues to rise.

4.2 Regression

In these experiments, noise is introduced into both the samples and labels. The noise ratio is set to $\varepsilon = 0.2, 0.4, 0.6, 0.8$. For each ε, we randomly select $\lfloor \varepsilon N \rfloor$ training samples and corrupt their labels by adding Gaussian noise drawn from $\mathcal{N}(\mu = 10, \sigma = 5)$. The ensemble size K is scaled to the noise level: $K = 15$ for $\varepsilon \in \{0.2, 0.4\}$, $K = 20$ for $\varepsilon = 0.6$, and $K = 25$ for $\varepsilon = 0.8$. The first-stage base model uses a linear predictor with bias, $f(\mathbf{x}; \theta) = \theta^\top \mathbf{x} + b$, and is trained using L_2 loss, where $\ell_i(\theta) = (y_i - f(\mathbf{x}_i; \theta))^2$. The second-stage learner is a two-layer MLP with ReLU activation in the hidden layer. Performance is evaluated at each noise level on held-out data using RMSE.

Table 1. Regression Dataset Summary

Dataset Name	Samples	Features	Description
Abalone	4177	8	Predict abalone age
QSAR	1055	41	Predict biodegradability
Traffic Flow	50000	11	Predict traffic volume
Obesity	2111	17	Predict obesity category
Pole Telecomm	10000	5	Predict power parameters
Concrete	1030	8	Predict concrete strength
Diamonds	53940	10	Predict the price
Household Power Consumption	2075	7	Predict electricity consumption
Garments Worker Productivity	1197	11	Predict worker efficiency
California Housing Prices	20640	8	Predict house prices

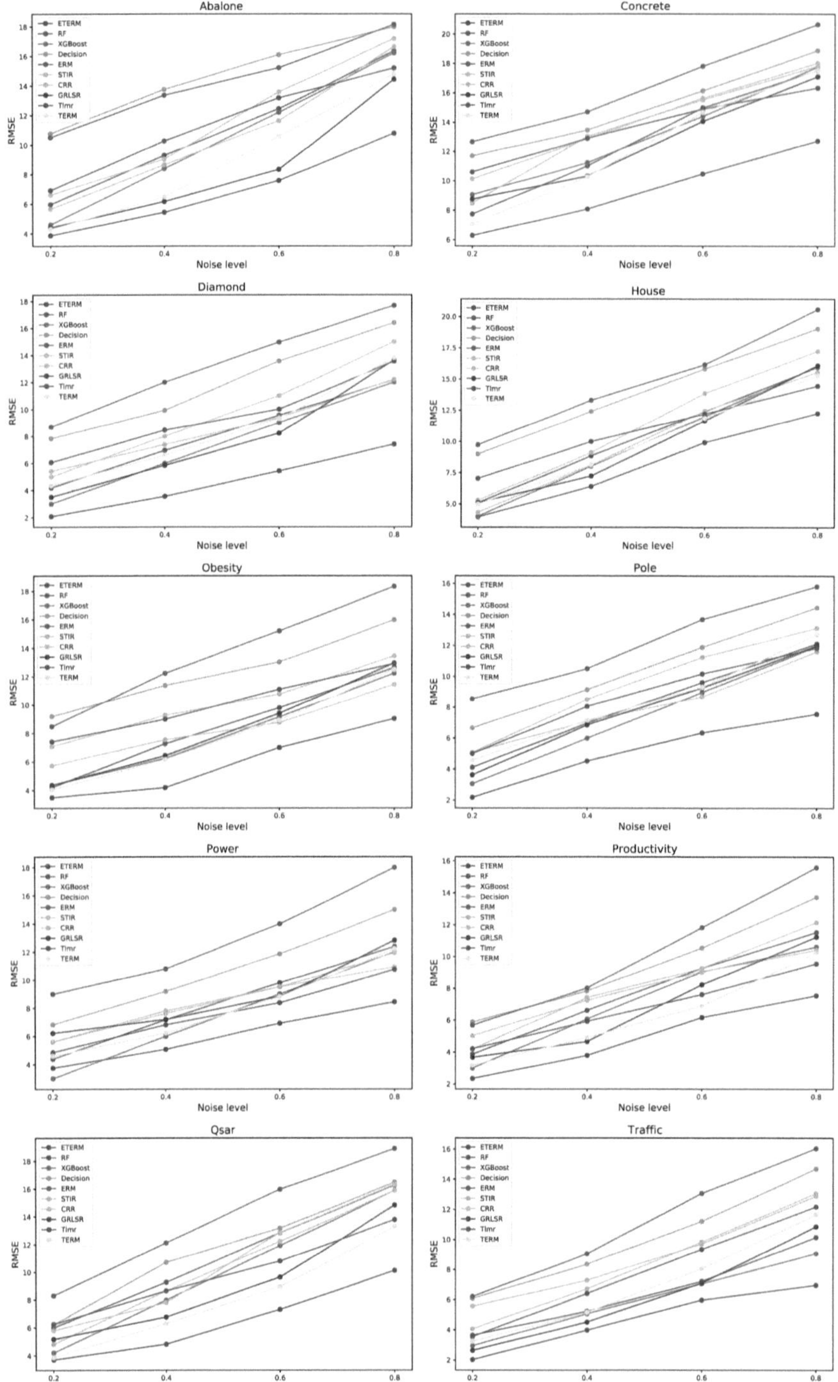

Fig. 4. Results of Regression Tasks.

The baseline algorithms in the experiments include both robust loss-based methods and classical ensemble algorithms. (1) Classical ensemble algorithms: Random Forest and XGBoost. (2) STIR [26]: stage-wise truncated iterative reweighting for robust least squares. (3) CRR [2]: iterative residual hard thresholding followed by pseudo-inverse least squares. (4) GRLSR [34]: least-squares regression with a concave loss and $\ell_{2,p}$-norm regularization solved via iterative optimization. (5) TLMR [14]: majorizationâĂŞminimization of a truncated loss by minimizing successive convex upper bounds. (6)ERM: a linear regression model trained via empirical risk minimization using the L_2 loss.(7)TERM [17]: it extends ERM by introducing a tilt parameter t for dynamic loss reweighting. In the original paper, t is set to -2, which we also adopt in our experiments. The detailed information about the datasets is summarized in Table 1.

According to the results in Fig. 4, ETERM maintains the lowest RMSE as the noise ratio increases, outperforming all baselines on all test datasets. First, we compare ETERM against state-of-the-art robust loss methods. Algorithms that rely solely on the loss function to suppress noise ignore the variations in sample distribution within the feature space. This effect is particularly pronounced for GRLSR on the QSAR and Traffic datasets: as the noise ratio increases from 0.2 to 0.8, its RMSE not only rises more rapidly but also fluctuates more widely. TERM similarly fails to address this limitation; however, after introducing ensemble learning in the second stage, ETERM's robustness to noise is significantly enhanced. For example, on the Abalone and Diamond datasets, when the noise ratio increases from 0.4 to 0.6, TERM's RMSE increases far more than ETERM's. Next, we compare ETERM with classical ensemble methods such as Random Forest and XGBoost. Although standalone ensemble methods, by combining multiple base learners, outperform certain robust loss algorithms (e.g., CRR and TMLR) under low-to-moderate noise conditions, their performance degrades sharply when the noise ratio reaches 0.6 or higher. For instance, on the Productivity dataset, Random Forest and XGBoost perform excellently at noise rates of 0.2 and 0.4; however, once noise increases to 0.6 or 0.8, their RMSE growth significantly exceeds that of ETERM. Therefore, whether relying solely on robust loss functions or using traditional ensemble algorithms, both struggle to maintain stable performance with diverse data and high noise ratios, whereas ETERM demonstrates superior robustness.

4.3 Classfication

For classification tasks, logistic regression is used in Stage 1 and XGBoost in Stage 2. Different datasets adopt different label processing strategies. For the MNIST dataset, specific label flips are applied, including $7 \rightarrow 1$, $2 \rightarrow 7$, $5 \leftrightarrow 6$, and $3 \rightarrow 8$. For the other datasets, which are originally binary classification tasks, only $0 \leftrightarrow 1$ label conversion is performed. Noise levels are set to $\varepsilon \in \{0.1, 0.2, 0.3, 0.4, 0.5\}$, and we scale the ensemble size K to the noise level: $K = 15$ for $\varepsilon \in \{0.1, 0.2\}$, $K = 20$ for $\varepsilon \in \{0.3, 0.4\}$, and $K = 25$ for $\varepsilon = 0.5$. Here, $\ell_i(\theta)$ denotes the cross-entropy loss.

Table 2. Classification Datasets

Dataset Name	Samples	Features	Description
Adult	48842	14	Predict income level
Mushroom	8124	22	Predict edibility
Mnist	70,000	784	Predict digit class
Gisette	13,500	5000	Predict digit recognition
Spambase	4601	58	Predict spam detection
Default of Credit Card	30000	23	Predict payment default
Student Academic	4424	36	Predict academic performance
Online Shopper Intention	12330	17	Predict purchase conversion
Bank	4522	16	Predict term deposit subscription
Bank-full	45211	16	Predict term deposit subscription

We conduct a systematic comparison between robust-loss algorithms and classical ensemble methods, as follows: (1)Adaboost, GBM, and Random Forest (RF): These are classical ensemble algorithms, all based on the Boosting framework, with RF being a distinct algorithm. (2)GCE [40]: smoothly interpolates between log-loss and 0âĂŞ1 loss via a tunable parameter, effectively decreasing the weight of low confidence (potentially noisy) examples. (3) CICE [6]: embeds a kernel-based similarity measure into the cross-entropy computation to suppress the influence of outliers on gradients. (4)AUL and AEL [42]: AUL asymmetrically scales positive and negative errors to reduce the impact of mislabeled samples, while AEL similarly adjusts the exponential loss to suppress gradients from noisy data. (5) FHSVM and FLSSVM [10]: FHSVM extends the standard hinge loss by raising slack variables to a fractional power, whlie FLSSVM integrates hinge loss into a regularized least-squares framework. (6)TERM: we also apply TERM as the baseline algorithms. These algorithms exhibit strong resistance to noise and perform exceptionally well on datasets with noisy or outlier-contaminated labels. The detailed information of the datasets is summarized in Table 2.

Table 3 displays the classification performance of the algorithms on ten datasets across six noise levels, highlighting that ETERM consistently outperforms the others. ETERM's average accuracy decreases from 92.7% in a noise-free scenario to 77.3% at a 50% noise level, a decline of 15.4% points—about 35%âĂŞ40% lower than AdaBoost or GBM. Nonetheless, at the highest noise level, ETERM outperforms the second-best by 4.2% points. ETERM shows robust performance on both high-dimensional datasets (e.g., Gisette) and smaller-scale benchmarks (e.g., Adult, Mushroom, and Bank). As the noise level reaches 0.3 or higher, ETERM's classification accuracy significantly surpasses that of standalone robust loss methods (e.g., TERM, CICE, AUL), with the performance gap widening even more. Moreover, ETERM maintains competitive training times and exhibits low variance across repeated runs, underscoring its practical feasibility. The integration of robust loss with ensemble learning enhances noise tolerance and consistently delivers superior classification performance in noisy, complex environments. ETERM also achieves low error variability and high accuracy in both regression and classification tasks across diverse data distributions and noise levels, demonstrating excellent generalization and wide applicability. Overall, ETERM proves to be a highly effective algorithm, offering robust performance and superior generalization across various tasks and noisy condition.

4.4 Ablation Experiments

To assess the benefits of combining robust loss with ensemble learning, we run ablation experiments on two fronts. In the regression experiments, we measured root-mean-square error under a 60% noise ratio. In the classification experiments, we measured accuracy under a 30% noise ratio. We compared (1) TERM applied alone in the base learner and (2) ETERM with its second stage replaced by simple averaging. Across both tasks and noise levels, the two-stage ETERM framework consistently outperformed both alternatives.

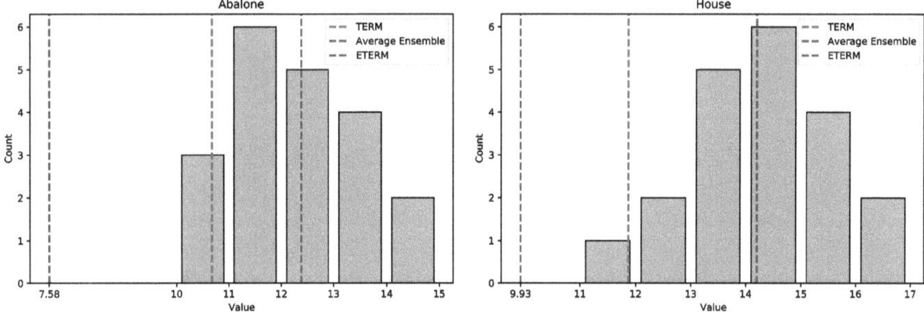

Fig. 5. Ablation Experiments on Regression Datasets.

Figure 5 illustrates the regression results on the Abalone and House datasets. We first summarize the distribution of base learners' predictions and display it as a bar chart. Then, we overlay dashed lines to indicate the RMSE of TERM, simple averaging and our ETERM method for direct comparison. By leveraging the second-stage ensemble in ETERM, the RMSE on Abalone decreases from approximately 12âĂŞ14 under simple averaging to 7.58—about 4.5 points lower than the best TERM-only result (10.67). On House, ETERM compresses the RMSE to 9.93, corresponding to reductions of around 16% and 30% relative to the best TERM (11.87) and simple averaging (14.24), respectively.

Figure 6 shows classification results on the Adult and Mushroom datasets, where ETERM consistently achieves the highest accuracy. On Adult it outperforms both TERM and simple averaging across all noise levels. On Mushroom it reaches a peak accuracy of about 85.5%, exceeding TERM's 81.6% by roughly 4% points and markedly outperforming simple averaging.

Table 3. Classification Performance on 10 Datasets

(a) Adult Dataset

Method	Noise Ratio					
	0	0.1	0.2	0.3	0.4	0.5
Adaboost	0.8867	0.8519	0.8037	0.7497	0.6756	0.6025
RF	0.8581	0.8369	0.7889	0.7292	0.6521	0.5984
GBM	0.8994	0.8648	0.8127	0.7612	0.7112	0.6209
GCE	0.8837	0.8629	0.8351	0.7932	0.7592	0.7084
AUL	0.8904	0.8636	0.8219	0.7921	0.7527	0.7062
AEL	0.9233	0.8957	0.8546	0.8139	0.7654	0.7038
FHSVM	0.8845	0.8571	0.8214	0.7759	0.7318	0.6917
FLSSVM	0.8967	0.8749	0.8483	0.8042	0.7561	0.7033
CICE	0.9014	0.8828	0.8562	0.8259	0.7748	0.7257
TERM	0.9036	0.8874	0.8495	0.8159	0.7648	0.7183
ETERM	**0.9329**	**0.9073**	**0.8724**	**0.8551**	**0.8279**	**0.7903**

(b) Mushroom Dataset

Method	Noise Ratio					
	0	0.1	0.2	0.3	0.4	0.5
Adaboost	0.9075	0.8849	0.8368	0.7991	0.7079	0.6386
RF	0.9153	0.8641	0.8270	0.7792	0.7143	0.6394
GBM	0.9182	0.8951	0.8463	0.7963	0.7243	0.6684
GCE	0.9327	0.9038	0.8651	0.8237	0.7635	0.6839
AUL	0.9363	0.9013	0.8654	0.8137	0.7742	0.7381
AEL	0.9368	0.8976	0.8617	0.8129	0.7683	0.7027
FHSVM	0.9275	0.8928	0.8615	0.8283	0.7624	0.7045
FLSSVM	0.9138	0.8881	0.8548	0.8216	0.7845	0.7236
CICE	0.9089	0.8853	0.8614	0.8372	0.8011	0.7628
TERM	0.9227	0.8976	0.8649	0.8251	0.7954	0.7546
ETERM	**0.9463**	**0.9177**	**0.8931**	**0.8552**	**0.8231**	**0.7839**

(c) MNIST Dataset

Method	**Noise Ratio**					
	0	0.1	0.2	0.3	0.4	0.5
Adaboost	0.9039	0.8736	0.8375	0.7877	0.7246	0.6595
RF	0.9163	0.8802	0.8237	0.7681	0.7039	0.6245
GBM	0.9185	0.8962	0.8547	0.8087	0.7305	0.6719
GCE	0.9132	0.8862	0.8405	0.8037	0.7501	0.7061
AUL	0.9246	0.9027	0.8615	0.8159	0.7572	0.6981
AEL	0.9064	0.8797	0.8507	0.8141	0.7672	0.7184
FHSVM	0.9184	0.8972	0.8645	0.8169	0.7623	0.7081
FLSSVM	0.9025	0.8916	0.8725	0.8319	0.7865	0.7264
CICE	0.9125	0.9013	0.8769	0.8352	0.7963	0.7382
TERM	0.9276	0.8952	0.8649	0.8152	0.7973	0.7491
ETERM	**0.9347**	**0.9186**	**0.8893**	**0.8516**	**0.8138**	**0.7638**

(d) Gisette Dataset

Method	Noise Ratio					
	0	0.1	0.2	0.3	0.4	0.5
Adaboost	0.9286	0.8871	0.8357	0.7871	0.7114	0.6257
RF	0.9142	0.8857	0.8514	0.8071	0.7529	0.6043
GBM	0.9201	0.8957	0.8643	0.7914	0.7214	0.6414
GCE	0.9137	0.8761	0.8468	0.7963	0.7502	0.6977
AUL	0.9343	0.8929	0.8416	0.8027	0.7641	0.7069
AEL	0.9129	0.8843	0.8527	0.8171	0.7746	0.7185
FHSVM	0.9187	0.8931	0.8682	0.8207	0.7693	0.7084
FLSSVM	0.9154	0.9003	0.8843	0.8582	0.8037	0.7586
CICE	0.8957	0.8763	0.8591	0.8174	0.7852	0.7349
TERM	0.9229	0.8814	0.8563	0.8223	0.7819	0.7382
ETERM	**0.9314**	**0.9129**	**0.8914**	**0.8757**	**0.8386**	**0.7814**

(e)Spambase Dataset

Method	Noise Ratio					
	0	0.1	0.2	0.3	0.4	0.5
Adaboost	0.9111	0.8821	0.8369	0.7787	0.7022	0.6163
RF	0.9284	0.8937	0.8561	0.8061	0.7448	0.6749
GBM	0.9271	0.8993	0.8452	0.7915	0.7368	0.6652
GCE	0.9087	0.8862	0.8641	0.8169	0.7538	0.6968
AUL	0.9147	0.8935	0.8671	0.8282	0.7789	0.7184
AEL	0.9137	0.8984	0.8693	0.8216	0.7631	0.7017
FHSVM	0.9261	0.8997	0.8628	0.8069	0.7561	0.6921
FLSSVM	0.9046	0.8835	0.8683	0.8267	0.7735	0.7141
CICE	0.9171	0.8902	0.8761	0.8237	0.7729	0.7292
TERM	0.9236	0.8959	0.8668	0.8217	0.7863	0.7282
ETERM	**0.9304**	**0.9195**	**0.8871**	**0.8473**	**0.7912**	**0.7584**

(f) Default Dataset

Method	Noise Ratio					
	0	0.1	0.2	0.3	0.4	0.5
Adaboost	0.8873	0.8418	0.8053	0.7489	0.6987	0.6241
RF	0.8923	0.8657	0.8135	0.7697	0.7023	0.6453
GBM	0.9074	0.8633	0.8257	0.7647	0.7081	0.6463
GCE	0.8972	0.8774	0.8309	0.7841	0.7423	0.6904
AUL	0.8927	0.8731	0.8469	0.8013	0.7862	0.7304
AEL	0.9074	0.8813	0.8457	0.8062	0.7639	0.7081
FHSVM	0.9107	0.8897	0.8659	0.8025	0.7583	0.7018
FLSSVM	0.9063	0.8752	0.8597	0.8173	0.7672	0.7151
CICE	0.8979	0.8781	0.8537	0.8265	0.7864	0.7382
TERM	0.9278	0.8931	0.8627	0.8245	0.7753	0.7228
ETERM	**0.9267**	**0.8951**	**0.8646**	**0.8276**	**0.7758**	**0.7407**

(g) Student Dataset

Method	Noise Ratio					
	0	0.1	0.2	0.3	0.4	0.5
Adaboost	0.8713	0.8543	0.8387	0.8045	0.7253	0.6739
RF	0.8846	0.8592	0.8019	0.7692	0.7017	0.6375
GBM	0.8912	0.8658	0.8446	0.8197	0.7617	0.6915
GCE	0.8943	0.8735	0.8472	0.8069	0.7594	0.7017
AUL	0.8924	0.8612	0.8253	0.7896	0.7343	0.6678
AEL	0.9084	0.8723	0.8462	0.8058	0.7561	0.7049
FHSVM	0.9014	0.8765	0.8334	0.7916	0.7557	0.7047
FLSSVM	0.8917	0.8727	0.8449	0.8014	0.7786	0.7326
CICE	0.9026	0.8839	0.8567	0.8286	0.7651	0.7065
TERM	0.8973	0.8649	0.8351	0.8086	0.7694	0.7168
ETERM	**0.9149**	**0.8981**	**0.8755**	**0.8413**	**0.8178**	**0.7583**

(h) Online Dataset

Method	Noise Ratio					
	0	0.1	0.2	0.3	0.4	0.5
Adaboost	0.9085	0.8781	0.8448	0.8016	0.7483	0.6955
RF	0.9027	0.8735	0.8229	0.7783	0.7197	0.6429
GBM	0.9168	0.8871	0.8554	0.8175	0.7397	0.6764
GCE	0.8924	0.8796	0.8472	0.8061	0.7538	0.7023
AUL	0.9016	0.8772	0.8478	0.8066	0.7786	0.7292
AEL	0.9084	0.8827	0.8524	0.8131	0.7616	0.7185
FHSVM	0.8908	0.8794	0.8431	0.8064	0.7529	0.7046
FLSSVM	0.8894	0.8608	0.8378	0.8153	0.7769	0.7294
CICE	0.8917	0.8725	0.8553	0.8294	0.7808	0.7381
TERM	0.9036	0.8892	0.8527	0.8186	0.7753	0.7234
ETERM	**0.9205**	**0.8924**	**0.8745**	**0.8408**	**0.8129**	**0.7745**

(i) Bank Dataset

Method	Noise Ratio					
	0	0.1	0.2	0.3	0.4	0.5
Adaboost	0.9013	0.8885	0.8579	0.8034	0.7598	0.7092
RF	0.8938	0.8761	0.8322	0.7849	0.7216	0.6681
GBM	0.9159	0.8742	0.8463	0.7907	0.7481	0.6874
GCE	0.9235	0.8961	0.8547	0.8129	0.7568	0.7017
AUL	0.9071	0.8836	0.8596	0.8239	0.7883	0.7582
AEL	0.9128	0.8859	0.8469	0.8154	0.7742	0.7328
FHSVM	0.9182	0.8896	0.8581	0.8173	0.7707	0.7188
FLSSVM	0.9027	0.8882	0.8647	0.8391	0.7818	0.7385
CICE	0.9027	0.8896	0.8682	0.8318	0.7968	0.7419
TERM	0.9015	0.8937	0.8546	0.8273	0.7861	0.7393
ETERM	**0.9207**	**0.9085**	**0.8735**	**0.8509**	**0.8333**	**0.7962**

(j) Bank-full Dataset

Method	Noise Ratio					
	0	0.1	0.2	0.3	0.4	0.5
Adaboost	0.9067	0.8798	0.8321	0.7885	0.7254	0.6724
RF	0.8992	0.8622	0.8027	0.7658	0.7028	0.6398
GBM	0.9091	0.8864	0.8416	0.7954	0.7495	0.6929
GCE	0.8972	0.8731	0.8465	0.8097	0.7436	0.6893
AUL	0.9049	0.8871	0.8527	0.8135	0.7764	0.7238
AEL	0.8991	0.8629	0.8216	0.7945	0.7572	0.7028
FHSVM	0.8932	0.8706	0.8484	0.8012	0.7656	0.7104
FLSSVM	0.8861	0.8632	0.8472	0.8239	0.7713	0.7337
CICE	0.9012	0.8837	0.8592	0.8263	0.7864	0.7215
TERM	0.9027	0.8826	0.8574	0.8261	0.7852	0.7369
ETERM	**0.9145**	**0.8889**	**0.8669**	**0.8373**	**0.8053**	**0.7849**

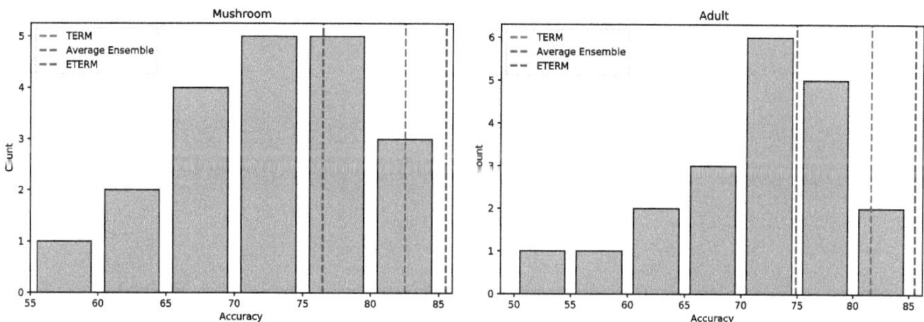

Fig. 6. Ablation Experiments on Classification Datasets.

Ablation experiments on both classification and regression dataset demonstrate the critical role of our two-stage ensemble learning framework. First, the random sampling of the tilted parameter t, combined with bootstrap-based data subsets, ensures substantial diversity among base learners, as evidenced by their varied predictive performance distributions. This heterogeneity allows the ensemble to capture a broad spectrum of noise patterns and data representations. Second, the proposed nonlinear stacking framework outperforms both averaging and best-t selection methods by learning optimal combinations of base predictions through their nonlinear correlations. The superior empirical results confirm that this hierarchical integration not only enhances noise robustness but also achieves consistently higher predictive accuracy compared to linear aggregation methods.

5 Conclusion

This paper presents ETERM, a two-stage noise-robust learning algorithm that combines ensemble learning with robust loss functions. It demonstrates clear advantages in both noise-free and noisy environments. ETERM utilizes diverse base learners to address different noise scenarios and enhances generalization through an adaptive fusion strategy. Future work could explore deep ensemble frameworks, such as multi-branch neural networks, to better handle more complex noise conditions.

Acknowledgments. This study work was funded by the National Natural Science Foundation of China (Grant No. 12201075).

Disclosure of Interests. The authors declare no conflict of interest.

References

1. Akhtar, M., Tanveer, M., Arshad, M.: Hawkeye: advancing robust regression with bounded, smooth, and insensitive loss function. arXiv preprint arXiv:2401.16785 (2024)

2. Bhatia, K., Jain, P., Kamalaruban, P., Kar, P.: Consistent robust regression. Adv. Neural Inf. Process. Syst. **30** (2017)
3. Bian, H.: Unveiling the evolution and impact of pretrained language models in natural language processing. In: Proceedings of the 3rd International Conference on Computer, Artificial Intelligence and Control Engineering, pp. 588–592 (2024)
4. Breiman, L.: Bagging predictors. Mach. Learn. **24**, 123–140 (1996)
5. Breiman, L.: Random forests. Mach. Learn. **45**, 5–32 (2001)
6. Deng, Q., et al.: Correntropy meets cross-entropy: a robust loss against noisy labels. Available at SSRN 4875114 (2025)
7. Introduction to Applied Optimization. SOIA, vol. 22. Springer, Cham (2020). https://doi.org/10.1007/978-3-030-55404-0
8. Dong, H., Yang, L.: Kernel based regression with robust loss function via iteratively reweighted least squares. arXiv preprint arXiv:1903.11202 (2019)
9. Freund, Y., Schapire, R.E.: A decision-theoretic generalization of on-line learning and an application to boosting. J. Comput. Syst. Sci. **55**(1), 119–139 (1997)
10. Fu, S., Wang, X., Tang, J., Lan, S., Tian, Y.: Generalized robust loss functions for machine learning. Neural Netw. **171**, 200–214 (2024)
11. Ghosh, A., Kumar, H., Sastry, P.S.: Robust loss functions under label noise for deep neural networks. In: Proceedings of the AAAI Conference on Artificial Intelligence, vol. 31 (2017)
12. He, H., Garcia, E.A.: Learning from imbalanced data. IEEE Trans. Knowl. Data Eng. **21**(9), 1263–1284 (2009)
13. Hendrycks, D., Mu, N., Cubuk, E.D., Zoph, B., Gilmer, J., Lakshminarayanan, B.: Augmix: a simple data processing method to improve robustness and uncertainty. arXiv preprint arXiv:1912.02781 (2019)
14. Huang, L.W., Shao, Y.H., Lv, X.J., Li, C.N.: Large-scale robust regression with truncated loss via majorization-minimization algorithm. Eur. J. Oper. Res. **319**(2), 494–504 (2024)
15. Jiang, L., Huang, D., Liu, M., Yang, W.: Beyond synthetic noise: deep learning on controlled noisy labels. In: International Conference on Machine Learning, pp. 4804–4815. PMLR (2020)
16. Li, J., Socher, R., Hoi, S.C.: Dividemix: learning with noisy labels as semi-supervised learning. arXiv preprint arXiv:2002.07394 (2020)
17. Li, T., Beirami, A., Sanjabi, M., Smith, V.: On tilted losses in machine learning: theory and applications. J. Mach. Learn. Res. **24**(142), 1–79 (2023)
18. Li, X.C., Xia, X., Zhu, F., Liu, T., Zhang, X.Y., Liu, C.L.: Dynamics-aware loss for learning with label noise. Pattern Recogn. **144**, 109835 (2023)
19. Liu, S., Zhu, Z., Qu, Q., You, C.: Robust training under label noise by over-parameterization. In: Chaudhuri, K., Jegelka, S., Song, L., Szepesvari, C., Niu, G., Sabato, S. (eds.) Proceedings of the 39th International Conference on Machine Learning. Proceedings of Machine Learning Research, vol. 162, pp. 14153–14172. PMLR (2022)
20. Liu, T., Tao, D.: Classification with noisy labels by importance reweighting. IEEE Trans. Pattern Anal. Mach. Intell. **38**(3), 447–461 (2015)
21. Liu, Y., Guo, H.: Peer loss functions: learning from noisy labels without knowing noise rates. In: III, H.D., Singh, A. (eds.) Proceedings of the 37th International Conference on Machine Learning. Proceedings of Machine Learning Research, vol. 119, pp. 6226–6236. PMLR (2020)
22. Ma, X., Huang, H., Wang, Y., Romano, S., Erfani, S., Bailey, J.: Normalized loss functions for deep learning with noisy labels. In: International Conference on Machine Learning, pp. 6543–6553. PMLR (2020)

23. Mehta, R., Roulet, V., Pillutla, K., Harchaoui, Z.: Distributionally robust optimization with bias and variance reduction. arXiv preprint arXiv:2310.13863 (2023)
24. Meyer, G.P.: An alternative probabilistic interpretation of the huber loss. In: Proceedings of the IEEE/CVF Conference on Computer Vision and Pattern Recognition, pp. 5261–5269 (2021)
25. Mienye, I.D., Jere, N.: Deep learning for credit card fraud detection: a review of algorithms, challenges, and solutions. IEEE Access (2024)
26. Mukhoty, B., Gopakumar, G., Jain, P., Kar, P.: Globally-convergent iteratively reweighted least squares for robust regression problems. arXiv preprint arXiv:2006.14211 (2020)
27. Pang, G., Shen, C., Cao, L., Hengel, A.V.D.: Deep learning for anomaly detection: a review. ACM Comput. Surv. (CSUR) **54**(2), 1–38 (2021)
28. Patrini, G., Rozza, A., Krishna Menon, A., Nock, R., Qu, L.: Making deep neural networks robust to label noise: a loss correction approach. In: Proceedings of the IEEE Conference on Computer Vision and Pattern Recognition, pp. 1944–1952 (2017)
29. Qi, Q., Guo, Z., Xu, Y., Jin, R., Yang, T.: An online method for a class of distributionally robust optimization with non-convex objectives. Adv. Neural. Inf. Process. Syst. **34**, 10067–10080 (2021)
30. Sun, H., Guo, C., Wei, Q., Han, Z., Yin, Y.: Learning to rectify for robust learning with noisy labels. Pattern Recogn. **124**, 108467 (2022)
31. Sun, X., Yang, Y., Liu, Y.: External knowledge enhancing meta-learning framework for few-shot text classification via contrastive learning and adversarial network. In: Web and Big Data (APWeb-WAIM 2024). Lecture Notes in Computer Science, vol. 14961, pp. 46–58. Springer, Heidelberg (2024). https://doi.org/10.1007/978-981-97-7232-2_4
32. Tang, H., Liu, L., Li, Z., Jia, Z., Zhang, Q.: Reducing influence of noise in regression problems on memristor computing-in-memory chips. IEEE Access (2025)
33. Tejasree, G., Agilandeeswari, L.: An extensive review of hyperspectral image classification and prediction: techniques and challenges. Multimedia Tools Appl. **83**(34), 80941–81038 (2024)
34. Wang, J., Xie, F., Nie, F., Li, X.: Generalized and robust least squares regression. IEEE Trans. Neural Netw. Learn. Syst. (2022)
35. Wang, Q., Xiao, Y., Tan, H., Mohamed, M.A.: Day-ahead scheduling of rural integrated energy systems based on distributionally robust optimization theory. Appl. Therm. Eng. **246**, 123001 (2024)
36. Wang, T., Lai, X., Cao, J.: A highly efficient admm-based algorithm for outlier-robust regression with huber loss. Appl. Intell. **54**(6), 5147–5166 (2024)
37. Xie, Y., Gu, Z., Tan, R., Luo, C., Song, X., Wang, H.: Generating adversarial texts by the universal tail word addition attack. In: Web and Big Data (APWeb-WAIM 2024). Lecture Notes in Computer Science, vol. 14961, pp. 310–326. Springer, Heidelberg (2024). https://doi.org/10.1007/978-981-97-7232-2_21
38. Yu, S., Ahn, J.H., Kang, J.: Fedefc: federated learning using enhanced forward correction against noisy labels. arXiv preprint arXiv:2504.05615 (2025)
39. Yu, X., Zhang, S., Jia, L., Wang, Y., Song, M., Feng, Z.: Noise is the fatal poison: a noise-aware network for noisy dataset classification. Neurocomputing **563**, 126829 (2024)
40. Zhang, Z., Sabuncu, M.: Generalized cross entropy loss for training deep neural networks with noisy labels. Adv. Neural Inf. Process. Syst. **31** (2018)

41. Zhou, T., Wang, S., Bilmes, J.: Robust curriculum learning: from clean label detection to noisy label self-correction. In: International Conference on Learning Representations (2021)
42. Zhou, X., Liu, X., Jiang, J., Gao, X., Ji, X.: Asymmetric loss functions for learning with noisy labels. In: International Conference on Machine Learning, pp. 12846–12856. PMLR (2021)
43. Zhu, D., Ying, Y., Yang, T.: Label distributionally robust losses for multi-class classification: Consistency, robustness and adaptivity. In: International Conference on Machine Learning, pp. 43289–43325. PMLR (2023)

A Multi-scale Dilated Convolution Model with Edge Optimization for Crack Detection

Ao Yang[1], Shaoqian Chen[1], Kangfei Yao[1], Xiaohui Huang[1], Yuewei Wang[1], Jianxin Li[2], and Yunliang Chen[1(✉)]

[1] School of Computer Science, China University of Geosciences, Wuhan, China
chenyunliang@cug.edu.cn

[2] Discipline of Business Systems and Operations, School of Business and Law, Edith Cowan University, Perth, Australia

Abstract. Crack detection is a key link to ensure the safety of building roads and the life of structures, and plays a crucial role in early warning and maintenance decision-making. However, cracks are often distributed in complex backgrounds as low contrast and irregular multi-scale. The down sampling-up sampling process is easy to cause information loss and spatial misalignment, resulting in disconnected artifacts of long cracks. The imbalance of categories makes it difficult for small cracks to get enough attention, which seriously weakens the recall rate and robustness of the model. Therefore, a crack detection model based on multi-scale dilated convolution and edge optimization (MDENet) is proposed. First, the multi-scale dilated Edge Module (MDEM) was used to parallel the multi-scale dilated convolution and edge algorithm, and the crack edge was refined to realize the complementary capture of global semantic information and local contour. Then, the deep features were divided into tokens by Tokenized KAN Phrase (Tok-KAN) and non-linear re-validation was performed to significantly improve the sensitivity to subtle cracks and suppress complex background noise. Finally, the residual channel attention module RCAM dynamically adjusted the channel weights in the skip connection layer, which kept key information and suppressed redundant interference. Experimental results show that MDENet achieves F1 scores of 87.43%, 74.29% and 73.09% on three public datasets, respectively, which are significantly better than mainstream models.

Keywords: Crack segmentation · Deep learning · Multi-scale dilated convolution · Edge optimization

1 Introduction

Civil infrastructure, such as roads, bridges, and tunnels, is prone to cracks and other structural damage during long-term service because of environmental erosion, material aging, and dynamic loads. Cracks are not only an early

J. Li et al. (Eds.): APWeb-WAIM 2025, LNCS 16115, pp. 231–245, 2026.
https://doi.org/10.1007/978-981-95-5719-6_15

manifestation of structural deterioration but also may cause chain damage and threaten public safety [1]. According to the American Society of Civil Engineers' 2021-Infrastructure-Report-Card, the United States boasts an inventory of over 617,000 bridges, 42% of which are at least 50 years old. Among these, 46,154 bridges (7.5% of the national total) are classified as structurally deficient, showing poor conditions characterized by prevalent cracks and potholes. It is estimated that the backlog of bridge maintenance needs in the U.S. amounts to $125 billion [2]. Therefore, the detection and analysis of cracks plays a key role in building safety assessment and maintenance. However, traditional crack detection is mainly based on artificial visual assessment, which has the problems of low efficiency, strong subjectivity and high cost [3].

In recent years, traditional models U-Net [4] and SegNet [5] have shown excellent performance in crack segmentation through their end-to-end learning framework. For example, MDAU-Net [6] enhances its ability to deal with irregular cracks by introducing a dual attention module. DeepCrack1 [7] uses multi-scale feature jump fusion to improve the segmentation accuracy. LLM [8] integrated the edge module to enhance the capture of crack edge details. However, current crack segmentation methods still have shortcomings in dealing with the challenges of low contrast, multi-scale, and irregular distribution in crack images. Specifically, there are three major challenges: (1) It is difficult for traditional convolutional frameworks to balance global context capture and edge preservation, especially for low-contrast and irregularly distributed cracks. (2) The down-sampling and up-sampling processes inevitably cause information loss and spatial dislocation, resulting in the fragmentation prediction of long continuous cracks. (3) The severe class imbalance between cracks and background biases training to dominant background features, which suppresses weak crack signals and reduces recall.

To address these challenges, MDENet collaborates three key dimensions: multi-scale context, edge refinement, and channel attention. Specifically, the Multi-scale Dilated Edge Module (MDEM) embedded in the first three network stages parallelizes the multi-scale dilated convolution to enlarge the receptive field. The edge extraction algorithm based on Laplacian of Gaussian and Difference of Gaussian accurately captures the edge information of cracks, and realizes the complementary capture of global semantic information and local contour. In the deepest stage, the Tokenized KAN (Tok-KAN) module divides high-level features into tokens for nonlinear recalibration, significantly amplifying sensitivity to tiny cracks while suppressing background noise. The Residual Channel Attention Module (RCAM) dynamically adjusted channel weights in skip connections to keep key information and to filter redundant interference. The contributions of this paper can be summarized:

- A novel crack segmentation network integrating multi-scale context learning, edge-aware refinement, and channel attention into a unified architecture. Unlike existing methods, MDENet resolves the inherent conflict between global semantic capture and local edge preservation, particularly for low-contrast and geometrically complex cracks.

- We introduce Multi-scale dilated Edge module (MDEM), Tokenized KAN (Tok-KAN) and Residual Channel attention module (RCAM) to enhance the global semantic understanding of cracks, the detection sensitivity of tiny cracks and the expression ability of key features of the model, respectively.
- MDEM, Tok-KAN, and RCAM work together. MDEM uses edge information to help Tok-KAN avoid over-smoothing and highlight subtle fractures. Tok-KAN then refines edge details, removing texture noise. Finally, RCAM combines features across different scales for continuous fracture geometry. A closed-loop optimization chain of "edge guidance, feature calibration, and cross-scale enhancement" is formed, which significantly improves the crack segmentation accuracy and robustness of the model in complex backgrounds.
- We achieve state-of-the-art performance on three benchmark datasets, and further show the effectiveness of the proposed module through ablation experiments.

2 Related Work

2.1 Methods Based On Edge Detection

In computer vision, edge detection serves as a critical technique for identifying structural defects such as cracks, with its core mechanism focusing on capturing local abrupt changes in pixel intensity [9]. In crack detection, the traditional gradient operator can effectively extract the local intensity change, but there are still differences in the uniformity of edge width and thickness. The frequency domain method improves the anti-noise performance through multi-resolution and direction selectivity, but often destroys the continuity of the crack because of reconstruction error. In recent years, the combination of deep learning and edge detection algorithm has made significant progress on the crack segmentation task, further improve the detection accuracy and adaptability [10]. PCDM-HED [11] effectively solves the problem of domain shift in heterogeneous 3D pavement data by fusing profile frequency decomposition and multi-level depth edge features, combined with the transfer learning mechanism. EfficientCrackNet [12] is a combination of depth of separable convolution MobileViT module, edge detection module and ultra-low weight subspace attention, significantly improve the crack complicated background segmentation accuracy and computational efficiency. These methods use multi-level feature fusion and a lightweight attention mechanism. This improves crack detection accuracy and noise immunity while also enhancing generalization and computational efficiency across different scenes.

2.2 Deep Learning-Based Approach

In recent years, deep learning methods based on U-Net architecture have made significant progress in crack segmentation tasks. By introducing attention mechanism, multi-scale feature fusion and dilated convolution techniques, the improved U-Net model shows stronger robustness and higher segmentation accuracy in complex backgrounds. For example, CrackFormerII [13] achieves efficient and accurate pixel-level segmentation of pavement cracks by integrating Transformer local self-attention mechanism and multi-scale feature fusion module. CT-crackseg [14] uses an expansion residual block, a boundary perception module, and a lightweight Transformer to improve crack detection. This improves accuracy and efficiency, especially for small cracks in complex settings. Besides the U-Net variant, other deep learning methods have also achieved remarkable success in crack segmentation. These deep learning methods significantly improve the accuracy and robustness of crack segmentation.

3 Model

In this section, the network architecture of the MDENet is detailed and its key modules: the Multi-scale Dilated Edge Module (MDEM), the Tokenized KAN (Tok-KAN) module, and the Residual Channel Attention Module (RCAM). Finally, the loss function employed in the model is discussed.

3.1 MDENet Network Architecture

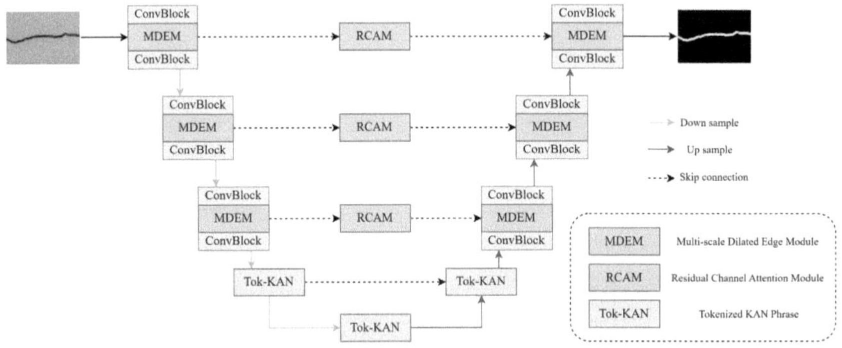

Fig. 1. MDENet Network Architecture. Multi-scale Dilated Edge Module (MDEM), Residual Channel Attention Module (RCAM), Tokenized KAN Phrase (Tok-KAN).

MDENet (Fig. 1), built upon the U-Net architecture, achieves high-precision crack segmentation through a multi-dimensional collaborative framework. In the first three encoder stages, the Multi-scale Dilated Edge Module (MDEM) performs parallel multi-scale dilated convolutions to expand receptive fields while integrating Laplacian-of-Gaussian (LoG) and Difference-of-Gaussian (DoG) edge detection algorithms. This design precisely captures crack boundaries and enables complementary fusion of global semantics with local contours, enhancing adaptability to complex crack patterns. At skip connections, the Residual

Channel Attention Module (RCAM) dynamically adjusts channel weights to amplify critical crack features and suppress background interference. At the deepest stage, Tokenized KAN (Tok-KAN) divides high-level features into tokens for nonlinear recalibration, which significantly improves the sensitivity to subtle cracks while filtering out complex background noise. MDENet uses progressive multi-scale fusion to solve "context-detail" conflicts, token-based recalibration to solve class imbalance, and channel attention to reduce spatial dissonance. This allows it to maintain geometric continuity when segmenting fragmented, discontinuous or intersecting cracks, outperforming other methods.

3.2 Multi-scale Dilated Edge Module

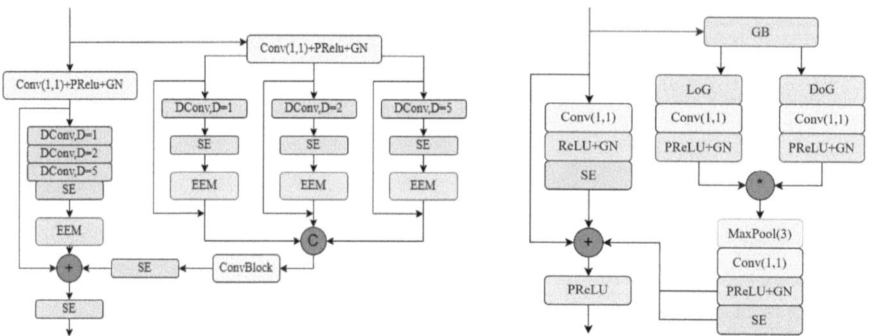

Fig. 2. Multi-scale Dilated Edge Module. **Fig. 3.** Edge Extraction Module [8].

First, MDEM (Fig. 2) was divided into serial and parallel multi-scale dilated convolution branches after dimensionality reduction by channel compression operation. The serial branch uses dilated convolutions (expansion rates 1, 2, and 5) to progressively expand its receptive field. This allows it to capture multi-scale context information, from fine to coarse. A parallel branch uses dilation rates of 1, 2, and 5 for dilated convolution. This extracts multi-scale features simultaneously, enriching feature expression. The outputs of both branches are fed into the Edge Extraction Module [8] (EEM (Fig. 3)). The EEM uses Difference of Gaussians (DoG) for mid-frequency edge detail extraction, Laplacian of Gaussian (LoG) for high-contrast boundary enhancement, and adaptive fusion with learnable channel weights to accurately preserve fine cracks and debris boundaries, even in low contrast or noisy conditions. Finally, Squeeze-and-Excitation (SE) recalibration later fine-tuned the fused features to amplify the signals related to cracks and suppress background interference.

MDEM achieves the complementary fusion of global semantics and local contour through the three-level collaboration of multi-scale receptive field expansion, traditional edge algorithm enhancement, and channel attention calibration. The design logic is: the serial dilated convolution gradually integrates the multi-level context to avoid the grid effect directly introduced by the large expansion rate.

Parallel dilated convolution extracts multi-scale information. Parallel LoG and DoG edge detection provide complementary strong prior information in the frequency domain. Channel attention solves the problem of feature redundancy. This collaborative mechanism enables MDEM to maintain the geometric continuity of cracks and significantly improve the segmentation robustness under complex textures, low contrast, and noise interference. The input feature map x is compressed and activated to get global spatial information:

$$X = \mathrm{GN}\Big(\mathrm{PReLU}\big(\mathrm{Conv}_{1\times1}(x)\big)\Big) \tag{1}$$

where $x \in \mathbb{R}^{c\times h\times w}$ is characterized by c channels, with h and w corresponding to its spatial dimensions. $\mathrm{Conv}_{1\times1}$ is the 1×1 convolution of channel compression, PReLU can learn the negative half axis slope to enhance the network fitting ability, GN is normalized by the mean and variance of the group calculation to get rid of the batch size limitation.

The serial branch gradually enlarges the receptive field while integrating edge priors via EEM, with residual connections aiding information preservation:

$$U = X + \mathrm{EEM}\Big(\mathrm{SE}(\mathrm{DConv}_5\big(\mathrm{DConv}_2(\mathrm{DConv}_1(X))\big))\Big) \tag{2}$$

where DConv_k represents the dilated convolution with dilation rate k, which can expand the receptive field without reducing the resolution. SE is Squeeze-and-Excitation. EEM combines DoG and LoG to extract the frequency domain edge prior and adaptively fuse it. + shows residual connections, which contribute to gradient flow and information retention.

The parallel branch applies dilated convolution and EEM, and then activates by ReLU to generate multi-scale feature M_i, to capture detail information of different context ranges in parallel.

$$M_i = \mathrm{ReLU}\Big(\mathrm{EEM}\big(\mathrm{SE}(\mathrm{DConv}_i(X))\big)\Big), \quad i \in \{1, 2, 5\} \tag{3}$$

Concat concatenates three features along the channel dimension, ConvBlock further fuses the context. Finally, the output of the serial branch U and the calibrated feature N of the parallel branch were added together, and then the module output Y was got by SE recalibration.

$$N = \mathrm{ConvBlock}\big(\mathrm{Concat}(M_1, M_2, M_3)\big), \quad Y = \mathrm{SE}(U + N) \tag{4}$$

Through the above design, MDEM can not only consider the global semantic information but also accurately keep the tiny crack structure under the collaboration of multi-scale receptive field expansion, frequency domain edge enhancement and channel attention recalibration, thus improving the segmentation robustness in scenes with complex textures, low contrast and noise interference.

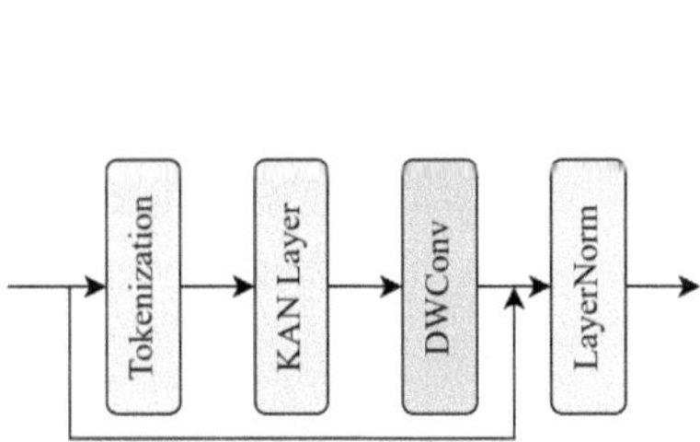

Fig. 4. Tokenized KAN Phrase [15].

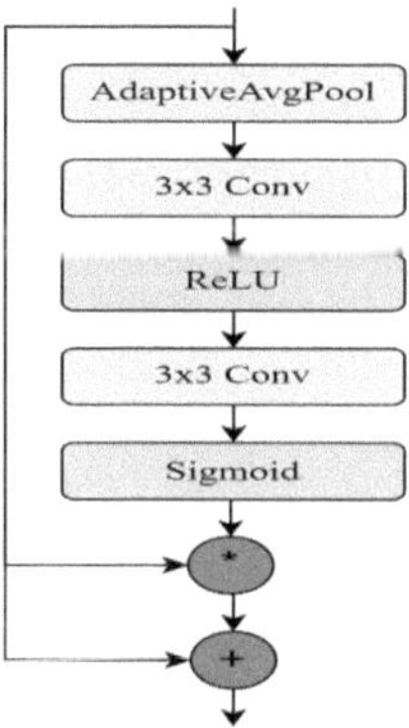

Fig. 5. Residual Channel Attention Module.

3.3 Tokenized KAN Phrase

At the deepest encoder stage, Tok-KAN [15] (Fig. 4) plays a key role in fine-grained recalibration of high-level semantic features. First, the feature map is divided into 2D blocks. These blocks are projected onto a high-dimensional embedding space via trainable linear maps to form intrinsic labels. Tokens are then processed sequentially through multiple nonblacks. Within each block, layer normalization stabilizes the feature distribution, which is then transformed non-linearly by KANLayer to adaptively model the crack geometry. Depthwise Separable Convolutions (DwConv) further refine local spatial details, while residual connections preserve and fuse the original information into the updated feature stream. This design enables Tok-KAN to filter out complex background noise while selectively amplifying weak signals in crack regions, achieving high sensitivity to tiny, fragmented, or crossed cracks. By addressing the limitations of traditional convolutional networks in balancing deep semantics and local details, Tok-KAN significantly improves MDENet's segmentation accuracy and geometric continuity under challenging environmental conditions. This process can be expressed as follows:

$$L_k = \mathrm{LN}\Big(L_{k-1} + \mathrm{DwConv}\big(\mathrm{KAN}(L_{k-1})\big)\Big) \tag{5}$$

where $\mathrm{LN}(\cdot)$ is layer normalization, L_{k-1} is the output of the previous layer, $\mathrm{DwConv}(\cdot)$ is depthwise separable convolution, $\mathrm{KAN}(\cdot)$ represents nonlinear feature transformation.

3.4 Residual Channel Attention Module

In the skip connection stage, RCAM (Fig. 5) optimizes cross-layer feature fusion by fusing residual learning and channel attention mechanism. Specifically, the shallow and deep features first extract multi-scale detail information through residual branches. These features are then fed into SE to dynamically calculate the channel correlation weights. The gating mechanism amplifies critical channel responses associated with cracks while suppressing redundant channels dominated by background noise. This design preserves the position sensitivity inherent in skip connections while removing the spatial misalignment between high-resolution shallow features and semantically rich deep features. RCAM improves the performance of MDENet by focusing on crack information and eliminating interference. This leads to better sensitivity and robustness, even in the presence of complex backgrounds, low contrast, and noise. This fine feature fusion ensures that precise crack perception information is propagated to the subsequent decoding stages.

3.5 Loss Function

Crack segmentation is difficult because crack regions are much smaller than the background, creating an extreme class imbalance. This imbalance makes accurate segmentation with a single loss function challenging. To address this issue, a composite loss function that merges Dice loss with a weighted binary cross-entropy term was employed to improve segmentation performance. Specifically, the Sigmoid activation is first applied to the model's output to get probabilities p_{i}. Subsequently, both the predicted values and the ground truth labels t_{i} are flattened, and Dice loss is expressed as:

$$L_{\mathrm{Dice}} = 1 - \frac{2\sum_{i=1}^{N} p_i\, t_i + s}{\sum_{i=1}^{N} p_i \;+\; \sum_{i=1}^{N} t_i \;+\; s} \tag{6}$$

where p_i and t_i represent the predicted probabilities and the accurate labels, respectively, and s is the smoothing factor. The BCE loss is calculated as:

$$L_{\mathrm{BCE}} = -\frac{1}{N}\sum_{i=1}^{N} w_i\big[t_i \ln(p_i) \;+\; (1-t_i)\ln(1-p_i)\big], \quad w_i = \begin{cases} \frac{|Y^+|}{|Y|}, & t_i = 1, \\ \frac{|Y^-|}{|Y|}, & t_i = 0, \end{cases} \tag{7}$$

where w_i represents the loss weight for the i pixel. $|Y^+|$ is the total number of positive class pixels. $|Y^-|$ is the total number of negative class pixels. Y is the total number of all pixels in the image. The final total loss is:

$$L = \lambda\, L_{\mathrm{BCE}} \;+\; \beta\, L_{\mathrm{Dice}}\,. \tag{8}$$

where λ and β are 1. This design effectively improves the robustness and accuracy of the model in complex backgrounds, while considering the region of overlap and pixel-level accuracy.

4 Experiment

The experimental study will be described in this chapter. Section 3.1 explains the experimental details and the implementation process. Section 3.2 describes the datasets used and their characteristics. Section 3.3 presents the evaluation metrics used in the experiments. Section 3.4 presents a comparative analysis between the proposed model and the existing methods based on the experimental results. Section 3.5 verifies the effectiveness of the model through ablation experiments.

4.1 Experimental Details

MDENet was implemented using the widely adopted PyTorch framework. During training, images and their corresponding labels were randomly cropped to 256×256 pixels to facilitate network learning. Besides random cropping, augmentation techniques such as random rotation, flipping, color jitter and motion blur applied to enhance performance, while a batch size of 4 and 100 training epochs were utilized. The AdamW optimizer was employed with a learning rate of 1e–4, weight decay of 0.01, and momentum (0.9, 0.999). The convolution dilation rates are 1, 2, and 5. All experiments were trained and tested on a computational platform equipped with an NVIDIA RTX 3090 GPU (24GB).

4.2 Datasets

DeepCrack [7]: The DeepCrack dataset serves as a publicly available reference dataset designed for structural crack analysis, containing 537 (300 training images and 237 test images) high-resolution samples paired with human-labeled pixel-wise annotations. All images are seized at 544×384 pixels. The dataset covers diverse crack morphologies, including varying perspectives and thin-to-wide fissures that occur on construction materials like concrete and asphalt, with occasional partial occlusions.

Crack500 [16]: The Crack500 dataset serves as a large-scale publicly available dataset for pavement crack analysis. Its original data, collected via smartphones, includes 500 raw images (with an approximate resolution of 2000ÃŮ1500 pixels), each meticulously labeled on a per-pixel basis. The 3,368 road crack images (1896 training images, 348 validation images and 1124 test images) were cropped and resized to 640×360 pixels.

CrackSegment: The CrackSegment dataset comprises all GAPS384 [17] dataset, all Volke dataset [18] and some Rissbilder [18] dataset, totaling 1,089 crack images (762 training images and 327 test images). Data samples with varying annotation standards and shooting scenes were fused. This comprehensive, real-world dataset improved model training and evaluation, leading to better generalization and robustness in complex settings.

4.3 Evaluation Metrics

In crack segmentation tasks, the target region usually occupies only a small part of the entire image. The traditional pixel accuracy is easily affected by the large number of background pixels, which is difficult to accurately reflect the extraction ability of the model for slender and sparse crack features. In view of this defect, an evaluation system based on a positive class (crack pixels) is proposed. Precision (Pr), recall (Re), and F1-score (F1) comprehensively evaluate the model performance.

4.4 Experimental Results

We compare eight models U-Net [4], SegNet [5], DeepCrack1 [7], DeepCrack2 [19], CrackFormerII [13], CT-crackseg [14], U-KAN [15], and LLM [8]. Among them, classical baselines include U-Net and SegNet, which establish fundamental encoder-decoder paradigms for semantic segmentation. Advanced competitors encompass DeepCrack1, DeepCrack2, CrackFormerII, and CT-crackseg, each integrating domain-specific designs for crack morphology learning, alongside LLM that combines traditional edge operators with deep networks. In addition, U-KAN is a Tok-KAN based UNet model, which is like our model. Experiments show that the performance of MDENet is better than the above eight models on three datasets of DeepCrack, Crack500 and CrackSegment.

As shown in Fig. 6, MDENet maintains complete crack continuity under different widths and morphologies while locating subtle cracks and suppressing background interference, which outperforms existing methods in complex scenes. MDENet (Fig. 7) uses its MDEM to accurately detect weak cracks. Tok-KAN enlarges details, and residual channel attention filters irrelevant interference, enabling continuous and accurate crack segmentation despite complex backgrounds (low contrast, texture noise, occlusion). However, in regions with extreme occlusion or abrupt change, local connectivity still needs to be improved.

DeepCrack Results: MDENet performs better than CT-crackseg on the DeepCrack dataset, achieving the highest precision (Pr = 0.9057) and F1-score (F1 = 0.8743), as shown in Table 1. The improvement is 2.78% in precision and 0.43% in F1-score. The precision and F1-score are improved by 2.78% and 0.43%, respectively. This improvement may come from MDEM, which improves the receptive field while enhancing edge information extraction for accurate segmentation. Compared with the LLM model, MDENet improves the precision by 2.63% and the F1-score by 1.21%. Compared with the traditional U-Net model, the accuracy is increased by 4.55% and the F1-score is increased by 1.67%. This limited improvement may stem from LoG/DoG edge detection in MDEM, where high-contrast noise amplifies false edges and limits pixel-level continuity modeling.

Crack500 Results: MDENet outperforms LLM on the Crack500 dataset, achieving the highest recall (0.7902) and F1-score (0.7429), as shown in Table 2. The improvement is 0.07% in recall and 0.21% in F1-score. The improved performance might come from MDEM's multi-branch dilated convolutions. These maintain crack continuity through multi-scale context aggregation, and Tok-KAN's nonlinear feature recalibration via orthogonal transformations in latent embedding space synergize with this. MDENet outperforms U-KAN by 5.01% in recall and 1.83% in F1-score, and exceeds SegNet by 2.31% in precision, 4.10% in

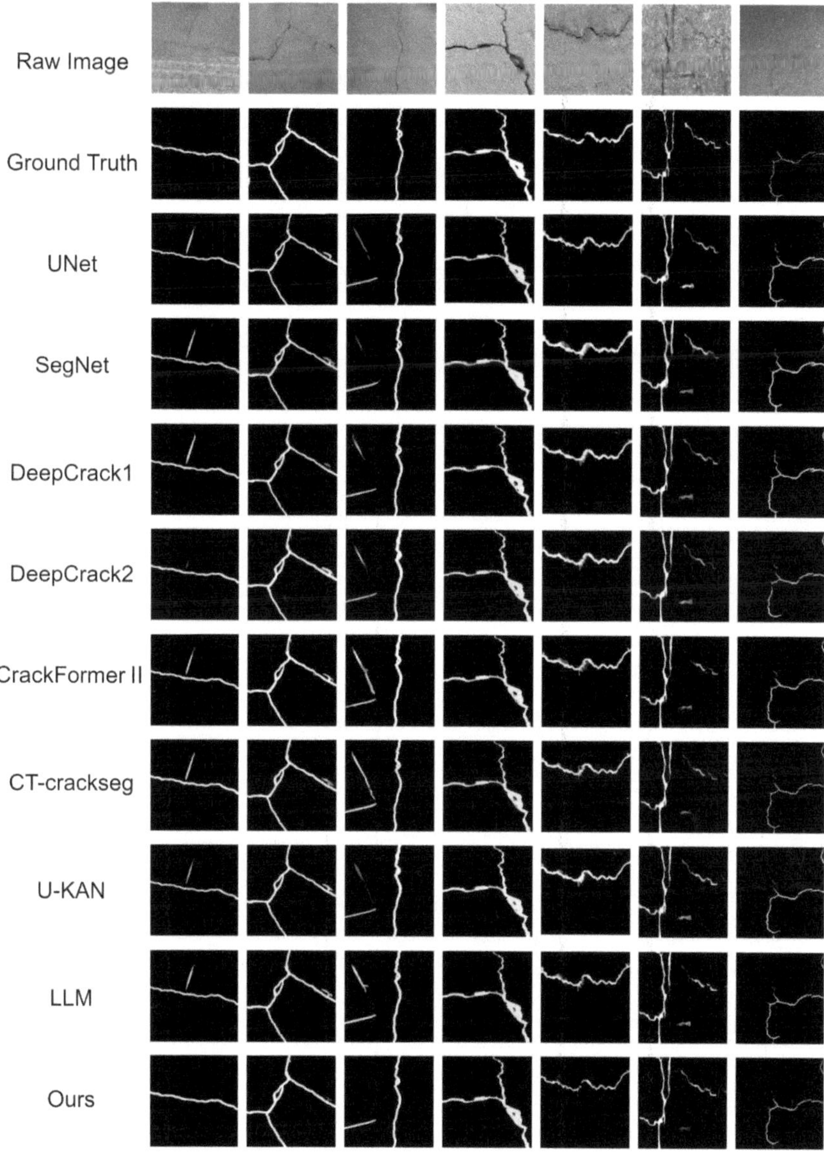

Fig. 6. Comparison of segmentation outcomes between the proposed model and other approaches. From the top row to the bottom, showing the original image, ground truth, UNet, SegNet, DeepCrack1, DeepCrack2, CrackFormerII, CT-crackseg, U-KAN, LLM, Ours.

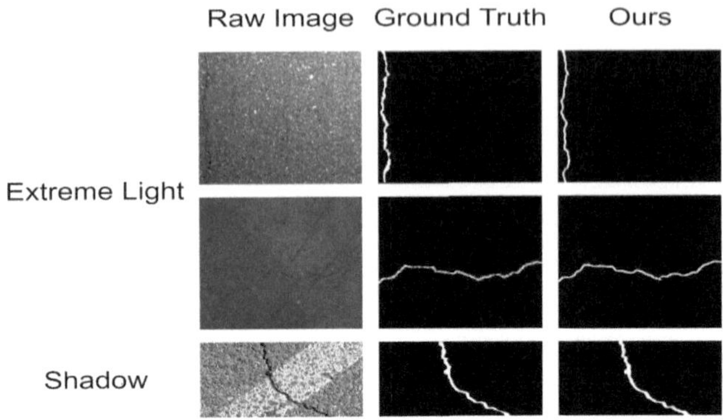

Fig. 7. Visualization results for scenes with extreme lighting and shadow.

Table 1. DeepCrack Dataset

Model	Metrics		
	Pr	Re	F1
U-Net (2015)	0.8602	0.8549	0.8576
SegNet (2017)	0.8579	0.8628	0.8603
DeepCrack1 (2019)	0.8631	0.8409	0.8518
DeepCrack2 (2019)	0.8656	0.8441	0.8547
CrackFomer II (2023)	0.8591	0.8489	0.8540
CT-crackseg (2023)	0.8779	0.8621	0.8700
U-KAN (2024)	0.8587	**0.8674**	0.8630
LLM (2024)	0.8789	0.8461	0.8622
MDENet	**0.9057**	0.8449	**0.8743**

Table 2. Crack500 Dataset

Model	Metrics		
	Pr	Re	F1
U-Net (2015)	0.6928	0.7492	0.7199
SegNet (2017)	0.6777	0.7591	0.7161
DeepCrack1 (2019)	0.6894	0.7806	0.7322
DeepCrack2 (2019)	0.6927	0.7446	0.7177
CrackFormer II (2023)	0.7004	0.7860	0.7408
CT-crackseg (2023)	0.6872	0.7890	0.7346
U-KAN (2024)	**0.7097**	0.7401	0.7246
LLM (2024)	0.6949	0.7895	0.7392
MDENet	0.7008	**0.7902**	**0.7429**

recall, and 2.68% in F1-score. While MDENet excels in crack continuity reconstruction, dynamic feature calibration could further improve robustness against high-intensity noise. This limited improvement may arise from the fixed dilation rates in MDEM exhibiting insufficient adaptability to abrupt crack scale variations, while Tok-KAN recalibration of weak crack signals under high-noise environments still requires further optimization.

CrackSegment Results: As summarized in Table 3, MDENet attains the best precision (Pr = 0.6928), recall (Re = 0.7735), and F1-score (F1 = 0.7309) on the CrackSegment dataset. It outperforms CT-crackseg (F1 = 0.7163) by 0.74% in precision, 2.34% in recall, and 1.46% in F1-score. Compared to CrackFormerII, MDENet improves precision by 2.56%, recall by 2.46%, and F1-score by 2.52%. These gains likely originate from DECrackNet's balanced design between receptive field expansion and edge feature extraction. In contrast, other models struggle to capture fine or fragmented crack edges under complex backgrounds and noise.

Table 3. CrackSegment Dataset

Model	Metrics		
	Pr	Re	F1
U-Net (2015)	0.6594	0.6988	0.6785
SegNet (2017)	0.6307	0.7470	0.6839
DeepCrack1 (2019)	0.6367	0.7628	0.6941
DeepCrack2 (2019)	0.6500	0.7510	0.6969
CrackFomer II (2023)	0.6672	0.7489	0.7057
CT-crackseg (2023)	0.6854	0.7501	0.7163
U-KAN (2024)	0.6649	0.7518	0.7057
LLM (2024)	0.6643	0.7471	0.7033
MDENet	**0.6928**	**0.7735**	**0.7309**

Table 4. Ablation studies results on CrackSegment

Model	Pr	Re	F1
Base line (B)	0.6594	0.6988	0.6785
B+DEM (u1)	0.6722	0.7695	0.7176
u1+Tok-KAN (u2)	0.6879	0.7719	0.7275
u2+RCAM (u3)	**0.6928**	**0.7735**	**0.7309**

Table 5. Ablation Studies on Dilation Rates

Configuration	Pr	Re	F1
DR=(1,1,1)	0.6923	0.7698	0.7290
DR=(1,2,2)	0.6799	0.7690	0.7217
DR=(1,2,5)	**0.6928**	**0.7735**	**0.7309**
DR=(2,3,4)	0.6709	0.7695	0.7168

4.5 Ablation Experiments

In the ablation experiments of MDENet, we used U-Net as the baseline model and gradually added each module to evaluate its contribution to the crack detection performance. All experiments were conducted using the CrackSegment dataset, with the resulting performance metrics summarized in Table 4. The experimental results with the baseline model yielding precision, recall, and F1 values of 0.6594, 0.6988, and 0.6785, respectively. After the addition of MDEM (u1), the precision improved by about 1.28%; the recall experienced an improvement of roughly 7.07%, and the F1 score saw an enhancement of approximately 3.91%. Further, after adding the Tok-KAN module (u2), the precision is improved by about 1.57%; the recall experienced an improvement of roughly 0.24%, and the F1 score saw an enhancement of approximately 0.99%. Finally, after adding the RCAM module (u3), the precision is improved by about 0.49%; the recall experienced an improvement of roughly 0.16%, and the F1 score saw an enhancement of approximately 0.34%. According to Table 5, the dilation configuration DR= (1,2,5) is chosen for its optimal balance between multi-scale feature coverage and artifact prevention. The full MDENet configuration achieves optimal metrics (Pr = 69.28%, Re = 77.35%, F1 = 73.09%), confirming the complementary roles of MDEM, Tok-KAN and RCAM in crack segmentation tasks.

5 Conclusion

This paper proposes MDENet, a crack detection model that addresses complex scenarios through a multi-dimensional collaborative framework. Three core modules comprise the architecture. MDEM captures global semantics and local crack details. RCAM optimizes cross-level feature fusion by noise suppression and crack feature amplification. Tok-KAN performs nonlinear recalibration of weak crack signals. These modules synergistically enable hierarchical refinement via multi-scale perception, channel optimization, and semantic enhancement, systematically resolving contextual loss, class imbalance, and spatial misalignment. Experimental results show MDENet achieves F1 scores of 87.43%, 74.29%, and 73.09% on the DeepCrack, Crack500, and CrackSegment datasets. This surpasses existing methods, especially regarding geometric continuity on fragmented and intersecting cracks. The model's adaptability to sudden cracks needs improvement. Future work will focus on dynamic receptive fields, multi-modal data fusion, and lightweight deployment for wider use.

Acknowledgements. This work is supported by the National Natural Science Foundation of China (No. 62076224).

References

1. Taheri, S.: A review on five key sensors for monitoring of concrete structures. Constr. Build. Mater. (2019). https://api.semanticscholar.org/CorpusID:139224276
2. of Civil Engineers, A.S.: 2021 infrastructure report card: a comprehensive assessment of America's infrastructure (2021). https://www.infrastructurereportcard.org/
3. O'Connell, H.M., Dexter, R.J., Bergson, P.M.: Fatigue evaluation of the deck truss of bridge 9340. Technical Report. MNmC - 2001-10, University of Minnesota, Department of Civil Engineering, Minneapolis, MN (2001). https://www.dot.state.mn.us/research/. Accessed 27 Feb 2024
4. Ronneberger, O., Fischer, P., Brox, T.: U-net: convolutional networks for biomedical image segmentation. ArXiv arxiv:1505.04597 (2015). https://api.semanticscholar.org/CorpusID:3719281
5. Badrinarayanan, V., Kendall, A., Cipolla, R.: Segnet: a deep convolutional encoder-decoder architecture for image segmentation. IEEE Trans. Pattern Anal. Mach. Intell. **39**, 2481–2495 (2015). https://api.semanticscholar.org/CorpusID:60814714
6. Al-Huda, Z., Peng, B., Al-antari, M.A., Algburi, R.N.A., Saleh, R.A.A., Moghalles, K.: Mdau-net: a multi-scale u-net with dual attention module for pavement crack segmentation. In: 2023 18th International Conference on Intelligent Systems and Knowledge Engineering (ISKE), pp. 170–177 (2023). https://api.semanticscholar.org/CorpusID:269026189
7. Zou, Q., Zhang, Z., Li, Q., Qi, X., Wang, Q., Wang, S.: Deepcrack: learning hierarchical convolutional features for crack detection. IEEE Trans. Image Process. **28**, 1498–1512 (2019). https://api.semanticscholar.org/CorpusID:53208814
8. Al-maqtari, O., Peng, B., Al-Huda, Z., Al-Malahi, A., Maqtary, N.: Lightweight yet effective: a modular approach to crack segmentation. IEEE Trans. Intell. Veh. (2024). https://api.semanticscholar.org/CorpusID:270083319

9. Ai, D., Jiang, G., Lam, S.K., He, P., Li, C.: Computer vision framework for crack detection of civil infrastructure - a review. Eng. Appl. Artif. Intell. **117**, 105478 (2023). https://api.semanticscholar.org/CorpusID:253068998
10. Guo, F., Qian, Y., Liu, J., Yu, H.: Pavement crack detection based on transformer network. Autom. Constr. **145** (2023). https://www.sciencedirect.com/science/article/pii/S0926580522005167
11. Gui, R., Sun, Q., Wu, W., Zhang, D., Li, Q.: Transfer learning for cross-scene 3d pavement crack detection based on enhanced deep edge features. Eng. Appl. Artif. Intell. **123**, 106452 (2023). https://api.semanticscholar.org/CorpusID:258873669
12. Zim, A.H., Iqbal, A., Al-Huda, Z., Malik, A., Kuribayashi, M.: Efficientcracknet: a lightweight model for crack segmentation. ArXiv arxiv:2409.18099 (2024). https://api.semanticscholar.org/CorpusID:272910747
13. Liu, H., Yang, J., Miao, X., Mertz, C., Kong, H.: Crackformer network for pavement crack segmentation. IEEE Trans. Intell. Transport. Syst. **24**, 9240–9252 (2023). https://api.semanticscholar.org/CorpusID:258368666
14. Tao, H., Liu, B., Cui, J., Zhang, H.: A convolutional-transformer network for crack segmentation with boundary awareness. In: 2023 IEEE International Conference on Image Processing (ICIP), pp. 86–90 (2023). https://api.semanticscholar.org/CorpusID:257102732
15. Li, C., Liu, X., Li, W., Wang, C., Liu, H., Yuan, Y.: U-kan makes strong backbone for medical image segmentation and generation. ArXiv arxiv:2406.02918 (2024). https://api.semanticscholar.org/CorpusID:270258333
16. Yang, F., Zhang, L., Yu, S., Prokhorov, D.V., Mei, X., Ling, H.: Feature pyramid and hierarchical boosting network for pavement crack detection. IEEE Trans. Intell. Transport. Syst. **21**, 1525–1535 (2019). https://api.semanticscholar.org/CorpusID:58028972
17. Eisenbach, M., et al.: How to get pavement distress detection ready for deep learning? A systematic approach. In: 2017 International Joint Conference on Neural Networks (IJCNN), pp. 2039–2047 (2017). https://api.semanticscholar.org/CorpusID:23870285
18. Kulkarni, S., Singh, S., Balakrishnan, D., Sharma, S., Devunuri, S., Korlapati, S.C.R.: Crackseg9k: a collection and benchmark for crack segmentation datasets and frameworks. In: ECCV Workshops (2022). https://api.semanticscholar.org/CorpusID:251903306
19. Liu, Y., Yao, J., Lu, X., Xie, R., Li, L.: Deepcrack: a deep hierarchical feature learning architecture for crack segmentation. Neurocomputing **338**, 139–153 (2019). https://api.semanticscholar.org/CorpusID:106407363

A Deep Reinforcement Learning Framework for Denial Constraint Discovery

Di Wu, Derong Shen(✉), Tiezheng Nie, and Yue Kou

Northeastern University, Shenyang, China
{shendr,nietiezheng,kouyue}@mail.neu.edu.cn

Abstract. Denial Constraint (DC) discovery aims to effectively and efficiently identify data quality issues. Nevertheless, balancing efficiency with task-specific applicability poses a substantial challenge. Unfortunately, most existing methods heavily rely on extensive enumeration and fail to adequately consider the requirements of downstream data cleaning tasks. To address these issues, we propose DCRer, a novel DC discovery framework based on deep reinforcement learning. DCRer models the DC discovery process as a Markov Decision Process (MDP) and utilizes a DC tree structure combined with a masking mechanism to guide predicate node selection. To improve training, we design a reward function and a Deep Q-Network (DQN). The reward function jointly considers the coverage, diversity, and completeness. Furthermore, the DQN integrates both Dueling DQN and Double DQN to improve model stability and mitigate estimation bias. Extensive experiments demonstrate the advantages of DCRer in terms of effectiveness, efficiency and scalability. Additionally, we integrate DCRer with existing data cleaning frameworks, validating its effectiveness in practical tasks.

Keywords: Denial constraint discovery · Deep reinforcement learning · Deep Q-Network

1 Introduction

Data-driven science, as the fourth paradigm following experimentation, theory, and computational science, leverages data analysis to uncover valuable insights, facilitating effective decision-making for businesses. Integrity constraints play a crucial role in data analysis tasks such as data mining, data cleaning, database design, and query optimization [1]. Among integrity constraints, Denial Constraints (DCs) [4] have recently gained significant attention due to their generality and expressiveness. DCs are sufficiently general to subsume many other data dependencies, such as Functional Dependencies (FDs) [5] and Conditional Functional Dependencies (CFDs) [6], and can express complex data quality rules that traditional constraints struggle to capture.

In recent years, substantial progress has been made in the field of DC discovery, including frameworks for data cleaning based on DCs [12]. DC discovery

J. Li et al. (Eds.): APWeb-WAIM 2025, LNCS 16115, pp. 246–260, 2026.
https://doi.org/10.1007/978-981-95-5719-6_16

typically involves a two-step process [3,4,8,10,11,14]: (1) building evidence sets, where an evidence set is constructed from the input data as an intermediate result, and (2) enumerating DCs, where algorithms such as set covering are applied to generate DCs from the evidence set. Although many DC discovery algorithms employ strategies such as pruning, and some methods have adopted deep reinforcement learning techniques, they still suffer from a large enumeration space and insufficient integration with downstream data cleaning tasks.

To address these issues, we propose a novel DC discovery framework called DCRer, which aims to discover DCs that are directly beneficial for downstream data cleaning tasks, such as error detection and correction. Our contributions are summarized as follows:

- We propose DCRer, a deep reinforcement learning-based framework for DC discovery. DCRer jointly considers coverage, diversity, and completeness to identify high-quality constraints.
- We model the DC discovery process as the growth of a DC tree. By introducing the DC tree for predicate node selection and employing a masking mechanism, we simplify the discovery process of DCs.
- We formalize DC discovery as a Markov Decision Process (MDP) and design a reward function and Deep Q-Network (DQN) to efficiently train an agent for intelligent constraint discovery.
- Experimental results demonstrate that DCRer improves the effectiveness of downstream data cleaning tasks compared to existing methods. Moreover, by leveraging prior learning, it enhances the efficiency of subsequent processing, saving substantial time and computational resources. At the same time, it also exhibits high scalability.

2 Related Work

In general, DC discovery consists of two main steps: building evidence sets and enumerating DCs. FastDC [4] is the first algorithm designed for DC discovery. It compares every pair of tuples in the input dataset to generate an intermediate evidence set, which is then used to guide a depth-first search for enumerating DCs. DCFinder [11] improves this process by combining data structures called position list indexes with predicate selectivity-based techniques, thereby reducing the number of evidence operations. More recently, [10] introduced a parallel pipeline architecture to efficiently compute intermediate data, significantly reducing the time needed for evidence set construction. In addition, inverted index, pruning, and parallel search strategies were proposed to further improve performance.

However, these methods still follow traditional DC discovery methodologies and thus suffer from high time complexity, especially due to their reliance on exhaustive enumeration. A more practical research direction focuses on how to efficiently discover DCs without enumerating all possible conditions. RLMiner [9] proposes a deep reinforcement learning-based algorithm for discovering efficient editing rules. RLMiner is capable of mining desirable rules for data repair, achieving comparable accuracy to enumeration-based methods while offering significantly higher efficiency and strong scalability. DCMiner [2] also adopts deep reinforcement learning to flexibly combine objective and subjective criteria, enabling the discovery of constraints that better align with user intent. It introduces an effective training procedure to mine concise, relevant, and diverse DCs, improving user validation and application. However, existing DC discovery methods primarily focus on constraint discovery and neglect integration with downstream data cleaning tasks.

3 Preliminary

Denial Constraints (DCs) are predicate conjunctions used to identify combinations of column values that conflict. Let A and B be two columns of a relation schema, and r is a relation instance. We define the predicate p_i as the expression $t.A\ op\ t'.B$, where t and t' are tuples of r, and $op \in \{=, \neq, >, \leq, <, \geq\}$ is a comparison operator. A DC φ is represented as the following:

$$\varphi : \forall t, t' \in r, \neg (p_1 \wedge \ldots \wedge p_m)$$

DCs represent multiple conjunctions of predicates. If these predicates are simultaneously satisfied, it indicates that tuples t and t', violate the DC. In other words, DC φ is satisfied only when at least one predicate is not satisfied.

We illustrate with the following example in Table 1, comprising five tuples and six column attributes: Name, Phone, City, State, Salary and Rate. We define the corresponding three DCs as follows:

(1) $\varphi_1 : \forall t, t' \in r, \neg (t.City = t'.City \wedge t.State \neq t'.State)$
(2) $\varphi_2 : \forall t, t' \in r, \neg (t.City = t'.City \wedge t.Phone = t'.Phone)$
(3) $\varphi_3 : \forall t, t' \in r, \neg (t.State = t'.State \wedge t.Salary < t'.Salary \wedge t.Rate > t'.Rate)$

The meanings of the three DCs are as follows: φ_1 specifies that no two tuples can have the same City and different States simultaneously. φ_2 specifies that no two tuples can have the same City and Phone. φ_3 specifies that for any two tuples with the same State, the Rate of the tuple with a higher Salary cannot be lower than the Rate of the tuple with a lower Salary.

Table 1. The Example Table.

Id	Name	Phone	City	State	Salary	Rate
t_1	Zhuo jun	984–5776	NEW YORK	NY	5000	4
t_2	Ingmar	459–7011	DOTHAN	AL	60000	5
t_3	Adriana	665–8462	DOTHAN	AL	35000	7
t_4	Wunnava	318–1834	NEW YORK	NI	90000	4.475
t_5	Naomichi	665–8462	DOTHAN	AL	90000	6.5

From Table 1, we can observe the following violations of DCs:

(1) The tuple pair $<t_1, t_4>$ violates φ_1 because t_1, t_4 have the same City but different States.
(2) The tuple pair $<t_2, t_5>$ violates φ_2 because t_2, t_5 have the same values for (City, Phone).
(3) The tuple pairs $<t_3, t_2>$ and $<t_3, t_5>$ violate φ_3 because when they have the same State, the tuple with lower Salary has a higher Rate.

4 DCRer

We propose a DC discovery framework based on deep reinforcement learning, called DCRer. Figure 1 illustrates the framework of DCRer. We perform DC discovery by constructing a DC tree and modeling it as a Markov decision process, denoted as SelP-MDP. The goal of SelP-MDP is to select predicate nodes to facilitate the construction of the DC tree. The agent selects an appropriate action a_t based on the current state s_t and updates the state to s_{t+1} in the environment, which includes the evidence set containing input data and the growing DC tree. To better train the agent, we evaluate the quality of discovered DCs through a reward function and choose the most appropriate predicate node p_i based on Q-values.

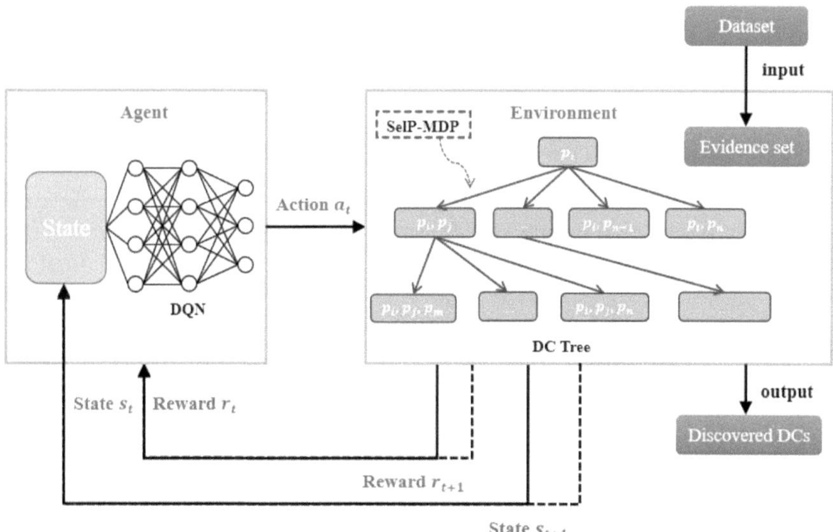

Fig. 1. Overall framework of DCRer.

4.1 Constructing the DC Tree

Predicate selection can reduce computational costs and uninteresting results [4]. The predicate selection methods for current DC discovery algorithms are as follows: for categorical columns, predicates use the operator set $\{=, \neq\}$; for numerical columns, $\{=, \neq, >, \leq, <, \geq\}$ are used. Predicates can only be applied to two different columns that share the same type and a certain proportion of common values. Additionally, predicates with the operator $\neq$ are generally less selective than those with the operator $=$ (unless for specific distributions, such as single-value columns) [10], and our algorithm follows the same principle. Table 2 illustrates the predicate space of the relations in Table 1.

Table 2. The Predicate Space of the Example Table in Table 1.

$p_1 : t.Id = t'.Id$	$p_2 : t.Id \neq t'.Id$
$p_3 : t.Name = t'.Name$	$p_4 : t.Name \neq t'.Name$
$p_5 : t.Phone = t'.Phone$	$p_6 : t.Phone \neq t'.Phone$
$p_7 : t.City = t'.City$	$p_8 : t.City \neq t'.City$
$p_9 : t.State = t'.State$	$p_{10} : t.State \neq t'.State$
$p_{11} : t.Salary = t'.Salary$	$p_{12} : t.Salary \neq t'.Salary$
$p_{13} : t.Salary \leq t'.Salary$	$p_{14} : t.Salary \leq t'.Salary$
$p_{15} : t.Salary \geq t'.Salary$	$p_{16} : t.Salary \geq t'.Salary$
$p_{17} : t.Rate = t'.Rate$	$p_{18} : t.Rate \neq t'.Rate$
$p_{19} : t.Rate \leq t'.Rate$	$p_{20} : t.Rate \leq t'.Rate$
$p_{21} : t.Rate \geq t'.Rate$	$p_{22} : t.Rate \geq t'.Rate$

To solve the issue of selecting appropriate nodes from the predicate space for DC discovery, we propose modeling the DC discovery process as the growth of a DC tree. Each node in the tree represents a predicate, and child nodes are generated by refining their parent nodes. Initially, high-probability predicates are selected from the predicate space as root nodes, and a child node is generated by selecting the next predicate through a Markov decision process. For each evidence e in evidence set E, it is used to check all candidate DCs in R. For each DC $\varphi \in R$, if $\varphi \subseteq e$, it is removed from R. To achieve this, for each predicate p_i not in e, it forms a new candidate $\varphi' = \varphi \bigcup p_i$, and if there does not exist a DC $\varphi'' \in R$ such that $\varphi'' \subseteq \varphi'$, i.e., φ' is minimal in R, then φ' is added to R.

Additionally, in predicate node selection, we perform a masking rule mechanism, which includes both local and global masking. Local masking indicates that in a DC, if a group of cells already contains an operator, predicate nodes containing other operators are masked. Global masking is used to avoid rediscovering DCs. If a predicate node has already been selected, it is masked.

Through the SelP-MDP process of predicate selection, new child nodes are generated, and the validity of the generated DCs is checked. If, at the current state, there are no nodes outside the evidence set, or there are nodes not in the evidence set but no selectable nodes after masking, then stop generating the DC tree. The leaf nodes of the DC tree represent the solution set R of our DCs.

4.2 SelP-MDP

The strategy for selecting DC tree nodes plays a crucial role in influencing subsequent selections and the final results. If we consider the DC discovery process as a decision-making process, reinforcement learning can be applied to train an agent to intelligently discover DCs, thereby avoiding extensive enumeration and significantly reducing time costs. To make decisions that maximize the overall effectiveness of the DC set obtained after the SelP-MDP process, we model this process as a Markov decision process, called SelP-MDP.

Agent: It is a DC discovery system. It first receives the state s_t and reward r_t from the environment and generates the next DC based on the current state update policy.

Environment: It includes the evidence set obtained from input data and the growing DC tree.

State: The state s_t is a combination of the DC tree and the solution set R, which consists of the discovered DCs. However, since the DC tree is continuously growing, its encoding increases over time. Encoding the growing tree as a state is challenging. Therefore, refining the nodes of the tree is necessary, and in this paper, we encode a DC (node) rather than the entire DC tree.

Action: The action a_t is to select a predicate node p_i from the DC tree. Specifically, action a_t will result in three possible outcomes:

(1) Add DC: If p_i, when combined with existing predicates, forms a new minimal non-trivial DC, it is added to the set of discovered DCs.
(2) Replace DC: If the new DC is a smaller subset of an existing one, it replaces the original constraint to ensure minimality.
(3) Prune: If the newly formed DC violates constraint conditions, the corresponding search path is discarded to avoid redundant computation.

Reward: Designing the reward is crucial as it directly affects the performance of the model. Since the states and actions are discrete, evaluating the goodness of a state is feasible. Therefore, the Q-learning method is suitable for the DC discovery scenario in this paper. We design an action-value $Q(s_t, p)$. Then, the policy selects the predicate node p_i with the maximum Q-value as the state s_t. The calculation of the specific Q-value and reward is described in 4.3.

Algorithm 1 demonstrates the SelP-MDP process. Its objective is to find the optimal set of DCs R. The algorithm first initializes an empty set of DCs R and sets $flag$ to false (Lines 1–2). Next, for each DC tree T_i, the algorithm resets the state s and iteratively performs the following steps while $flag$ is false (Line

Algorithm 1. Selp-MDP

Input: Evidence set E, DC tree T
Output: Optimal set of DCs R

1: $R \leftarrow \emptyset$
2: $flag \leftarrow$ ***False***
3: **for each** $T_i \in T$ **do**
4:     reset State s
5:     **while not** $flag$ **do**
6:         **if** all predicate nodes are masked **then**
7:             $flag \leftarrow$ ***True***
8:         **else**
9:             calculate Q-values
10:             $m \leftarrow mask_{global}$ **and** $mask_{local}$
11:             update Q-values with m
12:             select Action $a(p_i)$ with the maximum Q-value
13:             **if** $\varphi' = \varphi \cup \{p_i\}$ is valid **then**
14:                 $\varphi \leftarrow \varphi'$
15:             **else**
16:                 discard φ'
17:             **end if**
18:         **end if**
19:     **end while**
20:     $R \leftarrow R \cup \{\varphi\}$
21: **end for**
22: **return** R

3–5): if all predicate nodes are masked, set $flag$ to true and exit the loop (Lines 6–7); otherwise, the algorithm calculates the Q-value and selects the action with the maximum Q-value based on global and local masking (Lines 8–12). Next, the algorithm checks whether the newly generated DC is valid. If valid, update φ; if invalid, discard φ'(Lines 13–16). Finally, the algorithm returns the set of DCs R (Lines 22). This algorithm utilizes deep reinforcement learning to intelligently select predicate nodes to generate new child nodes, thereby obtaining the optimal set of DCs R.

4.3 Train Efficient Agent

Reward Function. Since our goal is to use DCs for subsequent data cleaning, we aim for DCs to be as concise, comprehensive, and diverse as possible. Therefore, we measure DCs comprehensively in terms of coverage, diversity, and completeness.

Coverage. We evaluate Coverage by measuring the ratio of g_1 to the number of predicates. g_1 represents the proportion of exceptional cases satisfied by DCs. The metric g_1 was initially proposed for FDs [13] and has been extended to DCs. $g_1(r, \phi)$ is defined as the ratio of the number of tuple pairs that violate the DC to the total number of tuple pairs. The formula is as follows:

$$g_1(r,\varphi) = \frac{|\{(t,t') \mid (t,t') \in r^2 \wedge (t,t')\ violates\ \varphi\}|}{(|r|^2 - |r|)} \tag{1}$$

We use $Cov(\varphi)$ to measure coverage, defined as follows:

$$Cov(\varphi) = \frac{g_1(r,\varphi)}{Len(\varphi)} = \frac{|\{(t,t') \mid (t,t') \in r^2 \wedge (t,t')\ violates\ \varphi\}|}{(|r|^2 - |r|) \times Len(\varphi)} \tag{2}$$

Diversity. The solution set R of DCs contains discovered DCs. To ensure the quality of DCs and the diversity of subsequent tasks, DCs within the solution set R should be diverse [7]. We use the Jaccard distance to measure the difference between two DCs φ_1 and φ_2:

$$Dis(\varphi_1,\varphi_2) = 1 - |\frac{\varphi_1 \cap \varphi_2}{\varphi_1 \cup \varphi_2}| \tag{3}$$

Completeness. Completeness ensures that the discovered DCs cover a broader range of attributes. This property is evaluated by measuring the attribute coverage ratio, which reflects how comprehensively the DC set covers the attributes in the dataset.The Completeness is defined as follows:

$$Com(R) = \frac{|A(R)|}{n} \tag{4}$$

where $|A(R)|$ denotes the number of distinct attributes covered by the DC set R, and n represents the R total number of attributes in the dataset.

Combining coverage, diversity, and completeness, we can further measure the overall quality and effectiveness of the solution set of DCs R. We define the comprehensive measure of R as $Mix(R)$, expressed as follows:

$$Mix(R) = \alpha \cdot Cov(R) + \beta \cdot Dis(R) + \gamma \cdot Com(R) \tag{5}$$

Deep Q-Network. As shown in Fig. 2, we design an action-value function $Q(s_t, p)$ using a Deep Q-Network (DQN), where the policy selects the predicate node p_i with the maximum Q-value as state s_t. Specifically, a deep neural network is used to estimate the value of the current DC's encoding vector, where the input is the current state encoding s_t, and the output is the estimated value of each action, i.e., predicates with higher values will be added to the current DC.

As an off-policy algorithm, DQN employs ε-greedy to balance exploration and exploitation when collecting data, storing the collected data for subsequent training. DQN also includes an experience replay module, which helps DQN achieve stable and outstanding performance. Specifically, this involves maintaining a replay buffer, where each four-tuple (state, action, reward, next state) sampled from the environment is stored. During Q-network training, a random batch of data is sampled from the replay buffer for training. This method ensures that the samples meet the independence assumption and allows each sample to be used multiple times, thereby improving sample efficiency.

Based on the standard DQN architecture, this work incorporates both Dueling DQN and Double DQN to enhance model stability and reduce estimation bias. Dueling DQN aims to decouple the state-value function and the action advantage function, thereby reducing Q-value estimation errors. Double DQN addresses the overestimation issue in Q-learning, improving training stability.

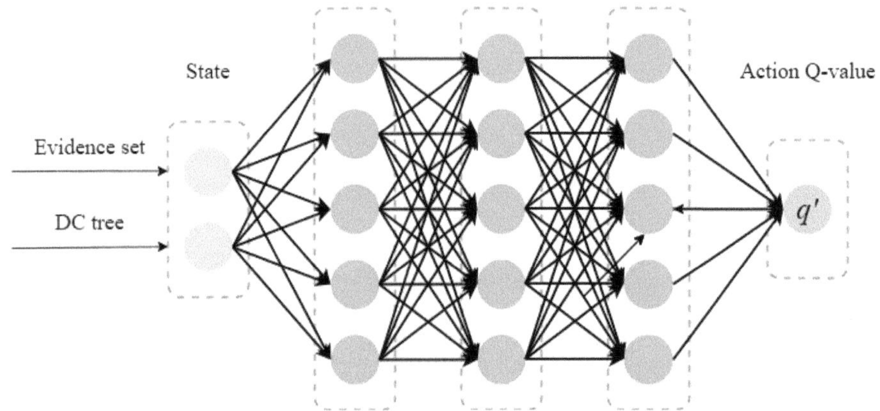

Fig. 2. Action-value network.

Dueling DQN separately models the state-value function $V(s)$ and the advantage function $A(s, a)$, enhancing the model's representational power and stability. The Q-value is decomposed as follows:

$$Q(s_t, a) = V(s_t) + \left(A(s_t, a) - \frac{1}{N} \sum_{a'} A(s_t, a') \right) \tag{6}$$

where $V(s_t)$ denotes the value of state s_t, and $A(s_t, a)$ represents the advantage of taking action a in state s_t relative to other actions. The mean subtraction operation ensures that Q-values are adjusted based on relative advantage only, avoiding unnecessary computations.

To mitigate the overestimation issue in DQN, we further adopt the Double DQN structure. Double DQN utilizes two separate neural networks—the online Q-network and the target Q-network—to decouple action selection from Q-value evaluation. The target Q-value is computed as:

$$Q_{target} = r_t + \gamma\, Q_{target}(s_{t+1}, \arg\max_{a'} Q_{eval}(s_{t+1}, a')) \tag{7}$$

where Q_{target} denotes the value from the target network, and $Q_{eval}(s_{t+1}, a')$ is the evaluation network's output for the next state. This separation prevents overoptimistic value estimates and improves learning reliability.

The masking mechanism assigns small negative values to disallowed actions at the action-value network's output, preventing their selection by greedy policies. The input to the masked action value network is the current state encoding s_t. The deep neural network then extracts features from the state encoding s_t to obtain the corresponding feature vector. For each node N of the DC tree, we denote Z_N as a vector capturing the feature information of that node. A linear layer and ReLU activation function are used for each node N to compute the final Q-value $q = \theta \cdot ReLU(W \cdot Z_N)$. Then, a designed masking layer is applied to limit the action space, resulting in q'. The appropriate predicate node is selected based on q'.

$$q' = q \odot m - inf * (1 - m) \tag{8}$$

5 Experiments

Datasets: We utilize three publicly available datasets Hospital, Flight, and Beers for evaluation.

Baseline: (1) FDCD [10]: The algorithm integrates the evidence context techniques and introduces late minimization and parallel execution for DC enumeration. Additionally, it demonstrates how to use these techniques to improve the previous DC enumeration algorithms.(2) FastADC [14]: This algorithm improves the evidence set construction by first building the clue set and then transforming the clue set to the evidence set, and studies parallel clue set construction. (3) DCMiner [2]: This algorithm leverages deep reinforcement learning to discover DCs, incorporating both objective and subjective reward function criteria to guide the learning process.

Evaluation Metrics: We assess the runtime of the discovered DCs application, as well as precision, recall, and F1-score for error repair using the discovered DCs.

Experimental Setup: We employ the discovered DCs for downstream data cleaning tasks and compare their effectiveness (Sect. 5.1). To visually demonstrate the efficiency of DC discovery, we compare the time taken to discover DCs (Sect. 5.2). To visually demonstrate the scalability of DCRer, we compare its accuracy on different data fractions across three datasets (Sect. 5.3). To visually demonstrate the importance of the reward function, we conduct ablation studies (Sect. 5.4).

5.1 Effectiveness of DC Discovery

The effectiveness of DC discovery is evaluated by measuring the accuracy, recall, and F1-score of dirty data repair after applying the discovered DCs for data cleaning. The input consists of a dataset containing dirty data and a set of DCs used for data repair. In this experiment, we compare the effectiveness of four methods by using the discovered DCs from DCRer, FastADC, FDCD, and DCMiner as inputs to the existing data cleaning framework HoloClean.

Figure 3 presents the comparison results of the effectiveness of DC discovery across three datasets. The comparative analysis shows that the proposed DCRer consistently outperforms the other methods across all datasets, achieving higher F1-scores. In particular, DCRer demonstrates the best performance on the Flights and Beers datasets, highlighting the practical utility of the discovered DCs in data cleaning tasks.

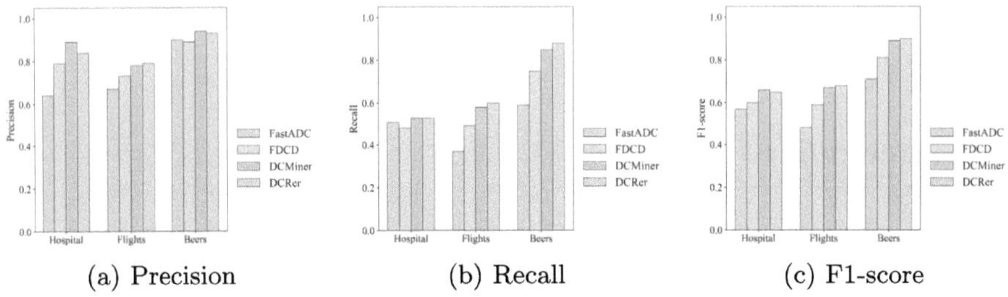

(a) Precision (b) Recall (c) F1-score

Fig. 3. Comparison results of effectiveness of DC discovery.

Although FastADC leverages multithreaded parallel acceleration and clue set optimization, it exhibits relatively low recall. FDCD, which combines evidence context techniques with parallel search strategies, achieves a more balanced performance between precision and recall, though its recall still leaves room for improvement. DCMiner, based on deep reinforcement learning, generally attains higher precision across the three datasets, but its recall is slightly lower than that of DCRer. Compared to the strong-performing DCMiner, DCRer achieves slight improvements on both the Flights and Beers datasets.

In summary, DCRer demonstrates an overall performance improvement in the DC discovery task compared to existing methods. The DCs discovered by DCRer not only exhibit strong structural expressiveness but also can be directly transformed into high-quality data cleaning operations.

5.2 Efficiency of DC Discovery

To intuitively demonstrate the efficiency of DC discovery, we compare the time taken by DCRer, FastADC, FDCD, and DCMiner in discovering DCs. Specifically, we measure the total time each method takes to complete the discovery process. To avoid the randomness of single-run results, each method is executed ten times, and the average runtime is calculated. Figure 4 presents the time cost comparison results (in seconds) across different datasets. Experimental results show that the runtimes of DCRer and DCMiner are generally lower than those of FDCD and FastADC, with deep reinforcement learning methods exhibiting a significant advantage in the later experimental rounds. Specifically, FDCD and FastADC, as traditional enumeration-based methods, still incur high computational overhead when processing larger datasets. Although these methods have improved their efficiency through parallelization strategies, their inherent reliance on enumeration leads to higher time complexity.

In contrast, the deep reinforcement learning strategies employed by DCMiner and DCRer demonstrate stronger adaptability. In each experiment, DCMiner and DCRer dynamically adjust their strategies based on historical data and quickly converge to optimal solutions, effectively mitigating the high computational complexity faced by traditional enumeration methods.

In summary, DCRer demonstrates high efficiency in DC discovery. Its iterative learning and optimization capabilities make DCRer well-suited for DC discovery tasks in complex environments.

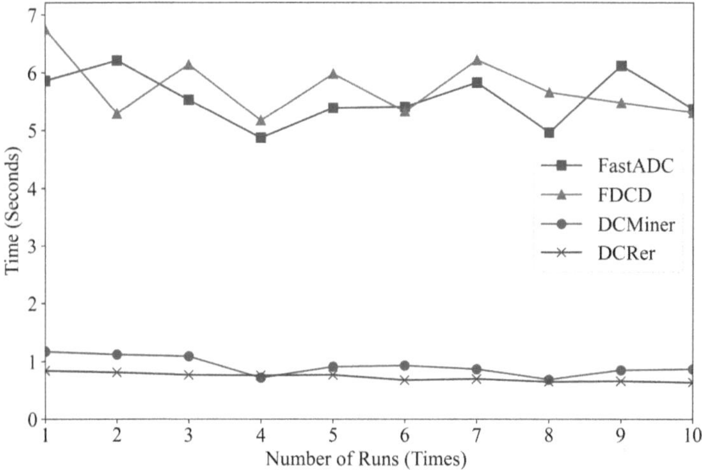

Fig. 4. Comparison results of efficiency of DC discovery.

5.3 Scalability of DC Discovery

To visually demonstrate the scalability of the DCRer model under different data scales, experiments on DC discovery were conducted on three datasets. The model's performance in terms of precision, recall, and F1-score is systematically evaluated across different data volumes.

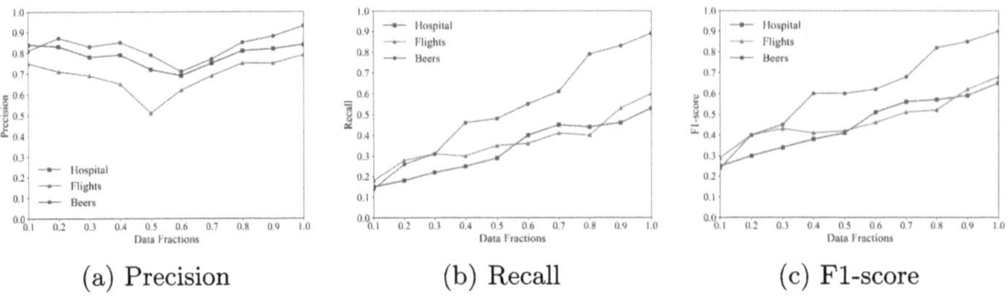

(a) Precision (b) Recall (c) F1-score

Fig. 5. Comparison results of scalability of DC discovery.

Figure 5 presents the performance of DCRer across varying data fractions. The experimental results indicate that, across the three datasets, precision, recall, and F1-score generally show an upward trend as the data volume increases. This suggests that DCRer exhibits good scalability and stability when extended to larger datasets.

As the data scale gradually increases, the overall performance of the Hospital dataset shows a slow upward trend. However, as the data volume grows, the model progressively accumulates information and improves its recognition ability, leading to a steady improvement in metrics. The Flights dataset demonstrates good stability during the expansion process, with all metrics showing steady growth, particularly recall and F1-score, which show a significant improvement. The Beers dataset overall shows an increasing trend, reaching a high level of stability in the later stages. These trends indicate that DCRer demonstrates good practicality and scalability across different application scenarios.

In summary, the performance of DCRer significantly improves with increasing data volume, indicating that DCRer has strong learning capabilities, scalability, and reliability when handling large-scale data. The algorithm's stability is high, and consistent performance improvements are observed across different types of datasets.

5.4 Ablation Study on the Importance of the Reward Function

This paper proposes a reward function that integrates coverage, diversity, and completeness, demonstrating how to efficiently train the agent. To intuitively illustrate the importance of the reward function, we compare five configurations: DCRer-NonR (completely removing the reward function), DCRer-Cov (retaining only the coverage reward), DCRer-Div (retaining only the diversity reward), DCRer-Com (retaining only the completeness reward), and the full DCRer. The performance of each method is evaluated using precision, recall, and F1-score.

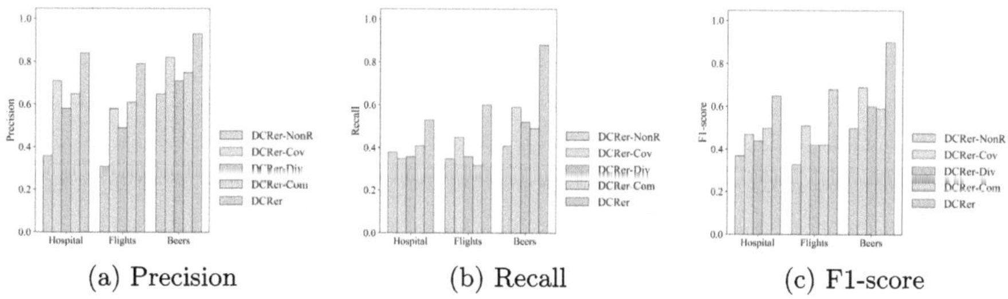

(a) Precision (b) Recall (c) F1-score

Fig. 6. Ablation experiments of the reward function.

Figure 6 presents the results of the ablation study. Experimental results show that DCRer with the complete reward function outperforms its variants across all datasets, indicating that the joint design of the three reward components is key to improving DCRer's capability in discovering high-quality DCs. DCRer-NonR performs the worst without a reward function, highlighting that the deep reinforcement learning model struggles to explore effectively and discover high-quality constraints without reward guidance. DCRer-Cov achieves relatively high precision but lower recall across datasets, suggesting that the coverage reward promotes the generation of more accurate DCs. DCRer-Div exhibits variable performance across datasets, implying that the diversity reward helps the model to generate structurally diverse constraints. DCRer-Com ranks second best, indicating that while the completeness reward assists in filtering low-quality constraints, it requires collaboration with other reward components to maximize its effectiveness on complex datasets.

In summary, the three components of the reward function—coverage, diversity, and completeness—exhibit strong complementarity and synergy. Although individual reward components can enhance performance in certain aspects, they are insufficient to fully address the comprehensiveness and accuracy required for effective DC discovery. In contrast, the complete reward design in DCRer consistently achieves superior performance across all three datasets, demonstrating the effectiveness and necessity of the proposed reward function in deep reinforcement learning-based DC discovery.

6 Conclusion

In this paper, we propose a novel framework, DCRer, for DC discovery based on deep reinforcement learning. We model the DC discovery process as a Markov decision process and utilize the DC tree for predicate node selection. To better train the agent, we employ a comprehensive measure of DCs based on coverage, diversity, and completeness. We then use Q-learning to greedily select action values. Based on experimental results, our framework DCRer demonstrates an improvement in effectiveness compared to enumeration methods in downstream data cleaning tasks. Moreover, through accumulated learning in earlier stages, subsequent processing efficiency increases significantly, saving considerable time and computational resources. In conclusion, DCRer demonstrates excellent performance in terms of effectiveness, efficiency and scalability. In the future, we continue to optimize the reward function, enhance the learning ability of the framework, and thereby improve the performance on downstream data cleaning tasks.

Acknowledgement. This work is supported by National Natural Science Foundation of China (62172082,62072084,62072086).

References

1. Abedjan, Z., Golab, L., Naumann, F.: Profiling relational data: a survey. VLDB J. **24**(4), 557–581 (2015)
2. Bian, L., Yang, W., Xu, J., Tan, Z.: Discovering denial constraints based on deep reinforcement learning. In: Proceedings of the 33rd ACM International Conference on Information and Knowledge Management (CIKM), pp. 120–129 (2024)
3. Bleifuß, T., Kruse, S., Naumann, F.: Efficient denial constraint discovery with hydra. PVLDB **11**(3), 311–323 (2017)
4. Chu, X., Ilyas, I.F., Papotti, P.: Discovering denial constraints. PVLDB **6**(13), 1498–1509 (2013)
5. Fan, W., Geerts, F., Jia, X., Kementsietsidis, A.: Conditional functional dependencies for capturing data inconsistencies. ACM Trans. Database Syst. **33**(6), 1–48 (2008)
6. Fan, W., Geerts, F., Li, J., et al.: Discovering conditional functional dependencies. IEEE Trans. Knowl. Data Eng. **23**(5), 683–698 (2011)
7. Li, S., Zhang, Y., Tan, Z., Ma, S.: Diversifying repairs of denial constraint violations. Inf. Syst. **108**, 102041 (2022)
8. Livshits, E., Heidari, A., Ilyas, I.F., Kimelfeld, B.: Approximate denial constraints. PVLDB **13**(10), 1682–1695 (2020). https://doi.org/10.14778/3401960.3401966
9. Mei, Y., Song, S., Fang, C., Wei, Z., Fang, J., Long, J.: Discovering editing rules by deep reinforcement learning. In: 2023 IEEE 39th International Conference on Data Engineering (ICDE), pp. 355–367. IEEE (2023)
10. Pena, H.M., Porto, F., Naumann, F.: Fast algorithms for denial constraint discovery. Proc. VLDB Endowment **16**(4), 684–696 (2022)
11. Pena, H.M., de Almeida, E.C., Naumann, F.: Discovery of approximate (and Exact) denial constraints. PVLDB **13**(3), 266–278 (2019)
12. Rekatsinas, T., Chu, X., Ilyas, I.F., Ré, C.: HoloClean: holistic data repairs with probabilistic inference. PVLDB **10**(11), 1190–1201 (2017)
13. Wyss, C., Giannella, C., Robertson, E.L.: FastFDs: a heuristic-driven, depth-first algorithm for mining functional dependencies from relation instances - extended abstract. In: Proceedings of the International Conference on Data Warehousing and Knowledge Discovery (DaWaK), pp. 101–110. Springer, Heidelberg (2001)
14. Xiao, R., Tan, Z., Wang, H., Ma, S.: Fast approximate denial constraint discovery. Proc. VLDB Endowment **16**(2), 269–281 (2022)

Information Retrieval and Knowledge Management II

Generating Difficulty Controllable Multiple-Choice Question by Iteratively Guiding the Large Language Model

Hao Zhou[1], Li Li[1(✉)], Xiaofei Xu[2], and Zhongwei Yin[1]

[1] School of Computer and Information Science, Southwest University, Chongqing 400715, China
lily@swu.edu.cn

[2] School of Information Technology, Murdoch University, Murdoch, WA 6150, Australia

Abstract. The automatic generation of Multiple-Choice Questions (MCQs) is an emerging task primarily applied in education. The goal is to generate MCQs based on a given context, including the question stem, answers, and distractors. In such application scenarios, the MCQ generation methods should provide MCQs with appropriate difficulties for individuals to enhance their reading comprehension abilities and learning experience. A few efforts of Difficulty-Controllable Question Generation(DCQG) have been made recently, however the previous definitions of difficulties in DCQGs failed to consider the potential relationships between the difficulties of MCQs and students' performances. In the paper, we propose the Difficulty-Controllable Multiple-Choice Question Generation (DCMCQG), a framework to generate MCQs dedicated to the students' abilities. Specifically, the definition of the difficulty is introduced from the Knowledge Tracking (KT) by dynamically modeling the difficulty as the error rate of students answering the MCQs. To be aware of the definition of the difficulty factor, we employed ten different reading comprehension models to simulate students answering MCQs, using the models' error rates as the difficulty labels for the MCQs. We further fine-tuned the ChatGLM3-6b [7] to understand the difficulty of MCQs. Subsequently, we proposed a difficulty feedback module to guide ChatGLM3-6b in generating MCQs that meet the specified difficulty levels. The automatic evaluation experiments demonstrate that our model ensures the quality of the generated MCQs and successfully aligns the generated MCQs with the specified difficulty levels. Additionally, supplementary human evaluation experiments validate the effectiveness of our method.

Keywords: Multiple-Choice Question · Large Language Model · Difficulty-Controllable

J. Li et al. (Eds.): APWeb-WAIM 2025, LNCS 16115, pp. 263–277, 2026.
https://doi.org/10.1007/978-981-95-5719-6_17

1 Introduction

Reading comprehension MCQs generation refers to the task of automatically generating MCQs that consist of the question, answer, and distractors from the given reading comprehension context. The generation of MCQs can be divided into two sub-tasks: Question-Answer Generation (QAG) [18,29] and Distractor Generation (DG) [9,25,30]. In early research, QAG and DG were often studied separately, with few studies combining the two tasks. In recent years, with the development of pre-trained language models, there has been a growing of work that integrates QAG and DG, resulting in a complete, end-to-end automatic MCQ generation system [12,24,28].

Reading comprehension MCQs help focus learners' attention on the reading context, thereby supporting the advancement of reading comprehension skills. To enhance this learning process, it is beneficial to provide MCQs that match the difficulty level appropriate for each learner's reading ability [27]. Difficulty-Controllable Question Generation (DCQG) [3,5,27] is a highly related task, it aims to control the difficulty of the generated questions by specifying different difficulty levels. However, previous research on DCQG for reading comprehension remains limited which restrict their practical application: 1). They ignore the relationship between the difficulty and the overall ability level of the learner, making it challenging to determine the appropriate difficulty for the learner. 2). They only control the difficulty of the question stem, but difficulty control should consider the entire MCQ, as difficulty usually depends on both the question and the distractors.

To address these issues, we propose a novel method for generating difficulty-controllable MCQs, which defines the difficulty of MCQs and considers the entire MCQ for difficulty control. In this approach, given a reading comprehension context and a specified difficulty level, the framework needs to generate MCQs related to the context and meet the difficulty level as closely as possible. To link the difficulty of MCQs with the students, we adopt the definition of question difficulty from Knowledge Tracing [23], where the accuracy rate of students answering the questions is used as the difficulty. To obtain the difficulty label for training our model, we used ten different reading comprehension models on the RACE [10] dataset to simulate students' performance, using the error rates of these models as the difficulty for the MCQs. Consequently, we obtained the D-RACE[1] dataset, which is the RACE dataset with difficulty labels. We fine-tuned ChatGLM3-6b on the D-RACE dataset using the LoRA [8] method to enable ChatGLM3-6b to understand how to generate MCQs at specified difficulty levels. However, the MCQ initially generated by the LLM often does not precisely match the specified difficulty. Therefore, we propose a difficulty feedback module to iteratively guide the generator to generate MCQ that meet the difficulty requirements. Our main contributions can be summarized as follows:

[1] The D-RACE dataset can be obtained at https://github.com/yichenchou/DCMCQG.

- We have proposed an innovative MCQ generation method with controllable difficulty, integrating the definition of difficulty from KT to achieve difficulty control.
- To fine-tune the LLM to understand the difficulty level, we utilized ten reading comprehension models to annotate the RACE dataset and obtained difficulty labels.
- We propose a feedback module for iteratively guiding the LLM to generate MCQs that conform to the specified difficulty level.

Extensive experiments show that our model generates high-quality MCQs that better match the specified difficulty labels. Additionally, human evaluation experiments demonstrate that our model effectively meets the needs of teachers in real-world scenarios.

2 Related Work

2.1 Difficulty-Controllable Question Generation

Question generation refers to generating questions based on a given context. The rise of pre-trained language models has had a profound impact on the field of question generation [11,19,20]. Yan et al. [17] proposed ProphetNet, they fine-tuned ProphetNet on the answer-aware QG task and achieved excellent results. Yoon et al. [31] proposed using the generated questions as input to iteratively generate more diverse questions. Dong et al. [4] proposed a novel unified framework that integrates unstructured contextual text and structured fact text to generate questions. Difficulty-controllable question generation is a relatively novel task. Previous question generation work did not consider difficulty, but providing questions with specified difficulty in educational applications is essential. Difficulty-controllable question generation was first proposed by Gao et al. [5] They categorized questions as either simple or difficult and then controlled the generation of simple or difficult questions. Cheng et al. [3] proposed to define the question difficulty as the number of reasoning steps required to answer the question and controlled question difficulty by adjusting the number of reasoning steps needed. Masaki et al. [27] used Item Response Theory to generate difficulty-controllable questions.

2.2 Distractor Generation

Distractor generation aims to generate incorrect options similar to the correct answer from a given context and question. Previous methods primarily used the seq2seq framework to generate distractors [9,14,25,30]. Gao et al. [6] adopted a hierarchical encoder-decoder framework and proposed static attention to penalize sentences related to the answer, thus generating lengthy distractors. Xie et al. [30] proposed a Multi-Selector Generation Network (MSG-Net), which uses a multi-selector mechanism to choose multiple different sentences from the article and then generate semantically rich distractors. Taslimipoor et al. [25] proposed a two-stage method, first generating combinations of answers and distractors, and then distinguishing and clustering them to obtain the final distractors.

2.3 MCQ Generation

The automatic generation of multiple-choice questions (MCQ) is a relatively recent task. Due to the limitations of previous model performance, Shuai et al. [24] proposed using two models to form an end-to-end MCQ generation system: one model for generating questions and another for generating distractors. Vachev et al. [28] and Rodriguez et al. [22] adopted a similar strategy. Unlike Shuai et al., their models do not require the correct answer as input. Although this results in some performance loss, the ability to generate MCQs without relying on the correct answer makes their models more applicable to real-world scenarios. With the success of large language models (LLMs) in various tasks, Subhankar et al. [12] proposed using multi-stage prompts to enhance the effectiveness of LLMs in generating MCQs. The output of each stage serves as the input for the next stage, iteratively generating high-quality MCQs. Our work introduces difficulty control in MCQ generation, an aspect that has not been considered in previous MCQ generation studies. We focus on linking difficulty to students' error rates when answering MCQs, and generating MCQs with controllable difficulty.

3 Method

3.1 Task Definition

The task of this study is to generate a reading comprehension MCQ given a reading passage and a target difficulty level. We use articles from the RACE dataset.

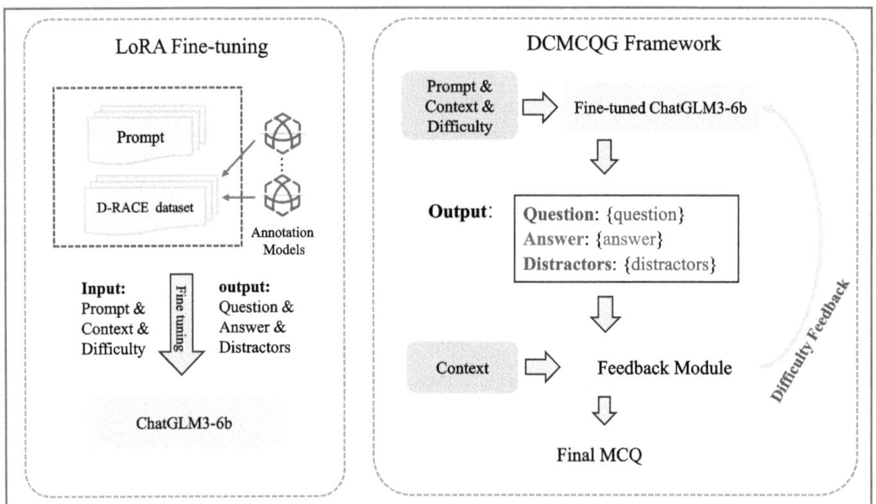

Fig. 1. An Overview of the Difficulty-Controllable Multiple-Choice Question Generation framework.

We propose a Difficulty-Controllable MCQ Generation(DCMCQG) framework. Formally, let C represent the reading context and d represent the specified difficulty level. Given C and d as inputs, our task is to generate a MCQ, including the question stem Q, answer A, and distractors D, with d as its difficulty level. Figure 1 outlines our proposed framework. The left part of the Fig. 1 shows our fine-tuning process.

We use the fine-tuned ChatGLM3-6b on the D-RACE dataset as the MCQ generator. The right part of the Fig. 1 illustrates the MCQ generation process. First, we input the context and difficulty, and the generator generates a MCQ that matches the specified difficulty based on the context and difficulty. Next, our designed difficulty feedback module evaluates the difficulty of the MCQ. If the MCQ does not match the specified difficulty, the difficulty feedback module provides feedback to the generator, prompting it to generate a MCQ of the specified difficulty. Below, we will provide a more detailed explanation of the entire generation process.

3.2 The Protocol of Difficulty Labeling

The RACE dataset is sourced from English reading comprehension exams tailored for Chinese students aged 12 to 18, encompassing both middle and high school levels. It covers a variety of topics and effectively assesses students' comprehension abilities. We use RACE to prepare our experimental dataset. Difficulty is a subjective concept, which in the real world manifests as the probability of students answering questions incorrectly. To better align with real-world scenarios, we propose directly defining difficulty as the probability of students answering questions incorrectly. Inspired by Gao et al. [16], we use ten different reading comprehension models to simulate students answering questions. The ten models are listed on GitHub[2] and they are all available on Huggingface[3]. The T5 models were proposed by Raffel et al. [21] The models prefixed with kda were proposed by Moon et al. [15] It is noteworthy that we did not utilize large language models, as their superior text comprehension capabilities enable them to easily answer middle and high school-level English reading comprehension test questions. Consequently, annotation results derived from such models would hold minimal reference value. The difficulty labeling protocol is as follows: these ten models are used to answer the MCQs in the RACE dataset, and the models' error rates are then calculated to serve as the measure of difficulty. The equation is:

$$d = 1 - \sum_{i=1}^{m} X_i/m \tag{1}$$

where d represents the difficulty, m is the number of models, and X_i is the output of the models (0 for incorrect, 1 for correct). Please note that we cannot directly use the train set of the RACE dataset for annotation because most of these

[2] https://github.com/yichenchou/DCMCQG.

[3] https://huggingface.co/.

models are trained on the RACE train set, making it very easy for the models to correctly answer the MCQs in the trainset. Therefore, we used the RACE test set for difficulty annotation. Then, we obtained the D-RACE dataset, which is the RACE test set with difficulty labels, comprising a total of 4,934 samples.

3.3 Controlled Prompting Template

Previous work on MCQG involved generating MCQs from a given input paragraph through simple prompts to LLMs. However, there has been no research on generating difficulty-controllable questions by prompting difficulty levels. One reason is that while LLMs possess strong language understanding capabilities, they cannot comprehend the difficulty level of a given MCQ. For example, if given a prompt: *"Please generate a MCQ with a difficulty level of 0.6 based on the provided context,"* the model often fails to generate a MCQ that matches the specified difficulty because it has not learned what a MCQ with a

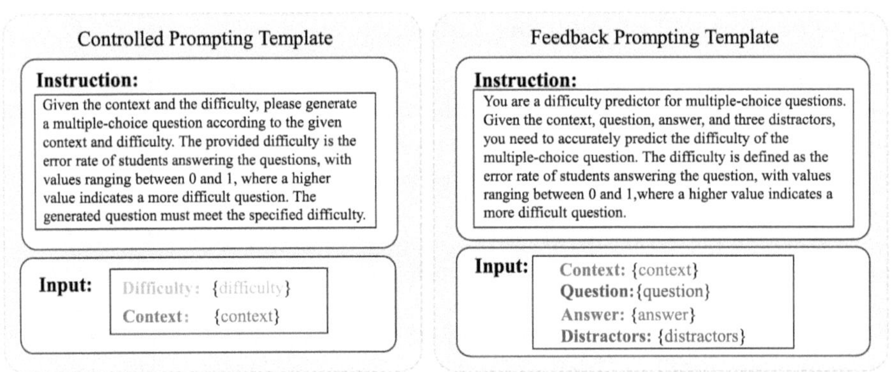

Fig. 2. The Construction of a Controllable Prompting Template and Feedback Prompting Template.

difficulty level of 0.6 looks like. Therefore, we propose fine-tuning LLMs to achieve difficulty control. The prompting template we set up is shown in Fig. 2. We have provided a detailed description of our definition of difficulty in the prompt to help the model better understand the concept of difficulty. We use the LoRA method to fine-tune ChatGLM3-6b. The inputs and outputs of the fine-tuning process are illustrated in Fig. 1. We specified the output format under this instruction: question, answer, distractors. This facilitates our experimental evaluation. The fine-tuned LLM can generate MCQs that match the specified difficulty based on the context and difficulty level.

3.4 The Difficulty Feedback Module

Although we fine-tuned ChatGLM3-6b using the D-RACE dataset, and ChatGLM3-6b tries to generate MCQs that match the specified difficulty, it often fails to generate multiple-choice questions that precisely match the difficulty level on the first attempt. Inspired by Yuan et al. [32], we found that iterative prompting of LLM can generate questions that meet the requirements. However, in practical use, iterative guidance should not be performed by teachers. We aim for this system to be an end to end fully automated system. Additionally, different teachers using the system may have varying perceptions of difficulty. To make our framework more automated and maintain consistency in difficulty definitions, we propose a difficulty feedback module to iteratively guide the generator in generating MCQ that match the difficulty level. Previous research [5,27] often used automatic QA systems to evaluate the difficulty of questions in experimental sections. We found that this method can be applied to generative models to pre-evaluate the difficulty of questions, thereby iteratively guiding the generator to generate MCQs that match the difficulty level. To effectively predict the difficulty of MCQs, we fine-tuned Qwen2-1.5b on the D-RACE dataset as the prediction model. We did not employ the ten annotation models introduced in Sect. 3.2 for difficulty prediction. This is because these models are reserved for experimental evaluation, and using them in difficulty prediction task would introduce bias in the evaluation process, compromising fairness. The MCQ difficulty prediction task can be considered the dual task of difficulty-controlled MCQ generation. After inputting the context and MCQ, the model outputs the predicted difficulty. The prompting template we set up is shown in Fig. 2.

To better illustrate our feedback process, our DCMCQG process is specifically described in Algorithm 1.

Algorithm 1. Procedure of Our DCMCQG Framework

Input: context C, difficulty level d
Output: (Q, A, D)

$(Q, A, D)_0 \Leftarrow$ `ChatGLM3-6b`(C, d)
$\hat{d}_0 \Leftarrow$ `QWen2-1.5b`$(C, (Q, A, D)_0)$
for each $i \in [0, 3]$ **do**
    if $\left|\hat{d}_i - d\right| <= 0.2$ **then** break
    else if $\hat{d}_i > d$ **then**
        $(Q, A, D)_{i+1} \Leftarrow$ `ChatGLM3-6b`(H_i, F_1)
    else
        $(Q, A, D)_{i+1} \Leftarrow$ `ChatGLM3-6b`(H_i, F_2)
    end if
    $\hat{d}_{i+1} \Leftarrow$ `QWen2-1.5b`$(C, (Q, A, D)_{i+1})$
end for
return $(Q, A, D)_i$

To clarify, the following symbols are defined:

- $(Q, A, D)_i$ denotes the MCQ generated in the ith iteration.
- $\hat{d}_i$ represents the difficulty predicted by the difficulty prediction model for $(Q, A, D)_i$.

- H_i indicates the conversation history.
- F_1 and F_2 represent feedback prompts. F_1: "The difficulty of the MCQ you generated is $\{\hat{d}\}$, which is higher than the specified difficulty $\{d\}$. Please generate a simpler question." F_2: "The difficulty of the MCQ you generated is $\{\hat{d}\}$, which is lower than the specified difficulty $\{d\}$. Please generate a more difficult question."

To generate the final MCQ with the desired difficulty level d, we first use the generator to generate an initial MCQ based on difficulty d and the context C. The difficulty of this MCQ is then predicted by the feedback module. Suppose the predicted difficulty is higher than the input difficulty, in that case, the difficulty feedback module will prompt the generator with *"The difficulty of the MCQ you generated is* $\{\hat{d}\}$*, which is higher than the specified difficulty* $\{d\}$*. Please generate a simpler question."* Conversely, if the difficulty is lower, a similar prompt is given to increase the difficulty. We allow for the predicted difficulty of the MCQ to deviate from the specified difficulty by a maximum of 0.2 and limit the iterations to three to prevent endless iterations. This stepwise guidance helps the generator generate MCQ that better match the specified difficulty.

4 Experimental Setup

4.1 DataSet

The original RACE dataset is derived from English reading comprehension exams designed for Chinese students aged 12 to 18, encompassing both middle and high school levels. It covers a wide range of topics and serves as a means to assess students' comprehension abilities. We utilize the D-RACE dataset, annotated with difficulty levels, as our experimental dataset. The specific annotation methods are described in Sect. 3.2. We divided the D-RACE dataset into training and testing sets in an 8:2 ratio.

4.2 Evaluation Metrics

We use both automatic and manual evaluations to assess our model.

- **Automatic Evaluation:** Previous work has used metrics like METEOR [1] for automatic evaluation, which are based on n-gram similarity. To better evaluate the quality of MCQs, we adopt the method proposed by Taslimipoor et al. [25] to evaluate the quality of the distractors. We employed the same embedding method as their work to calculate cosine similarity(CS). Additionally, we used the ten annotation models mentioned in Sect. 3.2 to automatically assess whether the difficulty of the MCQs generated by our model is accurate. We did not conduct separate ablation experiment because the zero-shot ChatGLM3-6b and the fine-tuned ChatGLM3-6b are essentially versions of DCMCQG with certain modules removed.

– **Human Evaluation:** Previous research has found that automatic evaluation metrics cannot fully assess the quality of MCQs, especially for tasks involving difficulty-controlled MCQ generation. Therefore, we designed human evaluation experiments to conduct the assessment.

4.3 Baselines

We use several baselines from previous literature. For evaluating the generation of distractors, we primarily employed some baselines mentioned by Taslimipoor et al. [25] These include T5 [13], zero-shot and one-shot GPT-3.5 [2], and two-step DG models [25]. Additionally, we set up zero-shot, one-shot, and fine-tuned versions of ChatGLM3-6b to compare with our model in terms of difficulty evaluation. We provided zero-shot and one-shot ChatGLM3-6b with the same prompt template as our model, with the one-shot ChatGLM3-6b being given a complete example (including context, difficulty, and MCQ). The fine-tuned ChatGLM3-6b is the DCMCQG without the feedback module. Additionally, we fine-tuned Llama2-7b [26] on the D-RACE dataset for comparison.

5 Experimental Result

5.1 Automatic Evaluation Result

Since the models compared in Tables 2 and 3 already include the DCMCQG model with partial modules removed, we don't conduct additional ablation experiments in this study. We employ the evaluation method proposed by Taslimipoor et al. [25]. This method primarily compares three aspects: i) the semantic similarity between the generated distractors and the correct answer (gd2c), ii) the semantic similarity between the generated distractors and the reference distractors in the dataset (gd2d), and iii) the semantic similarity among the generated distractors themselves (gd2gd). We report our results in Table 1. The first column (gd2c) shows the similarity between the generated distractors and the original

Table 1. The automatic evaluation results of our model are evaluated from three aspects: gd2c, gd2d, and gd2gd.

	gd2c	gd2d			gd2gd
		d1	d2	d3	
T5	49.25	56.26	37.90	17.73	58.55
zero-shot GPT3.5	42.21	48.06	46.79	46.29	51.99
one-shot GPT3.5	43.00	50.07	48.81	47.49	49.87
two-step DG	42.28	54.00	51.84	49.39	**43.56**
fine-tuned Llama2-7b	56.04	56.18	55.93	**55.87**	52.24
DCMCQG	53.25	**56.89**	**56.29**	55.86	53.63

correct answer. Given the debate over whether reasonable distractors should have higher similarity to the correct answer, we present this result without specific discussion. The following three columns display the semantic similarity of the three generated distractors to the ground-truth distractors. Higher similarity indicates better quality of the generated distractors. It can be observed that our model's generated distractors achieve higher scores than those from models such as one-shot GPT3.5 and two-step DG. The performance of fine-tuned Llama2-7b is similar to DCMCQG. Although it is slightly lower than DCMCQG, it still surpasses models like GPT-3.5. This is because Llama2-7b was also fine-tuned on the D-RACE dataset. The last column represents the semantic similarity among the generated distractors, lower scores indicate greater diversity among the generated distractors. Our model performs moderately in terms of diversity, The two-step DG performed the best, as two-step DG employs post-processing methods to enhance distractor diversity. Other LLMs also exhibited low diversity, possibly due to their tendency to generate similar distractors.

Table 2. Automatic evaluation results of the quality of questions generated by our model

Models	CS	METEOR
zero-shot ChatGLM3-6b	68.75	14.17
one-shot ChatGLM3-6b	69.54	14.54
fine-tuned ChatGLM3-6b	73.72	16.15
fine-tuned Llama2-7b	73.30	15.90
DCMCQG	**74.16**	**17.42**

Additionally, we conducted a simple evaluation of the quality of the generated questions, using cosine similarity(CS) and METEOR for the assessment. The results are shown in the Table 2. DCMCQG demonstrated the best performance, although the difference between it and the fine-tuned ChatGLM3-6b and fine-tuned Llama2-7b was not significant. The performance of ChatGLM3-6b in zero-shot and one-shot settings was slightly lower than fine-tuned models. This is because the model's performance improves after fine-tuning on the dataset.

5.2 Controllability Analysis

Additionally, we evaluated the accuracy of the difficulty levels of the MCQs generated by our model. Since our goal is to generate MCQs with controllable difficulty, it is essential to assess whether the generated MCQs' difficulty aligns with the input difficulty. We employed the ten annotation models mentioned in Sect. 3.2 for evaluation. After DCMCQG generates the MCQ, these ten reading comprehension models will answer the MCQ and use their error rates as the difficulty of the generated MCQ. This evaluation difficulty is then compared to

Table 3. Evaluation results of our model's difficulty control capability

models	MSE	MAE
zero-shot ChatGLM3-6b	0.2116	0.3671
one-shot ChatGLM3-6b	0.1953	0.3515
fine-tuned ChatGLM3-6b	0.1134	0.2681
fine-tuned Llama2-7b	0.1263	0.2836
DCMCQG	**0.0619**	**0.1825**

the input difficulty. Given that the difficulty levels are values between 0 and 1, we used two simple metrics for evaluation: Mean Squared Error (MSE) and Mean Absolute Error (MAE). The experimental results are shown in Table 3. It can be observed that our model achieved excellent performance. The zero-shot ChatGLM3-6b performed the worst, almost incapable of generating questions at the specified difficulty. Although the one-shot ChatGLM3-6b was provided with a complete example, including the difficulty, it still struggled to generate MCQs that matched the specified difficulty. The difficulty accuracy of the generated questions decreased after removing the difficulty feedback module from DCMCQG, indicating that the feedback module effectively serves as a post-processing step. While the fine-tuned ChatGLM3-6b is not as effective as the full DCMCQG, it is still significantly better than the other models. Similarly, the fine-tuned Llama2-7b, although slightly less effective than the fine-tuned ChatGLM3-6b, also outperformed both the zero-shot and one-shot ChatGLM3-6b. This indicates that the models fine-tuned on the D-RACE dataset are able to understand the specified difficulty levels.

5.3 Human Evaluation Result

We invited 5 annotators to evaluate the MCQs generated by our model. Due to the involvement of difficulty control, we provided the annotators with the definition of difficulty as described in this paper and informed them that the difficulty values in the dataset range from 0 to 1, with higher values indicating greater difficulty. We randomly selected 100 samples from the test set, where each sample contained a context, a question, an answer, and three distractors. In contrast to previous studies, we explicitly provided difficulty labels for the MCQs in these samples and asked annotators to judge whether the MCQs matched the specified difficulty. We considered three metrics: fluency (F), difficulty alignment (D), and relevance (R). The scoring is based on a five-point scale.

- **Fluency (F):** Evaluates the grammatical correctness and linguistic fluency of the generated MCQs.
- **Difficulty Alignment (D):** Evaluate whether the difficulty of the generated MCQs aligns with the input difficulty.

- **Relevance (R):** Evaluates the content relevance between the generated MCQs and the passage. Requires assessment based on the question, answer, and distractors.

Table 4. Human evaluation results of different models

models	F	D	R
zero-shot ChatGLM3-6b	4.42	3.14	4.31
one-shot ChatGLM3-6b	4.53	3.29	4.45
fine-tuned ChatGLM3-6b	4.67	3.56	4.52
fine-tuned Llama2-7b	4.64	3.51	4.49
DCMCQG	**4.75**	**3.91**	**4.57**

We use the average scores from five annotators as the final score. Table 4 presents the human evaluation results. The results indicate that our DCMCQG performs well in fluency. Even without task-specific fine-tuning on the D-RACE dataset, the zero-shot and one-shot ChatGLM3-6b demonstrated good fluency, which can be attributed to the strong generative capabilities inherent to LLMs. However, DCMCQG demonstrates superior performance in difficulty alignment, and there is a noticeable decrease in difficulty alignment after removing the feedback module, which proves the effectiveness of our feedback module. DCMCQG also performs well in relevance, meaning that the MCQs generated by DCMCQG are more contextually appropriate. In addition, we conducted a human evaluation without difficulty labels. Specifically, we randomly selected 100 samples without providing difficulty labels and asked annotators to assess the difficulty of the questions directly. The difficulty scoring range is from 0 to 10.

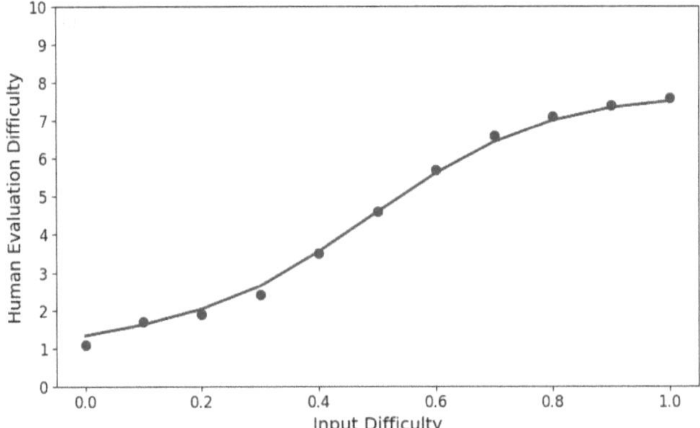

Fig. 3. The relationship between human difficulty evaluation and input difficulty.

Figure 3 shows the relationship between the difficulty values input to DCMCQG and the average difficulty assessed by humans. The horizontal axis represents the input difficulty values, while the vertical axis represents the manually assessed difficulty of the generated MCQs. It can be observed that the MCQs generated with higher input difficulty are considered more difficult by the annotators, while those with lower input difficulty are considered easier. This indicates that DCMCQG has good difficulty control capabilities.

6 Conclusion and Future Work

This paper presents a novel approach to generating MCQs with controllable difficulty. To our knowledge, previous work has not focused on difficulty control for MCQs as a whole. We propose using students' error rates as a difficulty definition to align with real-world scenarios where teachers manually generate MCQs. We employ ten reading comprehension models to simulate students' answering processes to annotate difficulty. Then, we fine-tune ChatGLM3-6b on the RACE dataset with difficulty labels, enabling it to understand the difficulty levels of MCQs. We also introduce a feedback module that answers the generated MCQ in advance to assess their difficulty, and then gradually guides ChatGLM3-6b to generate MCQ that meet the specified difficulty. Extensive evaluation experiments demonstrate the effectiveness of our method, especially in terms of difficulty control. However, this work has certain limitations. Since distractors are a crucial part of MCQ difficulty, we cannot ascertain whether the model adequately considers distractors during the rewriting process. In future work, we plan to focus on distractors to generate MCQs with more controllable difficulty.

References

1. Banerjee, S., Lavie, A.: METEOR: an automatic metric for MT evaluation with improved correlation with human judgments. In: Proceedings of the ACL Workshop on Intrinsic and Extrinsic Evaluation Measures for Machine Translation and/or Summarization, pp. 65–72. Association for Computational Linguistics, Ann Arbor, Michigan (2005)
2. Bitew, S.K., Deleu, J., Develder, C., Demeester, T.: Distractor generation for multiple-choice questions with predictive prompting and large language models. arXiv preprint: arXiv:2307.16338 (2023)
3. Cheng, Y., Li, S., Liu, B., Zhao, R., Lin, C., Zheng, Y.: Guiding the growth: difficulty-controllable question generation through step-by-step rewriting. In: Proceedings of the 59th Annual Meeting of the Association for Computational Linguistics and the 11th International Joint Conference on Natural Language Processing, vol. 1, pp. 5968–5978. Association for Computational Linguistics (ACL) (2021)
4. Dong, C., Shen, Y., Lin, S., Lin, Z., Deng, Y.: A unified framework for contextual and factoid question generation. IEEE Trans. Knowl. Data Eng. **36**(1), 21–34 (2024)
5. Gao, Y., Bing, L., Chen, W., Lyu, M.R., King, I.: Difficulty controllable generation of reading comprehension questions. In: Kraus, S. (ed.) Proceedings of the Twenty-Eighth International Joint Conference on Artificial Intelligence, IJCAI 2019, Macao, China, 10–16 August 2019, pp. 4968–4974 (2019)

6. Gao, Y., Bing, L., Li, P., King, I., Lyu, M.R.: Generating distractors for reading comprehension questions from real examinations. In: Proceedings of the AAAI Conference on Artificial Intelligence, vol. 33, pp. 6423–6430 (2019)
7. GLM, T., et al.: ChatGLM: a family of large language models from GLM-130B to GLM-4 all tools (2024)
8. Hu, E.J., et al.: LoRA: low-rank adaptation of large language models. arXiv preprint: arXiv:2106.09685 (2021)
9. Kumar, A.P., et al.: A novel approach to generate distractors for multiple choice questions. Expert Syst. Appl. **225**, 120022 (2023)
10. Lai, G., Xie, Q., Liu, H., Yang, Y., Hovy, E.: RACE: large-scale ReAding comprehension dataset from examinations. In: Proceedings of the 2017 Conference on Empirical Methods in Natural Language Processing, pp. 785–794. Association for Computational Linguistics, Copenhagen, Denmark (2017)
11. Lewis, M., et al.: BART: denoising sequence-to-sequence pre-training for natural language generation, translation, and comprehension. arXiv preprint: arXiv:1910.13461 (2019)
12. Maity, S., Deroy, A., Sarkar, S.: A novel multi-stage prompting approach for language agnostic MCQ generation using GPT. In: European Conference on Information Retrieval, pp. 268–277. Springer (2024)
13. Manakul, P., Liusie, A., Gales, M.J.: MQAG: multiple-choice question answering and generation for assessing information consistency in summarization. arXiv preprint: arXiv:2301.12307 (2023)
14. Maurya, K.K., Desarkar, M.S.: Learning to distract: a hierarchical multi-decoder network for automated generation of long distractors for multiple-choice questions for reading comprehension. In: Proceedings of the 29th ACM International Conference on Information & Knowledge Management, pp. 1115–1124 (2020)
15. Moon, H., et al.: Evaluating the knowledge dependency of questions. arXiv preprint: arXiv:2211.11902 (2022)
16. Moon, H., et al.: Evaluating the knowledge dependency of questions. In: Proceedings of the 2022 Conference on Empirical Methods in Natural Language Processing, EMNLP 2022, Abu Dhabi, United Arab Emirates, 7–11 December 2022, pp. 10512–10526. Association for Computational Linguistics (2022)
17. Qi, W., et al.: ProphetNet: predicting future N-gram for sequence-to-sequence pretraining. arXiv preprint: arXiv:2001.04063 (2020)
18. Qu, F., Jia, X., Wu, Y.: Asking questions like educational experts: automatically generating question-answer pairs on real-world examination data. In: Proceedings of the 2021 Conference on Empirical Methods in Natural Language Processing, EMNLP 2021, Virtual Event/Punta Cana, Dominican Republic, 7–11 November 2021, pp. 2583–2593. Association for Computational Linguistics (2021)
19. Radford, A., et al.: Language models are unsupervised multitask learners. OpenAI Blog **1**(8), 9 (2019)
20. Raffel, C., et al.: Exploring the limits of transfer learning with a unified text-to-text transformer. J. Mach. Learn. Res. **21**(1), 5485–5551 (2020)
21. Raffel, C., et al.: Exploring the limits of transfer learning with a unified text-to-text transformer. J. Mach. Learn. Res. **21**(140), 1–67 (2020)
22. Rodriguez-Torrealba, R., Garcia-Lopez, E., Garcia-Cabot, A.: End-to-end generation of multiple-choice questions using text-to-text transfer transformer models. Expert Syst. Appl. **208**, 118258 (2022)

23. Shen, S., Huang, Z., Liu, Q., Su, Y., Wang, S., Chen, E.: Assessing student's dynamic knowledge state by exploring the question difficulty effect. In: Proceedings of the 45th International ACM SIGIR Conference on Research and Development in Information Retrieval, pp. 427–437 (2022)
24. Shuai, P., Li, L., Liu, S., Shen, J.: QDG: a unified model for automatic question-distractor pairs generation. Appl. Intell. **53**(7), 8275–8285 (2023)
25. Taslimipoor, S., Benedetto, L., Felice, M., Buttery, P.: Distractor generation using generative and discriminative capabilities of transformer-based models. In: Proceedings of the 2024 Joint International Conference on Computational Linguistics, Language Resources and Evaluation (LREC-COLING 2024), pp. 5052–5063 (2024)
26. Touvron, H., et al.: Llama 2: open foundation and fine-tuned chat models. arXiv preprint: arXiv:2307.09288 (2023)
27. Uto, M., Tomikawa, Y., Suzuki, A.: Difficulty-controllable neural question generation for reading comprehension using item response theory. In: Proceedings of the 18th Workshop on Innovative Use of NLP for Building Educational Applications (BEA 2023), pp. 119–129 (2023)
28. Vachev, K., Hardalov, M., Karadzhov, G., Georgiev, G., Koychev, I., Nakov, P.: Leaf: multiple-choice question generation. In: European Conference on Information Retrieval, pp. 321–328. Springer (2022)
29. Willis, A., Davis, G., Ruan, S., Manoharan, L., Landay, J., Brunskill, E.: Key phrase extraction for generating educational question-answer pairs. In: Proceedings of the Sixth (2019) ACM Conference on Learning@ Scale, pp. 1–10 (2019)
30. Xie, J., Peng, N., Cai, Y., Wang, T., Huang, Q.: Diverse distractor generation for constructing high-quality multiple choice questions. IEEE/ACM Trans. Audio, Speech, Lang. Process. **30**, 280–291 (2021)
31. Yoon, H., Bak, J.: Diversity enhanced narrative question generation for storybooks. In: Proceedings of the 2023 Conference on Empirical Methods in Natural Language Processing, pp. 465–482. Association for Computational Linguistics, Singapore (2023)
32. Yuan, X., Wang, T., Wang, Y., Fine, E., Abdelghani, R.: Selecting better samples from pre-trained LLMs: a case study on question generation. In: Findings of the Association for Computational Linguistics: ACL 2023, Toronto, Canada, 9–14 July 2023, pp. 12952–12965. Association for Computational Linguistics (2023)

Research on a Multi-modal Entity Alignment Method Based on Neighborhood Matching

Zhanghui Wang, Fuzhuang Qian, Linlin Ding(✉), and Jinhua Wang

Faculty of Information, Liaoning University, Shenyang, China
dinglinlin@lnu.edu.cn

Abstract. The purpose of multi-modal entity alignment is to discover entities with the same meaning represented in two multi-modal knowledge graphs. Due to the heterogeneity of structures between different knowledge graphs, this paper proposes a multi-modal entity alignment model based on neighborhood matching. In structural embedding, this paper introduces long-distance neighbor information, uses a gating mechanism to aggregate direct and long-distance neighbor information, and the matching module is used to calculate the similarity between the neighborhood nodes. Meanwhile, multi-modal information such as relationships, attributes, and images are fused to enhance the effect of entity alignment. In this paper, experiments are conducted on DBP15K datasets and the results are significantly better than the baseline method.

Keywords: entity alignment · knowledge graph · multi-modal · neighborhood matching

1 Introduction

Entity Alignment (EA) aims to find equivalent entities between two different knowledge graphs (KGs) and is a key technology for knowledge fusion. However, entity alignment is not simple because real-life KGs are usually incomplete and different KGs usually have structural heterogeneity. Therefore, equivalent entities from two different KGs may have different expression forms or different neighborhood structures.

In recent years, entity alignment methods based on knowledge graph representation learning [1] have gradually become mainstream. Among them, the entity alignment method based on Graph Neural Networks (GNNs) is also widely used [2]. GNNs is a powerful model for learning vector representations of graph-structured data. GNNs takes the domain encoding structure and attributes of entities in the KG as input and learns the representation of a node by recursively aggregating the representation of its neighboring nodes. Different aggregation strategies will have different GNNs variants, including graph convolutional neural networks [3] (GCN) and graph attention networks [4] (GAT), etc. Research

J. Li et al. (Eds.): APWeb-WAIM 2025, LNCS 16115, pp. 278–292, 2026.
https://doi.org/10.1007/978-981-95-5719-6_18

[5] shows that GNNs has the same expressive power as the Weisfeiler-Leman (WL) test in identifying isomorphic subgraphs. GNNs has achieved good results in multiple embedding-based entity alignment method studies.

However, existing GNN-based entity alignment models still face a key problem that different KGs usually have structural heterogeneity [6], and the corresponding entities usually have different neighborhood structures. As shown in Fig. 1, two different KGs of Robert Downey Jr. have different neighborhood structures, and in KG_1 United States of America is Robert's two-hop neighbor. But in KG_2 United States of America is a one-hop neighbor. Different neighborhood structures can easily cause GNN to produce different representations of corresponding entities. Since relevant semantic information can appear in both direct neighbors and long-distant neighbors of the corresponding entity, this paper designs a module that aggregates both direct and long-distant neighbor information. In order to reduce noise information, the attention mechanism is further used to aggregate long-distant neighbors and find important neighbors in an end-to-end manner. Then, a gating mechanism is used to combine the output representations of multiple aggregate functions to obtain the hidden representation of the current layer. The matching module is used to calculate the neighborhood difference.

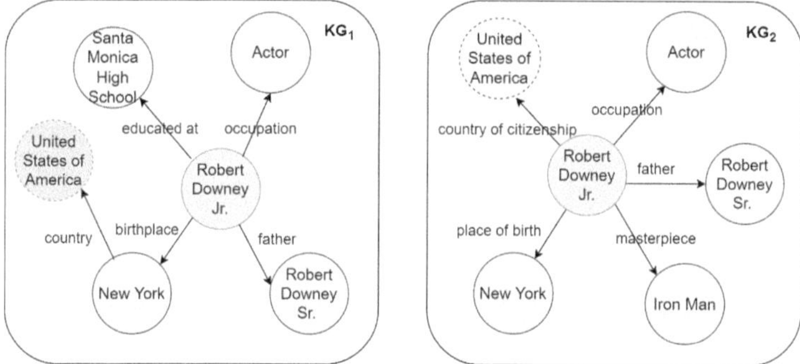

Fig. 1. Non - isomorphic relational neighborhoods of Robert Downey Jr. in different KGs.

However, existing entity alignment research largely ignores the multi-modal knowledge of real scenes. In real scenes, KGs usually consists of multi-modal knowledge, such as relationship triples, attributes and images. This additional information can effectively improve entity alignment. Therefore, this paper proposes Neighborhood Matching for Multi-modal Entity Alignment (NMEA), a multi-modal entity alignment model based on neighborhood matching. In addition to structure embedding, it also embeds relationships, attributes and image information. Then, entity alignment is performed after multi-modal fusion. This paper conducted experiments on the dataset DBP15K and conducted ablation research and analysis to prove the effectiveness of NMEA.

2 Related Work

Recent research on entity alignment mainly explores various additional information such as entity names [7], relationships [7–9], and attributes [7,9,10]. Most of these studies first use GNNs to map entities of different KGs into a unified low-dimensional vector space, then align entities through similarity measures of entity embedding. Research shows that the appropriate use of additional information as auxiliary proof can further improve the task performance of EA [11,12]. With the in-depth research on EA and the increasing popularity of multi-modal knowledge graphs, applying EA to multi-modal knowledge graphs, that is, multi-modal entity alignment, has attracted the research attention of scholars, but the scope of attempts is limited. At the beginning, Trisedya et al. proposed the AttrE [13] model, which is the first EA technology that uses attribute values and does not require seed alignment sets. It jointly embeds attributes and structures for learning, and embeds them in the same vector space for EA. Later, Chen et al. proposed MMEA [14] for entity alignment using similar entity pairs of heterogeneous multi-modal knowledge graphs using relationship embedding, numerical attribute embedding and image feature embedding. Liu et al. proposed EVA [15] creates initial seed pairs based on the visual similarity of entities, which can iteratively increase seed pairs through a guidance strategy, and utilize visual knowledge and other auxiliary information to implement EA. Cheng et al. proposed MultiJAF [16] using attention-based multi-modal fusion network to improve the complementarity of different embedding, and designed a numerical processing module. These methods mainly utilize additional information or multi-modal representation to enhance the contextual embedding of entities, but do not consider the structural heterogeneity of different KGs.

In order to solve the problem of structural heterogeneity, recent studies have also proposed solutions. The NMN [17] model designed a neighborhood matching module that uses graph sampling methods to effectively construct matching-oriented entity representations. The RNM [18] model proposed by Zhu et al. uses relational alignment to enhance the effect of entity alignment, while comparing the similarity of entities and relations. Relations play an important role both at the semantic level and in neighborhood matching through GCNs model mapping attributes. This model aims to use the results of relationship alignment and entity alignment to reinforce each other. Xie et al. proposed the GAEA [19] model and designed a simple entity-relationship encoder to generate potential representations of entities by jointly modeling comprehensive structural information and rich relational semantics. Two graph views are created using graph augmentation for edge-based alignment learning and contrastive entity representation learning, thereby alleviating structural heterogeneity and further improving alignment performance. These models address the issue of structural heterogeneity but do not consider multi-modal information to enhance entity alignment.

3 Proposed Method

Formally, a multi-modal KG is expressed as KG = (E, R, A, I, T), where E, R, A, I, T respectively represent the set of entities, relationships, attributes, images and triples. Given $KG_1=(E_1,R_1,A_1,I_1,T_1)$ and $KG_2=(E_2,R_2,A_2,I_2,T_2)$ as two knowledge graphs to be aligned, the goal is to find the aligned entity pairs P=$\{(e_1,e_2)|e_1\equiv e_2,e_1\in E_1,e_2\in E_2\}$ between KG_1 and KG_2. This article performs entity alignment based on a set of pre-aligned equivalent entities.

3.1 Overview of NMEA

In the multi-modal entity alignment model of this article, due to the structural heterogeneity of different KGs, k-hop neighborhood information is aggregated during structural embedding, and then neighborhood matching is used to calculate the similarity of neighborhood nodes. Then, we can obtain structural embedding representation. Embedding relational and attribute information using simple feed forward networks. Image embedding is obtained using residual networks. Finally, after integrating and embedding these multi-modal information, entity alignment is performed. Figure 2 shows the NMEA model.

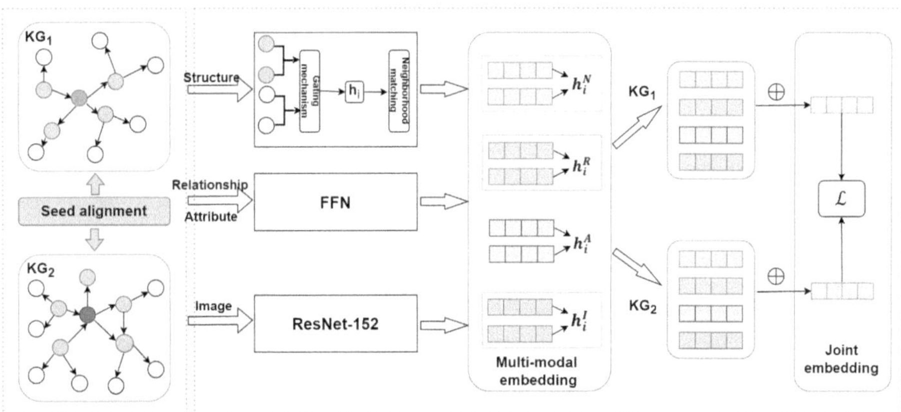

Fig. 2. Overall architecture of NMEA.

3.2 KG Structure Embedding

Figure 3 shows the structure embedding process without loss of generality. This figure shows the aggregation of one-hop and two-hop neighborhood information (k = 2).

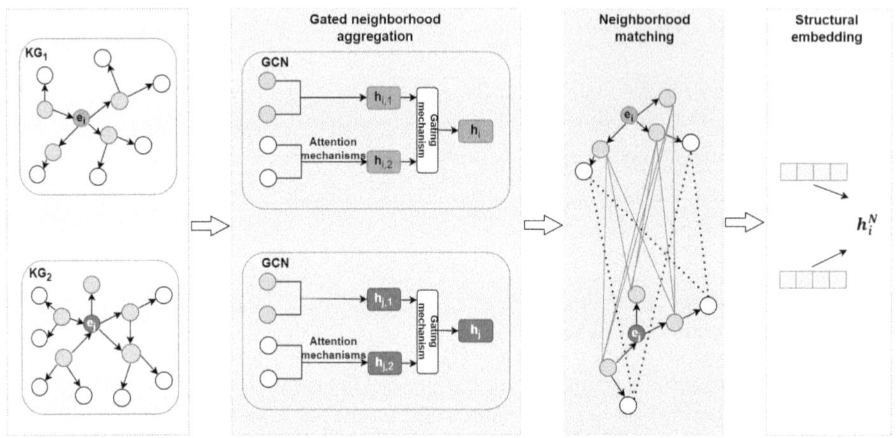

Fig. 3. Process of structure embedding.

Gated Neighborhood Aggregation. Neighborhood information within a two-hop range is aggregated through a gating mechanism. First, the one-hop neighborhood of an entity is the most important neighborhood, represented using ordinary GCN layer aggregation of one-hop neighbors. At the l-th layer, an entity e_i aggregates its one-hop neighbors to obtain its hidden representation $h_{i,1}^l$, which is calculated as follows:

$$h_{i,1}^l = \mathrm{Re}LU(\sum\nolimits_{j\in N_1(i)\cup\{i\}} \frac{1}{c_i} W_1^l h_j^{(l-1)}) \tag{1}$$

where $N_1(\cdot)$ represents a given one-hop neighbor set, c_i is a normalization constant, and W_1^l is a weight matrix.

To control the accumulated noise, a highway network [20] is introduced into the GCN layers, which can effectively control the noise propagation between GCN layers.

For two-hop neighborhood aggregation, directly using the original aggregation of GCN will lead to hierarchical propagation of noise information, so an attention mechanism is introduced here [21]. By aggregating the two-hop neighborhood information of the entity e_i at the l-th layer, the hidden representation of the entity e_i is obtained, denoted as $h_{i,2}^l$, and calculated as follows:

$$h_{i,2}^l = \mathrm{Re}LU(\sum\nolimits_{j\in N_2(i)\cup\{i\}} \alpha_{ij}^l W_2^l h_{j,2}^{(l-1)}) \tag{2}$$

where $N_2(\cdot)$ represents a given two-hop neighbor set, α_{ij}^l is the learnable attention weight of the entity e_i and its neighbors e_j. W_2^l is the weight matrix.

Not all long-distant neighbors contribute to describing the central entity. Therefore, for two-hop neighbor aggregation, this paper calculates attention weights between entities to highlight useful neighbors. This paper uses two matrices Z_1^l and Z_2^l for linear transformations for the central entity and its neighbors respectively. Formally, at the l-th layer, the attention weight $b_{ij}^l \in R$ between e_i and e_j is calculated as follows:

$$b_{ij}^l = Leakly\text{ReLU}[(Z_1^l h_i^l)^T (Z_2^l h_j^l)] \tag{3}$$

Finally, the attention weight is normalized using the softmax function to make them comparable across different entities:

$$\alpha_{ij}^l = softmax_j(b_{ij}^l) = \frac{\exp(b_{ij}^l)}{\sum_{k \in N_2(i) \cup \{i\}} \exp(b_{ik}^l)} \tag{4}$$

In order to aggregate two-hop neighbor information, this paper uses a gating mechanism to directly combine one-hop and two-hop neighbor information. Specifically, the hidden representation h_i^l of the entity e_i at the l-th layer is calculated as follows:

$$g(h_{i,2}^l) = \sigma(M h_{i,2}^l + b) \tag{5}$$

$$h_i^l = g(h_{i,2}^l) \cdot h_{i,1}^l + (1 - g(h_{i,2}^l)) \cdot h_{i,2}^l \tag{6}$$

where $g(h_{i,2}^l)$ represents the gate that controls the combination of one-hop and two-hop neighborhoods. M and b are the weight matrix and bias vector respectively.

Neighborhood Matching. The neighbor matching module calculates the cross-graph matching vector for each neighbor to measure the matching degree of the neighbor with the corresponding neighbor node [22]. Specifically, the neighborhood graph of the entity e_i in the given KG_1 is compared with each candidate entity in KG_2 to select the optimal entity pair. In order to reduce the matching overhead, this paper uses a low-cost approximation method. First, select the aligned entity set of the entity e_i to obtain the candidate entity set $S_i = \{s_{i1}, s_{i2}, ...s_{ik}...s_{it} | s_{ik} \in E_2\}$, and then calculate the similarity between the entity e_i and the candidate entity. Therefore, for an entity e_j in KG_2, its probability of being a candidate of e_j can be calculated as:

$$p(h_j | h_i) = \frac{\exp(h_i \cdot h_j)}{\sum_{k \in E_2} \exp(h_i \cdot h_k)} \tag{7}$$

Let (e_i,$s_i k$) be an entity pair to be measured, where $e_i \in E_1$ and $s_i k \in E_2$ is one of the candidate entities of e_i, e_s and e_t are the two neighbors of e_i and $s_i k$ respectively. First, calculate the cosine similarity between e_s and e_t in their representation space:

$$l_{s,t} = \cos ine(h_s, h_t) \tag{8}$$

where h_s and h_t are the GCN-output embedding representations of e_s and e_t respectively.

Then, these similarities are used as weights, and the candidate entity embedding is weighted and summed to obtain an attentive vector, and then the cross-matching vector is calculated:

$$h_s^{-1} = \frac{\sum_{t=1}^{N_{ik}} l_{s,t} \cdot h_t}{\sum_{t=1}^{N_{ik}} l_{s,t}} \quad (9)$$

$$m_s = h_s - h_s^{-1} \quad (10)$$

where h_s^{-1} is an attentive vector of the graph KG_2, m_s is the matching vector of e_s, measuring the difference between h_s and its nearest neighbors in KG_2, N_ik is the neighbor set of s_ik. Then, combining the weighted matching vectors m_s and the GCN-output embedding representation of e_s is:

$$h_s^{'} = h_s \oplus \beta * m_s \quad (11)$$

where $h_s^{'}$ is neighbor representations.

Neighborhood Aggregation. At this stage, we combine neighborhood information with the matched output representation to generate the final structural embedding. First, the neighbor representation of e_i is aggregated using the following aggregation method [23] to obtain the neighborhood representation of e_i:

$$g_i = (\sum\nolimits_{s \in N_i} \sigma(h_s^{'} W_{gate}) \cdot h_s^{'}) W_N \quad (12)$$

Then, the GCN-output representation h_i^l of the entity is concatenated with its neighborhood representation to construct the final structural embedding of e_i:

$$h_i^N = g_i \oplus h_i^l \quad (13)$$

3.3 Relationship and Attribute Embedding

Modeling relationships and attributes with GCN may contaminate entity representations due to noise from neighbors. In order to solve this problem, this paper treats the relationship of entity e_i as bag-of-word features [24], adopts a simple feed-forward network, and feeds it into a simple feed-forward layer to obtain the relationship embedding h_i^R. For simplicity and consistency, the same approach is adopted for attribute embedding h_i^A of entity e_i. Therefore, these embeddings are calculated as:

$$h_i^R = W_R u_i^R + b_R \quad (14)$$

$$h_i^A = W_A u_i^A + b_A \quad (15)$$

where W_R,W_A and b_R,b_A are learnable parameters, u_i^R is the bag-of-words relationship feature, and u_i^A is the bag-of-word attribute feature.

3.4 Visual Embedding

ResNet-152 [25] is used as feature extractor for all images. For each image, do a forward pass, using the final layer output before logits as image features. This feature is sent through a trainable feed-forward layer, resulting in the final image embedding:

$$h_i^I = W_I \cdot \mathrm{Res}Net(I) + b_I \tag{16}$$

where W_I and b_I are learnable parameters.

3.5 Joint Embedding

First, each feature matrix is L2 normalized, and then the multi-modal features are fused through a simple weighted concatenation:

$$\hat{h}_i = \bigoplus_{m \in M} [\frac{\exp(w_m)}{\sum_{j \in M} \exp(w_j)} h_i^m] \tag{17}$$

where M = N,R,A,I, w_m is the trainable attention weight of m modality.

3.6 Alignment Prediction

Since aligned entities have the same meaning in different KGs, aligned entities are theoretically closer in the common space. So measure the distance between two entities to determine if they should be aligned:

$$d(e_i, e_j) = \left\| \hat{h}_i - \hat{h}_j \right\|_{L_1} \tag{18}$$

Use the following loss function as the objective function of the NMEA model:

$$L = \sum_{(e_i, e_j) \in S} \sum_{(e_i^{'}, e_j^{'}) \in S'} [\gamma + d(e_i, e_j) - d(e_i^{'}, e_j^{'})]_+ \tag{19}$$

where [x]+= max{0, x}, γ >0 is the marginal hyperparameter, S is the candidate seed set, and $S^{'}$ is the negative sample set.

This paper performs alignment prediction through structure, relationship, attribute and visual embedding. The specific process is shown in Algorithm 1.

4 Experiments

4.1 Datasets

This paper evaluates NMEA model on the DBP15K [15]. DBP15K constructed three datasets from the multilingual DBpedia. Each dataset has 15,000 reference entity alignments and approximately 400,000 triples. Not all entities have corresponding images, but about 50–85 % of entities do, as shown in Table 1. For entities without images, a random vector sampled from a normal distribution is assigned, parameterized by the mean and standard deviation of the other images.

Algorithm 1. The training process of the NMEA

Require: Source knowledge graph KG_1; target knowledge graph KG_2; pre-aligned entity seed set S.
Ensure: Alignment results.
for the entities of KG_1 and KG_2 **do**
  The hidden representation of aggregated one-hop neighborhoods by Eq. (1)
  The hidden representation of aggregated two-hop neighborhoods by Eq. (2)
  Use the gating mechanism to aggregate one-hop and two-hop neighbor information by Eq. (6)
  Candidates for entities are calculated by Eq. (7)
  Calculate the crossgraph matching vector for each neighbor by Eq. (10)
  Calculate the match-oriented embedding of an entity by Eq. (13)
end for
for the relationship and attribute of KG_1 and KG_2 **do**
  Calculate relational embeddings by Eq. (14)
  Calculate attribute embeddings by Eq. (15)
end for
for the visual information of KG_1 and KG_2 **do**
  Calculate image embeddings by Eq. (16)
end for
for modal embedding **do**
  Perform L2 normalization on each feature matrix
  Fusing multi-modal features through trainable weighted concatenation by Eq.(17)
end for
Alignment training by Eq. (18) and Eq. (19)
Return alignment results

4.2 Experimental Setup

The configuration used in the DBP15K is:$\beta = 0.1$, $\gamma = 1.0$, using two layers of GCN, each layer combines one-hop and two-hop neighbor information (k = 2), the dimension of the hidden representation in the GCN layer is 300, The neighborhood representation has a dimension of 50, while the embedding dimension of the other modalities is 100. The learning rate is set to 0.001. The specific configuration of the experimental environment is shown in Table 2.

This article uses Hits@1 and Hits@10 as evaluation indicators to evaluate entity alignment performance. For each entity pair $(e_i, e_j) \in L$, calculate the

Table 1. Number of entities and images in DBP15K datasets

	$DBP15K_{ZH-EN}$		$DBP15K_{JA-EN}$		$DBP15K_{FR-EN}$	
	ZH	EN	JA	EN	FR	EN
All entities	19388	19572	19814	19780	19661	19993
Image covered	15912	14125	12739	13741	14174	13858

Table 2. Experimental environment

Experimental environment	Specific configurations
Operating system	Windows 64-bit
CPU	Intel(R)Core(TM)i5-1035G4CPU@1.10GHz
GPU	NVIDIA GeForce RTX 2080 Ti
Memory	64G
Programming language	Python
Development tools	PyCharm 2020

similarity and reliability of e_i and all entities in the corresponding graph. If e_j is in the top k most similar or reliable entity, then the counter H_k is increased by 1. Therefore, the evaluation index Hits@k is calculated as follows:

$$Hits@k = \frac{H_k}{|L|} \tag{20}$$

where $|L|$ is the number of test samples, and k is 1 or 10. The higher the value of Hits@1 and Hits@10, the better the performance.

4.3 Compare Model and Experimental Results

This paper compares recent entity alignment models based representation learning such as MuGNN, GMNN and RDGCN, among which, GMNN and RDGCN incorporate other information of KGs into their representations. Table 3 shows the entity alignment results of each model on the DBP15K datasets. It can be seen that the NMEA model performs better than other baseline entity alignment models on the three datasets of DBP15K. The Hits@1 results of the NMEA model are all above 70%, and the Hits@10 results are all above 85%, with the highest reaching 96.8%. This result demonstrates the superiority of the NMEA model proposed in this article.

Table 3. Model performance on DBP15K

Models	$DBP15K_{ZH-EN}$		$DBP15K_{JA-EN}$		$DBP15K_{FR-EN}$	
	Hits@1	Hits@10	Hits@1	Hits@10	Hits@1	Hits@10
MuGNN	49.4	84.4	50.1	85.7	49.5	87.0
GMNN	67.9	78.5	74.0	87.2	89.4	95.2
RDGCN	70.8	84.6	76.7	89.5	88.6	95.7
NMEA	73.4	86.8	78.7	91.4	90.5	96.8

In addition, this paper further considers the impact of different hop numbers on neighborhood information aggregation at each layer. The experimental results are shown in Fig. 4. As can be seen, considering two-hop neighborhoods leads to the best results. Aggregate neighborhood information of more than two hops, the more hops, the lower the performance of the model. This shows that aggregating two-hop neighbor information is sufficient.

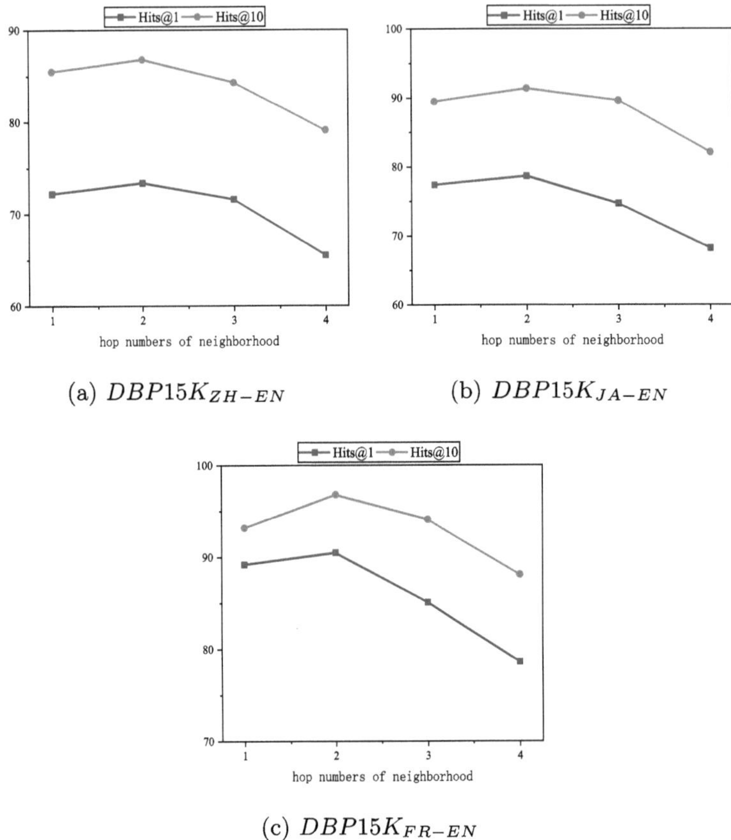

(a) $DBP15K_{ZH-EN}$ (b) $DBP15K_{JA-EN}$

(c) $DBP15K_{FR-EN}$

Fig. 4. Performance of models with different hop numbers on DBP15K.

4.4 Ablation Experiments

In the ablation study, this paper designed three variants of the model. The first is to replace the gating mechanism with additive operators (NMEA-G); the second is to remove the extra information embedding module such as relationships, attributes and images (NMEA-E); the third is to remove the matching module (NMEA-M). Table 4 shows the performance of NMEA and its variants.

When the additive operator is used instead of the gating mechanism, NMEA-G does not show very satisfactory results, and the results of both Hits@1

Table 4. Performance of NMEA and its variants on DBP15K

Models	$DBP15K_{ZH-EN}$		$DBP15K_{JA-EN}$		$DBP15K_{FR-EN}$	
	Hits@1	Hits@10	Hits@1	Hits@10	Hits@1	Hits@10
NMEA-G	69.4	84.7	75.3	89.7	85.3	95.3
NMEA-E	69.6	84.2	77.2	90.2	89.6	94.9
NMEA-M	71.3	86.1	76.5	90.5	87.7	96.1
NMEA	73.4	86.8	78.7	91.4	90.5	96.8

and Hits@10 drop significantly because the addition cannot selectively combine important representations across dimensions.

When comparing NMEA and NMEA-E, it can be observed that the average values of Hits@1 and Hits@10 dropped by approximately 2.1% and 1.9% respectively when only structures were embedded. Among them, on $DBP15K_{ZH-EN}$, the maximum difference in Hits@1 between NMEA and NMEA-E is 3.8%. These results demonstrate the effectiveness of embedding of additional information on entity alignment results.

When the neighborhood matching module is removed from NMEA, the results of Hits@1 and Hits@10 decrease to varying degrees. Among them, Hits@1 has the largest decrease on $DBP15K_{FR-EN}$, with a decrease of 2.8%. These results confirm the effectiveness of the neighborhood matching module in estimating neighborhood similarity.

During structure embedding, this paper designs two variants for two-hop neighbor aggregation. The first is to directly use GCN to aggregate two-hop neighbor information without using the attention mechanism (NMEA-Z); the second is to use GAT replaces the proposed attention mechanism (NMEA-T). The results are shown in Table 5. When NMEA aggregates two-hop neighbor information, directly using GCN aggregation like one-hop neighbors will cause the average performance of NMEA-Z on Hits@1 to drop by about 27.9% on the three datasets. The average performance drop of 16% on Hits@10. This result shows that directly aggregating two-hop neighborhoods will introduce a lot of noise, seriously affecting the performance of the model. The performance of NMEA-T is also slightly lower than NMEA, where the results of Hits@1 dropped by 1.8%-2.8% and the results of Hits@10 dropped by 0.2%-1.6%. These results show the effectiveness of our attention mechanism.

In addition, this paper also studies the impact of deleting different modalities, namely deleting structural information (NMEA-S), deleting relationship information (NMEA-R), deleting attribute information (NMEA-A), and deleting image information (NMEA-I). The results are shown in Fig. 5. The results show that deleting different modes leads to different degrees of performance degradation. When structural information is deleted, the model performance drops the most, with Hits@1 dropping by 33.1%-39.4%. Images, properties, and relationships are of similar importance. Deletion of images and attributes will decrease by 3%–4.3% on Hits@1, while deletion of relationships will decrease by

Table 5. The impact of attention mechanism

Models	$DBP15K_{ZH-EN}$		$DBP15K_{JA-EN}$		$DBP15K_{FR-EN}$	
	Hits@1	Hits@10	Hits@1	Hits@10	Hits@1	Hits@10
NMEA-Z	44.5	68.2	53.2	79.1	61.1	79.9
NMEA-T	71.2	86.6	76.9	89.8	87.7	95.7
NMEA	73.4	86.8	78.7	91.4	90.5	96.8

about 2.3%–3% on Hits@1. This demonstrates the importance of different modal information, especially structural information.

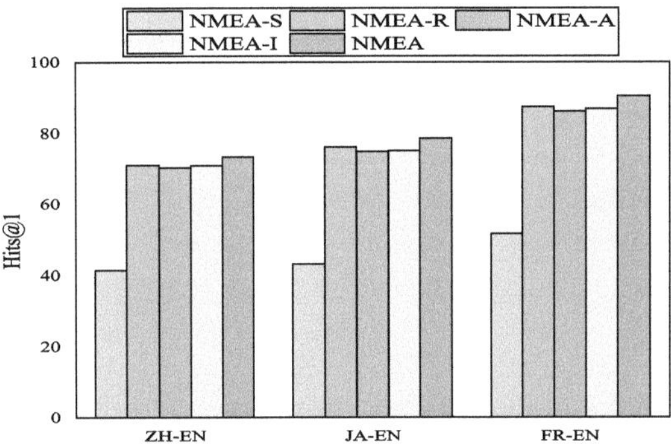

Fig. 5. The performance of deleting different modal models in Hits@1 on DBP15K.

Based on all the above results, it can be seen that multi-hop neighbor information does help entity alignment, and the gating mechanism and attention mechanism are crucial to capture important information in long-distant neighbors. In addition, the effectiveness of the matching module in estimating neighborhood similarity and the importance of different modal embeddings are also demonstrated.

5 Conclusions

In this paper, a multi-modal entity alignment model based on neighborhood matching(NMEA) is proposed. In the structure embedding stage, aiming at the structural heterogeneity between different knowledge graphs, the aggregation strategy of multi-hop neighborhood information was adopted, and the matching module was introduced to calculate the similarity of neighborhood nodes. In addition, multi-modal information is fully utilized to enhance entity alignment. The performance of the NMEA model was verified by conducting a large number of experiments on real datasets and comparing them with multiple entity alignment methods. Experimental results show that the NMEA model is always better than the baseline method in terms of dataset and evaluation index, and shows better performance and stronger robustness.

Acknowledgment. This study was funded by the Major Program of the National key research and development program (No.2022YFC3004603), the youth talent support program of 'Xing Liao Talent Program' (No. XLYC2203003), the National Natural Science Foundation of China (No.61802160, No.62072220 and No.62472204); and Natural Science Foundation of Liaoning Province (No.2022-KF-13-06).

References

1. Zhang, F., Yang, L., Li, J., Cheng, J.: A review of entity alignment studies. Chin. J. Comput. (006), 045 (2022)
2. Ma, H., Wang, H., Zhou, B., Sun, C., Xu, X.: A review of entity alignment methods based on representation learning. Comput. Eng. Sci. **45**, 554–564 (2023)
3. Kipf, T.N., Welling, M.: Semi-supervised classification with graph convolutional networks (2016)
4. Velikovi, P., Cucurull, G., Casanova, A., Romero, A., Liò, P., Bengio, Y.: Graph attention networks (2017)
5. Morris, C., et al.: Weisfeiler and leman go neural: Higher-order graph neural networks (2018)
6. Pujara, J., Miao, H., Getoor, L., Cohen, W.: Knowledge graph identification. In: Alani, H., et al. (eds.) ISWC 2013. LNCS, vol. 8218, pp. 542–557. Springer, Heidelberg (2013). https://doi.org/10.1007/978-3-642-41335-3_34
7. Cai, W., Wang, Y., Mao, S., Zhan, J., Jiang, Y.: Multi-heterogeneous neighborhood-aware for knowledge graphs alignment. Inf. Process. Manag. **59**(1), 102790 (2022)
8. Xin, K., Sun, Z., Hua, W., Hu, W., Zhou, X.: Informed multi-context entity alignment (2022)
9. Tam, N.T., et al.: Entity alignment for knowledge graphs with multi-order convolutional networks. IEEE Trans. Knowl. Data Eng. **34**(9), 4201–4214 (2020)
10. Su, M., Bu, G., Fan, Q., Liu, F.: Entity alignment algorithm based on attribute embedding and graph attention network. Comput. Syst. Appl. **32**, 202–208 (2023)
11. Sun, Z., et al.: A benchmarking study of embedding-based entity alignment for knowledge graphs. arXiv preprint arXiv:2003.07743 (2020)
12. Zhang, Z., et al.: An industry evaluation of embedding-based entity alignment. arXiv preprint arXiv:2010.11522 (2020)
13. Trisedya, B.D., Qi, J., Zhang, R.: Entity alignment between knowledge graphs using attribute embeddings. In: Proceedings of the AAAI Conference on Artificial Intelligence, vol. 33, pp. 297–304 (2019)
14. Chen, L., Li, Z., Wang, Y., Xu, T., Wang, Z., Chen, E.: MMEA: entity alignment for multi-modal knowledge graph. In: Li, G., Shen, H.T., Yuan, Y., Wang, X., Liu, H., Zhao, X. (eds.) KSEM 2020. LNCS (LNAI), vol. 12274, pp. 134–147. Springer, Cham (2020). https://doi.org/10.1007/978-3-030-55130-8_12
15. Liu, F., Chen, M., Roth, D., Collier, N.: Visual pivoting for (unsupervised) entity alignment. In: Proceedings of the AAAI Conference on Artificial Intelligence, vol. 35, pp. 4257–4266 (2021)

16. Cheng, B., Zhu, J., Guo, M.: Multijaf: multi-modal joint entity alignment framework for multi-modal knowledge graph. Neurocomputing **500**, 581–591 (2022)
17. Wu, Y., Liu, X., Feng, Y., Wang, Z., Zhao, D.: Neighborhood matching network for entity alignment. arXiv preprint arXiv:2005.05607 (2020)
18. Zhu, Y., Liu, H., Wu, Z., Du, Y.: Relation-aware neighborhood matching model for entity alignment. In: Proceedings of the AAAI Conference on Artificial Intelligence, vol. 35, pp. 4749–4756 (2021)
19. Xie, F., Zeng, X., Zhou, B., Tan, Y.: Improving knowledge graph entity alignment with graph augmentation. In: Pacific-Asia Conference on Knowledge Discovery and Data Mining, pp. 3–14. Springer, Heidelberg (2023). https://doi.org/10.1007/978-3-031-33377-4_1
20. Srivastava, R.K., Greff, K., Schmidhuber, J.: Highway networks. arXiv preprint arXiv:1505.00387 (2015)
21. Sun, Z., et al.: Knowledge graph alignment network with gated multi-hop neighborhood aggregation. In: Proceedings of the AAAI Conference on Artificial Intelligence, vol. 34, pp. 222–229 (2020)
22. Xu, K., et al.: Cross-lingual knowledge graph alignment via graph matching neural network. arXiv preprint arXiv:1905.11605 (2019)
23. Li, Y., Tarlow, D., Brockschmidt, M., Zemel, R.: Gated graph sequence neural networks. arXiv preprint arXiv:1511.05493 (2015)
24. Lin, Z., Zhang, Z., Wang, M., Shi, Y., Wu, X., Zheng, Y.: Multi-modal contrastive representation learning for entity alignment. arXiv preprint arXiv:2209.00891 (2022)
25. He, K., Zhang, X., Ren, S., Sun, J.: Deep residual learning for image recognition. In: Proceedings of the IEEE Conference on Computer Vision and Pattern Recognition, pp. 770–778 (2016)

Multi-granularity Knowledge Graph Entity Alignment via Semantic Clustering and Dynamic Collaborative Projection

Wei Yan[1,2](✉) and Tiantian Xu[1]

[1] School of Information, Liaoning University, Shenyang, China
yanwei@lnu.edu.cn
[2] School of Innovation and Entrepreneurship, Liaoning University, Shenyang, China

Abstract. Entity alignment, which identifies equivalent entities across source and target knowledge graphs, is essential for constructing comprehensive knowledge bases. Although TransE-based methods show effectiveness, they struggle to capture complex relations due to limited embedding expressiveness. The advanced TransD model uses dynamic mapping matrices but remains constrained by static relation modeling, semantic ambiguity, and insufficient generalization for low-frequency relations. To address these challenges, this paper proposes a Multi-Granularity Dynamic Projection Entity Alignment (MG-DPEA) model by integrating fine-grained and coarse-grained relation projections. Firstly, the fine-grained layer retains TransD's entity relation collaborative projection to capture specific relational features. Secondly, the coarse-grained layer uses hierarchical semantic clustering based on WordNet and the Stick-Breaking algorithm, grouping semantically similar relations that share projection matrices. Finally, an adaptive fusion unit dynamically integrates these multi granularity knowledge graphs. Extensive experiments demonstrate that MG-DPEA significantly improves alignment performance, especially for low-frequency relations, providing an interpretative and efficient approach for knowledge graph fusion under resource-constrained scenarios.

Keywords: knowledge graph · entity alignment · semantic clustering · dynamic collaborative projection · multi granularity

1 Introduction

With the development of information technology and the exponential increase in available data, knowledge-driven data services have emerged as fundamental tools for diverse applications. Applications such as intelligent question answering, semantic search, and recommendation systems use knowledge bases (KB) to improve the overall service quality. Large scale knowledge graphs (KGs), including YAGO, Wikidata, DBpedia, and FreeBase, serve as essential resources for constructing comprehensive KBs. These knowledge graphs systematically organize

J. Li et al. (Eds.): APWeb-WAIM 2025, LNCS 16115, pp. 293–308, 2026.
https://doi.org/10.1007/978-981-95-5719-6_19

substantial structured data in the form of triples (head entity, relation, tail entity), becoming the central mechanism for structured knowledge representation.

However, due to the variations in data sources and inconsistencies in construction criteria, multi source knowledge graphs often exhibit semantic heterogeneity and knowledge fragmentation problems. The widespread use of knowledge graphs necessitates effective fusion techniques of multi source knowledge graphs. The core technology of the fusion process is entity alignment, which is to identify and match entities in different knowledge graphs that represent the same objects in the real world.

Initial entity alignment methods relied on manually defined rules, symbolic logic reasoning, and traditional similarity metrics. These approaches rely on expert experience, are difficult to generalize to new fields, and fail to capture implicit semantic connections effectively. Recent advancements in knowledge representation learning, many embedding-based models solve the problem of heterogeneous knowledge graphs, such as: IPTransE [1], MTransE [2] and BootEA [3]. Entity alignment methods can be mainly divided into two categories, namely, relation-based methods and attribute-based enhancement methods. Relation-based methods assume that the topological similarity between entities can be used as the basis for alignment and rely on graph embedding techniques such as TransE [4] and Graph Neural Networks (GNNs) techniques to capture the global structural patterns of multi-hop paths and enhance the robustness of alignment through the constraints of relation triples. When the relationship definitions between graphs are very different or the structure is sparse, relying solely on relational information may lead to insufficient semantic coverage. Therefore, attribute-based enhancement methods further introduce multi-modal features of entities, such as GCN-Align [5], AttrE [6], JAPE [7] introduce attribute triples, ESEA [8] combines embedding-based and symbol-based methods and EASAE [9] uses BERT to learn summary embeddings as part of the symbol system to supplement local fine-grained information. JTMEA [10] combines type matching constraints to filter logical conflicts. DFMKE [11] uses early and late dual fusion to learn entity features under multimodality. TwoStage [12] uses a two-stage strategy to solve homogeneous and heterogeneous problems respectively to improve the alignment effect. With the development of knowledge applications, application scenarios that need to update knowledge over time have emerged, and temporal knowledge graphs have been derived. TEA [13] and CTEA [14] introduce time information when aligning entities to process dynamic knowledge graphs. LargeGNN [15] improves the scalability of entity alignment on large scale knowledge graphs.

Although existing methods have made some progress, these methods rely on information other than relation triplets, which is not conducive to low-resource entity alignment and the problem of long-tail entity alignment has not been fully solved. To address the above challenges, this paper proposes a Multi-Granularity Dynamic Projection Alignment Model (MG-DPEA). The core idea is to involve integrating hierarchical semantic clustering with dynamic collaborative projections to harmonize semantic specificity and generality. Our main contributions are summarized as follows:

- Multi-Granularity Projection Framework. Firstly, the fine-grained layer retains the uniqueness of high-frequency relations through the dynamic entity-relation collaborative projection from TransD [16]. Secondly, the coarse-grained layer uses a hierarchical clustering mechanism to cluster relation embedding. The first layer guides the root clustering based on the WordNet semantic dictionary, classifies relations into macro-semantic categories, and improves clustering interpretability. Subsequently, the second layer uses a differentiable Stick-Breaking process to dynamically infer the optimal number of sub-clusters for each root cluster. After clustering, similar relations share the projection matrix to enhance low-frequency generalization.
- Adaptive Projection Fusion Mechanism. To address the problem of insufficient semantic modeling of low-frequency relations in long-tail distribution, a context-aware attention fusion unit is designed. Multi-granularity Key-Value pools are used to jointly model coarse-grained cluster centers and fine-grained relational features, and projection weights are dynamically allocated through attention. Display frequency encoding, normalize the relation occurrence frequency and integrate it into the query generation process, guide low-frequency relations to focus on fine-grained local features, and high-frequency relations dominate the optimization of coarse-grained projection matrices.

The rest of this paper is organized as follows: Sect. 2 reviews related work. Section 3 explains the related definitions. Section 4 introduces our proposed model. Section 5 presents experiments and discusses the experimental results. Section 6 concludes this paper.

2 Related Work

2.1 Relation-Based Entity Alignment

Relationship triples establish the topological structure between entities. Relation-based entity alignment methods focus on the topological structure and relational semantics between entities and achieve matching by mining the similarity patterns of entity relationships across graphs. Its core assumption is that if two entities are connected to similar neighboring entities in different graphs through similar relationships, they may point to the same real object. Such methods usually rely on graph embedding techniques such as TransE and TransEdge [17] or graph neural networks such as KE-GCN [18] and MRAEA [19] to map entities and their relationships into a low-dimensional vector space, so that entities with similar structures are closer in the embedded space.

2.2 Embedding-Based Knowledge Representation

First, we define the mathematical notation (h, r, t) to represent a triple. The italic lowercase letters h, r and t represent the embedding vectors of the head entity h, relation r, and tail entity t, respectively.

TransE learns low-dimensional embeddings of entities and relations in knowledge graphs, regards relation r as the translation of the head and tail entities, and fundamentally proposes the triple relation hypothesis: if the triple (h, r, t) holds, then the embedding should satisfy $h+r \approx t$. A triple (h, r, t) corresponding to the real world should get a relatively high score, that is $h+t$ should be close to t. Define the following score function:

$$f_r(h,t) = -\left\|h + r - t\right\|_2^2 \tag{1}$$

The TransE model assumes that all relationships are simple linear transformations and can only efficiently handle one-to-one relationships, but has poor capabilities in handling one-to-many, many-to-one, and many-to-many relationships.

TransD maps entities and relationships into different semantic spaces through a dynamic projection mechanism, capturing complex semantic associations more flexibly. Two vectors are defined for each entity, one for representing entity features and one for generating projection matrices. Similarly, two vectors are defined for each relation r, one for representing relationship semantics and one for generating projection matrices. Given a triple (h, r, t), h, h_p, r, r_p, t, t_p is its vector representation, p is the projection vector flag, $h, h_p, t, t_p \in R^n, r, r_p \in R^m$. The projection matrices of entities and relations are dynamically generated by vector outer products:

$$M_{rh} = r_p h_p + I^{m \times n} \tag{2}$$

$$M_{rt} = r_p t_p^\top + I^{m \times n} \tag{3}$$

TransD defines the scoring function as follows:

$$f_r(h,t) = -\left\|M_{rh}h + r - M_{rt}t\right\|_2^2 \tag{4}$$

TransD proposes a dynamic projection matrix to improve flexibility, but the design of independently assigning a projection matrix to each relation faces two major bottlenecks: insufficient training of long-tail relationships can easily lead to underfitting of the projection matrix and weak generalization ability of low-frequency relationships; semantically similar relationships lack a parameter sharing mechanism, making it difficult to capture deep correlation features.

Recent research has integrated GNN to enhance embedding learning, such as GCN-Align, AliNet [20], RREA [21] and Dual-AMN [22], which uses graph attention to capture cross-graph structural similarities, but its relationship modeling still relies on traditional translation assumptions. Existing embedding methods generally assign independent parameters to each relationship, ignoring the potential semantic commonalities between relationships, resulting in the underfitting of long-tail relationships.

3 Related Definitions

3.1 Knowledge Graph

Knowledge graph is a structured semantic knowledge base that describes entities, attributes, concepts and their relationships in the real world in the form of a graph structure. It integrates scattered knowledge into an interconnected semantic network through symbolic representation and reasoning logic, enabling machines to understand and reason about complex semantics. Nodes represent entities or attributes, and edges represent relationships between entities or associations between entities and attributes. Triples are the basic units of knowledge, which are divided into relationship triples and attribute triples, namely: (h, r, t) and (h, a, v). Among them, h is the head entity, r is the relationship, t is the tail entity, a is the attribute and v is the attribute value. Knowledge graphs can store triples of graphs in formats such as Resource Description Framework (RDF) and graph databases. Table 1 shows triples stored in RDF format, using Uniform Resource Identifiers (URI) to uniquely identify entities, relations, and attributes.

Table 1. DBPedia Example

RDF triples		
dbr:Berlin	dbo:country	dbr:Germany
dbr:1984_novel	dbo:genre	dbr:Dystopian_fiction
dbr:Tesla_Inc.	dbo:founder	dbr:Elon_Musk
dbr:Marie_Curie	dbo:knownFor	dbr:Radioactivity

3.2 Entity Alignment

Entity alignment is the core task of knowledge graph fusion and integration, and its purpose is to identify entities in different knowledge graphs that point to the same object in the real world and establish their equivalent mapping relationship. Its goal is to eliminate the semantic ambiguity of heterogeneous knowledge graphs, build a unified knowledge base, and support semantic query, reasoning, and completion across graphs.

Given two knowledge graphs $KG_1 = (\varepsilon_1, r_1, \tau_1)$ and $KG_2 = (\varepsilon_2, r_2, \tau_2)$, the goal of entity alignment is to find a set of all equivalent entity pairs:

$$\mathcal{A} = \left\{ \left(e_i, e_j \right) | e_i \in \varepsilon_1, e_j \in \varepsilon_2, e_i \equiv e_j \right\} \tag{5}$$

Among them, $e_i \equiv e_j$ means that entities e_i and e_j point to the same object in the real world. ε_1 and ε_2 are entity sets. r_1 and r_2 are relation sets. τ_1 and τ_2 are relationship triple sets. Set a threshold β and when $sim(e_i, e_j) > \beta$, generate candidate entity pairs and enter the candidate pool.

4 Multi-granularity Dynamic Projection Model

4.1 Problem Definition and Motivation

This paper proposes a multi-granularity dynamic projection framework to solve the imbalance between commonality and specificity of relation representation in traditional knowledge graph embedding models. This method coordinates fine-grained relation specificity modeling and coarse-grained semantic commonality mining through hierarchical projection mapping and adaptive fusion mechanism, enhances the generalization ability of low-frequency relations, and improves the alignment quality of low-quality knowledge graphs. As shown in Fig. 1, the overall architecture of the MG-DPEA model.

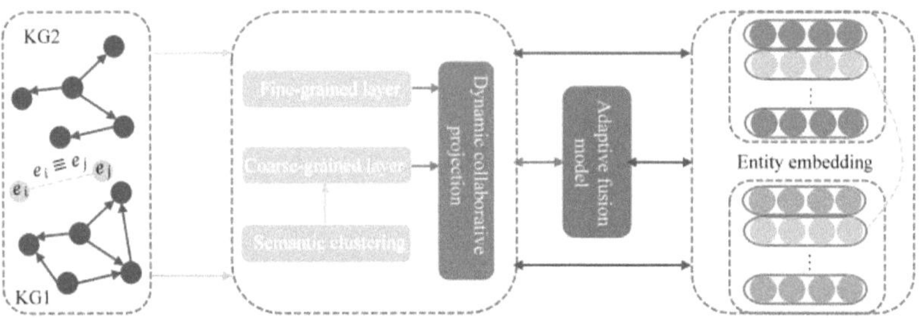

Fig. 1. Overall architecture of the proposed model MG-DPEA.

4.2 Coarse-Grained Projection Layer

The relations with complex semantic hierarchical structures are processed in layers. The first layer uses the hierarchical semantic network of WordNet as the prior knowledge of the relation type to guide the automatic division of the semantic clusters in the coarse-grained projection layer:

$$\begin{cases} C_j \leftarrow r_i, & hyper(r_i) \in D \\ C_j \leftarrow arg \max\limits_{r_j \rightarrow C_j} cos(r_i, r_j), & hyper(r_i) \notin D \end{cases} \tag{6}$$

where D is the dictionary in WordNet and C_j is the relation cluster. The relation sharing projection matrix $M_g \in R^{d \times d}$ is:

$$M_g = w_{rj} w_e^\top + I, w_{rj} \in R^d \tag{7}$$

where w_{rj} is the relation projection vector of cluster j, w_e is the entity projection vector, and I is the unit matrix.

The second layer performs semantic clustering and segmentation within each root cluster to avoid over-segmentation or under-segmentation caused by artificial presets. The Stick-Breaking method is used to adaptively adjust the number of clusters through end-to-end training, and the optimal number of sub-clusters K_g is dynamically inferred for each root cluster C_g. For the root cluster C_g, the weight sequence of sub-clusters c_{gk} is generated:

$$b_{gk} \sim Beta(1, \gamma_g), c_{gk} = b_{gk} \prod_{l=1}^{k-1} (1 - b_{gl}) \tag{8}$$

Among them, γ_g controls the sparsity of the root cluster, and c_{gk} is the cumulative weight of the k-th sub-cluster. The actual number of sub-clusters is truncated according to the cumulative weight:

$$K_g = min\left\{k | \sum_{m=1}^{k} c_{gm} \geq 0.99\right\} \tag{9}$$

Balance the sparsity of sub-cluster weights to prevent some sub-clusters from having too high or too low weights, define the loss function:

$$\mathcal{L}_{sparse} = \sum_{k=1}^{K} q(b_{gk}) ln \frac{q(b_{gk})}{p(b_{gk})} \tag{10}$$

Constrain the relationship embedding to gather towards the center of the sub-cluster to which it belongs, and define the loss function:

$$\mathcal{L}_{cluster} = \sum_{r \in C_g} \left\| r - \mu_{gk} \right\|^2 + \lambda \mathcal{L}_{sparse} \tag{11}$$

During the training process, gradient backpropagation optimizes the parameters:

$$\theta \leftarrow \theta - \eta \bigtriangledown_\theta \mathcal{L}_{cluster}, \theta \in \{b_{gk}, \mu_{gk}, r\} \tag{12}$$

Sub-cluster projection matrix:

$$M_{gk} = M_g + \triangle M_{gk} \tag{13}$$

where $\triangle M_{gk}$ is the residual matrix of sub-cluster k. In order to avoid semantic confusion and prevent the residual matrix from destroying the universality of the root matrix, an orthogonal constraint is introduced:

$$\mathcal{L}_{ortho} = \sum_{g=1}^{G} \left(\sum_{k \neq m} \| \triangle M_{gk} \triangle M_{gm}^{\top} \|_F^2 + \sum_{k=1}^{K_g} \| \triangle M_{gk} M_g^{\top} \|_F^2 \right) \tag{14}$$

4.3 Fine-Grained Projection Layer

Fine-grained projection follows the entity-relation collaborative mapping mechanism of TransD and generates a dynamic projection matrix M for each relation $r \in R$. The calculation form is:

$$M_r^f = w_r w_e^{\top} + I, w_r, w_e \in R^d \tag{15}$$

where w_r is the relation projection vector. This layer retains the fine-grained representation capability of high-frequency relations and captures semantic differences.

4.4 Adaptive Fusion Module

The attention mechanism is used to dynamically adjust the contribution weights of fine-grained and coarse-grained projections to meet the differentiated needs of low-frequency and high-frequency relationships. Relationship frequency is an important factor affecting the dependence on projections of different granularities. The number of times each relationship r appears $f(r)$ is counted, and the frequency of relationship r is normalized:

$$\widetilde{f}_{(r)} = \frac{f(r)}{\max_{r'} f(r'))} \tag{16}$$

where $\max_{r'} f(r'))$ is the maximum number of occurrences in all relations, making the frequency differences more obvious.

Given a triple (h, r, t), define a dynamic semantic query to capture the core semantics of the current relation:

$$q_r = W_Q \cdot [r \oplus \widetilde{f}_r] \tag{17}$$

where $\oplus$ represents vector concatenation, and $W_Q \in R^{(d+1)\times d}$ is a learnable parameter matrix. Multi-granularity feature pool:

$$Key/Value = \left\{\left(k_k^c, v_k^c\right)\right\}_{k=1}^{K} \cup \left(k_r^f, v_r^f\right) \tag{18}$$

Among them, $k_k^c = W_K \mu_k$, $v_k^c = W_V \mu_k$, $k_r^f = W_K r$, $v_r^f = W_V r$.
Coarse-grained projection layer attention weights:

$$\alpha_k = \frac{e^{\left(\frac{q_r^\top k_k^c}{\sqrt{d}} + \beta(1-\widetilde{f}_r)\right)}}{\sum_{i=1}^{K+1} e^{\left(\frac{q_r^\top k_i^c}{\sqrt{d}} + \beta(1-\widetilde{f}_r)\right)}}, k \in \{1, 2, ..., K\} \tag{19}$$

where K is the number of coarse-grained clusters and β is a parameter.
Fine-grained projection layer attention weights:

$$\alpha_{fine} = \frac{e^{\left(\frac{q_r^\top k_r^f}{\sqrt{d}}\right)}}{\sum_{i=1}^{K+1} e^{\left(\frac{q_r^\top k_i^f}{\sqrt{d}}\right)}} \tag{20}$$

Multi-granularity projection fusion based on attention weights:

$$M_{fusion} = \sum_{k=1}^{K} \alpha_k M_{gc_k} + \alpha_{fine} M_r^f \tag{21}$$

The entity projection:

$$e^{'} = e \cdot M_{fusion} \tag{22}$$

The weights are adaptively adjusted according to the relationship frequency and local context, and low-frequency relationships share coarse-grained semantic information to achieve semantic-driven multi-granularity fusion.

4.5 Dynamic Optimization Strategy for Entity Alignment

In order to improve clustering stability and stable learning of dynamic projection parameters, a two-stage training strategy is proposed. Use the TransE model to pre-train the embedding vector stage of entities and relations, and minimize the translation loss function:

$$\mathcal{L}_{TransE} = \sum_{(h,r,t)\in\tau,(h',r,t')\in\tau'} \left[\gamma + \left\|h + r - t\right\|_2^2 - \left\|h' + r - t'\right\|_2^2\right] \tag{23}$$

where (h', r', t') is a negative triplet, and τ' is a set of negative triples. We get the entity embedding set ε_{TransE} and the relation embedding set R_{TransE}.

The entity and relation embeddings obtained by TransE model training are used as the initialization weights of the MG-DPEA model to retain its semantic translation characteristics. However, after entering the MG-DPEA framework, the model over-adjusts the embedding vectors to adapt to new tasks, which causes the semantic information learned by TransE to be destroyed. In order to ensure that the optimization of the new structure is based on the original semantics, regularization is used to limit the degree of offset of the embedding vector:

$$\mathcal{L}_{embedding} = \lambda_e \left(\sum_e \left\|e - e_{TransE}\right\|_2^2 + \sum_r \left\|r - r_{TransE}\right\|_2^2\right) \tag{24}$$

Initialize the projection vectors of entities and relations to zero vectors, impose no prior constraints on the projections, and avoid excessive initial perturbations to the pre-trained TransE embedding space. To maintain the stability of entity embedding during training, the vector matrix is orthogonal constrained:

$$\mathcal{L}_{project} = \sum_{r\in R} \left\|M_r^f M_r^{f\top} - I\right\|_F^2 + \sum_{k=1}^{K} \left\|M_{gk} M_{gk}^{\top} - I\right\|_F^2 \tag{25}$$

Aligned entity pairs are closer, and non-aligned entities are farther away from each other. The entity alignment loss function is:

$$\mathcal{L}_{align} = \sum_{(i,j)\in\varepsilon} \sum_{(i',j')\in\varepsilon'} \left[\gamma + \left\|e_i^{'} - e_j^{'}\right\|_2^2 - \left\|e_{i'}^{'} - e_{j'}^{'}\right\|_2^2\right]_+ \tag{26}$$

As discussed above, the total loss function:

$$\mathcal{L}_{total} = \mathcal{L}_{align} + \mathcal{L}_{embedding} + \beta_1 \mathcal{L}_{cluster} + \beta_2 \mathcal{L}_{project} + \beta_2 \mathcal{L}_{ortho} \tag{27}$$

where β_1 and β_2 are hyperparameters, and the overall algorithm of the model is shown in Algorithm 1.

Algorithm 1. MG-DPEA algorithm

Input: triple set τ, ε_{TransE}, R_{TransE}, d

Output: candidate entity pair set $\mathcal{A} = \left\{ \left(e_i, e_j \right) | e_i, e_j \in \varepsilon \right\}$

for epoch=1 to MaxEpoch *do*:
  for batch in τ *do*:
    for each (h, r, t) in batch:
      $C_j \leftarrow WordNet(r_i)$
      $M_g = w_{rj} w_e^\top + I$
      for C_i in $\left\{ C_1, C_2, \cdots, C_k \right\}$:
        $c_{gk} = b_{gk} \prod_{l=1}^{k-1} (1 - b_{gl}), b_{gk} \sim Beta(1, \gamma_g)$
        $K_g = min \left\{ k | \sum_{m=1}^{k} c_{gm} \geq 0.99 \right\}$
        $M_{gk} = M_g + \triangle M_{gk}$
      endfor
      $M_r^f = w_r w_e^\top + I$
      $\alpha_k = \dfrac{exp\left(\frac{q_r^\top k_k^c}{\sqrt{d}} + \beta(1 - \widetilde{f}_r) \right)}{\sum_{i=1}^{K+1} exp\left(\frac{q_r^\top k_i^c}{\sqrt{d}} + \beta(1 - \widetilde{f}_r) \right)}$
      $\alpha_{fine} = \dfrac{exp\left(\frac{q_r^\top k_r^f}{\sqrt{d}} \right)}{\sum_{i=1}^{K+1} exp\left(\frac{q_r^\top k_i^f}{\sqrt{d}} \right)}$
      $e' = e \cdot \left(\sum_{k=1}^{K} \alpha_k M_{gc_k} + \alpha_{fine} M_r^f \right)$
      $\theta \leftarrow \theta - \eta \nabla_\theta \mathcal{L}_{total}$
    endfor
  endfor
endfor
$\mathcal{A} = \left\{ \left(e_i, e_j \right) | sim(e_i', e_j' > \tau) \right\}$

5 Experiments

5.1 Dataset

This experiment uses the DBP15k dataset from DBpedia, which includes three cross-language entity alignment sets: DBPzh-en, DBPfr-en, and DBPja-en. Table 2 shows the specific data. Supervised entity alignment is adopted, with 15,000 pairs of aligned entities. The dataset is divided into training set, validation set, and test set at a ratio of 30%, 10%, and 60%.

Table 2. Experimental data

DataSet	Language	Entity	Relation	Relation Triple
DBPzh-en	Chinese	19,388	1,701	70,414
DBPzh-en	English	19,572	2,133	95,142
DBPfr-en	French	19,661	903	105,998
DBPfr-en	English	19,993	1,208	115,722
DBPja-en	Japanese	19,814	1,299	77,214
DBPja-en	English	19,780	1,153	93,484

5.2 Evaluation Metrics

Following the conventions, we adopt $Hits@k$ (k=1, 10) and MRR as the evaluation metrics. $Hits@k$ represents the proportion of entities that appear correctly in the top k candidates. MRR represents the reciprocal meaning of the correct entity rankings, which is defined as:

$$MRR = \frac{1}{N}\sum_{i=1}^{|N|}\frac{1}{rank_i} \tag{28}$$

5.3 Experimental Setting and Results Analysis

All experiments are performed on NVIDIA GeForce RTX 3090 GPU. The embedding dimension is set to d=200, and the negative sampling ratio is 1:1. The Adam optimizer is used, the initial learning rate is 0.001, and the early stopping and learning rate decay strategies are adopted. When the effect of the validation set does not improve for 5 consecutive times, the learning rate is halved. Hyperparameter setting: $\lambda_e = 10^{-5}, \lambda = 0.3, \beta_1 = 0.3, \beta_2 = 0.01$.

To ensure the fairness of the experiment, we select baseline models that only use relation triplets to compare with MG-DPEA. As shown in Table 3, we select 10 state-of-the-art entity alignment models. MTransE and IPTransE are tested on non-DBP15k datasets in the original article, so they are re-verified on the dataset of this article. In the original papers of GCN-Align and RDGCN [23], the evaluation metrics are incomplete (no MRR), so we use the source codes provided by the authors for reproduction. We produce the TransD experiment on the DBP15k dataset. The remaining models use the experimental results in the original article. Table 3 compares the performance of the MG-DPEA model with other models, and the performance of this model has been greatly improved.

Table 3. Experimental results

Method	ZH-EN			JA-EN			FR-EN		
	Hits@1	Hits@10	MRR	Hits@1	Hits@10	MRR	Hits@1	Hits@10	MRR
MTransE	31.5	62.2	0.352	26.2	58.2	0.363	23.7	56.2	0.311
IPTransE	33.9	63.7	0.441	30.1	59.6	0.435	24.9	57.0	0.512
BootEA	62.9	84.8	0.703	62.2	85.4	0.701	65.3	87.4	0.731
TransEdge	73.5	90.2	0.801	71.9	93.2	0.795	71.0	94.1	0.796
TransD	38.4	64.3	0.503	35.6	63.3	0.434	33.1	63.1	0.459
GCN-Align	43.2	75.9	0.556	42.7	76.1	0.543	40.9	77.2	0.529
AliNet	53.9	82.6	0.628	54.9	83.1	0.645	55.2	85.2	0.657
MRAEA	63.8	88.6	0.736	64.6	89.1	0.735	66.4	91.1	0.765
RDGCN	69.7	83.4	0.753	75.9	89.7	0.812	80.1	95.0	0.882
KE-GCN	56.2	84.2	0.664	57.0	85.2	0.670	57.2	88.5	0.683
MG-DPEA	75.6	90.4	0.859	76.8	95.4	0.873	78.2	96.0	0.892

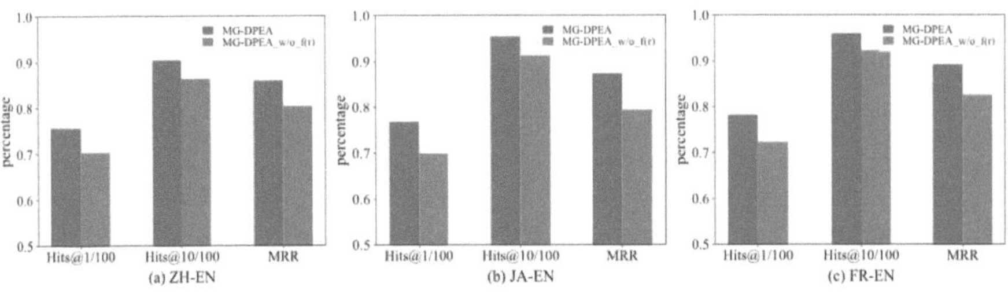

Fig. 2. The impact of relation frequency feature ablation on model performance.

Ablation Study. In the model, we explicitly introduced the relation frequency feature into the attention mechanism. To verify its contribution to the model performance, we conducted an ablation experiment and removed the frequency feature input. Remove $\widetilde{f_r}$ from the query generation and then adjust dimension

$W_Q \in R^{d\times d}$. The query vector is generated only with the relation vector $q_r = W_Q \cdot r$. The coarse-grained projection layer attention weights are modified as:

$$\alpha_k = \frac{e^{\left(\frac{q_r^\top k_k^c}{\sqrt{d}}\right)}}{\sum_{i=1}^{K+1} e^{\left(\frac{q_r^\top k_i^c}{\sqrt{d}}\right)}}, k \in \{1, 2, ..., K\} \tag{29}$$

As shown in Fig. 2, removing the frequency feature leads to a significant drop in performance, proving that the explicit frequency information is a key signal for dynamically adjusting the multi-granularity weights. This is because the frequency-aware attention mechanism can better distinguish the semantic modeling needs of high-frequency and low-frequency relationships. Specifically, the weights of low-frequency relationships tend to be fine-grained projections, capturing specific details through entity-relationship interactions; the weights of high-frequency relationships tend to be coarse-grained projections, which can stabilize semantic generalization. The frequency feature guides the model to achieve a precise balance between coarse-grained generalization and fine-grained specialization by quantifying the statistical priority of the relation-ship. The ablation of this ability undermines the effectiveness of multi-granularity collaboration and is the root cause of the decline in model performance.

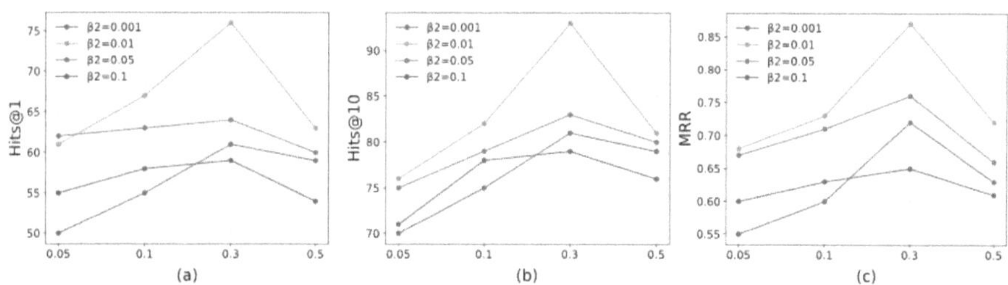

Fig. 3. The impact of parameters values on model performance.

Parameter Analysis. To further improve the expressive power of semantic clustering, we introduced a regular constraint of moving closer to the cluster center to the sub-cluster embedding when sub-dividing the root cluster. To ensure the stability of the projection, the projection matrix is orthogonally constrained. By adjusting parameters β_1 and β_2, the impact on the entity alignment performance is checked. As shown in Fig. 3, the horizontal axis represents β_1 and the broken lines represent different β_2. Figures 3 (a), (b) and (c) are the results of the three-evaluation metrics of entity alignment performance. The model is sensitive to both parameters, and there is an optimal combination: $\beta_1 = 0.3, \beta_2 = 0.01$. The data in the figure is all taken from the average of the three data sets.

Appropriate regularization weights can effectively improve model performance, while too small or too large β_1 values will lead to performance degradation. This shows that the regularization constraint of moving closer to the cluster center helps to improve the semantic consistency within the sub-cluster, but too strong constraints may inhibit the expressive power of the embedding, and too weak constraints will make it difficult to play the advantages of clustering. When β_2 is too small, the orthogonal constraint is not obvious, the model is prone to overfitting, and the embedding space structure is chaotic; when β_2 is too large, the projection matrix is forced to be approximately orthogonal, the model's expressive power is limited, and it is difficult to capture complex semantics, resulting in performance degradation. Therefore, the choice of β_2 has a significant impact on the model performance, and it is necessary to obtain the optimal value through experimental tuning so that the model can strike a balance between maintaining spatial structure and expression ability and obtain the best alignment effect.

6 Conclusion

In this paper, we propose MG-DPEA, a novel framework designed for entity alignment in knowledge graphs, which dynamically integrates coarse-grained and fine-grained semantic modeling through multi-granularity projection strategies. By leveraging frequency guided attention mechanism and hierarchical clustering with sparsity constraints, the key challenge of entity alignment in high-frequency and long-tail relations is effectively solved. Consequently, the proposed model ensures a consideration of generalization ability and semantic accuracy. MG-DPEA exclusively utilizes relation triple resources, which improves the accuracy of entity alignment under resource constrained conditions. Experiments show that this model is significantly better than mainstream methods that only use relation triples in both general and long-tail scenarios.

References

1. Zhu, H., Xie, R., Liu, Z., Sun, M.: Iterative entity alignment via joint knowledge embeddings. In: Proceedings of the Twenty-Sixth International Joint Conference on Artificial Intelligence, pp. 4258–4264 (2017)
2. Chen, M., Tian, Y., Yang, M., Zaniolo, C.: Multilingual knowledge graph embeddings for cross-lingual knowledge alignment. In: Proceedings of the Twenty-Sixth International Joint Conference on Artificial Intelligence, pp. 1511–1517 (2017)
3. Sun, Z., Hu, W., Zhang, Q., Qu, Y.: Bootstrapping entity alignment with knowledge graph embedding. In: Proceedings of the Twenty-Seventh International Joint Conference on Artificial Intelligence, pp. 4396–4402 (2018)
4. Bordes, A., Usunier, N., Garcia-Duran, A., Weston, J., Yakhnenko, O.: Translating embeddings for modeling multi-relational data. In: Proceedings of the 27th Annual Conference on Neural Information Processing Systems, pp. 2787–2795 (2013)

5. Wang, Z., Lv, Q., Lan, X., Zhang, Y.: Cross-lingual knowledge graph alignment via graph convolutional networks. In: Proceedings of the 2018 Conference on Empirical Methods in Natural Language Processing, pp. 349–357 (2018)
6. Trisedya, B.D., Qi, J., Zhang, R.: Entity alignment between knowledge graphs using attribute embeddings. In: Proceedings of the Thirty-Third AAAI Conference on Artificial Intelligence, pp. 297–304 (2019)
7. Sun, Z., Hu, W., Li, C.: Cross-lingual entity alignment via joint attribute-preserving embedding. In: Proceedings of the 16th International Semantic Web Conference, pp. 628–644 (2017)
8. Jiang, T., Bu, C., Zhu, Y., Wu, X.: Combining embedding-based and symbol-based methods for entity alignment. Pattern Recogn. **124**, 108433 (2022)
9. Munne, R.F., Ichise, R.: Entity alignment via summary and attribute embeddings. Log. J. IGPL **31**(2), 314–324 (2023)
10. Lu, G., Zhang, L., Jin, M., Li, P., Huang, X.: Entity alignment via knowledge embedding and type matching constraints for knowledge graph inference. J. Ambient. Intell. Humaniz. Comput. **13**(11), 5199–5209 (2022)
11. Zhu, J., Huang, C., Meo, P.D.: DFMKE: a dual fusion multi-modal knowledge graph embedding framework for entity alignment. Inf. Fusion **90**, 111–119 (2023)
12. Sun, Y., Lee, Y.: Embedding-based two-stage entity alignment for cross-lingual knowledge graphs. J. Inf. Sci. Eng. **40**(2), 317–339 (2024)
13. Zhu, L., Li, N., Bai, L.: Embedding-based entity alignment between multi-source temporal knowledge graphs. Eng. Appl. Artif. Intell. **133**, 108451 (2024)
14. Bai, L., Li, N., Li, G., Zhang, Z., Zhu, L.: Embedding-based entity alignment of cross-lingual temporal knowledge graphs. Neural Netw. **172**, 106143 (2024)
15. Xin, K., Sun, Z., Hua, W., Hu, W., Qu, J., Zhou, X.: Large-scale entity alignment via knowledge graph merging, partitioning and embedding. In: Proceedings of the 31st ACM International Conference on Information and Knowledge Management, pp. 2240–2249 (2022)
16. Ji, G., He, S., Xu, L., Liu, K., Zhao, J.: Knowledge graph embedding via dynamic mapping matrix. In: Proceedings of the 53rd Annual Meeting of the Association for Computational Linguistics and the 7th International Joint Conference on Natural Language Processing of the Asian Federation of Natural Language Processing, pp. 687–696 (2015)
17. Sun, Z., Huang, J., Hu, W., Chen, M., Guo, L., Qu, Y.: Transedge: translating relation-contextualized embeddings for knowledge graphs. In: Proceedings of the 18th International Semantic Web Conference, pp. 612–629 (2019)
18. Yu, D., Yang, Y., Zhang, R., Wu, Y.: Knowledge embedding based graph convolutional network. In: Proceedings of the WWW 2021: The Web Conference, pp. 1619–1628 (2021)
19. Mao, X., Wang, W., Xu, H., Lan, M., Wu, Y.: MRAEA: an efficient and robust entity alignment approach for cross-lingual knowledge graph. In: Proceedings of the Thirteenth ACM International Conference on Web Search and Data Mining, pp. 420–428 (2020)
20. Sun, Z., et al.: Knowledge graph alignment network with gated multi-hop neighborhood aggregation. In: Proceedings of the Thirty-Fourth AAAI Conference on Artificial Intelligence, pp. 222–229 (2020)
21. Mao, X., Wang, W., Xu, H., Wu, Y., Lan, M.: Relational reflection entity alignment. In: Proceedings of the 29th ACM International Conference on Information and Knowledge Management, pp. 1095–1104 (2020)

22. Mao, X., Wang, W., Wu, Y., Lan, M.: Boosting the speed of entity alignment 10×: dual attention matching network with normalized hard sample mining. In: Proceedings of WWW 2021: The Web Conference, pp. 821–832 (2021)
23. Wu, Y., Liu, X., Feng, Y., Wang, Z., Yan, R., Zhao, D.: Relation-aware entity alignment for heterogeneous knowledge graphs. In: Proceedings of Twenty-Eighth International Joint Conference on Artificial Intelligence, pp. 5278–5284 (2019)

MNS-EA: A Mixed Negative Sampling-Based Entity Alignment Model

Yong Feng[1], Han Yan[1], Xinliang Xia[1], Changshun Zhou[3], Yongxin Jia[1], Rongbing Wang[1], and Hongyan Xu[2](✉)

[1] School of Information Science and Engineering, Liaoning University, Shenyang, China

[2] School of Cyber Science and Engineering, Liaoning University, Shenyang 110036, China
xuhongyan@lnu.edu.cn

[3] School of Computer Science and Technology, Soochow University, Suzhou, China

Abstract. Entity alignment is the process of identifying and linking entities (like people, organizations, or locations) across different datasets or knowledge bases that refer to the same real-world object. Most entity alignment methods suffer from noise introduced when incorporating multi-hop neighborhood information and the neglect of interactions involving negative entity pairs, leading to suboptimal alignment performance. To address these limitations, we propose a Mixed Negative Sampling-based Entity Alignment model (MNS-EA). The model initially embeds entities into a unified vector space through multilingual training, subsequently employs a single-layer network to integrate one-hop neighborhood information, and constructs negative samples via a hybrid negative sampling algorithm to mitigate erroneous matches under information scarcity. Comparative experiments conducted on three DBP15K subsets (zh_en, ja_en, fr_en) demonstrate that the proposed model significantly enhances alignment accuracy. On the fr_en dataset, the proposed model demonstrates particularly notable metric improvements: Hits@1 achieves a 5.1% absolute gain over the suboptimal model HGCN, while Hits@10 outperforms RNMthe second-best baselineby 3.3%. Furthermore, comprehensive experiments conducted on the DWY100K dataset systematically validate both the component-wise effectiveness of our framework and its cross-dataset generalization capability.

Keywords: Knowledge Graph · Entity Alignment · Negative Samples · Mixed Negative Sampling · Multilingual Training

1 Introduction

Entity alignment requires comprehensive consideration of the structure, scale and semantic complexity of knowledge graphs(KGs). In recent years, mainstream models have typically embedded different KGs into a unified space using embedding models to address the problem of modality heterogeneity. However, there

J. Li et al. (Eds.): APWeb-WAIM 2025, LNCS 16115, pp. 309–324, 2026.
https://doi.org/10.1007/978-981-95-5719-6_20

are limitations in capturing multiple relationships among entities and contextual information when dealing with large-scale or sparse knowledge graphs. For this reason, many models employ graph neural network variants, such as graph convolutional networks (GCN) [1] and graph attention networks (GAT) [2], to capture one-hop and multi-hop neighbor information in the KGs in order to improve the accuracy of alignment. Despite this, pairs of entities that should be correctly aligned may not share the same neighborhood and their embedding results may not be similar. Moreover, incorrectly introducing too much multi-hop neighbor information can lead to non-equivalent entities being incorrectly matched, triggering cumulative errors. BootEA and RNM have certain limitations. BootEA primarily leverages the similarity of entity names and attributes, while RNM relies on graph neural network reasoning based on relational paths and structural dependencies. Both models focus on using positive examples to enhance performance metrics but fail to adequately consider negative samples. Our model addresses this limitation by effectively incorporating negative examples, which are not only readily available and easy to construct but also capable of introducing latent information about the KGs.

In summary, we propose an entity alignment model based on mixed negative sampling (MNS-EA), with the following innovations: the initial embedding module embeds the entities into a unified vector space through the LaBSE model to ensure cross-linguistic semantic consistency, and then employs the single-head single-layer graph attention network to aggregate one-hop neighborhood information to avoid the introduction of multihop noise; the entity alignment module: through the mixed negative sampling algorithm generates negative samples to reduce the probability of wrong matching when there is insufficient information.

The main contributions are summarized as follows: (1) A hybrid negative sampling based entity alignment model is proposed. The model reduces the complexity through a single-layer network and utilizes the limited single-hop neighborhood information to maximize the accuracy of the alignment. (2) A hybrid negative sampling algorithm is designed and implemented, which reduces the cost of manual labeling while generating effective negative samples, iteratively enhances the alignment effect, and reduces the probability of matching errors. (3) The idea of cost reduction and efficiency enhancement is introduced to cope with the bottleneck of the large-scale KG entity alignment task, and the model is verified to possess significant effectiveness and usability through comparative experiments on the public dataset, and the reasonableness of the model design is verified through ablation experiments.

2 Related Work

2.1 Embedding-Based Entity Alignment

In recent years, embedding-based alignment methods have become mainstream, the framework of such methods is shown in Fig. 1. First, the knowledge graphs are embedded (embedding module); then, based on the aligned entity pairs, the embedding spaces of different knowledge graphs are mapped to a unified vector space (interaction optimization module); finally, the entity alignment results are determined based on the distances or similarities between entities in the vector space (alignment module). In addition, some methods introduce an interaction iteration mechanism to add the alignment results to the set of aligned entity pairs to optimize the alignment accuracy.

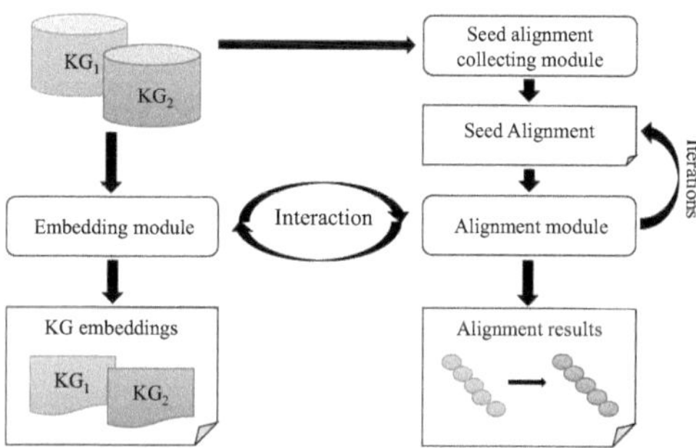

Fig. 1. A Generic Framework for Embedding-Based Entity Alignment.

High-quality embedding models are effective in enhancing the embedding effect. Some studies have utilized the BERT model for post-embedding re-alignment [3], which provides rich embedding representations for entity alignment through its powerful language comprehension and generation capabilities.GloVe [4] has also been applied to the initial embedding of entities, which improves the accuracy of entity alignment. Subsequently, scholars proposed the LaBSE [5] multilingual pre-training model, which is trained on a large-scale dataset of 109 different languages, and is able to embed KGs of different languages into the same vector space, providing strong support for cross-lingual entity alignment [6]. After the embedding is completed, researchers use some methods to exploit the neighbor information to enhance the alignment effect, such as GAT.

2.2 Positive and Negative Sample Construction Strategies and Semi-supervised Learning

In the entity alignment task, the construction of positive and negative samples is an important step that directly affects the training effect and performance. Positive samples typically consist of seed entity pairs representing entities that have been aligned. The acquisition of positive samples is relatively simple and is usually extracted from the alignment results or datasets. However, in order to improve the performance of the model, the positive samples need to be filtered or weighted to highlight the key relationships or entities and help the model better capture important patterns in the KG.

Adding negative samples to training aims to construct pairs of false entities to help the model recognize non-existent relationships. Construction methods include random sampling, generating negative samples using Generative Adversarial Networks (GANs) [7], and custom rule-based methods. When choosing positive and negative samples, it is necessary to consider the heterogeneity of the dataset and choose different strategies to generate positive and negative samples in order to optimize model effect.

In recent years, the research community has focused on the importance of seed entity pairs (positive samples). Many entity alignment models generate positive samples through different strategies to improve the alignment results, but ignore the role of negative samples.Additionally, most models for entity alignment are supervised [8], which, despite their excellent performance, incur high labor costs in large-scale KG alignment.

3 MNS-EA Model

The working principle of the MNS-EA model proposed in this paper is to capture one-hop neighborhood information through multilingual embedding in a uniform vector space, to combine with a single-layer network, and to design a hybrid negative sampling strategy to introduce effective samples and suppress noise interference. The overall framework of the model is shown in Fig. 2, which consists of two modules: the initial embedding module and the entity alignment module. The initial embedding module consists of two parts: initial entity embedding and single-hop neighbor information embedding. First, the entities of different knowledge graphs are initially embedded using the pre-trained language model LaBSE to generate the vector representation of each entity. Subsequently, a single-layer single-head graph attention network is introduced to aggregate the pre-trained embeddings of the single-hop neighbors, and the information of the neighboring entities is aggregated to the central entity to better capture the complex relationships and dependencies between the entities.

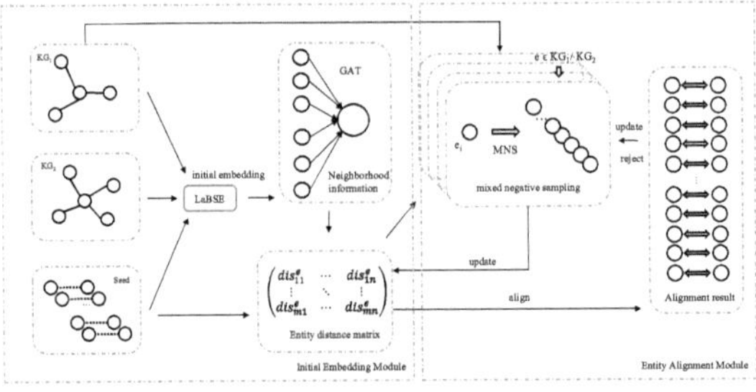

Fig. 2. Overall framework diagram of the MNS-EA model.

The entity alignment module consists of a hybrid negative sampling algorithm and an entity alignment training component. Since traditional alignment methods tend to ignore the role of negative samples, we proposes a mixed negative sampling algorithm (MNS), which is a negative sample generation method used in entity alignment.The MNS algorithm selects m entities that are not close to the input entities as additional negative samples, helping to reject the current match in each training batch. The process mainly consists of three steps: selecting opponent entities, self-negative sampling and iterative generation. By dynamically adjusting the number of negative samples and adaptively selecting negative samples, the MNS algorithm can improve the accuracy and efficiency of entity alignment. Finally, the inter-entity distance of self-negative sampling is utilized for entity alignment.

3.1 Initial Embedding

Entity Embedding. The structural information of KG (Knowledge Graph) provides a strong support for the entity alignment task, and the role of structural embedding is to map two original knowledge graph data into a unified vector space. The entity representation is initialized by the pre-trained LaBSE language model. LaBSE, as an advanced multilingual pre-trained model, can embed knowledge graphs of different languages into the same space, and it is one of the models with better embedding effect.

Single-Hop Neighbor Information Embedding. After the initial embedding, and combined with a single-layer single-head GAT network for the learning of structural embedding, GAT is able to capture the local information in the graph structure effectively, perform single-hop neighbor information aggregation, and aggregate the information in the central entity node. The input of GAT is the entity embedding matrix, and the initial embedding word vectors are shown in Eq.(1):

$$y = \{y_1, y_2, y_3, ..., y_n\} \;\; y \in \mathbb{R}^f \tag{1}$$

where y_n denotes the feature vector representation of the entity, n is the number of entities; F is the f-dimensional feature set of the node. The attention coefficient is calculated as shown in Eq.(2)

$$c_{i,j} = Leaky\text{Re}LU\left(a^T\left[Wy_i||Wy_j\right]\right) \tag{2}$$

In the above formula, y is the feature of the node; $LeakyReLU$ is a nonlinear activation function, a denotes a single-layer feed-forward neural network,a^T represents the transpose of the learnable parameters of a, and W is the parameter matrix; $||$ denotes the splicing for two node vectors; and then compute the attention coefficients from the entity e_i to the entity e_j, the computational process is shown in Eq.(3):

$$S_{i,j} = \frac{\exp\left(c_{i,j}\right)}{\sum_{k \in N_i} \exp\left(c_{i,k}\right)} \tag{3}$$

$S_{i,j}$ are the unnormalized attention coefficients, in order to better assign weights to the structural information of the node, it is necessary to normalize all the neighbor attribute vectors of the target node using the softmax function,it is necessary to aggregate the features of the nodes in the neighborhood to get the feature vector of the node's structure, which is computed as shown in Eq.(4):

$$y_i = Soft\max\left(\sum_{j\in N_i} s_{i,j}Wy_j\right) \tag{4}$$

where Wy_j denotes the features of the neighboring node j within the neighborhood. This part of the structure embedding, retains the semantic information of entity names,introduces lightweight effective neighborhood information, and the results prove that the method efficiently improves the accuracy of entity alignment. For two entities, e_i, e_j, the entity pair distance is calculated as shown in Eq.(5):

$$dis\left(e_i, e_j\right) = \|y_i, y_j\|_{L1} \tag{5}$$

where y_j denotes the embedding representation of e_i, y_j denotes the embedding representation of ej, and L1 denotes the L1 norm. The smaller the distance, the closer the embedding of entities e_1 and e_2, resulting in a higher alignment probability. The overall aggregation process is shown in Fig. 3

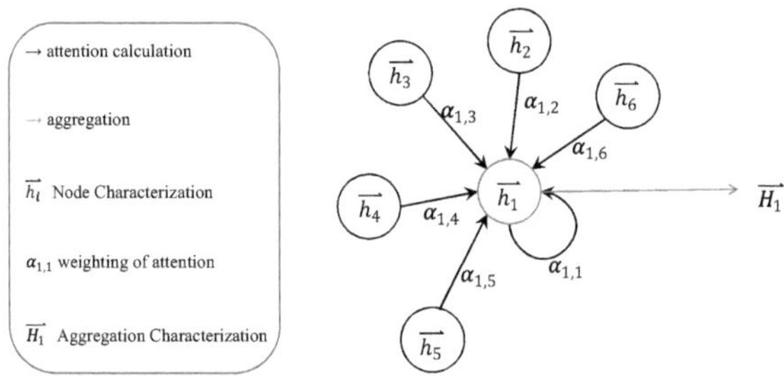

Fig. 3. Single-Hop Neighbor Information Aggregation Process.

3.2 Entity Alignment

Hybrid Negative Sampling Algorithm. When selecting negative samples from the opponent KG, the equivalent entities may be incorrectly selected, but it is difficult to ensure the diversity of negative samples by taking the opponent samples only from this KG. To overcome this problem, we propose the MNS hybrid negative sampling algorithm, which additionally selects m entities that are not close to the input entities as negative samples in each training batch for rejection matching. The algorithm introduces the concept of similarity threshold, which prioritizes the selection of samples with larger distance from each other's KGs to ensure higher representativeness of the selected negative samples, and then selects negative samples from its own KGs to ensure diversity.

During each training batch, our model maintains a negative sample pool. While selecting negative samples exclusively from the counterpart KG risks erroneous inclusion of equivalent entities, relying solely on intra-graph sampling from the source KG compromises negative sample diversity.

Experiments demonstrate that for each entity $e_i \in KG_1$ (or KG_2) within a training batch, our method prioritizes selecting negative samples from the counterpart graph with larger embedding distances. Specifically, entities $e_j \in KG_1$ (or KG_2) satisfying $\mathrm{d}(e_i, e_j) > \tau$ (where τ denotes the similarity threshold) are selected as negative samples. The similarity threshold is shown in Eq. (6):

$$Threshold = \frac{\sum_{i=1}^{10} \max\_10\_\mathrm{dis}\,[i-1]}{10} \tag{6}$$

The threshold τ is defined as the mean of the top-10 largest embedding distances between entity e_i and all entities e_j in the counterpart knowledge graph, where max_10_dis denotes the sorted list of maximum distances. Subsequently, the model selects intra-graph entities with the farthest embedding distances from the source knowledge graph as negative samples until reaching the predefined negative sample quota.The negative sample quantity is dynamically adjusted across training batches, with the actual number of training negative samples per batch determined by $\mathrm{m} = \min(k, |e|)$, where k denotes the current batch index and $|e|$ represents the cardinality of the entity set. As illustrated in Fig. 4, the algorithm primarily selects entity e_k from KG_2 as negative samples. When entities fail to satisfy the similarity threshold condition $\mathrm{d}(e_i, e_j) > \tau$, the model subsequently chooses entities e_p and e_q from KG_1 to fulfill the negative sample requirement.

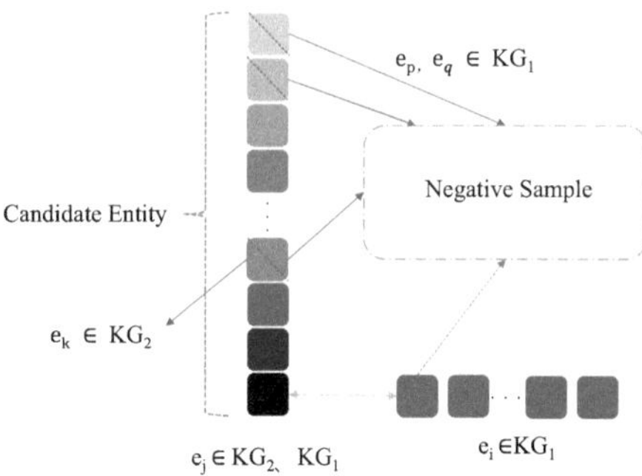

Fig. 4. Basic process of hybrid negative sampling algorithm

The negative sample selection process for counterpart KG entities follows an analogous procedure, as formally outlined in the following algorithmic workflow:

Step 1: For each entity in the training batch, prioritize selecting a negative sample from the counterpart KG. If no qualified candidates meeting the similarity threshold d(e_i, e_j) $> \tau$ are found in the counterpart KG, then select negative samples from the source KG.

Step 2:Let m denote the total entity count per batch, k represent the current batch index, and n indicate the number of generated negative samples. If n=m, proceed to Step 3; otherwise (if n<m), iteratively repeat Step 1 until n=k, then execute Step 3.

Step 3: Terminate the generation process and perform entity alignment based on candidate entity scores.

The complete hybrid negative sampling procedure is formally described in Table. 1.

Table 1. Hybrid Bootstrap Negative Sample Algorithm Flow.

Algorithm 1: Hybrid Bootstrap Negative Sampling Algorithm

Input: Current training batch k and entity $e_i \in KG_1$,$e_j \in KG_2$,Threshold

Output: TBootstrap negative sample set $S\left(h,r,t\right)^-$

initialization:$S\left(h,r,t\right)^- = [\,]$
For each $e_i \in E_1$:
    x=0
    While x <min(k,|e|):
        For each $e_j \in KG_2$:
            if $dis(e_j, e_j) >$ Threshold:
                $S(h,r,t)^-$ add e_j
                x+=1;Continue
        For each $e_k \in KG_1$:
            $S(h,r,t)^-$ add $e_k \in Max\left(dis\left(e_i, e_k\right)\right)$
            x+=1;Continue
    Return $S(h,r,t)^-$

Physical Alignment Training. The goal of entity alignment is to predict entity alignment by measuring the distances between entities in the uniform embedding space by reducing the distances between equivalent entities after generating valid negative samples and aggregating the equivalent entities of each input graph into a uniform vector space. Specifically, for entity e in G and entity e' in G', the distance between them is computed.

The output of the knowledge graph embedding module is a vector representation of the entities. For both entities e and e', this chapter uses a margin-based ranking loss function as the training objective. This loss function aims to make the distance between positive samples as small as possible while making the distance between negative samples as large as possible. In this way, the similarities and differences between the entities are effectively learned, thus improving the accuracy of entity alignment. The loss function is shown in Eq.(7).

$$L_{KG} = \sum_{(h,r,t)\in\triangle} \sum_{(h,r,t)\in\triangle^-} \max\left(0, f(h,t) - f(h,t)^- + \gamma\right) \tag{7}$$

where $\triangle$ denotes the set of correct triples,$\triangle^-$ denotes the score of the generated negative sample, and γ is a hyperparameter. The bootstrap method is first used to obtain negative samples. Then, the above loss function is used for training, and the model parameters are gradually optimized so that the model can better distinguish between equivalent and non-equivalent entities. Finally, the results of entity alignment are predicted by comparing the distances between entities in a unified vector space. The sum loss function is shown in Eq.(8).

$$L = L_{KG1} + L_{KG2} = L_{(h,r,t)_{KG1}} + L_{(h,r,t)_{KG2}} \tag{8}$$

4 Experiments

4.1 Dataset and Experimental Setup

Dataset. To evaluate the model performance and conduct comparisons, this study uses the DBP15K dataset with subsets divided into English, Chinese, Japanese and French versions. Each subset contains 15,000 aligned cross-language [9] entity pairs, and the dataset has been widely used in entity alignment [10] studies. The details of the dataset we used are shown in Table 2.

Table 2. Dataset DBP15K

	subdataset	entities	Relationships	triad
DBP15K	ZH	19388	1701	70414
	EN	19572	1323	95142
	FR	19661	903	105998
	EN	19993	1208	115722
	JA	19814	1299	77214
	EN	19780	1153	93484

The experiments in this section also use the large-scale dataset DWY100K [11], the statistics of which are detailed in Table 3. During the experiments, known equivalent entity pairs were used as seed sets during the execution of the entity alignment method. These seed sets provide the necessary initial alignment information for model training and evaluation.

The experimental compilation environment is Python3.7, which is realized by Pytorch. The dimension of entity embedding is 100, and the embedding hyperparameter γ =0.01. The initial learning rate is 1e-6, dropout is set to 0.3, and the number of GAT layers is set to 1. Epoch is 150, and the batch size is 64. In order to facilitate a fair comparison with other models, we take 30% of the pre-aligned entity pairs as training set, and 70% as test set.

Table 3. Dataset DWY100K

dataset	subdataset	source	entities	Relationships	triad
DWY100K	DBP-WD	DBpedia	100000	330	463294
		Wikidata	100000	220	448774
	DBP-YG	DBpedia	100000	302	428952
		YAGO3	100000	31	502563

4.2 Baseline Model and Evaluation Indicators

The evaluation metrics used in this experiment are Hits@k (k=1, 10) and Mean Reciprocal Rank (MRR). Hits@k denotes the percentage of correctly aligned entities among the similar entities in Top-k.The higher the value of Hits@k, the more accurately aligned entities are present among the Top-k candidates, leading to greater alignment accuracy.MRR, on the other hand, is the average of the inverted values of all the results, the higher the value of MRR, the higher the ranking of correctly aligned entities and the better the alignment performance.

This chapter selects mainstream relevant entity alignment models as benchmarks, including several competitive models:IPTransE [12], JAPE [13], BootEA [14]; and partially graph neural network-based models: RDGCN, AliNet [15], GCN-Align [16], HGCN, RNM. Certain models introduce multi-hop neighbor information, such as HGCN, RNM, and RDGCN; while others incorporate positive and negative sample alignment strategies, such as BootEA and RNM.The models listed above are trained using supervised or semi-supervised methods.

4.3 Experimental Results and Analysis

To verify the validity of the model, we conducted entity alignment prediction experiments, the results are shown in Table 4.The other base experimental results are taken from RNM [17], and the experimental results will be analyzed in depth in this section:

(1) From the results in Table 4, it is concluded that the MNS-EA model achieves better levels in both Hits@1 and Hits@10 evaluation metrics. Among them, the improvement of Hits@10 is more significant compared with Hits@1, furthur confirming that the global selection of negative samples through the hybrid negative sampling algorithm enables the model to more accurately identify the correct entities from the large set of potential entities, thereby improving the hit rate of entity alignment.

(2) Compared with models such as RDGCN, HGCN, NMN and RNM embedded with the Glove model, MNS-EA adopts the LaBSE model, and the metrics are all improved. This indicates that choosing a more suitable embedding model plays an important role in improving the alignment accuracy. The LaBSE model can be applied to datasets of more languages and provides richer global initial information, thus providing a basis for subsequent training.

Table 4. Comparison of experimental results

DataSet	$DBP15K_{zh\_en}$		$DBP15k_{ja\_en}$		$DBP15K_{fr\_en}$	
Metric	Hit@1	Hit@10	Hit@1	Hit@10	Hit@1	Hit@10
IPTransE	0.406	0.735	0.367	0.693	0.333	0.685
JAPE	0.412	0.745	0.363	0.685	0.324	0.667
BootEA	0.629	0.848	0.622	0.854	0.653	0.874
RDGCN	0.708	0.846	0.767	0.895	0.886	0.957
AliNet	0.539	0.826	0.549	0.831	0.552	0.852
GCN-Align	0.413	0.744	0.399	0.745	0.373	0.745
HGCN	0.720	<u>0.857</u>	0.766	0.897	0.892	<u>0.961</u>
RNM	**0.840**	**0.919**	<u>0.872</u>	<u>0.944</u>	<u>0.938</u>	0.954
MNS-EA	<u>0.839</u>	**0.919**	**0.879**	**0.951**	**0.943**	**0.987**

(3) On the zh_en dataset, MNS-EA exhibits a slightly lower Hit@1 compared to the RNM model. This occurs because RNM incorporates multi-hop relations through Graph Neural Networks (GNNs), while MNS-EA solely relies on single-hop neighborhood information. Consequently, RNM aggregates richer contextual information than MNS-EA, leading to its marginal superiority. Additionally, as revealed by analysis (2), although MNS-EA excels in global alignment, its performance in local alignment is slightly inferior due to insufficient capture of local features.

(4) BootEA, RDGCN, HGCN, and GCN-Align models all integrate the information of multi-hop neighbors to some extent, which enhances the entity alignment. However, the MNS-EA model only aggregates single-hop neighbor information, making the metrics much higher than the above baseline models, proving that significant alignment effects can still be achieved by optimizing the model structure and embedding strategy without relying on multi-hop information. In order to verify the effectiveness of using single-layer GAT to aggregate single-hop neighbor information in MNS-EA, the following experiments are conducted: the number of GAT layers is gradually increased from 1 to 3, so as to explore the impact of the number of GAT layers on the local alignment and global alignment performance. Figure 5 illustrates the effect of the number of GAT layers on the Hits@k (k = 1, 10) and MRR of local alignment.

In Fig. 5(a), the model's Hits@1 metric on the zh_en dataset improves when the number of GAT layers increases from 1 to 2. This may be attributed to the favorable local features provided by the two-hop neighbors, but Hits@1 does not show significant improvement on the other datasets.As the number of layers increases, Fig. 5(b) and Fig. 5(c) reveal a decreasing trend in Hits@10, suggesting that multi-hop information affects global judgment negatively, leading to a significant drop in both Hits@10 and MRR.

In order to work better with other components of our model, we finally choose to use a single-layer GAT. This can effectively aggregate the information of the

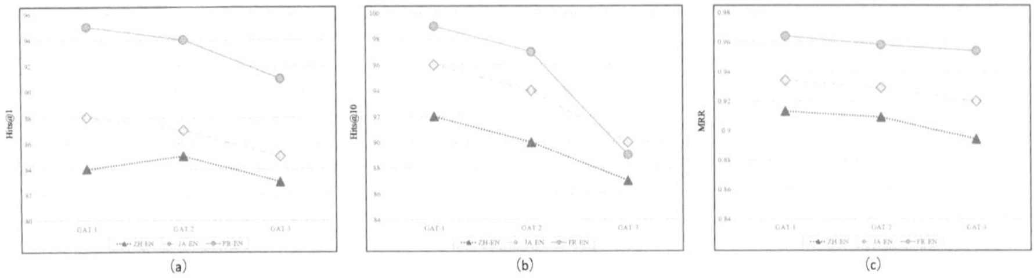

Fig. 5. Effect of the number of GAT layers on experimental metrics.

single-hop neighbors, avoid the potential noise effects of too many layers, and reduce the computational complexity.

4.4 Ablation Experiment

To evaluate the effect of each part of the model, we conduct experiments on the DBP15K zh_en dataset, and in the part of negative sampling, there are three cases 1) select from this graph; 2) select from the other graph; and 3) the mixed negative sampling.

The experimental results are shown in the Fig. 6, the horizontal coordinate is the ratio of the number of negative samples to the current batch number, and the vertical coordinate is hits@1, as the ratio increases, the Hits@1 metric continues to rise, in the ratio to reach the time of 1 tends to stabilize, the ratio of 1 when the upward trend becomes smaller, in order to reduce the burden of the model training to prevent the introduction of ineffective negative samples of information, the number of negative samples to increase the number of take m = min (k,|e|), k is the current training batch, |e| refers to the number of entities in the knowledge graph of the current batch.

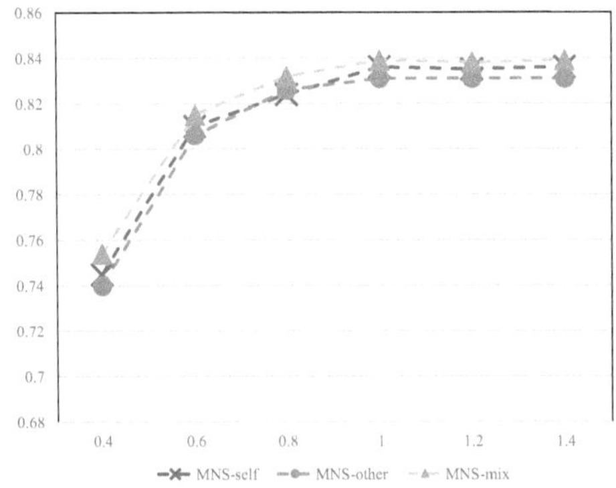

Fig. 6. Parametric ablation experiments.

And from the above figure, we can see that all the three negative sample generation schemes MNS-self, MNS-other, and MNS-mix can effectively improve the experimental indexes, due to the selection of negative samples from the opponent's knowledge graph, which may incorrectly select the equivalent entity, and only select the opponent's samples from this graph book, it is difficult to ensure the diversity of the negative samples, but the mix scheme improves the higher, because of its comprehensive consideration of the former two schemes, and the experimental results justify changing this scheme. Second, we provides the following variants of MNS-EA: MNS-a denotes the model without Labse, using Glove-based embedding; MNS-b denotes the model without incorporating single-hop neighborhood information; and MNS-c denotes the model without using mixed bootstrap negative sampling. The experimental results are shown in Table 5.

Table 5. Ablation experiment

Model	$DBP15K_{zh\_en}$		$DBP15k_{ja\_en}$		$DBP15K_{fr\_en}$	
Metric	Hit@1	Hit@10	Hit@1	Hit@10	Hit@1	Hit@10
MNS-a	<u>0.837</u>	<u>0.865</u>	<u>0.876</u>	<u>0.904</u>	0.937	<u>0.956</u>
MNS-b	0.835	0.863	0.873	0.902	<u>0.942</u>	0.952
MNS-c	0.832	0.860	0.868	0.899	0.932	0.950
MNS-EA	**0.839**	**0.869**	**0.879**	**0.906**	**0.943**	**0.958**

By comparing the experimental results of MNS-c with those of MNS-EA, the Hits@1 and MRR metrics of MNS-c in the three datasets showed a large decrease in the degradation. This decrease indicates that the improved alignment accuracy that can be obtained by using hybrid bootstrap negative sampling, and vertifies that the hybrid bootstrap negative sampling method is effective.

Observing the experimental results of MNS-a and MNS-b, it is found that the experimental data decreased compared to MNS-EA, but the indicators only decreased, not as significantly as MNS-c. This may be because the neighborhood structure in the knowledge graph is more complex, not avoiding the introduction of multi-hop neighbor noise, we only used a single-hop neighborhood less information, leading to therefore these variants of the experimental results with MNS-EA enhancement less. In future research, how to use multi-hop neighbor information more effectively should be considered. Taken together, the entity alignment of MNS-EA is optimal, proving that the model we proposed effectively improves the accuracy of entity alignment.

In order to elucidate the effectiveness of the embedding model selection and the generalization ability of our entity alignment model, further experiments were carried out, in which word vector models such as Glove, FastText, Word2vec, and BERT were used for embedding respectively, and the ablation study of the quality of graph embedding model was carried out on the DWY100K dataset.

The experimental results are shown in Table 6, with the best results are shown in bold and the second best results underlined.

Table 6. Ablation experiment

Model	$DWY100Kdbp\_wd$		$DWY100Kdbp\_yg$	
Metric	Hit@1	Hit@10	Hit@1	Hit@10
MNS-Word2vec	0.846	0.902	0.876	0.904
MNS-Glove	<u>0.974</u>	<u>0.989</u>	<u>0.981</u>	<u>0.994</u>
MNS-FastText	0.920	<u>0.989</u>	0.957	0.992
MNS-bert	0.897	0.954	0.912	0.965
MNS-EA	**0.981**	**0.996**	**0.996**	**0.998**

Experiments show that MNS-EA achieves the highest Hit@1 and Hit@10 on both subsets (dbp_wd and dbp_yg) of DWY100K, proving that MNS-EA is more robust and adaptive in handling different knowledge graphs. Other models Despite using other mainstream models, MNS-EA can still improve 0.7%-13.5% on Hit@1, compared with other models, proving that the combination of using LaBSE is effective. In addition, MNS-EA not only performs well on DBP15K, but also achieves excellent results on the larger scale DWY100K, proving the generalization ability of MNS-EA.

Since MNS-EA generates negative samples by distance thresholding, in order to explore the effectiveness of distance thresholding in defining negative samples, parametric ablation experiments are conducted. The distance threshold refers to Eq. (6) above, which is the average of the maximum distance in several sets of data. In this experiment, 5, 10, 15 and 20 groups were selected as inputs to the distance threshold to assess the effect of different threshold settings on negative sample generation. The results are shown in Fig. 6, when the number of groups selected is 5, all the indicators are lower because the higher distance thresholds calculated with fewer groups result in the generation of negative samples that are too far from the positive samples and lack of correlation, thus weakening the representativeness of the negative samples. On the contrary, when the number of groups selected is 15 or 20, the distance threshold is too low and the characteristics of the negative samples are not clear enough, in which case, if an error occurs in the previous step, the model will misclassify the data that should be positive samples as negative samples, leading to the accumulation of errors, which will have a negative impact on the model.

In addition, when the number of groups is 10, MNS-EA outperforms the other groups in all three datasets in terms of metrics. It shows that choosing 10 as the number of groups for the distance threshold can achieve a better balance between negative sample representativeness and feature clarity. Therefore, we choose 10 as the number of groups for the distance threshold, and a reasonable number of groups for the distance threshold is crucial for generating representative negative samples.

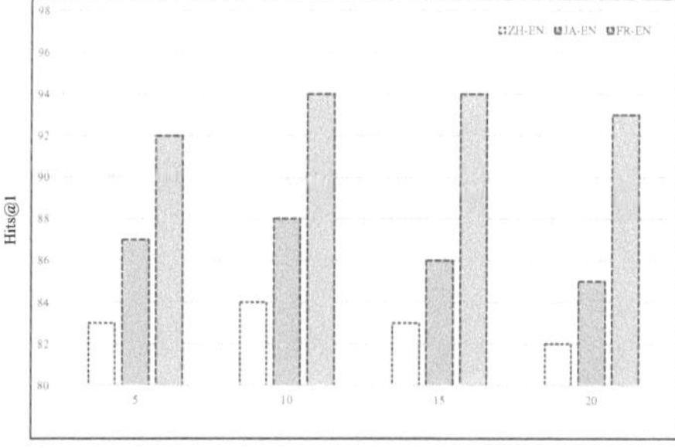

Fig. 7. The effect of distance thresholds generated by different group sizes on semi-supervised entity alignment.

5 Summary

For the knowledge graph fusion task, we propose an innovative two-way iterative entity alignment model based on multi-information graph attention networks. The model adopts a single-layer, single-head graph attention network architecture to effectively mine single-hop neighborhood information in the knowledge graph for embedded representations of entities, thus achieving embedded entities that maximize the capture of key information while maintaining lightweight. In addition, this study introduces a hybrid negative sampling algorithm, which makes full use of the dataset resources and enables the model to be effectively trained under a semi-supervised learning framework, which not only reduces the labor cost, but also improves the accuracy of entity alignment, and the experimental results on multiple benchmark datasets demonstrate superior performance. Looking ahead, future model will explore the integration of rich attribute information and attribute triples in the knowledge graph, with a view to further improving the accuracy of entity alignment.

Acknowledgments. This work was supported by the Natural Science Foundation General Project Science-Technology Plan Joint Program of Liaoning Provincial (2024-MSLH-196).

References

1. Li,J.R., Pan,Q.X., Gao,Z.L., Wei,K., Fan,Z.Q.: A crowdsourcing task recommendation method based on collaborative knowledge graph and hybrid neural network[J/OL].Computer Engineering,pp. 1-14 (2025)
2. Ren, M.L., Gong, R.: GAGAT:Global-aware graph attention network for knowledge graph reasoning[J/OL]. Data Analysis and Knowledge Discovery, pp. 1–18. (2025)
3. Chen,Z.Z.,Deng,Y.C.,Yu,D.H,Xiao,K.:Cross-language knowledge graph entity alignment based on meta-learning[J/OL]. Computer Science,1-12(2025)
4. Jeffrey,P.,Richard,S.,Christopher,M.:Glove: global vectors for word representation. Conference on Empirical Methods in Natural Language Processing (2014)

5. Han, L., et al.: Customised hLEPOR Metric Using LABSE Distilled Knowledge Model to Improve Agreement with Human **10.48550/arXiv**, 2108.09484 (Judgements[J].2021.)
6. Liu,X., et al.: SelfKG: self-supervised entity alignment in knowledge graphs (2022). https://doi.org/10.48550/arXiv.2203.01044
7. Feng,G.,et al.: Multimodal entity alignment based on dual-generatorshared-adversarial network. Application Research of Computers,pp. 1-10 (2025)
8. Chen,L.,Wang,J.Q.,Gao,Y.J.:An unsupervised entity alignment method and device for time-oriented knowledge graphs.https://xueshu.baidu.com/usercenter/paper/show?paperid=1s520ge08t190e70qv7p0mn0rx465778
9. Liu,C.M.,Gao,Y.B.,Yu,W.J.:Multi-embedding representation entity alignment method based on image fusion information. Computer Engineering and Applications,pp. 111-121 (2024)
10. Wang,J.L.,Zhang,H.,Zhang,Y.:Neighborhood information aggregation entity alignment method based on double layer graph attention network. Application Research of Computers, pp. 1686-1692 (Vol.41 No.6)
11. Sun,Z.Q.,Hu,W.,Zhang,Q.H.,Qu,Y.Z.:Bootstrapping entity alignment with knowledge graph embedding. In: Proceedings of the Twenty Seventh International Joint Conference on Artificial Intelligence, IJCAI 2018, July 13-19, 2018, Stockholm, Sweden, pp. 4396–4402
12. Zhu,H.,Xie,R.B,Liu,Z.Y.,Sun,M.S.:Iterative entity alignment via joint knowledge embeddings. In Proceedings of the 26th International Joint Conference on Artificial Intelligence (IJCAI'17). AAAI Press,pp. 4258–4264
13. Sun, Z., Hu, W., Li, C.: Cross-Lingual Entity Alignment via Joint Attribute-Preserving Embedding. In: d'Amato, C., et al. (eds.) ISWC 2017. LNCS, vol. 10587, pp. 628–644. Springer, Cham (2017). https://doi.org/10.1007/978-3-319-68288-4_37
14. Sun,Z.Q.,Hu,W.,Zhang,Q.H.,Qu,Y.Z.:Bootstrapping entity alignment with knowledge graph embedding. In: Proceedings of the 27th International Joint Conference on Artificial Intelligence (IJCAI'18). AAAI Press,pp. 4396–4402
15. Sun,Z., Wang,C., Hu,W., Chen,M., Dai,J., Zhang,W., Qu, Y.: Knowledge graph alignment network with gated multi-hop neighborhood aggregation. In: Proceedings of the AAAI Conference on Artificial Intelligence, 34(01),pp. 222-229
16. Xu,K.,et al.:Cross-lingual knowledge graph alignment via graph matching neural network. In: Proceedings of the 57th Annual Meeting of the Association for Computational Linguistics, pp. 3156–3161, Florence, Italy. Association for Computational Linguistics
17. Hart,G.A., et al.:ALINET: neural net automatic alignment of high energy laser resonator optical elements. IEEE, 1992. https://doi.org/10.1109/IJCNN.1992.226885

Improving Continual Relation Extraction via Parameter Regularization and Dynamic Memory

Lijie Li(✉), Rui Xue, Xiaodi Xu, Ye Wang, and Qilong Han

National Engineering Laboratory for Emulation in E-Government, Harbin Engineering University, Harbin, China

Abstract. Continual Relation Extraction aims to address catastrophic forgetting of knowledge about established relations in the task. The existing Continual Relation Extraction methods are set up on a sequence task, and the model is trained on each task to update the parameters, and the forgetting is alleviated by storing typical samples and replaying them. However, typical sample selection and storage methods employ clustering algorithm to store identical quantities of samples per relation class, failing to dynamically allocate more storage capacity to hard-to-learn relation classes. This simple strategy also causes unbounded growth of the memory space with sequential tasks. At the same time, the old relation knowledge is implicitly stored in the parameters of the model, which will undoubtedly cause forgetting when the model parameters are constantly updated with the task. To address these issues, we propose a novel Continual Relation Extraction model based on **P**arameter **R**egularization and **D**ynamic **M**emory (PRDM). Specifically, the dynamic memory method is used to allocate memory space more reasonably, and the test results of the previous task are used as the memory allocation basis for the relations of this task. We also introduce a parameter regularization mechanism to limit the variation of parameters by estimating the importance of the parameters. Experimental results on two public datasets demonstrate the superiority of the model in longer task sequences and validate the effectiveness of our method in alleviating catastrophic forgetting. The code and datasets are available from https://github.com/xueruisxf/PRDM.

Keywords: Continual Learning · Relation Extraction · Catastrophic Forgetting

1 Introduction

Relation Extraction aims to predict the relation between two entities within a sentence. For instance, given a sentence with the head entity e_1 and tail entity e_2 annotated with their respective positions, relation extraction aims to identify the relation between e_1 and e_2 correctly. It is a fundamental step for downstream

J. Li et al. (Eds.): APWeb-WAIM 2025, LNCS 16115, pp. 325–340, 2026.
https://doi.org/10.1007/978-981-95-5719-6_21

tasks such as question-answering systems [1], information retrieval [2], and others. Traditional relation extraction typically involves training with a fixed set of predefined relations [3,4], inadequate for handling new relation types that continuously emerge in real life.

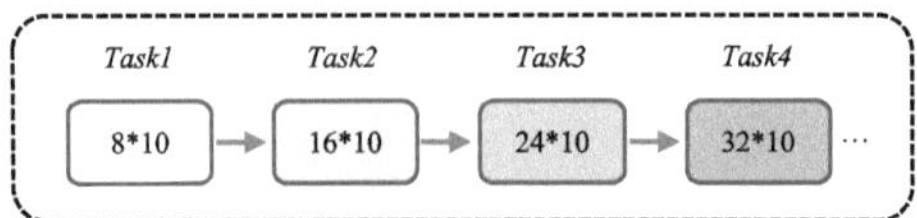

Fig. 1. Existing simple memory strategy.

To solve this situation, Continual Relation Extraction (CRE) is introduced [5]. In CRE, models are trained on a sequence of tasks where the set of relations varies dynamically across tasks, enabling the model to learn new relations. The expectation is for the model to perform well on new and old tasks. However, during continual learning, a significant issue known as catastrophic forgetting often arises [6]. Under this phenomenon, the model tends to forget relations learned from previous tasks after learning new ones.

Several recent works have proposed various methods to address the issue of catastrophic forgetting in the context of continual learning, with a focus on memory-based approaches [7–9]. These methods alleviate the model's forgetting of old relations by maintaining a memory that stores a small number of samples from previous tasks and replaying them during training. Wang et al. [10] have proposed an adversarial data augmentation mechanism to enhance the robustness of the model in learning representations of similar classes. However, this mechanism applies only to the first stage of model training. Xia et al. [11] have replaced the original linear classifiers with a progressive network architecture, effectively mitigating catastrophic forgetting. However, persistent parameter variation still exists in the model encoder layer, which can also lead to forgetting during continual learning.

By analyzing the existing research models, we find that they have shortcomings in typical sample selection and encoder parameter variation. In selecting memory samples, the same number of clusters is directly clustered for all samples, and each cluster center is used as a typical sample. In the storage strategy, the memory space corresponding to each relation of each task is the same and increases without limits, as shown in Fig. 1. For learning eight relation categories in a single time, each relation stores the same number of typical samples 10, and the memory space constantly increases. It cannot be optimized for samples with difficulty in recognition. As illustrated in Fig. 2, it can be observed that the representations of samples by the encoder are continuously altered during continual learning. When trained on new task instances, the model parameters change, resulting in a severe representation bias for the old task samples.

In response to the aforementioned issues, we propose a novel continual learning framework based on Parameter Regularization and Dynamic Memory

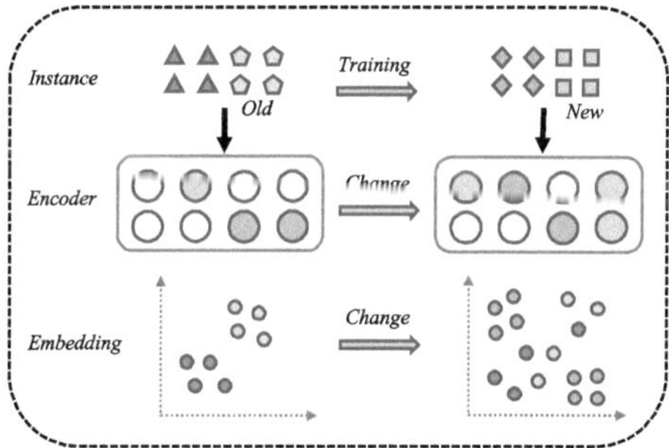

Fig. 2. An illustration of knowledge forgetting induced by parameter changes. In the encoder, the circle represents different parameters.

(PRDM). The model consists of four parts: Learning with New Data, Dynamic Memory, Memory Augmentation, and Memory Replay. In Learning with New Data, the weights of the regularization parameter are obtained by calculating the gradient after training a task. This weight is used in the new task learning phase of the next task. Specifically, parameter regularization evaluates the importance of different parameters based on the model's sensitivity to parameter changes. When a change in a particular parameter leads to a significant alteration in the representation of a relation sample, a weight of higher importance is assigned to that parameter. Aiming at the unreasonable problem of typical sample selection and storage, the Dynamic Memory method is used to allocate memory space more reasonably, and the test results of the previous task are used as the memory allocation basis for the relations of this task. Low-accuracy relations will be assigned more memory samples and the corresponding memory space. In addition, the model uses the rule-based data augmentation method before replaying memory to increase the diversity of memory samples, to alleviate the overfitting effect. Finally, Memory Replay uses the in-memory samples again to train the model and reinforce the old knowledge.

In summary, our contributions to this paper are as follows: Firstly, we propose solutions for the parameter variation in the encoder during the continual learning and the unreasonable selection and storage of typical samples. Second, we introduce a new CRE model that limits the variation of the model parameters and dynamically allocates memory. Lastly, the experimental results for the FewRel and TACRED datasets show that our proposed method outperforms the latest baselines and effectively reduces catastrophic forgetting.

2 Related Works

2.1 Relation Extraction

Traditional relation extraction focuses on extracting predefined relations between two given entities in a sentence, and this method judges the relation between these entities based on predefined rules by using techniques such as linguistic rules and pattern matching [12].In recent years, various deep neural networks have been proposed that are effective in extracting relational features from text, capturing global context information more comprehensively [13]. Previous methods can be divided into three areas based on how the data is used: supervised methods, distant supervised methods, and unsupervised methods.Supervised relation extraction methods consider the task as a multiclass text classification problem. The performance of supervised RE methods exceeds that of other methods, while they seriously rely on high-quality training data [14]. Distance supervision methods have also been widely applied in the field of relation extraction [15], incorporating a large amount of unlabeled data to augment relational learning. Unsupervised relation extraction methods have not been studied as extensively as fully or distantly supervised learning techniques. Unsupervised relation extraction does not require manually annotated data or a manually curated knowledge base, so it can be applied to domains and languages where annotated data and knowledge bases are not available [16].

2.2 Continual Learning

Continual learning aims to accumulate knowledge from a sequence of tasks continuously, and its primary challenge is catastrophic forgetting. To address this, existing continual learning methods can be roughly categorized into three types: (1) Memory-based methods [17], which maintain a memory that is continuously accessible, storing a small number of instances from old tasks and replaying them during the training phase. (2) Regularization-based methods [18], which constrain model changes through techniques such as elastic weights and knowledge distillation. (3) Dynamic architecture-based methods [19], which continuously modify the model architecture during the process of continual learning, using different networks for different tasks to reduce the interference between old and new tasks. The CRE method was proposed to continuously learn emerging new relations while overcoming catastrophic forgetting, which is a serious challenge in continual learning [7]. Memory-based methods are most effective for CRE scenarios among the continual learning methods. For example, EA-EMR [5] is a classical CRE model that leverages an explicit alignment model to mitigate sentence embedding distortion when the learned model is trained on new data and new relations. Memory-based methods have been the most studied methods in recent years, but memory size usually limits performance. Recently, to effectively use typical samples, RP-CRE had been proposed to enhance instance embeddings using memorized samples [8]. Moreover, recent work has increasingly adopted prototypical approaches to abstract relational information or directly for outcome prediction [9].

3 Methodology

This section formally defines the CRE problem and proposes the PRDM model. The overall model framework for the task is shown in Fig. 3, which employs a two-stage training approach. The part Learning with New Data in Fig. 3(a) represents the first stage of training, after which typical samples are selected and stored in memory by the Dynamic Memory allocation method. Then, Memory Augmentation is performed on the samples stored in memory. The part of Memory Replay in Fig. 3(d) represents the retraining of the model using the augmented memory samples, the second stage training, to mitigate the forgetting of the old task relation knowledge of the model. After the second stage of training, the regularization weights of the encoder parameter are calculated and used for training in the first stage of the next task, as shown in Fig. 3(e).

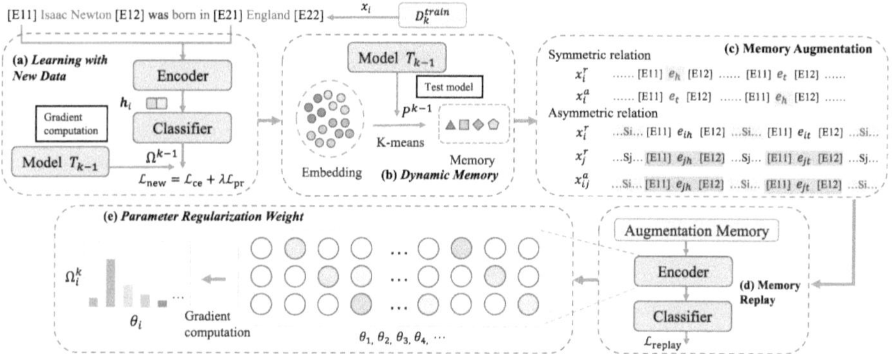

Fig. 3. A comprehensive model structure illustration for the $k-$th Task.

In CRE, the model is trained on a sequence of tasks $\{T_1, T_2, \ldots, T_k\}$, where the training set for the $k-$th task is D_k^{train}. The new task corresponds to learning new relations, denoted as R_k. Each task T_k is trained in isolation from all other tasks, aiming to correctly classify instances x_i to their corresponding relation labels y_i. The model needs to be tested on all previously known relations, denoted as $\tilde{R}_k$.Consistent with previous work, our model mitigates catastrophic forgetting by maintaining an accessible memory M. These samples are replayed after the model has learned the new task, prompting the model to review the knowledge of the old tasks.

3.1 Encoder and Classifier

The sentence encoder aims to extract generic word sense features from the input. The input can either be a labelled sentence or the name of a relation. Following the approach of earlier studies [8, 10, 11], the pre-trained language model BERT [20] as our encoder. Specifically, for an instance i in the data, the special tokens in the sentence represent the relation between entities, as shown in Fig. 3(a). Given an input sentence x that has been annotated with a pair of entity information, we use [E11]/E[12] and [E21]/E[22] to mark the start and end positions of the head and tail entities, respectively. The encoder processes the entire sentence, and the hidden layer representations of [E11] and [E21] are used as the relational representation between the sentences' entities. The representation of x is as follows:

$$h_i = \text{LayerNorm}(\mathbf{W}\text{Dropout}([h_{11}; h_{21}]) + \mathbf{b}) \quad (1)$$

where $h_{11}, h_{21} \in \mathbb{R}^h$ are the hidden layer representations of the start tokens for the head and tail entities, respectively. $\mathbf{W} \in \mathbb{R}^{d \times 2h}$ and $\mathbf{b} \in \mathbb{R}^d$ are weight and bias matrices,respectively.

For the representation h_i of instance i, the model requires a classification network to compute the probability distribution across all relations. Here, the model retains the network weights of the old tasks in the classifier layer and directly restores the weights of the corresponding old tasks to the previously stored weights after training the new task. Specifically, for the $k-$th task T_k, before the task begins training, the model first saves the old task classification network weights $\mathbf{W}_{\text{old}} \in \mathbb{R}^{|\tilde{R}_{k-1}| \times d}$ and add a classification network $\mathbf{W}_{\text{new}} \in \mathbb{R}^{|R_k| \times d}$ for the new task data. During the first stage of training, the classifier categorizes the relations corresponding to the new task, obtaining the probability distribution $P(x_i; \theta)$ as follows:

$$P(x_i; \theta) = \text{softmax}\left([\mathbf{W}_{\text{old}} h_i; \mathbf{W}_{\text{new}} h_i] + \mathbf{b}_c\right) \quad (2)$$

where $[\mathbf{W}_{\text{old}} h_i; \mathbf{W}_{\text{new}} h_i]$ denotes the concatenation of the outputs from the old task network and the new task network, and $\mathbf{b}_c \in \mathbb{R}^{|\tilde{R}_k|}$.

3.2 Parameter Regularization Weight

In CRE, a sequence of tasks shares the same neural network that contains many model parameters. The knowledge of old tasks is embedded within the parameter weights, and significant changes to essential parameter weights can result in catastrophic forgetting. In our approach, the importance of a parameter is approximated by the sensitivity of the model's output to changes in that parameter. Specifically, when a parameter in the model changes, the more significant the output change for the same sample, the more important the parameter is to the same sample. Formally, the model $f(\theta)$ after training for the current task is defined, and the output of the model for a given instance x_i is $f(x_i; \theta)$, applying a small perturbation δ_k to the parameters $\theta_k \in \theta$ will cause the model output to change, which can be expressed as follows:

$$\frac{f(x_i; \theta + \delta_k) - f(x_i; \theta)}{\delta_k} \approx \sum_i g_k(x_i) \quad (3)$$

where $g_k(x_i) = \frac{\partial f(x_i;\theta)}{\partial \theta_k}$ is the gradient of the parameter θ_k over an instance x_i and represents the importance of the parameter for that sample.

Based on the above Eq. (3), The parameter gradient of the model can measure the importance of the sample parameters, that is, the degree to which a small perturbation of the parameter will affect the representation output corresponding to the instance x_i. Then, the importance weight Ω_k of the parameter

θ_k for this task is obtained by accumulating the gradients over all instances in a task:

$$\Omega_k = \frac{1}{N} \sum_{i=1}^{N} g_k(x_i) \tag{4}$$

where N is the total number of task instances at that time, the calculated parameter with a small weight will not impact the output much.

3.3 Learning with New Data

When a new task T_k appears, to better understand the emerging relation R_k, PRDM trains the model on the new task data D_k^{train}. As shown in Fig. 3(a), the instance is first passed through the encoder to obtain the relation representation between the corresponding entities and then through the classifier to obtain the final classification distribution. **cross-entropy** loss is used to classify different relations:

$$\mathcal{L}_{ce} = \sum_{i}^{D_k^{train}} -\log P(y_i|x_i) \tag{5}$$

where $P(y_i|x_i)$ is the prediction score calculated by the classifier layer and (x_i, y_i) is the samples from D_k^{train}.

In order to alleviate the change of the old relations representation when the model learns a new task, the importance weights of the parameters to the previous training data are obtained by parameter estimation, and the important parameter pair changes are penalized. PRDM allows the new task to change parameters that are not important to the previous task (low Ω). Important parameters (high Ω) can also be reused through model sharing, but there is a penalty for changing them. Therefore, we introduce the **parameter regularization** loss:

$$\mathcal{L}_{pr} = \sum_{i} \Omega_i^{k-1} (\theta_i - \theta_i^*)^2 \tag{6}$$

where θ_i^* denotes the old encoder network parameters, Ω^{k-1} denotes the parameter regularization weight for the k-1 task.

Finally, the total loss function of the new task data learning stage is as follows:

$$\mathcal{L}_{\text{new}} = \mathcal{L}_{ce} + \lambda \mathcal{L}_{pr} \tag{7}$$

where λ is a hyperparameter.

3.4 Dynamic Memory

The model has different difficulty in identifying different relationships. Therefore, this model introduces the mechanism of dynamic memory allocation. Firstly, the results of the model on the test set at the end of the last task are obtained. For example, 10 relation categories are learned in each task, and the current test is at the end of the third task training, the test accuracy of 30 relation categories corresponding to the first three tasks can be obtained. The high and low accuracy represent the degree of the model's mastery of the relation learning. The higher the accuracy, the fewer samples can be stored in the memory of the relation category. At the same time, to solve the problem of unlimited memory increase, the model also sets a fixed memory size at the beginning of the task.

Specifically, a fixed memory size m is set before the start of the first task, and an equal amount of space $\lfloor M/|\tilde{R}_k| \rfloor$ is allocated to all samples at the $k-$th task. Therefore, to select a representative subset from the new task data set after each new task training, a part of the samples needs to be deleted from the existing fixed memory. The deletion is based on the test accuracy P^{k-1} of the model in the last task, and the ones with high accuracy are most likely to be deleted. At the same time, the lowest deletion lower bound is set, and each relation category must have no less than α samples in memory. Finally, dynamic allocation of memory space can be achieved.

3.5 Memory Augmentation

As mentioned earlier, due to the limitations of memory space, multiple samples in memory are constantly replayed, which may cause the model overfitting effect. Therefore, we increase the sample diversity by simple data augmentation. Firstly, the relation is divided into symmetric relation and asymmetric relation. Symmetric relation means that the exchange of the position of the head entity and the tail entity of the corresponding relation instance does not affect its correctness, such as the type of "spouse" relation. An asymmetric relation means that the position of the head entity and the tail entity of the corresponding relation cannot be swapped at will. The specific memory enhancement strategy is shown in Fig. 3(c). For symmetric relations, the head entity of the corresponding instance x_i^r of relation r is swapped with the tail entity to generate a new relation sample x_i^a. For asymmetric relation, two instances x_i^r and x_j^r are randomly selected from the corresponding instance of relation r, and the head entity and tail entity of instance x_j^r are replaced by the head entity and tail entity of instance x_j^r to generate a new relation sample x_{ij}^a. With the above strategy, the memory sample size can be expanded thrice.

3.6 Memory Replay

Since learning new relations can lead to catastrophic forgetting of prior knowledge, the model needs to learn from in-memory data to mitigate forgetting. During T_k tasks, the typical samples of the previous k tasks are stored in the memory, and the training set M_k for the memory replay stage is obtained after enhancing these data. The training loss is as follows:

$$\mathcal{L}_{\text{replay}} = \sum_{i}^{M_k} -\log P(y_i|x_i) \tag{8}$$

After the memory replay, the parameter importance weight Ω^k of the model encoder for the current task data will be calculated using Eq. (4), and the importance weight will be updated by accumulating the previously calculated Ω. When T_k tasks are performed, the final parameter weight $\tilde{\Omega}^k$ is:

$$\tilde{\Omega}^k = \left(\Omega^k + \tilde{\Omega}^{k-1} \times (k-1)\right) \times \frac{1}{k} \tag{9}$$

where Ω^k denotes all parameter weights after training for the k-th task, and $\tilde{\Omega}^k$ denotes all parameter weights for the previous k tasks.

After the training of the T_k task, the encoder and classifier are used to predict the relation label of a given test instance x_i, and the label with the largest probability among the classification results is selected as the final prediction result:

$$y_i = \underset{y_i \in \tilde{R}_k}{\arg\max} P(x_i; \theta_k) \tag{10}$$

4 Experiments and Results

This section mainly introduces the experimental setup and experimental results. Firstly, our model is compared with the baseline model. Secondly, the effectiveness of the proposed module is preliminarily verified through ablation experiments.

4.1 Experiment Setting and Baseline Models

We conduct experiments on two widely used datasets, FewRel and TACRED. FewRel is a popular relation extraction dataset originally built for few-shot learning. It contains 100 relations and 70,000 samples in total. To be consistent with previous work, we use 80 relations with 700 samples each and divide them into ten subsets to simulate ten mutually unrelated tasks. TACRED is a large-scale relation extraction dataset with 42 relations and 106,264 samples. Following the experimental setup of previous works, "no_relation" was removed from the relation set, and the other relations were divided into ten tasks. Meanwhile, to limit the sample imbalance of TACRED, the number of training samples per relation is limited to 320, and the number of testing samples is limited to 40.

In order to facilitate a fair comparison, we used the same experimental setup as RP-CRE [8], randomly divided all relations into ten groups, each containing the same number of relations and disjoint, constructed a task sequence composed of 10 tasks, and used the same random number seed as before to ensure the consistency of the task sequence. The average accuracy over five different sampled task sequences is reported. For all methods, the average number of instances held by memory for each relation is 10.

We pick the regularization loss for the hyperparameter values from the grid list $\lambda \in [500, 1000, \mathbf{2000}, \mathbf{3000}, 4000, 5000]$. The specific hyperparameter experimental data are shown in Table 2. The minimum number of samples $\alpha = 5$ in memory for each relation class. We used Bert-base-uncased as the encoder, and Adam as the optimizer, and set the learning rate for the BERT module to 1e−5 and for the classifier module to 1e−3. The batch size for our experiments was set to 32.

Compare our proposed framework model with the following baseline model:

EA-EMR (Wang [5]) was the first to combine lifelong learning with relation extraction and proposed memory replay and embedding alignment to mitigate catastrophic forgetting.

EMAR (Han [7]) was inspired by the human memory consolidation mechanism and proposed a three-stage training method involving memory activation and memory re-consolidation.

CML (Wu [21]) introduces curriculum learning and meta-learning, while also performing representation learning on different relations through the distribution of the main types of relations to alleviate order sensitivity and catastrophic forgetting in CRE.

RP-CRE (Cui [8]) is inspired by prototype networks and proposes a method of prototype refinement, designing an attention-based memory network to refine the embeddings of instances.

CRECL (Hu [9]) proposes a contrastive learning-based continuous relation extraction framework to ensure that relation embeddings are more discriminable.

CREST (Le [22]) through the combination of multi-task learning and CRE, the task of continuous learning is decomposed and multi-objective optimization is carried out to realize the efficient use of past information.

CDec (Xia [11]) introduces a simple and effective classifier decomposition framework that mitigates representation bias in the classifier layer through empirical initialization and adversarial fine-tuning.

4.2 Main Results

Table 1 shows the main experimental results of this paper, respectively, compared with the baseline model. The results of EMAR, RP-CRE, and CDec are reproduced from the local environment, and the other results directly refer to the original data in the corresponding papers. The encoder part of EMAR models is replaced by BERT, and the obtained data is much better than the results of the original papers. Although CREST is the latest model, its performance on longer sequences is not stable, it performs poorly on TACRED datasets, so our main comparison is the CDec model. Based on the above table, we can draw the following conclusions:

Our proposed model achieves overall optimal or suboptimal results on the FewRel dataset, especially when the task sequence is large, because our model can limit the change of important parameters, better maintain the knowledge of old tasks, and alleviate catastrophic forgetting. On the TACRED dataset, the model only improves the accuracy of relation recognition when the task sequence is longer. On the one hand, CRECL performs relatively well in the first few tasks on the TRACED dataset. In addition, we find that the data quality of TACRED is general, and the accuracy of the model is sometimes reduced when using the

Table 1. Accuracy (%) for all seen relations after learning the current task. * denotes our reproduced results from open source code. We show the best results in boldface and the second best ones in underlines.

FewRel										
Model	T1	T2	T3	T4	T5	T6	T7	T8	T9	T10
EA-EMR	89.0	69.0	59.1	54.2	47.8	46.1	43.1	40.7	38.6	35.2
CML	91.2	74.8	68.2	58.2	53.7	50.4	47.8	44.4	43.1	39.7
CRECL	97.8	94.9	92.7	90.9	89.4	87.5	85.7	84.6	83.6	82.7
CREST	**98.7**	93.6	**93.8**	**92.3**	91.0	89.0	87.6	86.7	86.0	**84.8**
EMAR(BERT)*	98.1	94.4	92.3	90.5	89.5	88.2	87.0	86.0	84.6	83.4
RP-CRE*	97.9	94.5	92.5	90.6	90.0	87.9	86.9	86.1	84.5	83.0
CDec*	97.9	95.2	93.1	91.3	91.1	89.3	87.9	87.1	86.2	84.4
PRDM(ours)	98.2	**95.5**	93.2	91.6	**91.5**	**89.9**	**88.6**	**87.9**	**86.8**	84.6
TACRED										
Model	T1	T2	T3	T4	T5	T6	T7	T8	T9	T10
EA-EMR	47.5	40.1	38.3	29.9	24.0	27.3	26.9	25.8	22.9	19.8
CML	57.2	51.4	41.3	39.3	35.9	28.9	27.3	26.9	24.8	23.4
CRECL	97.3	**93.6**	**90.5**	**86.1**	**84.6**	82.1	79.4	77.6	77.9	77.4
CREST	97.3	91.4	82.3	82.5	79.2	75.8	78.8	77.4	78.6	**79.4**
EMAR(BERT)*	**97.9**	92.9	88.4	84.9	83.4	82.2	79.4	77.9	77.6	76.9
RP-CRE*	96.2	92.5	89.7	83.8	82.7	80.9	78.0	77.0	76.4	75.9
CDec*	97.4	92.9	90.2	85.6	84.0	82.2	80.9	79.4	79.0	78.3
PRDM(ours)	97.3	92.6	89.8	85.9	85.2	**83.6**	**81.6**	**79.9**	**79.8**	78.8

replacement strategy for data enhancement, which may be caused by some too similar or even wrong samples generated in the data augmentation process. On the whole, it can be concluded from the above results that our model effectively alleviates catastrophic forgetting in CRE.

When comparing the performance of the models on the two datasets, all the models perform poorly on TRACED, mainly due to the data imbalance between the TRACED relations. Unlike the training samples that remain the same for the relations of FewRel, the number of training samples between different TRACED relations is quite different, which will further aggravate the forgetting in the learning process.

4.3 Ablation Study

This part aims to test the effectiveness of the three main modules of the PRDM model, and the experimental data are shown in Table 3. Since the model performs better when the task sequence is longer, and continual learning is also more focused on solving catastrophic forgetting, data from the sixth to the tenth

Table 2. Accuracy (%) of model with difference hyperparameter.

Dataset	λ	T6	T7	T8	T9	T10
FewRel	500	89.4	88.0	86.9	85.8	84.3
	1000	89.4	88.6	86.9	85.9	84.2
	2000	**89.9**	88.6	**87.9**	**86.8**	**84.6**
	3000	89.3	**88.9**	86.7	85.6	84.2
TACRED	1000	82.7	81.4	79.3	79.2	78.4
	2000	83.1	80.9	79.6	79.4	78.3
	3000	83.6	**81.6**	**79.9**	**79.8**	**78.8**
	4000	83.4	81.4	79.4	79.2	78.7
	5000	**83.7**	80.9	79.3	78.9	78.0

Table 3. Accuracy (%) of model with all ablation study results.

Dataset	Model	T6	T7	T8	T9	T10
FewRel	PRDM	89.9	88.6	87.9	86.8	84.6
	w.o.pr	89.4	88.1	87.3	85.9	84.4
	w.o.dm	89.7	88.4	87.6	86.6	84.6
	w.o.ma	89.9	88.5	87.9	86.6	84.5
TACRED	PRDM	83.6	81.6	79.9	79.8	78.8
	w.o.pr	82.7	81.0	79.4	79.2	78.4
	w.o.dm	83.3	81.4	79.5	79.4	78.5
	w.o.ma	83.4	81.5	79.7	80.1	78.7

task were analyzed. In w.o.pr, we remove the parameter regularization module. In w.o.ma, we remove the memory data augmentation module. In w.o.dm, we remove the dynamic memory modules. Our research data proves the necessity of each module of the model by showing the contribution of each component to the effect of relation recognition.

From Table 3, we can observe that the memory data augmentation method does not improve every task positively. Through the analysis of data samples, we believe that this rule-based method enriches the diversity of samples while, at the same time, It is also possible to produce some duplicate samples and even wrong samples. On the whole, this method improves the performance of the model on most tasks.

Comparing the two datasets horizontally, the improvement of PRDM on the TACRED dataset is more obvious, and the problems between the two modules rarely appear in the above FewRel dataset. The main reason is the imbalance of TACRED data, which has few relational data samples. Memory enhancement can effectively alleviate this situation.

4.4 Embedding Distribution and Long Task Sequence Study

In Fig. 4, we focus on a pair of relations, P156 and P361, which are susceptible to representation bias. The figure illustrates the evolution of the embedding distributions for two distinct relationship models across a sequence of tasks, from the second to the fourth task. The distributions of the two relationships are represented by green circles and blue crosses, respectively.

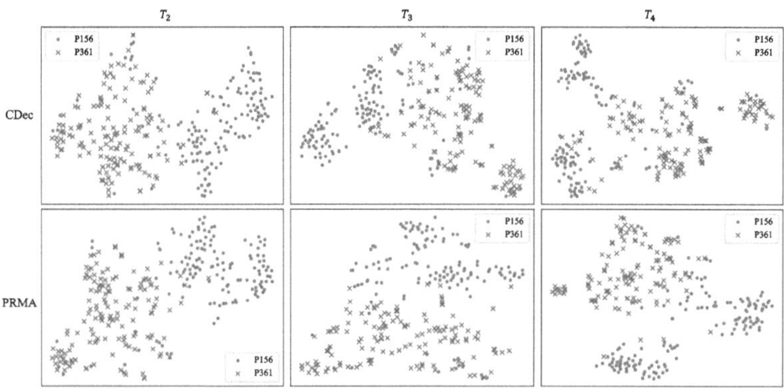

Fig. 4. Embedding distribution of relations over different task sequences. P156 and P361 are PIDs of "followed by" and "part of", respectively.

During the initial learning of these relations in the second task, both the CDec model and our proposed PRDM model yielded well-defined embedding distributions. However, as the third and fourth tasks are introduced, the embedding distributions for P156 and P361 in the CDec model start to diverge, and the distinction between them becomes increasingly blurred, potentially leading to confusion in the model's predictions. In contrast, in the PRDM model, it is evident that while the bias persists, it more effectively preserves the boundary information of the embedding distributions, thus mitigating the bias induced by the addition of new tasks.

In long task sequence performance, each task is set to learn five relation categories, the task length is extended to 16, and the forgetting broken line on the FewRel dataset is shown in Fig. 5. The performance of our model on long sequence tasks is significantly better than the existing models and shows effectiveness in mitigating catastrophic forgetting. Among them, EMAR and RP-CRE models directly replay typical samples or use memory sample information to strengthen the embedding, and the model performance is relatively general. At the same time, they are also sensitive to data. For example, the forgetting level of the model is low in the 8th to 9th task, but the forgetting level suddenly increases in the 9th to 10th task, indicating that the model is greatly affected by the data sequence. Compared with CDec, our model performs better.

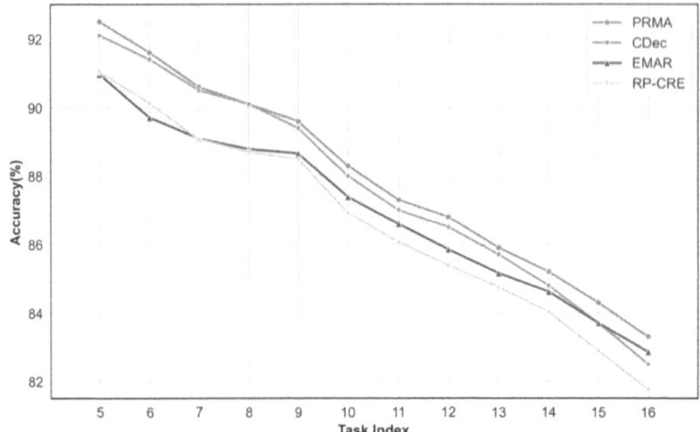

Fig. 5. Line chart of task accuracy for long task sequence.

5 Conclusion

In this paper, we propose a PRDM model to mitigate catastrophic forgetting during continuous relation extraction. In the model encoder, the changes of important parameters of the encoder are limited to keep more information related to the old task, and dynamic memory better optimizes the limited memory space. Finally, the memory samples are fully utilized through memory augmentation. Experimental results show that PRDM can effectively alleviate catastrophic forgetting and perform well on long-sequence tasks. We also explore the performance of the model on long sequence tasks and the sensitivity to memory size. Experiments further show the superiority of PRDM on longer task sequences and the better stability of the experimental results when the memory size changes.

Acknowledgments. This work was supported by the Fundamental Research Funds for the Central Universities under Grant No. 3072024LJ0603, the Heilongjiang Key R&D Program of China under Grant No. GA23A915, and the Industry-University-Research Innovation Fund for Chinese Universities under Grant No. 2024XL036.

References

1. Yu, M., Yin, W., Hasan, K.S., dos Santos, C.N., Xiang, B., Zhou, B.: Improved neural relation detection for knowledge base question answering. In: Barzilay, R., Kan, M. (eds.) Proceedings of the 55th Annual Meeting of the Association for Computational Linguistics (ACL), vol. 1, pp. 571–581 (2017)
2. Xiong, C., Power, R., Callan, J.: Explicit semantic ranking for academic search via knowledge graph embedding. In: Barrett, R., Cummings, R., Agichtein, E., Gabrilovich, E. (eds.) International Conference on World Wide Web, WWW 2017, pp. 1271–1279.https://doi.org/10.1145/3038912.3052558

3. Wang, L., Cao, Z., de Melo, G., Liu, Z.: Relation classification via multi-level attention CNNs. In: Proceedings of the 54th Annual Meeting of the Association for Computational Linguistics, ACL 2016, pp. 1298–1307 (2016). https://doi.org/10.18653/V1/P16-1123
4. Mandya, A., Bollegala, D., Coenen, F.: Contextualised graph attention for improved relation extraction. CoRR abs/2004.10624 (2020)
5. Wang, H., Xiong, W., Yu, M., Guo, X., Chang, S., Wang, W.Y.: Sentence embedding alignment for lifelong relation extraction. In: Conference of the North American Chapter of the Association for Computational Linguistics, NAACL 2019, Minneapolis, MN, USA, 2–7 June 2019, pp. 796–806 (2019).https://doi.org/10.18653/V1/N19-1086
6. French, R.M.: Catastrophic forgetting in connectionist networks. Trends Cogn. Sci. **3**(4), 128–135 (1999)
7. Han, X., et al.: Continual relation learning via episodic memory activation and reconsolidation. In: Proceedings of the 58th Annual Meeting of the Association for Computational Linguistics, ACL 2020, Online, 5–10 July, pp. 6429–6440 (2020) https://doi.org/10.18653/V1/2020.ACL-MAIN.573
8. Cui, L., et al.: Refining sample embeddings with relation prototypes to enhance continual relation extraction. In: Proceedings of the 59th Annual Meeting of the Association for Computational Linguistics and the 11th International Joint Conference on Natural Language Processing, ACL/IJCNLP 2021, pp. 232–243. Association for Computational Linguistics (2021). https://doi.org/10.18653/V1/2021.ACL-LONG.20
9. Hu, C., Yang, D., Jin, H., Chen, Z., Xiao, Y.: Improving continual relation extraction through prototypical contrastive learning. In: International Conference on Computational Linguistics, COLING 2022, Gyeongju, Republic of Korea, 12–17 October 2022, pp. 1885–1895 (2022)
10. Wang, P., et al.: Learning robust representations for continual relation extraction via adversarial class augmentation. In: Conference on Empirical Methods in Natural Language Processing, EMNLP 2022, Abu Dhabi, United Arab Emirates, 7–11 December, pp. 6264–6278 (2022)
11. Xia, H., Wang, P., Liu, T., Lin, B., Cao, Y., Sui, Z.: Enhancing continual relation extraction via classifier decomposition. In: The 63rd Annual Meeting of the Association for Computational Linguistics: ACL 2023, Toronto, Canada, 9–14 July, pp. 10053–10062 (2023)
12. Yang, Z., Yang, D., Dyer, C., He, X., Smola, A.J., Hovy, E.H.: Hierarchical attention networks for document classification. In: Conference of the North American Chapter of the Association for Computational Linguistics: Human Language Technologies, San Diego California, USA, 12–17 June 2016, pp. 1480–1489 (2016). https://doi.org/10.18653/V1/N16-1174
13. Wang, L., Cao, Z., de Melo, G., Liu, Z.: Relation classification via multi-level attention CNNs Annual Meeting of the Association for Computational Linguistics, ACL 2016, 7–12 August, Berlin, Germany (2016)
14. Xu, Y., Mou, L., Li, G., Chen, Y., Peng, H., Jin, Z.: Classifying relations via long short term memory networks along shortest dependency paths. In: Conference on Empirical Methods in Natural Language Processing, EMNLP 2015, Lisbon, Portugal, 17–21 September 2015, pp. 1785–1794 (2015). https://doi.org/10.18653/V1/D15-1206

15. Chen, T., Shi, H., Tang, S., Chen, Z., Wu, F., Zhuang, Y.: CIL: contrastive instance learning framework for distantly supervised relation extraction. In: Annual Meeting of the Association for Computational Linguistics and the 11th International Joint Conference on Natural Language Processing, ACL/IJCNLP 2021, pp. 6191–6200 (2021). https://doi.org/10.18653/V1/2021.ACL-LONG.483
16. Riedel, S., Yao, L., McCallum, A.: Modeling relations and their mentions without labeled text. In: Balcázar, J.L., Bonchi, F., Gionis, A., Sebag, M. (eds.) ECML PKDD 2010. LNCS (LNAI), vol. 6323, pp. 148–163. Springer, Heidelberg (2010). https://doi.org/10.1007/978-3-642-15939-8_10
17. Xiao, Z., Du, Z., Wang, R., Gan, R., Li, J.: Online continual learning with declarative memory. Neural Netw. **163**, 146–155 (2023)
18. Benzing, F.: Unifying importance based regularisation methods for continual learning. In: International Conference on Artificial Intelligence and Statistics, AISTATS 2022, Virtual Event, 28–30 March 2022, vol. 151, pp. 2372–2396. Proceedings of Machine Learning Research (PMLR) (2022)
19. Miao, Z., Wang, Z., Chen, W., Qiu, Q.: Continual learning with filter atom swapping. In: The Tenth International Conference on Learning Representations, ICLR 2022, Virtual Event, 25–29 April 2022. OpenReview.net (2022)
20. Devlin, J., Chang, M., Lee, K., Toutanova, K.: BERT: pre-training of deep bidirectional transformers for language understanding. In: Conference of the North American Chapter of the Association for Computational Linguistics, NAACL-HLT 2019, pp. 4171–4186. Association for Computational Linguistics (2019)
21. Wu, T., et al.: Curriculum-meta learning for order-robust continual relation extraction. In: Conference on Artificial Intelligence, AAAI 2021, pp. 10363–10369. AAAI Press (2021). https://doi.org/10.1609/AAAI.V35I12.17241
22. Le, T., Nguyen, M., Nguyen, T.T., Linh, N.V., Nguyen, T.H.: Continual relation extraction via sequential multi-task learning. In: Conference on Artificial Intelligence, AAAI 2024, pp. 18444–18452. AAAI Press (2024). https://doi.org/10.1609/AAAI.V38I16.29805

MultiRelE: Multi-relation Knowledge Graph Embedding Model

Hongyan Xu[1(✉)], Yongxin Jia[2], Han Yan[2], and Tingzhe Han[2]

[1] School of Cyber Science and Engineering, Liaoning University, Shenyang 110036, China
xuhongyan@lnu.edu.cn

[2] School of Information Science and Engineering, Liaoning University, Shenyang, China

Abstract. In order to solve the problems that knowledge graph embedding models increase the relationship size proportionally with the increase of entity dimension, resulting in a surge in the number of parameters, and it is difficult to identify relationship patterns in higher dimensions, this paper proposed a multi-relational knowledge graph embedding model, called MultiRelE. MultiRelE model uses matrix to represent entities and Kronecker product orthogonal matrix to represent relationships. It combines singular value thresholding and Grassmann manifold optimization to shrink the relationship matrix to reduce the number of parameters. Experimental results show that on WN18RR and FB15K-237 datasets, MultiRelE captures several relational patterns, and shows significant advantages over the suboptimal model DCNE while significantly reducing the number of parameters, with MRR increased by 7.72%and 8.19%respectively. The results show that the MultiRelE model has better indicators in dealing with multi-relational knowledge graphs and high-dimensional data scenarios, and provides a new solution for the field of knowledge graph embedding.

Keywords: Knowledge graph embedding · High-dimensional rotation · Multi-relation · Matrix representation · Contracting Grassmann Manifold Optimization

1 Introduction

Knowledge graph embedding technology [1] has demonstrated significant application value in several domains due to its ability to understand and represent complex relationships, such as Q&A system [2] utilizes knowledge graph embedding to provide more accurate information retrieval and Q&A services, and enhances question understanding through entity and relationship embedding. In recommender systems [3] knowledge graph embedding is used to understand user preferences and item characteristics to achieve personalized recommendations, thus enhancing user experience.

J. Li et al. (Eds.): APWeb-WAIM 2025, LNCS 16115, pp. 341–356, 2026.
https://doi.org/10.1007/978-981-95-5719-6_22

Currently, in the field of knowledge graph embedding, rotation-based knowledge graph embedding (KGE) models have made significant progress, among which RotatE [4] and QuatE [5] have been widely used because they can handle symmetric and asymmetric relations by introducing the rotation operation in the complex number space. However, rotation-based knowledge graph embedding models have limitations in generalizing the model to high-dimensional rotations and representing multiple relational patterns [6], leading to a proliferation of the number of parameters. Due to the computational complexity of high-dimensional rotations [7], exploring high-dimensional rotated KGE models becomes challenging.

For this reason, in this paper, a Multi-Relation Knowledge Graph Embedding (MultiRelE) model is proposed by using the Kronecker product orthogonal matrix representation of relations and an improved optimization algorithm to improve the rotation-based knowledge graph embedding model. The model consists of three modules, the entity representation module converts entity vectors into matrices, and optimizes the entity matrices by SGD; the multi-relationship matrix optimization module uses global orthogonal matrices with variable dimensions instead of rotation matrices to control the size of the relationship matrices, and introduces a self-attention mechanism, which enhances the model's ability to capture the complex interactions between entities and relationships, and employs the contraction of the Grassmann flow shape Optimization [8] technique is used to deal with the relation matrix, which reduces the number of parameters; the training objective module adopts a scoring function to calculate the correlation degree between entities and relations, and optimizes the parameters of the model by minimizing the loss function, which improves the model's generalization ability to complex relations. The experiments of the proposed model in this paper on the WN18RR and FB15K-237 datasets show that the model has higher generalization and flexibility in capturing multiple relational patterns [9], and the metrics outperform the baseline models, such as RotatE and QuatE, while drastically reducing the number of relational parameters. For example, on the WN18RR dataset, the MultiRelE model significantly outperforms baseline methods such as ComplEx, RotatE, and QuatE in terms of MRR and Hit@10 metrics, with metrics improvement of more than 4% points in each case.

The main contributions of this paper are summarized as follows:

1. this paper proposes a multi-relational knowledge graph embedding model MultiRelE, which adopts the Kronecker product orthogonal matrix to represent the relations, and adapts to different datasets by modifying the dimension m of the orthogonal matrix, which enhances the model's generalization ability.
2. A shrinkage Grassmann manifold optimization method is introduced, combining singular value thresholding with Grassmann manifold optimization for shrinkage optimization of the relation matrix to achieve the reduction of the number of parameters.

3. Through ablation experiments, we verify the contribution of key components such as self-attention mechanism and contraction Grassmann flow optimization to the model performance, and further validate the effectiveness of the components.

2 Related Work

2.1 Rotation-Based Knowledge Graph Embedding Model

Rotation-based knowledge graph embedding models can capture complex relationship patterns between entities by modeling relationships as rotation operations in complex space, which has pushed forward the development of knowledge graph embedding technology. ComplEx firstly embedded knowledge graph into complex space and modeled antisymmetric relationship patterns using Hermitian product, which laid the foundation for subsequent research. RotatE further defined relationships as rotation operations in complex vector space, which can simultaneously model multiple relationship patterns such as symmetry and inversion, and exchangeable combination. RotatE further defines relations as rotational operations in complex vector space, and is able to simultaneously model symmetry, antisymmetry, inversion, and exchangeable combinatorial relations, etc. QuatE extends the expressive capability of complex space by introducing quaternion operations, which further enhances the performance of the model in modeling complex relations. These models show strong modeling capabilities in multiplication operations in complex spaces. DensE, on the other hand, proposes an embedding method that can deal with non-exchangeable combinatorial relational patterns by introducing three-dimensional rotation [10] technique.

2.2 Grassmann Manifold Optimization Algorithm

The Grassmann manifold $G(k, d)$ is defined as the set of all k-dimensional subspaces in $\mathbb{R}^d$, whose elements are column-orthogonal matrices $U \in \mathbb{R}^{d\times k}$ (satisfying $U^T U = I_k$). In Knowledge Graph Embedding (KGE), if we parameterize the projection matrix of relation r as $M_r = U_r U_r^T$ (where $U_r \in G(k, d)$), the optimization problem can be formulated as:

$$\min_{U_r \in G(k,d)} L(U_r) = \sum_{(h,r,t)} [f_r(U_r h, U_r t) + \lambda R(U_r)] \tag{1}$$

where f_r is the triplet scoring function and $R(U_r)$ is the regularization term. Traditional methods update U_r via Riemannian gradient descent, with key steps as follows:

1. Compute the Euclidean gradient: $\nabla_{U_r} L$
2. Project onto the tangent space:

$$\mathrm{grad}_{U_r} L = (I - U_r U_r^T)\nabla_{U_r} L \tag{2}$$

3. Update via manifold retraction:

$$U_r^{(t+1)} = \mathrm{qf}(U_r^{(t)} - \eta \cdot \mathrm{grad}_{U_r} L) \quad (3)$$

3 MultiRelE Model

The MultiRelE model proposed in this paper achieves embedding and link prediction for knowledge graphs by transforming entities and relations into matrix form [11]. The ability of the model to capture complex interactions between entities and relations is enhanced by converting entities and relations into matrices and introducing a self-attention mechanism, where relations are represented by Kronecker product orthogonal matrices, and shrinking Grassmann manifold optimization techniques are used to reduce the number of relational parameters and to enhance the recognition of relational patterns. By stochastic gradient descent method [12]. The entity matrix is optimized to reduce the prediction error and improve the performance of the model on the link prediction task, which enables the model in this paper to handle multi-relational knowledge graphs and improve the accuracy of prediction.

3.1 Modeling Framework

The MultiRelE model consists of three core modules: the entity representation module, the multi-relationship matrix optimization module and the training objective module. The model framework is shown in Fig. 1, and the functions of each module are described in detail below.

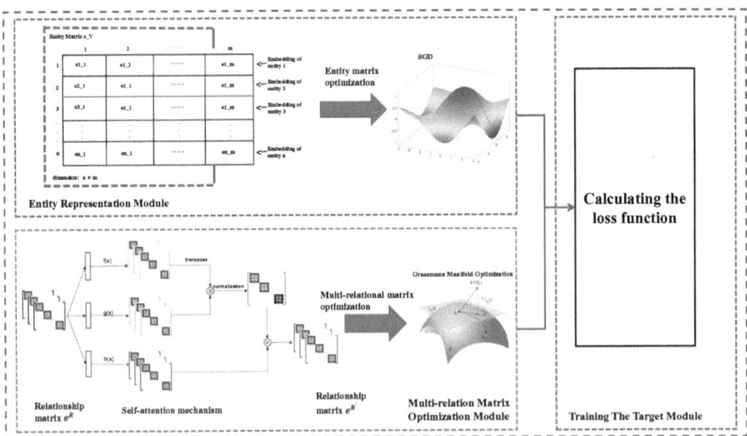

Fig. 1. MultiRelE model framework diagram

3.2 Entity Representation Module

Traditional entity vector embedding methods typically use a single vector to represent each entity (e.g., word vectors generated by Word2vec). These methods assign a fixed dimensional vector to each entity, which is suitable for representing static features. However, to enhance the expressive power of embeddings and the flexibility of the MultiRelE model, we transform vector embeddings into matrix embeddings. This is achieved by introducing a variable m to control the entity dimension, converting entity vectors $e \in \mathbb{R}^n$ into matrices $e \in \mathbb{R}^{n \times m}$. This transformation prevents unnecessary expansion of relation sizes while enabling optimization through stochastic gradient descent.

The conversion from vector embeddings to matrix embeddings is formulated as:

$$M = VV^T \tag{4}$$

where M represents the entity matrix and V denotes an entity vector embedding.

The entity matrix can be effectively optimized using stochastic gradient descent, which handles large-scale datasets by iteratively adjusting matrix values to minimize loss, thereby improving overall model performance:

$$W_{\text{new}} = W_{\text{old}} - \eta \nabla_W L \tag{5}$$

Here, W_{new} represents the updated weight matrix, W_{old} the previous weight matrix, η the learning rate, and $\nabla_W L$ the gradient of the loss function L with respect to the weight matrix.

This optimized approach enhances the model's generalization capability, leading to more accurate and stable performance on unseen data.

3.3 Multi-relation Matrix Optimization Module

In the MultiRelE model, the representation of relation matrices is based on the properties of orthogonal matrices. Traditional rotation-based KGE (Knowledge Graph Embedding) models use fixed-dimensional rotation matrices to represent relations, which limits the model's generalization capability when handling high-dimensional rotations. To overcome this limitation, the MultiRelE model employs Kronecker product orthogonal matrices to represent relations. Specifically, the relation matrix $e^R \in \mathbb{R}^{n \times n}$ is composed of multiple low-dimensional orthogonal matrices combined via Kronecker product, as shown in Eq. (6):

$$e^R = X_1 \otimes X_2 \otimes \cdots \otimes X_k \tag{6}$$

where each X_i is a $d_i \times d_i$-dimensional orthogonal matrix satisfying $X_i^T X_i = I_{d_i}$, and $\prod_{i=1}^{k} d_i = n$. This representation extends low-dimensional orthogonal matrices to high-dimensional ones through the Kronecker product, preserving the orthogonality while allowing flexible adjustment of each component's dimension to adapt to datasets of varying complexity, thereby improving the model's generalization capability.

To enhance the model's ability to capture complex interactions between entities and relations and to optimize the relation matrix e^R, we introduce a self-attention mechanism and employ the shrinking Grassmann manifold optimization method to obtain the relation matrix $e^{R'}$. The shrinking Grassmann manifold is used for structured learning of each Kronecker product component X_i. This geometric optimization method captures the local geometric properties of orthogonal matrices, thereby improving the precision of relation representation. During the joint optimization of entity and relation embeddings, the introduction of the Grassmann manifold enables the model to more accurately characterize complex interaction patterns between entities, such as symmetric, antisymmetric, inverse, and non-commutative composition relations.

By adjusting the dimensional configuration d of the Kronecker product, the model can adapt to the complexity of different datasets while maintaining its expressive power for various relation patterns.

3.4 Training Objective Module

The scoring function $f(h,r,t)$ measures the plausibility of factual triples (h,r,t) in a knowledge graph, where h and t represent the embedding matrices of the head and tail entities respectively, and r represents the relation embedding matrix. In the MultiRelE model, the scoring function is defined as Eq. (7):

$$f(h,r,t) = -\|RH - T\|_2 + b_h + b_t \tag{7}$$

where R denotes the relation embedding matrix, H the head entity embedding matrix, and T the tail entity embedding matrix. The notation $\|\cdot\|_2$ represents the Euclidean distance between matrices, which computes the distance between the transformed head entity (after applying the relation) and the tail entity. The terms b_h and b_t are bias terms for the head and tail entities respectively.

Furthermore, this work employs a uniform negative sampling approach by replacing the tail entity for given triples (h,r,t), rather than using alternative negative sampling techniques. The loss function is defined in Eqs. (8) and (9):

$$L = -\sum_{(h,r,t)\in D}\sum_{t'\sim p(t)} y_t \log \sigma(s(h,r,t')) \tag{8}$$

$$y_t = \begin{cases} -1, & \text{if } t' = t \\ 1, & \text{otherwise} \end{cases} \tag{9}$$

where D represents the training dataset, $p(t)$ is the negative sampling distribution used to select negative samples t' from all possible tail entities, and $\sigma(\cdot)$ denotes the sigmoid function that transforms the scoring function's output into probability values. This loss function is a variant based on logistic regression, which encourages the model to increase scores for correct factual triples while decreasing scores for incorrect ones. The scoring function's computation serves to measure the plausibility of triples in the knowledge graph, and optimizing this scoring function enhances the model's ability to identify correct triples.

3.5 Shrinking Grassmann Manifold Optimization Algorithm

To introduce a low-rank shrinkage mechanism, we embed Singular Value Thresholding (SVT) into the traditional Grassmann manifold optimization algorithm. The specific steps are as follows:

Step 1: Gradient Computation and Manifold Projection First compute the Euclidean gradient $\nabla_{U_r} L$ of the loss function L with respect to U_r, and project it onto the tangent space of the Grassmann manifold:

$$\text{grad}_{U_r} L = (I - U_r U_r^T) \nabla_{U_r} L \tag{10}$$

Step 2: Singular Value Decomposition and Threshold Shrinking

Perform Singular Value Decomposition (SVD) on the current iteration point $U_r^{(t)}$:

$$U_r^{(t)} = A \Sigma B^T, \quad \Sigma = \text{diag}(\sigma_1, \sigma_2, ..., \sigma_k) \tag{11}$$

where $\sigma_1 \geq \sigma_2 \geq ... \geq \sigma_k \geq 0$ are the singular values. Apply the soft-thresholding operator $S_\tau(x) = \text{sign}(x) \max(|x| - \tau, 0)$ to shrink the singular values:

$$\hat{\Sigma} = \text{diag}(S_\tau(\sigma_1), ..., S_\tau(\sigma_k)) \tag{12}$$

where the threshold τ is related to the regularization coefficient λ (e.g., $\tau = \lambda\eta$). Reconstruct the shrunk matrix:

$$\hat{U}_r = A \hat{\Sigma} B^T \tag{13}$$

Step 3: Re-orthogonalization and Manifold Retraction

Since thresholding may break orthogonality, perform QR decomposition on $\hat{U}_r$ to reproject it onto the Grassmann manifold:

$$U_r^{(t+1/2)} = \text{qf}(\hat{U}_r) \tag{14}$$

Further update the parameters by combining with the gradient direction:

$$U_r^{(t+1)} = \text{qf}(U_r^{(t+1/2)} - \eta \cdot \text{grad}_{U_r} L) \tag{15}$$

By optimizing the relation matrix on the shrinking Grassmann manifold, we can more easily handle the optimization of relation matrices, particularly for high-dimensional data and complex relations. This approach reduces the number of parameters and improves computational efficiency.

4 Experiments

4.1 Experimental Dataset

In the field of knowledge graph embedding, link prediction serves as an important benchmark task for evaluating the knowledge representation capability of models, and its commonly used benchmark datasets include FB15K [13], WN18 [14], WN18RR [15] &FB15K-237 [16]. Among them, WN18RR, as an improved subset of WN18, is constructed based on WordNet [17], which focuses on eliminating redundant relations between the training set and the test set; while FB15K-237, as an optimized subset of FB15K, is derived from the Freebase [18] commonsense knowledge base, which focuses on solving the problem of semantic overlap between relations. All the above datasets are designed for knowledge graph embedding tasks and do not contain personal privacy or sensitive content. In terms of data structure characterization, FB15K focuses on large-scale general knowledge, which is stored in (head entity ID, relation, tail entity ID) ternary format, covering complex associations among entities, while WN18 focuses on the semantic network of English vocabulary, whose entities cover lexical properties of nouns, verbs, adjectives and adverbs, and the relations characterize the semantic associations among vocabularies, and the data structure also adopts the standard ternary format. Both datasets are characterized by multiple relational patterns, including symmetric relations, asymmetric relations, relation inversion and relation combination. In this study, WN18RR and FB15K-237 are selected as the evaluation benchmarks, aiming to more accurately validate the model's knowledge reasoning ability through the de-redundantly processed dataset.

The description of the dataset is shown in Table 1, including the number of entities, the number of relationships, and the number of triples in the training, validation, and test sets. In terms of dataset characteristics, WN18RR has more number of entities and less number of relationships. While FB15k-237 has more number of relations and less number of entities, so it is more challenging to experiment on this dataset. Also the two datasets basically reflect the differences in the model's handling of data with different characteristics.

Table 1. Dataset Description (unit: units)

Dataset	Entities	Relations	Train	Validation	Test
WN18RR	40,943	11	86,835	3,034	3,134
FB15K-237	14,541	237	272,115	17,535	20,466

4.2 Evaluation Metrics

To predict tail entities given head entities and relations, we employ two established ranking metrics to evaluate the ranking of correct tail entities among all possible candidates.

The first metric is Mean Reciprocal Rank (MRR), which calculates the average of reciprocal ranks of correct entities. Higher values indicate better performance. The MRR is computed as:

$$\mathrm{MRR} = \frac{1}{n}\sum_{i=1}^{n}\frac{1}{\mathrm{rank}_i} \tag{16}$$

The second metric is Hits@K (where $K \in \{1, 3, 10\}$), which measures the frequency of correct entities appearing in the top-K ranked positions. It computes the proportion of correct entities in the top-N ranked results, with higher values indicating better performance. Typically, N values of 1, 3, and 10 are used for model evaluation:

$$\mathrm{Hits@}N = \frac{1}{n}\sum_{i=1}^{n} f(\mathrm{rank}_i, N) \tag{17}$$

$$f(\mathrm{rank}_i, N) = \begin{cases} 1 & \text{if } \mathrm{rank}_i \leq N \\ 0 & \text{if } \mathrm{rank}_i > N \end{cases} \tag{18}$$

4.3 Hyperparameter Settings

The key hyperparameters in the experimental setup include the learning rates for Grassmann and Adagrad, the number of negative samples, and the batch size. To determine the optimal hyperparameters, we conducted grid search on validation data. In Table 2, the Ir-entity values for DCNE, RotatE, and QuatE refer to the overall learning rate of each model. For the MultiRelE model, we use Grassmann manifold for relation optimization and Adagrad for entity optimization, as detailed in Table 2.

Table 2. Best Hyperparameters for MultiRelE and Baseline Models

Dataset	Model	Ir-entity	Ir-relation	Optimizer	Negative Samples
WN18RR (dim = 500)	DCNE	0.001	-	Grassmann	200
	RotatE	0.1	-	Adagrad	200
	QuatE	0.2	-	Adagrad	200
	MultiRelE(2x2)	0.2	0.02	-	200
	MultiRelE(3x3)	0.2	0.02	-	200
FB15k-237 (dim = 1000)	DCNE	0.05	-	Grassmann	200
	RotatE	0.1	-	Adagrad	200
	QuatE	0.2	-	Adagrad	200
	MultiRelE(2x2)	0.5	0.06	-	200
	MultiRelE(3x3)	0.5	0.06	-	200

4.4 Experimental Setup

The current model was compared with the baseline model, which includes TransE [19], DistMult [20], ConvE [21], MuRP [22], StAR [23], E-CP [24], and rotation-based KGE models such as ComplEx [25], RotatE, QuatE, DensE [26], and DCNE. MultiRelE discusses the performance differences by using different-sized orthogonal matrices, thereby further differentiating.

The link prediction experimental results based on the WN18RR and FB15K-237 datasets are shown in Table 3. The optimal values are bolded to highlight, and the suboptimal results are underlined. Based on the experimental results, the following conclusions can be drawn: The MultiRelE model exhibits outstanding performance indicators on the WN18RR and FB15K-237 datasets. Only the Hits@10 indicator under the WN18RR dataset achieves a result slightly lower than StAR. The StAR model has a stronger generalization ability for unseen entities and relations due to its text encoding part. On the WN18RR dataset, StAR can better handle entities and relations that did not appear during training, thus performing better in the Hits@10 indicator. The current model's superiority lies in its matrix representation of entities and relations and the introduction of self-attention mechanisms. The entity matrix is optimized using SGD, and the relation matrix is optimized using the contraction Grassmann manifold technology, resulting in superior performance in all indicators compared to all the other models. This highlights its outstanding representational ability.

Figures 2 and 3 respectively show the comparison of MRR accuracy of different entity size models of the MultiRelE model on the WN18RR and FB15K-237 datasets. The results show that as the entity size increases, the model performance gradually improves. However, when the entity size reaches a certain size, the performance improvement of the model will tend to stabilize, and the marginal effect of further increasing the size on performance gradually decreases, and even reduces performance. From the figures, it can be concluded that the MultiRelE (4×4) size model has a lower parameter quantity compared to larger size models, which directly reduces the model complexity. Moreover, the effect of representing entities in the low-dimensional entity vector space is better than other smaller-sized models, so the MultiRelE (4×4) size model is the best size model. This also suggests that researchers need to consider the trade-off between model complexity and experimental results when choosing the entity size, and optimize resource allocation. It indicates that MultiRelE can better capture complex relationship patterns by adjusting the matrix dimensions. Figures 4 and 5 respectively show the impact of changing m while keeping the constant entity size (n*m) on the WN18RR and FB15K-237 datasets. The results show that the MultiRelE (4×4) models with m = 1, 2, or 3 perform similarly and better than m = 10, and are significantly better than the DCNE model in all dimensions. And with the increase of low dimensions, the performance of MultiRelE further improves, but the performance of the high-dimensional m = 10 is lower than other dimensions. This indicates that the MultiRelE (4×4) model cannot fully represent its relationships by simply increasing the dimension, and an appropriate dimension needs to be selected to achieve the maximum performance. For

WN18RR, a larger dimension (such as m = 3) can better represent its complex relationships, while for FB15K-237, a smaller dimension (m = 1) can achieve stable performance. These experimental results collectively indicate that the MultiRelE model can adapt to datasets of different complexities by adjusting the dimension d of the matrix. Since the WN18RR and FB15K-237 datasets are relatively small, using the MultiRelE (4×4) model can achieve the optimal performance.

Table 3. Link Prediction Accuracy Comparison on WN18RR and FB15k-237 Datasets

Model	WN18RR				FB15k-237			
	MRR	Hits@1	Hits@3	Hits@10	MRR	Hits@1	Hits@3	Hits@10
TransE	.226	-	-	.501	.294	-	-	.465
DistMult	.430	.390	.440	.490	.241	.155	.263	.419
ComplEx	.440	.410	.460	.510	.247	.158	.275	.428
ConvE	.430	.400	.440	.520	.325	.237	.356	.501
RotatE	.470	.422	.488	.565	.297	.205	.328	.480
QuatE	.481	.436	.500	.564	.311	.221	.342	.495
DensE	.486	-	-	.572	.306	-	-	.481
MuRP	.481	.440	.495	.566	.335	.243	.367	.518
StAR	.401	.243	.491	**.709**	.296	.205	.322	.482
E-CP	.421	.382	.432	.511	.265	.193	.285	.511
DCNE	.492	.448	.510	.581	.354	.257	.393	.545
MultiRelE(2×2)	.515	.465	.535	.630	.375	.275	.405	.568
MultiRelE(3×3)	.518	.466	.540	.636	.380	.280	<u>.414</u>	.574
MultiRelE(4×4)	**.530**	**.470**	**.548**	<u>.642</u>	**.383**	**.284**	**.420**	**.582**
MultiRelE(10×**10**)	<u>.528</u>	<u>.468</u>	<u>.544</u>	.640	<u>.381</u>	<u>.281</u>	.413	<u>.579</u>

4.5 Ablation Study

In order to verify the influence of each key component in the MultiRelE model on the model's performance, ablation experiments were conducted to evaluate the contribution of the self-attention mechanism and the optimized technique of contracting the Grassmann manifold to the model's performance. The experimental comparison results are shown in Tables 4 and 5. The comparison models are as follows: 1) Remove the self-attention mechanism and only include the contracted Grassmann manifold optimization model MultiRelE-G; 3) Remove the contracted Grassmann manifold optimization and only include the self-attention mechanism model MultiRelE-A. From the experimental data, it can be found that all evaluation indicators of MultiRelE on the two datasets are superior to those of MultiRelE-G and MultiRelE-A. For example, on the WN18RR and

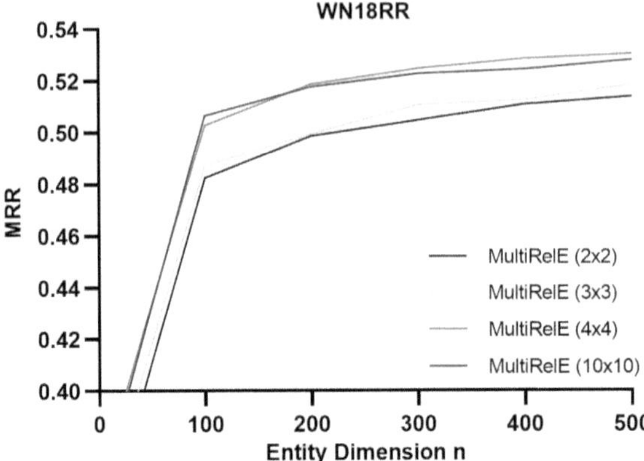

Fig. 2. Comparison of MRR accuracy of MultiRelE model for orthogonal matrices of different entity sizes under WN18RR dataset

FB15k-237 datasets, the MRR indicator has increased by 5.9%, 4.4%, and 5.2%, 4.1% respectively, and the Hits@3 indicator has increased by 1.5%, 3.7%, and 1.2%, 3.3% respectively, indicating that introducing the self-attention mechanism and using the contracted Grassmann manifold optimization method in the relationship matrix can improve the performance of the prediction model, further demonstrating the effectiveness of each key component in MultiRelE.

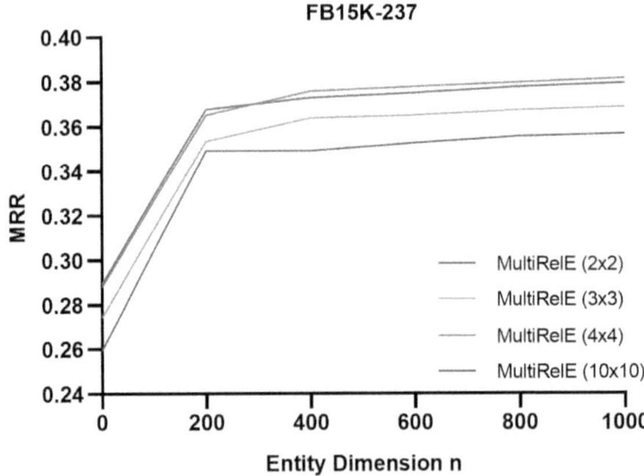

Fig. 3. Comparison of MRR accuracy of MultiRelE model for orthogonal matrices with different entity sizes under FB15K-237dataset

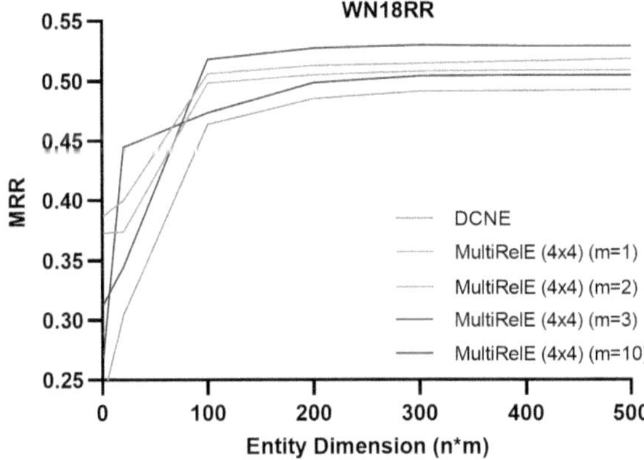

Fig. 4. A comparison of the MRR accuracy of the MultiRelE (4×4) and DCNE models on different dimensions of WN18RR

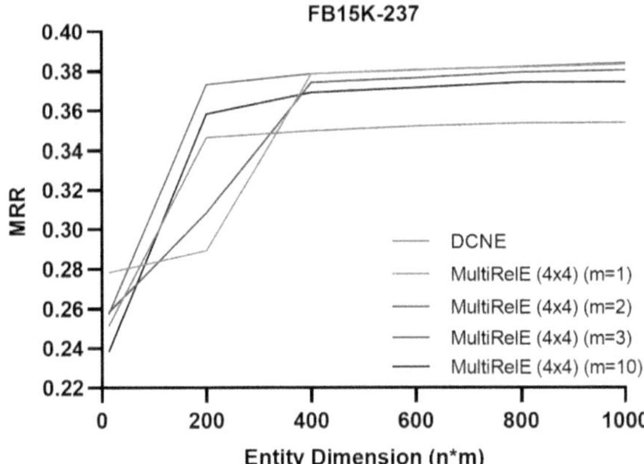

Fig. 5. A comparison of the MRR accuracy of the MultiRelE (4×4) and DCNE models on different dimensions of FB15K-237

Table 4. Results of ablation experiments on the WN18RR dataset

Model	MRR	Hits@1	Hits@3	Hits@10
MultiRelE-G	.471	.412	.493	.581
MultiRelE-A	.486	.430	.511	.602
MultiRelE	.530	.470	.548	.642

Table 5. Results of ablation experiments on the FB15K–237 dataset

Model	MRR	Hits@1	Hits@3	Hits@10
MultiRelE-G	.331	.234	.372	.535
MultiRelE-A	.342	.239	.385	.547
MultiRelE	.383	.284	.420	.582

5 Summary

In this paper, a novel knowledge graph embedding model MultiRelE is proposed, and its innovations are mainly reflected in the following aspects: firstly, the model adopts Kronecker product orthogonal matrices to represent different relational patterns, and this design not only can capture the diversity and complexity of relations, but also ensures the interpretability and stability of the matrices through orthogonal constraints; finally, the MultiRelE introduces the optimization method of shrinking Grassmann manifolds to optimize the relation matrix, thus ensuring that the number of covariates is reduced and the computational efficiency and convergence are ensured while expressing multiple relation patterns in high dimensions. The experimental results show that the model has a better link prediction effect compared with similar models. Although the model in this paper demonstrates significant improvement in expressing multiple relational patterns in high dimensions, its use of Kronecker product orthogonal matrices to represent relationships generates a relatively high complexity may lead to increased computational overhead in practical applications. This means that the actual operational efficiency of the model may be affected in real-time processing and application scenarios of large-scale knowledge graphs, especially when faced with high-dimensional data. Therefore, in future research, complexity optimization can be considered to achieve a better balance between accuracy and efficiency.

Acknowledgments. This work was supported by the Natural Science Foundation General Project Science-Technology Plan Joint Program of Liaoning Provincial (2024-MSLH-196).

References

1. Feng, W.L., Zhang, D., Li, G.Y.: MHAKGE: a knowledge graph embedding method using multi-head attention for fusing numerical attributes. Comput. Eng. Appl. 1–12 (2025). http://kns.cnki.net/kcms/detail/11.2127.TP.20241129.0946.007.html
2. Ren, H.Y., Liu, J.P., Wang, J., et al.: Research on intelligent question answering system based on large language model: a survey. Comput. Eng. Appl. 1–24 (2025). http://kns.cnki.net/kcms/detail/11.2127.TP.20241227.1952.011.html
3. Wu, G.H., Wang, X., Hao, G.S., et al.: Recommendation model integrating knowledge graph and high-order information aggregation mechanism. Comput.

Eng. Appl. 1–10 (2025). http://kns.cnki.net/kcms/detail/11.2127.TP.20241127.1756.025.html

4. Sun, Z., Deng, Z.H., Nie, J.Y., et al.: Rotate: knowledge graph embedding by relational rotation in complex space. arXiv preprint arXiv:1902.10197 (2019)
5. Zhang, S., Tay, Y., Yao, L., et al.: Quaternion knowledge graph embeddings. In: Advances in Neural Information Processing Systems, vol. 32 (2019)
6. Wang, J.H.: Research on knowledge graph completion based on knowledge graph embedding. University of Electronic Science and Technology of China (2024). https://doi.org/10.27005/d.cnki.gdzku.2024.000993
7. Xu, Z.H., Mao, C., Wang, L.Q., et al.: Knowledge graph completion with temporal and relational attention. J. Comput. Eng. Appl. **59**(17), 266–274 (2023)
8. Zhao, Y.W., Liu, Y.P.: Image set recognition based on subspace manifold. J. Comput. Appl. **43**(S1), 207–211 (2023)
9. Xiong, W., Chen, H., Su, H.Y.: QuatCNNEx: a knowledge graph embedding model for multiple relationship patterns. J. Comput. Sci. 1–11 (2024)
10. Cai, Q.H., Xu, B., Dong, X.D.: Knowledge graph completion model using semantic-enhanced prompts and structural information. J. Comput. Sci. 1–17 (2024). http://kns.cnki.net/kcms/detail/50.1075.TP.20241028.1439.034.html
11. Liu, H.C., Liu, L., Wang, H.L., et al.: A survey of link prediction in knowledge graph embedding methods. Comput. Eng. Appl. 1–21 (2025). http://kns.cnki.net/kcms/detail/11.2127.TP.20241111.1033.038.html
12. Wang, L., Yang, J., Zhang, C.Y., et al.: Generative adversarial network with dual discriminator and mixed attention. Comput. Eng. Appl. **60**(07), 212–221 (2024)
13. Wang, Z., Zhang, J.W., Feng, J.L., et al.: Knowledge graph embedding by translating on hyperplanes. In: Proceedings of the 28th AAAI Conference on Artificial Intelligence, Quebec City, 27–31 July 2014, pp. 1112–1119. AAAI, Menlo Park (2014)
14. Bordes, A., Usunier, N., Garcia-Duran, A., et al.: Translating embeddings for modeling multi-relational data. In: Proceedings of the 27th Annual Conference on Neural Information Processing Systems, Lake Tahoe, 5–8 December 2013, pp. 2787–2795. MIT Press, Cambridge (2013)
15. Xiao, H., Huang, M.L., Yu, H., et al.: TransA: an adaptive approach for knowledge graph embedding. arXiv:1509.05490 (2015)
16. Dettmers, T., Minervini, P., Stenetorp, P., et al.: Convolutional 2D knowledge graph embeddings. In: Proceedings of the 32nd AAAI Conference on Artificial Intelligence, the 30th Innovative Applications of Artificial Intelligence, and the 8th AAAI Symposium on Educational Advances in Artificial Intelligence, New Orleans, 2–7 February 2018, pp. 1811–1818. AAAI, Menlo Park (2018)
17. Miller, G.A.: WordNet: a lexical database for English. Commun. ACM **38**(11), 39–41 (1995)
18. Bollacker, K., Evans, C., Paritosh, P., et al.: Freebase: a collaboratively created graph database for structuring human knowledge. In: Proceedings of the ACM SIGMOD International Conference on Management of Data, pp. 1247–1250 (2008)
19. Antoine, B., Usunier, N., Garcia-Duran, A., et al.: Translating embeddings for modeling multi-relational data. In: Proceedings of the 26th International Conference on Neural Information Processing Systems, pp. 2787–2795 (2013)
20. Yang, B., Yih, W.T., He, X., et al.: Embedding entities and relations for learning and inference in knowledge bases. arXiv:1412.6575 (2014)
21. Dettmers, T., Minervini, P., Stenetorp, P., et al.: Convolutional 2D knowledge graph embeddings. In: Proceedings of the Thirty-Second AAAI Conference on Artificial Intelligence and Thirtieth Innovative Applications of Artificial Intelligence

Conference and Eighth AAAI Symposium on Educational Advances in Artificial Intelligence (AAAI 2018/IAAI 2018/EAAI 2018), pp. 1811–1818 (2018)
22. Fishberg, A., Quiter, B.J., How, J.P.: MURP: multi-agent ultra-wideband relative pose estimation with constrained communications in 3D environments. IEEE Robot. Autom. Lett. **9**(11), 10612–10619 (2024). https://doi.org/10.1109/LRA.2024.3451393
23. Wang, B., Shen, T., Long, G.D., et al.: Structure-augmented text representation learning for efficient knowledge graph completion. In: Proceedings of the Web Conference 2021 (WWW 2021), pp. 1737–1748 (2021). https://doi.org/10.1145/3442381.3450043
24. Zhao, B., Wang, Y.J., Ni, J.: Enhanced CP decomposition for link prediction in knowledge graphs. J. Comput. Appl. Res. **40**(05), 1396–1401 (2023). https://doi.org/10.19734/j.issn.1001-3695.2022.09.0498
25. Trouillon, T., Welbl, J., Riedel, S., et al.: Complex embeddings for simple link prediction. In: International Conference on Machine Learning, pp. 2071–2080 (2016)
26. Lu, H., Hu, H., Lin, X.: Dense: an enhanced non-commutative representation for knowledge graph embedding with adaptive semantic hierarchy. Neurocomputing **476**, 115–125 (2022)

LE^2C: LLM-Enhanced Event Evolutionary Graph for Explainable Classification

Jiayi Liang[1], Shuchun Wu[2], Xiaoling Wang[1(✉)], and Junyu Niu[2]

[1] School of Computer Science and Technology, East China Normal University, Shanghai, China
jyliang@stu.ecnu.edu.cn, xlwang@cs.ecnu.edu.cn
[2] Fudan University, Shanghai, China
20110240077@fudan.edu.cn, jyniu@fudan.edu.cn

Abstract. In the development of intelligent systems, multi-label event classification plays a vital role in enabling accurate decision-making across diverse scenarios such as incident response, customer service, and urban management. Although existing graph-based approaches for multi-label classification have shown potential, they struggle to model directed label dependencies and lack explainability, resulting in black-box decision-making processes. To address these issues, we propose a novel **L**LM-enhanced **E**vent Evolutionary graph for **E**xplainable **C**lassification (LE^2C) method. Specifically, we first leverage the powerful semantic learning capabilities of Large Language Models to construct an event evolutionary graph that models event dynamics. Furthermore, we introduce a co-occurrence probability matrix to enhance the expressivity and explainability of the graph, guiding explainable classification. Extensive experiments on two large real-world event classification tasks demonstrate the efficiency, effectiveness, and explainability of LE^2C. The code is available at https://github.com/NinaLiangjy/LE2C.

Keywords: Explainable Multi-label Classification · Event Evolutionary Graph · Knowledge Discovery · Large Language Model

1 Introduction

In the era of global intelligent cities, the ability to automatically identify and classify events from text is crucial for improving public opinion monitoring [33], risk warning [8], emergency response [2], and decision-making support [4]. By leveraging natural language processing (NLP) techniques, governments and related institutions can monitor social dynamics in real time, detect potential issues early, and allocate resources more efficiently. This enables more intelligent and precise urban management. Event classification, as a key task in this process, aims to assign each input text to its most appropriate event category based on

J. Liang and S. Wu—These authors contributed equally.

J. Li et al. (Eds.): APWeb-WAIM 2025, LNCS 16115, pp. 357–372, 2026.
https://doi.org/10.1007/978-981-95-5719-6_23

semantic content. Traditionally, event classification has been treated as a single-label task, where each instance belongs to only one event category. However, real-world events often involve multiple meanings or domains. Therefore, modeling this task as a multi-label classification problem is more reasonable, as it better captures the complexity and multidimensional nature of events.

Traditional methods for multi-label event classification tasks could generally be divided into two categories. The first category transforms the multi-label problem into one or more single-label problems [27,28]. However, this type of method ignores the dependencies between labels and cannot address the problem of label imbalance. The second category adapts existing classification algorithms to handle multi-label characteristics. For example, FastXML applies a novel node partitioning formulation which optimizes an normalized Discounted Cumulative Gain (nDCG) based ranking loss over all the labels [24], but it fails to adequately model the structured dependencies among labels. Recent studies [12,34] have introduced graph-based models to capture label co-occurrence relationships. [12] constructs a fully connected label graph to model correlations, while [34] further adopts message passing neural networks (MPNNs) to propagate features and label embeddings over the graph. These methods typically use undirected graphs, which limits their ability to capture joint probability distributions and directional dependencies between labels. Building on this, [23] proposes the Multi-relational Message Passing Network (MrMP), which integrates a Compositional Graph Convolutional Network (CompGCN) to capture various bidirectional semantic relationships among labels. Although this method achieves outstanding performance on several benchmark datasets, it is fundamentally a black-box model due to its deep neural network architecture and thus lacks explainability. When dealing with complex semantic relationships between labels, it remains unclear how the model utilizes input information and internal structures to make predictions.

Traditional information extraction (IE) methods typically adopt a pipeline architecture, which often leads to error propagation across stages. With the success of deep learning, neural network models have been widely applied to various IE subtasks. For instance, ONEIE employs an end-to-end neural IE framework that explicitly models cross-subtask and cross-instance dependencies [16]. However, such methods are generally tailored to specific tasks. To enable domain-general information extraction, UIE [18] introduces a structured extraction language to uniformly encode diverse extraction schemas, and leverages schema-based prompting mechanisms to adaptively generate target outputs. While these approaches have demonstrated strong performance in IE tasks, they still rely heavily on manually annotated data, making them difficult to train in low-resource scenarios. Recent advances address this limitation by employing large language models (LLMs) for information extraction in low-resource settings [19]. These LLM-based methods offer greater flexibility and generalization capabilities, making them more suitable for real-world applications where annotated data is scarce.

In order to address these challenges and classify events contained into correct labels, we propose LE^{2}C (**L**LM-Enhanced **E**vent Evolutionary Graph for **E**xplainable **C**lassification), an interpretable classification framework based on event evolutionary graphs. The core idea is to leverage Large Language Models (LLMs) to build event evolutionary graphs that link events with target labels. To overcome undirected graphs' limitations in modeling directional dependencies, we construct an event evolutionary graph to model the relationships between events and labels. This structure enhances the semantic expressiveness and the representations of event relations. Furthermore, in addressing overlapping labels and intersecting responsibilities, we design an interpretable classification algorithm based on the event evolutionary graph. We compute relevance scores between an event and its candidate labels, guiding the classification decision and generating explanation paths. This decision process significantly improves the explainability of automated event classification.

Our contributions are summarized as follows:

- **LLM Enhanced Event Element Extraction.** A method for element extraction based on a Large Language Model, which is designed to extract event elements from diverse textual content using a few-shot approach.
- **Event Evolutionary Graph Construction.** A method for constructing an event evolutionary graph, which is proposed to establish undirected and directed association graphs among events, geographic locations, and department groups in events.
- **A Novel Explainable Event Classification Algorithm.** An explainable event classification algorithm is proposed, which calculates the association scores of candidate labels and the contribution of event association information through a directed graph and displays the reasoning path.
- **Extensive Experiments on Real-world Datasets.** Experiments are conducted on two large real-world event classification datasets and validate the state-of-the-art performance and explainability of LE^{2}C.

2 Problem Definition

Problem 1. ***Multi-label Event Classification.*** *Given a set of events* $\mathcal{X} = \{x_1, x_2, \ldots, x_N\}$, *where each* $x_i \in \mathbb{R}^d$ *is a d-dimensional feature vector, and a set of event elements* $\mathcal{Y} = \{y_1, y_2, \ldots, y_L\}$ *representing semantic roles, as well as a set of labels* $\mathcal{D} = \{d_1, d_2, \ldots, d_M\}$ *responsible for executing events, the objective is to learn a function:*

$$f : \mathcal{X} \rightarrow 2^{\mathcal{D}},$$

that maps each event x_i *to a set of labels* $D_i \subseteq \mathcal{D}$.

Each event is annotated with a set of event elements $Y_i \subseteq \mathcal{Y}$, and each event element $y \in \mathcal{Y}$ is associated with a subset of labels via a many-to-many mapping $\phi : \mathcal{Y} \rightarrow 2^{\mathcal{D}}$. The classification function f must satisfy the following:

- The predicted labels D_i should semantically align with the corresponding event element set Y_i;
- The mapping ϕ between event elements and labels must be respected, i.e., $D_i \subseteq \bigcup_{y \in Y_i} \phi(y)$;
- The function supports multi-label and multi-target outputs, i.e., $|Y_i| \geq 1$ and $|D_i| \geq 1$ are common and expected.

Definition 1. ***Event Evolutionary Graph Construction.*** *Given a set of events $U = \{u_1, u_2, ..., u_n\}$, each event $u_p \in U$ consists of content description u_p^s, a event category u_p^c, and an associated label u_p^l. Based on the event data U, we construct an event evolutionary graph $G = (V, E)$. The vertex set V includes the events vertices $V^e \subset V$, extracted from event context u_p^s, the category vertices $V^c \subset V$, and label vertices $V^l \subset V$, derived from each event category u_p^c and label u_p^l, respectively. Edges E represent the relations among vertices.*

In this work, we propose an undirected event evolutionary graph $G = (V, E)$ and a directed event evolutionary graph $\dot{G} = (V, \dot{E})$, where directed edges $\dot{E}$'s weights are the normalized weights of edges E based on the same vertex categories.

Problem 2. ***Explainable Event Classification.*** *Given the directed event evolutionary graph $\dot{G} = (V, \dot{E})$ and the incoming event $\hat{U}$, the objective is to predict each event $\hat{u} \in \hat{U}$'s label $\hat{u}^d \subset V^d$, and generate its explanation $\phi_{\hat{u}}$.*

The explanation $\phi_{\hat{u}} \in \mathbb{R}^{|V^d|}$ is the explainable weights to represent the probability of event $\hat{u}$ classified into labels $V^d \subset V$.

3 Explainable Event Classification

In this section, we introduce the proposed LE^{2}C method in detail. Specifically, we first construct an undirected event evolutionary graph G, and a directed event evolutionary graph $\dot{G}$, and then perform the explainable event classification task. The framework is illustrated in Fig. 1. During the graph construction stage, we leverage a large language model, Qwen2.5-7B-Instruct[1], to extract event elements with semantic features from each event content u_p^s. The extracted elements of the event u_p^e, along with the associated category u_p^c and label u_p^l, serve as the vertices in the event evolutionary graphs, G and $\dot{G}$. Then, we construct the undirected event evolutionary graph G according to the proposed co-occurrence matrix of the vertices. Similarly, the directed graph $\dot{G}$ is built using a co-occurrence probability matrix to capture directional dependencies. Through the inference process, we apply the directed event evolutionary graph $\dot{G}$ to implement the event classification task. The details are as follows.

[1] https://huggingface.co/Qwen/Qwen2.5-7B-Instruct.

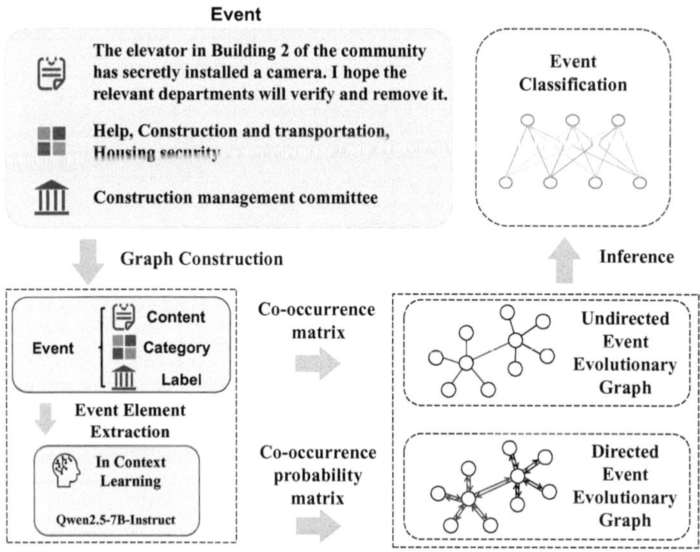

Fig. 1. Framework of LE^{2}C.

3.1 Event Evolutionary Graph Construction

To construct the directed and undirected event evolutionary graphs, $\dot{G}$ and G, we extract event elements u^e and category u^c from each event and organize them into the vertex sets V^e, V^c respectively. To capture richer semantic representations from the content description u^s, we adopt the advanced semantic modeling of a Large Language Model (Qwen2.5-7B-Instruct) in a few-shot learning manner. The instruction, as shown in Fig. 2, describes the extraction requirements and provides few-shot examples for event element identification. Given the few-shot instruction for event element extraction from the event content u^s, the powerful LLM will infer elements in the event. Moreover, to avoid the extracted elements from being too sparse, we merge synonyms within the extracted elements according to predefined patterns.

At this point, we have constructed the vertices $V = \{V^e \cup V^c \cup V^l\}$. Then, we update the edge weights by constructing the co-occurrence matrix and the co-occurrence probability matrix for the undirected event evolutionary graph $G = (V, E)$ and the directed event evolutionary graph $\dot{G} = (V, \dot{E})$.

3.2 Undirected and Directed Event Evolutionary Graphs

To construct an undirected event evolutionary graph G, we propose to use a co-occurrence matrix to represent the correlation relationships of two vertices. We propose calculating the co-occurrence matrix via Eq. 1 according to the linkage of related events in graph G.

$$Co(v_i, v_j) = |\{Source(v_p) \mid \forall v_p \in \mathcal{N}(v_i)\} \cap \{Source(v_q) \mid \forall v_q \in \mathcal{N}(v_j)\}| \quad (1)$$

Few-shot Instruction

Please help me extract elements from the event, Following is the requirements and example.
Extraction requirements:
1. Try to use 2 phrases to describe, and avoid using long paragraphs
2. Avoid repeated descriptions, and synonyms that have been used do not need to be described again
3. Do not extract meaningless events
4. Only need to reflect and describe the citizens' problems, no need to describe the demands
5. Avoid copying the original vocabulary, rewrite it appropriately, and try to summarize a phrase as the event
Extraction example:
Event description
At around 23:12 on December 28. 2023, there was road construction at the above address, and the noise affected their rest.
Event Extraction results
["Noise nuisance", "Nighttime construction"]
Event to extract:
The installation of the elevator at No. 4, Lane 235, *** Road will start as soon as possible, the contract will be signed on August 30, 2023. According to the contract, it will be completed in 210 working days, but it has not started yet. Request: Please verify and investigate, and hope that *** Co., Ltd. will fulfill the contract as soon as possible.

Fig. 2. Instruction-based event extraction for event evolutionary graph construction.

where $Co(v_i, v_j)$ is the co-occurrence value of vertices v_i and v_j. $Source(.)$ is the source event for each vertex, as the vertices are extracted from the events. $\mathcal{N}(.)$ represents the neighbor vertices set. The co-occurrence is calculated as the size of the intersection of the related event sets of the neighbor vertices of v_i and v_j. For example, we construct the undirected event evolutionary graph G and co-occurrence matrix as shown in Fig. 3 to analyze the correlation among the label vertices and the event element vertices. In the figure, the graph contains categories, event elements, and labels. The co-occurrence of the "Noise nuisance" event element and the "Construction management committee" label equals 2, which corresponds to the size of the intersection of their related event sets.

We utilize the proposed co-occurrence matrix to quantify the associations among vertices, where a higher co-occurrence weight indicates a stronger relationship between two vertices. However, the co-occurrence matrix is significantly influenced by vertex degrees and may introduce bias due to the imbalance in the number of different vertex types. For example, some generic terms, such as "inquiry", tend to appear with high frequency, resulting in inflated co-occurrence values on the graph. Consequently, these generic terms may be assigned disproportionate importance, which contradicts common semantic expectations.

To deal with this issue, we further propose a co-occurrence probability matrix to perform normalization, ensuring that the relationships among vertices are influenced not only by frequency but also by vertex type. Specifically, we normalize the co-occurrence value according to the types of vertices, as formulated mathematically in Eq. 2,

$$P(v_i, v_j) = \frac{Co(v_i, v_j)}{\sum Co(v_i, v_l),\ \forall v_l \in V^{type(v_j)}}, \tag{2}$$

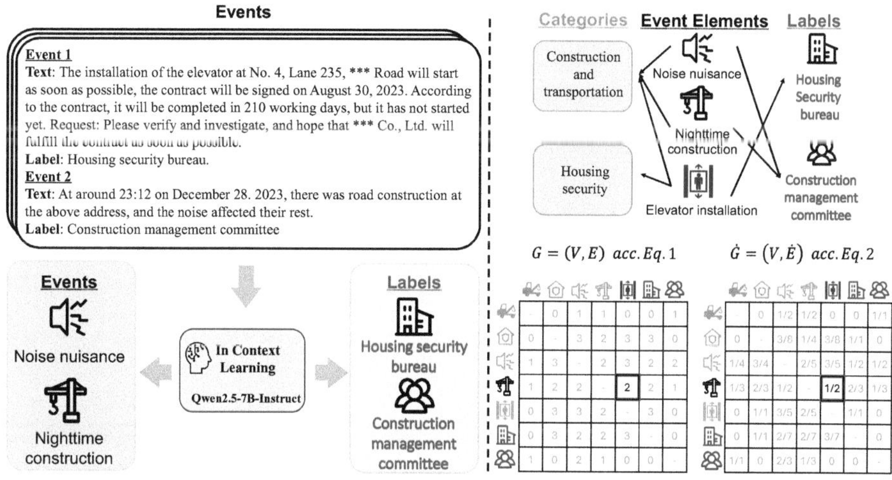

Fig. 3. Event evolutionary graphs.

where $Co(v_i, v_j)$ is the co-occurrence value of vertices v_i and v_j according to Eq. 1. The denominator is the sum of the frequency of the same type of vertices v_j, which is $V^{type(v_j)}$. For instance, in Fig. 3, when calculating the co-occurrence probability of event element vertex "Noise nuisance" and the label vertex "Construction management committee", the co-occurrence: $Co(Noise\ nuisance, Con\text{-}struction\ management\ committee) = 2$, according to Eq. 2. The denominator is the sum of the frequencies of "Noise nuisance" and its neighboring vertices that belong to the same vertex type. Through the above operations, we normalize the edge weights of each vertex to its neighbors under the same vertex type.

3.3 Explainable Classification

After constructing the event evolutionary graph, the classification of incoming events can be inferred based on the graph structure. For a new event $\hat{u}$, we extract its available fields, including the event content $\hat{u}^s$, category $\hat{u}^c$, and label $\hat{u}^l$. Then, we use the instruction learning of the Qwen2.5-7B-Instruct model to extract the related event elements $[v_1^e, v_2^e, ..., v_m^e]$. We concatenate the event elements with the event categories as the query list, as defined in Eq. 3:

$$Q = [v_1^e, v_2^e, ..., v_m^e, v_{m+1}^c, v_{m+2}^c, ..., v_{m+n}^c]. \tag{3}$$

For each event element $v_i^e \in Q$ and each event category $v_i^c \in Q$ in the directed event evolutionary graph $\dot{G}$, we obtain the edge weight from vertex v_i^e and v_i^c to all labels $V^l = [v_1^l, v_2^l, ..., v_k^l] \subset V$ on the directed graph $\dot{G}$, that is, the edge weight from each event vertex $v_i^e \in Q$ to each label vertex $v^l \in V^d$, and the edge weight from each category vertex $v_i^c \in Q$ to each label vertex $v^l \in V^d$. According to the co-occurrence probability matrix, we infer the probability matrix, as shown in Eq. 4:

$$P_{(m+n)\times k} = \begin{bmatrix} P_1 \\ \vdots \\ P_m \\ P_{m+1} \\ \vdots \\ P_{m+n} \end{bmatrix} = \begin{bmatrix} p_{v_1^e v_1^l} & \cdots & p_{v_m^e v_k^l} \\ \vdots & \ddots & \vdots \\ p_{v_m^e v_1^l} & \cdots & p_{v_m^e v_k^l} \\ p_{v_{m+1}^c v_1^l} & \cdots & p_{v_{m+1}^c v_k^l} \\ \vdots & \ddots & \vdots \\ p_{v_{m+n}^c v_1^l} & \cdots & p_{v_{m+n}^e v_k^l} \end{bmatrix}, \tag{4}$$

where the probability value in P is obtained according to the co-occurrence probability matrix in Eq. 4. After that, we calculate the rating score r for each label v^d for event classification. Specifically, taking the average of the co-occurrence probability of $m+n$ query event vertices to the current label v^l as the score of the label, as defined in Eq. 5,

$$r_{k,m+n} = \frac{1}{m+n}\left(\sum_{j=1}^{m} p_{v_j^e v_k^l} + \sum_{h=1}^{n} p_{v_h^c v_k^l}\right). \tag{5}$$

After sorting the rating scores of the labels, we obtain the candidate label results ranked from the highest to lowest relevance to the query list $[v_1^e, ..., v_m^e, v_{m+1}^c, ..., v_{m+n}^c] \subset V^e$, and the method can classify the event based on the rating score $r_{k,m}$. The rating scores are regarded as the explanation of the event classification results. To evaluate the explainability, we construct and visualize the inference process via a bipartite graph with labels list $[v_1^d, v_2^d, \ldots, v_k^d]$, event query list $[v_1^e, ..., v_m^e, v_{m+1}^c, ..., v_{m+n}^c]$ as vertices, and probability matrix $P_{(m+n)\times k}$ as edge weights in Sect. 4.4. We can observe the contribution of the query event vertices to the label score to determine whether the classification result is reliable. Therefore, this method is more explainable than the method of directly using black-box models such as neural networks for classification or retrieval.

4 Experiments

4.1 Dataset Description

We evaluate the effectiveness of the proposed LE^{2}C method for the event classification task on two large-scale datasets, as summarized in Table 1. The first dataset, named Citizen Work Order Dataset, includes 319,172 real work order records received by the government in a specific region from January 1, 2019 to March 29, 2024. The attributes of each record include ID, submission date, text description, category, and processing department. Among them, the ID is the only identifier of the work order. The work order text contains the description of it, mainly the sentences about the appeal, asking for help or work orders. The date shows the submission date, and the category briefly describes the type of the work order, such as "Inquiry".

For the multi-label event classification task, we define the patching of each work order as an individual event requiring classification. The textual content serves as the event content description in the LE^{2}C method. The original category of the work order is treated as the event type. The department assigned to process the work order is regarded as the classification target, that is, the label in our task.

Additionally, we use the public Consumer Financial Report Dataset[2], containing 22,000 consumer reports provided by the Consumer Financial Protection Bureau (CFPB). The attributes of each report include issue, company, and product. Each report in this dataset is labeled with a specific product category, resulting in a total of 75 distinct classification categories. Similarly, we define the process of selecting the corresponding product for each report as a multi-label event classification problem. The issue described in the report serves as the event content. The product category assigned to the report is used as the label for the event classification task.

Table 1. Data information.

Dataset	Events	Classification	Categories	Vertices	Edges
Citizen Event Dataset	41,121	51	250	20,069	474,756
Consumer Financial Report Dataset	22,000	75	381	12,036	318,658

4.2 Baselines

We use 4 baselines to compare the effectiveness of the proposed LE^{2}C for event classification. The baselines and the accomplishment of our methods are introduced as follows:

- **SVM** [6]**.** It is a classical prediction algorithm to separate data into different classes by finding the optimal hyperplane that maximizes the margin between the closest data points of each class.
- **BERT** [1]**.** It uses a transformer-based architecture with attention mechanisms to process text. It is pre-trained using two tasks: Masked Language Modeling (MLM) and Next Sentence Prediction (NSP), which allows BERT to capture deep bidirectional context.
- **Text level GNN** [9]**.** It treats words or sentences in a text as nodes in a graph. It uses graph neural networks to model relationships between these nodes, capturing dependencies between words to make classification.

[2] https://catalog.data.gov/dataset/consumer-complaint-database.

- **GPT-3.5 Turbo-16k** [22]. In-Context Learning (ICL) for classification tasks involves providing 35 examples of labeled data within the prompt, allowing the model to infer patterns and categorize new inputs based on those examples. The model uses the context of the examples to generate a relevant class label for unseen data.
- **LE^{2}C¬Element.** It is the variant that removes all the event vertices on the event evolutionary graph.
- **LE^{2}C¬Categories.** The variant removes all the category vertices on the event evolutionary graph.

Our algorithm is implemented using the Python programming language. The model inference and algorithmic components are built on the PyTorch framework. All experiments are conducted on a server equipped with six NVIDIA RTX A6000 GPUs.

4.3 Effectiveness of Event Classification

Table 2. LE^{2}C compares with baselines and ablation variants.

	City Management Dataset				Financial Dataset			
Baselines	acc@3	acc@5	acc@7	acc@10	acc@3	acc@5	acc@7	acc@10
SVM	0.862	0.938	0.961	0.976	<u>0.826</u>	<u>0.907</u>	0.930	0.947
Text level GNN	0.712	0.740	0.751	0.772	0.698	0.700	0.703	0.732
BERT	**0.947**	**0.966**	**0.975**	<u>0.982</u>	**0.903**	**0.951**	**0.969**	<u>0.981</u>
GPT-3.5 Turbo-16k	0.620	0.655	0.706	0.790	0.643	0.674	0.708	0.748
LE^{2}C¬Categories	0.753	0.812	0.873	0.881	0.771	0.839	0.894	0.927
LE^{2}C¬Element	0.805	0.902	0.922	0.944	0.714	0.801	0.857	0.931
LE^{2}C	<u>0.896</u>	<u>0.953</u>	<u>0.974</u>	**0.984**	0.776	0.863	<u>0.931</u>	**0.982**

Comparison with Baselines. In the event classification task, accuracy is employed as the evaluation metric to assess the effectiveness of assigning events to the correct target labels. *acc*@k is used as an indicator to evaluate the classification results, which indicates the accuracy of the model when predicting k candidate results. For example, *acc*@1 indicates the accuracy of the top-ranked prediction. The main results are shown in Table 2. When using the event evolutionary graph for event classification, the accuracy of the result with the top-3 predictions is 0.896. When the top 10 predictions are considered, the accuracy is 0.984, achieving state-of-the-art prediction results. From the result, we can find that: 1) GPT-3.5 Turbo is exhibiting fairly poor performance, typically because GPT-3.5 Turbo could not fully understand the rule information underlying event classification, duc to context limitations. 2) LE^{2}C outperforms Text

Level GNN because it focuses on global information, whereas Text Level GNN discards distant nodes during graph construction and relies solely on information from neighboring nodes for classification. 3) BERT outperforms SVM because it leverages deep contextualized embeddings to capture complex semantic relationships and global context, while SVM relies on static, hand-crafted features that lack the ability to model intricate language patterns and dependencies.

Ablation Study. We also conduct an ablation study to explore the importance of event element extraction in constructing the event evolutionary graph and its impact on classification results. In Table 2, $\text{LE}^2\text{C}\neg$Element is the event evolutionary graph that removes all the event vertices, and $\text{LE}^2\text{C}\neg$Categories removes all the category vertices in the original graph. As demonstrated in the table, the proposed LE^2C achieves the best results among all the evaluation metrics compared to the variants in both datasets. For the evaluation metrics $acc@\{3, 5, 7, 10\}$, the $\text{LE}^2\text{C}\neg$Categories obtain the worst results, since the graph removes all the categories. This indicates that the pre-defined categories of events are related to the target departments and therefore contribute significantly to the results. $\text{LE}^2\text{C}\neg$Categories does not achieve the performance of LE^2C because the event element vertices extracted from the event content summarize the most related content the event pays attention to. This will significantly assist event classification in the graph.

Efficiency of Event Classification. We also analyze the efficiency of LE^2C and the different baselines in the Citizen Event Dataset. We find that LE^2C has the shortest training time (121.1 s) and the second-highest accuracy with the highest score returned. Although BERT outperforms our proposed LE^2C in terms of accuracy, it requires the longest training time (7492.5 s), which is 62 times longer than that of LE^2C and over 3 times longer than that of the Text-level GNN (2109.7 s). Furthermore, the training time of LE^2C is even shorter than that of SVM, which takes 519.6 s. These results demonstrate the high efficiency of our proposed event classification method.

4.4 Explainability of Event Classification

To further demonstrate the explainability of the event classification procedure of LE^2C on the Citizen Event Dataset, we show the explainable graph of the process of the event classification procedure in Fig. 4.

In the visualization in Fig. 4, the larger the edge weight between the event element and the label, the closer the color of the edge to red, indicating that the event element vertex is more likely to be classified to a target label. These weight edges between the event element and the label with weights are considered the explanation for the classification. For instance, in the example event in Fig. 4, the extracted event elements are "Road construction" and "Noise nuisance".

For each type of vertex, such as the category type, the ticket in Fig. 5 contains two labels, "Road construction" and "Noise nuisance". From the directed graph

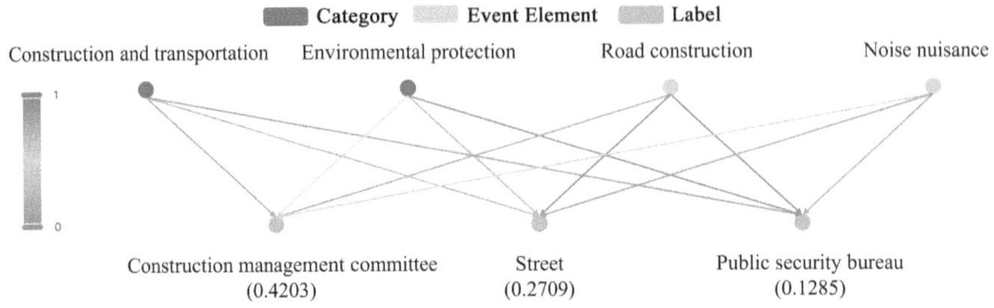

Fig. 4. Case study of explainable event classification.

Event ID: 197
Event content: At around 23:12 on December 28, 2023, there was road construction at the above address, and the noise affected their rest.
Event categories: Help, Construction and transportation type, Environmental protection
Event elements: "Road construction", "Noise disturbing residents"]

Fig. 5. A Random example of the event.

G, the edge weights of the "Road construction" and "Noise nuisance" vertices that point to the label vertices are taken as the edge weights in the reasoning bipartite graph. The edge weights from "Road construction" to "District construction management committee" is 0.944, and the edge weight from "Noise nuisance" to "District construction management committee" is 0.564. Therefore, the reason for classifying this ticket to the "District construction management committee" is "Road construction", which is also in line with common sense and verifies the explainability of LE^2C.

Similarly, the edge weight from each vertex pointing to each department vertex in the bipartite graph are calculated. The algebraic mean of the edge weights from all upper nodes pointing to the "District construction management committee" in the bipartite graph is obtained, and the classification score for the "District construction management committee" is 0.420.

5 Related Work

5.1 Graph-Based Explainable Classification

Knowledge Graphs store various knowledge and perform well in tasks such as classification [13,25], forecasting [7], and recommendation [17]. [13] applies knowledge embedding to vectorize medical texts before constructing a Medical Knowledge Graph. When classification results are ambiguous, a knowledge-based expert system is used to resolve inconsistencies, with results presented through Knowledge Graphs. To provide interpretable results, [25] proposes a binary node embedding technique to classify unseen entities and incorporate semantic information. When Knowledge Graphs characterize event evolution, they form Event Evolutionary Graphs. Integrating LLM-based graph reasoning models with eventuality-centric Knowledge Graphs [10], the Event Ground framework adopts a multi-stage approach to event representation by mapping events extracted from text to subgraphs. Recent works [5,11,35] explore using LLMs for complex event extraction. [35] improves event extraction by using LLMs to correct Small Language Models (SLMs)' prediction errors. However, as citizen events contain limited information, these methods struggle to construct graphs from events. Therefore, we first use LLMs to extract event elements from work order information and then construct a graph based on these extracted elements.

5.2 Multi-label Classification

Multi-label classification is a challenging problem which assigns each instance a set of labels [14]. Traditional methods utilize a unified text representation and predict different labels individually [21,29,31]. Early research [21] uses RNNs to address multi-label classification problems, focusing on the prediction of positive labels. However, this strategy would be ineffective when different labels concentrate on various tokens. Consequently, researches on label-specific learning [20,30,32] has been conducted to focus on labels' feature individually. [32] applies a multi-label attention mechanism and a shallow and wide probabilistic label tree to capture the most relevant part of text to each label in large quantity labels. Additionally, k nearest neighbor mechanism is utilized with multi-label contrastive learning strategy [26] to leverage the rich knowledge directly obtained from the existing training instances. Building on these insights, [15] extended contrastive learning with five specialized loss – functions—Strictly Contrastive Loss, Jaccard Similarity Contrastive Loss, Jaccard Similarity Probability Contrastive Loss, Stepwise Label Contrastive Loss, and Intra-label Contrastive Loss – to more effectively capture inter and intra label dependencies and improve classification performance. More recently, to enhance generalization to rare or compositional label combinations, [3] introduced a data augmentation framework using two novel text generation models to improve the compositional generalization ability of classifiers. Inspired by this, we adopt an in-context learning approach to extract structured event representations from text.

6 Conclusion

In this paper, we use a large language model to extract event elements from event content and combine them with structured attributes to build an interpretable event evolutionary graph. By inferring from the graph, we propose an explainable event classification method, named LE^{2}C. We conduct experiments on a public dataset and a real-world dataset, and achieve the state-of-the-art performance. In future work, we will consider using the geometry information for more accurate classification, and explore more valuable information from event dataset.

Acknowledgment. We would like to express our sincere gratitude to Tao Ji, Libin Cen, and Yicong Li for their insightful discussions and assistance. This work was supported by NSFC grant (No. 62136002 and 62477014), Ministry of Education Research Joint Fund Project (8091B042239), and Fundamental Research Funds for the Central Universities.

References

1. Botezatu, M.M., Bogojeska, J., Giurgiu, I., Voelzer, H., Wiesmann, D.: Multi-view incident ticket clustering for optimal ticket dispatching. In: Proceedings of the 21th ACM SIGKDD International Conference on Knowledge Discovery and Data Mining, pp. 1711–1720 (2015)
2. Bouramdane, A.A.: Enhancing disaster management in smart cities through MCDM-AHP analysis amid 21st century challenges. Inf. Syst. Smart City **3**(1) (2024)
3. Chai, Y., et al.: Compositional generalization for multi-label text classification: a data-augmentation approach. In: Proceedings of the AAAI Conference on Artificial Intelligence, vol. 38, pp. 17727–17735 (2024)
4. Charalabidis, Y.: Policy-related decision making in a smart city context: the polivisu approach. In: The Data Shake: Opportunities and Obstacles for Urban Policy Making, pp. 63–72 (2021)
5. Chen, R., Qin, C., Jiang, W., Choi, D.: Is a large language model a good annotator for event extraction? In: Proceedings of the AAAI Conference on Artificial Intelligence, vol. 38, pp. 17772–17780 (2024)
6. Cortes, C., Vapnik, V.: Support-vector networks. Mach. Learn. **20**(3), 273–297 (1995). https://doi.org/10.1007/BF00994018
7. Deng, S., Rangwala, H., Ning, Y.: Dynamic knowledge graph based multi-event forecasting. In: Proceedings of the 26th ACM SIGKDD International Conference on Knowledge Discovery & Data Mining, pp. 1585–1595 (2020)
8. Hodorog, A., Petri, I., Rezgui, Y.: Machine learning and natural language processing of social media data for event detection in smart cities. Sustain. Cities Soc. **85**, 104026 (2022)
9. Huang, L., Ma, D., Li, S., Zhang, X., Wang, H.: Text level graph neural network for text classification. In: Proceedings of the 2019 Conference on Empirical Methods in Natural Language Processing and the 9th International Joint Conference on Natural Language Processing (EMNLP-IJCNLP), pp. 3444–3450 (2019)
10. Jiayang, C., Qiu, L., Chan, C., Liu, X., Song, Y., Zhang, Z.: Eventground: narrative reasoning by grounding to eventuality-centric knowledge graphs. In: Proceedings of the 2024 Joint International Conference on Computational Linguistics, Language Resources and Evaluation (LREC-COLING 2024), pp. 6622–6642 (2024)
11. Kan, Z., Peng, L., Gao, Y., Liu, N., Qiao, L., Li, D.: LFDE: a lighter, faster and more data-efficient pre-training framework for event extraction. In: Proceedings of the ACM Web Conference 2024, pp. 3964–3975 (2024)
12. Lanchantin, J., Sekhon, A., Qi, Y.: Neural message passing for multi-label classification. In: Brefeld, U., Fromont, E., Hotho, A., Knobbe, A., Maathuis, M., Robardet, C. (eds.) ECML PKDD 2019. LNCS (LNAI), vol. 11907, pp. 138–163. Springer, Cham (2020). https://doi.org/10.1007/978-3-030-46147-8_9

13. Lei, Z., et al.: A novel data-driven robust framework based on machine learning and knowledge graph for disease classification. Futur. Gener. Comput. Syst. **102**, 534–548 (2020)
14. Lin, N., Fu, S., Lin, X., Wang, L.: Multi-label emotion classification based on adversarial multi-task learning. Inf. Process. Manag. **59**(6), 103007 (2022)
15. Lin, N., Qin, G., Wang, G., Zhou, D., Yang, A.: An effective deployment of contrastive learning in multi-label text classification. In: Findings of the Association for Computational Linguistics: ACL 2023, pp. 8730–8744 (2023)
16. Lin, Y., Ji, H., Huang, F., Wu, L.: A joint neural model for information extraction with global features. In: Proceedings of the 58th Annual Meeting of the Association for Computational Linguistics, pp. 7999–8009 (2020)
17. Liu, J.C., Chen, C.T., Lee, C., Huang, S.H.: Evolving knowledge graph representation learning with multiple attention strategies for citation recommendation system. ACM Trans. Intell. Syst. Technol. **15**(2), 1–26 (2024)
18. Lu, Y., et al.: Unified structure generation for universal information extraction. In: Proceedings of the 60th Annual Meeting of the Association for Computational Linguistics (Volume 1: Long Papers), pp. 5755–5772 (2022)
19. Ma, M.D., Wang, X., Kung, P.N., Brantingham, P.J., Peng, N., Wang, W.: Star: boosting low-resource information extraction by structure-to-text data generation with large language models. In: Proceedings of the AAAI Conference on Artificial Intelligence, vol. 38, pp. 18751–18759 (2024)
20. Ma, Q., Yuan, C., Zhou, W., Hu, S.: Label-specific dual graph neural network for multi-label text classification. In: Proceedings of the 59th Annual Meeting of the Association for Computational Linguistics and the 11th International Joint Conference on Natural Language Processing (Volume 1: Long Papers), pp. 3855–3864 (2021)
21. Nam, J., Loza Mencía, E., Kim, H.J., Fürnkranz, J.: Maximizing subset accuracy with recurrent neural networks in multi-label classification. In: Advances in Neural Information Processing Systems, vol. 30 (2017)
22. Ouyang, L., et al.: Training language models to follow instructions with human feedback. Adv. Neural. Inf. Process. Syst. **35**, 27730–27744 (2022)
23. Ozmen, M., Zhang, H., Wang, P., Coates, M.: Multi-relation message passing for multi-label text classification. In: 2022 IEEE International Conference on Acoustics, Speech and Signal Processing (ICASSP), ICASSP 2022, pp. 3583–3587. IEEE (2022)
24. Prabhu, Y., Varma, M.: Fastxml: a fast, accurate and stable tree-classifier for extreme multi-label learning. In: Proceedings of the 20th ACM SIGKDD International Conference on Knowledge Discovery and Data Mining, pp. 263–272 (2014)
25. Steenwinckel, B., Vandewiele, G., Weyns, M., Agozzino, T., Turck, F.D., Ongenae, F.: Ink: knowledge graph embeddings for node classification. Data Min. Knowl. Disc. **36**(2), 620–667 (2022)
26. Su, X., Wang, R., Dai, X.: Contrastive learning-enhanced nearest neighbor mechanism for multi-label text classification. In: Proceedings of the 60th Annual Meeting of the Association for Computational Linguistics (Volume 2: Short Papers), pp. 672–679 (2022)
27. Tsoumakas, G., Katakis, I., Vlahavas, I.: Random k-labelsets for multilabel classification. IEEE Trans. Knowl. Data Eng. **23**(7), 1079–1089 (2010)
28. Wang, R., Kwong, S., Wang, X., Jia, Y.: Active-labelsets ensemble for multi-label classification. Pattern Recogn. (2021)

29. Xiao, Y., Li, Y., Yuan, J., Guo, S., Xiao, Y., Li, Z.: History-based attention in seq2seq model for multi-label text classification. Knowl.-Based Syst. **224**, 107094 (2021)
30. Xu, P., Xiao, L., Liu, B., Lu, S., Jing, L., Yu, J.: Label-specific feature augmentation for long-tailed multi-label text classification. In: Proceedings of the AAAI Conference on Artificial Intelligence, vol. 37, pp. 10602–10610 (2023)
31. Yang, P., Sun, X., Li, W., Ma, S., Wu, W., Wang, H.: SGM: sequence generation model for multi-label classification. In: Proceedings of the 27th International Conference on Computational Linguistics, pp. 3915–3926 (2018)
32. You, R., Zhang, Z., Wang, Z., Dai, S., Mamitsuka, H., Zhu, S.: Attentionxml: label tree-based attention-aware deep model for high-performance extreme multi-label text classification. In: Advances in Neural Information Processing Systems, vol. 32 (2019)
33. Yue, A., Mao, C., Chen, L., Liu, Z., Zhang, C., Li, Z.: Detecting changes in perceptions towards smart city on Chinese social media: a text mining and sentiment analysis. Buildings **12**(8), 1182 (2022)
34. Zhao, W., Kong, S., Bai, J., Fink, D., Gomes, C.: Hot-VAE: learning high-order label correlation for multi-label classification via attention-based variational autoencoders. In: Proceedings of the AAAI Conference on Artificial Intelligence, vol. 35, pp. 15016–15024 (2021)
35. Zhu, M., et al.: Lc4ee: LLMs as good corrector for event extraction. In: Findings of the Association for Computational Linguistics ACL 2024, pp. 12028–12038 (2024)

Discrete Channel Mapping in Knowledge Distillation

Chong Zhang[1], Hongwei Liu[1], Hongzhi Wang[1(✉)], Wei Du[2], Jiaying Wang[2], and Sijia Zheng[2]

[1] Faculty of Computing, Harbin Institute of Technology, Harbin 150001, China
19B903094@stu.hit.edu.cn, {liuhw,wangzh}@hit.edu.cn
[2] State Grid Electric Power Space Technology Co., Ltd., Beijing, China

Abstract. Knowledge distillation methods provide task knowledge from complex teacher networks to compact student networks, aiming to improve the performance of the student network. Usually the knowledge is transferred through channel-wise feature mapping, from both final outputs and intermediate features of the student and teacher networks. When the number of channels in the feature maps of the student and teacher networks differs, previous methods predominantly employ feature transformation to align these channels. We propose a novel approach to discretely align intermediate feature channels by selecting discriminative features from the teacher network feature maps, rather than transforming them. Our new mapping mechanism achieves effectiveness by capturing instance-wise feature importance. Meanwhile, it is structurally simple and computationally cost-effective. Extensive experiments on classification and object detection tasks, across network architectures of similar and dissimilar design styles, clearly demonstrate the effectiveness and strong adaptability of our approach.

Keywords: Knowledge distillation · Model compression · Deep learning

1 Introduction

In recent years, deep convolutional neural networks (DCNN) have exhibited state-of-the-art performance on many tasks in the field of artificial intelligence and big data analysis, ranging from computer vision [1–3] to natural language processing [4,5]. However, the remarkable performance of DCNN comes with the cost of massive memory and computation consumption, making it challenging to apply these models to resource-limited devices such as smartphones or wearable devices. To overcome this hurdle, various schemes, including designing new architectures [6,7], network pruning [8,9], quantization [10], and knowledge distillation [11–13] have been proposed to obtain fast and compact neural networks.

Among these methods, knowledge distillation is a promising way to compress DCNN models. Specifically, It transfers task knowledge from teacher model to

J. Li et al. (Eds.): APWeb-WAIM 2025, LNCS 16115, pp. 373–385, 2026.
https://doi.org/10.1007/978-981-95-5719-6_24

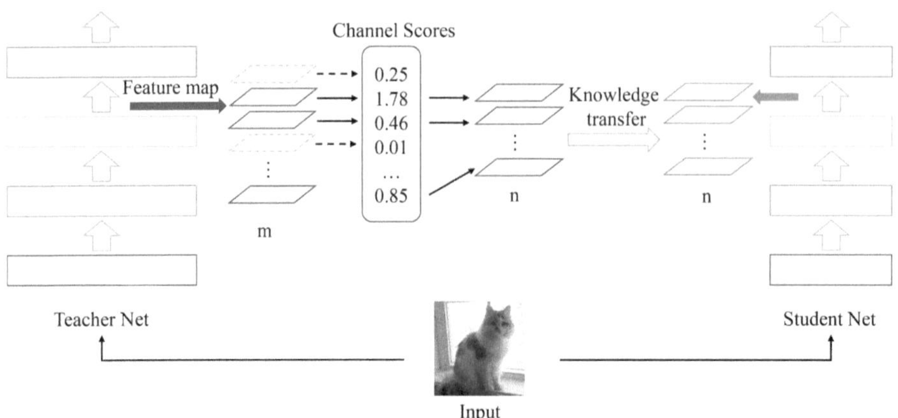

Fig. 1. Concept diagram of the proposed discrete channel mapping method.

student model, independent of the student structure, and could be combined with other compression strategies, making it more flexible and practical. In the first proposed version of knowledge distillation [11], the knowledge is distilled from the logits output by the teacher model. Then, the student model is trained under the supervision of both this knowledge and ground truth labels. Afterwards, especially for student models with more depth, intermediate feature maps have been added to the transferred knowledge to improve distillation effectiveness.

However, since the structure designs of different DCNN models vary, when the student and teacher models output intermediate feature maps with different numbers of channels, a feature transformation is usually needed to align these feature maps. For example, FitNet [12] proposed a regressor to transform the hint through convolution. AT [14] directly flattened the feature maps from 3D tensor to a 2D tensor to get ride of the channel dimension, through a spatial attention mapping function. These transformations make use of all the channel information to form the transferred knowledge. But from another perspective, the information with higher value and that with lower value are combined, which is not easy for an inexperienced student to distinguish and learn.

In this paper, we address the problem of intermediate feature alignment in a new way through discrete channel mapping. Specifically, for the channel transformation of teacher intermediate feature map, we evaluate the importance of each feature channel. Then, we select the important ones for distillation and discard the unimportant ones. As illustrated in Fig. 1, through a scoring mechanism, each feature channel gets an importance score. Subsequently, the same number of channels are selected as that of the student feature map for further learning.

There are two advantages of the proposed method. Firstly, the channels are directly selected from the teacher feature map, without any linear or nonlinear transformation, it is more interpretable and easy to learn for the student model. Secondly, the features are selected instance-wisely, which maximally preserve the characteristics of various inputs instead of making them transformed and assimilated. By doing so, useful knowledge is retained, while useless knowledge is discarded.

The key contributions of this paper are listed as follows:

- We proposed DCM, a discrete channel mapping mechanism, to directly select important channels from the intermediate features produced by the teacher model, so as to improve the quality of the transferred knowledge.
- We proposed an iterative two-stage learning procedure to train the student model with features selected by DCM, to maximize the utilization of intermediate feature maps and the final output digits.
- We empirically demonstrate the effectiveness of our method on knowledge distillation with representative DCNN models on different datasets and tasks.

The subsequent sections of the manuscript are structured as follows. In Sect. 2, we conduct a review of related works. Section 3 discusses the main idea of DCM, its scoring block and the learning procedure. In Sect. 4, we provide a series of experiments and present the experimental results along with analysis. Lastly, the manuscript is concluded in Sect. 5.

2 Related Works

The concept of Knowledge distillation was proposed by Hinton [11], where teacher output logits are used as soft target, combined with hard targets provided by the ground truth labels. Romero *et al.* [12] found that student models that are slim and deep, are usually hard to train even with the supervision from the teacher model, therefore they utilized one intermediate feature map to provide intermediate supervision. Following FitNet, many methods utilize one-stage intermediate feature information to transfer knowledge. RKD [15] used relations between outputs from multiply samples to guide the learning from the perspective of the linguistic structuralism. PKT [16] proposed a probabilistic knowledge transfer to transfer the teacher's probabilistic distribution knowledge to the student by modeling the data relationships via probability distributions.

Considering popular DCNN models are usually composed of multiple feature extracting stages, methods using multi-stage information are also studied. AT [14] transfer knowledge from multiple layer by extracting 3D feature maps into 2D attention maps. FSP [17] defined the flow of the solution procedure between different feature maps as FSP matrices to work as the soft target, but usually the channel number between student and teacher feature maps should be the same, since it forms the size of the FSP matrix. Through the use of input relationship, SP [18] transferred knowledge by preserving pairwise activation similarities within each mini-batch. KR [13] proposed a review mechanism to utilize the transferred knowledge in a cross stage way. In each stage, the student model not only gets knowledge from the current stage of the teacher model but also from previous stages. However, in order to handle feature maps from different stages with varying sizes, a substantial amount of feature transformation needs to be carried out prior to training.

All prior methods leveraging intermediate feature maps have to apply nonlinear transformation to the features. In this paper, we achieve this transformation through an effective but discrete way.

3 Methodology

The main concept of our discrete channel mapping is to select important channels from the feature maps of teacher model and discard the unimportant ones before transferring knowledge to the student model. In this section, we first formalize the discrete channel mapping mechanism. Then we introduce the specific way to select channels and the two-stage distillation process of our proposed method.

3.1 Proposed Discrete Channel Mapping

Deep Convolutional Neural Network (DCNN) models typically consist of multiple stages. The feature maps generated in higher stages usually have more channels and lower resolution. In the realm of knowledge distillation, it is generally necessary to align the intermediate feature maps originating from the same stage of the student and teacher models to keep the same feature resolution. But the channel dimension of teacher feature map $F_t \in R^{C_t \times H \times W}$ usually differs from that of the corresponding student feature map $F_s \in R^{C_s \times H \times W}$. In this scenario, we need to apply a mapping function $\mathcal{F}$ to the teacher feature map to align its dimension with that of the student feature map.

$$\mathcal{F} : R^{C_t \times H \times W} \rightarrow R^{C_s \times H \times W} \tag{1}$$

To achieve this, we present a scoring block inspired by squeeze-and-excitation net [24]. The main function of this block is illustrated in Fig. 1. This block is inserted to the end of each structural stage of the teacher net, it generates a score for each channel of the teacher feature maps ahead of knowledge distillation. This score can be used as an indication of the importance of channels, and the top C_s channels are selected for knowledge transfer. The implicit assumption that we make in this section is that the number of features channels of the teacher model C_t is bigger than that of the student model C_S.

The scoring block has two working phases, as shown in Fig. 2. In the pretraining of the teacher network, the scoring block works as an feature enhancer, the calculated channel scores are multiplied to the corresponding feature maps. In this way, the feature maps with more information are enhanced by higher scores and the ones with less information are suppressed by lower scores. There is no discrete channel choosing in this phase, therefore the gradients could be normally propagated in the back-propagation. When the scoring block works in the distillation, the multiply operation is replaced with a select operation, the channels with top C_s scores are for distillation. Figure 2(c) depicts the specific network structure of the scoring block. For the input feature map $F_t \in R^{C_t \times H \times W}$,

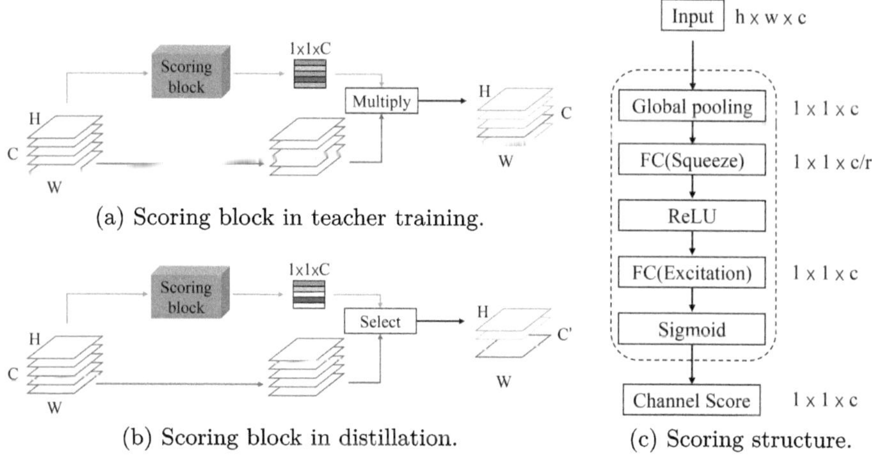

(a) Scoring block in teacher training.

(b) Scoring block in distillation.

(c) Scoring structure.

Fig. 2. Scoring block working in different phases of the knowledge distillation process and the specific schema of scoring block structure.

to mitigate the influence of spatial dimension, we use the global average pooling to generate channel-wise statistic $g \in R^{C_t}$, the c-th element of z could be represented as:

$$g_c = \frac{1}{H \times W} \sum_{i=1}^{H} \sum_{j=1}^{W} F_{tc}(i, j) \tag{2}$$

Then a bottleneck with two fully connected (FC) layers, nonlinear function ReLU with a sigmoid activation is used o learn the interaction between different channels, then the final scores of different channels are obtained:

$$S = \sigma(W_2 \delta(W_1 g)) \tag{3}$$

where σ stands for the sigmoid activation, δ stands for ReLU function, and $W_1 \in \frac{C_t}{r} \times C_t$ and $W_2 \in C_t \times \frac{C_t}{r}$ represent the fully connected layers, with the dimension reduction ratio r.

In the teacher training, the output of scoring block F_t^{score} is the channel-wise multiplication between teacher feature map and score S:

$$F_t^{score} = S_c \cdot F_{tc} \tag{4}$$

while in the distillation, the output of scoring block F_t^{select} is selected from the teacher feature map F_t according to score S and the choice number of C_s:

$$F_t^{select} = select(F_t, S, C_s) \tag{5}$$

Noting that the structure of scoring block is not restricted to the squeeze-and-excitation block, more sophisticated or simple scoring strategies for the channels could be employed here as well.

3.2 Iterative Two-Stage Learning Procedure

To fully utilize the intermediate information brought by discrete channel mapping, the final prediction from the teacher model and the ground truth of the training dataset, we adopt an iterative two-stage training procedure. In this procedure, we consider intermediate feature alignment separately, the final output of student and teacher model are considered together with the ground truth, as done in the tradition knowledge distillation.

For the intermediate feature alignment, the loss are calculated between student feature maps and the output of the discrete channel mapping from teacher feature maps:

$$L_{DCM} = \sum_{i \in I} D(F_c^i, F_t^{selecti}) \tag{6}$$

where I is the total number of stages used for discrete channel mapping and feature alignment, D is the distance function that measures the gap between the student and teacher features.

For the final output of student and teacher network a_s and a_t, they are firstly softened by a temperature parameter T before softmax:

$$P_t = softmax(\frac{a_t}{T}), P_s = softmax(\frac{a_s}{T}) \tag{7}$$

then the soft target are combined with the hard target, the distance between student output and the ground truth y_{true}, by a balancing parameter α:

$$L_{KD} = \alpha T^2 D(P_t, P_s) + D(P_s, y_{ture}) \tag{8}$$

In our learning procedure, we optimize these two objectives in an iterative way, details could be seen in Algorithm 1. In each training iteration, the features are selected from the teacher model from each intermediate layer (Line 2). Then the student network is firstly trained to minimize Eq. (6) only considering intermediate feature alignment (Line 3), then it is trained to minimize Eq. (8) to rectify its final output (line 4).

Algorithm 1. Iterative Two-stage Distillation Training

Input: Teacher network W_t, student network W_s, input images x and labels y
Output: Trained student Network W_s^*
1: **for** $e = 1, ..., E_{max}$ **do**
2: $F_t^{selecti} \leftarrow$ discrete channel mapping from W_t for $i \in I$
3: $W_s \leftarrow \arg\min_{W_s} L_{DCM}(W_s, F_t^{selecti})$
4: $W_s \leftarrow \arg\min_{W_s} L_{KD}(W_s, W_t)$
5: **end for**
6: Output W_s^*

4 Experiments

We conduct various experiments to evaluate the proposed method. In the classification experiments, we applied our method on varying architecture and datasets, transferring knowledge between similar and distinct network architectures. We also apply our method to the object detection task. And the results indicate that our method shows comparable or improved ability, compared to other state-of-the-art methods.

4.1 Classification

Implementation Details. We evaluated our method on many representative convolutional deep networks, including VGG-16 [19], ResNet [1], GoogLeNet [2], MobileNetV2 [7], WideResNet [20], and ShuffleNetV1 [21]. The details of these networks are summarized in Table 1. Since our method focus on channel mapping between different number of feature channels, we build our own slim student networks by shrinking the channel numbers of the teacher network when the teacher and student having architectures of the same style. This makes sense since slim and deep networks usually has fewer parameters with more potential then shallow ones, but they are hard to train from scratch which makes them suitable for evaluating a knowledge distillation method. We use two datasets in different scales. CIFAR-10 [22] consists of 50K 32×32 training images and 10K test images belong to 10 classes. Tiny-ImageNet [23] is composed of 100K 64×64 training images and 10K test images with 200 semantic classes.

In the training of each student model, the total epoch is set to be 300. The learning rate is set to be 0.1 and decreased by a factor of 10 at the 150th and 225th epochs. The batch size is 128 for all models. All the training is optimized using SGD with momentum of 0.9 and weight decay of 5×10^{-4}. All experiments are conducted on a NVIDIA GeForce RTX 3090 GPU.

Table 1. Network characteristics

Networks	Params (MB)	Flops($\times 10^6$)	Networks	Params (MB)	Flops($\times 10^6$)
VGG-16 [19]	14.99	313.46	Slim-VGG-16	3.80	113.54
ResNet56 [11]	0.85	126.55	Slim-ResNet56	0.33	50.47
MobileNetV2 [7]	2.24	27.84	Slim-MobileNetV2	0.71	15.65
GoogLeNet [2]	6.27	517.14	Slim-GoogLeNet	2.14	248.44
WRN40-2 [20]	2.24	328.87	WRN40-1	0.56	84.44
ResNet34 [2]	21.20	4612.53	slim-ResNet34	9.38	1566.39

Results on CIFAR-10. Firstly, we investigate the effectiveness of the proposed method. We compare the proposed method with traditional knowledge distillation using logits only, methods using single layer information, multi-layer information, and the multi-to-one method KR, to see how they improve the performance of DCNN student models. For the architecture of slim student models, we remove 40% to 50% channels from the teacher model's every convolutional layer, while preserving the first and last convolutional layers for sufficient feature extraction and smooth connection to the classifier.

As for intermediate feature alignment, we choose feature output from three intermediate layers, at the end of three structural stages, where the feature map sizes are halved. With input size of 32×32, we want these intermediate features with size of 16×16, 8×8 and 4×4. The features with the same resolution from student and teacher models are mapped through discrete channel mapping and aligned with the metric of MSE (mean-square error) between them. Table 2 summarizes the results on CIFAR-10 with the teacher and student having architectures of the same style. Our method outperforms other methods in most cases.

We further conduct experiments on the scenario where the student and teacher have different architectural styles. There's no requirement to adjust the teacher model's architecture to get the student model's architecture because the output channels of different models inherently differ. Therefore, we adopt the full version of the DCNN models as the student model. The results are summarized in Table 3. In these cases, the effectiveness of some methods has declined. Sometimes, they perform even inferior to student models trained from scratch. In contrast, our method outperforms all comparable methods across all architectures, which indicates the adaptability and generalization ability of our method.

Table 2. CIFAR-10 distillation between architectures of the same style

Methods	Teacher	VGG-16	ResNet56	GoogLeNet	WRN40-2	MobileNetV2
	Acc	93.90	93.12	94.08	93.89	91.90
	Student	Slim-VGG-16	Slim-ResNet56	Slim-GoogLeNet	WRN40-1	Slim-MobileNetV2
	Acc	92.55	91.36	93.50	92.37	91.24
KD [11]		92.74	91.52	93.55	92.21	90.98
FitNet [12]		92.36	91.54	93.48	92.40	91.05
AT [14]		92.59	92.44	**94.02**	93.06	91.36
FSP [17]		92.62	92.33	93.61	92.03	91.30
Review [13]		92.65	92.56	93.72	**92.68**	91.40
DCM		**93.04**	**92.72**	93.92	92.63	**91.41**

Results on Tiny-ImageNet. CIFAR-10 is a relatively small dataset with only ten categories. To verify the scalability and generalization ability of our method, we conduct experiments on Tiny-ImageNet dataset, which has more categories and the input images have a higher resolution. For the DCNN model, we choose

Table 3. CIFAR-10 distillation between architectures with different styles.

Methods	Teacher	VGG-16	GoogLeNet	VGG-16	WRN40-2
	Acc	93.90	94.08	93.90	93.89
	Student	ShuffleNetV1	ShuffleNetV1	MobileNetV2	MobileNetV2
	Acc	86.85	86.85	91.90	91.90
KD [11]		87.23	87.62	92.07	92.56
FitNet [12]		87.08	87.23	92.11	92.64
AT [14]		86.12	86.13	88.83	89.35
FSP [17]		87.92	87.73	91.32	91.46
DCM		**88.26**	**88.16**	**92.70**	**92.61**

ResNet34 for classification. As before, we set a slim version of ResNet34 as the student network. As we can see from Table 4, on the task requiring more detailed feature representation and knowledge transfer, our method consistently outperforms others.

Table 4. ResNet34 on Tiny-ImageNet

Methods	Teacher	Student	KD [11]	FitNet [12]	AT [14]	FSP [17]	Review [13]	DCM
Acc (%)	58.38	56.85	57.48	57.62	57.72	57.37	57.80	**57.98**

4.2 Object Detection

Table 5. Model performance on PASCAL VOC with 416 × 416 resolution

Models	Params (MB)	Flops ($\times 10^9$)	MAP
Teacher	19.82	9.52	76.80
Student	9.12	5.78	75.23
KD [11]	9.12	5.78	75.44
FitNet [12]	9.12	5.78	75.28
AT [14]	9.12	5.78	75.55
DCM	9.12	5.78	75.68

We further apply the proposed method on another object detection task on PASCAL VOC 2007 dataset. On this task, we use the famous detection model YOLOv2 [3] as the teacher and its slim version as the student, following the previous setting in Sect. 4.1. YOLOv2 is a famous CNN-based object detection framework that casts object detection tasks as a unified regression problem from image pixels to spatially separated bounding boxes and associated class probabilities. PASCAL VOC 2007 dataset is a well-known dataset for object detection, classification, and segmentation tasks, containing 20 different object classes, such as person, car, dog, and bird. Like the procedure for the classification task, we distill between the student and teacher's backbone output and intermediate features, on the CNN backbone of YOLOv2, which is composed of 19 convolutional layers. As shown in Table 5, the performance of the student model is obviously lower than that of the teacher model. With the help of different knowledge distillation methods, it is notably improved. Among these methods, DCM still gets better performance than others.

4.3 Abalation Study

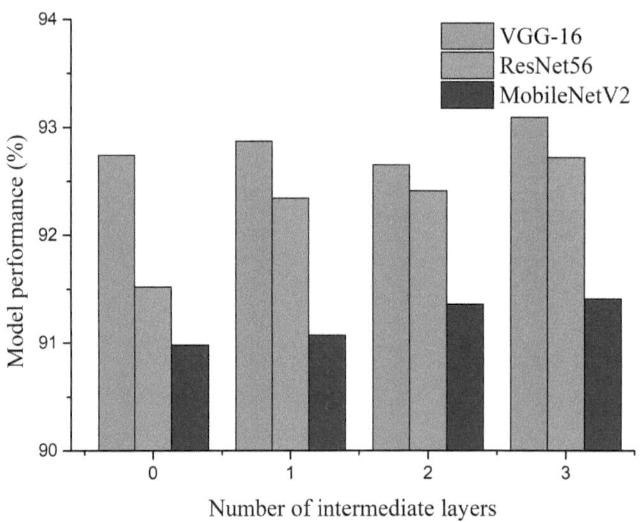

Fig. 3. DCM performance using different number of intermediate layers.

Number of Intermediate Layers. The experiments above show that selecting feature channels from the teacher network through discrete channel mapping could enhance the transferred information with higher value. However, on the other hand, discarding unimportant channels may also lead to information loss. Therefore, we have to determine whether it is beneficial to use more layers in the channel mapping process.

To verify the influence of the number of mapping layers, we conducted experiments on three different DCNN models on CIFAR-10, with the number of intermediate layers ranging from 0 to 3. Using 0 layers means that only the final digits output by the teacher are utilized in distillation, which is equivalent to the vanilla KD method. From the results shown in Fig. 3, we find that in general, using more intermediate layers will lead to greater performance improvement.

The Way to Select Channels. The channel selection of DCM relies on its internal channel scoring module, which needs to be embedded in the teacher network and involved in pre-training rather than being a simple plug-and-play component. This approach has two issues: first, it requires adjusting the teacher model's structure and re-conducting pre-training before knowledge distillation, complicating operations and consuming resources; second, if the teacher model's structure cannot be modified, DCM cannot be used to distill the student model.

To address these issues, we explore alternative efficient methods to directly evaluate the importance of intermediate feature channels in the teacher model, enabling effective channel selection for knowledge distillation. Specifically, we compare matrix rank and L2-norm based channel selection methods against DCM's channel scoring module.

Table 6. Effects of different channel selection methods

Accuracy	Teacher	Student	Rank	Le-norm	**DCM**
Top-1	VGG16(93.90)	slimVGG16(92.55)	36.61	37.76	**93.04**
Top-1	VGG16(93.90)	MobileNetV2(91.90)	42.52	44.38	**92.70**

Experimental results in Table 6 show that using matrix rank or L2-norm for intermediate feature channel selection in knowledge distillation leads to significant accuracy degradation in student models rather than performance improvement. This indicates that not all channel importance methods are suitable for guiding distillation. Although DCM's channel selection module is complex to implement, its performance remains irreplaceable.

Distillation Training Procedure. To verify the effectiveness of our proposed two-stage iterative training procedure, we compare this training procedure with direct training, in which intermediate feature alignment and digits supervision are jointly considered. Figure 4 depicts the variation of the training loss with respect to the number of training iterations. Relatively speaking, the iterative two-stage training procedure leads to a rapid decline in the training loss at the early stage of training, and the loss ends up at a lower point at the end of the training.

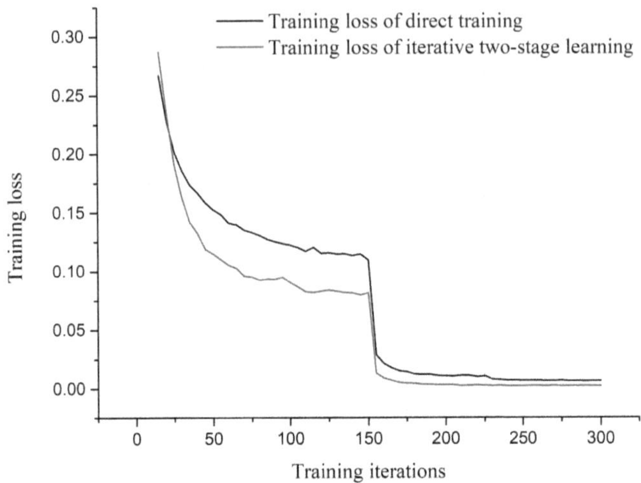

Fig. 4. Training loss curves using different training procedure.

5 Conclusion

This paper is focused on the field of knowledge distillation, and we have studied the feature mapping problem in knowledge distillation from a new perspective of discrete channel mapping. Specifically, we proposed a mapping mechanism based on a channel scoring block and an iterative two-stage training procedure for the distillation training. Extensive experiments demonstrate the effectiveness of discrete channel mapping, which achieve state-of-the-art performance on multiple computer vision tasks and various datasets. However, the way to select important feature channels is not restricted to the proposed method, and we will also seek other efficient ways to achieve this goal.

Acknowledgments. This work is supported by National Natural Science Foundation of China (NSFC) (62232005, 62202126); the National Key Research and Development Program of China (2021YFB3300502).

Disclosure of Interests. The authors have no competing interests to declare that are relevant to the content of this article.

References

1. He, K., Zhang, X., Ren, S., Sun, J.: Deep residual learning for image recognition. arXiv preprint arXiv:1512.03385 (2015)
2. Szegedy, C., et al.: Going deeper with convolutions. In: Proceedings of the IEEE Conference on Computer Vision and Pattern Recognition, pp. 1–9 (2015)
3. Redmon, J., Farhadi, A.: YOLO9000: better, faster, stronger. In: CVPR 2017, pp. 6517–6525 (2017)

4. Antol, S., et al.: VQA: visual question answering. In: Proceedings of the IEEE International Conference on Computer Vision, pp. 2425–2433 (2015)
5. Noh, H., Seo, P.H., Han, B.: Image question answering using convolutional neural network with dynamic parameter prediction. arXiv preprint arXiv:1511.05756 (2015)
6. Cui, J., Chen, P., Li, R., Liu, S., Shen, X., Jia, J.: Fast and practical neural architecture search. In: ICCV (2019)
7. Sandler, M., Howard, A.G., Zhu, M., Zhmoginov, A., Chen, L.-C.: Mobilenetv 2: inverted residuals and linear bottlenecks. In: CVPR (2018)
8. Frankle, J., Carbin, M.: The lottery ticket hypothesis: finding sparse, trainable neural networks. In: ICLR (2019)
9. Liu, Z., Sun, M., Zhou, T., Huang, G., Darrell, T.: Rethinking the value of network pruning. In: ICLR (2019)
10. Jacob, B., et al.: Quantization and training of neural networks for efficient integer-arithmetic-only inference. In: CVPR (2018)
11. Hinton, G.E., Vinyals, O., Dean, J.: Distilling the knowledge in a neural network. CoRR, abs/1503.02531 (2015)
12. Romero, A., Ballas, N., Kahou, S.E., Chassang, A., Gatta, C., Bengio, Y.: Fitnets: hints for thin deep nets. In: Bengio, Y., LeCun, Y. (eds.) ICLR (2015)
13. Chen, P., Liu, S., Zhao, H., Jia, J.: Distilling knowledge via knowledge review. In: CVPR 2021, pp. 5008–5017 (2021)
14. Zagoruyko, S., Komodakis, N.: Paying more attention to attention: improving the performance of convolutional neural networks via attention transfer. In: ICLR (2017)
15. Park, W., Kim, D., Lu, Y., Cho, M.: Relational knowledge distillation. In: CVPR, pp. 3967–3976 (2019)
16. Passalis, N., Tefas, A.: Probabilistic knowledge transfer for deep representation learning. CoRR, abs/1803.10837 (2018)
17. Yim, J., Joo, D., Bae, J.-H., Kim, J.: A gift from knowledge distillation: fast optimization, network minimization and transfer learning. In: CVPR (2017)
18. Tung, F., Mori, G.: Similarity-preserving knowledge distillation. In: ICCV (2019)
19. Simonyan, K., Zisserman, A.: Very deep convolutional networks for large-scale image recognition. In: ICLR (2015)
20. Zagoruyko, S., Komodakis, N.: Wide residual networks. In: BMVC (2016)
21. Zhang, X., Zhou, X., Lin, M., Sun, J.: Shufflenet: an extremely efficient convolutional neural network for mobile devices. In: CVPR (2018)
22. Krizhevsky, A., Hinton, G.: Learning multiple layers of features from tiny images. Technical report, Citeseer (2009). https://www.cs.toronto.edu/~kriz/learning-features-2009-TR.pdf, April 2022
23. Le, Y., Yang, X.: Tiny imagenet visual recognition challenge. CS 231N **7**(7), 3 (2015)
24. Jie, H., Shen, L., Sun, G.: Squeeze-and-excitation networks. In: CVPR, pp. 7132–7141 (2018)

Uncertainty-Aware Semantic Decoding for LLM-Based Sequential Recommendation

Chenke Yin, Fan Li, Jia Wang(✉), Dongxiao Hu, Haichao Zhang, Chong Zhang, and Yang Xiang

Xi'an Jiaotong-Liverpool University, Suzhou, China
Jia.Wang02@xjtlu.edu.cn

Abstract. Large language models have been widely applied to sequential recommendation tasks, yet during inference, they continue to rely on decoding strategies developed for natural language processing. This creates a mismatch between text-generation objectives and recommendation next item selection objectives. This paper addresses this limitation by proposing an Uncertainty-aware Semantic Decoding (USD) framework that combines logit-based clustering with adaptive scoring to improve next-item predictions. Our approach clusters items with similar logit vectors into semantic equivalence groups, then redistributes probability mass within these clusters and computes entropy across them to control item scoring and sampling temperature during recommendation inference. Experiments on Amazon Product datasets (six domains) gains of 18.5% in HR@3, 11.9% in NDCG@3, and 10.8% in MRR@3 compared to state-of-the-art baselines. Hyperparameter analysis confirms the optimal parameters among various settings, and experiments on H&M, and Netflix datasets indicate that the framework can adapt to differing recommendation domains. The experimental results confirm that integrating semantic clustering and uncertainty assessment yields more reliable and accurate recommendations.

Keywords: LLM for data management · Uncertain data · Information retrieval

1 Introduction

Large Language Models (LLMs) have proven valuable for recommendation systems by enhancing personalized suggestion generation across diverse domains [10,25]. Their strong natural language capabilities support efficient handling of multi-modal data like text descriptions, visual features, and categorical attributes. LLMs unify various information sources under one framework, enabling flexible, high-quality recommendations that adapt to complex user preferences [11]. Figure 1 shows how these models [26] process user histories and item

C. Yin and F. Li—These authors contributed equally to this work.

J. Li et al. (Eds.): APWeb-WAIM 2025, LNCS 16115, pp. 386–401, 2026.
https://doi.org/10.1007/978-981-95-5719-6_25

metadata in an autoregressive manner. However, current decoding strategies, inherited from natural language generation, can be inefficient for recommendation tasks that only require a single item identifier [43]. Beam search often entails unnecessary overhead, while greedy decoding may miss high-probability alternatives [11]. This mismatch stems from framing item recommendations like text generation instead of recognizing unique structural requirements. Thus, specialized decoding methods are needed to address these domain-specific challenges.

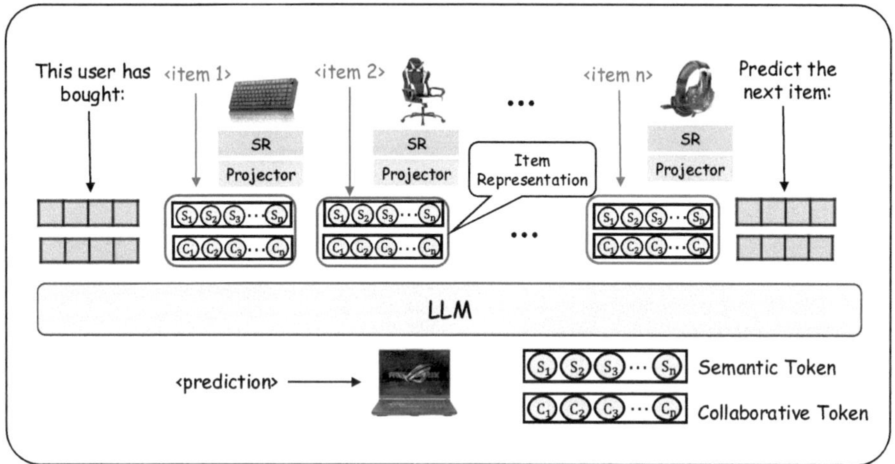

Fig. 1. LLM-Based Sequential Recommendation Framework, which integrates sequential recommender (SR) and projector (e.g., a trainable MLP). These embeddings jointly form a collaborative token prompt (e.g., "This user has bought: [item1], [item2], ... [item$_n$]. Predict the next item this user will buy.").

This limitation leads us to examine recommendation tasks through the lens of semantic uncertainty, drawing inspiration from recent advances in natural language generation [23] and recent work on uncertainty in recommender systems [42,51]. In sequential recommendation, we observe that user preferences often exhibit semantic equivalence patterns—different items or sequences can satisfy identical user needs despite having distinct representations. For instance, a user seeking wireless headphones might be equally satisfied with several similar products across different brands. This phenomenon parallels semantic equivalence in natural language, where different expressions can convey identical meanings. Standard decoding methods like beam search focus exclusively on token-level probabilities without considering these semantic relationships, potentially overestimating uncertainty when probability mass is distributed across semantically equivalent items. By explicitly modeling semantic uncertainty in user preferences, we can develop more effective decoding strategies that aggregate probabilities within semantic equivalence classes, leading to more accurate preference estimation and better recommendations.

Based on these insights, we propose an **U**ncertainty-aware **S**emantic **D**ecoding (**USD**) framework specifically designed for LLM-based sequential recommendation. Our framework consists of two key components: (1) A logit-based semantic clustering module that identifies semantically equivalent item groups by analyzing the similarity of their probability distributions in the user's preference space, significantly reducing redundant computations during decoding. (2) A semantic uncertainty estimation component that extends entropy calculation to capture uncertainty over preference patterns rather than individual tokens. By computing entropy over the meaning-distribution rather than token sequences, our approach provides a more accurate measure of recommendation uncertainty. The entire framework operates with minimal computational overhead, as semantic clustering is performed efficiently on a small set of candidate items, and uncertainty estimation is integrated seamlessly into the decoding process. Importantly, our method maintains compatibility with different LLM architectures and can be easily extended to handle multi-modal inputs through appropriate encoder designs.

The main contributions of this work are summarized as follows:

- We identify fundamental limitations in conventional decoding strategies for LLM-based recommendation systems and introduce the Uncertainty-aware Semantic Decoding (USD) framework to address the misalignment between standard text generation approaches and recommendation requirements.
- We develop a logit-based semantic clustering algorithm that identifies preference equivalence patterns among candidate items and design an uncertainty-guided scoring mechanism that quantifies semantic entropy over clustered items rather than individual tokens.
- Extensive experiments on Amazon Product, H&M, and Netflix datasets demonstrate that our method significantly outperforms state-of-the-art baselines, achieving improvements of 18.5% in HR@3, 11.9% in NDCG@3, and 10.8% in MRR@3.

2 Related Work

2.1 LLM for Recommendation

Recent research shows that there is increasing interest in LLM4Rec. Several studies have examined the use of LLMs to predict user feedback through in-context learning [7] and fine-tuning [1]. These methods usually instruct LLMs to produce predictions directly without showing their intermediate reasoning steps, which limits the use of LLMs' reasoning ability. Additionally, recent work has used the reasoning capabilities of LLMs for recommendation tasks with prompting strategies such as chain-of-thought [46] and self-reflection [45]. Despite these efforts, they often prioritize improving LLM performance through training enhancements, overlooking a crucial aspect: the detailed examination of the models' recommendation outputs and the considerations for the decoding phase.

2.2 LLM Uncertainty Quantification

Uncertainty quantification (UQ) in Large Language Models (LLMs) is crucial for addressing model confidence and reliability [4,9]. Token-level methods derive uncertainty from the probability distribution over generated tokens, often using entropy metrics to estimate response confidence [14,36]. Such approaches detect errors and improve interpretability. Another line of research, self-verbalized UQ, lets LLMs articulate their confidence, showing alignment with actual correctness [27,31]. Additionally, semantic similarity UQ checks multiple outputs for contradictions or hallucinations [8,37,53], while mechanistic interpretability examines neuron-level decisions to illuminate model reasoning [6,22,39,41].

2.3 LLM Decoding Generation

LLMs employ varied decoding strategies to balance fluency, coherence, and factual soundness. A common approach is Maximum a Posteriori (MAP) decoding, selecting the most probable sequence [35] but risking repetitive outputs. Self-refinement mechanisms iteratively revise generated text for improved coherence [24,29], while Minimum Bayes Risk (MBR) decoding focuses on minimizing expected risk [2]. Recent work also explores compute-efficient solutions to lower inference cost [50]. Another key line is guided decoding, relying on external knowledge to steer outputs toward factual correctness [5,12]. Meta-search and ensemble-based methods further enhance diversity and accuracy by merging multiple generation paths [13,40].

3 Problem Formulation

In this section, we establish the mathematical foundations for our semantic uncertainty-based decoding approach to LLM-powered sequential recommendation systems.

Sequential Recommendation. Let $\mathcal{U}$ denote the set of users and $\mathcal{I}$ the set of items. For each user $u \in \mathcal{U}$, their historical interaction sequence is denoted as $\mathcal{H}_u = \langle i_1, i_2, \ldots, i_n \rangle$, where each $i_j \in \mathcal{I}$ represents an interacted item. Given $\mathcal{H}_u$, the sequential recommendation task aims to predict the next item i_{n+1} that the user is likely to interact with from $\mathcal{I} \setminus \mathcal{H}_u$, which represents the set of items the user has not yet interacted with.

LLM-Based Decoding for Recommendation. In LLM-based sequential recommendation, an item i is represented through its contextual information $\mathcal{M}_i$ (e.g., title, category) and the prediction process uses an autoregressive formulation:

$$p_\theta(i_{n+1}|\mathcal{H}_u) = \prod_{t=1}^{T} p_\theta(y_t|y_{<t}, \mathcal{H}_u) \tag{1}$$

where p_θ is the LLM with parameters θ, and y_t represents tokens in the output sequence. Traditional LLM approaches employ beam search decoding, which maintains multiple hypotheses throughout the generation process:

$$g(y|\mathcal{H}_u; p_\theta, \phi) \in \mathcal{P}(\mathcal{Y}) \tag{2}$$

where g represents the generation algorithm with parameters ϕ, and $\mathcal{P}(\mathcal{Y})$ is the space of probability distributions over possible outputs.

Semantic Equivalence in Item Space. We formalize this through a semantic equivalence relation $E(s, s')$ between items:

$$E(s, s') = \mathbb{I}[\mathrm{Sim}(s, s') > \tau] \tag{3}$$

where $\mathrm{Sim}(s, s')$ measures similarity between items based on their logit vectors, and τ is a threshold parameter. This relation partitions the item space into semantic clusters $C = \{c_1, c_2, ..., c_m\}$, where each cluster contains items that are functionally equivalent in satisfying specific user preferences.

4 Methodology

In this section, we introduce our Uncertainty-aware Semantic Decoding (USD) framework, whose aim is to bridge the gap between standard text-generation-oriented decoding methods and the unique needs of sequential recommendation. We begin with an overview of the main components and then detail each submodule: (i) **Logit-based Semantic Clustering** defines how candidate items form equivalence groups; (ii) **Semantic Uncertainty Estimation** quantifies user preference ambiguity by measuring entropy over these clusters; (iii) **Uncertainty-guided Adaptive Decoding** integrates semantic entropy information to balance exploration and exploitation. As depicted in Fig. 2, our framework is designed to cluster candidate items based on their logit similarities, estimate uncertainty across these clusters, and then provide final item suggestions guided by an adaptive scoring mechanism.

4.1 Logit-Based Semantic Clustering

Standard decoding processes seldom differentiate between closely related items that satisfy an identical user need. To alleviate such redundancy, we introduce a similarity measure:

$$\mathrm{Sim}(s, s') = \frac{\mathbf{l}_s \cdot \mathbf{l}_{s'}}{\|\mathbf{l}_s\| \, \|\mathbf{l}_{s'}\|}. \tag{4}$$

In this equation, s and s' are two candidate items drawn from the model's output space, $\mathbf{l}_s$ and $\mathbf{l}_{s'}$ denote their respective logit representations (i.e., pre-softmax activations) conditioned on the user history $\mathcal{H}_u$, and $\|\mathbf{l}_s\|$ represents the Euclidean norm of $\mathbf{l}_s$. The dot product $\mathbf{l}_s \cdot \mathbf{l}_{s'}$ therefore captures alignment in their

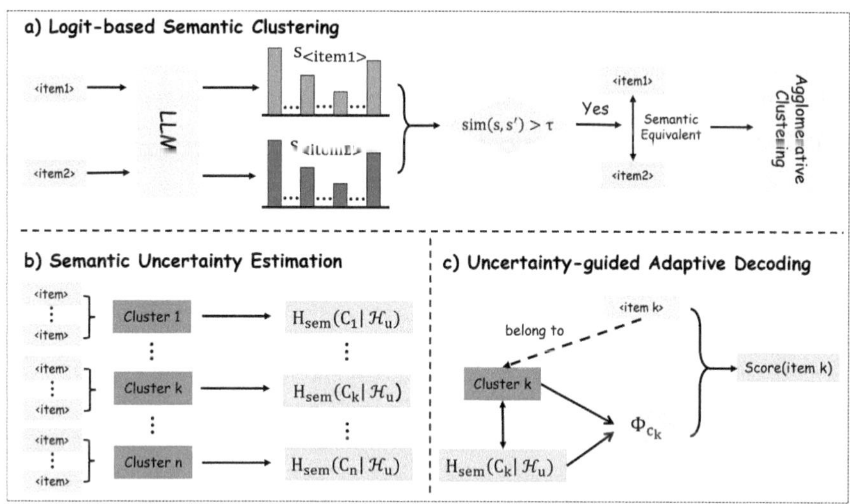

Fig. 2. An overview of the proposed algorithmic framework for semantic clustering and uncertainty-guided decoding.

logit-level embeddings. We then declare s and s' to be semantically equivalent if $\text{Sim}(s, s')$ exceeds a threshold:

$$E(s, s') = \mathbb{I}\big[\text{Sim}(s, s') > \tau\big], \tag{5}$$

where $\tau \in [0, 1]$ is the similarity threshold and $\mathbb{I}[\cdot]$ is the indicator function that returns 1 if the condition is true, 0 otherwise. We use an agglomerative procedure to cluster items satisfying $E(s, s')$, yielding a set of semantic clusters $C = \{c_1, c_2, \ldots, c_m\}$ whose members fulfill comparable user intents.

4.2 Semantic Uncertainty Estimation

Based on these clusters, we measure preference ambiguity across clusters rather than individual items. Let $p_\theta(s \mid \mathcal{H}_u)$ be the LLM's probability of item s, given user history $\mathcal{H}_u$. We sum these probabilities over each cluster c:

$$p(c \mid \mathcal{H}_u) = \sum_{s \in c} p_\theta(s \mid \mathcal{H}_u). \tag{6}$$

Here, c represents a single cluster and s enumerates the items residing within c, while $p_\theta(s \mid \mathcal{H}_u)$ comes directly from the original language model with parameters θ. We then define the semantic entropy:

$$H_{\text{sem}}(C \mid \mathcal{H}_u) = -\sum_{c \in C} \big[p(c \mid \mathcal{H}_u) \log p(c \mid \mathcal{H}_u)\big]. \tag{7}$$

In this definition, $H_{\text{sem}}(C \mid \mathcal{H}_u)$ quantifies the overall uncertainty of user interests at the cluster level, $p(c \mid \mathcal{H}_u)$ is the probability assigned to each cluster, and the summation extends over all clusters $c \in C$. By concentrating probability mass on c, we avoid excessive dilution by semantically duplicative items. Monte Carlo sampling of K candidate items helps compute H_{sem} efficiently during inference.

4.3 Uncertainty-Guided Adaptive Decoding

Where standard beam search or greedy strategies may misallocate computational effort, we propose a scoring function that incorporates semantic entropy. For each candidate item s in the sampled set S, we define

$$\text{Score}(s) = (1-\alpha)\, p_\theta(s \mid \mathcal{H}_u) + \alpha\, \Phi\big(s, C, H_{\text{sem}}\big). \tag{8}$$

In this formula, s is a single candidate item, $\alpha \in [0,1]$ is a hyperparameter that tunes the extent to which we trust item-level model probabilities versus cluster-level reasoning, and $p_\theta(s \mid \mathcal{H}_u)$ is the item's base probability. The function $\Phi(s, C, H_{\text{sem}})$ is defined as

$$\Phi(s, C, H_{\text{sem}}) = \frac{p(c_s \mid \mathcal{H}_u)}{|c_s|} \Big(1 - \beta\, H_{\text{sem}}(C \mid \mathcal{H}_u)\Big), \tag{9}$$

where c_s is the semantic cluster containing item s, $|c_s|$ denotes the size of that cluster, $\beta \in [0,1]$ specifies how much to factor in the entropy term, and $H_{\text{sem}}(C \mid \mathcal{H}_u)$ is the previously mentioned cluster-level entropy. Additionally, we adapt the sampling temperature:

$$\tau = \tau_0\big(1 + \gamma\, H_{\text{sem}}(C \mid \mathcal{H}_u)\big), \tag{10}$$

where $\tau_0 > 0$ is a base temperature, $\gamma \geq 0$ regulates how strongly uncertainty drives exploration, and H_{sem} is the same semantic entropy. In this manner, high uncertainty pushes the system to broaden candidate exploration, while low uncertainty narrows focus for precision.

5 Experiments

In this section, we evaluate our proposed Uncertainty-aware Semantic Decoding (USD) framework for sequential recommendation through comprehensive experiments across multiple real-world datasets. Our evaluation aims to answer the following research questions: **RQ1:** How does USD perform compared to state-of-the-art recommendation methods? **RQ2:** How much does each component contribute to USD's overall performance? **RQ3:** How does USD compare with alternative decoding strategies? **RQ4:** How well does USD generalize across different recommendation domains and datasets? **RQ5:** How do different hyperparameter settings affect USD's effectiveness?

5.1 Experimental Setup

Datasets. We evaluate our approach on multiple large-scale datasets from the Amazon Product Dataset[1], spanning six diverse domains: Baby, Beauty, Clothing, Grocery, Sports, and Toys. For each product, we extract attributes including titles, descriptions, categories, and brand attributes. We filter out users and items with fewer than 10 interactions to ensure data quality. For evaluation, we adopt the leave-one-out strategy, using each user's last interaction for testing, second-to-last for validation, and the remaining interactions for training.

Implementation Details. We implement our USD framework using RedPajama-INCITE-Instruct-3B as the backbone model, which comprises 2.8B parameters with a decoder-only transformer architecture (32 layers). To optimize memory usage while maintaining numerical stability, we employ mixed precision training (FP16). For our USD framework hyperparameters, we set semantic similarity threshold $\tau = 0.8$, uncertainty weight $\alpha = 0.5$, and uncertainty parameter $\beta = 0.3$ based on validation performance. For candidate generation, we use $K = 10$ items with a temperature of $\tau_0 = 0.95$. We implement our model using PyTorch 2.0 and the Accelerate library for distributed evaluation on 8 NVIDIA RTX 3090 GPUs.

Baselines. We compare against four categories of baselines, all baselines undergo identical data preprocessing and follow the same evaluation protocol:

- Non-LLM methods: Traditional collaborative filtering (MF [21,34], LightGCN [16]), and sequential models (HGN [28], GRU4Rec [19], SASRec [20], S^3-Rec [54], MACR [47], UltraGCN [30]);
- LLM-based approaches: Language models (BERT4Rec [38], UniSRec [18], P5 [10], VIP5$^+$ [11]), and multi-modal variants (VBPR [15], CausalRec [33], MM-GCL [52], MMSSL [49], UniMP [48]).

5.2 Performance Comparison(RQ1)

Our extensive evaluation demonstrates that USD effectively addresses the fundamental mismatch between standard LLM decoding strategies and recommendation requirements.

Table 1 presents comparisons against various state-of-the-art methods across six diverse domains from the Amazon Product Dataset. USD consistently outperforms all baselines, achieving average improvements of 18.5% on HR@3, 11.9% on NDCG@3, and 10.8% on MRR@3 compared to the strongest baseline. Non-LLM methods like MF and LightGCN show limited performance due to their inability to leverage rich semantic information, while sequential models (SASRec, GRU4Rec) capture temporal patterns but fall short in modeling semantic relationships. Even advanced LLM-based methods (P5, UniMP) underperform USD as they rely on decoding strategies originally designed for text generation rather

[1] https://huggingface.co/datasets/McAuley-Lab/Amazon-Reviews-2023..

Table 1. Performance Comparison of Different Models

Type	Method	HR@3	NDCG@3	MRR@3	HR@5	NDCG@5	MRR@5
Non-LLM	MF	0.0105	0.0077	0.0065	0.0165	0.0093	0.0078
	MACR	0.0110	0.0080	0.0068	0.0170	0.0105	0.0091
	LightGCN	0.0142	0.0103	0.0088	0.0206	0.0129	0.0094
	UltraGCN	0.0151	0.0111	0.0095	0.0215	0.0134	0.0102
	HGN	0.0167	0.0113	0.0113	0.0231	0.0153	0.0117
	GRU4Rec	0.0132	0.0101	0.0086	0.0201	0.0128	0.0096
	SASRec	0.0189	0.0124	0.0102	0.0276	0.0175	0.0126
	S^3-Rec	0.0205	0.0149	0.0133	0.0311	0.0193	0.0156
LLM-based	BERT4Rec	0.0121	0.0092	0.0079	0.0198	0.0127	0.0105
	UniSRec	0.0201	0.0146	0.0135	0.0281	0.0191	0.0158
	P5	0.0086	0.0056	0.0042	0.0124	0.0074	0.0061
	$VIP5^+$	0.0175	0.0125	0.0108	0.0262	0.0163	0.0127
	VBPR	0.0114	0.0084	0.0071	0.0181	0.0102	0.0086
	CausalRec	0.0143	0.0105	0.0088	0.0229	0.0146	0.0121
	MMGCL	0.0151	0.0112	0.0095	0.0241	0.0159	0.0130
	MMSSL	0.0181	0.0132	0.0112	0.0281	0.0194	0.0164
	UniMP	0.0248	0.0194	0.0176	0.0337	0.0231	0.0196
	USD (Ours)	**0.0294**	**0.0217**	**0.0195**	**0.0388**	**0.0257**	**0.0214**

than recommendation tasks. These results confirm our motivation that standard decoding approaches fundamentally misalign with recommendation objectives. By explicitly modeling semantic relationships between items and incorporating uncertainty estimation, USD effectively bridges this gap, providing more accurate recommendations by recognizing when probability mass distributed across similar items represents a single strong preference rather than genuine uncertainty.

5.3 Ablation Studies(RQ2)

Table 2. Ablation study on key components of USD framework.

Method Variant	HR@3	NDCG@3	MRR@3	HR@5	NDCG@5	MRR@5
Complete USD	**0.0294**	**0.0217**	**0.0195**	**0.0388**	**0.0257**	**0.0214**
USD w/o UE	0.0273	0.0203	0.0182	0.0361	0.0240	0.0198
USD w/o SC	0.0263	0.0195	0.0176	0.0346	0.0230	0.0190

Table 2 reveals that removing any component significantly degrades performance, confirming their complementary nature. The semantic clustering (**SC**) component provides the most substantial contribution (10.5% decrease in HR@3 when removed), followed by uncertainty estimation (7.1% decrease). Removing semantic clustering causes the model to treat semantically similar items as distinct alternatives, leading to diluted probability estimates and suboptimal rankings. This confirms our core motivation that standard decoding methods fail to capture semantic relationships between items, resulting in probability mass being distributed across functionally equivalent items without appropriate aggregation. Similarly, disabling uncertainty estimation(**UE**) reduces the model's adaptability in ambiguous preference scenarios, particularly when users exhibit interest across multiple distinct categories. These findings validate our theoretical understanding of semantic equivalence in recommendation spaces and demonstrate the importance of explicitly modeling uncertainty in user preferences.

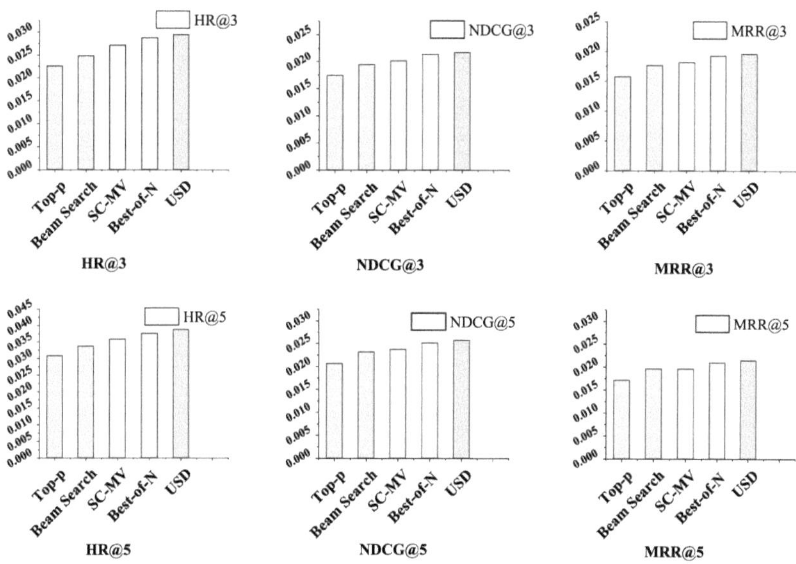

Fig. 3. Decoding Strategies Comparison.

5.4 Decoding Strategies Comparison(RQ3)

To demonstrate how USD addresses the mismatch between standard decoding strategies and recommendation requirements, we implement and compare four alternative decoding algorithms: Beam Search, Nucleus (Top-p) Sampling [17], Best-of-N [3,32]. Self-consistency [44]. Figure 3 shows that USD outperforms all alternatives across all metrics. Across multiple datasets, USD outperforms these baselines with HR@3 improvements ranging from 2.4% to 23.5%. Concretely,

Beam Search (HR@3 around 0.0248) and Nucleus Sampling (0.0225) struggle to reassign probability among semantically similar items, while Best-of-N (0.0287) and Self-consistency (0.0271) improve coverage but lack explicit semantic modeling. By contrast, USD (0.0294) consolidates probabilities within logit-based clusters and leverages uncertainty-driven cues to more effectively produce the next recommendation.

5.5 Cross-Domain Generalization Analysis(RQ4)

Beyond our primary validation on the Amazon dataset, we examine USD's transferability to distinct recommendation domains: H&M[2] and Netflix[3] in Table 3. These datasets present fundamentally different challenges—H&M with its complex retail ecosystem and hierarchical product relationships, and Netflix with its content-centric preference patterns and temporal dynamics.

Table 3. Performance Comparison on H&M and Netflix Datasets

	H&M			Netflix		
	HR@5	NDCG@5	MRR@5	HR@5	NDCG@5	MRR@5
P5	0.0101	0.0063	0.0046	0.0742	0.0413	0.0316
VIP5	0.0122	0.0118	0.0093	0.0936	0.0589	0.0395
S3-Rec	0.0185	0.0121	0.0102	0.1155	0.0632	0.0511
UniSRec	0.0196	0.0139	0.0107	0.1324	0.0856	0.0644
UniMP	0.0313	0.0206	0.0172	0.1723	0.1196	0.1024
USD	**0.0368**	**0.0242**	**0.0203**	**0.1835**	**0.1271**	**0.1091**

The results reinforce our key findings from earlier experiments. USD consistently outperforms all baselines across both domains, achieving improvements of 17.6% in HR@5, 17.5% in NDCG@5, and 18.0% in MRR@5 over UniMP on the H&M dataset. For Netflix, USD shows improvements of 6.5% in HR@5, 6.3% in NDCG@5, and 6.5% in MRR@5 over the same baseline. This cross-domain evaluation directly tests USD approach to addressing decoding policy mismatch can be generalized in the recommended environment.

5.6 Hyperparameter Analysis (RQ5)

We conduct extensive hyperparameter sensitivity analyses to identify optimal configurations for USD across different domains in Fig. 4. For the uncertainty weight parameter α, which balances item-specific probability and semantic cluster information, performance peaks at $\alpha = 0.5$ and declines symmetrically toward

[2] https://www.kaggle.com/competitions/h-and-m-personalized-fashion-recommendations/data..

[3] https://www.kaggle.com/datasets/netflix-inc/netflix-prize-data..

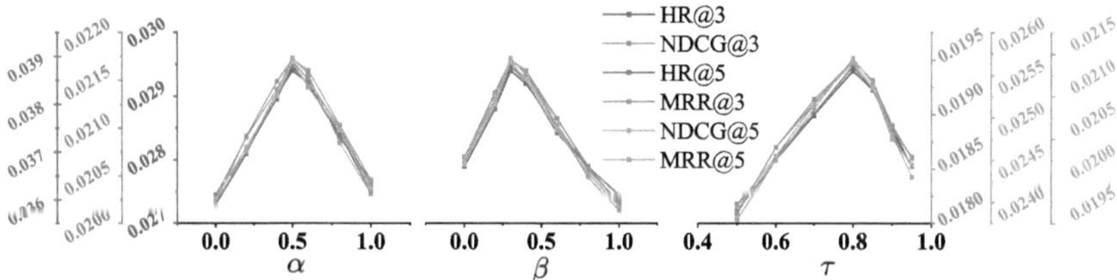

Fig. 4. Hyperparameter Analysis.

extremes. This pattern confirms our hypothesis that both individual item probabilities and semantic cluster information provide complementary signals for effective recommendation. When $\alpha = 0$ (relying solely on item-specific probabilities), the model fails to capture semantic relationships between items—precisely the limitation of standard decoding approaches that motivated our work. Conversely, when $\alpha = 1$ (relying solely on semantic clustering), the model loses precision by overlooking item-specific nuances. The uncertainty parameter β achieves optimal results at $\beta = 0.3$, representing an ideal balance between confidence in established preferences and exploration of alternatives under uncertainty. And the semantic similarity threshold $\tau = 0.8$ creates clusters with optimal granularity. These parameter studies not only identify optimal configurations but also validate our core motivation: standard decoding approaches ($\alpha = 0$) significantly underperform when they fail to account for semantic relationships, while our balanced approach ($\alpha = 0.5$) effectively bridges the gap between token-level decoding and semantic-aware recommendation.

6 Conclusion

In this work, we presented an Uncertainty-aware Semantic Decoding (USD) framework that addresses the core mismatch between traditional text-generation decoding and the specialized structure of sequential recommendation. By clustering semantically equivalent items at the logit level and quantifying uncertainty through semantic entropy, USD better allocates probability mass among near-duplicate candidates and refines exploration via an adaptive temperature mechanism. Extensive empirical evaluations reveal consistent improvements over state-of-the-art baselines, with gains exceeding 10% on key metrics such as HR@3 and NDCG@3. Ablation analyses confirm that both semantic clustering and uncertainty estimation are crucial contributors to robust performance, while hyperparameter studies demonstrate the stability of the approach under varying threshold and entropy-weight settings. Future avenues may explore integrating domain-specific knowledge or multimodal signals, leveraging the framework's capacity to seamlessly incorporate diverse contextual features for more personalized, efficient, and explainable recommendations.

Acknowledgments. This study was funded by the National Natural Science Foundation of China (Grant No. 72401232), the Natural Science Foundation of the Jiangsu

Higher Educational Institution of China (Grant No. 23KJB520037), the XJTLU Research Development Fund (RDF-21-01-053), and Liaoning Liaohe Lab (Grant Nos. LLL24ZZ-02-01 and LLL24ZZ-02-02).

References

1. Bao, K., Zhang, J., Zhang, Y., Wang, W., Feng, F., He, X.: Tallrec: an effective and efficient tuning framework to align large language model with recommendation. In: Proceedings of the 17th ACM Conference on Recommender Systems, RecSys 2023, Singapore, Singapore, 18–22 September 2023, pp. 1007–1014 (2023)
2. Bertsch, A., Xie, A., Neubig, G., Gormley, M.: It's MBR all the way down: modern generation techniques through the lens of minimum Bayes risk. In: Elazar, Y., Ettinger, A., Kassner, N., Ruder, S., A. Smith, N. (eds.) Proceedings of the Big Picture Workshop, pp. 108–122. Association for Computational Linguistics (2023). https://doi.org/10.18653/v1/2023.bigpicture-1.9
3. Charniak, E., Johnson, M.: Coarse-to-fine n-best parsing and MaxEnt discriminative reranking. In: Knight, K., Ng, H.T., Oflazer, K. (eds.) Proceedings of the 43rd Annual Meeting of the Association for Computational Linguistics (ACL 2005). Association for Computational Linguistics, Ann Arbor, Michigan (2005)
4. Chen, J., Mueller, J.: Quantifying uncertainty in answers from any language model and enhancing their trustworthiness (2023)
5. Chen, X., Lin, M., Schärli, N., Zhou, D.: Teaching large language models to self-debug (2023)
6. Chiang, W.L., et al.: Vicuna: an open-source chatbot impressing GPT-4 with 90%* chatgpt quality. **2**(3), 6 (2023). https://vicunalmsys.org. Accessed 14 Apr 2023
7. Dai, S., et al.: Uncovering chatgpt's capabilities in recommender systems. In: RecSys, pp. 1126–1132. ACM (2023)
8. Dunefsky, J., Chlenski, P., Nanda, N.: Transcoders find interpretable LLM feature circuits (2024)
9. Fadeeva, E., et al.: Fact-checking the output of large language models via token-level uncertainty quantification (2024)
10. Geng, S., Liu, S., Fu, Z., Ge, Y., Zhang, Y.: Recommendation as language processing (RLP): a unified pretrain, personalized prompt & predict paradigm (p5). In: Proceedings of the 16th ACM Conference on Recommender Systems, pp. 299–315 (2022)
11. Geng, S., Tan, J., Liu, S., Fu, Z., Zhang, Y.: Vip5: towards multimodal foundation models for recommendation. arXiv preprint arXiv:2305.14302 (2023)
12. Hao, S., et al.: LLM reasoners: new evaluation, library, and analysis of step-by-step reasoning with large language models. arXiv preprint arXiv:2404.05221 (2024)
13. Havrilla, A., et al.: Glore: when, where, and how to improve LLM reasoning via global and local refinements. arXiv preprint abs/2402.10963 (2024)
14. He, P., Liu, X., Gao, J., Chen, W.: Deberta: decoding-enhanced BERT with disentangled attention (2021)
15. He, R., McAuley, J.: VBPR: visual Bayesian personalized ranking from implicit feedback. In: Proceedings of the AAAI Conference on Artificial Intelligence, vol. 30 (2016)
16. He, X., Deng, K., Wang, X., Li, Y., Zhang, Y., Wang, M.: LightGCN: simplifying and powering graph convolution network for recommendation. In: Proceedings of the 43rd International ACM SIGIR Conference on Research and Development in Information Retrieval, pp. 639–648 (2020)

17. Holtzman, A., Buys, J., Du, L., Forbes, M., Choi, Y.: The curious case of neural text degeneration. In: International Conference on Learning Representations (2020)
18. Hou, Y., Mu, S., Zhao, W.X., Li, Y., Ding, B., Wen, J.R.: Towards universal sequence representation learning for recommender systems. In: Proceedings of the 28th ACM SIGKDD Conference on Knowledge Discovery and Data Mining, pp. 585–593 (2022)
19. Jannach, D., Ludewig, M.: When recurrent neural networks meet the neighborhood for session-based recommendation. In: Proceedings of the Eleventh ACM Conference on Recommender Systems, pp. 306–310 (2017)
20. Kang, W.C., McAuley, J.: Self-attentive sequential recommendation. In: 2018 IEEE International Conference on Data Mining (ICDM), pp. 197–206. IEEE (2018)
21. Koren, Y., Bell, R., Volinsky, C.: Matrix factorization techniques for recommender systems. Computer **42**(8), 30–37 (2009)
22. Krause, L., Tufa, W., Baez Santamaria, S., Daza, A., Khurana, U., Vossen, P.: Confidently wrong: exploring the calibration and expression of (un)certainty of large language models in a multilingual setting. In: Gatt, A., et al. (eds.) Proceedings of the Workshop on Multimodal, Multilingual Natural Language Generation and Multilingual WebNLG Challenge (MM-NLG 2023). Association for Computational Linguistics, Prague, Czech Republic (2023)
23. Kuhn, L., Gal, Y., Farquhar, S.: Semantic uncertainty: linguistic invariances for uncertainty estimation in natural language generation. In: The Eleventh International Conference on Learning Representations (2023)
24. Kumar, A., et al.: Training language models to self-correct via reinforcement learning (2024)
25. Li, J., et al.: Text is all you need: learning language representations for sequential recommendation. In: Proceedings of the 29th ACM SIGKDD Conference on Knowledge Discovery and Data Mining, KDD 2023, pp. 1258–1267. Association for Computing Machinery (2023). https://doi.org/10.1145/3580305.3599519
26. Liao, J., et al.: LLaRA: large language-recommendation assistant. In: Proceedings of the 47th International ACM SIGIR Conference on Research and Development in Information Retrieval, pp. 1785–1795. ACM. https://doi.org/10.1145/3626772.3657690. https://dl.acm.org/doi/10.1145/3626772.3657690
27. Lieberum, T., et al.: Gemma scope: open sparse autoencoders everywhere all at once on Gemma 2 (2024)
28. Ma, C., Kang, P., Liu, X.: Hierarchical gating networks for sequential recommendation. In: Proceedings of the 25th ACM SIGKDD International Conference on Knowledge Discovery & Data Mining, pp. 825–833 (2019)
29. Madaan, A., et al.: Self-refine: iterative refinement with self-feedback. In: Thirty-Seventh Conference on Neural Information Processing Systems (2023)
30. Mao, K., Zhu, J., Xiao, X., Lu, B., Wang, Z., He, X.: UltraGCN: ultra simplification of graph convolutional networks for recommendation. In: Proceedings of the 30th ACM International Conference on Information & Knowledge Management, pp. 1253–1262 (2021)
31. Nikitin, A., Kossen, J., Gal, Y., Marttinen, P.: Kernel language entropy: fine-grained uncertainty quantification for LLMs from semantic similarities (2024)
32. Pauls, A., Klein, D.: K-best A* parsing. In: Su, K.Y., Su, J., Wiebe, J., Li, H. (eds.) Proceedings of the Joint Conference of the 47th Annual Meeting of the ACL and the 4th International Joint Conference on Natural Language Processing of the AFNLP. Association for Computational Linguistics, Suntec, Singapore (2009)

33. Qiu, R., Wang, S., Chen, Z., Yin, H., Huang, Z.: Causalrec: causal inference for visual debiasing in visually-aware recommendation. In: Proceedings of the 29th ACM International Conference on Multimedia, pp. 3844–3852 (2021)
34. Rendle, S., Freudenthaler, C., Gantner, Z., Schmidt-Thieme, L.: BPR: Bayesian personalized ranking from implicit feedback. arXiv preprint arXiv:1205.2618 (2012)
35. Stahlberg, F., Byrne, B.: On NMT search errors and model errors: cat got your tongue? In: Proceedings of the 2019 Conference on Empirical Methods in Natural Language Processing and the 9th International Joint Conference on Natural Language Processing (EMNLP-IJCNLP), pp. 3356–3362. Association for Computational Linguistics (2019). https://doi.org/10.18653/v1/D19-1331
36. Stengel-Eskin, E., Hase, P., Bansal, M.: Lacie: listener-aware finetuning for confidence calibration in large language models (2024)
37. Su, Y., Lan, T., Wang, Y., Yogatama, D., Kong, L., Collier, N.: A contrastive framework for neural text generation (2022)
38. Sun, F., et al.: Bert4rec: sequential recommendation with bidirectional encoder representations from transformer. In: Proceedings of the 28th ACM International Conference on Information and Knowledge Management, pp. 1441–1450 (2019)
39. Tang, H., et al.: Time series forecasting with LLMs: understanding and enhancing model capabilities. SIGKDD Explor. Newsl. **26**(2), 109–118 (2025)
40. Tyen, G., Mansoor, H., Cărbune, V., Chen, P., Mak, T.: LLMs cannot find reasoning errors, but can correct them given the error location (2024)
41. Wang, C., Jia, D., Wang, W., Ngoduy, D., Peng, B., Wang, J.: A knowledge-informed deep learning paradigm for generalizable and stability-optimized car-following models. arXiv preprint arXiv:2504.14241 (2025)
42. Wang, C., Feng, F., Zhang, Y., Wang, Q., Hu, X., He, X.: Rethinking missing data: aleatoric uncertainty-aware recommendation (2023). https://arxiv.org/abs/2209.11679
43. Wang, H., et al.: Rethinking Large Language Model Architectures for Sequential Recommendations
44. Wang, X., et al.: Self-consistency improves chain of thought reasoning in language models. In: The Eleventh International Conference on Learning Representations (2023)
45. Wang, Y., Liu, Z., Zhang, J., Yao, W., Heinecke, S., Yu, P.S.: DRDT: dynamic reflection with divergent thinking for LLM-based sequential recommendation. CoRR abs/2312.11336 (2023)
46. Wei, J., et al.: Chain-of-thought prompting elicits reasoning in large language models. In: NeurIPS (2022)
47. Wei, T., Feng, F., Chen, J., Wu, Z., Yi, J., He, X.: Model-agnostic counterfactual reasoning for eliminating popularity bias in recommender system. In: Proceedings of the 27th ACM SIGKDD Conference on Knowledge Discovery & Data Mining, pp. 1791–1800 (2021)
48. Wei, T., et al.: Towards unified multi-modal personalization: large vision-language models for generative recommendation and beyond. In: The Twelfth International Conference on Learning Representations (2024)
49. Wei, W., Huang, C., Xia, L., Zhang, C.: Multi-modal self-supervised learning for recommendation. In: Proceedings of the ACM Web Conference 2023, pp. 790–800 (2023)
50. Wu, Y., Sun, Z., Li, S., Welleck, S., Yang, Y.: An empirical analysis of compute-optimal inference for problem-solving with language models (2024)
51. Xiang, Y., Fan, L., Yin, C., Kong, M., Ji, C.: Exploiting epistemic uncertainty in cold-start recommendation systems (2025). https://arxiv.org/abs/2502.16256

52. Yi, Z., Wang, X., Ounis, I., Macdonald, C.: Multi-modal graph contrastive learning for micro-video recommendation. In: Proceedings of the 45th International ACM SIGIR Conference on Research and Development in Information Retrieval, pp. 1807–1811 (2022)
53. Zhang, C., Jin, M., Shu, D., Wang, T., Liu, D., Jin, X.: Target-driven attack for large language models. arXiv preprint arXiv:2411.07268 (2024)
54. Zhou, K., et al.: S3-rec: self-supervised learning for sequential recommendation with mutual information maximization. In: Proceedings of the 29th ACM International Conference on Information & Knowledge Management, pp. 1893–1902 (2020)

Dual-Stream Adaptive Retrieval and Hierarchical Agent Collaboration for Document Visual QA

Qin Fang[1], Ruixue Gou[1], Shiqi Liu[1,2], Minqi Song[3], Pan Yuan[1], and Xian Peng[1(✉)]

[1] National Engineering Research Center of Educational Big Data, Central China Normal University, Wuhan, China
{fangqin,augyuki,liushiqi,yuanpan}@mails.ccnu.edu.cn, pengxian@ccnu.edu.cn

[2] Key Laboratory of Big Data Research and Application for Basic Education, Hunan Normal University, Changsha, China

[3] Faculty of Artificial Intelligence in Education, Central China Normal University, Wuhan, China
piscesminqi@mails.ccnu.edu.cn

Abstract. Document Visual Question Answering (DocVQA) is critical for automating the comprehension of visually rich documents in domains such as finance, healthcare, education, and law. However, existing retrieval-augmented generation (RAG) methods, such as TextRAG and VisRAG, face significant challenges in handling complex document layouts and large-scale document corpora. TextRAG, reliant on OCR-based text extraction, often fails to capture essential visual structures like tables and diagrams, resulting in incomplete semantic representations. VisRAG, while incorporating visual cues, suffers from performance degradation due to accumulated visual noise when increasing document length. To address these challenges, we propose a novel two-stage framework comprising dual-stream adaptive retrieval and hierarchical agent collaboration. The retrieval module integrates textual and visual retrievers, guided by a Wasserstein-based Compact Adaptive Breakpoint Selection (WCABS) algorithm, which dynamically optimizes the selection of top-k evidence pages to minimize noise across multi-page documents. The reasoning module employs a hierarchical agent system, where a Selector Agent performs distributed evidence extraction and an Integrator Agent aggregates the extracted information to generate the final answer, ensuring robust and structured reasoning. Experiments on the ViDoSeek dataset demonstrate the effectiveness of our approach, showcasing robust multimodal retrieval and structured reasoning capabilities for complex document queries.

Keywords: Document Visual Question Answering · Retrieval-Augmented Generation · Large Vision-Language Models

J. Li et al. (Eds.): APWeb-WAIM 2025, LNCS 16115, pp. 402–416, 2026.
https://doi.org/10.1007/978-981-95-5719-6_26

1 Introduction

Documents are one of the fundamental forms of information preservation and exchange. Each year, tens of millions of documents are created, read, saved, and dispatched [1]. Document Visual Question Answering (DocVQA) is a fundamental task with broad applications in information retrieval and automated document understanding [2,3]. Accurately understanding complex documents and answering user queries over intricate layouts is crucial for various real-world domains, including finance, healthcare, education, and law [4–6]. Current DocVQA approaches typically adopt one of two strategies: (1) TextRAG, which extracts text via techniques such as optical character recognition (OCR) [7] and processes it through retrieval-augmented generation (RAG) [8]. In this approach, a retrieval model identifies relevant text segments, which a large language model (LLM) utilizes to generate precise responses. (2) VisRAG, which employs visual retrieval to select pertinent document pages, is subsequently processed by a large vision-language model (LVLM) to produce accurate responses [9]. Figure 1 depicts the workflows of these two DocVQA approaches.

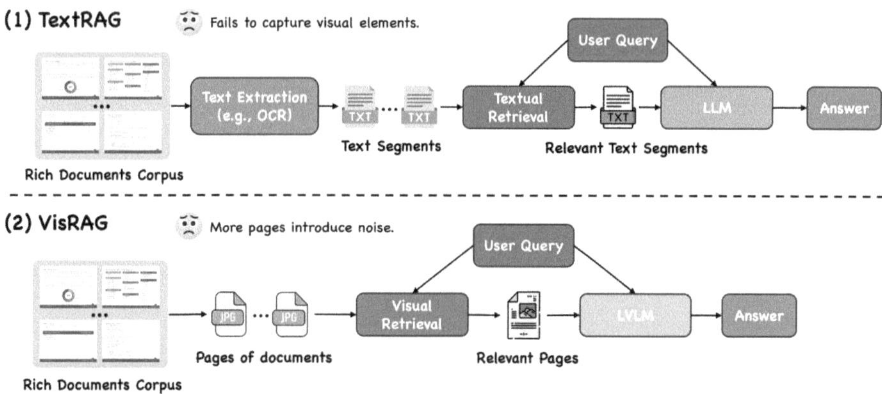

Fig. 1. Workflows of Current DocVQA Approaches: TextRAG and VisRAG.

However, existing Retrieval-Augmented Generation (RAG) methods, such as TextRAG and VisRAG, face significant limitations when processing visually complex documents and large-scale document corpora. For TextRAG, OCR-based text extraction often fails to capture multimodal elements such as diagrams, tables, and charts, resulting in incomplete semantic representations and limited performance on layout-rich queries [6]. This indicates that relying solely on textual signals is insufficient for answering document questions in visually rich scenarios. Nevertheless, textual features can still play a valuable role in guiding coarse-grained page retrieval. In contrast, VisRAG directly leverages visual inputs. However, experiments on the ViDoSeek dataset [10] reveal that increasing the number of input pages to a large vision-language model (LVLM) leads to a noticeable decline in answer accuracy due to the accumulation of irrelevant visual noise. This degradation, as shown in Fig. 2, highlights the necessity of adaptive filtering strategies to reduce irrelevant content and improve reasoning precision.

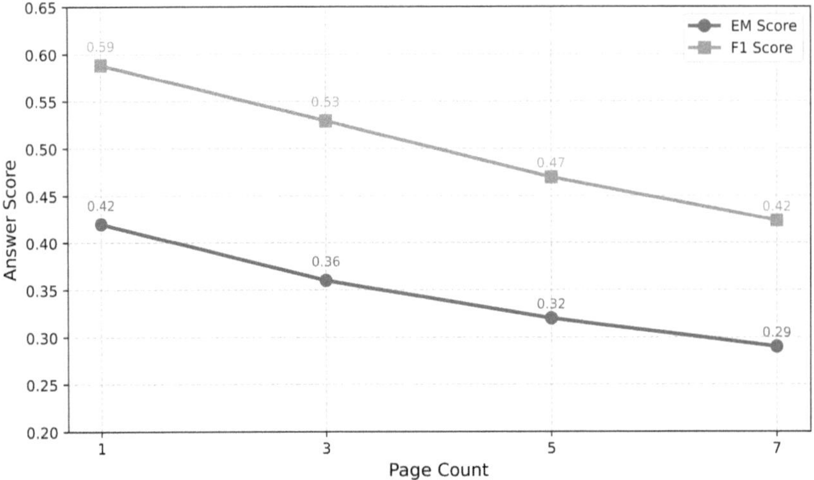

Fig. 2. Impact of total page count (including the presence of ground-truth page) on answer quality. The experiments were conducted on the ViDoSeek dataset, using a random selection of 200 samples for $k \in \{1, 3, 5, 7\}$. Results reveal that increasing the number of retrieved pages, even when ground-truth ones are present, leads to performance degradation due to the inclusion of irrelevant content. This highlights the LVLM's sensitivity to input noise and the importance of precise evidence selection in DocVQA.

To overcome the limitations of existing DocVQA approaches, we propose a two-stage framework comprising dual-stream adaptive retrieval and hierarchical agent collaboration. The retrieval module integrates both textual and visual retrievers to dynamically identify salient evidence pages, effectively filtering out irrelevant pages across multi-page documents. Based on the retrieved evidence, the reasoning module employs two specialized agents in a hierarchical manner: a Selector Agent that performs distributed evidence extraction, and an Integrator Agent that aggregates the extracted information to generate the final answer. This hierarchical collaboration further enhances the generation and reasoning capabilities of the large vision-language model.

Our major contributions are as follows:

1. We propose the Wasserstein-based Compact Adaptive Breakpoint Selection (WCABS) algorithm for dynamically determining the optimal number of retrieved document pages.

2. We design a dual-stream retrieval module that integrates textual and visual signals for multimodal evidence selection.
3. We introduce a hierarchical agent collaboration mechanism for structured reasoning and answer generation.
4. We perform comprehensive experiments to demonstrate the effectiveness of our approach.

2 Related Work

2.1 DocVQA Tasks

Document Visual Question Answering (DocVQA) focuses on answering natural language questions by leveraging both structured and unstructured information within documents. Early research primarily targeted single-page documents or image-level question answering tasks [3,11,12]. Most current approaches remain constrained to modeling within a single document or fixed context window, making them less effective in large-scale document collections [13]. Furthermore, integrating diverse modalities, including charts, tables, and natural images, poses significant challenges in synthesizing semantic information across these modalities while preserving retrieval efficiency [14]. Additionally, real-world documents often exhibit complex structures, comprising multi-page layouts, extensive textual content, and heterogeneous multimodal components, which amplify the limitations of existing approaches [4]. With the growing capacity of modern models to handle longer contexts and advances in multimodal retrieval techniques, recent studies have started to explore question-answering over multi-page documents. Increasing interest in multimodal embeddings has notably enhanced performance in visual retrieval tasks [15,16]. Consequently, there is a pressing need for a unified and efficient mechanism capable of modeling multimodal content and enabling reasoning across documents.

2.2 Vision-Language Models

In recent years, with the development of the transformer architecture and multimodal pretraining techniques, vision-language models(VLMs) have demonstrated impressive performance on tasks such as cross-modal retrieval and visual question answering(VQA) [17]. For example, ColPali introduces a visual-language model-based concept indexing space for document visual features, enabling efficient end-to-end retrieval on the ViDoRe dataset and demonstrating the potential of VLMs in structured document scenarios [18]. In document-related scenarios, structural understanding and semantic aggregation are particularly critical. For instance, LLaVA integrates a language model with visual features to guide the question-answering process, exhibiting a certain level of reasoning ability on tasks involving complex layouts [19]. Qwen-VL employs robust cross-modal alignment and instruction tuning to achieve strong generalization across various image-text question answering tasks [20]. Meanwhile, GPT-4V offers native support for image input, marking a paradigm shift toward general-purpose multimodal intelligence [21]. Despite significant progress in document image understanding, existing VLMs still face clear challenges in long-document reasoning, joint modeling of visual and textual content, and efficient cross-document retrieval [22].

2.3 Retrieval-Augmented Generation

Traditional retrieval-augmented generation (RAG) methods primarily rely on the textual modality, enhancing the generation capability of language models by retrieving relevant information from external knowledge bases [8]. However, such approaches face limitations when dealing with multimodal documents rich in visual content, as they struggle to effectively leverage non-textual information such as images and layout [18]. To address this issue, recent work has introduced the Multimodal RAG framework, which integrates textual and visual modalities to enhance generation quality. For instance, the VisRAG model incorporates vision-language models (VLMs) to directly encode and retrieve from document images, thereby avoiding the information loss typically introduced during traditional text parsing [9]. This approach preserves both the visual and textual information of the original document, significantly enhancing retrieval and generation performance. Despite the promising potential of multimodal RAG methods in handling visually rich documents, several challenges remain, such as effective cross-modal information fusion, understanding of complex layouts, and efficient retrieval [23].

3 Task Formulation

Given a text query q and a corpus $D = \{D_1, D_2, \ldots, D_M\}$ comprising M documents, where each document D_m is composed of N pages represented as $D_m = \{p_1, p_2, \ldots, p_N\}$, the objective is to retrieve relevant pages and generate an answer a using Retrieval-Augmented Generation (RAG) framework. The task comprises two stages: (1) page-level retrieval, where a retriever $R : (q, D) \rightarrow P_R$ selects a subset of relevant pages $P_R \subset D$ from the corpus; (2) answer generation, where a generator $G : (q, P_R) \rightarrow a$ takes the query q and retrieved pages P_R as input to prompt a large vision-language model(LVLM) to generate the answer a.

4 Methodology

In this section, we provide a detailed explanation of our two-stage framework, which combines dual-stream adaptive retrieval with hierarchical agent collaboration, building on key insights and foundational concepts. Figure 3 illustrates the structure and flow of this framework, offering a visual representation of how the dual-stream retrieval and agent collaboration components interact within the system.

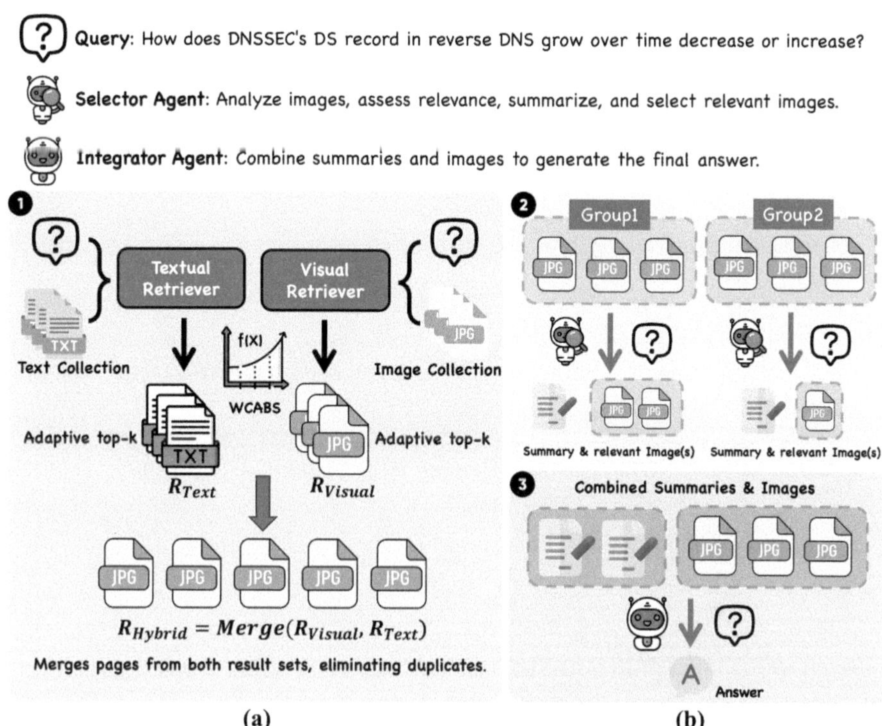

Fig. 3. Illustration of the two-stage framework integrating dual-stream adaptive retrieval with hierarchical agent collaboration. (a) depicts the dual-stream adaptive retrieval process, while (b) shows the hierarchical agent collaboration component of the framework.

4.1 Dual-Stream Adaptive Retrieval

Dual-Stream Relevance Scoring. For a query q and a document collection $C = \{p_1, p_2, \ldots, p_n\}$, we compute relevance scores to quantify the similarity between the query and each page. The textual and visual pipelines employ distinct scoring mechanisms tailored to their respective data modalities, enabling effective multimodal evidence retrieval.

In the textual pipeline, we extract text from each document page $p_i \in C$ using PPOCR [24] and segment it into a set of text chunks $\{t_{i,j}\}$, where $t_{i,j}$ denotes the j-th text segment from page p_i. Each text segment $t_{i,j}$ is indexed using a sentence embedding model. For a query q and text segment $t_{i,j}$, we compute their embeddings $E_q \in \mathbb{R}^D$ and $E_{t_{i,j}} \in \mathbb{R}^D$, respectively, where D is the embedding dimension. The textual relevance score $s_{i,j}^{\text{text}}$ is defined as the cosine similarity between the query and text segment embeddings:

$$s_{i,j}^{\text{text}} = \cos(E_q, E_{t_{i,j}}) = \frac{E_q \cdot E_{t_{i,j}}}{\|E_q\| \, \|E_{t_{i,j}}\|} \quad (1)$$

To construct the set of all textual relevance scores between the query and the corpus, we define:

$$S_{\text{text}}(q, C) = \left\{ s_{i,j}^{\text{text}} \;\middle|\; t_{i,j} \in \bigcup_{p_i \in C} \{t_{i,j}\}_j \right\} \tag{2}$$

In the visual pipeline, each page p_i is treated as an image, and visual features are extracted using ColPali [18], a Vision Language Model trained for document image understanding. ColPali generates multi-vector embeddings for both the query q and page p_i, denoted as $E_q \in \mathbb{R}^{N_q \times D}$ and $E_{p_i} \in \mathbb{R}^{N_d \times D}$, respectively, where N_q and N_d are the number of vectors for the query and page, and D is the embedding dimension.

To compute the relevance score s_i^{visual}, we use a late-interaction mechanism [25]. The score is defined as the sum of maximum dot products between query and page embedding vectors:

$$s_i^{\text{visual}} = \sum_{j=1}^{N_q} \max_{k=1}^{N_d} (E_q^{(j)} \cdot E_{p_i}^{(k)}) \tag{3}$$

where $E_q^{(j)}$ and $E_{p_i}^{(k)}$ denote the j-th and k-th embedding vectors of the query and page, respectively. The set of visual relevance scores is:

$$S_{\text{visual}}(q, C) = \{s_i^{\text{visual}} \mid p_i \in C\} \tag{4}$$

Wasserstein-Based Compact Adaptive Breakpoint Selection (WCABS). Conventional information retrieval methods often employ a fixed hyperparameter k to specify the number of retrieved pages. However, a static k is suboptimal: a small k risks omitting relevant content, while a large k introduces irrelevant noise and increases computational cost. Manual tuning of k across diverse queries and modalities is both impractical and inefficient.

To address these challenges, we propose the Wasserstein-based Compact Adaptive Breakpoint Selection (WCABS) algorithm, which dynamically selects the optimal k for each modality based on the distribution of relevance scores (S_{text} or S_{visual}). WCABS hypothesizes that relevance scores exhibit a distributional shift between highly relevant and less relevant pages. To detect this shift, WCABS employs the 1-Wasserstein distance [26], which quantifies the separation between score distributions before and after a candidate breakpoint.

The 1-Wasserstein distance is selected for its sensitivity to the ranked structure of relevance scores and its robustness to non-standard score distributions, in contrast to divergence-based metrics (e.g., KL or Jensen-Shannon divergence) [27]. For one-dimensional score distributions, it provides a computationally efficient closed-form solution based on cumulative distribution differences, enabling real-time dynamic k-selection. Combined with an exponential length penalty to favour compact result sets and statistical validation for robustness,

WCABS ensures adaptive and precise retrieval tailored to query and document characteristics.

The algorithm proceeds as follows:

1. **Score Extraction and Sorting**: For each modality-specific retrieval pipeline, we extract the top-m relevance scores $S = \{s_1, s_2, \ldots, s_m\}$, already ranked in descending order ($s_1 \geq s_2 \geq \cdots \geq s_m$), along with their corresponding pages $\mathcal{P} = \{p_1, p_2, \ldots, p_m\}$, where m is a hyperparameter.
2. **Quantile-based Candidate Breakpoints**: To dynamically optimize the retrieval set size, we compute candidate breakpoints $K = \{k_1, k_2, \ldots, k_l\}$ using quantile thresholds $Q = \{q_1, q_2, \ldots, q_l\}$, where $q_i \in [0, 1]$. Each breakpoint is defined as:
$$k_i = \max\left(1, \lfloor q_i \cdot m \rfloor\right), \tag{5}$$
We select breakpoints satisfying $k_i \leq k_{\max}$, with $k_{\max}$ as the maximum allowable size. If no k_i meets this criterion, we default to $K = \{k_{\min}\}$, where $k_{\min} \leq k_{\max}$ is a predefined minimum size. These breakpoints facilitate the adaptive selection of the optimal retrieval set size.
3. **Wasserstein Distance and Objective Function**: For each candidate breakpoint $k_i \in K$, partition the sorted scores into two subsets: $S_1 = \{s'_1, \ldots, s'_{k_i}\}$ (high-relevance) and $S_2 = \{s'_{k_i+1}, \ldots, s'_m\}$ (low-relevance). Compute the 1-Wasserstein distance $W(S_1, S_2)$ between the empirical distributions of S_1 and S_2:
$$W(S_1, S_2) = \int_{-\infty}^{\infty} |F_1(x) - F_2(x)| \, dx, \tag{6}$$
where F_1 and F_2 are the cumulative distribution functions of S_1 and S_2, and x represents a score value on the real axis. To balance relevance and retrieval set size, we define the objective function:
$$O(k_i) = W(S_1, S_2) - \lambda \exp(\beta k_i), \tag{7}$$
where $\lambda > 0$ controls the penalty weight and $\beta > 0$ governs the decay rate. The optimal breakpoint k^* is selected as:
$$k^* = \arg\max_{k_i \in K} O(k_i), \tag{8}$$
4. **Statistical Validation**: To ensure the robustness of the selected breakpoint k^*, we validate the separation between the relevance scores $S_1 = \{s_i \mid i \leq k^*\}$ (high-relevance) and $S_2 = \{s_i \mid i > k^*\}$ (low-relevance) using the Mann-Whitney U test. The test evaluates the alternative hypothesis that S_1 stochastically dominates S_2, with a significance threshold α. If the p-value exceeds α, indicating insufficient evidence of dominance, we update k^* to the smallest k from the candidate set $K \cup \{k_{\min}\}$.

Textual and Visual Hybrid Retrieval. After applying WCABS, the textual pipeline yields R_{text}, containing k_{text} text chunks, and the visual pipeline yields R_{visual}, containing k_{visual} page images. We merge the pages associated with these results into a hybrid set:

$$R_{\text{Hybrid}} = \text{Merge}(R_{\text{visual}}, R_{\text{text}}), \tag{9}$$

where Merge$(\cdot)$ maps text chunks to their source pages, combines them with the visual pages, and removes duplicates to produce a unified set of unique pages.

4.2 Hierarchical Agent Collaboration

Despite the effectiveness of our dual-stream adaptive retrieval in selecting relevant pages, large vision-language models (LVLMs) often struggle with degraded reasoning performance when processing multiple page images simultaneously due to visual noise and information overload. In order to address this issue, we propose a novel multi-agent framework that augments multimodal reasoning and evidence analysis through hierarchical agent collaboration. The framework under consideration consists of two specialized agents: the Selector Agent and the Integrator Agent. These agents collaborate to extract relevant information, mitigate noise, and generate precise answers from a set of input images in response to user queries. By integrating adaptive page grouping, parallel evidence extraction, and summary synthesis, our framework significantly improves the accuracy and efficiency of question answering, outperforming single-model approaches that directly process large page sets.

Selector Agent. The Selector Agent is tasked with identifying images relevant to a given query from a potentially large input set, thereby reducing noise and computational overhead. Given a set of hybrid retrieval input images $R_{\text{Hybrid}} = \{p_1, p_2, \ldots, p_n\}$ and a query q, the Selector Agent employs an adaptive grouping strategy to partition the images into manageable subsets of size k. This grouping is defined as:

$$\mathcal{G} = \{R_{\text{Hybrid}}[i : i + k] \mid i = 0, k, 2k, \ldots, \lfloor n/k \rfloor \cdot k\}, \tag{10}$$

This strategy balances computational efficiency with the need to preserve the model's performance by processing smaller subsets. The action space of the Selector Agent includes both the selection of relevant images and the generation of concise summaries to facilitate subsequent processing. For each group $\mathcal{G}_j \in \mathcal{G}$, the Selector Agent evaluates the images in parallel, producing a structured output comprising a summary and a subset of selected images. The selection process is formalized as:

$$(s_j, \mathcal{S}_j) = \Phi(\mathcal{G}_j, q), \tag{11}$$

where Φ is the agent's processing function, s_j is a textual summary of relevant information in $\mathcal{G}_j$, and $\mathcal{S}_j \subseteq \mathcal{G}_j$ is a subset of pages selected based on their relevance to q. These summaries and selected pages are passed to the Integrator Agent for answer synthesis.

Integrator Agent. The Integrator Agent enhances multimodal reasoning and evidence synthesis by processing the structured outputs from the Selector Agent, ultimately generating a concise, query-specific answer. It receives selected image sets $\{\mathcal{S}_j\}$ and their corresponding textual summaries $\{s_j\}$ for all groups $\mathcal{G}_j \in \mathcal{G}$, along with the original query q. The final answer generation process is formalized as:

$$A_{\text{final}} = \Psi(q, \{s_j\}, \{\mathcal{S}_j\}), \tag{12}$$

where Ψ denotes the integration function that jointly leverages contextual cues from the textual summaries and visual semantics from the selected image sets. By grounding the reasoning process in query-relevant evidence, the Integrator Agent generates accurate and succinct responses, effectively mitigating noise and addressing scalability challenges in multimodal question answering.

5 Experiments

5.1 Experiment Setup

Dataset. ViDoSeek is the first dataset explicitly curated to facilitate question-answering over large-scale document collections [10]. It consists of 1142 questions spanning diverse domains and is designed to evaluate model performance across four distinct content types: Text, Layout, Chart, and Table.

Evaluation Metric. For evaluation, we report Exact Match (EM) and F1 scores. EM measures the proportion of predictions that exactly match any of the reference answers. The F1 score, defined as the harmonic mean of precision and recall, captures the token-level overlap between predicted and ground-truth answers, balancing correctness and completeness.

Baselines and Oracle. We adopt Nv-embedV2 [28] and ColQwen2 [18] as retrievers for the TextRAG and VisualRAG baselines, respectively. We select the top-7 retrieved results for generation, aligning with the average page length used in our dual-stream adaptive retrieval strategy. This setup ensures a fair comparison and effectively highlights the benefits of our approach. Additionally, we include an Oracle setting, where the LVLM generates answers based on the ground-truth page without retrieval, serving as an upper-bound reference.

Implementation Details. We employ Qwen2.5-VL-7B [29] as the large vision-language model for both the Selector and Integrator Agents. To handle the document pages retrieved by the dual-stream retrieval pipeline, we adopt a multi-page processing strategy in which each page is encoded independently. This design preserves structural and contextual integrity, mitigating the potential information loss introduced by spatial image concatenation. For the WCABS algorithm, we configure the following parameters: the number of top candidate breakpoints $m = 20$, quantile thresholds for score distribution analysis $Q = [0.1, 0.2, 0.3]$, minimum retrieval size $k_{\min} = 5$, and maximum retrieval size $k_{\max} = 10$. All experiments are conducted on 2 NVIDIA A800 GPUs.

5.2 Experiment Results

We compare our method against established baselines for document understanding, as summarized in Table 1. Overall, our approach achieves an Exact Match (EM) score of 0.32 and an F1 score of 0.49, outperforming TextRAG (EM: 0.28, F1: 0.43) by 14.3% and 14.0%, and VisualRAG (EM: 0.29, F1: 0.44) by 10.3% and 11.4%, respectively. Notably, our method yields significant gains in complex modalities such as Chart and Table, where purely TextRAG or VisualRAG methods struggle. In particular, our performance on Chart (EM: 0.39, F1: 0.46) approaches the oracle upper bound (EM: 0.41, F1: 0.47). These improvements are attributed to the synergy among WCABS's dual-stream adaptive retrieval, hybrid page merging strategy, and the noise-resilient reasoning enabled by the hierarchical multi-agent framework. Although the Oracle setting represents the upper-bound performance, our approach narrows the gap significantly, validating the effectiveness of our Dual-Stream Adaptive Retrieval and Hierarchical Agent Collaboration framework.

Table 1. Overall Generation Performance Comparison of Different Methods and Types

Method	Text		Layout		Chart		Table		Overall	
	EM	F1	EM	F1	EM	F1	EM	F1	EM	F1
Upper Bound	0.26	0.58	0.32	0.55	0.41	0.47	0.57	0.64	0.37	0.56
TextRAG	0.19	0.45	0.25	0.44	0.29	0.35	0.41	0.48	0.28	0.43
VisualRAG	0.20	0.47	0.26	0.44	0.32	0.37	0.43	0.50	0.29	0.44
Ours	**0.23**	**0.50**	**0.28**	**0.48**	**0.39**	**0.46**	**0.50**	**0.57**	**0.32**	**0.49**

5.3 Retrieval Evaluation

In Table 2, we report the detailed performance for various retrievers, including text-based and visual-based. Figure 4 depicts the recall trends across different retrievers, including an ablation study on WCABS adaptivity. The results show that adaptive retrieval achieves superior recall performance with fewer pages, while hybrid adaptive retrieval delivers improved performance by combining the outputs of two pipelines.

Table 2. Retrieval Performance on ViDoSeek Across Retrievers.

Retriever	Recall@1	Recall@3	Recall@5	Recall@7	MRR@7
BGE-M3 [30]	0.6042	0.7881	0.8608	0.8967	0.7095
NV-Embed-V2 [28]	0.6550	0.8380	0.9072	0.9308	0.7558
ColPali [18]	0.7093	0.8862	0.9273	0.9510	0.8026
ColQwen2 [18]	0.7487	0.9081	0.9466	0.9615	0.8319

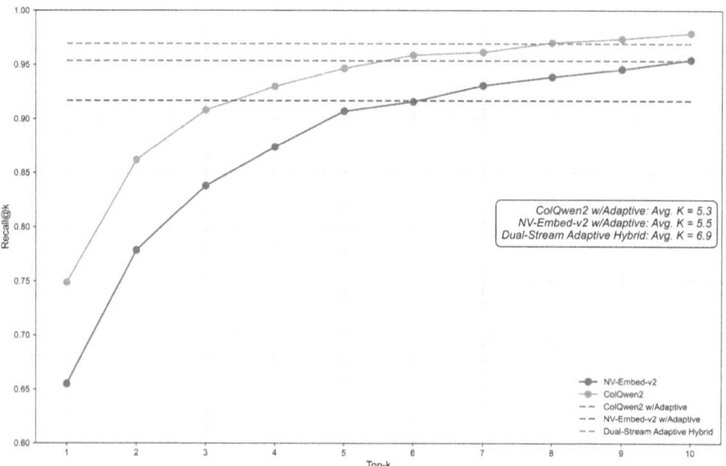

Fig. 4. Retrieval Performance Across Textual, Visual, and Hybrid Retrievers, with Ablation on WCABS Adaptivity.

5.4 Ablation Study

Table 3 presents the results of our ablation study on the ViDoSeek benchmark, evaluating the individual and combined contributions of the retrieval and generation components. We examine three ablated configurations:

- **(a) Baseline**: A standard VisualRAG setup without adaptive retrieval or multi-agent reasoning components.
- **(b) Hybrid Adaptive Retrieval**: Extends (a) by introducing the Hybrid Adaptive Retrieval module, while maintaining the base generator.
- **(c) Multi-Agent Generation**: Builds upon (a) by incorporating the Multi-Agent Generation strategy, using the original retriever.

Our proposed method consistently outperforms all ablated variants, highlighting the complementary strengths and scalability of both the retrieval and generation components. Specifically, while variants (b) and (c) individually outperform the baseline (a) by primarily enhancing precision and recall, respectively, their overall improvements are constrained when applied independently. In contrast, the complete method, which synergistically integrates both components,

Table 3. Performances of ablated models on ViDoSeek benchmark.

Retrieval	Generation	Metrics			
Hybrid Adaptivity	Multi-Agent	EM	F1	Precision	Recall
		0.2916	0.4425	0.4803	0.4439
✓		0.2951	0.4579	0.5017	0.4570
	✓	0.2986	0.4548	0.4843	0.4606
✓	✓	0.3214	0.4910	0.5247	0.4975

yields substantially greater performance gains, underscoring their interdependent contributions. We attribute these results to the following observations:

- (b) **Hybrid Adaptive Retrieval**: While the Hybrid Adaptive Retriever retrieves more relevant content, the increased page length introduces additional noise and reasoning overhead for the generator, ultimately constraining the performance improvements.
- (c) **Multi-Agent Generation**: The Multi-Agent generation strategy improves answer quality when provided with sufficiently relevant context. However, in the absence of the Hybrid Adaptive Retrieval mechanism, the quality of the retrieved pages is suboptimal, thereby limiting the generation effectiveness.

These findings highlight the complementary roles of the two components: the Hybrid Adaptive Retrieval improves cross-modal evidence recall, while the Multi-Agent generator enhances answer precision through structured reasoning. Their combination yields clear synergistic gains, resulting in a more robust and performant end-to-end system.

6 Conclusion

In this paper, we introduce a two-stage DocVQA framework that combines Dual-Stream Adaptive Retrieval with Hierarchical Agent Collaboration. Our Wasserstein-based Compact Adaptive Breakpoint Selection (WCABS) algorithm enables dynamic top-k page selection. The dual-stream retrieval module jointly incorporates textual and visual results, expanding the evidence search space to uncover more potential supporting pages. On top of this, the Selector and Integrator Agents collaboratively perform structured reasoning and response synthesis, enabling more accurate answer generation. Experiments on ViDoSeek demonstrate state-of-the-art performance, surpassing existing TextRAG and VisRAG approaches. In future work, we plan to explore fine-grained layout-aware representations to capture complex document structures, and develop dynamic task-routing mechanisms to adaptively coordinate between textual and visual pathways, further improving adaptability and accuracy in diverse document understanding scenarios.

Acknowledgments. This work was supported by the National Key Research and Development Program of China (2024YFC3308200), National Natural Science Foundation of China (Grant Nos. 62293555, 62293554), Special Projects of Major Science and Technology Programs in Yunnan Province (202402AD080002), and the Fundamental Research Funds for the Central Universities (No. CCNU25ZZ100).

References

1. Bornmann, L., Mutz, R.: Growth rates of modern science: a bibliometric analysis based on the number of publications and cited references. J. Am. Soc. Inf. Sci. **66**(11), 2215–2222 (2015)
2. Han, S., et al.: Mdocagent: a multi-modal multi-agent framework for document understanding. arXiv preprint arXiv:2503.13964 (2025)
3. Tanaka, R., Nishida, K., Nishida, K., Hasegawa, T., Saito, I., Saito, K.: Slidevqa: a dataset for document visual question answering on multiple images. In: Proceedings of the AAAI Conference on Artificial Intelligence, vol. 37, pp. 13636–13645 (2023). https://doi.org/10.1609/aaai.v37i11.26598
4. Chia, Y.K., et al.: M-longdoc: a benchmark for multimodal super-long document understanding and a retrieval-aware tuning framework. arXiv preprint arXiv:2411.06176 (2024)
5. Mathew, M., Karatzas, D., Jawahar, C.: Docvqa: a dataset for vqa on document images. In: Proceedings of the IEEE/CVF Winter Conference on Applications of Computer Vision, pp. 2200–2209 (2021)
6. Cho, J., Mahata, D., Irsoy, O., He, Y., Bansal, M.: M3docrag: multi-modal retrieval is what you need for multi-page multi-document understanding. arXiv preprint arXiv:2411.04952 (2024)
7. Memon, J., Sami, M., Khan, R.A., Uddin, M.: Handwritten optical character recognition (ocr): A comprehensive systematic literature review (slr). IEEE Access **8**, 142642–142668 (2020)
8. Lewis, P., et al.: Retrieval-augmented generation for knowledge-intensive nlp tasks. Adv. Neural. Inf. Process. Syst. **33**, 9459–9474 (2020)
9. Yu, S., et al.: Visrag: vision-based retrieval-augmented generation on multi-modality documents. arXiv preprint arXiv:2410.10594 (2024)
10. Wang, Q., et al.: Vidorag: visual document retrieval-augmented generation via dynamic iterative reasoning agents. arXiv preprint arXiv:2502.18017 (2025)
11. Tito, R., Karatzas, D., Valveny, E.: Hierarchical multimodal transformers for multipage docvqa. Pattern Recogn. **144**, 109834 (2023). https://doi.org/10.1016/j.patcog.2023.109834
12. Mishra, A., Shekhar, S., Singh, A.K., Chakraborty, A.: Ocr-vqa: visual question answering by reading text in images. In: 2019 International Conference on Document Analysis and Recognition (ICDAR), pp. 947–952. IEEE (2019). https://doi.org/10.1109/ICDAR.2019.00155
13. Ding, Y., et al.: V-doc: visual questions answers with documents. In: Proceedings of the IEEE/CVF Conference on Computer Vision and Pattern Recognition (CVPR), pp. 21492–21498 (2022)
14. Zhang, Y., et al.: Motiongpt: finetuned llms are general-purpose motion generators. In: Proceedings of the AAAI Conference on Artificial Intelligence, pp. 7368–7376 (2024)

15. Liu, H., Li, C., Li, Y., Lee, Y.J.: Improved baselines with visual instruction tuning. In: Proceedings of the IEEE/CVF Conference on Computer Vision and Pattern Recognition, pp. 26296–26306 (2024)
16. Tong, H., et al.: Mj-video: fine-grained benchmarking and rewarding video preferences in video generation. arXiv preprint arXiv:2502.01719 (2025)
17. Wang, W., et al.: Image as a foreign language: Beit pretraining for vision and vision-language tasks. In: Proceedings of the IEEE/CVF Conference on Computer Vision and Pattern Recognition, pp. 19175–19186 (2023)
18. Faysse, M., et al.: Colpali: efficient document retrieval with vision language models (2025). https://arxiv.org/abs/2407.01449
19. Liu, H., Li, C., Wu, Q., Lee, Y.J.: Visual instruction tuning. Adv. Neural. Inf. Process. Syst. **36**, 34892–34916 (2023)
20. Bai, J., et al.: Qwen technical report. arXiv preprint arXiv:2309.16609 (2023)
21. Achiam, J., et al.: Gpt-4 technical report. arXiv preprint arXiv:2303.08774 (2023)
22. Zhu, D., Chen, J., Shen, X., Li, X., Elhoseiny, M.: Minigpt-4: enhancing vision-language understanding with advanced large language models. arXiv preprint arXiv:2304.10592 (2023)
23. Abootorabi, M.M., et al.: Ask in any modality: a comprehensive survey on multimodal retrieval-augmented generation. arXiv preprint arXiv:2502.08826 (2025)
24. Du, Y., et al.: Pp-ocr: a practical ultra lightweight ocr system. arXiv preprint arXiv:2009.09941 (2020)
25. Khattab, O., Zaharia, M.: Colbert: efficient and effective passage search via contextualized late interaction over bert. In: Proceedings of the 43rd International ACM SIGIR Conference on Research and Development in Information Retrieval, pp. 39–48 (2020)
26. Panaretos, V.M., Zemel, Y.: Statistical aspects of wasserstein distances. Ann. Rev. Stat. Appl. **6**(1), 405–431 (2019)
27. Weng, L.: From gan to wgan. arXiv preprint arXiv:1904.08994 (2019)
28. Lee, C., et al.: Nv-embed: improved techniques for training llms as generalist embedding models. arXiv preprint arXiv:2405.17428 (2024)
29. Bai, S., et al.: Qwen2. 5-vl technical report. arXiv preprint arXiv:2502.13923 (2025)
30. Chen, J., Xiao, S., Zhang, P., Luo, K., Lian, D., Liu, Z.: Bge m3-embedding: multi-lingual, multi-functionality, multi-granularity text embeddings through self-knowledge distillation. arXiv preprint arXiv:2402.03216 (2024)

Retrieval and Distill: A Temporal Data Shift-Free Paradigm for Online Recommendation System

Lei Zheng[1], Ning Li[1], Chengguang Gan[2], Yong Yu[1], and Weinan Zhang[1(✉)]

[1] Shanghai Jiao Tong University, Shanghai, China
{zhenglei2016,lining01,yyu,wnzhang}@sjtu.edu.cn
[2] Yokohama National University, Yokohama, Japan
ganchnegguan@yahoo.co.jp

Abstract. Current recommendation systems are significantly affected by a serious issue of temporal data shift, which is the inconsistency between the distribution of historical data and that of online data. Most existing models focus on utilizing updated data, overlooking the transferable, temporal data shift-free information that can be learned from shifting data. We propose the Temporal Invariance of Association theorem, which suggests that given a fixed search space, the relationship between the data and the data in the search space keeps invariant over time. Leveraging this principle, we designed a retrieval-based recommendation system framework that can train a data shift-free relevance network using shifting data, significantly enhancing the predictive performance of the original model in the recommendation system. However, retrieval-based recommendation models face substantial inference time costs when deployed online. To address this, we further designed a distill framework that can distill information from the relevance network into a parameterized module using shifting data. The distilled model can be deployed online alongside the original model, with only a minimal increase in inference time. Extensive experiments on multiple real datasets demonstrate that our framework significantly improves the performance of the original model by utilizing shifting data.

Keywords: Temporal Data Shift · Retrieval-Enhanced Methods · Knowledge Distillation · Pretraining · Click-Through Rate

1 Inroduction

Click-through rate (CTR) prediction models play a significant role in modern recommendation systems. To enhance the accuracy of CTR models, deep learning-based approaches have been extensively employed [3,28,33,34]. However, the dynamic environment faced by the recommendation systems, with the data distribution evolving over time, poses significant challenges to the effectiveness of these models [47].

J. Li et al. (Eds.): APWeb-WAIM 2025, LNCS 16115, pp. 417–435, 2026.
https://doi.org/10.1007/978-981-95-5719-6_27

To tackle this challenge, prior research has undertaken investigations from two distinct perspectives, namely incremental learning and behavior sequence modeling. On one hand, incremental learning techniques delve into updating the models that make these predictions as new data comes in, without having to start from scratch every time [15,19,40]. This means the models learn and improve gradually as they get access to more recent data. However, the process of learning neural network parameters depends on iterative updates based on gradients, which slowly infuse supervision data into the model weights using a minimal learning rate. This poses a significant challenge for large parametric recommendation models in swiftly adapting to shifts in distribution. On the other hand, behavior sequence modeling focuses on understanding how users' behaviors change over time by looking at the sequence of actions they take. In this area, various network structures have been proposed, including recurrent neural networks (RNNs) [9,10], convolutional neural networks (CNNs) [31,41], and memory networks [21,26]. Moreover, the attention mechanism has emerged as the predominant approach for modeling item dependencies, with several notable contributions such as SASRec [14], DIN [46], DIEN [45], and BERT4Rec [29]. These studies aim to identify sequential patterns in user behavior, thereby facilitating the prediction of future preferences based on historical activities. However, these studies fail to directly tackle the issue of distribution shift during training time, and these high-capacity models significantly increase the online workload and inference burden.

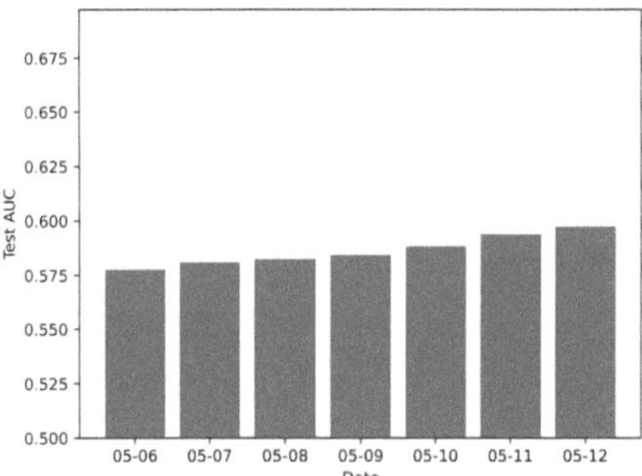

Fig. 1. The phenomenon of temporal data shift on a real dataset collected from Tmall. The test set consists of data after Nov. 10, 2015. The x-axis represents the date from which we add all data up to Nov. 10 to train a CTR model, and the y-axis represents the model's performance on the test set. We observed that model performance peaked when trained on temporally adjacent data, with performance degrading as the training period extended further from the test set timeframe.

All of the above-mentioned models either update the model using the latest data [6,33] or use past shifting data as a reference for retrieval [22,23], without directly using the shifting data for training model parameters. However, directly using the temporally shifting data for model training is challenging, as an example illustrated in Fig. 1 based on a public dataset of Tmall, an international e-commerce platform. In this dataset, data spanning Nov. 11–12, 2015 is employed as the test set. The x-axis represents the training set from the indicated date to Nov. 10, 2015. We train a common deep CTR model PNN [25] using different training sets to make predictions. The y-axis indicates the AUC performance of the model on the test set. We can observe that utilizing data over Nov. 1–10, 2015 for predictions on the test set yields the best results, whereas adding data from earlier time periods will negatively impact the results due to data shift. Therefore, it is crucial to find an effective method that can directly utilize these data for model training.

Inspired by the recent proposed retrieval-based tabular data prediction models [24,44], we found that similar data from historical records can significantly enhance the predictive capability and generalizability. In other words, although the probability distribution modeled by the CTR is time-variant, the probability distribution of the association between current user behavior data and similar historical data can remain invariant over time if the search space is fixed. If we design a neural network to model the probability distribution of data similar to the current query, this neural network is temporal data shift-free. Thus, the shifting data can be used to train such a neural network. By incorporating this neural network with the original CTR model, we can obtain an aggregated prediction model that has been trained with shifting data.

In this paper, we propose the Retrieval and Distill paradigm (RAD) to address the challenge of ineffective training of a CTR model over shifting data. The RAD paradigm generally consists of two major components, namely the Retrieval Framework and the Distill Framework. We first establish a Retrieval Framework to assist the original model in making predictions using similar data within the shifting data. We refer to the neural network in Retrieval Framework that retrieves and outputs the logits of similar data as the relevance network. By pre-training this relevance network using shifting data and then merging the original CTR model and relevance network, we can significantly enhance the predictive capability of the original CTR model. However, the added relevance network in the Retrieval Framework, due to its retrieval process (such as BM25 [27]), is difficult to deploy online due to its inference time, similar to other retrieval-based CTR models [24,44]. To address this difficulty, we further build the Distill Framework to distill knowledge from the relevance network using shifting data, obtaining a parameterized student network called search-distill module. By aggregating the original CTR model and the search-distill module, we finetune the Distill Framework with unshifting data, e.g., the latest training data. This yields the final model that can be deployed online for light workload and efficient inference.

In sum, the technical contributions of this paper are threefold.

- We highlight the significant impact of the data shift phenomenon in recommendation systems, which is not addressable by simply increasing training data or the model capacity. To deal with this issue, we propose the Retrieval

and Distill (RAD) paradigm, where the recommendation model is enhanced by incorporating shifting data into the model. To the best of our knowledge, RAD is the first paradigm that successfully utilizes shifting data for model training and lightweight deployment.
- As the rationale of RAD, we raise the theorem of Temporal Invariance of Association, which provides effective guidance on how to utilize shifting data.
- We design an innovative distillation approach that distills information from the retrieval framework of RAD. This approach optimizes both the time complexity and space complexity of the retrieval process to $O(1)$, which largely pushes forward the practical usage of retrieval-based models for online recommendation systems.

Extensive experiments on multiple real datasets demonstrate that RAD significantly improves the performance of the original model via effective training over shifting data. RAD offers a new paradigm in the field of recommendation systems, enabling models to train using both shifting and unshifting data, opening up a new pathway for enhancing the performance of CTR models by increasing the amount of training data.

2 Preliminaries

In this section, we formulate the problem and introduce the notations. In the context of recommendation systems, we represent the dataset as a tabular structure, denoted by $\mathcal{D}$, comprising F feature columns $\mathcal{C} = \{C_i\}_{i=1}^{F}$ alongside a singular label column $\mathcal{Y}$. The feature columns encapsulate attributes such as "Age," "City," and "Category." Each individual entry within table $\mathcal{D}$ corresponds to a sample s_z. A sample is characterized by an amalgamation of multiple features along with a label, articulated as $s_z = (x_z, y_z)$, where $x_z = \{c_i^z\}_{i=1}^{F}$. Accordingly, table $\mathcal{D}$ is defined as an ensemble of N samples, expressed as $\mathcal{D} = \{s_z\}_{z=1}^{N}$.

A click-through rate (CTR) model can be mathematically represented as a conditional probability, $P(y|x)$, where y is the event of a click, and x represents the features. The goal of the model is to accurately estimate this probability given the features x, which can include information about the item, the user, and the context.

Theorem 1. *Temporal Invariance of Association.*

In the paper, we model $P(y|x)$ as $P(y|x, x_s)$, where x_s represents documents similar to x within a fixed search space $\mathcal{E}$. Given that the probability distribution of $P(y|x, x_s)$ changes over time, while the probability distribution of $P(x_s|x)$ remains constant, we can utilize the data come from the time-varying $P(y|x, x_s)$ to train a model that represents $P(x_s|x)$. This process allows us to capture the temporal dynamics in $P(y|x)$ while leveraging the time-invariant properties of $P(x_s|x)$, thereby enhancing the model's adaptability to temporal changes in the future.

We partition the dataset by date into three segments. The last few days, denoted as $\mathcal{D}_{[t+1,t+\Delta]}$, serve as the test set, $\mathcal{D}_{\text{test}}$. Data within a window of d

days prior to the test dates is considered unshifting data, which is $\mathcal{D}_{[t-d+1,t]}$ and is used as the training set, denoted by $\mathcal{D}_{\text{train}}$. The remaining portion, $\mathcal{D}_{(-\infty,t-d]}$, is designated as the search space, $\mathcal{D}_{\text{shifting}}$.

The **Retrieval and Distill (RAD)** framework comprises two components. The first component, the Retrieval Framework, employs a retrieval-based method to assist any original model in addressing the data shift issue. However, retrieval-based models face significant efficiency challenges. Therefore, the second component, the Distill Framework, utilizes distillation to eliminate the retrieval process. We will introduce these two components separately in the following.

Retrieval Framework. The objective of the Retrieval Framework is to employ a relevance network, which incorporates non-parametric retrieval, to assist any original model $F(x)$ in predicting the label. The formulation of the Retrieval Framework is as follows:

$$\hat{y_R} = f_\theta(F(x), x, R(x)), \tag{1}$$

where $R(x)$ is designed to fit $P(x_s|x)$ and is referred to as the *relevance network* and f_θ which approximate the $P(y|x, x_s)$ is data shift sensitive.

To obtain a model, $R(x)$, that approximates the probability distribution $P(x|x_s)$, we employ a Retrieval Framework, devoid of $F(x)$, named the teacher network. The formulation of the teacher network is as follows:

$$\hat{y_T} = T_\gamma(x, R(x)). \tag{2}$$

According to Theorem 1, The $R(x)$ component within T_γ, trained using shifting data, is invariant to data shift. Therefore, to obtain an $R(x)$ that has been trained with shifting data, T_γ can be minimized by the following loss function:

$$\mathcal{L}_{\text{pretrain}} = \sum_{x_z \in \mathcal{D}_{\text{shifting}}} \text{CE}(y^z, \hat{y}_T^z), \tag{3}$$

where CE is binary cross-entropy. This step obtains the model $R(x)$ that approximates $P(x_s|x)$.

Once we have obtained an $R(x)$ that has been pretrained with shifting data, we can utilize $R(x)$ in the training of the Retrieval Framework. We use unshifting data to minimize the following loss function:

$$\mathcal{L}_{\text{retrieval}} = \sum_{x_z \in \mathcal{D}_{\text{train}}} \text{CE}(y^z, \hat{y}_R^z), \tag{4}$$

where CE is binary cross-entropy. In this step, we obtain the Retrieval Framework, f_θ, which approximates $P(y|x, x_s)$.

Distill Framework. Although the Retrieval Framework can leverage shifting data to significantly enhance the original model, the deployment of retrieval-based methods presents substantial challenges in terms of storage space and inference time in an online environment. Therefore, we have designed the Distill Framework to eliminate the non-parametric search process.

Distill Framework can be formulated as:

$$\hat{y}_D = f'_\phi(F(x), x, r(x)), \tag{5}$$

where $r(x)$ is distilled from $R(x)$ pretrained using loss function (3), which we refer to as the *search-distill module.* Similar to f_θ, f'_ϕ approximates $P(y|x, x_s)$ and can also only be trained using unshifting data.

We assume

$$w_R = R(x), \tag{6}$$

where w_R is the last layer logits of $R(x)$ and assume

$$w_r = r(x), \tag{7}$$

where w_s is the last layer logits of $r(x)$. The loss function used to distill knowledge from $R(x)$ to $r(x)$ can be written as:

$$\mathcal{L}_{\mathrm{KD}} = \sum_{x_z \in \mathcal{D}_{\mathrm{shifting}}} \mathrm{MSE}(r(x), R(x)) = \sum_{x_z \in \mathcal{D}_{\mathrm{shifting}}} \mathrm{MSE}(w_r^z, w_R^z), \tag{8}$$

where MSE is the Mean Squared Error loss function.

Once we obtain the search-distill module, we can use unshifting data to derive a final Distill Framework using the following loss function:

$$\mathcal{L}_{\mathrm{distill}} = \sum_{x_z \in \mathcal{D}_{\mathrm{train}}} \mathrm{CE}(y^z, \hat{y}_D^z), \tag{9}$$

where CE is binary cross-entropy loss.

3 The RAD Paradigm

In this section, the details of RAD will be presented. We start with an overview of the entire paradigm's structure at Sect. 3.1, followed by detailed expositions of the Retrieval Framework and Distill Framework in Sects. 3.2 and 3.3, respectively.

3.1 Overview

Traditional CTR models have not accounted for the data shift issue, and they cannot enhance performance by merely adding shifting data [5,12,18]. Training only with unshifting data neglects a significant amount of information. Our proposed Retrieval and Distill paradigm aims to devise a universal solution that utilizes shifting data to enhance the performance of existing models. RAD is generally divided into two parts. The first part incorporates a Retrieval Framework to introduce shifting data into the datastore during training. Concurrently, as per Theorem 1, we pretrain the model's relevance network with shifting data and then transfer it for use. This approach substantially improves the model's

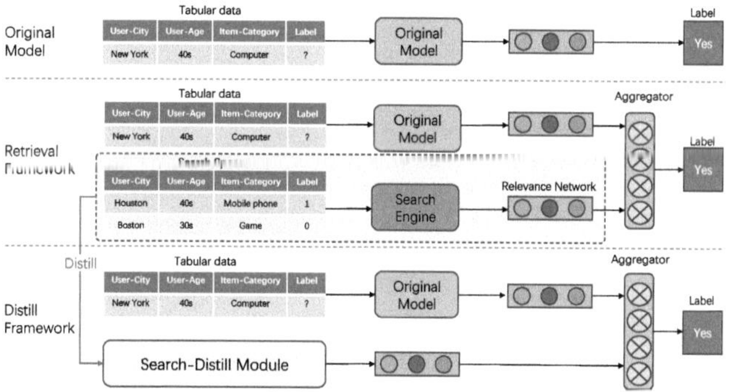

Fig. 2. This figure illustrates the original model and its combination with the two components of the RAD paradigm. In CTR tasks, the original model typically takes tabular data as input and outputs a probability indicating the likelihood of a click. The RAD paradigm initially employs a retrieval framework to assist the original model in making predictions using shifting data. However, considering the performance requirements of the CTR model, we designed the RAD's distill framework to eliminate the search process in the retrieval framework, thereby meeting the online inference time requirements.

performance without altering its original structure. However, including a non-parametric search component in the relevance network poses deployment challenges for online recommendation systems. Therefore, the second part is a Distill Framework tasked with transforming the relevance network into a parametric neural network model. We distill a simple neural network (search-distill module) using shifting data and the relevance network as the teacher network. Ultimately, we merge the search-distill module with the original model and finetune it using unshifting data to yield the final online deployable model. The following sections will elucidate these modules in detail.

3.2 Retreival Framework

The Retrieval Framework aims to employ a relevance network that utilizes shifting data in conjunction with the original model for CTR prediction. According to Theorem 1, the relevance network is temporal data shift-free; therefore, as an initial step, we pretrain the relevance network using shifting data with a teacher network, which is a Retrieval Framework that does not contain the original model. In the second step, we jointly train the relevance network and original model using unshifting data. Next, we will detail the neural network structure of the Retrieval Framework, followed by its training method.

Framework Model Structure. The neural network structure of the Retrieval Framework can be seen in Fig. 3. The Retrieval Framework aggregates the outputs of both the teacher network and the original model, where the teacher

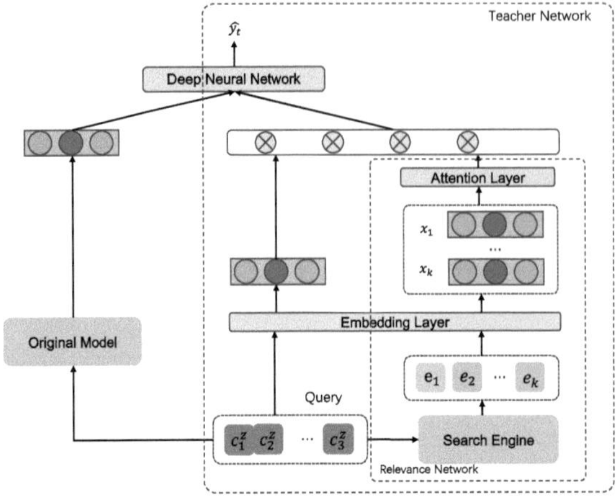

Fig. 3. Retrieval framework.

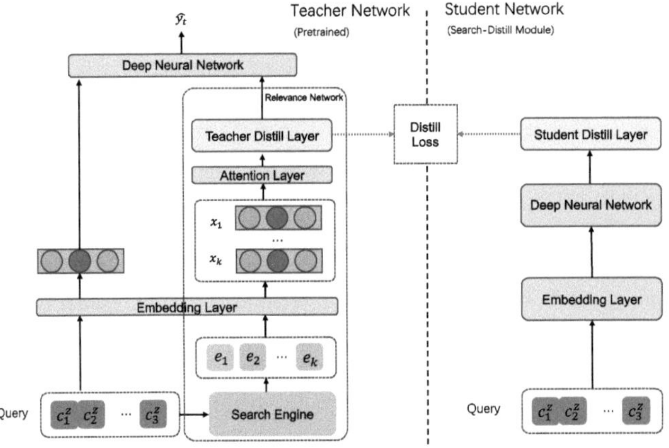

Fig. 4. Distill Process.

network specifically combines the original input with the relevance network. We shall now explicate the original model, relevance network, and teacher network.

Original Model. We denote s_z as any tabular data entry within the dataset $\mathcal{D}$, where the feature part of s_z is represented as x_z, and the label part as y_z, with $x_z = \{c_z^i\}_{i=1}^F$ comprising F features. Traditional CTR models take such an x_z as input and output a probability. We represent the original model as O, with the last layer logit denoted by w_o.

In the traditional model, the probability prediction is given by

$$\hat{y_O^z} = O(x_z) = \text{sigmoid}(w_o), \tag{10}$$

where w_o is the input of the aggregation layer of the Retrieval Framework.

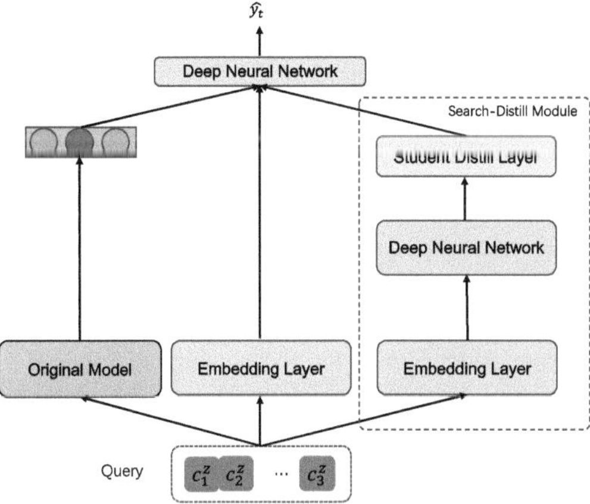

Fig. 5. Distill Framework.

Relevance Network. The relevance network features an embedding layer shared with input x_z, a search engine, and an attention-based aggregation layer. Within our framework, we utilize shifting tabular data entries as the search space, with BM25 [27] serving as our search algorithm.

In the BM25 algorithm, we treat any sample x_z as the query and a key x_d in the datastore as the document. As such, the ranking score can be calculated as

$$\text{RankScore}(x_z, x_d) = \sum_{j=1}^{M} \text{IDF}(a_j^z) \cdot \mathbf{1}(x_j^z = x_j^d), \tag{11}$$

$$\text{IDF}(x_j^z) = \log \frac{N - N(a_j^z) + 0.5}{N(a_j^z) + 0.5}, \tag{12}$$

where $\mathbf{1}(\cdot)$ is the indicator function, N is the number of data samples in $\mathcal{D}_{\text{shifting}}$, and $N(a_j^z)$ is the number of data samples that have the categorical feature value x_j^z. By ranking the candidate samples using BM25, we obtain the top K entries as the retrieved set $\mathcal{S}(x_z)$.

For each item within $\mathcal{S}(x_z)$, an attention mechanism is applied to calculate its aggregation parameter

$$\alpha_k = \frac{\exp(x_k^\top W x_z)}{\sum_{j=1}^{K} \exp(x_j^\top W x_z)}, \tag{13}$$

The elements of $\mathcal{S}(x_z)$ are then consolidated into a logit w_R :

$$w_R = \sum_{k=1}^{K} \alpha_k \cdot x_k, \quad s_k \in \mathcal{S}(x_z), \tag{14}$$

where w_s is the input of the aggregation layer of the teacher network.

Teacher Network. The teacher network is a Retrieval Framework that does not include the original model. From Fig. 3, we can observe that the teacher network forms the right portion of the diagram. The teacher network serves as an intermediary bridge for training the relevance network. The teacher network takes x_z and the relevance network output as inputs, producing a probability as output. Drawing inspiration from RIM [24], we incorporate a factorization machine module within the aggregation layer of the teacher network. This aggregation layer is designed to effectively merge the input x_z with the aggregated w_R, thus improving the teacher network's capability to discover the hidden relationships between x_z and the returned $S(x_z)$ from the search engine.

Pretrain with Shifting Data. The relevance network models the probability distribution $P(w_R|x)$, where w_R is the logit representation of x_s. As established by theorem 1, the probability distribution represented by the relevance network is time-invariant, which allows us to pretrain it using shifting data. To obtain the relevance network, we initialize a separate teacher network. The teacher network is trained using the dataset $\mathcal{D}_{\text{shifting}}$ and with loss function (3). Although the separate teacher network trained in this manner performs poorly on the test set $\mathcal{D}_{\text{test}}$ due to data shift—often hovering around 0.5 in our experiments—the relevance network is transferable.

Finetune with Unshifting Data. After obtaining the pretrained relevance network, we integrate it with the original model and the target query x_z to form the Retrieval Framework. This framework is then trained using $\mathcal{D}_{\text{train}}$ with loss function (4), essentially finetuning it.

3.3 Distill Framework

To optimize the time complexity of the Retrieval Framework, we propose a Distill Framework that distills the relevance network (pretrained via the Retrieval Framework) into a search-distill module by removing its computationally intensive BM25 search component. This module is then integrated with the original model through a multilayer neural network, aggregated, and finetuned using $\mathcal{D}_{\text{training}}$, enabling efficient deployment in online environments.

Framework Model Structure. The neural network structure of the Retrieval Framework can be seen in Fig. 5. The network architecture of the Distill Framework is similar to that of the Retrieval Framework. We replace the relevance network with the search-distill module.

From Fig. 4, we can observe the form of the teacher network in the Distill Framework. The teacher network in the Distill Framework differs somewhat from that in the Retrieval Framework. We removed the cross layer from the teacher network in the Retrieval Framework to distill only the relevance network portion and added two neural network layers after the attention layer. We use this teacher network to obtain a relevance network for distillation.

The search-distill module is a multilayer neural network equipped with an embedding layer. Akin to the original model, the search-distill module takes the feature portion of tabular data x_z as its input. The output of the search-distill module is a logit of the same size as that of the final output from the relevance network.

Pretrain and Distill with Shifting Data. From Theorem 1, we understand that the relevance network operates as a temporal data shift-free module. Like the relevance network, the search-distill module is also used to approximate the probability $P(x_s|x)$, which can be trained using shifting data. We first obtain the relevance network using the teacher network and loss function (3). Then, we employ $\mathcal{D}_{\text{shifting}}$ and loss function (8) to perform distillation on the final logit layer of the search-distill module. The distillation process can be observed in Fig. 4. We employ the mean squared error loss function to align the final logit layer of the search-distill module with that of the relevance network.

Finetune with Unshifting Data. After obtaining a distilled search-distill module, we integrate the original model, the input x_z, and the search-distill module using a multilayer neural network for aggregation. This network is then trained with unshifting data and loss function (9), allowing us to finetune and enhance the original model with insights gleaned from shifting data without significantly increasing the deployment overhead of the original model.

4 Experiments

In this section, we evaluate the RAD paradigm across multiple datasets using various traditional CTR models. We measure the efficacy of the RAD paradigm using the conventional CTR prediction task. We select two sets of classic CTR models: one representing factorization models and the other representing sequence prediction models. Each set of models is tested on three real-world datasets.

This section starts with five research questions (RQs) guiding the subsequent discourse.

RQ1 Does the RAD paradigm enhance the performance of existing CTR prediction models?
RQ2 Can distillation functions be applied to the distillation of non-parametric models?
RQ3 Can the relevance network, trained using shifting data, be transferred to predict future data?
RQ4 How does the RAD paradigm affect the run time of the original model?
RQ5 How do different distillation loss functions affect the RAD paradigm?

4.1 Datasets

In order to evaluate the performance of RAD, we conduct extensive experiments for CTR prediction tasks on three real-world large-scale recommendation datasets from Alibaba and Ant Group, i.e., Taobao, Tmall and Alipay[1]. These datasets consist of sequential user-item interactions in e-commerce scenes. The datasets contain timestamped user behaviors. We split them chronologically: the newest data for testing, the oldest for retrieval ($\mathcal{D}_{\text{shifting}}$), and the middle segment for training ($\mathcal{D}_{\text{training}}$). This mimics real-world scenarios where models must adapt to evolving preferences while leveraging historical data.

4.2 Evaluation Metrics

In the CTR prediction task, the area under the ROC curve (AUC) and negative log-likelihood (LogLoss) are widely used metrics. AUC measures the probability that a randomly chosen positive sample will be ranked higher than a randomly chosen negative sample, while Logloss quantifies the difference between the predicted probability and the actual label. We choose these two metrics to evaluate the model performance.

4.3 Compared Methods

To evaluate our framework, we select six strong baseline models grouped into two categories: (1) **Feature interaction models**: DNN (MLP), DeepFM [6] (combines FM and DNN), and PNN [25] (product-based feature interaction); (2) **Sequential models**: Transformer encoder [32], DIN [46], and DIEN [45] (DIN with RNN), which model user behavior sequences via attention mechanisms.

4.4 Overall Performance (RQ1).

The results are listed in Table 1. The results reveal the following insights. i) In our experiments, sequence models, except the original Transformer model, outperformed factorization models. This indicates that increasing data volume is beneficial for recommendation systems. ii) The Retrieval Framework utilizes shifting data as a search space and pretrains the relevance network with shifting data, significantly enhancing performance beyond the original model. This demonstrates the substantial benefit of shifting data for the original model. iii) The Distill Framework employs the distilled relevance network to assist the original model. While predictive performance surpasses the original model, it falls short of models augmented by the Retrieval Framework, suggesting that the distilled relevance network retains valuable information, albeit with less incremental information than the retrieval model. iv) The performance of feature interaction-based models within the Distill Framework has already surpassed

[1] https://tianchi.aliyun.com/dataset/x, where ‘x’ is ‘649’, ‘42’, and ‘53’ for Taobao, Tmall, and Alipay, respectively.

Table 1. Performance comparison of CTR prediction task. Rel.Impr means relative AUC improvement rate against each original model. Improvements are statistically significant with $p < 0.01$.

Models		Taobao			Tmall			Alipay		
		LogLoss	AUC	Rel. Impr.	LogLoss	AUC	Rel. Impr.	LogLoss	AUC	Rel. Impr.
Original	DNN	0.6454	0.6744	–	0.4259	0.8890	–	0.6230	0.7011	-
	DeepFM	0.6591	0.6545	–	0.4264	0.8885	–	0.6375	0.6803	–
	PNN	0.6469	0.6787	–	0.4274	0.8949	–	0.6253	0.7130	–
	Transformer	0.6757	0.5990	–	0.4644	0.8609	-	0.6761	0.6523	–
	DIN	0.6267	0.7040	–	0.4301	0.8820	-	0.6257	0.7333	–
	DIEN	0.6328	0.6947	–	0.3930	0.9037	-	0.6295	0.7218	–
Retrieval	DNN	0.4525	0.8633	28.00%	0.2985	0.9446	6.26%	0.4897	0.8455	20.60%
	DeepFM	0.4566	0.8614	31.61%	0.3016	0.9443	6.27%	0.4694	0.8583	26.16%
	PNN	0.4576	0.8606	26.81%	0.3054	0.9468	5.80%	0.4429	0.8748	22.68%
	Transformer	0.4614	0.8557	42.86%	0.3459	0.9249	7.44%	0.5606	0.7984	21.23%
	DIN	0.5558	0.7906	12.30%	0.3239	0.9354	6.05%	0.5626	0.7826	6.72%
	DIEN	0.5733	0.7702	10.87%	0.3226	0.9371	3.10%	0.5810	0.7684	6.46%
Distill	DNN	0.7201	0.7224	7.11%	0.4100	0.8961	0.80%	0.5972	0.7423	5.88%
	DeepFM	0.6144	0.7192	9.88%	0.4108	0.8961	0.86%	0.5900	0.7532	10.72%
	PNN	0.6106	0.7269	7.10%	0.4061	0.9026	0.87%	0.5686	0.7713	8.17%
	Transformer	0.6263	0.6953	16.09%	0.4237	0.8940	3.85%	0.6227	0.7196	10.3%
	DIN	0.5956	0.7420	5.40%	0.3812	0.9152	3.76%	0.5927	0.7425	1.25%
	DIEN	0.6099	0.7176	3.29%	0.3690	0.9157	1.33%	0.6230	0.7562	4.77%

that of the original sequence models. Moreover, as illustrated in Fig. 7, the distillation method can enhance model performance without significantly increasing the inference burden

4.5 Applying Knowledge Distillation to Non-parametric Models (RQ2)

Knowledge distillation is traditionally employed for transferring knowledge between parametric models, typically from a complex, larger model to a simpler, smaller one. In this context, we extend the application of knowledge distillation to transfer knowledge from a non-parametric model (BM25 search) to a simple neural network. As illustrated in Table 1, distilling information from the retrieval-based relevance network into the search-distill module demonstrates that the distilled student model can still significantly enhance the performance of the original model. However, compared to the direct use of the non-parametric model, performance is considerably reduced. There is significant room for improvement in distilling information from non-parametric models into parametric models.

Table 2. Performance comparison of pretrained relevance network in Retrieval Framework.

Models		Taobao		Tmall		Alipay	
		LogLoss	AUC	LogLoss	AUC	LogLoss	AUC
pretrained with $\mathcal{D}_{\text{train}}$	DNN	0.6210	0.7139	0.3373	0.9291	0.6227	0.7070
	DeepFM	0.6239	0.7109	0.3337	0.9320	0.6300	0.6966
	PNN	0.6188	0.7226	0.3272	0.9405	0.6063	0.7339
pretrained with $\mathcal{D}_{\text{shifting}}$	DNN	0.5224	0.8163	0.3141	0.9398	0.5006	0.8396
	DeepFM	0.5183	0.8169	0.3103	0.9405	0.4724	0.8564
	PNN	0.5087	0.8256	0.3179	0.9438	0.4446	0.8744

4.6 Temporal Invariance of Association (RQ3)

Table 2 showcases a group of experiments designed to validate the Theorem 1 of Temporal nvariance of Association. The relevance network aids the original model in prediction in two ways: the additional information provided by the retrieved similar data x_s, and the information gain brought by pretraining with shifting data. To eliminate the influence of x_s on the results during testing, we added D_{train} pretraining for comparison. Similarly, to rule out the impact of finetuning on the relevance network, we fixed the parameters of the relevance network during the finetuning phase. By comparing the data in the table, we find that: i) The relevance network pretrained with shifting data performs better than the model pretrained only with train data. This indicates that the relevance network trained with shifting data indeed learns time-invariant information in the time-varying data distribution. Theorem 1 is validated. ii) The relevance network trained with $\mathcal{D}_{\text{shifting}}$ performs better because whether using $\mathcal{D}_{\text{shifting}}$ or $\mathcal{D}_{\text{train}}$, both are fitting $P(x_s|x)$, and shifting data has a much larger volume. Hence, the trained relevance network performs better. Thus, we obtain a network that enhances model training effectiveness by increasing the volume of data, unlike the network in Fig. 1, where increasing the volume of data would decrease model performance.

4.7 Performance Efficiency Study (RQ4)

Recently, a range of retrieval-based models have been introduced in the field of recommender systems, some of which utilize discrete features for retrieval, such as SIM [21] and RIM [24], while others employ continuous features, like DERT [44]. Due to the significant time overhead associated with retrieval, these models face challenges in being directly deployed online. In Fig. 6, we compare three methods for augmenting relevant information. As RAD employs distillation to bypass the retrieval process, it incurs no retrieval time. On the other hand, directly aggregating the search-distill module with the original model increases the inference burden on the original model. However, as shown in Fig. 7, the additional inference load introduced by incorporating the search-distill module is not significant, and the time overhead it introduces is considerably less than the burden added by using sequence models for model inference.

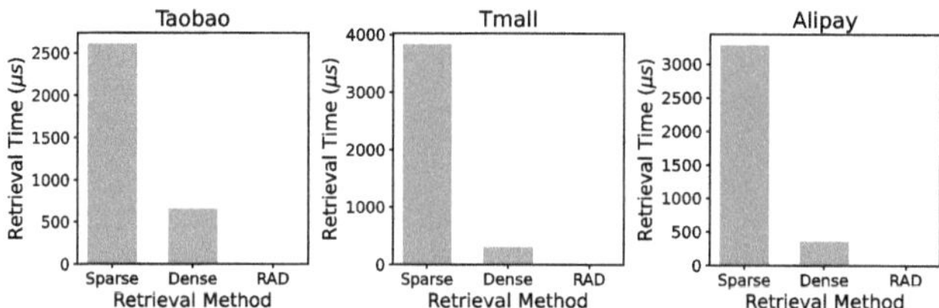

Fig. 6. Comparison of Retrieval time.

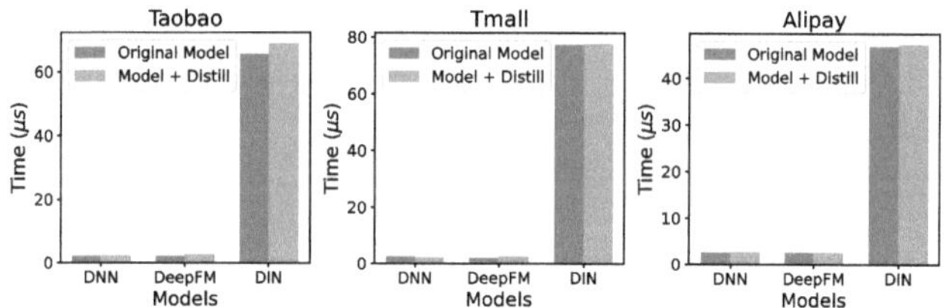

Fig. 7. Comparison of Inference time.

5 Related Work

Click-through Rate (CTR) Prediction. is crucial in the fields of online advertising, recommendation systems, and information retrieval. Many deep learning models for CTR prediction primarily concentrate on investigating the feature interactions within a single instance [6,8,17,25]. The Wide&Deep network [2] constructs fully connected (FC) layers based on field feature embeddings to extract feature interactions implicitly. Recently, graph neural networks have also shown great potential in recommendation scenes by constructing data into graph structures and performing message passing [7,16,35–37]. Despite the numerous models proposed in this direction, the model capacity might be constrained as the model's input is a single instance, necessitating the model to encode all knowledge into the parameters. Our work employs these deep models as the base model of the framework.

Retrieval-based CTR prediction methods, adapted from sequential recommendation, often replace RNNs when processing long user behavior sequences, as RNNs struggle with early pattern recall [21], offering a more efficient alternative to recurrence and attention mechanisms. RIM [24] expands the research scenario from sequential recommendation to generic tabular data prediction. The query is the target row data, and the retrieved data instances are the relevant rows in the table, with BM25 [27] serving as the predefined relevance function between two rows. DERT [44] is the pioneering work to incorporate dense retrieval into recommendation systems. Retrieval-enhanced machine learning is now considered a significant frontier in machine learning research [42].

Knowledge Distillation. (KD) [11] seeks to transfer the 'dark knowledge' from a teacher model to a student model and is extensively used in model compression and knowledge transfer [4]. Recent studies have also employed KD in various recommendation tasks, such as click-through rate (CTR) prediction [48], topology distillation [13], and multi-task transfer [38]. Prior theoretical analyses [1,20,30] have indicated that the teacher's predictions, also referred to as soft labels, are typically viewed as more informative training signals compared to binary hard labels. KD can adaptively adjust the training dynamics of the student model based on the values of the soft labels. Knowledge distillation is typically employed to transfer knowledge from a larger parameterized model to a smaller one. Recent studies have applied knowledge distillation to transfer knowledge from KNN to parameterized models [39,43], demonstrating the potential of knowledge distillation in non-parametric models.

6 Conclusion

In current recommendation systems, temporal data shift poses a significant challenge. The presence of data shift prevents the system from simply enhancing the CTR model's adaptability to new data by adding more training data. We observed that although the correlation between features and labels in recommendation systems changes over time, if a fixed search space is established, the relationship between the data and the search space remains invariant. Therefore, we designed a framework that uses retrieval techniques to leverage shifting data for training a relevance network. However, due to the use of BM25 as a retrieval method, this framework is challenging to deploy in online recommendation systems. We then designed a distillation method using knowledge distillation to transfer knowledge from the relevance network to a parameterized module, the search-distill module. We refer to this entire process as the Retrieval and Distill paradigm (RAD). With the RAD paradigm, we have an effective method for leveraging shifting data to enhance the performance of CTR models. In future research directions, we aim to incorporate a wider variety of data into the CTR model using RAD. On the other hand, enhancing the performance of the distillation method is also a significant area of focus.

References

1. Chandrasegaran, K., Tran, N.T., Zhao, Y., Cheung, N.M.: Revisiting label smoothing and knowledge distillation compatibility: what was missing? In: International Conference on Machine Learning, pp. 2890–2916. PMLR (2022)
2. Cheng, H.T., et al.: Wide & deep learning for recommender systems. In: 1st DLRS Workshop, pp. 7–10 (2016)
3. Covington, P., Adams, J., Sargin, E.: Deep neural networks for youtube recommendations. In: Proceedings of the 10th ACM Conference on Recommender Systems, pp. 191–198 (2016)
4. Gou, J., Yu, B., Maybank, S.J., Tao, D.: Knowledge distillation: a survey. Int. J. Comput. Vision **129**, 1789–1819 (2021)
5. Gu, Y., Ding, Z., Wang, S., Zou, L., Liu, Y., Yin, D.: Deep multifaceted transformers for multi-objective ranking in large-scale e-commerce recommender systems. In: Proceedings of the 29th ACM International Conference on Information & Knowledge Management, pp. 2493–2500 (2020)
6. Guo, H., Tang, R., Ye, Y., Li, Z., He, X.: Deepfm: a factorization-machine based neural network for ctr prediction. In: IJCAI (2017)
7. He, X., Deng, K., Wang, X., Li, Y., Zhang, Y., Wang, M.: Lightgcn: simplifying and powering graph convolution network for recommendation. In: Proceedings of the 43rd International ACM SIGIR Conference on Research and Development in Information Retrieval, pp. 639–648 (2020)
8. He, X., Liao, L., Zhang, H., Nie, L., Hu, X., Chua, T.S.: Neural collaborative filtering. In: WWW, pp. 173–182 (2017)
9. Hidasi, B., Karatzoglou, A., Baltrunas, L., Tikk, D.: Session-based recommendations with recurrent neural networks. arXiv preprint arXiv:1511.06939 (2015)
10. Hidasi, B., Quadrana, M., Karatzoglou, A., Tikk, D.: Parallel recurrent neural network architectures for feature-rich session-based recommendations. In: Proceedings of the 10th ACM Conference on Recommender Systems, pp. 241–248 (2016)
11. Hinton, G., Vinyals, O., Dean, J.: Distilling the knowledge in a neural network. arXiv preprint arXiv:1503.02531 (2015)
12. Juan, Y., Zhuang, Y., Chin, W.S., Lin, C.J.: Field-aware factorization machines for ctr prediction. In: Proceedings of the 10th ACM Conference on Recommender Systems, pp. 43–50 (2016)
13. Kang, S., Hwang, J., Kweon, W., Yu, H.: Topology distillation for recommender system. In: Proceedings of the 27th ACM SIGKDD Conference on Knowledge Discovery & Data Mining, pp. 829–839 (2021)
14. Kang, W.C., McAuley, J.: Self-attentive sequential recommendation. In: 2018 IEEE International Conference on Data Mining (ICDM), pp. 197–206. IEEE (2018)
15. Katsileros, P., Mandilaras, N., Mallis, D., Pitsikalis, V., Theodorakis, S., Chamiel, G.: An incremental learning framework for large-scale ctr prediction. In: Proceedings of the 16th ACM Conference on Recommender Systems, pp. 490–493 (2022)
16. Li, Z., Cui, Z., Wu, S., Zhang, X., Wang, L.: Fi-gnn: modeling feature interactions via graph neural networks for ctr prediction. In: CIKM (2019)
17. Liu, B., et al.: Autofis: automatic feature interaction selection in factorization models for click-through rate prediction. In: KDD (2020)
18. Naumov, M., et al.: Deep learning recommendation model for personalization and recommendation systems. arXiv preprint arXiv:1906.00091 (2019)
19. Peng, D., Pan, S.J., Zhang, J., Zeng, A.: Learning an adaptive meta model-generator for incrementally updating recommender systems. In: Proceedings of the 15th ACM Conference on Recommender Systems, pp. 411–421 (2021)

20. Phuong, M., Lampert, C.: Towards understanding knowledge distillation. In: International Conference on Machine Learning, pp. 5142–5151. PMLR (2019)
21. Pi, Q., Bian, W., Zhou, G., Zhu, X., Gai, K.: Practice on long sequential user behavior modeling for click-through rate prediction. In: Proceedings of the 25th ACM SIGKDD International Conference on Knowledge Discovery & Data Mining, pp. 2671–2679 (2019)
22. Qi, P., et al.: Search-based user interest modeling with lifelong sequential behavior data for click-through rate prediction. In: Proceedings of the 26th ACM SIGKDD International Conference on Knowledge Discovery & Data Mining (2020)
23. Qin, J., Zhang, W., Wu, X., Jin, J., Fang, Y., Yu, Y.: User behavior retrieval for click-through rate prediction. In: Proceedings of the 43rd International ACM SIGIR Conference on Research and Development in Information Retrieval (2020)
24. Qin, J., et al.: Retrieval & interaction machine for tabular data prediction. In: Proceedings of the 27th ACM SIGKDD Conference on Knowledge Discovery & Data Mining, pp. 1379–1389 (2021)
25. Qu, Y., et al.: Product-based neural networks for user response prediction over multi-field categorical data. TOIS **37**(1), 1–35 (2018)
26. Ren, K., et al.: Lifelong sequential modeling with personalized memorization for user response prediction (2019)
27. Robertson, S.E., Walker, S., Jones, S., Hancock-Beaulieu, M.M., Gatford, M., et al.: Okapi at trec-3. Nist Special Publication Sp **109**, 109 (1995)
28. Shan, Y., Hoens, T.R., Jiao, J., Wang, H., Yu, D., Mao, J.: Deep crossing: web-scale modeling without manually crafted combinatorial features. In: Proceedings of the 22nd ACM SIGKDD International Conference on Knowledge Discovery and Data Mining, pp. 255–262 (2016)
29. Sun, F., Liu, J., Wu, J., Pei, C., Lin, X., Ou, W., Jiang, P.: Bert4rec: sequential recommendation with bidirectional encoder representations from transformer. In: Proceedings of the 28th ACM International Conference on Information and Knowledge Management, pp. 1441–1450 (2019)
30. Tang, J., et al.: Understanding and improving knowledge distillation. arXiv preprint arXiv:2002.03532 (2020)
31. Tang, J., Wang, K.: Personalized top-n sequential recommendation via convolutional sequence embedding. In: Proceedings of the eleventh ACM International Conference on Web Search and Data Mining, pp. 565–573 (2018)
32. Vaswani, A., et al.: Attention is all you need. In: Advances in Neural Information Processing Systems, vol. 30 (2017)
33. Wang, R., Fu, B., Fu, G., Wang, M.: Deep & cross network for ad click predictions. In: ADKDD, pp. 1–7 (2017)
34. Wang, R., et al.: Dcn v2: Improved deep & cross network and practical lessons for web-scale learning to rank systems. In: Proceedings of the Web Conference 2021, pp. 1785–1797 (2021)
35. Wang, X., He, X., Cao, Y., Liu, M., Chua, T.S.: Kgat: knowledge graph attention network for recommendation. In: Proceedings of the 25th ACM SIGKDD International Conference on Knowledge Discovery & Data Mining, pp. 950–958 (2019)
36. Wang, X., He, X., Wang, M., Feng, F., Chua, T.S.: Neural graph collaborative filtering. In: Proceedings of the 42nd International ACM SIGIR Conference on Research and Development in Information Retrieval. pp. 165–174 (2019)
37. Wu, J., Wang, X., Feng, F., He, X., Chen, L., Lian, J., Xie, X.: Self-supervised graph learning for recommendation. In: Proceedings of the 44th international ACM SIGIR Conference on Research and Development in Information Retrieval, pp. 726–735 (2021)

38. Yang, C., Pan, J., Gao, X., Jiang, T., Liu, D., Chen, G.: Cross-task knowledge distillation in multi-task recommendation. In: Proceedings of the AAAI Conference on Artificial Intelligence, vol. 36, pp. 4318–4326 (2022)
39. Yang, Z., Sun, R., Wan, X.: Nearest neighbor knowledge distillation for neural machine translation. arXiv preprint arXiv:2205.00479 (2022)
40. Ye, M., et al.: Future gradient descent for adapting the temporal shifting data distribution in online recommendation systems. In: Uncertainty in Artificial Intelligence, pp. 2256–2266. PMLR (2022)
41. Yuan, F., Karatzoglou, A., Arapakis, I., Jose, J.M., He, X.: A simple convolutional generative network for next item recommendation. In: Proceedings of the Twelfth ACM International Conference on Web Search and Data Mining, pp. 582–590 (2019)
42. Zamani, H., Diaz, F., Dehghani, M., Metzler, D., Bendersky, M.: Retrieval-enhanced machine learning. arXiv preprint arXiv:2205.01230 (2022)
43. Zhang, H., et al.: Decoupled non-parametric knowledge distillation for end-to-end speech translation. In: ICASSP 2023-2023 IEEE International Conference on Acoustics, Speech and Signal Processing (ICASSP), pp. 1–5. IEEE (2023)
44. Zheng, L., Li, N., Chen, X., Gan, Q., Zhang, W.: Dense representation learning and retrieval for tabular data prediction. In: Proceedings of the 29th ACM SIGKDD Conference on Knowledge Discovery and Data Mining, pp. 3559–3569 (2023)
45. Zhou, G., et al.: Deep interest evolution network for click-through rate prediction. In: Proceedings of the AAAI Conference on Artificial Intelligence, vol. 33, pp. 5941–5948 (2019)
46. Zhou, G., et al.: Deep interest network for click-through rate prediction. In: KDD (2018)
47. Zhu, J., Cai, G., Huang, J., Dong, Z., Tang, R., Zhang, W.: Reloop2: building self-adaptive recommendation models via responsive error compensation loop. arXiv preprint arXiv:2306.08808 (2023)
48. Zhu, J., Liu, J., Li, W., Lai, J., He, X., Chen, L., Zheng, Z.: Ensembled ctr prediction via knowledge distillation. In: Proceedings of the 29th ACM International Conference on Information & Knowledge Management, pp. 2941–2958 (2020)

Retrieval-Based Knowledge Consistency Validation for Fake News Detection

Ruize An[1], Jingyuan Wang[1], Richong Zhang[1](✉), Jing Zhang[2], and Ruipeng Luan[3]

[1] Beihang University, Beijing, China
{anruize,wangjingyuan03}@buaa.edu.cn, zhangrc@act.buaa.edu.cn

[2] Research Institute of Systems Engineering, The Academy Military Science, Beijing 100850, China

[3] Unit 91550 of the PLA, Dalin 116023, China

Abstract. Fake news detection, which is typically based on text classification of news content, is crucial for the accurate dissemination of information on the Internet. Previous methods have demonstrated that incorporating auxiliary information, such as user comments, can enhance detection performance. In this paper, we argue that related content retrieved from the Internet is also a considerable source of information, which aids in verifying the authenticity of news. Therefore, we introduce an adaptive multi-source information integration framework that selectively incorporates news content, user comments, and retrieval information, which is generated by **R**etrieval-based **K**nowledge **C**onsistency **V**alidation (**R-KCV**). Specifically, we begin by searching the Internet for richer external information and refining the search results using a knowledge-based information collection strategy to reduce redundancy. Next, we introduce an inconsistency critique generation strategy and a self-check mechanism, which reorganize the retrieved information to generate critically analyzed supplementary insights. Finally, we propose an adaptive attention mechanism to dynamically balance the importance of information from different sources, enabling the generation of a fused multi-source detection result. Experiments on three representative datasets demonstrate the effectiveness of our model.

Keywords: Fake News Detection · Retrieval-Augmented Generation · Attention

1 Introduction

Fake news detection [2,19] plays a crucial role in ensuring the accurate dissemination of information on the Internet. Traditional fake news detection starts from news text and determines whether a piece of text contains false information based on important features extracted from the text. Naturally, this makes traditional fake news detection a type of text classification task. Subsequently, information such as news comments [16,20], news propagation structures [18],

J. Li et al. (Eds.): APWeb-WAIM 2025, LNCS 16115, pp. 436–451, 2026.
https://doi.org/10.1007/978-981-95-5719-6_28

and user retweet time sequences [21] has been proven to be effective evidence for determining the authenticity of news.

However, we find that in some cases, the auxiliary information used by these methods is limited. At the same time, language models may struggle to effectively summarize the viewpoints expressed in these information and establish valid logical connections with the original text. To address these issues, we consider to gather additional prior knowledge from Internet, summarize the retrieved content, and analyze it in conjunction with the original news, leveraging advanced techniques such as large language models (LLMs). We emphasize that it will improve the accuracy of certain cases in fake news detection. Below is a specific example.

Consider the following news: *Katy Perry was exposed to be crying while dating Suki Waterhouse, and rumors suggest that they may have broken up.* A well-developed encoder can extract and encode the key pieces of information, "crying" and "breaking up". Using special techniques, such as cross-attention mechanisms, the encoder can calculate the correlation between these two features, making it easy to determine that the news is true.

In reality, a careful examination of relevant reports about these two celebrities reveals that, in addition to the information about their breakup, there are also reports indicating that Suki Waterhouse had previously purchased a ring and stated that it would be given to Katy Perry. If this relevant information is incorporated into the judgment of the original news, combined with appropriate human reasoning: *purchasing a ring* → *as a gift* → *moved to tears*. If a human detective were to analyze this situation, would they conclude that the two might be preparing for an engagement?

While this may seem like a dramatic gossip news story, it actually highlights the necessity of retrieving external information and the importance of discerning this information. It implies that, access to auxiliary information should be expanded and a human-like ability to summarize and generalize needs to be applied. It will facilitate the integration of the retrieved information to obtain the final information useful for judging the original news. However, current auxiliary information-based approaches have yet to achieve this.

Fortunately, the Retrieval-Augmented Generation (RAG) [9] excels at extracting relevant information during retrieval and synthesizing it into coherent summaries. This makes RAG particularly well-suited for the reasoning process discussed earlier, especially in the contexts of evidence retrieval and information summarization. Building on this strength, we propose a novel multi-source framework for fake news detection, designed to integrate and filter information from three key sources: news text, user comments, and retrieval-based insights obtained through RAG. To obtain reliable retrieval information, we first extract keywords from the original news content to formulate retrieval queries, which are then used to search for relevant information online. For the large volume of retrieved data, we leverage LLMs to extract key concepts and structure the information within knowledge reports. This structured representation shifts LLMs' focus on entities and their logical relationships instead of the textual information similar to the original news, enhancing the quality of the generating insights.

Furthermore, we argue that identifying discrepancies between relevant information and the original news is crucial, as such differences can indicate that the news is fake. Inspired by this, we propose a novel critical comment generation strategy that specifically highlights contradictions between retrieved information and the news content. By pinpointing inconsistencies and cross-referencing the generated outputs, our method provides robust evidence for fake news detection. Moreover, to mitigate the risk of errors caused by hallucinations in LLMs, we reinforce the generated evidence through a self-check mechanism. This mechanism performs a secondary verification of contradictions between the retrieved information and the news content, reducing the likelihood of misinformation due to hallucinations. In summary, the credibility of the evidence used for misinformation detection is further strengthened by the dual protection of critical comment generation and the self-check mechanism.

Finally, we acknowledge that retrieval-based information may not always be necessary and absolutely accurate for every news item. In some cases, user comments, as a complementary perspective to retrieval-based information, can also provide sufficient context for verification. To address this, we introduce an adaptive multi-score mechanism that dynamically determines whether to rely on retrieved information or user comments, optimizing the detection process based on the specific characteristics of each case.

In short, our contributions are as follows:

- We propose a novel multi-source framework for fake news detection, integrating and filtering information from three sources: news contents, user comments, and retrieval information. We develop an adaptive attention mechanism that selectively utilizes features from either the final retrieval information or user comments.
- We introduce R-KCV to get the retrieval information. Specifically, a knowledge-based information collection strategy is proposed to handle the retrieved results. Meanwhile, in the generation stage, we present an inconsistency critique generation strategy coupled with a self-check mechanism to generate more effective evidence for detecting fake news while reducing hallucinations.
- Experimental results demonstrate R-KCV's superior performance compared to baselines. In comparison experiments with single-source methods and ablation experiments based on our own approach, our method achieved good results. It indicates that adding retrieval information obtained through knowledge-based collection and inconsistency critique generation leading to a more robust and interpretable fake news detection system.

2 Related Works

2.1 Fake News Detection

Fake news detection has been explored in multiple dimensions. The most fundamental approach involves classification of characteristics by extracting lexical [14] and sentimental characteristics from the texts of news articles [13]. Building on this, many methods improve the accuracy of news veracity prediction by incorporating auxiliary features. Specifically, user comments [16,20] are one of such feature. They have been widely used in news veracity detection and have been well-proven as an effective approach. News propagation structure [18] and user social graph [21] are also commonly utilized to improve classification performance. In addition, there are cases where knowledge bases [4] have been applied in news detection. These cases can be seen as preliminary attempts to explore the role of auxiliary information and reasoning processes in fake news detection. Our approach builds upon this foundation and further develops it by leveraging RAG technology.

Large language models (LLMs) have demonstrated exceptional reasoning capabilities. Utilizing their commonsense reasoning ability to obtain supplementary explanations from LLMs can significantly enhance detection accuracy [6]. Unlike these studies, in this research, the LLM serves as a tool for extracting keyword information and summarizing retrieval results. The auxiliary information comes from retrieved results rather than the LLM itself, effectively mitigating the uncontrolled interference of LLM hallucinations in the auxiliary information.

2.2 Retrieval-Augmented Generation

The concept of Retrieval-Augmented Generation (RAG) was initially proposed by Lewis et al. [9]. It aims to leverage large language models (LLMs) to answer queries that exceed their context window limitations [11]. The core idea is to retrieve relevant content from an external large-scale text corpus and provide these retrieved texts as additional context to the LLM, enabling it to generate more accurate responses [8]. This process forms a standard setup for RAG, also known as Naïve RAG. Subsequently, different aspects of the RAG framework have been explored and optimized for various scenarios [15]. To enhance the summarization capabilities of large language models, techniques such as knowledge graphs [1] have been introduced. This improvement is specifically designed to optimize performance on sensemaking queries [7], which require a global understanding of the entire dataset. Such a requirement has significant real-world applications. For instance, in the field of fake news retrieval, we aim to summarize and determine evidence for news authenticity from as much information as possible.

Inspired by this, this paper proposes a GraphRAG technique tailored for fake news detection. Unlike MUSER [10], which simply classifies retrieved results by perspective, our approach excels in constructing knowledge reports, segmenting key themes, and summarizing retrieved content.

3 Method

3.1 Problem Formulation

We focus on enhancing fake news detection by incorporating three sources of information. As shown in the Fig. 1, three sources include news content N, user comments C and retrieval information R. Specifically, C and R are regarded to provide additional insights for detecting fake news. And we define the fake news detection problem as a classification task:

$$f(N, R, C) \rightarrow y, \quad y \in \{0, 1\}, \tag{1}$$

where f is a multi-source fake news detector that takes N, R, and C as input and predicts whether N is fake or real.

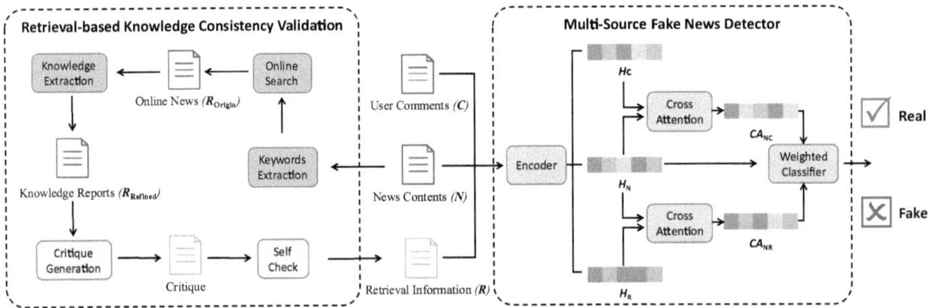

Fig. 1. Our proposed framework involves three sources: news contents N, user comments C, and retrieval information R. We pass N through the retrieval module, which consists of **online knowledge collection** (blue) and **inconsistency critique generation** (yellow), to get R. Then N, R and C are input into the **multi-source fake news detector** (gray) to obtain the detection results.

Moreover, since news content and user comments are readily available and fit well within the input window of classification models, we focus on methods for obtaining retrieval information. Since the results obtained directly through retrieval cannot be guaranteed in terms of quality, we utilize R-KCV to obtain final retrieval information. And we define the retrieval module as a function g:

$$g(N, I_{online}) \rightarrow R, \tag{2}$$

where I_{online} means the information in the Internet.

3.2 Online Knowledge Collection

As shown in Fig. 1, to obtain retrieval information R, we extract keywords from N and use Google Search to retrieve k relevant articles, forming the set R_{Origin}.

However, due to the length constraints of classification models, directly using all k articles is infeasible, necessitating summarization and compression.

A standard RAG approach segments each retrieved article into multiple text chunks, aggregates chunks across all k articles, and applies a secondary filtering step based on keyword relevance. Common techniques include vector similarity, BM25, and re-ranking models. However, this approach often introduces redundancy, overemphasizing certain key facts while neglecting others.

To enhance retrieval efficiency, we introduce an approach of knowledge-based collection. For each article in R_{Origin}, we prompt LLMs to construct a knowledge report that represents entities and their relationships, enabling fine-grained comparisons. This prompt helps shift the LLMs' attention toward the key entities in the news and their logical relationships between R_{Origin} and N, rather than redundant information shared by both.

This process lays the groundwork for generating a global summary that concisely captures core ideas. The structured output from this method forms R_{Refined}, which serves as an effective auxiliary input to the generation model.

3.3 Inconsistency Critique Generation

In contrast to consistent information, identifying discrepancies between the retrieved information and the original news is crucial, as such differences may signal that the news is fake. However, large language models (LLMs) often focus primarily on the similarities between the R_{Refined} and the N, frequently failing to detect contradictions. This limitation makes it challenging to extract meaningful insights. To address this, we implement an inconsistency critique generation strategy, explicitly prompting LLMs to critique N based on discrepancies between N and R_{Refined}.

Criticism should, of course, be moderate to avoid misjudging the news. That is, sometimes, retrieving information consistent with news content, but the LLMs criticizes it, which is regarded as LLMs' hallucination. Therefore, a self-check mechanism is placed after the criticism is generated, prompting the LLMs to reconsider and ensure that the criticism is fair.

The final retrieval information (R) was obtained through the two generations using LLMs mentioned above, making it more effective.

3.4 Prompt Presentation

Here we display some of our prompts as follows. Among them, the examples have been omitted due to space reasons.

Knowledge Report Generation

> Given a news article and a related webpage, extract the relevant knowledge from the webpage that pertains to the news. Generate a knowledge report that includes entities, events, findings and analysis, and a summary...
> [Examples]

Critique Generation

> You are a news critic. Given a news article and a related knowledge report, your task is to carefully identify any inconsistencies between the news and the report. Based on the report, critique any errors found in the news. However, keep in mind that the news is not always incorrectâĂŤyou should also acknowledge instances where the news aligns with the report... [Examples]

Self Check

> Given a news article and related commentary, carefully review the commentary to identify any misunderstandings of the news or factual errors. Correct any inaccuracies and output both the error-free commentary and the revised versions of the corrected commentary... [Examples]

3.5 Multi-source Fake News Detection

So far, we have obtained the final retrieval information, denoted as R. We incorporate this into a multi-source framework. As shown in Fig. 1, each of N, R, and C is processed through separate encoders to generate hidden representations H_N, H_C and H_R.

Next, to capture the relationships between the different sources, we apply a cross-attention (CA) mechanism to further enhance the interaction between these sources, defined as:

$$\text{CA}(X, Y) = \text{Softmax}\left(\frac{Q'K'^{\top}}{\sqrt{d_{\text{k}}}}\right)V', \tag{3}$$

where $Q' = W_{\text{Q}} \cdot X$, $K' = W_{\text{K}} \cdot Y$, and $V' = W_{\text{V}} \cdot Y$ represent the query, key, and value projections, respectively. Here, $\text{CA}(X, Y)$ denotes the cross-attention operation, which enables information flow between two different input sources. Later we use CA_{XY} to represent the result of $\text{CA}(X, Y)$

As additional information, both C and R should establish relationships with N. So, we incorporate two cross-attention modules: $CA(N, C)$ and $CA(N, R)$, to obtain fusion representations CA_{NR} and CA_{NC}. In $CA(N, R)$, queries originate from N, while keys and values are derived from R, allowing the model to compare N with the retrieved content to extract supporting or conflicting evidence. Similarly, $CA(N, C)$ enables the model to assess user perspectives in relation to N.

Since the importance of each source varies in different cases, we employ an adaptive weighting mechanism using a multi-layer perceptron (MLP) with softmax activation:

$$H_{\text{Sources}} - \text{Concat}(H_{\text{N}}, CA_{\text{NC}}, CA_{\text{NR}}) \tag{4}$$

$$[w_{\mathrm{N}}, w_{\mathrm{NC}}, w_{\mathrm{NR}}] = \mathrm{Softmax}(\mathrm{MLP}(H_{\mathrm{Sources}})) \quad (5)$$

$$W_{\mathrm{Sources}} = w_{\mathrm{N}} \cdot H_{\mathrm{N}} + w_{\mathrm{NC}} \cdot CA_{\mathrm{NC}} + w_{\mathrm{NR}} \cdot CA_{\mathrm{NR}} \quad (6)$$

$$\hat{y} = \mathrm{Softmax}(\mathrm{MLP}(W_{\mathrm{Sources}})) \quad (7)$$

where H_{N} represents the hidden states of News N obtained after passing through the BERT layer, and $[w_{\mathrm{N}}, w_{\mathrm{NC}}, w_{\mathrm{NR}}]$ represents the weight of $[H_N, CA_{\mathrm{NC}}, CA_{\mathrm{NR}}]$.

Here, we have completed the explanation of our framework. Next, for convenience, we will refer to the entire framework as R-KCV in the experimental and analysis sections.

4 Experiments

This section first introduces the datasets used in our experiments, emphasizing their characteristics and significance. We then outline the baseline methods for comparison, followed by a detailed explanation of the experimental setup, including implementation specifics and evaluation criteria. Lastly, we present and analyze the experimental results, providing in-depth insights into the performance of our proposed method.

4.1 Dataset

As shown in Table 1, we selected two English datasets and one Chinese dataset for testing, covering news from different domains with variations in style, deception characteristics, and other aspects to comprehensively evaluate the proposed method.

Table 1. Dataset Statistics

Dataset	Train		Valid		Test	
	Fake	Real	Fake	Real	Fake	Real
GossipCop	1980	1978	992	987	986	993
PolitiFact	117	108	54	58	54	59
Weibo	1141	1172	594	562	578	579

These datasets are widely used in the field of fake news detection. Specifically:

- **GossipCop** [17]: Primarily covering entertainment news, with data sourced from social media platforms, including news reports and corresponding fact-checking results.
- **PolitiFact** [17]: Focused on political news, containing extensive analyses of politicians' statements and policy interpretations, with high demands for detail accuracy.

- **Weibo** [12]: A Chinese dataset from the Weibo platform, which includes not only the news content but also user interaction information, allowing evaluation of model generalization across different language environments.

Dataset statistics are shown in Table 1. The ratio of the training set to the validation set to the test set is approximately 2:1:1, and the ratio of fake to real news is about 1:1.

4.2 Baselines

dEFEND [16]: A model that leverages sentiment information for fake news detection. Early research focused on using sentiment as a key feature for distinguishing fake news.

DualEmo [20]: A model that uses social relationship modeling, relying on emotions and social interactions to detect fake news.

BERT [3]: A pre-trained transformer model that has set a new standard in natural language processing. When applied to fake news detection, BERT significantly outperforms traditional methods, using only news content N as input and classifying it via an MLP.

DeBERTa [5]: An improved version of BERT that introduces disentangled attention mechanisms for better handling of linguistic nuances. We include it to compare performance with the standard BERT.

MUSER [10]: Another recent method designed for fake news detection, which conducts multi-step retrieval on wikipedia to enhance BERT model. This method is included to contrast the utility of information sourced from Wikipedia with that from the Internet.

Qwen2.5-32B: A powerful open-source large language model that has demonstrated state-of-the-art performance among open-source models in many benchmark tests.

GPT-4o: A representative large language model from the GPT series. As a state-of-the-art LLM, GPT-4o brings a different approach, offering a new perspective on fake news classification.

4.3 Implementation Details

We choose **BERT** as the encoder of our proposed model. We set the batch size, learning rate, and number of epochs based on the dataset size. For **GossipCop** and **Weibo**, we used a batch size of 32, learning rate 3×10^{-5}, and trained for 10 epochs. For **PolitiFact** (smaller dataset), we used a batch size of 8, learning rate 1×10^{-5}, and trained for 5 epochs.

For the sake of execution efficiency, the Qwen2.5-7B-Instruct model—moderate in both size and performance—was utilized for online knowledge collection and inconsistency critique generation. If R-KCV's effectiveness can be demonstrated using Qwen2.5-7B-Instruct, then larger and more powerful models should be equally capable. Specifically, it was configured with a temperature of 0.9 and a maximum output length of 512 tokens when generating inconsistency critique. This configuration was chosen to ensure that the generated keywords are diverse yet concise, and the output length is compatible with the input requirements of BERT models.

4.4 Main Results

As shown in the Table 2, the experimental results demonstrate the performance of various methods across three datasets. On the GossipCop and Politifact datasets, our model achieved accuracies of 0.901 and 0.917, with corresponding F1 scores of 0.903 and 0.920, significantly outperforming other methods. Specifically, compared to MUSER, which achieved accuracies of 0.867 and 0.896, our model shows substantial improvement. This discrepancy suggests that network information plays a crucial role in the detection of fake news, particularly in datasets such as GossipCop, which focuses on gossip news, and Politifact, which deals with political news. These types of news often involve intricate background information, public debates, and policy discussions, all of which are frequently discussed and shared across the internet. Thus, network retrieval can provide valuable contextual information and factual support for fake news detection, enhancing the model's ability to identify deceptive claims.

Table 2. Experimental results

Method	GossipCop		Politifact		Weibo	
	Acc.	F1	Acc.	F1	Acc.	F1
dEFEND	0.713	0.702	0.824	0.822	/	/
DualEmo	0.762	0.760	0.881	0.892	/	/
BERT	0.755	0.749	0.869	0.870	0.902	0.917
DeBERTa	0.760	0.757	0.896	0.903	0.901	0.915
MUSER	0.867	0.886	0.896	0.908	0.912	0.922
Qwen2.5-32B	0.655	0.574	0.692	0.612	0.738	0.701
GPT-4o	0.793	0.743	0.825	0.806	0.828	0.818
R-KCV	**0.901**	**0.903**	**0.917**	**0.920**	**0.914**	**0.926**

In contrast, on the Weibo dataset, while our model still performs well, achieving an accuracy of 0.914 and an F1 score of 0.926, the improvement is less pronounced compared to other models. This phenomenon can be attributed to the nature of the fake news in the Weibo dataset, which tends to be more explicit and straightforward. Weibo news articles are often direct in their presentation, with exaggerated headlines or sensationalized language, which makes them easier to detect using text classification alone. As a result, methods like BERT, which rely solely on textual features, can perform effectively without the need for additional network information. Consequently, despite incorporating external network information, our model does not experience significant performance gains, as the fake news in Weibo is often evident from the text itself.

4.5 Ablation Study

To verify the necessity of each module, we conducted an ablation study, comparing the performance when fewer information sources were utilized (Table 3).

Table 3. Ablation Study Results: R-KCV$_X$ denotes the classification results on single-source information X. R-KCV$_{XY}$ indicates the dual-source classification with X and Y.

Method	GossipCop		Politifact		Weibo	
	Acc.	F1	Acc.	F1	Acc.	F1
R-KCV$_N$	0.755	0.749	0.869	0.870	0.902	0.917
R-KCV$_R$	0.689	0.633	0.703	0.674	0.705	0.696
R-KCV$_C$	0.727	0.719	0.685	0.696	0.806	0.805
R-KCV$_{NC}$	0.840	0.845	0.881	0.889	0.906	0.920
R-KCV$_{NR}$	0.833	0.835	0.884	0.887	0.908	0.921
R-KCV	0.901	0.903	0.917	0.920	0.914	0.926

In single-source detection, R-KCV$_R$ and R-KCV$_C$ perform relatively well, although the effect is not as good as R-KCV$_N$, still suggesting the value of auxiliary information R and C. At the same time, we can see that R-KCV$_R$ and R-KCV$_C$ behaves differently on different datasets, which implies that the two types of information have different emphasis. For example, R-KCV$_C$ exhibits significant performance variation across datasets, primarily relying on direct emotions and opinions present in the data. The evidence for this is that it performs well on datasets containing a large amount of such information, such as the GossipCop dataset, where it achieves an accuracy of 0.806 and an F1 score of 0.805. In contrast, its performance deteriorates on datasets with fewer direct emotional expressions, with the worst-case accuracy dropping to 0.685 and the F1 score to 0.696. In comparison, R-KCV$_R$ focuses more on deeper-level information. By leveraging its ability to critique news, it can extract information across different datasets, leading to more stable performance. For instance, its highest performance on the Weibo dataset results in an accuracy of 0.705 and an F1 score of 0.696. Even in the GossipCop dataset, its lowest accuracy remains at 0.689, with an F1 score of 0.633. All in all, this is exactly what we hope, because two kinds of auxiliary information with different focus will make the model robust.

Compared to single-source detection, dual-source detection generally shows obvious advantages. For example, in the GossipCop dataset, R-KCV$_{NC}$ improves accuracy by 0.085 and F1 score by 0.096 compared to R-KCV$_N$. Similarly, R-KCV$_{NR}$ improves accuracy by 0.078 and F1 score by 0.086 compared to R-KCV$_N$. These results indicate that both direct comment-based attention and in-depth retrieval-based information contribute more effectively to fake news detection than relying solely on the original news content. Finally, our proposed comprehensive framework achieves significant improvements over dual-source detection, with accuracy and F1 score on GossipCop increasing by up to 0.068. This demonstrates the superiority and necessity of incorporating both direct and in-depth auxiliary information.

4.6 Weight Allocation Study

In our fake news detection model, N, CA_{NR} and CA_{NC} are integrated through weighted fusion to enhance classification performance. Here we investigated the weight information of the fusion and used the weight of CA_{NR}, CA_{NC} on datasets to measure the importance of R, C to a certain degree.

Table 4. Weight Allocation Cases: Four cases from our datasets. The weight assigned to each source is marked in brackets.

News Contents (*N*)	User Comments (*C*)	Retrieval Information (*R*)	Pred: Target
VIDEO: Special Preview Of Jersey Shore In Miami!,"They're baaaaaackkk!!! A preview of the second season of the breakout hit Jersey Shore aired prior to the MTV Movie Awards on Sunday night... **(0.246)**	New post: VIDEO: Special Preview Of Jersey Shore In Miami! AM gossip links: Special video preview of 'Jersey Shore' in Miami **(0.331)**	Miami: The new location for the second season of Jersey Shore, including time spent in both South Florida and New Jersey... **(0.423)**	**Real: Real**
Just one day after a report surfaced that Katy Perry and Robert Pattinson were spied making out...It's nothing serious at this point, although Rob would definitely love to take things to the next level... **(0.139)**	...It's claimed that Robert Pattinson has had a crush on Katy Perry for a long time, but she preferred to keep their relationship platonic...**(0.360)**	The article's assertion that "Rob wasn't going to take no for an answer" and that he was "determined to win her over" is speculative and lacks concrete evidence...**(0.501)**	**Fake: Fake**
Reality TV star Kris Jenner is repo rtedly working on a new spin-off s how about her grandchildren calle d "Keeping Up with the Kids"... **(0.135)**	Is Kris Jenner Developing Kar dashian Kids Spinoff Show? Kris Jenner is not developing a Kardashian kids spinoff—yet. **(0.409)**	...However, none of the provided reports m ention any plans for such a show...which do not discuss any conflict or controversy reg arding a potential show involving Kanye W est's children...**(0.358)**	**Fake: Fake**
...John Mccain to vote no on Graham-Cassidy health care bill... **(0.258)**	...John Mccain to vote no on Graham-Cassidy health care bill... **(0.540)**	... The news accurately reflects senator John Mccain's opposition to the Graham-Cassidy healthcare bill... **(0..202)**	**Real: Fake**

Some representative cases are shown in Table 4. Analysis shows that the weight of N is typically low, approximately ranging from 0.1 to 0.3, primarily because the discriminative power of news content itself is limited in fake news detection. News content is often easily manipulated or lacks contextual support, making the information it provides insufficient for high-confidence classification decisions. The weight of C and R are influenced by factors such as the style of the dataset and the quality of the specific retrieval. In the fourth case, C: R achieved an extremely high ratio of 0.540:0.202, which may be due to the fact that C had a nearly identical central sentence to N. In contrast, in the second case, C:R had a ratio of only 0.360:0.501, which may be attributed to the presence of some explicit doubts in R.

4.7 Retrieval Number Study

To optimize performance across datasets, we study the critical parameter k in online search, representing the number of relevant articles selected. As shown in Fig. 2, accuracy initially increases with k, suggesting that more information enhances generation. However, this improvement plateaus for the GossipCop dataset at $k = 8$, stabilizing around 0.901, while accuracy declines for the PolitiFact and Weibo datasets. This indicates that excessive data can be counterproductive due to the LLM's input window limitations.

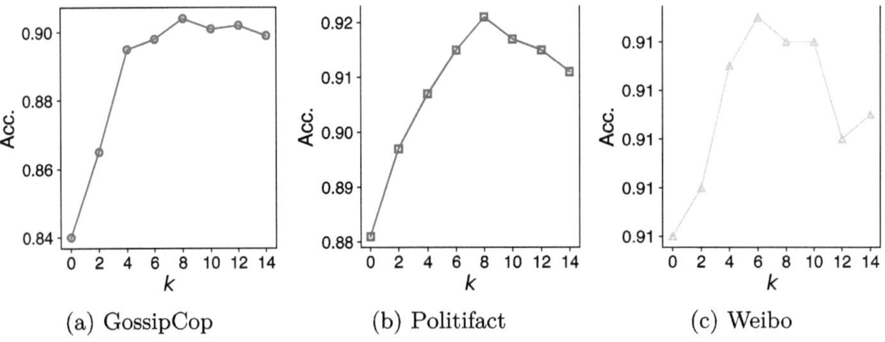

(a) GossipCop (b) Politifact (c) Weibo

Fig. 2. Accuracy of each dataset on the top-k most relevant retrieved articles.

Additionally, we observe that for the GossipCop and PolitiFact datasets, $k = 8$ represents the peak value, while for Weibo, the optimal point occurs earlier at $k = 6$. This can be explained by the aforementioned analysis. For the GossipCop and PolitiFact datasets, our architecture relies more heavily on retrieved data, so a larger number of articles is beneficial. In contrast, for Weibo data, comments provide more effective information, reducing the need for extensive data retrieval.

4.8 Case Study

To better demonstrate the effectiveness of our approach, we present a case study. Case is shown in Fig. 3. The news content reports on a rumor about Katy Perry and Robert Pattinson, claiming that they were spotted making out and suggesting that they have been "secretly dating" for a long time. We first extracted keywords such as *Katy Perry Robert Pattinson dating January 2023* and got online search results. The titles of these search results are shown in Fig. 3, including *Katy Perry and Robert Pattinson seen making out in Los...* and *A Look*

At Robert Pattinson's Girlfriends And Dating History.... Subsequently, we utilized knowledge-guided prompt to generate knowledge reports for each searched news. Each knowledge report includes entities, events, analysis, and a summary. For example, it mentions the event of the sighting and provides an analysis of their relationship. Finally, we generated inconsistency critique and prompted the model to self-check. The initially generated critique contained overly sharp opinions and some possible hallucinatory contents, which may mislead our detector. After self-checking, a softer version was generated.

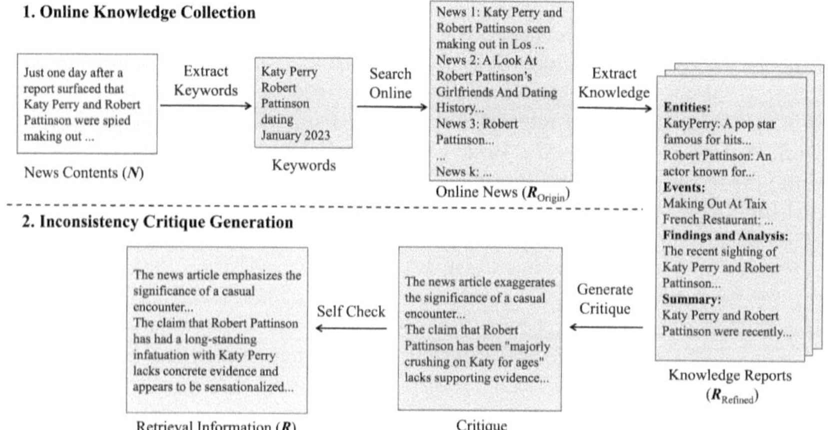

Fig. 3. A case that news N goes through **online knowledge collection** and **inconsistency critique generation**, and the final result R is obtained.

5 Conclusion

We proposed a retrieval-based knowledge consistency validation method, named R-KCV, to enhance the effectiveness of LLMs in fake news detection. We used the idea of knowledge-focused generation to refine raw search engine results, extracting key information and reducing redundancy to help the model better understand online knowledge. At the same time, the knowledge inconsistency critique strategy leverages the text generation capability of LLMs to focus on inconsistencies between news content and online knowledge. A self-check mechanism is also introduced to minimize hallucinations and improve detection accuracy. Our experimental results demonstrated the superiority of R-KCV.

Acknowledgments. This work was supported by the National Science and Technology Major Project under Grant 2022ZD0120202, in part by the National Natural Science Foundation of China (No. U23B2056), in part by the Fundamental Research Funds for the Central Universities, and in part by the State Key Laboratory of Complex & Critical Software Environment.

References

1. Baek, J., Aji, A.F., Saffari, A.: Knowledge-augmented language model prompting for zero-shot knowledge graph question answering. CoRR **abs/2306.04136** (2023). https://doi.org/10.48550/arXiv.2306.04136
2. Chen, Y., et al.: Cross-modal ambiguity learning for multimodal fake news detection. In: WWW '22: The ACM Web Conference 2022, Virtual Event, Lyon, France, 25–29 April 2022, pp. 2897–2905. ACM (2022). https://doi.org/10.1145/3485447.3511968
3. Devlin, J., Chang, M., Lee, K., Toutanova, K.: BERT: pre-training of deep bidirectional transformers for language understanding. In: Proceedings of the 2019 Conference of the North American Chapter of the Association for Computational Linguistics: Human Language Technologies, NAACL-HLT 2019, Minneapolis, MN, USA, 2–7 June 2019, Volume 1 (Long and Short Papers), pp. 4171–4186. Association for Computational Linguistics (2019). https://doi.org/10.18653/v1/n19-1423
4. Dun, Y., Tu, K., Chen, C., Hou, C., Yuan, X.: KAN: knowledge-aware attention network for fake news detection. In: Thirty-Fifth AAAI Conference on Artificial Intelligence, AAAI 2021, Thirty-Third Conference on Innovative Applications of Artificial Intelligence, IAAI 2021, The Eleventh Symposium on Educational Advances in Artificial Intelligence, EAAI 2021, Virtual Event, 2–9 February 2021, pp. 81–89. AAAI Press (2021). https://doi.org/10.1609/aaai.v35i1.16080
5. He, P., Liu, X., Gao, J., Chen, W.: DeBERTa: decoding-enhanced BERT with disentangled attention. In: 9th International Conference on Learning Representations, ICLR 2021, Virtual Event, Austria, 3–7 May 2021. OpenReview.net (2021). https://openreview.net/forum?id=XPZIaotutsD
6. He, X., Bresson, X., Laurent, T., Perold, A., LeCun, Y., Hooi, B.: Harnessing explanations: LLM-to-LM interpreter for enhanced text-attributed graph representation learning. In: The Twelfth International Conference on Learning Representations, ICLR 2024, Vienna, Austria, 7–11 May 2024. OpenReview.net (2024). https://openreview.net/forum?id=RXFVcynVe1
7. Klein, G., Moon, B.M., Hoffman, R.R.: Making sense of sensemaking 1: alternative perspectives. IEEE Intell. Syst. **21**(4), 70–73 (2006). https://doi.org/10.1109/MIS.2006.75
8. Laskar, M.T.R., Hoque, E., Huang, J.X.: Query focused abstractive summarization via incorporating query relevance and transfer learning with transformer models. In: Advances in Artificial Intelligence - 33rd Canadian Conference on Artificial Intelligence, Canadian AI 2020, Ottawa, ON, Canada, 13–15 May 2020, Proceedings. Lecture Notes in Computer Science, vol. 12109, pp. 342–348. Springer (2020). https://doi.org/10.1007/978-3-030-47358-7_35
9. Lewis, P.S.H., et al.: Retrieval-augmented generation for knowledge-intensive NLP tasks. In: Advances in Neural Information Processing Systems 33: Annual Conference on Neural Information Processing Systems 2020, NeurIPS 2020, 6–12 December 2020, virtual (2020). https://proceedings.neurips.cc/paper/2020/hash/6b493230205f780e1bc26945df7481e5-Abstract.html
10. Liao, H., et al.: MUSER: A multi-step evidence retrieval enhancement framework for fake news detection. In: Proceedings of the 29th ACM SIGKDD Conference on Knowledge Discovery and Data Mining, KDD 2023, Long Beach, CA, USA, 6–10 August 2023, pp. 4461–4472. ACM (2023). https://doi.org/10.1145/3580305.3599873

11. Liu, N.F., et al.: Lost in the middle: how language models use long contexts. Trans. Assoc. Comput. Linguistics **12**, 157–173 (2024). https://doi.org/10.1162/tacl_a_00638
12. Ma, J., et al.: Detecting rumors from microblogs with recurrent neural networks. In: Kambhampati, S. (ed.) Proceedings of the Twenty-Fifth International Joint Conference on Artificial Intelligence, IJCAI 2016, New York, NY, USA, 9-15 July 2016, pp. 3818–3824. IJCAI/AAAI Press (2016). http://www.ijcai.org/Abstract/16/537
13. Potthast, M., Kiesel, J., Reinartz, K., Bevendorff, J., Stein, B.: A stylometric inquiry into hyperpartisan and fake news. In: Proceedings of the 56th Annual Meeting of the Association for Computational Linguistics, ACL 2018, Melbourne, Australia, 15–20 July 2018, Volume 1: Long Papers, pp. 231–240. Association for Computational Linguistics (2018). https://aclanthology.org/P18-1022/
14. Rashkin, H., Choi, E., Jang, J.Y., Volkova, S., Choi, Y.: Truth of varying shades: analyzing language in fake news and political fact-checking. In: Proceedings of the 2017 Conference on Empirical Methods in Natural Language Processing, EMNLP 2017, Copenhagen, Denmark, 9–11 September 2017, pp. 2931–2937. Association for Computational Linguistics (2017). https://doi.org/10.18653/v1/d17-1317
15. Shi, Z., et al.: Generate-then-ground in retrieval-augmented generation for multi-hop question answering. In: Proceedings of the 62nd Annual Meeting of the Association for Computational Linguistics (Volume 1: Long Papers), ACL 2024, Bangkok, Thailand, 11–16 August 2024, pp. 7339–7353. Association for Computational Linguistics (2024). https://doi.org/10.18653/v1/2024.acl-long.397
16. Shu, K., Cui, L., Wang, S., Lee, D., Liu, H.: dEFEND: Explainable fake news detection. In: Proceedings of the 25th ACM SIGKDD International Conference on Knowledge Discovery & Data Mining, KDD 2019, Anchorage, AK, USA, 4–8 August 2019, pp. 395–405. ACM (2019). https://doi.org/10.1145/3292500.3330935
17. Shu, K., et al.: FakeNewsNet: a data repository with news content, social context, and spatiotemporal information for studying fake news on social media. Big Data **8**(3), 171–188 (2020). https://doi.org/10.1089/big.2020.0062
18. Sun, T., Qian, Z., Dong, S., Li, P., Zhu, Q.: Rumor detection on social media with graph adversarial contrastive learning. In: WWW '22: The ACM Web Conference 2022, Virtual Event, Lyon, France, 25–29 April 2022, pp. 2789–2797. ACM (2022). https://doi.org/10.1145/3485447.3511999
19. Verma, P.K., Agrawal, P., Amorim, I., Prodan, R.: WELFake: word embedding over linguistic features for fake news detection. IEEE Trans. Comput. Soc. Syst. **8**(4), 881–893 (2021). https://doi.org/10.1109/TCSS.2021.3068519
20. Zhang, X., Cao, J., Li, X., Sheng, Q., Zhong, L., Shu, K.: Mining dual emotion for fake news detection. In: WWW '21: The Web Conference 2021, Virtual Event/Ljubljana, Slovenia, 19–23 April 2021, pp. 3465–3476. ACM/IW3C2 (2021). https://doi.org/10.1145/3442381.3450004
21. Zhu, J., Gao, C., Yin, Z., Li, X., Kurths, J.: Propagation structure-aware graph transformer for robust and interpretable fake news detection. In: Proceedings of the 30th ACM SIGKDD Conference on Knowledge Discovery and Data Mining, KDD 2024, Barcelona, Spain, 25–29 August 2024, pp. 4652–4663. ACM (2024). https://doi.org/10.1145/3637528.3672024

Graph Data Management and Analytics II

DCS-GCN: A Dual-Channel Social Graph Convolutional Network for Recommendation

Bin Li(✉) and Shuangyou Li

School of Computer Science, Northeast Electric Power University, Jilin 132012, China
libinjlu5765114@163.com

Abstract. Graph Convolutional Networks (GCNs) have been widely used in recommendation systems due to the graph-structured nature of recommendation data. However, existing GCN-based recommendation methods face two key challenges: 1) data sparsity problem, where sparse datasets make it hard for algorithms to extract useful information; 2) over-smoothing problem, where stacking convolutional layers makes embedding representations too similar, causing dissimilar users to have similar interests and weakening recommendation performance. To address these problems, we propose a novel dual-channel social graph convolutional networks, dubbed DCS-GCN, for recommendation. Building on traditional GCN-based recommendation frameworks, DCS-GCN enriches user information through social graph-based message passing to alleviate data sparsity problem. It also diversifies the aggregation mechanism by mining and passing social relationship information in the user-item interaction graph, to mitigate over-smoothing problem. Finally, the model fuses these features from two social channels at each graph convolutional layer to generate final user and item representations for preference prediction. Experiments on two public datasets show that DCS-GCN outperforms several state-of-the-art recommendation methods (Our code is available at https://github.com/anonymity73/DCS-GCN).

Keywords: Recommendations · Social networks · Graph convolution networks · Data sparsity problem · Over-smoothing problem

1 Introduction

Recommender systems have permeated every aspect of people's lives [1–3], including short video, music, movie, and shopping platforms, etc. A common strategy for recommendation typically involves the following steps: First, the recommendation algorithm learns the embedding representations of users and items. Then, it computes the similarity scores between users and items through inner-product operations. Based on the ranking of these scores, the user's behaviors and preferences are analyzed, and items that the users may be interested in are recommended [4, 5].

Recent studies have shown that Graph Convolutional Networks (GCNs), due to their powerful capabilities in processing graph-structured data, have been widely applied to research on collaborative filtering recommendation models and have achieved many satisfactory results [6, 7]. For instance, NGCF [8] explicitly incorporates high-order

J. Li et al. (Eds.): APWeb-WAIM 2025, LNCS 16115, pp. 455–470, 2026.
https://doi.org/10.1007/978-981-95-5719-6_29

connectivity information into the embedding learning of users and items by performing embedding propagation on the user-item interaction graph. However, He et al. [9] demonstrated through extensive ablation studies that the linear transformations and nonlinear activation functions in NGCF not only fail to impact recommendation performance positively but also increase computational complexity. Therefore, they removed these two components and proposed a lightweight GCN model for recommendation, which has achieved satisfactory results and become one of the more advanced recommendation models currently available.

The aforementioned GCN-based recommendation models have achieved promising results. However, these models primarily focus on model optimization and concentrate on enhancing the performance of the models themselves, with less consideration given to the practical state of recommendation systems. As a result, they have limited effectiveness in mitigating the data sparsity problem, and it is difficult to fundamentally improve the impact of data sparsity on recommendation quality. Moreover, due to the aggregation mechanism of graph convolution, existing models are prone to over-smoothing when stacking convolutional layers. This causes the embedding representations of different users to become increasingly similar, thereby restricting further improvements in recommendation performance.

To address the challenges of data sparsity and over-smoothing problems, this paper proposes DCS-GCN, a novel dual-channel social graph convolutional network for recommendation. DCS-GCN performs message passing through two channel social graph convolutional networks. The first channel conducts convolution operations on the inherent social graph, and the second channel performs friend clustering analysis on the user-item interaction graph and conducts message passing on the resulting social subgraphs. We utilize the inherent social graph for information propagation to enrich the original user information, thereby to alleviate the data sparsity problem in recommendation systems. To enable the embedding representations to absorb information in multiple manners, we also explore social relationships in the user-item interaction graph. Finally, we fuse the features learned from the two social channels to generate the final representations of users and items for subsequent preference prediction.

In summary, the main contributions of this paper are summarized as follows:

(1) We present DCS-GCN, a novel dual-channel social graph convolutional recommendation method. It uses explicit social network graphs to reduce data sparsity impact and mines implicit social relationships in the user-item interaction graph to mitigate over-smoothing problem.
(2) DCS-GCN fuses embedding features from both social and user-item interaction graphs to generate robust user and item representations, enhancing recommendation performance.
(3) Extensive experiments on two public datasets show DCS-GCN outperforms state-of-the-art methods on key metrics, proving its effectiveness and feasibility.

2 Related Works

In the field of shallow computation, SBPR model [10], based on Bayesian Personalized Ranking (BPR) [11], integrates social relationships and preference feedback via "social feedback" to better predict users' preference rankings. TrustMF [12] incorporates trust relationships and rating data, using "trustor" and "trustee" feature vectors to characterize bidirectional user influence, and shows advantages in cold-start and sparse data scenarios. TrustSVD [13] integrates user trust and item rating information, considering both explicit and implicit influences of ratings and trust.

In the field of deep learning, GraphRec [14] model represents user-item and user-user interactions as graph data and employs Graph Attention Networks to learn the embeddings of users and items. DGRec [15] proposes a dynamic graph attention network-based social recommendation model that optimizes recommendations by capturing both dynamic user interests and context-dependent social influences within a session-based framework. DiffNet [16] proposes a neural network-based social recommendation model that optimizes user and item embeddings by simulating the recursive influence diffusion process of users in social networks. DiffNet++ [17] enhances social recommendation by jointly modeling recursive influence diffusion in social networks and interest diffusion in user-item interactions. ESRF [18] uses GCNs for social recommendation via alternative neighborhood generation, denoising, and social attention, unified by adversarial training. MSGCN [19] proposes a multi-social graph convolutional network for friend recommendation, integrating multiple social relationships to enhance user representation and improve recommendation accuracy. SocialLGN [20] proposes a social recommendation model based on LightGCN [9], which propagates the representations of users and items simultaneously in the user-item interaction graph and the social graph and designs a graph fusion operation to aggregate user representations from the two graphs. Although existing methods are actively attempting to mitigate the data sparsity problem, their performance enhancement is still somewhat limited due to the insufficient handling of social relationships and user interests.

3 Problem Formulation

In this section, we will formalize the proposed DCS-GCN. Let $\{u_1, u_2, u_3, ..., u_{|\mathcal{U}|}\} \in \mathcal{U}$ and $\{i_1, i_2, i_3, ..., i_{|\mathcal{I}|}\} \in \mathcal{I}$ denote the sets of users and items in the dataset, respectively. The message passing operations of the proposed recommendation model will conduct on two graphs, namely the social graph and the user-item interaction graph. The specific details are described as follows:

The social graph is constructed by connecting the users from set $\mathcal{U}$, representing the network of friendships among users. It is defined as $\mathcal{G}_s = \{u_m, s_{mn}, u_n | u_m, u_n \in \mathcal{U}\}$, where u_m and u_n denote any two users in set $\mathcal{U}$, and s_{mn} indicates whether u_m and u_n are friends. If $s_{mn} = 1$, it means that there is a friendship between the two users (typically manifested as mutual following on the platform). If $s_{mn} = 0$, it means that there is no friendship between the two users. It should be noted that $\mathcal{N}_u^s$ represents the set of all users who are friends with a user u in the social network.

The user-item interaction graph is constructed by connecting users from set $\mathcal{U}$ with items from set $\mathcal{I}$, representing the interaction relationships between users and items. It is defined as $\mathcal{G}_{u-i} = \{u, s_{ui}, i | u \in \mathcal{U}, i \in \mathcal{I}\}$. Here, u represents a user from set $\mathcal{U}$, i represents an item from set $\mathcal{I}$, and s_{ui} indicates whether the user u has interacted with the item i. If $s_{ui} = 1$, it means that there is an interaction between the user and the item (typically manifested as clicks, collections, or purchases on the platform). Otherwise, it means that there is no interaction between the user and the item. $\mathcal{N}_u^{u-i}$ represents the set of all users who have interacted with an item i in the user-item interaction graph. $\mathcal{N}_i^{u-i}$ represents the set of all items that have interacted with a user u in the user-item interaction graph.

Input: A social graph $\mathcal{G}_s$ and a user-item interaction graph $\mathcal{G}_{u-i}$.

Output: A function to compute the interaction probabilities between any user u and a set of items $\mathcal{I}$.

4 Design of DCS-GCN

As shown in Fig. 1, the proposed DCS-GCN recommendation model in this study conducts message passing through a dual-channel social graph convolutional network. The first channel performs convolution operations on the inherent social graph to mine user features. The essence of this process is to integrate additional information, thereby alleviating the data sparsity problem. The second channel conducts friend clustering analysis in the user-item interaction graph and performs message passing on the resulting social subgraphs. This multi-graph message passing method can enrich the aggregation process, thereby mitigating the over-smoothing problem. Moreover, after each convolution operation, the model fuses the features output from the two channels for the final recommendation score calculation. The specific model computation process of DCS-GCN will be introduced in Sects. 4.1 to 4.6.

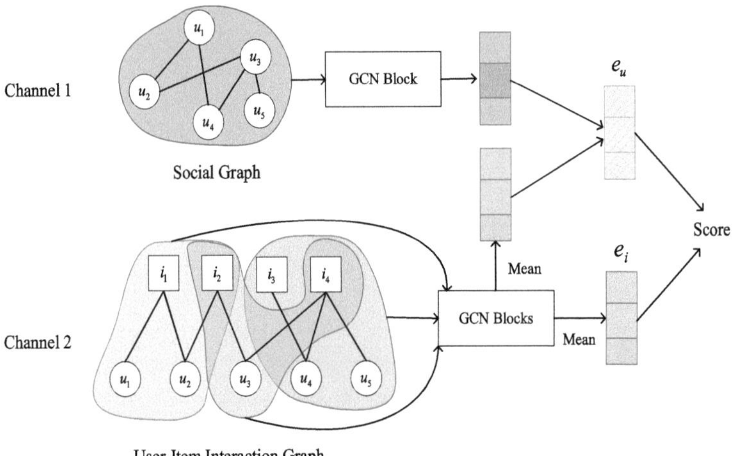

Fig. 1. System architecture of DCS-GCN

4.1 Embedding Layer

The primary function of the embedding layer is to initialize the embedding representations for all users and items. In this paper, we initialize the embedding $e_u^{(0)} \in R^d$ for any user and $e_i^{(0)} \in R^d$ for any item using a normal distribution. The number in the superscript of the embedding indicates the number of graph convolutional layers the embeddings have passed through, for example, "(0)" denotes that these embeddings are the initial embeddings without any graph convolutional layer processing. d represents the dimensionality of the embeddings for all users and items.

By transposing and stacking the embeddings of all M users output from the embedding layer, we can obtain a user embedding matrix $E_U^{(0)} \in R^{M \times d}$. Similarly, by transposing and stacking the embeddings of all N items output from the embedding layer, we can obtain an item embedding matrix $E_I^{(0)} \in R^{N \times d}$.

4.2 The First Social Channel

As shown in Fig. 2, in the first social channel, we employ a lightweight GCN model (i.e., a GCN model without linear transformations and nonlinear activation functions) to conduct message passing on the user feature vectors initialized by the embedding layer. This process focuses solely on learning user embeddings through the inherent social graph. After layers of convolution, the user embeddings integrate information from higher-order neighbors, and these embeddings serve as the user representations for the first social channel.

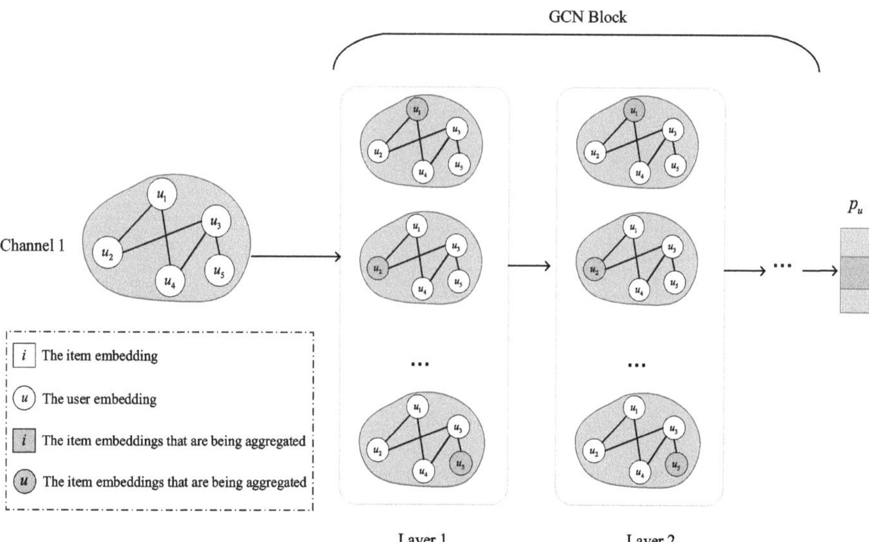

Fig. 2. Workflow of the first social channel

Take the k-th layer of convolution as an example, $k \in (1, 2, ..., K)$. e_u^{k-1} represents the user feature of a particular user output from the k-1-th layer. The k-th convolution layer can be formulated as follows:

$$p_u^{(k)} = \sum_{v \in \mathcal{N}_u^s} \frac{1}{\sqrt{|\mathcal{N}_u^s|}\sqrt{|\mathcal{N}_v^s|}} e_u^{k-1} \tag{1}$$

Here, $p_u^{(k)}$ represents the user embedding obtained after the k-th layer of message passing. $1/(\sqrt{|\mathcal{N}_u^s|}\sqrt{|\mathcal{N}_v^s|})$ is used to normalize each user's feature vector to prevent the embedding representation from continuously increasing due to vector superposition.

4.3 The Second Social Channel

As shown in Fig. 3, in the second social channel, unlike the first social channel, the embeddings of both users and items can be learned. We first conduct unsupervised clustering analysis on the user embeddings in the user-item interaction graph through the subgraph generation component to capture the social relationships among users. In each social subgraph, we also use a lightweight GCN model to perform message passing on the feature vectors initialized by the embedding layer. After multiple layers of convolution operations, the embeddings of users and items fully integrate information from higher-order neighbors. Finally, by averaging the subgraph features, we can obtain the representations of users and items for the second social channel.

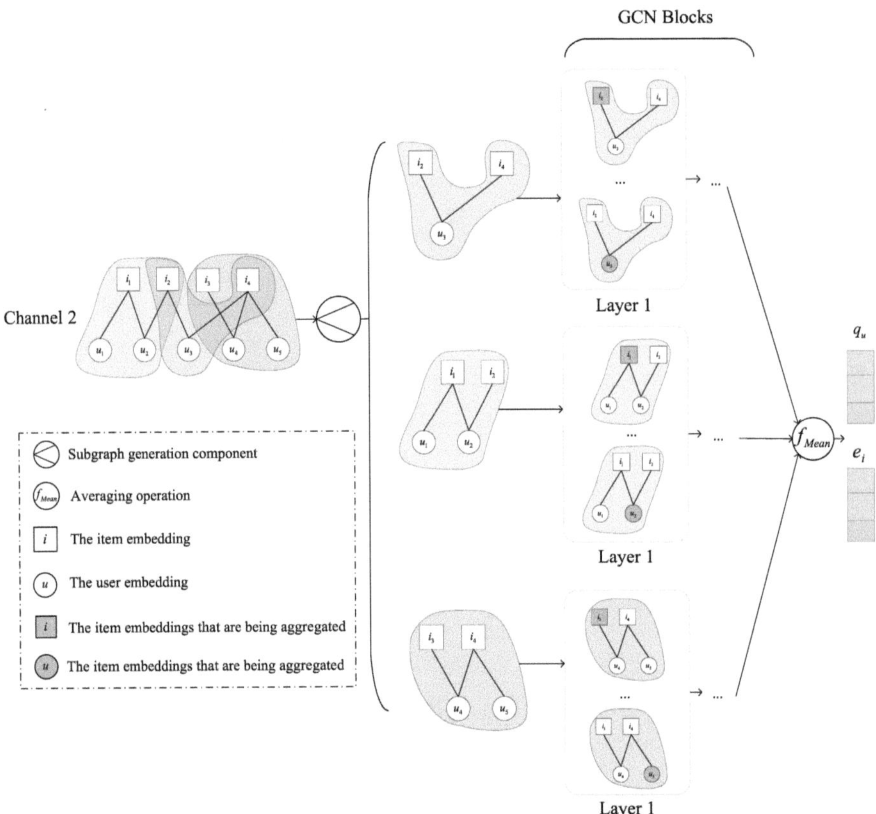

Fig. 3. Workflow of the second social channel

The main function of the second social channel is to reduce the homogeneity of users' embeddings (to alleviate the over-smoothing problem). This study employs a subgraph generation component to conduct clustering analysis on users in the user-item interaction graph. The specific process of the subgraph generation is: Firstly, the initialized user embeddings are mapped to a feature space with the low dimensionality as the number of subgraphs. This work selects two fully connected layers for computation (Compared to standard methods like K-means, they can learn the complex nonlinear relationships of data). Secondly, in mapped feature space, each user corresponds to a low-dimensional feature vector. The position of the maximum value in this feature vector is then taken as the category subgraph label for users, the workflow is as shown below:

$$Y_1 = \sigma(W_1 e_u^{(0)} + b_1) \tag{2}$$

$$Y_2 = W_2 Y_1 + b_2 \tag{3}$$

Here, $W_1 \in R^{d\times d}$ and $W_2 \in R^{N\times d}$ represent the weight matrices of the two fully connected layers, while $b_1 \in R^d$ and $b_2 \in R^N$ are the bias terms of these layers. σ denotes the ReLU function. It is important to note that the number of categories for all users is directly related to the first dimension of the weight matrix W_2—that is, N.

For each decomposed social subgraph, we employ a lightweight GCN model to learn the embeddings of users and items. Similarly, taking the k-th layer of convolution as an example, $k \in (1, 2, ..., K)$, where $e_u^{(k-1)}$ and $e_i^{(k-1)}$ represent the user and item features at the k-1-th layer, respectively, the k-th convolution layer can be formulated as follows:

$$q_u^{(k)} = \frac{1}{|G|}\sum_{g\in G}\sum_{i\in \mathcal{N}_i^{u-i}} \frac{1}{\sqrt{|\mathcal{N}_{gu}^{u-i}|}\sqrt{|\mathcal{N}_{gi}^{u-i}|}} e_i^{k-1} \tag{4}$$

$$e_i^{(k)} = \frac{1}{|G|}\sum_{g\in G}\sum_{i\in \mathcal{N}_i^{u-i}} \frac{1}{\sqrt{|\mathcal{N}_{gu}^{u-i}|}\sqrt{|\mathcal{N}_{gi}^{u-i}|}} e_u^{k-1} \tag{5}$$

Here, $q_u^{(k)}$ and $e_i^{(k)}$ represent the user and item embedding obtained after the k-th layer of message passing. G denotes the set of subgraphs, and g represents a specific subgraph within the set. $1/(\sqrt{|\mathcal{N}_{gu}^{u-i}|}\sqrt{|\mathcal{N}_{gi}^{u-i}|})$ is used to normalize the feature vectors of users and items to prevent the embeddings from continuously increasing due to vector superposition. Note that the embeddings from multiple subgraphs finally will be averaged to represent the embeddings at each layer.

4.4 Feature Fusion and Rating Prediction

After K layers of graph convolutional message passing, we obtain two sets of user embeddings $\{p_u^{(0)}, p_u^{(1)}, ..., p_u^{(K)}\}$ and $\{q_u^{(0)}, q_u^{(1)}, ..., q_u^{(K)}\}$, as well as one set of item embeddings $\{e_i^{(0)}, e_i^{(1)}, ..., e_i^{(K)}\}$. Given that user embeddings are divided into two sets with a significant scale difference between them and considering the demand for lightweight models, this paper employs a simple weighting method to fuse these features. The fusion formula is as follows:

$$e_u^{(k)} = \partial(W_3 p_u^{(k)} + W_4 q_u^{(k)}) \tag{6}$$

Here, W_3 and $W_4 \in R$ are the learnable fusion weight, and ∂ is the ReLU function.

The final embeddings for users and items are as follows:

$$e_u = \frac{1}{K+1} \sum_{k=0}^{K} e_u^{(k)} \tag{7}$$

$$e_i = \frac{1}{K+1} \sum_{k=0}^{K} e_i^{(k)} \tag{8}$$

The preference score of a user for a particular item can be described as:

$$Score = e_u^T e_i \tag{9}$$

4.5 Loss Function

During the model training process, we randomly sample many triplets (u, i^+, i^-) from the training set to adjust the model parameters. The elements of these triplets represent: user u, item i^+ that the user has interacted with, and item i^- that the user has not interacted with. The model uses the Bayesian Personalized Ranking (BPR) function as the loss function, aiming to make the user's score for interacted items $Score^+$ much higher than the score for non-interacted items $Score^-$. The BPR loss function can be expressed as follows:

$$\ell_{BPR} = \sum_{(u,i^+) \in \mathcal{N}^{u-i} and (u,i^-) \notin \mathcal{N}^{u-i}} - \ln \sigma(Score^+ - Score^-) + \lambda ||E^{(0)}||_2^2 \tag{10}$$

Here, $\lambda ||E^{(0)}||_2^2$ represents the L2 regularization, which is used to prevent overfitting problem during the training process.

4.6 Matrix Form and Complexity of DCS-GCN

Let $\tilde{S} \in R^{M \times M}$ denote the message passing matrix for the first social channel, and $\tilde{G}_1, \tilde{G}_2, ..., \tilde{G}_z \in R^{M \times N}$ denote the message passing matrix for the second social channel's subgraphs. Also, let $E_U^{(k-1)}$ and $E_I^{(k-1)}$ represent the user and item embedding matrices output at the k-1-th layer, respectively. The matrix form of DCS-GCN is as follows:

$$E_U^{(k)} = \partial(W_3 \tilde{S} E_U^{(k-1)} + W_4 \frac{1}{z}(\tilde{G}_1 E_I^{(k-1)} + \tilde{G}_2 E_I^{(k-1)} + ... + \tilde{G}_z E_I^{(k-1)})) \tag{11}$$

$$E_I^{(k)} = \frac{1}{z}(\tilde{G}_1^T E_U^{(k-1)} + \tilde{G}_2^T E_U^{(k-1)} + ... + \tilde{G}_z^T E_U^{(k-1)}) \tag{12}$$

(1) Time complexity

The time complexity brought by user embedding updates mainly consists of two parts: the time complexity of matrix multiplication $\tilde{S}E_U^{(k-1)}$ is $O(M^2d)$, and the matrix multiplication $\tilde{G}_1E_I^{(k-1)} \mid \tilde{G}_2E_I^{(k-1)} \mid \ldots \mid \tilde{G}_zE_I^{(k-1)}$ is $O(zMNd)$. Similarly, the time complexity brought by item embedding updates is $O(zMNd)$. Therefore, the total time complexity of K-layer convolutions is $O(KM^2d + 2zKMNd)$. Although subgraph computation brings additional overhead, we still make it feasible in terms of time due to using lightweight GCN components as the basic architecture and a simple feature fusion mechanism.

(2) Space complexity

The learnable parameters of the model presented in this paper include: $\{E_U^{(0)} \in R^{M\times d}, E_I^{(0)} \in R^{N\times d}, W_1 \in R^{N\times d}, W_2 \in R^{N\times d}, b_1 \in R^d, b_2 \in R^N, W_3 \in R, W_4 \in R\}$. The parameter storage space required by the model is $(M + N + d + N)d + N + d + 2$, Traditional recommendation algorithms based on GCNs also typically involve parameter update operations for $E_U^{(0)}$ and $E_I^{(0)}$, their complexity is $(M + N)d$. The additional space mainly occupied by our model is $(d + N)d$, which is contributed by the cluster components.

5 Experiments

5.1 Datasets

Two widely used recommendation system datasets, LastFM[1] and Filmtrust[2], were selected for the experiments in this study. Both datasets contain rich social relationship information. LastFM is a music recommendation dataset that includes interaction records between 1,892 users and 17,632 music items, as well as social relationship data among users. Filmtrust is a movie recommendation dataset that includes interaction records between 1,508 users and 2,071 movie items, as well as social relationship data among users. Detailed information about the datasets is shown in Table 1.

Table 1. Description of the dataset details

Datesets	LastFM	Filmtrust
Number of users	1892	1508
Number of items	17632	2071
Number of user-item interactions	92834	35496
Number of social interactions	223711	13860

[1] https://grouplens.org/datasets/hetrec-2011/.

[2] https://guoguibing.github.io/librec/datasets.html.

5.2 Experimental Baselines

We selected two state-of-the-art GCN-based recommendation algorithms (NGCF and LightGCN) and three current advanced social recommendation models (SBPR, DiffNet, and SocialLGN) to conduct comparative experiments with our DCS-GCN. The following is a detailed description of these experimental baselines:

NGCF [8]: A method that uses graph convolutional networks to spread user and item embeddings on an interaction graph, adding higher-order connections.

LightGCN [9]: A simple graph network for recommendations that only keeps neighbor aggregation, removing complex operations.

SBPR [10]: A recommendation method that uses friends' preferences to improve accuracy by considering positive, social, and negative feedback.

DiffNet [16]: A social recommendation model that simulates influence spreading in social networks, capturing user interests through user-item and social graph.

SocialLGN [20]: A social recommendation model based on a lightweight GCN model, spreading user and item representations in both interaction and social graphs to improve performance, especially for new users or items.

5.3 Evaluation Metrics

To comprehensively evaluate the performance of the proposed DCS-GCN model in this paper, we selected Recall@K, Precision@K, and Normalized Discounted Cumulative Gain (NDCG@K) as the experimental metrics. The suffix "@K" in the metric names indicates the specific value of the metric when the length of the recommendation list is K. Suppose the set of items recommended to a user is denoted as $R(u)$, and the set of items that the user is actually interested in, as indicated in the test set, is denoted as $T(u)$. The following is a detailed introduction to each metric:

Recall shows if the recommendation system can suggest items users actually like. Simply put, it's the percentage of correctly recommended items in the test set. A higher recall means the system can better find items users might like. The formula for Recall is:

$$\mathrm{Re}\,call@K = \frac{|R(u) \cap T(u)|}{|T(u)|} \tag{13}$$

Precision measures how accurate the recommendation system's results are. It shows the percentage of recommended items that the user is actually interested in. The formula for Precision is:

$$\mathrm{Pr}\,ecision@K = \frac{|R(u) \cap T(u)|}{|R(u)|} \tag{14}$$

NDCG is a metric that considers both the number of relevant items in the recommendation list and their positions. Relevant items at the top of the list contribute more to the NDCG score. Thus, NDCG provides a more complete picture of the recommendation quality. The formula for NDCG is:

$$NDCG@K = \frac{\sum_{i=1}^{K} \frac{relevance_i}{\log_2(i+1)}}{\sum_{j=1}^{|R(u)\cap T(u)|} \frac{1}{\log_2(j+1)}} \tag{15}$$

Here, $relevance_i$ takes a value of 0 or 1. If $relevance_i = 0$, it indicates that the i-th item in the recommendation list was not clicked by the user. If $relevance_i = 1$, it indicates that the i-th item in the recommendation list was clicked by the user.

5.4 Parameter Configuration

In the experimental design, for the five baseline models, this paper directly adopted the optimal parameter configurations determined in their respective studies. For the proposed DCS-GCN model in this paper, we chose a three-layer graph convolutional structure to compare with the baseline models, as most of the baseline models also adopted a three-layer convolutional structure. Regarding the number of subgraphs in the second social channel, we found through extensive experiments that the optimal number of subgraphs for both datasets was 3 thereby we set it to 3. We speculate that this result may be related to the similar user scales of the two datasets.

In terms of hardware configuration, all experiments were run on an NVIDIA Tesla T4 GPU with 16GB of memory. Regarding the software environment, the experiments utilized CUDA version 11.8 and were developed with Python 3.10.

In model training, the dimension of the embedding vectors was set to 64. The L2 regularization parameter, learning rate, batch size, and number of training epochs were set to 1×10^{-4}, 1×10^{-2}, 2048, and 10,000, respectively. For the optimizer, we selected the Adam optimizer for parameter optimization.

5.5 Comparative Experiments

During the experiments, we divided the interaction data of each recommendation dataset into training and test sets at a ratio of 80% and 20%, respectively. To more accurately evaluate the model's performance in the face of data sparsity problem, we specifically selected user data with fewer than 20 interaction records in the test set for evaluation. This setting aims to test whether our model can effectively alleviate the data sparsity problem and enhance the performance of recommendation systems in practical applications.

Table 2. Performance comparison of our model vs. competitors

Model	LastFM			Filmtrust		
	Recall @10	Precision @10	NDCG @10	Recall @10	Precision @10	NDCG @10
NGCF [8]	0.1169	0.0333	0.1070	0.5042	0.1495	0.3913
LightGCN [9]	0.1727	0.0417	0.1374	0.5902	0.1681	0.4592
SBPR [10]	0.1123	0.0209	0.0828	0.4963	0.1212	0.3507
DiffNet [16]	0.1713	0.0417	0.1107	0.5880	0.1576	0.4305
SocialLGN [20]	0.1974	0.0458	0.1419	0.5923	0.1701	0.4641
DCS-GCN	**0.2423**	**0.0583**	**0.1568**	**0.6040**	**0.1902**	**0.4859**
Improve.	22.74%	27.29%	10.50%	1.97%	11.81%	4.49%

Table 2 shows the performance comparison results between our proposed DCS-GCN model and the five state-of-the-art baseline models. In the experiments, we uniformly set the recommendation list length to 10 and calculated the Recall, Precision, and NDCG for all models. The results clearly demonstrate that our DCS-GCN model outperforms the other advanced baseline models in multiple key metrics, showing significant performance advantages. Specifically, on the LastFM dataset, DCS-GCN achieved remarkable improvements of 22.74%, 27.29%, and 10.50% in Recall, Precision, and NDCG, respectively, compared with the current state-of-the-art social recommendation model SocialLGN. On the Filmtrust dataset, DCS-GCN also exhibited excellent performance. Compared with SocialLGN, it achieved increases of 1.97%, 11.81%, and 4.49% in Recall, Precision, and NDCG, respectively. These results fully illustrate the powerful performance of the DCS-GCN model in the field of recommendation systems.

5.6 Ablation Study

To verify the rationality of the DCS-GCN model structure, we further explored the performance differences between single-channel and dual-channel social recommendation models. To this end, we designed two single-channel social recommendation models as comparison baselines to comprehensively evaluate the advantages and effectiveness of the dual-channel structure in recommendation systems.

SCS-GCNg: This model removes the social graph in the first channel of DCS-GCN and only mines social relationships in the second channel. It learns the embeddings of users and items through the user-item interaction graph.

SCS-GCNs: This model eliminates the social message passing in social subgraphs of DCS-GCN and only retains the convolutional propagation mechanism of the social graph and the user-item interaction graph. This model also integrates social relationships through a single channel.

Table 3. Performance comparison of our model vs. single-channel social GCN models

Model	LastFM			Filmtrust		
	Recall @10	Precision @10	NDCG @10	Recall @10	Precision @10	NDCG @10
SCS-GCNg	0.1522	0.0399	0.0999	0.4030	0.1617	0.3900
SCS-GCNs	0.1755	0.0433	0.1367	0.4955	0.1622	0.4566
DCS-GCN	**0.2423**	**0.0583**	**0.1568**	**0.6040**	**0.1902**	**0.4859**

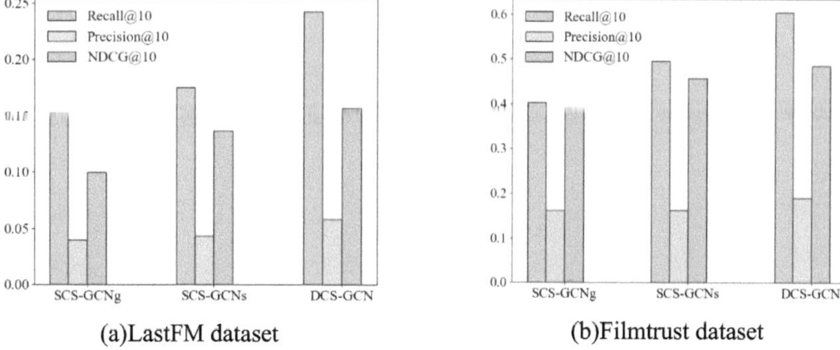

(a)LastFM dataset (b)Filmtrust dataset

Fig. 4. Performance comparison of our model vs. single-channel social GCN models

The experimental results on the two datasets are shown in Table 3 and Fig. 4. The results indicate that the dual-channel social recommendation model outperforms the two single-channel social recommendation models in terms of Recall, Precision, and NDCG. This finding fully demonstrates the rationality of the structural design of the proposed DCS-GCN model. Meanwhile, we observed that SCS-GCNs performed better than SCS-GCNg. This suggests that integrating social graphs for recommendations is more promising than relying solely on the user-item interaction graph, further proving the necessity of incorporating social network information in recommendation systems.

5.7 Validation Experiments for Over-Smoothing Problem

In this section, we verify the effectiveness of DCS-GCN in alleviating the over-smoothing problem. To this end, we set the number of model layers to range from 1 to 7 and observed whether there was a significant decline in their performance in terms of Recall, Precision, and NDCG.

Figure 5 shows the test results of the DCS-GCN model on the two datasets. It can be noted that as the number of graph convolutional layers in the model increases, the recommendation performance does not deteriorate but continues to improve. This indicates that our proposed model does not suffer from over-smoothing problem but can effectively mitigate the catastrophic failure mode through a diverse message passing mechanism. After 3 to 4 layers, the performance tends to reach saturation. Our analysis suggests that 3 to 4 layers of convolution are sufficient to extract most of the valuable information from the data, which also demonstrates the effectiveness of our model.

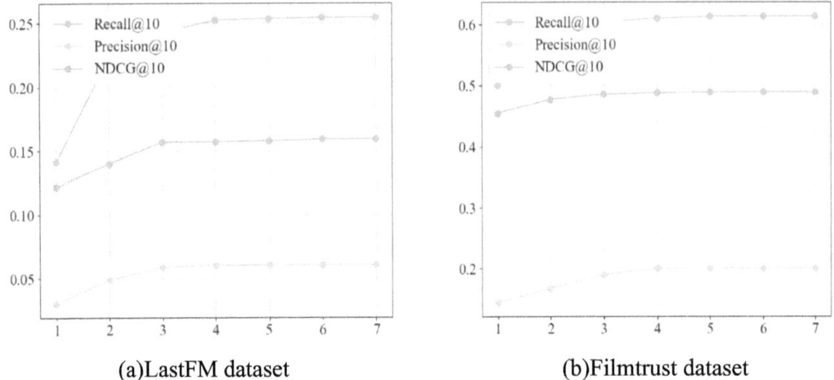

(a)LastFM dataset (b)Filmtrust dataset

Fig. 5. The impact of increasing model layers on model performance

To more intuitively observe the alleviation effect of DCS-GCN on the over-smoothing problem of user representations, we selected 7-layer graph convolution training on both the SocialLGN and DCS-GCN models and selected the embeddings of the top 100 users (each with a dimension of 64) from the LastFM and Filmtrust datasets for visualization. Figure 6 and Fig. 7 show the specific visualization results. It can be clearly seen that the traditional GCN model (represented by SocialLGN) exhibits significant over-smoothing phenomena after multiple layers of graph convolution, and the user embeddings become more similar. In contrast, our model does not show obvious homogenization in the feature representations on both datasets. This is clearly beneficial for recommendation results and directly demonstrates that our model can effectively alleviate the over-smoothing problem.

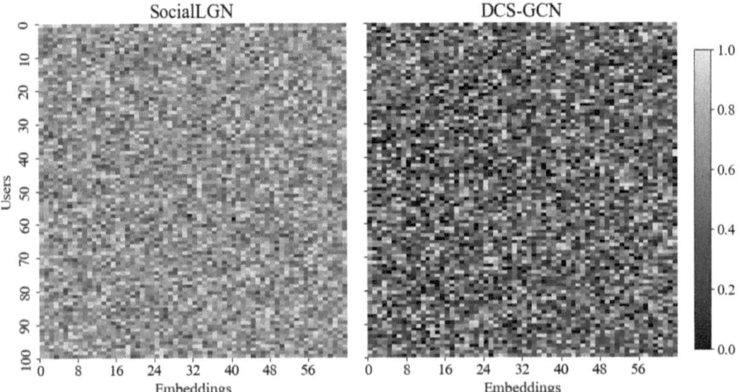

Fig. 6. Heatmaps of embeddings on the LastFM dataset

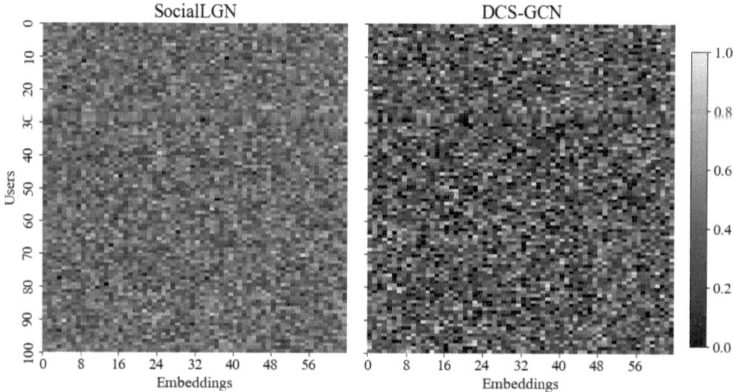

Fig. 7. Heatmaps of embeddings on the Filmtrust dataset

6 Conclusion

In this paper, we propose a recommendation model based on dual-channel social graph convolutional network—DCS-GCN. This model effectively addresses two common issues in recommendation systems, data sparsity problem and over-smoothing problem, by conducting message passing on a dual-channel social network. We evaluated the performance of DCS-GCN on two widely used datasets. The results demonstrate that our model has surpassed several state-of-the-art recommendation methods in sparse data environments. Additionally, through ablation studies, we further validated the rationality of the model structure. We also conducted validation experiments for the over-smoothing problem. The experimental results show that the performance of our model does not deteriorate with the increase in the number of layers. Moreover, the visualization results indicate that the embedding do not tend to become similar after multiple layers of convolutional operations. The above experimental results fully demonstrate the necessity of incorporating social network information into recommendation systems. However, the introduction of the component concept in this paper may bring additional overhead. In the future, we will tend to explore lighter recommendation networks to enhance the real-time capabilities of recommendation algorithms and further better serve social media platforms.

Acknowledgement. This study was funded by the Jilin Provincial Department of Education under Grant no. JJKH20240153KJ.

References

1. Ko, H., Lee, S., Park, Y., Choi, A.: A survey of recommendation systems: recommendation models, techniques, and application fields. Electronics **11**(1), 141 (2022)
2. Zhang, J., Wang, Y., Yuan, Z., Jin, Q.: Personalized real-time movie recommendation system: practical prototype and evaluation. Tsinghua Sci. Technol. **25**(2), 180–191 (2019)

3. Schedl, M., Knees, P., McFee, B., Bogdanov, D.: Music recommendation systems: techniques, use cases, and challenges. In: Recommender Systems Handbook, pp. 927–971(2021)
4. Zhao, Y., Wang, Y., Liu, Y., Cheng, X., Aggarwal, C.C., Derr, T.: Fairness and diversity in recommender systems: a survey. ACM Trans. Intell. Syst. Technol. **16**(1), 1–28 (2025)
5. Aljunid, M.F., Manjaiah, D.H., Hooshmand, M.K., Ali, W.A., Shetty, A.M., Alzoubah, S.Q.: A collaborative filtering recommender systems: Survey. Neurocomputing **617**, 128718 (2025)
6. Mao, K., Zhu, J., Xiao, X., Lu, B., Wang, Z., He, X.: UltraGCN: ultra simplification of graph convolutional networks for recommendation. In: Proceedings of the 30th ACM International Conference on Information and Knowledge Management, pp. 1253–1262(2021)
7. Peng, S., Sugiyama, K., Mine, T.: SVD-GCN: a simplified graph convolution paradigm for recommendation. In: Proceedings of the 31st ACM International Conference on Information and Knowledge Management, pp. 1625–1634 (2022)
8. Wang, X., He, X., Wang, M., Feng, F., Chua, T.S.: Neural graph collaborative filtering. In: Proceedings of the 42nd International ACM SIGIR Conference on Research and Development in Information Retrieval, pp. 165–174 (2019)
9. He, X., Deng, K., Wang, X., Li, Y., Zhang, Y., Wang, M.: LightGCN: simplifying and powering graph convolution network for recommendation. In: Proceedings of the 43rd International ACM SIGIR Conference on Research and Development in Information Retrieval, pp. 639–648 (2020)
10. Zhao, T., McAuley, J., King, I.: Leveraging social connections to improve personalized ranking for collaborative filtering. In: Proceedings of the 23rd ACM International Conference on Information and Knowledge Management, pp. 261–270 (2014)
11. Rendle, S., Freudenthaler, C., Gantner, Z., Schmidt-Thieme, L.: BPR: Bayesian personalized ranking from implicit feedback. arXiv preprint, arXiv-1205 (2012)
12. Yang, B., Lei, Y., Liu, J., Li, W.: Social collaborative filtering by trust. IEEE Trans. Pattern Anal. Mach. Intell.Intell. **39**(8), 1633–1647 (2016)
13. Guo, G., Zhang, J., Yorke-Smith, N.: A novel recommendation model regularized with user trust and item ratings. IEEE Trans. Knowl. Data Eng.Knowl. Data Eng. **28**(7), 1607–1620 (2016)
14. Fan, W., et al.: Graph neural networks for social recommendation. In: The World Wide Web Conference, pp. 417–426 (2019)
15. Song, W., Xiao, Z., Wang, Y., Charlin, L., Zhang, M., Tang, J.: Session-based social recommendation via dynamic graph attention networks. In: Proceedings of the Twelfth ACM International Conference on Web Search and Data Mining, pp. 555–563 (2019)
16. Wu, L., Sun, P., Fu, Y., Hong, R., Wang, X., Wang, M.: A neural influence diffusion model for social recommendation. In: Proceedings of the 42nd International ACM SIGIR Conference on Research and Development in Information Retrieval, pp. 235–244 (2019)
17. Wu, L., Li, J., Sun, P., Hong, R., Ge, Y., Wang, M.: Diffnet++: a neural influence and interest diffusion network for social recommendation. IEEE Trans. Knowl. Data Eng.Knowl. Data Eng. **34**(10), 4753–4766 (2020)
18. Yu, J., Yin, H., Li, J., Gao, M., Huang, Z., Cui, L.: Enhancing social recommendation with adversarial graph convolutional networks. IEEE Trans. Knowl. Data Eng.Knowl. Data Eng. **34**(8), 3727–3739 (2020)
19. Chen, L., Xie, Y., Zheng, Z., Zheng, H., Xie, J.: Friend recommendation based on multi-social graph convolutional network. IEEE Access **8**, 43618–43629 (2020)
20. Liao, J., et al.: SocialLGN: light graph convolution network for social recommendation. Inf. Sci. **589**, 595–607 (2022)

DED: Integrating Degree Entropy and Dynamic Delay Mechanisms for Influence Maximization in Multilayer Networks

Zhongxia Li, Weidong Chen(✉), and Yao Chen

School of Computer Science, South Normal China University, Guangzhou, China
chenwd@scnu.edu.cn

Abstract. Traditional single-layer network models exhibit fundamental limitations in characterizing multilayer interaction within complex social systems, leading to inadequately address the evolving complexities of modern social networks. This limitation has driven the extension of the Influence Maximization (IM) problem to multilayer networks, where identifying influential nodes is challenged by intricate structural properties and cross-layer node interactions. In this paper, we propose a novel Degree-Entropy-Delay (DED) algorithm with a hybrid seed selection strategy. The algorithm combines layer weights, node degree, and information entropy to quantify node importance. To mitigate overlapping influence caused by clustered high-degree nodes, we incorporate the delay mechanism to optimize seed node selection. Comprehensive experiments conducted on eight publicly available real-world networks demonstrate the effectiveness of our algorithm in maximizing influence spread within multilayer networks. The DED algorithm achieves up to 33% higher influence coverage than state-of-the-art methods in large-scale dense networks under the SIR model.

Keywords: Multilayer networks · Influence maximization · Seed selection · Information entropy · Delay mechanism

1 Introduction

The advancement of internet infrastructure has enabled the rise of online social platforms such as Weibo, WeChat, and Facebook. These platforms connect billions of users globally and introduce critical challenges in social network analysis, particularly for viral marketing [16] and public opinion monitoring [13]. Identifying influential spreaders has become a critical task for optimizing information dissemination in such contexts. This study examines a representative scenario in social network diffusion modeling, where a startup enterprise seeks to implement a cost-effective marketing strategy for its newly developed social media application. During the initial deployment phase, the organization faces budget

J. Li et al. (Eds.): APWeb-WAIM 2025, LNCS 16115, pp. 471–485, 2026.
https://doi.org/10.1007/978-981-95-5719-6_30

constraints that necessitate the optimal selection of seed users to initiate viral propagation. The core challenge constitutes the Influence Maximization (IM) problem [6], defined as the problem of finding a set of seed nodes in a social network that can maximize the spread of influence under the diffusion model.

Existing IM research predominantly focuses on single-layer networks [1,4]. However, real-world social systems typically exhibit multilayer interactions. Social networks often consist of multiple interconnected layers [10], each representing distinct types of interactions with users playing different roles. For instance, users engage in a multilayer social network through various behaviors such as following, content sharing, and commenting on Facebook. Accurately identifying influential nodes in such multilayer networks remains a significant challenge. Furthermore, the "rich-club" phenomenon [14] complicates influence analysis in large and dense networks, as densely connected high-degree nodes dominate information flow, resulting in influence overlap among nodes. Existing methods have limitations because these approaches overlook the relationships between layers and fail to effectively address the overlap of seed influence. To address these challenges, this paper proposes the DED algorithm for IM in multilayer networks. The proposed algorithm consists of three sequential phases: 1) the separation of overlapping and non-overlapping nodes, 2) the selection of candidate seed nodes by integrating node weights with a delay mechanism from both categories of nodes, and 3) the final selection of seed nodes from candidate seed nodes. The primary contributions of this work are summarized as follows:

- We design a delay mechanism that effectively alleviates influence overlap through dynamic adjustments.
- We propose the DED algorithm by integrating node weights with a delay mechanism. The node weights, which incorporate layer weights, node degree centrality, and information entropy, are dynamically adjusted with the delay mechanism to quantify influence potential.
- Empirical validation using eight real-world datasets demonstrates superior performance in terms of both effectiveness and efficiency.

The rest of this paper is organized as follows. In Sect. 2, we discuss the related work. The problem definition is presented in Sect. 3. The proposed algorithm is presented in Sect. 4. Experimental results and analysis are presented in Sect. 5. The paper is summarized in Sect. 6.

2 Related Work

Researchers [9] have proven the IM problem to be NP-hard and proposed a greedy algorithm framework based on Monte Carlo simulations, which iteratively selects nodes offering the maximum marginal gain. The Cost-Effective Lazy Forward (CELF) [12] refined this approach by leveraging the submodularity property, significantly reducing computational overhead while maintaining solution quality. Recent research on multilayer networks has focused on extending single-layer approaches through various methodologies, including greedy algorithms, heuristic strategies, and community-based techniques. The Knapsack (KSN) [11] approach addresses this challenge by running parallel approximation algorithms on individual network layers and then merging the resulting seed sets using a multiple-choice knapsack formulation. The structure of network analysis methods has demonstrated particular promise in this domain. The Clique-Based Influence Maximization (CIM) [8] demonstrates effectiveness by identifying key seed nodes from maximal cliques, while Community-Based Influence Maximization (CBIM) [18] achieves comparable results through community detection, similarity-based merging, and targeted seed selection from merged communities.

Recent innovations build upon established techniques, with K++ Shell algorithm [5] enhancing traditional k-shell decomposition through sophisticated analysis of node connectivity patterns and neighbor significance metrics. The Adaptive Coupling Degree (ACD) algorithm [21] introduces a novel dimension by incorporating cross-layer neighborhood information, employing an iterative selection process that prioritizes nodes with both high propagation potential and minimal influence overlap. Another study [2] employs advanced layer-weighting mechanisms that simultaneously consider intra-layer connection density and user activity patterns for more accurate influence assessment. The Discrete Particle Swarm Optimization (DPSOMIM) [19] method utilizes the random connectivity centrality metric based on the discrete particle swarm algorithm and incorporates a neighborhood optimization strategy. Existing multilayer IM algorithms face limitations: high computational complexity and insufficient network structure utilization.

3 Problem Definition

3.1 Influence Maximization in Multilayer Networks

A multilayer network $M = \{G_1, G_2, \ldots, G_L\}$ consists of L layers, where each layer $a \in \{1, \ldots, L\}$ represents a graph $G_a = (V, E_a)$. All layers share a common node set V, while each layer maintains its distinct edge set E_a. As illustrated in Fig. 1, the multilayer network comprises two layers. The IM problem in multilayer networks aims to identify an optimal set $S \subseteq V$ of k seed nodes that maximizes the spread of influence across all layers under the specified diffusion model. Mathematically, the optimization problem is defined as:

$$S^* = \underset{S \subseteq V, |S|=k}{\arg\max} \, (\bigcup_{l=1}^{\mathrm{L}} V_l(S)) \tag{1}$$

As shown in Eq. (1), where $V_l(S)$ denotes the set of nodes influenced by seed set S within layer l, the multilayer IM problem exhibits fundamental similarities to the classical IM problem. The additional complexity emerges from the multilayer topological structure. A crucial distinction can be made between nodes that active in multiple layers and those active in only one layer. These roles can be formally defined as follows:

Definition 1 (Overlapping Node). *A node i in a multilayer network M is defined as an overlapping node if it has at least one active connection ($d_i^l \geq 1$) in two or more distinct layers, where d_i^l denotes the degree of node i in layer l.*

Definition 2 (Non-Overlapping Node). *A node i in a multilayer network M is defined as a non-overlapping node if it has at least one active connection ($d_i^l \geq 1$) in exactly one layer and has no active connections ($d_i^l = 0$) in all other layers.*

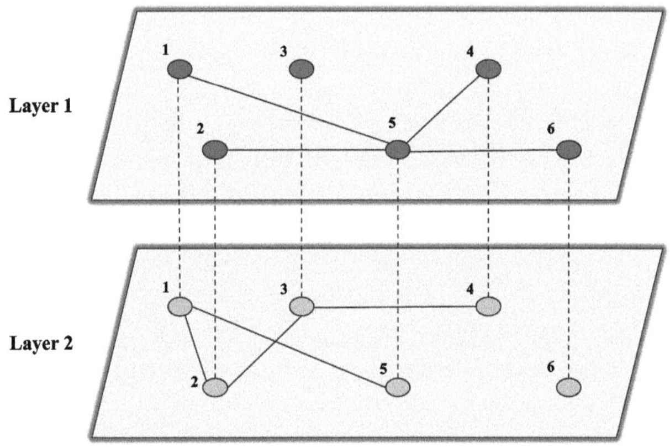

Fig. 1. A multilayer network consisting of two layers.

3.2 Diffusion Model

MIC Model. The Independent Cascade (IC) model [3] is a foundational propagation model widely applied to the IM problem. During the propagation process, activated nodes attempt to influence each of their neighbors with probability $\rho \in (0, 1]$. If an activation attempt fails, no further attempts are made by that node towards the same neighbor. The traditional IC model, however, does not account for the structural complexities inherent in multilayer networks, which prompt researchers to develop the Multilayer Independent Cascade (MIC) model [19,21]. While the MIC model allows active nodes to simultaneously propagate influence to neighbors across different layers, it neglects the role of edge weights in influence diffusion. To address this limitation, we adapt the MIC model by incorporating edge weight parameters into its propagation mechanism to better capture real-world network characteristics.

SIR Model. The Susceptible-Infected-Recovered model [15] has seen widespread application in influence maximization studies. In this model, network nodes are classified into three states: Susceptible (S), Infected (I), and

Recovered (R). A susceptible node transitions to the infected state with probability α (infection rate) upon interaction with an infected node. Infected nodes transition to the recovered state with probability β.

4 Proposed Algorithm

4.1 Layer Weights

In multilayer networks, each layer represents different types of interactions, resulting in unique sets of nodes and edges between layers. To assess the relative significance of each layer l, we compute layer weights w_l using Eq. (2), which measures the proportion of shared nodes and edges between layer l and other layers relative to the entire network and prioritizes the layers that play a more significant role in multilayer networks.

$$w_l = 2^{\frac{n_o(l)+e_o(l)}{\sum_{l_1=1}^{L}(n_o(l_1)+e_o(l_1))}} \tag{2}$$

$$n_o(l) = \sum_{l_1 \neq l}^{L} |V_l \cap V_{l_1}| \tag{3}$$

$$e_o(l) = \sum_{l_1 \neq l}^{L} |E_l \cap E_{l_1}| \tag{4}$$

where $n_o(l)$ denotes the number of nodes in layer l that also appear in at least one other layer, while $e_o(l)$ counts edges connecting these overlapping nodes across different layers.

4.2 Node Weights

In our proposed method, nodes are classified as either overlapping or non-overlapping. As illustrated in Fig. 1, nodes $\{1, 2, 4, 5\}$ are classified as overlapping nodes, while node $\{3, 6\}$ are identified as non-overlapping nodes. The degree of a node represents the number of connections it has with other nodes and serves as a fundamental metric for assessing its importance. Specifically, the multilayer degree $D(i)$ is computed via Eq. (5) as the total number of unique neighbors, where $N_l(i)$ represents the direct neighbors of i in layer l and $N_l^{\text{out}}(i)$ represents its outgoing neighbors in layer l.

$$D(i) = \begin{cases} \left|\sum_{l=1}^{L} N_l(i)\right|, & \text{for undirected graphs} \\ \left|\sum_{l=1}^{L} N_l^{\text{out}}(i)\right|, & \text{for directed graphs} \end{cases} \tag{5}$$

Previous studies [17] introduced the concept of information entropy $E(i)$ for evaluating node importance. While node degree is a critical metric, the topological quality of neighboring nodes also significantly influences information diffusion potential. Specifically, $E(i)$ quantifies the diversity of decisions made by a node during the diffusion process, reflecting the heterogeneity in the distribution of information outflow from node i to its neighboring nodes. The symbol p_{ij} denotes the probability of information transmission from node i to node j. To quantify an influential node and address the limitations of degree centrality, we calculate degree entropy $E(i)$ using Eq. (6). The information entropy $E(i)$ reflects the capacity of a node to propagate information through diverse connection pathways, with higher values indicating greater potential for widespread dissemination. The node weights are then calculated using Eq. (8).

$$E(i) = \sum_{l=1}^{L} \sum_{j \in N_l(i)} -p_{ij} \log(p_{ij}) \tag{6}$$

$$p_{ij} = \frac{D(j) \times w_l}{\sum_{l_1=1}^{L} \sum_{k \in N_l(i)} (D(k) \times w_{l_1})} \tag{7}$$

$$weight(i) = D(i) \times E(i) \tag{8}$$

4.3 Delay Mechanism

The "rich-club" phenomenon, where high-degree nodes form tightly connected clusters, hinders influence propagation. To mitigate this issue, we introduce a delay mechanism reducing influence overlap among seed nodes, promoting broader information spread and enhancing coverage. This mechanism dynamically adjusts node degree and information entropy by incrementally applying a base delay of 1 to the neighbors of selected candidate seeds. As shown in Eq. 9, $(\mathbf{A}_l^n)_{s,i}$ denotes paths of length n from node s to i. The base delay value are first propagated to immediate neighbors, then to their neighbors, extending its effect over iterations. Since overlapping nodes may occupy central positions, exacerbating the rich-club effect, we propagate the delay value three times versus twice for non-overlapping nodes. Once a candidate node is selected, its delay value will not be altered.

$$dl_i^l = \begin{cases} \sum_{n=1}^{3} (\mathbf{A}_l^n)_{s,i}, & \text{if } s \text{ is an overlapping node} \\ \sum_{n=1}^{2} (\mathbf{A}_l^n)_{s,i}, & \text{if } s \text{ is a non-overlapping node} \end{cases} \tag{9}$$

When node 5, an overlapping node, is selected as the candidate seed node in Fig. 1, the delay values d_i^l in Layer 1 are $dl_1^1 = 5$, $dl_2^1 = 5$, $dl_3^1 = 0$, $dl_4^1 = 5$, $dl_5^1 = 0$, and $dl_6^1 = 5$. In Layer 2, the delay values are $dl_1^2 = 3$, $dl_2^2 = 1$, $dl_3^2 = 1$, $dl_4^2 = 0$, $dl_5^2 = 0$, and $dl_6^2 = 0$. Based on these delay values, we update the node degree $d_{dl}(i)$ and the information entropy $E_{dl}(i)$ using the formulas given in Eq. (10) and (11), respectively.

$$D_{dl}(i) = D(i) - \sum_{l}^{L} dl_i^l \times w_l \tag{10}$$

$$E_{dl}(i) = \begin{cases} \sum\limits_{l=1}^{L} \sum\limits_{j \in N_l(i)} -p_{dl_{ij}} \log(p_{dl_{ij}}), & \text{if } p_{dl_{ij}} > 0 \\ 0, & \text{if } p_{dl_{ij}} \leq 0 \end{cases} \tag{11}$$

$$p_{dl_{ij}} = \begin{cases} \dfrac{D_{dl}(j)}{\sum\limits_{l_1=1}^{L} \sum\limits_{k \in N_l(i)} D_{dl}(k)}, & \text{if } \sum\limits_{l_1=1}^{L} \sum\limits_{k \in N_l(i)} D_{dl}(k) > 0 \\ 0, & \text{otherwise.} \end{cases} \tag{12}$$

$$weight(i) = D_{dl}(i) \times E_{dl}(i) \tag{13}$$

4.4 Seed Node Selection

After classifying node into overlapping and non-overlapping nodes, we compute three key metrics: layer weights, node degree, and information entropy. These metrics are then integrated to calculate composite node weights, and the node with the maximum weight is selected as the initial candidate seed node. Once the initial candidate seed node is identified, we implement the delay mechanism to the candidate seed, which triggers updates to both the node degree and information entropy based on the assigned delay value. The node weights are then recomputed using Eq. (13). This process is repeated iteratively to select subsequent candidate seeds. Finally, we ranks all candidate seeds and selects the top-k nodes with the highest scores using Eq. (15). The term $cs_w(i)$ denotes the normalized weight of candidate seed node i, while $\hat{D}_{dl}(i)$ and $\hat{E}_{dl}(i)$ represent the normalized degree centrality and normalized information entropy of node i within the candidate seed set.

$$cs_w(i) = \hat{D}_{dl}(i) \times \hat{E}_{dl}(i) \tag{14}$$

$$score(i) = c_w(i) \times \hat{D}_{dl}(i) \tag{15}$$

4.5 Time Complexity Analysis

The Degree-Entropy-Delay algorithm employs a three-phase strategy. In the first phase, we initialize the overlapping nodes, non-overlapping nodes, and candidate seed set S' (Line 1–3), then calculates layer weights (Lines 4–6). In the second phase, the node with the highest node weights is selected as the candidate seed node separately from both overlapping and non-overlapping nodes based on our delay mechanism. The node weights are computed by integrating node degree and information entropy metrics. This process continues until a total of $2k$ candidate seed nodes are selected (Lines 7–16). Finally, the top-k seed nodes are ranked from the candidate seed set S' and designated as the final seed nodes S (Lines 17–18).

Algorithm 1. Degree-Entropy-Delay Algorithm (DED)

Input: Multilayer network $M = \{G_1, G_2, \ldots, G_L\}$, Seed set size $k \in \mathbb{N}^+$
Output: Seed node set $S \subseteq V$

```
ON ← {v ∈ V | active nodes in multiple layers}   //Overlapping nodes
NON ← V \ ON   //Non-overlapping nodes
S' ← ∅   //Candidate seed set
for each layer l ∈ {1, ..., L} do
    w_l ← Compute by Eq. (2)
end for
for each subset 𝒳 ∈ {ON, NON} do
    for i ← 1 to k do
        D_dl(i) ← Compute by Eq. (10)
        E_dl(i) ← Compute by Eq. (11)
        weights(i) ← Compute by Eq. (13)
        u ← arg max_{i∈𝒳}(weights(i))
        𝒳 ← 𝒳 − {u}
        S' ← S' ∪ {u}
    end for
end for
S ← Select top-k nodes from S' ordered by Eq. (15)
return S
```

The time complexity of the proposed algorithm is as follows: Calculating network layer weights has a complexity of $O(L^2 \cdot (|\overline{E}| + |\overline{V}|))$, while node degree calculations take $O(L \cdot |\overline{E}| + |\overline{V}|)$, where L denotes the number of layers, and $|\overline{E}|$ and $|\overline{V}|$ represent the average number of edges and nodes per layer. Candidate seed node selection runs in $O(L \cdot (|\overline{E}| + |\overline{V}|) + k \cdot (L + |\overline{V}|))$, and determining the final seed nodes from the candidate set S' has a complexity of $O(k)$. Given the constraints $L \ll |V|$ and $k \ll |V|$, the overall complexity reduces to $O(L^2 \cdot (|\overline{E}| + |\overline{V}|))$. Assuming a uniform distribution of nodes across layers, the complexity further simplifies to $O(L \cdot (|E| + |V|))$.

Table 1. Details of datasets

Network	Nodes	Edges	Layers	Type
Celegans multiplex GPI network	3879	8181	6	Directed
Homo multiplex GPI network	18222	170899	3	Directed
Moscow Athletics 2013	88804	210250	7	Directed
NYClimate March 2014	102439	353495	3	Directed
London Multiplex Transport Network	369	441	3	Undirected
Sacchpomb multiplex GPI network	6570	231496	7	Undirected
Drosophila multiplex GPI network	8215	39327	7	Undirected
Arxiv netscience multiplex	14489	59026	13	Undirected

5 Experiments

5.1 Experiments Setup

In this paper, we use the MIC model and the SIR model to evaluate the performance of our proposed algorithm. To ensure robust and valid results, we conducted hundreds to thousands of repeated experiments for each algorithm. Eight real-world network datasets are utilized for comprehensive validation, including four weighted undirected networks and four weighted directed networks. The structural properties of these datasets are quantitatively summarized in Table 1. To evaluate the effectiveness of DED, we compared it with six benchmark methods: ACD [21], DD [3], DPSOMIM [19], ECRM [20], EnRenew [7], and KSN [11].

5.2 MIC Model Performance Analysis

To evaluate algorithm performance under the MIC model, we conducted influence propagation experiments using 1,000 Monte Carlo simulations for each seed set size k, with a propagation probability of $\rho = 0.05$. In each trial, the cumulative count of activated nodes was used as the primary evaluation metric. For seed set sizes $k = 10, 20, 30, 40$, and 50, the influence spread of each algorithm across datasets is illustrated in Fig. 2.

In small-scale sparse networks, such as Celegans, London, Drosophila, and Arxiv, most algorithms achieve comparable performance levels, with minimal differentiation in influence spread. However, the advantages of DED algorithm become particularly evident in large-scale dense networks. As shown in Fig. 2(h) and Fig. 2(g), DED shows superior performance on the NYClimate and Moscow datasets, achieving a 5% and 3% increase in influence coverage over the state-of-the-art ACD method, respectively. On the Sacchpomb network, baseline methods exhibit plateaued performance as the seed set size k increases, showing no statistically significant improvement. In contrast, the DED algorithm achieves a consistent 2.7% higher influence coverage than the all baseline methods. This superior performance demonstrates our proposed algorithm's ability to reduce influence overlap while effectively utilizing network structural complexity for scalable diffusion (Table 2).

5.3 SIR Model Performance Analysis

To evaluate algorithm performance under the SIR model in multilayer networks, we conducted 100 independent propagation simulations for each network, with each simulation initialized using 200 seed nodes. The infection rate α and recovery rate β were adaptively adjusted based on network size. During each simulation, we track the number of infected ($n_{I(t)}$) and recovered ($n_{R(t)}$) nodes at each time step t. The evaluation metric $F(t)$, shown in Eq. (16), quantifies the cumulative infection scale at time t, where n is the total number of nodes.

$$F(t) = \frac{n_{I(t)} + n_{R(t)}}{n} \tag{16}$$

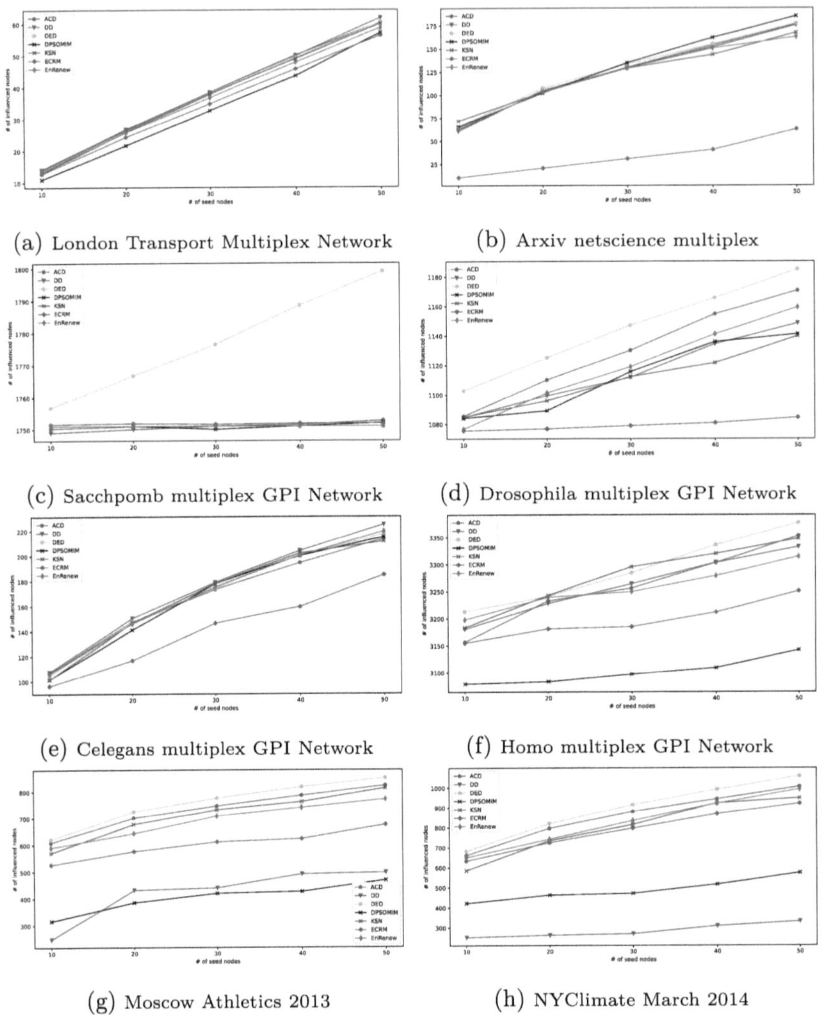

(a) London Transport Multiplex Network

(b) Arxiv netscience multiplex

(c) Sacchpomb multiplex GPI Network

(d) Drosophila multiplex GPI Network

(e) Celegans multiplex GPI Network

(f) Homo multiplex GPI Network

(g) Moscow Athletics 2013

(h) NYClimate March 2014

Fig. 2. Influence spread comparison under the MIC model.

The propagation performance of all datasets under the SIR model is presented in Figs. 3 and 4. The proposed DED algorithm demonstrates superior performance of all eight networks. As shown in Figs. 3(d) and 4(b), DED achieves 8% and 3% improvements over the best ACD algorithm on the Drosophila and Homo networks. Particularly, DED achieves a 33% increase compared to the state-of-the-art ACD algorithm on the Sacchpomb network, as demonstrated in Fig. 3(c). The performance results not only validate the effectiveness of the delay mechanism but also confirm the robustness of our seed node selection strategy. Among the baseline methods, ACD demonstrates superior performance to other algorithms while remaining inferior to DED. The EnRenew, KSN, and

Table 2. The influence spread of algorithms at $k = 50$ under the MIC model

Datasets	Algorithms						
	ACD	DED	DD	DPSOMIM	ECRM	EnRenew	KSN
London	60.395	60.486	**61.808**	57.107	56.277	58.669	60.552
Arxiv	176.157	177.213	175.504	**185.160**	62.731	162.679	167.255
Sacchpomb	1752.669	**1799.165**	1751.558	1752.653	1751.849	1751.051	1751.179
Drosophila	1170.571	**1185.014**	1148.407	1141.122	1084.354	1159.251	1139.703
Celegans	213.549	217.463	**224.972**	215.477	184.767	219.652	211.516
Moscow	823.015	**850.979**	496.930	468.165	675.288	771.551	812.812
NYClimate	1006.008	**1058.650**	332.154	574.289	921.310	992.548	949.065
Homo	3352.505	**3377.257**	3332.154	3141.903	3250.520	3314.244	3347.692

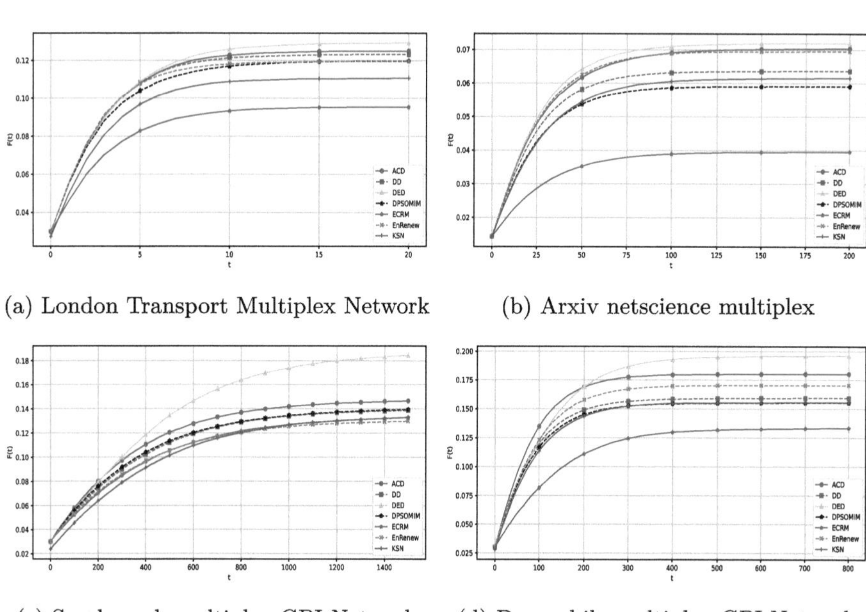

(a) London Transport Multiplex Network (b) Arxiv netscience multiplex

(c) Sacchpomb multiplex GPI Network (d) Drosophila multiplex GPI Network

Fig. 3. Influence spread comparison of undirected networks under the SIR model.

DPSOMIM algorithms exhibit different performance across networks, achieving strong results on the Homo network but performing significantly poorer on the Sacchpomb network.

5.4 Ablation Experiments Analysis

To evaluate the effectiveness of the proposed DED algorithm framework, we compare four variants: (1) DED, (2) DED-ND (excluding degree centrality), (3)

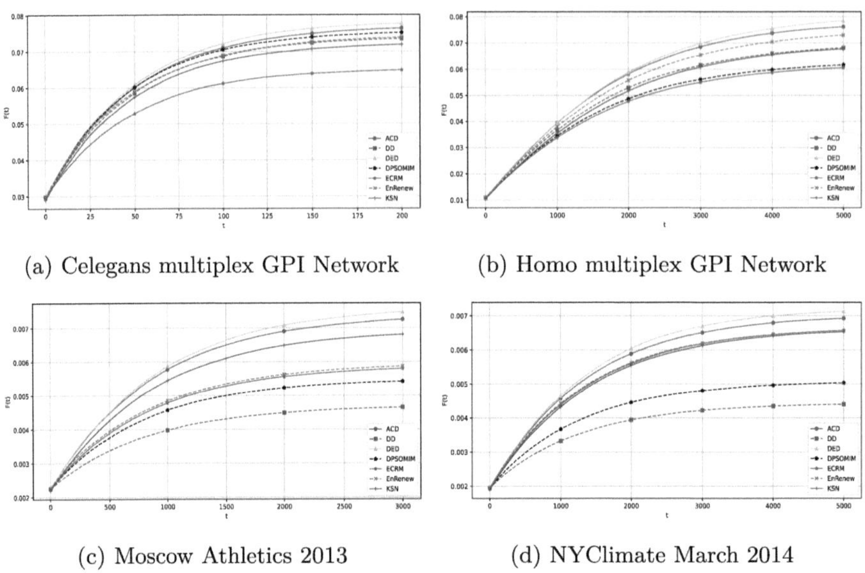

(a) Celegans multiplex GPI Network (b) Homo multiplex GPI Network

(c) Moscow Athletics 2013 (d) NYClimate March 2014

Fig. 4. Influence spread comparison of directed networks under the SIR model.

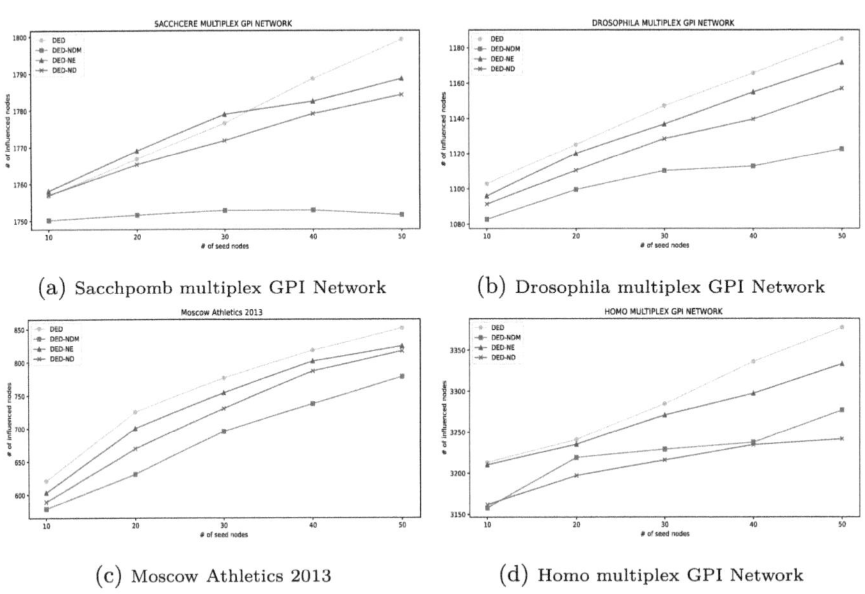

(a) Sacchpomb multiplex GPI Network (b) Drosophila multiplex GPI Network

(c) Moscow Athletics 2013 (d) Homo multiplex GPI Network

Fig. 5. Ablation study on DED variants under the MIC model.

DED-NE (excluding entropy), and (4) DED-NDM (excluding delay mechanism) under the MIC model.

As illustrated in Fig. 5, the experimental results demonstrate the effectiveness of the key components of DED. The delay mechanism significantly improves influence propagation, with the DED algorithm outperforming the DED-NDM variant across different networks. Furthermore, the combination of degree centrality and information entropy proves crucial for optimal node selection, as evidenced by the superior performance of the complete DED algorithm compared to both DED-ND and DED-NE variants that lack either component.

5.5 Algorithm Running Time Analysis

The running time of various algorithms for selecting 50 seed nodes is shown in Fig. 6. The KSN and DPSOMIM algorithms show the highest computational complexity across all networks, making them unsuitable for large-scale networks. Conversely, the DD and EnRenew algorithms consistently maintain the shortest computational durations across all networks.

Our proposed DED algorithm is orders of magnitude faster than the KSN and DPSOMIM algorithms while maintaining performance advantages. When compared to other heuristic algorithms, DED exhibits a marginally longer runtime, but still remains within an acceptable range. Our analysis identifies

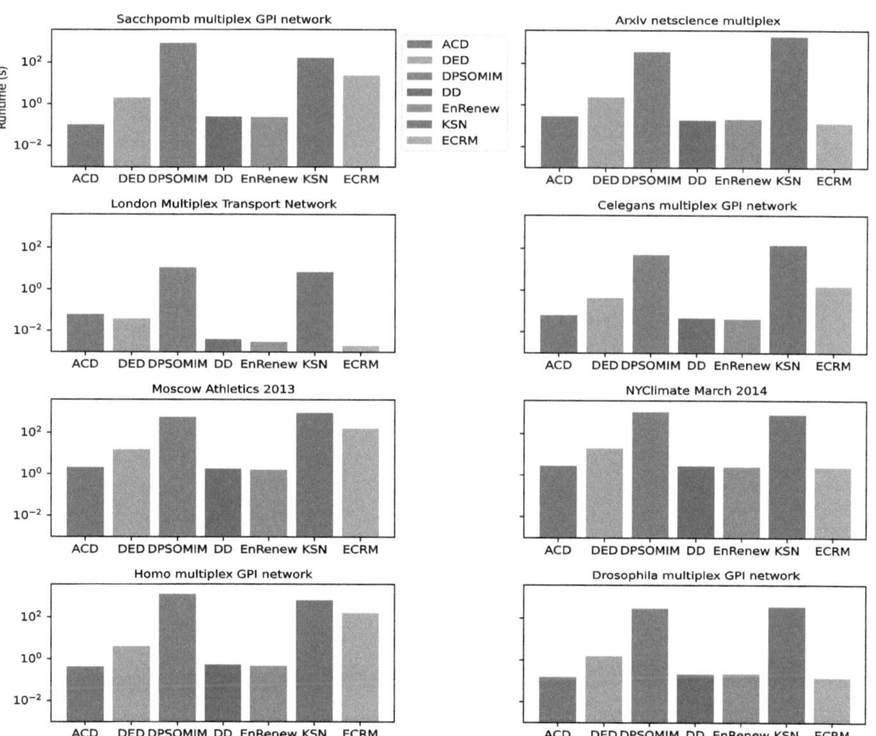

Fig. 6. Runtime comparison of algorithms for selecting 50 seed nodes.

several limitations in existing approaches: the DD and ACD algorithms neglect the influence of nodes on multi-hop neighborhoods; the EnRenew algorithm employs information entropy for node evaluation, but fails to comprehensively capture node significance; meanwhile, the ECRM algorithm relies on k-shell decomposition for hierarchy determination, making it difficult to distinguish core node influence in highly centralized networks. By integrating heuristic initialization with a greedy selection strategy, the proposed DED algorithm iteratively selects the node with the highest weight and subsequently updates node weights through the delay mechanism, effectively reducing influence overlap and identifying influential nodes.

6 Conclusions

In this paper, we focus on the problem of influence maximization in multilayer networks. Although significant progress has been made in developing solutions for single-layer networks in recent years, existing approaches remain inadequate for efficiently handling the complexities of multilayer structures. To address this limitation, we propose the DED algorithm comprising three phases. The algorithm first classifies nodes into overlapping and non-overlapping categories, then selects candidate nodes from both categories by integrating node weights with the delay mechanism, and ultimately determines the final seed nodes from the candidate set. By explicitly calculating cross-layer interactions and dynamically adjusting seed selection priorities, our algorithm effectively identifies influential nodes while maintaining computational scalability. Experimental evaluations demonstrate that the proposed DED algorithm outperforms the state-of-the-art methods in terms of both influence spread and efficiency across diverse multilayer networks. Future work will extend the proposed framework to generalized influence maximization scenarios, with particular emphasis on its application in dynamic networks.

References

1. Borgs, C., Brautbar, M., Chayes, J., Lucier, B.: Maximizing social influence in nearly optimal time. In: Proceedings of the Twenty-Fifth Annual ACM-SIAM Symposium on Discrete Algorithms, pp. 946–957. SIAM (2014)
2. Bouyer, A., Mohammadi, M., Arasteh, B.: Identifying influential nodes based on new layer metrics and layer weighting in multiplex networks. Knowl. Inf. Syst. **66**(2), 1011–1035 (2024)
3. Chen, W., Wang, Y., Yang, S.: Efficient influence maximization in social networks. In: Proceedings of the 15th ACM SIGKDD International Conference on Knowledge Discovery and Data Mining, pp. 199–208 (2009)
4. Cheng, S., Shen, H., Huang, J., Zhang, G., Cheng, X.: StaticGreedy: solving the scalability-accuracy dilemma in influence maximization. In: Proceedings of the 22nd ACM International Conference on Information & Knowledge Management, pp. 509–518 (2013)

5. Chowdary, C.R., et al.: K++ shell: influence maximization in multilayer networks using community detection. Comput. Netw. **234**, 109916 (2023)
6. Domingos, P., Richardson, M.: Mining the network value of customers. In: Proceedings of the Seventh ACM SIGKDD International Conference on Knowledge Discovery and Data Mining, pp. 57–66 (2001)
7. Guo, C., Yang, L., Chen, X., Chen, D., Gao, H., Ma, J.: Influential nodes identification in complex networks via information entropy. Entropy **22**(2), 242 (2020)
8. Katukuri, M., Jagarapu, M., et al.: CIM: clique-based heuristic for finding influential nodes in multilayer networks. Appl. Intell. **52**(5), 5173–5184 (2022)
9. Kempe, D., Kleinberg, J., Tardos, É.: Maximizing the spread of influence through a social network. In: Proceedings of the ninth ACM SIGKDD International Conference on Knowledge Discovery and Data Mining, pp. 137–146 (2003)
10. Kivelä, M., Arenas, A., Barthelemy, M., Gleeson, J.P., Moreno, Y., Porter, M.A.: Multilayer networks. J. Complex. Netw. **2**(3), 203–271 (2014)
11. Kuhnle, A., Alim, M.A., Li, X., Zhang, H., Thai, M.T.: Multiplex influence maximization in online social networks with heterogeneous diffusion models. IEEE Trans. Comput. Soc. Syst. **5**(2), 418–429 (2018)
12. Leskovec, J., Krause, A., Guestrin, C., Faloutsos, C., VanBriesen, J., Glance, N.: Cost-effective outbreak detection in networks. In: Proceedings of the 13th ACM SIGKDD International Conference on Knowledge Discovery and Data Mining, pp. 420–429 (2007)
13. Li, Y., Ma, S., Zhang, Y., Huang, R., et al.: An improved mix framework for opinion leader identification in online learning communities. Knowl. Based Syst. **43**, 43–51 (2013)
14. McAuley, J.J., da Fontoura Costa, L., Caetano, T.S.: Rich-club phenomenon across complex network hierarchies. Appl. Phys. Lett. **91**(8) (2007)
15. Pastor-Satorras, R., Vespignani, A.: Epidemic dynamics and endemic states in complex networks. Phys. Rev. E **63**(6), 066117 (2001)
16. Peng, S., Zhou, Y., Cao, L., Yu, S., Niu, J., Jia, W.: Influence analysis in social networks: a survey. J. Netw. Comput. Appl. **106**, 17–32 (2018)
17. Qiao, T., Shan, W., Zhou, C.: How to identify the most powerful node in complex networks? A novel entropy centrality approach. Entropy **19**(11), 614 (2017)
18. Rao, K.V., Chowdary, C.R.: CBIM: Community-based influence maximization in multilayer networks. Inf. Sci. **609**, 578–594 (2022)
19. Wang, S., Liu, W., Chen, L., Zong, S.: Influence maximization based on discrete particle swarm optimization on multilayer network. Inf. Syst. **127**, 102466 (2025)
20. Zareie, A., Sheikhahmadi, A., Jalili, M., Fasaei, M.S.K.: Finding influential nodes in social networks based on neighborhood correlation coefficient. Knowl. Based Syst. **194**, 105580 (2020)
21. Zhang, S.S., Xie, M., Liu, C., Zhan, X.X.: Influence maximization in multilayer networks based on adaptive coupling degree. Chaos Interdiscip. J. Nonlinear. Sci. **35**(3) (2025)

ComIVY: Community-Driven Budgeted Influence Maximization via IVY Optimization

Yao Chen, Weidong Chen(✉), and Zhongxia Li

School of Computer Science, South China Normal University, Guangzhou, China
chenwd@scnu.edu.cn

Abstract. The Budgeted Influence Maximization (BIM) problem aims to maximize social influence under cost constraints, yet existing methods struggle with computational complexity and adaptability to diverse cost models. We propose ComIVY, a novel approach integrating community structure detection with the IVY algorithm which is a new bio-inspired modeling variant drawing inspiration from the growth patterns of Ivy plants. ComIVY dynamically allocates budgets across communities, selects seed nodes via IVY optimization, and reduces influence overlap through a two-hop neighbor filtering mechanism. We evaluate ComIVY on six real-world networks, demonstrating up to 25% higher influence spread compared to six state-of-the-art baselines across varying budgets, while maintaining reasonable runtime efficiency.

Keywords: Social networks · Budgeted influence maximization · Community structure · IVY algorithm · Dynamic budget allocation

1 Introduce

Social networks, formed through social interactions, underpin modern information dissemination and interaction, playing a crucial role in large-scale information propagation, opinion diffusion, innovation stimulation, and rumor spreading [5]. The network-based propagation mechanism, particularly in viral marketing, demonstrates significant practical value [7]. The Influence Maximization (IM) problem strategically selects initial nodes and diffusion models to maximize the number of affected nodes [17]. Typically, social networks are abstracted as graph models, with users as vertices and social connections as edges. The core of IM is to select a set of k seed nodes whose initial activation maximizes the propagation range, aiding in understanding propagation patterns, optimizing marketing strategies, and controlling harmful information. However, traditional IM problems face limitations in cost function flexibility, failing to meet dynamic real-world requirements. For instance, in advertising, selection costs vary across platforms and users, requiring rational decision-makers to balance costs and benefits within a budget. Seed node selection must account for incentive factors,

J. Li et al. (Eds.): APWeb-WAIM 2025, LNCS 16115, pp. 486–500, 2026.
https://doi.org/10.1007/978-981-95-5719-6_31

with each node associated with specific costs under a total budget constraint, rendering the traditional IM assumption of "uniform node selection costs" inadequate. To address this, the Budgeted Influence Maximization (BIM) problem has emerged [21]. By solving BIM, it is possible to optimize the allocation of propagation resources within a limited budget, enhance propagation efficiency and coverage, and maximize return on investment.

1.1 The IM Problem

Many algorithms have been developed for the Influence Maximization (IM) problem. Approximation algorithms provide solution quality guarantees but face scalability issues. Greedy-based algorithms (e.g., Basic Greedy [17], CELF++ [11]) rely on extensive Monte Carlo simulations (MCS), resulting in high time complexity. Sampling-based algorithms (e.g., TIM [25], IMM [24]) use reverse reachable sampling to avoid costly MCSs. Heuristic algorithms (e.g., centrality-based, PageRank [4], SIMPATH [12]) lack approximation bounds but offer high scalability and efficiency by leveraging network topology. Metaheuristic algorithms (e.g., Simulated Annealing [16], Discrete Particle Swarm [10]) lack approximation guarantees but find satisfactory solutions within acceptable time. Community-based algorithms (e.g., CIM [8], CoFIM [23]) enhance scalability by detecting communities and selecting seed sets at the community level. With advances in deep learning, learning-based methods (e.g., ToupleGDD [6], CoreQ [1]) estimate influence areas using learnable parameter functions, avoiding high simulation and sampling costs.

1.2 The BIM Problem

Although various IM algorithms exist, most perform poorly when directly applied to the BIM problem. To address cost-effective selection, Nguyen et al. [21] proposed an approximation algorithm with a guaranteed ratio of $1 - 1/e$. Zhan et al. [29] extended CELF by selecting nodes with the highest influence-to-cost ratio;. Wang et al. [26] employed a greedy algorithm considering cost, influence spread, and their ratios. Han et al. [15] introduced the BSSA algorithm using simulated annealing. Xu et al. [28] proposed a PageRank-based cost model (PRBC) and the BRMDN algorithm. Banerjee et al. [2] developed ComBIM, incorporating community detection, budget allocation, seed selection, and budget transfer. Xiao et al. [27] addressed sparse communities with a flexible budget-based algorithm using Reverse Influence Sampling (RIS). Lozano-Osorio et al. [19] applied a GRASP framework to solve BIM. Existing BIM algorithms face limitations: high computational complexity, insufficient utilization of network structures, and lack of adaptability to diverse scenarios.

1.3 Contribution and Organization

To tackle the above-mentioned challenges for BIM, we propose ComIVY by combining network community structure with the IYV algorithm, a very recent powerful modeling variant of bio-inspired algorithms [9]. ComIVY dynamically adjusts the budget allocation across communities, ensuring efficient resource utilization and adaptability to varying community sizes and budget requirements. The main contributions of this paper are as follows:

(1) The IVY algorithm is effectively applied to the BIM problem for the first time, expanding its application scope;
(2) A community structure-based IVY algorithm is proposed, improving cost-benefit balance by combining community structure and IVY population optimization capabilities;
(3) The sum of two-stage neighbor node influence is adopted as the reward function to reduce computational complexity while ensuring accuracy, and the effectiveness of ComIVY is validated on six real networks, demonstrating superior performance and strong generalization.

The paper is organized as follows: Sect. 2 outlines Problem Definitions; Sect. 3 describes the ComIVY algorithm; Sect. 4 details experiments and results; Sect. 5 concludes and discusses future work.

2 Problem Definitions

This section systematically explores the BIM problem, first formalizing it through a mathematical language, then introducing common diffusion models, and finally describing the cost model.

2.1 Formulation of the BIM Problem

In the BIM problem, given a fixed budget B and a cost function C, C assigns non-uniform selection costs to each vertex in the network. The objective is to find a seed set S such that the total cost does not exceed B, while maximizing the number of influenced nodes. In the graph $G(V, E)$, $C(v)$ denotes the cost for node v to adopt a product or idea, $\sigma(S)$ denotes the number of nodes eventually affected by seed set S. The BIM problem can be formally defined as follows:

$$\arg\max_{S \subseteq V} \sigma(S) \quad \text{subject to} \quad \sum_{v \in S} C(v) \leq B \tag{1}$$

Note that when the cost per node is set to 1, the BIM problem reduces to the traditional IM problem. Since traditional IM problem is NP-hard, the BIM problem remains NP-hard. We have to resort to heuristics for solutions.

2.2 Diffusion Model

Evaluating Seed Sets on Networks G requires the definition of an influence diffusion model (IDM). The independent cascade model (IC model) and the Linear Threshold Model (LT model) proposed by Kempe et al. [17] provide the basis for subsequent research. The IC model emphasizes the independence of individual behavior. In the BIM problem, the most widely used Influence Diffusion Models (IDMs) include the Independent Cascade Model (IC) [17], the Weighted Cascade Model (WC) [17], and the Trivalent Model (TV) [13]. In this paper, we use WC models for experiments. The IC model assumes that each edge has the same influence probability (e.g., 0.1), while the WC model defines the probability that user v is influenced by user u as inversely proportional to the in-degree of v, expressed as $1/d_{\text{in}}(v)$, where $d_{\text{in}}(v)$ is the in-degree of user v. The TV model randomly selects influence probabilities from the set (0.1, 0.01, 0.001).

2.3 Cost Model

Assigning costs to nodes is a critical step in BIM problems. This section outlines two commonly used node cost function models.

Cost Model Based on Positive Real Numbers: In this model, the cost of node v is randomly drawn from a set of positive real numbers, reflecting cost diversity and randomness, and better modeling real-world information diffusion. Nguyen et al. [21] use the interval [1,3] with a budget of [10,100]; Banerjee et al. [2] and Lozano-Osorio et al. [19] use [50,100] with a budget of [2000,26000]. This model is widely adopted due to its simplicity and lack of need for node categorization or sorting.

Cost Model Based on Out-Degree and Diffusion Probability: In this model, the cost of node v is related to its out-degree and diffusion probability [15]. For the IC model, the cost function is defined as:

$$C(v) = d_{\text{out}}(v) \cdot W + 1 \tag{2}$$

where $d_{\text{out}}(v)$ is the out-degree of v and W is the diffusion probability. Han et al. [15] employed this cost function.To adapt it to the WC model, we refine the formula as:

$$C(v) = \sum_{s \in N_{\text{out}}(v)} W_{v,s} + 1 \tag{3}$$

where $N_{\text{out}}(v)$ is the set of out-degree neighbors of v, and $W_{v,s}$ is the edge influence probability from v to s. The addition of the constant 1 ensures a base cost for each node, preventing zero-cost nodes. In this paper, experiments were conducted using both models separately, the first setting the cost interval to [50,100] and the budget to [2000,26000], the second setting for Eq. 3

3 ComIVY Algorithm

This section details the proposed ComIVY algorithm, which consists of three phases: community division and budget allocation, intra-community seed set selection, and budget transfer. Figure 1 shows the overall framework of the algorithm. The input to the algorithm is a given budget and social network, and after three phases, the output is a selected set of seed nodes and the used budget.

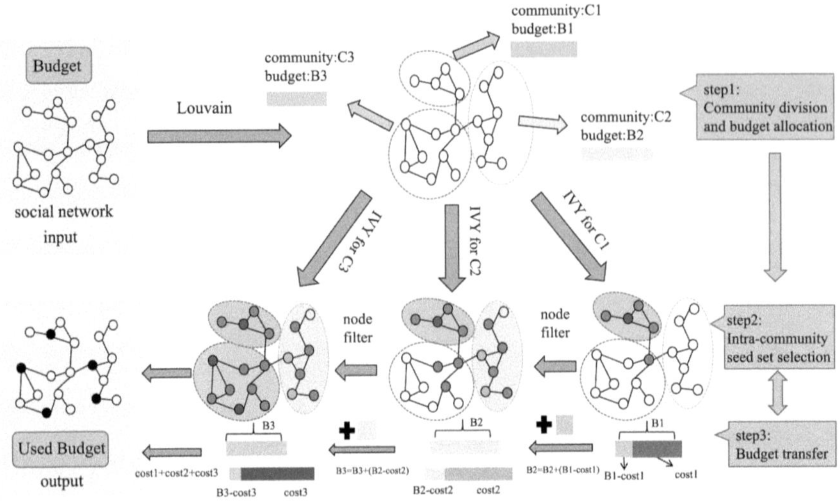

Fig. 1. ComIVY algorithm framework.

3.1 Community Division and Budget Allocation

In this phase, the input social network is divided into communities. We employ the community detection method based on modularity optimization (Louvain algorithm) proposed by Blondel et al. [3], which iteratively moves nodes to neighboring communities to maximize modularity until no further optimization is possible. Due to its efficiency and scalability, this algorithm is widely used for community detection in large-scale networks. After community detection, budget allocation is performed. Budgets are allocated based on the number of nodes in each community, with larger communities prioritized by sorting communities in descending order of node count. The budget allocation formula is:

$$B_i = \frac{|V_i| \cdot B}{|V|} \tag{4}$$

where B_i is the budget for the community i, $|V_i|$ is the number of nodes in the community i, B is the total budget and $|V|$ is the total number of nodes in the graph.

3.2 Intra-Community Seed Set Selection

After obtaining sorted communities and budgets, we optimize seed selection within each community using the IVY algorithm. The IVY algorithm is a bionic optimization algorithm based on the growth behavior of ivy in nature, which performs an efficient search in the solution space by simulating the climbing, spreading, and growth mechanisms of ivy. The basic process includes population initialization, growth and climbing, diffusion branching, solution updating and selection, etc., and gradually approaches the global optimal solution through iterative optimization. The core advantage of this algorithm is that it can effectively maintain the population diversity while converging quickly, and it also has the characteristics of simple structure and easy expansion, which is suitable for solving complex optimization problems [9]. For the BIM problem, the diversity preservation mechanism of the IVY algorithm can effectively avoid premature convergence and ensure the exploration of a wider solution space under limited budget constraints.

The IVY algorithm is originally designed for optimization problems in continuous search spaces. To adapt it for discrete search spaces in the BIM problem, we need to modify it for optimizing the seed selection process. In the algorithm, each individual in the population possesses:

A vector of position representing a seed set:

$$I_i = (I_i^1, I_i^2, \ldots, I_i^d) \tag{5}$$

A growth velocity vector controlling the search dynamics:

$$G_v = (G_v^1, G_v^2, \ldots, G_v^d) \tag{6}$$

- d denotes the solution dimension (corresponding to the seed set size in IM problem)
- I_i represents a candidate seed set where each component I_i^j indicates a node

We adapt it to the BIM problem, retaining the original population update formulas and using the sum of two-step neighbor influence as the reward function. Guo et al. [14] shows that this method optimally balances computational complexity and influence evaluation accuracy, since the information propagation probability decays with distance and two-step propagation covers the main influence range of nodes. The reward function is expressed as:

$$I(S) = \frac{1}{R}\sum_{i=1}^{R}\left(|S| + \sum_{v\in S}\sum_{u\in N_1(v)} II(v \to u) + \sum_{u\in N_1(v)}\sum_{w\in N_1(u)} II(u \to w)\right) \tag{7}$$

where R is the number of simulations, S is the seed set, $N_1(v)$ denotes the set of direct neighbors of node v, and $II(v \to u)$ is an indicator function that represents whether node v successfully activates node u. The value of $II(v \to u)$ is defined as:

$$II(v \to u) = \begin{cases} 1, & \text{if random}(0,1) \le W_{v,u}, \\ 0, & \text{otherwise.} \end{cases} \tag{8}$$

3.3 Budget Transfer

After selecting the seed set for each community, any unused budget is transferred to the next community. Once all communities are processed, the IVY algorithm is rerun on the remaining nodes if budget remains. Note that in the algorithm, after each round of seed set selection, the two-hop neighbors of the selected seed set are calculated using the following formula:

$$F(S) = S \cup \left(\bigcup_{v \in S} N(v) \right) \cup \left(\bigcup_{u \in \bigcup_{v \in S} N(v)} N(u) \right) \tag{9}$$

where S is the current seed set, $N(v)$ is the set of direct neighbors of node v, and $F(S)$ contains S and its two-hop neighbors. After obtaining $F(S)$, the selected seed nodes and their two-hop neighbors are filtered before selecting the seed set for the next community. The filtering formula is as follows:

$$V_i' = V_i \setminus F(S) \tag{10}$$

where V_i is the node set of community i, and V_i' is the filtered node set. This design effectively reduces influence range overlap between seed sets of different communities. Before executing the IVY algorithm to select the seed set for each community, we preprocess to calculate the average population length L_i for the community:

$$L_i = \left\lceil \frac{|V_i| \cdot B_i}{\sum_{v \in V_i} C(v)} \right\rceil \tag{11}$$

where $|V_i|$ is the number of nodes in community i, B_i is the budget allocated to community i, $C(v)$ is the cost function for node v, and $\lceil \cdot \rceil$ denotes the ceiling operation. This formula calculates the average length of the seed set for each community (i.e., the population length for the IVY algorithm), providing initialization parameters for seed selection.

The Algorithm 1 takes as input a social network $G(V, E, W)$, sorted communities SC, community budgets CB, a cost function $Cost(G)$, and a total budget B. It outputs the selected seed set S and the used budget UB. For each community, the algorithm filters out the selected seed nodes and their two-hop neighbors to reduce overlap (line 5), selects the candidate nodes V_i (line 6), and calculates the average length L_i to guide seed selection (line 7). The IVY algorithm is then called to select the seed set $Seeds$, and S and UB are updated (lines 8–11). If the current community budget is not fully used and is not the last community, the remaining budget is transferred to the next community (lines 12–14). If the final UB is less than B, the IVY algorithm is called again to select additional seeds within the remaining budget (lines 16–24). The algorithm achieves efficient budget utilization and influence maximization by dynamically adjusting community budget allocation and filtering overlapping nodes. It demonstrates strong generality and robustness by adapting to different community sizes and budget allocations.

The time complexity of the reward function is $O(R \cdot |S| \cdot d^2)$. The time complexity of the IVY algorithm is $O(T \cdot N \cdot R \cdot |S| \cdot d^2)$. The time complexity of the ComIVY algorithm is $O(n \cdot T \cdot N \cdot R \cdot |S| \cdot d^2)$. Since T, R, and N are constants, the time complexity of the ComIVY algorithm can be simplified to $O(n \cdot |S| \cdot d^2)$.

Algorithm 1. Community IVY

Require: A social network $G(V, E, W)$, sorted communities SC, community budgets CB, cost function $\text{Cost}(G)$, total budget B.
Ensure: Seed set S, used budget UB.

```
S ← ∅
UB ← 0
n ← len(SC)
for i ← 1 to n do
    F(S) ← Compute by Eq. 9
    V_i ← Compute by Eq. 10 // Filter two-hop neighbors to reduce overlap
    L_i ← Compute by Eq. 11 //Calculate the average length of the population
    Seeds ← IVY-algorithm(V_i, CB[i], L_i) //Use IVY algorithm select seed set
    S ← S ∪ Seeds
    cost ← Σ_{s∈Seeds} Cost(s)
    UB ← UB + cost
    if cost < CB[i] and i < n then
        CB[i + 1] ← CB[i + 1] + (CB[i] − cost)
    end if
end for
if UB < B then
    F(S) ← Compute by Eq. 9
    V_i ← Compute by Eq. 10
    L_i ← Compute by Eq. 11
    Seeds ← IVY-algorithm(V_i, B − UB, L_i)
    S ← S ∪ Seeds
    cost ← Σ_{s∈Seeds} Cost(s)
    UB ← UB + cost
end if
return S, UB
```

Here, n is the number of communities, $|S|$ is the size of the seed set, d is the average degree of nodes, T is the number of iterations, N is the population size, and R is the number of simulations.

4 Experiment

We conducted experiments using the ComIVY algorithm on six real networks of varying sizes to evaluate its effectiveness in solving BIM problems, compare its efficiency with existing methods, and statistically demonstrate the differences in results. Additionally, we examined its generalization under different cost functions, parameter analysis, and ablation experiments.

4.1 Experiment Setup

This section describes hyperparameter setting, datasets, comparison methods.

Hyperparameter Setting: We adopt the WC diffusion model and two cost functions: the first randomly samples node costs from the interval $[50, 100]$, and the second is defined by Eq. 3. For the IVY algorithm, we set N_{pop} (population size) to 30 and I_{max}(iterations) to 100. All our experimental results are averaged from 10,000 simulations using Monto Carlo.

Datasets: Table 1 provides a summary of the basic information of the networks used in our experiments, including the number of nodes $|V|$, the number of edges $|E|$, the average degree d_{avg}, and the number of communities C.

Table 1. Information of Networks

Datasets	$\|V\|$	$\|E\|$	d_{avg}	C	Reference
LastFM	7624	27806	7.29	26	[18]
CA-HepPh	11204	117649	21	29	[18]
Fb-Pages-Sport	13865	86858	12.5	28	[22]
Facebook	22470	171002	15.2	60	[18]
CA-CondMat	23133	91342	7.89	623	[18]
Deezer	28281	92752	6.55	85	[18]

Comparison Methods: We compare ComIVY with six representative algorithms: the CELF++ greedy algorithm based on cost-budgeted [29], the degree-based heuristic degree based on degree centrality [20], the degree-cost ratio-based heuristic degree cost [12], the BSSA based on simulated annealing combining Billboard and Handbill strategies [15], the ComBIM community-based heuristic method allocating budgets across detected communities [2], and the GRASP based on greedy randomized adaptive search [19].

4.2 Experimental Results

Figures 2 and 3 show the results of the seven algorithms on six networks, with the x-axis denoting the budget and the y-axis denoting the influence range. In Fig. 2, we use a positive real cost function model with a cost interval of [50,100] and a budget interval of [2000,26000], which shows that ComIVY outperforms all other algorithms in all datasets except the Dezzer dataset, where it slightly lags behind CELF++. Under this cost model, influence propagation performs worst as Degree and Degree-Cost only consider the degree of the node. GRASP outperforms the other algorithms, lagging behind only our proposed ComIVY algorithm. In Fig. 3, we use a cost model as in Eq. 3 with a budget interval of [100, 350]. The results indicate that ComIVY consistently achieves the highest influence diffusion across all datasets, further validating its robustness and adaptability to different cost models.

Table 2 shows the statistical results of the seven algorithms in six networks under the positive real cost function model when the budget value is 1000 (the results have been rounded).

In summary, by effectively integrating the network community structure and the population optimization capability of the IVY algorithm, ComIVY significantly outperforms other methods in medium to large networks and shows excellent performance across different cost functions, which proves the effectiveness and generalizability of the ComIVY algorithm.

Figure 4 presents the running time (in seconds) of seven algorithms on six networks under the cost model based on positive real numbers, which is recorded for budget = 2000, 10000, and 18000. Due to the significantly slower performance of CELF++, results are displayed on a logarithmic scale. CELF++ exhibits the longest running time across all datasets, while Degree and Degree-Cost show the shortest. ComIVY's running time is slightly longer than that of BSSA, ComBIM, and GRASP, as it executes the IVY algorithm once per community. Experimental results demonstrate that ComIVY can generate high-quality solutions within a reasonable timeframe.

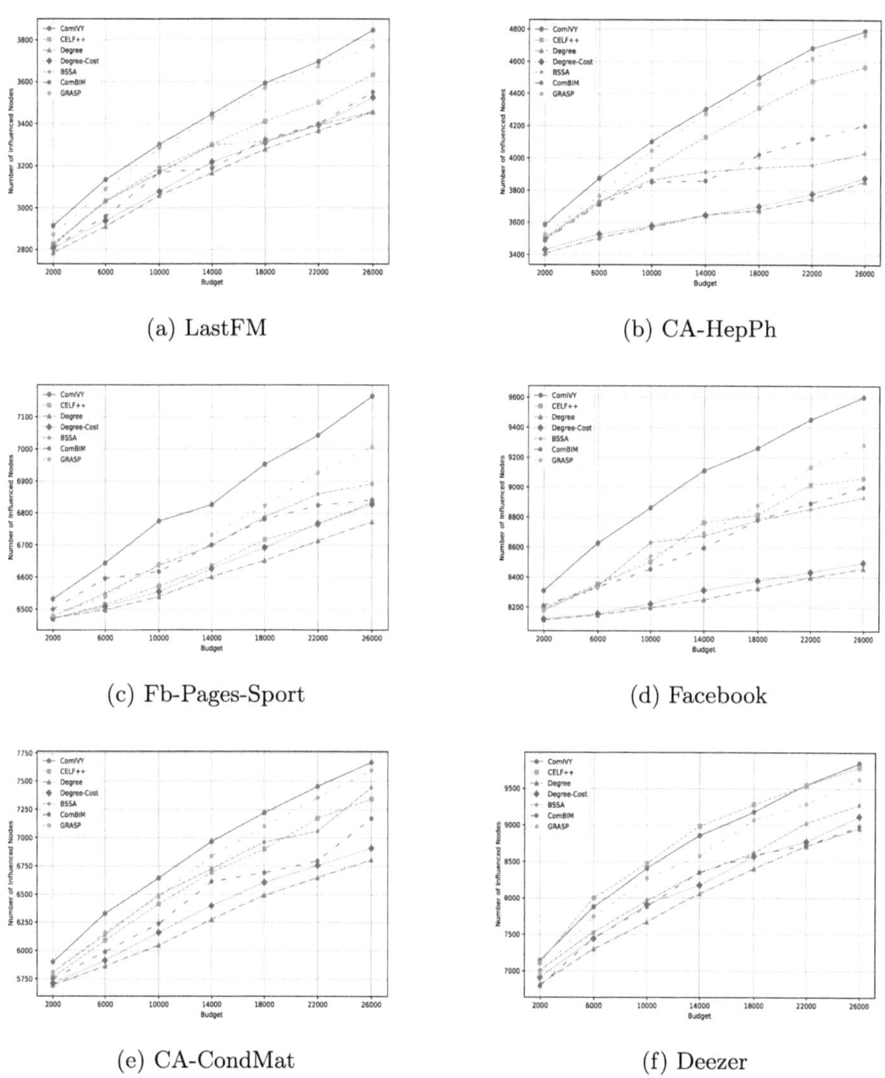

(a) LastFM

(b) CA-HepPh

(c) Fb-Pages-Sport

(d) Facebook

(e) CA-CondMat

(f) Deezer

Fig. 2. Influence spread comparison under the positive real cost model (cost [50, 100]).

Table 2. Influence Spread Comparison (Budget = 1000)

Dataset	ComIVY	CELF++	Degree	DegreeCost	BSSA	ComBIM	GRASP
LastFM	**3302**	3190	3060	3078	3168	3173	3285
CA-HepPh	**4102**	3931	3569	3579	3864	3851	4045
Fb-Pages-Sport	**6775**	6573	6540	6555	6637	6618	6641
Facebook	**8863**	8502	8198	8223	8632	8467	8540
CA-CondMat	**6645**	6414	6048	6160	6494	6257	6479
Deczer	8411	**8479**	7674	7911	7964	7891	8273

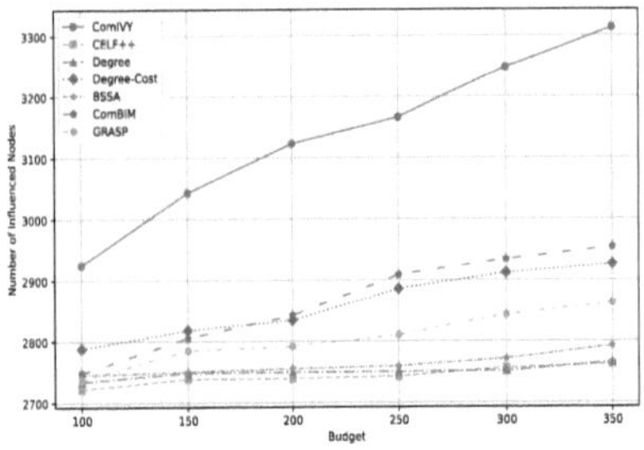

(a) LastFM

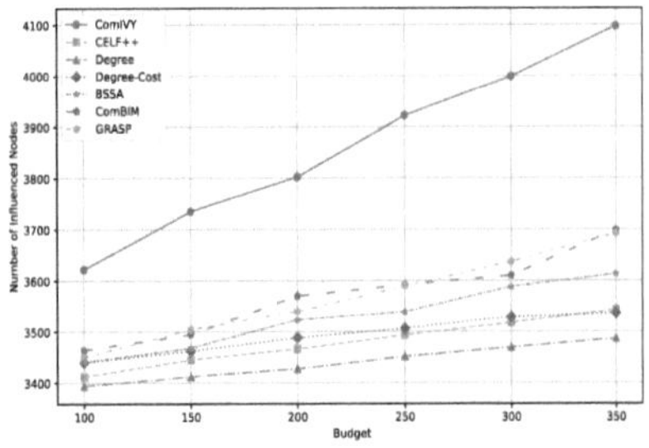

(b) CA-HepPh

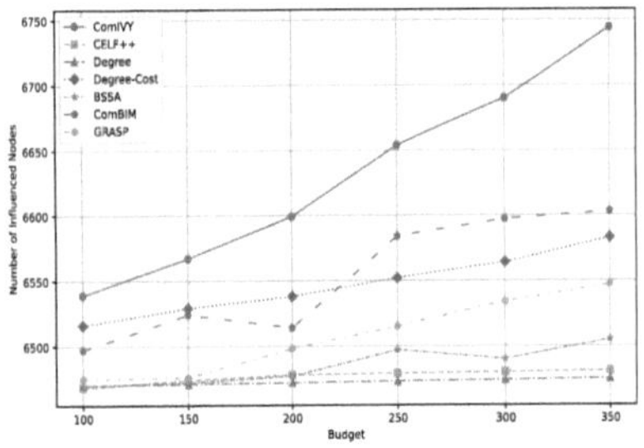

(c) Fb-Pages-Sport

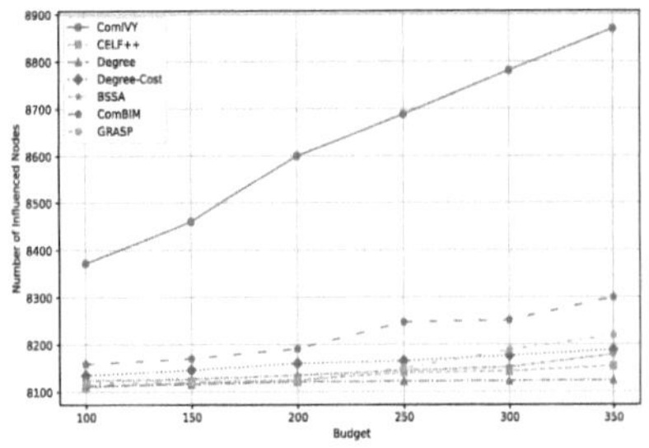

(d) Facebook

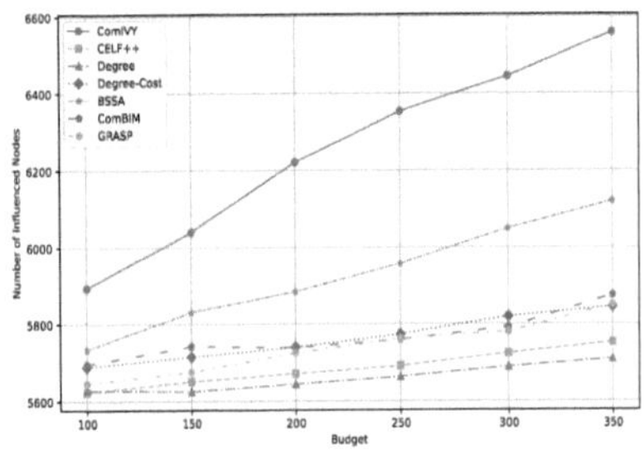

(e) CA-CondMat

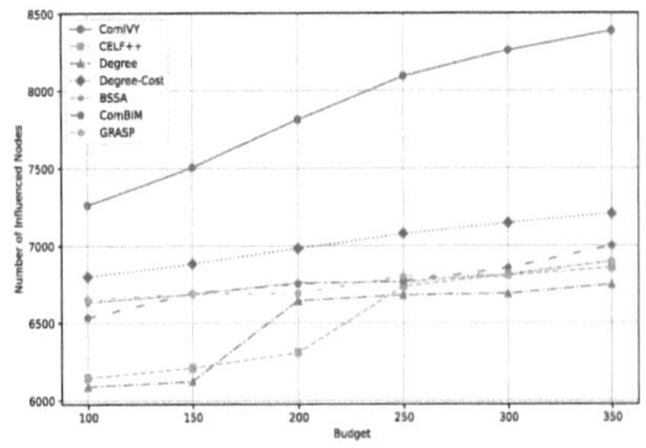

(f) Deezer

Fig. 3. Influence spread comparison under the cost model of Eq. 3.

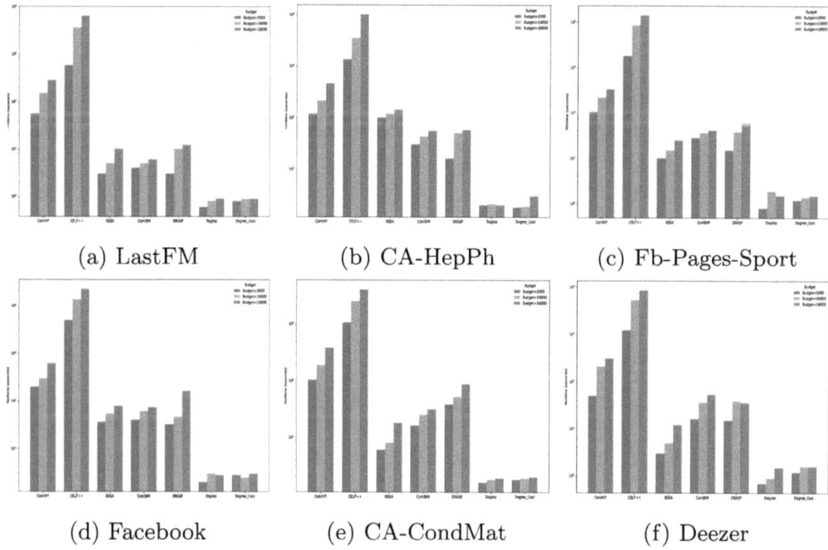

(a) LastFM (b) CA-HepPh (c) Fb-Pages-Sport

(d) Facebook (e) CA-CondMat (f) Deezer

Fig. 4. The comparison on running time of different algorithms under WC model.

4.3 Parameter Analysis

To evaluate the impact of parameters on ComIVY's performance, we conducted sensitivity experiments on four datasets, focusing on the population size N_{pop} and the number of iterations $I_{\max}$. The population size is the number of populations (number of feasible solutions) in a single optimization, which affects the algorithm performance and the diversity of the search space. Smaller populations may fall into local optimality, while larger populations may incur higher computational costs. The parameter $I_{\max}$ indicates the number of evolutionary steps performed by the ComIVY algorithm, which affects the depth of exploration and the computational cost. Therefore, our goal is to find the optimal parameters that strike a balance between efficiency and performance through experimental analysis. Figure 5a shows that $N_{\text{pop}} = 30$ achieves the optimal balance between solution quality and computational efficiency. Figure 5b shows that when the number of iterations exceeds 100, the range of influence improvement tends to level off, which indicates that $I_{\max} = 100$ achieves optimal computational efficiency while ensuring performance.

4.4 Ablation Experiments

To evaluate the effectiveness of the proposed algorithmic framework, we also conducted ablation experiments to develop two variants, ComSA (Community Simulated Annealing) and IVV (without community division), which are community simulated annealing algorithms and IVY algorithms used directly without partitioning the communities, respectively, and compared them with ComIVY.

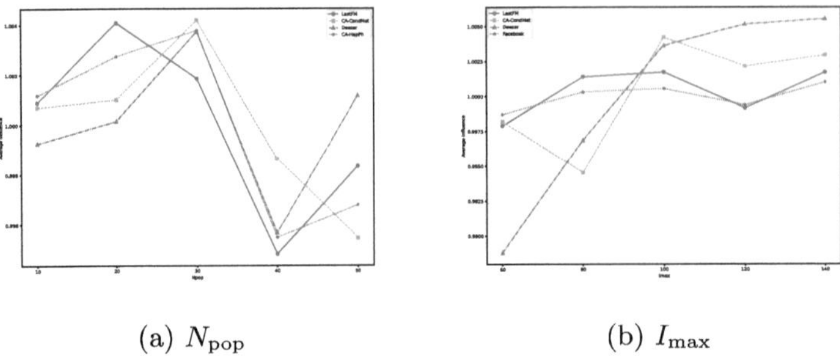

(a) N_{pop} (b) I_{max}

Fig. 5. The results of parameter analysis.

Figures 6a and b illustrate their performance in the LastFM and CA-HepPh datasets under the WC model. It is clear that ComIVY, which integrates the community structure and the IVY algorithm, outperforms the other variants under different budget conditions. These experimental results show that combining the community structure with the IVY algorithm can effectively improve the quality of the seed set and the performance of the algorithm.

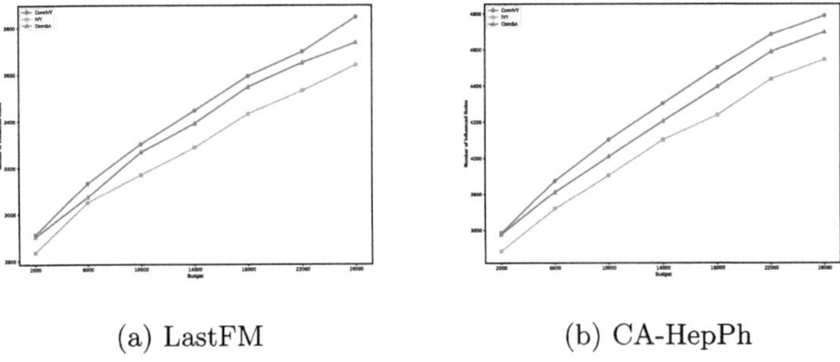

(a) LastFM (b) CA-HepPh

Fig. 6. The results of ablation experiments.

5 Conclusion and Future Research

We propose the ComIVY algorithm, which integrates graph community structure with the IVY algorithm to optimize seed node selection for solving the Budgeted Influence Maximization (BIM) problem. Through comparative experiments with six existing algorithms on six networks of varying sizes, we validate the effectiveness and generalization capability of ComIVY under different cost functions. Ablation experiments further demonstrate that combining community structure with the IVY algorithm significantly improves seed set quality and algorithm performance. However, ComIVY has some limitations: its performance is dependent on the quality of community detection, which may vary from network to network; it is more sensitive to hyperparameter population sizes and the number of iterations, and may require careful parameter tuning to obtain optimal results. Future research could focus on improving computational efficiency or leveraging distributed computing frameworks to enhance scalability for very large networks, optimizing the reward function of the IVY algorithm to reduce runtime while maintaining high-quality solutions, and extending the application of the algorithms to BIM problem variants, such as multi-objective optimization scenarios (e.g., simultaneously optimizing influence propagation and fairness) and BIM problems in multi-layer social network environments. Through these efforts, we aim to expand the applicability of ComIVY to broader scenarios and advance the field of network influence maximization.

References

1. Ahmad, W., Wang, B.: A learning-based influence maximization framework for complex networks via k-core hierarchies and reinforcement learning. Expert Syst. Appl. **259**, 125393 (2025)
2. Banerjee, S., Jenamani, M., Pratihar, D.K.: Combim: a community-based solution approach for the budgeted influence maximization problem. Expert Syst. Appl. **125**, 1–13 (2019)
3. Blondel, V.D., Guillaume, J.L., Lambiotte, R., Lefebvre, E.: Fast unfolding of communities in large networks. J. Stat. Mech: Theory Exp. **2008**(10), P10008 (2008)
4. Brin, S., Page, L.: Reprint of: The anatomy of a large-scale hypertextual web search engine. Comput. Netw. **56**(18), 3825–3833 (2012)
5. Centola, D.: The spread of behavior in an online social network experiment. science **329**(5996), 1194–1197 (2010)
6. Chen, T., Yan, S., Guo, J., Wu, W.: Touplegdd: a fine-designed solution of influence maximization by deep reinforcement learning. IEEE Trans. Comput. Soc. Syst. **11**(2), 2210–2221 (2023)
7. Chen, W., Wang, C., Wang, Y.: Scalable influence maximization for prevalent viral marketing in large-scale social networks. In: Proceedings of the 16th ACM SIGKDD International Conference on Knowledge Discovery and Data Mining, pp. 1029–1038 (2010)
8. Chen, Y.C., Zhu, W.Y., Peng, W.C., Lee, W.C., Lee, S.Y.: Cim: community-based influence maximization in social networks. ACM Trans. Intell. Syst. Technol. (TIST) **5**(2), 1–31 (2014)
9. Ghasemi, M., Zare, M., Trojovský, P., Rao, R.V., Trojovská, E., Kandasamy, V.: Optimization based on the smart behavior of plants with its engineering applications: Ivy algorithm. Knowl.-Based Syst. **295**, 111850 (2024)
10. Gong, M., Yan, J., Shen, B., Ma, L., Cai, Q.: Influence maximization in social networks based on discrete particle swarm optimization. Inf. Sci. **367**, 600–614 (2016)
11. Goyal, A., Lu, W., Lakshmanan, L.V.: Celf++ optimizing the greedy algorithm for influence maximization in social networks. In: Proceedings of the 20th international conference companion on World wide web, pp. 47–48 (2011)
12. Goyal, A., Lu, W., Lakshmanan, L.V.: Simpath: an efficient algorithm for influence maximization under the linear threshold model. In: 2011 IEEE 11th International Conference on Data Mining, pp. 211–220. IEEE (2011)

13. Granovetter, M.: Threshold models of collective behavior. Am. J. Sociol. **83**(6), 1420–1443 (1978)
14. Guo, J., Liu, Y., Shen, J., Wei, Z., Lv, J.: Influence maximization algorithm based on genetic algorithm. J. Comput. Inf. Syst. **10**(21), 9255–9262 (2014)
15. Han, S., Zhuang, F., He, Q., Shi, Z.: Balanced seed selection for budgeted influence maximization in social networks. In: Tseng, V.S., Ho, T.B., Zhou, Z.-H., Chen, A.L.P., Kao, H.-Y. (eds.) PAKDD 2014. LNCS (LNAI), vol. 8443, pp. 65–77. Springer, Cham (2014). https://doi.org/10.1007/978-3-319-06608-0_6
16. Jiang, Q., Song, G., Gao, C., Wang, Y., Si, W., Xie, K.: Simulated annealing based influence maximization in social networks. In: Proceedings of the AAAI Conference on Artificial Intelligence, vol. 25, pp. 127–132 (2011)
17. Kempe, D., Kleinberg, J., Tardos, É.: Maximizing the spread of influence through a social network. In: Proceedings of the ninth ACM SIGKDD International Conference on Knowledge Discovery and Data Mining, pp. 137–146 (2003)
18. Leskovec, J., Krevl, A.: Snap datasets: Stanford large network dataset collection (2014). http://snap.stanford.edu/data
19. Lozano-Osorio, I., Sánchez-Oro, J., Duarte, A.: An efficient and effective grasp algorithm for the budget influence maximization problem. J. Ambient. Intell. Humaniz. Comput. **15**(3), 2023–2034 (2024)
20. Narayanam, R., Narahari, Y.: A shapley value-based approach to discover influential nodes in social networks. IEEE Trans. Autom. Sci. Eng. **8**(1), 130–147 (2010)
21. Nguyen, H., Zheng, R.: On budgeted influence maximization in social networks. IEEE J. Sel. Areas Commun. **31**(6), 1084–1094 (2013)
22. Rossi, R.A., Ahmed, N.K.: The network data repository with interactive graph analytics and visualization. In: AAAI (2015). https://networkrepository.com
23. Shang, J., Zhou, S., Li, X., Liu, L., Wu, H.: Cofim: a community-based framework for influence maximization on large-scale networks. Knowl.-Based Syst. **117**, 88–100 (2017)
24. Tang, Y., Shi, Y., Xiao, X.: Influence maximization in near-linear time: a martingale approach. In: Proceedings of the 2015 ACM SIGMOD International Conference on Management of Data, pp. 1539–1554 (2015)
25. Tang, Y., Xiao, X., Shi, Y.: Influence maximization: near-optimal time complexity meets practical efficiency. In: Proceedings of the 2014 ACM SIGMOD International Conference on Management of Data, pp. 75–86 (2014)
26. Wang, Y., Huang, W., Zong, L., Wang, T., Yang, D.: Influence maximization with limit cost in social network. SCIENCE CHINA Inf. Sci. **56**, 1–14 (2013)
27. Xiao, M., Li, P., Huang, W., Xiao, J., Nie, L.: Community influence maximization based on flexible budget in social networks. In: Gao, H., Wang, X. (eds.) CollaborateCom 2021. LNICSSITE, vol. 406, pp. 534–553. Springer, Cham (2021). https://doi.org/10.1007/978-3-030-92635-9_31
28. Xu, X., Zhang, Y., Hu, Q., Xing, C.: A balanced method for budgeted influence maximization. In: SEKE. pp. 250–255 (2015)
29. Zhan, Q., Yang, H., Wang, C., Xie, J.: Cpp-sns: a solution to influence maximization problem under cost control. In: 2013 IEEE 25th International Conference on Tools with Artificial Intelligence, pp. 849–856. IEEE (2013)

Enhancing Partial Evaluation Subgraph Matching Through Vertex Hotness Caching

Hui Wang, Xin Wang(✉), Jinshuo Zhao, and Yang Liu

College of Intelligence and Computing, Tianjin University, Tianjin, China
{wanghui025,wangx,zhaojinshuo,liruxru}@tju.edu.cn

Abstract. The distributed subgraph matching algorithm based on the partial evaluation framework significantly improves subgraph matching efficiency by partitioning graph data across multiple computing nodes and executing query tasks in parallel. However, despite its parallel advantages in handling large-scale graph data, data partitioning also poses challenges. Specifically, since graph data is divided into multiple partitions, for highly selective queries, some partitions struggle to utilize specific vertex information to narrow the search space, resulting in a large number of invalid intermediate results. Therefore, this paper proposes an optimization method for distributed subgraph matching based on vertex hotness caching. This method leverages the principle of query locality, identifies frequently accessed vertices through analyzing query logs, and designates them as high-hotness vertices. It then caches these high-hotness vertices and their multi-hop neighborhood information on the master node. This allows highly selective queries that can be covered by the cache to be directly computed on the master node, avoiding the difficulty that the partial evaluation framework has in utilizing high-selectivity vertices to narrow the search space.

Keywords: Subgraph matching · Partial evaluation · Distributed computing

1 Introduction

With the widespread application of graph data in fields such as social networks [1], bioinformatics [10], and financial analysis [16], the subgraph matching problem has gradually become a key task in graph computing. The subgraph matching problem is NP-Hard [9], and as the scale of graph data continues to grow, traditional single-machine subgraph matching algorithms struggle to efficiently process large-scale graph data. Therefore, distributed subgraph matching algorithms have emerged to address this challenge.

Distributed subgraph matching algorithms exhibit significant advantages in processing large-scale graph data. However, partitioning the data across multiple nodes also introduces new challenges. Specifically, the distributed storage

J. Li et al. (Eds.): APWeb-WAIM 2025, LNCS 16115, pp. 501–515, 2026.
https://doi.org/10.1007/978-981-95-5719-6_32

of graph data necessitates cross-partition node access during query processing, thereby incurring substantial message-passing overhead. In contrast, distributed subgraph matching algorithms based on partial evaluation frameworks [4,5] effectively reduce this overhead by independently computing partial matches on each partition.

However, this approach introduces a new issue: poor support for highly selective queries. A highly selective query refers to a query in which certain query vertices specify concrete URIs. These query vertices that specify concrete URIs are termed high-selectivity vertices. Such queries can quickly locate specific data vertices through high-selectivity vertices, significantly narrowing the search space. However, under the partial evaluation framework, the algorithm needs to expand partial matches for the query as much as possible within each partition. If a partition does not contain the specified URI information from the query, only partial matching results for other parts of the query can be obtained. Lacking the pruning capability of high-selectivity vertices, algorithms based on the partial evaluation framework have to compute partial matches across the entire graph data in each partition, greatly expanding the query search space.

To address the issues mentioned above, the main contributions of this paper are summarized as follows:

(1) Propose a vertex hotness caching method. This method caches high-hotness subgraphs on the master node, allowing some highly selective queries to be computed directly on the master node.
(2) Propose a vertex hotness identification algorithm based on query logs. By leveraging the principle of query locality, this algorithm mines frequently accessed vertices from query logs and designates them as high-hotness vertices to improve the cache hit rate.
(3) Propose a cache coverage checking method to quickly determine whether the cache can meet the query requirements.
(4) Experiments on LUBM datasets of varying scales were conducted to validate our methods. Our methods show significant advantages in improving the execution efficiency of highly selective queries under the partial evaluation framework.

2 Related Work

In this section, several existing major distributed computing models and the corresponding distributed subgraph matching algorithms are introduced.

2.1 Pregel

Pregel is a distributed graph computing framework by Google for large-scale graph data processing. It employs a superstep-based model with compute, communicate, and synchronize phases. Pregel follows a vertex-centric approach, dividing the graph into subgraphs across computing nodes. In each superstep, all vertices execute user-defined computation logic in parallel, communicate through message passing, and synchronize globally at the end of each phase.

Based on the Pregel model, Xu et al. [14] proposed a distributed subgraph matching method called SP-Tree. This method transforms the query graph into a shortest-path-based spanning tree and then matches the SP-Tree in a bottom-up manner using the Pregel model. By filtering out invalid local computations and message passing, as well as deferring Cartesian product operations, this method significantly reduces the number of intermediate results. Zhang et al. [15] implemented a hybrid subgraph matching framework based on Pregel that combines the advantages of both join-based and exploration-based algorithms. The framework decomposes the query graph into path sketches, first enumerates the path sketches through exploration, and then joins the path sketches to obtain the final matching results.

2.2 MapReduce

MapReduce is a distributed computing framework for processing large datasets. It works in two stages: Map and Reduce. In the Map stage, input data is split into key-value pairs and processed to generate intermediate results. These results are then sorted by key and grouped together. In the Reduce stage, the grouped data is aggregated to produce the final output.

TwinTwigJoin [3] adopts the MapReduce framework and introduces TwinTwig (a single edge or two connected edges) as the basic join unit. Combined with a left-deep join framework, it achieves efficient subgraph matching on large-scale graph data. S2X [6] decomposes the query graph into a set of triple patterns for matching and reduces redundant computation by discarding invalid intermediate results. The remaining matching results are then joined to form the final query results. DSsearch [14] employs graph partitioning and optimizes neighbor vertices during the data graph preprocessing phase to reduce communication costs between distributed computing nodes. It also designs the DSgraph storage structure to defer Cartesian product operations and minimize redundant intermediate results. StarMR [11] breaks down the query graph into multiple star structures and matches these structures step by step in MapReduce iterations to generate complete subgraph matching results. Su et al. [8] decompose star structures and compute their optimal query sequences to reduce the generation of intermediate results, thereby minimizing redundant computations

2.3 Partial Evaluation

The partial evaluation framework breaks down tasks into subtasks that run in parallel on distributed nodes. Intermediate results are then sent to a central node for final computation. In distributed subgraph matching, each node computes partial results independently, which are aggregated at the master node. This reduces message overhead and boosts performance.

For example, gStoreD leverages gStore [17] as the underlying computing engine to calculate partial matching results. It improves computational efficiency by extracting LEC features based on the similarity of partial matching results and filtering partial matches through early communication of candidate vertices. BN-Index [7] constructs a boundary neighbour index (BN-Index) using the boundary properties of partial matches to reduce the number of partial matches. PM-Index [13] builds a partial matching index structure using in-edge and out-edge vertices to enhance search efficiency during the assembly phase. Wang et al. [12] proposed a regular path query method based on partial evaluation. PEG [2] rewrites the query into a set of local subqueries, each of which can be independently computed on sub-nodes to produce local matching results.

3 Preliminaries

In this section, we will introduce the concepts necessary for understanding the content of this paper.

Definition 1 (RDF Graph). *An RDF graph $G = (V, E, \Sigma, \Lambda)$ is represented by a set of triples. A triple $t = \langle s, p, o\rangle \in U \times U \times (U \cup L)$ consists of three parts: subject (s), predicate (p), and object (o). Here, U denotes an infinite set of Uniform Resource Identifiers (URIs), and L denotes a set of literals.* $V = \{s \mid \langle s, p, o\rangle \in G\} \cup \{o \mid \langle s, p, o\rangle \in G\}$ *denotes the set of vertices.* $E = \{(s, o) \mid \langle s, p, o\rangle \in G \wedge s \in V \wedge o \in V\}$ *denotes the set of edges.* $\Sigma : E \rightarrow U$ *is a mapping such that for each edge* $(s, o) \in E$, $\Sigma(s, o)$ *represents the URI of the predicate p associated with that edge.* $\Lambda : V \rightarrow U$ *is a mapping such that for each vertex* $v \in V$, $\Lambda(v)$ *represents the URI of the entity associated with that vertex.*

Definition 2 (Subgraph Matching Query). *Given two RDF graphs: a data graph* $G = (V, E, \Sigma, \Lambda)$ *and a query graph* $Q = (V_q, E_q, \Sigma_q, \Lambda_q)$, *where V and* V_q *are the sets of vertices of the data graph and query graph, respectively, E and* E_q *are their respective sets of edges,* $\Sigma : E \rightarrow U$ *and* $\Sigma_q : E_q \rightarrow U$ *are the mappings from edges to predicates for the data graph and query graph, respectively, and* $\Lambda : V \rightarrow U$ *and* $\Lambda_q : V_q \rightarrow U$ *are the mappings from vertices to URIs for the data graph and query graph, respectively. If there exists an injective function* $f : V_q \rightarrow V$ *that satisfies the following conditions, then Q is said to have a subgraph match in G:*

1. ***Edge Matching****: For each* $(u, v) \in E_q$, $(f(u), f(v)) \in E$.
2. ***Vertex URI Matching****: For each* $u \in V_q$, $\Lambda_q(u) = \Lambda(f(u))$. *If a vertex is a variable, it can match any URI.*
3. ***Edge Predicate Matching****: For all* $(u, v) \in E_q$, $\Sigma_q(u, v) = \Sigma(f(u), f(v))$.

Definition 3 (Distributed RDF Graph). *An RDF graph* $G = (V, E, \Sigma, \Lambda)$ *is partitioned into n subsets* $\{P_1, P_2, \ldots, P_n\}$, *where* $P_i = (V_i, E_i, \Sigma_i, \Lambda_i)$. *For any* $i \neq j$, $V_i \cap V_j = \emptyset$ *and* $E_i \cap E_j = \emptyset$, *and* $V = \bigcup_{i=1}^{n} V_i$. *The vertex set* V_i *is also referred to as the internal vertex set of* P_i, *and the edge set* E_i *is also referred to as the internal edge set of* P_i.

4 Vertex Hotness Caching

This section introduces the basic concepts and related knowledge of the query optimization method based on vertex hotness caching. First, we elaborate on an important concept in this chapter—cache coverage, which is employed to determine whether the existing cached information can cover the complete results of the query. Subsequently, we introduce the vertex hotness identification algorithm and describe the construction method of the vertex hotness caching, as well as its application in the distributed subgraph matching method based on the partial evaluation framework.

4.1 Cache Coverage Check

Cache coverage is an important concept in this paper, which is utilized to determine whether the existing cached information can meet the query requirements. This method examines the high-selectivity vertices in the query that belong to the vertex hotness caching and marks these vertices and their multi-hop neighbors to determine whether the cache can cover the query.

Definition 4 (Cache Coverage). *Given a query* $Q = (V_q, E_q, \Sigma_q, \Lambda_q)$*, for any vertex* $u \in V_q$*, if* u *specifies a concrete URI, then* $u.selective = true$*, and* $match(u)$ *denotes the data vertex that* u *matches. Meanwhile, given a set of vertices* V_c *in the vertex hotness caching, for any vertex* $v \in V_c$*,* $C_h[v]$ *represents the coverage range of vertex* v*. The definition of cache coverage is as follows:*

1. *For each vertex* u *in the query graph* Q*, if* u *is a high-selectivity vertex and* $match(u) \in V_c$*, then mark* u *and all its neighbors within* $C_h[match(u)] - 1$ *hops in* Q*.*
2. *After traversing all vertices in the query graph* Q*, if there are no two adjacent unmarked vertices in* Q*, then the query* Q *is considered to be covered by the vertex hotness caching.*

Algorithm 1 provides a detailed description of the cache coverage check algorithm. The inputs of this algorithm include the query Q, the set of vertices V_c in the vertex hotness caching, and the shortest distance matrix D between query vertices. The shortest distance matrix D is utilized to quickly obtain the undirected shortest distance between any two query vertices. The algorithm first initializes an empty set V_{mark} to record the marked query vertices (line 1). Subsequently, it checks each vertex u_i in the query Q to determine whether it is a high-selectivity vertex. For each high-selectivity vertex u_i, it further checks whether its matching vertex $match(u_i)$ belongs to V_c (lines 2–3). If the condition is satisfied, u_i and all its neighboring query vertices within the coverage hop count minus one are marked as covered (lines 4–7). During the marking process, the algorithm checks whether the marked set V_{mark} covers all vertices in the query graph Q. If the number of vertices in V_{mark} is equal to the number of vertices in Q, it indicates that the existing cache data can fully cover the current query, and the algorithm returns True (lines 8–9). If, after the marking phase, the marked set V_{mark} still fails to cover all query vertices, the algorithm further examines the connections between the unmarked vertices. If there are two unmarked vertices that are connected, it indicates that the cache cannot cover the query (lines 10–13). If all unmarked vertices in the query graph Q are not connected to each other, it can be concluded that the existing cache data can fully cover the current query, and the algorithm returns True; otherwise, it returns False.

Algorithm 1: Cache Coverage Check Algorithm

```
Input: Query Q, set of vertices V_c in the vertex hotness caching, shortest
       distance matrix D between query vertices
Output: Coverage status (Boolean value)
1  Initialize the set of marked vertices V_mark = ∅;
2  foreach u_i ∈ V_q do
3      if u_i.selective = true ∧ match(u_i) ∈ V_c then
4          V_mark ← V_mark ∪ {u_i}
5          foreach u_j ∈ V_q do
6              if i ≠ j ∧ D[u_i][u_j] ≤ C_h[match(u_i)] − 1 then
7                  V_mark ← V_mark ∪ {u_j}
8      if |V_q| = |V_mark| then
9          return True
10 foreach u_i ∈ V_q \ V_mark do
11     foreach u_j ∈ V_q \ V_mark do
12         if D[u_i][u_j] = 1 then
13             return False
14 return True
```

Complexity Analysis : The time complexity of Algorithm 1 is $O(|V_q|^2)$, where $|V_q|$ is the number of query vertices in Q.

Example 1. Fig. 1a provides an example of a highly selective query, where the query vertices u_2 and u_3 specify the data vertices v_2 and v_3. Figure 1a illustrates the cache coverage example for this query. Assuming that vertices v_2 and v_3 are high-frequency vertices with a coverage hop count of 2 each, the cache coverage check process for Fig. 1a is shown in Fig. 1b. The query vertices u_2 and u_3 are mapped to the data vertices v_2 and v_3, respectively.

The cache coverage algorithm traverses all highly selective vertices in the query, identifying the query vertices that match the high-frequency vertices, namely u_2 and u_3. Starting from these two query vertices, the algorithm checks the shortest distances between these vertices and other vertices in the query

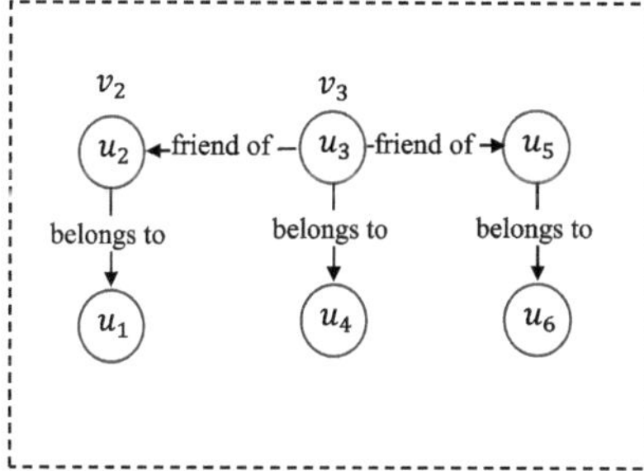

(a) Highly selective query example

Query Vertex	u_1	u_2	u_3	u_4	u_5	u_6
High-Selectivity Vertex	-	v_2	v_3	-	-	-
Cache Coverage	-	u_1	-	-	-	-
	-	u_2	u_2	-	-	-
	-	u_3	u_3	-	-	-
	-	-	u_4	-	-	-
	-	-	u_5	-	-	-
	-	-	-	-	-	-

(b) Cache coverage example

Fig. 1. Cache coverage example

graph, marking vertices with distances less than or equal to 1. For u_2, the covered query vertices are u_1 to u_3; for u_3, the covered query vertices are u_2 to u_5. Therefore, after the marking phase, query vertices u_1 to u_5 are marked, while query vertex u_6 remains unmarked. Since there are no other unmarked vertices connected to u_6 in the graph, this query can be fully covered by the cache.

4.2 Vertex Hotness Identification

The proposed method evaluates the vertex hotness based on the frequency of data vertices in the query log and the contribution of their β-hop neighbors to the query. It calculates a weight for each vertex appearing in the query log and identifies the vertex hotness according to the magnitude of the weights.

It is worth noting that low-selectivity queries often yield a large number of query results. Identifying high-hotness vertices for low-selectivity queries often does not lead to significant performance improvements and may instead cause cache pollution, reducing the cache hit rate. Consequently, this method only analyzes the result sets of high-selectivity queries to ensure that the vertices stored in the cache have high reuse value, thereby effectively improving cache utilization and query performance. Unless otherwise stated, the query set referred to in the subsequent sections of this chapter specifically denotes the high-selectivity query set.

Algorithm 2 describes the process of the vertex hotness identification algorithm. For each query Q_i in the query set, an undirected shortest distance matrix D_i is computed to quickly obtain the shortest distance between any two vertices later (lines 2–3). The `computeShortestDist` function calculates the undirected shortest distances between all pairs of nodes in the input query graph and outputs the shortest distance matrix. For each data vertex v in each result of query Q_i, the corresponding query vertex u is found, and the number of neighbors within β hops of this vertex u is counted as the weight (lines 4–9). The function $M(v)$ represents obtaining the query vertex u corresponding to the data vertex v. The weights are sorted in descending order, and the vertex sequence sorted by weight is returned. A threshold can also be provided to prevent recording too many vertices (lines 10–15). Here, the *sort* function indicates sorting the sequence in descending order. The *getNext* function indicates sequentially retrieving an element from a sequence.

Algorithm 2: Vertex Hotness Identification Algorithm

Input: Query set $\mathbb{Q} = \{Q_1, \ldots, Q_m\}$, query result set $\mathbb{R} = \{\mathbb{R}(Q_1), \ldots, \mathbb{R}(Q_m)\}$, hop number β, threshold ε

Output: Vertex hotness sequence V_h

1 Initialize weight function $W : V \rightarrow \mathbb{N}$

2 **foreach** $Q_i \in \mathbb{Q}$ **do**

3     $D_i \leftarrow$ computeShortestDist(Q_i) `// Compute the undirected shortest distance matrix` D_i `for query` Q_i

4   **foreach** $R_j \in \mathbb{R}(Q_i)$ **do**

5   **foreach** $v \in R_j$ **do**

6             $u = M(v)$ `// Obtain the query vertex` u `corresponding to data vertex` v

7   **foreach** $u' \in V_{Q_i}$ **do**

8   **if** $D_i[u][u'] \leq \beta$ **then**

9                     $W(v) \leftarrow W(v) + 1$

10 sort(W) `// Sort by weight in descending order`;

11 $V_h \leftarrow \emptyset$;

12 **while** $\varepsilon > 0$ **do**

13     $\eta \leftarrow getNext(W)$

14     $V_h \leftarrow V_h \cup \{\eta\}$

15     $\varepsilon \leftarrow \varepsilon - 1$ `// Continuously obtain the next highest-weight vertex until the threshold is reached`

16 **return** V_h

Complexity Analysis : The time complexity of Algorithm 2 is $O(|\mathbb{Q}||\overline{\mathbb{R}(Q_i)}||V_{Q_i}|^2 + |W|\log(|W|) + |\varepsilon|)$, where $|\mathbb{Q}|$ is the number of queries, $|\overline{\mathbb{R}(Q_i)}|$ is the average number of result sets for each query, $|V_{Q_i}|$ is the number of vertices in query Q_i, $|W|$ is the number of vertices with counted weights, and $|\varepsilon|$ is the threshold for high-heat vertices.

4.3 Vertex Hotness Caching Construction

In this subsection, we have introduced in detail the construction method of the vertex hotness caching. This cache is stored on the master node and is mainly optimized for high-selectivity queries. The method caches high-hotness vertices and their multi-hop neighbor information on the master node. When the query results can be completely covered by the vertices in the vertex hotness caching, the query results can be directly computed using the cache, thereby avoiding the additional overhead of distributed computation and improving query performance. In addition, the cache only records the high-hotness vertices and their multi-hop neighbor information. Compared with the complete graph data, the amount of data is significantly reduced, which further improves query efficiency. Therefore, the vertex hotness caching is essentially a local subgraph of the query graph. To ensure that the vertex hotness caching can independently support high-selectivity queries that meet the conditions, the cache needs to preserve the complete information of high-hotness vertices and their neighbors within the multi-hop range.

Algorithm 3: Vertex Hotness Caching Construction Algorithm

Input: Graph partition $S = \{S_1, \ldots, S_k\}$, set of high-hotness vertices V_h, hop number β

Output: vertex hotness caching and the mapping C_h from cached vertices to covered hop numbers

Initialize the set of cached vertices $V_c \leftarrow \emptyset$
Initialize the set of pending vertices $V_{pending} \leftarrow V_h$
Initialize the mapping from vertices to covered hop numbers $C_h \leftarrow \emptyset$
for $t = 1$ **to** β **do**
    Initialize the set of new neighbor vertices $V_{new} \leftarrow \emptyset$
    Initialize the partition vertex array $P_t \leftarrow \{\emptyset, \ldots, \emptyset\}$ // One empty set for each partition
    foreach $v \in V_{pending}$ **do**
        $C_h[v] \leftarrow \beta - t + 1$ // Mark the covered hop number for the current pending vertex
        $P_t[S(v)] \leftarrow P_t[S(v)] \cup \{v\}$ // Assign vertex v to its corresponding partition
    // Send requests to each partition
    foreach $S_i \in S$ **do**
        if $P_t[i] \neq \emptyset$ **then**
            $N_i = GetNeighbours(S_i, P_t[i])$ // Send request to partition S_i to collect 1-hop neighbors of all vertices in $P_t[i]$
            $cache(N_i)$ // Cache the collected 1-hop neighbor information on the master node
            foreach $v \in P_t[i]$ **do**
                foreach $u \in N_i[v]$ **do**
                    if $u \notin V_c$ **then**
                        $V_{new} \leftarrow V_{new} \cup \{u\}$ // Add unrecorded neighbors to the set of new neighbor vertices
    // Update the set of cached vertices and the set of pending vertices
    $V_c \leftarrow V_c \cup V_{pending}$
    $V_{pending} \leftarrow V_{new}$ // Utilize the new neighbor vertices as the pending set for the next round
return C_h

Algorithm 3 presents the construction algorithm of the vertex hotness caching, which iteratively collects the multi-hop neighbor information of each high-hotness vertex. The inputs include the graph partition S, the set of high-hotness vertices V_h, and the predefined maximum hop number β. The algorithm finally yields the vertex hotness caching, which includes the mapping C_h from cached vertices to covered hop numbers, as well as the 1-hop neighbor information of all cached vertices, except for vertices with a cache hop number of 0.

Complexity Analysis : The time complexity of Algorithm 3 is $O(|V_h|d^\beta)$, where $|V_h|$ is the number of high-hotness vertices, d is the average degree of vertices, and β is the predefined hop number.

4.4 Query Processing

Figure 2 illustrates the overall workflow of the vertex hotness caching. The method based on the vertex hotness caching preprocesses high-selectivity queries on the master node. This allows high-selectivity queries that can be covered by the cache to be computed on the master node, thereby fully utilizing the pruning capability of high-selectivity vertices.

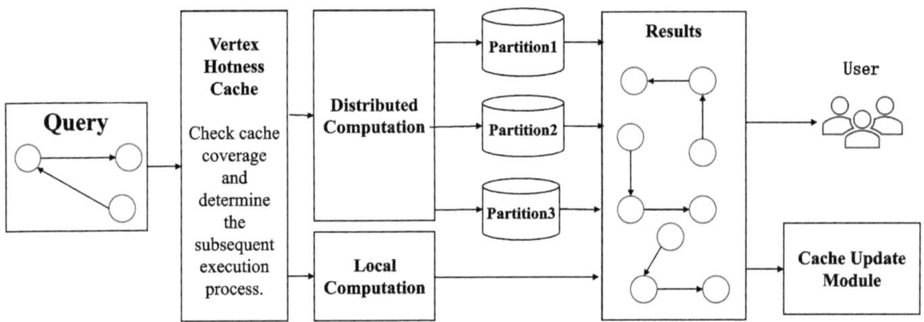

Fig. 2. Vertex Hotness Caching Overall Process

Algorithm 4 outlines the detailed procedure of a distributed subgraph matching algorithm that leverages vertex hotness caching to optimize query processing. The inputs of the algorithm include the partition set S, the query graph Q, and the vertex hotness caching C_h. After the query arrives at the master node, the master node first computes an undirected shortest distance matrix for the query to be utilized in subsequent cache coverage calculations (lines 1–2). Then, through Algorithm 1, i.e., the function *checkCacheCoverage*, it checks whether the current query can be covered by the vertex hotness caching. For queries that can be covered by the cache, subgraph matching is completed on the master node using a single-machine algorithm (lines 3–4). Otherwise, the subgraph matching computation is completed using a partial evaluation framework, with partial matches computed independently on each partition, i.e., the function *getPartialMatch*, and then the partial matches are assembled on the master node, corresponding to the function *assemble* (lines 5–9). Finally, the assembled final result is returned (line 10).

Algorithm 4: Subgraph Matching Algorithm Based on Vertex Hotness Caching

---

Input: Partition set $S = \{S_1, \ldots, S_i\}$, query graph Q, vertex hotness caching V_c
Output: Query result set $\mathbb{R}_G(Q)$

1 Initialize the query result set $\mathbb{R}_G(Q) \leftarrow \emptyset$
2 Compute the undirected shortest distance matrix of query graph Q: $D \leftarrow \text{computeShortestDist}(Q)$
3 **if** *checkCacheCoverage*(Q, V_c, D) **then**
4     $\mathbb{R}_G(Q) \leftarrow \text{singleNodeCompute}(Q)$ `// If the specific vertices in the query can be covered by the cache, complete subgraph matching on the master node`
5 **else**
6   **foreach** $S_i \in S$ **do**
7         $P_{S_i}(Q) \leftarrow \text{getPartialMatch}(S_i, Q)$
8         $P_G(Q) \leftarrow P_G(Q) \cup P_{S_i}(Q)$
9     $\mathbb{R}_G(Q) \leftarrow \text{assemble}(P_G(Q))$
10 **return** $\mathbb{R}_G(Q)$

---

5 Experiments

In this section, we implemented our method and validated the effectiveness and efficiency of the hot vertex cache. We also compared it with the baseline methods on LUBM datasets at different scales.

5.1 Experimental Settings

This experiment integrated the vertex hotness caching by modifying the source code of gStoreD. The system was deployed on a server equipped with a 64-core Intel Xeon Silver 4216 @ 2.10 GHz CPU, 512 GB of memory, and a 1920 GB solid-state drive, running CentOS 7.6. Three Docker containers were created on the server to serve as distributed nodes.

Data Sets. We ran experiments on four LUBM datasets of different sizes, with statistics in Table 1. To evaluate the vertex hotness caching, we implemented high-selectivity queries divided into three categories based on vertex count: 4, 5, and 6 vertices. Each category had 6 queries with different structures and selective vertex positions. By changing the URI values of selective vertices, each query was expanded into 10 versions, totaling 180 queries.

Table 1. Statistics of data sets.

Data set	#Triples	#Vertices	#Edges
LUBM20	2,688,046	437,569	1,795,325
LUBM40	5,307,458	864,236	3,546,175
LUBM60	8,003,821	1,302,478	5,347,519
LUBM80	10,728,220	1,744,940	7,166,392

Baselines. To verify the efficiency and effectiveness of the vertex hotness caching, we compared it with the mainstream RDF graph query system gStoreD based on the partial evaluation framework. The default hop number for the cache was set to 3.

Evaluation Process. To verify the effectiveness of the proposed method, this experiment conducted tests from two aspects: first, evaluating the acceleration effect of the vertex hotness caching on high-selectivity queries; and second, testing the cache hit rate. In terms of evaluating the acceleration effect on high-selectivity queries, the acceleration effect was quantified by comparing the execution time of queries in cases of cache hit and cache miss. The experiment selected three sets of queries and measured their execution times on datasets of different sizes. For each set of queries, the average query time was calculated as the basis for performance evaluation. Regarding the evaluation of the cache hit rate, the results of the aforementioned 180 high-selectivity queries were employed as query logs to identify high-hotness vertices, and the hit rates of the 6 types of queries proposed in Table 2 were tested on the LUBM20 dataset.

Table 2. Query sets.

Query	#Vertices	Type
$Q_1 \sim Q_3$	4	chain
$Q_4 \sim Q_6$	4	tree
$Q_7 \sim Q_9$	5	chain
$Q_{10} \sim Q_{12}$	5	tree
$Q_{13} \sim Q_{15}$	6	chain
$Q_{16} \sim Q_{18}$	6	tree

5.2 Experimental Results

Exp 1. Query Efficient. The average query time of the baseline gStoreD and the vertex hotness caching method on four LUBM datasets of different sizes (LUBM20, LUBM40, LUBM60, LUBM80) is shown in Fig. 3.

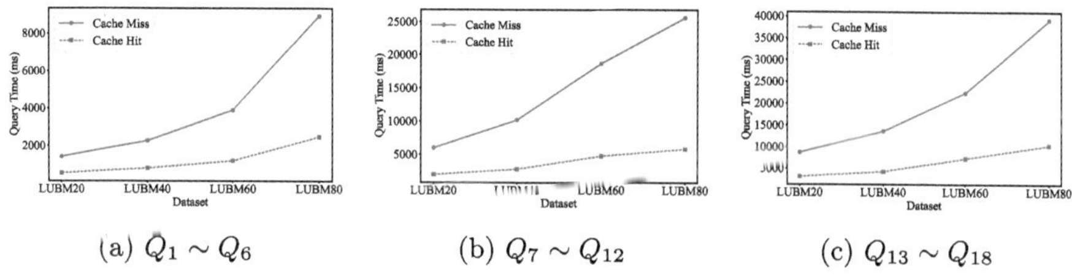

(a) $Q_1 \sim Q_6$ (b) $Q_7 \sim Q_{12}$ (c) $Q_{13} \sim Q_{18}$

Fig. 3. Average Execution Time with Vertex Hotness Caching Hits

Figure 3 shows the difference in query time between cache hits and cache misses for high-selectivity queries. The figure provides the average execution time for three groups of queries divided by the number of vertices, under both cache hit and cache miss conditions. As the scale of the dataset increases, the query time for cache misses grows rapidly, primarily because the time gStoreD spends computing the candidate set for each vertex also increases quickly with the growing data scale.

The increase in the number of query vertices also leads to longer query times. On the one hand, this is because more candidate vertices need to be computed for the additional vertices. On the other hand, the increased number of expansion operations adds to the search time for matching results. In contrast, the query time for cache hits in the vertex hotness caching is significantly reduced, and its growth trend is relatively stable as the data scale increases. This is because queries that hit the cache can directly locate the specific data vertices through indexing and start expanding from those vertices, without the need to compute the global candidate vertex set. Therefore, the search space does not grow rapidly with the increase in dataset size. Moreover, since the vertex hotness caching is a subset of the complete dataset with a smaller overall data volume, the computational overhead is further reduced. Although an additional cache coverage check is required, the time for this check is negligible compared to the subgraph matching query time.

Exp 2. Cache Hit Rate. Figure 4 shows the hit rate of different types of queries in the vertex hotness caching.

As shown in Fig. 4, when the number of query vertices is 4, both chain and tree queries achieve high cache hit rates. This is because for queries containing 4 vertices, regardless of their structure or the location of selective vertices, high-hotness vertices can cover all vertices in the query. However, when the number of query vertices increases to 5, the hit rate for chain queries ($Q_7 \sim Q_9$) drops significantly. This is due to the fact that when selective vertices are located at the ends of the chain queries, they do not hit the cache regardless of their URI variations. Furthermore, when the number of query vertices is 6, this situation becomes more pronounced ($Q_{13} \sim Q_{15}$). At this point, the cache only hits when selective vertices are located in the middle of the query. This indicates that as the

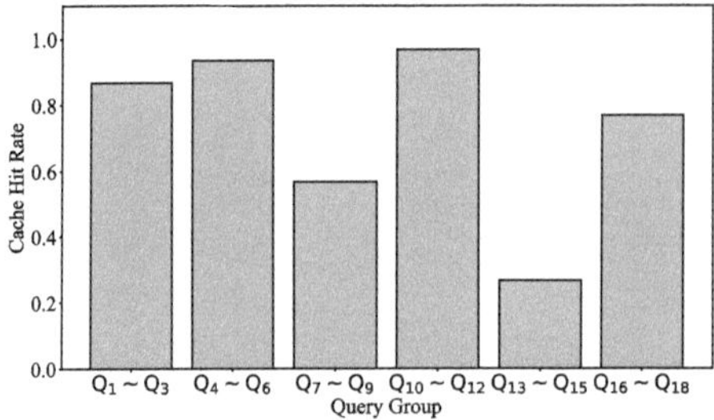

Fig. 4. Hit Rates of Different Types of Queries in the Vertex Hotness Caching

number of query vertices increases, the sensitivity of the cache hit rate to query structure and the location of selective vertices becomes significantly stronger.

6 Conclusion

This paper proposes the vertex hotness caching method to optimize subgraph matching methods based on partial evaluation frameworks. This method caches high-hotness vertices and their multi-hop neighbors on the master node. For high-selectivity queries that can be covered by the cache, single-machine computation using the cache is performed on the master node, thereby alleviating the issue of poor utilization of the pruning capability for high-selectivity vertices in partial evaluation frameworks. The effectiveness of the vertex hotness caching has been verified through extensive experiments. The experimental results show that, in the case of cache hits, the vertex hotness caching can effectively reduce the execution time of high-selectivity queries.

Acknowledgement. This work was supported by the National Natural Science Foundation of China (62472311).

References

1. Galluzzo, Y.: A comprehensive review of the data and knowledge graphs approaches in bioinformatics. Comput. Sci. Inf. Syst. **00**, 27–27 (2024)
2. Ji, S., Peng, P., Hu, J., Zou, L., Huang, Z., Qin, Z.: Peg: a partial evaluation-based distributed rdf graph system. In: International Conference on Database Systems for Advanced Applications, pp. 658–662. Springer, Heidelberg (2023). https://doi.org/10.1007/978-3-031-30678-5_51
3. Lai, L., Qin, L., Lin, X., Chang, L.: Scalable subgraph enumeration in mapreduce. Proc. VLDB Endow. **8**(10), 974–985 (2015)
4. Peng, P., Zou, L., Guan, R.: Accelerating partial evaluation in distributed sparql query evaluation. In: 2019 IEEE 35th International Conference on Data Engineering (ICDE), pp. 112–123. IEEE (2019)

5. Peng, P., Zou, L., Özsu, M.T., Chen, L., Zhao, D.: Processing sparql queries over distributed rdf graphs. VLDB J. **25**, 243–268 (2016)
6. Schätzle, A., Przyjaciel-Zablocki, M., Berberich, T., Lausen, G.: S2X: graph-parallel querying of RDF with GraphX. In: Wang, F., Luo, G., Weng, C., Khan, A., Mitra, P., Yu, C. (eds.) Big-O(Q)/DMAH -2015. LNCS, vol. 9579, pp. 155–168. Springer, Cham (2016). https://doi.org/10.1007/978-3-319-41576-5_12
7. Song, Y., et al.: Optimizing subgraph matching over distributed knowledge graphs using partial evaluation. World Wide Web **26**(2), 751–771 (2023)
8. Su, Q., Huang, Q., Wu, N., Pan, Y.: Distributed subgraph query for rdf graph data based on mapreduce. Comput. Electr. Eng. **102**, 108221 (2022)
9. Ullmann, J.R.: An algorithm for subgraph isomorphism. J. ACM (JACM) **23**(1), 31–42 (1976)
10. Wang, C., Zhu, H.: Representing fine-grained co-occurrences for behavior-based fraud detection in online payment services. IEEE Trans. Dependable Secure Comput. **19**(1), 301–315 (2020)
11. Wang, X., Chai, L., Xu, Q., Yang, Y., Li, J., Wang, J., Chai, Y.: Efficient subgraph matching on large rdf graphs using mapreduce. Data Sci. Eng. **4**, 24–43 (2019)
12. Wang, X., Wang, J., Zhang, X.: Efficient distributed regular path queries on rdf graphs using partial evaluation. In: Proceedings of the 25th ACM International on Conference on Information and Knowledge Management, pp. 1933–1936 (2016)
13. Xing, J., Liu, B., Li, J., Choudhury, F.M., Wang, X.: Optimal subgraph matching queries over distributed knowledge graphs based on partial evaluation. In: Zhang, W., Zou, L., Maamar, Z., Chen, L. (eds.) WISE 2021. LNCS, vol. 13080, pp. 274–289. Springer, Cham (2021). https://doi.org/10.1007/978-3-030-90888-1_22
14. Xu, Q., Wang, X., Li, J., Zhang, Q., Chai, L.: Distributed subgraph matching on big knowledge graphs using pregel. IEEE Access **7**, 116453–116464 (2019)
15. Zhang, Y., Zheng, W., Zhang, Z., Peng, P., Zhang, X.: Hybrid subgraph matching framework powered by sketch tree for distributed systems. In: 2022 IEEE 38th International Conference on Data Engineering (ICDE), pp. 1031–1043. IEEE (2022)
16. Zhao, X., Jiang, R., Han, Y., Li, A., Peng, Z.: A survey on cybersecurity knowledge graph construction. Comput. Secur. **136**, 103524 (2024)
17. Zou, L., Mo, J., Chen, L., Özsu, M.T., Zhao, D.: gStore: answering sparql queries via subgraph matching. Proc. VLDB Endow. **4**(8), 482–493 (2011)

Fetan: Enhancing Few-Shot Classification on Text-Attributed Graphs with In-Context Learning of LLMs

Yun Zhang[1], Minghe Yu[2](✉), Jintong Sun[2], Tiancheng Zhang[1], and Ge Yu[1]

[1] School of Computer Science and Engineering, Northeastern University, Shenyang, Liaoning, China
{tczhang,yuge}@mail.neu.edu.cn

[2] Software College, Northeastern University, Shenyang, Liaoning, China
yuminghe@mail.neu.edu.cn

Abstract. Classification on text-attributed graphs (TAGs) is crucial in data mining but challenging due to limited labeled data. Few-shot graph learning helps by utilizing sparse annotations to extract meta-knowledge, but still struggles with insufficient reference information for query nodes. Large Language Models (LLMs) offer a potential solution with their strong generalization and textual understanding. However, integrating LLMs into TAGs classification introduces challenges such as using information from well-labeled graph parts, capturing node structure, comparing query nodes with classes from a small labeled support set, and designing effective prompts. To address these, we propose Fetan, a method that enhances FEw-shot classification on Text-Attributed graphs with iN-context learning of LLMs. Fetan constructs rich prompts by first generating a prototype-free label representation via an encoder-based LLM, producing representative keywords for each label as semantic anchors. It then selects diverse contextual examples—including neighbours and structurally similar nodes identified via motif-based matching—to embed relational and structural cues. Additionally, Fetan incorporates local label distributions for statistical context augmentation. Finally, Fetan compresses verbose node attributes into salient keyword sequences via an encoder-based LLM to construct concise and informative prompts. Experimental results demonstrate Fetan's effectiveness, outperforming existing methods under label-scarce conditions.

Keywords: Few-shot learning · Text-attributed graphs · Large language models · In-context learning

1 Introduction

Text-attributed graphs (TAGs), which integrate node textual features with graph structures, are widespread in real-world applications such as social networks,

J. Li et al. (Eds.): APWeb-WAIM 2025, LNCS 16115, pp. 516–532, 2026.
https://doi.org/10.1007/978-981-95-5719-6_33

recommendation systems, and academic graphs [44]. This rich combination supports a variety of downstream tasks and has become a critical research focus in data mining and machine learning. Among these tasks, classification is particularly crucial, enabling applications like user profiling, product categorization, and knowledge discovery [47]. However, TAG classification models often suffer from the scarcity of labeled data [17,32], as obtaining abundant labels across categories is impractical in real-world settings. To address the problem of sparse labels, few-shot learning has been introduced into graph domains as a promising solution, where the few-shot graph contains only sparsely labeled nodes. As illustrated in Fig. 1, few-shot graph learning aims to enable models to generalize from a few labeled instances by extracting transferable meta-knowledge [48]. Specifically for TAGs, models must learn to classify nodes based on both textual features and structural information, even under limited supervision [3,4,9,34,45].

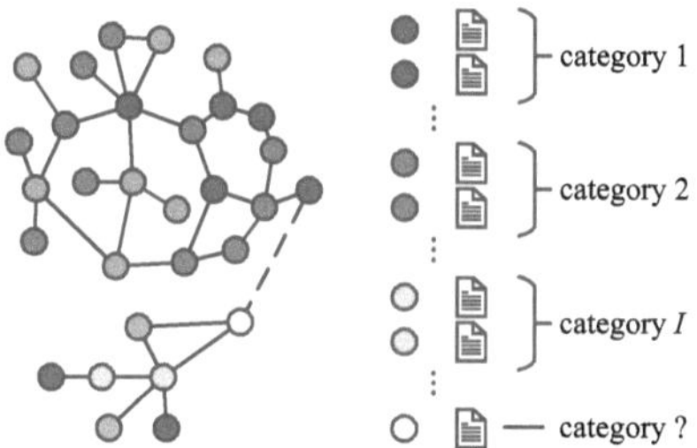

Fig. 1. Schematic diagram of node classification in the case of sparse labels on TAGs.

Traditional graph few-shot classification methods [11,21,23,41,46] have made some progress. A popular method is to build **prototypes** from a support set (*a small set of labeled nodes*) as label representations and classify query nodes by similarity comparing similarities with these prototypes. However, for TAGs, these methods often lack sufficient semantic understanding, leading to low accuracy. Recent work explores large models for graph classification. Large language models (LLMs), pre-trained on massive data, exhibit strong generalization and can be adapted to new tasks with simple fine-tuning. Inspired by LLMs, large graph models (LGMs) [19,43] pre-train on large graphs and fine-tune on downstream tasks to transfer learned knowledge. Yet, these models do not have the same power and generality as LLM, which prevents them from performing graph tasks efficiently. There are also some methods that combine graph neural networks (GNNs) with LLMs to address the problem of insufficient understanding of traditional GNNs [8,24,36,39], while using **in-context learning (ICL)** methods [8,16,26,29,37] to integrate examples and instructions into the input, thereby activating the internal knowledge of LLM to improve classification accuracy. However, these GNN-LLM hybrids still rely heavily on fine-tuning, demanding large labeled datasets. In contrast, in NLP, it has been shown that accurate classification can be achieved through well-designed prompts without fine-tuning [30], but similar advances have yet to appear for graph data.

We aim to leverage the excellent understanding and generalization capabilities of LLMs for few-shot classification on TAGs. However, this objective introduces four main challenges: (1). **Effectively utilizing information from well-labeled parts of the graph with LLMs.** Traditional few-shot learning methods rely on abundant labeled data from non-target categories to teach models how to learn rapidly. However, LLMs may have already acquired such generalization abilities and only require appropriate prompts to activate them. The key challenge lies in extracting and leveraging relevant information from the subset of nodes with sufficient labels to assist in downstream tasks. (2). **Capturing structural information of nodes.** LLMs are designed to process sequential textual input, yet TAGs contain not only textual attributes but also structural dependencies between nodes. Thus, it is crucial to encode node information in a way that simultaneously preserves node features and captures their structural relationships to support graph-based reasoning within LLMs. (3). **Comparing query nodes with support set classes in a graph context.** Few-shot classification requires models to effectively compare query instances with candidate classes to determine the correct label. Prototypical Networks [33], for instance, represent each label as the centroid of its support examples in the embedding space, and classify the query node by selecting the nearest label prototype. (4). **Transforming TAGs into text-based prompts suitable for LLM input.** Since LLMs cannot directly process graph structures, it becomes necessary to translate TAGs into textual prompts that encode both attribute and structural information. This transformation must retain critical graph semantics while adapting the format to the LLM's input requirements to ensure effective downstream reasoning.

To address these challenges, we propose **Fetan**: a method that enhances **FE**w-shot classification on **T**ext-**A**ttributed graphs with i**N**-context learning of LLMs. **Fetan** tackles the challenges through four core strategies:

- **Prototype-free label representation:** Instead of constructing vector-based label prototypes, we use an encoder-based LLM to generate representative keywords for each label (Sect. 4.1). These keywords serve as semantic anchors to align query nodes with labels, tackling Challenge (3).
- **Contextual example selection:** We build informative prompts by selecting diverse examples (Sect. 4.2)-including neighbours from few-shot and well-labeled graph parts, and motif-matched structural analogs——to provide rich relational and structural cues for Challenges (1) and (2).
- **Statistical context augmentation:** We augment prompts with local label distribution statistics around the query node Sect. 4.3, bridging the modality gap between structured graph data and natural language. This supports Challenges (1) and (3), enhancing robustness in sparse scenarios.
- **Attribute compression for prompt optimization:** We compress verbose node attributes into salient keywords using an encoder-based LLM, and design a structured prompt format that integrates examples and statistical signals (Sect. 4.4). This directly addresses Challenge (4).

We evaluate **Fetan** on multiple TAG datasets and show that it achieves superior few-shot classification performance without fine-tuning the LLM.

2 Related Work

2.1 Graph Few-Shot Classification

Graph few-shot classification involves classifying query set nodes with few labeled examples from a support set. CGNet [11] introduces the Cross-Feature Module to refine and integrate features by exploring correlations between support and query images. AMGNN [41] uses an adaptive fusion strategy to integrate semantic and visual information, improving generalization in few-shot tasks. Yayong et al. [21] propose a method that combines topology-based class augmentation and prototype calibration to enhance node classification, addressing class integration and mitigating catastrophic forgetting. DouN-GNN [46] optimizes graph updates and reduces redundancy by introducing gray image features and an orthogonal transformation module, boosting performance in few-shot scenarios. SMART [23], an unsupervised method, replaces meta-learning with transfer learning, using a graph-specific mixup strategy and prompt-tuning to outperform supervised models. Nevertheless, existing methods remain limited by scarce labeled data and a shallow understanding of textual node attributes in TAGs. Our method leverages the language understanding and prior knowledge embedded in LLMs to address these limitations.

P2TAG [47] bridges GNNs and language models through mixed graph-text prompts. However, extracting hidden embeddings for node classification via LLM fine-tuning diverges from pre-training objectives, increasing complexity and risking catastrophic forgetting [18]. In contrast, our method leverages pre-trained LLMs directly, preserving both reasoning capabilities and model stability.

2.2 ICL of Graph Plus LLMs

Recent efforts have combined GNNs and LLMs for tasks such as molecular property prediction [8,24,39], yet fine-tuning large models remains costly, data-intensive, and fragile under label scarcity. In NLP, for tasks like text classification and prediction, generating task-specific instructions has been shown to improve performance [30,42]. This is where in-context learning (ICL) comes in: a prompt engineering technique where task demonstrations are embedded as natural language examples within the prompt.

For graph-related tasks, Wang et al. [36] propose feeding nodes, after GNN embedding, into an LLM alongside instructions, allowing the LLM to predict graph properties. KICGPT [37] focuses on link prediction by integrating structured knowledge graphs with LLMs, converting triples into a natural language format suitable for LLM input, and employing a retrieval-re-ranking mechanism. GRACE [26] encodes code into a graph structure and inputs it into LLMs along with text-based examples. PRODIGY [16] introduces a pre-trained LGM that mimics LLM strategies, treating each N-way K-shot graph as an ICL example. However, as noted earlier in this paper, no LGM has yet been pre-trained to the scale of Llama, BART [20], or T5 [5]. Fifty et al. [8] combine few-shot learning and ICL by encoding molecules with message-passing neural networks before inputting them into a transformer encoder, a method better suited for molecular graphs than general node classification. Mosbach et al. [29] find that well-designed ICL can rival fine-tuning, suggesting a viable alternative when labeled data are scarce.

Existing ICL methods applied to graphs with LLMs have notable limitations: (1) they inherit issues discussed in Sect. 2.1, including catastrophic forgetting caused by the mismatch between the fine-tuning and pre-training objectives, or insufficiently optimized pre-trained parameters, leading to reduced accuracy; (2) they are not specifically designed for classifying entities with text attributes that are associated with other entities. In contrast, our method specifically targets TAGs, avoids introducing excessive noise from inconsistent fine-tuning, and provides a more accurate solution for node classification.

3 Preliminaries

Given a TAG $\mathcal{G} = (\mathcal{V}, \mathcal{E})$, where $\mathcal{V}$ and $\mathcal{E}$ denote the node and edge sets, we partition $\mathcal{V}$ into two subsets based on label availability. $\mathcal{V}_s \subset \mathcal{V}$ contains categories with sufficient labeled nodes and defines the *source graph* $\mathcal{G}_s = (\mathcal{V}_s, \mathcal{E}_s)$ with label set $\mathcal{Y}_s$. Conversely, $\mathcal{V}_f \subset \mathcal{V}$ includes categories with sparse labels, forming the *few-shot graph* $\mathcal{G}_f = (\mathcal{V}_f, \mathcal{E}_f)$ with label set $\mathcal{Y}_f$. By construction, the label sets are disjoint, i.e., $\mathcal{Y}_s \cap \mathcal{Y}_f = \emptyset$.

The objective is to classify sparsely labeled nodes in $\mathcal{V}_f$. In each few-shot classification task, an unlabeled node $v \in \mathcal{V}_f$ is classified using a small set of labeled nodes, forming the *support set* $\mathcal{S} = \{(x_i, y_i)\}_{i=1}^{N \times K}$, where x_i denotes the text attributes of node v_i, $N = |\mathcal{Y}_f|$ is the number of distinct labels, and K is the number of nodes per label. The set of nodes to be classified forms the *query set* $\mathcal{Q}$. This setting defines the **N-way K-shot graph classification problem**.

ICL enables LLMs to perform tasks using a few text-based examples provided in the prompt without fine-tuning. Rather than updating model parameters, ICL leverages pre-trained knowledge and generalization ability. In our setting, given a support set $\mathcal{S}$, the LLM predicts the label of a query x_q based on task instructions and examples derived from $\mathcal{S}$.

4 Methodology

LLMs possess strong text understanding and reasoning abilities, making them a natural choice for classifying nodes in TAGs. We initially tested this by inputting text descriptions of six Ele-Computers [40] entities from the Amazon Review dataset into Llama2-Chat [35], using nine candidate categories. Llama2-Chat correctly classified three nodes, while the remaining three were misclassified: one node from the *Computer Components* category was assigned to *Computer Accessories & Peripherals*, another from *Laptop Accessories* was misclassified as *Computer Accessories & Peripherals*, and a third from *Computer Components* was labeled as *Networking Products*. This indicates that while Llama2 Chat exhibits some classification capability, its accuracy remains suboptimal.

We hypothesize that this is due to insufficient input information, as we only provided textual descriptions without incorporating relationship and structural data from the TAG. Moreover, LLMs perform best with well-structured textual input. To address these limitations, we propose **Fetan**, a method that enhances FEw-shot classification on Text-Attributed graphs with iN-context learning of LLMs for node classification, as illustrated in Fig. 2. Specifically, we first generate representative keywords for labels via an encoder-based LLM. Next, we augment the prompt with diverse contextual examples, including neighbours and structurally similar nodes. Additionally, we incorporate statistical label distributions around the target node to provide additional cues about its neighbourhood context. Then, we refine the raw textual attributes by extracting salient keywords using an encoder-based LLM to reduce redundancy. Finally, the classification is performed by prompting Llama2 and Llama3 with the enriched input, enabling effective generalization to unseen categories.

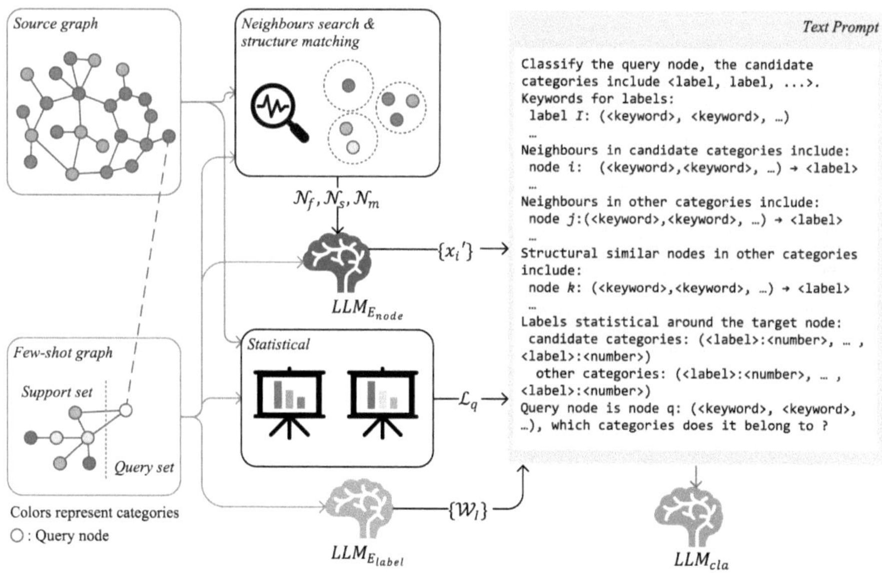

Fig. 2. Framework for generating text prompts in the proposed Fetan. An LLM extracts keywords from node text attributes. The prompt incorporates support set nodes, their neighbours in both the support set and source graph, structurally similar nodes and statistical information for node classification.

4.1 Keywords for Labels

Conventional few-shot classification methods construct a prototype for each candidate label by encoding its support examples into a representative vector [25, 33]. In contrast, as our method does not rely on explicit node embeddings, we do not directly form label prototypes. Instead, we generate a set of keywords to serve as a semantic proxy for each prototype.

We employ an encoder-based LLM, denoted as $LLM_{E_{label}}$, to extract n_k keywords per label. Models like BERT [6], RoBERTa [22], and DeBERTaV3 [13, 14] are well-suited for this task due to their strong semantic capabilities.

For a candidate label $y_I \in \mathcal{Y}_f$, the corresponding nodes set is $\mathcal{V}_I \subset \mathcal{V}_f$, with the associated text attribute set defined as $\mathcal{X}_I = \{x_i\}^K$, where x_i denotes the text attributes of node $v_i \in \mathcal{V}_I$. The keywords set $\mathcal{W}_I$ is then generated using $LLM_{E_{label}}$ as follows:

$$\mathcal{W}_I = LLM_{E_{label}}(\text{Prompt}||\mathcal{X}_I), \tag{1}$$

where the prompt is *"Extract n_k keywords based on the following content"*. These keywords function analogously to label prototypes in guiding classification.

4.2 Example Nodes

To construct a prompt that captures both the contextual and structural semantics of the query node, we select three types of example nodes from complementary perspectives. These nodes are chosen to be representative in terms of relational relevance or structural similarity. Below, we describe each type and the motivation for its inclusion:

Neighbours in the Few-shot Graph. Given the relational nature of graphs, adjacent nodes often share semantic or structural similarities. We thus include the neighbours of the query node within the few-shot graph, forming a neighbour set $\mathcal{N}_f$ to enrich the prompt with relevant relational context. Formally, the neighbour set is defined as:

$$\mathcal{N}_f(v_q) = \{v \in \mathcal{V}_f \mid (v_q, v) \in \mathcal{E}_f\}. \tag{2}$$

Neighbours in Source Graph. The query node may also be connected to nodes in the source graph that are not part of candidate categories. These neighbours, denoted as set $\mathcal{N}_s$, provide additional context. To prevent these nodes from overwhelming information from candidate categories, we limit their number to a maximum of n_s. When the number of such neighbours exceeds this threshold, we retain only the top n_s nodes with the highest degree. Then:

$$\mathcal{N}_s(v_q) = \text{Top}_{n_s}\left(\{v \in \mathcal{V}_s \mid (v_q, v) \in \mathcal{E}_s\}\right), \tag{3}$$

where Top_{n_s} selects up to n_s neighbours with the highest degrees.

Motif-Based Local Structure Matching. To capture structural insights, we retrieve nodes with similar local structures to the query node. Using motif-based subgraphs [27], we identify patterns such as triangles, stars, and squares within the k-hop neighbourhood. We focus on triangle, 2-star, and square motifs due to their prevalence in social and citation networks and their tractable computation. These motifs capture essential local connectivity patterns such as clustering, hub-spoke structures, and cyclic relations. Prior work [2,27] has shown these patterns are sufficient proxies for higher-order topological signals in low-resource scenarios.

Specifically, motif counts are computed using the adjacency matrix $\boldsymbol{A}$ of the graph $\mathcal{G}$ as follows: (1) Triangle count $\boldsymbol{T} = \frac{1}{6}\mathrm{Tr}(\boldsymbol{A}^3)$, summing all length-3 closed walks; (2) 2-star count $\boldsymbol{S} = \boldsymbol{A}\mathbf{1}$, where $\mathbf{1}$ is the all-ones vector and $\boldsymbol{S}$ gives the degree of each node; (3) Square count $\boldsymbol{C_4} = \frac{1}{8}\mathrm{Tr}(\boldsymbol{A}^4) - \frac{1}{4}\|\boldsymbol{S}\|_2^2$, adjusting length-4 closed walks by subtracting repeated paths. Each node i forms a motif frequency vector $\boldsymbol{m}_i = (T_i, S_i, C_{4,i})$, which is L2-normalized as $\hat{\boldsymbol{m}}_i = \frac{\boldsymbol{m}_i}{\|\boldsymbol{m}_i\|}$ with $\|\boldsymbol{m}_i\| = \sqrt{T_i^2 + S_i^2 + C_{4,i}^2}$. Similarity between nodes is measured via cosine similarity between normalized vectors. Formally, the motif-based neighbour set is defined as:

$$\mathcal{N}_m(v_q) = \mathrm{Top}_{n_m}\left(\{v \in \mathcal{V} \setminus \{v_q\} \mid \mathrm{cosine}(\hat{\boldsymbol{m}}_v, \hat{\boldsymbol{m}}_{v_q}) \text{ is high}\}\right), \tag{4}$$

where Top_{n_m} selects the n_m most similar nodes to v_q in terms of motif structure.

4.3 Statistical Information Around the Target Node

To further enhance the prompt, we incorporate statistical cues that summarize the local label distribution around the query node. This is particularly useful for bridging the modality gap between structured graphs and pretrained language models, where few-shot examples alone may be insufficient without fine-tuning.

Specifically, we compute the label distribution of the query node's neighbours. Given a query node v_q, let $\mathcal{N}_f(v_q)$ and $\mathcal{N}_s(v_q)$ denote its neighbour sets in the few-shot graph and source graph, respectively. We define the label frequency function over a node set $\mathcal{N}$ as:

$$f_y(\mathcal{N}) = \sum_{v \in \mathcal{N}} \mathbb{I}[y_v = y], \tag{5}$$

where $\mathbb{I}[\cdot]$ is the indicator function and y_v denotes the label of node v.

We extract the top k_f labels with the highest frequency from $\mathcal{N}_f(v_q)$:

$$\{(y_1, n_1), \ldots, (y_{k_f}, n_{k_f})\}, \quad \text{where } n_i = f_{y_i}(\mathcal{N}_f(v_q)). \tag{6}$$

Similarly, we extract the top k_s labels from $\mathcal{N}_s(v_q)$:

$$\{(y_{k_f+1}, n_{k_f+1}), \ldots, (y_{k_f+k_s}, n_{k_f+k_s})\}, \quad \text{where } n_j = f_{y_j}(\mathcal{N}_s(v_q)). \tag{7}$$

These label statistics are included in the prompt as a distributional summary:

$$\mathcal{L}_q = \{(y_i, n_i)\}_{i=1}^{k_f+k_s}, \tag{8}$$

which serves as contextual prior knowledge to guide the language model in generating label predictions for the query node.

4.4 Graph to Text Prompt

To enable ICL with LLMs, we transform structured graph data into a well-formed natural language prompt. This process involves three key components: label-level semantic guidance, example node representations, and statistical context.

Label-Level Semantic Guidance. To construct the prompt, we first incorporate label-level semantics. As described in Sect. 4.1, we extract a keyword set $\mathcal{W}_I$ for each candidate label y_I using an encoder-based LLM. These keywords act as lightweight semantic prototypes, helping the LLM better align query nodes with possible labels. We integrate these keywords into the prompt by appending each label with its associated $\mathcal{W}_I$ set in natural language format. The format is:

```
label I: (<keyword>, <keyword>, ...)
```

This structured prototype is inserted before node examples in the final prompt.

Example Node Encoding. Then we convert graph nodes into natural language format. Nodes in the TAG typically include verbose textual attributes—for instance, in the Ele-Computers dataset [40], the average node has 94 word-level tokens. Feeding such lengthy inputs into the LLM risks noise, token overflow, and degraded performance.

To address this, we introduce an encoder-based LLM, denoted as $LLM_{E_{node}}$, to extract n_k salient keywords per node—matching the number used for label keywords. For each $v_i \in \mathcal{N}_f \cup \mathcal{N}_o \cup \mathcal{N}_s$, we obtain a compact representation $x'_i = LLM_{E_{node}}(x_i)$, which is then formatted as:

```
node i: (<keyword>, <keyword>, ...) → <label>
```

Statistical Context Modeling. To further enrich the prompt, we include local statistical context surrounding the query node. These are appended as auxiliary information in the following format:

```
Labels statistical around the target node:
candidate categories: (<label>:<number>, ..., <label>:<number>)
other categories: (<label>:<number>, ..., <label>:<number>)
```

Final Prompt Structure. The complete prompt $\mathcal{P}_q$ for query node v_q is:

$$\mathcal{P}_q = \texttt{Instruction} \| \underbrace{\texttt{Label Keywords}}_{\mathcal{W}_I, \forall y_I} \| \underbrace{\texttt{Examples}}_{\mathcal{S}, \mathcal{N}_f, \mathcal{N}_s, \mathcal{N}_m} \| \underbrace{\texttt{Statistical Info}}_{\mathfrak{L}_q} \tag{9}$$

The final query is structured as:

> **`Query node is node` q`: (<keyword>, <keyword>, ...), which categories does it belong to?`**

LLM-based Classification. Finally, the prompt $\mathcal{P}_q$ is passed to an LLM-based classifier LLM_{cla}. Unlike models such as RoBERTa and DeBERTaV3 that require fine-tuning, Llama-based models can perform classification in a zero-shot manner using natural language prompts. Specifically, we use **instruction-tuned** Llama models—`Llama2-Chat` [35] and `Llama3-Instruct` [1,12]—which are optimized to follow task instructions out-of-the-box. These models are trained with a large set of instruction-response pairs, enabling better adherence to classification task formats. Thus, $\mathcal{P}_q$ is formatted as a plain-text instruction and directly fed to LLM_{cla} for prediction:

$$\hat{y}_q = LLM_{cla}(\mathcal{P}_q) \tag{10}$$

5 Experiments

5.1 Experimental Setup

Dataset and Metrics. We conduct experiments on TAG datasets from the CS-TAG benchmark [40], derived from the Amazon Review dataset. In these datasets, nodes represent items, edges indicate frequent co-purchases or co-browsing, and each node has an associated text description. The datasets are publicly available[1]. Following Zhao et al. [47], we use four subsets: *Children*, *History*, *Computers*, and *Photo*. To assess model performance, we employ standard classification metrics, with accuracy as the evaluation measure.

Environment and Configuration. Our experiments are implemented using PyTorch [31], and all LLMs are obtained from Huggingface [38]. The LLM used for keyword extraction is DeBERTaV3, while LLMs for classification are the instruction-tuned versions of LLaMA models, specifically `Llama2-Chat` [35] and `Llama3-Instruct` [1,12]. We use NVIDIA A100 SXM4 GPUs for all experiments. Few-shot classification is performed with $N = \{3, 5\}$-way $K = \{1, 3, 5\}$-shot tasks. Each task is evaluated over five random runs, and the average accuracy is reported. The hyperparameters are as follows: the maximum number of neighbours from other categories is $n_s = 3$; motif-based local structure matching selects $n_m = 5$ similar nodes; and $n_k = 20$ keywords are extracted per node.

[1] CS-TAG.

Baselines. We compare our method with several representative baselines. **GPN** [7] classifies query nodes by measuring their proximity to label prototypes computed via weighted averaging of support nodes. **G-Meta** [15] leverages local subgraphs to learn transferable patterns, enabling rapid adaptation to new tasks with minimal data. Both methods adopt lightweight neural networks. **P2TAG** [47] jointly trains language models and graph neural networks with masked language modeling and employs graph-text mixed prompts to enhance few-shot classification on text-attributed graphs. We further include LLM-based baselines using **Llama2-Chat** (7B) and **Llama3-Instruct** (8B), which classify nodes solely based on textual attributes in an N-way, 0-shot setting. Since they do not utilize support examples, their performance is reported once, independent of the shot number K. Our method variants, **Fetan-l2** and **Fetan-l3**, correspond to final classifications by Llama2-Chat and Llama3-Instruct, respectively.

5.2 Performance Evaluation

The experimental results are summarized in Table 1. As shown, our proposed **Fetan-l3**, which employs llama3-Instruct as the final classifier, consistently outperforms all baseline methods across all datasets and few-shot configurations. Moreover, **Fetan-l2** achieves the second-best performance on the History dataset, further validating the effectiveness of integrating few-shot classification with ICL.

We observe that increasing the number of shots consistently improves performance across all methods, as expected. However, **Fetan-l3** exhibits a smaller performance gap between 1-shot and 5-shot settings, especially in challenging 4-way classification tasks. For example, in the *Children* dataset, **Fetan-l3** improves only 2.5% from 1-shot (88.3%) to 5-shot (90.8%), while P2TAG improves 14.0% (66.5% to 80.8%). This suggests that **Fetan-l3** requires fewer examples to generalize well, showcasing strong few-shot adaptability.

Notably, using an LLM alone yields competitive results, suggesting strong inherent classification ability without fine-tuning. While Llama3 independently achieves surprisingly strong performance on datasets such as Children and History, the contextual learning strategy introduced by **Fetan** further enhances classification accuracy, surpassing the nearest baseline, P2TAG, and achieving the best overall performance.

Compared to traditional methods such as GCN or GAT, which require full retraining for new tasks and rely heavily on structural information, **Fetan** offers a plug-and-play solution with zero retraining overhead. This makes it highly suitable for cold-start scenarios and rapidly evolving domains. By incorporating task-specific context, **Fetan** boosts accuracy, improves generalization, and significantly reduces training cost, showcasing the potential of few-shot classification with state-of-the-art LLMs.

These results highlight three key advantages of **Fetan**: (1) strong performance even in extremely few-shot settings, (2) excellent generalization across domains and task difficulties, and (3) practical deployment potential due to zero

Table 1. Few-shot classification accuracy (%) on the four sub-datasets of the CS-TAG benchmark, with the best performance highlighted in bold.

Dataset	Children								
Setting	2-way			3-way			4-way		
	1-shot	3-shot	5-shot	1-shot	3-shot	5-shot	1-shot	3-shot	5-shot
GPN	59.7±2.3	68.8±1.2	72.6±1.2	46.0±1.7	54.7±0.4	60.1±1.1	41.3±1.7	49.2±1.6	53.3±1.2
G-Meta	59.0±2.0	67.2±0.9	69.5±1.7	46.2±2.9	54.0±2.3	57.7±1.4	40.8±2.3	48.7±1.7	51.7±1.3
P2TAG	81.6±1.3	86.9±0.9	88.7±1.2	66.5±1.4	77.9±1.0	80.8±1.1	61.6±1.3	72.2±1.8	75.5±1.2
Llama2	62.3±1.4 (0-shot)			55.6±3.2 (0-shot)			42.0±2.0 (0-shot)		
Llama3	86.4±2.2 (0-shot)			78.0±3.1 (0-shot)			71.6±1.8 (0-shot)		
Fetan-l2	80.5±1.5	85.9±1.0	86.7±0.4	74.3±2.2	76.5±1.9	80.3±1.2	61.2±1.6	67.1±2.0	72.5±1.0
Fetan-l3	**88.3±1.6**	**89.9±1.5**	**90.8±0.4**	**85.8±1.7**	**88.0±1.4**	**89.5±1.0**	**74.5±1.9**	**76.2±1.5**	**78.9±1.1**
Dataset	Computers								
Setting	2-way			3-way			4-way		
	1-shot	3-shot	5-shot	1-shot	3-shot	5-shot	1-shot	3-shot	5-shot
GPN	70.6±2.3	76.0±2.3	79.5±2.3	63.3±1.4	71.7±1.6	70.4±1.7	55.3±2.5	65.8±1.6	67.1±0.9
G-Meta	71.3±2.3	76.7±2.3	80.2±2.3	64.1±1.5	71.5±2.1	71.1±2.5	56.3±1.9	67.7±1.5	69.0±1.0
P2TAG	87.3±1.1	92.8±0.5	94.2±0.4	81.4±1.2	88.6±1.1	89.6±0.4	73.7±1.3	83.6±0.7	86.6±0.8
Llama2	57.3±2.7 (0-shot)			45.7±4.7 (0-shot)			42.7±2.5 (0-shot)		
Llama3	87.2±2.4 (0-shot)			81.3±2.3 (0-shot)			75.9±2.3 (0-shot)		
Fetan-l2	75.2±2.5	82.7±1.3	85.2±1.4	70.7±3.8	76.0±1.5	79.3±1.4	68.2±1.7	74.6±1.3	77.8±0.7
Fetan-l3	**89.5±1.5**	**93.3±1.2**	**94.5±0.6**	**85.5±2.0**	**89.6±1.7**	**90.4±1.4**	**81.5±1.3**	**86.0±1.0**	**88.2±1.5**
Dataset	History								
Setting	2-way			3-way			4-way		
	1-shot	3-shot	5-shot	1-shot	3-shot	5-shot	1-shot	3-shot	5-shot
GPN	53.7±1.6	55.2±1.3	56.3±1.2	36.9±1.6	38.4±0.7	40.6±0.8	30.4±0.6	32.6±0.7	33.4±0.8
G-Meta	55.0±1.5	56.5±1.8	57.8±0.6	37.5±1.5	40.4±1.3	41.1±0.7	31.6±1.2	33.0±1.3	34.8±1.1
P2TAG	66.9±2.6	77.1±1.5	80.5±1.5	52.9±0.8	64.4±1.0	68.5±1.6	44.6±0.7	56.9±1.7	61.7±1.6
Llama2	68.8±1.5 (0-shot)			54.6±0.8 (0-shot)			43.7±3.9 (0-shot)		
Llama3	89.0±2.1 (0-shot)			76.4±3.4 (0-shot)			67.8±1.0 (0-shot)		
Fetan-l2	79.1±1.2	82.6±1.1	84.8±0.6	67.0±1.6	71.0±1.1	75.6±0.4	57.4±1.3	59.2±0.8	63.9±0.5
Fetan-l3	**90.3±1.7**	**91.7±1.0**	**92.0±0.5**	**81.5±2.7**	**84.3±1.6**	**85.0±1.4**	**69.8±1.7**	**70.0±1.0**	**73.7±0.6**
Dataset	Photo								
Setting	2-way			3-way			4-way		
	1-shot	3-shot	5-shot	1-shot	3-shot	5-shot	1-shot	3-shot	5-shot
GPN	78.6±2.8	82.2±0.7	84.5±1.1	68.2±2.1	74.7±1.7	76.0±1.1	63.4±2.3	71.8±1.6	73.9±1.6
G-Meta	72.6±2.6	77.6±1.1	77.6±1.2	77.6±1.2	69.6±1.1	72.4±1.0	57.3±1.9	68.1±1.8	70.0±1.5
P2TAG	87.2±0.9	93.1±0.5	94.2±1.1	78.9±2.1	88.4±1.4	89.8±0.9	74.4±0.5	84.1±1.0	86.7±0.3
Llama2	55.8±2.3 (0-shot)			50.8±2.4 (0-shot)			44.5±3.9 (0-shot)		
Llama3	84.7±2.0 (0-shot)			82.4±1.4 (0-shot)			71.2±1.5 (0-shot)		
Fetan-l2	81.0±1.6	86.2±1.7	88.8±0.8	74.4±2.1	78.5±0.8	79.2±0.9	66.7±3.0	73.9±1.9	76.0±1.4
Fetan-l3	**89.7±1.2**	**94.5±1.3**	**94.9±1.0**	**87.6±1.7**	**89.9±1.0**	**90.9±1.3**	**81.2±1.6**	**86.6±2.0**	**88.4±0.6**

retraining. The consistent outperformance over both traditional graph learners and LLM baselines confirms the efficacy of integrating graph structure and statistics via prompt-driven few-shot learning.

5.3 Ablation Study

Impact of Prompt Components. To evaluate the contribution of individual components in the prompt design, we perform ablation experiments using several variants of Fetan-l3 on a 3-way 3-shot classification task from the *Children* dataset. Each variant disables one or more specific components from the original Fetan-l3 prompt. The ablated components include:

- **w/o** $\mathcal{W}_I$: Replacing the label keyword set $\mathcal{W}_I$ with plain label names.
- **w/o** $\mathcal{N}_f(v_q)$: Removing few-shot graph neighbours.
- **w/o** $\mathcal{N}_s(v_q)$: Removing source graph neighbours.
- **w/o** $\mathcal{N}_m(v_q)$: Removing motif-based neighbours.
- **w/o** $\mathcal{L}_q$: Removing label statistics.
- **w/o all neighbours**: Removing all above three kinds of neighbours, and only label keywords and statistics are retained.
- **Text-only** (Llama3): Plain attribute text without any graph-based or statistical augmentation.

As shown in Fig. 3, all prompt components contribute positively to the final performance. The full version of Fetan-l3 achieves the highest accuracy (88.0%), while the text-only baseline drops to 78.0%, demonstrating that all components work together to significantly improve performance.

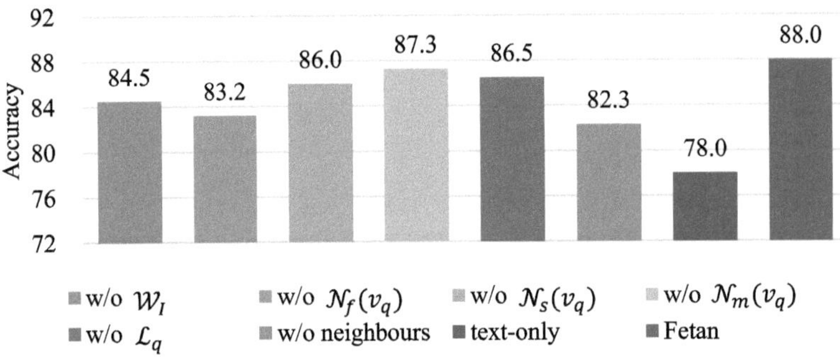

Fig. 3. Impact of prompt components.

Among individual components, the removal of few-shot neighbours $\mathcal{N}_f(v_q)$ causes the most significant drop (to 83.2%), highlighting the central role of contextual example selection. Similarly, removing label keywords $\mathcal{W}_I$ reduces performance to 84.5%, showing the effectiveness of prototype-free label representation.

In contrast, the removal of source-graph neighbours $\mathcal{N}_s(v_q)$ and motif-based neighbours $\mathcal{N}_m(v_q)$ causes smaller degradations (to 86.0% and 87.3%, respectively), suggesting they provide complementary but less dominant benefits. Notably, eliminating label statistics $\mathcal{L}_q$ only slightly impacts performance (86.5%), indicating that statistical context plays a supportive role.

The most severe drop after removing all neighbour sets (accuracy 82.3%) demonstrates that the combination of different types of structural context yields stronger representation than any single component alone.

Overall, this ablation confirms that all the components work in a synergistic manner to enhance few-shot graph classification under Fetan.

5.4 Hyperparameter Analysis

Impact of Keyword Number on Classification Performance. We explore how the number of extracted keywords n_k affects performance on a 3-way 3-shot classification task using Fetan-l3 on the *Computers* dataset. Accuracy is measured as n_k varies from 1 to 50. As shown in Fig. 4, performance improves rapidly with more keywords, peaking at $n_k = 19$ (89.6%), after which it declines slightly, suggesting that excessive keywords may introduce noise.

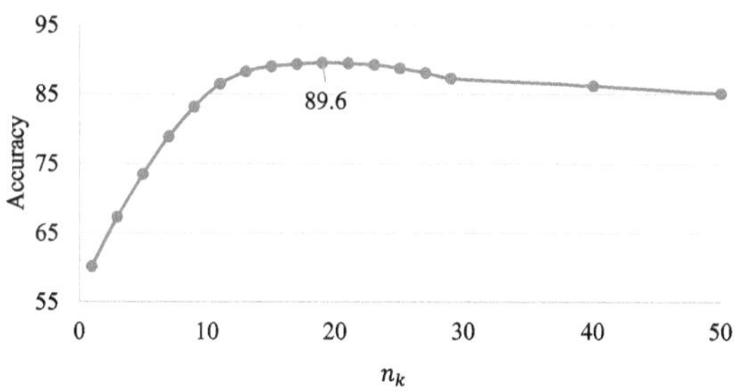

Fig. 4. Accuracy vs. number of keywords n_k.

5.5 Generalization to Other LLMs

Although Fetan is primarily evaluated using Llama2-Chat and Llama3-Instruct, its design is inherently model-agnostic and compatible with a broad range of LLMs. As our method leverages prompt-based inference without requiring fine-tuning or modification of the base model, it can be readily applied to other LLMs across different architectures.

In preliminary trials, we tested Fetan with ChatGLM3 [10] and MiniMax-M1-80k [28], both of which yielded promising results, demonstrating the framework's adaptability. A more comprehensive evaluation across a wider variety of LLMs—including multilingual and instruction-tuned models—will be explored as part of our future work.

6 Conclusion

We propose Fetan, a novel method for few-shot node classification on text-attributed graphs, leveraging in-context learning with large language models.

By constructing prompts that integrate textual, structural, and relational information, Fetan enables accurate classification under sparse labeling conditions. Experimental results show that Fetan consistently outperforms existing baselines, achieving notable improvements in classification accuracy.

Acknowledgments. This study was funded by the National Natural Science Foundation of China (grant number 62272093, 62137001, and 62461146205).

Disclosure of Interests. The authors have no competing interests to declare that are relevant to the content of this article.

References

1. AI@Meta: Llama 3 model card (2024). https://github.com/meta-llama/llama3/blob/main/MODEL_CARD.md
2. Benson, A.R., Gleich, D.F., Leskovec, J.: Higher-order organization of complex networks. Science **353**(6295), 163–166 (2016). https://doi.org/10.1126/science.aad9029. https://www.science.org/doi/abs/10.1126/science.aad9029
3. Chen, J., et al.: Zero-shot and few-shot learning with knowledge graphs: a comprehensive survey. Proc. IEEE **111**(6), 653–685 (2023)
4. Cheng, H., Zhou, J.T., Tay, W.P., Wen, B.: Graph neural networks with triple attention for few-shot learning. IEEE Trans. Multimedia **25**, 8225–8239 (2023)
5. Chung, H.W., et al.: Scaling instruction-finetuned language models. JMLR **25**(70), 1–53 (2024)
6. Devlin, J., Chang, M.W., Lee, K., Toutanova, K.: BERT: pre-training of deep bidirectional transformers for language understanding. In: NAACL (2019)
7. Ding, K., Wang, J., Li, J., Shu, K., Liu, C., Liu, H.: Graph prototypical networks for few-shot learning on attributed networks. In: CIKM, pp. 295–304 (2020)
8. Fifty, C., Leskovec, J., Thrun, S.: In-context learning for few-shot molecular property prediction. CoRR arxiv:2310.08863 (2023)
9. Gharoun, H., Momenifar, F., Chen, F., Gandomi, A.H.: Meta-learning approaches for few-shot learning: a survey of recent advances. ACM Comput. Surv. **56**(12), 1–41 (2024)
10. GLM, T., et al.: Chatglm: a family of large language models from glm-130b to glm-4 all tools (2024)
11. Gong, W., et al.: Cgnet: few-shot learning for intracranial hemorrhage segmentation. Comput. Medical Imaging Graph. **121**, 102505 (2025)
12. Grattafiori, A., et al.: The llama 3 herd of models. arXiv preprint arXiv:2407.21783 (2024)
13. He, P., Gao, J., Chen, W.: Debertav3: improving deberta using electra-style pre-training with gradient-disentangled embedding sharing (2021)
14. He, P., Liu, X., Gao, J., Chen, W.: Deberta: decoding-enhanced bert with disentangled attention. In: ICLR (2021)
15. Huang, K., Zitnik, M.: Graph meta learning via local subgraphs. In: NeurIPS 2020 (2020)
16. Huang, Q., et al.: PRODIGY: enabling in-context learning over graphs. In: NeurIPS (2023)
17. Ju, W., et al.: A survey of data-efficient graph learning. In: IJCAI, pp. 8104–8113 (2024)

18. Kirkpatrick, J., et al.: Overcoming catastrophic forgetting in neural networks. Proc. Natl. Acad. Sci. **114**(13), 3521–3526 (2017)
19. Lang, S., et al.: Aifs-ecmwf's data-driven forecasting system. arXiv preprint arXiv:2406.01465 (2024)
20. Lewis, M., et al.: Bart: denoising sequence-to-sequence pre-training for natural language generation, translation, and comprehension. In: ACL (2019)
21. Li, Y., Moghadam, P., Peng, C., Ye, N., Koniusz, P.: Inductive graph few-shot class incremental learning. In: WSDM, pp. 466–474 (2025)
22. Liu, Y., et al.: Roberta: a robustly optimized bert pretraining approach (2019). arxiv:1907.11692
23. Liu, Y., et al.: A simple but effective approach for unsupervised few-shot graph classification. In: WWW, pp. 4249–4259 (2024)
24. Liu, Y., Ding, S., Zhou, S., Fan, W., Tan, Q.: Moleculargpt: open large language model (llm) for few-shot molecular property prediction. arXiv preprint arXiv:2406.12950 (2024)
25. Lu, B., Gan, X., Yang, L., Zhang, W., Fu, L., Wang, X.: Geometer: graph few-shot class-incremental learning via prototype representation. In: SIGKDD, pp. 1152–1161 (2022)
26. Lu, G., Ju, X., Chen, X., Pei, W., Cai, Z.: GRACE: empowering llm-based software vulnerability detection with graph structure and in-context learning. J. Syst. Softw. **212**, 112031 (2024)
27. Milo, R., Shen-Orr, S., Itzkovitz, S., Kashtan, N., Chklovskii, D., Alon, U.: Network motifs: simple building blocks of complex networks. Science **298**(5594), 824–827 (2002). https://doi.org/10.1126/science.298.5594.824
28. MiniMax: Minimax-m1: Scaling test-time compute efficiently with lightning attention (2025). https://arxiv.org/abs/2506.13585
29. Mosbach, M., Pimentel, T., Ravfogel, S., Klakow, D., Elazar, Y.: Few-shot fine-tuning vs. in-context learning: a fair comparison and evaluation. In: ACL, pp. 12284–12314 (2023)
30. Pan, F., Wu, X., Li, Z., Luu, A.T.: Are LLMs good zero-shot fallacy classifiers? In: EMNLP, pp. 14338–14364 (2024)
31. Paszke, A.: Pytorch: an imperative style, high-performance deep learning library. arXiv preprint arXiv:1912.01703 (2019)
32. Rakaraddi, A., Siew-Kei, L., Pratama, M., de Carvalho, M.V.: Graph mining under data scarcity. IJCNN 1–7 (2024)
33. Snell, J., Swersky, K., Zemel, R.S.: Prototypical networks for few-shot learning. In: NeurIPS, pp. 4077–4087 (2017)
34. Song, Y., Wang, T., Cai, P., Mondal, S.K., Sahoo, J.P.: A comprehensive survey of few-shot learning: evolution, applications, challenges, and opportunities. ACM Comput. Surv. **55**(13s), 1–40 (2023)
35. Touvron, H., et al.: Llama 2: open foundation and fine-tuned chat models. arXiv preprint arXiv:2307.09288 (2023)
36. Wang, D., Zuo, Y., Li, F., Wu, J.: Llms as zero-shot graph learners: alignment of gnn representations with llm token embeddings. In: NeurIPS, vol. 37, pp. 5950–5973 (2024)
37. Wei, Y., Huang, Q., Zhang, Y., Kwok, J.T.: KICGPT: large language model with knowledge in context for knowledge graph completion. In: EMNLP, pp. 8667–8683 (2023)
38. Wolf, T., et al.: Transformers: state-of-the-art natural language processing. In: EMNLP, pp. 38–45 (2020)

39. Xu, J., Wu, Z., Lin, M., Zhang, X., Wang, S.: Llm and gnn are complementary: distilling llm for multimodal graph learning. arXiv preprint arXiv:2406.01032 (2024)
40. Yan, H., et al.: A comprehensive study on text-attributed graphs: benchmarking and rethinking. In: NeurIPS, vol. 36, pp. 17238–17264 (2023)
41. Yang, J., Dong, Y., Li, G.: An adaptive dual-channel multi-modal graph neural network for few-shot learning. Knowl. Based Syst. **310**, 112845 (2025)
42. Yao, B., et al.: More samples or more prompts? Exploring effective few-shot in-context learning for llms with in-context sampling. In: NAACL, pp. 1772–1790 (2024)
43. Ying, C., et al.: Do transformers really perform bad for graph representation? CoRR arxiv:2106.05234 (2021)
44. Yu, J., Ren, Y., Gong, C., Tan, J., Li, X., Zhang, X.: Leveraging large language models for node generation in few-shot learning on text-attributed graphs. In: AAAI, vol. 39, pp. 13087–13095 (2025)
45. Yu, M., Zhang, Y., Sun, J., Huang, M., Zhang, T., Yu, G.: Hg-scc: a subgraph-aware convolutional few-shot classification method on heterogeneous graphs. IEEE Trans. Knowl. Data Eng. **37**(4), 1871–1884 (2025)
46. Zhang, Y., Zhou, X., Wang, N., Tang, J., Xuan, T.: Doun-gnn: double nodes graph neural network for few-shot learning. Neurocomputing **617**, 128970 (2025)
47. Zhao, H., et al.: Pre-training and prompting for few-shot node classification on text-attributed graphs. In: KDD, pp. 4467–4478 (2024)
48. Zhu, Y., et al.: Graphclip: enhancing transferability in graph foundation models for text-attributed graphs. In: WWW, pp. 2183–2197 (2025)

Graph Contrastive Anomaly Detection Based on Beta Wavelet Multi-GNNs

Yifan Song[1], Yu Yang[2], Kangzheng Liu[1], and Feng Zhao[1(✉)]

[1] School of Computer Science and Technology, Huazhong University of Science and Technology, Hubei 430074, China
{songyf,frankLuis,zhaof}@hust.edu.cn

[2] Centre for Learning, Teaching and Technology (LTTC), The Education University of Hong Kong, Hong Kong SAR, China
yangyy@eduhk.hk

Abstract. Graph anomaly detection (GAD) serves to distinct unusual patterns markedly differ from the norm. Recently, the integration of graph neural networks (GNNs) and contrastive learning for GAD has attracted significant attention. Graph contrastive anomaly detection (GCAD) techniques have primarily emphasized enhancing detection capabilities by integrating multiscale comparison modules. However, as the general backbone of GCAD methods, GNNs derive node representations by smoothing signals from neighboring nodes, which may lead to indistinguishable representations for anomalous nodes. Furthermore, detection outcomes often lack stability due to the inherent randomness of the GCAD pipeline. In our study, we tackle these challenges by proposing a novel approach BWMGNN-GCAD, termed Beta Wavelet Kernel GNN (BWGNN), coupled with a Multi-GNN module. BWGNN mitigates the low-pass issue inherent in traditional GNNs, while employing multiple GNNs enhances result stability. Experiments performed on three popular datasets demonstrate that our method outperforms current state-of-the-art techniques. Ablation studies further confirm that the BWMGNN-GCAD methodology, leveraging multiple GNN modules, significantly boosts detection efficacy. Our research underscores the potential efficacy of employing multiple neural networks and graph augmentation techniques in anomaly detection tasks.

Keywords: Contrastive learning · graph augmentation · beta wavelet kernel graph neural network · multi-GNN

1 Introduction

Graph anomaly detection (GAD) refers to find objects within a graph that exhibit significant deviations from the majority of other objects (edges, subgraphs, or nodes). GAD plays an important role in discerning aberrant patterns and mitigating potential risks, thus garnering widespread interest across various industries such as network intrusion [16,18,28], money laundering [5,15,20],

J. Li et al. (Eds.): APWeb-WAIM 2025, LNCS 16115, pp. 533–548, 2026.
https://doi.org/10.1007/978-981-95-5719-6_34

and financial fraud detection [23,30]. Earlier, shallow learning techniques like ANOMOLOUS [29] and Radar [14] leveraged residual analysis methodologies, yielding some advancements in anomaly detection. However, GAD faces significant hurdles when dealing with the complexities of nonlinear, high-dimensional data and intricate interaction patterns inherent. While the emergence of the graph neural networks (GNNs) has provided a potent tool for GAD, anomaly detection remains a vital task primarily due to the scarcity and complexity of anomalous instances, which are often sparse and challenging to label accurately. [1,17,37]. To address the challenge, contrastive learning techniques, with their nature that suitable for learning under lack of labels, have been integrated into GNN-based models for GAD. Notably, existing methodologies in graph contrastive anomaly detection (GCAD), leverage graph enhancement and multiscale comparison modules to refine model performance and improve anomaly detection accuracy. Representative methods are ANEMONE [11], SL-GAD [38], and GRADATE [4], etc. These developments reflect continuous improvements aimed at strengthening the reliability and effectiveness of GAD techniques for practice.

However, aforementioned GCAD approaches primarily augment the model's representation by incorporating various multiscale comparisons or graph enhancement strategies without adequately addressing the limitations of the underlying backbone. Most graph neural networks (GNNs) are constrained to utilizing low-pass filters, which accentuate low-frequency signals (resulting in smoother signals) while dampening high-frequency signals (resulting in more oscillatory signals), as illustrated in Fig. 1. While effective in graphs adhering to the homophily assumption, where nodes with similar features tend to connect, GNNs encounter challenges in graphs containing anomalies. In these graphs, normal nodes usually display similar characteristics to their neighboring nodes (low-frequency patterns), whereas anomalies tend to show distinct features compared to their neighbors (high-frequency patterns). This discrepancy undermines the efficacy of GNNs, as their low-pass property mismatches the characteristics of graphs containing anomalies. GNNs inadvertently blur the distinction between representations of normal and anomalous nodes by filtering out high-frequency signals, potentially leading to suboptimal performance in GAD. In addition, the randomness of graph augmentation methods and random walk algorithm could lead to unstable calculation results of GCAD, thus affect the credibility of the method. Meanwhile, the impact of multi-GNN module on GCAD has not been widely studied.

To address these issues, this paper conbined GCAD with beta wavelet kernel, thus, a beta wavelet kernel multi-GNN module-based GCAD method (BWMGNN-GCAD) is proposed to detect node anomalies in attributed graphs. For the problem that traditional GNNs are limited to low-pass filters, different from previous methods, in BWMGNN-GCAD, the original GNN model is replaced with the beta wavelet kernel graph neural network (BWGNN) model. The BWGNN utilizes beta kernel wavelets to generate bandpass filters with good locality in both spectral and spatial domains; therefore, it can effectively capture abnormal information from the graph [33]. To enhance the reliability

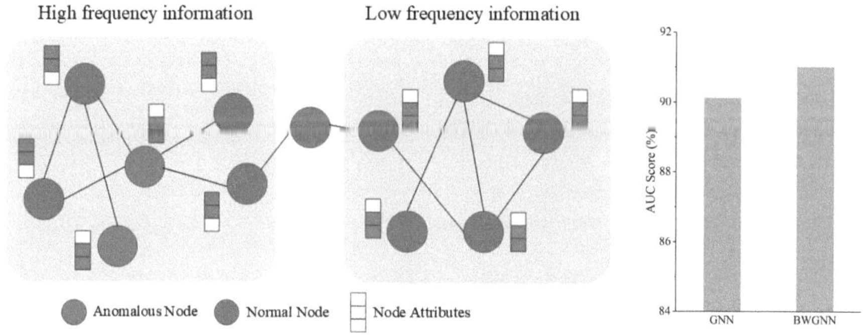

Fig. 1. The nature of GNN leads to sub-optimal performance. (a) An illustration of graphs in GAD. Anomalies typically exhibit distinct features from their neighbors, characterized by high-frequency information. Conversely, normal nodes tend to share similar attributes with their neighboring normal nodes, reflecting low-frequency information. (b) The detection performance of traditional GNN and BWGNN on the Cora dataset.

of the final outcomes, drawing on the advantages of ensemble learning, a multi-GNNs module is introduced to minimize detection errors and boost overall model effectiveness. The proposed approach achieves relatively high evaluation scores in experiments based on three datasets. An ablation study of the multi-GNN modules verified their effectiveness. Specifically, our contributions are as follows:

- To alleviate the limitations that GNNs could produce confused representations as a low-pass filter for GAD, the contrastive learning is combined with a BWGNN backbone to form a novel method named BWMGNN-GCAD.
- To improve the model performance and obtain stable experimental results, multi-GNN modules are used.
- Experiments on widely-used datasets are performed to validate the superior performance of BWMGNN-GCAD.

The paper's framework consists of five main sections. Section 2 provides an in-depth analysis of existing research in graph anomaly detection (GAD), setting the stage for the proposed approach. Section 3 details the key elements of our method and explains the anomaly detection process. Section 4 showcases experimental outcomes on various attributed graph datasets, highlighting the efficacy of our proposed method. Finally, Sect. 5 provides a summary of the key findings and suggests potential future research directions in graph anomaly detection.

2 Related Works

2.1 Methods Based on Shallow Learning Methods and GNNs

For anomaly detection, Radar [14] proposed a learning framework based on residual analysis to characterize the difference between attribute information and network information and verify their consistency. In addition, ANOMALOUS [29] fused a novel matrix decomposition approach and residual analysis with anomaly detection, thus, the resulting approach display excellent robustness for noisy features. However, these methods are based on anomaly detection with tabular data and are not relevant for graph structures. Therefore, they usually yield relatively inferior metrics in GAD. Similar to GNN classification methodologies [19,33,36], these methods are also suitable for GAD. They could typically employ a GNN Mapping function to derive node representations, which could be based on models such as GCN [12], GAT [34], GraphSAGE [8], or others. Tang et al. [33] conducted spectral analysis and devised spectral and spatial local bandpass filters to effectively tackle anomaly detection tasks utilizing these steps. Similarly, Zhang et al. [36] proposed a methodology wherein they interconnected intermediate representations and introduced specialized modules for graph inconsistency and imbalanced characteristics in anomaly detection scenarios.

2.2 Methods Based on Reconstruction Error

The work of Song et al. [32] has demonstrated that normal nodes tend to exhibit greater coherence with their neighboring nodes compared to nodes further away in the graph. Consequently, reconstructing normal nodes tends to be less complex compared to reconstructing anomalous nodes [21,22]. Leveraging reconstruction error, the original graphs can be utilized to generate new graphs, facilitating the identification of abnormal nodes based on their similarity [26]. To address issues caused by sparse network structures and a lack of labeled data, DOMINANT [3] was introduced as a classic reconstruction algorithm, formalizing the reconstruction process as described earlier. However, Fan et al. [7] highlighted that earlier approaches fail to account for the complex interactions between graph structures and node attributes. To address this, AnomalyDAE integrates attention mechanisms to evaluate the importance of neighboring nodes and utilizes dual autoencoders to improve the representation of cross-modal data.

2.3 Methods Based on Contrastive Learning

The conventional GCAD model CoLA [25] performs graph comparisons of nodes at a single scale, and it operates as described above. Notably, Jin et al. [11] modeled only instance pairs at a single scale, thereby limiting the capturing of complex anomaly patterns. Duan et al. [4] propose a new multi-scale contrastive learning approach, incorporating subgraph-subgraph contrast to enhance the framework, aiming to enhance GAD performance by incorporating subgraph comparison information. By leveraging graph augmentation techniques and conducting comprehensive experiments, the proposed method outperforms existing state-of-the-art techniques, proving its effectiveness in tackling anomaly detection challenges.

3 Methodology

This section begins by defining the notations employed throughout the paper, followed by an explanation of the research problem under investigation. In addition, the proposed method is described in detail, spanning graph augmentation, the BWGNN backbone and the final BWMGNN-GCAD method. The complete workflow is presented in Fig. 2, offering a straight visualization of the methodological approach used in this research.

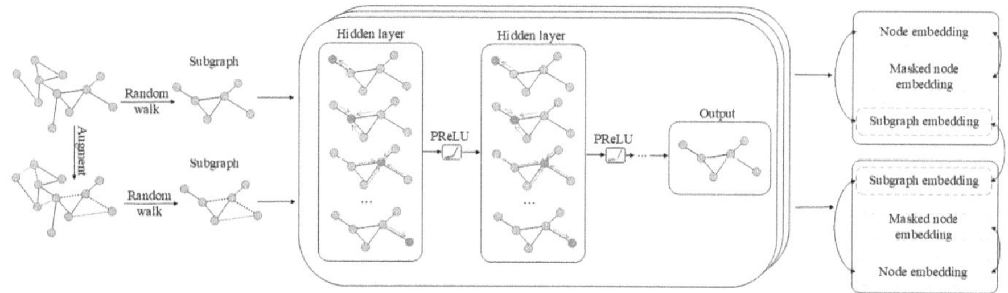

Fig. 2. Overview of BWMGNN-GCAD

3.1 Graph Augmentation

To perform graph contrastive learning, the original graph must first undergo augmentation for subsequent operations. Feature masking is a widely-used strategy in graph-based anomaly detection, aimed at minimizing the effects of irrelevant or noisy features. By selectively masking specific node or edge attributes, the model can focus on the most essential information for detecting anomalies. This strategy improves the robustness and effectiveness of anomaly detection algorithms by eliminating less significant features.

Additionally, edge removal is a preprocessing step aimed at simplifying the graph structure by selectively removing edges based on certain criteria. This can involve removing edges with low weights, edges connecting nodes with different attributes, or edges that do not conform to specific patterns or constraints. Edge removal helps in reducing noise and complexity in the graph, making it easier for anomaly detection algorithms to identify meaningful patterns and anomalies. In line with Jin et al. [11], we not only eliminate edges from the adjacency matrix but also simultaneously introduce an equal number of new edges.

3.2 BWGNN Backbone

To address the problem of smoothing abnormal features by using the original GNN backbone, we integrate graph contrastive anomaly detetion, with the beta wavelet graph neural network that delicately extracts graph data features using its unique frequency analysis capability [33].

Beta Graph Wavelet. In computer vision applications, the beta distribution is typically used as a wavelet basis [13], but it has not yet been used to mine graphical data [6,10]. In this paper, the beta distribution is chosen to establish the kernel function of the graph, and the probability density function of the beta distribution is

$$\beta_{p,q}(w) = \begin{cases} \frac{1}{B(p+1,q+1)w^p(1-w)^q} & if w \in [0,1] \\ 0 & otherwise \end{cases} \tag{1}$$

Given that the eigenvalues of the normalized graph Laplacian L lie in the range $[0,2]$, we define $\beta^*_{p,q} = \frac{1}{2}\beta_{p,q}(\frac{w}{2})$ to cover the entire spectral range of L. Additionally, the restrictions $p, q \in \mathbb{N}^+$ is imposed to ensure that $\beta^*(p,q)$ is a polynomial, allowing for efficient computation. Consequently, the beta wavelet transform $W_{p,q}$ can be expressed as:

$$W_{p,q} = U\beta^*_{p,q}(\Gamma)UT = \beta^*_{p,q}(L) = \frac{(\frac{L}{2})^p(I-\frac{L}{2})^q}{2B(p+1,q+1)} \tag{2}$$

Given that $p+q=C$ remains constant, the beta wavelet transform W is structured from a collection of $C+1$ wavelets of equivalent order. Thus, the beta wavelet kernel $W = (W_{0,C}, W_{1,C-1}, ..., W_{C,0})$ is constructed.

Beta Wavelet Graph Neural Network. Unlike traditional GNN models that stack multiple layers in a cascading manner [12], the BWGNN employs distinct wavelet kernels in parallel and aggregates the resultant filtering outcomes. The propagation process utilized in the BWGNN unfolds as follows:

$$\begin{aligned} Z_i &= W_{i,C-i}(\mathrm{MLP}(X)) \\ H &= \mathrm{AGG}([Z_0, Z_1, ..., Z_C]) \end{aligned} \tag{3}$$

where, $\mathrm{MLP}(\cdot)$ denotes a multilayer perceptron, $\mathrm{AGG}(\cdot)$ represents a basic aggregation function like summation or concatenation, and $W_{i,C-i}$ signifies the wavelet kernel utilized in this study. H is then processed through another MLP, culminating in the computation of the anomaly probability p_i via a sigmoid function. The BWGNN is optimized using a weighted cross-entropy loss function, which facilitates efficient learning for anomaly detection tasks.

The BWGNN is optimized using a weighted cross-entropy loss function, which facilitates efficient learning for anomaly detection tasks. In addition, the complexity of BWGNN is $O(C|E|)$, where $C = p+q$, E refers to the number of edges, as $\beta^*_{p,q}(L)$ is a polynomial function that can be computed recursively [2].

3.3 Multi-GNN Comparisons

In GCAD, multiscale comparisons can be abstracted into three types: node-node comparisons, subgraph-subgraph comparisons, the remaining one is node-subgraph comparisons. Each type of comparison focuses on different interaction modes. Based on the previous GCAD methods [4,11,25,38], G can be used to generate several views for node v_i, subgraph feature b_i, node feature C_i, and masked node feature $(C_i^m)_i$, respectively. Figure 2 demonstrates these views in detail, and the followings are three comparison views.

Node-Node Comparison This approach uses node features C_i and masked node features $(C_i^m)_i$ to compute similarity scores between nodes. A bilinear function is applied to compute the positive and negative similarity scores $y_i = Bilinear(C_i, (C_i^m)_i))$ and $\hat{y}_i = Bilinear(C_i, (C_j^m)_j)$, respectively. The loss function L_{nn} is then designed to maximize the agreement between similar node pairs and minimize it for dissimilar pairs. The L_{nn} is formalized as :

$$L_{nn} = \frac{1}{n} \cdot \sum_{i}^{n} \log y_i + \log(1 - \hat{y}_i) \tag{4}$$

Subgraph-Subgraph Comparison A new GNN mapping is introduced to extract subgraph views for each node. Positive and negative instance pairs are established using bilinear functions on subgraph representations. The loss function L_{ss} is formulated similarly to the node-node comparison, encouraging the model to maximize similarity for positive pairs and minimize it for negative pairs. The L_{ss} can be formalized as :

$$\begin{aligned} g_i &= Bilinear(b_i, \hat{b_i}), \quad \hat{g}_i = Bilinear(b_i, \hat{b_j}) \\ L_{ss} &= \frac{1}{n} \cdot \sum_{i}^{n} \log g_i + \log(1 - \hat{g}_i) \end{aligned} \tag{5}$$

where b_i, $\hat{b_i}$ form the positive instance pairs, while b_i , $\hat{b_j}$ are negative instance pairs.

Node-Subgraph Comparison Two variations are introduced for node-subgraph comparisons. In the standard case, the node features C_i are compared with subgraph representations, while in the masked case, the masked node features $(C_i^m)_i$ are used. Bilinear functions compute the positive and negative similarity scores, with corresponding loss functions L_{ns} and L_{ns}' to optimize node-subgraph matching. The formulas are as follows:

$$\begin{aligned} h_i &= Bilinear(C_i, b_i), \quad \hat{h_i} = Bilinear(C_i, b_j) \\ L_{ns} &= \frac{1}{n} \cdot \sum_{i}^{n} \log h_i + \log(1 - \hat{h_i}) \\ h_i' &= Bilinear((C_i^m)_i, b_i), \quad \hat{h_i}' = Bilinear((C_i^m)_i, b_j) \\ L_{ns}' &= \frac{1}{n} \cdot \sum_{i}^{n} \log h_i' + \log(1 - \hat{h_i}') \end{aligned} \tag{6}$$

Together, these methods leverage both direct node features and graph-level subgraph representations to refine node and subgraph embeddings through contrastive learning.

Multi-GNN Modules. This module encodes augmented graphs through different channels, which actually means encoding graphs from different perspectives. This refers to feature extraction and entity pruning. First, it generates corresponding relational permissions based on several modes (self attention and cross graph attention), with each type of attention mechanism corresponding to a GNN channel, which shares parameters in graphs to achieve structural features transfer. Then, the graph structure is encoded and the embedding of each entity is optimized through its neighboring nodes, so that aligned seed pair information can propagate throughout the entire graph. Finally, by ensuring that the embedding of seed entity pairs is as identical as possible, several anomaly features will be embedded into the same space.

3.4 Inference Phase for BWMGNN-GCAD

Throughout the training process, the contrastive loss function is employed to optimize and update the entire network, ensuring effective learning. Subsequently, for the inference, the consistency scores is computed, and the positive and negative pairs for node v_i are represented as y_i and $\hat{y_i}$. For normal nodes, the predicted score for positive instance pairs y_i approaches 1, indicating high confidence in their classification as normal. Conversely, the score of negative pairs $\hat{y_i}$ approaches 0, reflecting the low likelihood of normal nodes being incorrectly classified as anomalies. On the other hand, for anomalous nodes, both y_i and $\hat{y_i}$ converge towards 0.5, indicating a balance between positive and negative pairs. Consequently, the final anomaly score can be calculated as $(\hat{y_i} - y_i)$. Following [38], we perform sampling T times to ensure stability and compute the mean and standard deviation. This process can be formalized as follows:

$$
\begin{aligned}
f_1(v_i) &= \frac{\sum_{r=1}^{T}(\hat{y_i}^{(r)} - y_i^{(r)})}{T} = \bar{x} \\
f_2(v_i) &= \sqrt{\sum_{r=1}^{T}((\hat{y_i}^{(r)} - y_i^{(r)}) - \bar{x})^2/T} = s \\
f(v_i) &= \bar{x} + s
\end{aligned} \tag{7}
$$

where, the anomaly score $f(v_i)$ for node v_i as a final outcome is determined as the sum of the mean $f_1(v_i)$ and standard deviation $f_1(v_i)$. To mitigate the influence of randomness, we introduce a hyperparameter T, which we set to 256 for stability and to mitigate computational costs. This parameter facilitates the aggregation of stable results, ensuring reliable inference outcomes.

4 Experiments

In this section, various experiments with BWMGNN-GCAD and empirical evidence supporting the superior performance of the proposed method are presented. To facilitate a comprehensive understanding of this approach, we establish four research questions (RQs) of significant value.

- RQ1: Is it possible for the proposed BWMGNN-GCAD to surpass existing methods in terms of performance?
- RQ2: Does the BWGNN backbone alleviate the problem that GNNs are low pass filters?
- RQ3: Could the multi-GNN modules used be capable of getting stable experiment results?
- RQ4: Is it possible for graph enhancement methods to function effectively?

4.1 Experimental Settings

Datasets. According to previous studies [9,35], we utilize three common used networks, Cora, Citeseer, and Pubmed [31]. As for the negative samples, abnormal nodes are established through disrupting the graph's structure and modifying node features, and the injection algorithm is based on that used in previous work [11,25]. Thus, the injected graph comprises nodes with structural and contextual anomalies. The statistical details can be found in Table 1, and the total number of anomalies for each dataset is shown in the last column.

Table 1. Key statistical details of the datasets

Datasets	Nodes	Edges	Attributes	Anomalies
Cora	2708	5429	1433	150
Citeseer	3327	4732	3703	150
Pubmed	19717	44338	500	600

Baselines. We compare the BWMGNN with classic shallow learning methods, the Radar method, and anomaly learning methods, considering their relative performance. Explicit and heterotopic methods are based on reconstruction errors, which are used to identify anomalies, and comparative methods such as CoLA, ANEMONE, SL-GAD, and GRADATE are considered.

To simplify the implementation of the Radar and ANEMONE methods, we adopt the PyGOD Python library [24], specifically designed for graph outlier detection. For the remaining algorithms, we replicate their functionality using open-source models. It's important to note that we maintain consistency by setting hyperparameters to identical values across all methods, ensuring a fair comparison in our experiments.

Evaluation Metrics. The range of scores that are considered abnormal in this article does not constitute a probability value between 0 and 1. Hence, it is not appropriate to establish a threshold to distinguish normal from abnormal nodes. Thus, the commonly used measures of accuracy, precision, and recall rate are not considered in this study. The Area Under the Curve (AUC) is a widely used metric for evaluating classification models, providing a quantitative measure of the relationship between FPR and TPR [27]. It effectively summarizes the performance of a model across different classification thresholds. The formula for AUC is given by:

$$AUC = \frac{\Sigma(p_i, n_j)_{pi>nj}}{P \times N} \tag{8}$$

Parameter Setting. For the BWMGNN-GCAD method across all datasets, the number of training epochs and learning rate are uniformly set to 100 and 0.001, respectively. Additionally, we fix the hidden dimension and batch size at 64 and 300, respectively. During the reasoning process, we conduct sampling over 256 rounds and set the size of the sampled subgraph to 4, as suggested by prior research [11,25]. Moreover, we set the balance factor of the model to (0.3, 0.7) to ensure optimal performance.

4.2 Experimental Results and Discussion

Comparison with Baseline Methods. To address RQ1, we conducted a comparative analysis of our experimental results with several baseline methods, including CoLA, ANEMONE, and GRADATE. While these methods share similarities in their utilization of contrast loss, it's essential to note that the implementation details may vary. To ensure a fair comparison, we maintained consistency in hyperparameters such as the number of epochs, learning rate, and balance factor across all methods. In the graph enhancement module of the BWMGNN-GCAD method, we employed a combination of feature masking and edge removal, which consistently demonstrated stable performance across most cases. The experimental findings, as presented in Table 2, indicate that the performance of the compared learning methods consistently surpasses that of shallow learning methods. Notably, for the Cora dataset, our proposed method achieved the optimal AUC value, indicative of its strong detection performance. However, slight discrepancies were observed for other datasets, likely attributable to variations in graph enhancement strategies and the randomness of seeds. Nevertheless, these minor deviations underscore the versatility and adaptability of our proposed model. Importantly, our model exhibits high flexibility, allowing for the derivation of different contrast losses solely by adjusting hyperparameters.

Ablation Study. To answer RQ2 and RQ3, we conducted several ablation experiments with three datasets. The symbol w/o represents the method without the corresponding component. Specifically, Ours means the proposed

Table 2. Comparing BWGNN-GCAD with baseline methods (AUC score)

Models	Cora	Citeseer	Pubmed
Radar [14]	0.6481	0.6229	0.5450
ANOMALOUS [29]	0.6784	0.6641	0.5412
DOMINANT [3]	0.8102	0.8314	0.8053
AnomalyDAE [7]	0.7622	0.7214	0.7882
CoLA [25]	0.8914	0.9062	0.9514
ANEMONE [11]	0.9083	0.9181	**0.9540**
GRADATE [4]	0.9012	**0.9233**	0.9482
BWMGNN-GCAD (ours)	**0.9140**	0.9040	0.9381

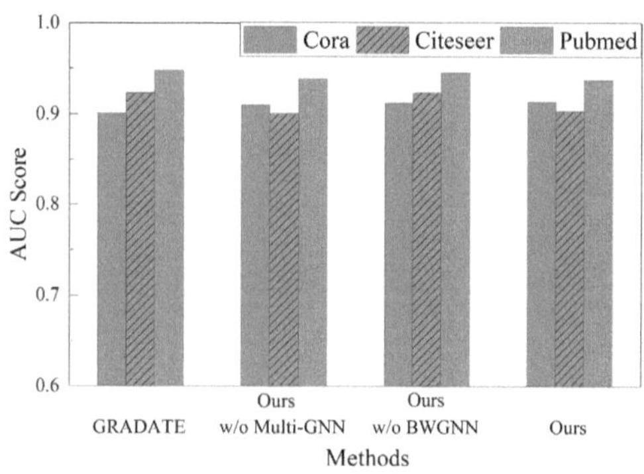

Fig. 3. Ablation study of BWMGNN-GCAD

BWMGNN-GCAD, w/o BWGNN represents the method in which the BWGNN backbone is replaced with a vanilla GNN, while w/o multi-GNN represents there are only one GNN module is used, not the multi-GNN framework. Figure 3 shows the ablation experiment results. In response to RQ2, where we compared our method with the baseline, we observed a relatively high performance, which underscores the effectiveness of the BWGNN backbone. This finding suggests that the BWGNN architecture contributes significantly to the overall performance improvement compared to traditional GNNs, highlighting its superiority in capturing intricate graph structures and anomaly patterns. For RQ3, our analysis indicates that the multi-GNN module plays a crucial role in maintaining the stability of the final results. The absence of this module led to inferior performance, which can be attributed to several factors. Firstly, the use of fewer training parameters in a single GNN model limits its capacity to capture complex patterns within the graph data. Additionally, the statistical instability inherent in a single GNN model contributes to fluctuations in the results, leading to inconsistent performance. These insights emphasize the importance of leveraging a multi-GNN framework for enhancing stability and robustness in graph anomaly detection tasks.

Table 3. Comparison of different graph augmentation methods (AUC score)

Graph augmentation Methods	GRADATE	BWMGNN-GCAD
Feature Masking	0.9091	0.9123
Edge Removal	0.9091	0.9182
Feature Masking+Edge Removal	0.9103	0.9165
Hot Kernel	0.7622	0.9204
Personalized PageRank	0.7538	0.9024

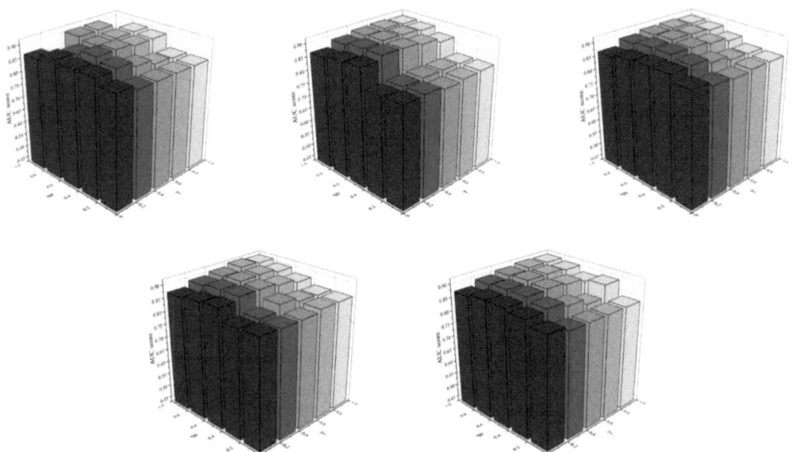

Fig. 4. Sensitivity analysis for the balance parameters α, β and γ on Cora dataset (a) $\alpha = 0.1$, (b) $\alpha = 0.3$, (c) $\alpha = 0.5$, (d) $\alpha = 0.7$, (e) $\alpha = 0.9$

Effects of Graph Augmentation Methods. To answer RQ4, we evaluated various methods including feature masking, edge removal, feature masking combined with edge removal, personalized PageRank diffusion, and hot kernel diffusion for image enhancement. We set the ratio of masking to removal at 0.2 to enhance modeling complexity. Our findings, as depicted in Table 3, indicate that the model's performance with feature masking combined with edge removal exhibited the most stable performance. This result suggests that integrating both feature masking and edge removal techniques can effectively mitigate noise and irrelevant information, leading to improved stability in the enhancement process. Additionally, personalized PageRank diffusion and hot kernel diffusion methods also showed promising results, albeit with slightly less stability compared to the combined approach. These observations underscore the importance of carefully selecting and combining preprocessing techniques to optimize graph augmentation performance.

Sensitivity of Parameters. The sensitivity analysis of the balance parameters α, β, and γ in the loss function was conducted to assess their collective influence on detection performance. As depicted in Fig. 4, the hyperparameters α, β and γ improve detection performance for Cora dataset. Specifically, fine-tuning α, β, and γ collectively can slightly contribute to enhanced detection accuracy. The interaction between these parameters is crucial, as changes in one parameter may necessitate adjustments to others to maintain optimal performance. In practice, setting α to 0.7, β to 0.9, and γ to 0.9 for Cora reflects a balanced configuration that maximizes detection efficacy. This highlights the importance of considering the interaction of these parameters to achieve optimal performance in graph anomaly detection tasks.

5 Discussion

The experimental results and analyses presented in this study demonstrate the effectiveness and versatility of the proposed BWMGNN-GCAD method for graph anomaly detection (GAD). In addressing RQ1, our comparative analysis with baseline methods such as CoLA, ANEMONE, and GRADATE revealed that the proposed method consistently outperforms shallow learning approaches, particularly on the Cora dataset, where it achieved the highest AUC value. This superior performance can be attributed to the integration of the BWGNN backbone and the multi-GNN framework, which collectively enhance the model's ability to capture complex graph structures and anomaly patterns. However, minor performance discrepancies observed across other datasets highlight the influence of graph enhancement strategies and random seed variations, underscoring the need for further refinement in these areas.

Regarding RQ2 and RQ3, ablation experiments confirmed the critical role of the BWGNN backbone and the multi-GNN module in improving detection performance and stability. The BWGNN backbone's ability to model intricate graph relationships and the multi-GNN module's capacity to reduce statistical instability were key factors in achieving robust results. These findings suggest that leveraging advanced architectures and ensemble techniques can significantly enhance the reliability of GAD methods.

For RQ4, our evaluation of graph enhancement techniques revealed that combining feature masking and edge removal yielded the most stable performance. This approach effectively mitigates noise and irrelevant information, further validating the importance of preprocessing in GAD tasks. Additionally, sensitivity analysis of the balance parameters α, β, and γ emphasized the need for careful parameter tuning to optimize detection performance.

6 Conclusion

This paper presents a new framework for graph anomaly detection (GAD), named the Beta Wavelet Kernel Multi-GNN Graph Contrastive Anomaly Detection method (BWMGNN-GCAD). The BWMGNN-GCAD approach integrates multi-contrast patterns and multi-GNN modules, unifying traditional GCAD techniques. In particular, the BWMGNN-GCAD variant utilizes a BWGNN backbone, with multiple GNN modules further improving detection performance. By conducting multiscale comparisons and evaluating the use of GNN modules, we show that employing multiple GNN modules provides greater benefits than additional node comparisons. Our proposed method outperforms state-of-the-art GAD methods on the Cora dataset while maintaining lower computational overhead. For graph enhancement, feature masking and edge removal prove to be effective techniques. Looking ahead, we highlight the ensemble of diverse GNN modules as a promising direction for future research. Furthermore, we recommend extending our method to more practical scenarios, such as heterogeneous or dynamic graphs, to further assess its applicability and effectiveness. In the future, we envision several promising directions for advancing the BWMGNN-GCAD framework. First, exploring the integration of adaptive mechanisms to dynamically adjust the contributions of different GNN modules could further enhance detection accuracy and robustness. Second, extending the method to handle heterogeneous graphs, where nodes and edges may represent diverse types of data, could broaden its applicability to real-world scenarios such as social networks or knowledge graphs. Additionally, adapting the framework to dynamic graphs, which evolve over time, would address the growing need for anomaly detection in temporal data. Given the current stage of research, further investigations are needed to fully explore BWMGNN-GCAD's potential versatility and applicability across different domains, especially on more complex heterogeneous or dynamic graphs.

Acknowledgement. This work was supported in part by the National Key R&D Program of China under Grant 2023YFF0905503, National Natural Science Foundation of China under Grants No.62472188, and EdUHK project under Grant No. RG 67/2024-2025R.

References

1. Chen, T., Tsourakakis, C.: Antibenford subgraphs: unsupervised anomaly detection in financial networks. In: Proceedings of the 28th ACM SIGKDD Conference on Knowledge Discovery and Data Mining, pp. 2762–2770 (2022)
2. Defferrard, M., Bresson, X., Vandergheynst, P.: Convolutional neural networks on graphs with fast localized spectral filtering. In: Proceedings of the 30th International Conference on Neural Information Processing Systems, NIPS'16, pp. 3844–3852. Curran Associates Inc., Red Hook (2016)
3. Ding, K., Li, J., Bhanushali, R., Liu, H.: Deep anomaly detection on attributed networks. In: Proceeding of the 2019 SIAM International Conference on Data Mining (SDM), pp. 594–602 (2019)
4. Duan, J., et al.: Graph anomaly detection via multi-scale contrastive learning networks with augmented view. In: Proceedings of the AAAI Conference on Artificial Intelligence, vol. 37, pp. 7459–7467 (2023)
5. Dumitrescu, B., Baltoiu, A., Budulan, S.: Anomaly detection in graphs of bank transactions for anti money laundering applications. IEEE Access **10**, 47699–47714 (2022)

6. ElAdel, A., Zaied, M., Ben Amar, C.: Fast beta wavelet network-based feature extraction for image copy detection. Neurocomputing **173**(2), 306–316 (2016)
7. Fan, H., Zhang, F., Li, Z.: Anomalydae: dual autoencoder for anomaly detection on attributed networks. In: Proceeding of the IEEE International Conference on Acoustics, Speech, and Signal Processing (ICASSP), pp. 5685–5689 (2020)
8. Hamilton, W.L., Ying, R., Leskovec, J.: Inductive representation learning on large graphs. In: Proceedings of the 31st International Conference on Neural Information Processing Systems, pp. 1025–1035 (2017)
9. Hassani, K., Khasahmadi, A.H.: Contrastive multi-view representation learning on graphs. In: International Conference on Machine Learning, pp. 4116–4126 (2020)
10. Jemai, O., Zaied, M., Amar, C.B., Alimi, A.M.: Fbwn: an architecture of fast beta wavelet networks for image classification. In: The 2010 International Joint Conference on Neural Networks (IJCNN), pp. 1–8 (2010)
11. Jin, M., Liu, Y., Zheng, Y., Chi, L., Li, Y.F., Pan, S.: Anemone: graph anomaly detection with multi-scale contrastive learning. In: Proceeding of the 30th ACM International Conference on Information & Knowledge Management, pp. 3122–3126 (2021)
12. Kipf, T.N., Welling, M.: Semi-supervised classification with graph convolutional networks. In: International Conference on Learning Representations (2017)
13. Lai, Y., et al.: Positive data modeling using a mixture of mixtures of inverted beta distributions. IEEE Access **7**, 38146–38156 (2019)
14. Li, J., Dani, H., Hu, X., Liu, H.: Radar: residual analysis for anomaly detection in attributed networks. In: Proceeding of the 26th International Joint Conference on Artificial Intelligence (IJCAI), pp. 2152–2158 (2017)
15. Li, X., et al.: Flowscope: spotting money laundering based on graphs. In: Proceeding of the AAAI Conference on Artificial Intelligence, vol. 34, no. 4, pp. 4731–4738 (2020)
16. Li, Z., Rios, A.L.G., Trajkovic, L.: Machine learning for detecting anomalies and intrusions in communication networks. IEEE J. Sel. Areas Commun. **39**(7), 2254–2264 (2021)
17. Liu, K., Zhang, Y.: A temporal knowledge graph completion method based on balanced timestamp distribution. arXiv preprint arXiv:2108.13024 (2021)
18. Liu, K., Zhao, F., Chen, H., Li, Y., Xu, G., Jin, H.: Da-net: distributed attention network for temporal knowledge graph reasoning. In: Proceedings of the 31st ACM International Conference on Information & Knowledge Management, pp. 1289–1298 (2022)
19. Liu, K., Zhao, F., Jin, H.: Fs-net: frequency statistical network for temporal knowledge graph reasoning. Int. J. Softw. Inf. **34**(10), 4518–4532 (2023)
20. Liu, K., Zhao, F., Xu, G., Wang, X., Jin, H.: Temporal knowledge graph reasoning via time-distributed representation learning. In: 2022 IEEE International Conference on Data Mining (ICDM), pp. 279–288 (2022)
21. Liu, K., Zhao, F., Xu, G., Wang, X., Jin, H.: Retia: relation-entity twin-interact aggregation for temporal knowledge graph extrapolation. In: 2023 IEEE 39th International Conference on Data Engineering (ICDE), pp. 1761–1774 (2023)
22. Liu, K., Zhao, F., Xu, G., Wu, S.: Ie-evo: internal and external evolution-enhanced temporal knowledge graph forecasting. In: 2023 IEEE International Conference on Data Mining (ICDM), pp. 408–417 (2023)
23. Liu, K., Zhao, F., Yang, Y., Xu, G.: Dysarl: dynamic structure-aware representation learning for multimodal knowledge graph reasoning. In: Proceedings of the 32nd ACM International Conference on Multimedia, pp. 8247–8256 (2024)

24. Liu, K., et al.: Pygod: a python library for graph outlier detection. J. Mach. Learn. Res. **25**(141), 1–9 (2024)
25. Liu, Y., Li, Z., Pan, S., Gong, C., Zhou, C., Karypis, G.: Anomaly detection on attributed networks via contrastive self-supervised learning. IEEE Trans. Neural Netw. Learn. Syst. **33**(6), 2378–2392 (2022)
26. Luo, X., et al.: Comga: community-aware attributed graph anomaly detection. In: Proceeding of the 15th ACM International Conference on Web Search and Data Mining (WSDM), pp. 657–665 (2022)
27. Ma, X., Wu, J., Yang, J., Sheng, Q.Z.: Towards graph-level anomaly detection via deep evolutionary mapping. In: Proceeding of the 29th ACM SIGKDD Conference on Knowledge Discovery and Data Mining, pp. 1631–1642 (2023)
28. Miao, K., Shi, X., Zhang, W.A.: Attack signal estimation for intrusion detection in industrial control system. Comput. Secur. **96**, 101926 (2020)
29. Peng, Z., Luo, M., Li, J., Liu, H., Zheng, Q.: Anomalous: a joint modeling approach for anomaly detection on attributed networks. In: Proceeding of the 27th International Joint Conference on Artificial Intelligence (IJCAI), pp. 3513–3519 (2018)
30. Pourhabibi, T., Ong, K.L., Kam, B.H., Boo, Y.L.: Fraud detection: a systematic literature review of graph-based anomaly detection approaches. Decis. Supp. Syst. **133**, 113303 (2020)
31. Sen, P., Namata, G., Bilgic, M., Getoor, L., Gallagher, B., Eliassi-Rad, T.: Collective classification in network data. AI Mag. **29**(3), 93–106 (2008)
32. Song, C.M., Havlin, S., Makse, H.A.: Self-similarity of complex networks. Nature **433**(7024), 392–395 (2005)
33. Tang, J., Li, J., Gao, Z., Li, J.: Rethinking graph neural networks for anomaly detection. In: Proceeding of the 39th International Conference on Machine Learning (ICML), pp. 21076–21089 (2022)
34. Veličković, P., Cucurull, G., Casanova, A., Romero, A., Liò, P., Bengio, Y.: Graph attention networks. In: Proceeding of the International Conference on Learning Representations (2018)
35. Veličković, P., Fedus, W., Hamilton, W.L., Liò, P., Bengio, Y., Hjelm, R.D.: Deep graph infomax. In: Proceeding of the International Conference on Learning Representations (2019)
36. Zhang, G., et al.: Fraudre: fraud detection dual-resistant to graph inconsistency and imbalance. In: Proceeding of the 21st IEEE International Conference on Data Mining (ICDM), pp. 867–876 (2021)
37. Zhang, Z., Zhao, L.: Unsupervised deep subgraph anomaly detection. In: Proceeding of the 2022 IEEE International Conference on Data Mining (ICDM), pp. 753–762 (2022)
38. Zheng, Y., Jin, M., Liu, Y., Chi, L., Phan, K.T., Chen, Y.P.P.: Generative and contrastive self-supervised learning for graph anomaly detection. IEEE Trans. Knowl. Data Eng. **35**(12), 12220–12233 (2021)

Adaptive Graph Contrastive Learning for Blockchain Smart Contract Vulnerability Detection

Junjie Zhou[1], Xiangguo Zhao[1(✉)], Xin Yao[1], Xin Bi[2], and Ye Yuan[3]

[1] College of Software, Northeastern University, Shenyang 110819, China
zhaoxiangguo@mail.neu.edu.cn, yaoxin@stumail.neu.edu.cn

[2] State Key Laboratory of Intelligent Deep Metal Mining and Equipment, Northeastern University, Shenyang 110819, China
bixin@mail.neu.edu.cn

[3] School of Computer Science and Technology, Beijing Institute of Technology, Beijing 100081, China
yuan-ye@bit.edu.cn

Abstract. Detecting vulnerabilities in smart contracts is essential for ensuring the security and reliability of blockchain applications. However, existing graph neural network based methods often rely on expert-crafted features or function call surfaces. And the long-tail distribution in vulnerability datasets causes biased learning toward majority classes. Contrastive learning has been explored as a way to alleviate this issue. But existing augmentation strategies often introduce noise in contrastive learning, degrading representation quality. To address these issues, we propose the Adaptive Graph Contrastive Learning (AGCL) framework. AGCL utilizes the unsupervised multi-level structural attention (UMSA) mechanism to extract the similarity between nodes from semantic, structure and nested function calls. It includes mask degree-free GCN (MDR-GCN) and harmonic distance loss (HDL) to improve the separation between positive and negative representations. Experimental results on ESC and VSC datasets for Reentrancy and Infinite Loop detection surpasses the existing SOTA methods. This performance gain is achieved with full consideration of complex code, such as semantic, structure and nested function calls.

Keywords: Graph contrastive learning · Adaptive graph augmentation · Graph representation learning · Blockchain smart contract vulnerability detection

1 Introduction

Blockchain technology [1] has revolutionized transaction execution, with smart contracts [2] enabling automated, decentralized agreements. Owing to their adoption in domains such as finance [3] and digital asset exchange [4], and their

J. Li et al. (Eds.): APWeb-WAIM 2025, LNCS 16115, pp. 549–563, 2026.
https://doi.org/10.1007/978-981-95-5719-6_35

inherently open-source nature, smart contracts are increasingly exposed to critical security vulnerabilities.

Two prevalent vulnerabilities in smart contracts are Reentrancy Attacks and Infinite Loops [5]. Reentrancy Attacks exploit asynchronous execution, allowing repeated function calls to drain funds, as seen in the 2022 Qubit Finance incident, which led to losses exceeding $80 million [6]. Infinite Loop vulnerabilities trap contracts in endless cycles, disrupting operations; for instance, the 2020 Bitcoin Gold attack exploited this flaw for double-spending, resulting in the loss of approximately 18,000 Bitcoin [7]. To mitigate such risks, researchers have developed systematic approaches for analyzing and securing smart contract implementations.

Current vulnerability detection methods mainly include symbolic execution, fuzz testing, and deep learning. Symbolic execution tools like Oyente [9] are highly automated but limited by path explosion and constraint solving. Fuzzing tools such as ContractFuzzer [12] can discover unexpected bugs but often suffer from low path coverage and sparse input data. Intermediate representation techniques, e.g., Slither [13], enable rule-based analysis but lack runtime memory insights. Consequently, deep learning approaches like DR-GCN [15] have emerged as a complementary solution.

However, existing deep learning methods still face the following challenges.

- **Limited modeling of nested function calls.** Existing methods mainly depend on manual rules and shallow call features, failing to capture interprocedural control and data dependencies, thus weakening their ability to represent complex behaviors.
- **Long-tail distribution.** Smart contract vulnerability datasets exhibit severe class imbalance, with rare types (e.g., Infinite Loop, Reentrancy) severely underrepresented. This skews training toward majority classes and hinders detection of minority-class vulnerabilities.

To solve these challenges, we propose the **A**daptive **G**raph **C**ontrastive **L**earning (AGCL). We first build structured representations of contracts using unsupervised multi-level structural attention (UMSA) to capture logical order and hierarchical dependencies. To mitigate feature loss and noise in traditional contrastive learning, we design a dual-graph fusion strategy that integrates original structures with denoised representations via edge pruning. We further introduce mask degree-free GCN (MDR-GCN), which masks less relevant nodes to enhance detection efficiency. Lastly, we develop harmonic distance loss (HDL) to jointly learn structural and node-level features. The main contributions are summarized as follows.

- We propose a novel graph generation module based on UMSA, which reduces reliance on prior knowledge and effectively uncovers latent relationships.
- We design a graph contrastive learning framework with a tailored loss function to address long-tail distributions, and introduce an adaptive augmentation module to preserve essential graph information.

- Extensive experiments on two public datasets show that AGCL outperforms state-of-the-art methods.

The Sect. 2 deals with the research-related work, the Sect. 3 focuses on the definition of the research problem, the Sect. 4 describes our method, the Sect. 5 deals with the experiments we conducted and finally the conclusion.

2 Related Work

2.1 Smart Contract Vulnerability Detection

Vulnerability detection in smart contracts is crucial for blockchain security, using symbolic execution, fuzz testing, intermediate representation, and deep learning [8]. Symbolic execution tools like Oyente [9], Securify [10], and Mythril [11] improve efficiency but often underreport and require human intervention. Fuzz testing tools like ContractFuzzer [12] reduce false alarms but struggle with path coverage, causing incomplete detection. Intermediate representation tools like Slither [13] and Smartcheck [14] depend on predefined rules, limiting comprehensive analysis. Deep learning methods, such as DR-GCN [15], address these challenges but focus on direct function calls, neglecting implicit relationships, which limits their ability to detect vulnerabilities fully.

2.2 Graph Augmentation

Graph augmentation methods are classified into graph-level, node-level, and edge-level. Graph-level enhancement manipulates the entire graph structure, with techniques like graph sampling improving model robustness through diverse configurations. Node-level enhancement, such as feature shuffling (used by DGI [16] and further research [17] [18]) and node dropping (used in graph classification [20] and node tasks [21]), enriches data diversity. Edge-level enhancement alters graph connectivity through edge removal, addition, and rewiring, like in GROC [22], enhancing robustness to adversarial transformations.

3 Problem Definition

Given a set of smart contract codes $C = \{c_1, c_2, ..., c_n\}$, each c_i is transformed into a contract graph $G_i = \{V_i, E_i\}$, where nodes V_i represent code elements and edges E_i indicate their relationships (e.g., function calls, conditions, or latent links). Each node $v_i \in V_i$ is associated with a feature vector x_i and a label y_i. Nodes are further categorized into three types:

Definition 1 (Main Nodes). *Functions critical to vulnerability detection, including user-defined and built-in ones, are defined as a set* $M_i\{i = 1, 2, 3, ..., n\}$.

Definition 2 (Secondary Nodes). *Security-sensitive variables, representing key program states like balances, access flags, and critical parameters, are denoted as the set* $S_i\{i = 1, 2, 3, ..., n\}$.

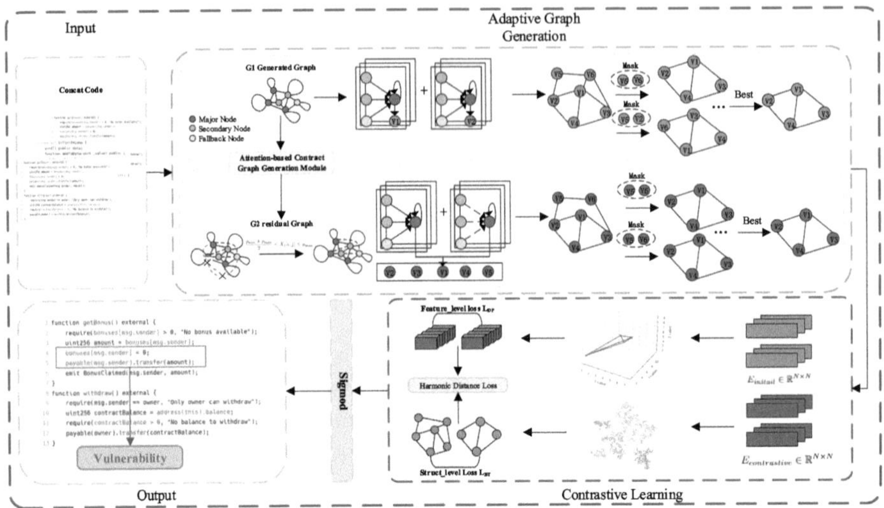

Fig. 1. Red nodes indicate main nodes, green for secondary, and yellow for fallback nodes. The framework consists of three modules: Attention-based Graph Generation, Adaptive Graph Augmentation, and Contrastive Learning. (Color figure online)

Definition 3 (Fallback Nodes). *Fallback functions are invoked during external calls and often serve as the root cause of vulnerabilities. These functions are denoted by the set F.*

We view smart contract vulnerability detection as a node classification task. Define a classifier f, the output node labels can be expressed as $\hat{y} = f(\cdot)$. If there is a vulnerability in the smart contract then $\hat{y} = 1$, otherwise $\hat{y} = 0$.

4 Method

The AGCL (Fig. 1) includes three key modules: the Attention-based Contract Graph Generation Module, which uses unsupervised multi-level structural attention (UMSA) to construct optimized graphs; the Adaptive Graph Augmentation Module, which applies subtle perturbations for improved generalization; and the Contrastive Learning Module, which ensures better attention to minority class samples through resampling or weighting, enhancing performance on imbalanced datasets.

4.1 Attention-Based Contract Graph Generation

Existing methods primarily rely on direct function call dependencies in contract graphs, often overlooking the deeper relationships within invocation chains. To address this, we propose a Contract Graph Generation Module (Fig. 2) based on unsupervised multi-level structural attention (UMSA), which explores contract graph information as implicit relations from semantic, structure and nested function calls, and treats implicit relations as weak relations. By distinguishing strong and weak edges, our method captures inter node dependencies more comprehensively.

Strong relational edges are defined by direct invocation or dependency between nodes, reflecting the temporal dynamics inherent to contract execution. These edges are formally represented as:

$$E_{strong} = \{f_i, f_j \mid f_i \text{ calls } f_j \text{ or } f_i \text{ depends on } f_j\} \tag{1}$$

Weak relational edges are inferred through multi-modal structural-semantic correlations, forming the adjacency matrix X_{mined}. This matrix, generated by the Unsupervised Multi-level Structural Attention (UMSA), includes latent feature similarities. As shown in Eq. 2, each entry $X_{mined}[i, j]$ denotes the implicit association strength between nodes i and j.

$$X_{mined} = clip(\underbrace{\sum_{m=1}^{3} softmax([S_{sem}, S_{struct}, S_{path}] \cdot w_g)_m \cdot S_m \odot (1 - A_{init})}_{\text{Gated Fusion}}) \tag{2}$$

where the gated fusion function dynamically integrates three similarity measures: S_{sem}, S_{struct}, and S_{path}, each weighted by the gate vector w_g. Each $S_m(i, j)$ represents the correlation between nodes (i, j) across different modalities. Element-wise masking $\odot(1 - A_{\text{init}})$ suppresses existing edges in A_{init}, ensuring that the inferred weak edges remain complementary. The function clip$(\cdot)$ performs scaling and truncation.

S_{sem} captures semantic similarity, computed as the cosine similarity between transformed node features $W_q x_i$ and $W_k x_j$.

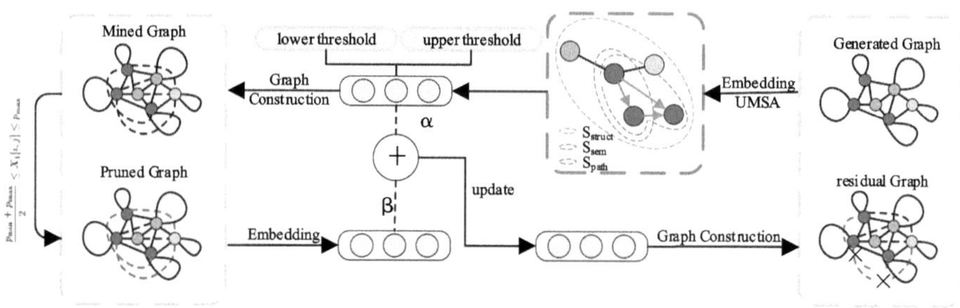

Fig. 2. Detailed process of the attention-based contract graph generation module.

$$S_{sem}(i, j) = \frac{(W_q x_i)^T (W_k x_j)}{\|W_q x_i\| \|W_k x_j\|} \tag{3}$$

S_{struct} reflects the dependence on the overall structure around the node, derived from the diffusion of node features through the normalized adjacency matrix $A_{\text{norm}} = D^{-1/2} A_{\text{init}} D^{-1/2}$.

$$S_{struct}(i,j) = (A_{\text{norm}} W_s x_i)^T (A_{\text{norm}} W_s x_j) \tag{4}$$

S_{path} captures dependencies along multiple paths between nodes. Traditional path methods are often static and discrete representations, which are difficult to adapt to dynamic scenarios such as multiple entry points, inconsistent levels, and fallback path reentry in function call graphs. To solve this problem, we designed the Multi-path Bidirectional Gated Graph Recurrent Unit (Mp-BiGGRU) (Fig. 3). For main nodes, depth is defined by the call hierarchy tree; secondary nodes inherit the depth of their associated main nodes. Fallback nodes, as independent entries triggered externally (e.g., via transactions), are decoupled from the primary call tree and assigned separate depths. The main equation is as follows.

$$S_{path}(i,j) = \sum_{m=1}^{|Paths(i,j)|} \alpha_m \cdot \left(\Gamma(\overrightarrow{H}_{\mathcal{P}_m}, \overleftarrow{H}_{\mathcal{P}_m}) \odot \Omega\left(\mathcal{G}_{\mathcal{P}_m}\right) \right) \tag{5}$$

where the $\Gamma(\cdot)$ function achieves cross-timestep parameter sharing through tensor product operations $\prod$ and includes the stitching of bidirectional encoded matrices. α_m represents the attention weight assigned to the $m-th$ path between nodes i and j, which is computed by normalizing the relevance of each path through a softmax function. α_m is defined as Eq. 6.

$$\alpha_m = \frac{\exp\left(q^T GeLU\left(W_a\left[\overrightarrow{H_{\mathcal{P}_m}}, \overleftarrow{H_{\mathcal{P}_m}}\right]\right)\right)}{\sum_{k=1}^{|Paths(i,j)|} \exp\left(q^T GeLU\left(W_a\left[\overrightarrow{H_{\mathcal{P}_k}}, \overleftarrow{H_{\mathcal{P}_k}}\right]\right)\right)} \tag{6}$$

where the matrix W_a maps bi-directional features to the attention space, and the query vector q learns the path importance assessment criteria through end-to-end training.

The path representation $\left[\overrightarrow{H_{\mathcal{P}_m}}, \overleftarrow{H_{\mathcal{P}_m}}\right]$ in Eq. 6 captures bidirectional dependencies. The forward propagation $\overrightarrow{H}_{\mathcal{P}}$ is computed through gated recursion along the path sequence, using trainable transformation matrices and nonlinear activations to aggregate node features (Eq. 7):

$$\overrightarrow{H}_{\mathcal{P}} = \prod_{k=1}^{n} \left(W_{\overrightarrow{r}} \sigma(W_{\overrightarrow{z}}[h_k, \overrightarrow{h}_{k-1}]) + W_{\overrightarrow{h}}[h_k, \overrightarrow{h}_{k-1} \sigma(W_{\overrightarrow{z}}[h_k, \overrightarrow{h}_{k-1}])] \right) \tag{7}$$

The backward propagation representation $\overleftarrow{H}_{\mathcal{P}}$ is similarly derived by reverse sequential processing, enabling capture of inverse dependencies:

$$\overleftarrow{H}_{\mathcal{P}} = \prod_{k=n}^{1} \left(W_{\overleftarrow{r}} \sigma(W_{\overleftarrow{z}}[h_k, \overleftarrow{h}_{k+1}]) + W_{\overleftarrow{h}}[h_k, \overleftarrow{h}_{k+1} \sigma(W_{\overleftarrow{z}}[h_k, \overleftarrow{h}_{k+1}])] \right) \tag{8}$$

where the weight matrices $W_{\overrightarrow{r}}$, $W_{\overrightarrow{z}}$, $W_{\overrightarrow{h}}$ and their backward counterparts correspond to the reset gate, update gate, and candidate hidden states in forward and backward propagation.

The gating modulation factor $\Omega(\mathcal{G}_{\mathcal{P}})$ encodes topological features (e.g., nesting depth, branching factor) using a graph structure encoder, as shown in Eq. 9.

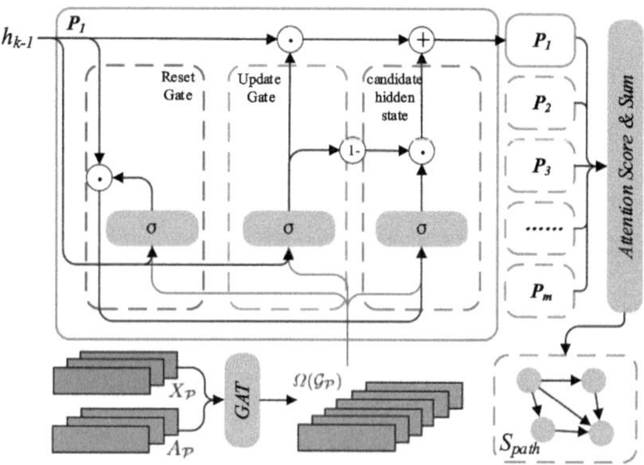

Fig. 3. Multi-path Bidirectional Gated Graph Recurrent Unit (Mp-BiGGRU).

$$\Omega(\mathcal{G}_{\mathcal{P}}) = ReLU\left(\sum_{l=1}^{L} W_{\mathcal{G}}^{(l)} \cdot GAT^{(l)}(A_{\mathcal{P}}, X_{\mathcal{P}})\right) \tag{9}$$

where the graph attention network (GAT) stacks L-layers, $W_{\mathcal{G}}^{(l)}$ fuses multilayer GAT features, and $A_{\mathcal{P}}$ encodes node connectivity within path $\mathcal{P}$, while $X_{\mathcal{P}}$ contains structural attributes like node degrees and nesting levels. The output serves as gating coefficients for the Hadamard product with GRU states, enabling dynamic path influence adjustment.

To address gradient instability caused by unbounded values in the mined graph G_{mined}, we truncate its adjacency matrix X_{mined} to the range $[p_{\min}, p_{\max}]$. Edges with weights in $[(p_{\min} + p_{\max})/2, p_{\max}]$ are identified as weak edges E_{weak}. These, together with strong edges and key nodes (major, secondary, fallback), form the initial graph G_1. A pruned graph G_{pruned} is obtained by partially removing E_{weak}, and we stabilize graph structure using a weighted fusion:

$$X_{\text{comparison}} = \alpha \cdot X_{\text{mined}} + \beta \cdot X_{\text{pruned}}. \tag{10}$$

To simplify the graph, secondary and callback nodes are merged into their nearest major nodes. The feature of each major node V_{M_i} is updated by aggregating both direct and path-based neighbor features:

$$V_{M_i} = f\left(Self_{M_i}, \sum_{N_j \in Neighbors(M_i)} V_{N_j}, \sum_{N_k \in PathNeighbors(M_i)} V_{N_k}\right). \tag{11}$$

To further enhance structural representation, we propose the UMSA. UMSA captures multi-level connectivity patterns and models cross-function and cross-contract propagation paths, overcoming limitations of local semantic attention. Its unsupervised nature enables adaptation to scenarios with scarce labels, providing a highly discriminative graph structure for downstream learning modules.

4.2 Adaptive Graph Augmentation

To refine the initial graph structure, we propose MDR-GCN (Fig. 4), an enhanced DR-GCN variant. The original propagation is defined as:

$$H^{(l+1)} = ReLU\left(\hat{D}^{-\frac{1}{2}}\hat{X}\hat{D}^{-\frac{1}{2}}H^{(l)}W^{(l)}\right) \tag{12}$$

where the $\hat{X} = X + I$ is the self-loop augmented adjacency matrix, $\hat{D}$ is its degree matrix, and $W^{(l)}$ is the learnable weight. Given preprocessing in Sect. 4.1, we simplify this as:

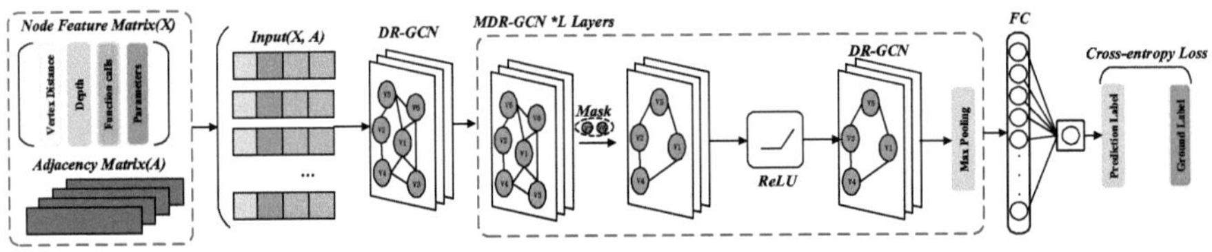

Fig. 4. Detailed process of the adaptive augmentation module.

$$H^{(l+1)} = ReLU\left((X_n^2 + I)H^{(l)}W^{(l)}\right) \tag{13}$$

However, DR-GCN treats all nodes and features equally, risking noise propagation. So we propose the MDR-GCN, which alleviates this by a node-level mask vector M, guiding attention to informative nodes. The updated propagation is:

$$H^{(l+1)} = ReLU\left((X_n^2 + I)(H^{(l)} \odot M)W^{(l)}\right) \tag{14}$$

This selective mechanism prioritizes vulnerable nodes, improves feature focus, and enhances structural learning. Final predictions are compared to ground truth using cross-entropy loss:

$$CrossEntropy(Y, \hat{Y}) = -\sum_i Y_i \log \widehat{Y_i} \tag{15}$$

We then optimize structure of G_1 in the Adaptive Augmentation Module, updating its embedding for downstream contrastive learning with graph G_2.

4.3 Contrastive Learning

This module utilizes MDR-GCN to extract embedding matrices X_1 and X_2 from the original graph G_1 and the augmented graph G_2, which are mapped into a shared embedding space for vulnerability prediction via a Sigmoid function. To improve both robustness and discrimination, we propose a contrastive learning framework that incorporates positive and negative sample pairs. Positive pairs originate from different augmented views of the same node, preserving semantic consistency, while negative pairs are sampled from semantically unrelated nodes or distinct contracts, enhancing inter-class separability.

To further address the challenges of representation collapse, semantic drift, and noise sensitivity inherent in graph augmentation, we introduce the Harmonic Distance Loss (HDL), which synergistically combines Barlow Twins Loss (BTL) and Double Positive Loss (DPL).

The Barlow Twins Loss (BTL) explicitly encourages feature decorrelation and invariance across augmented views, formulated as:

$$\mathcal{L}_{BT} = \frac{1}{D}\sum_{i=1}^{D}\left((1-C_{ii})^2 + \lambda\sum_{k\neq i}^{D} C_{ik}^2\right) \tag{16}$$

where C is the cross-correlation matrix of normalized features $\hat{z}_a$ and $\hat{z}_b$ from two augmented views. Diagonal terms C_{ii} promote consistency, while off-diagonal terms C_{ik} $(i \neq k)$ penalize feature redundancy. This design mitigates overfitting to spurious patterns introduced by augmentation.

While BTL focuses on global feature decorrelation, it overlooks fine-grained distance relations critical for graph-level tasks. Therefore, we complement it with Double Positive Loss (DPL), defined as:

$$\mathcal{L}_{\mathrm{DP}} = \frac{1}{|\mathcal{B}|}\sum_{(anc,pos)\in\mathcal{B}}\left[(1-\tau)\cdot\frac{\tilde{d}_{\mathrm{Euc}}}{1+\tilde{d}_{\mathrm{Euc}}} + \tau\cdot\frac{\tilde{d}_{\mathrm{Man}}}{1+\tilde{d}_{\mathrm{Man}}}\right] \tag{17}$$

where $\tau \in [0,1]$ balances the precision of Euclidean distance d_{Euc} and the robustness of Manhattan distance d_{Man}. Both distances are batch-normalized to ensure stable optimization. $\mathcal{B}$ denotes the set of positive node pairs, with anc and pos as their ℓ_2-normalized embeddings. Meanwhile, negative pairs are implicitly integrated by penalizing high similarity among unrelated nodes, thus enhancing structural discriminability.

The overall loss is a weighted combination:

$$\mathcal{L}_{\mathrm{HD}} = \gamma\cdot\mathcal{L}_{\mathrm{BT}} + (1-\gamma)\cdot\mathcal{L}_{\mathrm{DP}} \tag{18}$$

where $\gamma \in [0,1]$ controls the balance between global decorrelation and local alignment.

In summary, integrating Barlow Twins Loss and Double Positive Loss mitigates feature correlation and enhances feature alignment. By jointly leveraging both positive and negative samples, HDL promotes discriminative and generalizable representations, making the unified loss effective for optimizing contrastive learning performance.

Table 1. Performance comparison in terms of accuracy, recall, precision, and F1-score. A total of fourteen methods are investigated, including existing vulnerability detection methods, neural network-based methodes, and our method AGCL. '–' denotes not applicable.

Model	Infinite Loop				Reentrancy Attack			
	Acc.	Prec.	Recall	F1	Acc.	Prec.	Recall	F1
Jolt	0.4325	0.2134	0.3756	0.2765	–	–	–	–
PDA	0.4534	0.2124	0.4304	0.2847	–	–	–	–
Bolt	0.5152	0.3857	0.5514	0.4522	–	–	–	–
Looper	0.5913	0.4692	0.6121	0.5286	–	–	–	–
Smartcheck	–	–	–	–	0.5256	0.3165	0.2467	0.2786
Oyente	–	–	–	–	0.5963	0.5270	0.3812	0.4522
Mythril	–	–	–	–	0.6124	0.7243	0.4011	0.5139
Securify	–	–	–	–	0.7214	0.5672	0.5115	0.5403
Vanilla-RNN	0.4625	0.4521	0.4132	0.4411	0.5055	0.5715	0.4824	0.4986
LSTM	0.5055	0.5831	0.4534	0.5025	0.5294	0.6710	0.5104	0.5791
GRU	0.5093	0.5002	0.4468	0.4500	0.5667	0.7210	0.5380	0.6137
GCN	0.6371	0.5342	0.5342	0.5427	0.7492	0.7263	0.6987	0.7350
GraphCL	0.6444	0.5521	0.6031	0.5531	0.7961	0.7684	0.7248	0.7511
DR-GCN	0.6642	0.5511	0.6325	0.5676	0.8147	0.8089	0.7236	0.7639
AGCL	**0.6804**	**0.5723**	**0.6536**	**0.5869**	**0.9565**	**0.9543**	**0.9264**	**0.9377**

5 Experiment

5.1 Datasets

Extensive experiments were conducted on datasets comprising smart contracts sourced from both the Ethereum and VNT Chain platforms. These datasets, referred to as ESC (Ethereum Smart Contracts) and VSC (VNT Chain Smart Contracts), are acquired from reputable sources for reference [15].

- **ESC dataset**: 40,932 Ethereum contracts with 307,396 functions, including 5,013 using `call.value`. This dataset is used for studying reentrancy vulnerability detection.
- **VSC dataset**: 4,170 VNT Chain contracts with 13,761 functions. This dataset is used for studying infinite loop vulnerability detection.

5.2 Experimental Settings

Experiments were conducted with carefully selected parameters to ensure reliability and reproducibility. Models were trained for 500 epochs using a learning rate of 0.004, weight decay of 1e–4, and a dropout rate of 0.25. The Adam optimizer and a batch size of 32 were used, with 256 hidden units in the final fully connected layer. Five-fold cross-validation was applied, with 20% of contracts for training and 80% for testing. Evaluation metrics included accuracy, recall, precision, and F1-score. The ESC dataset was used for Reentrancy detection and VSC for Infinite Loop analysis

5.3 Baseline

We compared our method to fourteen smart contract vulnerability detection methods, which included Jolt [25], PDA [26], Bolt [28], and Looper [27], which could detect Infinite Loop, and Smartcheck [14], Oyente [9], Mythril [11], and Securify [10], which could detect Reentrancy Attack, as well as the more cutting-edge deep learning methods Vanilla-RNN [32], LSTM [29], GRU [30], GCN [31], GraphCL [33] and DR-GCN [15].

5.4 Experiment Results

We evaluated AGCL on the detection of Reentrancy Attack and Infinite Loop Vulnerabilities and compared its performance against traditional and deep learning-based methods.

For Reentrancy Attack detection, AGCL was compared with Smartcheck, Oyente, Mythril, and Securify. Performance metrics, including accuracy, recall, precision, and F1-score, are presented in the right section of Table 1. AGCL achieved 95.65% accuracy, significantly outperforming the best traditional method, Securify, which reached 72.14%. This represents a 23.51% improvement, while AGCL's recall exceeded existing methods by 38.71%, highlighting the advantages of applying graph neural networks to this task. This improvement from reentrancy attack vulnerability is reliance on complex call chains. AGCL captures similarities across multiple execution paths via contrastive learning, making it better at identifying such vulnerabilities than traditional tools.

For Infinite Loop detection, AGCL was compared with Jolt, PDA, Bolt, and Looper. The results in the left section of Table 1 demonstrate that AGCL outperformed these methods, achieving an 8.91% accuracy improvement. This enhancement is attributed to AGCL's ability to embed fallback information and capture the similarity between fallback functions and other nodes. Infinite Loop vulnerability is more reflected in the control flow errors within a single function rather than the complex cross-function call chain dependencies, so the improvement is not very obvious.

We also compared AGCL with deep learning-based methods, including Vanilla-RNN, LSTM, GRU, GraphCL, GCN and DR-GCN, for both tasks. As shown in the left section of Table 1, deep learning methods outperformed traditional approaches, with DR-GCN achieving accuracies of 81.47% for Reentrancy Attack and 66.42% for Infinite Loop detection. Nevertheless, AGCL surpassed DR-GCN, with accuracy improvements of 14.18% and 1.62%. These results demonstrate AGCL's robustness and effectiveness in detecting smart contract vulnerabilities.

5.5 Ablation Study

Table 2. Ablation Study Results (Before the addition of HDL, the cross-entropy loss function was used)

Model	Infinite Loop				Reentrancy Attack			
	Acc.	Prec.	Recall	F1	Acc.	Prec.	Recall	F1
AGCL	0.6804	0.5723	0.6536	0.5869	0.9565	0.9543	0.9264	0.9377
w/o HDL	0.6751	0.5659	0.6453	0.5826	0.9466	0.9445	0.9133	0.9294
w/o CL	0.6735	0.5622	0.6412	0.5711	0.9316	0.9431	0.9082	0.9216
w/o AGA	0.6711	0.5634	0.6408	0.5701	0.9305	0.9414	0.9078	0.9175
w/o AGG	0.6642	0.5511	0.6325	0.5676	0.8147	0.8089	0.7236	0.7639

To evaluate the effectiveness of each key module within our proposed model, we conducted a series of ablation studies for the scenarios of Infinite Loop Vulnerability and Reentrancy attacks, demonstrating the efficacy of the Attention-based Contract Graph Generation Module (AGG), Adaptive Graph Augmentation Module (AGA), Contrastive Learning (CL), and Harmonic Distance Loss (HDL). The results are shown in Table 2.

For Infinite Loop detection, the left section of Table 2 shows a significant performance drop when modules are removed. The AGG module is essential for identifying structural features of loops, while the AGA module balances Precision and Recall by adjusting the graph structure, preventing overfitting. The CL module improves generalization by enhancing sample discriminability.

For Reentrancy detection, the right section of Table 2 shows that removing AGG and AGA modules leads to a marked decrease in Recall, highlighting their importance in understanding complex node interactions critical for detecting reentrancy. AGG is key for identifying important interactions, while AGA strengthens adaptability to graph changes. The CL module further enhances model performance by improving recognition of subtle attack patterns.

In conclusion, the ablation studies confirm that AGG, AGA, and CL are vital for model performance. AGG captures critical graph interactions, AGA prevents overfitting by adapting the graph structure, and CL boosts discriminative power and generalization. Additionally, HDL refines the loss function and stabilizes performance, equipping the model to address complex vulnerabilities effectively.

5.6 Hyperparametric Analysis

In this section, we analyzed the effect of key parameters on model performance using five-fold cross-validation to ensure fair comparisons across datasets. The evaluated parameters included $p_{\min}$, $p_{\max}$, α, β, and γ. These experiments were conducted to identify parameter settings that balance performance across diverse conditions.

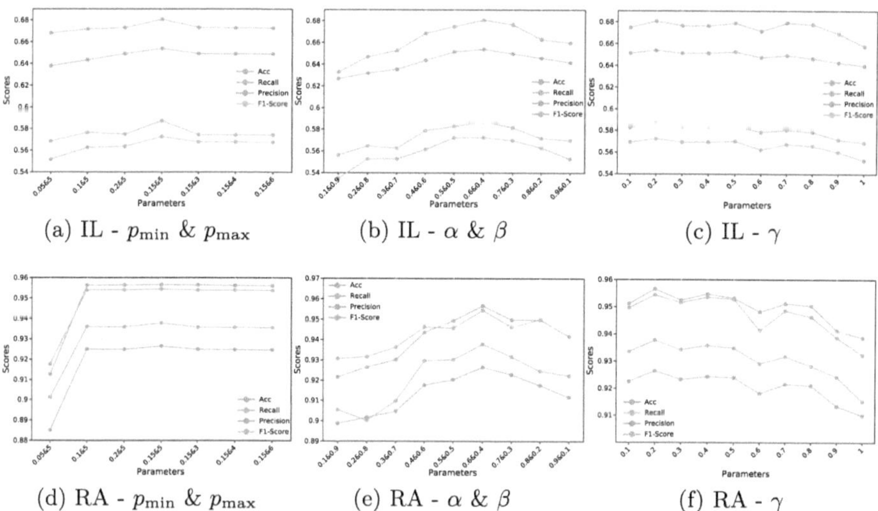

(a) IL - $p_{\min}$ & $p_{\max}$ (b) IL - α & β (c) IL - γ

(d) RA - $p_{\min}$ & $p_{\max}$ (e) RA - α & β (f) RA - γ

Fig. 5. IL: Infinite Loop, RA: Reentrancy Attack. (a) & (b) & (c) are all parameter analyses for the upstream task of Infinite Loop, and (d) & (e) & (f) are all parameter analyses for the upstream task of Reentrancy Attack. (a)&(d) are parameter analysis for $p_{\min}$ & $p_{\max}$, (b) & (e) are parameter analysis for α & β, and (c) & (f) are parameter analysis for γ.

For $p_{\min}$ and $p_{\max}$, we tested combinations: 0.05 & 5, 0.1 & 5, 0.2 & 5, 0.15 & 5, 0.15 & 3, 0.15 & 4, and 0.15 & 6, while keeping other parameters constant. Results shown in Fig. 5(a) & (d) indicated the best values were $p_{\min} = 0.15$ and $p_{\max} = 5$. The superior performance is due to these values maintaining a robust representation of the feature distribution while avoiding overfitting.

For α and β, combinations from 0.1 & 0.9 to 0.9 & 0.1 were tested in increments of 0.1, with results shown in Fig. 5(b) & (e). The optimal settings of $\alpha = 0.6$ and $\beta = 0.4$ balance the contributions of the two loss components, enhancing the model's ability to capture key features and improve discrimination.

Finally, γ was varied between 0.1 and 1 in increments of 0.1 while keeping other parameters fixed. Results, presented in Fig. 5(c) & (f), identified $\gamma = 0.2$ as optimal. This setting ensures effective integration of the two loss functions, avoiding dominance by either component and improving stability during training.

The optimal parameter combination ($p_{\min} = 0.15$, $p_{\max} = 5$, $\alpha = 0.6$, $\beta = 0.4$, $\gamma = 0.2$) enhances the model's ability to balance robustness and generalization. These findings underscore the importance of careful parameter tuning in achieving high stability and effectiveness across diverse experimental conditions.

6 Conclusion

This paper proposes AGCL, an advanced smart contract vulnerability analyzer that overcomes key limitations of existing approaches. AGCL employs a unified multi-level structural attention (UMSA) module to capture nested function dependencies while reducing reliance on expert rules and retaining implicit semantics. To mitigate long-tail data challenges, a tailored contrastive learning strategy is introduced to balance sample distributions. AGCL further incorporates a mask degree-free GCN (MDR-GCN) to suppress noise and maintain contextual integrity, along with harmonic distance loss (HDL) to enhance feature separability. Experimental results show that AGCL achieves SOTA performance, particularly in Reentrancy detection, demonstrating its effectiveness in graph-based vulnerability analysis.

Acknowledgments. This work was supported by the National Key R&D Program of China (No. 2022YFB2702100) and the National Natural Science Foundation of China (No. 62072087). The funding agencies had no role in the study design, data collection, analysis, interpretation, manuscript writing, or the decision to publish the results.

References

1. Zhou, Y., et al.: Blockchain challenges and opportunities: a survey. Int. J. Web Grid Serv. **14**(4), 352–375 (2018)
2. Buterin, V.: A Next Generation Smart Contract & Decentralized Application Platform (2015)
3. Javaid, M., Haleem, A., Singh, R.P., Suman, R., Khan, S.: A review of blockchain technology applications for financial services. BenchCouncil Trans. Benchmarks Stand. Eval. **2**(3), 100073 (2022)
4. de Vos, M., Ileri, C.U., Pouwelse, J.: XChange: a universal mechanism for asset exchange between permissioned blockchains. World Wide Web **24**(5), 1691–1728 (2021)
5. Qian, P., Liu, Z., He, Q., Huang, B., Tian, D., Wang, X.: Smart contract vulnerability detection technique: a survey. arXiv preprint arXiv:2209.05872 (2022)
6. CoinTelegraph: Qubit Finance suffers $80 million loss following hack (2022)
7. CoinTelegraph: Bitcoin Gold Blockchain Hit by 51% Attack Leading to $70K Double Spend (2020)
8. Chu, H., Zhang, P., Dong, H., Xiao, Y., Ji, S., Li, W.: A survey on smart contract vulnerabilities: data sources, detection and repair. Inf. Softw. Technol. **159**, 107221 (2023)
9. Luu, L., Chu, D.-H., Olickel, H., Saxena, P., Hobor, A.: Making smart contracts smarter. In: Proceedings of ACM CCS, pp. 254–269 (2016)
10. Tsankov, P., Dan, A., Drachsler-Cohen, D., Gervais, A., Bünzli, F., Vechev, M.: Securify: practical security analysis of smart contracts. In: *Proceedings of ACM CCS*, pp. 67–82 (2018)
11. Mythril: Mythril: A framework for bug hunting on the Ethereum blockchain (2017). https://mythx.io/. Accessed 08 May 2024

12. Jiang, B., Liu, Y., Chan, W.K.: ContractFuzzer: fuzzing smart contracts for vulnerability detection. In: Proceedings of IEEE/ACM ASE, pp. 259–269 (2018)
13. Feist, J., Grieco, G., Groce, A.: Slither: a static analysis framework for smart contracts. In: WETSEB, pp. 8–15 (2019)
14. Tikhomirov, S., et al.: SmartCheck: static analysis of ethereum smart contracts. In: WETSEB, pp. 9–16 (2018)
15. Zhuang, Y., et al.: Smart contract vulnerability detection using graph neural networks. In: Proceedings of IJCAI, pp. 454–461 (2020)
16. Veličković, P., et al.: Deep graph infomax. arXiv preprint arXiv:1809.10341 (2018)
17. Jing, B., Park, C., Tong, H.: HDMI: high-order deep multiplex infomax. In: WWW, pp. 2414–2424 (2021)
18. Li, K., et al.: Reliable representations make a stronger defender: unsupervised structure refinement for robust GNN. In: Proceedings of ACM KDD, pp. 925–935 (2022)
19. Opolka, F.L., et al.: Spatio-temporal deep graph infomax. arXiv preprint arXiv:1904.06316 (2019)
20. Pinheiro, G.A., et al.: SMICLR: Contrastive learning on multiple molecular representations. J. Chem. Inf. Model (2022)
21. Feng, W., et al.: Graph random neural networks for semi-supervised learning on graphs. In: Proceedings of NeurIPS, pp. 1–12 (2020)
22. Jovanović, N., et al.: Towards robust graph contrastive learning. arXiv preprint arXiv:2102.13085 (2021)
23. Veličković, P., et al.: Graph attention networks. In: ICLR (2018)
24. Zbontar, J., et al.: Barlow twins: self-supervised learning via redundancy reduction. arXiv preprint arXiv:2103.03230 (2021)
25. Carbin, M., et al.: Detecting and escaping infinite loops with jolt. In: ECOOP, pp. 609–633 (2011)
26. Ibing, A., Mai, A.: A fixed-point algorithm for automated static detection of infinite loops. In: IEEE HASE, pp. 44–51 (2015)
27. Burnim, J., et al.: Looper: lightweight detection of infinite loops at runtime. In: ASE, pp. 161–169 (2009)
28. Kling, M., et al.: Bolt: on-demand infinite loop escape in unmodified binaries. SIGPLAN Not. **47**(10), 431–450 (2012)
29. Hochreiter, S., Schmidhuber, J.: Long short-term memory. Neural Comput. **9**(8), 1735–1780 (1997)
30. Chung, J., et al.: Empirical evaluation of gated recurrent neural networks on sequence modeling. arXiv preprint arXiv:1412.3555 (2014)
31. Kipf, T., Welling, M.: Semi-supervised classification with graph convolutional networks. arXiv preprint arXiv:1609.02907 (2016)
32. Zaremba, W., et al.: Recurrent neural network regularization. arXiv preprint arXiv:1409.2329 (2014)
33. Hafidi, H., et al.: GraphCL: contrastive self-supervised learning of graph representations. arXiv preprint arXiv:2007.08025 (2020)

CPGCN: Evolutionary Relationship Mining Framework for Ethnic Costume Elements

Shan Huang[1,2,3], Yanuo Li[1,2,3], Siheng Wu[1,2,3], Xiaodong Duan[1,2,3(✉)], and Ruibo Li[4]

[1] College of Computer Science and Technology, Dalian Minzu University, Dalian 116650, China
[2] State Ethnic Affairs Commission Key Laboratory of Big Data Applied Technology, Dalian 116650, China
[3] Dalian Key Laboratory of Digital Technology for National Culture, Dalian 116650, China
duanxd@dinu.edu.cn
[4] College of Letters and Science, University of California, Davis, USA
rboli@ucdavis.edu

Abstract. Ethnic costumes serve as a significant medium for material and cultural exchange and integration among different ethnic groups. The correlations between their elements and the evolutionary patterns are of great importance in uncovering the historical connotations of ethnic fusion. However, existing research has predominantly focused on classification and recognition tasks, with limited exploration into the deep interconnections among elements and their implications for ethnic integration. To solve this problem, we propose a new framework for mining the evolutionary relationships of ethnic costume elements, namely Community-Preserving Graph Convolutional Network (CPGCN). This end-to-end framework adaptively integrates link information and attribute information while specifically considering community structures. By predicting relationships between nodes in the feature network of ethnic costume elements, it obtains characteristic foundations of ethnic integration processes. Furthermore, we propose a new ethnic costume element extraction model, Xception-DL. By mining the features of various parts in the ethnic costume element data and calculating the similarity between each feature node, a feature network of ethnic costume elements is constructed. Extensive experiments on multiple common datasets show that CPGCN significantly outperforms existing methods.

Keywords: Link Prediction · Feature Extraction · Graph Neural Network

1 Introduction

In recent years, research on ethnic costumes has mainly focused on classification and identification tasks, while the exploration of correlation and evolution

J. Li et al. (Eds.): APWeb-WAIM 2025, LNCS 16115, pp. 564–580, 2026.
https://doi.org/10.1007/978-981-95-5719-6_36

laws among different ethnic costumes is still insufficient. When the network is constructed with dress samples as nodes and feature similarity as edges, its complexity is reflected in two aspects: first, the network structure level (the large number of nodes and complex connectivity relationships), and second, the data attribute level (the high-dimensionality and diversity of the dress elements), which poses a challenge to the traditional analytical methods [13]. Data mining techniques provide a feasible path to analyze such complex data. Graph Neural Networks (GNN), as one of the methods to deal with graph-structured data, is able to utilize both network topology and node attribute information. Under this framework: first, attribute network link prediction can quantify the likelihood of potential associations among costume nodes and assist in identifying cultural associations that are not explicitly recorded; second, community structure analysis can identify costume groups with similar attributes (e.g., specific shapes and patterns) and strong internal connections that may correspond to regional cultural branches; third, by tracking the evolution of community structure (e.g., changes in inter-community connections) and node Third, by tracking the evolution of community structure (e.g., changes in connection between communities) and the migration of node attributes, it is expected to provide data references for the dissemination paths and technological inheritance of costume elements [18].

The main contributions of this paper are as follows:

- We propose a framework for mining the evolutionary relationships of ethnic costume elements, CPGCN. Designed with an end-to-end architecture and joint training strategy, CPGCN adaptively integrates both link information and attribute information while specifically incorporating community structures.
- We propose a new ethnic costume element extraction model, Xception-DL. By mining the features of various parts in the data of ethnic costume elements and calculating the similarity between each feature node according to the characteristics of graph data, a feature network of ethnic costume elements is constructed.
- The effectiveness of the CPGCN framework proposed is evaluated. Many experiments are conducted on multiple common datasets, and comparisons and analyses are made with existing methods. CPGCN demonstrates superior performance.

2 Related Work

2.1 Link Prediction

Link prediction, as a core task of network analysis, shows a three-stage development in its methodological evolution: early similarity-based methods (e.g., Common Neighbors (CN), Adamic-Adar (AA)) relied on heuristic assumptions but were difficult to adapt to the complex network structure; the subsequent rise of network embedding methods improves the performance by learning from the low-dimensional representations, where three major schools, namely matrix decomposition (e.g. M-NMF [11]), random wandering (e.g., node2vec [3]), and deep learning models (e.g., GCN) have their own breakthroughs, but generally suffer from information integration flaws - either ignoring attribute information (DeepWalk [5]), or ignoring community structure (GraphSAGE [19]), or limited by non-attribute networks (M-NMF). Due to more powerful representation learning capabilities, GNNs are becoming increasingly popular for link prediction in attribute networks. Current GNN methods (e.g., EdgeConvNorm [17], LGLP [15]), although enabling end-to-end prediction through graph classification frameworks, still suffer from a twofold limitation: the lack of community-structure modeling leads to the invalidation of topology constraints, and the simple splicing of attribute-links hinders deep association mining, and may even cripple GNNs in graph data mining tasks.

2.2 Clothing Feature Extraction

Feature extraction is a core task in the field of computer vision, aiming to transform high-dimensional visual data into machine-recognizable feature representations. Traditional methods rely on manually designed rules: global features (color, shape, texture) versus local features (e.g., LBP, HOG, SIFT). Local Binary Pattern (LBP) encodes texture information, Histogram of Gradient Orientation (HOG) describes shape features, and Scale-Invariant Feature Transform (SIFT) enables rotational invariant extraction. These methods are interpretable, but there are limitations in feature representation capabilities.

The application of deep learning enhances the feature extraction. For example, MSFN [12] enhances the representation capability through multi-scale feature fusion. Compared to traditional methods, deep learning achieves better feature representation through end-to-end learning, which significantly improves the performance of tasks such as image classification. Current research is devoted to optimizing the network architecture to enhance robustness and generalization.

2.3 Research on Study on the Digital Preservation of Chinese National Costumes and the Cultural Association of Elements

Current research on the digital preservation of ethnic costumes primarily focuses on applying digital archiving and intelligent processing technologies. For example, Qi Xiaoli [6] explored the digital reproduction and innovative design of intangible cultural heritage costumes; Tang Xin [9] proposed a grayscale image colorization method integrating style and content features; Zheng Xingren et al. [14] improved algorithms for precise costume classification and recognition.

At the level of costume element application, existing studies predominantly address the modern adaptation of individual elements. For instance, Chen Xiaomei [1] analyzed strategies for integrating traditional costume elements into contemporary fashion design; Liu Xiaohan et al. [4] incorporated Mongolian motifs into sports footwear design. Notably, ethnic costume elements are interdependent; their cultural interrelationships are essential to deciphering the Semiotics of ethnic attire and revealing its profound cultural heritage and national spirit. Nevertheless, very few studies have systematically investigated the cultural relationships between these elements.

3 CPGCN

3.1 Framework Overview

First, multiple images of ethnic costumes, such as Manchu and Mongolian costumes, are acquired and cover different styles, such as Manchu dragon patterned flat collar and Mongolian floral patterned stand-up collar. Then, the complete costume images are segmented into sub-images based on the neckline, cuffs, hemline and front chest. These sub-images are fed into a pre-trained Xception-DL model for feature extraction and similarity comparison to construct a feature network. Finally, the link prediction between nodes yields a feature base for the gradual fusion of clothing elements. The framework diagram is shown in Fig. 1.

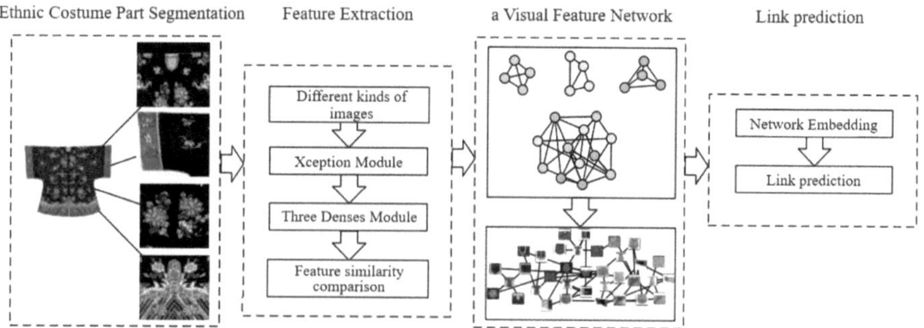

Fig. 1. The framework of CPGCN.

3.2 Feature Extraction Network

The ethnic costume feature extraction network Xception-DL proposed in this paper is shown in Fig. 2. Xception-DL retains the structure of the original Xception except for the fully connected layer and takes the parameters of the pre-trained Xception model as the initial values. To meet the requirements of feature extraction of ethnic costume, a Flatten layer is newly added to convert the multi-dimensional input into a one-dimensional one, which facilitates the transfer of feature information to the subsequent fully connected layer for classification. In the final stage of the Three Denses module, the one-dimensionalized image data output from the Flatten layer is first transferred to the dropout layer and the fully connected layer. Then, after fine-tuning the model for the ethnic clothing elements data environment, the Softmax layer is used to obtain the results of feature extraction.

In terms of parameter optimization, in order to improve the Xception-based feature extraction model for ethnic clothing to adapt to migration learning, the effects of dropout value, dimensionality of fully connected layers, and the number of layers on the performance of the model are discussed.

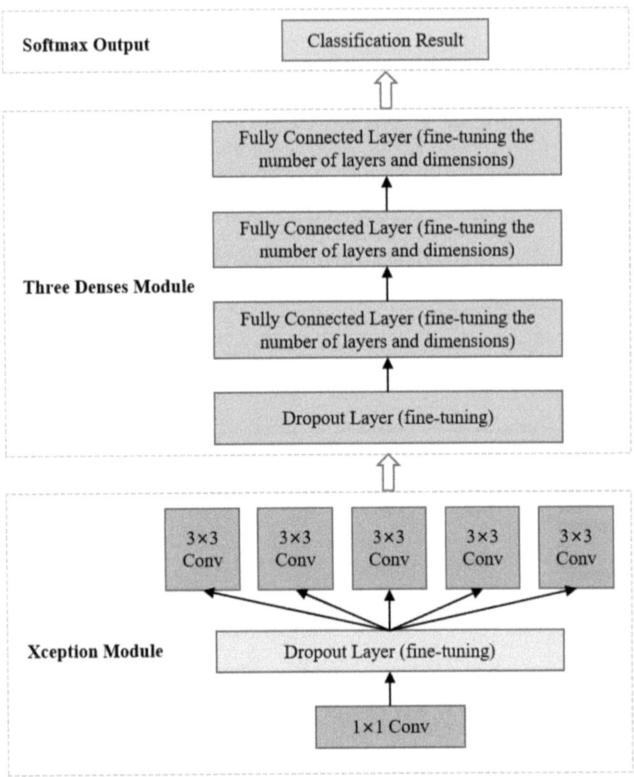

Fig. 2. Feature extraction network.

3.3 Link Prediction Model

The structure of the link prediction model is shown in Fig. 3. The method consists of a network embedding module and a link prediction module, which are then organically connected using a joint training strategy. The network embedding module uses AGCN to fuse link information and attribute information, generating a node representation matrix $H \in R^{n \times d}$ (where d is the dimensionality of node representations). It preserves the community structure by reconstructing the input graph $\mathcal{G}^{Training}$ with the BigCLAM overlapping community detection model and generates a graph reconstruction loss $\mathcal{L}_{Rec}$. The link prediction module takes the node representation H as input and computes the link probability between nodes using MLP, generating a prediction loss $\mathcal{L}_{Pre}$. Finally, $\mathcal{L}_{Rec}$ and $\mathcal{L}_{Pre}$ are combined through a weighted unified loss function to jointly train the AGCN and MLP, optimizing the node representation H to improve the link prediction performance.

Network Embedding Based on AGCN. Considering that link generation may be influenced by attribute information, link information, or both, this paper utilizes a network embedding module to adaptively fuse these two types of information for node representation. To achieve this, an AGCN is designed. The process is as follows.

Attribute Information Processing. Compute an attribute similarity matrix $S = [S_{ij}]^{n \times n}$ among the n nodes, where S_{ij} is defined as:

$$S_{ij} = \frac{x_i \times x_j}{||x_i||||x_j||} \tag{1}$$

Construct a k-nearest neighbor (kNN) graph $\mathcal{G}_F = (\mathcal{V}, \mathcal{E}_F, A_F, X)$ by selecting the top k similar node pairs for each node, where $\mathcal{E}_F$ and A_F represent the corresponding link set and binary adjacency matrix, respectively Learn hierarchical representations for each node v_i in $\mathcal{G}_F$ using a multi-layer GCN with a mean aggregator (MGCN):

$$H_{F_i}^{(l)} = \sigma\left(W^l Mean\left(\left\{H_{F_i}^{(l-1)}\right\}\left\{H_{F_j}^{(l-1)}, \forall v_i \in \mathcal{N}_F(i)\right\}\right)\right) \tag{2}$$

Here, W^l is the weight matrix for the l-th layer of MGCN, $\mathcal{N}_F(i)$ denotes the neighbors of v_i in $\mathcal{G}_F$, $\sigma(\cdot)$ is the activation function, and $Mean(\cdot)$ aggregates node representations by averaging their components. The final node representation $H_F \in R^{n \times d}$ is obtained for $\mathcal{G}_F$.

Link Information Processing. Use the original input graph $\mathcal{G}$ as the topological graph $\mathcal{G}_T$. Obtain the node representation $H_T \in R^{n \times n}$ for $\mathcal{G}_T$ in the same manner as $\mathcal{G}_F$.

Community-Preserving Network Embedding. To enable the node representation H to simultaneously preserve community structures, we employ the BigCLAM model to constrain H in reconstructing the training graph $\mathcal{G}^{Training}$. The generation of $\mathcal{G}^{Training}$ is modeled as:

$$P(\mathcal{G}^{Training}|H) = \prod_{e_{ij} \in \varepsilon^{Training}} P(e_{ij} \in \varepsilon^{Training}) \times \prod_{e_{ij} \notin \varepsilon^{Training}} P(e_{ij} \notin \varepsilon^{Training}) \tag{3}$$

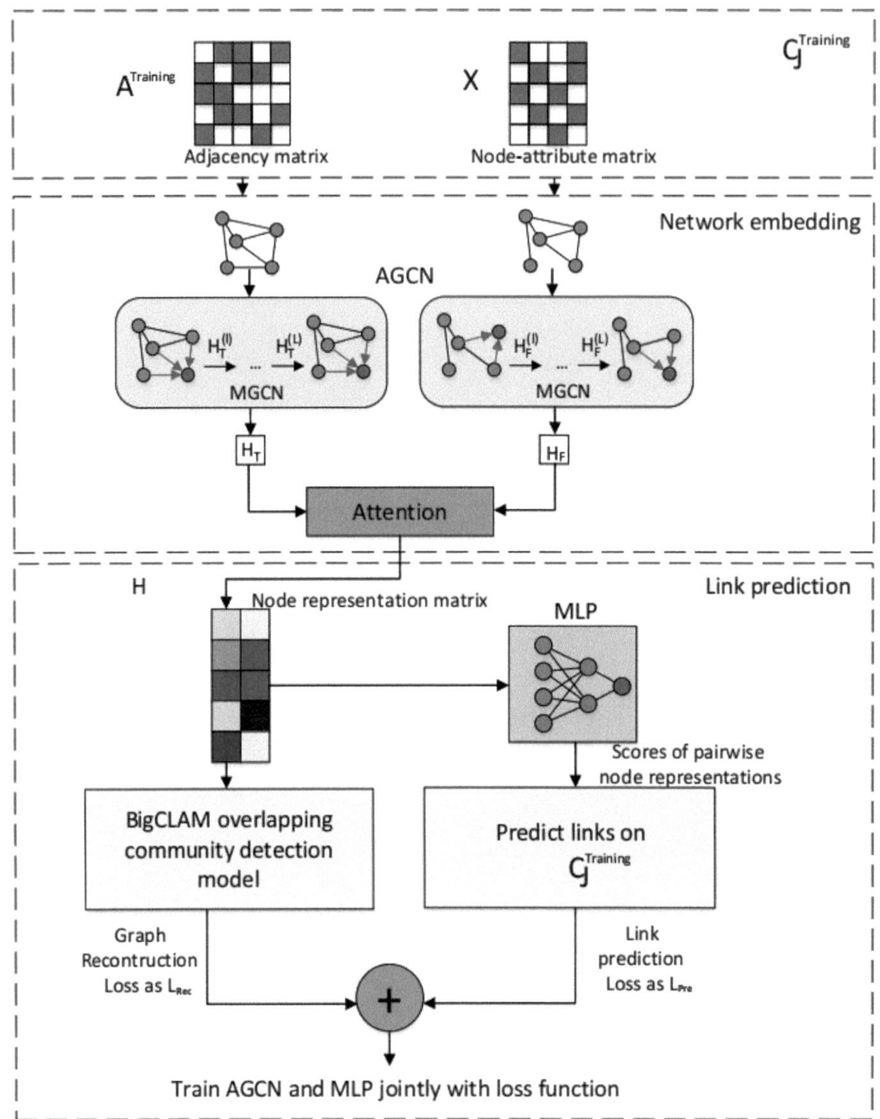

Fig. 3. Link prediction model.

Link Prediction. We predict unobserved links by estimating their existence probabilities. We employ a MLP that processes the concatenated representations of node pairs (H_i and H_j):

$$S_{ij} = MLP(H_i \| H_j) \tag{4}$$

Samples are drawn from the training set (positive samples) and unobserved edges (negative samples). The MLP computes scores for both sample types, and the model is optimized by minimizing the loss $\mathcal{L}_{Pre}$, enabling the MLP to learn pairwise node relationships through nonlinear transformations.

3.4 Unified Loss Function

The network embedding and link prediction modules are connected through node representations. To make network embedding learning more conducive to link prediction characterization, this paper jointly trains AGCN and MLP in the two modules. To this end, the prediction loss $\mathcal{L}_{Pre}$ and graph reconstruction loss $\mathcal{L}_{Rec}$ are combined to construct a unified loss function:

$$\mathcal{L} = \mathcal{L}_{Rec} + \alpha \mathcal{L}_{Pre} \tag{5}$$

where α is a positive hyperparameter that regulates the contribution of $\mathcal{L}_{Rec}$. By minimizing $\mathcal{L}$, AGCN and MLP can be jointly trained to enhance each other to form an end-to-end deep learning method for attribute network link prediction.

4 Experiments

4.1 Experiment Settings

The experiments are conducted on a computer equipped with an Intel(R) Core(TM) i7-9700K CPU, 16 GB memory, and a GeForce RTX2080Ti GPU, implemented in the Ubuntu 18.04 system using the Python-based Pytorch deep learning framework (version 1.8). All methods used optimal parameters. For CPGCN, the layer configurations of AGCN and MLP are set as n-256-d and 2d-d-1, respectively, with $k = 10$ and $a = 10$. Each method is tested by repeating the experiment 10 times, and the average results are recorded.

4.2 Datasets

We select five real-world attributed networks and the proposed Ethnic Costume Element Feature Network (EF) as datasets for empirical analysis. These include two widely used benchmark networks, Cora and PubMed, as well as networks proposed in the literature [7]. All these networks have well-defined ground-truth communities. For Cora and PubMed, their ground-truth community partitioning is obtained using the Louvain algorithm rather than the associated classification labels. Additionally, the ground-truth communities in Cora and PubMed are non-overlapping, while the communities in the other four networks may overlap to some extent. Among them, the proportions of networks with at least one overlapping community in Fb1684, Fb1912, and CS are 52.9%, 97.8%, and 100%, respectively.

4.3 Performance Analysis of Structural Optimization of Feature Extraction Model

Through systematic optimization experiments on fully connected layers (dimension D, quantity L) and Dropout layers (value T), the performance of the Xception model for ethnic costume element feature extraction was significantly improved. Results are shown in Figs. 4 and 5: With $L = 3$, $D = 1024$, the model (Xception-DL) achieved peak accuracy 0.908, substantially enhancing nonlinear feature representation. Under a two-layer structure ($L = 2$) with $T = 0.4$, overfitting was most effectively suppressed, yielding 0.902 accuracy and optimal generalization capability-surpassing the original model. These targeted parameter adjustments effectively resolved issues of insufficient accuracy and weak generalization, establishing a more reliable foundation for subsequent tasks.

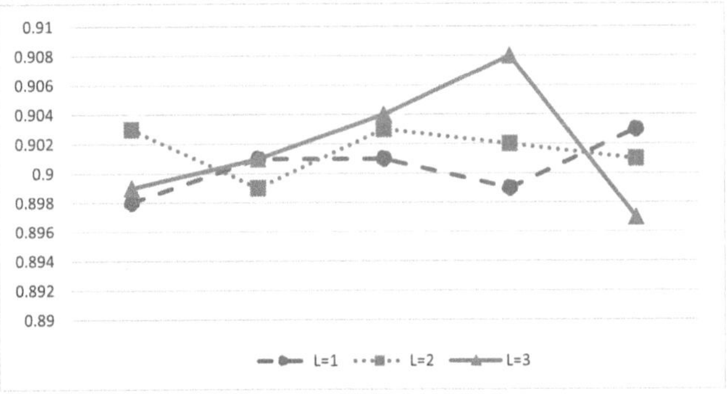

Fig. 4. The impact of the number and dimension of fully connected layers.

4.4 Comparison Experiment

Comparing CPGCN with the existing methods on various datasets, the area under the ROC curve (AUC) and average precision (AP) results in Tables 1 and 2 show that CPGCN outperforms the existing methods in most networks, especially in the scenario of small training sets. For example, when the Cora dataset has 20% of training set, its AUC and AP are improved by 8.66%, 6.81%, 3.41% and 2.72%, respectively, compared with other methods, and other networks also have similar performance. The results show that CPGCN can maintain good prediction performance even with limited training samples when dealing with overlapping community structure networks.

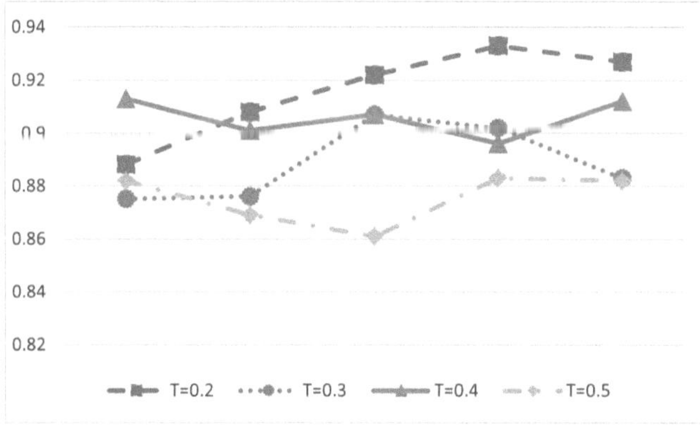

Fig. 5. The impact of dropout values on the model under two fully connected layers.

Table 1. AUC results of CPGCN and other convolutional methods on different training sets.

Dataset	TSS%	GCN	GraphSAGE	GAT	VGAE	SEAL	Ours
Cora	20%	0.766	0.717	0.765	0.762	0.641	**0.803**
	80%	0.930	0.887	0.954	0.918	0.884	**0.972**
PubMed	20%	0.867	0.732	0.884	0.891	0.827	**0.937**
	80%	0.951	0.873	0.916	**0.964**	0.949	0.962
Fb1684	20%	0.916	0.809	0.862	0.905	0.910	**0.928**
	80%	0.937	0.845	0.943	0.946	**0.951**	0.950
Fb1912	20%	0.951	0.889	0.955	0.955	0.946	**0.971**
	80%	0.964	0.918	0.963	0.973	0.972	**0.977**
CS	20%	0.915	0.892	0.908	0.908	0.889	**0.932**
	80%	0.963	0.946	0.958	0.963	0.958	**0.974**
EF	20%	0.792	0.821	0.809	0.834	0.794	**0.886**
	80%	0.888	0.863	0.876	0.893	0.896	**0.902**

Table 2. AP results of CPGCN and other convolutional methods on different training sets.

Dataset	TSS%	GCN	GraphSAGE	GAT	VGAE	SEAL	Ours
Cora	20%	0.747	0.708	0.802	0.770	0.669	**0.864**
	80%	0.942	0.870	0.959	0.901	0.899	**0.969**
PubMed	20%	0.888	0.728	0.897	0.897	0.820	**0.929**
	80%	0.958	0.851	0.908	**0.967**	0.953	0.964
Fb1684	20%	0.904	0.771	0.836	0.888	0.901	**0.904**
	80%	0.927	0.798	0.921	0.920	0.922	**0.934**
Fb1912	20%	0.931	0.856	0.931	0.938	0.943	**0.961**
	80%	0.949	0.886	0.950	0.966	**0.972**	0.971
CS	20%	0.906	0.880	0.908	0.896	0.770	**0.935**
	80%	0.966	0.926	0.960	0.958	0.970	**0.966**
EF	20%	0.825	0.794	0.803	0.783	0.842	**0.855**
	80%	0.884	0.849	0.878	0.881	0.901	**0.904**

4.5 Stability Experiment

In the experiments, we introduced attribute noise by randomly selecting $P\%$ of nodes and swapping their attribute vectors, thereby simulating inaccurate data or deliberate interference. As shown in Figs. 6 and 7, when the noise ratio increased from 0% to 50%, the performance of all methods (CPGCN, SEAL, LGLP, and ECN) declined, as the added noise distorted the authenticity of node attributes and structural information of links. However, CPGCN demonstrated significantly superior noise resistance compared to baseline models. At $P =$ 50%, CPGCN exhibited only 9.54% and 11.2% reductions in AUC and AP, respectively, while other models suffered decreases of at least 19.2% and 21.8%. This demonstrates CPGCN's capability to adaptively integrate noisy data while maintaining high robustness.

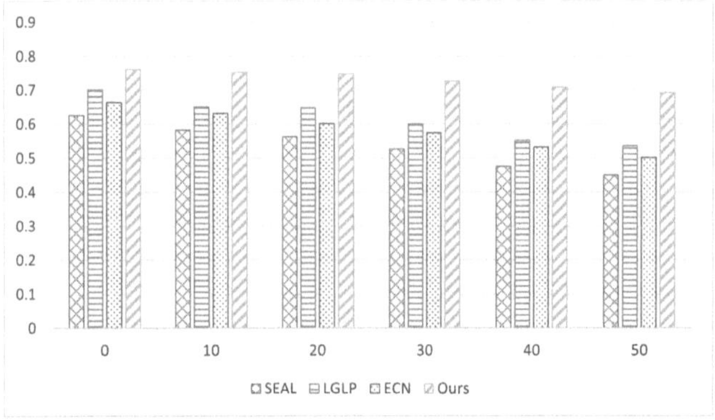

Fig. 6. AUC comparison of cora performance under different exchange attribute vector ratios.

4.6 Analysis of Ablation of Community Structures

To explore the effect of community structure on link prediction on attribute networks, we propose the simplified model CPGCN-COM ($\alpha = 0$ in CPGCN) that ignores the community factor. Experiments on six real attribute networks show that CPGCN significantly outperforms CPGCN-COM in both AUC and AP, especially in sparse networks (as shown in Figs. 8 and 9). For example, AUC and AP are improved by 5.29% and 5.52% on Cora dataset, and similar advantages are verified on PubMed and CS datasets. The results confirm that the community structure can effectively improve the link prediction accuracy, reflecting the superiority of CPGCN.

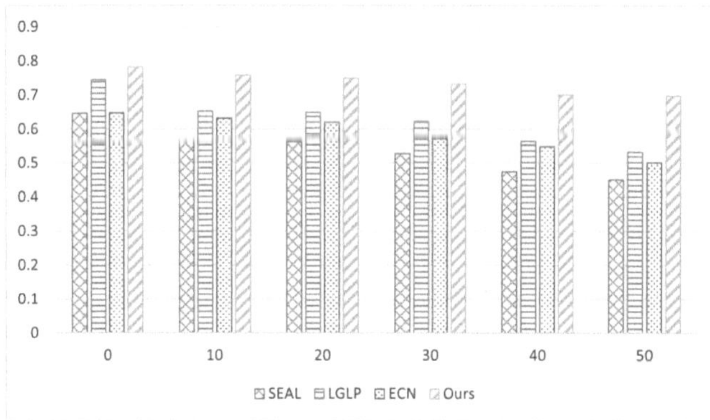

Fig. 7. AP comparison of cora performance under different exchange attribute vector ratios.

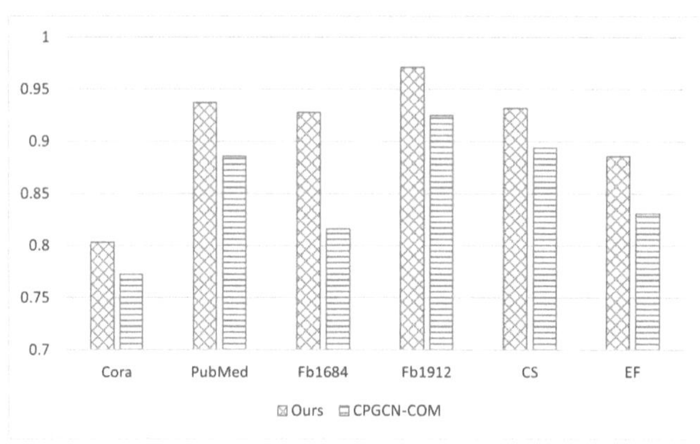

Fig. 8. Comparison of AUC between CPGCN and CPGCN-COM methods on different datasets.

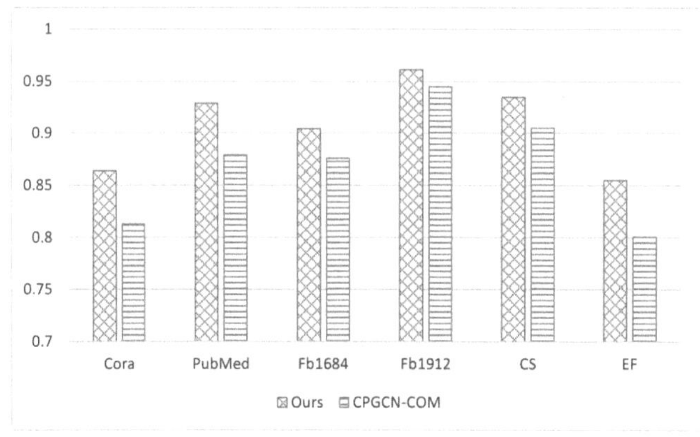

Fig. 9. Comparison of AP between CPGCN and CPGCN-COM methods on different datasets.

4.7 Comparison Results with Its Variants

The CPGCN framework is highly flexible and extensible, and its core modules (e.g., MGCN, BigCLAM, and MLP) can be replaced with similar models according to the task requirements. To validate the effectiveness of MGCN, we conduct comparison experiments by replacing MGCN in CPGCN with GCN, GAT and GIN respectively on a dataset with 80% training samples (other parameters remain unchanged). As shown in Figs. 10 and 11, CPGCN with MGCN slightly outperforms the other variants in both AUC and AP metrics, indicating that MGCN can fuse link information and node attributes more effectively.

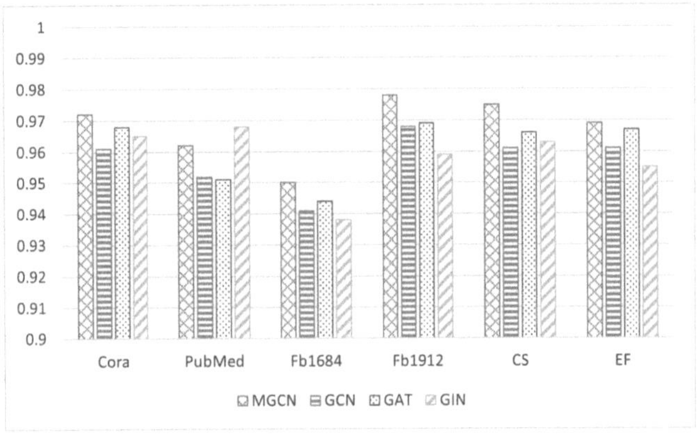

Fig. 10. Comparison of AUC performance of different GNN models.

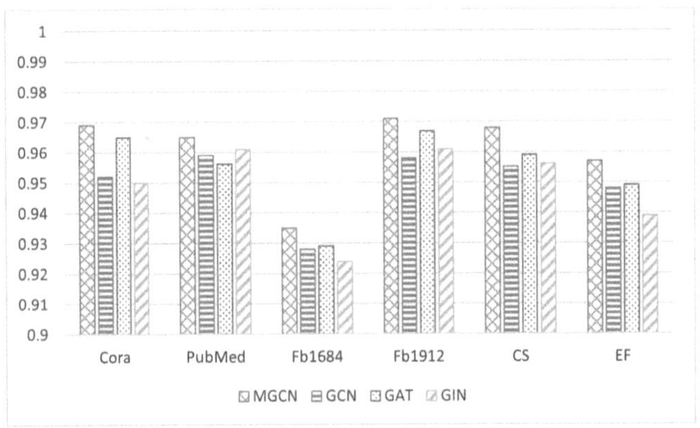

Fig. 11. Comparison of AP performance of different GNN models.

4.8 Analysis of the Evolutionary Relationship of Ethnic Costume Elements

Based on the final predictive information of ethnic costume elements obtained from CPGCN, we conducted the following analysis. The elements of Manchu and Mongolian ethnic costumes have maintained cultural continuity while demonstrating mutual influence during their evolutionary process.

During the Yuan Dynasty, cultural exchanges between the main nomadic peoples, the Manchus and the Mongols, were quite frequent. Costumes of this period were usually characterized as wide and comfortable, featuring loose cuffs to facilitate horseback riding and other activities. Manchu and Mongolian costumes share many similarities and reflect the typical characteristics of nomadic lifestyles [10].

In the Ming Dynasty, while Manchu costumes retained their overall loose structure, details such as narrower cuffs began to adapt to non-equestrian activities. Meanwhile, Mongolian costumes incorporated embroidery techniques, marking a significant stylistic transformation [16].

By the Qing Dynasty, the Manchu "Magua" jacket with its iconic "horse-hoof sleeves" became a defining feature of their attire, profoundly influencing the design of Mongolian costumes [2,8] (as shown in Fig. 12).

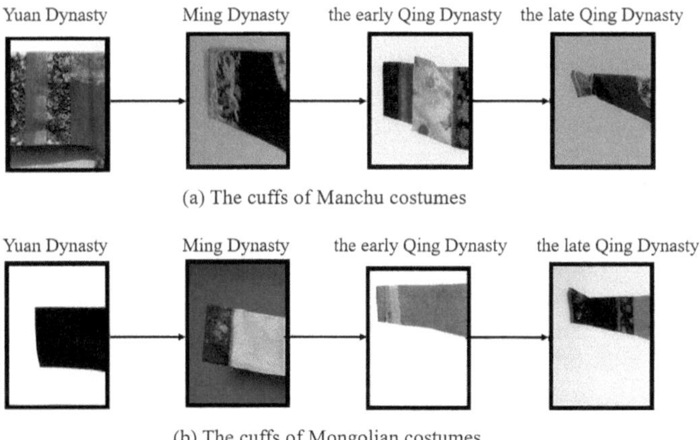

Fig. 12. Historical evolution of cuffs in Manchu and Mongolian clothing.

From a diachronic perspective, the elements in the costumes of the Manchu and Mongolian ethnic groups not only have their own unique regional and ethnic characteristics but also reflect the historical process of mutual integration and influence. The relationship node diagram is shown in Fig. 13.

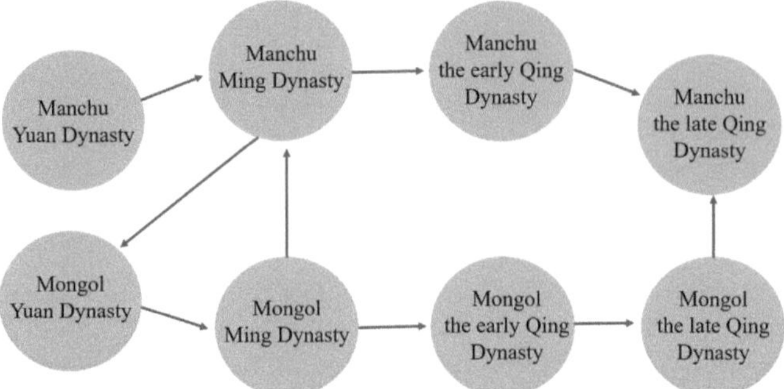

Fig. 13. The relationship between full and Mongolian clothing cuffs.

5 Conclusion

As an important carrier of cultural exchange and integration of various ethnic groups, the elemental evolution law of national costumes is of great significance in revealing the history of ethnic integration. Aiming at the shortcomings of existing studies, we propose a new framework CPGCN for mining the evolutionary relationship of ethnic clothing elements. CPGCN is trained by AGCN fusing node attributes and topological information, combined with community detection to preserve structural features, and joint MLP link prediction for multi-tasking. Concurrently, we develop the Xception-DL element extraction model and optimized the network structure through migration learning to significantly improve the feature extraction capability. We provide new perspectives and methods for mining the evolutionary relationship of costume elements, which helps to deepen the research on the connotation of ethnic integration. In the future, we will combine multi-dimensional information such as multi-region costume data and historical craftsmanship to further expand the depth of research.

Acknowledgment. This study was supported by "Fundamental Research Funds for the Central Universities" (grant number 044420250025).

Disclosure of Interests. The authors have no competing interests to declare that are relevant to the content of this article.

References

1. Chen, X.: Inheritance and innovation of traditional ethnic clothing elements in modern fashion design. Shanghai Apparel **07**, 51–53 (2024)
2. Gao, M., Ming, Q.: A comparative study on manchu and mongolian clothing culture from the perspective of semiotics. People's TribuneAcademic Front (13), 88–91 (2019). https://doi.org/10.16619/j.cnki.rmltxsqy.2019.14.011

3. Grover, A., Leskovec, J.: node2vec: scalable feature learning for networks. In: Proceedings of the 22nd ACM SIGKDD International Conference on Knowledge Discovery and Data Mining, KDD 2016, pp. 855–864. ACM, New York, NY, USA (2016). https://doi.org/10.1145/2939672.2939754
4. Liu, X., Cui, L.: Application of mongolian clothing elements in outdoor sports shoe design. China Leather **54**(05), 63–69+74 (2025). https://doi.org/10.13536/j.cnki.issn1001-6813.2025-005-014
5. Perozzi, B., Al-Rfou, R., Skiena, S.: Deepwalk: online learning of social representations. In: Proceedings of the 20th ACM SIGKDD International Conference on Knowledge Discovery and Data Mining, KDD 2014, pp. 701–710. ACM, New York, NY, USA (2014). https://doi.org/10.1145/2623330.2623732
6. Qi, X.: Research on digital representation and innovative design of intangible cultural heritage clothing from the perspective of artificial intelligence. Dyeing Finishing Technol. **46**(05), 70–75 (2024)
7. Shchur, O., Günnemann, S.: Overlapping community detection with graph neural networks (2019). https://arxiv.org/abs/1909.12201
8. Suqi Tian, Qi Dong, H.S., Duan, T.: The influence of the political system of the qing dynasty on the dress of horqin women. Fashion China (Z1), 115–121 (2022)
9. Tang, X.: Deep learning based gray scale image coloring research on ethnic costumes. Master's thesis, Yunnan Normal University (2023). https://doi.org/10.27459/d.cnki.gynfc.2023.000958
10. Tian, S.: Evolution and innovative design of mongolian tribal costume forms under the league banner system in the qing dynasty. Master's thesis, Inner Mongolia University of Technology (2022). https://doi.org/10.27225/d.cnki.gnmgu.2022.000064
11. Wang, X., Cui, P., Wang, J., Pei, J., Zhu, W., Yang, S.: Community preserving network embedding. In: Proceedings of the Thirty-First AAAI Conference on Artificial Intelligence, AAAI 2017, pp. 203–209. AAAI Press (2017). https://doi.org/10.5555/3298239.3298270
12. Wu, T., Wang, S.: Multi-scale feature extraction and fusion network for single image deblurring. Journal of Nanjing University of Posts and Telecommunications (Natural Science Edition), pp. 1–13 (2025)
13. Xiao, A.: The consciousness of the chinese national community from the perspective of the evolution of ethnic costume culture. Footwear Technol. Des. **3**(03), 46–48 (2023)
14. Zheng, X., Zihou Yuan, Y.D., Zhang, H.: Clothing classification and recognition based on improved resnet50 and transfer learning. Textile Eng. J. **2**(05), 51–62 (2024). https://doi.org/10.20150/j.cnki.fzgcxb.2024.05.006
15. Zhang, M., Chen, Y.: Link prediction based on graph neural networks. In: Proceedings of the 32nd International Conference on Neural Information Processing Systems, NIPS 2018, pp. 5171–5181. Curran Associates Inc., Red Hook, NY, USA (2018). https://doi.org/10.5555/3327345.3327423
16. Zhang, P.: Research on Mongolian costumes under China's traditional craft revitalization plan. Master's thesis, Changchun University of Technology (2021). https://doi.org/10.27805/d.cnki.gccgy.2021.000420
17. Zhang, Z., Cui, L., Wu, J.: Exploring an edge convolution and normalization based approach for link prediction in complex networks. J. Netw. Comput. Appl. **189**, 103113 (2021). https://doi.org/10.1016/j.jnca.2021.103113

18. Zhou, Y.: The value of ethnic costume research in sichuan-tibet-yunnan-qinghai regions for strengthening the consciousness of the chinese national community. Res. China Natl. Museum **00**, 45–54 (2023)
19. Zhuang, C., Ma, Q.: Dual graph convolutional networks for graph-based semi-supervised classification. In: Proceedings of the 2018 World Wide Web Conference, pp. 499–508. WWW '18, International World Wide Web Conferences Steering Committee, Republic and Canton of Geneva, CHE (2018). https://doi.org/10.1145/3178876.3186116

Shilling Attacks on GNN-Based Recommender Systems with Graph Contrastive Learning

Qixin Guan[1], Shunmei Meng[2(✉)], Qianmu Li[2], and Xuyun Zhang[3]

[1] Department of Cyber Science and Engineering, Nanjing University of Science and Technology, Nanjing, China
gqx@njust.edu.cn

[2] Department of Computer Science and Engineering, Nanjing University of Science and Technology, Nanjing, China
{mengshunmei,qianmu}@njust.edu.cn

[3] School of Computing, Macquarie University, Sydney, Australia
xuyun.zhang@mq.edu.au

Abstract. As Graph Neural Networks (GNN) have become increasingly popular in recommender systems (RSs) due to their ability to capture complex user-item relationships, they have also introduced new vulnerabilities. Specifically, the reliance on graph-structured data makes these systems particularly susceptible to shilling attack, where attackers can manipulate recommendation outcomes by injecting fake users or fabricating interactions. However, existing shilling attacks for GNN-based RSs often fail to fully exploit the graph structure, limiting their effectiveness. In this paper, we propose GraphFaux, a shilling attack for GNN-based RSs that uses graph structural learning to optimize fake interactions, affecting the recommendations of more users. It combines Generative Adversarial Networks (GANs) and Graph Structure Contrastive Learning (GSCL) to generate fake users that closely resemble real users. We use GANs to generate fake user features by combining the target item features with real user behavior. A scoring model then calculates the interaction probabilities for the edges, resulting in a more realistic and effective attack. Additionally, through structural learning, we construct two distinct views and employ contrastive learning to capture fine-grained user-item relationships within the graph. This multi-perspective refinement enhances the fake interactions, optimizing the connections between fake users and target items. Extensive evaluations across three datasets and different recommendation models demonstrate that GraphFaux achieves an average improvement of 11.7%, even compared to state-of-the-art shilling attack methods.

Keywords: Shilling Attack · Recommender System · Structure Learning

J. Li et al. (Eds.): APWeb-WAIM 2025, LNCS 16115, pp. 581–595, 2026.
https://doi.org/10.1007/978-981-95-5719-6_37

1 Introduction

With the rapid advancement of deep learning, GNN-based RSs have become integral to modern web applications, including e-commerce, social networking, and content recommendation. Their ability to capture graph-structured data allows them to model complex interactions between users and items, generating precise, personalized recommendations [4,9]. However, this strong reliance on graph structures also introduces new security vulnerabilities. In particular, shilling attacks, where adversaries inject fake users or interactions to manipulate item embeddings, can significantly distort recommendation results, increasing the exposure of targeted items [17,18]. Such attacks pose serious threats to the security, reliability, and fairness of recommender systems, potentially leading to misleading recommendations that degrade user experience and undermine the commercial integrity of online platforms.

Early research on shilling attacks primarily focused on heuristic methods, which rely on rules to generate fake user profiles, such as random attacks, popular item attacks, and love/hate attacks [11,12,16]. However, these traditional attack methods are often model-agnostic and lack a deep understanding of the internal mechanisms of recommender systems, making it difficult to maximize their effectiveness. Consequently, more targeted attack methods have emerged, tailored to RSs, such as those designed for matrix factorization-based RSs [12] and graph-based RSs [3]. However, in graph-based RSs, these methods typically generate fake user profiles by considering only item interactions and not the users' own features, which makes them easier to detect. Recently there has been a growing interest in exploring attacks on GNN-based RSs by injecting fake user nodes, but these approaches often fail to fully leverage the potential of the graph structure, which they tend to rely on simply adding fake users or edges without optimizing or fine-tuning the graph structure. In particular, these approaches often fail to fully exploit the unique capabilities of GNNs for node embeddings [22], which limits the effectiveness of the attack. This suggests that current methods have not adequately accounted for the complexities of GNN structures. Thus, there is a need for more refined attack strategies that can better exploit the graph characteristics of GNN, revealing their vulnerabilities and improving the effectiveness of malicious attacks. It is important to emphasize that the primary goal of this research is to expose vulnerabilities in GNN-based RSs rather than to facilitate malicious activities. By understanding the mechanisms of such attacks, we can develop more robust defense strategies [24–26], such as combining behavioral analysis with graph-based anomaly detection, to protect recommender systems from exploitation.

In this paper, we propose GraphFaux, an innovative shilling attack method designed for GNN-based RSs, which uses graph structural learning to optimize the interactions of fake users, strengthening the attack's ability. This approach leverages GANs to craft fake users harder to detect through adversarial training, significantly enhancing the stealthiness and effectiveness of the attack. Then by integrating prior knowledge of item popularity, we use a scoring model to calculate interaction probabilities to generate fake interactions, increasing the exposure and recommendation weight of the target item. Furthermore, by using graph structure learning to construct different contrastive views, we optimize the interactions of fake users. To the best of our knowledge, this is the first study to apply graph structural learning in a shilling attack on GNN-based RSs, effectively improving the camouflage of fake users and boosting the target item's visibility to influence more users.

The main contributions of GraphFaux are as follows:

- We propose a shilling attack method tailored for GNN-based RSs, named GraphFaux. It considers both user feature information and structural feature, leveraging GANs to generate fake user features and a scoring model to create fake interactions, significantly enhancing the ability of attack.
- To further enhance the attack's precision, we introduce a graph structure contrastive learning approach, which generates different views for comparison. This novel application of contrastive learning in shilling attacks significantly improves its ability to manipulate the recommender system undetected.
- Extensive experiments conducted on three datasets show that GraphFaux consistently surpasses state-of-the-art shilling attack methods, presenting a heightened threat to GNN-based RSs.

2 Related Work

GNN-Based Recommender System. Graph Neural Networks have gained significant attention in RSs due to their ability to effectively model complex relationships in graph-structured data. GNN-based RSs represent a cutting-edge approach in modern online platforms, leveraging high-order structural information in user-item graphs to capture intricate dependencies between users and items, which enhances recommendation accuracy. Unlike traditional methods like neighborhood-based approaches [20], matrix factorization [10], and association rule-based techniques [1], GNN-based RSs excel at modeling non-linear relationships and interactions within graph structures, making them more capable of handling the complexity of modern recommendation tasks. However, their reliance on graph representations also exposes them to vulnerabilities, making them susceptible to malicious attacks that can manipulate graph structures and compromise the quality of recommendations.

Shilling Attack in Recommendations. Shilling attacks, also known as data poisoning or profile injection attacks, aim to manipulate RSs by injecting fake user profiles to promote or demote specific items. Early heuristic methods, such as random and average attacks, were model-agnostic and their performance is often suboptimal. The advancement of adversarial attack research has spurred the exploration of novel shilling attack methods, including optimization-based attacks using gradient methods, as well as approaches leveraging GANs [15], reinforcement learning [2], and knowledge distillation techniques. Deep learning's advancement has spurred the evolution of increasingly sophisticated attack strategies. Methods like WGAN, which uses Wasserstein distance, create highly authentic fake user profiles with effective attack outcomes. Techniques like AUSH [13] and Leg-UP [14] further enhance stealth by generating templates based on known information to create profiles. Recent research has expanded shilling attacks to graph-based RSs, such as GSPAttack [19], which specifically targets GNN-based RSs. AutoAttack [5] focuses on promoting items to specific user groups, significantly increasing their visibility.

Unlike existing methods, GraphFaux introduces a novel combination of Generative Adversarial Networks and Graph Structure Contrastive Learning. While prior GAN-based approaches focus solely on generating realistic user features, GraphFaux goes a step further by leveraging GSCL to optimize the interactions between fake users and target items. This multi-perspective refinement ensures that fake users are not only structurally similar to real users but also semantically aligned with the target items, maximizing the attack's impact.

3 Problem Definition

Our work assumes a black-box attack scenario, where the attacker has no access to the internal parameters of the recommendation model but can inject fake users and interactions into the system. This type of attack is classified as a data poisoning attack, as it manipulates the training data to influence the model's recommendations. Unlike evasion attacks, which aim to alter the model's predictions at inference time, our approach focuses on corrupting the training process to achieve long-term manipulation of the recommendation outcomes.

Consider a recommender system consisting of a user set U, an item set I and interaction edges E, where the graph structure is represented as $G = (U \cup I, E)$. When performing a shilling attack, the attacker creates a group of fake users U_F and establishes malicious interactions E_F. The attacked graph structure becomes $G_m = (U_m \cup I, E_m)$, where $U_m = \{U \cup U_F\}$ and $E_m = \{E \cup E_F\}$. The goal of the attack is to manipulate RSs in such a way that the target item I_t is recommended to a broader audience. For this purpose, we generate U_F and E_F to increase the likelihood of the target item being recommended to normal users. Details are as follows:

$$\max_{u \in U, i_t \in I_t} gRS\left(u, i_t \mid U_m, I, E_m, I_t, \theta\right) \tag{1}$$

where $gRS(\cdot)$ is the recommendation function, which calculates the probability that item i_t will appear in the recommendation list for user u, and model parameters θ.

4 Methodology

Figure 1 illustrates the proposed GraphFaux framework, which consists of three key steps. First, fake user features are generated using GANs, ensuring high stealth. Next, interaction edges are created by simulating the behaviors and characteristics of real users. These interactions are then optimized using Graph Structure Contrastive Learning to strengthen the relationships between fake users and target items. Finally, through joint optimization, GraphFaux maximizes the attack's effectiveness while minimizing its impact on the recommendation system.

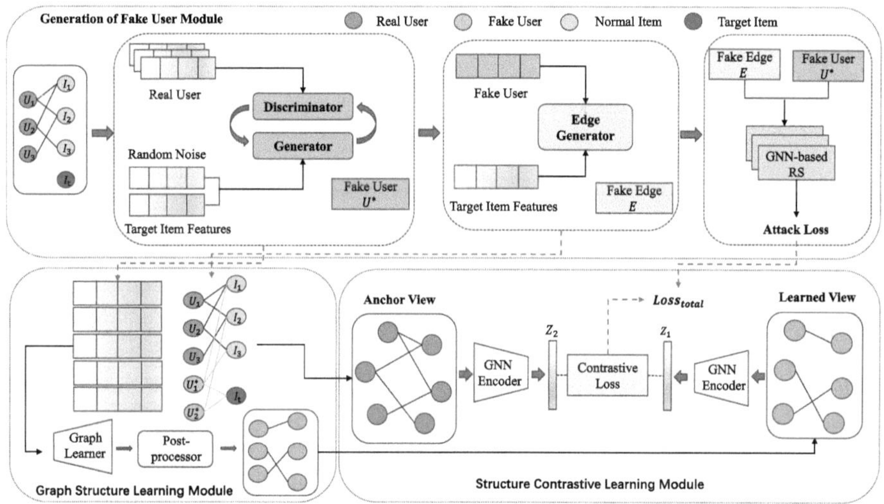

Fig. 1. The framework of GraphFaux

4.1 Generation of Fake User

Fake Feature Generation. In GNN-based RSs, user preferences are captured through user features and user-item interaction graphs. Attackers can exploit both these components to craft fake users for shilling attacks. To make fake user features resemble real ones and remain harder to detect, we leverage GAN for feature generation.

Consider a user feature matrix $X_{real} \in R^{n \times d}$, with the goal of generating m fake users to produce an updated feature matrix $X' = \begin{bmatrix} X_{real} \\ X_{\text{fake}} \end{bmatrix}$. To achieve this, we adopt the concept of adversarial training to generate fake user features. The generator G uses random noise $z \in R^{z_{\text{dim}}}$, where z_{dim} is the dimension of the random noise, and a target item feature vector $y_j \in R^d$ to produce fake user features $X_{\text{fake}} = G(z, y_j)$. The discriminator D, implemented as a neural network, takes a user feature vector $X \in R^d$ as input and outputs a probability $D(X')$. This probability indicates the likelihood that x represents a real user feature.

$$D(X') = \sigma((X'W_0)W_1) \tag{2}$$

where W_0, W_1 is the weight matrix and σ is the sigmoid function, which outputs $D(X') \in [0, 1]$.

To maximize its ability to correctly classify real and fake user features, the discriminator employ binary cross-entropy loss, which is defined as:

$$\mathcal{L}_{fusr} = \sum_{u \in U_F \cup U} L(\hat{p}_u, q_u) \tag{3}$$

where $L(\hat{p}_u, q_u) = -(q_u \log(\hat{p}_u) + (1 - q_u)\log(1 - \hat{p}_u))$, q_u is a binary indicator representing the ground truth label, and $\hat{p}_u$ represents the prediction probability of user u.

Fake Edge Generation. In shilling attacks, structural similarity is crucial for success. To ensure fake users mimic real user behavior, we use a scoring model to compute interaction probabilities with popular items. By leveraging high interaction frequencies, fake users' behavior becomes more realistic, enhancing attack stealth. Specifically, we firstly obtain feature representations e^u and e^{i_t} for fake users and target items via a surrogate model. We then utilize a two-layer neural network F to calculate connection probabilities with candidate items. Finally, we apply the Gumbel-Top-k technique $\mathcal{G}$ to convert these probabilities into actual connections. The process is as follows:

$$\begin{aligned} e_{\text{mal}} &= \mathcal{G}(F(i_t, u, G; \theta^*)) \\ F(i_t, u, G; \theta) &= \sigma([e^u \| e^t] W_0 + b_0) W_1 + b_1 \end{aligned} \tag{4}$$

where σ is the activation function, $[e^u \| e^{i_t}]$ is the concatenation of the fake user and target item features, and $\theta = W_0, W_1, b_0, b_1$ are learning parameters.

To tackle the issue of edge discretization, we employ the Gumbel-Softmax technique to convert the connection probability $F_{\text{u,i}}$ of a fake user into an edge e_{mal}. The Gumbel distribution effectively represents the distribution of sample extrema, defined as $G_i = -\log(-\log(U_i))$, where $U_i \sim \text{Uniform}(0, 1)$. The discretized connection probability $F_{\text{u,i}}$ for an edge using the Gumbel distribution is expressed as:

$$\text{Gumbel - Softmax } (F_{u,i}) = \frac{\exp(F_{u,i} + G_i)}{\sum_{j=1}^{|I|} \exp(F_{u,j} + G_j)} \tag{5}$$

If $F_{\text{u,i}}$ exceeds a predefined threshold (set at 0.5), an edge is generated between the user u and item i.

4.2 Graph Structure Contrastive Learning

Graph Structure Learning. In this section, we employ a graph learner to roughly model the graph-structured data and then use a post-processor to refine it into a more effective adjacency matrix.

The graph learner p_θ models graph-structured data by extracting node embeddings $\mathrm{E}_m \in R^{n\times d}$ and generating an adjacency matrix $\mathrm{S}' \in R^{n\times n}$ based on node similarity. The details are as follows:

$$\mathrm{S}' = p_\theta^{ML}(\mathrm{X}', \mathrm{A}) = \varphi\left(g_\theta(\mathrm{X}', \mathrm{A})\right) = \varphi(\mathrm{E_m}), \tag{6}$$

where $g_\theta(\cdot)$ is a neural network-based embedding function parameterized by θ, $\varphi(\cdot)$ computes pairwise similarities using a non-parametric metric, and $A \in [0,1]^{n\times n}$ represents the weighted adjacency matrix.

The post-processor refines the adjacency matrix by applying sparsification (via k-nearest neighbors), symmetrization, and normalization. This ensures the matrix is sparse, symmetric, non-negative, and the edge weights are within the range $[0, 1]$, better aligning the structure with real-world graphs.

Structural Contrastive Learning. After above processing, a graph structure is obtained with an adjacency matrix S' and a feature matrix X'. Two views are then constructed: the learner view $G_1 = (\mathrm{S}', \mathrm{X}')$, which combines the learned adjacency matrix S' and feature matrix X', and the anchor view $G_2 = (\mathrm{S}, \mathrm{X}')$, which combines the original adjacency matrix S and feature matrix X'.

To enhance robustness, data augmentation techniques are applied, including feature masking and edge dropout, which are controlled by two hyperparameters. Feature Masking Rate (p_m), which determines the proportion of node features that are randomly masked (set to zero) during augmentation. For example, if $p_m = 0.2$, 20% of the features for each node are masked. Edge Dropout Rate (p_d), which specifies the probability of dropping edges from the graph during augmentation. For instance, if $p_d = 0.3$, each edge has a 30% chance of being removed.

These augmentation techniques produce augmented views $\tilde{G}_1$ and $\tilde{G}_2$, which are then processed through a GNN encoder to derive the embeddings Z_1 and Z_2. Contrastive learning is then employed to optimize the model, using the InfoNCE loss function:

$$\mathcal{L}_{\mathrm{gscl}} = -\frac{1}{N}\sum_{i=1}^{N} \log \frac{\exp\left(\mathrm{sim}\left(Z_1^i, Z_2^i\right)/\tau\right)}{\sum_{j=1}^{N} \exp\left(\mathrm{sim}\left(Z_1^i, Z_2^j\right)/\tau\right)} \tag{7}$$

where N is the total number of sample pairs, Z_1^i and Z_2^i are the embeddings of the i-th sample in view $\tilde{G}_1$ and $\tilde{G}_2$, $\mathrm{sim}(\cdot,\cdot)$ represents the similarity function, and τ denotes a temperature hyperparameter. This approach improves the efficiency of graph structure learning. Minimizing the loss strengthens the similarity of related node pairs while reducing it for unrelated pairs.

4.3 Optimization

In promotion attacks, fake users interact with the target item to boost its ranking and increase its visibility. We use the following loss function to achieve this:

$$\mathcal{L}_{\text{target}} = -\sum_{u \in U_F, t \in I_t} \log r_{u,t} \tag{8}$$

where $r_{u,t}$ represents the prediction probability of user u and item t.

Shilling attacks can cause a significant decline in recommendation performance, which, in turn, increases the likelihood of the attack being detected. To ensure the system's performance, we incorporate a constraint function:

$$\mathcal{L}_{mrp} = -\sum_{u \in U \cup U_F, i \in I} r_{u,i} \log \hat{r}_{u,i} + (1 - r_{u,i}) \log (1 - \hat{r}_{u,i}), \tag{9}$$

where $\hat{r}_{u,i}$ represents the prediction probability of interaction between user u on item i.

Considering all the attacks and constraints mentioned above, we employ the following unified loss function for joint training:

$$\mathcal{L}_{total} = \mathcal{L}_{fuser} + \alpha \mathcal{L}_{target} + \beta \mathcal{L}_{mrp} + \gamma L_{gscl} \tag{10}$$

where α, β, and γ are hyperparameters that regulate the influence of each optimization objective on the overall attack outcome.

5 Experiments

5.1 Experimental Settings

Datasets. To demonstrate the effectiveness of our method, we use three publicly available datasets—Automotive[1], ML-100K[2] and Yelp[3] used in prior research on shilling attacks and recommender systems. Table 1 summarizes the dataset statistics.

Table 1. Statistics of datasets.

Dataset	Users	Items	Interactions	Sparsity
Automotive	2,928	1,835	20,473	99.62%
ML-100K	943	1,682	100,000	93.70%
Yelp	2,762	10,477	119,237	99.59%

Baseline. We compare GraphFaux to traditional shilling attack methods random [11], bandwagon [16], and the state-of-the-art deep learning-based approaches such as AUSH [13], Leg-UP [14], and GSPAttack [19].

1 http://jmcauley.ucsd.edu/data/amazon/.
2 https://grouplens.org/datasets/movielens/100k/.
3 https://www.kaggle.com/yelp-dataset/yelp-dataset.

Victim RSs. We perform shilling attacks on popular RSs, targeting both a traditional model (WRMF [8]) and deep learning based recommendation models (NCF [7], NGCF [21], LightGCN [6]and SimGCL [23]).
Evaluation Metric. Shilling attack effectiveness is assessed using Hit Ratio (HR@k), which calculates the percentage of users whose top-k recommendations contain the target item. Additionally, normalized discounted cumulative gain (NDCG@k) evaluates the recommender system's performance under attack.

5.2 Comparison and Analysis

We evaluate GraphFaux on three datasets and five different recommendation models to assess its attack performance and recommendation quality.

Table 2. Evaluating attack performance in different recommendation models. Top results highlighted in bold, second-best underlined.

Dataset	Victim	Attack Method (HR@50)					
		Random	Bandwagon	AUSH	Leg-UP	GSPAttack	GraphFaux
Automotive	WRMF	0.2556	0.3198	0.1968	0.2857	<u>0.3362</u>	**0.3547**
	NCF	0.2219	0.3069	0.2932	0.3218	<u>0.3546</u>	**0.4015**
	NGCF	0.2544	0.3094	0.3165	0.3608	<u>0.4013</u>	**0.4866**
	LightGCN	0.2036	0.3530	0.2536	<u>0.3868</u>	0.3036	**0.4274**
	SimGCL	0.2158	0.3101	0.3293	0.3208	<u>0.3564</u>	**0.3841**
ML-100K	WRMF	0.3017	0.3632	0.3154	0.3354	<u>0.3743</u>	**0.4216**
	NCF	0.3773	0.4331	<u>0.4858</u>	0.4532	0.4742	**0.5289**
	NGCF	0.3533	0.4121	0.4258	<u>0.4605</u>	0.4553	**0.4721**
	LightGCN	0.3311	0.3600	0.4595	0.4258	<u>0.4637</u>	**0.4854**
	SimGCL	0.1840	0.2029	0.2092	0.2870	<u>0.3427</u>	**0.3501**
Yelp	WRMF	0.1049	0.1142	0.1161	<u>0.1552</u>	0.1384	**0.2007**
	NCF	0.0738	0.0695	0.0989	0.0876	<u>0.1148</u>	**0.1315**
	NGCF	0.0629	0.0724	0.0849	0.0787	<u>0.0993</u>	**0.1584**
	LightGCN	0.0603	0.0441	0.0763	0.0854	<u>0.1050</u>	**0.1240**
	SimGCL	0.0986	0.0861	0.1015	0.1236	<u>0.1280</u>	**0.1528**

Attack Performance: Our proposed GraphFaux method significantly enhances the likelihood of target items appearing in recommendation lists. As shown in Table 2, GraphFaux consistently outperforms baseline methods in terms of HR@50. On the Yelp dataset, it achieves an improvement of over 51.3% compared to traditional methods. For GAN-based approaches like AUSH and Leg-UP, our method demonstrates an average performance boost of 34.7%. Even when compared to GSPAttack, which is specifically designed for GNN, GraphFaux achieves a 15.2% improvement. These enhancements are attributed to the use of GAN for generating high-quality fake users and the introduction of structural contrastive learning, which significantly improves the quality of fake user interactions, making RSs more vulnerable to shilling attacks.

Recommendation Performance: Traditional shilling attacks typically lead to a noticeable decline in overall recommendation performance, making such anomalies easy to detect. Consequently, preserving the integrity of recommendation quality is critical to ensure that shilling attacks remain undetected. As shown in Table 3, we use NDCG@50 to evaluate recommendation performance. Compared to the best-performing baseline methods, GraphFaux achieves a 12.6% improvement, indicating that it has the least impact on recommendations and enhances its stealthiness, making it more difficult to detect. This improvement suggests that GraphFaux not only minimizes the degradation in recommendation quality but also cleverly manipulates the graph structure to avoid detection, offering a more sophisticated and effective attack strategy.

Table 3. Recommendation performance after being attacked by different attack methods on three datasets.

NDCG@50	Automotive	ML-100K	Yelp
Random	0.0519	0.0481	0.0147
Bandwagon	0.0660	0.0514	0.0100
AUSH	0.0689	0.0577	0.0239
Leg-UP	0.0641	0.0586	0.0177
GSPAttack	0.0750	0.0670	0.0366
GraphFaux	**0.0800**	**0.0723**	**0.0484**
BeforeAttack	0.1290	0.2741	0.0925

5.3 Ablation Study

We conducted ablation experiments to assess how various modules affect the effectiveness of our attack. Specifically, we created several variants by selectively removing components from our attack framework:

- **Our-target**: We removed the constraint $\mathcal{L}_{target}$, which is responsible for boosting the target item's prominence.
- **Our-constraint**: We omitted the constraint $\mathcal{L}_{mrp}$, which ensures the overall performance of the recommender system is maintained.
- **Our-gscl**: We used interaction probabilities calculated by a scoring model to establish connections without optimizing the overall graph structure, thus removing the graph structure contrastive learning module $\mathcal{L}_{gscl}$.

The ablation study in Table 4 demonstrates that removing the module enhancing the target item significantly drops attack performance, highlighting

Table 4. Ablation Study

Attack Method	HR@50	NDCG@50
Ours-target	0.5309	0.0663
Ours-constraint	0.6137	0.0402
Ours-gscl	0.4659	0.0622
Our attack	**0.6861**	**0.0737**

its role in generating effective fake users. Eliminating the constraint to maintain overall recommendation performance impacts system quality the most. Additionally, removing the graph structure contrastive learning module notably affects attack efficiency, demonstrating the importance of optimizing graph structures for fake users. For example, Our-gscl uses contrastive learning to find the best interaction structure, and removing this component results in a sharp performance decline, underscoring the value of a well-designed graph structure in boosting attack success.

5.4 Impact of Profile Size

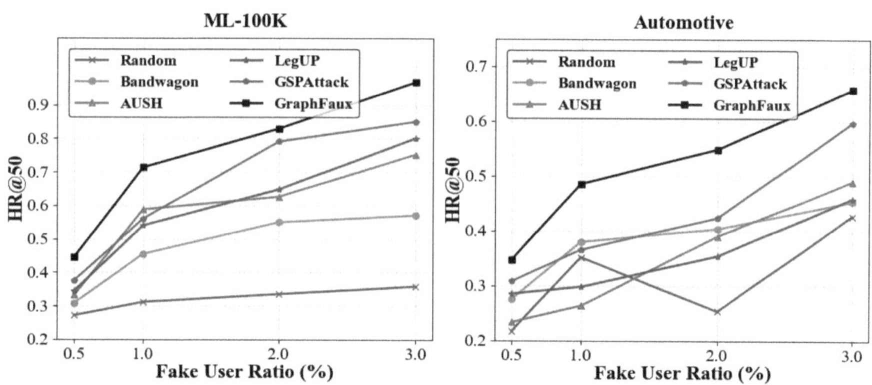

Fig. 2. The influence of fake user quantities on attack performance

We analyze the impact of shilling attacks on RSs by introducing varying numbers of fake users across two datasets. Specifically, we tested four injection ratios: 0.5%, 1%, 2%, and 3%. By gradually increasing the proportion of fake users, we observed changes in attack effectiveness and recommendation performance. As shown in Figs. 2 and 3, the hit rate of the target item increases with more fake users, but the overall recommendation performance gradually declines. This degradation may be due to the noise introduced by excessive fake users,

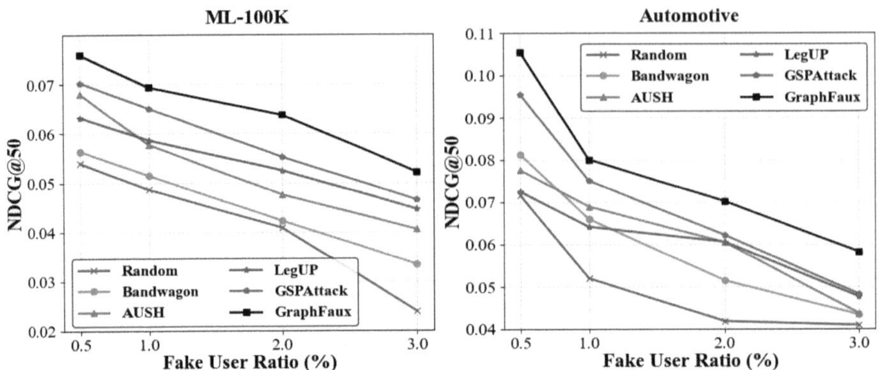

Fig. 3. The influence of fake user quantities on recommendation performance

which disrupts the system's recommendation quality. GraphFaux, by incorporating structural contrastive learning and performance-preserving constraints, achieves a better balance between attack effectiveness and recommendation performance.

5.5 Visualization of Fake User Distribution

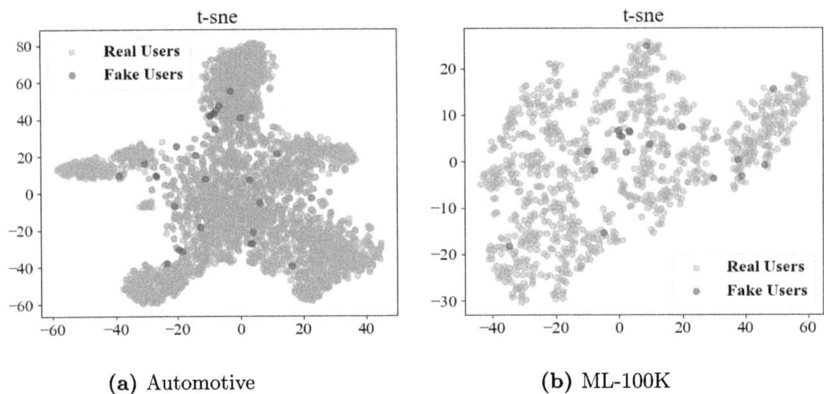

(a) Automotive **(b)** ML-100K

Fig. 4. Fake User Distribution across Different Datasets: (a) Automotive and (b) ML-100K

To further investigate the stealthiness of the attack, we use t-SNE to visualize user representations. Figure 4 shows the user projection after LightGCN is attacked by GraphFaux. As seen in the figure, the fake users generated by GraphFaux are randomly distributed in the feature space and seamlessly blend with the real user data. This dispersed distribution demonstrates that our combined approach of GAN and structural optimization not only improves attack effectiveness but also enhances the stealthiness of the fake users, making the attack more difficult to detect. Notably, the fake users exhibit no distinct clustering patterns compared to traditional attack methods, which often leave detectable traces due to their homogeneous interaction behaviors. Furthermore, the overlap between fake and real user embeddings suggests that GraphFaux successfully mimics the natural diversity of real user preferences, posing significant challenges to existing anomaly detection algorithms that rely on feature or structural outliers.

5.6 Hyperparameter Sensitivity Analysis

Table 5. Evaluating the Impact of Feature Masking and Edge Dropout Rates on GraphFaux's Attack Performance

p_m	HR@50	NDCG@50	p_d	HR@50	NDCG@50
0.1	0.3533	0.0413	0.1	0.3175	0.0340
0.2	0.4854	0.0723	0.2	0.3575	0.0471
0.3	0.4121	0.0556	0.3	0.4854	0.0723
0.4	0.3491	0.0398	0.4	0.3891	0.0532
0.5	0.3659	0.0378	0.5	0.3343	0.0367

In this experiment, we studied the effects of hyperparameters p_m and p_d on the performance of the recommendation system, and used HR@50 and NDCG@50 as evaluation indexes. Table 5 indicate that moderate feature masking ($p_m = 0.2$) and edge dropout ($p_d = 0.3$) effectively enhance attack performance while maintaining high recommendation quality. However, excessive masking can degrade user feature information, leading to a decline in both attack effectiveness and recommendation performance. Similarly, insufficient edge dropout fails to improve model robustness, whereas excessive dropout disrupts the graph structure, negatively impacting both attack effectiveness and recommendation quality. These findings highlight the importance of carefully tuning p_m and p_d to balance attack performance and recommendation quality.

6 Conclusion

In this paper, we introduce GraphFaux, a novel shilling attack method for GNN-based RSs. By combining GAN with Graph Structure Contrastive Learning, GraphFaux generates unnoticeable fake user profiles and optimizes their interactions with target items, enhancing attack effectiveness while maintaining stealth. Experiments show that GraphFaux outperforms existing methods in both effectiveness and stealth. In the future, we will focus on developing defenses to limit the spread of such malicious users and designing targeted strategies to safeguard the security and integrity of GNN-based RSs.

Acknowledgments. This work is supported in part by the project of Frontier Technologies R&D Program of Jiangsu (No. BF2025004), the project of Frontier Technologies R&D Program of Jiangsu (No. BF2024071), the Science and Technology Project of State Grid Jiangsu Electric Power Company Ltd (No. J2023179), the State Key Laboratory of Novel Software Technology (No. KFKT20 24A03), National Natural Science Foundation of China (No. 61702264).

References

1. Davidson, J., et al.: The youtube video recommendation system. In: Proceedings of the Fourth ACM Conference on Recommender Systems, pp. 293–296 (2010)
2. Du, L., et al.: Parl: poisoning attacks against reinforcement learning-based recommender systems. In: Proceedings of the 19th ACM Asia Conference on Computer and Communications Security, pp. 1331–1344 (2024)
3. Fang, M., Yang, G., Gong, N.Z., Liu, J.: Poisoning attacks to graph-based recommender systems. In: Proceedings of the 34th Annual Computer Security Applications Conference, pp. 381–392 (2018)
4. Gao, C., et al.: A survey of graph neural networks for recommender systems: challenges, methods, and directions. ACM Trans. Recommender Syst. **1**(1), 1–51 (2023)
5. Guo, S., Bai, T., Deng, W.: Targeted shilling attacks on gnn-based recommender systems. In: Proceedings of the 32nd ACM International Conference on Information and Knowledge Management, pp. 649–658 (2023)
6. He, X., Deng, K., Wang, X., Li, Y., Zhang, Y., Wang, M.: Lightgcn: simplifying and powering graph convolution network for recommendation. In: Proceedings of the 43rd International ACM SIGIR conference on Research and Development in Information Retrieval, pp. 639–648 (2020)
7. He, X., Liao, L., Zhang, H., Nie, L., Hu, X., Chua, T.S.: Neural collaborative filtering. In: Proceedings of the 26th International Conference on World Wide Web, pp. 173–182 (2017)
8. Hu, Y., Koren, Y., Volinsky, C.: Collaborative filtering for implicit feedback datasets. In: 2008 Eighth IEEE International Conference on Data Mining, pp. 263–272. Ieee (2008)
9. Ibrahim, O.A.S., Younis, E.M., Mohamed, E.A., Ismail, W.N.: Revisiting recommender systems: an investigative survey. Neural Comput. Appli., 1–29 (2025)
10. Koren, Y., Bell, R., Volinsky, C.: Matrix factorization techniques for recommender systems. Computer **42**(8), 30–37 (2009)
11. Lam, S.K., Riedl, J.: Shilling recommender systems for fun and profit. In: Proceedings of the 13th International Conference on World Wide Web, pp. 393–402 (2004)
12. Li, B., Wang, Y., Singh, A., Vorobeychik, Y.: Data poisoning attacks on factorization-based collaborative filtering. Adv. Neural Inform. Process. Syst. **29** (2016)
13. Lin, C., Chen, S., Li, H., Xiao, Y., Li, L., Yang, Q.: Attacking recommender systems with augmented user profiles. In: Proceedings of the 29th ACM International Conference on Information & Knowledge Management, pp. 855–864 (2020)
14. Lin, C., Chen, S., Zeng, M., Zhang, S., Gao, M., Li, H.: Shilling black-box recommender systems by learning to generate fake user profiles. IEEE Trans. Neural Netw. Learn. Syst. **35**(1), 1305–1319 (2022)

15. Liu, S., Yu, S., Li, H., Yang, Z., Duan, M., Liao, X.: A novel shilling attack on black-box recommendation systems for multiple targets. Neural Comput. Appl. **37**(5), 3399–3417 (2025)
16. Mobasher, B., Burke, R., Bhaumik, R., Williams, C.: Toward trustworthy recommender systems: an analysis of attack models and algorithm robustness. ACM Trans. Internet Techno. (TOIT) **7**(4), 23–es (2007)
17. Nawara, D., Aly, A., Kashef, R.: Shilling attacks and fake reviews injection: principles, models, and datasets. IEEE Trans. Comput. Soc. Syst. (2024)
18. Nguyen, T.T., et al.: Manipulating recommender systems: a survey of poisoning attacks and countermeasures. ACM Comput. Surv.**57**(1), 1–39 (2024)
19. Nguyen Thanh, T., et al.: Poisoning gnn-based recommender systems with generative surrogate-based attacks. ACM Trans. Inform. Syst. **41**(3), 1–24 (2023)
20. Sarwar, B., Karypis, G., Konstan, J., Riedl, J.: Item-based collaborative filtering recommendation algorithms. In: Proceedings of the 10th International Conference on World Wide Web, pp. 285–295 (2001)
21. Wang, X., He, X., Wang, M., Feng, F., Chua, T.S.: Neural graph collaborative filtering. In: Proceedings of the 42nd international ACM SIGIR conference on Research and development in Information Retrieval, pp. 165–174 (2019)
22. Wang, Z., Yu, J., Gao, M., Yin, H., Cui, B., Sadiq, S.: Unveiling vulnerabilities of contrastive recommender systems to poisoning attacks. In: Proceedings of the 30th ACM SIGKDD Conference on Knowledge Discovery and Data Mining, pp. 3311–3322 (2024)
23. Yu, J., Yin, H., Xia, X., Chen, T., Cui, L., Nguyen, Q.V.H.: Are graph augmentations necessary? simple graph contrastive learning for recommendation. In: Proceedings of the 45th International ACM SIGIR Conference on Research and Development in Information Retrieval, pp. 1294–1303 (2022)
24. Zayed, R.A., Ibrahim, L.F., Hefny, H.A., Salman, H.A., AlMohimeed, A.: Experimental and theoretical study for the popular shilling attacks detection methods in collaborative recommender system. IEEE Access **11**, 79358–79369 (2023)
25. Zhang, F., Chan, P.P., He, Z.M., Yeung, D.S.: Unsupervised contaminated user profile identification against shilling attack in recommender system. Intell. Data Analy. **28**(6), 1411–1426 (2024)
26. Zhang, Y., Hao, Q., Zheng, W., Xiao, Y.: User similarity-based graph convolutional neural network for shilling attack detection. Appl. Intell. **55**(5), 340 (2025)

Big Data Management

DC-Storage: A Fast Permissioned IoT Blockchain Storage with Decoupled Index

Haoyi Ding, Zeshun Peng(✉), Gang Wang, Xiaohua Li, Xiaomei Dong, and Ge Yu

Northeastern University, Shenyang 110819, China
{dinghy,pengzeshun,wanggang}@stumail.neu.edu.cn,
{lixiaohua,dongxiaomei,yuge}@mail.neu.edu.cn

Abstract. Permissioned blockchain has emerged as an effective solution to IoT data security challenges. With its decentralization, immutability, and transparency, integrating blockchain with IoT enhances security and improves data availability. Due to the performance limitations of underlying blockchains in handling massive IoT data, existing IoT blockchains typically adopt a two-layer architecture. In this architecture, the actual data is stored off-chain (e.g., in cloud servers or cloud storage) while only lightweight proofs are maintained on-chain. However, this approach faces several challenges. First, off-chain storage introduces vulnerability issues such as data loss and leaks. Second, synchronization between the off-chain data and the on-chain proofs becomes a performance bottleneck. To address these limitations, we propose DC-Storage, a fast permissioned IoT blockchain with a dual-chain architecture. We identify index construction as the primary performance bottleneck and decouple the index chain from the data chain to enable fast data chain construction with asynchronous indexing. Since transactions are considered committed after modifying the data chain, this significantly improves system throughput. Furthermore, we enable parallel index construction, substantially accelerating the indexing process. Experimental results show that DC-Storage outperforms its baseline with 5.03× higher throughput.

Keywords: permissioned blockchain · IoT data · storage · tree index

1 Introduction

Permissioned blockchains offer decentralization, immutability, and auditability, making them an effective solution to enhance data security [8,32], particularly in Internet of Things (IoT) applications [19]. By storing IoT data on-chain, enterprises can ensure data integrity and availability while eliminating the risks of storage failures and data tampering. However, the exponential growth in IoT devices poses significant performance challenges for blockchain-based IoT storage. Industry projections indicate that the number of IoT devices will surpass 75 billion by 2025 [24], representing a threefold increase from 2019 levels. This

J. Li et al. (Eds.): APWeb-WAIM 2025, LNCS 16115, pp. 599–615, 2026.
https://doi.org/10.1007/978-981-95-5719-6_38

massive scale of IoT data is common in real-world scenarios. For instance, in smart grid IoT platforms [2], each device generates real-time telemetry data from 800,000 measurement points. With the connection of 50,000 such devices, an IoT blockchain must store over 4 billion new records daily.

To address these performance challenges, existing IoT blockchains typically adopt a hybrid storage architecture, combining on-chain storage and off-chain storage [15,30]. In this architecture, the actual data is stored off-chain (e.g., in cloud storage services) while only lightweight proofs (i.e., cryptographic hash values) are maintained on-chain. This design allows users to verify data authenticity by comparing the off-chain data with the corresponding on-chain proofs. While this design improves system throughput by reducing on-chain storage overhead, it also introduces several challenges:

First, the off-chain storage lacks data availability. [15] utilizes cloud servers as off-chain storage. Although data integrity can be verified through on-chain proofs, cloud server failures may lead to data loss, preventing users from accessing the original IoT data. Even with data replication mechanisms, cloud servers cannot achieve the same level of availability as blockchain storage. Second, off-chain storage may compromise data privacy. While cloud storage services (e.g., Amazon S3 [20]) offer higher availability, they introduce additional security risks. Cloud storage services typically operate under a shared responsibility model, making them vulnerable to unauthorized access and breaches. Similarly, IPFS-based solutions [17,34,35] suffer from availability and privacy issues, as data accessibility depends on node availability and sensitive information is exposed across public nodes. Third, data persistence introduces significant latency overhead. Before recording the proofs on-chain, the on-chain storage must ensure that the corresponding data is persisted in the off-chain storage. This synchronization process involves multiple round-trip communications between the on-chain and off-chain storage, significantly increasing the overall latency.

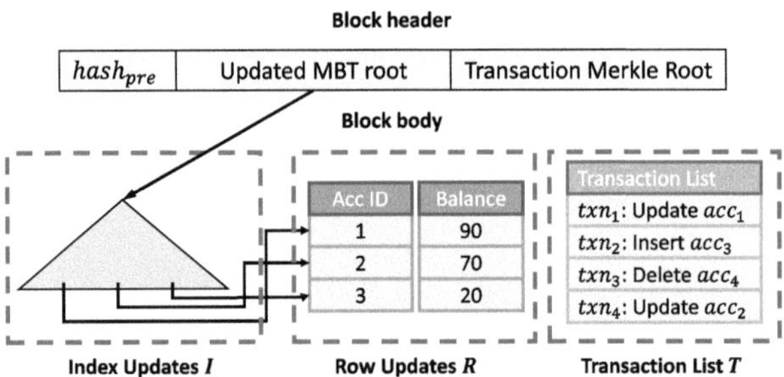

Fig. 1. Block Structure of Permissioned IoT blockchain.

Although existing approaches reduce on-chain storage overhead, they fail to address the fundamental performance bottleneck. Through systematic analysis, we identify that index construction during block creation is the primary performance bottleneck. Specifically, each node maintains a copy of the blockchain ledger, which is stored as a chain of blocks that stores both transactions (for audit) and the latest ledger state (for query), as shown in Fig. 1. The blockchain also creates an index tree (e.g. Merkle B+ tree) for each specific column to speed up queries, with the tree root's hash stored in the block header. For instance, Ethereum [9] employs a Merkle Patricia Trie for account balances to accelerate balance queries. Since blocks are generated sequentially and all indices must be constructed before creating each block, index construction becomes a bottleneck, particularly in IoT scenarios with high transaction rates.

We validate the above analysis using a synthetic IoT workload on NeuChain [21]. Since the ledger of NeuChain is stored in a hash table, we modify its code to store the ledger in blocks and build a Merkle B+ Tree as the account index for the ledger (detailed setup in Sect. 4). As shown in Fig. 2, as the number of transactions per block increases from 100 to 1500, the index building time consumes 37.4% to 57.9% of the total block building time. This high proportion of index-building time is primarily attributed to the hashing operations, which are necessary for ensuring index verifiability [18]. The increasing proportion of index building overhead occurs because as the number of transactions per block increases, the number of rows that need to be modified increases nonlinearly (due to the $O(n\log(n))$ complexity of tree building operation), increasing the proportion of the index building overhead.

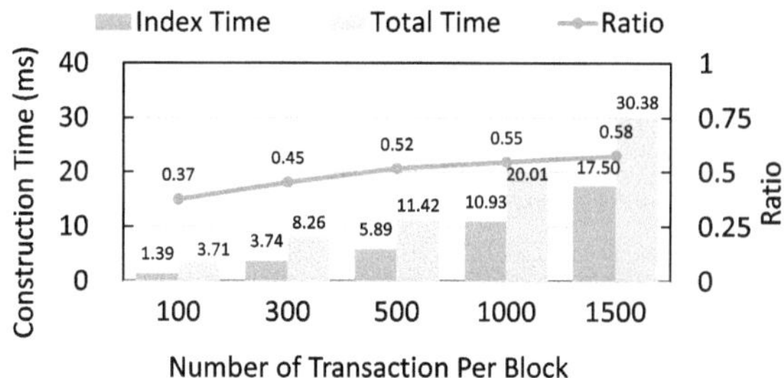

Fig. 2. Index construction time of total time with increasing block size.

To address these challenges, we propose DC-Storage, a fast permissioned IoT blockchain with a dual-chain architecture. Its core idea is to decouple indexing from block building and enable asynchronous index construction, thereby reducing the sequential block-building overhead in traditional IoT blockchains.

Decoupling index construction from block building is not trivial. First, transactions must be executed before returning results to clients. Since index construction (i.e., the index chain) is asynchronous to the blockchain (i.e., the data chain), when a node executes block b_{i+1}, the indexing of its previous block b_i may not yet be completed. Consequently, executing transactions based solely on index chains could result in stale reads, violating transaction consistency. To address this issue, we propose a double indexing technique. Given that transaction execution accesses the local ledger without requiring proofs (as correct nodes will produce identical execution results), each node maintains a fast in-memory hash table to index the latest updates that have not yet been included in the index chain. During transaction execution, this hash table is queried before the index chain to prevent stale reads.

Second, since index chain construction is time-consuming, its building speed may be slower than that of the data chain. This could prevent clients from obtaining verifiable queries for the most recently modified rows. To address this issue, we introduce parallel index chain construction. When the index chain significantly lags behind the data chain, we fork the index chain to enable concurrent construction, thereby accelerating the index chain building process. This forking process is deterministic to prevent malicious attacks.

In summary, the contributions of this paper are as follows:

1. We propose a novel dual-chain architecture that decouples index construction from block building while ensuring transaction execution consistency and query accuracy through a double indexing technique.
2. We introduce parallel index chain construction to accelerate indexing while maintaining correctness through consensus.
3. We implemented DC-Storage, a fast permissioned IoT blockchain using the above techniques. Experiments show that DC-Storage outperforms its baseline with 5.03× higher throughput.

2 Background and Related Work

2.1 Authenticated Blockchain Index

Permissioned blockchains typically accelerate ledger queries and transaction execution by indexing specific columns (e.g., account). For example, a node can leverage account indices to efficiently query account attributes (e.g., name or balance) without traversing the entire ledger during transaction execution. Most permissioned blockchains, such as Hyperledger Fabric [3] and NeuChain [21], employ traditional database indexes, such as Log Structured Merge Tree [1] or in-memory hash tables. However, these indices lack authentication capabilities. Since Byzantine nodes can tamper with ledgers or query results, light clients cannot verify the authenticity of returned values as they only maintain block headers. In contrast, authenticated blockchain indices, such as Merkle B+ tree (MBT) and Merkle Patricia Trie [9], provide cryptographic proofs with query results. Light clients can thus verify returned values by validating these proofs using their block headers, preventing Byzantine attacks.

However, constructing authenticated indices [25] requires a higher overhead than traditional indices due to proof generation. Several research efforts have focused on accelerating index construction and query performance. vChain [31] extends verifiable query semantics and designs intra-block and inter-block index structures to improve query performance. However, it has poor index construction performance, making it unsuitable for high-throughput IoT scenarios. vChain+ [26] improves query performance over vChain at the cost of longer index construction time. Experiments show that vChain+ takes over 250 ms to construct indices for 50 data objects. To support verifiable multi-dimensional aggregation queries, [36] proposes an accumulator-based index structure. However, the computational overhead of constructing these accumulators is also heavy.

While these prior works focus mainly on query performance, they do not address the high index construction overhead. To handle high-throughput IoT applications, we decouple index construction from block construction and propose parallel index construction.

2.2 Permissioned IoT Blockchain

Table 1. Comparison of permissioned IoT blockchains

Scheme	Off-Chain Storage	Data Availability	Data Sync Overhead
[15]	Cloud Server	Low	Medium
[28]	Database	Vary	LoW
[17]	IPFS	Medium	High
[34]	IPFS	Medium	High
[35]	IPFS	Medium	High
DC-Storage (ours)	Blockchain	High	Zero

Permissioned IoT blockchains typically adopt a hybrid architecture combining on-chain and off-chain storage. Table 1 summarizes the characteristics of existing solutions. [15] employs blockchain to record IoT parameters while utilizing cloud servers to store the data for data mining. However, cloud servers exhibit significantly lower availability than permissioned blockchains, making them susceptible to failures resulting in data loss and reduced availability. Moreover, synchronization overhead between cloud servers and blockchain networks also reduces performance. Similarly, [28] utilizes databases to store data. Data availability varies depending on the underlying database architecture (e.g., standalone or cloud databases). However, the high performance of databases helps reduce data synchronization overhead. To enhance availability, [17,34,35] leverage IPFS for off-chain storage, where the blockchain stores only the hash values of IPFS files containing IoT data. Nevertheless, IPFS also faces availability challenges [23]. Furthermore, IPFS incurs higher synchronization overhead than cloud server or database solutions. In contrast, DC-Storage stores data directly in the blockchain, achieving high availability with zero synchronization overhead.

2.3 Merkle B+ Tree

The Merkle B+ tree (MBT) extends the traditional B+ tree by incorporating cryptographic hash functions to enable authentication capabilities. As shown in Fig. 3, leaf nodes store a set of key-value pairs, where each key represents an indexed attribute (e.g., account) and the corresponding value is the hash pointer of the row (e.g., hash(account||balance)) to ensure data integrity. Each non-leaf node contains multiple key-pointer pairs and a hash value. The hash value of a non-leaf node is computed by concatenating and hashing its children's hash values. This hierarchical hashing structure ensures that any modification to the indexed attributes or the underlying data will propagate up to the root hash, enabling efficient verification of query results.

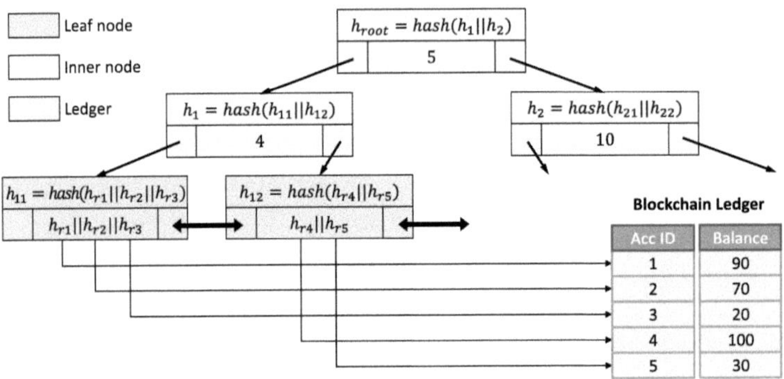

Fig. 3. The structure of Merkle B+ Tree (MBT).

As shown in Fig. 1, the block of IoT blockchains typically comprises three components: (1) a transaction list $\mathcal{T}$ for auditing purposes, (2) incremental row updates $\mathcal{R}$ containing the updated ledger, and (3) incremental index updates $\mathcal{I}$ constructed based on $\mathcal{R}$. While existing research has primarily focused on extending query semantics based on MBTs, they overlook the significant overhead of index construction. By storing all components within the same block, these approaches substantially reduce block generation efficiency.

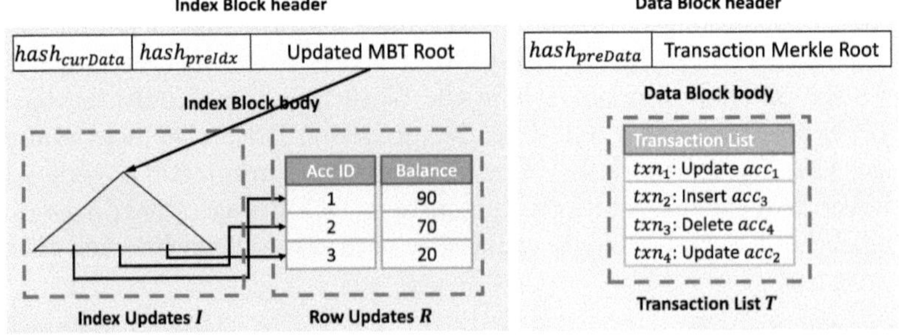

Fig. 4. Block Structure of DC-Storage.

Specifically, EthMB+ [13] introduces a tamper-proof data query model based on MBT to expand blockchain query primitives. EthMB+ employs an extractor to retrieve transaction records from Ethereum and insert them into the MBT. The MBT then processes user query requests and returns results through the query interface. Similarly, EBTree [29] employs MBT to facilitate real-time queries (including top-k, range, and exact-match searches) on Ethereum blockchain data, while utilizing RLP encoding to optimize storage efficiency.

ChainDB [14] adopts the hybrid storage architecture (Sect. 2.2) and utilizes MBTs to provide verifiable range queries. Similarly, [12] adopts the hybrid storage architecture and employs MBT as the index structure to support skyline and top-k queries. This approach addresses multi-dimensional data query challenges by constructing separate MBTs for different attributes of on-chain data. Furthermore, by incorporating bloom filters into each block to streamline the query verification process, the system significantly enhances verification efficiency for light nodes.

3 DC-Storage Design

To prevent index construction from becoming a performance bottleneck, we propose a dual-chain structure that decouples index construction from block generation. The dual-chain structure consists of a data chain containing transaction list $\mathcal{T}$ and an index chain comprising rows updates $\mathcal{R}$ and index updates $\mathcal{I}$, as shown in Fig. 4. Our key observation is that transaction commitment only requires the transaction to be stored on the blockchain (i.e., executing t, adding it to $\mathcal{T}$, and reaching consensus on the block containing $\mathcal{T}$), while $\mathcal{R}$ and $\mathcal{I}$ are constructed solely to support verifiable queries. Honest nodes can maintain lightweight, non-verifiable versions of $\mathcal{R}$ and $\mathcal{I}$ locally for transaction execution while constructing authenticated indices asynchronously to enhance performance. Since $\mathcal{R}$ and $\mathcal{I}$ are irrelevant to building $\mathcal{T}$, the data chain can be generated asynchronously from the index chain, thereby improving performance.

3.1 DC-Storage Overview

The dual-chain structure of DC-Storage is shown in Fig. 5. The nodes first achieve consensus (e.g., PBFT [11]) on the next data block containing a list of transactions from clients. Then, each node executes the block and generates an index block containing the ledger and index updates. To maintain the authenticity of the index chain, the nodes subsequently reach consensus on the index block. Since executing transactions in the $(i+1)$-th block requires looking up the index of the i-th block, each node maintains a local hash table that caches recent ledger updates to prevent transaction execution from being blocked by index chain generation. Finally, to enable verifiable queries for the latest updates, we introduce a concurrent index chain construction scheme.

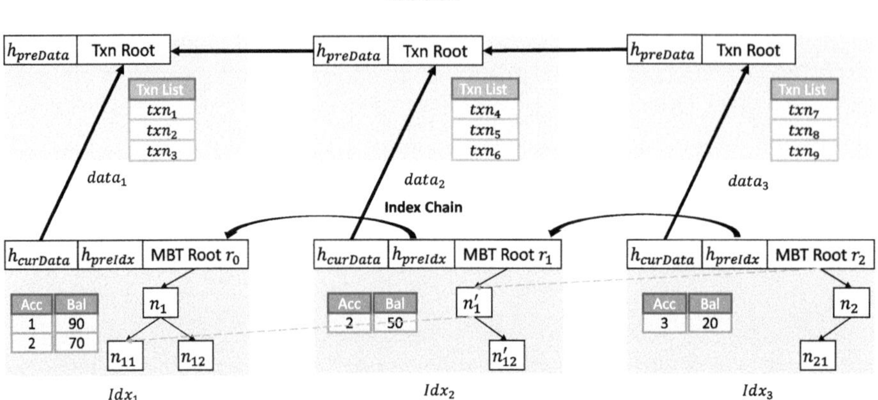

Fig. 5. The dual chain structure of DC-Storage.

3.2 Fast Decoupled Data Chain Construction

Since the construction of the index chain may be slower than that of the data chain, the latest updates may not be indexed immediately. This asynchronicity could lead to stale reads when querying through the index chain, violating transaction consistency. To address this issue, we propose a double indexing mechanism. By maintaining a local hash table for the latest updated rows, each node ensures that transaction execution always accesses the most recent version of the row. The workflow of transaction execution is shown in Algorithm 1.

Specifically, during transaction execution, read operations first query the local hash table. If a hit occurs, the latest row is returned directly. Otherwise, the node proceeds to query its index chain. Since each node maintains and trusts its local hash table and index chain, read operations do not require proof of authenticity during transaction execution. Write operations directly add the key-value pair to the row update map and the local hash table.

Delta-Based Hash Table Maintenance. The local hash table may consume excessive memory and impact query performance if it grows unbounded. To address this, we employ a delta approach for hash table maintenance, as shown in Algorithm 2. Let data_i and idx_i denote the i-th data block and index block.

Specifically, after executing the transaction list $\mathcal{T}$ from the latest data block data_i, the node appends the updates of the committed transactions to the row updates list $\mathcal{R}$ (which will subsequently be stored in the corresponding index block idx_i) and updates the hash table indices accordingly. Upon receiving an index block idx_j, the node iterates through the $\mathcal{R}$ within the block and removes each row update r from the hash table. To prevent incorrect deletion of the latest version, a row is removed from the hash table only when r exactly matches the most recent version r' indexed in the hash table.

An Example of Transaction Execution. Consider a ledger state where block data_1 and idx_1 have achieved consensus. The ledger contains a table with

Algorithm 1. Transaction Execution

```
Require: Txn list 𝒯 in data block, local hash table lt, MBT of index chain mbt
Ensure: Execution results ℰ, row updates ℛ
ℰ ← ∅; ℛ ← ∅                     ▷ Initialize empty result set and row updates set
for each transaction t ∈ 𝒯 do
    (e, r) ← EXECUTE(t)          ▷ Get the execution result and updated rows of t
    ℰ ← ℰ ∪ {e}                  ▷ Add execution result e to result set ℰ
    ℛ ← ℛ ∪ r                    ▷ Add updated rows to row updates ℛ
return (ℰ, ℛ)
function EXECUTE(t)                              ▷ Execute single transaction
    r ← ∅                                        ▷ Initialize empty row updates map
    for each operation op ∈ t.operations do      ▷ Process read and write operations
        if op.type = READ then
            if op.key ∈ lt then                  ▷ Query the local hash table first
                read(lt[op.key])
                continue
            if op.key ∈ mbt then                 ▷ Then query the index chain
                read(mbt[op.key])
                continue
            rollback()
            return (ABORT, ∅)                    ▷ The read row does not exist, abort
        else if op.type = WRITE then
            r[op.key] ← op.value                 ▷ Add to row updates
            lt[op.key] ← op.value                ▷ Update local hash table
    return (COMMIT, r)
```

Algorithm 2. Prune Hash Table

```
Require: Row updates ℛ in index block, local hash table ht
Ensure: Pruned local hash table
for each row r ∈ ℛ do
    if r.key ∉ ht then continue          ▷ Skip if key does not exist in hash table
    if ht[r.key] ≠ r.value then
        continue                         ▷ Skip if row was updated after this version
    ht.remove(r.key)                     ▷ Remove entry from hash table
```

account ID and balance columns, comprising two initial records: $\langle \text{acc}_1, 100\rangle$ and $\langle \text{acc}_2, 50\rangle$. A node receives and executes block data_2 containing transactions txn_4: $\text{acc}_1.\text{bal} - 10$ and txn_5: $\text{acc}_2.\text{bal} + 10$. During the read operations for acc_1 and acc_2, since the local hash table is empty, the node queries the index chain. The execution results in the updated row list $\mathcal{R}_2$ containing $\langle \text{acc}_1, 90\rangle$ and $\langle \text{acc}_2, 70\rangle$, which are subsequently cached in the local hash table.

Subsequently, the node executes data_3 containing transaction txn_6: $\text{acc}_1.\text{bal} - 20$. Following a similar process, this generates $\mathcal{R}_3$ containing $\langle \text{acc}_1, 70\rangle$. At this point, when idx_2 (containing $\mathcal{R}_2$ and $\mathcal{I}_2$) reaches consensus and is received by the node, it can safely remove acc_2 from the hash table since its pointed value matches that in $\mathcal{R}_2$. However, acc_1 must be retained in the hash table as it has been updated by txn_6 in $data_3$.

Recall that, during transaction execution, read operations only need to access the most recent version of rows and do not require proof of authenticity. Therefore, entries in the hash table can be safely removed when their pointed values match those in $\mathcal{R}$.

3.3 Concurrent Index Construction

To enable verifiable queries of the latest ledger state for clients, the index chain construction must keep pace with the data chain, even though transaction execution can access the latest state without relying on the index chain. To address this, we propose a concurrent index chain construction strategy.

The leader node monitors the construction progress of both chains. When the gap between the data chain and index chain exceeds a predefined threshold δ, DC-Chain triggers a forking mechanism to accelerate index chain construction. Specifically, DC-Chain forks a temporary side chain to construct the lagging index blocks. We only construct one side chain for each index to prevent unlimited fork attacks. Moreover, to prevent a malicious leader node, the fork request must achieve consensus before execution.

Query Processing. For query processing, a naive approach would be to merge the side chain back into the main chain upon completion, allowing clients to query a single, up-to-date index chain. However, merging two MBTs incurs substantial computational overhead and could block the construction of the main chain. Therefore, we propose a pragmatic solution where nodes query both the main chain and side chain simultaneously, selecting the most recent version of records and returning the corresponding records and proofs to clients.

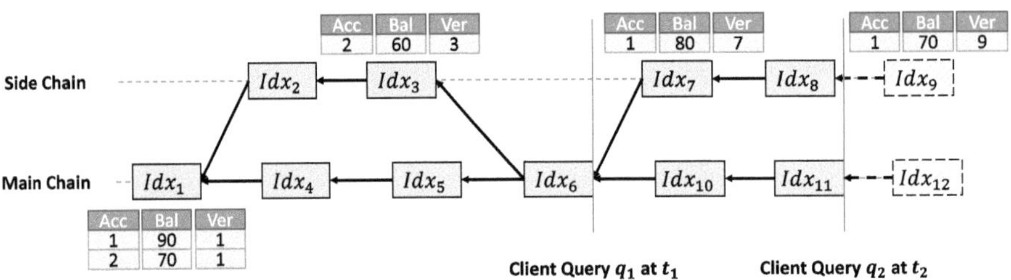

Fig. 6. Example of concurrent index construction.

To ensure consistency during side chain construction, queries can only be processed based on the last block with *all its predecessor blocks constructed*, rather than the latest blocks in either the main chain or side chain. As shown in Fig. 6, when block idx_9 and idx_{12} are being constructed concurrently in the index chain, queries must be based on block idx_8. This is necessary because block

idx_9 has not been constructed yet. Querying based on block idx_{11} would omit the ledger updates in block idx_9, resulting in incorrect results. In other words, a node can provide authenticated queries up to block height 8.

Since clients maintain lightweight block headers of the index chain, rows stored in both the side chain and main chain can be authenticated. Moreover, each row maintains a version number to prevent Byzantine nodes from returning stale versions. The most recent row is determined by comparing versions of the rows retrieved from both chains.

An Example. As shown in Fig. 6, the ledger initially contains two records stored in index block idx_1: $\langle \text{acc}_1, 90\rangle$ and $\langle \text{acc}_2, 70\rangle$. At time t_1, when a client queries acc_2, the node performs a search based on block height 6, retrieving $\text{acc}_2 = 60$ from the side chain and $\text{acc}_2 = 70$ from the main chain. By comparing the version numbers of these two results, the client determines the final value as $\text{acc}_2 = 60$, which represents the most recent update.

Since idx_9 is still under construction at time t_2, query q_2 for acc_1 cannot be done based on block height 11. Therefore, the node process q_2 is based on block height 8 (main chain up to idx_6 and side chain up to idx_8). The value of acc_1 is 80 in the side chain and 90 in the main chain. The client determines the final value as 80 by comparing their version numbers (1 and 7).

3.4 Security Analysis

This section analyzes the system's security mechanism when facing Byzantine behavior in the query processing and index construction.

Verifiable Query Processing. In the traditional model, users trust the query results returned by the service node by default, but in the Byzantine environment, the node may return tampered or incomplete data due to program failure, security vulnerabilities or malicious motives, which seriously threatens the security of the system. To this end, the system introduces the Verification Object (VO) as a structured proof of each query result, which is generated by an authenticated data structure (such as a Merkle tree or Merkle B tree). At the same time, the user maintains a trusted root hash value (Root Hash) locally as a light node. After receiving the query results and VO, the user can independently reconstruct and compare the root hash to verify the integrity and legitimacy of the results. This mechanism effectively prevents Byzantine behaviors such as tampering and omissions of service nodes, and enhances the credibility of queries.

BFT During Index Construction. The index construction process also faces the problem of malicious nodes forging index structures, such as tampering with data ranges or inserting wrong paths, leading to misleading queries. To prevent such attacks, the system introduces a consensus mechanism in the index proposal stage. Algorithms represented by PBFT require more than 2/3 of the nodes to reach a consensus before accepting the index submitted by a node. This mechanism ensures that even if there are Byzantine nodes, incorrect or maliciously constructed indexes cannot be adopted by the system, ensuring the correctness of the index structure and network consistency.

Limitations. The dual-chain architecture introduces additional consensus instances and chain structure maintenance costs, but in the context of the Internet of Things, which emphasizes real-time applications, this overhead is acceptable, and compared to the improvement in the overall system throughput, its benefits significantly outweigh the costs.

4 Experimental Evaluation

In this section, we evaluate the performance of DC-Storage.

Implementation. We implemented a blockchain prototype in C++ based on NeuChain [21]. We employ MBTs as authenticated indices. We utilize PBFT as the consensus protocol. To tolerate at most f Byzantine nodes, the total number of nodes must exceed $3f+1$. We use ED25519 for digital signatures and SHA256 for hash-based data integrity verification. To optimize system performance, we incorporate pipelining and batching techniques. Each node participates in two concurrent PBFT consensus processes, one for the data chain and the other for the index chain. For optimal performance, blocks are stored in memory.

Experimental Setup. We built a cluster with three nodes and a client on one virtual machine equipped with a 2.10GHz, 8-core Intel Xeon Silver 4110 CPU and 24GB of RAM. The nodes are connected through a local network to simulate a distributed environment. To evaluate the performance benefits of our approach, we compare our system against the following baselines:

- NeuChain: Serves as *an upper bound* for performance as it does not require authenticated index construction.
- NeuChain-MBT: A baseline implementation that only uses MBTs for index authentication.

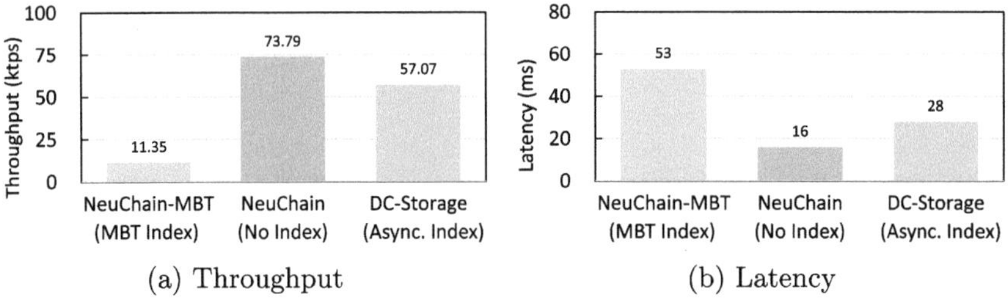

(a) Throughput (b) Latency

Fig. 7. Overall performance comparison.

Workload. Smallbank [10] workload simulates a simple banking application with basic account operations such as balance checking, deposits, and transfers. To simulate IoT workloads, we extend the ledger schema with a timestamp column and build an MBT index on it. The timestamp is updated whenever a transaction modifies the corresponding row. If not explicitly stated, the block size of all competitors is 1000.

4.1 Overall Performance

As shown in Fig. 7, DC-Storage achieves performance comparable to NeuChain while providing the same authenticated query as NeuChain-MBT. Specifically, DC-Storage achieves a 5.02× performance improvement compared to the baseline NeuChain-MBT. This is primarily attributed to the asynchronous index construction mechanism. By decoupling index construction from block creation, DC-Storage approaches the high performance of NeuChain while providing MBT-authenticated queries. The slightly lower performance compared to NeuChain is due to the additional computational overhead of maintaining a separate consensus instance for the index chain. Moreover, transaction execution incurs higher latency as it requires querying both the hash table and the MBT index, instead of directly accessing the state database in NeuChain.

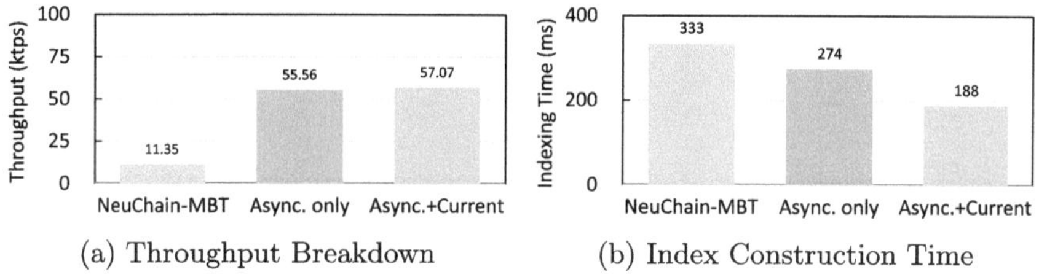

(a) Throughput Breakdown (b) Index Construction Time

Fig. 8. Performance breakdown.

4.2 Performance Breakdown

We present a performance breakdown to analyze the individual impact of index decoupling and concurrent index construction. Figure 8a compares the performance of the baseline (NeuChain-MBT), DC-Storage with only decoupled indexing (Async. only), and DC-Storage with both optimizations (Async.+Concurrent). The results show that decoupling indexing significantly improves throughput, as index construction was the primary bottleneck (as discussed in Sect. 1). Concurrent index construction, however, does not impact throughput since transaction execution proceeds independently of index chain construction.

Figure 8b shows the time consumed to execute and index 15,000 transactions. Async. only is faster compared to NeuChain-MBT. DC-Storage further reduces the construction overhead through parallel MBT construction. When the number of accounts is 1,000,000 and the size is 44 bytes, the delta hash table consumes about 42 MB of DRAM.

4.3 Performance Varying Block Size

In this experiment, we vary the block size from 100 to 1000 transactions to observe the system performance under different workloads. As shown in Fig. 9, the performance of all systems increases as the block size increases, due to different reasons. For NeuChain-MBT, the performance bottleneck lies in MBT construction. Larger batch sizes improve performance because batch insertion can avoid constructing unnecessary intermediate nodes during tree reorganization. NeuChain's performance is primarily limited by network round-trips required for PBFT consensus. therefore, larger block sizes reduce the coordination, leading to better performance. DC-Storage combines the advantages of both approaches and shows consistent performance improvements with increased block sizes.

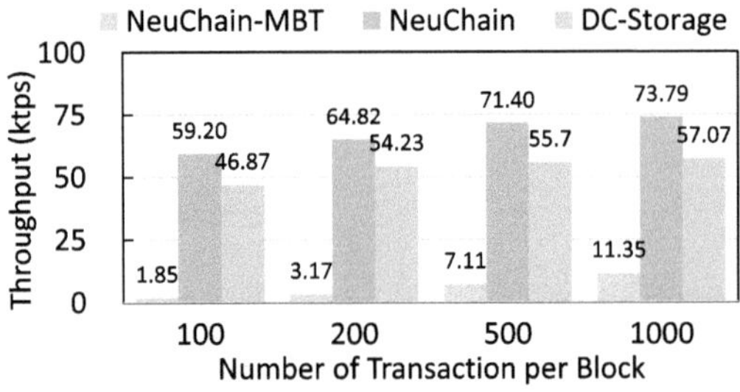

Fig. 9. Throughput varying block size.

4.4 Overhead of Authenticated Index Construction

To show indexing performance, we compare DC-Storage index chain construction performance with vChain [31] and vChain+ [26]. The results are shown in Table 2, where the baseline results are obtained from [26].

Table 2. ADS Construction Cost

DataSet	ETH		4SQ	
	T	S	T	S
vChain-acc1	260	125.6	390	28.1
vChain-acc2	40	126.1	40	29.3
vChain+	110	451.5	250	1209.1
DC-Storage	2	8.5	2	7.1

T: Index construction time(ms/block)
S: Index size(KB/block)

In the ETH [27] and 4SQ [33] workloads, DC-Storage achieves significantly faster index construction, requiring only 2 ms per block, while other solutions are substantially slower (e.g., vChain-acc1 takes 260-390 ms per block). This superior performance is attributed to the concurrent index construction design of DC-Storage. Moreover, the MBT index consumes only 8.5 KB per block for ETH and 7.1 KB per block for 4SQ. This represents a 99.41% reduction in storage overhead compared to vChain+, which is about 1209.1 KB per block.

5 Future Work

Many IoT applications (e.g., temperature, humidity, and pressure) involve processing complex, high-dimensional data that spans multiple attributes (e.g., time, location, device ID, and sensor readings). While this article focuses on the design and implementation of single-column indexes, future work should address more advanced indexing strategies capable of supporting multi-attribute and multidimensional queries, which are increasingly common in real-world IoT scenarios.

To this end, a variety of multidimensional index structures can be considered. R-tree [16] and their variants (e.g., R*-trees [5] and R+-tree [22]) are widely used for spatial data indexing and support efficient range and nearest-neighbor queries. K-D Tree [6] is suitable for low-dimensional point data and is effective for applications involving small to moderate dimensions. For higher-dimensional data, X-tree [7] can be employed to mitigate the performance degradation caused by the "curse of dimensionality" by avoiding excessive node overlap. Similarly, UB-tree [4], which uses space-filling curves to linearize multidimensional data into a one-dimensional space, is another viable option for building multidimensional indexes atop traditional B+-trees.

Beyond performance, future research should also consider verifiable indexing mechanisms to ensure the integrity and trustworthiness of query results in distributed and potentially untrusted environments. By integrating Merkle trees into multidimensional index structures, it is possible to construct verifiable indexes that allow clients to verify the correctness and completeness of query results without trusting the data source. This is especially relevant in edge computing, cloud-assisted IoT systems, and blockchain-integrated platforms.

6 Conclusion

This paper presents DC-Storage, a fast permissioned IoT blockchain with a novel dual-chain architecture. By employing a double indexing technique, DC-Storage ensures transaction execution consistency and query accuracy. Additionally, DC-Storage introduces concurrent index chain construction, significantly accelerating index building. Experimental results show that DC-Storage achieves a 5.03× higher throughput than its baseline. In the future, we will continue to study how to generalize the proposed dual-chain approach to handle more advanced query types and more complex data models.

Acknowledgement. This work is supported by the National Natural Science Foundation of China (62372097), the National Social Science Foundation of China (21&ZD124), and the Fundamental Research Funds for the Central Universities (N2416003). Zeshun Peng is the corresponding author.

References

1. Leveldb (2024). http://code.google.com/p/Leveldb/
2. Tdengine user case (2024). https://www.taosdata.com/tdengine-user-cases
3. Androulaki, E., et al.: Hyperledger fabric: a distributed operating system for permissioned blockchains. In: Proceedings of the Thirteenth EuroSys Conference, pp. 1–15 (2018)
4. Bayer, R., Markl, V.: The ub-tree: Performance of multidimensional range queries (1998)
5. Beckmann, N., Kriegel, H.P., Schneider, R., Seeger, B.: The r*-tree: an efficient and robust access method for points and rectangles. In: Proceedings of the 1990 ACM SIGMOD International Conference on Management of Data, pp. 322–331 (1990)
6. Bentley, J.L.: Multidimensional binary search trees used for associative searching. Commun. ACM **18**(9), 509–517 (1975)
7. Berchtold, S., Keim, D.A., Kriegel, H.P.: The x-tree: An index structure for high-dimensional data (1996)
8. Bertino, E.: Data security and privacy in the iot. In: EDBT, vol. 2016, pp. 1–3 (2016)
9. Buterin, V., et al.: Ethereum white paper. GitHub Repository **1**(22–23), 5–7 (2013)
10. Cahill, M.J., Röhm, U., Fekete, A.D.: Serializable isolation for snapshot databases. ACM Trans. Database Syst. (TODS) **34**(4), 1–42 (2009)
11. Castro, M., Liskov, B., et al.: Practical byzantine fault tolerance. OsDI **99**, 173–186 (1999)
12. Ding, H., et al.: Efficient and verifiable skyline computation on blockchain system with merkle b+ tree index. In: 2024 IEEE International Symposium on Parallel and Distributed Processing with Applications (ISPA), pp. 2113–2120. IEEE (2024)
13. Du, P., Liu, Y., Li, Y., Yin, H.: Ethmb+: a tamper-proof data query model based on b+ tree and merkle tree. In: CCF China Blockchain Conference, pp. 49–59. Springer (2022). https://doi.org/10.1007/978-981-19-8877-6_4
14. Gao, J., et al.: Chaindb: ensuring integrity of querying off-chain data on blockchain. In: Proceedings of the 2022 5th International Conference on Blockchain Technology and Applications, pp. 175–181 (2022)
15. Goyat, R., et al.: Blockchain-based data storage with privacy and authentication in internet of things. IEEE Internet Things J. **9**(16), 14203–14215 (2020)
16. Guttman, A.: R-trees: a dynamic index structure for spatial searching. In: Proceedings of the 1984 ACM SIGMOD International Conference on Management of Data, pp. 47–57 (1984)
17. Haque, E.U., Shah, A., Iqbal, J., Ullah, S.S., Alroobaea, R., Hussain, S.: A scalable blockchain based framework for efficient iot data management using lightweight consensus. Sci. Rep. **14**(1), 7841 (2024)
18. Jing, S., Zheng, X., Chen, Z.: Review and investigation of merkle tree's technical principles and related application fields. In: 2021 International Conference on Artificial Intelligence, Big Data and Algorithms (CAIBDA), pp. 86–90. IEEE (2021)
19. Khan, A.A., Laghari, A.A., Shaikh, Z.A., Dacko-Pikiewicz, Z., Kot, S.: Internet of things (iot) security with blockchain technology: a state-of-the-art review. IEEE Access **10**, 122679–122695 (2022)
20. Palankar, M.R., Iamnitchi, A., Ripeanu, M., Garfinkel, S.: Amazon s3 for science grids: a viable solution? In: Proceedings of the 2008 International Workshop on Data-Aware Distributed Computing, pp. 55–64 (2008)

21. Peng, Z., et al.: Neuchain: a fast permissioned blockchain system with deterministic ordering. Proc. VLDB Endowment **15**(11), 2585–2598 (2022)
22. Sellis, T., Roussopoulos, N., Faloutsos, C.: The r+-tree: A dynamic index for multi-dimensional objects (1987)
23. Shi, R., Cheng, R., Han, B., Cheng, Y., Chen, S.: A closer look into ipfs: accessibility, content, and performance. Proc. ACM Measurem. Anal. Comput. Syst. **8**(2), 1–31 (2024)
24. Statista, R.: Internet of things-number of connected devices worldwide 2015-2025. Statista Research Department. statista. com/statistics/471264/iot-number-of-connected-devices-worldwide (2019)
25. Tamassia, R.: authenticated data structures. In: Di Battista, G., Zwick, U. (eds.) ESA 2003. LNCS, vol. 2832, pp. 2–5. Springer, Heidelberg (2003). https://doi.org/10.1007/978-3-540-39658-1_2
26. Wang, H., Xu, C., Zhang, C., Xu, J., Peng, Z., Pei, J.: vchain+: optimizing verifiable blockchain boolean range queries. In: 2022 IEEE 38th International Conference on Data Engineering (ICDE), pp. 1927–1940. IEEE (2022)
27. Wood, G., et al.: Ethereum: a secure decentralised generalised transaction ledger. Ethereum Project Yellow Paper **151**(2014), 1–32 (2014)
28. Wu, H., Peng, Z., Guo, S., Yang, Y., Xiao, B.: Vql: efficient and verifiable cloud query services for blockchain systems. IEEE Trans. Parallel Distrib. Syst. **33**(6), 1393–1406 (2021)
29. XiaoJu, H., XueQing, G., ZhiGang, H., LiMei, Z., Kun, G.: Ebtree: a b-plus tree based index for ethereum blockchain data. In: Proceedings of the 2020 Asia Service Sciences and Software Engineering Conference, pp. 83–90 (2020)
30. Xiong, Z., Zhang, Y., Luong, N.C., Niyato, D., Wang, P., Guizani, N.: The best of both worlds: a general architecture for data management in blockchain-enabled internet-of-things. IEEE Network **34**(1), 166–173 (2020)
31. Xu, C., Zhang, C., Xu, J.: vchain: enabling verifiable boolean range queries over blockchain databases. In: Proceedings of the 2019 International Conference on Management of Data, pp. 141–158 (2019)
32. Yaga, D., Mell, P., Roby, N., Scarfone, K.: Blockchain technology overview. arXiv preprint arXiv:1906.11078 (2019)
33. Yang, D., Zhang, D., Qu, B.: Participatory cultural mapping based on collective behavior data in location-based social networks. ACM Trans. Intell. Syst. Technol. (TIST) **7**(3), 1–23 (2016)
34. Zheng, Q., Li, Y., Chen, P., Dong, X.: An innovative ipfs-based storage model for blockchain. In: 2018 IEEE/WIC/ACM International Conference on Web Intelligence (WI), pp. 704–708. IEEE (2018)
35. Zhou, E., et al.: Mstdb: qhybrid storage-empowered scalable semantic blockchain database. IEEE Trans. Knowl. Data Eng. **35**(8), 8228–8244 (2022)
36. Zhu, Y., Zhang, Z., Jin, C., Zhou, A.: Enabling generic verifiable aggregate query on blockchain systems. In: 2020 IEEE 26th International Conference on Parallel and Distributed Systems (ICPADS), pp. 456–465. IEEE (2020)

zkHARPS: A Decentralized Method for Cross-Chain Identity Aggregation and Privacy Proof

Hanyu Mao[1], Tiezheng Nie[1](✉), Minghe Yu[2], Xiaomei Dong[1], Xiaohua Li[1], and Ge Yu[1]

[1] School of Computer Science and Engineering, Northeastern University, Shenyang, China
nietiezheng@mail.neu.edu.cn

[2] School of Software, Northeastern University, Shenyang, China

Abstract. As the blockchain ecosystem evolves from single-chain systems to multi-chain collaboration, decentralized cross-chain identity authentication has become a critical challenge for ensuring system interoperability and privacy protection. Existing identity verification schemes often suffer from identity fragmentation, privacy leakage risks, and insufficient data consistency. To address these issues, we propose zkHARPS, a decentralized method for cross-chain identity aggregation and privacy proof that integrates secure multi-party computation with zero-knowledge proofs. Specifically, we design a novel cross-chain identity aggregation protocol that enables secure global identity computation from distributed fragments via multi-party computation. In addition, we develop HARPS, a recursive hash-based ZKP framework that compactly encodes multi-attribute identity proofs using zkSNARK. Furthermore, to ensure consistent and efficient identity synchronization across heterogeneous blockchains, we design a lightweight cross-chain verification mechanism that leverages event-driven listeners and embedded light clients. The proposed method is implemented and validated on both Hyperledger Fabric and Ganache, and compared with mainstream zero-knowledge proof methods, including Bulletproofs, Scalable zk, and ZK-STARK. Experimental results demonstrate that zkHARPS achieves significant advantages in proof generation time, verification latency, gas cost, storage overhead, and identity aggregation stability, making it well-suited for privacy-preserving applications in complex multi-chain environments.

Keywords: Blockchain · Cross-chain identity · Zero-knowledge proof · Secure multi-party computation · Privacy protection

1 Introduction

Decentralized Identity (DID), as one of the key applications of blockchain technology, aims to address the issues of privacy leakage and centralization inherent in traditional identity authentication systems [1]. DID enables users to create and manage their own identities on blockchains, removing dependence on centralized identity providers.

J. Li et al. (Eds.): APWeb-WAIM 2025, LNCS 16115, pp. 616–632, 2026.
https://doi.org/10.1007/978-981-95-5719-6_39

However, most existing DID systems are restricted to single-chain environments. As blockchain applications continue to evolve, the limitations of single-chain systems in terms of performance and functionality are becoming increasingly evident, and the coexistence of multiple heterogeneous blockchains has become an inevitable trend. The isolation across chains has resulted in fragmentation of data, assets, and identities, significantly hindering interoperability and user experience within the blockchain ecosystem [2], and making it difficult to achieve unified identity management and verification across chains [3].

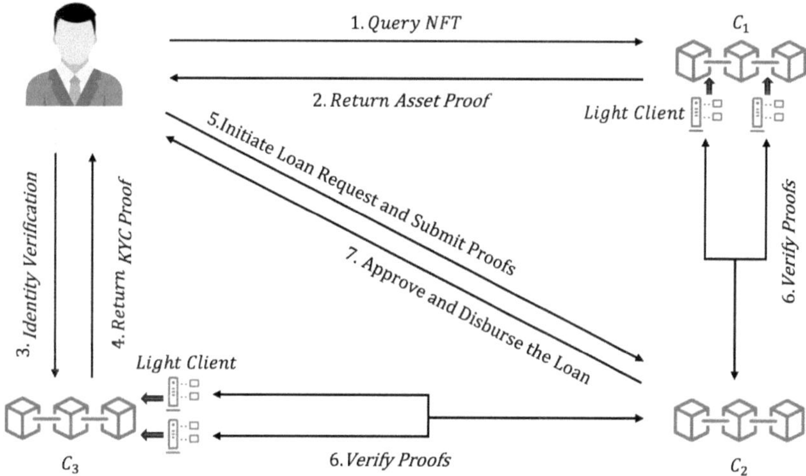

Fig. 1. Traditional Cross-chain Identity Authentication Workflow.

In a multi-chain financial ecosystem, trustworthy cross-chain identity authentication becomes critical for enabling secure operations between heterogeneous blockchains [4, 5]. As illustrated in Fig. 1, this paper presents an example where the user U applies for a loan on the chain C_2 (a lending chain). To obtain the loan, the user must satisfy two conditions: (1) they must hold a specific NFT on the chain C_1 (an asset chain), and (2) they must have completed KYC verification on the chain C_3 (an identity verification chain). In traditional solutions, this process is usually achieved by combining light clients and cross-chain state proofs [6]. The authentication process [7] is as follows: the user first queries C_1 and generates a proof of NFT ownership; then completes KYC verification on C_3 and obtains a corresponding certification proof; finally, the user submits both proofs to C_2, where the lending platform verifies their validity via a light client. Upon successful verification, the loan is issued.

Although the workflow enables basic cross-chain identity verification, it faces several key challenges: (1) identity fragmentation and redundant verification, as users must register separately on each chain, leading to data duplication and increased overhead; (2) risk of privacy leakage, since sensitive information is transmitted without robust privacy protection; (3) absence of standardized cross-chain identity protocols, with most current solutions focusing on assets rather than identity management; and (4) difficulty in maintaining consistency, as identity updates may not be synchronized across chains, resulting in potential authentication failures.

To address these challenges, we propose zkHARPS, a decentralized cross-chain identity aggregation and privacy-preserving method based on zero-knowledge proofs. Our solution integrates: (1) secure identity aggregation via multi-party computation (MPC) to unify fragmented identities across blockchains; (2) privacy-preserving verification using ZKP techniques [8]; (3) a dynamic update mechanism to ensure consistency across chains; and (4) optimized computation and communication for efficient cross-chain performance. We use enhanced Shamir secret sharing for secure identity aggregation and propose HARPS, a hash-based attribute range proof model, to encode verification conditions. Integrated with a zkSNARK verifier, this model supports selective disclosure of identity attributes across chains, ensuring interoperability and privacy-preserving computation within multi-chain environments. The main contributions of this paper are summarized as follows:

1. We introduce HARPS, a recursive hash-based structure that enables efficient zkSNARK proofs with selective attribute disclosure.
2. We design a trustless cross-chain verification mechanism using blockchain listeners, Merkle proofs, and light clients, ensuring synchronization and modularity.
3. We propose zkHARPS, a decentralized method for cross-chain identity aggregation and privacy proof. To the best of our knowledge, this is the first method that combines MPC with zkSNARK to support secure, scalable, and privacy-preserving identity verification across heterogeneous blockchains. The experiments of zkHARPS demonstrate superior performance.

2 Background and Related Work

This section begins with an overview of decentralized identity and proceeds to examine recent advances in zero-knowledge proofs and secure multi-party computation.

2.1 Decentralized Identity

Decentralized Identity (DID) is a novel identity management paradigm that gives users full control over their personal identity data, eliminating reliance on centralized authorities. The DID architecture enhances privacy and security by returning identity ownership to individuals. Many existing DID systems operate on a single blockchain. For instance, uPort [9], based on Ethereum, enables users to create and manage digital identities with encrypted on-chain storage, controlled entirely by the user. Hyperledger Indy [10], built on the Sovrin network, also supports on-chain DID generation and verification, ensuring identity privacy and security. While these systems address centralization issues, they are confined to single-chain contexts. In multi-chain environments, identity data is fragmented across heterogeneous blockchains lacking interoperability, making unified identity verification and aggregation across chains difficult. This poses a significant limitation to decentralized identity systems in cross-chain scenarios.

2.2 Zero-Knowledge Proof

Zero-Knowledge Proof (ZKP) enables a prover to convince a verifier of validity without revealing any additional information—ideal for privacy-preserving identity authentication. The ZKP can be represented by the following verification equation:

$$g^z \cong c \cdot h^k (modp) \tag{1}$$

where g and h are cryptographic generators, p is a large prime modulus, z and k are private values held by the prover. The verifier sends a challenge c, and the prover responds in a way that proves knowledge of the secret without revealing it. Despite strong privacy guarantees, traditional ZKPs facc limitations in efficiency, storage, trusted setup, and multi-chain scalability. To address these, researchers have proposed several optimized ZKP variants, which can be categorized into four main types:

Scalable Recursive Zero-Knowledge Proof. To improve zkSNARK scalability, recursive proof systems [11] and elliptic curve cycles [12], enabling scalable zkSNARKs without trusted setup. Systems like Halo and Aurora support recursive verification for large constraint systems, significantly reducing on-chain verification cost and storage overhead. However, [11] relies on trusted setup and raises security concerns, while [12] increases system complexity and demands high computational resources.

Short Proofs without Trusted Setup. To remove the need for trusted setup, Bulletproofs [13] use inner product arguments and polynomial compression to produce short, efficient zero-knowledge proofs. Ideal for range proofs and confidential transactions, Bulletproofs have been adopted by privacy-focused systems like Monero, offering a compact and setup-free ZKP solution. However, proof generation is time-consuming and unsuitable for general-purpose computations.

Application-Oriented ZKP for Cross-Chain Interoperability. In heterogeneous blockchain environments, ZKP is employed to remove dependency on trusted relays. zkBridge [14] is a trustless cross-chain bridge that uses zkSNARK to generate verifiable state proofs. It enables secure and traceable cross-chain communication, significantly improving decentralization and security in interoperability scenarios. However, its system implementation is complex and may suffer from cross-chain latency.

Transparent and Quantum-Resistant ZK-STARK. ZK-STARKs is transparent (requiring no trusted setup) and secure against quantum attacks. Designed for scalable data verification, they support large computations efficiently. Arade and Pise [15] further analyzed their mathematical foundations and demonstrated their practical use in supply chain privacy, highlighting both scalability and real-world applicability. However, their proofs are relatively large, leading to higher communication costs.

3 zkHARPS Architecture

This section provides a detailed introduction to the architecture of the proposed zkHARPS method. The architecture design encompasses four key functionalities: cross-chain identity aggregation, dynamic updates, privacy protection, and cross-chain verification. The overall workflow of the architecture is illustrated in Fig. 2, and the architecture is composed of the following core modules:

3.1 Decentralized Identity

The Identity Aggregation Module uses a secure multi-party computation protocol to aggregate user identity data from multiple blockchains and generate a unified global identity, denoted as ID_{global}. This module contains an update component that continuously monitors identity information across different chains to maintain consistency.

Inputs to this module include identity fragments from different chains (e.g., ID_{A} on chain C_1, ID_{B} on chain C_2), newly updated identity attributes (e.g., a new identity ID_D or a change in KYC verification status on an existing chain). The module computes the global identity using the aggregation function f as follows: $ID_{\text{global}} = f(ID_{\text{A}}, ID_{\text{B}}, \ldots)$. This ensures unified identity representation across chains. When a user updates their identity on a specific chain (e.g., chain C_4), the update component detects the change via cross-chain monitoring and synchronizes the update to the module. The global identity ID'_{global} is then recalculated and passed to the Privacy Proof Module for downstream processing.

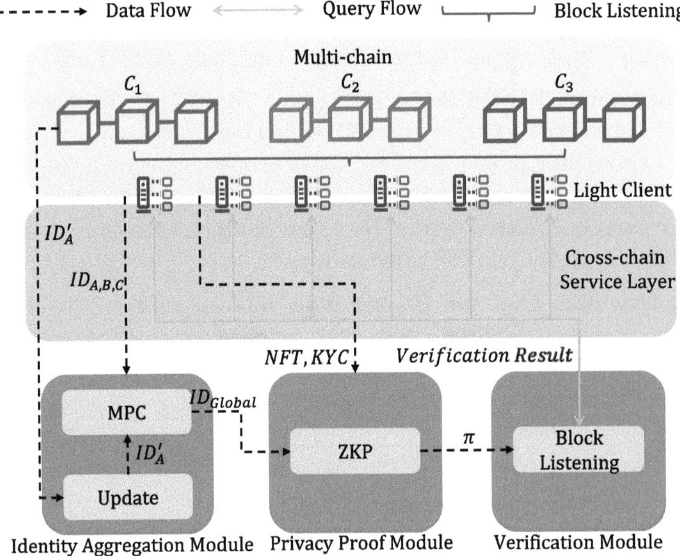

Fig. 2. Overall Workflow and Module of zkHARPS Architecture.

3.2 Privacy Proof Generation

The Privacy Proof Module leverages zero-knowledge proof techniques to generate privacy-preserving proofs for identity verification. The goal of this module is to allow users to demonstrate compliance with certain predefined conditions such as holding specific access permissions, completing KYC, or owning sufficient assets without disclosing the actual identity data.

Inputs to this module include ID_{global} and user-specified verification conditions. We construct a privacy proof π using ZKP, ensuring that users can verify their identity attributes without revealing any sensitive information. The generated proof π is submitted to the target chain and can be verified by any authorized verifier using preset verification algorithms.

The typical workflow involves the user selecting the attributes they wish to prove (e.g., token ownership on a specific chain). A zero-knowledge proof π is generated accordingly and submitted to the verifier on the target chain. Thanks to the properties of ZKP, the verifier can confirm the eligibility of user without accessing the underlying data, thus ensuring data confidentiality and cross-chain identity reliability.

3.3 Verification

The Verification Module is responsible for verifying the outputs of both the Identity Aggregation Module and the Privacy Proof Module. It ensures the correctness and consistency of identity verification across chains by using a block listener (BL) mechanism that monitors identity-related events and verification requests in real-time. The module enhances both the scalability and reliability of the method.

Inputs include aggregated ID_{global} and corresponding privacy proof π. When a user submits a verification request on a target chain (e.g., an identity management platform on C_3), this module retrieves the input data and performs validation. It first accesses relevant identity data via cross-chain protocols and then checks the validity of the proof π. If the proof is valid, the verification result is broadcast to all relevant blockchains, ensuring global identity consistency. If the proof fails, the verification module returns to the denial and blocks further access or transactions.

3.4 zkHARPS Workflow

The zkHARPS system operates in three core stages. First, during the Initialization Stage, users register identity fragments on multiple blockchains. The Identity Aggregation Module applies MPC to compute a unified global identity ID_{global}. Next, in the Identity Verification Stage, users submit a verification request with specified attributes. The Privacy Proof Module generates zero-knowledge proof π, , which is then verified on the target chain by the Cross-Chain Verification Module. Upon successful verification, the result is broadcast across all involved blockchains to ensure global consistency. Finally, in the Dynamic Update Stage, any identity changes on a single chain automatically trigger the update mechanism. The new data is sent to the aggregation module, which recalculates an updated global identity (ID'_{global}), regenerates a corresponding privacy proof π', and re-verifies it—ensuring all chains maintain an up-to-date and consistent view of the user's identity.

4 Algorithm Design

In this section, we present a detailed description of the proposed decentralized cross-chain identity aggregation and privacy-proof algorithms. The core components include identity aggregation, privacy-preserving verification, identity update, and cross-chain communication mechanisms.

4.1 Identity Aggregation Algorithm

Identity Modeling. Assume that a user holds identity data across n different blockchains, denoted as $ID_1, ID_2, ..., ID_n$. The identity on chain C_i is represented as:

$$ID_i = H(P_i, S_i) \tag{2}$$

where P_i is the public key on chain C_i of user, S_i represents the identity attributes stored on-chain (e.g., asset snapshot), and $H(\cdot)$ is a cryptographic hash function ensuring data integrity and tamper-resistance.

Secret Sharing and Encrypted Fragmentation. To protect the privacy of identity data across chains, we employ an enhanced Shamir's Secret Sharing Scheme. Each identity ID_i is encoded as a secret value in a $(t-1)$-degree polynomial:

$$f_i(x) = a_0 + a_1x + \cdots + a_{t-1}x^{t-1}, a_0 = ID_i \tag{3}$$

Each participating chain C_j receives a share of this polynomial evaluated at a predefined point:

$$S_{i\to j} = f_i(x_j), j = 1,2, \ldots, n \tag{4}$$

That is, chain C_j distributes encrypted shares $S_{i\to j}$ to other chains while retaining its own share. No single chain can reconstruct ID_i independently. Only when at least t chains collaborate can the original identity be recovered using Lagrange Interpolation:

$$ID_i = f_i(0) = \sum_{j=1}^{t} S_{i\to j} \cdot \lambda_j \tag{5}$$

where the Lagrange coefficient λ_j is computed as:

$$\lambda_j = \prod_{\substack{1 \leq k \leq t \\ k \neq j}} \frac{x_k}{x_k - x_j} \tag{6}$$

This ensures that identity data is recoverable only under the cooperation of at least t chains and remains private against any single-chain adversary.

Two-Chain and Multi-chain Reconstruction Feasibility. In the two-chain setting ($n = 2, t = 2$), the identity share ID_i is split into two fragments S_A and S_B. After mutual exchange, the original identity can be reconstructed via:

$$ID_i = f(0) = S_A \cdot \frac{x_B}{x_B - x_A} + S_B \cdot \frac{x_A}{x_A - x_B} \tag{7}$$

To ensure fairness and synchronization, a bidirectional commitment mechanism is introduced. Chains A and B exchange encrypted fragments simultaneously and validate fragment hash of each other before performing reconstruction. This prevents refusal to send or injection of malicious fragments.

In multi-chain scenarios ($n > 2$), the recovery adopts a threshold policy where any $t \leq n$ chains can reconstruct the identity. This improves fault tolerance and supports partial availability (e.g., in case of offline or unstable nodes). The global identity is constructed as:

$$ID_{\text{global}} = F(ID_1, ID_2, \ldots, ID_n) = H(w_1 \cdot ID_1, w_2 \cdot ID_2, \ldots, w_n \cdot ID_n) \quad (8)$$

where w_i is a weight factor assigned to chain C_i, which can be dynamically adjusted based on trust level or security rating of the chain.

Update Mechanism. When a user updates their identity on a specific chain C_k (e.g., from ID_k to $ID_{k'}$), the system regenerates a new polynomial $f_{k'}(x)$ and updates the corresponding fragments. The identity aggregation module is notified to recompute the new global identity:

$$ID'_{\text{global}} = F\left(ID_1, ID_2, \ldots, ID_k', \ldots, ID_n\right) \quad (9)$$

Robustness Mechanisms. To further enhance the robustness, reliability, and privacy of the identity aggregation process, we incorporate several auxiliary mechanisms. First, a hash commitment reconciliation mechanism ensures that every identity fragment exchanged across chains is accompanied by an on-chain hash record, providing tamper-evident logging and enabling verifiable integrity checks. Second, the method is designed to be delay-tolerant, requiring only a threshold t of n chains to be online for successful identity reconstruction, thus supporting fault-tolerant operation in asynchronous or unstable multi-chain environments. Finally, a collaborative validation model is implemented, where a threshold signature must be jointly produced by participating chains before any global identity is accepted. This prevents malicious fragment injection and ensures that only verified identity components are included in the aggregated result.

4.2 Privacy-Proof Construction Based on Hashed Attribute Chains

To address the limitations of traditional zero-knowledge proof (ZKP) techniques in large-scale identity verification—such as poor composability, rigid structures, and low efficiency—we propose a novel proof construction method based on hash chain validation, called the Hashed Attribute Range Proving Scheme (HARPS). Unlike existing recursive constructions, arithmetic circuits, or algebraic intermediate representations, HARPS builds a chain-based cryptographic commitment system that compresses multiple verification attributes into a single verifiable state. This enables the generation of efficient privacy-preserving proofs under zero-knowledge conditions.

Attribute Modeling and Verification Goals. Assume that a user has m verifiable identity attributes across multiple blockchains, denoted as:

$$\overrightarrow{s} = (s_1, s_2, \ldots, s_m), s_i \in \mathbb{Z}_p \tag{10}$$

Each attribute s_i reflects an identity state on a specific chain (e.g., asset value, KYC level, trust score). The corresponding verification condition for s_i is defined by a predicate:

$$C_i(s_i) = \begin{cases} 1, & if s_i satisfies condition p_i \\ 0, & otherwise \end{cases} \tag{11}$$

Typical predicates C_i include: threshold constraints (e.g., $s_i \geq T_i$), bounded intervals (e.g., $L_i \leq s_i \leq U_i$), set membership ($s_i \in G$), or binary flag matching ($s_i \in$ BinaryFlags). The goal of HARPS is to prove the existence of $\overrightarrow{s}$ such that all $C_i(s_i) = 1$, and the resulting hash chain commitment matches the on-chain stored state.

Construction of the Hash Commitment Chain. To conceal individual attribute values and compress verification results, we construct the attribute hash chain as follows:

$$H_i = H(H_{i-1}||C_i(s_i)||r_i),\ i = 1, .., m,\ H_0 = H(init||nonce) \tag{12}$$

where, H is a collision-resistant hash function (Poseidon), chosen for its ZKP-friendly characteristics; $C_i(s_i) \in \{0,1\}$ denotes the binary outcome of condition evaluation; $r_i \in Z_p$ is a randomly generated salt for each step. The final commitment value H_m is recorded on-chain and submitted to the verifier. This design ensures the combined result of all conditions is non-invertibly encoded, individual conditions are not discernible, and the entire state is compact and tamper-proof.

Zero-Knowledge Proof Objective. The ZKP statement is modeled as:

$$\exists \vec{s} such that \forall i,\ C_i(s_i) = 1 \wedge H_m = H^*(\vec{s}) \tag{13}$$

where $H^*\left(\overrightarrow{s}\right)$ denotes the final hash commitment calculated from the attribute chain. The proof is constructed as a non-interactive ZKP:

$$\pi_{harps} = ZK - Prove\left[\bigwedge_{i=1}^{m} C_i(s_i) = 1 \wedge \& H_m = H(H_{m-1}||1||r_m)\right] \tag{14}$$

This method is compatible with generic ZKP systems and does not rely on a specific recursive or circuit encoding, making it easily extensible and combinable with other privacy modules.

HARPS Integrate with zkSNARK: zkHARPS Model. O further validate the generality and adaptability of the HARPS model, this paper integrates it with the mainstream zero-knowledge proof system zkSNARK [16, 17] (Zero-Knowledge Succinct Non-Interactive Argument of Knowledge), resulting in a privacy-preserving proof system that combines structural security with practical verifiability. In the following sections, this integrated approach is referred to as zkHARPS. To implement the HARPS proof system within a zkSNARK framework, we model the proof target using an R1CS [18] (Rank-1 Constraint System), which represents all verification conditions as a set of multiplication constraints:

$$\forall j \in [1, N], \left(a_j \cdot x\right) \cdot \left(b_j \cdot x\right) = c_j \cdot x \tag{15}$$

where, x includes the identity attributes s_i, random salts r_i, auxiliary variables t_i, z_i, b_j, and intermediate hash states. Each predicate $C_i(s_i)$ is transformed into Boolean constraints, such as Threshold condition:

$$s_i \geq T_i \Rightarrow s_i - T_i = t_i, t_i \cdot z_i = 1 \tag{16}$$

And Interval condition:

$$s_i \in [L_i, U_i] \Rightarrow (s_i - L_i) \cdot (U_i - s_i) = t_i, t_i \cdot z_i = 1 \tag{17}$$

where, z_i is a Boolean auxiliary variable used to implement inverse multiplication logic (i.e., $t_i \cdot z_i = 1$ only if $t_i \geq 1$). All multiplication gates and constraints for the hash chain are constructed accordingly from Eq. (12).

Circuit Composition and Proof Generation. The full constraint system $\mathcal{R}$ is composed of both the attribute verification logic and the hash commitment chain. The complete variable vector is defined as:

$$x = \left(s_1, \ldots, s_m, r_1, \ldots, r_m, b_{ij}, t_i, z_i, H_0, \ldots, H_m\right) \tag{18}$$

The circuit output is H_m , which, along with the ID_{global} computed in Sect. 4.1, is considered a public input. All other values are private. Given this input, the prover uses a zkSNARK compiler (e.g., SnarkJS + Groth16) to translate the constraint system RRR into a QAP (Quadratic Arithmetic Program) and generate a proof based on the trusted setup:

$$\pi_{harps} = Prove_{zkSNARK}(\mathcal{R}, x_{witness}, CRS) \tag{19}$$

where, $x_{witness}$ is the actual witness satisfying all constraints; and $\pi_{harps} = (A, B, C)$ is the final zkSNARK proof consisting of three elliptic curve group elements.

4.3 Identity and Proof Verification Method

Under the zkHARPS model, the verifier responsibility is not only to confirm that attributes of user satisfy all designated privacy-preserving conditions, but also to verify the consistency and authenticity of the cross-chain identity ID_{global}. Specifically, it must be ensured that ID_{global} corresponds to a legitimate global identity collaboratively constructed by multiple chains and that it is cryptographically bound to the final attribute hash commitment H_m. To achieve this, we bind the zkSNARK verification mechanism with the MPC-generated identity output, such that the soundness of the zero-knowledge proof relies on the consistency of the global identity. This enhances the verifiability and anti-forgery capability of the entire system.

The verifier receives a set of inputs necessary for the validation process, including the zero-knowledge proof π_{harps}, which demonstrates that private attributes of user satisfy all specified verification conditions; the attribute hash chain commitment H_m, which serves as the public digest of the verification logic; the global identity ID_{global}, aggregated through MPC across multiple blockchains; and relevant on-chain audit records for traceability and integrity verification.

The necessary and sufficient condition for successful verification is that the proof π_{harps} must demonstrate the existence of an attribute vector $\overrightarrow{s}$, such that all predicates $C_i(s_i) = 1$ are satisfied, and the resulting final hash value computed from $\overrightarrow{s}$ equals the public commitment H_m . Moreover, H_m must be the privacy-preserving digest of the attribute set represented by ID_{global}, ensuring a binding consistency between identity and the privacy proof.

Since both ID_{global} and H_m are part of the public input to π_{harps}, they naturally form a binding privacy proof. Thus, it suffices to check that the attribute commitment matches the public identity and satisfies the encoded constraints. This is directly verified using the public zkSNARK verifier as follows:

$$zkSNARK.Verify\left(\pi_{harps}, H_m, ID_{global}\right) \rightarrow TrueorFalse \tag{20}$$

If the verification succeeds, the system proceeds to validate the signature set of the identity aggregation nodes and the associated MPC authorization certificate linked to ID_{global}. Only when all steps pass is the identity and its corresponding attribute set considered valid and the verification process successfully completed.

4.4 Cross-Chain Transmission and Light Client Deployment

To synchronize identity data across blockchains and support privacy-preserving attribute verification, the cross-chain transmission module acts as a vital bridge between source and target chains. It comprises three core components: an event-listening mechanism, on-chain authenticity verification, and seamless integration with the MPC-based identity aggregation scheme, alongside light client deployment. This section details their design and coordination within the zkHARPS system.

Event Listening Mechanism Design. When identity updates occur on the source chain (e.g., KYC completion, asset changes), a predefined event is emitted by an Identity Update smart contract. To capture these updates, the system deploys an off-chain listener that subscribes to events via RPC and filters them using event hashes. Upon detecting an update, the listener wraps the block height, transaction index, and raw data into a Merkle proof, which is transmitted to the target chain via a light client. This ensures reliable and verifiable cross-chain delivery of identity events for secure aggregation and verification.

Data Authenticity Verification on the Target Chain. To validate that identity updates originate from a legitimate source chain state, the system uses a light client combined with Merkle path verification. The event hash h_{event} is treated as a Merkle leaf, and the off-chain agent generates a corresponding Merkle path. The light client of target chain synchronizes source chain headers to obtain the latest Merkle root h_{root}. The verification contract checks whether h_{event} is included in h_{root}. If the proof is valid, the event is deemed authentic. Importantly, this module does not reconstruct user identity directly but serves as a verifiable data source for the MPC-based identity aggregation process.

Light Client Deployment Strategy. To avoid the overhead of replicating full source-chain consensus on the target chain, the system adopts a lightweight deployment approach. For Ethereum, the light client includes a block header synchronization module and a consensus verification module. Only recent block headers are retained, with older data pruned to reduce on-chain storage. For example, integrating the Ethereum Beacon Light Client enables efficient tracking and verification of source-chain states, supporting EIP-1186-compliant Merkle Patricia proofs. This design ensures lightweight, scalable, and interoperable identity synchronization across chains.

5 Evaluation

All experiments were conducted on a server equipped with an Intel(R) Xeon(R) Gold 6354 CPU @ 3.00 GHz and 504 GB RAM. The smart contracts (chaincode) were developed and deployed on both Hyperledger Fabric and the Ethereum testnet (Ganache), using Go and Solidity respectively. Gas cost analysis was carried out with the Hardhat Gas Reporter, while zero-knowledge proof circuits were written in Circom v2 and compiled and executed using the SnarkJS + Groth16 proving system. The event listener and light client prototype were implemented in Node.js with Web3.js. To simulate realistic cross-chain identity verification, we built a dataset comprising: (1) 500 users with identity fragments (assets, reputation, KYC) across 2–3 blockchains; (2) 1–5 diverse verification conditions per user (e.g., range, Boolean, threshold).

5.1 Proof Generation Time Comparison

This experiment aims to evaluate the proof generation efficiency of the proposed zkHARPS scheme under varying numbers of verification conditions, and to compare it against representative zk-proof systems such as Bulletproofs, Scalable zk, and ZK-STARK. The number of verification conditions was set to {1, 5, 10, 20, 50}, and all schemes were executed under identical circuit structures and hardware environments.

As shown in Fig. 3(a), the experimental results demonstrate that the proposed zkHARPS scheme exhibits excellent linear scalability in proof generation time. Even in the case of 50 verification conditions, the proof can be generated in under 1.3 s, significantly outperforming Bulletproofs, Scalable zk, and ZK-STARK. This performance advantage stems from zkHARPS circuit-level aggregation design, where multiple logical predicates are compiled into a single R1CS constraint system, greatly reducing the workload during the proving phase.

In contrast, while Bulletproofs and ZK-STARK eliminate the need for trusted setup, their proving phases typically exhibit O(nlogn) or higher complexity, which leads to performance degradation in high-dimensional verification scenarios. In conclusion,

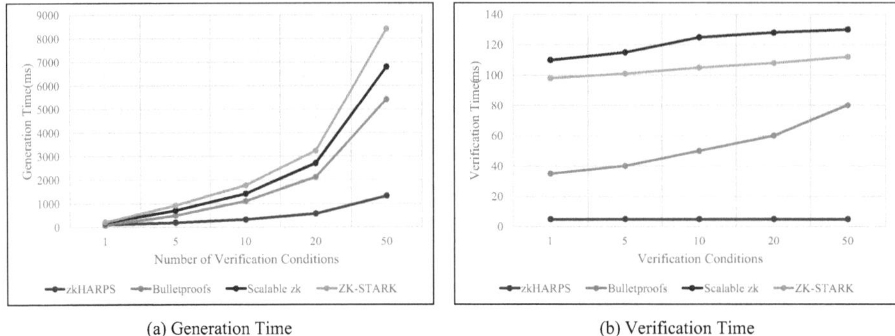

(a) Generation Time (b) Verification Time

Fig. 3. Comparison of Proof Generation and Verification Time Across Different Methods.

zkHARPS demonstrates superior scalability and robustness in complex multi-attribute proof generation tasks.

5.2 Proof Verification Time Comparison

This experiment compares the on-chain verification performance of various zero-knowledge systems, with a particular focus on how verification time scales with the number of verification conditions. By deploying the verification smart contracts to the Ganache test environment, we measured the average verification time for each system across a range of 1 to 50 verification conditions, in order to evaluate their practical execution efficiency on-chain.

As shown in Fig. 3(b), the results indicate that zkHARPS maintains a stable verification time of approximately 5 ms, significantly outperforming other systems. This advantage arises from the fact that zkHARPS relies on a fixed-size pairing operation for verification, which is independent of the number of verification conditions.

In contrast, Bulletproofs and ZK-STARK require handling multiple constraints or challenge values during verification, leading to higher complexity compared to SNARKs. Although Scalable zk uses recursive structures to compress verification logic, making it suitable for large-scale off-chain aggregation, it is not optimized for low-latency single proof verification on-chain.

Therefore, in high-TPS consortium chains or Layer-2 networks where low-latency response is critical, zkHARPS ability to maintain a consistently short verification time helps avoid on-chain congestion and performance bottlenecks.

5.3 Gas Cost Comparison

To comprehensively evaluate the on-chain resource consumption of different zero-knowledge proof systems, this experiment breaks down Gas costs into three key dimensions: contract deployment cost, proof data upload cost, and verification function execution cost. For each system, we set the number of verification conditions to $\{5, 10, 50\}$ and measure the gas usage for both deployment and verification procedures.

As shown in Fig. 4, zkHARPS consistently achieves the lowest Gas consumption across all metrics. Its contract deployment cost remains around 940,000 Gas due to its efficient circuit design. Proof upload costs grow linearly with the number of conditions, but zkHARPS benefits from a fixed proof size of 192 bytes, making its overhead much smaller than Bulletproofs and STARK, which generate larger and variable-length proofs. In verification, zkHARPS maintains a stable cost between 330,000–370,000 Gas, far outperforming Bulletproofs (>1M) and STARK (>2.5M), whose high costs stem from complex polynomial and commitment operations. Even Scalable zk, though better than STARK, still incurs noticeable overhead due to recursive proof unfolding. Overall, zkHARPS proves to be the most efficient option, especially for high-frequency smart contract scenarios and storage-sensitve cross-chain identity systems.

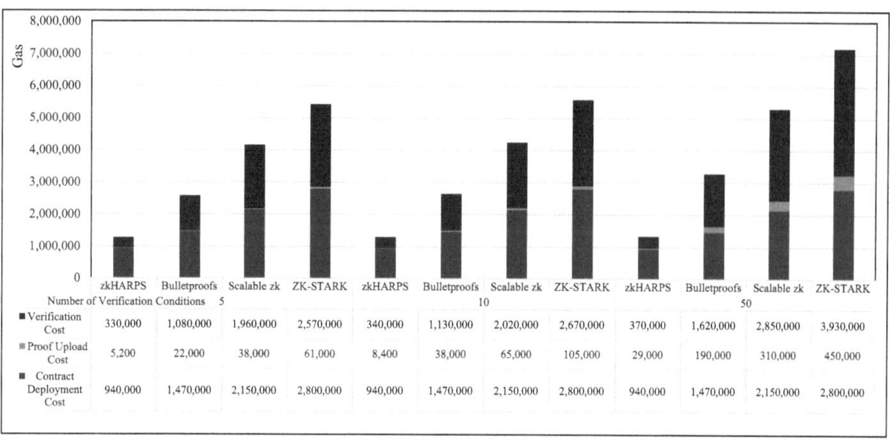

Fig. 4. Comparison of Gas Cost Across ZKP Methods.

5.4 Storage Overhead Comparison

To compare the on-chain storage burden of different zk methods, this experiment compiles and exports the proof files under identical circuit logic and records their original sizes (in bytes) to evaluate their impact on blockchain storage consumption. Table 1 presents the proof sizes for each method.

Table 1. Proof Sizes of Different ZKP Methods.

Method	zkHARPS	Bulletproofs	Scalable zk	ZK-STARK
Size (bytes)	192	672	1024	2500+

The results indicate that zkHARPS produces the smallest proof size at 192 bytes, outperforming all other schemes. In contrast, Bulletproofs, which lack proof compression, exhibit linearly increasing storage requirements as conditions grow. ZK-STARK, due to its use of transparent hash extensions, typically produces proofs exceeding 2 KB. While Scalable zk theoretically supports recursive compression, its initial verifier remains relatively large, with R1CS-generated proofs averaging around 1 KB.

In blockchain environments, smaller proof sizes directly translate into lighter-weight contract verifications, reduced block space usage, and lower on-chain storage costs. This makes zkHARPS particularly suitable for integration into Layer 1 environments or even resource-constrained mobile on-chain systems.

5.5 Identity Aggregation Consistency Testing

To validate the system fault tolerance and identity consistency in asynchronous multi-chain environments, we designed an Identity Aggregation Consistency Test to evaluate whether the system can correctly and stably reconstruct ID_{global} under varying numbers of nodes, synchronization delays, and data integrity conditions. This test specifically focuses on the robustness of the system against data offset and node failures, demonstrating the adaptability of zkHARPS in dynamic multi-chain settings.

The experiment is based on a multi-node cross-chain identity collaboration scenario, with the following variables defined: number of participating nodes {5, 10, 20, 50}; maximum block offset $\{\pm 1, \pm 5, \pm 10, \pm 20\}$ to simulate desynchronization; node synchronization ratios $\{100\%, 80\%, 60\%, 50\%\}$ to represent partial updates; and random fragment loss ranging from 0% to 30% to simulate node failures. The threshold for aggregation is set to $t = n/2$. The fragments are aggregated using the MPC protocol and the HARPS commitment mechanism to reconstruct the global identity ID_{global}. . The system then checks whether the aggregation was successful and records the aggregation latency (ms) and the reconstruction success rate. The experimental results are presented in Table 2.

Table 2. Success Rate and Latency of Identity Aggregation Consistency.

Number of Nodes	Max Offset	Synchronization Ratio	Reconstruction Success Rate	Aggregation Latency (ms)
5	±1	100%	100.0%	65
10	±5	80%	100.0%	88
20	±10	70%	98.9%	122
50	±10	60%	95.7%	310
20	±20(offline)	50%	91.2%	490

The experimental results show that zkHARPS consistently achieves high identity aggregation accuracy and low latency, even under asynchronous and partially chain offline conditions. In small networks (≤10 nodes) or with minimal block offset (±5), the system maintains a 100% aggregation success rate and latency below 100 ms. In larger networks (20–50 nodes), if ≥60% of nodes are synchronized, zkHARPS reconstructs global identities with >95% accuracy, while maintaining latency under 500 ms. Even under extreme conditions—only 50% node synchronization and ±20 block offset—zkHARPS achieves a 91.2% success rate, confirming its robustness in unstable environments.

This resilience is attributed to threshold-based MPC protocol of system, which supports partial reconstruction if the minimum number of valid shares is met. The HARPS hash chain structure enforces version consistency by verifying tail hashes before aggregation. Additionally, timestamp and snapshot mechanisms allow consistent identity reconstruction at specific time points. The update process, coupled with the cross-chain listener, buffers delayed inputs, allowing the system to tolerate temporary chain desynchronization. Overall, zkHARPS demonstrates strong fault tolerance and reliable identity consistency.

6 Conclusion

This paper presents zkHARPS, a decentralized cross-chain identity aggregation and privacy-proof scheme that combines MPC, ZKP, and hashed attribute structures. It enables unified identity aggregation and privacy-preserving verification across blockchains. The system supports multi-chain synchronization, data privacy, and efficient validation. Experiments on Hyperledger Fabric and Ethereum testnet confirm its practical applicability and performance advantages. Results show that zkHARPS outperforms existing methods in generation speed, verification efficiency, storage, and gas cost. Future work will focus on anonymous identity authentication.

Acknowledgments. This work was supported by the National Natural Science Foundation of China (grant number 62372097 and 62072086) and the National Social Science Foundation of China (grant number 21&ZD124).

References

1. Wood, G.: POLKADOT: vision for a heterogeneous multi-chain framework. White paper **21**(2327), 4662 (2016)
2. Buterin, V.: Ethereum white paper. GitHub Reposit. **1**(22–23), 5–7 (2013)
3. Hardjono, T., Lipton, A., Pentland, A.: Toward an interoperability architecture for blockchain autonomous systems. IEEE TEM **67**(4), 1298–1309 (2019)
4. Narayanan, A., Bonneau, J., Felten, E., Miller, A.: Bitcoin and Cryptocurrency Technologies: A Comprehensive Introduction. Princeton University Press (2016)
5. Sasson, E.B., Chiesa, A., Garman, C., Green, M., Miers, I., Tromer, E.: ZEROCASH: decentralized anonymous payments from bitcoin. In: Symposium on Security and Privacy, Berkeley, USA, 18–21 May, 2014, pp. 459–474 (2014)
6. Liu, Y., He, D., Obaidat, M., Kumar, N., Khan, M.: Blockchain-based identity management systems: a review. J. Netw. Comput. Appl. **166**, 102731 (2020)
7. Dunphy, P., Petitcolas, F.: A first look at identity management schemes on the blockchain. IEEE Secur. Priv. **16**(4), 20–29 (2018)

8. Kosba, A., Miller, A., Shi, E., Wen, Z.: HAWK: the blockchain model of cryptography and privacy-preserving smart contracts. In: Symposium on Security and Privacy, San Jose, USA, 22–26 May, 2016, pp. 839–858 (2016)
9. Lundkvist, C., Heck, R., Torstensson, J., Mitton, Z., Sena, M.: UPORT: a platform for self-sovereign identity [EB/OL] (2017). https://whitepaper.uport.me/uPort_whitepaper_DRAFT20170221.pdf
10. Bhattacharya, M., Zavarsky, P., Butakov, S.: Enhancing the security and privacy of self-sovereign identities on hyperledger indy blockchain. In: International Symposium on Networks, Computers and Communications, Montreal, Canada, 20–22 October, 2020, pp. 1–7 (2020)
11. Ben-Sasson, E., Chiesa, A., Tromer, E., et al.: Scalable zero knowledge via cycles of elliptic curves. Algorithmica **79**, 1102–1160 (2017)
12. Ben-Sasson, E., Bentov, I., Horesh, Y., Virza, M.: Scalable zero knowledge with no trusted setup. In: Advances in Cryptology–CRYPTO 2019: 39th Annual International Cryptology Conference, Santa Barbara, CA, USA, August 18–22, 2019, Proceedings, Part III 39. Springer International Publishing, 2019, pp. 701–732 (2019)
13. Bünz, B., Bootle, J., Boneh, D., et al.: BulletProofs: short proofs for confidential transactions and more. In: 2018 IEEE Symposium on Security and Privacy (SP). IEEE, 2018, pp. 315–334 (2018)
14. Xie, T., Zhang, J., Cheng, Z., et al.: ZKBRIDGE: trustless cross-chain bridges made practical. In: SIGSAC Conference on Computer and Communications Security, pp. 3003–3017 (2022)
15. Arade S, Pise N. ZK-STARK: Mathematical Foundations and Applications in Blockchain Supply Chain Privacy. Cybernetics and Information Technologies, 2025, 25(1)
16. Ben-Sasson, E., Chiesa, A., Tromer, E., et al.: Succinct {Non-Interactive} zero knowledge for a von neumann architecture. In: USENIX Security Symposium, pp. 781–796 (2014)
17. Groth, J.: On the size of pairing-based non-interactive arguments. In: Advances in Cryptology–EUROCRYPT, Vienna, Austria, May 8–12, 2016, pp. 305–326(2016)
18. Ben-Sasson, E., Chiesa, A., Riabzev, M., et al.: AURORA: transparent succinct arguments for R1CS. In: Advances in Cryptology–EUROCRYPT, Darmstadt, Germany, May 19–23, 2019, pp. 103–128 (2019)

FLAR: Fibonacci-Assisted Lightweight Anonymous Revocable Authentication Scheme in Industrial Internet of Things

Junfeng Tian[1,2], Jian Geng[1,2(✉)], and Siyi Zhang[1,2]

[1] Key Lab on High Trusted Information System in Hebei Province, Hebei University, Baoding, China
JianGeng1210@163.com

[2] School of Cyber Security and Computer, Hebei University, Baoding, China

Abstract. The data-centric paradigm promoted by Industry 4.0 is accelerating Industrial Internet of Things (IIoT), resulting in increasingly frequent inter-departmental data interaction. Secure and efficient sharing therefore depends on reliable authentication among smart devices. Current schemes, however, do not jointly satisfy dynamic anonymity, traceability, and low overhead. Consequently, pseudonym management is cumbersome, revocation mechanisms are inflexible and costly. Therefore, we propose a Fibonacci-assisted lightweight anonymous revocable authentication (FLAR) scheme. By integrating a Fibonacci sequence with a hash chain, the scheme enables rapid signature verification. We design a dual parameter derivation algorithm to support swift pseudonym generation while maintaining data traceability and facilitating flexible revocation. Security is rigorously proven: existential unforgeability under chosen-message attacks (EU-CMA) is established in Random-Oracle Model (ROM), and Burrows-Abadi-Needham (BAN) logic plus *ProVerif* analyses confirm that all specified security properties hold. Performance evaluation shows that, FLAR markedly lowers than the other related schemes both computational and communication overhead, better fulfilling the lightweight and real-time demands of IIoT environments.

Keywords: Authentication · Fibonacci Sequence · Industrial Internet of Things (IIoT) · Information Security

1 Introduction

Industry 4.0 has driven the Industrial Internet of Things (IIoT) toward a data-centric collaborative model, enhancing interconnectivity across industrial sectors [1]. In the IIoT ecosystem, smart devices subscribe to diverse services—such as production and management tasks—and collect corresponding data in shared environments like Production-on-Demand Park (PoD Park) [2]. While this data-driven approach optimizes industrial planning and boosts productivity, it also

J. Li et al. (Eds.): APWeb-WAIM 2025, LNCS 16115, pp. 633–648, 2026.
https://doi.org/10.1007/978-981-95-5719-6_40

Fig. 1. Data interaction between industrial departments in PoD Park.

exposes sensitive information (e.g., customer details, production metrics) to significant privacy risks [3]. Given the resource constraints of IIoT devices, there is a critical need to balance stringent privacy protection with minimal computational overhead [4]. Figure 1 depicts a typical PoD Park data-exchange scenario: the Edge Server authorizes and revokes service access for smart devices, enabling real-time interactions within and between departments, yet frequent communications over insecure networks amplify privacy concerns [5,6]. To address these challenges, numerous IIoT authentication schemes offering anonymous credentials and flexible revocation have been proposed, demonstrating practical effectiveness [7,8].

Despite the success in achieving inter-departmental security management and operational efficiency, existing schemes face increasingly severe security and performance challenges due to frequent information exchanges between devices. On one hand, some schemes implement fixed pseudonym or incomplete pseudonym updating mechanisms [9], allowing attackers to intercept or analyze exchanged information and link it to real identity. While some solutions achieve strict anonymity, they overly depend on trusted third parties, introducing security vulnerabilities. On the other hand, most schemes incur high overhead in anonymity mechanisms and offer single-function revocation mechanisms [10], resulting in resource waste within the system and making them unsuitable for IIoT scenarios where high data density and real-time data requirements are critical, thereby failing to meet the need for flexible device revocation in PoD Park.

To address the challenges, we propose FLAR, a secure and lightweight authentication scheme that enables dynamic anonymity for smart devices, along with flexible revocation. The contributions of FLAR are as follows:

1. Based on concept of Fibonacci sequences, we design a lightweight authentication scheme called FLAR that allows for rapid authentication and revocation of smart devices. FLAR ensures the anonymity and unlinkability of devices, eliminates high-latency operations, and guarantees data traceability.
2. We design a dual parameter derivation algorithm, which combined with hash chain, enables efficient parameter management for smart devices. The approach significantly reduces both computational and storage overheads of system while maintaining its security.
3. We validate EU-CMA security of FLAR based on ROM and conduct formal security analysis using BAN logic and *ProVerif*. The results show that FLAR significantly outperforms other schemes in terms of security. Besides,

we comprehensively test the performance of FLAR in real-world applications. The experimental results demonstrate that FLAR provides the minimal computational and communication overhead compared to other solutions.

The rest of the paper is organized as follows: Sect. 2 reviews related work. Section 3 outlines the system model. Section 4 describes detailed FLAR. The security and performance analysis are provided in Sect. 5. Finally, Sect. 6 concludes the paper.

2 Related Work

In [11], He et al. proposed a lightweight authentication scheme for IoT devices, which combines elliptic curve cryptography (ECC) and hash operations to achieve device anonymity, aiming to improve the efficiency and security of IoT systems. Similarly, Bai et al. designed an efficient anonymous authentication scheme based on Rabin cryptosystem, leveraging the Rabin encryption algorithm to ensure device anonymity and significantly enhance privacy of data [12]. However, like most traditional schemes [13], these solutions rely on fixed pseudonyms to support communication between devices, failing to achieve complete device anonymity. Attackers can still link the transmitted information between channels to user's real identity, resulting in privacy data leakage. Consequently, Ren et al. introduced the ACLAP protocol [14], an authentication scheme based on certificateless approach, which incorporates a one-time random factor combined with hash operations to generate dynamic pseudonyms for devices. Additionally, Cao et al. applied group signature technology to design a revocable anonymous authentication scheme [15], enabling traceable anonymous access and revocation management for edge smart controllers through anonymous certificate management. Li et al. proposed a real-time key update strategy in [16], generating temporal keys for all devices and achieving anonymity and revocation mechanisms based on temporal information. Yadav et al. proposed a symmetric key authentication protocol for IIoT devices, which dynamically hides device identities by updating identity masks with symmetric keys before each session [17].

However, anonymity provided by [14–17] requires a key generation center (KGC) to generate or store parameters, and a failure in KGC could severely impact device privacy. The heavy reliance on KGC not only makes the system vulnerable to security threats but also creates bottlenecks in performance due to large-scale generation of pseudonyms in the system. Moreover, while anonymity mechanisms ensure secure data transmission, absolute anonymity may lead to malicious data sharing. Malicious devices can use pseudonyms to send erroneous production data, misguiding other devices, which could severely hinder production efficiency. Therefore, a flexible traceable revocation mechanism is crucial. Similar to [15,16], Lin et al. designed the privacy-preserving authentication scheme EBCPA [18], which uses blockchain and smart contracts to maintain an anonymous public key list, enabling a flexible revocation mechanism by monitoring malicious information. Further, Wang et al. pro-posed a revocable anonymous authentication protocol based on Okamoto [19], which combines key derivation algorithms and blockchain to achieve flexible revocation of device anonymous certificates. Yang et al. introduced TSA-IPFE, an authentication scheme that implements authorization revocation and dynamic pseudonym allocation, embedding "edge cloud identity" into keys and cipher-texts to enable dynamic authorization management and an efficient revocation mechanism [20].

The revocation mechanisms in [18–20] have made significant progress, achieving flexible revocation for smart devices without relying on KGC. However, the traceable revocation mechanisms based on blockchain smart contracts place a significant resource burden on the system due to frequent query accesses. Especially frequent on-chain queries and blockchain storage operations, which is not suitable for DoP Park. Therefore, there is an urgent need for a lightweight authentication protocol that can implement dynamic anonymity without relying on KGC and achieve a flexible traceable revocation mechanism with low overhead.

3 System Design

3.1 Fibonacci Sequence

The Fibonacci sequence, a classic mathematical series introduced by Leonardo Fibonacci [21], is defined by the recurrence relation: $F_n = F_{n-1} + F_{n-2}$, where each term in the sequence is the sum of the two preceding terms, with initial values F_0 and F_1 being user-defined random seeds. The unique theoretical advantages of Fibonacci sequence in cryptography are as follows:

- **Dynamic and Unpredictable Values**: Since Fibonacci sequence is generated by a recurrence relation, it is extremely difficult for attackers to predict any value in the sequence without knowing initial seed and starting state.
- **Computational Lightweight**: The computation in the sequence involves simple integer addition, with a computational complexity of $O(n)$, making it highly suitable for IIoT devices with limited computational capabilities.
- **State Traceability and Granularity Control**: Each value in the sequence corresponds to a unique index, which is used for tracking in revocation.

3.2 System Model

Figure 2 illustrates the DoP Park scenario in an IIoT setting. In DoP Park, smart devices—both within and across departments—may subscribe to multiple services, but only those holding valid service authorization credentials are deemed trustworthy. The system model comprises three entities: the Key Generation Center (KGC), Smart Devices (SD), and Edge Servers (ES).

KGC: A trusted third-party entity responsible for system initialization and registration of IIoT entities.

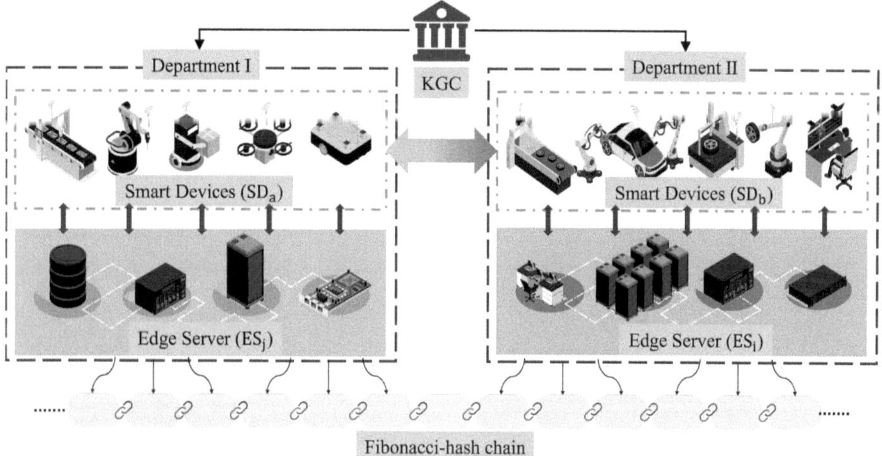

Fig. 2. Fibonacci-assisted system model for PoD Park.

SD: An entity with limited resources within the system. It uses Fibonacci-hash chains to achieve dynamic anonymity and key pair generation.

ES: A server node with abundant computational and storage resources within the system. It is responsible for maintaining the parameter hash table of SDs and acts as the manager of industrial departments.

In the model, three key factors are considered: 1) SD can subscribe to multiple services. 2) Before utilizing a service, SD must join the corresponding department. 3) As the manager, ES must authorize an SD's join request.

3.3 Threat Model

We evaluate the security of FLAR using widely adopted Dolev-Yao and CK-Adversary threat models [22]. In this threat model, attacker A is categorized into two types: internal and external. Internal attackers include legitimate system entities (SD and ES) that are authorized to participate in FLAR. External attackers refer to any unauthenticated external entities. A possesses the following capabilities:

1. A can fully control messages transmitted over public channels, including actions like eavesdropping, modification, impersonation, and replay attacks.
2. A can intercept information from multiple sessions and, through data analysis, deduce real identity of the signer.

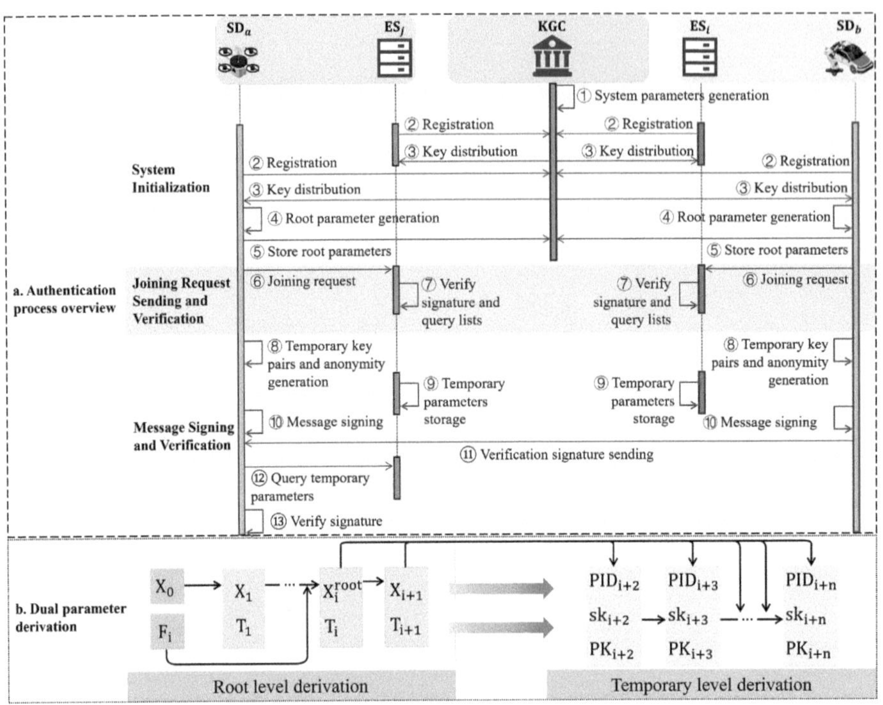

Fig. 3. Authentication process overview and dual parameter derivation.

3.4 Security Objectives

In the subsection, we outline the security property objectives of FLAR:

1. **Message Integrity and Authentication**: To ensure security of the system, the integrity of messages must be guaranteed, and the receiver should be able to verify the validity of messages.
2. **Anonymity**: To effectively protect the privacy of SDs, dynamic anonymity generation for SDs must be ensured.
3. **Traceability**: The KGC or ES should be able to trace the identity of SDs based on specific requirements.
4. **Unlinkability**: Attackers should not be able to link two different messages belonging to the same SD.
5. **Perfect Forward Security**: An attacker who gains access to the current session key should not be able to decrypt past messages.
6. **Resistance to Various Attacks**: To ensure privacy preservation, FLAR must be resilient against like replay attacks, impersonation attacks, and man-in-middle attacks.

4 Proposed Scheme FLAR

This section details FLAR's four phases: system initialization, join request sending and verification, message signing and verification, and traceability and revocation—as summarized in Fig. 3(a).

4.1 System Initialization

System Parameter Generation: 1) Given ECC parameters $(\mathbb{G}, q, P)$, KGC selects a random number $msk \in \mathbb{Z}_q^*$ as system's master key and computes the corresponding public key $K_{pub} = msk \cdot P$. 2) Two hash functions are randomly chosen: $H_1 : \{0,1\}^* \to \mathbb{Z}_q^*$, $H_2 : \{0,1\}^* \to \{0,1\}^*$. 3) KGC ensures that msk is kept secret and publishes $(\mathbb{G}, q, \mathbb{Z}_q^*, K_{pub}, H_1, H_2)$ over public channel. Notations used are shown in Table 1.

Table 1. Notations Description

Notations	Description
KGC	Key generation center
SD_i	i–th smart device
ES_j	j–th edge server
K_{pub}/msk	System public/master/master key
$seed$	Initial seed of Fibonacci-hash chain
$\mathbb{Z}_q^*$	The interval $[1, q-1]$
q	A large prime
F_i	i–th value on the Fibonacci-hash chain
Z_i^0	Head element of i–th device on the Fibonacci-hash chain
Enc/Dec	Symmetric encryption/decryption

Service Seed Generation: IIoT system offers various types of services. For each service, KGC generates a service seed and keeps it secret. The service seed is defined as $Ser_s \in \{0,1\}^*$, and random values $e_s, r_s \in \mathbb{Z}_q^*$ are chosen. The service commitment C_s is defined as $C_s = e_s \cdot P + r_s \cdot K_{pub}$, where r_s is service seed, and e_s, r_s are combined in a Pedersen commitment to protect the service secret. The auxiliary key $\text{aser}_s = H_1(Ser_s||msk)$ is generated to verify the legitimacy of service authorization credentials during subsequent device registrations.

IIoT Entity Registration: To ensure user and device privacy protection in the system, the registration process takes place over a secure channel.

- ES_j submits a registration request $\{ID_{Ej}, Ser_s\}$ to KGC, where ID_{Ej} represents the identity of ES_j, and Ser_s represents the requested service type. KGC randomly selects $x_j \in \mathbb{Z}_q^*$ as private key and computes public key $X_j = x_j \cdot P$. KGC then sends the key pair to ES_j, which stores $(x_j, X_j, aser_s, C_s)$.

- SD_i submits a registration request $\{ID_{Si}, Ser_s\}$ to KGC, where ID_{Si} represents the identity of SD_i, and Ser_s represents the requested service type. KGC randomly selects $y_i \in \mathbb{Z}_q^*$ as private key and computes long-term public key $Y_i = y_i \cdot P$ to protect the privacy of SD, authentication credential for the service must be kept in use. Thus, SD_i randomly selects $seed \in \mathbb{Z}_q^*$ as the initial random seed for Fibonacci sequence, where $F_0 = seed$ and $F_1 = seed$, and Fibonacci sequence is defined by $F_n = F_{n-1}+F_{n-2}$. Fibonacci-hash chain is constructed, with first element $Z_i^0 = H_1(ID_{Si}||seed)$, and subsequent elements $Z_i^n = H_1(Z_i^{n-1}||F_n)$. Based on SD_i's unique Fibonacci-hash chain, the auxiliary key $as_i = H_1(Z_i^0||aser_s)$ is calculated. The values $e_i = e_s \cdot as_i$, and $r_i = r_s \cdot as_i$ are then computed. SD_i stores $\{y_i, Z_i^0, e_i, r_i\}$. The service authorization credential changes according to Fibonacci-Hash chain, meaning the device discards the authorization credential once it is used. Additionally, while the service seed Ser_s remains the same for the service, the Z_i^0 values differ across devices. Thus, revoking the SD's authorization will not affect other devices' authorization certificates for the same service.

Dynamic Anonymous Identity Generation for Device: To ensure dynamic anonymity of SDs, before joining a new department, it needs to use a new temporary anonymous identity and temporary public-private key pair. A novel dual parameter derivation algorithm is designed to allow SDs to independently generate a large number of temporary identities and anonymous keys without frequently requesting KGC. As shown in Fig. 3(b), the algorithm is used to generate temporary anonymous identity and temporary public-private key pair for SD_i. The chain's first element Z_n^0, unique to each SD, serves as the root derivation. The pseudonym used for each device authentication is defined as: $PID_i^t = H_1(Z_i^t||T_i^1)$, where Z_i^t represents $t-th$ node in SD_i's Fibonacci-hash chain, and T_i^1 is the timestamp for current authentication session, ensuring the uniqueness of pseudonym and preventing replay attacks.

Each time a new temporary identity is needed, SD_i locally updates $t = t+1$, computes $F_{t+1} = F_t + F_{t-1}$, and generates $Z_i^{t+1} = H_1(Z_i^t||F_{t+1})$. The new pseudonym is defined as $PID_i^{t+1} = H_1(Z_i^{t+1}||T_{t+1})$, and corresponding temporary private key $sk_i^{t+1} = H_1(y_i||Z_i^{t+1})$ and temporary public key $pk_i^{t+1} = sk_i^{t+1} \cdot P$ are calculated. To revoke corresponding temporary parameters, the system simply marks the invalidity of Z_i^{t+1}.

The chain first elements for each SD are stored in system's hash table, with lookup and insertion/deletion operations having a time complexity of $O(1)$. For storage of temporary identities and temporary public-private key pairs for devices, each device maintains a hash table locally, storing only the Z_n^i values.

4.2 Joining Request Sending and Verification

In the phase, SD_i wishes to join a new department and must send a join request to corresponding ES_j. Upon receiving the request, ES_j validates the legitimacy of SD_i and checks whether it has corresponding service authorization.

Sending Join Request: Take SD_i as an example. SD_i selects three random numbers $a_i, l_{1i}, l_{2i} \in \mathbb{Z}_q^*$ and computes following values: $f = H_2(a_i \cdot X_j)$, $C_i = e_i \cdot P + r_i \cdot K_{pub}$, $C_i^{'} = l_{1i} \cdot P + l_{2i} \cdot K_{pub}$, where $C_i^{'}$ is the blinded commitment, and $\delta_i = H_1(f||C_i||C_i^{'}||T_i^1)$ is verification factor. Then, SD_i computes $\beta_i^1 = l_{1i} + e_i \cdot \delta_i$ and $\beta_i^2 = l_{2i} + r_i \cdot \delta_i$, which are used to construct a zero-knowledge proof, combining the device's secret value with the randomly chosen blinding factors and the verification factor to ensure that any tampering can be detected. SD_i computes $A_i = a_i \cdot P, b = Enc(\beta_i^1||\beta_i^2||C_i||C_i^{'}||PID_i^t||pk_i^t||Ser_s||Z_i^0)$ and generates signature factor: $\varepsilon_i = H_1(A_i||b||pk_i^t||T_i^1)$. Finally, request signature is computed as: $\zeta_i = a_i + sk_i^t \cdot \varepsilon_i$, SD_i sends message $M_i^1 = \left\{\zeta_i, T_i^1, b, A_i\right\}$ to ES_j.

Verifying Join Request: Upon receiving M_i^1, ES_j checks validity of T_i^1, computes: $f' = H_2(A_i \cdot x_j)$ and decrypts: $Dec(c) = (\beta_i^1||\beta_i^2||C_i||C_i^{'}||PID_i^t||pk_i^t||Ser_s||Z_i^0)$. After this, ES_j checks the legitimacy of Z_i^0. If legal, ES_j computes $\varepsilon_i^{'} = H_1(A_i||b||pk_i^t||T_i^1)$ and verifies whether the following equation holds:

$$\zeta_i \cdot P = A_i + pk_i^t \cdot \varepsilon_i^{'} \tag{1}$$

If Eq. (1) holds, the process continues. ES_j computes: $as_i^{'} = H_1(Z_i^0||aser_s)$ and then calculates the service commitment $C_s^{'} = \frac{C_i}{as_i^{'}}$. It queries the database to check if there is a matching $\left\{C_s^{'}, Ser_s\right\}$. If a match exists, ES_j computes $\delta_i^{'} = H_1(f^{'}||C_i||C_i^{'}||T_i^1)$ and verifies whether the following equation holds:

$$\beta_i^1 \cdot P + \beta_i^2 \cdot K_{pub} = C_i^{'} + \delta_i^{'} \cdot C_i \tag{2}$$

If Eq. (2) holds, the verification is successful, and SD_i's request is approved. The phase ensures that a device can participate in multiple departments for various tasks, with the design ensuring both verification and flexible revocation.

4.3 Message Signing and Verification

In the phase, each SD_i derives a fresh anonymous identity and temporary key pair from its Fibonacci-hash chain, enabling flexible revocation via dual parameter derivation algorithm. For example, once SD_i joins a department using Z_i^t, all messages are signed and verified to guarantee data-source authenticity and integrity: SD_i signs outgoing data, and ES validates the signature upon receipt.

Dual Parameter Derivation: Based on the current temporary root derivation parameter Z_i^t, a new dynamic anonymous identity is generated: update $t = t+1$, $Z_i^{t+1} = H_1(Z_i^t||F_{t+1})$, $PID_i^{t+1} = H_1(Z_i^{t+1}||T_{t+1})$. Then, SD_i Compute the corresponding temporary public-private key pair: $sk_i^{t+1} = H_1(y_i||Z_i^{t+1})$ and $pk_i^{t+1} = sk_i^{t+1} \cdot P$. The Z_i^{t+1} used in the phase serves as temporary certificate for the service requested by SDs. ES can verify SD's identity and its valid status by querying the certificate's validity.

Message Signing: Assume the message is c_i and requested service Ser_s is authorized by corresponding ES_j, with the timestamp T_i^2. SD_i selects a random number $d_i \in Z_q^*$, computes $D_i = d_i \cdot P$ and $f_i = H_1(c_i||PID_i^{t+1}||pk_i^{t+1}||X_j \parallel D_i||T_i^2)$. Then, SD_i generates the signature $\eta_i = d_i + sk_i^{t+1} \cdot f_i$ and sends $M_i^2 = \{\eta_i, c_i, Ser_s, D_i, PID_i^{t+1}, pk_i^{t+1}, X_j, T_i^2, Z_i^{t+1}\}$ to the verifier SD_j.

Message Verification: Upon receiving M_i^2, SD_j performs the following checks: First, it checks the timestamp T_i^2. If T_i^2 is valid, it proceeds to the next step. It then queries the status of temporary certificate Z_i^{t+1}, and computes $f_i^{'} = H_1(c_i||PID_i^{t+1}||pk_i^{t+1}||X_j||D_i \parallel T_i^2)$. The following equation is then verified:

$$\eta_i \cdot P = D_i + pk_i^{t+1} \cdot f_i^{'} \tag{3}$$

If Eq. (3) holds, the verification is successful.

4.4 Traceability and Revocation

In FLAR, revocation operations can be implemented based on different needs. The phase divides revocation into three categories:

- **Root-Level Derivation Traceability and Revocation**: When the root-level derivation used by SD for a particular service becomes invalid or reaches its expiration, all authorizations corresponding to the within the industrial department need to be revoked. This means revoking the root-level derivation for that device. Based on the root-level parameter Z_n^0 and corresponding Ser_s, the system marks the root-level parameter in the hash table as revoked and stops using all temporary parameters based on Z_n^0.
- **Temporary Root Derivation Traceability and Revocation**: When a SD, such as SD_i, wishes to exit the $j-th$ department, ES_j queries the table for the entry corresponding to SD_i's temporary root-level derivation Z_i^t, and marks Z_i^t in the chain as revoked. This revokes the temporary root derivation the corresponding communication authorizations for future sessions. Thus, SD_i still retains authorization but can no longer use the dynamically generated anonymous identity based on the revoked temporary root derivation.
- **Real Identity Traceability and Revocation**: When a device behaves maliciously and sends unauthorized or malicious messages, the system needs to trace the real identity of device and revoke all its authorization credentials within the system. Take SD_i as example, its corresponding root derivation is Z_i^0. The system simply needs to monitor and identify any parameters derived from Z_i^0 involved in the propagation of illegal information. Once detected, the system marks Z_i^0 and its corresponding entries in the hash table as revoked. This effectively revokes all of SD_i's privileges within the system, thereby implementing a flexible traceability and revocation mechanism.

5 Security Analysis and Performance Analysis

5.1 ROM-Based Security Proof

In the section, we provide a proof to prove EU-CMA security of FLAR [23].

Definition 1. ***EU-CMA***: *For a digital signature scheme, if, within a given time t, any attackers A, even after making q adaptive signature queries, cannot forge a valid signature for a new message with advantage ε, then the scheme is secure under EU-CMA.*

Theorem 1. ***ECDLP Reduction Statement***: *Suppose that Elliptic Curve Discrete Logarithm Problem (ECDLP) on $\mathbb{G}$ is $(\varepsilon^{'}, \zeta^{'})$ − hard, meaning that any algorithm solving ECDLP in time $\zeta^{'}$ has a success rate of at most $\varepsilon^{'}$. Then, in ROM, if there is an attacker capable of forging a signature with advantage ε in time ζ (using at most q_1 signature queries and q_2 hash queries), an algorithm can be constructed to solve ECDLP in time at most $\zeta^{'} \leq 2\zeta + q_1(2t_m + t_a)$, with success probability $\varepsilon^{'} \geq \varepsilon_1(\frac{\varepsilon_1}{q_2} + \frac{1}{q})$, where t_m is time for scalar multiplication, and t_a is time for point addition. Thus, the unforgeability of FLAR is strictly reduced to the difficulty of solving ECDLP in terms of advantage and runtime.*

Proof. Assume that A can break FLAR with advantage ε. Then, challenger C can solve ECDLP with probability $\varepsilon^{'}$ based on the execution of A.

- Initialization: Given an ECDLP instance $\{P, Q = aP\}$, where $a \in \mathbb{Z}_q^*$, $P, Q \in \mathbb{G}$ (with group order q), C receives the instance and sets public key $PK_i = Q$, then sends $\{\mathbb{G}, P, PK_i\}$ to A.
- ROM Simulation: C simulates H_1 and H_2 in ROM. For any query x (for example, in the form $x = (m||t_i||PID||PK||V||LPK)$, where m is message, t_i is timestamp, PID is forged identity, V is a random value from the signature, and LPK is long-term public key), C checks the internal mapping table Map_{H_1}. If x already exists, C returns previously programmed random value. If x does not exist, C selects $r_x \in \mathbb{Z}_q^*$, adds (x, r_x) to Map_{H_1}, and returns r_x. To reduce probability of "abort" events due to repeated queries, C uses pre-programming: after the first occurrence of a signature query for some x, it fixes the random output to return the same value for subsequent queries. The same procedure is used for H_2.
- Signature Query Simulation: If A issues a signature query asking for a signature on message m, C constructs the query string $x = (m||t_i||PID||PK||V||LPK)$, checks Map_{H_1}, and if x is not present, returns r_x. Then, C randomly selects $\sigma \in \mathbb{Z}_q^*$ and constructs the signature response as: $V = \sigma \cdot P - r_x \cdot PK$. The pair (σ, V) is then returned to A, and mapping for x is recorded to ensure consistent responses for the same query.
- Forging Output and Forking Process: Using Forking Lemma, C replays A's execution twice independently. During the first execution, for the forged input $x^* = (m^*||t_i^*||PID^*||PK^*||V^*||LPK)$, C stores the value returned by $H_1(x^*)$. C replays A's execution while keeping internal randomness unchanged, but at x^*, it reprograms it to return a different random value $r^*(r^* \neq r)$. Thus, A outputs two forged signatures (σ^*, V^*) and $(\sigma^{*'}, V^{*'})$ corresponding to the same message M^* but with differences.
- Solving ECDLP: For the first forged signature, we have: $V^* = \sigma^* \cdot P - r \cdot PK$. For the second forged signature, we have: $V^{*'} = \sigma^{*'} \cdot P - r^* \cdot PK$. Since

V^* for the same m^* remains unchanged, we can set: $\sigma^* \cdot P - r \cdot PK = \sigma^{*'} \cdot P - r^* \cdot PK$, which simplifies to: $(\sigma^* - \sigma^{*'}) \cdot P = (r - r^*) \cdot PK$. Thus: $(\sigma^* - \sigma^{*'}) = (r - r^*) \cdot a \ (mod\ q)$. This leads to:

$$a = \frac{(\sigma^x - \sigma^{x'})}{(r - r^*)} \ (mod\ q) \tag{4}$$

If A forges with advantage ε, then C solves ECDLP with probability: $\varepsilon' \geq \varepsilon_1(\frac{\varepsilon_1}{q_2} + \frac{1}{q})$ within time at most $2\zeta + q_1(2t_m + t_a)$. A non-negligible advantage ε thus yields a non-negligible ECDLP-solving probability ε', contradicting the ECDLP hardness. Therefore, FLAR achieves EU-CMA security.

5.2 Fromal Security Analysis

Using BAN logic and *ProVerif*, we formally analyze FLAR's security, focusing on the Join Request Sending and Verification phase—since signature verification is similar. We model three principals: Smart Device (S), Edge Server (E), and Key Generation Center (KGC). Statements (X, Y) and keys (K) adhere to the notation and inference rules in Table 2. The proof proceeds as follows:

Table 2. BAN Notations and Rules

Notations	Description	Rules	Description
$S \mid\equiv X$, $S \lhd X$	S believes X, S receives X	$\frac{S\mid\equiv S \overset{K}{\leftrightarrow} E,\ S \lhd (X)_K}{S\mid\equiv E\mid\sim X}$	R_1: Message meaning rule
$S \mid\sim X$, $S \Rightarrow X$	S once sent X, S has jurisdiction over X	$\frac{S\mid\equiv\#(X)}{S\mid\equiv\#(X,Y)}$	R_2: Freshness rule
$\#(X)$, $\langle X\rangle_K$	X is fresh, X is combined with K	$\frac{S\mid\equiv\#(X),\ S\mid\equiv E\mid\sim X}{S\mid\equiv E\mid\equiv X}$	R_3: Nonce verification rule
$(X)_K$, $S \overset{K}{\leftrightarrow} E$	X is encrypted with K, K is shared between S and E	$\frac{S\mid\equiv E\mid\Rightarrow X,\ S\mid\equiv E\mid\equiv X}{S\mid\equiv X}$	R_4: Jurisdiction rule

- **Initialization**: For FLAR's initial state, the assumptions apply: $A_1 : E| \equiv S \overset{pk_i^t}{\leftrightarrow} E$, $A_2 : S| \equiv \#(T_i^1)$, $A_3 : E| \equiv \#(T_i^1)$, $A_4 : S| \equiv S \overset{pk_i^t}{\leftrightarrow} E$, $A_5 : S| \equiv E \Rightarrow K_i, A_6 : E| \equiv S \Rightarrow K_i$. Idealized form is: $M_1 - idl : S \rightarrow E : (A_i, T_i^1)_{K_i}$, and FLAR's security goals are: $G_1 : S| \equiv S \overset{K_i}{\leftrightarrow} E, G_2 : E| \equiv S \overset{K_i}{\leftrightarrow} E$.
- **Validation**:
  1) E sees the encrypted message: $E \lhd M_1 - idl$.
  2) Based on A_1 and apply rule $R_1 : E| \equiv S| \sim (A_i, T_i^1)_{K_i}$.
  3) Based on A_3 and apply rule $R_3 : E| \equiv S| \equiv (A_i, T_i^1)_{K_i}$.

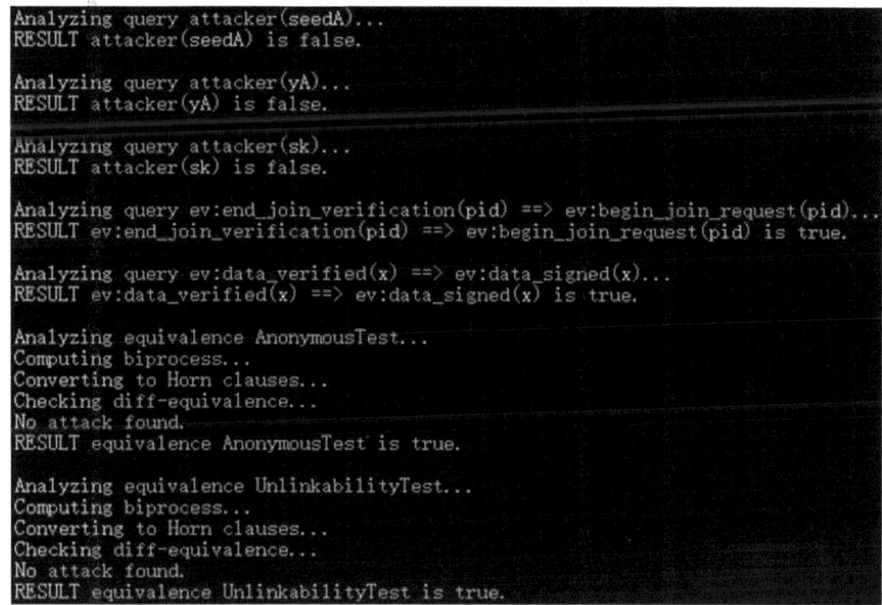

Fig. 4. Experimental results of *Proverif*.

4) Since E can derive the session key K_i from its private key and A_i, and by A_6 together with the jurisdiction rule R_4, we obtain: $E| \equiv S \overset{K_i}{\leftrightarrow} E$, which establishes $\boldsymbol{G_2}$.
5) Similarly, S sees and verifies the same message, derives K_i from A_i, and by A_5 and R_4 obtains: $S| \equiv S \overset{K_i}{\leftrightarrow} E$, which establish $\boldsymbol{G_1}$.

Therefore, both S and E believe they share the session key K_i. This completes the BAN-logic proof of session-key security. Moreover, we employed $ProVerif$ to validate FLAR's security, and the results are shown in Fig. 4.

- **Message Integrity and Authentication**: BAN logic proves secure negotiation of session keys, ensuring **Message Integrity and Authentication**.
- **Anonymity**: 'RESULT equivalence **AnonymousTest** is true' indicates that the query AnonymousTest is succeed, thus confirming **Anonymity**.
- **Traceability**: Our proposed FLAR scheme fulfills a flexible device-based revocation mechanism that guarantees **Traceability**.
- **Unlinkability**: 'RESULT equivalence UnlinkabilityTest is true' indicates that query **UnlinkabilityTest** is succeed, thus confirming **Unlinkability**.
- **Perfect Forward Security**: The unreachability of **Attacker(sk)** shows that, even if private keys are compromised, the session key cannot be recovered, which guarantees **Perfect Forward Security**.
- **Resistance to Various Attacks**: The unreachability of **Attacker(seedA)** ensures device seeds remain confidential, mitigating impersonation attacks. The unreachability of **Attacker(yA)** confirms private keys remain

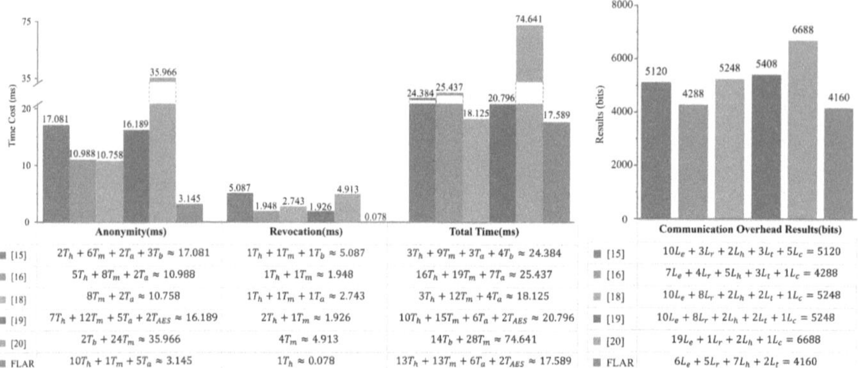

	Anonymity(ms)	Revocation(ms)	Total Time(ms)
[15]	$2T_h + 6T_m + 2T_a + 3T_b \approx 17.081$	$1T_h + 1T_m + 1T_b \approx 5.087$	$3T_h + 9T_m + 3T_a + 4T_b \approx 24.384$
[16]	$5T_h + 8T_m + 2T_a \approx 10.988$	$1T_h + 1T_m \approx 1.948$	$16T_h + 19T_m + 7T_a \approx 25.437$
[18]	$8T_m + 2T_a \approx 10.758$	$1T_h + 1T_m + 1T_a \approx 2.743$	$3T_h + 12T_m + 4T_a \approx 18.125$
[19]	$7T_h + 12T_m + 5T_a + 2T_{AES} \approx 16.189$	$2T_h + 1T_m \approx 1.926$	$10T_h + 15T_m + 6T_a + 2T_{AES} \approx 20.796$
[20]	$2T_b + 24T_m \approx 35.966$	$4T_m \approx 4.913$	$14T_b + 28T_m \approx 74.641$
FLAR	$10T_h + 1T_m + 5T_a \approx 3.145$	$1T_h \approx 0.078$	$13T_h + 13T_m + 6T_a + 2T_{AES} \approx 17.589$

	Communication Overhead Results(bits)
[15]	$10L_e + 3L_r + 2L_h + 3L_t + 5L_c = 5120$
[16]	$7L_e + 4L_r + 5L_h + 3L_t + 1L_c = 4288$
[18]	$10L_e + 8L_r + 2L_h + 2L_t + 1L_c = 5248$
[19]	$10L_e + 8L_r + 2L_h + 2L_t + 1L_c = 5248$
[20]	$19L_e + 1L_r + 2L_h + 1L_c = 6688$
FLAR	$6L_e + 5L_r + 7L_h + 2L_t = 4160$

(a) Comprehensive comparison of computational overhead. (b) Comparison of communication overhead.

Fig. 5. Comprehensive comparison of scheme performance.

secure, countering insider-privilege attacks. Successful triggering of **ev:begin_join_request(pid)** demonstrates resilience to man-in-middle attacks. Overall, FLAR is effectively against various attacks.

5.3 Performance Analysis

Experiments were conducted on Ubuntu 20.04 with an Intel i7-3.10 GHz CPU and 8 GB RAM. We evaluated FLAR against existing schemes by measuring real-world computational and communication overhead. Computational cost—broken down into anonymity, revocation, and total overhead—was based on actual runtimes. Using the public BN254-curve benchmark (with linear frequency correction), we measured primitive timings as follows: Hash operation $T_h = 0.049$ ms, symmetric encryption $T_{AES} = 0.061$ ms, ECC scalar multiplication $T_m = 1.21$ ms, ECC point addition $T_a = 0.089$ ms, and Bilinear pairing $T_b = 2.840$ ms.

Computational Overhead: Figure 5(a) shows the results of FLAR versus existing schemes. FLAR exhibits significantly lower anonymity overhead, revocation-mechanism overhead, and total computation cost. While [20] offers flexible anonymity and revocation, its high overhead renders it impractical for IIoT. By contrast, our Fibonacci-hash-chain–based approach achieves secure, flexible anonymity and revocation at the lowest cost; only [18] approaches similar performance, demonstrating that FLAR successfully balances security and efficiency.

Communication Overhead: we compare communication costs in detail. We define: hash output L_h, timestamp L_t, random and verification data L_r as 160 bits, encrypted data block $L_c = 320$ bits, and ciphertext block $L_c = 128$ bits. In FLAR, the registration, join, and revocation phases incur 2240 bits, 1280 bits, and 640 bits, respectively, for a total of 4160 bits. Figure 5(b) demonstrates that FLAR achieves the lowest communication cost among all comparisons, with only [16] coming close. In summary, FLAR remains lightweight in both computational and communication, making it well suited for IIoT environments.

6 Conclusions

To achieve an effective balance between strict privacy protection and low overhead in PoD Park—characterized by high data density and stringent real-time requirements—we propose a lightweight authentication scheme called FLAR. FLAR guarantees anonymity while providing a low-overhead, flexible revocation mechanism. By integrating Fibonacci sequence with hash chain, we design a dual parameter derivation algorithm that underpins a lightweight anonymity mechanism and a flexible revocation mechanism, thereby satisfying both anonymity and traceability requirements. FLAR's EU-CMA is proven in ROM, and formal security analysis via BAN logic and *ProVerif* confirms that all specified security properties are met. Performance analysis show that, compared to existing approaches, FLAR incurs minimal computational and communication overhead—especially in its anonymity and revocation mechanisms—making it particularly suited for IIoT systems with high security and efficiency demands.

In future work, we will focus on extending the scheme with fault-localization–capable, efficient batch verification, which is expected to further increase edge-side throughput and leverage inherent parallelism of large-scale IoT deployments.

Acknowledgement. This work was supported in part by the Natural Science Foundation of Hebei Province (F2021201049, F2021201058) and the Funds of the Central Government for Local Science and Technology Development (236Z0701G).

References

1. Piccialli, F., Bessis, N., Jung, J.J.: Data science challenges in industry 4.0. IEEE Trans. Ind. Inform. (2020)
2. Liu, Y., Chi, C., Zhang, Y., Tang, T.: Identification and resolution for industrial internet: architecture and key technology. IEEE Internet Things J. **9**(18), 16780–16794 (2022)
3. Shang, W., Wen, X., Chen, Z., Xiong, W., Chang, Z., Cao, Z.: Lightweight authentication scheme for edge control systems in Industrial Internet of Things. Front. Inf. Technol. Electron. Eng. **25**(11), 1466–1478 (2024)
4. Huang, Y., Xu, G., Song, X., Xu, Y.: An efficient RLWE-based privacy-preserving authentication scheme based on edge computing in Industrial Internet of Things. IEEE Trans. Serv. Comput. (2024)
5. Niu, H., Zhang, X., Chu, Z., Shi, W.: DSFL: a blockchain-based data sharing and federated learning framework. Appl. Intell. **55**(6), 474 (2025)
6. Lingga, P., Jeong, J., Yang, J., Kim, J.: SPT: Security policy translator for network security functions in cloud-based security services. IEEE Trans. Dependable Secure Comput. (2024)

7. Brown, L., et al.: An architecture for edge networking services. In: Proc. ACM SIGCOMM 2024 Conf., pp. 645–660 (2024)
8. Liu, Y., He, D., Luo, M., Wang, H., Liu, Q.: ATRC: an anonymous traceable and revocable credential system using blockchain for VANETs. IEEE Trans. Veh. Technol. **73**(2) (2024)
9. Xie, D., Yang, J., Bian, W., Chen, F., Wang, T.: An improved identity-based anonymous authentication scheme resistant to semi-trusted server attacks. IEEE Internet Things J. **10**(1), 734–746 (2023). https://doi.org/10.1109/JIOT.2022.3203991
10. Hu, Y., Bian, W., Xie, D., Xu, Z., He, P.: Secure user authentication scheme using revocable biometrics based on secret sharing for smart home. IEEE Internet Things J. **12**(8), 10885–10898 (2025). https://doi.org/10.1109/JIOT.2024.3514821
11. He, D., Zhao, Z., Chan, S., Guizani, M.: A novel authentication protocol for IoT-enabled devices. IEEE Internet Things J. **10**(1), 867–876 (2023). https://doi.org/10.1109/JIOT.2022.3204410
12. Bai, L., Hsu, C., Harn, L., Cui, J., Zhao, Z.: A practical lightweight anonymous authentication and key establishment scheme for resource-asymmetric smart environments. IEEE Trans. Dependable Secure Comput. **20**(4), 3535–3545 (2023)
13. Li, Y., Cheng, Q., Liu, X., Li, X.: A secure anonymous identity-based scheme in new authentication architecture for mobile edge computing. IEEE Syst. J. **15**(1), 935–946 (2021)
14. Ren, S., Liu, Y., Yu, B., Liu, J., Li, D.: Provable secure anonymous device authentication protocol in IoT environment. IEEE Internet Things J. **11**(7), 12266–12277 (2024). https://doi.org/10.1109/JIOT.2023.3332943
15. Cao, Z., Chen, Z., Shang, W., Zhu, Y.: Efficient revocable anonymous authentication mechanism for edge intelligent controllers. IEEE Internet Things J. **10**(12), 10357–10367 (2023)
16. Li, X., Jiang, C., Du, D., Fei, M., Wu, L.: A novel revocable lightweight authentication scheme for resource-constrained devices in cyber-physical power systems. IEEE Internet Things J. **10**(6), 5280–5292 (2023). https://doi.org/10.1109/JIOT.2022.3221943
17. Yadav, A.K., Misra, M., Pandey, P.K., Liyanage, M.: An EAP-based mutual authentication protocol for WLAN-connected IoT devices. IEEE Trans. Ind. Inform. **19**(2), 1343–1355 (2023). https://doi.org/10.1109/TII.2022.3194956
18. Lin, C., Huang, X., He, D.: EBCPA: efficient blockchain-based conditional privacy-preserving authentication for VANETs. IEEE Trans. Dependable Secure Comput. **20**(3), 1818–1832 (2023)
19. Wang, F., Cui, J., Zhang, Q., He, D., Zhong, H.: Blockchain-assisted flexible revocable anonymous authentication in Industrial Internet of Things. IEEE Trans. Netw. Sci. Eng. **12**(1), 518–532 (2025). https://doi.org/10.1109/TNSE.2024.3503996
20. Yang, H., Peng, C.: TSA-IPFE: a secure solution for authorization revocation and dynamic identity assignment in IoT. IEEE Internet Things J. (2025)
21. Nazish, M., Banday, M.T.: A novel Fibonacci-sequence-based chaotification model for enhancing chaos in one-dimensional maps. IEEE Internet Things J. (2024)
22. Ammann, M., Hirschi, L., Kremer, S.: DY fuzzing: formal Dolev-Yao models meet cryptographic protocol fuzz testing. In: 2024 IEEE Symposium on Security and Privacy (SP), pp. 1481–1499 (2024). https://doi.org/10.1109/SP54263.2024.00096
23. Yang, N., Tang, C., He, D.: A lightweight certificateless multi-user matchmaking encryption for mobile devices: enhancing security and performance. IEEE Trans. Inf. Forensics Secur. **19**, 251–264 (2024)

RL-ABO: Adaptive Blockchain Control Parameter Optimization Method Based on Reinforcement Learning

Yunze Li[1,2,3], Shuyi Miao[1,2,3], Zishuai Zhang[1,2,3], Xinwei Xu[1,2,3], Wangjie Qiu[1,2,3(✉)], and Zhiming Zheng[1,2,3]

[1] The Institute of Artificial Intelligence, Beihang University, Beijing 100191, China
wangjieqiu@buaa.edu.cn

[2] Beijing Advanced Innovation Center for Future Blockchain and Privacy Computing, Beihang University, Beijing 100191, China

[3] Zhongguancun Laboratory, Beijing 100191, China

Abstract. Blockchain technology has emerged as a cornerstone of the Web3.0 ecosystem with its decentralized, traceable, and immutable properties. However, the exponentially growing demand for transaction processing in the new-generation Internet scenario is still restricted by the performance bottleneck of blockchain. Therefore, effective performance optimization strategies are urgently needed to improve the efficiency and scalability of blockchain systems. Although existing optimization methods improve the performance of blockchain by adjusting the blockchain configuration parameters, they still have the problem of poor performance in the environment of limited blockchain node resources and fluctuating network environment. To overcome these challenges, we propose RL-ABO, an adaptive blockchain control parameter optimization method based on reinforcement learning, designed to dynamically adjust the blockchain parameters according to the real-time network environment and transaction load demand under the premise of limited node resource consumption. Specifically, we design a new reward function to jointly optimize performance and resource utilization, and introduces the clip mechanism and experience replay mechanism to enhance the training efficiency and dynamic adaptability. Experimental results show that, compared with existing methods, RL-ABO shortens the convergence time by 32.7%, improves the throughput by 8.3%, and significantly decreases the utilization of the central processing unit (CPU) and memory. Furthermore, RL-ABO shows outstanding performance in scenarios with fluctuating network delays, effectively addressing the limitations of traditional blockchain performance optimization methods.

Keywords: Blockchain · Performance optimization · Dynamic adaptive · Reinforcement learning

J. Li et al. (Eds.): APWeb-WAIM 2025, LNCS 16115, pp. 649–663, 2026.
https://doi.org/10.1007/978-981-95-5719-6_41

1 Introduction

With the advent of the Web3.0 era, the Internet architecture is undergoing profound transformations. Blockchain technology has become a key component of building a new network infrastructure, subverts the established pattern of the traditional centralized system, and triggers a wave of innovation in various fields such as finance, supply chain and digital rights confirmation [9,12,14]. However, with the continuous expansion of blockchain application scenarios, the transaction processing pressure on the blockchain is increasing exponentially, and the performance bottleneck is becoming increasingly prominent, restricting its further development. Among the numerous metrics used to measure blockchain performance, transactions per second (TPS) serves as a key metric, directly reflecting the processing capacity of the transaction system. Currently, mainstream blockchain systems have a significant TPS gap compared to traditional centralized transaction systems [20]. This not only results in slow transaction responses and poor user experience, but also makes it difficult for blockchain to be applied in commercial scenarios such as high-frequency trading and real-time data processing.

To break through the performance bottleneck of blockchain, existing studies implement dynamic parameter optimization of blockchain based on reinforcement learning [6,10,11,18], with the aim of improving the transaction processing ability. These studies improve the throughput of the blockchain to a certain extent by constructing an intelligent decision model to dynamically adjust the parameters of the consensus algorithm or network configuration according to the state of the system. However, due to the limited node resources in the distributed architecture of the blockchain system, coupled with the complex and changeable network environment, the existing optimization methods still face two principal challenges:

- **Excessive resource consumption.** Existing solutions often focus on a single performance optimization goal, ignoring excessive consumption of resources such as central processing unit (CPU) and memory that accompany performance improvement. Especially in the blockchain consensus nodes, this resource-intensive optimization strategy not only raises the operation requirements of hardware devices and the user threshold but also exacerbates the imbalance of decentralization degree due to the difference of node resources, thereby introducing potential security risks.
- **Insufficient dynamic adaptability.** Due to the lack of full consideration of dynamic changes in the operating environment of the blockchain, the existing methods are difficult to quickly adjust the optimization strategy in the face of sudden conditions such as network fluctuations and node failures, resulting in a sharp decrease in system performance and unable to adapt to the complexity and variability of real-world application scenarios [1,16].

To address the aforementioned challenges, we formulate the blockchain performance optimization process as a Markov decision process (MDP) [15] and propose an adaptive blockchain control parameter optimization method based on reinforcement learning (RL-ABO). We aim to achieve dynamic optimization of blockchain performance under the premise of limited node resource consumption in a complex dynamic environment. RL-ABO constructs a complete performance optimization framework, which covers three core modules: the real-time performance evaluation module, the dynamic adaptive optimization module, and the parameter modification module. Different from the existing methods, RL-ABO focuses on enhancing resource utilization efficiency. By devising a novel reward function, RL-ABO effectively restricts the upper bound of resource utilization, thereby striking an optimal balance between system efficiency and resource consumption. Moreover, by introducing the clip mechanism and experience replay mechanism [2,3] in the reinforcement learning training process, the training efficiency and dynamic adaptability of the model are significantly improved. In summary, our main contributions are as follows:

- We propose RL-ABO, a novel blockchain performance optimization method that dynamically optimizes blockchain parameters according to the current running state of the blockchain. This real-time optimization method breaks the limitation of traditional static parameter setting and lays a solid foundation for improving blockchain performance.
- To minimize computing resource consumption, we design a reward function that jointly optimizes performance and resource utilization. In addition, we incorporate a clip mechanism and an experience replay mechanism into the reinforcement learning training process, significantly enhancing the training efficiency and dynamic adaptability of RL-ABO.
- Extensive evaluations demonstrate that RL-ABO reduces the convergence time by 32.7%, improves throughput by 8.3%, and exhibits lower CPU and memory utilization compared to existing methods. Moreover, RL-ABO outperforms competitors in environments with fluctuating network delays.

The remaining parts of this paper are arranged as follows: Sect. 2 systematically reviews related work on blockchain performance optimization. Section 3 describes the framework design and the essential algorithm of RL-ABO. In Sect. 4, the effectiveness of RL-ABO is verified by sufficient experiments and compared with existing methods. Finally, we conclude in Sect. 5.

2 Related Work

The successful application of reinforcement learning (RL) in the field of database provides new ideas to optimize blockchain performance [7,19]. The Athena method proposed by Li et al. employs a policy-based multi-agent deep deterministic policy gradient technique to optimize the heterogeneous parameters of Fabric, significantly improving the system performance [8]. However, this system only focuses on a single performance goal and fails to fully consider the security risks faced by blockchains in the performance optimization process. Liu et al. constructed a blockchain performance optimization framework based on RL and used the dual deep Q-Network (DDQN) to dynamically select and adjust key parameters such as the block producer, the consensus mechanism, the block size, and the generation interval [10]. This approach enhances the scalability and performance of blockchains without compromising the decentralization, latency, and security of the system. The AdaChain framework designed by Wu et al. is a dynamic and adaptive permission blockchain structure [17]. It leverages reinforcement learning to adapt to changes in workload and switch to a more optimized architecture in real time, securely, and accurately. The DRLPB method proposed by Gadiraju et al. applies RL to dynamically optimize the Prism blockchain parameters to enhance the consensus performance [4]. Li et al. proposed a PBFT dynamic adaptive framework based on multi-agent architecture named DA-PBFT, which divided the dynamic adaptive process into two sub-processes: optimization and decision-making [6]. In the optimization process, a PBFT optimization model based on deep reinforcement learning was constructed to generate optimization strategies for the consensus nodes. In the decision-making process, the PBFT optimization decision consensus mechanism is constructed based on the Borda counting method [13].

Some existing work has shown that the real-time adjustment of blockchain control parameters based on RL can effectively improve system throughput. However, existing approaches generally overlook the substantial increase in resource consumption that accompany performance improvements. This not only inflates operational costs but also leads to efficiency bottlenecks in resource-constrained environments. Additionally, there is a notable lack of research on dynamic adaptability to real-world uncertainties. In the real network environment, unexpected events, such as network latency fluctuations occur frequently. However, most current blockchain performance optimization methods are based on the assumption of a relatively stable network environment. As a result, these methods may not be able to cope with complex and variable network conditions in practical applications, thus affecting the performance and stability of the blockchain.

3 Framework

3.1 Overview of RL-ABO

RL-ABO is a real-time optimization framework for blockchain parameters. It is designed to achieve performance optimization by dynamically adjusting key parameters of the blockchain while effectively managing resource utilization. As shown in Fig. 1, the framework consists of three modules. (1) Performance evaluation module: This module continuously monitors the throughput of the blockchain network as well as the utilization rates of CPU and memory resources. It sends transaction loads to the blockchain and analyzes block information, generating a comprehensive performance score through weighted calculations based on real-time data, which provides data support for parameter optimization. (2) Dynamic adaptive optimization module: This module constructs MDP based on the state information and performance scores collected in the previous module. It uses a reinforcement learning algorithm to interact with the blockchain and tries to find the optimal parameter optimization strategy. This strategy can balance resource utilization and maximize processing performance. (3) Parameter modification module: It loads the parameter optimization strategy obtained by the previous module, interacts with the blockchain to obtain the optimal parameter combination, and writes these parameters into the configuration file. We then submit the updated configuration file to the blockchain in the form of transactions, thereby facilitating the dynamic modification of the parameter. Overall, RL-ABO enables blockchain systems to adapt to actual operating conditions, optimize performance, and maintain efficient and sustainable computational resources.

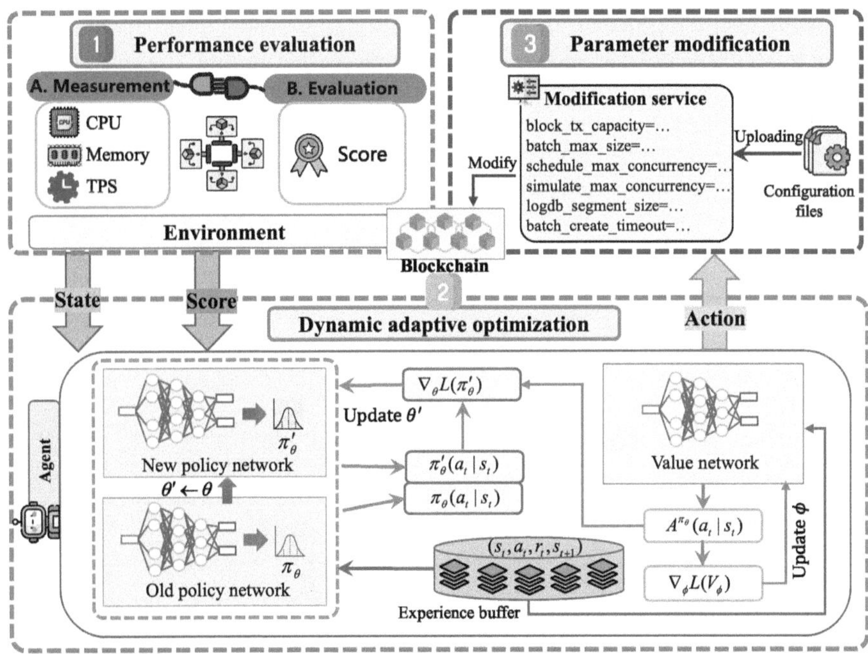

Fig. 1. Overall framework of RL-ABO.

3.2 Workflow

The workflow of the RL-ABO framework is divided into the distributed deployment of the underlying blockchain architecture and the centralized parameter optimization training module based on reinforcement learning. The parameter optimization training module calls the blockchain smart contract in the form of sending transactions to realize the interaction functions between the two modules such as performance monitoring and parameter modification, so as to reduce the coupling between the parameter optimization service and the underlying blockchain.

As shown in Fig. 2, in the underlying blockchain architecture, the distributed deployed blockchain nodes continuously receive the transaction load (step 1). The performance evaluation module monitors the transaction load of the blockchain in real time (step 2), and stores the status information such as performance, computing resource utilization, and performance score, together with the current blockchain parameter settings, into the database (step 3). In the centralized module based on reinforcement learning, the dynamic adaptive optimization module reads data from the database (step 4), and uses the deep reinforcement learning algorithm to explore the parameter optimization strategy to balance resource utilization and maximize network performance. After obtaining the optimization strategy, the parameter modification module interacts with the blockchain to obtain the optimal parameter combination, writes it into the configuration file (step 5), and then submits it to the blockchain in the form of transactions to update the blockchain parameters to complete the dynamic parameter modification and perform the performance optimization (step 6).

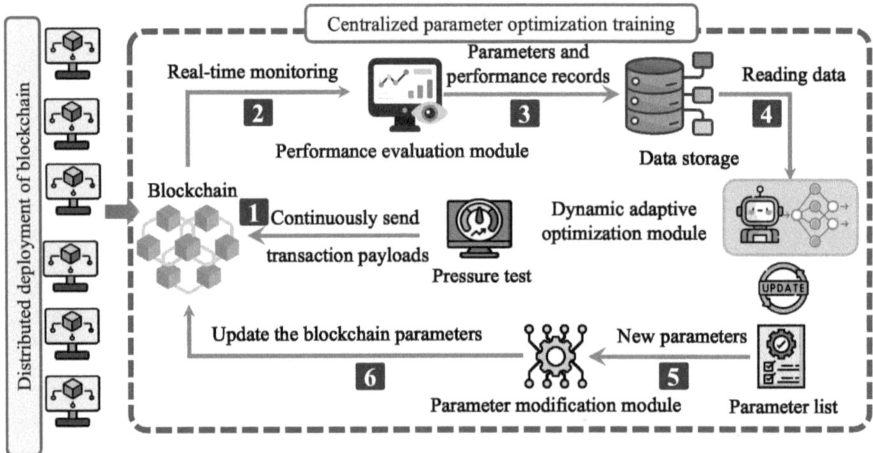

Fig. 2. RL-ABO workflow.

3.3 Performance Evaluation

To comprehensively evaluate the processing performance of blockchain systems under actual loads, we design a performance evaluation module that integrates transaction throughput calculation and resource utilization analysis, with each evaluation conducted within a mini-batch.

In the experimental process, the master node first continuously sends transaction loads to the blockchain network. Let t_{init} denote the initial timestamp, which is accurately recorded as the time reference for the performance evaluation. By subscribing to the block messages of the blockchain network, the process of packing and uploading transaction loads to the blockchain is monitored in real time. Key information such as block height and block generation time for each block generation is recorded in detail until all injected transaction loads are successfully packed into blocks. At this point, the final timestamp, denoted as t_{final}, is recorded.

In the performance calculation stage, based on the initial timestamp t_{init} and the final timestamp t_{final}, combined with the total transaction load size L within the mini-batch, the real-time transaction throughput of the blockchain, denoted as TPS, is obtained through the formula:

$$TPS = \frac{L}{t_{\text{final}} - t_{\text{init}}} \tag{1}$$

Meanwhile, within the time period T of packing and generating blocks for the transaction loads, CPU and memory utilization data of each node in the blockchain are collected at a frequency of once per second, forming the CPU utilization sequence $U_{cpu} = [u_1, u_2, \ldots, u_T]$ and the memory utilization sequence $U_{mem} = [v_1, v_2, \ldots, v_T]$ respectively. Then, the average CPU utilization $\bar{U}_{cpu}$ and average memory utilization $\bar{U}_{mem}$ for the mini-batch are calculated by taking the mean of the sequences:

$$\bar{U}_{cpu} = \frac{1}{T}\sum_{i=1}^{T} u_i \quad \text{and} \quad \bar{U}_{mem} = \frac{1}{T}\sum_{i=1}^{T} v_i \tag{2}$$

We introduce weight coefficients α, β, and γ ($\alpha + \beta + \gamma = 1$), and calculate the performance score *score* for each mini-batch:

$$score = \alpha\left(1 - \frac{\bar{U}_{cpu}}{100}\right) + \beta\left(1 - \frac{\bar{U}_{mem}}{100}\right) + \gamma\left(\frac{TPS - TPS_{min}}{TPS_{max} - TPS_{min}}\right) \tag{3}$$

where TPS_{min} and TPS_{max} represent the minimum and maximum transaction throughput values observed specifically within the current mini-batch.

3.4 Dynamic Adaptive Optimization

This section details the design of the dynamic adaptive optimization module in RL-ABO, which transforms the blockchain performance optimization process into MDP to construct the state space, action space, and reward function for performance optimization. Then, a deep reinforcement learning algorithm based on actor-critic architecture [5] is used to construct a dynamic adaptive optimization model. The model aims to provide an optimal parameter configuration for the blockchain, in order to cope with dynamic changes of transaction load and network environment on the blockchain, maximize blockchain performance, and reduce CPU and memory utilization.

State Space. The state space S^t of the dynamic adaptive optimization module at the t-th epoch can be defined as a multi-dimensional vector:

$$S^t = \left[\text{TPS}, \overline{U}_{\text{cpu}}, \overline{U}_{\text{mem}}, N, P\right]^t \tag{4}$$

where TPS, $\overline{U}_{\text{cpu}}$, and $\overline{U}_{\text{mem}}$ are obtained from performance evaluation module. N denotes the total number of nodes that participate in the consensus process. P represents the parameter configuration currently applied in the blockchain.

Action Space. The action space $\mathcal{A}$ of the dynamic adaptive optimization module is composed of Block_tx_capacity, Max_txpool_size, Batch_max_size, Batch_create_timeout, Schedule_max_concurrency, Simulate_max_concurrency and Logdb_segment_size. These are the key control parameters that affect the performance of the blockchain. The specific descriptions of each control parameter are summarized in Table 1.

Table 1. List of blockchain control parameters.

Parameter	Description
Block_tx_capacity	Number of transactions that a block can contain.
Max_txpool_size	Transaction pool storage capacity.
Batch_max_size	Upper limit of the transactions per batch.
Batch_create_timeout	Maximum time interval for creating a batch.
Schedule_concurrency	Max concurrent executions for executing schedule.
Simulate_concurrency	Max concurrent executions for executing simulate.

Reward Function. The core optimization objective of the dynamic adaptive optimization module is to maximize the transaction throughput of the blockchain, while the optimization process must meet the constraints of CPU and memory resource utilization. The specific reward function r is constructed to guide the optimization strategy as follows:

$$r = \begin{cases} score, & \text{if } \bar{U}_{\text{cpu}} \leq \varphi_{\text{cpu}} \text{ and } \bar{U}_{\text{mem}} \leq \varphi_{\text{mem}} \\ 0, & \text{otherwise} \end{cases} \tag{5}$$

where φ_{cpu} and φ_{mem} represent the pre-set thresholds of CPU and memory resource utilization respectively, serving as the safety boundaries for the system's resource usage. $\bar{U}_{\text{cpu}}$, $\bar{U}_{\text{mem}}$ and *score* are the average CPU utilization, average memory utilization and performance score respectively, all of which are obtained from the performance evaluation module. Through this binary decision-making mechanism, this reward function enforces the optimization process to pursue performance improvement while satisfying resource constraints, thereby achieving the dual objectives of efficient system resource utilization and maximization of transaction processing performance.

Training Algorithm. The RL-ABO training algorithm focuses on optimizing the policy network π_θ and the value network V_{θ_v}. In each training round r, the agent makes observations of the environment state s based on S^t, then interacts with the environment over T time steps. During this interaction, it stores experiences in the form of (s, a, r, s') into a buffer.

The experience replay mechanism randomly samples experiences from the buffer. This mechanism not only breaks the temporal correlations that exist in the sequence of experiences collected during the agent-environment interaction but also significantly enhances the algorithm's dynamic adaptability. In real-world scenarios, the environment can change over time and new patterns or situations may emerge. By storing experiences in the buffer, the algorithm can retain information about different environmental states and agent behaviors. This allows the agent to quickly adapt to new situations because it can learn from both recent and older experiences.

Algorithm 1. RL-ABO Training Algorithm

Input: Policy π_θ, Training rounds R, Number of epochs E, Mini-batch size M, Clip parameter ϵ, Discount factor γ, Entropy coefficient c
Output: Optimized policy network π_θ and value network V_{θ_v}

Initialize policy network π_θ, value network V_{θ_v}, experience buffer $buf \leftarrow \emptyset$
for $r = 1$ to R **do**
  Observe state s according to $S^t = [TPS, \bar{U}_{cpu}, \bar{U}_{mem}, N, P]^t$
  for $t = 1$ to T **do**
    Sample action a from action space $\mathcal{A}$
    Execute action a in environment, obtain reward r and next state s'
    Store (s, a, r, s') in buf
  end for
  Let $G_t = 0$
  for $t = T - 1$ downto 0 **do**
    $G_t = r_t + \gamma G_{t+1}$
  end for
  for $e = 1$ to E **do**
    Sample mini-batch of size M from buf
    for $i = 0$ to $M - 1$ **do**
      Let (s, a, G) be the i-th element of mini-batch
      Advantage $A = G - V_{\theta_v}(s)$
      Ratio $r(\theta) = \frac{\pi_\theta(a|s)}{\pi_{\theta_{old}}(a|s)}$
      Clipped surrogate loss $L_{clip}(\theta) = \min\left(r(\theta)A, \text{clip}(r(\theta), 1 - \epsilon, 1 + \epsilon)A\right)$
      Entropy term $H(\pi_\theta) = -\sum_a \pi_\theta(a|s) \log(\pi_\theta(a|s))$
      Value function loss $L_v(\theta_v) = \frac{1}{2}(V_{\theta_v}(s) - G)^2$
      Update policy network and value network:
      $\theta \leftarrow \theta + \alpha\left(L_{clip}(\theta) + cH(\pi_\theta)\right)$
      $\theta_v \leftarrow \theta_v - \beta L_v(\theta_v)$
    end for
  end for
end for

The clip mechanism is a crucial part of this algorithm, as it controls the magnitude of policy updates. It is defined by the formula

$$L_{\text{clip}}(\theta) = \min\left(r(\theta)A, \text{clip}(r(\theta), 1-\epsilon, 1+\epsilon)A\right). \tag{6}$$

where A is the advantage function that represents how much better an action a in state s is compared to the average action in that state, ϵ is a hyperparameter that determines the allowable range for policy updates.

The clip mechanism ensures that the policy does not change too drastically during the training process. It works by comparing two values: one is the product of the policy ratio and the advantage function, and the other is obtained by first clipping the policy ratio to be within the range $[1-\epsilon, 1+\epsilon]$ and then multiplying it by the advantage function. The smaller of these two values is then used for policy updates, which helps to maintain the stability of the training process.

A detailed training process of the RL-ABO is presented in Algorithm 1.

3.5 Parameter Modification

The blockchain parameter modification module is designed to optimize the parameters of the blockchain system in an adaptive and consistent manner, and the detailed process is shown in Algorithm 2.

Algorithm 2. Blockchain Parameter Modification

Require:

π_θ: Optimized policy network generated by algorithm 1
$Voting(transaction)$: Function to conduct voting on the parameter update results
$UpdateConfigFile(file, new\_params)$: Function to update configuration file
$ModifyService(file)$: Function to package the configuration file into a transaction
$SubmitTrans(transaction)$: Function to submit transactions to the blockchain

Ensure: Successful application of new parameters to the blockchain

Load π_θ
Interact with $BlockchainAPI$
loop
  $S^t \leftarrow PerformanceEvaluation$
  $a_{selected} \leftarrow$ Sample action from $\pi_\theta(a|S^t)$
  $vote\_result \leftarrow Voting(a_{selected})$
  if $vote\_result > \frac{2}{3}$ **then**
    $UpdateConfigFile(config\_file, a_{selected})$
    $transaction \leftarrow ModifyService(config\_file)$
    Submit $transaction$ to the blockchain network:
    $is\_validated \leftarrow SubmitTrans(transaction)$
    if $is\_validated$ **then**
      Apply new parameters to the blockchain
      Break
    end if
  end if
end loop

The algorithm begins by loading π_θ and connecting to the blockchian to access real-time system data. In an iterative loop, it evaluates the current state S^t of the blockchain system through the performance evaluation module. Based on this state, the policy network samples a proposed set $a_{selected}$ of parameter modifications. These proposals are then put to a vote, and if the result exceeds the two-thirds threshold, indicating strong support, the configuration file is updated with the selected parameters. The modified configuration is then packaged as a transaction and submitted to the blockchain network. Once the transaction is successfully validated, the new parameters are applied, and the iterative process is completed. This ensures that parameter changes are informed by data and endorsed by the community, improving the blockchain's adaptability and operational efficiency while upholding network-wide consensus.

4 Evaluation

4.1 Experimental Setup

We built the RL-ABO underlying blockchain system based on the Go programming language, using four devices with uniform configuration for distributed deployment, each equipped with an Intel (R) Xeon (R) Gold 5218R CPU (2.10 GHz) and 32 GB memory and runs the CentOS 7 operating system. Meanwhile, the dynamic adaptive optimization module based on reinforcement learning is implemented using Python programming language and deployed on a standalone device equipped with an Intel (R) Xeon (R) Gold 6248R CPU (3.00 GHz) and 128 GB memory. It is equipped with NVIDIA RTX A6000 GPU (48 GB memory), supports CUDA 12.3, and runs the Ubuntu 20.04.6 operating system. The experimental comparison methods include DA-PBFT [6] and the method proposed by Liu et al. [10], which aims to comprehensively evaluate the advantages of RL-ABO in terms of performance, resource utilization, and network adaptability by comparing multiple methods.

4.2 Performance Evaluation

Figure 3 shows the convergence performance of RL-ABO and the other two methods. In the initial stage, the throughput of RL-ABO increases rapidly after optimization, which is significantly faster than the other two methods, showing its efficient learning and adaptation ability in training. With increasing training rounds, RL-ABO keeps a high-throughput growth trend and reaches a relatively stable and high level in a short number of rounds, which verifies the convergence performance of RL-ABO. Compared to DA-PBFT, the convergence time of RL-ABO is reduced by 32.7%, and the throughput of RL-ABO is increased by 8.3% when it reaches the steady state. Compared with the optimization method proposed by Liu et al., the throughput of RL-ABO increases by 37.5%.

The excellent performance of RL-ABO is largely attributed to the clip mechanism in the training process, which avoids excessive or unreasonable policy updates caused by the anomaly of the advantage function, thereby enhancing

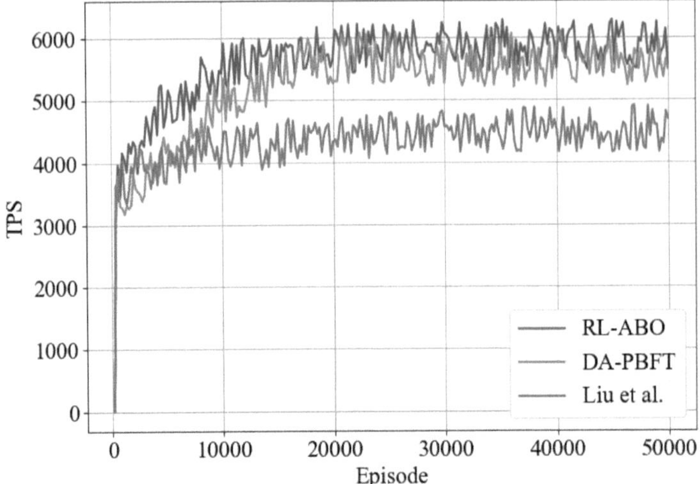

Fig. 3. Performance evaluation.

the stability and convergence speed of the algorithm in the training process, making RL-ABO show significant advantages in performance optimization.

4.3 Resource Utilization Evaluation

In order to comprehensively evaluate the resource utilization efficiency of the RL-ABO when dealing with different sizes of transaction loads, this experiment compared RL-ABO with other methods to monitor CPU and memory utilization with the change in transaction load, aiming to verify the advantages and effectiveness of the RL-ABO in resource management.

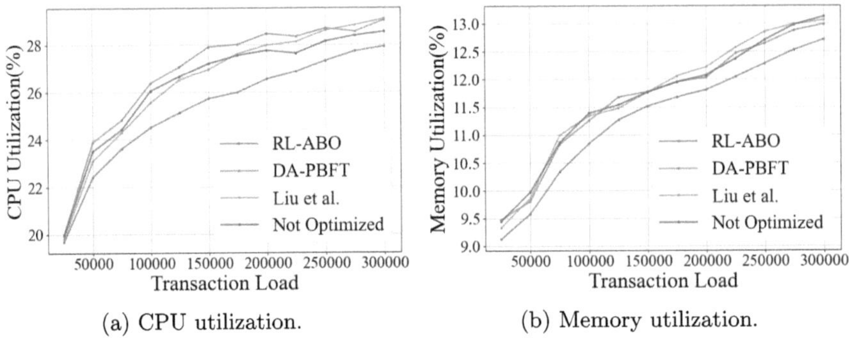

(a) CPU utilization.

(b) Memory utilization.

Fig. 4. Resource utilization evaluation.

CPU Utilization Evaluation. Figure 4a shows the change in average CPU utilization of each consensus node with transaction load under different methods. As the transaction load increases, the CPU utilization of each method shows an upward trend. Compared with DA-PBFT and Liu et al. methods, the CPU utilization of RL-ABO has a lower starting value and a relatively moderate growth rate. The CPU utilization of the RL-ABO grows more smoothly and always stays at a relatively low level, which indicates that RL-ABO can allocate CPU resources more efficiently in high-load scenarios, and effectively avoid the system performance bottleneck that may be caused by excessive resource consumption.

Memory Utilization Evaluation. Figure 4b shows how the average memory utilization of each consensus node changes with transaction load under different methods. As the transaction load gradually increases, the memory utilization of each method continues to increase. RL-ABO consistently achieves lower memory utilization than DA-PBFT and Liu et al. throughout the test interval. Especially in the high-load stage, the memory utilization growth of RL-ABO is significantly lower than that of other comparison methods, indicating that RL-ABO has higher efficiency and stability in memory usage.

Through comparative analysis of CPU and memory utilization of different methods under different transaction loads, the results show that RL-ABO has significant advantages in resource management, which is attributed to the unique design of our method for resource utilization in the reinforcement learning reward function. Whether faced with low-load or high-load transaction scenarios, RL-ABO can make more efficient use of CPU and memory resources under the premise of ensuring the normal operation of the system.

4.4 Network Latency Adaptability Evaluation

In order to fully evaluate the ability of RL-ABO to adapt to network delay fluctuations, this experiment simulates network fluctuation events in real application scenarios by injecting delay into the communication ports of each consensus node in the blockchain. As shown in Fig. 5, under different network delay conditions, the TPS of each method shows different changing trends. The transaction throughput of RL-ABO is significantly higher than that of other methods when the network latency is low, showing its efficiency under good network conditions. With an increase in network latency, the transaction throughput of RL-ABO decreases, but the decline speed is relatively slow and the performance is always significantly better than other methods. At the same time, RL-ABO can still maintain a certain transaction processing capacity in a high-latency environment, compared with the non-optimized method, which can hardly maintain effective transaction processing.

In conclusion, RL-ABO shows stronger network delay adaptation ability, which is attributed to the unique experience replay mechanism of RL-ABO, which allows RL-ABO to make full use of historical experience to quickly make decisions in the face of network delay fluctuations, showing the characteristics of RL-ABO dynamic adaptation.

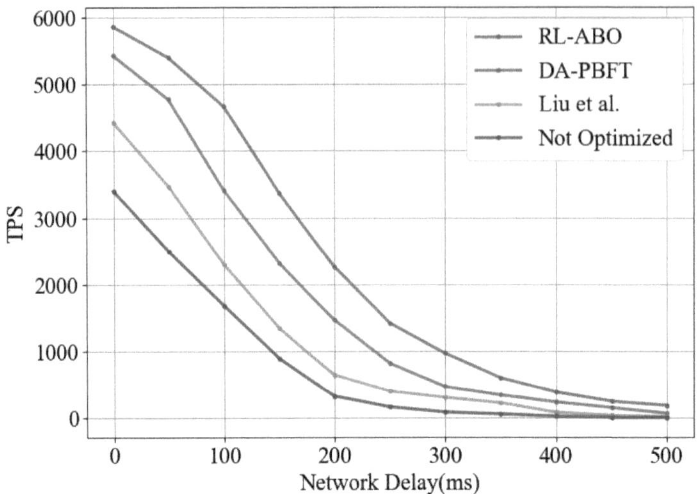

Fig. 5. Network latency adaptability evaluation.

5 Conclusion

In this paper, we propose RL-ABO, an adaptive blockchain parameter optimization method. Specifically, we model the blockchain performance optimization process as MDP and design a novel reward function that can simultaneously optimize performance and resource utilization. In addition, we not only speed up the training process, but also significantly improve the adaptability of the blockchain in the face of dynamic network environments by introducing clip and experience replay techniques. Comprehensive experimental evaluation demonstrates the effectiveness of the RL-ABO. Compared with the existing methods, the convergence time of our method is reduced by 32.7%, the throughput is increased by 8.3%, and the CPU and memory usage are greatly reduced. In addition, RL-ABO outperforms other methods in scenarios with fluctuating network latency, demonstrating its robustness and reliability. Furthermore, future research will focus on extending the applicability of our method to a wider range of complex and heterogeneous blockchain ecosystems.

Acknowledgement. This work was supported by the Beijing Natural Science Foundation (Z230001) and the Beijing Advanced Innovation Center for Future Blockchain and Privacy Computing (GJJ-23-001, GJJ-23-002).

References

1. Antwi, R., et al.: A survey on network optimization techniques for blockchain systems. Algorithms **15**(6), 103 (2022)
2. Arulkumaran, K., Deisenroth, M.P., Brundage, M., Bharath, A.A.: Deep reinforcement learning: a brief survey. IEEE Signal Process. Mag. **34**(6), 26–38 (2017)
3. Fedus, W., et al.: Revisiting fundamentals of experience replay. In: Proceedings of the 37th International Conference on Machine Learning. Proceedings of Machine Learning Research, vol. 119, pp. 3061–3071 (2020)
4. Gadiraju, D.S., Lalitha, V., Aggarwal, V.: An optimization framework based on deep reinforcement learning approaches for prism blockchain. IEEE Trans. Serv. Comput. **16**(4), 2451–2461 (2023)
5. Grondman, I., et al.: A survey of actor-critic reinforcement learning: standard and natural policy gradients. IEEE Trans. Syst. Man Cybernet. Part C (Appl. Rev.) **42**(6), 1291–1307 (2012)
6. Li, C., Qiu, W., Li, X., Liu, C., Zheng, Z.: A dynamic adaptive framework for practical byzantine fault tolerance consensus protocol in the internet of things. IEEE Trans. Comput. **73**(7), 1669–1682 (2024)
7. Li, G., Zhou, X., Li, S., Gao, B.: QTune: a query-aware database tuning system with deep reinforcement learning. Proc. VLDB Endow. **12**(12), 2118–2130 (2019)
8. Li, M., et al.: Auto-tuning with reinforcement learning for permissioned blockchain systems. Proc. VLDB Endow. **16**(5), 1000–1012 (2023)
9. Li, X., Jiang, P., Chen, T., Luo, X., Wen, Q.: A survey on the security of blockchain systems. Futur. Gener. Comput. Syst. **107**, 841–853 (2020)
10. Liu, M., et al.: Performance optimization for blockchain-enabled industrial internet of things (IIoT) systems: a deep reinforcement learning approach. IEEE Trans. Industr. Inf. **15**(6), 3559–3570 (2019)
11. Liu, Z., Hou, L., Zheng, K., Zhou, Q., Mao, S.: A DQN-based consensus mechanism for blockchain in IoT networks. IEEE Internet Things J. **9**(14), 11962–11973 (2021)
12. Liu, Z., et al.: Make web3. 0 connected. IEEE Trans. Depend. Secure Comput. **19**(5), 2965–2981 (2021)
13. Miao, S., et al.: Know your account: double graph inference-based account deanonymization on ethereum. In: 2025 IEEE 41st International Conference on Data Engineering (ICDE), pp. 1305–1319. IEEE Computer Society (2025)
14. Monrat, A.A., Schelén, O., Andersson, K.: A survey of blockchain from the perspectives of applications, challenges, and opportunities. IEEE Access **7**, 117134–117151 (2019)
15. Puterman, M.L.: Markov decision processes. Handbooks Oper. Res. Management Sci. **2**, 331–434 (1990)
16. Rao, I.S., Kiah, M.M., Hameed, M.M., Memon, Z.A.: Scalability of blockchain: a comprehensive review and future research direction. Clust. Comput. **27**(5), 5547–5570 (2024)
17. Wu, C., et al.: AdaChain: a learned adaptive blockchain. Proc. VLDB Endow. **16**(8), 2033–2046 (2023)
18. Yang, Z., et al.: Sharded blockchain for collaborative computing in the internet of things: combined of dynamic clustering and deep reinforcement learning approach. IEEE Internet Things J. **9**(17), 16494–16509 (2022)
19. Zhang, J., et al.: CDBTune+: an efficient deep reinforcement learning-based automatic cloud database tuning system. VLDB J. **30**(6), 959–987 (2021)
20. Zheng, Z., Xie, S., Dai, H.N., Chen, X., Wang, H.: Blockchain challenges and opportunities: a survey. Int. J. Web Grid Serv. **14**(4), 352–375 (2018)

ByzTierFL: A Tiered Approach to Byzantine Robust and Decentralized Federated Learning

Haokai Xu, Xiaomei Dong(✉), Gang Wang, Zeshun Peng, Xiaohua Li, and Ge Yu

School of Computer Science and Engineering, Northeast University, Shenyang, China
xmdong@mail.neu.edu.cn

Abstract. Federated Learning (FL) enables privacy-preserving, collaborative model training across massive populations of edge devices. However, its practical deployment is impeded by device-network heterogeneity, Byzantine adversaries, and the scalability bottleneck of centralized coordination. We propose ByzTierFL, a fully decentralized, Byzantine-robust, tier-aware FL framework that addresses these challenges in a unified manner. ByzTierFL dynamically stratifies clients into tiers based on latency and data quality. ByzTierFL then performs inter-tier aggregation using ByzShield, a novel consensus mechanism that combines multi-model screening and reputation-driven filtering to suppress malicious updates. Built on a hybrid IPFS Hyperledger Fabric substrate, ByzTierFL supports auditable provenance and scalable storage, reducing on-chain communication overhead by 85%. Experiments on non-IID image and text benchmarks show that ByzTierFL reduces per round latency by 65.8% relative to PBFL baselines and maintains over 90% accuracy even when 20% of clients are Byzantine. The framework demonstrates strong scalability and resilience, providing robust and efficient federated learning for real-world heterogeneous and adversarial environments.

Keywords: Federated Learning · Byzantine Robustness · Tiered Architecture · Blockchain · IPFS

1 Introduction

Federated Learning (FL) empowers decentralized devices to collaboratively train a global model while keeping raw data local, addressing privacy concerns in sensitive domains such as healthcare and finance [1–4]. FL is increasingly deployed in domains such as autonomous driving, smart healthcare, finance, and IoT, where data privacy, regulatory compliance, and operational scale are critical. In these real-world scenarios, participating devices often exhibit highly diverse hardware, fluctuating network conditions, and intermittent connectivity. Moreover, adversarial threats are heightened due to the open and distributed nature of FL,

J. Li et al. (Eds.): APWeb-WAIM 2025, LNCS 16115, pp. 664–680, 2026.
https://doi.org/10.1007/978-981-95-5719-6_42

making robust, scalable, and privacy-preserving learning essential for practical adoption. As FL moves from concept to deployment, addressing these intertwined challenges becomes increasingly urgent. However, practical FL systems are confronted with three fundamental challenges.

Heterogeneity Induced Efficiency Accuracy Conflict. Devices participating in FL often differ significantly in computational capacity, battery life, and network reliability. Stragglers slow clients delay training, while non-IID, imbalanced local data increases model bias and slows convergence. Synchronous aggregation is bottlenecked by slow clients; fully asynchronous methods may cause communication congestion and model inconsistency at scale [5,6]. This persistent heterogeneity creates a difficult balance between system efficiency and the accuracy or fairness of the learned model.

Byzantine Threats and Model Integrity. FL is vulnerable to adversarial attacks: any participant might upload malicious or corrupted model updates. A single compromised client can poison the global model, causing severe performance degradation or targeted misclassification. While robust aggregation algorithms such as Krum [7] and Median [8] filter some malicious updates, they often struggle to distinguish diverse honest updates from adversarial ones, especially with heterogeneous data [9,10]. Most methods also ignore client history, limiting adaptability and incentives for honest behavior.

Communication Bottlenecks and Centralization Risks. Traditional FL frameworks rely on a central server for coordination and aggregation. As client numbers grow, the server becomes a communication and computation bottleneck, limiting scalability and introducing a single point of failure. Blockchain-based FL [11] offers decentralization but suffers from high storage and consensus costs.

To address these challenges, we propose ByzTierFL, a two-layer, tiered aggregation architecture that clusters clients by communication latency and data quality. This enables synchronous aggregation within homogeneous groups and asynchronous, weighted aggregation across tiers, thereby balancing efficiency and fairness. We introduce ByzShield, a Byzantine-resilient protocol that incorporates multi-model screening, secondary aggregation, and dynamic reputation tracking to filter malicious updates while preserving legitimate heterogeneous contributions. To ensure scalability and auditability, ByzTierFL leverages a hybrid decentralized storage backend, utilizing IPFS for off-chain storage and Hyperledger Fabric to anchor cryptographic hashes, thus achieving transparent, tamper-evident, and efficient federated learning. These innovations collectively result in notable improvements in efficiency, robustness, and decentralization, as detailed in the following key aspects:

- **Superior Efficiency and Fairness:** ByzTierFL's tiered aggregation reduces per-round latency by 65.8% compared to PBFL [15], while preserving accuracy and fairness among heterogeneous clients.

- **Enhanced Byzantine Robustness:** ByzShield's multi-model screening and reputation enable ByzTierFL to maintain over 90% accuracy under 20% Byzantine attack, outperforming advanced robust aggregation schemes.
- **Scalable and Auditable Decentralization:** The IPFS-Fabric hybrid architecture reduces on-chain communication cost by 85%, secures model update traceability, and removes central points of failure.

2 Related Work

Table 1 provides a comparison of representative FL frameworks across six core dimensions. Attack resilience refers to the ability to defend against Byzantine or malicious clients; Non-IID adaptation denotes robustness to heterogeneous data distributions across clients; distributed operation indicates support for decentralized systems without single points of failure; dynamic efficiency refers to flexibility in handling system dynamics such as stragglers and variable participation; historical contribution covers mechanisms to record and leverage clients' past behaviour; and blockchain integration involves the use of blockchain for security, transparency, or auditability.

Table 1. Comparative summary of ByzTierFL and related schemes

Schemes	Attack Resilience	Non-IID Adaptation	Distributed	Dynamic Efficiency	Historical Contribution	Blockchain
Krum [7]	✓	×	×	×	×	×
Trimmed Mean [8]	✓	×	×	×	×	×
BAFFLE [13]	×	×	✓	×	×	✓
BlockFL [11]	×	×	✓	×	×	✓
PBFL [15]	✓	×	✓	×	×	✓
TiFL [16]	✓	✓	×	×	×	×
BlockDFL [20]	✓	✓	✓	✓	×	✓
ByzTierFL (Ours)	✓	✓	✓	✓	✓	✓

The main challenges and limitations of existing FL frameworks are discussed below, focusing on Byzantine robustness, Non-IID adaptation, decentralization and blockchain integration, dynamic efficiency, and historical adaptation.

Byzantine Robustness. Classic robust aggregators such as Krum, Median, and Trimmed Mean [8] are designed to withstand malicious updates. Krum selects the update closest to its $n-f-2$ nearest neighbours, while Median and Trimmed Mean apply coordinate-wise outlier filtering. Despite their theoretical resilience to up to $f < n/2$ Byzantine clients, these methods often discard benign but diverse updates, cannot fuse multiple trustworthy models, and lack adaptability to evolving attacks or heterogeneous data. Moreover, they operate in a centralised setting and do not consider clients' historical reliability.

Non-IID Adaptation. Addressing statistical heterogeneity remains a key challenge. Most robust aggregators (e.g., Krum, Trimmed Mean) exhibit sensitivity to Non-IID data. TiFL [16] seeks to mitigate straggler effects and Non-IID bias via client tiering, aggregating updates within homogeneous subgroups. However, synchronous intra-tier aggregation may bias learning toward faster but less representative clients, and its Byzantine defense is limited to Krum-like filters.

Decentralisation and Blockchain Integration. Blockchain-based federated learning frameworks, including BAFFLE [13], BlockFL [11], and BlockDFL [20], integrate on-chain storage of model updates and logs to enhance transparency, traceability, and system resilience. Although these approaches leverage blockchain to provide tamper-evident records and decentralised coordination, reliance on consensus mechanisms such as Proof-of-Work (PoW) or Proof-of-Stake (PoS) often lead to high latency and significant energy consumption, which limits deployment in resource-constrained environments. In addition, PBFL overlays homomorphic encryption on blockchain to enhance privacy, but its scalability is constrained by dependence on small trusted datasets. Other solutions, such as FedChain [14], prioritises device-side learning but incur substantial on-chain storage overhead, which may impact overall system efficiency. While blockchain integration introduces promising benefits for decentralised federated learning, existing methods, including BlockDFL, continue to face challenges in balancing transparency, scalability, and resource efficiency.

Dynamic Efficiency and Historical Adaptation. Most existing schemes lack mechanisms for dynamic adaptation or tracking of historical client behaviour, which limits their ability to reward reliability or penalise adversaries over time. Only a few recent works partially address historical contributions, and those approaches remain centralised or are not scalable.

ByzTierFL for Robust and Decentralised Federated Learning. ByzTierFL addresses these limitations through a two-layer hierarchical architecture and a lightweight ByzShield consensus mechanism. In contrast with previous approaches, ByzTierFL combines Byzantine robustness with Non-IID adaptation by screening multiple candidate models and supporting diverse data distributions. Full decentralisation is realised through integration with Hyperledger Fabric and IPFS, thereby eliminating the overhead associated with PoW or PoS. The framework also enhances dynamic efficiency by adapting flexibly to system changes and supporting asynchronous updates. Historical contributions are recorded on-chain, which enables effective incentive and trust management. A modular and distributed design ensures that scalability, security, and efficiency are balanced in large-scale deployments.

In summary, ByzTierFL is the only framework that simultaneously achieves robustness against Byzantine attacks, Non-IID adaptability, full decentralisation, dynamic efficiency, historical contribution tracking, and blockchain-based security, thus advancing the state of the art.

3 ByzTierFL Architecture

ByzTierFL adopts a hierarchical federated learning framework that integrates two-layer aggregation with decentralized storage and consensus mechanisms (see Fig. 1). By integrating hierarchical aggregation with decentralized storage and consensus mechanisms, the architecture systematically mitigates the challenges of heterogeneous FL environments. Hierarchical aggregation reduces the impact of device diversity and network variability, while decentralized storage and consensus frameworks ensure accountability, integrity, and scalability throughout the learning process.

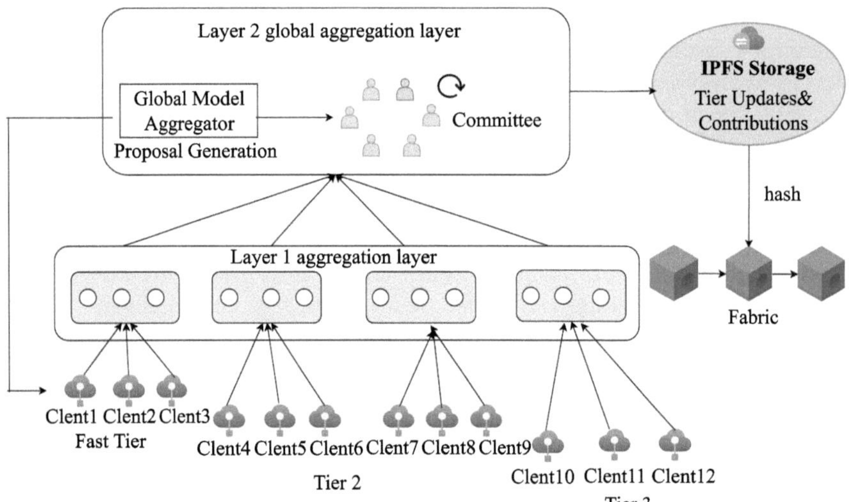

Fig. 1. System architecture of ByzTierFL.

3.1 Hierarchical Aggregation

To balance efficiency and robustness, ByzTierFL introduces a two-layer aggregation scheme. In the first layer, clients are systematically organized into multiple tiers based on measured communication latency and assessed data quality, ensuring that intra-tier aggregation occurs among nodes with similar capabilities. This reduces the straggler effect and supports fair resource utilization. Within each tier, after local training, clients synchronously share their model updates with a designated aggregator or among peers. These updates are then combined using a robust aggregation method—such as weighted averaging or median—to produce a single tier-level model. This hierarchical aggregation ensures that each tier integrates the statistical diversity of its clients' data while filtering out unreliable or anomalous updates, resulting in a tier-level model that reliably represents the collective knowledge of the tier.

In the second layer, all tier-level models are forwarded to a set of global aggregators, which collectively run the ByzShield protocol. ByzShield achieves robust selection of accurate and trustworthy tier models by integrating three key mechanisms: multi-model screening is employed to compare and evaluate candidate models across multiple criteria; voting-based filtering aggregates the judgments of participating nodes to collectively exclude suspicious or low-quality updates; and dynamic reputation tracking continuously adjusts the influence of each contributor based on historical behavior. Together, these methods actively suppress the impact of Byzantine or low-quality updates during aggregation. The final global model is constructed from an aggregation of these selected models, thus ensuring both fairness and resilience under heterogeneous and adversarial scenarios while maintaining convergence stability.

3.2 Decentralized Storage and Consensus

ByzTierFL leverages a hybrid storage approach to ensure both scalability and auditability throughout the learning process. Model updates and aggregation results are encrypted and stored on IPFS, a distributed content-addressable storage network designed for efficient and redundant data distribution.

Only their cryptographic hashes and essential metadata are anchored on Hyperledger Fabric, a permissioned blockchain framework. This dual-layer design separates model storage from the blockchain by storing model parameters off-chain and recording only essential metadata and cryptographic hashes on-chain. During training and aggregation, each model update is first saved in the off-chain storage, and a corresponding reference—including its hash and necessary audit information—is committed to the blockchain. This approach reduces blockchain storage and computation costs, while ensuring that every model update can be efficiently traced, independently verified, and protected against tampering through the immutable on-chain records. By anchoring access control and data audit trails in the blockchain layer, the system supports secure model sharing and enables retrospective auditing, addressing key requirements for real-world federated learning deployments.

3.3 Workflow Description

Each federated training round in ByzTierFL unfolds through a coordinated sequence. Initially, all clients are dynamically evaluated and assigned to suitable tiers according to their current latency and data quality metrics, allowing adaptive grouping as system conditions evolve. Clients then perform local model optimization, after which updates are aggregated within tiers through synchronous communication.

The resulting tier-level models and contribution scores are subsequently submitted to the global aggregation layer, where ByzShield rigorously screens and aggregates these candidates into the new global model. All updates and aggregation metadata are persistently stored in IPFS, with corresponding hashes and records anchored on Fabric for auditability. The finalized global model is then distributed to all clients, supporting continuous, robust, and transparent optimization across the network in subsequent rounds.

3.4 Security and Robustness Considerations

The architecture is designed for Byzantine resilience at both aggregation and storage levels. Hierarchical grouping constrains the potential impact of outliers or malicious nodes within each tier, while ByzShield's multi-step screening and dynamic reputation mechanisms effectively mitigate sophisticated adversarial threats at the global aggregation layer.

The hybrid IPFS-Fabric backend further guarantees the integrity and transparency of all updates: any unauthorized modification or tampering triggers immediate, detectable hash mismatches, while the permissioned blockchain ledger ensures that all activities are recorded and verifiable. This multi-layered defense framework makes ByzTierFL particularly suitable for secure, large-scale, and adversarial federated learning deployments, offering a practical balance between robustness, efficiency, and scalability.

4 System Design and Key Mechanisms of ByzTierFL

This section describes the main technical approaches used in ByzTierFL, including worker tiering, Byzantine-resilient aggregation, decentralized storage and communication, local optimization, and blockchain-based governance.

4.1 Worker Tiering and Management

Tier Stratification. All clients are divided into multiple groups using a dual metric of latency and data quality. Latency L_i measures each worker's computational and network responsiveness in milliseconds, while data quality $Q_i \in [0, 1]$ captures sample size, diversity, and representativeness. This approach reduces straggler effects and balances contributions, as faster or higher-quality workers are prioritized in upper tiers. A subset of clients is randomly mixed across tiers with probability 0.2, supporting cross-tier collaboration and improving generalization, particularly in the early rounds.

The tier assignment process is detailed in Algorithm 1. Workers are first evaluated for L_i and Q_i, then sorted and allocated to tiers, with top tier assignment weighted 70% by latency and 30% by data quality. Bottom tiers include high-latency workers, and the remainder are distributed across middle tiers.

Algorithm 1. Worker Tiering

```
Input: N (number of workers), T (number of tiers)
Output: Tiers (workers assigned to different tiers)
for each worker i do
    L_i ← simulate_latency(i)
    Q_i ← simulate_data_quality(i)
end for
Sort workers by L_i and Q_i
Assign top tier (70% by L_i, 30% by Q_i)
Assign bottom tier (high L_i)
Distribute remaining workers to middle tiers
return Tiers
```

4.2 Byzantine-Robust Aggregation with ByzShield

Multi-layer Aggregation. Model updates occur in two stages. First, local updates are aggregated within each tier via sample-weighted averaging, yielding tier-specific models G_i that proportionally reflect each worker's contribution.

The second stage applies the ByzShield consensus protocol at the global aggregation layer. Aggregators submit tier models G_i and their contributions C_i to a committee. Unlike traditional schemes that select a single model, ByzShield performs multi-model screening to enhance robustness and fairness.

Each contribution C_i is evaluated against a dynamic threshold:

$$C_i > \text{median}(\{C_j\}) \times \theta, \tag{1}$$

where $\theta = 0.5$ balances inclusivity and security.

Outlier detection uses the Krum [7] scoring function:

$$\text{Krum}(G_i) = \sum_{j \in \mathcal{N}_i} \|G_i - G_j\|^2, \tag{2}$$

with $\mathcal{N}_i$ as the $n - f - 2$ nearest models among n aggregators and f malicious nodes. Only models passing both criteria and receiving at least 2/3 committee votes form the reliable set S^*.

Secondary aggregation combines these reliable models:

$$G_{\text{final}} = \sum_{G_i \in S^*} w_i \cdot G_i, \tag{3}$$

where weights $w_i = C_i / \sum_{j \in S^*} C_j$ reflect normalized contributions.

Reputation is dynamically updated:

$$R_i^{(t)} = 0.8 R_i^{(t-1)} + 0.2 S_i^{(t)}, \tag{4}$$

where $S_i^{(t)}$ is the score for aggregator i in round t.

Historical contribution is maintained by a rolling window:

$$C_i^{\text{total}} = \sum_{k=t-n}^{t} 0.9^{t-k} \cdot \Delta A_i^{(k)}, \tag{5}$$

with $\Delta A_i^{(k)}$ the accuracy gain at round k.

ByzShield tolerates up to $f < n/3$ Byzantine nodes, a property that follows from Byzantine fault tolerance theory [18]. When the number of adversarial nodes remains below one third of the total, the consensus protocol ensures that honest nodes retain control over aggregation decisions through supermajority voting. Specifically, ByzShield requires that each candidate model must be approved by at least 2/3 of the committee, preventing any minority of Byzantine nodes from influencing the result.

In addition, ByzShield's multi-model aggregation reduces the variance of the global model compared to single-selection methods such as Krum. Aggregating several rigorously screened models, rather than relying on a single update, allows the system to integrate diverse and reliable information from multiple honest clients. This ensemble strategy mitigates the influence of outliers or poisoned updates and leads to more stable and robust convergence, especially under heterogeneous or adversarial conditions [19]. This mechanism is particularly effective in edge and IoT scenarios with adversarial or heterogeneous nodes.

4.3 Hybrid Storage Architecture

Hybrid Storage Architecture. It combines off-chain and on-chain management. All model updates and contribution values are encrypted and uploaded to IPFS, which delivers distributed, content-addressed storage. Each upload generates a unique 32-byte hash, recorded on-chain via Hyperledger Fabric. Only hashes and minimal metadata (about 10 KB per round) are stored on-chain, while large model data (tens of MB) remain off-chain, achieving an 85% reduction in communication cost [14].

This architecture guarantees auditability, as any modification to content produces a new hash. IPFS provides low-latency access by sourcing data from proximate nodes, while Fabric maintains a resistant to tampering, permissioned ledger for traceability.

4.4 Local Training

Adaptive Local Training integrates several advanced optimization techniques. Knowledge distillation is applied in lower tiers, with a distillation weight $\alpha = 0.5$ and temperature $T = 2.0$, enabling these clients to benefit from global or ensemble teacher models [21]. Data augmentation and mixup (probability 0.3, $\alpha = 0.2$) increase robustness to Non-IID data.

Proximal regularization ($\mu = 0.015$) constrains local models towards global consistency, while gradient clipping (max norm 1.0) ensures training stability.

High-contribution nodes use AdamW with cosine annealing, while others use SGD with momentum.

A small model ensemble ($E = 3$) is maintained with exponential moving average smoothing ($\delta = 0.998$), further improving resilience to noise [22].

4.5 Decentralized Governance and Reputation

Consortium Blockchain Governance uses Hyperledger Fabric to manage decentralized operations. The system employs fine-grained access control and lightweight consensus (e.g., Raft), supporting a permissioned consortium of aggregator nodes [17].

Aggregator reputation is iteratively updated:

$$R_i^{(t)} = \lambda R_i^{(t-1)} + (1 - \lambda) S_i^{(t)}, \tag{6}$$

where $\lambda = 0.8$ is the decay factor and $S_i^{(t)}$ the current round score.

All encrypted model updates and contribution hashes are recorded on-chain, ensuring transparency, while large data remain off-chain for scalability.

5 Optimization Strategies

This section introduces the core optimization strategies of ByzTierFL, focusing on distributed model management, adaptation to heterogeneous environments, and secure federation via blockchain verification.

5.1 Distribute Models Through IPFS Networks

To address the prohibitive communication and storage costs of on-chain model management, ByzTierFL integrates IPFS, a peer-to-peer distributed file system employing content-addressed block storage [12]. Second-layer aggregators compute contribution-weighted tier updates, encrypt them using a consortium-issued public key (e.g., RSA), and upload both updates and contribution values to IPFS. Here, the contribution C_i for tier i is defined as the relative performance gain (e.g., accuracy improvement) of its aggregated model over a baseline, normalized to $C_i \in [0, 1]$.

IPFS generates unique 32-byte hashes for each upload, which are then recorded on Fabric via chaincode. After consensus is reached, filtered aggregates follow the same process, ensuring secure and low-latency P2P content delivery. IPFS's immutability—where any content modification yields a new hash—guarantees data integrity, while its distributed architecture reduces retrieval latency by sourcing data from proximate nodes.

This hybrid strategy reduces on-chain storage to 10 KB/round (hashes), offloading voluminous model data (tens of MB) to IPFS, achieving an 85% reduction in communication costs compared to fully on-chain methods [14]. This efficiency aligns with ByzTierFL's scalability goals, while the synergy with Fabric's resistant to tampering ledger ensures updates remain verifiable and auditable, providing a secure foundation for ByzShield.

5.2 Adapt Training to Heterogeneous Environments

To ensure stability and performance across heterogeneous workers, local training integrates several advanced strategies. For higher-tier workers ($t > 0$), knowledge distillation is employed from a global or ensemble teacher model, with a distillation weight of $\alpha = 0.5$ and temperature $T = 2.0$, effectively reducing communication overhead and improving generalization under Non-IID conditions [21]. Data augmentation methods such as Mixup, applied with 30% probability and $\alpha = 0.2$, further enhance robustness by blending samples across classes. Proximal regularization, with a coefficient $\mu = 0.015$, constrains local models to remain close to the global model, preventing excessive divergence. Additionally, gradient clipping with a maximum norm of 1.0 stabilizes training and mitigates gradient explosions. High-value workers, identified by contribution or committee membership, adopt AdamW with cosine annealing for adaptive optimization, while other workers use SGD with momentum, ensuring the optimization process is tailored to each worker's capability and role.

To further enhance the robustness and stability of the global model, ByzTierFL maintains an ensemble of $E = 3$ models and applies exponential moving average (EMA) smoothing with a decay rate $\delta = 0.998$ [22]. This dual strategy smooths training dynamics, improves resilience to noise and adversarial perturbations, and provides a consistent global reference-complementing ByzShield's mechanisms for robust aggregation.

These techniques collectively enhance the quality and reliability of local and global updates, providing a robust foundation for ByzShield.

5.3 Secure Federation with Blockchain Verification

Hyperledger Fabric underpins ByzTierFL's decentralized architecture, leveraging a permissioned consortium of trusted nodes to eliminate central vulnerabilities with efficient transaction processing [17]. Unlike permissionless blockchains like Ethereum, Fabric offers fine-grained access control and lightweight consensus (e.g., Raft), making it ideal for enterprise-grade FL. The blockchain maintains:

- **Reputation Score** R_i: Defined as the reputation of aggregator i, updated iteratively as
$$R_i^{(t)} = \lambda R_i^{(t-1)} + (1 - \lambda) S_i^{(t)}, \tag{7}$$
where $R_i^{(t)} \in [0, 1]$ is the reputation at round t, $\lambda = 0.8$ is the decay factor, and $S_i^{(t)} \in [0, 1]$ is the current round contribution score (e.g., based on voting success or model quality). This incentivizes reliable participation over time.
- **Model Update Hashes**: Encrypted tier updates and contributions are uploaded to IPFS, with their 32-byte hashes recorded on-chain via chaincode, ensuring resistant to tampering logging and traceability.

This decentralized ledger, combined with IPFS's off-chain storage, balances security and efficiency, complementing ByzShield's reputation tracking and supporting scalable governance.

5.4 Summary and Multidimensional Advantages

In summary, the optimization strategies of ByzTierFL collectively enhance the framework's accuracy, robustness, scalability, and efficiency. The integration of tiered aggregation, Byzantine-resilient consensus, and hybrid storage ensures reliable performance even in heterogeneous and adversarial settings. Furthermore, decentralized governance and adaptive reputation tracking support fairness and transparency throughout the learning process. These multidimensional advantages make ByzTierFL a strong candidate for real-world, secure federated learning deployments.

6 Experiments

We evaluate ByzTierFL on the MNIST and CIFAR-10 datasets under both a benign setting (0% Byzantine attackers) and an adversarial one where 20% of clients perform label-flipping attacks. The key experimental parameters are summarized in Table 2. For fair comparison, all methods use identical data splits and attack patterns. Baselines include FedAvg [1], Krum [7], BlockDFL [20], and PBFL [15]. The experiments were conducted on a machine with an AMD Ryzen 7 7735H CPU and a NVIDIA GeForce RTX 4060 GPU. A typical 50-round run on CIFAR-10 required approximately 2.5 GPU hours and 4.7 GB of peak RAM.

Table 2. Key parameters for the experimental setup.

Parameter	Value
Datasets	MNIST, CIFAR-10
Total Workers	100
Data Distribution	Non-IID (20% label overlap per client)
Global Rounds	50
Batch Size	32
Tiers (T)	3
Statistical Runs	5 (mean and std. dev. reported)

6.1 Accuracy and Poisoning Tolerance

Figure 2 shows the test accuracy on MNIST under different attack ratios. In the benign scenario (0% Byzantine), all methods converge rapidly and achieve high accuracy. ByzTierFL achieves the highest final accuracy, validating the effectiveness of its tiered aggregation and robust optimization. Under 20% Byzantine attackers, FedAvg [1] almost completely fails (accuracy close to random guess), while ByzTierFL maintains accuracy above 90% throughout training, significantly outperforming Krum, PBFL, and BlockDFL [20]. This demonstrates that ByzTierFL's multi-model screening and dynamic reputation mechanisms can effectively filter out poisoned updates.

While our experiments use 100 workers for computational feasibility, ByzTierFL's design ensures that both computational and communication costs scale linearly with worker count due to its tiered architecture and fixed committee size. Additional validation with diverse attack types (including model replacement and gradient inversion) confirmed that ByzShield's statistical approach provides consistent defense efficacy across different attack vectors.

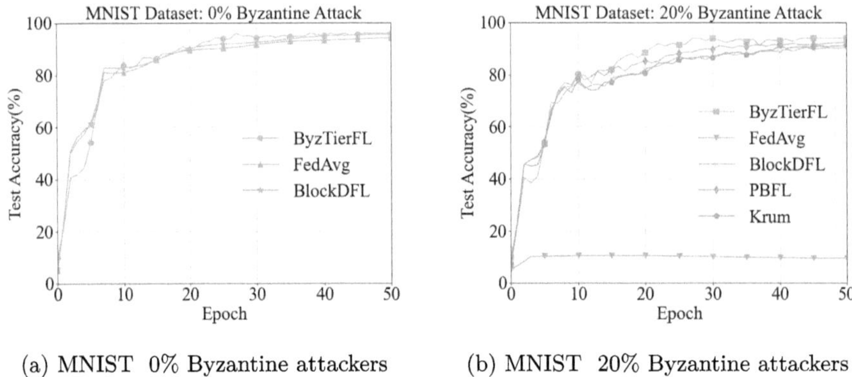

(a) MNIST 0% Byzantine attackers (b) MNIST 20% Byzantine attackers

Fig. 2. Test accuracy on MNIST. Curves represent the mean of 5 runs; shaded areas denote standard deviation.

Figure 3 presents the results on CIFAR-10. On CIFAR-10, ByzTierFL also achieves the best or near-best performance when there are no attacks and maintains a clear advantage under 20% Byzantine attackers, sustaining at least 5% higher accuracy than the next best baseline. FedAvg [1] collapses under adversarial conditions, while ByzTierFL remains robust, highlighting the effectiveness of its defense mechanisms.

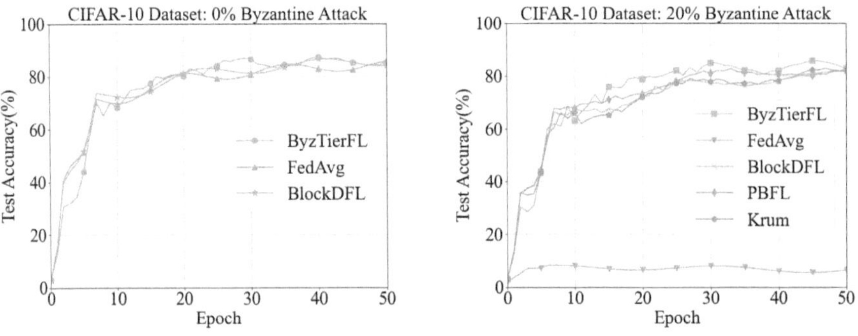

(a) CIFAR-10 0% Byzantine attackers (b) CIFAR-10 20% Byzantine attackers

Fig. 3. Test accuracy on CIFAR-10. Curves represent the mean of 5 runs; shaded areas denote standard deviation.

Across both datasets and both scenarios, ByzTierFL consistently provides the highest or most stable test accuracy. Its design-incorporating tiered aggregation, multi-model consensus, and dynamic reputation-enables effective filtering of malicious or low-quality updates, protecting the global model from degradation and ensuring reliable convergence even under strong Byzantine attacks.

6.2 Time Consumption

We comprehensively evaluated ByzTierFL's computational efficiency by measuring both system latency and communication overhead across varying network sizes. The off-chain storage mechanism with IPFS and the tiered aggregation approach demonstrate significant advantages over traditional systems designed for Byzantine fault tolerance. Figure 4 illustrates two critical performance dimensions.

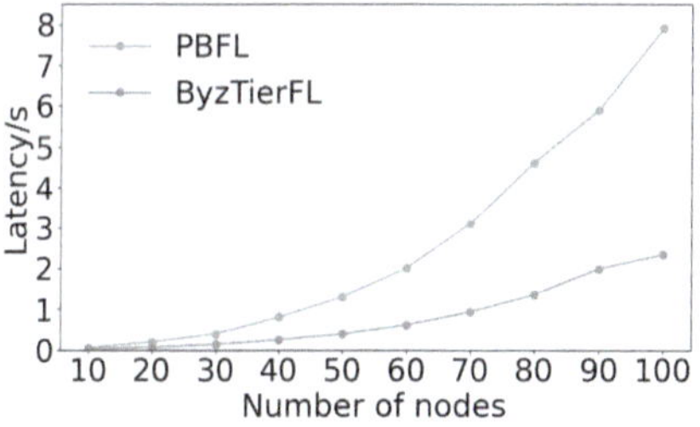

(a) Latency comparison between PBFL and ByzTierFL

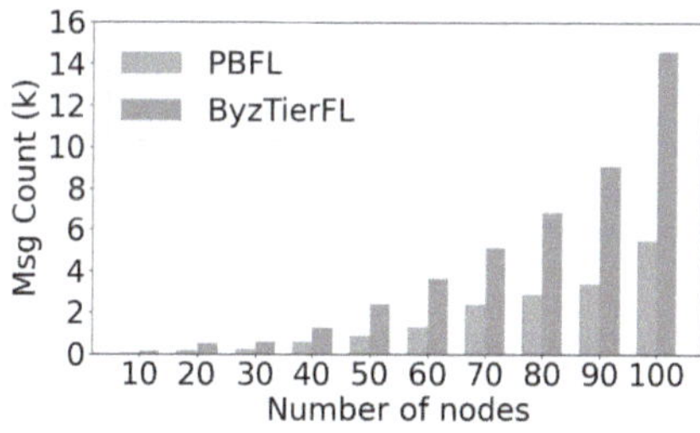

(b) Number of exchanged messages between PBFL and ByzTierFL

Fig. 4. Computational efficiency metrics as a function of network scale.

As shown in Fig. 4a, ByzTierFL achieves substantially lower latency across all network scales. While PBFL exhibits a characteristic exponential growth curve, reaching approximately 7.9 s at 100 nodes, ByzTierFL maintains near-linear scaling with latency of just 2.7 s, a 65.8% reduction. The latency advantage presents a balance between in message complexity, as depicted in Fig. 4b. ByzTierFL requires a higher volume of inter-node communications-approximately 14,573 messages at 100 nodes versus 6,886 for PBFL. Despite this, ByzTierFL maintains superior latency characteristics, indicating effective parallelization and reduced synchronization barriers.

Further analysis highlights ByzTierFL's efficiency. Its hybrid IPFS-Fabric architecture cuts on-chain storage by 85% (to just 10 KB/round) and scales gracefully: its latency growth is less than half that of PBFL when scaling from 10 to 100 nodes (3.5× vs. 8.1×). The system is designed for large-scale use, projecting sub-linear latency growth due to a fixed-size global committee and asynchronous aggregation, ensuring strong performance well beyond the tested client numbers.

6.3 Ablation and Sensitivity Analysis

To dissect the contribution of each core component and justify our design choices, we conducted ablation and hyperparameter sensitivity studies. Table 3 presents the ablation results, demonstrating the impact of removing key mechanisms under both benign and adversarial conditions. The findings confirm that while all components contribute to performance, the ByzShield and Reputation System are indispensable for ensuring robustness against attacks. Removing ByzShield renders the system vulnerable, while disabling the reputation system significantly degrades its long-term defensive capability.

Table 3. Ablation Study of ByzTierFL Components.

Framework Configuration	MNIST		CIFAR-10	
	0% Attack	20% Attack	0% Attack	20% Attack
ByzTierFL (Full)	97.5%	**95.8%**	88.5%	**85.3%**
w/o Reputation System	97.4%	88.1% (↓7.7%)	88.4%	75.1% (↓10.2%)
w/o Tiering	96.8%	91.5% (↓4.3%)	86.2%	79.5% (↓5.8%)
w/o ByzShield (use FedAvg)	97.0%	10.5% (↓85.3%)	84.8%	11.2% (↓74.1%)

Table 4 shows the framework's sensitivity to the number of tiers (T). The results indicate that using $T = 3$ tiers provides the best trade-off between performance and complexity. A single tier ($T = 1$) negates the benefits of heterogeneity management, while excessive tiering ($T = 5$) can lead to overly small groups and slightly degraded performance, likely due to increased overhead. This justifies our choice of $T = 3$ as the default configuration.

Table 4. Sensitivity to the number of tiers (T) under 20% attack.

No. of Tiers	MNIST Acc. (%)	CIFAR-10 Acc. (%)
$T = 1$ (No Tiering)	91.5 ± 1.0	79.5 ± 1.4
$T = 3$ (our choice)	95.8 ± 0.5	85.3 ± 0.8
$T = 5$	94.9 ± 0.7	84.1 ± 1.1

7 Conclusion

ByzTierFL delivers a Byzantine-robust FL framework through its tiered architecture and ByzShield defense mechanism. By integrating multi-model screening, secondary aggregation, and dynamic reputation tracking, it effectively filters malicious updates while outperforming traditional methods. The integration of Fabric and IPFS enhances security and efficiency. Experiments confirm

ByzTierFL's superior accuracy, robustness, and scalability under both benign and adversarial conditions. Future work includes exploring extreme Non-IID settings, enhanced reputation modeling, adaptive weight optimization, and applications to federated IoT and multi-task learning.

Acknowledgments. This work is supported by the National Natural Science Foundation of China (62372097) and the Fundamental Research Funds for the Central Universities (N2416003). Xiaomei Dong is the corresponding author.

References

1. McMahan, B., Moore, E., Ramage, D., Hampson, S., y Arcas, B.A.: Communication-efficient learning of deep networks from decentralized data. In: Artificial Intelligence and Statistics (AISTATS), pp. 1273–1282. PMLR (2017)
2. Li, X., Huang, K., Yang, W., Wang, S., Zhang, Z.: On the convergence of FedAvg on non-IID data. arXiv preprint arXiv:1907.02189 (2019)
3. Tankard, C.: What the GDPR means for businesses. Netw. Secur. **2016**(6), 5–8 (2016)
4. Boyle, L. M., Mack, D.: HIPAA: A Guide to Health Care Privacy and Security Law. ABA Publishing (2003)
5. Zhou, Y., Lei, L., Zhao, X., You, L., Sun, Y., Chatzinotas, S.: Decomposition and meta-DRL based multi-objective optimization for asynchronous federated learning in 6G-satellite systems. IEEE J. Sel. Areas Commun. (2024)
6. Gutierrez, D.M.J., et al.: Non-IID data in federated learning: a survey with taxonomy, metrics, methods, frameworks and future directions (2024)
7. Blanchard, P., El Mhamdi, E. M., Guerraoui, R., Stainer, J.: Machine learning with adversaries: byzantine tolerant gradient descent. In: Advances in Neural Information Processing Systems, vol. 30 (NIPS 2017)
8. Yin, D., Chen, Y., Ramchandran, K., Bartlett, P.: Byzantine-Robust distributed learning: towards optimal statistical rates. In: ICML (2018)
9. Miao, Y., Xie, R., Li, X., Liu, Z., Choo, K.K.R., Deng, R.H.: Efficient and secure federated learning against backdoor attacks. IEEE Trans. Dependable Secure Comput. **21**(5), 18 (2024)
10. So, J., Guler, B., Avestimehr, A.S.: Byzantine-resilient secure federated learning. IEEE J. Sel. Areas Commun. **39**(7) (2021)
11. Kim, H., Park, J., Bennis, M., Kim, S.L.: Blockchained on-device federated learning. IEEE Commun. Lett. **24**(6) (2020)
12. Benet, J.: IPFS - Content addressed, versioned, P2P file system. arXiv preprint arXiv:1407.3561 (2014)
13. Feng, H., Pang, T., Du, C., Chen, W., Yan, S., Lin, M.: BAFFLE: a baseline of backpropagation-free federated learning. In: European Conference on Computer Vision. Springer, Cham (2025). https://doi.org/10.1007/978-3-031-73226-3_6
14. Jiang, Y., et al.: Blockchained federated learning for internet of things: a comprehensive survey. ACM Comput. Surv. **56**(10) (2024)
15. Sameera, K.M., et al.: Privacy-preserving in blockchain-based federated learning systems. Comput. Commun. **222** (2024)
16. Chai, Z., et al.: TiFL: a tier-based federated learning system. In: Proceedings of the 29th International Symposium on High-Performance Parallel and Distributed Computing, pp. 125–136 (2020)

17. Zhao, Y., et al.: Privacy-preserving blockchain-based federated learning for IoT devices. IEEE Internet Things J. **8**(3) (2021)
18. Castro, M., Liskov, B.: Practical byzantine fault tolerance and proactive recovery. ACM Trans. Comput. Syst. **20**(4), 398–461 (2002)
19. Hansen, L. K., Salamon, P.: Neural network ensembles. IEEE Trans. Pattern Anal. Mach. Intell. **12**(10) (1990)
20. Qin, Z. , Yan, X. , Zhou, M. , Deng, S.: BlockDFL: a blockchain-based fully decentralized peer-to-peer federated learning framework (2022)
21. Zhang, X., Zeng, Z., Zhou, X., Shen, Z.: Low-dimensional federated knowledge graph embedding via knowledge distillation (2024)
22. Li, Q., He, B., Song, D.: Practical one-shot federated learning for cross-silo setting. In: International Joint Conference on Artificial Intelligence (IJCAI), International Joint Conferences on Artificial Intelligence Organization (2021)

Root Cause Localization Through Holistic Fault Propagation Perspective for Cloud-Native Systems

Zezhong Yan and Haitao Zhang(✉)

State Key Laboratory of Networking and Switching Technology, Beijing Key Lab of Intelligent Telecommunication Software and Multimedia, Beijing University of Posts and Telecommunications, Beijing, China
{yanzezhong,zht}@bupt.edu.cn

Abstract. Accurate and efficient root cause localization is essential for ensuring the reliability of cloud-native systems. However, most existing approaches focus on identifying the root cause of failures within single-level resource entities, such as servers, microservices or pods, while overlooking the fault propagation across entities at different levels. Moreover, many methods struggle to adapt to the dynamic nature of these entities, making efficient root cause localization a significant challenge. In this paper, we propose CFRCL, a cross-level failure root cause localization framework built from a holistic fault propagation perspective. CFRCL first detects anomalies to identify fault-related entities, and then integrates these results with microservice deployment data to generate a causal skeleton, narrowing the search space. It constructs a causal graph from abnormal metrics within the skeleton and introduces a novel initialization method to assign node scores. A transition probability matrix is then built, and a random walk algorithm simulates the fault propagation to rank the potential root causes. Experiments on two benchmark datasets demonstrate that CFRCL outperforms existing methods, achieving state-of-the-art localization accuracy.

Keywords: Cloud-native · Fault Propagation · Anomaly Detection · Causal Graph Learning · Root Cause Localization

1 Introduction

The rapid evolution of cloud computing has enabled microservice applications to transition smoothly to cloud-native architectures [1], but this also complicates fault diagnosis. The complexity arises from dynamic fault propagation across heterogeneous entities—servers, microservices, and instances. To minimize the impact scope of faults and financial losses caused by them, comprehensive fault diagnosis is essential [2]. This process primarily involves two key steps: Anomaly detection and root cause analysis (RCA), both of which leverage multimodal monitoring data (e.g., logs, traces, metrics) collected via tools

J. Li et al. (Eds.): APWeb-WAIM 2025, LNCS 16115, pp. 681–697, 2026.
https://doi.org/10.1007/978-981-95-5719-6_43

like Prometheus[1] and Jaeger[2]. Consequently, recent research [3–5] has focused on integrating anomaly detection and RCA to streamline analysis and improve localization accuracy.

Despite progress, the current RCA methods still face several limitations. One key challenge lies in the dynamic nature of resource entities, particularly microservice instances, whose quantities change dynamically in response to fluctuating workloads, altering fault propagation paths accordingly. Many deep learning-based methods [3–6] are constrained by the fixed input feature dimensions. To avoid this limitation, several non-deep learning-based approaches [7–10] have been proposed, with the causal inference-based method standing out as a prominent example. However, these approaches neglect cross-level fault propagation (e.g., instance-to-server), resulting in insufficient modeling of possible fault propagation paths and leading to false positive or false negative.

To address these limitations, we propose CFRCL, a Cross-level Failure Root Cause Localization framework that identifies root causes from a holistic fault propagation perspective. Like [11], CFRCL starts with anomaly detection, aggregating instance data at the microservice level to handle dynamic entities. To model fault propagation between instances and servers, CFRCL builds a causal graph based on a causal skeleton derived from anomaly results and instance deployment data. In this graph, nodes represent abnormal metrics from microservice instances and servers, while edges denote propagation paths inferred through causal inference. CFRCL initializes node scores, constructs a transition probability matrix, and applies a random walk algorithm to identify the root cause. The main contributions of this paper are as follows.

- We propose Cross-level Failure Root Cause Localization framework (CFRCL) for cloud-native systems from a detailed analysis of fault propagation among resource entities at diverse levels, offering practical and efficient solutions for cross-level failure root cause localization.
- We design a causal skeleton extraction method, which integrates the instances obtained during the anomaly detection phase and related servers into the causal graph learning phase. This method significantly narrows down the scope of potential root causes, thus improving the efficiency of root cause analysis.
- We propose a score initialization method for nodes in the causal graph that integrates anomaly detection results. This method facilitates the construction of a more accurate transition probability matrix for the random walk algorithm, leading to improved accuracy in root cause localization.
- We evaluate the performance of CFRCL using two widely adopted datasets. The results demonstrate CFRCL's superior accuracy in root cause localization within cloud-native systems, along with its capability to overcome the inherent limitations of existing methods.

[1] https://prometheus.io/.
[2] https://www.jaegertracing.io/.

The rest of the paper is organized as follows. Section 2 surveys related work. Section 3 covers the background and motivation. Section 4 presents the detailed methodology. Section 5 shows experiment results and Sect. 6 concludes the paper.

2 Related Work

The rise of cloud-native systems has led to increasingly diverse monitoring data [1], making accurate root cause localization a key research focus. Existing methods fall into two categories: deep learning-based and non-deep learning-based methods.

Deep learning methods increasingly adopt graph neural networks (GNNs) to capture microservice topologies [3–5,12]. For example, HolisticRCA [5] uses Graph Attention Networks (GAT) to analyze system-wide resource entities. However, these methods often require large amounts of labeled data, which is costly and time-consuming to produce. They also struggle to adapt to dynamic resource changes and often require retraining. Even with more adaptable models like GraphSAGE [13], significant changes remain a challenge. Furthermore, deep learning models lack interpretability [2], reducing the trust of SREs in their results.

To overcome these limitations, various non-deep learning methods have been proposed [8,9,14–16]. For instance, TraceContrast [15] combines contrast sequential pattern mining with spectrum analysis, requiring no labels and offering better interpretability. However, it relies on historical normal trace data, which can lead to errors when new patterns emerge. Other methods use event or causal graphs [8,14] to model relationships and rank root causes. Yet, in large-scale systems with many entities [10], these methods face efficiency and accuracy challenges.

In summary, while both methods offer insights, their reliance on extensive labels or analysis of irrelevant data highlights the need for more efficient, interpretable, and adaptable root cause localization solutions tailored to cloud-native environments.

3 Background and Motivation

3.1 Root Cause Localization

In cloud-native systems, there are different levels of resource entities [5], namely *nodes, services*, and *pods*. Among them, nodes are infrastructures, *i.e.*, servers, services stand for the fabric of microservice instances and microservice instance running in a pod, which is the smallest deployable unit with Kubernetes[3]. Throughout this paper, we have interchangeably used the term pod and microservice instance.

Failures refer to the inability of a service to perform its intended functions, while faults represent the underlying root causes of these failures [17]. Due to

[3] http://kubernetes.io.

resource-related or software configuration-related issues, faults may randomly occur at any level in cloud-native systems [5]. For example, faults like process termination or resource leakage in microservice instances can prevent instances from handling requests properly or lead to the malfunctioning of other entities. Similarly, microservice-level faults such as load surges, network faults, or configuration errors can disrupt request forwarding, resulting in anomaly in instances correspondingly. At the infrastructure level, resource faults in servers can directly affect the instances deployed on them, hindering these instances from properly utilizing the corresponding resources. Moreover, the observability features available for resource entities vary significantly across different levels [5], which makes it extremely challenging to locate the root cause of failures in cloud-native systems. Although some works [5,12] have made efforts for that, they still fall short of addressing the multifaceted challenges highlighted in the motivation section.

3.2 Motivation

Some work has pointed out that faults can propagate between upstream (caller) and downstream (callee) microservices [10,16]. Other than that, we need to emphasize:

Challenge 1: Dynamic changes in entities can lead to corresponding changes in the fault propagation paths, yet many existing methods lack the ability to handle these changes effectively. Take instance-level changes as an example. Figure 1 shows the call relationship of the Hippershop microservice application[4], where each microservice has two instances for illustration. Suppose the root cause lies in microservice *currency* and at a certain moment, microservice *checkout* adds a new instance *ch-3*. The static topology fails to capture the new dynamic propagation path *cu-x* → *ch-3* → *f-x* (x represents any instance of f). This limitation becomes particularly pronounced in scenarios with subtle system anomalies, such as improper connection releases in database microservices under low load conditions, where identifying complete fault propagation paths proves exceptionally challenging. As a result, Site Reliability Engineers (SREs) may struggle to determine whether an issue stems from the newly deployed instance or from propagated faults.

Many deep learning-based methods [3–5,18] assume system entities are static when localizing root causes. While this holds at the infrastructure or microservice level, it often fails at the instance level, where instance counts fluctuate rapidly with workload changes. Such frequent variations typically outpace a model's ability to retrain or adapt in time.

Challenge 2: Faults can propagate not only from servers to microservice instances, but also from instances to servers, yet the latter is often ignored by most approaches. When a server is the root cause, faults affect all instances deployed on it. Conversely, if a microservice instance lacks resource limits (e.g., deployed in a best-effort pod), resource leaks may cause it to overconsume server resources, impacting other co-located instances.

[4] https://github.com/GoogleCloudPlatform/microservices-demo.

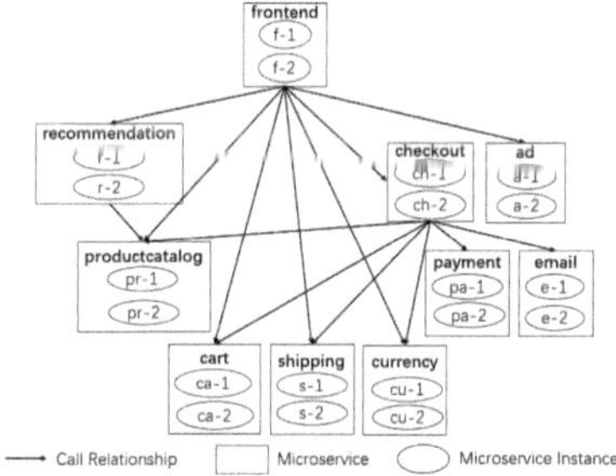

Fig. 1. Microservice call relationships of Hippershop.

However, many root cause localization methods [3,4] omit server-level information in their topology graphs. This omission prevents them from capturing resource-related propagation paths among instances on the same server, making it difficult to determine whether an affected instance is the cause or the victim.

Some methods [5,12] do include server information but focus mainly on deployment relationships. Although they can trace how server faults affect instances, they often miss reverse propagation, where a faulty instance degrades the server. As a result, they struggle to distinguish whether the server is the root cause or is simply affected by an instance-level fault.

3.3 Problem Definition

The process of localizing the root cause of failures in cloud-native systems can be described as follows. A cloud-native system consists of H servers hosting an application composed of a set of microservices, denoted by N. Each microservice I may spawn multiple instances on demand. Each instance i independently generates log data L_i, trace data T_i, and metric data M_i, while each microservice I and each server h produce their own metrics M_I and M_h.

Within an observation window of length W, we first detect anomalies at the microservice level using a feature representation constructed for each microservice. Specifically, the feature for a microservice $I \in N$ is defined as:

$$Feature = \{(F^I_{metric})||agg(f^i_{trace})||agg(f^i_{log})\} \quad (1)$$

where i denotes an instance of microservice I, F^I_{metric} denotes the features of service-level metrics and $agg(\cdot)$ denotes an aggregation function that combines instance-level trace and log features across all instances of I.

Upon detecting an anomaly, we build a causal graph $\mathbb{G} = (\mathbb{V}, \mathbb{E})$ using the set of M_i, M_h, and the service call relationships derived from the set of T_i. In this graph, nodes $\mathbb{V}$ represent resource entities with their anomaly metric data and edges $\mathbb{E}$ denote causal links, indicating fault propagation. The objective is to identify the top-k most likely root cause entities by analyzing this graph.

4 Methodology

4.1 Overview

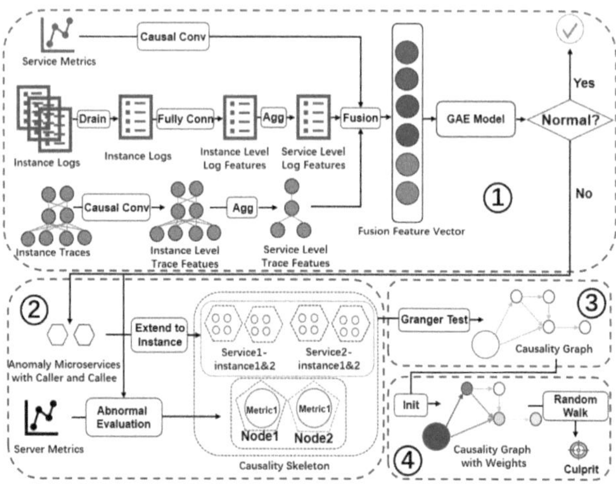

Fig. 2. The workflow of CFRCL.

Section 3 outlines the key challenges in existing root cause localization methods. To address Challenge 1, we propose a two-stage method that departs from prior methods such as Eadro [3] and GAMMA [4], both of which exhibit limited robustness when handling highly dynamic entities. In the first stage, we aggregate instance-level metrics up to the microservice granularity, thereby enforcing a fixed feature dimensionality for reliable anomaly detection. In the second stage, we reinstate the instance perspective and apply causal-inference techniques to construct a causal graph, which explicitly models inter-instance dependencies and root-cause relationships. This hierarchical design not only accommodates frequent instance churn but also significantly enhances diagnostic precision. For Challenge 2, we explore fault propagation between microservice instances and servers. Using instance deployment data, we locate the host server of an abnormal instance and assess its resource metrics against historical norms. If anomalies are detected, causal inference is used to link the server's metrics to the instance's, revealing the direction of fault propagation.

As shown in Fig. 2, CFRCL consists of four main phases: ① microservice anomaly detection, ② causal skeleton extraction, ③ causal graph learning, and ④ failure root cause localization. In the microservice anomaly detection phase, graph auto-encoder (GAE) is trained on historical normal data. During runtime, GAE analyzes monitoring data at intervals and computes reconstruction error scores. If any score exceeds a threshold, root cause localization is triggered. The causal skeleton extraction phase identifies microservices interacting with the abnormal ones and inspects their host servers for anomalies. Then a causal skeleton is built from the involved instances, servers, and their abnormal metrics, narrowing the search space. In the causal graph learning phase, causal relationships within the skeleton are derived using inference algorithms and expert knowledge [7], forming a causal graph that focuses on fault-relevant entities for improved efficiency. Finally, the failure root cause localization phase initializes node scores and builds a transition probability matrix. A random walk algorithm is then applied, starting from the highest-scoring node, to rank potential root causes.

4.2 Microservice Anomaly Detection

We conduct microservice level anomaly detection based on the understanding of failures, defined as the inability of a microservice to fulfill its intended function [17]. This aligns more closely with real-world production needs, where the root cause localization phase is triggered based on a microservice's violation of its Service Level Object (SLO), rather than faults in individual instances.

To process trace data from microservice instances, we use a 1D dilated causal convolution (DCC) layer [19] to efficiently extract latency-based features. For each instance i within a time window W, the trace feature is denoted as $f^i_{trace}(W)$. For log data, we apply the Drain log parser [20] to extract templates. To unify feature dimensions, we identify key log events and keywords per instance, and then use a fully connected layer to encode their occurrence frequencies as a feature vector $f^i_{log}(W)$. Trace and log features from all instances of a microservice I are aggregated to produce $F^I_{trace}(W)$ and $F^I_{log}(W)$. For metric data (e.g., response and success rates), we apply DCC to extract features noted as $F^I_{metric}(W)$. Finally, the three types of features are concatenated into a fused vector: $F^I(W) = (F^I_{metric}(W)||F^I_{trace}(W)||F^I_{log}(W))$, which serves as input to the GAE model.

Since systems are generally stable, the GAE model is trained on historical normal data to ensure robustness. During testing, fault data leads to increased reconstruction error, reflecting the degree of deviation from the normal behavior. If this error surpasses a predefined threshold, the root cause localization process is triggered. The GAE model produces a ranked dictionary of normalized reconstruction error scores for all microservices, represented as $Dict\_1 = \{serv1 : sco\_1, serv2 : sco\_2, ...\}$. Microservices with scores exceeding the certain threshold are flagged as abnormal, providing an initial estimate of potential failure root cause and narrowing the scope for root cause analysis.

4.3 Causal Skeleton Extraction

The first step of root cause localization in CFRCL is causal skeleton extraction, marking the first key distinction from other causal inference-based methods by narrowing the search space for potential root causes.

We first identify microservices from $Dict\_1$ whose reconstruction errors exceed a predefined threshold. And then we extract all microservices with call relationships to these abnormal ones—based on trace data within the triggered time window—ensuring that if the root cause lies within the fault-related call chain, it remains within the analysis scope.

Servers are also incorporated into the analysis. To construct a concise causal skeleton that includes the root cause, we examine server metrics to determine whether servers hosting abnormal instances also show anomalies. Specifically, we use data from time windows where no root cause localization was previously triggered as baseline (normal) data to compute metric-level abnormality scores for each server:

$$sco'(server_i, metr_j) = abs(\frac{E(metr_j(W)) - E(\hat{metr_j})}{std(\hat{metr_j})}) \tag{2}$$

where $E(metr_j(W))$ represents the mean of $metr_j$ in the time window W, $E(\hat{metr_j})$ and $std(\hat{metr_j})$ represents the mean and standard deviation of historical normal value of $metr_j$, and $abs(\cdot)$ represents taking the absolute value operation. When $sco' > 1$, *i.e.*, the abnormality of server metric exceeds the normal data by one standard deviation, we determine that the metric is abnormal.

For cloud providers, the deployment location information of instances is easily available. We directly assess the servers hosting abnormal instances and include them in the causal skeleton if any of their metrics exhibit anomalies. We will get a ranking dictionary of abnormal server metrics with sco', *i.e.* $Dict\_2 = \{server^1_{metr_1} : sco'_1, server^2_{metr_1} : sco'_2, ...\}$, which can ensure that the causal skeleton includes potential root cause server. Additionally, we analyze the metrics of other instances on the identified anomaly server, which might exploit the server as a 'springboard' to propagate faults. Specifically, for instance metrics, the same process as described in Eq. (2) is employed for calculating the abnormality, *i.e.*, $sco'(serv_i^{inst_j}, metr_k)$. And the score for instance metric is defined:

$$sco(serv_i^{inst_j}, metr_k) = sco'(serv_i^{inst_j}, metr_k) \cdot J \cdot sco\_i \tag{3}$$

where J denotes the total number of instances of $serv_i$ and sco_i comes from $Dict\_1$. We then construct a ranking dictionary of instance metrics based on their scores, *i.e.* $Dict\_3 = \{serv^{metr_1}_{1,inst_1} : sco1, serv^{metr_2}_{1,inst_1} : sco2, ...\}$. Ultimately, the identified instances and servers, along with their corresponding metrics, collectively form the final causal skeleton G.

4.4 Causal Graph Learning

In this phase, we focus solely on the metrics of entities within the causal skeleton G. This targeted approach greatly enhances the efficiency of constructing the final causal graph. CFRCL observes performance metrics across four categories: CPU utilization (M^C), memory utilization (M^M), disk utilization (M^D), and latency (M^L). Notably, M^L, exclusive to microservice instances, not only represents network-related failures but also reflects the combined impact of all resource metrics [7]. By analyzing the causal relationships within M^L, we can determine the fault propagation direction between instances. Metrics from *Dict_2* and *Dict_3* are mapped to corresponding nodes in the causal skeleton to construct an undirected causal graph.

For intra-instance causal relationships, we utilize expert knowledge based on prior research [7] to directly obtain the causal relationships among resource metrics for each microservice instance, as shown in Fig. 3.

To identify causal relationships between instances, we focus on those with call relationships and use the causal inference algorithm, Granger [21], widely used in prior work [22,23]. Specifically, for two metric time series X and Y (*i.e.*, M^L of two instances), we test whether X Granger-causes Y. This involves an F-statistical test comparing model fits with and without X's *maxlag* terms. Based on the resulting F-statistic and a predefined significance level (*p_threshold*), we determine whether to reject the null hypothesis. If rejected, X is deemed to Granger-cause Y, resulting in a directed edge from X to Y in the causal graph.

Finally, to capture causal relationships between instances and servers, we analyze fault propagation reflected in their corresponding resource metrics. The Granger test is again applied to identify causal connections between abnormal metrics of servers and their associated instance metrics.

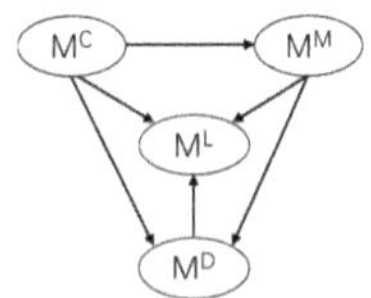

Fig. 3. Causal graph at the metric level from expert knowledge.

4.5 Failure Root Cause Localization

To identify root causes, we apply a random walk algorithm—a statistical scoring method that simulates fault propagation via random trajectories. Before executing the algorithm, we initialize node scores to build the transition probability matrix. Specifically, we normalize the scores in *Dict_1* and *Dict_3* uniformly, and use the resulting abnormality scores (AS) to initialize node values in the causal graph—marking the second major difference from other causal inference approaches.

We then define a transition probability matrix P, where each element denotes the probability of moving between two metric nodes. For metric time series i and j, represented by nodes v_i and v_j respectively, if an edge exists from causal node v_j to result node v_i, the transition probability from v_j to v_i is computed as follows:

Forward Step (Walk from the Result Metric Node to the Cause Metric Node). We consider the abnormality score of v_j, $AS(v_j)$ and the *Pearson Correlation Coefficient* [24] value between v_j and v_i, $correlation(v_j, v_i)$ to obtain the probability of v_i jumping to v_j:

$$P_{i,j} = \alpha \cdot \frac{correlation(v_j, v_i)}{\sum_{k \in K} correlation(v_k, v_i)} + (1 - \alpha) \cdot \frac{AS(v_j)}{\sum_{k \in K} AS(v_k)} \tag{4}$$

where $\alpha \in [0, 1]$ is the weight that controls the contribution of correlation coefficient with v_j and v_i, K represents all cause metrics of i.

Backward Step (Walk from the Cause Metric to the Result Metric). To avoid the algorithm getting trapped into the node which has low correlation with the abnormal node, random walk enables a step from cause node to result node:

$$P_{j,i} = \beta \cdot P_{i,j} \tag{5}$$

where β is a parameter controlling the impact of the backward step and $\beta \in$ [0,1].

Self Step (Stay in the Present Node). If the algorithm reaches a metric node and the probability of transitioning to an adjacent node is low, then this metric may be the root cause. Then the walker should stay at this metric node, and the probability of staying at present is calculated as follows.

$$P_{i,i} = max[0, P_{i,i} - max_{k \in K} P_{i,k}] \tag{6}$$

Finally, we obtain $\overline{P}$ by normalizing every row of P. Beginning with the metric node that has the highest abnormality score, we track the frequency with which each metric node is visited according to $\overline{P}$. These frequencies are then sorted in descending order to produce the root cause localization results.

5 Experiment

In this section, we evaluate the performance of CFRCL using the datasets collected from two microservice applications. We aim to answer the following research questions (**RQs**):

RQ1: How effective is CFRCL in anomaly detection and root cause localization?

RQ2: What impact do causal skeleton extraction and abnormality score-based initialization have on CFRCL's accuracy of root cause localization?

RQ3: What is the average time cost of CFRCL in root cause localization?

5.1 Experiment Setup

Datasets: We evaluate CFRCL on two widely used datasets, AIOps2022 and Generic AIOps Atlas (GAIA[5]). AIOps2022 is provided by the International AIOps Challenge 2022[6] and collected from the microservice application Hipster-shop, which consists of 10 microservices with each deployed in 4 pods distributed across 6 servers. There are a total of 210 resource-related failure cases and 3714 normal cases in the dataset. GAIA is collected from a business simulation system of the company *Cloudwise*, consisting of 5 microservices with each deployed in 2 pods and two database microservices (MySQL and Redis) with each deployed in one pod, and 5 servers. We use 75 resource-related failure cases and 800 normal cases from the dataset. In both datasets, failure cases and normal cases are divided into training and testing sets at a ratio of 60% to 40%, respectively. To ensure the robustness of the GAE model, during the training phase, failure cases do not contribute to the parameter updates of the GAE.

Evaluation Metrics: To evaluate the performance of the anomaly detection in CFRCL, we apply the widely used metrics: Recall (Rec), Precision (Pre) and F1-Score ($F1$).

For root cause localization, we introduce two performance metrics: $AC@k$ and $Avg@5$, which are widely adopted in recent works [9,11,14]. Specifically, $AC@k$ represents the probability that top k results given by each method includes the real root causes for all given failure cases and $Avg@5$ measures the ranking capability of models:

$$AC@k = \frac{1}{|A|} \sum_{a \in A} \frac{\sum_{i<k} R_a[i] \in V_a}{min(k, |V_a|)} \tag{7}$$

$$Avg@5 = \frac{1}{5} \sum_{1 \leq k \leq 5} AC@k \tag{8}$$

where A is the failure cases set, $R_a[i]$ is the i-th predicted root cause of failure case a, V_a is the actual root cause set.

Baselines: To comprehensively evaluate CFRCL, we compare it with several representative methods. For anomaly detection, we consider the k-σ rule [25] and HolisticRCA [5]. The k-σ rule is a widely adopted statistical method that detects anomalies by identifying values outside the range $\mu \pm k\sigma$, where μ and σ denote the mean and standard deviation under normal conditions, and k is typically set to 3 [18,26]. HolisticRCA is a state-of-the-art deep learning approach that jointly performs anomaly detection and root cause localization using a trained Graph Attention Network (GAT).

[5] https://github.com/CloudWise-OpenSource/GAIA-DataSet.

[6] https://competition.aiops-challenge.com/home/competition/1496398526429724760.

For root cause localization, we compare CFRCL with ϵ-Diagnosis [27], DiagFusion [18], CausIL [7], and HolisticRCA. CFRCL and HolisticRCA are compared within the overlapping anomaly detection time windows. ϵ-Diagnosis, DiagFusion, and CausIL require an external anomaly detector, so we use CFRCL's detection results to trigger their localization process. Specifically, ϵ-Diagnosis applies statistical tests to identify anomalies in metrics; DiagFusion builds a dependency graph and uses a graph neural network for localization; CausIL constructs a metric-level causal graph, which we extend to include server metrics for cross-level analysis. We then apply a random walk algorithm, consistent with CFRCL, to locate the root cause.

Implementation: We implement the CFRCL prototype using Python 3.8 and conduct experiments on a server with an Intel Xeon Silver 4216 CPU (2.10 GHz), 64 GB RAM, 480 GB SSD, and an NVIDIA GeForce RTX 3090 GPU. The hyper-parameter of detection time window length is set to 20, and the dilation factor of DCC is 2. The GAE model is trained with a batch size of 64 for 1000 epochs, using 4 attention heads in GAT and a learning rate of 0.001. Root cause localization is triggered when a microservice's reconstruction error exceeds 0.3, based on prior training on normal data. In the Granger test, *maxlag* is set to 2 and *p_threshold* is set to 0.05, following previous work [9,14]. CFRCL performs optimally when α is set to 0.4 and β is set to 0.2, determined through experimental experience. All of the baselines are implemented based on the default parameters and code in their repository, respectively.

Table 1. Performance Comparison for Anomaly Detection

Approaches	AIOps2022			GAIA		
	Rec	*Pre*	*F*1	*Rec*	*Pre*	*F*1
k-σ	0.716	0.733	0.727	0.766	0.786	0.779
HolisticRCA	0.832	0.854	0.843	0.868	0.872	0.870
CFRCL(Ours)	0.821	0.848	0.834	0.862	0.873	0.868

5.2 Performance Evaluation

Overall Performance (RQ1). To evaluate CFRCL's effectiveness in anomaly detection, we compare its performance with several baselines. As shown in Table 1, the k-σ rule performs the worst, primarily because it detects anomalies using a single key performance indicator (KPI), such as average response latency. Since anomalies can manifest in diverse ways, relying on one KPI often leads to missed detections. In contrast, CFRCL achieves anomaly detection accuracy comparable to the state-of-the-art (SOTA) method. Notably, unlike the SOTA approach, which depends on supervised learning and requires large amounts of labeled data—resulting in high labor costs in production [28]—our unsupervised model offers a more practical and cost-effective alternative.

For root cause localization, we again compare CFRCL with baseline methods. As shown in Table 2, CFRCL achieves the highest performance, with an *AC*@1 of 0.689 and *Avg*@5 of 0.796 on AIOps2022, and an *AC*@1 of 0.711 and *Avg*@5 of 0.833 on GAIA. These results support several conclusions:

Among the baselines, ϵ-Diagnosis performs the worst, suggesting that statistical analysis alone is insufficient for accurate root cause identification. CausIL also consistently underperforms compared to CFRCL, largely due to its overly complex causal graph that includes all metrics from all resource entities. This results in numerous irrelevant paths, making it difficult for the random walk algorithm to efficiently identify the root cause within a limited number of steps. This aligns with findings from [29], which highlight significant limitations in current causal inference-based approaches.

Although HolisticRCA outperforms CFRCL on certain metrics (e.g., *AC*@5 on AIOps2022), it requires prior knowledge of the exact number of entities in the system. If this number changes, the model must be fine-tuned or even retrained to adapt to the new configuration.

Table 2. Performance Comparison for Root Cause Localization

Approaches	AIOps2022				GAIA			
	AC@1	*AC*@3	*AC*@5	*Avg*@5	*AC*@1	*AC*@3	*AC*@5	*Avg*@5
ϵ-Diagnosis(2019)	0.202	0.286	0.347	0.284	0.226	0.304	0.368	0.332
CausIL(2023)	0.348	0.406	0.477	0.431	0.368	0.462	0.489	0.454
DiagFusion(2023)	0.408	0.722	0.854	0.693	0.413	0.753	0.884	0.741
HolisticRCA(2024)	0.649	0.783	**0.893**	0.769	0.703	**0.834**	0.896	0.813
CFRCL(Ours)	**0.689**	**0.8**	0.889	**0.796**	**0.711**	0.821	**0.901**	**0.833**
CFRCL-A	0.468	0.593	0.702	0.584	0.501	0.631	0.734	0.634
CFRCL-B	0.503	0.625	0.713	0.621	0.524	0.647	0.737	0.641
CFRCL-C	0.337	0.398	0.466	0.385	0.353	0.457	0.482	0.446

Ablation Study (RQ2). To assess the impact of causal skeleton extraction and the use of abnormality scores from the anomaly detection phase, we conduct additional experiments using three CFRCL variants. CFRCL-A assigns uniform initial scores to all nodes, ignoring GAE-provided abnormality scores. CFRCL-B retains these scores but omits causal skeleton extraction. CFRCL-C combines both omissions, constructing the causal graph without either component.

As shown in Table 2, both CFRCL-A and CFRCL-B perform worse than the full CFRCL model, with CFRCL-C showing the most significant drop. The performance decline in CFRCL-A highlights the importance of leveraging anomaly detection results for initializing node scores. CFRCL-B's degradation demonstrates the value of causal skeleton extraction in narrowing the candidate root cause set. Notably, while performance drops for all methods on the larger AIOps2022 dataset compared to GAIA, CFRCL and CFRCL-B degrade the least—further underscoring the importance of incorporating abnormality scores to maintain localization accuracy at scale.

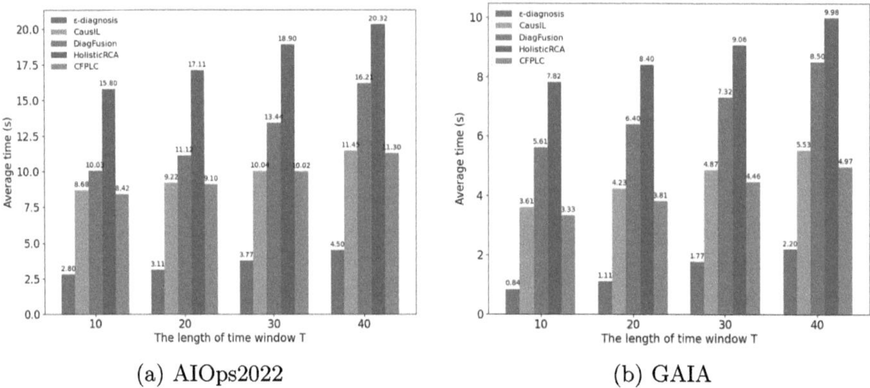

(a) AIOps2022

(b) GAIA

Fig. 4. Average time to localize a single root cause in different detection time window lengths.

Average Time Cost of Localization (RQ3). We compare the average time required by different methods to locate a single root cause across varying time window lengths in two datasets, measuring from the end of anomaly detection. As shown in Fig. 4, the results demonstrate that the average time required for all methods increases as the time window lengthens. This is intuitive as longer time windows contain more data to be analyzed. Among the methods, ϵ-Diagnosis achieves the shortest time due to its relatively straightforward statistical analysis. In contrast, HolisticRCA examines all data features across every entity within the system, resulting in increased model complexity and taking the most time. Additionally, while CausIL is the SOTA method for constructing metric-level causal graphs, CFRCL achieves a slightly faster localization speed. This advantage stems from CFRCL's causal skeleton extraction phase, which reduces the scope of potential root causes involved in constructing causal graphs—the primary time cost of causal inference-based methods.

In summary, CFRCL excels in overall localization performance by achieving high accuracy with relatively low time cost—an advantage that baselines lack.

6 Conclusion

This paper identifies two key limitations in existing root cause localization methods for cloud-native systems. To address them, we propose CFRCL, an end-to-end, cross-level framework designed from a fault propagation perspective. CFRCL leverages anomaly detection results to improve localization accuracy and models potential fault propagation across resource levels using causal relationships. It introduces a novel approach to initialize the causal graph with abnormality scores from anomaly detection and applies a random walk algorithm to identify likely root causes. Experiments on two widely used datasets demonstrate CFRCL's effectiveness and its ability to overcome limitations of existing methods.

Acknowledgement. This work is supported by the National Natural Science Foundation of China (NSFC) under Grant No. 62172050.

Disclosure of Interests. The authors have no competing interests to declare that are relevant to the content of this article.

References

1. Kratzke, N., Quint, P.C.: Understanding cloud-native applications after 10 years of cloud computing-a systematic mapping study. J. Syst. Softw. **126**, 1–16 (2017)
2. Soldani, J., Brogi, A.: Anomaly detection and failure root cause analysis in (micro) service-based cloud applications: a survey. ACM Comput. Surv. (CSUR) **55**(3), 1–39 (2022)
3. Lee, C., Yang, T., Chen, Z., Su, Y., Lyu, M.R.: Eadro: an end-to-end troubleshooting framework for microservices on multi-source data. In: 2023 IEEE/ACM 45th International Conference on Software Engineering, pp. 1750–1762 (2023)
4. Somashekar, G., Dutt, A., Adak, M., Lorido Botran, T., Gandhi, A.: Gamma: graph neural network-based multi-bottleneck localization for microservices applications. In: Proceedings of the ACM on Web Conference 2024, pp. 3085–3095 (2024)
5. Han, Y., et al.: Holistic root cause analysis for failures in cloud-native systems through observability data. IEEE Trans. Serv. Comput. (2024)
6. Cheng, H., Li, Q., Liu, B., Liu, S., Pan, L.: DGERCL: a dynamic graph embedding approach for root cause localization in microservice systems. IEEE Trans. Serv. Comput. 1–12 (2024)
7. Chakraborty, S., Garg, S., Agarwal, S., Chauhan, A., Saini, S.K.: Causil: causal graph for instance level microservice data. In: Proceedings of the ACM Web Conference 2023, pp. 2905–2915 (2023)
8. Zheng, L., Chen, Z., He, J., Chen, H.: Mulan: multi-modal causal structure learning and root cause analysis for microservice systems. In: Proceedings of the ACM on Web Conference 2024, pp. 4107–4116 (2024)
9. Wu, Z., et al.: Flowrca: enhancing microservice reliability with non-invasive root cause analysis. In: 2024 IEEE International Conference on Web Services, pp. 1251–1258 (2024)
10. Tao, L., et al.: Diagnosing performance issues for large-scale microservice systems with heterogeneous graph. IEEE Trans. Serv. Comput. **17**(5), 2223–2235 (2024)
11. Wang, Y., Zhu, Z., Fu, Q., Ma, Y., He, P.: MRCA: metric-level root cause analysis for microservices via multi-modal data. In: Proceedings of the 39th IEEE/ACM International Conference on Automated Software Engineering, pp. 1057–1068 (2024)

12. Zhu, Y., et al.: Microirc: instance-level root cause localization for microservice systems. J. Syst. Softw. **216**, 112145 (2024)
13. Hamilton, W., Ying, Z., Leskovec, J.: Inductive representation learning on large graphs. In: Advances in Neural Information Processing Systems, vol. 30, pp. 1024–1034 (2017)
14. Zhang, S., et al.: Illuminating the gray zone: non-intrusive gray failure localization in server operating systems. In: Companion Proceedings of the 32nd ACM International Conference on the Foundations of Software Engineering, pp. 126–137 (2024)
15. Zhang, C., Dong, Z., Peng, X., Zhang, B., Chen, M.: Trace-based multi-dimensional root cause localization of performance issues in microservice systems. In: Proceedings of the IEEE/ACM 46th International Conference on Software Engineering, pp. 1–12 (2024)
16. Xie, R., Yang, J., Li, J., Wang, L.: Impacttracer: root cause localization in microservices based on fault propagation modeling. In: 2023 Design, Automation & Test in Europe Conference & Exhibition, pp. 1–6 (2023)
17. Saltzer, J.H., Kaashoek, M.F.: Principles of cOmputer System Design: An Introduction. Morgan Kaufmann (2009)
18. Zhang, S., et al.: Robust failure diagnosis of microservice system through multimodal data. IEEE Trans. Serv. Comput. **16**(6), 3851–3864 (2023)
19. Lea, C., Vidal, R., Reiter, A., Hager, G.D.: Temporal convolutional networks: a unified approach to action segmentation. In: Hua, G., Jégou, H. (eds.) ECCV 2016. LNCS, vol. 9915, pp. 47–54. Springer, Cham (2016). https://doi.org/10.1007/978-3-319-49409-8_7
20. He, P., Zhu, J., Zheng, Z., Lyu, M.R.: Drain: an online log parsing approach with fixed depth tree. In: 2017 IEEE International Conference on Web Services, pp. 33–40 (2017)
21. Arnold, A., Liu, Y., Abe, N.: Temporal causal modeling with graphical granger methods. In: Proceedings of the 13th ACM SIGKDD International Conference on Knowledge Discovery and Data Mining, pp. 66–75 (2007)
22. Lin, C.M., Chang, C., Wang, W.Y., Wang, K.D., Peng, W.C.: Root cause analysis in microservice using neural granger causal discovery. In: Proceedings of the AAAI Conference on Artificial Intelligence, vol. 38, pp. 206–213 (2024)
23. Lin, W., Ma, M., Pan, D., Wang, P.: Facgraph: frequent anomaly correlation graph mining for root cause diagnose in micro-service architecture. In: 2018 IEEE 37th International Performance Computing and Communications Conference, pp. 1–8 (2018)
24. Abe, H., Tsumoto, S.: Analyzing behavior of objective rule evaluation indices based on a correlation coefficient. In: International Conference on Knowledge-Based and Intelligent Information and Engineering Systems, pp. 758–765 (2008)
25. Lin, J., Chen, P., Zheng, Z.: Microscope: pinpoint performance issues with causal graphs in micro-service environments. In: Pahl, C., Vukovic, M., Yin, J., Yu, Q. (eds.) ICSOC 2018. LNCS, vol. 11236, pp. 3–20. Springer, Cham (2018). https://doi.org/10.1007/978-3-030-03596-9_1
26. Yu, G., et al.: Microrank: end-to-end latency issue localization with extended spectrum analysis in microservice environments. In: Proceedings of the Web Conference 2021, pp. 3087–3098 (2021)
27. Shan, H., et al.: ϵ-diagnosis: unsupervised and real-time diagnosis of small-window long-tail latency in large-scale microservice platforms. In: The World Wide Web Conference, pp. 3215–3222 (2019)

28. Zhang, S., et al.: Failure diagnosis in microservice systems: a comprehensive survey and analysis. ACM Trans. Softw. Eng. Methodol. (2024)
29. Pham, L., Ha, H., Zhang, H.: Root cause analysis for microservices based on causal inference: how far are we? In: 2024 39th IEEE/ACM International Conference on Automated Software Engineering, pp. 706–718 (2024)

Author Index

J. Li et al. (Eds.): APWeb-WAIM 2025, LNCS 16115, pp. 699–701, 2026.
https://doi.org/10.1007/978-981-95-5719-6

If you have any concerns about our products,
you can contact us on
ProductSafety@springernature.com

In case Publisher is established outside the EU,
the EU authorized representative is:
Springer Nature Customer Service Center GmbH
Europaplatz 3, 69115 Heidelberg, Germany

Printed by Libri Plureos GmbH
in Hamburg, Germany